FROMMER'S

ENGLAND

ON $50 A DAY

DARWIN PORTER

Assisted by
**Danforth Prince
and Margaret Foresman**

1990

Published by Prentice Hall Trade Division
A Division of Simon & Schuster Inc.
15 Columbus Circle
New York, NY 10023

ISBN 0-13-279639-2
ISSN 1042-8399

Manufactured in the United States of America

CONTENTS

Introduction. ENGLAND ON $50 A DAY   1

     Frommer's Dollarwise Travel Club—How to Save Money on
     All Your Travels   3

I. GETTING TO AND AROUND ENGLAND   9

     1. Plane Economics   9
     2. Traveling Within England   12

II. INTRODUCING ENGLAND   20

     1. The English   21
     2. The Culture   24
     3. Food and Drink   28
     4. Alternative and Special-Interest Travel   30
     5. The ABCs of England   37

III. SETTLING INTO LONDON   44

     1. Orientation   45
     2. Belgravia   55
     3. Victoria   56
     4. Earl's Court   60
     5. Brompton and South Kensington   61
     6. Knightsbridge   63
     7. Chelsea   63
     8. Kensington   64
     9. Shepherd's Bush   67
     10. Notting Hill Gate   67
     11. Paddington and Bayswater   67
     12. St. Marylebone   71
     13. Leicester Square   73
     14. Bloomsbury   73
     15. In and Around Hampstead   76
     16. Blackheath   76
     17. On the Fringe   77
     18. Airport Hotels   77
     19. An Accommodation Round-up   79

IV. LONDON: RESTAURANTS, PUBS, AND
     WINE BARS   81

     1. West End   83
     2. Westminster and St. James's   93
     3. The City   95
     4. Holborn and Bloomsbury   98
     5. Belgravia and Knightsbridge   99
     6. Chelsea   101

7. Kensington   105
8. West London   107
9. East End   108
10. South of the Thames   109
11. Hampstead Heath   110
12. Thames Dining   111
13. For Fish and Chips   112
14. Time Out for Tea   113

V. LONDON: WHAT TO SEE AND DO   115
1. Seeing the Sights   115
2. Shopping   140
3. London After Dark   151
4. Taking the Tours   163
5. London for Children   165
6. One-Day Trips from London   168

VI. WINDSOR, OXFORD, AND THE HOME
     COUNTIES   174
1. Windsor   175
2. Ascot   183
3. Henley-on-Thames   184
4. Oxford   185
5. Woodstock (Blenheim Palace)   196
6. Hertfordshire   197
7. Buckinghamshire   200
8. Bedfordshire (Woburn Abbey)   203

VII. KENT, SURREY, AND SUSSEX   206
1. Canterbury   213
2. Dover   219
3. Royal Tunbridge Wells   222
4. Richmond   224
5. Haslemere   225
6. Rye and Winchelsea   228
7. Hastings and St. Leonards   231
8. Battle   234
9. Alfriston and Lewes   236
10. Brighton   238
11. Arundel   243
12. Chichester   245

VIII. HAMPSHIRE AND DORSET   249
1. Portsmouth and Southsea   250
2. Southampton   255
3. New Forest   257

4. Isle of Wight   259
5. Winchester   262
6. Bournemouth   265
7. Shaftesbury   268
8. Wareham   269
9. Dorchester   270
10. Bridport   272
11. Chideock   273
12. Charmouth   274
13. Lyme Regis   274
14. Donyatt   276
15. Sherborne   276

IX. DEVON   278

1. Exeter   279
2. Dartmoor   284
3. Chagford   287
4. Torbay (Torquay)   289
5. Totnes   291
6. Dartmouth   293
7. Salcombe   294
8. Plymouth   295
9. Clovelly   300
10. Combe Martin and Lynton-Lynmouth   301

X. CORNWALL   304

1. Looe   305
2. Polperro   307
3. Fowey   310
4. Truro   311
5. St. Mawes   312
6. Falmouth   313
7. Penzance   316
8. The Isles of Scilly   318
9. Newlyn, Mousehole, and Land's End   322
10. St. Ives   324
11. Port Isaac   327
12. Tintagel   328
13. Bolventor   330

XI. WILTSHIRE, SOMERSET, AND AVON   331

1. Salisbury   332
2. Castle Combe   342
3. Exmoor National Park   344
4. Dunster   345
5. Glastonbury   347
6. Wells   350

    7. The Caves of Mendip 353
    8. Bath 355
    9. Bristol 363

XII. THE COTSWOLDS   367
    1. Wotton-under-Edge 368
    2. Tetbury 369
    3. Malmesbury 369
    4. Cirencester and Painswick 370
    5. Cheltenham 373
    6. Sudeley Castle 375
    7. Bibury 376
    8. Burford and Minster Lovell 376
    9. Shipton-under-Wychwood 378
  10. Chipping Norton 378
  11. Bourton-on-the-Water 379
  12. Stow-on-the-Wold and Lower Swell 381
  13. Moreton-in-Marsh 383
  14. Broadway 384
  15. Chipping Campden 386

XIII. STRATFORD AND THE HEART OF ENGLAND   390
    1. Stratford-upon-Avon 390
    2. Warwick 404
    3. Kenilworth Castle 408
    4. Coventry 409
    5. Hereford and Worcester 412

XIV. CAMBRIDGE AND EAST ANGLIA   420
    1. Cambridge 420
    2. Ely 431
    3. Thaxted 434
    4. Saffron Walden 434
    5. Finchingfield 435
    6. Dedham 436
    7. Newmarket 437
    8. Clare 438
    9. Long Melford 438
  10. Lavenham 440
  11. Woodbridge and Aldeburgh 441
  12. East Bergholt 443
  13. Norwich 444
  14. North Norfolk 447

XV. EAST MIDLANDS   451
    1. Northamptonshire 451
    2. Leicestershire 455

    3. Derbyshire   457
    4. Nottinghamshire   461
    5. Lincolnshire   466

XVI. CHESHIRE, SHROPSHIRE, AND THE
     POTTERIES   473
    1. Chester   473
    2. Nantwich   478
    3. Shrewsbury   479
    4. Stoke-on-Trent   483
    5. Stafford   486
    6. Lichfield   487

XVII. LIVERPOOL AND BLACKPOOL   489
    1. Liverpool   489
    2. Blackpool   494

XVIII. THE LAKE DISTRICT   498
    1. Kendal   499
    2. Windermere   500
    3. Ambleside   505
    4. Rydal   507
    5. Grasmere   508
    6. Hawkshead and Coniston   510
    7. Keswick   512
    8. Bassenthwaite   514
    9. Penrith   515
  10. Borrowdale   516

XIX. YORKSHIRE AND NORTHUMBRIA   517
    1. York   518
    2. North Yorkshire   528
    3. West Yorkshire   538
    4. Durham   540
    5. Tyne and Wear   544
    6. Northumberland   546

Index   553

MAPS AND CHARTS

Mileage Chart   18
England   32
London   58–59
The West End   66
Kensington   68
Piccadilly   84
The City   97
Chelsea/Knightsbridge   102–103
The London Underground   117
Covent Garden   145
Soho and Russell Square   159
Oxford   189
Kent, Surrey, and the Sussexes   211
Southwestern Counties   251
Cornwall and Devon   282
Salisbury   334
Gloucester, Worcester, and Warwick   392
Cambridge   423
East Anglia   433
The Lake District   501
Yorkshire/Derbyshire/Lincolnshire/Lancaster   520–521
Durham and Northumberland   543

A DISCLAIMER

I don't have to tell you that whatever the level of inflation, prices do rise. In researching this book, I have made every effort to obtain up-to-the-minute prices, but even the most conscientious researcher cannot keep up with the constantly changing prices of the travel industry. As this guide goes to press, I believe I have obtained the most reliable data possible. Nonetheless, in the lifetime of this edition the wise traveler will add 15% to the prices quoted throughout these pages.

BRITAIN'S VAT

Great Britain has a standard Value Added Tax (called VAT for short) of 15%. Most European Community countries already have a tax similar to VAT (France, for example, has a paralyzing one of 23%). This extra VAT charge will show up on your bill unless otherwise stated. It is in addition to the service charge. Should the service charge in a restaurant be 15%, you will, in effect, be paying 30% higher than the prices quoted. The service charges, if included as part of the bill, are also taxable.

As part of an energy-saving scheme, the British government has also added a special 25% tax on gasoline (petrol).

For more information on taxes, see "The ABCs of England" in Chapter II.

ENGLAND ON $50 A DAY

The aim of this book is to bring you closer to the heart of England.
In the pages that follow, I'll invite you to live—among other places—in a timbered, 17th-century home one hour from London; to sleep in a four-poster wooden bed; to enjoy multicourse meals while seated at a polished black oak refectory table before a 15-foot-wide fireplace in which logs burn brightly.

I'll take you to the cottage of an English sea captain where you can experience genial country hospitality and hear tales of the deep—or to a hillside farm, perched on a wild moor, where you'll be served a four o'clock tea accompanied by home-churned butter and crusty bread, warm from the oven, and thick cream piled high on a bowl of tiny strawberries that you yourself have just picked in a nearby field.

Such experiences as these have two characteristics in common: they represent the best way to live in England—and they are inexpensive, for the inns, guesthouses, and restaurants recommended in this book are those designed for and primarily patronized by Britishers.

You'll be taken to pubs dating back to the days of Shakespeare and Queen Elizabeth I that offer complete luncheons for £5.50 ($9.65). You'll be guided deep into the English countryside to a stone manor house that stands proudly at the end of an avenue of old trees. Here, for only £15 ($26.25) daily, you'll receive bed and breakfast.

The budget details start in just a few pages. First, I'll outline the order of our discussion, then tell you a bit about the $50-a-day limit I've placed on basic expenditures.

THE ORGANIZATION OF THIS BOOK

Here's how *England on $50 a Day* sets forth its information:

Chapter I, directly ahead, deals with getting to England—mainly by air—and then with the various modes of transportation within the country. Naturally, our focus is on the least expensive means of transport—on such items as excursion fares and off-season discounts.

Chapter II discusses where you can go in England for the most interesting visits, and it gives a condensed view of the country's history, its people, its culture, and its food and drink. It concludes with some vital data on the ABCs of life that will help your adjustment to traveling here.

Chapters III through V turn the spotlight on London, giving some practical information and documenting first the budget and moderately priced hotels, then the restaurants, pubs, and wine bars, concluding with data on the major sights (including my personal list of the Top Ten), shopping bargains, nightlife, and one-day trips within Greater London.

Chapter VI explores some of the most history-rich sights within easy reach of London: Windsor Castle, Woburn Abbey, and the university city of Oxford.

Chapters VII through XI move away from London to the south of England: Kent, Surrey, Sussex, then Hampshire and Dorset (Thomas Hardy country), followed by "The West"—Devon, Cornwall, Wiltshire, Somerset, and Avon. Here you'll find my descriptions of thatched cottages, hillside farms, and Georgian manor houses, which you can use for exploring this varied English countryside.

Chapters XII and XIII do the same with respect to the most tourist-trodden district of England, the Shakespeare Country, and the hamlets of the Cotswolds.

Chapter XIV focuses on some less-visited, magnificent points for exploration —East Anglia (Cambridge, of course, but also Ely, Norwich, and the fen and broads country), and the pink villages of Suffolk.

Chapter XV cuts through unknown England, ferreting out the attractions of the East Midlands, including the cathedral city of Lincoln.

Chapters XVI through XIX travel across the entire northern sweep of England, from the wilds of Northumbria to the cathedral city of York, to Liverpool and Cheshire, all the way to the beautiful Lake District, immortalized by the poets.

$50 A DAY—WHAT THAT MEANS

You can live in England on a number of price levels. The unknowing can lavish huge sums on sterile holidays, but comfort and charm are not necessarily priced so high at all. I aim to establish that fact by showing you exactly what you can get for $50 a day.

The specific aim of this book—as it is in all its companion books—is to show you clearly how to keep *basic living costs* (room and three meals a day) down to $50 per person per day. There is nothing gimmicky about this goal, as readers of my other books have found. Since the cost of entertainment, sightseeing, shopping, and transportation is all *in addition* to that basic $50-a-day figure, I prescribe reasonable standards for the budget-minded.

Half of this book is devoted to recommendations for comfortable rooms and well-prepared meals—within a $50-a-day budget. You'll find comfortable rooms in London and in the country, usually with innerspring mattresses and almost always with hot and cold running water. None of the rooms in this price bracket, unless otherwise stated, has a private bath.

The $50-a-day budget roughly breaks down this way—$29 per person (based on double occupancy) for a room and breakfast, $6 for lunch, and $15 for dinner.

You'll note also that I do include in these pages recommendations sometimes far above our allowances—to enable you a wider range of choices where few budget establishments are available and also to give you opportunities for a good old-fashioned splurge.

Many of the accommodations recommended were chosen because of a unique historical, cultural, or architectural feature that gives them special value. This is truer for the country than it is for London, where the $50-a-day hotels were selected more for their facilities, comfort, and conveniences than for any spectacular charm.

SOME DISCLAIMERS

No restaurant, inn, hotel, guesthouse, or shop paid to be mentioned in this book. What you read are entirely personal recommendations—in many cases, proprietors never knew that their establishments were being visited or investigated for inclusion in a travel guide.

A word of warning: Unfortunately, prices change, and they rarely go downward. England has no governmental control of hotel prices, as is the practice in countries such as Spain. "Mine host" can charge a guest anything he or she "bloody well chooses." Competition is what keeps the rates down. Always, when checking into a hotel or guesthouse, inquire about the price and agree on it. This can save much embarrassment and disappointment when it comes time to settle the tab.

Hotel owners sometimes complain that $50-a-day travelers have arrived at their establishments and demanded to be charged prices quoted in an earlier edition of this guide. Your chances of pulling off this stunt are about as good as they would be in the United States. *England on $50 a Day* is revised every year at considerable expense, involving not only travel research but heavy printing costs. It is foolish economy to travel with a copy that your brother-in-law and his wife used on their trip abroad some years ago. That cozy little family dining room of a year ago can change colors, blossoming out with cut-velvet walls and dining tabs that include the decorator's fee and the owner's new Rolls.

Finally, even in a book revised annually, it may develop that some of the people, animals, or settings I've described are no longer there. Viennese chefs have nervous breakdowns, red-cheeked English maids elope with charming Italians, overstuffed sofas are junked in favor of streamlined modern ones, and 19-year-old dogs go to heaven—so any and all of these things may be different. But while people, dogs, and sofas come and go, many of the old inns and pubs recommended have weathered the centuries intact, and barring war, fire, or flood, should be standing proudly to greet you on your visit.

FROMMER'S DOLLARWISE® TRAVEL CLUB—HOW TO SAVE MONEY ON ALL YOUR TRAVELS

In this book we'll be looking at how to get your money's worth in England, but there is a "device" for saving money and determining value on *all* your trips. It's the popular, international Frommer's Dollarwise Travel Club, now in its 29th successful year of operation. The club was formed at the urging of numerous readers of the $-A-Day and Frommer Guides, who felt that such an organization could provide continuing travel information and a sense of community to value-minded travelers in all parts of the world. And so it does!

In keeping with the budget concept, the annual membership fee is low and is immediately exceeded by the value of your benefits. Upon receipt of $18 (U.S. residents), or $20 U.S. by check drawn on a U.S. bank or via international postal money order in U.S. funds (Canadian, Mexican, and other foreign residents) to cover one year's membership, we will send all new members the following items.

(1) Any two of the following books
Please designate in your letter which two you wish to receive:

Frommer $-A-Day® Guides
Europe on $40 a Day
Australia on $30 a Day
Eastern Europe on $25 a Day
England on $50 a Day
Greece on $30 a Day
Hawaii on $60 a Day
India on $25 a Day
Ireland on $35 a Day
Israel on $40 a Day
Mexico (plus Belize and Guatemala) on $30 a Day
New York on $50 a Day
New Zealand on $40 a Day
Scandinavia on $60 a Day
Scotland and Wales on $40 a Day

South America on $35 a Day
Spain and Morocco (plus the Canary Is.) on $40 a Day
Turkey on $30 a Day
Washington, D.C., & Historic Virginia on $40 a Day

($-A-Day Guides document hundreds of budget accommodations and facilities, helping you get the most for your travel dollars.)

Frommer Guides

Australia
Austria and Hungary
Belgium, Holland & Luxembourg
Bermuda and The Bahamas
Brazil
Canada
Caribbean
Egypt
England and Scotland
France
Germany
Italy
Japan and Hong Kong
Portugal, Madeira & the Azores
South Pacific
Switzerland and Liechtenstein
Alaska
California and Las Vegas
Florida
Mid-Atlantic States
New England
New York State
Northwest
Skiing USA—East
Skiing USA—West
Southern Atlantic States
Southeast Asia
Southwest
Texas
USA

(Frommer Guides discuss accommodations and facilities in all price ranges, with emphasis on the medium-priced.)

Frommer Touring Guides

Australia
Egypt
Florence
London
Paris
Scotland
Thailand
Venice

(These new, color illustrated guides include walking tours, cultural and historic sites, and other vital travel information.)

Gault Millau

Chicago
France

Italy
London
Los Angeles
New England
New York
San Francisco
Washington, D.C.

(Irreverent, savvy, and comprehensive, each of these renowned guides candidly reviews over 1,000 restaurants, hotels, shops, nightspots, museums, and sights.)

Serious Shopper's Guides
Italy
London
Los Angeles
Paris

(Practical and comprehensive, each of these handsomely illustrated guides lists hundreds of stores, selling everything from antiques to wine, conveniently organized alphabetically by category.)

A Shopper's Guide to the Caribbean
(Two experienced Caribbean hands guide you through this shopper's paradise, offering witty insights and helpful tips on the wares and emporia of more than 25 islands.)

Beat the High Cost of Travel
(This practical guide details how to save money on absolutely all travel items—accommodations, transportation, dining, sightseeing, shopping, taxes, and more. Includes special budget information for seniors, students, singles, and families.)

Bed & Breakfast—North America
(This guide contains a directory of over 150 organizations that offer bed & breakfast referrals and reservations throughout North America. The scenic attractions, and major schools and universities near the homes of each are also listed.)

California with Kids
(A must for parents traveling in California, providing key information on selecting the best accommodations, restaurants, and sightseeing attractions for the particular needs of the family, whether the kids are toddlers, school-age, preteens, or teens.)

Frommer's Belgium
(Arthur Frommer unlocks the treasures of a country overlooked by most travelers to Europe. Discover the medieval charm, modern sophistication, and natural beauty of this quintessentially European country.)

Frommer's Cruises
(This complete guide covers all the basics of cruising—ports of call, costs, fly-cruise package bargains, cabin selection booking, embarkation and debarkation and describes in detail over 60 or so ships cruising the waters of Alaska, the Caribbean, Mexico, Hawaii, Panama, Canada, and the United States.)

Frommer's Skiing Europe
(Describes top ski resorts in Austria, France, Italy, and Switzerland. Illustrated with maps of each resort area. Includes supplement on Argentinian resorts.)

Guide to Honeymoon Destinations
(A special guide for that most romantic trip of your life, with full details on planning and choosing the destination that will be just right in the U.S. [California, New England, Hawaii, Florida, New York, South Carolina, etc.], Canada, Mexico, and the Caribbean.)

Marilyn Wood's Wonderful Weekends
(This very selective guide covers the best mini-vacation destinations within a 200-mile radius of New York City. It describes special country inns and other accommodations, restaurants, picnic spots, sights, and activities—all the information needed for a two- or three-day stay.)

Manhattan's Outdoor Sculpture
(A total guide, fully illustrated with black and white photos, to more than 300 sculptures and monuments that grace Manhattan's plazas, parks, and other public spaces.)

Motorist's Phrase Book
(A practical phrase book in French, German, and Spanish designed specifically for the English-speaking motorist touring abroad.)

Paris Rendez-Vous
(An amusing and *au courant* guide to the best meeting places in Paris, organized for hour-to-hour use: from power breakfasts and fun brunches, through tea at four or cocktails at five, to romantic dinners and dancing 'til dawn.)

Swap and Go—Home Exchanging Made Easy
(Two veteran home exchangers explain in detail all the money-saving benefits of a home exchange, and then describe precisely how to do it. Also includes information on home rentals and many tips on low-cost travel.)

The Candy Apple: New York for Kids
(A spirited guide to the wonders of the Big Apple by a savvy New York grandmother with a kid's-eye view to fun. Indispensable for visitors and residents alike.)

The New World of Travel
(From America's #1 travel expert, Arthur Frommer, an annual sourcebook with the hottest news and latest trends that's guaranteed to change the way you travel—and save you hundreds of dollars. Jam-packed with alternative new modes of travel that will lead you to vacations that cater to the mind, the spirit, and a sense of thrift.)

Travel Diary and Record Book
(A 96-page diary for personal travel notes plus a section for such vital data as passport and traveler's check numbers, itinerary, postcard list, special people and places to visit, and a reference section with temperature and conversion charts, and world maps with distance zones.)

Where to Stay USA
(By the Council on International Educational Exchange, this extraordinary guide is the first to list accommodations in all 50 states that cost anywhere from $3 to $30 per night.)

(2) Any one of the Frommer City Guides
Amsterdam
Athens
Atlantic City and Cape May
Boston

Cancún, Cozumel, and the Yucatán
Chicago
Dublin and Ireland
Hawaii
Las Vegas
Lisbon, Madrid, and Costa del Sol
London
Los Angeles
Mexico City and Acapulco
Minneapolis and St. Paul
Montréal and Québec City
New Orleans
New York
Orlando, Disney World, and EPCOT
Paris
Philadelphia
Rio
Rome
San Francisco
Santa Fe, Taos, and Albuquerque
Sydney
Washington, D.C.

(Pocket-size guides to hotels, restaurants, nightspots, and sightseeing attractions covering all price ranges.)

(3) A one-year subscription to *The Dollarwise Traveler*

This quarterly eight-page tabloid newspaper keeps you up to date on fastbreaking developments in low-cost travel in all parts of the world bringing you the latest money-saving information—the kind of information you'd have to pay $35 a year to obtain elsewhere. This consumer-conscious publication also features columns of special interest to readers: **Hospitality Exchange** (members all over the world who are willing to provide hospitality to other members as they pass through their home cities); **Share-a-Trip** (offers and requests from members for travel companions who can share costs and help avoid the burdensome single supplement); and **Readers Ask . . . Readers Reply** (travel questions from members to which other members reply with authentic firsthand information).

(4) Your personal membership card

Membership entitles you to purchase through the club all Frommer publications for a third to a half off their regular retail prices during the term of your membership.

So why not join this hardy band of international budgeteers and participate in its exchange of travel information and hospitality? Simply send your name and address, together with your annual membership fee of $18 (U.S. residents) or $20 U.S. (Canadian, Mexican, and other foreign residents), by check drawn on a U.S. bank or via international postal money order in U.S. funds to: Frommer's Dollarwise Travel Club, Inc., 15 Columbus Circle, New York, NY 10023. And please remember to specify which *two* of the books in section (1) and which *one* in section (2) you wish to receive in your initial package of members' benefits. Or, if you prefer, use the order form at the end of the book and enclose $18 or $20 in U.S. currency.

Once you are a member, there is no obligation to buy additional books. No books will be mailed to you without your specific order.

AN INVITATION TO READERS

Like all the books in this series, *England on $50 a Day* hopes to maintain a continuing dialogue between its author and its readers. All of us share a common aim—to travel as widely and as well as possible, at the lowest possible cost. In achieving that goal, your comments and suggestions can be of aid to other readers. Therefore, if you come across a particularly appealing hotel, restaurant, shop, or bargain, please don't keep it to yourself. And this applies to any comments you may have about the existing listings. The fact that a hotel or restaurant is recommended in this edition doesn't mean that it will necessarily appear in future editions if readers report that its service has slipped or that its prices have risen too drastically. You have my word that each and every letter will be read by me personally, although I find it well-nigh impossible to *answer* each and every one. Be assured, however, that I'm listening. Send your comments or finds to Darwin Porter, c/o Prentice Hall Travel, 15 Columbus Circle, New York, NY 10023.

TIME OUT FOR A COMMERCIAL

Even in a book as fat as this one, I don't pretend to have covered the British Isles in just one volume. One book can hardly do justice to the treasures and lore of England. For that reason, we have since 1969 published a companion book, *Frommer's England & Scotland,* for those visitors who often want to break up their economizing at times and patronize some of the more medium-priced hotels and restaurants of England, particularly its old manor houses and charming restaurants. Over the years, thousands of readers have traveled with both guides, economizing in London, splurging in York, and so forth, since each guide offers a substantially different set of recommendations. Only the sights remain the same. They don't change, regardless of what price bracket you travel in.

Many budget travelers to England, however, will want to venture beyond its borders and discover Scotland to the north and Wales to the west. With those people in mind, and after hundreds of written requests from readers, we now offer a separate guide, *Scotland and Wales on $50 a Day,* which covers the two countries sharing the same island with England. How close they are geographically, but how different they are once you get there.

Like its older sister guide to England, the book on Scotland and Wales is written on the same theme, describing hundreds of budget hotels and inns, B&B houses, restaurants, tea rooms, and pubs—often offbeat favorites that offer the most authentic and enriching travel experience.

In addition, budget-conscious travelers will find all the information needed on low-cost transportation, sightseeing, shopping bargains, and inexpensive nightlife throughout these other two fascinating countries.

So if you plan to travel not only to England, but also to "take the high road" north to Scotland, stopping off in such beautiful cities as Edinburgh, or if you intend to seek out that special magic that is Wales, take along our younger sister. You'll need her help.

GETTING TO AND AROUND ENGLAND

1. PLANE ECONOMICS
2. TRAVELING WITHIN ENGLAND

The deregulation of the airline industry made world headlines in 1979, and since that time any vestiges of uniformity in price structures for transatlantic flights have disappeared. Airlines compete fiercely with one another, offering a confusing barrage of pricing systems and package deals, each straining the capacities for anyone trying to sort the system into a coherent whole. Travel agents refer to the masses of documentation they receive daily as "chaos." However, that can mean beneficial chaos to the alert traveler willing to study and consider all the options available.

1. Plane Economics

The best strategy for securing the least expensive airfare is to shop around and, above all, remain as flexible as possible. Keep calling the airlines. Sometimes you can purchase a ticket that is lower in price at the last minute. If the flight is not fully booked, an airline might discount the price of tickets in an attempt to achieve a full passenger load.

Many passengers, however, find themselves locked into already defined vacation dates and rigid itineraries that require a prearranged departure and return date.

Most airlines charge different fares according to the season. For the pricing of flights to Europe, midsummer months are the peak travel times and fares are the most expensive at that time. Basic season, which falls (with just a few exceptions) into the winter months, offers the least expensive fares. Travel during Christmas and Easter weeks is usually more expensive than in the weeks just before or after those holidays. The periods between basic and peak seasons is called the shoulder season.

Even within the various seasons, airlines offer a variety of seating arrangements, ranging from first class through business and economy classes. Most airlines also offer heavily discounted promotional fares available erratically according to last-minute market plans. But, be warned: the less expensive your ticket is, the more stringent the restrictions. These restrictions will most often include advance purchase, a minimum stay abroad, and cancellation or alteration penalties. The most common and frequently used such fare is the APEX or advance purchase excursion (see below).

Also note that prices tend to be higher in many classes on weekends, which, depending on the airline, are usually defined as Friday, Saturday, and Sunday.

THE AIRLINES

Several airlines fly the enormously popular routes from North America to Great Britain. In fact, you have a greater choice of flights to Britain than you do to any other country in Europe. These airlines include British Airways, American Airlines, Delta, Pan Am, TWA, and such smaller airlines as Virgin Atlantic.

Many passengers prefer to fly the national carrier of the nation they intend to visit as an advance preview of their trip abroad. **British Airways** is the premier airline of the United Kingdom. It offers the most frequent flights from North America to Great Britain. Today, BA flies to London (usually nonstop) from at least 18 different U.S. cities. That fact makes transfers through New York unnecessary for many visitors coming from such cities as Boston, Washington, D.C., Atlanta, Dallas, Houston, Miami, Chicago, Detroit, Philadelphia, Seattle, Los Angeles, San Francisco, Anchorage, Orlando, Tampa, and Pittsburgh.

At New York's JFK Airport, British Airways is the only non–U.S. based carrier to have its own terminal. Likewise, at Heathrow in London, its Terminal 4 is considered the most up-to-date in the world.

From Canada, BA services Toronto, Montréal, and Vancouver. The airline is unique in offering service useful for business travelers, a daily nonstop flight from New York to Manchester. And for the tourist, this flight can often serve as an efficient launching pad for tours of the Midlands and Shakespeare Country.

TWA offers connections out of New York from each of the more than 60 cities it services in the United States.

American Airlines offers daily service to Gatwick Airport (on the periphery of London) from Dallas. It also features daily service from Chicago's O'Hare Airport to Manchester.

Pan Am makes nonstop runs from New York to London three times a day, landing at Heathrow Airport. Pan Am also offers daily nonstop service from Detroit, Miami, Los Angeles, San Francisco, and Washington, D.C., as well as five-times-a-week nonstop service from Seattle to London.

Delta Airlines, depending on the season, makes either one or two nonstop flights every day between its headquarters in Atlanta and London's Gatwick Airport. Seasonal discounts often apply, so residents of American's Southeast are well advised to research carefully the affairs of this particular carrier.

Northwest Airlines flies nonstop from both Minneapolis and Boston to London's Gatwick Airport, which is connected directly to the heart of London by train.

Canadians, for the most part, prefer **Air Canada,** whose aircraft depart from London on nonstop flights from Vancouver, Toronto, and Montréal, after connecting with dozens of Canadian cities.

Long considered a no-frills alternative to Western Europe's larger airlines, **Virgin Atlantic Airways** now offers services and amenities comparable to those offered by major carriers. Owned by the same people (Virgin Atlantic Records) who gave the world Boy George and the Culture Club, the airline offers competitive prices for its daily flights between New Jersey's Newark Airport and London's Gatwick Airport. The airline also offers five-times-a-week nonstop flights between Miami and Gatwick and audio entertainment that is arguably better (according to electronic music buffs) than the competition's.

TYPES OF FARES

Generally your cheapest option on a regular airline is to book a **Super APEX** fare. This is now the most heavily used fare to London from North America. On most airlines, British Airways included, APEX tickets are valid for a stay abroad for at least 21 days in advance. Travel dates in both directions must be reserved at the time of purchase, with a $100 penalty assessed for alterations or cancellations.

To give you a rough idea of prices, BA's APEX fares from New York to London in high season cost $776 midweek and $832 weekends. The same fare from Chicago to London goes for only $12 more per category, a small difference considering the greater air miles. High season APEX tickets from Los Angeles to London are $899 midweek and $953 weekends. Round-trip low season midweek passage from New York to London is $511 and between Chicago and London $533. British Airways also matches its competitors by offering "giveaway" fares. For example, in 1989 for a short time it featured a $300 round-trip ticket from New York to London. But these fares come and go and you must always check with the airline or a reputable travel agent. On certain flights and in certain seasons, BA also offers a 10% senior citizen discount and youth fares for passengers under 25.

Predictably, the other airlines follow suit. Also in 1989 for a period, Pan Am offered a "giveaway ticket" of $298.50 round trip between JFK and Heathrow. The ticket, of course, carried many restrictions.

In high season, with stringent qualifiers on the conditions of flight, TWA offers a round-trip APEX fare of $608 from New York to London, with favorable terms for add-on flights from other cities served by that carrier.

From Dallas, American Airlines offers a high-season round-trip fare of $776 to London if travel in both directions occurs on a weekday. On weekends, the price of a ticket goes up by $50.

On Virgin Atlantic Airways, fares can range from as low as $99 one way in low season to $669 (plus tax) for a round-trip midsummer crossing. Delta also comes through with discounts. In May 1989 it featured a $421 round-trip, nonrefundable, fare from Atlanta to London with a 30-day advance booking. Otherwise, its round-trip passage goes up to $744 with a 21-day advance purchase and a stay abroad of between 7 and 180 days.

These fares are only cited to give you an idea of what is available. They will surely change in the lifetime of this edition.

CHARTER FLIGHTS

Strictly for reasons of economy, some travelers may wish to accept the numerous restrictions and possible uncertainties of a charter flight to England. Charters require that passengers strictly specify departure and return dates, and full payment is required in advance. Any changes in flight date are possible (if at all) only upon payment of a stiff penalty. Any reputable travel agent can advise about fares, cities of departure, and the reputation of the charter company.

Buyer Beware

With careful advance research, the much-vaunted discounts of the charter carriers can frequently be matched with an APEX ticket from one of the major carriers. A bit of advance telephone work and allegiance to the better-established carriers can often save you time, hassle, money, and heartbreak.

There are many charter specialists but three of the more reputable ones include **Council Travel,** a division of the Council on International Educational Exchange (CIEE), 205 East 42nd St., 16th floor, New York, NY 10017 (tel. 212/661-1450); **LTU,** 10 East 40th St., Suite 3705, New York, NY 10016 (tel. 212/532-0207 or toll free 800/888-0200); and **Access International,** 250 West 57th St., Suite 511, New York, NY 10107 (tel. 212/333-7280) or toll free 800/825-3633. For additional assistance, check with a travel agent.

2. Traveling Within England

BY AIR

Most of the airports of the United Kingdom are connected by British Airways into one almost continuous network. The most popular routes (between London and Manchester, Glasgow, Edinburgh, and Belfast) benefit from shuttle services, leaving Heathrow Terminal 1 on more than 35 flights daily. More information, of course, can be obtained from a travel agent or by getting in touch with British Airways directly.

BY TRAIN

There is something magical about traveling on a train in Britain. You sit in comfortable compartments on upholstered seats, next to the British. You're served your meal in the dining car like an aristocrat, and the entire experience can be a relaxing interlude.

You should, of course, be warned that *your Eurailpass is not valid on trains in Great Britain.* The cost of rail travel here can be quite low, particularly if you take advantage of certain cost-saving travel plans, some of which can only be purchased in North America, before leaving for England.

BritRail Pass

This pass gives unlimited rail travel in England, Scotland, and Wales and is valid on all British Rail routes. It is not valid on ships between Great Britain and the continent, in the Channel Islands, or in Ireland. Gold (first-class) and silver (economy-class) passes are sold for travel periods of varying lengths. An eight-day gold pass costs $250 as of 1989; a silver ticket goes for $179. For 15 days, a gold pass costs $370; a silver, $259. For 22 days, gold is $470; silver, $339. For one month, gold is $540; silver, $389. Children up to 5 years of age travel free, and those 5 to 15 go for $125 gold and $90 for silver for eight days; $185 gold and $130 silver for 15 days; $235 gold and $170 silver for 22 days; and $270 gold and $195 silver for one month.

Youth passes, all silver, are $149 for eight days, $219 for 15 days, $289 for 22 days, and $329 for one month. The youth pass is available for persons 16 through 25 years of age, but they must pay the full adult fare if they choose to go first class.

BritRail also offers a **Senior Citizen gold pass** to those age 60 and over, costing less than the regular gold pass. Prices are $210 for eight days, $310 for 15 days, $400 for 22 days, and $460 for one month.

Prices for BritRail Passes are higher for Canadian travelers.

BritRail Passes cannot be obtained in England but should be secured before leaving North America, either through travel agents or by writing to or visiting BritRail Travel International in the U.S. at 630 Third Ave., New York, NY 10017; Suite 603, 800 S. Hope St., Los Angeles, CA 90017; or Cedar Maple Plaza, 2305 Cedar Springs, Dallas, TX 75201. Canadians can write to 94 Cumberland St., Toronto M5R 1A3, ON, or 409 Granville St., Vancouver V6C 1T2, BC.

BritRail Passes do not have to be predated. Validate your pass at any British Rail station when you start your first rail journey. Travel can be made on all scheduled BritRail trains, including intercity high-speed 125-mph trains. The passes are all good for trips made on consecutive days from the time of validation. Seat reservations, usually obtainable on the day you travel, cost an additional $3 per person per trip. They are essential for some trains on certain peak days such as holidays and on Saturdays in summer.

BritRail Flexipass

The Flexipass allows the traveler the same unlimited access to the British Rail network as the regular BritRail Pass, with these differences: The Flexipass is available only for either 8 days or for 15 days. The 8-day Flexipass can be used for any 4 nonconsecutive days. The 15-day Flexipass can be used for any 8 nonconsecutive days of travel out of 15. The 8-day pass costs $210 in first class, $149 in economy. Children 5 to 15 are charged $105 first class, $75 economy. Seniors pay $180 first class, and youths 16 through 25 pay $129 to travel economy class. The 15-day Flexipass costs $310 first class, $219 economy. For children, the charges are $155 first class, $110 economy. First class for seniors is $270, and economy class for youths is $189.

With Flexipass, you get your money's worth. For example, to travel to York and Bath from London without the pass would cost at least $154 in economy class, round trip. However, for only $149, the 8-day BritRail Flexipass buys 4 whole days of rail travel to any destination you choose.

Remember, you cannot purchase your Flexipass in Great Britain. You must secure it from either your travel agent or from BritRail Travel International in the U.S.

Capital Travel Pak

The Capital Travel Pak is a package offered by BritRail for purchase before you leave home, to let you see all the best of London and take easy rail trips to many nearby attractions for four days or a full week. The package combines a four- or seven-day rail pass with a four- or seven-day London Visitor Travelcard (see "Transportation in Greater London," Chapter III). The four-day Travel Pak costs $99 for adults, $60 for children 5 to 15. The price of a seven-day package is $129 for adults, $65 for children 5 to 15. The passes and Travelcards are for consecutive days from the day of validation. Gatwick or Heathrow Airport transfers are included.

Special Bargain Fares

British Rail from time to time offers special round-trip fares for optional travel and weekend travel that may only be purchased in Great Britain. Because of the changing nature of these fares and facilities, it is not possible to give information about them to travelers from abroad. Information may be obtained from travel agents and British Rail stations in Great Britain.

If you're in London and want more information on transportation rates, schedules, or facilities, go to the **British Travel Centre,** Rex House, 4-12 Lower Regent St., S.W.1 (tel. 01/730-3400), only a few minutes' walk from Piccadilly Circus. This office deals only with inquiries made in person. Don't try to telephone for information. The office is open from 9 a.m. to 6:30 p.m. Monday to Saturday, and from 10 a.m. to 4:30 p.m. Sunday. You can also make reservations and purchase rail tickets there and at the British Travel Centres at Oxford Street, Victoria Station, the Strand, King William Street, Heathrow Airport, and the main London stations— Waterloo, King's Cross, Euston, Victoria, and Paddington—where each deals mainly with its own region. For general information, call the appropriate station. All numbers are listed in the telephone directory.

The Britainshrinkers

This is a bonanza for travelers who want to make several quick trips into the heart of England without having to check out of their hotel room in London. Scheduled full-day tours are offered from April 1 to October 31, as well as several overnight excursions into Scotland and Wales. The journeys are operated by British Rail. You're whisked out of London by train to your destination, where you hop on a waiting bus to visit the various sights during the day. You have a light lunch in a local pub, and there is also free time to shop or explore. A guide accompanies the tour from London and back. Your return is in time for dinner or the theater. Included in the rates are entrance fees and VAT.

On a one-day trip, you can visit Warwick Castle, Stratford-upon-Avon, and Coventry Cathedral at a cost of $79 for adults, $63 for children up to 16 years old, but holders of BritRail Passes pay only $56 for adults, $51 for children. One of the most heavily booked tours is to Bath and Stonehenge, taking in Salisbury Cathedral, costing $79 for adults and $62 for children for regular tickets, and $51 for adults and $46 for children for BritRail Pass holders.

CAR RENTALS

Once you get over the initial awkwardness of driving on the left-hand side of the road, you will quickly discover that the best way to see the real Britain is to have a car while you're there. There is, quite simply, no substitute for the freedom and flexibility that only your own vehicle can provide.

Partly because of the huge number of visitors to the United Kingdom, the British car-rental market is among the most competitive in all of Europe, with many different companies bidding avidly for the U.S.-based business. The company that you eventually select will depend on your age and the category of car you're seeking.

For example, younger drivers usually gravitate to **Hertz** because that company allows 18-year-old drivers to rent its less expensive cars if they present a credit card in their own name. Drivers must be 21 at **Avis** and 23 at Budget.

In overall pricing, however, in the small and medium-size categories, **Budget Rent-a-Car** is usually the least expensive choice. For example, Budget's Fiat Panda (a small car suitable for two passengers and a modest amount of luggage) costs, as of this writing, £79 ($138.25) a week with unlimited mileage. Similar or comparable cars at Avis and Hertz rent for £91 ($159.25) and £98 ($171.50), respectively. Budget tends to be the most competitively priced in the medium-size market as well. However, as the size, power, accessories, and extra features of rental vehicles increase, the price advantages at all three major chains become blurred.

In brief, it's best to shop around, compare prices, and have a clear idea of your automotive needs before you reserve a car. All three companies give the best rates to clients who reserve at least two business days in advance and who agree to return the car to its point of origin. It is also an advantage to keep the car for at least one week, as opposed to three or four days. Be warned that all car rentals in the U.K. attach a 15% extra government tax.

When you reserve a car, ask about the availability of a 24-hour-a-day number within Britain that you can call for emergency assistance if your vehicle breaks down.

For reservations and information, you can call either of the major players by dialing the following toll-free numbers from within the U.S.: Budget at 800/527-0700, Avis at 800/331-2112, and Hertz at 800/654-3001.

A less well known car-rental company, which enjoys strong sales in the U.K., is **Kenning Car Rental,** affiliated in North America with General Rent-a-Car. This company sometimes offers attractive promotional rates that merit a second look. For reservations and information, contact their Florida sales office by dialing toll free 800/227-8990.

Car Insurance

With the rise in inflation and a staggering increase in the cost of car repairs, the price of insurance premiums is on the rise worldwide. Several years ago, far more insurance protection was automatically factored into the average car-rental contract. Today, however, many benefits have been decreased, and it's more important than ever to purchase additional insurance to avoid financial liability in the event of an accident.

In other words, it pays to ask questions—lots of them—before renting a car. You can purchase an optional collision damage waiver at each of the major car-rental companies for around £10 ($17.50) a day. Without it, you might be responsible for up to the full cost of the eventual repairs to the vehicle. Considering the unfamiliarity of driving on the left, different road practices, and roads that tend to be narrow and sometimes thickly congested, I consider the purchase of a waiver to be almost essential. Additional personal accident insurance (which covers unforeseen medical costs in the event of an accident) costs around £2 ($3.60) a day.

Driving Requirements

To drive a car in Britain, your passport and your own driver's license must be presented with your deposit; no special British license is needed. The prudent driver will secure a copy of the *British Highway Code,* available from almost any stationer or news agent.

Although not mandatory, a membership in one of the two major auto clubs in England can be helpful: the **Automobile Association** and the **Royal Automobile Club.** The headquarters of the AA are at Fanum House, Basingstoke, Hampshire RG21 2EA (tel. 0256/20123); the RAC offices are in London at RAC House, Landsdowne Road, Croydon, Surrey CR9 2JA (tel. 01/686-2525). Membership in one of these clubs is usually handled by the agent from whom you rent your car. Upon joining, you'll be given a key to the many telephone boxes you see along the road, so that you can phone for help in an emergency.

Warning: Pedestrian crossings are marked by striped lines (zebra striping) on the road. Also, flashing lights near the curb indicate that drivers must yield the right of way if a pedestrian has stepped out into the zebra zone to cross the street.

Wearing seat belts is mandatory in the British Isles.

Fuel

Gasoline, called petrol by the British, is usually sold by the liter, with 4.5 liters making up their imperial gallon. Most pumps show a list of prices and measures. The prices, incidentally, will be much higher than you are used to paying. You'll probably have to serve yourself at the petrol station. In some remote areas, especially in Scotland, stations are few and far between, and many all over the country are closed on Sunday.

BUSES IN ENGLAND

For the traveler who wants to see the country as even a train cannot reveal it but who can't afford to rent a car or doesn't trust his or her driving skills on British roads, the old, reliable, and inexpensive (about half the cost of rail travel) bus, or "coach" as it's called here, offers a fine form of transportation. While the trains do go everywhere, passing through towns and villages, they rarely bring you into contact with country life, and they almost never carry you across the high (main) streets of the villages, as the buses do. Moreover, distances between towns in England are usually short, so your chances of tiring are lessened. Every remote village is reachable by bus.

The **express motorcoach network,** operated by National and Scottish Citylink Coaches, covers the greater part of Britain. It links many villages and most towns and cities with frequent schedules, convenient timetables, and efficient operation in all seasons. Most places off the main route can be easily reached by stopping and switching to a local bus. Fares are relatively cheap, making travel on the express motorcoach network economical.

The departure point from London for most of the bus lines is **Victoria Coach Station,** 164 Buckingham Palace Rd., S.W.1 (tel. 01/730-0202), which is a block up from Victoria Railroad Station. You need reservations for some express buses. The locals can usually be boarded on the spot.

Britexpress Card

This offers one-third off all adult journey tickets purchased on Britain's Express Coach Network of National Express and Scottish Citylink coaches, valid for a

30-day period throughout the year. You may travel where and when you wish with a choice of 1,500 destinations. All it costs is £9 ($15.75). The Britexpress Card can be purchased from your U.S. travel agent or on your arrival in London at Victoria Coach Station at 164 Buckingham Palace Rd., S.W.1 (tel. 01/730-0202). Examples of some approximate one-way fares and travel times are: London to Edinburgh (Cordon Bleu service), £17 ($29.75), time 7 hours, 45 minutes; London to Stratford-upon-Avon, £9 ($15.75), time 3 hours, 5 minutes; London to York (Rapide service), £16 ($28), time 4 hours, 20 minutes; London to Cambridge, £6 ($10.50), time 1 hour, 50 minutes. Travel tickets can be purchased in the United Kingdom from 2,500 agents nationwide.

Tourist Trail Pass

This provides unlimited travel on the nationwide National Express and Scottish Citylink bus network and is available for five, eight, 15, 22, or 30 days. Prices start at £48 ($84), with a one-third discount for senior citizens and children. The pass can be purchased as for the Britexpress Card (above).

Other Bus Service

For journeys within a roughly 35-mile radius of London, including such major attractions as Windsor, Hampton Court, Chartwell, and Hatfield House, try the **Green Line** bus service. Personal callers can go to the Green Line Enquiry Office at Eccleston Bridge, Victoria, London, S.W.1 (off Buckingham Palace Road), or phone 01/668-7261 for more information.

Golden Rover tickets cost £4.50 ($7.90) per person, and they are available for one day's travel on most London Country and Green Line routes, but not their Jetlink and Flightline buses connecting London and the airports. It is possible to cover quite a large area around London and into the country for a very small cost. For more precise information on routes, fares, and schedules, write to **Green Line Travel Ltd.,** Lesbourne Road, Reigate, Surrey RH2 7LE (tel. 01/668-7261). The Country Bus Lines ring the heart of London. They never go into the center of the capital, although they hook up with the routes of the red buses and the Green Line coaches that do.

BICYCLES

If you choose this form of transportation, you may want to join the **Cyclists' Touring Club,** Cotterell House, 69 Meadrow, Godalming, Surrey GU7 3HS (tel. 04868/7217). It costs £17.50 ($30.65) to join, with membership being good for one year. The club helps with information and provides maps, insurance, touring routes, and a list of low-cost accommodations, including farmhouses, inns, guesthouses, and even private homes that cater especially to cyclists.

MOTORCYCLES

These are real money-savers in this land of steep petrol (gas) prices, if you don't mind getting drenched occasionally. **Scootabout Limited,** 59 Albert Embankment, S.E.1 (tel. 01/582-0055), just a minute's walk from the Vauxhall Underground station, is the only motorcycle-rental company in London insured to rent to North Americans. They can also arrange for European travel on their vehicles. You can pick up a Moped by the day, week, or month. These are four-stroke, fully automatic motors with a kick-start and a twist throttle grip. They get more than 150 miles to the gallon, and prices are inclusive of VAT, insurance, helmet rental, and carrier, as well as unlimited mileage and RAC membership. A Moped costs £10.95 ($19.15) for the day, decreasing to £7.80 ($13.75) per day on a weekly rental. For vehicles from 125cc (cubic centimeters) to 750cc, renters must possess valid motorcycle licenses from their own countries. A £50 ($87.50) deposit is required for vehicles of 50cc, 70cc, and 125cc. A £100 ($175) deposit is required for vehicles of

200cc, 500cc, and 750cc. The deposit is refunded on a no-damage-done return of the vehicle.

BACKPACKING

For those who prefer to rely on their own two legs and savor the countryside at close quarters, the **Backpackers' Club,** P.O. Box 381, 7-10 Friar St., Reading, Berkshire RG3 4RL (tel. STD-04917/739), has information concerning the main routes—along Offa's Dyke, the border between England and Wales, the North and South Downs Ways, and the Pennine Way through the Yorkshire Dales and across Hadrian's Wall, to name only a few. You can write to them at the above address.

HITCHHIKING

It is not illegal in Britain and is normally quite safe and practical. It is, however, illegal for pedestrians to be on motorways. The cleaner and tidier you look, the better your chance. Have a sign with your destination written on it. It helps, of course, not to be overloaded with backpacks and luggage.

WHERE TO GO

It takes weeks to tour England thoroughly, and many readers do just that, either by car, train, or bus. However, others are much more rushed and will need to direct their limited sightseeing time carefully. **London** is targeted at the top of every first-time visitor's list. Even those on the most rushed of schedules generally fit in **Windsor Castle,** lying about an hour's train ride from central London. For many, that's it. Then they're off to Paris or other places on the continent.

However, those with more time will want to go to the south of England, the very cradle of English history, centering their exploration around the cathedral city of **Canterbury**, some 65 miles to the southeast of London. It can be done on a rushed day trip. I'd suggest two nights there, however: one day for Canterbury, another day for exploring some of the historic homes of Kent, including Knole, a showplace of England lying in the village of Sevenoaks, about 25 miles from Central London, and Churchill's home, Chartwell, 1½ miles south of Westerham. Those with yet a third night to spend in the south can go to **Rye,** the old Cinque port near the English Channel, 65 miles south of London.

The second most popular jaunt is to **Stratford-upon-Avon** and the university city of **Oxford.** At the very minimum this should take up to two nights. The first night can be spent at Oxford, 57 miles northwest of London, and the second night at Stratford-upon-Avon, 40 miles northwest from Oxford, a total distance of 92 miles from London. Those with one or two more nights to spend in Stratford-upon-Avon can use it as a base for day trips to Warwick Castle, Kenilworth Castle, Sulgrave Manor (ancestral home of George Washington), and Coventry Cathedral.

My favorite tour—and perhaps yours too—might be to the fabled **West Country** of England, taking in Winchester, Salisbury, the New Forest, and the old spa at Bath. Bath is considered by many to be the most outstanding place to visit in the west of England. Your first night can be spent in Salisbury, which is a base for exploring the prehistoric ruins of Stonehenge on the Salisbury Plain. Salisbury is an 83-mile drive from London. From Salisbury, you can head north to Bath, that Georgian city on a bend of the River Avon, a distance of some 115 miles from London.

After that, those with three or four days remaining can either head southwest of Bath, taking in Devon and Cornwall, perhaps the single two most charming counties of England, or can head north to the Cotswolds, the rolling hills and old wool towns that always seem to enchant. I've left out the Lake District, Cambridge, East Anglia, the cathedral city of York, and many, many more places. But that's what this book is about. As I said, it will take weeks.

MILEAGE BETWEEN CITIES AND TOWNS

From \ To	Birmingham	Blackpool	Bournemouth	Brighton	Bristol	Cambridge	Carlisle	Dover	Exeter	Gloucester	Land's End	Leeds	Leicester	Lincoln	Liverpool	LONDON	Norwich	Nottingham	Oxford	Plymouth	Portsmouth	Sheffield	Shrewsbury	Southampton	York
Berwick-upon-Tweed	264	193	412	390	352	294	89	409	428	318	552	156	252	224	175	337	329	258	329	474	401	203	265	388	148
Birmingham																									
Blackpool	121																								
Bournemouth	147	270																							
Brighton	163	286	92																						
Bristol	81	204	82	137																					
Cambridge	100	208	154	106	144																				
Carlisle	196	154	353	353	277	264																			
Dover	176	297	174	82	200	125	372																		
Exeter	157	174	82	166	76	220	353	248																	
Gloucester	56	82	133	76	35	123	237	180	111																
Great Yarmouth	180	252	241	191	248	82	309	180	297	205															
Harwich	167	176	191	120	220	67	336	135	248	178															
Kingston-upon-Hull	152	127	282	233	231	158	158	277	309	198															
Land's End	281	405	205	289	198	334	477	366	123	235															
Leeds	113	72	260	260	206	145	119	270	270	159	394														
Leicester	39	140	158	171	136	68	206	202	196	85	320	68													
Lincoln	90	128	209	202	178	85	181	202	247	128	371	68	51												
Liverpool	93	49	234	256	161	168	120	273	237	126	320	75	100	118											
LONDON	105	234	100	54	121	54	301	71	172	109	287	196	97	131	202										
Newcastle upon Tyne	207	129	347	345	288	230	57	345	364	253	488	92	187	159	155	274									
Norwich	166	232	214	161	223	57	289	174	287	186	421	176	119	100	202	114									
Nottingham	50	111	183	168	155	83	181	221	202	110	345	70	25	35	98	114	122								
Oxford	64	187	99	83	74	83	260	126	142	52	274	168	73	124	150	57	145	98							
Plymouth	203	328	128	212	123	263	399	289	46	157	89	316	242	293	234	218	355	274	181						
Portsmouth	191	264	31	48	99	124	337	152	118	108	303	244	150	201	218	70	174	186	70	150					
Sheffield	76	86	211	211	163	120	152	230	237	126	361	33	62	46	72	159	166	37	135	283	234				
Shrewsbury	45	98	185	179	82	145	176	221	179	79	303	109	84	117	58	150	205	82	106	225	185	82			
Southampton	128	251	31	61	77	131	324	143	105	93	228	232	137	188	221	77	193	162	64	151	21	199	170		
York	130	96	269	245	211	150	121	264	287	176	411	24	108	75	99	193	181	77	181	333	258	58	133	245	

BARGAIN SIGHTSEEING TIP

If you plan to do extensive sightseeing in Britain, consider the **Great Britain Heritage Pass**. Information about it can be obtained by calling 01/846-9000. The pass grants you entrance to 600 properties within the country, including Edinburgh Castle, Churchill's Chartwell, Woburn Abbey, Hampton Court Palace, and Windsor Castle. The ticket covers all properties in care of the National Trust and those run by the Department of the Environment. It is estimated that anyone visiting as many as five of these sightseeing attractions will get back the initial outlay of £16 ($28) for a 15-day pass and £24 ($42) for a one-month pass. In the United States you can purchase this pass at any branch office of British Airways or its specially appointed travel agents. In Great Britain, it can be purchased at any tourist office in the country.

TOURS

Many questions arise for persons planning their first trip to the British Isles as well as to other European destinations. Sometimes a prospective traveler isn't sure what he or she really wants to see in England, aside, of course, from the Tower of London and Big Ben. Troublesome thoughts that arise often are: How do I plan my trip to be sure of seeing the most outstanding sights of the country? How much of a problem will I have in trying to get from place to place, complete with luggage? Am I too old to embark on such a journey, perhaps alone? Will I meet people who share my interests with whom to chat and compare notes?

My answer to all these questions, indeed, my advice to many people going to England and/or other European countries for the first time is simply: Go on a good tour. By this I don't mean simply a tour of one city or of one building. I refer to a vacation tour where you and your needs will be looked after from your arrival at Heathrow or Gatwick in England or wherever to your departure en route back to the United States. Choose a tour suited to the time you have for your trip, the money you can spend, and the places you want to go. Check with your travel agent for the latest and most appealing offers.

INTRODUCING ENGLAND

1. THE ENGLISH
2. THE CULTURE
3. FOOD AND DRINK
4. ALTERNATIVE AND SPECIAL-INTEREST TRAVEL
5. THE ABCs OF ENGLAND

Why go to England? This is an easy and difficult question to answer. Millions of words have been written by some of the world's greatest writers who share my conviction that among all the countries of the world that one needs to savor and explore in a lifetime, England ranks near the top. I must speak of my own indelible enthusiasm. I have cultural roots in the heritage of England—as do many other readers of this book—but my affection for England goes beyond my own "roots." In fact, many of the world's greatest Anglophiles have no ancestral link to England at all.

The cultural side of England is a powerful lure. These islanders have shaped much of the character and customs of the world and have given it a great language. This in itself is surprising, since the English live in a cramped space and lack many natural resources. Perhaps for that very reason, they learned early to rely on a special resource: their wits.

Fortunately for latter-day pilgrims to England, the years and centuries have left a clear trail of former glory. Traveling around the country is similar to experiencing a living, illustrated history book. This is true whether you stop and ponder over the ancient mystery of Stonehenge, relive the days of the Romans when you walk through an excavated villa, hear the influence of the Celtic language in the accent of the Cornish people, or witness evidence of the cultures brought by the Danes, the Normans, the Germans, and now the Americans and Canadians. I find it amazing how these islanders have handled the outside forces brought to bear on them. In their own way and in their own time, they have absorbed them and made them distinctly English.

There is so much to thrill you. You can stand in the inner courtyard of the Tower of London and see where Lady Jane Grey was beheaded, or you can walk through Westminster Abbey, treading on the stone grave-markers of such unforgettable men as Disraeli, Newton, Darwin, Chaucer, and Kipling. You can visit the homes of many of the legendary figures of literary history, including Samuel Johnson, Charles Dickens, William Shakespeare, and Emily Brontë. Attending an English court of law will give you a firsthand experience with one of the greatest systems of justice the world has ever known. The country's innumerable museums bring you quickly in touch with history-making events of the past. You can see and almost feel the treasures (or plundered loot, as critics have called it) from Greece and Egypt, and the important documents of musical, literary, and political figures. Here are the early Bibles, the Magna Carta, and the personal letters of Shelley. Here in England are two of the world's foremost universities, Oxford and Cambridge, which can be visited for a view of that unique educational system that has produced some of the world's greatest leaders and thinkers.

You will like the convenience of seeing so much in such a small area. America has treasures of history and geography, but the vastness of the United States can make it a lifetime project to visit them all. But in England, as you travel through fishing hamlets, villages, country lanes, and cathedral cities, in an hour you can have moved into a different region. For one thing, this is an island of widely varying geography, from the mountainous Lake District, the rolling hills of the Cotswolds, the Holland-like canals in Lincoln, and the marsh areas of the Norfolk Broads, to the moody Lorna Doone country with its rugged hills and coastline.

England is marked by fascinating building styles, from the most imposing and romantic of moated castles to splendid country manor houses with their highly cultivated gardens, to churches and cathedrals that are an art in themselves. The architecture of England is a direct reflection of its inner spirit. Soaring Gothic-arched churches with their stained-glass windows have been erected in nearly every city. People living in the country have built houses native to their surroundings that are sheer perfection in their combination of beauty and utility, be it a thatched cottage in a flower-filled lane in Devon or a half-timbered house in Stratford-upon-Avon.

Whether you're sports-oriented or a more contemplative traveler, you'll find the English calendar loaded with events. You can attend one of the Bard's plays at Stratford-upon-Avon, go on a canal ride through the Midlands, take a trip on a houseboat, or spend a week at a farm in the West Country, riding over hills and dales, perhaps joining a fox hunt. There is boat racing to watch at Cambridge and Henley-on-Thames, or you can walk across a Yorkshire moor. You can sample true English fare at hundreds of ancient inns and pubs or visit one of the stately homes of England, later strolling through spectacular gardens (the English, as the world knows, are great gardeners). Perhaps a swim in one of the hidden coves on the Cornish coast will lead you into a summer day. Whatever your interests or desires, England can usually accommodate you.

Best of all are the English people themselves. Like all the peoples of the world, they have their share of devils, but you are likely to be surprised by the warmth and graciousness of the average man or woman. Added to this is their amazing variety of artistic accomplishment—not only in their literature, but in their art, as exemplified by the sculpture of Henry Moore. The theater of London is stimulating and refreshing. You'll want to attend concerts, festivals, even country fairs, and you'll find that both the ballet and opera are alive, vital, and worth experiencing. You'll be intrigued by the English fascination with their sports—with cricket, football, racing, tennis, skating, sailing, hockey, or hiking.

Certainly, you won't be able to do everything in just one trip. You'll want to come back for a second, a third, and most definitely a fourth visit.

1. The English

The British Isles have been a melting pot of races since prehistoric times, as attested by artifacts and traces of settlements.

HISTORY

Until about 6,000 years before Christ, Britain was probably part of the continent of Europe. It was split off by the continental drift and other natural forces, but even after the split people on the mainland could look across to what was now a big island. Pressed by marauders from the east or simply seeking living room for their increasing tribes, some brave souls made their way across the often wild waters of the channel. Some came, too, simply seeking plunder.

The earliest inhabitants of the British Isles—of whom archeologists are certain were a small, dark people known as the Iberians, also called pre-Celts. They are believed to have created Stonehenge before 500 B.C., when the early Celts, who were blond and often blue-eyed, poured in from the coastal areas of Europe, settling from Denmark to northern Italy. The Iberians who survived the bloody assaults of these invaders fled to the Scottish Highlands and the mountain fastnesses of Wales, where some of their descendants live today.

In 54 B.C., the Romans, led by Julius Caesar, invaded Britain, where they believed they would find precious metals. The land was heavily wooded from the south of what is today England to the north coast of Scotland, with treeless areas around marshes and on hills and moors. The Britons resisted the onslaught of Roman troops but lacked the leadership and war experience to prevent the takeover. The Romans took all of the southern part of the island, from the Cheviot Hills in Scotland to the English Channel, and added it to the Roman Empire by A.D. 43. During almost four centuries of occupation, they built roads, villas, towns, walls, and fortresses, farmed the land, and introduced first their pagan religions and then Christianity. Agriculture and trade flourished, and the lives of the people were lastingly influenced.

After the withdrawal of the Roman legions around A.D. 410, waves of Jutes, Angles, and Saxons flocked in from German lands, establishing themselves in small "kingdoms" throughout the formerly Roman colony. From the 8th through the 11th centuries, the newcomers came into conflict with Danish raiders for control of the land.

The Battle of Hastings in 1066, when William the Conqueror invaded from Normandy and defeated the last Anglo-Saxon king, Harold, has probably become familiar to almost every American schoolchild.

The Norman rulers were on the throne from 1066 to 1154, when the first of the Plantagenets, Henry II (that "friend" of Thomas à Becket), was crowned. That line held power until 1399. During this period, in 1215 King John was forced by his nobles to sign the Magna Carta, guaranteeing rights and the rule of law, and laying the foundations of the parliamentary system.

In 1399, the Lancastrians took the throne. Their reign was marked by defeat in the Hundred Years' War, in which they tried to cement claims to lands in France. Opposing the Lancastrians at home and wanting the crown also was the House of York. Dissension between these claimants led to the War of the Roses, the red rose representing Lancaster and the white rose York. By 1461, the House of York had seized power, but the war continued. It was during this time that the boy king, Edward V, and his younger brother were murdered in the Tower of London, a crime still laid by some at the door of their uncle, Richard III, who later became king.

In 1485, Richard III was slain at the Battle of Bosworth Field, ending the War of the Roses and placing the first Tudor on the throne. That king, Henry VII, was followed by his son, Henry VIII, whose daughter, Elizabeth I, eventually succeeded to the crown. Henry VII curbed the powers of the barons, established reforms of the legal system, gave more importance to the landed gentry, and improved England's economic situation. Henry VIII's excesses and exploits are well known: He married six times, and he split with the Roman Catholic church, establishing the Church of England. Of his wives, two were beheaded, two were set aside, one died in childbirth, and one survived him. The dissolution of the monasteries brought the riches of the abbots and bishops pouring into the coffers of Henry and his associates, and the property formerly owned by the church was placed mostly in lay hands.

Elizabeth I managed to walk a risky line between Catholic and Protestant dissidents but held to the latter faith. During her reign England became a major naval power, defeating the Spanish Armada, founding the first colonies in the New World, and establishing a vigorous trade with the Orient and Europe. Also, Scotland was united with England, and the son of Mary Queen of Scots came to the throne as James I of England and James VI of Scotland.

Thus ended the Tudor dynasty. The Stuarts came to power in the year 1603, holding it until Charles I was beheaded in 1649. During this era, the *Mayflower* sailed for the New World, and dissatisfaction with the established Church of England, as well as with what many saw as Papist leanings by the monarchs, created a time of great stress in England. Parliament and the Stuart kings came into conflict, resulting in a bloody civil war between Parliamentarian troops led by Oliver Cromwell and Royalists who were on the side of King Charles. The Royalists lost the war, the king lost his head, and in 1649 the Puritan Commonwealth was established, with Cromwell as Lord Protector.

The Commonwealth lasted until 1660, when Stuart King Charles II came to the throne. The monarchy was restored, but troubles still beset the people of the country. The Great Plague wiped out thousands of lives in 1665–1666, and the Great Fire destroyed large portions of London in 1666.

In 1688, the so-called Glorious Revolution removed Catholic King James II from the throne and crowned in his place William of Orange and his wife, Mary, James's daughter. A Bill of Rights was signed by the monarchs, settling once and for all the question that had been at the very root of the Civil War: the king was king by will of Parliament, not by divine right from God.

The Hanoverian dynasty came into power in 1727. Britain had many ups and downs under the House of Hanover. Canada was won from the French, the British Indian Empire was firmly entrenched through the redoubtable Clive of India, the Boston Tea Party marked the start of the American Revolution, Captain Cook claimed Australia and New Zealand for England, and the British became embroiled in the Napoleonic Wars. This was a time of glory for two of the country's great leaders: Admiral Lord Horatio Nelson and the Duke of Wellington, the one at Trafalgar and the other at Waterloo.

Perhaps the single most important change in all this period, from the point of view of the "commoner," was the Industrial Revolution, which transformed forever the lives of the laboring class and brought great wealth to persons of the middle class. Comparatively, the loss of the American colonies probably had little effect on the day-by-day pursuits of the average English person.

The reign of Queen Victoria, which began in 1837, saw great progress in the country. Trade unions were formed, a universal public school system was developed, industrialization and urbanization spread, and railroads swept to almost every section of the British Isles. So impressed was Parliament with the glories of the empire that it declared Victoria empress, not just queen, reigning over large parts of Africa and Asia. When Edward VII succeeded to the throne in 1901, the country entered the 20th century with the advent of the telephone and the motorcar, which again changed the lifestyle and thinking of everybody.

In 1910, the Windsors took the sovereignty, leading the nation through World War I (George V), the abdication before his coronation of the man who would have been King Edward VIII (he became the Duke of Windsor in order to marry the American divorcée, Wallis Simpson), and on through World War II (George VI).

During these years came the blitz, the Dunkirk evacuation in 1941, and the successful D-Day operation that placed the Allies firmly on the road to defeating Hitler. These events have been kept alive through documentaries, movies, and the memories of those who participated. Winston Churchill had his finest hour as prime minister in those perilous times.

Queen Elizabeth II came to the throne after the death of her father in 1952. Since then, Britain has joined the NATO alliance and the Common Market—and Big Ben still chimes the hours outside the Houses of Parliament.

GOVERNMENT

The United Kingdom of Great Britain and Northern Ireland (that's its name), comprises England, Wales, Scotland, and Northern Ireland. It is governed by a constitutional monarchy, the head of state being Queen Elizabeth II. The head of government, however, is the prime minister, who is selected by the majority party in Parliament but is then requested by the queen to form a government, i.e., to take charge and name cabinet members to head the various branches of that government.

Parliament is technically three separate entities: the sovereign, the House of Lords, and the House of Commons. The "government" consists of the prime minister and the cabinet members (who must be members of Parliament). The queen's function is chiefly ceremonial. There are two main political parties, Conservative and Labour. The Conservatives present themselves as champions of free enterprise and freedom of the individual to make his or her own decisions, with some government support. Labour tends toward more state ownership and control, with the state providing a good deal of support for the individual. The Liberals and the Social Democrat Party have joined in an uneasy alliance to form the Social Democratic and Liberal Party, which is beginning to have some impact.

---

2. The Culture

The English are a hospitable people, happy to share their music, art, literature, and other cultural benefits with people who come from what was, after all, once a colonial possession of Great Britain (and Canada still is a member of the Commonwealth). With no language barrier—except for a dialect now and then—this is an opportunity for great cultural experiences.

LITERATURE

The most outstanding figure of all in England's literary tapestry is—who dare say me nay?—William Shakespeare (1564–1616). But if England had had no Shakespeare, that tapestry would still be a rich and glowing panoply of artists with words—oral, written, sung, in poetry, in prose, in drama. From the Old English epic poem *Beowulf,* almost surely the result of centuries of verse recited down the ages by tribal bards, to the works of the post–World War II "angry young men," English literature is vast.

Old English poetry and prose yielded to the language now called Middle English, in which the culture and tongue of the Normans enriched the speaking and writing of the old Anglo-Saxon language. Middle English was used by philosophers, historians, and romance writers from the 13th and 14th centuries. Greatest of the writers of this period was Geoffrey Chaucer, whose *Canterbury Tales* is masterfully told. The literary highlight of the 15th century was *Morte d'Arthur,* Sir Thomas Malory's epic based on the legend of King Arthur and his court. Ballads were also popular storytelling devices in that century, a sort of continuation of the bardic epic tradition.

During the Tudor era, stars in the literary sky were Sir Thomas More *(Utopia),* Edmund Spenser *(The Faerie Queen),* and Christopher Marlowe *(The Tragical History of Dr. Faustus).* It was in this era that the sonnet form was adopted from an Italian verse model, attracting as users a number of poets, such as Sir Philip Sidney and the greatest of them all, Shakespeare (remember "Shall I compare thee to a summer's day"?).

With the coming to the throne of the Stuarts came "Rare Ben Jonson," writer of satirical comedies and leader of poets who met at the Mermaid Tavern in London, and John Donne ("Never send to know for whom the bell tolls . . . "). It was during this time that the great translation of the Bible under the auspices of King James I, called the King James Bible, took its immortal position in literature. During this Jacobean period, the Cavalier poets, of whom Robert Herrick heads the list, wrote romantic verse and backed the king against Cromwell and Parliament.

The literary giant of the mid-17th century was John Milton, a pro-Parliamentarian who was also considered one of the country's great geniuses. In view of *Paradise Lost,* who will argue? This was a period—during the Commonwealth—when many writers were imbued with Puritanism, resulting in some rather dull reading. A memorable exception was John Bunyan (*Pilgrim's Progress*), who was imprisoned for his pains after the restoration of the monarchy but whose powerful writing transcends theological differences. After Charles II was returned to the throne, theaters closed by Cromwell reopened and literature took on a lighter and more lively tone, as reflected in such works as the famous *Diary* of Samuel Pepys.

Through the 18th century, the literary world of England was crowded with the output of geniuses and near-geniuses from the rising middle class, much of whose work was aimed at social reform. Among these were Daniel Defoe (*Robinson Crusoe* and *Moll Flanders*), Alexander Pope (*An Essay on Man*), and a host of essayists and novelists—Henry Fielding (*Tom Jones*), Samuel Richardson (*Pamela*), and a number of others. Most memorable of this period, however, is Samuel Johnson, whose *Dictionary of the English Language* made him England's premier lexicographer and man of letters, and whose *Rasselas* speaks to readers as well now as it did then. His association with James Boswell from Scotland resulted in Johnson's becoming a major figure in literary annals, albeit through Boswell's writings. In Dr. Johnson's circle of close friends was another notable literary figure of the time, Oliver Goldsmith.

To enter into a dissertation on the 19th-century literary scene in England and to try to expound on the stars in that galaxy in limited space would be to bog down utterly. So I'll just mention several names known to everyone who has ever studied literature in school: William Blake, William Wordsworth, Samuel Taylor Coleridge, George Gordon (Lord) Byron, John Keats, Percy Bysshe Shelley, Jane Austen, and Charles Lamb—but there are so many more. As you travel through the country, you will see birthplaces, familiar haunts, habitations, and burial places of many such writers.

Now to a period that challenges a student of literature—the Victorian. The great middle class had learned to read, printing was flourishing, and the union of these forces produced a literary thrust that took the country at a gallop into the 20th century. In this letters-rich age, readers devoured the works of Charles Dickens, William Makepeace Thackeray, the Brontë sisters, Matthew Arnold, Alfred Lord Tennyson, the Brownings, Lewis Carroll, George Eliot, George Meredith, Thomas Hardy, and Algernon Charles Swinburne, with a little heavier reading from John Ruskin thrown in.

Coming at the turn of the century, but usually considered literary figures of modern times, are such notables as Rudyard Kipling, H. G. Wells, John Galsworthy, Arnold Bennett, Somerset Maugham, A. E. Houseman, and Walter de la Mare. Among the better known writers of the 20th century are Robert Graves, Stephen Spender, W. H. Auden, Rupert Brooke, Siegfried Sassoon, Virginia Woolf, D. H. Lawrence, Evelyn Waugh, Aldous Huxley, Kingsley Amis, J. B. Priestley, Graham Greene, George Orwell, E. M. Forster, A. A. Milne, Noël Coward, Daphne du Maurier, Nancy Mitford, C. P. Snow, Antonia Fraser, Norah Lofts, and not to be forgotten, Winston Churchill. Although the literary merit of the many British writers we could name varies, they all provide "a good read," as the British say.

In this category—good reads—are some of the best mystery and suspense novels to be found. From these you can learn about life in England from cottages to castles, in the cities and in the remote country, in the past and in the present, and a lot about the police and the crime scene from even before the Bow Street Runners to today's New Scotland Yard. Ellis Peters makes you feel at home at Shrewsbury in the 12th century, Dorothy Sayers places you in the fen country in the 1920s, and Agatha Christie brings to life village atmosphere in Miss Marple's St. Mary Mead. There are many other writers of this ilk, such as P. D. James, E. X. Ferrars, and Ruth Rendell, whose stories, whether you're a mystery fan or not, can enrich your visit to England by giving you a personal word tour of all the country.

I could, of course, go on and still manage to leave out your favorite English writer. In fact, I'm sure someone will ask, "But what about Jonathan Swift? George Bernard Shaw? Sir Walter Scott? Robert Burns? Robert Louis Stevenson? Oscar Wilde? Joseph Conrad? Dylan Thomas?" My answer is that although these novelists and poets are usually included and indeed made their mark in "English" literature, they are not English-born, being from Ireland, Scotland, Wales, or elsewhere, and I have tried to keep this within the limitations of literary figures of England. Even Sir Arthur Conan Doyle, creator of that quintessential Londoner, Sherlock Holmes, was born in Edinburgh.

No question about it—the British Isles are rich in literary greats, and I've only reminded you of *some* of them.

MUSIC

From the time the English monks' choirs surpassed those of Germany and France in singing the Gregorian chant (brought to this country by St. Augustine, Pope Gregory's missionary) and were judged second only to the choirs of Rome, music has been heard throughout England. Polyphonic music developed after the simple chant, and sacred vocal music was early accompanied by the organ. The first organ at Winchester was installed in the 10th century. One of the earliest written compositions was a polyphonic piece (a round), *Sumer is icumen in,* with six parts.

Instruments commonly used in the Middle Ages, besides the organ found only in churches, were the fiddle, the lute, and the rebeck, used in court circles for the entertainment of royalty and hangers-on. Kings had musicians at court through the Plantagenets and into the time of the Tudors, with Henry VIII in particular making himself known as a composer. The sonnets Henry wrote for his lady loves were set to music, the best known being "Greensleeves." The British Museum contains some 34 manuscripts of Henry's compositions. So flourishing was music in England in the 16th century that Erasmus of Rotterdam reported, after one of his visits: "They are so much occupied with music here that even the monks don't do anything else."

Music among the common people of the time may have been less polished but was no less enthusiastic, with ditties and rounds being composed and heard in taverns and fields, the richness of the tunes compensating for the frequent vulgarity of the words. Some of the songs Shakespeare had his characters sing attest to the general coarseness of lyrics.

It was during the Tudor dynasty that English cathedral music came into full flower. It was during these years, too, that the forerunners of the opera and operetta came into being, with spectacles, called masques, being accompanied by music. These combined instrumental and vocal music, dancing, satire, recitations, and elaborate scenic accompaniment—the beginning of stage design.

Musicians were persecuted in the 1600s during the Commonwealth, but they came back into glory with the restoration of the monarchy under the Stuarts, with Henry Purcell writing the first English opera, *Dido and Aeneas,* in 1689. From this point on, a veritable galaxy of musical talent was inspired and appreciated in London and thence in all England. Operas were written, influenced by Italian works, with Sir John Gay satirizing such productions in *The Beggars' Opera* in 1728. Handel, who became an English subject, composed many oratorios here, including *Messiah,* and other musicians followed (sometimes haltingly) in his train.

All of this doubtless led to the totally English musical productions, the operettas of the 19th century, with those by Gilbert and Sullivan being at the top of the heap then and for all the years since.

Many great names in the music world are English: Sir Edward Elgar, Ralph Vaughan Williams, Sir William Walton, Sir Benjamin Britten, to name just a few.

But English music has not stood still. Paul McCartney and John Lennon of The Beatles began what has been called "the British invasion"—British rock music's invasion of America. Since the 1960s, English rock musicians have often dominated the American music charts. Vocalists such as Phil Collins, David Bowie, and Sting, and guitarists such as Eric Clapton have been leading forces in popular music. But England's biggest musical influence has come from its rock bands: The Rolling Stones, The Who, Pink Floyd, The Sex Pistols, and XTC. The influence of British rock on Western popular music and culture has been and still is tremendous.

ART

From the first carved and jewel-bedecked baubles, utensils, and even weapons of prehistoric man, the craze for ornamentation continued and grew. Intricately wrought crosses, religious statuary, and illuminated manuscripts led the way to stained-glass windows, ecclesiastical paintings, and other art forms connected first with the abbeys and cathedrals that came into being over the centuries throughout the country. Soon these were followed by decorative glorification and expansion of the homes of royal and noble personages. The same trend affected the gentry and whoever could afford to have their persons and structures beautified.

Ornate tombs with sculptured effigies of the dead marked the resting places of the nobility and the princes of the church in the Middle Ages, and the cathedrals became art galleries of awesome beauty. Medieval painting consisted mostly of illumination of manuscripts by monks who took as models work they had done in European monasteries. Other art by the 13th century included the embroidering of tapestries, metalwork, and carving, with panel painting, stained glass, and frescoes being among the mediums of expression.

Art, and even beauty, were considered the work of the devil during the religious upheavals of the 16th and 17th centuries, but when peace of a sort returned, sculpture came into vogue again, and painting reached an enviable grandeur. The name of Grinling Gibbons looms large for his baroque work in the late 17th and early 18th centuries, but it was not really until the 20th century that sculpture became a serious competitor to painting in England. Names such as Henry Moore, Barbara Hepworth, Sir Jacob Epstein, and Kenneth Armitage are only a few of the greats connected with English sculpture today.

By the time interest in art revived after the Reformation, painting in oils was being done on the European continent, and from this arose the wealth of fine pictures, from miniatures to vast murals, which you can see today. This art reached great heights in England, and your visits to the island's many museums and galleries will make you conversant with the masters.

At first, portraiture was the "done thing," as the British put it, with everybody who was anybody being depicted—alone, with family, with pets, whatever. The early leader in this field was Hans Holbein the Younger, a Swiss-born artist who had moved to England and who became painter for Henry VIII. Among the leading painters of the Tudor and Stuart periods, two who were outstanding were Sir Anthony Van Dyck and Sir Peter Lely, neither of them English-born.

Native English painters came into their own by the 18th century, during the same era that landscape and animal painting and social satire began to vie with portraiture as recognized art forms. A roll call of the greats of that time resounds even today: Thomas Gainsborough, William Hogarth, Sir Joshua Reynolds, George Romney, and many more. It was in that era that the Royal Academy of Arts was formed (1768), which you can visit in Piccadilly.

Painters of the 19th and 20th centuries whose supremacy is recognized include John Constable, Joseph Mallord William Turner, Aubrey Beardsley, Sir Edward Burne-Jones, Dante Gabriel Rossetti, W. Holman Hunt, Ben Nicholson, Augustus John, Francis Bacon, and Graham Sutherland, to name a few. Some of these, it is true, are felt to be too cloyingly romantic or too iconoclastically avant-garde for all tastes, but each has earned a place in art history.

Whatever your preferences may be—Old Masters or latter 20th-century artists —you can find something to please you (and probably something to complain about) in the hundreds of galleries large and small throughout England.

ARCHITECTURE

From ancient man-made ceremonial sites such as Stonehenge, which are seen as "prehistoric cathedrals," through the great minsters and more recognizable cathedrals of the Middle Ages, up to the modern places of worship at Coventry and Liverpool, the art of humanity has ever sought to bring a functional shape to the site where a higher power is invoked, as well as to places of human habitation.

Architecture in England has moved through many periods, examples of most of which can be seen today in preserved, restored, and reconstructed form. Separate architectural periods came after untitled eons in which mankind made do with caves or huts of wattle and daub and whatever was at hand to work with. These designated architectural periods include the Anglo-Saxon, 6th to mid-11th century; the Norman, 11th and 12th centuries; Gothic (actually including four phases: Early English, Decorated, Perpendicular, and Tudor), 12th to 16th centuries; Renaissance (including Elizabethan, Jacobean, Palladian, and Byzantine), mid-16th to early 18th centuries; Georgian, early 18th to 19th; Regency, early 19th; Victorian, mid-19th to 20th; and the architecture of the present century, which has taken many forms.

Many examples exist of work from all periods since the Norman, so that the interested visitor has little difficulty in finding them among the sights of England. The names of the architects responsible for many of these lasting monuments to human genius have not survived, but enough are known to make a formidable roster of greatness. From the monk, Gandulf, a stonemason credited with construction of the White Tower, the list reads through Inigo Jones, Sir Christopher Wren, Nicholas Hawksmoor, Sir John Vanbrugh, James Gibbs, John Nash, Sir Edwin Lutyens, and countless others. (Robert Adam, whose name is synonymous with handsome interiors and some exterior work, was a Scotsman, but much of his work can be seen in England.)

Not a builder of houses but a landscape architect was Lancelot ("Capability") Brown, whose work also lives on, framing the beauty of many palaces and manor houses.

The rich legacy of a millennium of builders is an integral part of the visitor's enjoyment of England.

3. Food and Drink

Understanding British traditional dishes will help you enjoy your visit even more. The following comments will explain a few; other "surprises" you must seek out for yourself. Many good old-fashioned dishes are available in restaurants, wine bars, and pubs, which are sometimes called inns or taverns, a name going back to the Middle Ages.

The most common pub meal is based on the food a farm worker took with him to work, a ploughman's lunch. Originally a good chunk of local cheese, a hunk of homemade crusty white or brown bread, some butter, and a pickled onion or two, it was washed down with ale. You will now find such variations as pâté and chutney replacing the onions and cheese. Cheese is still, however, the most common ingredient. There are many regional variations, the best known being Cheddar, a good solid mature cheese, as is Cheshire. Another is the semismooth-textured Caerphilly from a beautiful part of Wales, and also Stilton, a softer tangy cheese, popular with a glass of port.

Dishes with names so perplexing you have no hint of their ingredients are found on the little tea shop menu or in pubs and the like. Perhaps the most popular is shepherd's pie, a deep dish of chopped cold lamb mixed with onions and seasoning and covered with a layer of mashed potato and served hot. Another version is cottage pie, which is minced beef covered with potatoes and served hot.

Traveling in the southeast part of England around Colchester, you will find a most prized British dish, the oyster, for which, it is suggested, Julius Caesar really invaded Britain in 54 B.C.

As you move about England, you will come across dishes that were developed to fill a particular need. The Cornish pasty was made from the remains of the family's Sunday lunch in a Cornish fishing village: minced meat, chopped potato, carrot, onion, and seasoning mixed together and put into a pastry envelope, ready to be taken to sea by the fisherman on Monday for his lunch. In Grasmere you can buy gingerbread cookies made from a recipe more than 125 years old, coming in the same alphabet shapes used to teach children to read in the 19th century. A "flitting dumpling," northern in origin, is made of dates, walnuts, and syrup mixed with other ingredients into a pudding. It was cut into slices and could feed a family when they were "flitting" from one area to another. It is said that "hurry pudding," or "hasty pudding" in some areas, was invented by people avoiding the bailiff. This dish from Newcastle uses up stale bread (some dried fruit and milk were added in a dish that was put into the oven). In the northeast you'll come across Lancashire hotpot, a stew of mutton, potatoes, kidneys, and onions (sometimes carrots). This concoction was originally put into a deep dish and set on the edge of the stove to cook slowly while the family went to work in a local mill.

Among the most well known and traditional of English dishes is roast beef and Yorkshire pudding. The pudding is made with a flour base and cooked under the joint, allowing the fat from the meat to drop onto it. The beef could easily be a large "sirloin" (rolled loin) that, so the story goes, was named by King James I (not Henry VIII as some claim) when a guest at Hoghton Tower, Lancashire; "Arise Sir Loin," he cried as he knighted the joint with his dagger. Meat left over would be eaten the next day in "bubble and squeak," which is made with cabbage and potatoes chopped and fried together. Another dish that makes use of a batter similar to Yorkshire pudding is "toad-in-the-hole," in which sausages are cooked in batter.

On the west coast you'll find a delicacy not to be missed, the Morecambe Bay shrimp. Of course, the whole coast of Britain provides a feast of dishes, the champions being cod, haddock, herring, plaice, and the aristocrat of flat fish, Dover sole. Cod and haddock are the most popular fish used in the making of that curious British tradition, "fish and chips" (chips, of course, are fried potatoes or french fries). The true British cover this dish with salt and vinegar. In the past the wrapping was newspaper, but now hygiene has removed the added—some say indispensable—taste of newsprint from the dish!

Kipper, a smoked herring, is a popular breakfast dish. The finest are from the Isle of Man, Whitby, or Loch Fyne in Scotland. Herrings are split open and placed over oak chips and smoked slowly to produce a nice pale brown smoked fish. The British eat large breakfasts, or at least many of them do. "Ham and eggs" is said to have originated in Britain. Kedgeree is another popular dish (haddock, egg, and rice). Some B&Bs (bed and breakfasts) still serve black pudding with breakfast items (it's made of pig's blood, oatmeal, barley, or groats and suet—rather repulsive-sounding, but loved by many).

High tea, almost unknown in the south, is common in the north of England and in Scotland. It is a meal that is a mix of hot and cold, giving the worker on his return home a combination of tea and supper. The word "dinner," in the north describes the midday meal (lunch), while in the south it means the evening meal. Supper by tradition is a meal taken late at night, usually after the theater.

Incidentally, real English mustard is simply the fine ground seed mixed with water, nothing else.

The East End of London has quite a few interesting old dishes, among them tripe and onions. Dr. Johnson's favorite tavern, the Cheshire Cheese on Fleet Street, still offers a steak, kidney, mushroom, and game pudding in a suet case in winter and a pastry case in summer. The typical East Ender will be seen at the Jellied Eel stall on Sunday by Petticoat Lane, eating eel or perhaps cockles, mussels, whelks, and winkles, all small shellfish eaten with a touch of vinegar. The eel pie and mash shop can still be found in London. The name "eel pie," however, is misleading, because it is really a minced beef pie topped with flaky pastry, served with mashed potatoes, and accompanied by a portion of jellied eel.

It is a misconception to believe that "everything" stops for tea. People in Britain drink an average of four cups of tea a day, mainly at work. The real delight is to visit the little country tea shops where you can enjoy a pot of tea, some toasted tea cake (currant bun), a crumpet (sometimes confused with the rarely found muffin), bread and butter, or sandwiches and good homemade cakes, all enjoyed while listening to the conversation at the next table.

A word about the wine of the country: Britain does not produce much real wine. It does produce some very pleasant white wine that is on the medium sweet side and quite fruity in taste. The real "wines" are cider and beer, both of which go well with the traditional dishes mentioned earlier.

Beer is served in all pubs. Draft beer is traditionally served at cellar temperature; as the British like to taste their beer, they prefer it on the warm side of cold. Most bottled beer, however, is similar to light lager beers and is served cold. Draft beer comes in two basic types: lager, mild and carbonated, and ale, stronger and uncarbonated. In the south ale is called "bitter," but it doesn't really taste bitter. A half pint is the equivalent in strength to a single measure of Scotch. Others are mild ale, which is full flavored, and brown ale, which is dark and flavorsome. Stout is a strong, rich dark beer, often mixed with champagne to make "Black Velvet." Guinness is the most famous stout, strong tasting and very dark, with a good white head (froth). Cider made from apples can be stronger than expected.

However, after reading all the above, you can still be assured that the food and drink (including French and Italian wines) served in most restaurants will be international in scope, with some traditional British dishes. The reputation that Britain had for years for its soggy cabbage and tasteless dishes is no longer deserved. If you pick and choose carefully and use this guide to help you seek out the finer dining rooms, you can enjoy some of the finest food in Europe while touring the British Isles.

4. Alternative and Special-Interest Travel

Mass tourism of the kind that has transported vast numbers of North Americans to the most obscure corners of the map has been a by-product of the affluence, technology, and democratization that only the last half of the 20th century was able to produce.

With the advent of the 1990s and the changes they promise to bring, some of America's most respected travel visionaries have perceived a change in the needs of many of the world's most experienced (and sometimes jaded) travelers. There has emerged a demand for specialized travel experiences whose goals and objectives are clearly defined well in advance of an actual departure. There is also an increased demand for organizations that can provide like-minded companions to share and participate in increasingly esoteric travel plans.

This yearning for a special-interest vacation might be especially intense for a frequent traveler whose expectations have already been defined by earlier exposure to foreign cultures.

With that in mind, the author of this guide hopes to enhance the quality of his readers' travel experiences by including the following section.

Caveat: Under no circumstances is the inclusion of an organization to be interpreted as a guarantee either of its credit-worthiness or its competency. Information about the organizations coming up is presented only as a preliminary preview, to be followed by your own investigation should you be interested.

INTERNATIONAL UNDERSTANDING

About the only thing the following organizations have in common is reflected by the headline. These organizations not only promote trips to increase international understanding, but they often encourage and advocate what might be called "intelligent travel."

The Friendship Force was founded in Atlanta, Georgia, under the leadership of former President Jimmy Carter during his tenure as governor of that state. This nonprofit organization exists for the sole purpose of fostering and encouraging friendship among disparate peoples around the world. The dozens of branch offices lie throughout North America, meet regularly for meetings of goodwill, and appoint a volunteer director whose responsibility it is to recruit new members and cultivate potential destinations for en masse visits.

These visits usually occur once a year. Because of group bookings by the Friendship Force, the price of air fare to the host country is usually less than what a volunteer would pay if he or she bought an APEX ticket individually. Each participant is required to spend two weeks in the host country (host countries are primarily in Europe, but also throughout the world). One stringent requirement is the need for a participant to spend one full week in the home of a family as a guest, supposedly to further the potential for meaningful friendships between the host family and the participants. Most volunteers spend the second week traveling in the host country.

It should be noted that no particular study regime or work program is expected of participants, but only a decorum and interest level that speaks well of America and its residents. Again, the goal and aim of this group is to further friendship in a nonpolitical, nonreligious context of cooperation and good will. For more information, contact The Friendship Force, 575 South Tower, 1 CNN Center, Atlanta, GA 30303 (tel. 404/522-9490).

People to People International, 501 E. Armour Blvd., Kansas City, MO 64109 (tel. 816/531-4701), defines its purpose as the promotion of world peace through increased understanding among individuals. This philanthropic nonprofit organization was established in the early 1950s by Dwight D. Eisenhower. Each of its programs is administered from its headquarters in Kansas City. This organization, however, was never intended as an inexpensive way for participants to travel. People to People organizes collegiate ambassador programs, where participants spend a month in Europe studying with an American professor for college credit. Similar programs exist for high school students as well. Programs have been offered, for example, for students of corporate or public administration to spend two unpaid months watching the interior workings of a British corporation or a British government agency.

There is also a department to facilitate visits by North American professionals to their counterparts in countries around the world. This usually occurs in a convention setting, requires time away of two or three weeks, and might include doctors, lawyers, farmers, experts on aging, and a bewildering array of representatives of highly specialized careers. Membership in this organization qualifies newcomers to a newsletter and costs $15 a year for individuals, $25 for families, and $10 for students.

World Wide Christian Tours, P.O. Box 506, Elizabethtown, KY 42701 (tel. 502/769-5900, or toll free 800/732-7920), focuses on Christian travel. These

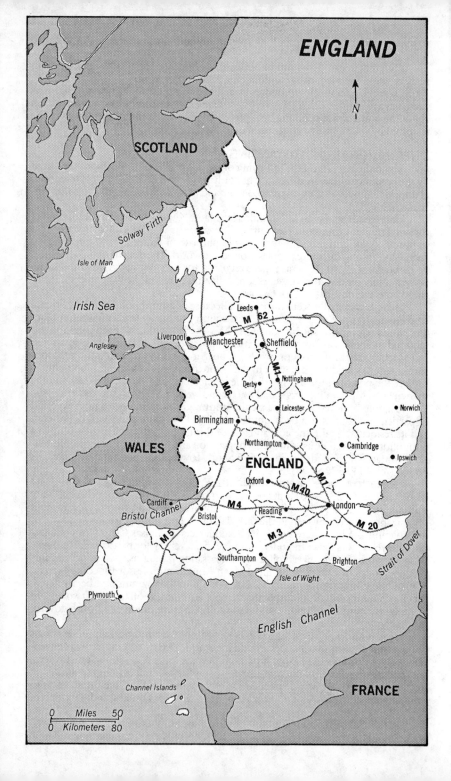

travels include ecumenical tours of England, golf-related tours of Scotland, senior citizen tours of Western Europe, and the ever-popular Holy Land trip. This is the largest organization of its kind in Kentucky and will tailor-make tours for special-interest and church groups of two to well over 200. World Wide Christian Tours is bonded and approved by ARC and IATA and also has a bus brokerage license.

Servas, 11 John St., New York, NY 10038 (tel. 212/267-0252), was founded in 1948 by an American-born conscientious objector living in Denmark. This organization grew slowly from a collection of index cards kept in a friend's kitchen to one of the most prominent collections of people of goodwill in the world. Servas (translated from the Esperanto, it means "to serve") is a nonprofit/nongovernmental/international/interfaith network of travelers and hosts whose goal is to help build world peace, goodwill, and understanding. They do this by providing opportunities for deeper, more personal contacts among people of diverse cultural and political backgrounds.

Servas travelers are invited to share living space in a privately owned home within a community, normally staying without charge for visits lasting a maximum of two days. This is unquestionably geared to more thoughtful and peace-oriented travelers who want to share common experiences above and beyond what they might find in a typical bed-and-breakfast establishment. Visitors pay a $45 annual membership fee, fill out an application, and are interviewed for suitability by one of more than 200 Servas interviewers throughout the country. They then receive a Servas directory listing the names and addresses of Servas hosts who will allow (and encourage) visitors in their homes.

Visitors can also request simply a day visit or a shared meal instead of the actual overnight in the host home. What's amazing is that with all the potential problems that an organization this diverse might have, there seem to be surprisingly few trouble zones. Hosts eager to meet other members of Servas live throughout the world, including all the countries of Europe. This is, frankly, one of the best opportunities for a visiting North American to spend quality time in the homes of families on all six continents, who will probably be sympathetic to visions of world peace and global understanding.

International Visitors Information Service, 733 15th St., N.W., Suite 300, Washington, DC 20005 (tel. 202/783-6540), will mail anyone a booklet for $4.95 listing opportunities someone might use for contact with local residents in foreign countries. Europe is heavily featured. Checks should be made out to Meridian House/IVIS.

Staying with a British Family

An ideal way to find out about the British way of life is provided by a number of hosts operating under a code of conduct set up by the British Tourist Authority. For information on this program, a booklet is available published by the BTA listing dozens of agencies and services offering help in finding the place where you might like to stay for a happy British holiday. If possible, interested persons should call in person at the **British Travel Centre,** 12 Regent Street, Piccadilly Circus, in London. In the U.S., write to any of the following **British Tourist Authority** offices: Third Floor, 40 West 57th St., New York, NY 10019; John Hancock Center, Suite 3320, 875 North Michigan Ave., Chicago, IL 60611; Cedar Maple Plaza, 2305 Cedar Springs Rd., Dallas, TX 75201-1814; or World Trade Center, 350 South Figueroa St., Suite 450, Los Angeles, CA 90071.

ADVENTURE/WILDERNESS TRAVEL

Whether by bicycle or on foot, the following organizations offers tours for athletic types who want to explore "the wilds," or at least country roads, before they disappear forever.

Outward Bound, 383 Field Point Rd., Greenwich, CT 06830 (tel. 203/661-

0797, or toll free 800/243-8520 outside Connecticut), is considered the oldest and most experienced wilderness survival school in America. Outward Bound was founded in 1941 by a German-English educator, Kurt Hahn. Its goal is to help people "go beyond their self-imposed limits, to use the wilderness as a metaphor for personal growth and self-discovery." Training sessions last from three days to three months. A three-month course will sometimes be accepted for college credits toward a degree. The location of these courses is usually in a wilderness setting near the sea or high in the mountains. Outward Bound maintains 35 different schools and centers throughout the world, at least six of which are in Western Europe.

Wilderness Travel, Inc., 801 Allston Way, Berkeley, CA 94710 (tel. 415/548-0420, or toll free 800/247-6700 outside California), is one of the largest tour operators in California that specializes in mountain tours and bicycle tours of Europe, offering at least 16 different outdoors-oriented trips to Europe. About a quarter of its clientele comes from California, while the rest are from around the United States. It specializes in bicycle tours of France, mountain-climbing tours of the Alps, walking tours of Tuscany, Cornwall, and the Cotswolds, as well as Wales and Scotland, and sailing trips along the Aegean coast of Turkey. Call or write for more information.

Country Cycling Tours, 140 W. 83rd St., New York, NY 10024 (tel. 212/874-5151), is one of New York's largest tour operators for bicycles. This company has tours in England, Ireland, and France, as well as walking tours in England and France. New bicycling regions are sometimes added to the list of destinations. Tours, costing from $1395 to $1795, include overnight accommodations in three-star hotels, breakfast, and most dinners. Luggage precedes you in a van. Tours are designed for energetic beginners, stress back roads, and include accommodations that offer the regional charm of the district. Cyclists can bring their own bicycles or rent them on site. Tours offer ten to 13 days of cycling.

The American company referred to as "the granddaddy of cycle tour operators" is **Vermont Bicycle Touring,** P.O. Box 711, Bristol, VT 05443 (tel. 802/453-4811). Tours range from 25 to 40 miles a day, and a van transports luggage. The tours allow flexibility for individual levels of cycling experience, but additional guidance, assistance, and services are always available. Most of this group's European tours are sent to England.

For trekking and backpacking tours, get in touch with **Outdoor Bound,** 18 Stuyvesant Oval, No. 1A, New York, NY 10009 (tel. 212/505-1020). Founded by Seth Steiner, this group leads walking tours through the Lake District of England, Yugoslavia, and the Sinai Desert. Tours last up to two weeks, covering five to ten miles a day. In England, accommodations are in a 17th-century country inn near Ambleside and Windermere. A minibus takes walkers to an embarkation point noted for scenic beauty. Depending on the tour and options, charges are $1000 to $2000.

INLAND WATERWAYS

For a completely new angle on travel in the British Isles, visitors can take boat trips on the network of inland waterways threading through the country. You can choose between a skipper-yourself boat, equipped with food, comprehensive instructions, and suggested routes, or else a hotel boat, where you get good food, a helpful crew, and the companionship of fellow passengers. Waterways holidays make sightseeing easy, allowing you to leave your luggage aboard as you spend the days exploring. Some places allow you to take your boat right into the center of a city, as at Chester, Stratford-upon-Avon, Norwich, Cambridge, York, and Windsor.

Cruising areas include the Norfolk Broads, canals, the River Thames, Scottish and Irish lochs, and the fascinating Cambridgeshire rivers: Ouse, Cam, and Nene. For information and reservations, contact **UK Waterway Holidays Ltd.,** Welton Hythe, Daventry, Northamptonshire NN11 5LG (tel. 0327/843773).

SENIOR CITIZEN VACATIONS

One of the most dynamic organizations in the world of postretirement studies for senior citizens is **Elderhostel,** 80 Boylston St., Boston, MA 02116 (tel. 617/426-7788). Established in 1975 by Martin Knowlton, a retired engineer and professor of political science, it is, quite simply, one of the most creative forces in the lives of senior citizens. During a four-year backpacking tour of Europe that he began in his mid-50s, Knowlton noticed an inefficient summer use of college dormitories. He became inspired to try to fill them with crowds of what many universities consider their most avid students, senior citizens. Today, Elderhostel maintains a dazzling array of programs throughout the world, including England, Scotland, and all major countries on the continent. Most courses last around three weeks, representing remarkable value, considering that air fare, hotel accommodations in student dormitories or modest inns, all meals, and tuition are included. Currently, three weeks with all of these included cost a surprisingly low $1992 for a program in England, for example. Courses involve no homework, are ungraded, and are especially intensive in liberal arts. Even field trips are related to the academic discipline being studied in the classroom.

In no way is this to be considered a luxury vacation, but rather an academic fulfillment of a type never possible for senior citizens until several years ago. Participants must be more than the age of 60. However, if a pair of members goes as a couple, only one member needs to be older than 60. Meals are the kind of solid, no-frills fare most college undergraduates know only too well. But most graduates would consider gourmet cuisine of relatively unimportant merit because of the multiple additional benefits. A frequently unpublicized side benefit of this program is the safety in which many older single women can travel. Some 70% of the participants are women, who understandably prefer to travel with a goal and an orientation, amid like-minded individuals waiting for them at the end of their transatlantic airplane ride.

Anyone interested in participating in one of Elderhostel's programs should write for their free newsletter and a list of upcoming courses and destinations.

One company that has made a reputation exclusively because of its quality tours for senior citizens is **Saga International Holidays.** Established in the 1950s as a sensitive and highly appealing outlet for mature tour participants, this group prefers that joiners be at least 60 years of age or older. Insurance and air fare are included in the net price of any of their tours, all of which encompass dozens of locations in Europe and usually last for an average of 17 nights. For more information, get in touch with Saga International Holidays, 120 Boylston St., Boston, MA 02116 (tel. toll free 800/343-0273).

EDUCATIONAL AND STUDY TRAVEL

University vacations, or **UNIVAC,** offers a wealth of study at Oxford and Cambridge, where participants find themselves surrounded by history in a rich atmosphere of culture and academic excellence spanning more than 700 years. These cultural vacations combine relaxation with the stimulus of an academic purpose, wherein you can explore history, literature, and the arts through lectures, excursions, and guided walking tours, with no pressures such as exams or papers to prepare. There are no formal academic requirements for participation in UNIVAC—all adults over 18 are invited to share in the programs, living in one of the colleges, eating in an elaborate dining hall or intimate private Fellows' dining rooms.

Programs, lasting seven to 12 days, include university architecture, history, art, and literature, among other troves of English treasures. North American headquarters for UNIVAC is the International Building, 9602 N.W. 13th St., Miami, FL 33172 (tel. 305/591-1736, or toll free 800/792-0100). In the United Kingdom, headquarters is at 8 Beaufort Pl., Cambridge CB5 8AG; in summer, Brasenose College, Oxford OX1 4AJ, or Corpus Christi College, Cambridge CN2 1RH.

British Universities Summer Schools, University of Oxford, Department for External Studies, Rewley House, Wellington Square, Oxford OX1 2JA, England, offers academic programs in literature and history related to the cultural resources of the universities of Birmingham (at its Stratford-upon-Avon center), London, and Oxford. These schools are designed for graduates, particularly teachers, for graduating seniors, and some undergraduates.

The **Institute of International Education,** the largest U.S. organization in the field of international higher education, administers a variety of postsecondary academic, training, and grant programs. It is best known for administering the USIA predoctoral and collaborative Fulbright grants. For information on IIE-administered programs for U.S. citizens, contact the U.S. Student Programs Division of IIE, 809 United Nations Plaza, New York, NY 10017 (tel. 212/984-5330). College students, teachers, university faculty, adults, and professionals looking for study opportunities abroad can visit the IIE Information Center in New York at 809 United Nations Plaza, First Avenue at 45th Street.

If you're interested in scientific discoveries in Europe, you might investigate **Earthwatch,** P.O. Box 403N, Watertown, MA 02271 (tel. 617/926-8200). It organizes scientific projects throughout the world, including several in Europe. Most expeditions are organized into two-week work teams, where participants interested in a "hands-on study project" each contribute to the cost of that project. Examples of studies include surveys of birds, glaciers, architectural history, and marine ecology, as well as archeological excavations.

Earthwatch is a nonprofit organization to which university professors from around the world apply for paying volunteers for their research projects. Payments that volunteers make are considered tax-deductible contributions to a scientific project. Only 7% of the volunteers are students. A work project with Earthwatch offers a "chance to pursue for a brief while the path not taken." It has also been defined as a "scientific short-term Peace Corps." About a third of the 350 college professors who apply yearly are accepted on the basis of the research merits of their projects. Tasks include everything from weighing a wolf pup to measuring turtle eggs to researching genealogical records. The organization publishes a magazine six times a year, listing the dozens of unusual opportunities.

HEALTH AND FITNESS FACILITIES

A wide range of health and fitness facilities is offered at a number of hotels in England and Scotland, together with sporting amenities, such as golf, riding, and fishing at some places. Included in the hotels' offerings are saunas, solariums, gymnasiums, whirlpools, steam cabinets, massage facilities, slimming and beauty treatments, jogging tracks, squash and tennis courts, and indoor or outdoor heated swimming pools. Health farms and hydros are also available, with a selection of therapies and treatments, such as Swedish, gyratory, and underwater massages, deep-cleansing facials, hair removal by waxing, manicure, and pedicure.

For information on locations and offerings, write to the **British Tourist Authority,** 64 St. James's St., London SW1A 1NF, and ask for the brochure they publish on these facilities, or ask at any BTA office.

OPERA TOURS

On a cultural note, **Dailey-Thorp,** 315 W. 57th St., New York, NY 10019 (tel. 212/307-1555), has been in business since 1971. It's probably the best-regarded organizer of music and opera tours in America. Because of its "favored" relations with European box offices, it's often able to purchase blocks of otherwise unavailable tickets to such events as the Salzburg Festival, the Vienna, Milan, Paris, and London operas, or the Bayreuth Festival in Germany. Tours range from seven to 21 days, including first-class or deluxe accommodations and meals in top-rated European restaurants. Dailey-Thorp is also known for its breakthrough visits to operas in Eastern Europe and the regional operas of Italy.

A TRAVEL COMPANION

A recent American census showed that 77 million Americans more than 15 years of age are single. However, the travel industry is far better geared for double occupancy of hotel rooms. One company that has made heroic efforts to match single travelers with like-minded companions is now the largest and best-listed company in the United States, thanks to a rash of acquisitions of its former competitors across the country. Jens Jurgen, the German-born founder, charges between $29 and $66 for a six-month listing in his well-publicized records. New applicants desiring a travel companion fill out a form stating their preferences and needs. They then receive a mini-listing of the kinds of potential partners who might be suitable for travel. Companions of the same or opposite sex can be requested. Because of the large number of listings, success is often a reality.

For an application and more information, get in touch with Jens Jurgen, **Travel Companion,** P.O. Box P-833, Amityville, NY 11701 (tel. 516/454-0880).

---

5. The ABCs of England

The aim of this "grab bag" section—dealing with the minutiae of your stay—is to make your adjustment to the English way of life easier. For more specific information on London, refer to "Practical Facts" under the Orientation section on the British capital, Chapter III.

BABYSITTERS: These are very hard to find, and the only safe way would be to get your hotel to recommend someone—possibly a staff member. Expect to pay the going fee as well as the cost of travel to and from your hotel, although in suburban areas most babysitters have their own cars, in which case you will be expected to reimburse them for the gasoline used. A number of organizations advertised in the yellow pages of the telephone directory provide sitters, using registered nurses, teachers, housewives, and other experienced persons for this service.

BANKS: Hours, generally, are from 9:30 a.m. to 3:30 p.m. Monday to Friday. There are also Bureaux de Change, which charge for cashing traveler's checks or personal checks (limited to checks drawn on United Kingdom banks only). They also change dollars into sterling. Bureaux are often open 18 hours a day, seven days a week. There are also branches of the main banks at the international airports that offer a 24-hour service to travelers. As a word of warning, you should note that the little change bureaus have nothing to do with the main banks and tend to give lower rates of exchange. They are open for long hours, and you pay for this convenience. If you use one of the big banks—Midland, National Westminster, Barclays, Lloyds, Royal Bank of Scotland, Clydesdale, American Express, or Thomas Cook—you will get the best rate.

CIGARETTES: Most U.S. brands are available in major towns. *Warning:* Smoking is banned at an increasing number of places. Make sure you enter a "smoker" on the train or Underground, and smoke only on the upper decks of buses or in the smoking area of single-deckers, in theaters, and at other public places. Some restaurants restrict smoking.

CLIMATE: English temperatures can range from 30°F to 110°F. It is, however, a temperate country with no real extremes, and even in summer evenings are cool. No Britisher will ever really advise you about the weather—it's far too uncertain. However, if you come from a hot area, bring some warm clothes. If you come from the cooler climes, you should be all right.

CRIME: Theft is not as bad, perhaps, as in the U.S. In the main, mugging is limited to the poor areas. Use discretion and a little common sense, and stay in well-lit areas. It's always wise to lock your car and protect your valuables.

CURRENCY EXCHANGE: As a general guideline, the price conversions in this book have been computed at the rate of £1 (one pound sterling) for each $1.75 U.S. There are now £1 coins as well as banknotes, plus coins of 20p (pence), 10p, 2p, and 1p. The ½p coin has been officially killed, although they'll still be seen around for a while. Bear in mind, however, that international exchange rates are far from stable, and this ratio might be hopelessly outdated by the time you actually arrive in Britain.

CUSTOMS: Overseas visitors may import 400 cigarettes and one quart of liquor. But if you come from the Common Market (EEC) area, you're allowed 300 cigarettes and one quart of liquor, provided you bought them and paid tax in that EEC country. If you have obtained your allowance on a ship or plane, then you may only import 200 cigarettes and one liter of liquor. There is no limit on money, film, or other items that are for your own use. Obviously, commercial goods, such as video films and nonpersonal items, will require payment of a bond and will take a number of hours to clear and deal with. Do not try to import live birds or animals. You may be subjected to heavy fines, and the pet will be destroyed. Upon leaving England, citizens of the United States who have been outside the country for 48 hours or more are allowed to bring back to their home country $400 worth of merchandise duty free—that is, if they haven't claimed such an exemption within the past 30 days. Beyond that free allowance, you'll be charged a flat rate of 10% duty on the next $1000 worth of purchases. If you make purchases in Britain, it is most important to keep your receipts. On gifts, the duty-free limit is $50.

DENTISTS: You can find one listed in the yellow pages of the telephone book or else you can ask at your hotel. Appointments are usually necessary, but if you are in pain a dentist will generally fit you in. The **Emergency Dental Service** (tel. 01/ 584-1008) will put you in touch with a dentist in your area.

DOCTORS: Hotels have their own list of local practitioners, for whom you'll have to pay. (Look under "Hospitals" in the yellow pages for 24-hour emergency service.) If out of town, dial "0" (zero) and ask the operator for the local police, who will give you the name, address, and phone number of a doctor in your area. Emergency treatment is free, but if you're admitted to a hospital, referred to an outpatient clinic, or treated for an already-existing condition, you will be required to pay. You will also pay if you visit a doctor in his or her office or if the doctor makes a "house call" to your hotel. Be safe. Take out adequate medical/accident insurance or extend your existing insurance to cover you while you're abroad.

DOCUMENTS FOR ENTRY: U.S. citizens, Canadians, Australians, New Zealanders, and South Africans all fall under the same category for entry into the United Kingdom. A passport is definitely required, but no visa is necessary. Immigration officers prefer to see a passport with two months' remaining validity. Much depends on the criteria and observations of immigration officers. The one checking you through will want to be satisfied that you have the means to return to your original destination (usually a round-trip ticket) and visible means of support while you're in Britain. If you are planning to fly from, say, the U.S. to the U.K. and then on to a country that requires a visa, India, for example, it's wise to secure the India visa before your arrival in Britain. Even the amount of time spent in the British Isles depends for holiday-makers on the immigration officer.

DRUGSTORES: In Britain they're called "chemist" shops. Every police station in the country has a list of emergency chemists. Dial "0" (zero) and ask the operator for the local police. Emergency drugs are normally available at most hospitals, but you'll be examined to see that the drugs you request are really necessary.

ELECTRICAL APPLIANCES: The electrical current is 240 volts, AC (50 Hz). Some international hotels are specially wired to allow North Americans to plug in their appliances, but you'll usually need a transformer plus an adapter for your electric razor, hairdryer, or soft contact lens sterilizer. Ask at the electrical department of a large hardware store for the size converter you'll need.

EMBASSY AND HIGH COMMISSION: For passport or other problems, you can visit the **U.S. Embassy,** 24 Grosvenor Square, London W1A 1AE (tel. 01/499-9000). The **Canadian High Commission** is at MacDonald House, 1 Grosvenor Square, London W1X 0AB (tel. 01/629-9492). The entrance for visitors is around the corner at 38 Grosvenor Street. The tube station is Bond Street.

EMERGENCY: For police, fire, or ambulance, dial 999. Give your name and address, plus your telephone number, and state the nature of the emergency. Misuse of the 999 service will result in a heavy fine. (So cardiac arrest, yes; dented fender, no.)

FILM: All types are available, especially in large cities. Processing takes about 24 hours, and many places, particularly in London, will do it almost while you wait. There are few restrictions on the use of your camera, except when notices are posted, as in churches, theaters, and certain museums. If in doubt, ask.

HAIRDRESSING: Ask at your hotel. You should tip the "hairwasher" at least 50p (90¢) and the stylist £1 ($1.75) or so, more if you have a tint or permanent. Hairdressing services are available in most department stores, and for men at the main railway stations in London.

HOLIDAYS AND FESTIVALS: These are Christmas Day, Boxing Day (December 26), New Year's Day, Good Friday and Easter Monday, May Day, and the spring and summer bank holidays.

LAUNDRY AND DRY CLEANING: Most places take two days to complete the job, and most hotels require the same length of time. London and most provincial towns have launderettes where you can wash and dry your own clothes, but there are no facilities for ironing. Many launderettes also have dry-cleaning machines. Otherwise, there are establishments that will do dry cleaning for you with one-day service. The **Association of British Laundry Cleaning and Rental Services,** 7 Churchill Court, 58 Station Rd., North Harrow, Middlesex HA2 7SA, will give you a list if you can't find a facility close to you. For information about dry cleaners, phone 01/863-8658, and about launderers, 01/863-9178.

LIBRARIES: Every town has a public library, and as a visitor you can use the reference sections. The lending of volumes, however, is restricted to local citizens.

LIQUOR LAWS: No alcohol is served to anyone under the age of 18. Children under 16 are not allowed in pubs except in special rooms. In 1988, laws that had been on the books since the Industrial Revolution were altered. (It was about time, serious beer-drinkers said.) Before that time, British drinking laws were considered hopelessly antiquated, at least by continental standards. Today, there is confusion in the land. Opening hours in England are left to the discretion of the innkeeper, although he or she can't exceed certain prescribed limits. The law allows a pub to serve liquor or beer from 11 a.m. to 11 p.m. Monday to Saturday, and noon to 2 p.m. and 7 to 10:30 p.m. on Sunday. Guests are expected to "drink up" and leave the premises within 20 minutes of the last order. Many publicans in the countryside of England have decided to retain some semblance of the older and more limited pub hours. Hours in Scotland are more "flexible" and have always been more enlightened and liberal than those in England. Hotel residents can usually purchase alcoholic drinks outside the regular pub hours.

LOST PROPERTY: For help in finding items lost in London, see "Practical Facts," Chapter III. Wherever you are in England, report your loss to the nearest police station, which will help you if possible. For items lost on British Rail, go to the Euston Station Lost Property Office (tel. 01/922-6477).

For lost passports, credit cards, or money, report the loss and circumstances immediately to the nearest police station. For lost passports, you should then go directly to your embassy. The address will be in the telephone book (and see "Embassy and High Commission," above). For lost credit cards, report to the appropriate organization; the same holds true for lost travelers' checks.

LUGGAGE STORAGE: You may want to make excursions throughout Britain, taking only your essentials along. Very few B&B hotels in London have space to store lots of luggage, and you might want to return to a different hotel. It's possible to store suitcases at most railway stations. At stations you must be prepared to allow luggage to be searched for security reasons. Be warned that if you object, you could be viewed with suspicion.

MAIL DELIVERY: You can have your mail addressed Poste Restante (General Delivery) at any of the big towns, or give your hotel address. A letter generally takes about seven to ten days to arrive in the U.S. When claiming personal mail, always carry along identification.

MEDICAL SERVICES: Medical treatment is free only for unforeseen emergency conditions that arise during your stay in the United Kingdom. You'll need to consult a physician privately for any other medical treatment you require. The larger hotels will get in touch with their house doctor should you need one.

NEWSPAPERS: *The Times* is the top, then the *Telegraph,* the *Daily Mail,* and the *Guardian,* all papers carrying the latest news. Others have some news, but rely on gimmicks to sell. The *International Herald Tribune,* published in Paris, and an international edition of *USA Today* are available daily.

OFFICE HOURS: Business hours are from 9 a.m. to 5 p.m. Monday to Friday. The lunch break lasts an hour, but most places stay open all day.

PETS: See "Customs." It is illegal to bring in pets, except with veterinary documents, and even then they are subject to a quarantine of six months. Hotels have their own rules but generally do not allow dogs in restaurants or public rooms and often not in the bedrooms either.

POLICE: The best source of help and advice in emergencies is the police (dial 999). If the local police can't assist, they will have the address of a person who can. Losses, theft, and other crimes should be reported immediately to the police.

POST OFFICE: Post offices and sub-post offices are centrally situated and are open from 9 a.m. to 5 p.m. Monday to Friday. On Saturday, the hours are 9 a.m. to noon.

RADIO AND TELEVISION: There are 24-hour radio channels operating throughout the United Kingdom, with mostly pop music and talk shows during the night. TV starts around 6 a.m. with breakfast TV and educational programs. Lighter entertainment begins around 4 or 5 p.m., after the children's programs, and continues until around midnight. There are now four television channels—two commercial and two BBC channels without commercials.

RELIGIOUS SERVICES: Times of services are posted outside the various places of worship. Almost every form of worship is catered to in London and other large cities. But in the smaller towns and villages you are likely to find only Anglican (Episcopalian), Roman Catholic, Baptist, and Nonconformist houses of worship.

REST ROOMS: These are usually found at signs saying "Public Toilets." Expect to pay a 5p (10¢) tip for women; men are free. Hotels can be used, but they discourage nonresidents. Garages (filling stations) also have facilities for use of customers only, and the key is often kept by the cash register. There's no need to tip except in hotels where there is an attendant.

SENIOR DISCOUNTS: These are only available to holders of a British pension book.

SHOE REPAIRS: Many of the large department stores of Britain have "Shoe Bars" where repairs are done while you wait.

STORE HOURS: In general, stores are open from 9 a.m. to 5:30 p.m. Monday to Saturday. In country towns, there is usually an early-closing day when the shops shut down at 1 p.m. The day varies from town to town.

TAXES: As part of an energy-saving program, the British government has added a special 25% tax on gasoline (petrol). There is no local sales tax in cities and towns, but a 15% Value Added Tax (VAT) is added to all hotel and restaurant bills. VAT is also included in the cost of many of the items you purchase to take home with you.

At shops that participate in the Retail Export Scheme, it is possible to get a refund sent to you at home for the amount of the VAT tax on your purchases. Ask the salesperson for a Retail Export Scheme form (Form VAT 407) and a stamped, pre-addressed envelope in which to return it.

Save the VAT form along with your sales receipt to show at customs. You may also have to show the actual purchases to customs officials at airports or other ports of departure. After the form has been stamped by customs, mail it back to the shop in the envelope provided.

Here are three organizing tips to help you through the customs procedures: Keep your VAT forms with your passport as customs is often located near passport control; pack your purchases in a carry-on bag so you will have them handy after you've checked your other luggage; and allow yourself enough time at your departure point to find a mailbox.

TELEGRAMS: Depending on the destination you wish your message to reach, you can send a telegram, telemessage, or a mailgram. Any of these forms can be arranged by dialing 190, 193, or 100 from any phone in Britain. Costs for these messages can be debited from any private or business phone or paid through your hotel switchboard. Less conveniently, the cost can be paid at once by dropping coins in most pay phones (an employee of the phone company will give you the costs). Most visitors find that a mailgram (delivered the next day if received before 10 at night) to be less expensive. You'll probably be advised at the post office that it's less expensive simply to call home if you keep your message brief enough.

TELEPHONES: British Telecom is carrying out a massive improvement program to its public pay phone service. During the transitional period, you may encounter four types of pay phones. The old style (gray) pay phone is being phased out, but there are a few still in use. You will need 10p (20¢) coins to operate such phones, but you should not use this type for overseas calls. Its replacement is a blue and silver push-button model that accepts coins of any denomination. The other two types of phones require cards instead of coins to operate. The Cardphone uses distinctive green cards especially designed for it. They are available in five values—£1 ($1.75), £2 ($3.50), £4 ($7), £10 ($17.50), and £20 ($35)—and they are reusable until the total value has expired. Cards can be purchased from newsstands and post offices. Finally, the Creditcall pay phone operates on credit cards—Access, VISA, American Express, and Diners—and is most common at airports and large railway stations.

Phone numbers in Britain outside of the major cities consist of an exchange number plus telephone number. To dial the number, you will need the code of the exchange being called. Information sheets on call box walls give the codes in most instances. If your code is not there, however, call the operator by dialing 100. In major cities, phone numbers consist of the exchange code and number (seven digits in all). These seven digits are all you need to dial if you are calling from within the same city. If you are calling from elsewhere, you will need to prefix them with the dialing code for the city. Again, you will find these codes on the call box information sheets. If you do not have the telephone number of the person you want to call, dial 192 or 142 either for London or elsewhere in the country. Give the operator the name of the town and then the person's name and address.

The guide to telephone costs: A call at noon from London to Reading, 40 miles away and lasting three minutes, costs 80p ($1.40). This charge is almost halved between 6 p.m. and 8 a.m. and on weekends. A local call costs 20p (35¢) for almost three minutes at all times. Unused coins are refunded at the end of a call. The charges quoted are for pay phones. You will have to pay far more if you use a hotel operator at any time.

TELEX AND FAX: Telexes are very common in offices and hotels. If your hotel has a telex, they will send it for you. Fax is less common, but can be found, for instance at large post offices. Refer to the yellow pages for telex bureaux, and dial 100 and ask for Freefone Intelpost for information on fax.

TIME: England is based on Greenwich Mean Time with BST—British Standard Time (GMT + 1 hour)—during the summer (roughly April to October). When London is 12 noon, New York is 7 a.m., Chicago is 6 a.m., Denver is 5 a.m., and Los Angeles an early 4 a.m.

TIPPING: Many establishments add a service charge. If service has been good, it is usual to add an additional 5% to that. If no service is added to the bill, give 10% for poor service; otherwise, 15%. If service is bad, tell them and don't tip! Taxi drivers expect about 20%.

TOURIST INFORMATION: The British Tourist Authority has a **British Travel Centre** at Rex House, 4-12 Lower Regent St., London S.W.1 (tel. 01/730-3400). This center, which deals only with inquiries made in person, offers a full information service on all parts of England. For various sources of information on London, see Part I of Chapter III.

WEATHER: For London, telephone 01/246-8091; for Devon and Cornwall, 0392/8091; and for the Midlands, 021/8091.

WEIGHTS AND MEASURES: England has converted to the metric system for the most part. Below is a list of equivalents for quick reference and formulas if you feel the need to convert.

Length
    1 millimeter = 0.04 inches (*or* less than 1/16 in)
    1 centimeter = 0.39 inches (*or* just under ½ in)
    1 meter   = 1.09 yards (*or* about 39 inches)
    1 kilometer   = 0.62 mile (*or* about ⅔ mile)

To convert kilometers to miles, take the number of kilometers and multiply by .62 (for example, 25 km × .62 = 15.5 mi).

To convert miles to kilometers, take the number of miles and multiply by 1.61 (for example, 50 mi × 1.61 = 80.5 km).

Capacity
    1 liter = 33.92 ounces
            = 1.06 quarts
            = 0.26 gallons

To convert liters to gallons, take the number of liters and multiply by .26 (for example, 50 l × .26 = 13 gallons).

To convert gallons to liters, take the number of gallons and multiply by 3.79 (for example, 10 gal × 3.79 = 37.9 l).

Weight
    1 gram   = 0.04 ounces (*or* about a paperclip's weight)
    1 kilogram = 2.2 pounds

To convert kilograms to pounds, take the number of kilos and multiply by 2.2 (for example, 75 kg × 2.2 = 165 pounds).

To convert pounds to kilograms, take the number of pounds and multiply by .45 (for example, 90 lb × .45 = 40.5 kg).

Area
    1 hectare (100m²) = 2.47 acres

To convert hectares to acres, take the number of hectares and multiply by 2.47 (for example, 20 ha × 2.47 = 49.4 acres).

To convert acres to hectares, take the number of acres and multiply by .41 (for example, 40 acres × .41 = 16.4 hectares).

Temperature

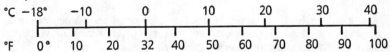

To convert degrees C to degrees F, multiply degrees C by 9, divide by 5, then add 32 (for example 9/5 × 20°C + 32 = 68°F).

To convert degrees F to degrees C, subtract 32 from degrees F, then multiply by 5, and divide by 9 (for example, 85°F − 32 × 5/9 = 29°C).

III

SETTLING INTO LONDON

1. ORIENTATION
2. BELGRAVIA
3. VICTORIA
4. EARL'S COURT
5. BROMPTON AND SOUTH KENSINGTON
6. KNIGHTSBRIDGE
7. CHELSEA
8. KENSINGTON
9. SHEPHERD'S BUSH
10. NOTTING HILL GATE
11. PADDINGTON AND BAYSWATER
12. ST. MARYLEBONE
13. LEICESTER SQUARE
14. BLOOMSBURY
15. IN AND AROUND HAMPSTEAD
16. BLACKHEATH
17. ON THE FRINGE
18. AIRPORT HOTELS
19. AN ACCOMMODATION ROUND-UP

London is a hybrid, a gathering place of people from the far corners of a once-great empire. The country gentleman and the factory worker from the provinces visit London somewhat in the mood of going abroad.

The true Londoner, usually from the East End, is called a Cockney. He or she is a person born within the sound of "Bow Bells," the chimes of a church in Cheapside. But the city is also the home of the well-bred English lady who has had to sell her family estate of 400 years and take meager lodging in Earl's Court; of the expatriate Hollywood actress living in elegance in a Georgian town house; of the islander from Jamaica who comes seeking a new life and ends up collecting fares on one of London's red double-decker buses; and of the young playwright from Liverpool whose art reflects the outlook of the working class.

Cosmopolitan or not, Europe's largest city is still like a great wheel, with Piccadilly Circus at the hub and dozens of communities branching out from it. Since London is such a conglomeration of sections—each having its own life (hotels, restaurants, pubs)—the first-time visitor may be intimidated until he or she gets the hang of it. In this chapter, I'll concentrate mainly on the so-called West End. For the most part, a visitor will live and eat in the West End, except when he or she ventures into the old and historic part of London known as "The City" or goes on a tour to the Tower of London or seeks lodgings in the once-remote villages such as Hampstead.

1. Orientation

London is a city that has never quite made up its mind about its own size. The "City of London" proper is merely one square mile of (very expensive) real estate around the Bank of England. All the gargantuan rest is made up of separate cities, boroughs, and corporations called Westminster, Chelsea, Hampstead, Kensington, Camden Town, and so forth, each with its own mayor and administration and ready to fight for its independent status at the drop of an ordinance. These sections started life as individual villages entirely, but through the centuries the growth of Greater London has filled in the fields and woods that once separated them. Together, they add up to a mammoth metropolis—once the largest city on the globe, now dropped to 16th in a United Nations survey of population. The millions of people here live spread out over 609 square miles. Luckily, only a minute fraction of this territory need concern us—the rest is simply suburbs, stretching endlessly into the horizon, red-roofed and bristling with TV antennas.

But the heart, the brick-and-mortar core of this giant, is perhaps the most fascinating area on earth. For about a century, one-quarter of the world was ruled here. And with every step you take, you'll come across some sign of the tremendous influence this city has exerted over our past thoughts and actions—and still wields today.

HISTORY

London is a very old city, even by European standards. The Roman conquerors of Britain founded Londinium in A.D. 43 by settling and fortifying two small hills on the north bank of the River Thames and linking them via a military road network with the rest of the island.

More than a thousand years later, another conqueror turned the city into his capital. This was William of Normandy, who defeated the last Saxon ruler of England, Harold Godwin, in 1066. There isn't much left of the Roman period, but William the Conqueror left his imprint on London for all time to come. For a start, he completed and had himself crowned in Westminster Abbey. Every British monarch has been crowned there since, right up to the present Queen Elizabeth II. He also built the White Tower, which today forms part of the Tower of London. William did more to transform London (or rather, Westminster) into a royal capital. He and his nobles superimposed their Norman French onto the country's original Anglo-Saxon language and thus concocted English as we speak it today. Both the richness and the maddening illogicality of our tongue are direct results of that transplant.

The Normans weren't exactly gentle rulers, but the nation they created did pretty well. No one, for instance, has ever successfully invaded Britain since William's time—unless you count North American visitors and others from all over.

Royal but Democratic

London is a mass of contradictions, some of them dating far back in the city's history. On the one hand, London is a decidedly royal city, studded with palaces, court gardens, coats-of-arms, and other royal paraphernalia. Yet it is also the home of mankind's second-oldest parliamentary assembly (Iceland has the oldest). When handsome and rash King Charles I tried to defy its representatives, he found himself swept off his throne and onto a scaffold long before the French got around to dealing likewise with their anointed monarch.

The huge, gray building that houses the "Mother of Parliaments," with its famous clock, Big Ben, is more truly symbolic of London than Buckingham Palace. For it was there that Prime Minister William Pitt intoned, "You cannot make peace with dictators—you have to defeat them," at a time when England stood alone against the might of Napoleon. It was there too that Sir Winston Churchill repeated these sentiments in even better phrases when England—alone again—held out against Hitler. It was also in Parliament that "His Majesty's Loyal Opposition" stood up to give a rousing cheer for General Washington's army, which had just whipped His Majesty's Hessian mercenaries—whom they detested every ounce as much as did the American colonists.

Nevertheless, London was largely shaped by the monarchs who ruled her—imposingly by the tough Tudors, beautifully by the wicked Georges, clumsily by the worthy Victoria.

Bouncing Back from Disasters

Much of London is also the result of disasters, both accidental and premeditated. The first was the Great Fire of 1666, which swept away most of the old wooden Tudor houses and resulted in a new city built of brick. The cause of the fire—like that of the great Chicago conflagration—remains unknown. Considering the fire hazards of those tightly packed timbered dwellings, the remarkable thing is that the town didn't burn down annually. As it was, the blaze gutted three-quarters of London—about 13,300 homes, churches, and public buildings. But it also gave England's greatest architect, Christopher Wren, the chance to design St. Paul's Cathedral as it stands today, as well as 51 other superb churches, plus the magnificent Royal Hospitals in Chelsea and Greenwich.

The blitz that Hitler unleashed on the city during 1940–1941 also had one unexpected result. Along with beautiful structures, the rain of incendiary bombs demolished vast patches of the pestilential slum areas around Whitechapel in the East End. The region—made equally famous by Charles Dickens and Jack the Ripper—had been London's festering sore, boasting possibly the worst housing conditions in the western world. With slum clearance courtesy of the Luftwaffe, the L.C.C. rebuilt some of the area into rather drab but infinitely superior apartment blocks. There was something else the blitz gave London: a world image as the embattled fortress of freedom, caught unforgettably by the wartime news photo showing the white dome of St. Paul's silhouetted against the black smoke of a dozen simultaneous fires.

The postwar building boom may have made London a little less "quaint," but it also made her a very much healthier, happier place to live in, and it provided the overture of her present phase, which is that of a lively cosmopolitan city.

A BIT OF GEOGRAPHY

There is, fortunately, an immense difference between the sprawling vastness of Greater London and the pocket-size chunk that might be called "Tourist Country." For a start, all of the latter is *north* of the River Thames. Except for a couple of quick excursions, we'll never have to penetrate the southern regions at all.

Our London begins at Chelsea, on the north bank of the Thames, and stretches for roughly five miles up to Hampstead. Horizontally, its western boundary runs through Kensington, while the eastern lies five miles away at Tower Bridge. Within this five- by five-mile square, you'll find all the hotels and restaurants and nearly all of the sights that are usually of interest to visitors. Make no mistake—this is still a hefty portion of land to cover, and a really thorough exploration of it would take a couple of years. But it has the advantage of being flat and eminently walkable, besides boasting one of the best public transport systems ever devised.

The local, but not the geographical, center of this area is **Trafalgar Square,** which we'll therefore take as our orientation point. The huge, thronged, fountain-splashed square was named after the battle in which Admiral Nelson destroyed the combined Franco-Spanish fleets and lost his own life. His statue tops the towering pillar in the center, and local residents maintain that the reason he's been up there all these years is that nobody has told him the lions at the base are made of stone. If you stand facing the steps of the imposing National Gallery, you're looking northwest. That is the direction of **Piccadilly Circus,** which, as mentioned, is the real core of tourist London, as well as the maze of streets that make up **Soho.** Farther north runs **Oxford Street,** London's gift to shopping, and still farther northwest lies **Regents Park** with its zoo.

At your back—that is, south—runs **Whitehall,** which houses or skirts nearly every British government building, from the Ministry of Defence to the official residence of the prime minister on Downing Street. In the same direction, a bit farther south, stand the Houses of Parliament and Westminster Abbey.

Flowing southwest from Trafalgar Square is the table-smooth **Mall,** flanked by magnificent parks and mansions and leading to Buckingham Palace, residence of the Queen. Farther in the same direction lie **Belgravia** and **Knightsbridge,** the city's plushest residential areas, and south of them, **Chelsea,** with its chic flavor, plus **Kings Road,** the boutique-filled shopping drag.

Due west from where you're standing stretches the superb and distinctly high-priced shopping area bordered by **Regent Street** and **Piccadilly** (the street, *not* the Circus). Farther west lie the equally elegant shops and even more elegant homes of **Mayfair.** Then comes **Park Lane,** and on the other side, **Hyde Park,** the biggest park in London and one of the largest in the world.

Running north from Trafalgar Square is **Charing Cross Road,** past **Leicester Square** and intersecting with **Shaftesbury Avenue.** This is London's theaterland, boasting an astonishing number of live shows as well as first-run movie houses. A bit farther along, Charing Cross Road turns into a browser's paradise, lined with new and secondhand bookshops. Finally it funnels into **St. Giles Circus.** This is where you enter **Bloomsbury,** site of the University of London, the awesome British Museum, some of our best budget hotels, and erstwhile stamping ground of the famed "Bloomsbury Group," led by Virginia Woolf. Northeast of your position lies **Covent Garden,** known for its Royal Opera House.

Follow **The Strand** eastward from **Trafalgar Square** and you'll come into **Fleet Street.** Beginning in the 19th century, this corner of London became the most concentrated newspaper district in the world, but over the decades during this century, the newspapers either folded or moved away. The last newspaper was published on Fleet Street in 1989. At the end of Fleet Street lies **Ludgate Circus**—and only there do you enter the actual City of London. This was the original walled settlement and is today what the locals mean when they refer to **"The City."** Its focal point and shrine is the Bank of England on Threadneedle Street, with the Stock Exchange next door and the Royal Exchange across the road.

"The City" is unique insofar as it retains its own separate police force (distinguished by a crest on their helmets) and lord mayor. Its 677 acres are an antheap of jammed cars and rushing clerks during the week and totally deserted on Sunday, because hardly a soul lives there. Its streets are winding, narrow, and fairly devoid of charm. But it has more bankers and stockbrokers per square inch than any other place on the globe. And in the midst of all the hustle rises St. Paul's Cathedral, a monument to beauty and tranquility. At the far eastern fringe of the City looms the

Tower of London, shrouded in legend, blood, and history. It's permanently besieged by battalions of visitors.

Designed to Confuse

I'd like to tell you that London's thoroughfares follow a recognizable pattern in which, with a little intelligence, even a stranger can find his or her way around. Unfortunately, they don't and you can't. London's streets follow *no* pattern whatsoever, and both their naming and numbering seems to have been perpetrated by a group of xenophobes with an equal grudge against postmen and foreigners.

Be warned that the use of logic and common sense will get you nowhere. Don't think, for instance, that Southampton Row is anywhere near Southampton Street and that either of these places has any connection with Southampton Road. This is only a mild sample. London is checkered with innumerable squares, mews, closes, and terraces, which jut into or cross or overlap or interrupt whatever street you're trying to follow, usually without the slightest warning. You may be walking along ruler-straight Albany Street and suddenly find yourself flanked by Colosseum Terrace (with a different numbering system). Just keep on walking and after a couple of blocks you're right back on Albany Street (and the original house numbers), without having encountered the faintest reason for the sudden change in labels.

House numbers run in odds, evens, clockwise, or counterclockwise as the wind blows. That is, when they exist at all—and frequently they don't. Every so often you'll come upon a square that is called a square on the south side, a road on the north, a park on the east, and possibly a something-or-other close on the west side. Your only chance is to consult a map or ask your way along. Most of the time you'll probably end up doing both.

But there are a couple of consoling factors. One is the legibility of the street signs. The other is the extraordinary helpfulness of the locals, who sometimes pass you from guide to guide like a bucket in a fire chain.

TRANSPORTATION IN GREATER LONDON

If you know the ropes, transportation within London can be unusually easy and inexpensive, because London enjoys one of the best Underground (subway) and bus systems in the world, operated by London Regional Transport, with Travel Information Centres in the Underground stations at King's Cross, Oxford Circus, and Piccadilly Circus, and also in the British Rail stations at Euston and Victoria and each of the terminals at Heathrow Airport.

Travelcards, for use on bus, Underground, and British Rail services and available in any combination of adjacent zones, are offered by the London Regional Transport. The cost of a Travelcard good for 7 days in the Central Zone is £6.40 ($11.20) for adults, £2.50 ($4.40) for children. For two zones, the charge is £6.80 ($11.90) for adults, £2.50 ($4.40) for children; for three zones, £11.20 ($19.60) for adults, £2.80 ($4.90) for children; for four zones, £14 ($24.50) for adults, £5 ($8.75) for children; and for all zones, £17.70 ($31) for adults, £5 ($8.75) for children.

To purchase a Travelcard, you must present a **Photocard.** For persons 16 years old or older, the Photocard is easy to get. Just take a passport-type picture of yourself when you buy your first Travelcard, and the Photocard will be issued free. Child-rate Photocards are only issued at main post offices in the London area, and in addition to a passport-type photograph, proof of age is required (for example, a passport or a birth certificate). Travelcards are not issued at child rates unless supported by a Photocard. Older children (14 or 15) are charged adult fares on *all* services unless in possession of one of the cards. A child-rate Photocard is not, however, required for tours.

For shorter stays in London, you may want to consider the **One-Day Off-Peak Travelcard.** This ticket can be used on most bus, Underground, and British Rail services throughout Greater London after 9:30 a.m. Monday to Friday and at any time on bank holidays. The ticket is available from Underground ticket offices, bus garages, Travel Information Centres, and some newsstands. It costs £2.30 ($4.05) for adults, 80p ($1.40) for youths 14 or 15.

These fares, although valid at the time of writing, will very likely change during the lifetime of this edition and are therefore only presented for general background information so that you will know the range of travel options open to you.

The London Transport Information Centres provide information on a wide range of facilities and places of interest in addition to data on most bus and Underground services. They take reservations for London Transport's guided tours (see "Taking the Tours," Chapter V, Section 4), and have free Underground and bus maps and other information leaflets. A 24-hour telephone information service is available (tel. 01/222-1234).

In addition to the information obtainable from any of the Travel Information Centres, information is also available from London Regional Transport, Travel Information Service, 55 Broadway, London SW1H 0BD.

Airports

London has two main airports, **Heathrow** and **Gatwick**. It takes 35 to 45 minutes by Underground train from Heathrow Central to central London, costing £1.70 ($3) for adults and 60p ($1.05) for children. From Heathrow, you can also take an airbus, which gets you into central London in about an hour. The cost is £4 ($7) for adults, £2 ($3.50) for children.

Gatwick Airport, where many charter and some scheduled flights come in, lies 30 miles south of London. Trains leave from there every 15 minutes until midnight and every hour after midnight. Also, there is an express bus from Gatwick to Victoria Station every half hour from 6:30 a.m. to 8 p.m. and every hour from 8 to 11 p.m. This is Flightline bus 777, and it costs £4 ($7) per person.

The Underground, airbus, and train are, of course, far cheaper means of transport than a private taxi. For example, a taxi from Heathrow into central London is likely to cost more than £20 ($35).

A bus service connects the two airports, leaving every hour for the 70-minute trip. In addition, there is an expensive helicopter service that takes only 15 minutes between airports.

For flight information, telephone Heathrow at 01/759-4321, or Gatwick at 0293/31299.

London's newest airport is called **London City Airport** (tel. 01/474-5555), lying about six miles from "The City." It's reached by the District Line of the Underground (get off at Plaistow). Once leaving the Underground, you can take a taxi the rest of the way to the airport. This airport specializes in STOL (short takeoff and landing), and flights whisk you to Amsterdam, Brussels, or Paris like a commuter flight. Leading airlines using this airport include Euro City Express (linked with Sabena) and Brymon Airways (with ties to Air France). The airport lies in the old Docklands along the Thames, east of London.

The Underground

Londoners usually refer to the Underground as the "tube." Stations are identified by a distinctive sign, a red circle with blue crossbar, and the words "London Underground." (If you ask for a "subway," you risk ending up in a tunnel for pedestrians running beneath the road.) Destinations are listed on ticket machines, or you can buy your tickets from a booking office if you don't have the correct change. Maps showing the Underground network are displayed in every station, on each platform, and in Underground train cars. You can transfer as many times as you like, so long as you stay in the Underground and don't leave the network on ground level.

The electric subways are, to begin with, comfortable, the cars having cushioned seats, no less. The flat fare for one journey within the central zone is 50p (90¢). Trips from the central zone to destinations in the suburbs range from 80p ($1.40) to

£2.50 ($4.40). *Be sure to keep your ticket;* it must be presented when you get off. If you owe extra, you'll be billed by the attendant. Each subway line has its own distinctive color, and all you need do is follow the clearly painted arrows, which are on every stairway and at every corridor turning.

Note: If you're out on the town and are dependent on the Underground, watch your time carefully. Many of the trains stop running at midnight (11:30 p.m. on Sunday).

The line serving Heathrow Airport to central London has trains with additional luggage space, as well as moving walkways from the airport terminals to the Underground station.

Buses

The comparably priced bus system is almost as good as the Underground— and you have a better view. To find out about current routes, pick up a free bus map at one of the London Transport Travel Information Centres listed above. The map is available to personal callers only, not by mail.

After you've queued up for the red double-decker bus and selected a seat downstairs or on the upper deck (the best seats are on top, where you'll see more of the city), a conductor will come by to whom you'll tell your destination. He or she then collects the fare and gives you a ticket. As with the Underground, the fare varies according to the distance you travel. If you want to be warned when to get off, simply ask the conductor.

Bus Terminals: Victoria Coach Station, Buckingham Palace Road, S.W.1 (tel. 01/750-0202), is the main bus terminal. Tube: Victoria. Other bus stations are at King's Cross Coach Station and at Gloucester Road beside the Forum Hotel. The green single-decker buses you see on London streets link the center with outlying towns and villages.

Taxis

You can pick up a cab in London either by heading for a cab rank (stand), by hailing one on the streets, or by telephoning 01/253-5000, 01/272-0272, or 01/272-3030 for a radio cab. The minimum fare is £1 ($1.75) for the first 1305 yards, or four minutes and 21 seconds, with increments of 20p (35¢) thereafter, based on distance or time. Each additional passenger is charged 20p (35¢). From 8 p.m. to midnight Monday to Friday and from 6 a.m. to 8 p.m. on Saturday, after the minimum fare, increments are 40p (70¢). From midnight to 6 a.m. Monday to Friday and between 8 p.m. on the day before until 6 a.m. on the day after Sunday or public holidays, the meter clicks over at 60p ($1.05). From 8 p.m. December 24 to 6 a.m. December 27 and from 8 p.m. December 31 to 6 a.m. January 1, the flag still drops at £1 ($1.75), but increments are £2 ($3.50). Passengers are charged 10p (20¢) for each piece of luggage in the driver's compartment and any other item more than two feet long. All these tariffs include VAT. It's recommended that you tip about 20% of the fare and never less than 15%. If you have a complaint about the taxi service you get, or if you leave something in a cab, phone the Public Carriage Office, 15 Penton St., N.1 (tel. 01/278-1744), from 9 a.m. to 4:30 p.m. Monday to Friday. For complaints, you must know the cab number, which is displayed in the passenger compartment.

Be warned: If you phone for a cab, the meter starts running when the taxi receives instructions from the dispatcher, so you could find £1 ($1.75) or more on the meter when you get into the vehicle.

Cab sharing is now permitted in London, as British law allows cabbies to offer shared rides for two to five passengers. The taxis accepting ride sharing display a notice of yellow plastic with the words "Shared Taxi." These shared rides are mainly available at Heathrow Airport, main train stations, and the some 200 taxi stands in London. The savings per person is as follows: Each of two riders sharing is charged

65% of the fare a lone passenger would be charged. Three persons pay 55% each, four are charged 45% each, and five (the seating capacity of all new London cabs) pay 40% of the single-passenger fare.

The journey between Heathrow and central London costs £20 ($35) or more. If you are traveling between central London and Gatwick Airport, you must negotiate a fare with the driver before you get in the cab, as the meter does not apply. This is necessary because Gatwick is outside the Metropolitan Police District.

Bikes

You can rent bikes by the day or by the week from a number of businesses, one of the most popular being **Savile's Bike Rental,** 97 Battersea Rise, Battersea, S.W.11 (tel. 01/228-4279), which has been renting out bicycles for some 75 years. Stan Savile's father started the company back in 1912. Prices are £30 ($52.50) per week, which is much lower than the charge of many of its competitors. The firm is not only one of the cheapest but also one of the most reliable bike companies I have found. A deposit of £25 ($43.75) is required with a passport. Padlocks are provided free. The shop is open daily except Sunday from 9 a.m. to 5:30 p.m. Take the Northern Line tube from central London to Clapham Common and change to bus 35 or 37, getting off at Clapham Junction.

PRACTICAL FACTS

Besides the general information on England given in "The ABCs of England," Chapter II, some facts pertaining mainly to London may help make your visit here better.

AMERICAN EXPRESS: It has its main office at 6 Haymarket, S.W.1 (tel. 01/930-4411). Tube: Piccadilly Circus. There are some five other London locations, including the British Travel Centre, 4 Regent St., S.W.1, all open seven days a week.

BABYSITTERS: To find a babysitter in London, your hotel may be able to help you. A good possibility is **Childminders,** 9 Paddington St., W.1 (tel. 01/935-2049). Tube: Baker Street. Visitors to London can pay £4 ($7) temporary booking fee each time they hire a sitter from the agency. Or, if they prefer, the annual membership fee is £25 ($43.75), plus VAT. The membership fee or booking charge is paid to the agency, while pay for the job goes to the employee. Evening sitters cost £2.20 ($3.85) to £2.95 ($5.15) per hour, depending on the day of the week. The daytime charge is £3.50 ($6.15) per hour.

BANKS: Hours are generally from 9:30 a.m. to 3:30 p.m. Monday to Friday, although some banks in the suburbs are open from 9:30 a.m. to 12:30 p.m. Saturday. There are also Bureaux de Change, which charge for cashing traveler's checks or personal (United Kingdom) checks and for changing foreign currency into pounds sterling. Bureaux are often open seven days a week, 12 hours a day. There are branches of the main banks at London's airports. You'll always get the best rates at banks.

CHURCH SERVICES: The interdenominational **American Church in London** is at 79 Tottenham Court Rd., W.1 (tel. 01/580-2791). Established in 1969, it is staffed largely by Americans and is housed within a red-brick church constructed by a Congregationalist group in the 1950s. Two services are usually held on Sunday, one at 9:45 a.m., another at 11:45 a.m. Tube: Goodge Street.

DENTIST: Need emergency dental treatment? To find the dentist nearest you, phone 01/677-6363 or 01/584-1008 in London. You will be directed to whichever dental surgery in or near your area can attend to your needs.

DOCTORS: Ask at your hotel, which probably has a list of practitioners available.

DRUGSTORE: A 24-hour drugstore ("chemist" in Britain) operation is maintained in London by **Bliss the Chemist,** 50-56 Willesden Lane, Kilburn, N.W.6 (tel. 01/624-8000; tube: West Hampstead), and 5 Marble Arch, W.1 (tel. 01/723-6116; tube: Marble Arch. Emergency drugs are normally available at most hospitals, but you'll be examined to see that the medication you request is really necessary.

EMERGENCIES: In order to call **police, fire,** or **ambulance** in London, dial 999.

EYEGLASSES: If your glasses get lost or broken, try **Selfridges Optical** in Selfridges Department Store, 400 Oxford St., W.1 (tel. 01/629-1234, ext. 3889). Most prescriptions can be filled within one or two hours. More complicated prescriptions may take up to 24 hours to prepare. Cost, including examination, will be around £76 ($133). You will pay more for elaborate frames. It's always wise to take a copy of your lens prescription with you when you travel. Tube: Bond Street.

HOSPITALS: Among hospitals offering emergency care in London 24 hours a day are the **Royal Free Hospital,** Pond Street, N.W. 3 (tel. 01/794-0500; tube: Belsize Park), and the **University College Hospital,** Gower Street, W.C. 1 (tel. 01/387-9300; tube: Euston Square or Warren Street). The first treatment is free under the National Health Service. Many other London hospitals also have accident and emergency departments, including St. Mary's Hospital, Paddington; London Hospital, Whitechapel; King's College Hospital, Denmark Hill; Charing Cross Hospital; and St. Bartholomew's Hospital. Only emergency treatment is free.

LOST PROPERTY: For finding property lost in London on the tube or in a taxi—or elsewhere—report the loss to the police first, and they will advise you where to apply for its return. Taxi drivers are required to hand property left in their vehicles to the nearest police station. London Transport's Lost Property Office will try to assist personal callers only at their office at the Baker Underground station. For information on items lost on British Rail trains, lost passports, and lost credit cards, see "Lost Property" in the ABCs of England section of Chapter II.

LUGGAGE SHIPPING: This can relieve you of a lot of worry about how to get all your souvenirs home. **London Baggage Company Ltd.,** 262 Vauxhall Bridge Rd., S.W.1 (tel. 01/828-2400), offers worldwide service for shipping unaccompanied luggage, at rates usually below the normal excess baggage charges of airlines. They collect your extras from your London hotel and deal with all documentation and shipping. Prices vary according to weight and destination, but the charge for picking up your parcels, doing the paperwork, and delivering everything to the airport is about £18 ($31.50), plus insurance. Tube: Pimlico Station.

MEDICAL SERVICE: You can go to **Medical Express,** Chapel Place, W.1 (tel. 01/499-1991), just off Oxford Street, almost equidistant between the Oxford Circus and Bond Street tube stations. It's a medical center where you can have a consultation and full medical/clinical examination, such as a blood-pressure check, an EKG, and X-rays. The cost is £45 ($78.75) for a general consultation. For £20 ($35), you can get the British equivalent of your U.S. prescription here, if they decide that it is bona fide. The center is open Monday to Friday from 9 a.m. to 7 p.m., Saturday from 10 a.m. to 5 p.m. Full specialist services available by appointment include EG, gynecology, ENT, dermatology, and cardiology, among others, at consultation fees of £50 ($87.50).

POST OFFICES: Hours for the **Chief Post Office** in London at King Edward Street, EC1A 1AA, near St. Paul's Cathedral, are from 8:30 a.m. to 6:30 p.m. Monday to Friday and to 9 p.m. Wednesday; closed Saturday and Sunday. Tube: St. Paul's. The **Trafalgar Square Post Office**, 24-28 William IV St., London WC2N 4DL, operates as three separate businesses: inland and international postal services and banking, open from 8 a.m. to 8 p.m. Monday to Saturday; postage stamp sales, open from 10 a.m. to 7 p.m. Monday to Friday and 10 a.m. to 4:30 p.m. Saturday; and the post shop, selling greeting cards and stationery, open from 9 a.m. to 6:30 p.m. Monday to Friday and 9:30 a.m. to 5 p.m. Saturday. Tube: Charing Cross. Other post offices and sub–post offices are open from 9 a.m. to 5:30 p.m. Monday to Friday and 9 a.m. to 12:30 p.m. Saturday. Many sub–post offices and some main post offices close for one hour at lunchtime.

TELECOMMUNICATIONS: To make telephone calls: The **Westminster Communications Center,** 1A Broadway, S.W. 1, is open daily from 9 a.m. to 7 p.m., except Sunday. Here you can call all countries not available from a call box. Receptionists are available to help you in case of difficulty and to take your payment once your call is finished. You can pay in cash, check, credit card, or traveler's checks in pounds sterling. A range of other services is also available, including telex, telegrams, telemessages, word processing, photocopying, radio paging, voice bank, cellular radio rental, and facsimile. Call 01/222-4444 for details. The phone area code for London is 01, but of course, as in the U.S. and Canada, you don't use the area code while you're in the city, only when you're calling from elsewhere within the country. Tube: St. James's Park.

LONDON INFORMATION

Tourist information is available from the London Visitor and Convention Bureau's facilities. The **London Tourist Information Centre,** Victoria Station Forecourt, S.W. 1, can and will help you with almost anything of interest to a tourist in the U.K. capital. Staffed by courteous, tactful, sympathetic, patient, and understanding men and women, the center deals chiefly with accommodations in all size and price categories, from single travelers, family groups, and students to large-scale conventions. They also arrange for tour ticket sales and theater reservations and operate a bookshop. Hours are from 9 a.m. to 8:30 p.m. daily from early April to the end of October, from 9 a.m. to 7 p.m. Monday to Saturday, and from 9 a.m. to 5 p.m. Sunday from November to April. The bookshop is open from 9 a.m. to 6 p.m. Monday to Saturday and from 9 a.m. to 4 p.m. Sunday, and these hours are extended in July and August. For most types of service, you must apply in person. Tube: Victoria Station.

The bureau also has offices at the following locations:

Harrods, Knightsbridge, S.W. 3, on the fourth floor. Open during store hours. Tube: Knightsbridge.

Selfridges, Oxford Street, W.1, basement services area, Duke Street entrance. Open during store hours. Tube: Bond Street.

The Tower of London, West Gate, E.C.3. Open early April to the end of October, from 10 a.m. to 6 p.m. daily. Tube: Tower Hill.

Heathrow Airport Terminals 1, 2, and 3, Underground Concourse, open from 9 a.m. to 6 p.m., and Terminal 2, Arrivals Concourse, open from 9 a.m. to 7 p.m. daily.

Telephone inquiries may be made to the bureau by calling 01/730-3488 Monday to Friday from 9 a.m. to 5:30 p.m. (For riverboat information, call 01/730-4812.) Written inquiries should be addressed to the London Tourist Board and Convention Bureau, Correspondence Assistant, 26 Grosvenor Gardens, London SW1W ODU.

The British Tourist Authority has a **British Travel Centre** at Rex House, 4-12

Lower Regent St. (tel. 01/730-3400). This center offers a full information and hotel booking service for all parts of Britain, a British Rail ticket office, a travel agency, a theater ticket agency, hotel booking service, a bookshop, and a souvenir shop, all under one roof. Hours are from 9 a.m. to 6:30 p.m. Monday to Friday and from 10 a.m. to 4 p.m. Saturday and Sunday. Tube: Piccadilly Circus.

B&B HOTELS—WHAT TO EXPECT

Since London is one of the gateway cities to Europe, some basic points about low-budget accommodations should be covered to avoid disappointing the first-timer abroad.

The majority of budget hotels aren't hotels at all (in the sense of having elevators, porters, and private baths). Rather, they are old (averaging between 75 and 200 years), family-type guesthouses masquerading under the name "hotel." When the street pump ceased to supply the water, many of these homes for Victorian families were hastily, and often badly, converted.

London still contains hundreds of these four- and five-story hotels, even though many blocks are being razed to make way for skyscrapers and commercial buildings. Some of the former town houses are attached in rows in the Georgian style and open onto a square. At first glance, most of them look the same, but once inside, you'll find widely varying degrees of cleanliness, service, and friendliness.

Most bed-and-breakfast hotels (B&Bs) serve an English breakfast, or at least a continental one, usually in a converted servants' room in the basement, and they rarely serve any other meal. The rooms on higher floors tend to be smaller. The rooms have sinks (except in the most rock-bottom establishments), innerspring mattresses (occasionally), closet and dresser space (hopefully), and a desk and armchair (maybe). The bathroom may be a half flight down, two flights down, or (miracle of miracles) on the same floor.

It can even be in your bedroom. There is no longer the shortage of baths and showers as in days of yore. Most B&B establishments now have adequate baths. Ask first what is included in the room rate, and in the case of a B&B, ask to see the room before accepting. You'll probably be asked to pay in advance in B&B establishments. Incidentally, the designation of a private shower (or bath) on the tariff sheet presented to you doesn't always include a toilet in smaller places or in made-over old hotels.

A Traveler's Advisory

If you've arrived in London as a first-time visitor and, because of a limited budget, must seek low-cost lodgings, you should know that decent accommodations are hard to find. Since the last edition of this book was researched, I have received more complaints about B&B hotels in London than in any destination on the continent of Europe.

Chances are, you won't like what you get, and you will feel with some justification that you're being overcharged for a poor room, indifferent service, and often a surly reception.

I have selected a list of what I consider adequate B&B lodgings for London. Most of them are presented without any particular enthusiasm. Dozens and dozens were rejected as being total disasters.

If you make out better than I have warned, then be happily surprised.

Because of the poor state of many of central London's B&B establishments and low-budget hotels, I have in this edition included a number of "big splurge" hotels, and in some cases "super splurge" choices where you'll break our very limited budget but will be assured of comfort and value. This was done at the request of hundreds of readers who did not want to compromise a certain standard of living—that is, moderate comfort and a private bath—when traveling to London. But be warned: to get a good moderately priced hotel, especially a decent room with private bath, you may want to pay two to three times our room allowance. However, once you leave London, one of the world's most expensive cities, you can often find very good accommodations at moderate prices throughout all the counties.

For those who don't mind taking the tubes or trains for about 20 or 30 minutes every day, I've also included several B&B selections on the fringes of London, where establishments offer more reasonable tabs for quite good accommodations.

Reservations by Mail

Most hotels require at least a day's deposit before they will reserve a room for you. This can be accomplished either by an international money order or a personal check. Usually you can cancel a room reservation one week ahead of time and get a full refund. A few hotelkeepers will return your money three days before the reservation date. It's no trouble if you reserve well in advance, but if you send off several deposits at the last minute, you may lose money. Many hotel owners operate on such a narrow margin of profit that they find just buying stamps for airmail replies too expensive by their standards. Therefore, it's most important that you enclose a prepaid International Reply Coupon.

SOUTHWEST LONDON

During the most crowded periods already referred to, the wise budget visitor heads for the southwestern portion of the city—by which I mean the area south of Piccadilly and below Hyde Park but still on the north bank of the Thames. Although the hotels here are not as numerous as in other sections of town, they are plentiful enough, and more likely than the others to have vacancies, even at the height of the season.

Most of the southwestern hotels are in the moderately expensive **Victoria** section (around Victoria Station), on the fringes of **Belgravia,** and in the less expensive **Earl's Court** area (where large numbers of Canadian and Australian visitors stay). Scattered, and most reasonably priced, hotels and guesthouses are also to be found in the museumland of **South Kensington** and the neighboring middle-class district of **Brompton.**

---

2. Belgravia

Belgravia, south of Hyde Park, is the aristocratic quarter of London, challenging Mayfair for grandness. It reigned in glory along with Queen Victoria, but today's aristocrats are likely to be the top echelon in foreign embassies, along with a rising new-money class of actors and models.

Belgravia is near Buckingham Palace Gardens and Brompton Road. Its center is Belgrave Square, one of the more attractive plazas in London. A few town houses once occupied by eminent Edwardians have been discreetly turned into moderately priced hotels (others were built specifically for that purpose). For those who prefer a residential address, Belgravia is choice real estate.

For best all-around value, the **Diplomat Hotel,** 2 Chesham St., London SW1X 8DY (tel. 01/235-1544), is a leader in its field. Part of its allure lies in its status as a small, reasonably priced family-operated hotel in an otherwise prohibitively expensive neighborhood. It was originally built by one of the neighborhood's most famous architects in the 19th century on a wedge-shaped street corner near the site of the Belgravia Sheraton.

Each of the 28 comfortable bedrooms contains a modern bath, color TV, phone, a high ceiling, and well-chosen wallpaper in vibrant Victorian-inspired colors. Each comes with such extra touches as a hairdryer and morning newspapers. Singles rent for £49.95 ($87.40) daily and doubles for £64.95 ($113.65). A sumptuous English buffet breakfast is served in a private dining room. Tube: Sloane Square.

3. Victoria

Directly south of Buckingham Palace is a section in Pimlico often referred to as Victoria, with its namesake, sprawling Victoria Station, as its center. Known as the "Gateway to the Continent," Victoria Station is where you get boat-trains to Dover and Folkestone for that trip across the Channel to France.

The section also has many other advantages from the standpoint of location, as the British Airways Terminal, the Green Line Coach Station, and the Victoria Coach Station are all just five minutes from Victoria Station. From the bus stations, you can hop aboard many a Green Line Coach fanning out to the suburbs. In addition, an inexpensive bus tour of London departs from a point on Buckingham Palace Road just behind the Victoria Railroad Station.

As you gaze down Belgrave Road, looking at the hotels that line the street, you'll find few recommendable choices, as many are now occupied by welfare recipients. With some exceptions, you'll find the pickings better on the satellite streets jutting off Belgrave Road.

Your best bet, however, is to walk about Ebury Street, which lies directly to the east of Victoria Station and Buckingham Palace Road. There you will find some of the best moderately priced lodgings in central London. My favorite recommendations along this street follow.

Collin House, 104 Ebury St., London SW1W 9QD (tel. 01/730-8031), provides a good, clean B&B under the watchful eye of its resident proprietors, Mr. and Mrs. D. L. Thomas. Everything is maintained here, and the majority of bedrooms have private showers and toilets, something of a rarity for a B&B. Single rooms with private bath/shower and toilet cost £30 ($53.50) per night; doubles rent for £36 ($63) without bath, rising to £42 ($73.50) with a private bath and toilet. All rates are inclusive of a full English breakfast, VAT, and the use of showers and toilets for those who don't have private facilities. There are also a number of family rooms. The main bus, rail, and Underground terminals are about a five-minute walk from the hotel. Tube: Victoria Station.

Ebury House, 102 Ebury St., London SW1W 9QD (tel. 01/730-1350), is a comfortable and straightforward guesthouse where visitors are as likely to be greeted by Lola, the longtime manager, as by owners Marilyn and David Davies. All of the 13 bedrooms contain color TV and hairdryers, and there is one full bath per floor and a pay phone on one of the stairwells. Accommodations, with breakfast included, cost £28 ($49) daily in a single, rising to £38 ($66.50) in a double. The pine-paneled breakfast room is the establishment's morning rendezvous point, where anyone wanting to discuss the weekend's rugby scores will find an avid connoisseur in David. Tube: Victoria Station.

Lewis House Hotel, 111 Ebury St., London SW1W 9QU (tel. 01/730-2094), is a town house that was the home of playwright Sir Noël Coward from 1917 to 1930. During World War II, military leaders were housed here, each with a direct phone link to the Admiralty and the War Office. This family-run hotel, today managed by John Evans, offers rooms with or without showers, costing £38 ($66.50) to £42 ($73.50) daily for two persons, including a full English breakfast and VAT. The family suite, for four or five persons, rents for £85 ($148.75) and has bath facilities. Breakfast is taken in the large Noël Coward room, which has many pictures of "the master" and assorted memorabilia on the walls. Tube: Victoria Station.

Sir Gar House, 131 Ebury St., London SW1W 9QU (tel. 01/730-9378), is one of a row of Victorian brick-fronted town houses along Ebury Street, three minutes' walk from Victoria Station (the nearest tube stop). Unusual for the area, the hotel has a walled-in manicured garden. Annie Evans, the resident owner, offers a total of 11 comfortably furnished rooms, each with tea- and coffee-making facilities, color TV, and hot and cold running water. About half the rooms contain showers and toilets. These cost £44 ($77) daily for two persons, with VAT, service, and a full English breakfast included. Bathless rooms rent for £38 ($66.50) in a double, £25 ($43.75) in a single.

Elizabeth Hotel, 37 Eccleston Square, London SW1V 1PB (tel. 01/828-6812), is an intimate, privately owned establishment overlooking the quiet gardens of a stately square. It is an excellent place to stay, convenient to Belgravia, Chelsea, and Westminster, and not far from Buckingham Palace. Of its 24 rooms, three have baths or showers, and good facilities are available for the bathless rooms, which have hot and cold water basins. Singles without bath cost from £26 ($45.50) daily, and bathless doubles or twins go from £40 ($70). A double with a sink and shower but no toilet is priced from £44 ($77). A large double with a full bathroom, color TV, and refrigerator rents from £57 ($99.75). Prices include a full English breakfast and VAT. The reception staff will help guests find good pubs and restaurants in the neighborhood. Tube: Victoria Station.

Astors Hotel, 110-112 Ebury St., London SW1W 9QU (tel. 01/730-3811), is a brick-fronted Victorian house in the popular Belgravia area of Ebury Street. Victoria main line and tube stations are a five-minute walk away. The resident manager offers 20 comfortably furnished rooms, each with hot and cold running water, color TV, and radio. Some have full baths or showers, and for these you pay £45 ($78.75) daily for two persons, with VAT, service, and a full English breakfast included. Singles cost from £25 ($43.75), and bathless doubles rent for £38 ($66.50).

Chesham House Hotel, 64-66 Ebury St., London SW1 W9Q (tel. 01/730-8513), has a stone facade flanked by a pair of old-fashioned carriage lamps, and its interior is more modernized than you'd expect from a glance at the outside. Each of the 23 rooms contains a TV and running water; none has a private bath. Coffee is served continuously after 5 p.m. every day, and breakfast is served in a functional basement room. The director, Major Eric J. Fletcher, rents singles from £26 ($45.50) nightly, doubles and twins from £40 ($70) to £44 ($77), and family rooms from £50 ($87.50) to £54 ($94.50). A full English breakfast is included in the room price. Tube: Victoria Station.

Harcourt House, 50 Ebury St., London SW1W OLU (tel. 01/730-2722) is tall, narrow, and fronted with white stucco. This pleasant hotel was originally built in the 1840s as a private house. Today, a confusing labyrinth of steep stairs leads to 10 comfortably cozy twin bedrooms, only a few with private bath. Bathless rooms rent for £40 ($70) nightly, rising to £48 ($84) and £50 ($87.50) with bath. Included in the price is a generous English breakfast, served within a Victorian-inspired, cellar-level breakfast room. The tube is Victoria Station, which lies within a three-minute walk of the front entrance.

Caswell Hotel, 25 Gloucester St., London SW1V 2DB (tel. 01/834-6345), was built in 1850. The hotel contains four floors, a chintz-filled lobby, and understated but comfortable room furnishings. Accommodations don't contain TV or phone, but many visitors consider the calm and proximity to Victoria Station (the nearest tube stop) worth the lack of electronic comforts. The quiet of the 20 bedrooms derives from the location on a cul-de-sac with little traffic. Mr. and Mrs. Hare, the owners, charge rates of £26 ($45.50) daily for a bathless single, £37 ($64.75) for a bathless double, and £48 ($84) for a double with bath.

Enrico Hotel, 79 Warwick Way, London SW1V 1QP (tel. 01/834-9538), is clean, well scrubbed, and decorated in a comfortable but functional style. The hotel's 26 bedrooms are often filled with a repeat clientele who know of its good value. Bathless singles cost £22 ($38.50) daily, with bathless doubles going for £28 ($49). Doubles with shower peak at £34 ($59.50), including breakfast. Discounts of £2 ($3.50) per room are made for stays of two nights or more. Tube: Victoria Station.

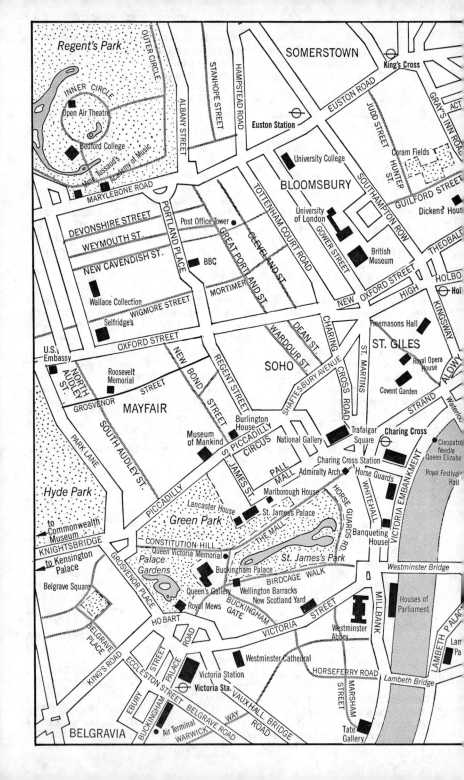

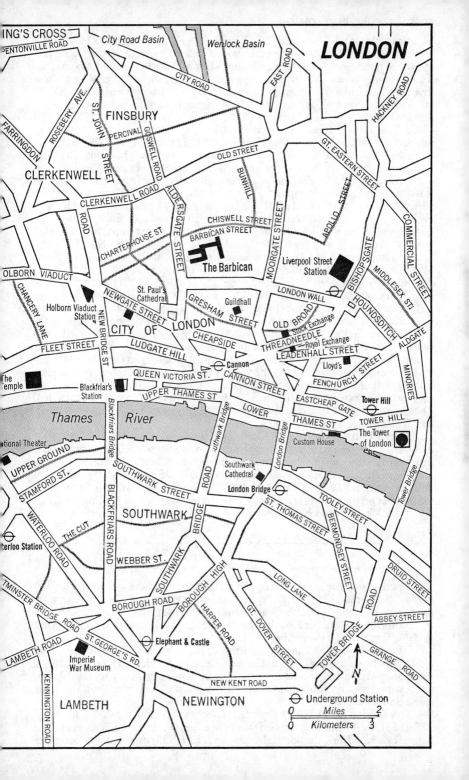

Granada Hotel, 73 Belgrave Rd., London SW1V 2BG (tel. 01/834-6560), is set into a row of identical houses, each with a protruding Adam-style porch. This renovated hotel offers comfortable accommodations. Each of the 16 bedrooms contains its own shower, TV and video, a phone, and radio and cassette. Most of them have complete baths. The Spanish-born owner, José Gil, has installed a ground-floor sauna, Jacuzzi, sunbed, and bar. Breakfast is the only meal served. The bedrooms rent for £26 ($45.50) daily in a single, £40 ($70) in a double, and £44 ($77) to £50 ($87.50) in a triple. Tube: Victoria Station.

Oxford House Hotel, 92-94 Cambridge St., London SW1V 4QG (tel. 01/834-6467), is set on a quiet one-way street (which taxi drivers have difficulty finding), only a few blocks from Victoria Station (the nearest tube stop). This 150-year-old Victorian town house is sheltered by a facade which is half brick and half stucco. It is owned and operated by an India-born interior designer, Mr. Kader, and his Irish wife, Terry. The hotel maintains 18 bedrooms, none of which has a private bath. Each, however, is cozily decorated with flowery fabrics and coordinated bedspreads and carpets. A copious English breakfast (Mr. Kader is known for his scrambled eggs) is served in a cozy cellar-level room and is included in the price of a room. Small, cramped, and relatively inconvenient single rooms lie on the fourth floor. Singles rent for £22 ($38.50) daily, with doubles costing £32 ($56).

Romany House Hotel, 35 Longmore St., London SW1V 1JQ (tel. 01/834-5553), was established as a hotel in 1937 when a 500-year-old cottage was joined to a 200-year-old Georgian white-fronted town house. The name came out of a vision by a psychic. The owners, Mary and Peter Gulbitis, have owned the property for some 20 years and are honest about its shortcomings. "We don't want to sell it too lavishly, because we want people to know what they are getting," Mrs. Gulbitis explains. The place is old-fashioned but filled with a certain corny charm, and many visitors are repeat. None of the bedrooms has a private bath, but there are adequate hallway facilities. The two singles are priced at £18 ($31.50) nightly, whereas the eight doubles or twins rent for £28 ($49). Breakfast, VAT, and service are included. The breakfast room in the cellar is reached by the narrow staircase of the former cottage. Tube: Victoria Station.

Melita House Hotel, 33-35 Charlwood St., London SW1V 2DU (tel. 01/828-0471), sits on a residential street near Victoria Station. Originally built more than a century ago as a private house, it contains 18 comfortable bedrooms. In summer, depending on the plumbing, singles cost £20 ($35) to £28 ($49) daily, with doubles going for £30 ($52.50) to £40 ($70). In winter, discounts of around £2 ($3.50) per person nightly are granted. Included in the price is a full English breakfast. Tube: Victoria Station.

---

4. Earl's Court

Another popular hotel and rooming-house district is the area in and around Earl's Court, below Kensington, bordering the western half of Chelsea. A 15-minute subway ride from the Earl's Court station will take you into the heart of Piccadilly, via either the District or Piccadilly Lines. The area is convenient to both the West End Air Terminal and the Exhibition Halls.

Incidentally, Earl's Court was for years a staid residential district, drawing genteel ladies who wore pince-nez, but I haven't seen one of those for a long time. Now a new young crowd is attracted to the district at night, principally to a number of pubs, wine bars, and coffeehouses. In summer, Australians virtually fill up all the cheap B&B houses.

The Beaver Hotel, 57-59 Philbeach Gardens, London W14 8RS (tel. 01/373-4553), comprises 40 rooms on four floors. Built in the typical Victorian town house fashion in 1887, the hotel offers singles at £20 ($35) daily and doubles at £15

($26.25) per person for a bed and a full English breakfast, including service and tax. A few rooms have three beds, and these are suitable for families with children. More than half of the units contain private baths and rent for £22 ($38.50) per person, based on double occupancy, £18.50 ($32.40) per person for three occupants. All the rooms are centrally heated and contain water basins, radios, and telephones. A bar serves drinks and snacks in the evening. Tube: Earl's Court.

Hotel Halifax, 65 Philbeach Gardens, London SW5 9EE (tel. 01/373-4153), is a well-appointed Victorian house that has been brought up to date with such amenities as central heating. The hotel rents out 15 bedrooms, each with hot and cold running water, color TV, and a radio and intercom unit. Some accommodations contain a private shower as well. In summer, with breakfast and taxes included, bathless singles cost £22 ($38.50) daily, with bathless doubles going for £32 ($56). However, doubles with private bath peak at £38 ($66.50). Guests are given their own keys. The hotel opens onto a tree-lined crescent near the Earl's Court tube stop.

Merlyn Court Hotel, 2 Barkston Gardens, London SW5 0EN (tel. 01/370-1640), is a red-brick, turn-of-the-century hotel offering 18 rooms, with a cellar-level breakfast room and a TV lounge for viewing or socializing. None of the bedrooms has a private toilet, although a few of them contain private showers. Depending on the plumbing, singles cost from £22 ($38.50) to £24 ($42.90) daily, with doubles costing £30 ($52.50) to £34 ($59.50). In winter, these tariffs are discounted by about £2 ($3.50) per person nightly. Tube: Earl's Court.

Kensington Court Hotel, 33 Nevern Pl., London SW5 9NP (tel. 01/370-5151), lies just off Earl's Court Road, standing on a quiet residential street of Victorian-era town houses. It presents one of the few modern facades on the street. The owners rent a total of 35 clean, well-kept bedrooms, each with private bath, color TV, and coffee-making equipment. Singles cost £45 ($78.75) daily, doubles or twins £55 ($96.25). Some family units for three or four guests rent from £59 ($103.25) to £63 ($110.25). Bar snacks are available throughout the day and evening in the lounge bar. Tube: Earl's Court.

Hogarth Hotel, Hogarth Rd., London SW5 0QQ (tel. 01/370-6831), is in its second decade. Rising five floors near the Earl's Court Exhibition Centre, the hotel has a well-appointed restaurant and contains 85 rooms, each with private bath, color TV, and coffee-making facilities. With a continental breakfast included, singles cost £45 ($78.75) to £50 ($87.50) daily, and doubles or twins go for £60 ($105) to £65 ($113.75), including service and tax. Tube: Earl's Court.

Concord Hotel, 155-157 Cromwell Rd., London SW5 0TQ (tel. 01/370-4151), offers one of the best values along this busy traffic artery. Frankly, many of the hotels along Cromwell Road are disasters, but this one is suitable. It stands behind a brown brick facade with neoclassical detailing and a garden and children's sandboxes. There's a sunken TV lounge with leather couches. Rooms are modestly furnished but clean and comfortable. In all, the owner rents out 40 rooms, 12 of which contain a private shower or bath. Depending on the plumbing, the B&B rates range from £25 ($43.75) to £33 ($57.75) daily, and doubles cost £34 ($59.50) to £50 ($87.50). The hotel is not licensed for alcohol but does offer breakfast. Tube: Earl's Court.

5. Brompton and South Kensington

Brompton and South Kensington (S.W.7), south of Kensington Gardens and Hyde Park, are essentially residential areas, not as elegant as bordering Belgravia and Knightsbridge. The section is, however, rich in museums—in fact, it is often dubbed "museumland"—and it has a number of colleges and institutes, which draw large numbers of students.

Staying in this section of London has much to recommend it. In addition to the nearby Kensington museums, such as the Victoria and Albert, Albert Hall is within the district, and Kensington Gardens and Harrods department store are within walking distance.

One of the best streets in London for hotels is the gracefully charming Sumner Place in South Kensington. However, all of these hotels are over our budget, but they represent such good value, nevertheless, that I've decided to include them. Sumner Place was a rundown street filled with roughly similar Victorian houses, but today the street has been considerably upgraded. The rental income from the buildings along the street goes into a charitable trust. Any of the street's hotels can be reached via the South Kensington tube stop.

Number Sixteen, 16 Sumner Pl., London SW7 3EG (tel. 01/589-5232), is an elegant luxury "pension" made up of four early Victorian town houses. Built in 1848 and opened as Number Sixteen in 1970, the hotel has beautiful gardens, and the 33 rooms, reached by elevator, contain an eclectic mix of English antiques and modern paintings. Singles cost £40 ($70) to £60 ($105) daily, and doubles go for £95 ($166.25) to £110 ($192.50). Taxes and a continental breakfast served in the rooms are included. There's an honor-system self-service bar in one of the elegantly formal sitting rooms. Tube: South Kensington.

Aster House, 3 Sumner Pl., London SW7 3EE (tel. 01/581-5888), is the smallest hotel on this unusual street of hotels and is located behind an early Victorian facade. Peter Carapiet, the owner, has built "l'Orangerie" over the adjacent garage, with a glassed-in conservatory that doubles as a breakfast room and lounge. All 12 of the hotel's rooms have private baths, color TV, mini-bars, direct-dial phones, and central heating. Two of the attractive units are on the ground floor, one with a fireplace and a curtained four-poster. Singles cost £42 ($73.50) to £52 ($91), while doubles and twins go for £68 ($119) to £82 ($143.50). Tube: South Kensington.

Eden Plaza Hotel, 68-69 Queensgate, London SW7 5TJ (tel. 01/370-6111), stands on a broad, tree-lined boulevard that gets a lot of traffic. It is especially reasonable in price considering its fine neighborhood. Double-glazed windows help keep out the traffic noise. The hotel rents out 64 small but well-maintained bedrooms. Each has private bath or shower, direct-dial phone, color TV, and hairdryer. An elevator services all floors. A single rents for £48 ($84) daily and doubles or twins from £60 ($105) to £65 ($113.75). Breakfast is included in the price, along with VAT and service. A cocktail bar is a good rendezvous point, and a restaurant, the Plaza, serves both British and continental dishes. Tube: Gloucester Road.

Adelphi Hotel, 127-129 Cromwell Rd., London SW7 4DT (tel. 01/373-7177), is one of the best value hotels in the neighborhood. It rents 71 comfortably furnished bedrooms. All but three of these contain private baths. Singles rent for £54.90 ($96.10) daily, doubles or twins for £69.90 ($122.35), triples and four-bedded units for £89.90 ($157.35). Rates include an English breakfast, service, and tax, and all accommodations are equipped with phone, color TV, radio, video, hairdryer, and trouser-press. The large bow window of the front parlor has been transformed into a stylish lounge with a bar, which serves hot snacks in the evening. Tube: Gloucester Road.

Sorbonne Hotel, 39 Cromwell Rd., London SW7 2DH (tel. 01/589-6636), was built in 1840 and was once the private residence of the aunt of Sir Winston Churchill. Nowadays, standing opposite the Natural History Museum and near Harrods department store, it is an appealing choice. The owners rent out 20 pleasant rooms, a dozen of which contain private shower or bath, along with a phone and radio. Accommodations, naturally, depend on the plumbing: singles from £20.50 ($35.90) to £31 ($54.25), doubles from £30.50 ($53.40), rising to a high of £41 ($71.75) in a twin with bath. Some triples with bath are also rented for £50 ($87.50), these tariffs including VAT and a continental breakfast. Tube: South Kensington.

6. Knightsbridge

Adjoining Belgravia is Knightsbridge, a top residential and shopping district of London. Just south of Hyde Park, Knightsbridge is close in character to Belgravia. Much of this section to the west of Sloane Street is older, dating back in architecture and layout to the 18th century. Several of the major department stores, such as Harrods, are here.

Executive Hotel, 57 Pont St., London SW1X 0BD (tel. 01/581-2424), was built in 1870 as a private house behind an ornate neo-Romanesque facade of red brick. From the front you see only a discreet metal plaque announcing the establishment's status as a hotel. But once inside, you find 29 comfortable, modernized, and unfrilly bedrooms. Each of these contains simple built-in furniture, a high ceiling, radio, color TV, phone, private bath, and central heating. With a full English breakfast included, singles cost £49.95 ($87.40) daily, with a double or twin costing £64.95 ($113.65). An extra bed can be added to a double for £19.95 ($34.90). An elevator takes guests to one of the five upstairs floors. A cozy modern bar occupies one of the rooms off the lobby, and the location, near the attractions of Knightsbridge (the nearest tube stop), make the Executive very, very central.

Knightsbridge Green Hotel, 159 Knightsbridge, London SW1X 7PD (tel. 01/584-6274), is an unusual establishment that was constructed a block from Harrods in the 1920s. Later, when it was converted into a hotel, the developers were careful to retain the wide baseboards, cove molding, high ceilings, and spacious proportions of the dignified old structure. None of the accommodations contains a kitchen, but the result comes close to apartment-style living. Many of the doubles or twins are suites, each well furnished, with access to the second-floor "club room," where coffee and pastries are available throughout the day. Each of the accommodations contains a private bath, phone, and TV set. Singles rent for £55 ($96.25) daily, and doubles cost from £70 ($122.50). The hotel offers 16 suites for two persons for £85 ($148.75). VAT is included. Reservations are important here. Tube: Knightsbridge.

Knightsbridge Hotel, 10 Beaufort Gardens, London SW3 1FT (tel. 01/589 9271), stands on a treelined square that is peaceful and tranquil and free from traffic, and it has a subdued Victorian charm. The place is small, only 20 bedrooms. Each of the accommodations has phone, radio, and central heating, and there's a lounge with a color "telly" and a bar on the premises. Rooms come with and without bath, with singles costing £29 ($50.75) to £40 ($70) daily, and doubles going for £41 ($71.75) to £65 ($113.75). Each price includes a continental breakfast, VAT, and service. Tube: Knightsbridge.

7. Chelsea

This fashionable district stretches along the Thames, south of Hyde Park, Brompton, and South Kensington. Beginning at Sloane Square, it runs westward toward the periphery of Earl's Court and West Brompton. Its spinal cord is King's Road. The little streets and squares on either side of the King's Road artery have hundreds of tiny cottages used formerly by the toiling underprivileged of the 18th and 19th centuries. By now, except maybe for Mayfair or Belgravia, Chelsea couldn't be more chic. Hence, the visitor seeking reasonably priced accommodations should follow Greeley's sage advice to go west. However, those who can afford a splurge may want to settle in here.

The Willett, 32 Sloane Gardens, Sloane Square, London SW1W 8DJ (tel. 01/824-8415), is one of the nuggets of Chelsea, a 19th-century town house opening onto gardens. The hotel has been fully renovated with new furnishings, but the traditional charm of the place remains. Singles with private bath cost £49.95 ($97.40) daily, with a double or twin-bedded room, also with bath, renting for £59.95 ($104.91). An extra bed can be added to a bedroom for £19.95 ($34.91) per person. VAT is added to all tariffs. Tube: Sloane Square.

Blair House Hotel, 34 Draycott Pl., London SW3 2SA (tel. 01/581-2323), lies deep in the heart of Chelsea, an old-fashioned building of architectural interest. It has been modernized and completely refurnished. Rooms are usually small but still comfortable, and contain such conveniences as direct-dial phone, radio, and facilities for making tea or coffee, along with a TV set. Most rooms contain a private bath or shower, and naturally, these are more expensive. Singles range in price from £33 ($57.75) to £47 ($82.25) daily, and twins or doubles cost from £48 ($84) to £60 ($105), including a continental breakfast and VAT. Tube: Sloane Square.

Oakley Street Hotel, 73 Oakley St., London SW3 5HF (tel. 01/352-5599), lies north of the Chelsea Embankment and is best reached by buses. Singles rent for £15 ($26.25) daily, and twins and doubles cost £25 ($43.75) to £29 ($50.75). Accommodations shared with two other people are priced at £8.50 ($14.90) per person. Rates include a full English breakfast, free tea and coffee whenever you want it, and use of kitchen facilities, including a refrigerator and a cooker. Everything but food is provided for preparing your own meals. Tube: Sloane Square.

Flaxman House, 104-105 Oakley St., London SW3 5NT (tel. 01/352-0187), is a clean bright 22-room town house decorated with contemporary furniture (painted white). There are eight singles, eight doubles, as well as four twin-bedded rooms and one reserved for families. Charges for B&B are £13 ($22.72) to £18 ($31.50) daily in a single, rising to £23 ($40.25) to £32 ($56) in a double. Breakfast is included. Tube: Sloane Square.

WEST LONDON

This district is a potential bonanza for finding a room. There are literally dozens of private hotels scattered over a wide and attractive section of the West End. I'll first list the guesthouses in the Royal Borough of Kensington (west of Kensington Gardens and Hyde Park).

In the same vicinity is another hunting ground, Bayswater, encompassing within its undefined borders Queensway and Notting Hill Gate. The already-mentioned Paddington district, surrounding Paddington Station, north of Hyde Park, is one of the major sections for budget hotels in London, with the prized Sussex Gardens in its lair. This section also includes St. Marylebone, a district that touches one corner of Hyde Park and is next to Regent's Park in the east and Edgeware Road in the west.

8. Kensington

The Royal Borough (W 8) draws its greatest number of visitors from shoppers (Kensington High Street), but it also contains a number of fine middle-class guesthouses, lying, for the most part, west of Kensington Gardens. The district can be a convenient place to stay—so near the Kensington Palace where Queen Victoria was once a resident. Of course, in Victoria's day the rows of houses along Kensington Palace Gardens were inhabited by millionaires (yet Thackeray also lived here). Today the houses are occupied in part by foreign ambassadors.

Hotel Lexham, 32-38 Lexham Gardens, London W8 5JU (tel. 01/373-6471), a Victorian terrace hotel, is owner-operated, facing on an attractively quiet garden square with a cast-iron fence out front. Of the 60 comfortably furnished bed-rooms, more than half contain a private bath or shower. Depending on the plumb-ing, singles cost from £25.50 ($44.65) to £31.50 ($55.15) daily, and twins or doubles rent for £34.50 ($60.40) to £49.50 ($86.65). Several large family rooms are popular, with extra beds for children priced at £10.50 ($18.40) each. Units also contain phones, radios, electric shaver points, and central heating, and families with children receive a special welcome. Guests have use of two well-appointed lounges, and a restaurant overlooking a walled garden serves a traditional English breakfast (included with VAT in the tariffs) along with moderately priced lunches or dinners. Tube: Gloucester Road.

Atlas Hotel, 24-30 Lexham Gardens, London W8 5JU (tel. 01/373-7873), along with the nearby Apollo Hotel (see below), offers a total of 130 rooms between the two, 70% of which contain private baths. This long-established hotel offers rooms ranging from £24 ($42) to £37 ($64.75) daily in a single and £24 ($42) per person in a twin- or double-bedded unit. Three adults can also rent a triple-bedded room with bath at £19 ($33.25) per person. One child of 12 or under can share a room with parents free. Elevators service all floors. Tube: Gloucester Road.

Apollo Hotel, 18-22 Lexham Gardens, London W8 5JU (tel. 01/835-1133), shares much in common with its just-recommended sister, the Atlas. The owner op-erates these Victorian buildings on a quiet residential street in Kensington, just off Cromwell Road. Both hotels have elevators servicing all floors, and guests of both hotels use the bar at the Atlas. The Apollo, however, has more rooms with baths (there are more showers in the Atlas). All rooms in the Apollo have color TV and direct-dial phones. The tariffs are the same, however: from £24 ($42) to £37 ($64.75) daily in a single and £24 ($42) per person in a twin- or double-bedded unit. Tube: Gloucester Road.

Vicarage Private Hotel, 10 Vicarage Gate, London W8 4AG (tel. 01/229-4030), is the domain of Eileen and Martin Diviney, who charge £20 ($35) daily in a single, £38 ($66.50) in a double, and £46 ($80.50) in a triple. None of the rooms have private baths. All rates include breakfast, individually prepared by Mrs. Diviney. The rooms have pleasant furnishings, water basins, and shaver points, and there is a good supply of showers. The house is centrally heated. Vicarage Gate is handy for boutiques and restaurants on Kensington Church Street, and a self-serve laundry is nearby. Parking is likely to be a major problem in case you bring a car into London. Tube: Kensington High Street and Notting Hill Gate.

Clearlake Hotel, 19 Prince of Wales Terrace, London W8 5PQ (tel. 01/937-3274), is a family hotel on a residential street facing Kensington Gardens. You can, of course, rent the comfortable single and double rooms, but the real finds here are the one-, two-, and three-room apartments with private baths and gas or electric kitchenettes. Some apartments also have a full-size kitchen and two bathrooms. The larger apartments can accommodate as many as eight, with plenty of closet space to go around. Rates range from £18 ($31.50) daily for a single up to £120 ($210) for a large apartment capable of housing four or more. All units have phones, color TV, and firm beds. Tube: Kensington High Street or Gloucester Road.

Avonmore Hotel, 66 Avonmore Rd., London W14 8RS (tel. 01/603-4296), is easily accessible to West End theaters and shops yet is located in a quiet neighbor-hood, only two minutes from the West Kensington station of the Underground's District Line. It's also reached by bus numbers 9, 27, or 73. The Avonmore, a pri-vately owned bright friendly place, boasts wall-to-wall carpeting, color TV sets, re-frigerators, phones, radio alarms, and central heating in each room. An English breakfast, VAT, and service are included in the price of £28 ($49) daily in a single, £38 ($66.50) in a double. There is a ratio of two rooms per clean, tiled bath. The owner of the Avonmore, Margaret McKenzie, provides friendly, personal service. Her hotel is a winner of the National Award for the best small private hotel in Lon-don.

Abbey House, 11 Vicarage Gate, London W8 4AG (tel. 01/727-2594), was

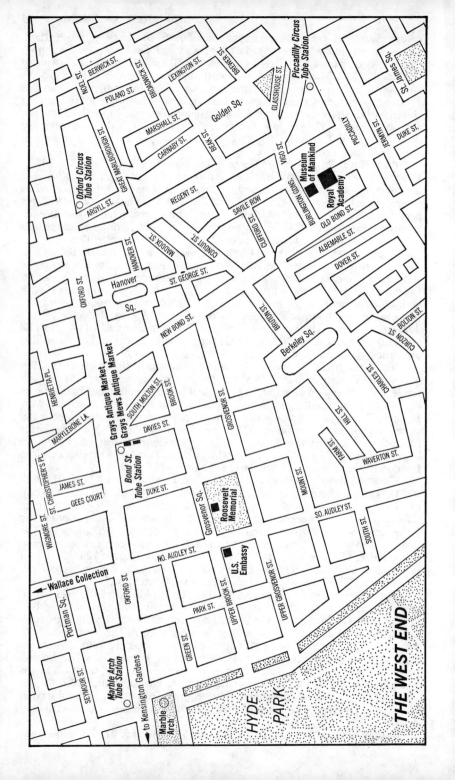

THE WEST END

built about 1860 on a typical Victorian square. It is modern, thanks to renovations, yet it has many original features. The 15 spacious bedrooms have central heating, color TV, shaver points, vanity lights, and hot and cold water basins. The hotel offers shared baths, one to each two to four lodging units. The rooms are all refurbished annually. Singles rent for £20 ($35) daily, doubles for £35 ($61.25), and triples for £44 ($77), with VAT and a hot English breakfast included. Tube: Kensington High Street.

9. Shepherd's Bush

Reeve's Private Hotel, 48 Shepherd's Bush Green, London W12 8PJ (tel. 01/740-1158), caters primarily to women, offering nine bedrooms, extra security locks, double glazing, a sympathetic female staff, and a cozy, comfortable decor that is neither excessively florid nor excessively ruffled. There is a bar and restaurant where only residents, many loyal repeat clientele, and their invited guests or outsiders who reserve in advance are welcomed. Each of the bedrooms contains a color TV, private toilet and shower, and phone. With breakfast and taxes included, singles range from £38 ($66.50) to £45 ($78.75), with doubles costing £56 ($98). Tube: Shepherd's Bush.

10. Notting Hill Gate

Increasingly gaining in fashion and frequented by such persons as the Princess of Wales, Notting Hill Gate is bounded on the south by Bayswater Road and on the east by Gloucester Terrace. It is hemmed in on the north by West Way and on the west by the Shepherd's Bush ramp leading to the M40. It has many turn-of-the-century mansions and small houses sitting on quiet, leafy streets.

Pembridge Court Hotel, 34 Pembridge Gardens, London W2 4DX (tel. 01/229-9977), presents a neoclassically elegant, cream-colored facade to a residential neighborhood that is making gains toward gentrification. Its brick-lined restaurant, where full meals with wine cost from £15 ($26.25), is popular and well recommended. The 25 bedrooms have color TV, radios, direct-dial phones, hairdryers, and trouser-presses. A full English breakfast is included in the price of £50 ($87.50) daily in a single, from £70 ($122.50) to £100 ($175) in a double. The hotel was awarded a certificate of distinction in 1988 by the British Tourist Authority, which was presented by Lord and Lady Spencer. Tube: Notting Hill Gate.

11. Paddington and Bayswater

Another popular hotel area, jammed with budget housing, is the Paddington section, around Paddington Station, just to the northwest of Kensington Gardens and Hyde Park. Slightly to the west of Hyde Park, Bayswater is an unofficial district with a number of decently priced lodgings.

Again, you'd be well advised to telephone ahead. If you have not obtained a reservation, then begin your trek by taking the Underground to either Paddington or Edgware Road and walking to Sussex Gardens, a long avenue flanked by bed-and-breakfast houses, many of which are dreadfully run down. That's not all: Many of the budget hotels in the Paddington and Bayswater areas now deal mostly with homeless persons sent from the local authorities. Postbreakfast hours, when guests have just checked out, are your best time for finding a vacancy.

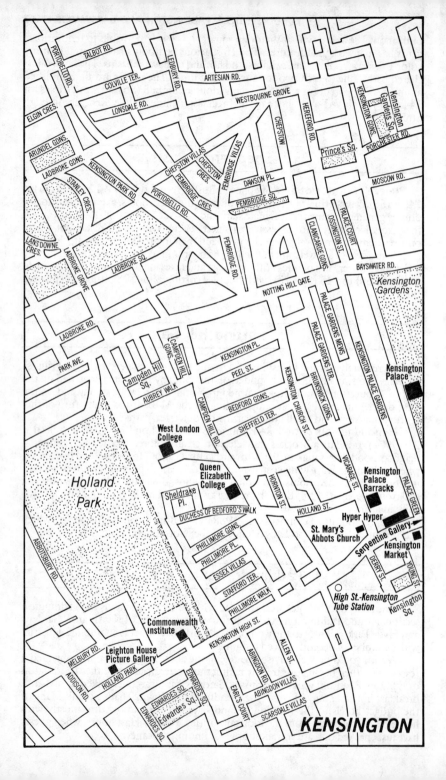

KENSINGTON

If you're unable to find a room on Sussex Gardens, then try the satellite Norfolk Square, which lies near Sussex Gardens (even closer to Paddington Station).

Tube stops serving the Bayswater and Paddington areas are Paddington, Bayswater, Queensway, Notting Hill Gate, and Ladbroke.

Coburg Hotel, 129 Bayswater Rd., London W2 4RJ (tel. 01/229-3654), is a moderately priced accommodation overlooking Kensington Gardens, around the corner from one of the most popular budget restaurant streets of London, Queensway. There you can take either the Queensway or Bayswater tubes to the West End in minutes. The hotel, a landmark on the Bayswater skyline, has been massively renovated. Its motto is "Delivering value for money," and in that it succeeds admirably, as evidenced by many repeat customers.

A large number of accommodations are offered, 125 bedrooms in all, including some family rooms. Most of the accommodations have a color TV, private bath, and an electric trouser-press, and all have phone and radio. Rooms overlooking Bayswater Road are double-glazed for tranquility's sake. Depending on the plumbing, rates in a single range from £39.95 ($69.90) to £59.95 ($105.91) daily and from £59.95 ($105.91) to £79.95 ($139.90) in a double or twin, including a large buffet English breakfast. VAT is extra. The hotel also offers a good restaurant downstairs.

Columbia Hotel, 85-99 Lancaster Gate, London W2 3NS (tel. 01/402-0021), overlooks Kensington Gardens and Hyde Park, and offers one of the best deals in the neighborhood. Originally constructed as five town houses in 1853, the hotel has 92 well-furnished bedrooms, each with private shower or bath and color TV. Prices, including VAT, service, and a continental breakfast, range from £35 ($61.25) daily in a single, from £46 ($80.50) in a double or twin, and are £60 ($105) in a triple. Guests enjoy the Regency-style residents' lounge or the Trafalgar Cocktail Bar. An in-house restaurant serves good, straightforward cookery, with dinners costing from £10 ($17.50). Tube: Paddington Station or Lancaster Gate.

Delmere Hotel, 130 Sussex Gardens, London W2 1UB (tel. 01/706-3344), is considered a safe and dependable hotel for the area. Renovated and upgraded in 1988, it today offers 40 traditionally decorated bedrooms, each with private shower or bath. With a continental breakfast included, singles rent for £56 ($98) daily in summer, rising to £68.50 ($119.90) in a double. Winter rates are reduced to £48 ($84) daily in a single, with doubles going for £58 ($101.50). Tube: Paddington Station.

Craven Gardens Hotel, 16 Leinster Terrace, London W2 3EF (tel. 01/262-3167), lies north of Kensington Gardens and Bayswater Road and offers a total of 45 modestly furnished but well-kept bedrooms, all with a private bath. Each unit has a color TV, phone, and radio. Singles cost £39 ($68.25) daily, and doubles or twins go for £49.50 ($86.65). Only breakfast is served. A few steps from the modern reception area is a bar outfitted with cane furnishings that's popular with residents. Tube: Paddington Station or Lancaster Gate.

Parkwood Hotel, 4 Stanhope Pl., London W2 2HB (tel. 01/402-2241), occupies one of the best locations for a good value hotel in London, standing near Oxford Street and Marble Arch on a fairly quiet street just 50 yards from Hyde Park, in a section of London known as Connaught Village. It has 18 well-furnished bedrooms, mainly with private baths. Only breakfast is served, and tariffs include VAT. Singles cost £30 ($52.50) to £40 ($70) daily, doubles or twins £40 ($70) to £54 ($94.50), and some triple-bedded units £58 ($101.50) to £65 ($113.75). All accommodations contain color TV and coffee-making equipment. Tube: Marble Arch.

Colonnade Hotel, 2 Warrington Crescent, London W9 1ER (tel. 01/286-1052), is an imposing town house built in 1853 as two private homes in a residential area. The 53 bedrooms are spacious, some with balconies, and are equipped with either private baths and showers or hot and cold water basins. All have TV, video, radios, phones, hairdryers, and trouser-presses. There are 16 special rooms with four-poster beds. Some are air-conditioned and some have Jacuzzis. The rates are £35 ($61.25) to £50 ($87.50) daily in a single, and from £65 ($113.75) to £85 ($148.75) in a double. Tariffs depend on the plumbing. A full English breakfast and VAT are included. Mr. Richards, owner since 1948, emphasizes: "Every bedroom, bathroom, and corridor is centrally heated 24 hours a day of every day from the first chill wind of autumn until the last breath of retreating winter, even in summer if necessary." He's installed a water-softening plant as well. The hotel has a licensed restaurant and a cocktail piano bar called Cascades, which has become so popular that you need a reservation even to get a martini. Tube: Warwick Avenue Station.

Mornington Hotel, 12 Lancaster Gate, London W2 3LG (tel. 01/262-7361), lies just north of Hyde Park and Kensington Gardens and has been completely re-decorated with a Scandinavian-designed interior. Each of the bedrooms, which number 70 in all, is also complete with private bath and shower, color TV, a phone, and a radio. Rates are from £59 ($103.25) daily in a single, rising to £70 ($122.50) to £78 ($136.50) in a double or twin. If you're traveling with a child, the Swedish-speaking staff will place an extra bed in your room for an additional charge. Tariffs include a Scandinavian buffet breakfast, service, and VAT. Naturally, there's a genu-ine Finnish sauna. Tube: Lancaster Gate.

Averard Hotel, 10 Lancaster Gate, London W2 3LH (tel. 01/723-8877), was originally built late in the 19th century. This five-story elevator building, one block from Hyde Park, contains 60 conservatively modern bedrooms. Each offers a pri-vate bath, color TV, and phone. The only meal served is breakfast, although many restaurants lie within the neighborhood, and a bar is open for residents and their guests. All year, singles rent for £42 ($73.50) daily, doubles £54 ($94.50), triples, £62 ($108.50), and quads £70 ($122.50). A continental breakfast is included in the price. Tube: Lancaster Gate.

Camelot Hotel, 45-47 Norfolk Square, London W2 1RX (tel. 01/723-9118), is a former town house standing at the corner of an old, tree-filled square, only two minutes from Paddington Station. The hotel was recently refurbished and now has an elevator. Most rooms have their own private showers and toilet facilities, and rent ranges from £27.50 ($48.15) to £39.50 ($69.15) daily in a single and from £45 ($78.75) to £52 ($91) in a double, depending on the plumbing. Some triple rooms cost from £59 ($103.25) to £66 ($115.50), with a family room renting for £80 ($140). All units have color TV, radio, and coffee-making facilities, and prices in-clude an English breakfast and tax.

King's Hotel, 60-62 Queensborough Terrace, London W2 3SH (tel. 01/229-7055), is a family-owned hotel containing 28 bedrooms, each with a color TV, phone, simple built-in furniture, fitted carpets, and private baths. The most appeal-ing rooms overlook a string of private gardens. With VAT and an English breakfast included, rooms with bath cost £40 ($70) daily for a single and £50 ($87.50) for a double. Bathless accommodations rent for £35 ($61.25) in a single and £45 ($78.75) in a double. Tube: Paddington or Queensway.

Slavia Hotel, 2 Pembridge Square, London W2 4EW (tel. 01/727-1316), of-fers 31 simple but clean accommodations, each with private bath. In a neighbor-hood popular with upwardly mobile young families, Slavia (named for the owner's homeland, Yugoslavia) sits across from the private gardens of Pembridge Square. A full cooked breakfast is served in the rustic, Yugoslav-inspired breakfast room in the cellar. With VAT and breakfast included, singles cost £35 ($61.25) daily, doubles £48 ($84). None of the rooms contain a TV (a conscious decision on the part of management), but each has a phone and simple furniture. Tube: Notting Hill Gate.

Tregaron Hotel/Ashley Hotel/Oasis Hotel, 13-17 Norfolk Square, London W2 1RU (tel. 01/723-9966), is a combination of three mid-Victorian buildings, and since many repeat clients prefer to use the names they learned many years ago, this hotel maintains three separate signs (and three small depictions in neon of Welsh dragons) above each of the trio of front doors. You register, however, at 15

Norfolk Square for one of the 52 small but comfortable bedrooms. Depending on the plumbing, double rooms cost from £16.50 ($28.90) to £18.50 ($32.40) per person. Bathless singles rent for £17.50 ($30.65) daily. Included in the price is a cooked English breakfast served in a cellar-level room. Tube: Paddington.

St. David's Hotel, 16 Norfolk Square, London W2 1RX (tel. 01/723-3856), is run by George Neokleous, who offers not only clean and comfortably furnished bedrooms but good English breakfasts and pleasant service. Rates are from £18 ($31.50) per person daily. Most rooms are furnished with private showers, and some have toilets as well. There is central heating, and rooms have TV as well. Guests have found the owner helpful and courteous. The hotel stands one minute from the Paddington and Lancaster Gate tube stations.

Gower Hotel, 129 Sussex Gardens, London W2 2RX (tel. 01/262-2262), is a clean, comfortable hotel set on a street lined with less-desirable accommodations. Renovated in 1988, it contains 21 rooms, most of which contain a private toilet, shower, sink, color TV, and phone. A full English breakfast is included. Rooms with bath cost £25 ($43.75) daily in a single, rising to £35 ($61.25) in a double and £45 ($78.75) in a triple. For a bathless room (there are only three), the rate is £18 ($31.50) in a single and £28 ($49) in a double. Tube: Paddington Station.

Fairways Hotel, 186 Sussex Gardens, London W2 1TU (tel. 01/723-4871), is near Hyde Park, a black and white town house easily recognized by its colonnaded front entrance with carved iron balustrade stretching across the front second-floor windows. The majority of the 17 bright and clean bedrooms contain private baths. Color TV and tea- or coffee-making facilities are in all the units. An English breakfast is included. Singles cost from £24 ($42) daily, while doubles run from £36 ($63) to £46 ($80.50) for two, depending on the plumbing. Tube: Paddington Station.

Garden Court Hotel, 30-31 Kensington Gardens Square, London W2 4BG (tel. 01/727-8304), is situated opposite the iron fence that rings the gardens in the center of Kensington Gardens Square. It has nearly 40 economically furnished but well kept bedrooms. Each has a dresser, wardrobe, and hot and cold running water (some with private shower and toilet). With an English breakfast included charges are £21 ($36.75) daily in a single without bath and £30 ($52.50) for a similar double. However, with bath tariffs go up to £28 ($49.90) daily in a single and £42 ($73.50) in a double. Tube: Bayswater.

St. Charles Hotel, 66 Queensborough Terrace, London W2 3SH (tel. 01/221-0022), originally a private home, is set a stone's throw from Kensington Gardens on a street dotted with private houses and hotels. A few of the ornate plaster ceilings and much of the original oak paneling still remain. The 16 modestly furnished bedrooms all contain a private shower and hot and cold running water, although only a few of them offer a private toilet. The rooms cost from £20 ($35) to £25 ($43.75) daily in a single and from £32 ($56) to £35 ($61.25) in a double (full English breakfast included). Tube: Queensway.

12. St. Marylebone

Below Regent's Park, lying northwest of Piccadilly Circus, is the principally Georgian district of St. Marylebone (pronounced Mar-li-bone), a residential section facing Mayfair to the south and extending north of Marble Arch at Hyde Park. A number of simple but gracious town houses in this section have been converted into private hotels, and little discreet bed-and-breakfast signs appear in the windows.

If you have arrived in London without a reservation in the peak months, then start at Edgware Road and walk past Seymour and Great Cumberland Place. Let the summer crowds fight it out in Bloomsbury.

Bryanston Court Hotel, 56-60 Great Cumberland Pl., London W1H 8DD (tel. 01/262-3141), is one of the most elegant hotels on the street. Each of the three individual houses that were joined together into this hotel was built almost 200 years ago. Each of the 56 bedrooms contains a private bath, color TV, phone, and radio. The opulently red dining room, the Brunswick Restaurant, is furnished in an early 19th-century style with antiques and oil portraits. The charge is £55 ($96.25) daily in a single, £60 ($105) to £68 ($119) in a double, with VAT and a continental breakfast included. Tube: Marble Arch.

Hotel Concorde, 50 Great Cumberland Pl., London W1H 8DD (tel. 01/402-6316), is a small hotel with style. The reception desk, the nearby chairs, and part of the tiny bar area were at one time a part of a London church. A display case in the lobby contains an array of reproduction English silver, each piece of which is for sale. Each of the 28 rooms is modern and stylish. They all have color TV, direct-dial phones, and private baths. Singles rent for £55 ($96.25) daily and doubles for £65 ($113.75), with VAT and a continental breakfast included in the tariffs. Tube: Marble Arch.

Edward Lear Hotel, 28-30 Seymour St., London W1H 5WD (tel. 01/402-5401), is a popular hotel one city block from Marble Arch in a pair of brick town houses, both of which date from 1780. The western house was the London home of the 19th-century artist and poet Edward Lear, whose illustrated limericks and original lithographs adorn the walls of one of the sitting rooms. Steep stairs lead to the 30 bedrooms, 11 of which contain private baths, all of which have color TV, radios, beverage facilities, hairdryers, free luggage storage, and ironing facilities. Singles start at £29 ($50.75) daily, doubles and twins at £39 ($68.25), and triples at £48 ($84). Tube: Marble Arch.

Hart House Hotel, 51 Gloucester Pl., London W1H 3PE (tel. 01/935-2288), is a well-preserved building, part of a group of Georgian mansions occupied by the French nobility during the French Revolution, in the heart of the West End. It is within a few minutes' walking distance of the theaters, Oxford Street, Selfridges, Marble Arch, Hyde Park, Regent's Park, and the zoo, as well as Madame Tussaud's and the Planetarium. Hart House is centrally heated, and all of the 15 rooms have hot and cold running water, color TV, radio, and phone. The clean, comfortable rooms rent for £26 ($45.50) daily for a single, £39 ($68.25) for a twin or double, and £57 ($99.75) to £65 ($113.75) for a triple (depending on the plumbing), including English breakfast. Tube: Marble Arch or Baker Street.

Kenwood House Hotel, 114 Gloucester Pl., London W1H 3DB (tel. 01/935-3473), is a 16-room hotel in a 200-year-old Adam-style building. The owners maintain the Georgian ceiling and ashwood fireplace of the reception area and have installed matching curtains, wallpaper, and carpets within their renovated bedrooms. With an English breakfast included, bathless rooms cost £24 ($42) daily in a single and £35 ($61.25) in a double. Double rooms with bath rent for £40 ($70) a night. A handful of triples go for £42 ($73.50), and a room for four occupants rents for £50 ($87.50). Tube: Baker Street.

Hallam Hotel, 12 Hallam St., Portland Place, London W1N 5LJ (tel. 01/580-1166), is a heavily ornamented stone and brick Victorian house, one of the only ones on the street to escape bombing in World War II. There is a bar for residents. An elevator leads to the 23 simple but comfortable bedrooms, each with TV, phone, radio, and 24-hour room service. VAT and a light English breakfast are included in the price of the rooms, costing from £34 ($59.50) to £43 ($75.25) daily in a single, £57 ($99.75) to £62 ($108.50) in a double. Tube: Oxford Circus.

NORTHERN LONDON

London's most numerous cluster of budget hotels is to be found in the northern part of the city, a geographical designation that shouldn't discourage you. By northern I refer to an area that has as its southern border Oxford Street, New Oxford Street, and High Holborn. Its western border touches Regent's Park; its northern border, the terminals of Kings Cross, St. Pancras, and Euston Stations; and its eastern border, Farringdon Road, the beginning of Finsbury. Most of the accommodations are centered in the southern part, known as Bloomsbury.

During the warmer months, June through mid-September, the hotels here are heavily booked, so be sure to obtain advance reservations, or phone the hotels that sound attractive to you before appearing on their doorsteps.

13. Leicester Square

Vistors flock to this area for its theaters, restaurants, and nightlife, but almost no one thinks of it as a hotel district. However, there is one closely guarded secret. **Manzi's,** 1-2 Leicester St., off Leicester Square, London WC2 H7BL (tel. 01/734-0224), is the oldest seafood restaurant in London (see the next chapter). Right above its second floor are 18 well-kept and comfortable bedrooms, each with private bath or shower. Prices are reasonable, too: £28 ($49) daily in a single and £48 ($84) in a double. Guests climb a flight of steps and check in at a postage-stamp-size reception desk, right at the entrance to the busy restaurant. Unloading luggage might be a bit of a problem here, but many readers like to be right in the heartbeat of London life. One saves a lot of transportation costs this way. Tube: Leicester Square.

14. Bloomsbury

Northeast of Piccadilly Circus, beyond Soho, lies a world within itself. It is, among other things, the academic heart of London, where you'll find London University, several other colleges, the British Museum, and many bookstores. Despite its student overtones, the section is fairly staid and quiet. Its reputation has been fanned by such writers as Virginia Woolf, who lived within its bounds (it figured in her novel *Jacob's Room*). The novelist and her husband, Leonard, were once the unofficial leaders of a group of artists and writers known as "the Bloomsbury group" —nicknamed "Bloomsberries." At times, this intellectual camaraderie reached out to embrace Bertrand Russell.

The heart of Bloomsbury is **Russell Square,** and the streets jutting off from the square are lined with hotels and bed-and-breakfast houses. If you have not found a hotel room by phoning first and prefer to make your search on foot, you might try the following itinerary: From the Russell Square Underground station (whose exit is on Bernard Street), walk first along Bernard Street, which contains many hotels. Then, one long block north of Bernard Street, try Coram Street, another hotel-lined block, and after that sample Tavistock Place, running one block north of Coram and parallel to it. North of Tavistock Place is Cartwright Gardens, which has a number of old converted town houses catering to overnight guests.

The Bernard Street–Coram Street–Tavistock Place hotels are, however, the most likely Russell Square establishments to be booked in summer. You'll have a better chance on the other side of Russell Square (opposite Bernard Street), where you'll find the relatively high-priced hotels of Bloomsbury Street (lined with publishing houses) and those on the less expensive Gower Street, where you'll be at the midpoint of the London University area. On Gower Street, for instance, you'll find the Royal Academy of Dramatic Art, across from which are a number of B&B houses.

Hotel President, Russell Square, London WC1N 1DB (tel. 01/837-8844), is a larger and more substantial hotel than any of the B&B establishments I've recommended so far. Part of the Imperial Hotel grouping, it dates from the 1960s, when it opened in Bloomsbury with a total of 450 rooms, each with private bath, shower, and phone. However, its rates are reasonable, costing £44 ($77) daily in a single and £54 ($94.50) in a double or twin, including breakfast and VAT. Rooms are centrally heated and are reached by elevator. They are clean and comfortable, but not stylish in any way. If you can't find a room here, then the Imperial grouping takes in a total of 4500 beds in other Central London establishments, including the Imperial and the Bedford. The hotel also has vast public areas, including an arcade of shops, a hairdresser, and a coffee shop serving till 2 a.m. Tube: Russell Square.

Academy Hotel, 17-21 Gower St., London WC1E 6HG (tel. 01/634-4115), is for the visitor who wants something different from the standard chain hotel and who is tired of paying four-star prices for two-star comforts. Originally built in 1776, the hotel is three separate Georgian row houses joined together. It was modernized and completely refurbished in 1987, but many architectural details left by the original builders remain, including mahogany and teak decoration and marble fireplaces. It stands within walking distance of the theater section, Covent Garden, and other points of interest in the West End. Facilities include an elegant bar, library room, and a secluded patio garden. The hotel offers 24-hour room service, and each accommodation is not only well furnished but contains a color TV and radio, direct-dial phone, and beverage-making equipment. Most rooms have private showers and toilets, but public plumbing is adequate. Singles rent for £55 ($96.25) daily, with doubles going for £70 ($122.50), including tax and a continental breakfast. Tube: Euston Square.

"Y" Hotel, 112 Great Russell St., London WC1B 3NQ (tel. 01/636-8616), is a modern 168-room hotel in the heart of London. Single rooms, with VAT and service included, rent for £39 ($68.25) daily, with doubles and twins going for £59 ($103.25). All the units have private showers, central heating, color TV, and radios. The furnishings are up to date and comfortable, and there's even wall-to-wall carpeting. Built at the Oxford Street end of Tottenham Court Road by the London Central Young Men's Christian Association for men and women of all ages, this "Y" Hotel may be unlike any you've ever seen. Its facilities include squash courts, a gymnasium, a swimming pool, a shop, and an underground parking garage. Other facilities are a lounge and bar, plus a restaurant. Tube: Tottenham Court Road.

Morgan Hotel, 24 Bloomsbury St., London WC1B 3QJ (tel. 01/636-3735), is one of a long row of similar buildings but distinguished by its gold-tipped iron fence railings. Several of the 14 rooms overlook the British Museum, and the whole establishment is very much part of the international scholastic scene of Bloomsbury. Bedrooms, three to a floor, vary in size, some being rather large. All of the bedrooms in this completely refurbished hotel are well carpeted and have private showers and toilets, big beds (by British standards), dressing tables with mirrors, and ample wardrobe space, as well as central heating. Singles cost £30 ($52.50) daily, and doubles go for £45 ($78.75). Prices include a full English breakfast and VAT. Book well in advance. The nearest tubes are Russell Square and Tottenham Court Road.

Devon House Hotel, 56 Cartwright Gardens, London, WC1H 9EL (tel. 01/387-1719), is a five-minute walk from the British Museum. It contains 15 bedrooms, only three of which offer a full private bathroom. With a full English breakfast, rates range from £25 ($43.75) daily for a bathless single and £36 ($63) for a bathless double to doubles with private bath costing £40 ($70). In winter, tariffs are reduced by about £2 ($3.50) per person nightly. The centrally heated bedrooms do not have TVs or phones but represent a price-conscious and well-scrubbed refuge in a desirable neighborhood in Bloomsbury. Tube: Russell Square or Euston Station.

Crescent Hotel, Cartwright Gardens, London WC1H 9EL (tel. 01/387-1515), is a good economy choice in Bloomsbury. Rooms are well maintained, costing £23 ($40.25) per day in a single, rising to £37 ($64.75) for a twin- or double-bedded room, including a full English breakfast and tax. In addition, there are family rooms, consisting of two single beds and one double bed beginning at £49.50 ($86.65) daily. Children under 14 years of age pay half price in a family room. There's a TV lounge as well. Tube: Russell Square.

Avalon Private Hotel, 46 Cartwright Gardens, London WC1H 9EL (tel. 01/387-2366), is set behind the brick facade of a Georgian town house. With a full English breakfast and VAT, prices range from £23 ($40.25) daily in a single, £36 ($63) in a double, £45 ($78.75) in a triple, and £50 ($87.50) for a quad, all bathless, to £42 ($73.50) for a double and £50 ($87.50) in a triple with bath. Each room has beverage-making equipment. Guests can request a key that opens the iron gate leading into a semiprivate, horseshoe-shaped garden across the street, where a tennis court is available. Tube: Russell Square.

George Hotel, 58-60 Cartwright Gardens, London WC1H 9EL (tel. 01/387-6789), is part of this famous Georgian crescent. Well run and decidedly well maintained, it is one of the best of the B&Bs along this highly competitive crescent. Several of the 40 rooms are quite small, with an exposed sink with hot and cold running water. Only three contain a private bath or shower. Singles cost £22 ($38.50) to £25 ($43.75) daily, and doubles go for £35 ($61.25) to £38 ($66.50), including VAT and an English breakfast. The George must be one of the few central London hotels with tennis courts available for use of the guests. Tube: Russell Square.

Gower House Hotel, 57 Gower St., London WC1E 6HJ (tel. 01/636-4685), is a clean and suitable hotel run by P. and J. Borg, its owners, who cater to families. In all, they offer 14 bedrooms, including some large family rooms, adequate for three to five persons. In these the rate is £12.50 ($21.90) per person nightly. Otherwise, singles cost £20 ($35), and doubles or twins go for £30 ($52.50). All tariffs include a full English breakfast and tax. Each room contains hot and cold running water, and there is a breakfast room as well as a TV lounge. Tube: Goodge Street.

Ruskin Hotel, 23-24 Montague St., London WC1 5BN (tel. 01/636-7388), stands next to the British Museum, within walking distance of London's shopping district and major West End theaters. Listed as a building of historical interest, the hotel has retained many of its original architectural features. The elevator-serviced bedrooms have hot and cold running water, shaver points, intercoms, hot beverage facilities, and electrical outlets. The rooms also are centrally heated, and several contain showers. The cost of a room, including a full English breakfast served in the dining room, is £24 ($42) daily in a single and £36 ($63) in a double, including VAT. Tube: Holborn or Tottenham Court Road.

Maree Hotel, 25-27 Gower St., London WC1E 6HG (tel. 01/636-4868), stands on a quiet street near the British Museum, and offers 31 bedrooms, only three of which have a private toilet and shower. With a continental breakfast included, bathless rooms cost £20 ($35) daily in a single and £30 ($52.50) in a double. In winter, bathless rooms rent for £18 ($31.50) in a single and £26 ($45.50) in a double. Rooms with bath cost about £2 ($3.50) per person more per night. Tube: Goodge Street.

St. Athans Hotel, 20 Tavistock Pl., London WC1H 9RE (tel. 01/837-9140), comprises five interconnected buildings linked with a labyrinth of staircases, fire doors, and not-quite-parallel hallways. It offers 77 simple and functional bedrooms. None of the bedrooms contains a private bath, and the hotel has no bar and serves no meals other than breakfast. With an English breakfast included, singles cost £24 ($42) nightly, doubles £34 ($59.50), and triples £48 ($84). St. Athans is not named after a saint but is a humorous play on the phrase "Stay at Hans." Tube: Russell Square.

Harlingford Hotel, 61-63 Cartwright Gardens, London WC1H 9EL (tel. 01/387-1551), is composed of three early Victorian buildings and offers 44 simple but comfortable bedrooms, 30 of which have private toilet and shower. The buildings, connected via a bewildering array of staircases and meandering hallways, are on the corner of Marchmont Street in the heart of Bloomsbury. Rooms with private facilities cost £34 ($59.50) nightly in a single and £45 ($78.75) in a double. Rooms that are bathless go for £27 ($47.25) in a single and £39 ($68.25) in a double. Breakfast and VAT are included in the price. Tube: Russell Square.

Langland Hotel, 29-31 Gower St., London WC1E 6HG (tel. 01/636-5801), lies close to the British Museum behind a 200-year-old facade constructed of the soot-encrusted yellow bricks known as "London stock," and it contains 30 simple but comfortable bedrooms. Bathless accommodations cost £23 ($40.25) daily in a single, £33 ($57.75) in a double, £36 ($63) in a triple, and £51 ($89.25) in a quad. Rooms with private bath rent for £38 ($66.50) in a twin, £45 ($78.75) in a triple, and £55 ($96.25) in a quad, with an English breakfast included. Because of the traffic, the quieter rooms lie in back. Tube: Goodge Street, Russell Square, or Euston Station.

15. In and Around Hampstead

Sandringham (Igar) Hotel, 3 Holford Rd., London NW3 1AD (tel. 01/435-1569), stands on a residential street in one of the best parts of London. Coming out of the Hampstead tube station on Heath Street, turn right and walk up toward the hill. At the fourth right, you enter Hampstead Square, which leads to Holford Road. From the upper rooms, you will have a view over Hampstead Heath and the heart of London. The B&B charges without bath are £23 ($40.25) in a single, £39 ($68.25) in a double, and £48 ($84) for a four-bedded room. A room with a private bath or shower costs £45 ($78.75) in a double, £50 ($87.50) in a triple, and £55 ($96.25) in a four-bedded room. VAT is included. Breakfast is served in a pretty room that has a view of the well-kept garden.

At **Frognal Lodge,** 14 Frognal Gardens, London NW3 6UX (tel. 01/435-8238), the easygoing and charming staff of this attractive hotel has received several glowing reader reports, and I concur. The late 19th-century house offers 17 rooms, 7 with full private baths and color TV. All have phones. A generous English breakfast and VAT are included in the prices, which are £47.75 ($83.55) daily in a double with bath or else £37.50 ($65.65) in a small double with a shared bath. The single rate is £23.50 ($41.15) with a shared bath, rising to £36 ($63) with a private bath. The attic room, which has a sloped ceiling and exposed beams, is a favorite. Tube: Hampstead.

In West Hampstead, a somewhat offbeat accommodation is provided by the **Charlotte Restaurant,** 221 West End Lane, London NW6 1XJ (tel. 01/794-6476), an old established and inexpensive restaurant with a tasteful decor that offers B&B and a three-course dinner. The ten rooms rent for £14 ($24.50) daily in a bathless single, £20 ($35) in a single with bath. Doubles range from £22 ($38.50) to £30 ($52.50), depending on the plumbing. A full English breakfast, prepared and served in the Charlotte Restaurant, is included in the price. The accommodations are one minute from public transport, 15 minutes from Piccadilly. Tube: West Hampstead.

16. Blackheath

Bardon Lodge Hotel, 15-17 Stratheden Rd., London SE3 7TH (tel. 01/853-4051), was a British Tourist Authority award-winner in 1987 and is composed of two grand Victorian houses joined together and refurbished. All rooms have private showers, tea- and coffee-making facilities, hairdryers, trouser-presses, color TV, and direct-dial phones. A double costs £57 ($99.75) daily, including a substantial English breakfast and taxes. The hotel is five miles from London's center, in a quiet residential area a short walk from Greenwich Park and the National Maritime Museum. From Greenwich Pier, a boat will take you to the Tower of London and Westminster. It is also close to a convenient bus line.

---

17. On the Fringe

Worcester House, 38 Alwyne Rd., Wimbledon, London SW19 7AE (tel. 01/946-1300), was built around 1910. This hotel has nine rooms, each of which has its own shower and toilet, color TV, radio, phone, hairdryer, and tea- or coffee-making facilities. The charge is £34.50 ($60.40) to £42.50 ($74.40) daily in a single, £49.45 ($86.55) to £54 ($94.50) in a double, with VAT and an English breakfast included. It is only ten minutes from the tennis courts at Wimbledon. Tube: Wimbledon.

Justin James Hotel, 43 Worple Rd. (corner of Malcolm Road), Wimbledon, London SW19 4JA (tel. 01/947-4271), is located only about 30 minutes by train from Waterloo or Victoria Stations (passengers coming from Victoria will have to change trains once). All but two of the 14 bedrooms contain private bath. With VAT and an English breakfast included, rooms with bath cost £30 ($52.50) daily in a single and £45 ($78.75) in a double. Bathless rooms are £35 ($61.25) in a single and £40 ($70) in a double. Tube: Wimbledon.

Solana, 18 Golders Rise, Hendon, London NW4 2HR (tel. 01/202-5321), is a small private guesthouse for non smokers only. In this clean, terraced house, most rooms have water basins, and there is a public shower/bathroom. Prices range from £10 ($17.50) in a single to £18 ($31.50) for two persons sharing a twin-bedded room. The rates cover bed and breakfast, which can be either continental or English. Guests can sit in the little garden in summer. The guesthouse is in a pleasant area off the main road, and it is possible to park your car if you stay at Solana. It's close to the end of the M1, A406, A41, and A1 motorways and is easily reached via the Northern Line Tube and buses from the city, ten minutes' walk from Hendon Central tube stop.

Mrs. Betty Merchant, 562 Caledonian Rd., Holloway, London N7 9SD (tel. 01/607-0930), has a small, comfortable private guesthouse with unrestricted parking on the street for guests. The bedrooms—one single, one double, and one family unit—rent for £10 ($17.50) nightly per adult, £8 ($14) for children under 12, with two nights' stay required. A full English breakfast is included. The house has central heating. Guests are asked to phone, not write, for reservations at this small, popular guesthouse. Mrs. Merchant's house is connected to the West End by buses that stop quite near the house. Tube: Caledonian Road.

---

18. Airport Hotels

Most regularly scheduled planes will land at Heathrow, and charter flights are likely to go to Gatwick, which more and more is becoming the gateway to London. If you need to be near either airport, close to your point of departure, consider some of the following suggestions instead of the well-advertised and more expensive operations at both airports.

HEATHROW
Close to the airport are several worthwhile suggestions.

The Swan, The Hythe, Staines, Middlesex TW18 3JB (tel. 0784/452494), lies beside the Thames. It is an attractive old inn with a reputation for good food ranging from bar snacks to a limited à la carte choice of traditional English "fayre." A three-course meal costs £10 ($17.50), featuring simple wholesome no-frills cookery. Food is served from 12:30 p.m. to 2 p.m. and from 7:30 p.m. to 9:30 p.m daily. On Saturday and Sunday, last orders go in at 10 p.m. The six bedrooms have central heating, color TV, and tea- or coffee-makers. Singles cost £27 ($47.25) daily, and doubles go for £37 ($64.75).

Upton Park Guest House, 41 Upton Park, Slough, Berkshire, SL1 2DA (tel. 0753/28797), is about a 15-minute cab ride from Heathrow. Jan and Pete Jones, who run the place, can arrange for a local cab to meet you if you preplan. The rate is cheaper than taking a cab at the airport. All rooms have central heating, hot and cold running water, color TV, and complimentary tea and coffee. A pleasant bar is available for residents. Bed and a full English breakfast costs £24 ($42) per night.

GATWICK

Since this airport is so far from London, you may want to find a convenient perch nearby while waiting for the departure of your flight. Some suggestions follow.

Gatwick Skylodge Hotel, London Road, County Oak, Crawley, West Sussex RH11 0PF (tel. 0293/54411), is a busy airport hotel within easy reach of Gatwick by courtesy bus. The bus operates regularly from 6:15 a.m. to 11:45 p.m. All rooms have a private bath, color TV, tea- or coffee-maker, and direct-dial phone. Rates, including VAT and a continental breakfast, are £45 ($78.75) daily in a single, £52 ($91) in a twin or double, and from £66 ($115.50) to £77 ($134.75) for three to four persons. Rooms are held on 6 p.m. release unless a deposit of £10 ($17.50) is prepaid. There is a restaurant where evening meals are served. An English breakfast is available if required.

Oakleigh House, Copthorne, West Sussex RH10 3HG (tel. 0342/712703), is a small but choice guesthouse about five miles from Gatwick, offering B&B accommodations in single, double, twin, or family rooms, some with private shower and toilet, but all with color TV and courtesy beverage trays. Charges range from £20 ($35) daily in a single to £30 ($52.50) and up in a double. The hotel is a short drive from the Gatwick Airport Railway Station, from which an express train travels every 15 minutes to London's Victoria Station. Taxi service to and from Gatwick Airport costs about £5 ($8.75) per journey.

Brooklyn Hotel, Bonnetts Lane, Ifield, Crawley, West Sussex RH11 0NY (tel. 0293/546024), is an old, well-cared-for Victorian house set in the lovely English countryside, only five minutes from Gatwick Airport. A phone call from the airport will bring a car from the hotel to collect you and your luggage free and take you to the hotel, or if you're staying there prior to departure, they'll take you to Gatwick in time for your flight, another free service. The hotel, set in five acres of rural parkland, offers full central heating, color TV, and beverage-making facilities. Martin Davis charges £15 ($26.25) to £25 ($43.75) daily for a single, £28 ($49) to £34 ($59.50) in a double. Breakfast is extra, and if a guest wishes, a light snack will be served in the evening. However, a free courtesy service takes guests to and from a nearby restaurant, and there are two pubs within about a ten-minute walk, both serving inexpensive meals. The hotel does not have a bar, but it is licensed, so that you can have drinks served in the lounge if you wish. The proprietors will help guests plan trips into London by public transport.

About eight miles east of Dorking, near Reigate, in the little town of Redhill, about 500 yards from the Redhill Railway Station on the A25 to Sevenoaks, stands the **Ashleigh House Hotel,** 39 Redstone Hill, Redhill, Surrey RH1 4BG (tel. 0737/764764). The gracious hosts, Jill and Michael Warren, serve a good English breakfast in the dining room overlooking a garden. Some of the accommodations have private showers. Singles rent for £20 ($35) daily and doubles for £32 ($56) to £34 ($59.50) for B&B. There's a heated swimming pool for use of guests in summer, plus a TV lounge. The hotel is only about 15 minutes by car from Gatwick and 30 minutes by train from London.

A good B&B—discovered by several readers—is **Lynwood House,** 50 London Rd., Redhill, Surrey RH1 1LN (tel. 0737/766894), which offers clean and comfortable accommodations, most with showers, all with hot and cold running water. The tariff is from £32 ($56) for two persons nightly. Breakfast is generous and well prepared. The location, just under 15 minutes from Gatwick Airport by either car or train, is 200 yards from the Redhill Railway Station.

19. An Accommodation Round-up

STAYING WITH A FAMILY

Many agencies in Britain can arrange stays with a private family, either in London or in the country. As much as possible, interests are matched. This program is an intriguing way to involve yourself in the social life of a country, seeing it from the inside. Also, it's a bargain when compared to hotels. Some agencies limit themselves to teenagers; others welcome older readers. Try one of the following:

Family Holidays, 42 Walton Rd., Sidcup, Kent, DA14 4LN (tel. 01/300-5444), under the direction of Michael and Geraldine Kenney, has a well-screened list of British families who will welcome you into their homes as paying guests. The choice includes numerous professional people and others who live in attractive town, country, and seaside locations all around Great Britain. Upon application, you'll receive information about your hosts, such as interests, ages, and family. The cost of accommodation is less than $100 (U.S.) per person per week for full board. There is a booking fee of £10 ($17.50), and operating costs are covered by a 15% service charge. There's even an arrangement for what to do if you and your host don't get on too well.

Ball Tourist Services, 82 Newlands Rd., Norbury, London SW16 4SU (tel. 01/653-8467), will arrange for accommodations with selected families living in the southwest suburbs of London, including Streatham, Norbury, and Thornton Heath. Only about 15 to 20 minutes by train to the center of London, the area is convenient for all sorts of recreational and sightseeing activities. Host-family accommodation is also available in Paignton (Devon), Edinburgh, Canterbury, the Isle of Wight, Cambridge, and the Lake District. Accommodation with an English breakfast is from £10 ($17.50) daily. With an English breakfast and an evening meal, the cost goes up to £13 ($22.75). Prices include the booking fee and tax.

B&B IN PRIVATE HOMES

S. K. Opperman and R. L. Lumb run **Bed and Breakfast Nationwide,** Admirals House, Heckford Road, Great Bentley, Colchester, Essex COQ 8RS (tel. 0206/251540), an agency specializing in B&B accommodations in private homes all over Great Britain. Host homes range from small cottages to large manor houses, and the prices vary accordingly. You can write, stating your requirements and the general price range you're interested in. Owners have been selected for their wish to entertain visitors from overseas in their own homes. Even working farms are included. You, too, can vary your travel plans, spending a night in an Elizabethan manor, perhaps the following night in a thatched cottage near the sea. Remember, these are private homes, and hotel-type services are not available. You will, however, be virtually guaranteed a comfortable room, a hearty breakfast, and a glimpse into the British way of life.

YOUTH HOSTELS

In London youth hostels, reservations are imperative—and must be made months or even a year in advance. In one season alone, the youth hostels of London turned away 33,000 written applications with deposits! You must, of course, comply with each hostel's restrictions, such as a membership card and in many cases a curfew. A great number also carry limitations on the number of nights you can stay.

Britain is an ideal choice for those who want to put some action in their holidays. The activities are widely varied, ranging from underwater swimming off the coast of Devon, to canoeing on the River Wye, climbing, walking, and gliding.

One way to find out information about these adventure holidays is to go to the London office of the **Youth Hostels Association,** 14 Southampton St., London WC2E 7HY (tel. 01/836-8541). The yearly membership fee is £7.50 ($13.15) for adults.

For a full list, write to YHA, Trevelyan House, 8 St. Stephen's Hill, St. Albans, Hertfordshire AL1 2DY (tel. 0727/55215).

In the United States, you can join the **American Youth Hostels Association** (contact them at: American Youth Hostels, P.O. Box 37613, Washington, DC 20013-7613, or call 202/783-6161). To join, mail a check for the yearly membership fee of $20 plus $1 postage and handling if you're between the ages of 18 and 54. A two-year membership costs $30 plus $1. If you are 17 or younger, or 55 or older, you can obtain a youth or senior citizen membership, each of which costs $10 plus $1. A life membership costs $200, regardless of age. A family membership is available for $30 plus $1 for one year for parent(s) and accompanying children age 17 and under. Parents can use a family membership without being accompanied by children, although children under 17 who arrive without their parents are required to have a junior membership of their own. Membership in AYH is honored at youth hostels in England as well as in more than 70 other countries.

Quest Hotel, 45 Queensborough Terrace, London W2 3SY (tel. 01/229-7782), is operated as a student hostel for travelers from all over the world. Fun and laughter can be shared with the staff, and worldwide budget travel hints are passed around by guests from all over, with a large Australian contingent. They cater mostly to young people in the 18 to 30 age range, but they also enjoy the company of spirited, more mature travelers. The hostel is in the heart of London, close to all major sights and attractions, only a stone's throw from Kensington Gardens and Hyde Park. The price ranges from £7 ($12.25) to £8.50 ($14.90) per person daily in a room shared with four to five other people and £11 ($19.25) per person in a twin-bedded room. There are no singles. A continental breakfast is included in the prices. Tube: Bayswater or Queensway.

Earl's Court Youth Hostel, 38 Bolton Gardens, London SW5 0AQ (tel. 01/373-7083), is an old five-story mansion providing dormitory-style living in an establishment with 111 beds, hot showers, ten bathrooms, a launderette for the use of hostel members staying here, and a cafeteria, plus a reception and common room that are open from 7 a.m. to midnight. In the dormitory rooms, which are open from 7 a.m. to 11 a.m. and from 5 p.m. to midnight, prices are: senior (age 21 and over), £7 ($12.25) daily; junior (16 to 20 years old), £5.60 ($9.80); and young (5 to 15), £4.70 ($8.25). Sheet sleeping bag rental is 70p ($1.25). Cafeteria service is available for breakfast, snacks, and evening meals. Tube: Earl's Court.

IV

LONDON: RESTAURANTS, PUBS, AND WINE BARS

1. WEST END

2. WESTMINSTER AND ST. JAMES'S

3. THE CITY

4. HOLBORN AND BLOOMSBURY

5. BELGRAVIA AND KNIGHTSBRIDGE

6. CHELSEA

7. KENSINGTON

8. WEST LONDON

9. EAST END

10. SOUTH OF THE THAMES

11. HAMPSTEAD HEATH

12. THAMES DINING

13. FOR FISH AND CHIPS

14. TIME OUT FOR TEA

With the pressure of tourism and the influx of foreign chefs, the local cuisine picture has brightened considerably. There also exists now a current wave of English-born, -bred, and -trained chefs who have set a superb standard of cookery, using high-quality ingredients. One food writer called this new breed "the very professional amateur."

In the snackeries of suburbia the vegetables may still taste as if they had a grudge against you, and the soup remains reminiscent of flavored tapwater. But in the central sections of London—where you'll do your eating—the fare has improved immeasurably. This is largely because of intense competition from foreign establishments, plus the introduction of espresso machines, which made English coffee resemble—well, coffee.

In the upper brackets, London has always boasted magnificent restaurants, several of which have achieved world renown. But these were the preserve of the middling wealthy. The lower orders enjoyed a diet akin to parboiled blotting paper. For about a century the staple meal of the working class consisted of fish 'n' chips—and in my opinion they still haven't learned how to properly fry either the fish *or* the chips (potatoes).

There are some dishes—mostly connected with breakfast—at which the English have always excelled. The traditional morning repast of eggs and bacon (imported from Denmark) or kippers (smoked herring, of Scottish origin) is a tasty starter, and the locally brewed tea beats any American bag concoction. It's with the other meals that you have to use a little caution.

The prevailing mealtimes are much the same as in the U.S. You can get lunch from about midday onward and dinner until about 11 p.m.—until midnight in the Soho area. The difference is that fewer Londoners go in for the "business person's lunch." They'll either make do with sandwiches or take a snack in a pub. The once-hallowed custom of taking afternoon tea for many years became the preserve of matrons unworried about their waistlines. However, over the past few years it has been having a renaissance.

What may astonish you is the profusion of international restaurants. London offers a fantastic array of Italian, Indian, Chinese, French, German, Swiss, Greek, Russian, Jewish, and Middle Eastern dineries, which probably outnumber the native establishments. You'll find them heavily represented on my list.

Most of the restaurants I mention serve the same meals for lunch or dinner, so they're easily interchangeable. Most—but not all—add a 10% to 15% service charge to your bill. You'll have to look at your check to make sure of that. If nothing has been added, leave a 12% to 15% tip.

All restaurants and cafés in Britain are required to display the prices of the food and drink they offer, in a place where the customer can see them before entering the eating area. If an establishment has an extensive à la carte menu, the prices of a representative selection of food and drink currently available must be displayed, as well as the table d'hôte menu if one is offered. Charges for service and any minimum charge or cover charge must also be made clear. The prices shown must be inclusive of VAT.

Finally, there's the matter of location. Once upon a time London had two traditional dining areas: Soho for Italian and Chinese fare, Mayfair and Belgravia for French cuisine.

Today the gastronomical legions have conquered the entire heart of the metropolis. You're likely to find any type of eatery anywhere from Chelsea to Hampstead. The majority of my selections are in the West End region, but only because this happens to be the handiest for visitors.

First, I'll survey the downtown district of London, by which I refer to a broad area embracing not only the theater district, but Piccadilly Circus, Soho, Covent Garden, The Strand, Trafalgar Square, and Leicester Square, as well as the elegant residential district of Mayfair and "Little America." South of here is the seat of government, Westminster and Whitehall, and the heart of royal and aristocratic London, St. James's (Buckingham Palace). To the east is the older part of London, which includes the financial square mile known as "The City," as well as the newspaper and publishing empire centered around Fleet Street.

Finally, I'll fan out to such residential districts as Bloomsbury (budget hotels and the British Museum), Chelsea, St. Marylebone, Brompton, and Kensington. And then, at the end of the chapter, I'll set forth my more remote recommendations —the pubs and bistros in Hampstead Heath, and a few scattered, but famous, inns, restaurants, and pubs either in the East End or along the Thames.

1. West End

PICCADILLY CIRCUS

Garish, overneoned, crowded, but exciting, Piccadilly Circus keeps time with the heartbeat of a mighty city. If you're intrigued by Times Square at night, you'll find that Piccadilly Circus carries an equal fascination. Here from all sections of the city come the aristocrat, the housewife, the punk, the government official, the secretary, the pimp, the financier. They converge around the statue of Eros, named for love, about the only thing that occasionally unites these diverse elements of life that descend on Piccadilly.

The following restaurants and pubs have been selected not only for the quality of their food but because they offer the best value for the money.

Criterion Brasserie, 222 Piccadilly, W.1 (tel. 01/839-7133), stands right in the heart of London, overlooking the famous statue of Eros, next door to the Criterion Theatre. The long, neo-Byzantine dining room is a riot of gold and mosaic ceilings, and you expect the prices to match the decor. But they don't. From noon to 3 p.m. daily (on Sunday from 12:30 p.m.), they serve a good value at lunch at only £7.95 ($13.90), including a three-course meal and a glass of wine. At night expect to pay at least £10 ($17.50) from the à la carte menu. Specialties include a savory bourride, cassoulet Criterion, or a selection of grills. For the vegetarian, there is feuillette de legumes. Dinner hours are 6 to 11 p.m. daily and on Sunday from 7 to 10 p.m. Tube: Piccadilly Circus.

The Carvery, Regent Palace Hotel, Glasshouse St., W.1 (tel. 01/734-7000), just 20 feet from Piccadilly Circus, will fool you. Who'd think that for only £11.50 ($20.15) you could have all that your plate can hold of fabulous roasts and be able to go back for seconds—even thirds for those who suffer from one of the seven deadly sins? Yet that's the famous policy of this renowned all-you-can-eat establishment, a winner with those seeking rib-sticking "joints," for which the English are known. There is a wide range of appetizers. The buffet carving table offers prime rib with Yorkshire pudding, roast leg of Southdown lamb with mint sauce, and a roast leg of English pork with apple sauce.

You carve the meat yourself, slicing off as much as you want. Carvers stand by to assist and give instructions on how to wield the knife. Serve yourself with buttered peas, roast potatoes, new carrots, and gravy. In another area is a display of cold joints and assorted salads, whatever is in season. Desserts might include pineapple cake, perhaps a strawberry mousse. Well-brewed coffee for "afters" is included in the price. The Carvery is open Monday through Saturday from noon to 2:30 p.m. and 5:15 to 9 p.m., and on Sunday from 12:30 to 2:30 p.m. and 6 to 9 p.m. Tube: Piccadilly Circus.

Pappagalli's Pizza, Inc., 9 Swallow St., W.1 (tel. 01/734-5182), features an old-timey New York saloon decor in which you can enjoy reasonably priced Italian fare in the heart of London. Full meals cost from £8 ($14), and service is daily, except Sunday, from noon to 3 p.m. and 5 to 11 p.m. Happy hour, when drinks are reduced, is from 5:30 to 7 p.m. You can select from an array of sauces and from several different pastas. Pizzas come in two sizes, serving from two to four persons, and you can compose your own pizza from a selection of toppings. There is also a serve-yourself fresh salad bar ("Only one helping, please"). Tube: Piccadilly Circus.

The Granary, 39 Albemarle St., W.1 (tel. 01/493-2978), serves a variety of dishes, all of which have a real home-cooked flavor. An inexpensive meal of, say, meat pie, vegetables, chocolate cake, a glass of wine, and coffee, will cost from £7 ($12.25). The fare might include avocado stuffed with spinach, cheese, and shrimps, warm calves' liver salad, and steak-and-mushroom pie with bubble and squeak. Desserts are tempting, especially the tipsy cake and the upside-down cake. All portions

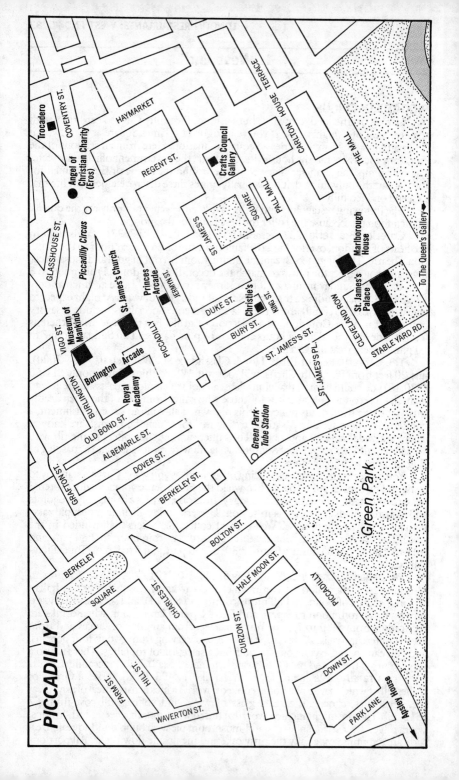

are large. Hours are from 11 a.m. to 8 p.m. Monday to Friday and from noon to 2:30 p.m. Saturday; closed Sunday. Tube: Green Park.

Wren at St. James's Coffee House, 35 Jermyn St., S.W.1 (tel. 01/437-9419). At this enterprising church, a two-minute walk from Piccadilly Circus, visitors can do brass rubbings. It also boasts a cheerful coffeeshop right within its walls with courtyard service in fair weather. There is always a fresh soup of the day, along with cold appetizers. They specialize in large potatoes baked in their "jackets," as the British say, and filled with a variety of stuffings such as cheese and tuna. A bill isn't likely to run more than £5.50 ($9.60). It's busy at lunchtime, when hot dishes are served. Teatime specialties include homemade cakes and large scones with cream and jam. The coffeehouse is open Monday to Friday from 8 a.m. to 8 p.m., on Saturday from 10 a.m. to 8 p.m., and on Sunday from 10 a.m. to 4 p.m. Tube: Piccadilly Circus.

AROUND LEICESTER SQUARE

Named for the second Earl of Leicester, and once the site of the home of Sir Joshua Reynolds, Leicester Square has changed its colors today, bursting out as the cinema center of London. The 19th-century square is a congested area of stores, theaters, cinemas, even churches. And beyond those, it has some inexpensive restaurants and pubs in its little offshoot lanes and alleyways, where West End actors discreetly select their "local."

There's now a large paved pedestrian precinct rivaling Piccadilly Circus and *Eros* as a meeting place for travelers and locals. It's less dangerous than Piccadilly Circus for many reasons, among which is that there's no traffic.

Stockpot, 40 Panton St., S.W.1 (tel. 01/839-5142), suggests good wholesome fare and lives up to its promise. Penny for penny, I'd hazard a guess that this cozy little member of a popular chain offers one of the best dining bargains in London. (Others are at 6 Basil St., S.W.3, and at 98 King's Rd., S.W.3.) Meals include a bowl of minestrone, spaghetti bolognese (the eternal favorite), a plate of braised lamb, and the apple crumble (or other desserts). Meals cost from £5 ($8.75) up. Offering two levels of dining in a Scandinavian-style atmosphere, the Stockpot has a share-the-table policy during peak dining hours. Hours are from 8 a.m. to 11:30 p.m. Monday to Saturday and from noon to 10 p.m. on Sunday. The little restaurant lies off Haymarket, opposite the Comedy Theatre. Tube: Piccadilly Circus.

If it's a charming ambience you're seeking, you'll find it in the heart of the theater district at the pubs and wine bars recommended below.

Manzi's, 1-2 Leicester St., off Leicester Square (tel. 01/734-0224), is London's oldest seafood restaurant, famous for fish, oysters, and other seafood specialties. Try the legendary Whitstable or Colchester oysters, or the less expensive grilled sardines. Main course selections include grilled king prawns, and various versions of Dover sole (the English like to eat it "on the bone"). The house also has a good selection of wines and sherries. You can dine either on the ground floor or in the Cabin Room upstairs. Since fish is expensive these days, a meal will cost from £20 ($35). The ground floor is open from noon to 3 p.m. and 5:30 to 11:45 p.m., and the Cabin Room serves from noon to 3 p.m. and 6 to 11:30 p.m. No lunch is offered on Sunday. Tube: Leicester Square.

China China, 38 Panton St., S.W.1 (tel. 01/925-0311), serves Hong Kong–style cuisine in the heart of theater and cinema land, close to both Piccadilly Circus and Leicester Square (the nearest tube stops). It serves set menus for £7 ($12.25) to £9 ($15.75) per person. You can also order à la carte from an extensive menu that includes Cantonese fried steak, deep-fried squid with prawn balls, and sizzling chicken with chiles and black bean sauce. Hours are daily, except Sunday, from noon to 3 p.m. and 5:30 to 11:45 p.m. On Saturday the restaurant is open all day, from noon to 11:45 p.m.

Cork and Bottle Wine Bar, 44-46 Cranbourn St., W.C.2 (tel. 01/734-7807), is in the theater district, just off Leicester Square. The most successful dish is a raised cheese-and-ham pie. It has a cream-cheesy filling, and the well-buttered pastry is crisp—not your typical quiche. Don Hewitson, the owner, also offers a mâchon Lyonnaise, a traditional worker's lunch in Lyon. He imports his own saucisson from a charcuterie in Lyon, serving it hot with warm potato salad, a mixed green salad, spicy Dijon mustard, and french bread. Meals cost from £9 ($15.25). Don has an extensive wine list. In fact, Don, a New Zealander, has been called "the Kiwi guru of the modern wine bar movement." The bar is open Monday to Saturday from 11 a.m. to 3 p.m. and 5:30 to 11 p.m., and on Sunday from noon to 2 p.m. and 7 to 10:30 p.m. Tube: Leicester Square.

Woodlands, 37 Panton St., S.W.1 (tel. 01/839-7258), offers the famed vegetarian cuisine from the south of India in the heart of London. It has several branches, of which the Panton Street "restaurant row" address is the most central. You can order Thalis (a variety plate), classic uthappan, iddlys, and dosas (spicy vegetarian concoctions). Service is from noon to 3 p.m. and 5:30 to 10:45 p.m. daily, except on Sunday when it opens only for dinner. Count on spending from £10 ($17.50) per person. Tube: Leicester Square.

The **Salisbury,** 90 St. Martin's Lane, W.C.2 (tel. 01/836-5863), one of the most famous Victorian pubs of London, is ably run by Kevin and Patsy Lee. Its glittering cut-glass mirrors reflect the faces of English stage stars (and would-be stars) sitting around the curved buffet bar, having a cold joint snack. A plate of the roast leg of pork at the buffet, plus a salad, costs from £4 ($7). In the saloon, you'll see and hear the Oliviers of yesterday and tomorrow. The place is open Monday to Saturday from 11 a.m. to 11 p.m., and Sunday from noon to 3 p.m. and 7 to 10:30 p.m. Tube: Leicester Square.

TRAFALGAR SQUARE AND THE STRAND

Between Leicester Square and Westminster, a former marshy meadow is known today as Trafalgar Square. The square is dominated by a monument honoring Lord Nelson, who died in the Battle of Trafalgar on October 21, 1805.

Beginning at the square, The Strand, south of Covent Garden, runs east into Fleet Street. Londoners used to be able to walk along The Strand and see the Thames, but the river, of course, has receded now. In the 17th century, the wealthy built their homes on The Strand, and their gardens stretched to the Thames itself. But today it is in transition to something less grand—flanked as it is with theaters (the Savoy, for example), shops, hotels, and such landmarks as Somerset House.

Peaceful lanes jut off from The Strand, leading to the Victoria Embankment Gardens along the river. Opposite the gardens is Cleopatra's Needle, an Egyptian obelisk, London's oldest monument. If the weather permits, you might want to stroll along the river.

Sherlock Holmes, 10 Northumberland St., W.C.2 (tel. 01/930-2644), is a favorite of devotees of the legendary English detective and his creator, Arthur Conan Doyle. You can have your mug of beer and then look at the upstairs re-creation of the living room of 221B Baker Street, where get-togethers of "The Baker Street Irregulars" are held. Such Holmesiana are included as the cobra of *The Speckled Band* and the head of *The Hound of the Baskervilles*. The food served upstairs reflects both an English and a continental influence. Main-dish specialties include roast beef with Yorkshire pudding, the chef's homemade steak-and-kidney pie, and veal Cordon Bleu. A three-course meal with coffee comes to around £11 ($19.25). In the snackbar downstairs, you can have a salad with a wide variety of traditional English pies, or choose a hot dish from one of the chef's specialties. Hours are from 11 a.m. to 11 p.m. Monday to Saturday, and from noon to 3 p.m. and 7 to 10:30 p.m. Sunday. Tube: Charing Cross or Embankment.

Clarence Inn, 53 Whitehall, S.W.1 (tel. 01/930-4808), just down from Trafalgar Square, is the haunt of civil servants from the nearby ministry offices. They enjoy such lunchtime food as braised oxtail, Oriental pork chops, or traditional shepherd's pie. There are always at least four hot dishes of the day, plus a range of cold dishes and salads. A serve-yourself buffet there costs about £6 ($10.50). The 18th-century inn offers blackened beams, a sawdust-strewn floor, church pews, and uncovered tables lit by flickering gaslights, and in the evening from Monday to Thursday a strolling minstrel makes light music in the bar. Food service in the downstairs pub is from 11:30 a.m. to 10 p.m. Monday to Saturday, and from noon to 2 p.m. and 7 to 10 p.m. on Sunday. The pub remains open from 11 a.m. to 11 p.m. Monday to Saturday, and from noon to 3 p.m. and 7 to 10:30 p.m. on Sunday. The buffet restaurant upstairs is open only from noon to 2:30 p.m. daily. Tube: Charing Cross or Embankment.

National Gallery Restaurant, Trafalgar Square, W.C.2 (tel. 01/930-5210), offers lunch in a comfortable basement before you explore the gallery. Juicy quiches and flans are presented before you, along with a line-up of fresh, crisp salads. Hot daily specials are likely to include chili with rice, coq au vin, and beef bourguignon. Count on spending from £5 ($8.75). The restaurant is open Monday to Saturday from 10 a.m. to 5 p.m. and on Sunday from 2 to 5 p.m. Hot food is served only at lunch from noon to 3 p.m. After that, drinks and snacks are available. Tube: Charing Cross.

Val Taro, 32 Orange St., W.C.2 (tel. 01/930-2939), popular as an after-theater dining spot, offers an Italy-inspired menu that includes at least six superb veal dishes, grilled double filet of sole, excellent beefsteaks, and an array of pastas and antipasti. Meals cost from £15 ($26.25). Hours are from noon to 3 p.m. and 6 to 11 p.m. Monday to Friday, but only from 6 to 11 p.m. Saturday. It is closed Sunday. The wine bar has the same lunchtime hours, but it is open in the evening from 5:30 to 11 p.m. You can order a plate of pasta or a salad to accompany your glass of wine. Tube: Leicester Square.

COVENT GARDEN

In 1970, London's flower, fruit, and "veg" market celebrated its 300th anniversary. But "Auld Lang Syne" might have been the theme song. Once a district of gambling dens and bawdy houses east of Piccadilly Circus and north of the Strand, the historic but congested market was transferred in 1974 to a $7.2-million, 64-acre site at Nine Elms, in the suburb of Vauxhall, South London, 2½ miles away, across the Thames.

Covent Garden dates from the time when the monks of Westminster Abbey dumped their surplus homegrown vegetables here. Charles II in 1670 granted the Earl of Bedford the right to "sell roots and herbs, whatsoever" in the district. The king's mistress, Nell Gwynne, once peddled oranges on Drury Lane (later appearing on the stage of the Drury Lane Theatre).

Before that, in the 1630s Inigo Jones designed the square, hoping to have a plaza in the Florentine style, but the work bogged down. Even his self-tabbed "handsomest barn in England," St. Paul's Covent Garden, burned down in the late 18th century and was subsequently rebuilt. The English actress, Dame Ellen Terry (noted in particular for her letters to G. B. Shaw), is buried here.

St. Paul's eastern face looks down on the market where Professor Higgins in *Pygmalion* met his "squashed cabbage leaf," Eliza Doolittle, and later got reacquainted in *My Fair Lady.* Also in the area is the Royal Opera House on Bow Street, housing the Royal Ballet and the Covent Garden Opera Company. On nearby Russell Street, Samuel Johnson met his admirer, Boswell, and coffeehouses in the district were once patronized by Addison and Steele. Just as chicly dressed people of fashion once flocked to Les Halles in Paris to have onion soup with butchers in blood-soaked smocks, so London revelers have dropped in at Covent Garden's pubs to drink with Cockney barrow boys in the early dawn hours. The tradition will be sadly missed.

The old central market has reopened with expensive stores selling exclusive products jostled by the more temporary stalls in the center peddling unremarkable souvenirs, jewelry, baskets and wickerwork, clothing, and T-shirts. Occasional groups enliven the place with impromptu music.

The area attracts art galleries, such as the Acme, the Hammond Lloyd, the Covent Garden, and the William Drummond. It's appropriate that art galleries should be returning to Covent Garden. In the 18th century it was a beehive of artists, including Sir Peter Lely and Sir Godfrey Kneller (famous portrait painters, the latter of whom is buried at St. Paul's Church, around the corner). Others who lived here were Sir James Thornhill, Richard Wilson, Henry Fuseli, Daniel Mytens, the sculptor Roubiliac, Johann Zoffany, and John Flaxman. The American painter Benjamin West also lived here after he got out of jail, where he was sent for trying to study in London during the Revolution.

In the popular Covent Garden complex is **Plummers Restaurant,** 33 King St., W.C.2 (tel. 01/240-2534). It is an informal sort of place where a woman can go on her own without attracting attention and where there is room enough between the tables so that you don't have to listen to someone else's conversation. Appetizers include avocado vinaigrette or clam chowder. Then there is a wide selection of main dishes, including halibut and spinach in a parmesan cheese sauce, traditional steak-and-kidney pie, and vegetarian dishes, including vegetable cottage pie. There are Scottish beefburgers (100% meat) ranging from plain to Plummers Superburger topped with bacon, egg, and melted cheese. Desserts include various flavors of ice cream and sorbet, and there is apple and blackberry pie and cream. Coffee—as much as you can drink—finishes off the meal. A meal will cost around £14 ($24.50), but you can get away with £8 ($14) for a beefburger and coffee. VAT is included, but a 12% service charge is added to all bills. Hours are from 12:30 to 2:30 p.m. and 6 to 11 p.m. The place is closed at lunchtime Saturday and all day Sunday. Tube: Covent Garden.

Diana's Diner, 39 Endell St., W.C.2 (tel. 01/240-0272), is a busy, noisy place, with no pretensions to elegance but with a well-deserved reputation among local office workers for serving satisfying meals at very reasonable prices. The most expensive dish is sirloin steak with chips. There are also steak pie and a selection of pasta dishes. Breakfast offers excellent deals. Meals cost around £8 ($14). The diner is open from 7:30 a.m. to 7 p.m. Monday to Friday and from 9 a.m. to 7 p.m. Saturday. Tube: Covent Garden.

Magno's, 65a Long Acre, W.C.2 (tel. 01/836-6077), is useful for before- and after-theater meals if you're in the area. It offers a fixed-price menu of appetizer, a main course, a glass of wine, and coffee for only £8.45 ($14.80), including VAT and service. This meal is served from 6 to 7 p.m. However, should you miss the pretheater meal, your regular à la carte tab could easily rise to £18 ($31.50) or more. The brasserie is open Monday to Friday for lunch and dinner and on Saturday for dinner only, offering a selection of modern French cuisine, grills, and salads. It has a friendly atmosphere and good service. Hours are noon to 2:30 p.m. Monday to Friday and 6 to 11:30 p.m. Monday to Saturday. Tube: Covent Garden.

Smith's Restaurant, 33 Shelton St., W.C.2 (tel. 01/379-0310), is part of a converted old Covent Garden brewery. The food is predominantly in the new English style, simple cooking using high-quality ingredients. Try, for example, grilled radicchio with Gruyère cheese, venison sausages with black pudding, and English cheeses from Neal's Yard. The daily specials and dessert selection reflect seasonal foods and always include a vegetarian dish. The pretheater menu is a popular feature, as Smith's is opposite the Donmar Theatre and close to others. Served from 6 to 8 p.m., the menu of two courses costs £8.95 ($15.65), including VAT and service. At other times, meals cost from £12 ($21). Hours are from noon to midnight Monday to Saturday, with last orders at 11:30 p.m.

Food for Thought, 31 Neal St., W.C.2 (tel. 01/836-0239), serves some of the best and least expensive vegetarian food in the neighborhood, with meals costing from £5 ($8.75). During the peak dining hours, it is likely to be crowded, so it's advised that you go after the rush. After leaving the tube at Covent Garden, stroll along Neal Street toward Shaftesbury Avenue. The restaurant is on the left in the second block. The food selections change twice a day, but they include good soups with whole-meal bread, freshly made salads, quiches, curries, and casseroles, including hot pie. It is open from noon to 8 p.m. Monday to Friday, from 11:30 a.m. to 4:30 p.m. Saturday; closed Sunday. Take-away service is also provided.

MAYFAIR

Mayfair (W.1), bounded by Piccadilly, Hyde Park, and Oxford and Regent Streets, is the elegant, fashionable section of London. Luxury hotels exist side by side with Georgian town houses and swank shops. Here are all the parks, names, and streets that have snob associations the world over. Grosvenor Square (pronounced Grov-nor) is nicknamed "Little America" because it contains the American Embassy and a statue of Franklin D. Roosevelt. Berkeley (pronounced Barkley) is the home of the English Speaking Union.

At least once you'll want to dip into the exclusive Mayfair section, or even make repeated trips to Carnaby, which lies only one block from Regent Street.

Casper & Giumbini's, 6 Tenterden St., W.1 (tel. 01/493-7923), is nestled just off the northwest corner of Hanover Square in the heart of Mayfair. The original Casper & Giumbini's opened in Dublin many years ago. The same atmosphere has been re-created in London, with a hand-carved mahogany bar, burnished brass, Tiffany lamps, and stained glass. Resident piano players and convivial crowds usually keep the place jumping. The menu is Anglo-American, with an occasional French influence. There is a large, reasonably priced wine list, and a selection of beers from around the world. Brunch is good value at £6 ($10.50), including an alcoholic drink of your choice. A bar lunch is only £4 ($7), and a meal in the restaurant costs from £10.50 ($18.40) for three courses, plus your drink. It is open seven days a week, from noon to 3 p.m. and 5:30 p.m. to midnight. Tube: Bond Street.

Chicago Pizza Pie Factory, 17 Hanover Square, W.1. (tel. 01/629-2669), specializes in deep-dish pizza covered with cheese, tomato, and a choice of sausage, pepperoni, mushrooms, green peppers, onions, and anchovies. The regular-size pizza is enough for two or three diners, and the large one is suitable for four or five persons. It's one of the few places where a doggy bag is willingly provided. There are smoking and nonsmoking tables. The menu also includes stuffed mushrooms, garlic bread, salads, and homemade cheesecakes served with two forks. The cost begins at £8 ($14). A video over the bar shows continuous American baseball, football, and basketball games. The 275-seat restaurant is full of authentic Chicago memorabilia, and the waitresses wear *Chicago Tribune* newspaper-sellers' aprons. The Factory is just off Oxford Street in Hanover Square, opposite John Lewis and within easy reach of Regent Street as well. It is open Monday to Saturday from 11:45 a.m. to 11:30 p.m. Tube: Bond Street.

Shampers, 4 Kingly St., W.1 (tel. 01/437-1692), created by New Zealander Don Hewitson, serves a superb selection of wines and imaginatively prepared food. Wines from Australia and New Zealand are a specialty. Full meals in the street-level bar cost from £5 ($8.75) each, and typical dishes include cheese and ham pie, pastas, and a vegetarian dish of the day. At lunch only from noon to 3 p.m. Monday to Friday, the cellar serves as a Provençal-inspired brasserie. Here it costs around £10 ($17.50) for a meal of, perhaps, sausages and ratatouille. Hours for the wine bar are Monday to Friday from 11 a.m. to 11 p.m. and on Saturday from 11 a.m. to 3 p.m. Closing is Saturday night and all day Sunday. Tube: Oxford Circus.

Cranks Health Food Restaurant, 8 Marshall St., W.1 (tel. 01/437-9431), around the corner from Carnaby Street, took its name from "cranks." But instead of the colloquial meaning of an eccentric, impractical person, the restaurant defines the word as those "who have the courage to pursue a line of thinking against the general stream of orthodox belief." Their "line," by the way, is excellent—the best of natural soups, salads, and breads made from 100% organic, stoneground whole wheat flour. Hot savory dishes, quiche, flan, pizza, and a whole array of salads cater to every appetite and every pocket. Main courses cost as little as £3 ($5.25), and substantial snacks are less. Cranks is open from 8 a.m. to 7 p.m. Monday to Saturday. An evening menu is served until 10:30 p.m., with meals costing from £7 ($12.25). At lunchtime it gets crowded. Tube: Oxford Circus. For details of other Cranks London restaurants, phone 01/607-4474 during regular office hours.

Widow Applebaum's Deli & Bagel Academy, 46 South Molton St., W.1 (tel. 01/629-4649), is a useful place for those who don't wish to go to the East End of London to enjoy New York Jewish food in the strict environment of Bloom's (see the "East End" section later in this chapter). It's good for a before-theater meal, but avoid it during office lunch hours. The pastrami is flown in fresh daily from New York. Sandwiches, including roast beef and turkey, are topped with cole slaw and pickled cucumbers and are accompanied by potato salad. Count on spending from £8 ($14) for a meal here. The deli is open daily, except Sunday, from 9 a.m. to 10 p.m. The place also features a full English breakfast for £2 ($3.50), and it is served daily except Sunday from 8 to 11 a.m. South Molton Street is a pedestrian precinct, and tables are set outside in fair weather. Tube: Bond Street.

Justin de Blank, 54 Duke St., W.1 (tel. 01/629-3174), just off Oxford Street, offers breakfast, lunch, and dinner, and is a haven for tired shoppers. They serve a variety of foods. You might begin with a soup of the day or a fresh salad, then follow with such main courses as lamb and apricot casserole, or seafood with a mushroom and saffron sauce, or various vegetarian dishes. For dessert, you might try an individual apple strudel. A three-course meal costs from £10 ($17.50). Justin is open from 8:30 a.m. to 3:30 p.m. and 4:30 to 9 p.m. Monday to Friday, and from 9 a.m. to 3:30 p.m. Saturday; closed Sunday. Tube: Bond Street.

Hard Rock Café, 7 Old Park Lane, W.1 (tel. 01/629-0382), is a down-home southern-cum-midwestern American roadside diner with good food at reasonable prices and service with a smile. Almost every night, there is a line waiting to get in, as this is one of the most popular places in town with young people. It is also the favorite of visiting rock stars, film stars, and tennis players from America. The café gives generous portions of all food items, and the price of a main dish includes not only salad but fries. Naturally, you can get corn on the cob, and specialties include various steaks. The dessert menu is equally tempting, including homemade apple pie and thick, cold shakes. There is also a good selection of beer. The place is open seven days a week, charging from £9 ($15.75) up for a complete meal. Food is served from 11:30 a.m. to 12:30 a.m. Sunday to Thursday and from 11:30 a.m. to 1 a.m. Friday and Saturday. *People* magazine called this place "the Smithsonian of rock 'n' roll." Tube: Green Park or Hyde Park Corner.

Shepherd Market

One of the curiosities of Mayfair is Shepherd Market, a tiny village of pubs, two-story inns, book and food stalls, and restaurants, all sandwiched between the slices of Mayfair grandness. At one corner you might be contemplating whether to buy that antique Rolls-Royce, then you suddenly turn down a street and are transplanted to a remnant of a village of old England, where the peddlers are hawking their wares. While here, you may want to drop in for a drink at one of London's best-known pubs.

Shepherd's Tavern, 50 Hertford St., W.1 (tel. 01/499-3017), is a nugget, considered *the* pub of Mayfair. It attracts a congenial mixture. There are many luxurious touches, including a collection of antique furniture. Chief among these is a sedan chair that once belonged to the son of George III, the Duke of Cumberland. Bar snacks and hot dishes include shepherd's pie or fish pie with vegetables. Upstairs, the owners operate a cozy restaurant, Georgian in style with cedar paneling. There they serve staunchly British food, with a three-course fixed meal costing £14 ($24.50). You can also order à la carte. Meals are served from noon to 3 p.m. and 6 to 10:30 p.m. Monday to Saturday. On Sunday, only dinner is offered from 6 to 10:30 p.m. The street-level pub is open 11 a.m. to 11 p.m. Monday to Saturday, and from noon to 3 p.m. and 7 to 10:30 p.m. on Sunday. Tube: Green Park.

Bunch of Grapes, 16 Shepherd Market, W.1 (tel. 01/629-4989), is a pub that is all bustle at lunchtime. It's a period piece from 1882, with a fireplace, lace curtains, turn-of-the-century chandeliers, hunting trophies, and Staffordshire figurines. Join the locals and order real ale at 65p ($1.15) per half pint. Hot and cold snacks and steak sandwiches are served at the snack bar 11 a.m. to 3 p.m. Monday to Saturday. In the restaurant upstairs, an à la carte menu is available, offering traditional English fare, with meals costing from £12 ($21). The restaurant is open from noon to 3 p.m. Monday to Friday. The pub is open from 11 a.m. to 11 p.m. Monday to Saturday, and from 11 a.m. to 3 p.m. and 7 to 10:30 p.m. Sunday. Tube: Green Park.

SOHO

This section (W.1) of crisscrossed narrow lanes and crooked streets is the main foreign quarter of London, site of many of the city's best foreign restaurants. The unanglicized life of the continent holds forth in Soho: great numbers of French people are found here, and so are Italians and all other European nationalities, as well as Orientals. Traditionally, it has been known as the center of vice and prostitution in London.

Soho starts impudently at Piccadilly Circus, spreading out like a peacock and ending at Oxford Street. One side borders the theater center on Shaftesbury Avenue. From Piccadilly Circus, walk northeast and you'll come to Soho, to the left of Shaftesbury. This jumbled section can also be approached from the Tottenham Court Road tube station. Walk south along Charing Cross Road, and Soho will be to your right.

Of Gerrard Street, a correspondent wrote that "the smell of pickled ginger and roast duckling seeps from restaurant doors. The men scurry into stores from afternoon games of fan-tan and mah-jongg. A lilting twang of Chinese rock 'n' roll envelops the downtown street." The East End's Limehouse made a small pretense, but Gerrard Street has succeeded in becoming London's first Chinatown. Strip shows have given way to Chinese restaurants and bookstores keeping you informed of the latest developments in Hong Kong or China.

Soho in a sense is a Jekyll and Hyde quarter. In daytime it's a paradise for the searcher of spices, continental food, fruits, fish, and sausages, with at least two street markets offering fruit and vegetables, often at bargain prices. At night it's a dazzle of strip joints, gay clubs, porno movies, sex emporiums, and titillating bookshops, all intermingled with international restaurants that, because of the competition, are on their toes to offer value for money.

Red Fort, 77 Dean St., W.1 (tel. 01/437-2115), is considered one of the finest Indian restaurants in London, where the competition is keen. If you're on the tightest of budgets, go only for their help-yourself Sunday buffet at £9.95 ($17.40), where a spread of Indian delicacies is placed before you. Otherwise, count on spending from £10.95 ($19.15) for a superb meal. The waiters are helpful in explaining the menu. Hours are from noon to 3 p.m. and 6 to 11 p.m. daily. Tube: Leicester Square or Tottenham Court Road.

Kettner's Restaurant, 29 Romilly St., W.1 (tel. 01/734-6112), has had a long and topsy-turvy history, dating back to 1869. Once it was patronized by King Edward VII, then Prince of Wales. Today it's pizza time, as this is the flagship restaurant of the Pizza Express chain. However, its standards of service and the quality of its food are far above the standards of a typical chain emporium. It's also a center for live jazz, usually offered every night and at lunch on Sunday. You can begin your evening in the champagne bar on the ground floor. The restaurant is open seven days a week from noon to midnight. Reservations are not taken. Tube: Leicester Square.

Dumpling Inn, 15a Gerrard St., W.1 (tel. 01/437-2567), in the small Chinese district of Soho, attracts a number of devoted regulars. Don't be fooled by the name or the Venetian murals—this is an elegant Chinese restaurant serving classical Mandarin dishes. The haute cuisine of China, Mandarin cooking dates back nearly 3000 years and employs a number of unique cooking rituals. The somewhat small portions allow you to sample a variety of this delectable cuisine. Try the shark's fin soup, the beef in oyster sauce, or the grilled pork or beef dumplings, and many Pekinese and Cantonese specialties are also served. Meals cost from £10 ($17.50). Dinner reservations are recommended, and you should allow plenty of time for dining here, since most dishes are prepared to your special order. Hours are nonstop, every day of the year except Christmas, from noon to 11:45 p.m. Tube: Leicester Square.

Pasticceria Amalfi, 31 Old Compton St., W.1 (tel. 01/437-7284), is a crowded good bargain-priced Italian restaurant. Italian chefs prepare dishes in the traditional way, including spaghetti, pizzas, veal in white wine, minestrone, and lasagne. Dinners cost from £10 ($17.50) to £12 ($21). A pâtisserie turns out excellent Italian pastries. It is open seven days a week, serving lunch from noon to 3 p.m. and dinner from 6 p.m. to midnight. On Sunday it stays open continuously from 10 a.m. to midnight. Tube: Leicester Square.

Venus Kebab House, 2 Charlotte St., W.1 (tel. 01/636-4324), is a zesty choice on a highly competitive street. It's a winner for Greek specialties and good food in the low-price range. Avgolemono, the Greek national soup, is made with chicken stock, rice, egg, lemon, and spices. The standard specialties are dolmades (vine leaves stuffed with lamb, beef, rice, tomatoes, and spices) and moussaka. Four-course meals begin at £8 ($14). A corner restaurant, the Venus has outdoor tables in summer. It's open from noon to 3 p.m. and 5:30 to 11:30 p.m. Monday to Saturday. Tube: Goodge Street or Tottenham Court Road.

Chiang Mai, 48 Frith St., W.1 (tel. 01/437-7444), in the center of Soho, is named after the ancient northern capital of Thailand, a region known for its rich, spicy foods. Try their hot and sour dishes, their chili-laced specials, even their special vegetarian menu. Meals cost from £10 ($17.50) and up and are served daily except Sunday from noon to 3 p.m. and 6 to 11:30 p.m. The location is next door to Ronnie Scott's, the most famous jazz club in England. Tube: Leicester Square.

Anemos, 32 Charlotte St., W.1 (tel. 01/636-2289), is the place for breaking plates, dancing, and joining the waiters in a rip-roaring Greek song. They also have a magic show and a floor show with Greek dancing. A typical meal of taramosalata, hummus, and kebabs, plus dessert, cheese, coffee, and a half bottle of wine, will run as much as £15 ($26.25). The restaurant is closed on Sunday so the staff can clean up the mess. Otherwise, it's open from noon to 3 p.m. and 6 to 11:45 p.m. Tube: Goodge Street.

Gabys Continental Bar, 30 Charing Cross Rd., W.C.2 (tel. 01/836-4233), is really just a snackbar but is open from 9 a.m. to midnight daily, and can satisfy your needs whatever the time of day, particularly after the theater. The service is quick. Salt beef (corned, to us) sandwiches are a featured selection, as are hearty soups such as bean and barley. The house specialties are donner kebabs, which are spit-roasted lamb served in pita bread with relish and shredded salad. Meals cost from £6 ($10.50) at this fully licensed restaurant. Tube: Leicester Square.

Le Beaujolais Wine Bar, 25 Litchfield St., W.C.2 (tel. 01/836-2277), stands at Cambridge Circus. You get some good wines here at reasonable prices: for example, a bottle of house wine costs from £5.25 ($9.20). Meals start from £7 ($12.25) per person. There is cold food to accompany your wine, including French pâtés, cheeses, and chicken and ham, and a hot dish of the day such as a classic coq au vin. Le Beaujolais is open Monday to Friday from noon to 11 p.m. without interruption, on Saturday from 5:30 to 11 p.m., and is closed on Sunday. Tube: Leicester Square.

North of Soho, in a section of London called "Fitzrovia," **Auntie's,** 126 Cleveland St., W.1 (tel. 01/387-3226), serves an array of dishes that many of its diners remember from childhood: beef and mushroom pie with Guinness gravy, "toad in the hole," even Auntie's bangers and mash. Rabbit hotpot is served with a white mustard-seed sauce, and for dessert you can order a tipsy fruit trifle. A set lunch or dinner costing £15 ($26.25) is served from noon to 2:45 p.m. and 6 to 10:45 p.m. Monday to Saturday (closed Saturday for lunch and all day Sunday). The service, food, and surroundings make this a worthy choice. It's very intimate, so reservations are imperative. Tube: Great Portland Station.

---

2. Westminster and St. James's

This section (S.W.1) has been the seat of the British government since the days of Edward the Confessor. Dominated by the Houses of Parliament and Westminster Abbey, Parliament Square is the symbol of the soul of England. Westminster is a big name to describe a large borough of London, including Whitehall itself, the headquarters of many government offices. In addition, the sprawling area in and around Victoria Station (with many budget hotels) is also a part of Westminster. Sections of it fall into Pimlico.

Westminster College, 76 Vincent Square, S.W.1, offers a complete midday meal, coffee included, for around £6.20 ($10.85), including VAT. The secret is that this is the finest school for hotel and restaurant catering in England, and the nonprofit meals are cooked and served by undergraduates. It's really not amateur hour, as there is strict supervision. The food is of a high standard, but you must order whatever their "assignment" is for the day. You can reserve space by phone (tel. 01/828-1222) between noon and 2 p.m. only, up to ten days in advance, or just arrive around noon to see whether there is space, have a drink in the lounge if you wish, and then be shown to your seat. If you are alone, you'll probably have to share. Naturally, the dining room is closed on Saturday and Sunday and for a variable six-week period every summer. Tube: St. James's Park.

Grandma Lee's Bakery and Restaurant, 2 Bridge St., S.W.1 (tel. 01/839-1319), is a bright and cheerful place across the street from the Houses of Parliament and the tower of Big Ben. Bread, buns, and rolls are freshly baked on the premises, later to appear at the ground-floor service counter filled with your choice of an array of ingredients. Everything comes in a bun, including breakfast, a bacon-and-egg bun served from 7 to 11 a.m. Along with juice, tea, and coffee, it comes to £2 ($3.50). They also serve beef casserole with bread and chili with bread. Meals cost from £4 ($7). It's open daily from 7 a.m. to 9 p.m. Tube: Westminster.

ST. JAMES'S

This section (S.W.1), the beginning of Royal London, starts at Piccadilly Circus, moving southwest. It's frightfully convenient, as the English say, enclosing a number of locations, such as American Express on Haymarket and many of the leading department stores, eventually encompassing Buckingham Palace.

But don't be scared off. There are luncheon bargains available in an atmosphere ranging from the world's most exclusive grocery store to a posh Victorian pub.

At **Fortnum and Mason,** 181 Piccadilly, W.1 (tel. 01/734-8040), pause, first, to look at the famous Fortnum and Mason clock outside, then enter the refined precincts of the world's most elegant grocery store (more about this in the shopping section coming up). It's well known historically that this store has supplied "takeout" treasures to everybody from the Duke of Wellington to Florence Nightingale in the Crimea, even Mr. Stanley while he pursued Dr. Livingstone. What is lesser known is that you can also order a sandwich here prepared by grocers who hold the Royal Warrant or else partake of a proper sitdown meal, and not just caviar, truffles, or rich chocolates.

There are three places at which to eat or dine. The **Fountain Restaurant,** with its own entrance in Jermyn Street, opens at 9:30 a.m. daily, when English or continental breakfasts are available at £5.50 ($9.65) and £3.25 ($5.70), respectively. The restaurant is open until 11:30 p.m. Famous for its extravagant ice cream sundaes, it is also an ideal venue for a pre- or after-theater supper. An evening grill menu is offered, costing from £10 ($17.50).

The **Patio & Buttery** restaurant on the mezzanine is also open from 9:30 a.m., providing cheerful surroundings in which to meet friends for morning coffee, a light lunch, or cream teas, costing around £3.25 ($5.70) and served from 2:30 to 5 p.m.

The elegant **St. James's Restaurant** on the fourth floor is open from 9 a.m. to 5 p.m. Traditional roast beef with all the trimmings, carved from the trolley, is just one of the popular dishes available for lunch, costing from £12 ($21). Also available is the ultimate in afternoon teas, with fresh sandwiches, scones and cream, and cakes for £5.50 ($9.65).

Also recommended is a picnic in London park. Fortnums offers a choice of seven menus, packed in picnic baskets, at prices beginning at £12.05 ($21.10) and extending upward. The store is closed on Sunday. Tube: Green Park or Piccadilly Circus.

Red Lion, 2 Duke of York St., St. James's Square, S.W.1 (tel. 01/930-2030), is only a short walk from Piccadilly Circus, near American Express on Haymarket. Ian Nairn compared its spirit to that of Edouard Manet's painting *A Bar at the Folies-Bergère* (see the collection at the Courtauld Institute Galleries). A simple pub luncheon costs from £4 ($7). Everything is washed down with a pint of lager or cider in the jewel-like little Victorian pub with its posh turn-of-the-century decorations, such as patterned glass and deep-mahogany curlicues that recapture the gin-palace atmosphere. Food is more copious at lunch than at dinner, with only sandwiches and "pasties" being offered in the evening. The Red Lion roars from 11 a.m. to 11 p.m. Single women can be at ease here. Tube: Piccadilly Circus.

NEAR VICTORIA STATION

On one of London's most popular streets for budget hotels, **Ebury Wine Bar,** 139 Ebury St., S.W.1 (tel. 01/530-5447), is most convenient for dining or drinking in the area. Wine is sold by either the glass or bottle. A cold table is offered daily, and you can always get an enticing plat du jour. The menu invariably includes grilled steaks and lamb cutlets. All the food is prepared fresh daily. Sunday lunch costs £7.95 ($13.90). Otherwise, meals go for around £12 ($21). The wine bar is open seven days a week, serving food from noon to 2:45 p.m. and 6 to 10 p.m. Monday to Saturday, and from noon to 2:30 p.m. and 7 to 10 p.m. on Sunday. Tube: Victoria Station.

Methuselah's, 29 Victoria St., S.W.1 (tel. 01/222-1750), is owned by Don Hewitson, a New Zealander credited with changing the face of London wine bars. (All of them that have shown his magic touch over the years are recommended in this guide.) Opposite New Scotland Yard, his latest venture, which is exclusively his, is popular with MPs from the House of Commons. Mr. Hewitson also provides a sophisticated menu. He calls his food "Bourgeois," and it shows a devotion to Provence. The day's specialties are written on the blackboard. There is a ground-floor bar, along with a cellar buffet and wine bar, plus a more formal restaurant, the Burgundy Room, on the mezzanine. Meals cost from £11 ($19.25) and are served Monday to Friday only from 11:30 a.m. to 3 p.m. and 5:30 to 11 p.m. Tube: Victoria.

Albert, 52 Victoria St., S.W.1 (tel. 01/222-5577), once named "pub of the year," is a real bit of Victorian England near Victoria Station. From 8 to 10:30 a.m. Monday to Friday, it serves a copious English breakfast for £4.95 ($8.65) to £6.95 ($12.15). You can come back for lunch at the carvery with sumptuous roasts traditionally prepared and carved for you. Meals cost from £11.95 ($20.90) per person and are served continuously, seven days a week, from noon to 9:30 p.m. The pub is open Monday to Friday from 11 a.m. to 10:30 p.m., on Saturday from 11 a.m. to 3 p.m. and 6 to 10:30 p.m., and on Sunday from noon to 2:30 p.m. and 7 to 10:30 p.m.

PIMLICO

Still the choice for taking a maiden aunt to lunch, the **Tate Gallery Restaurant,** Millbank, S.W.1 (tel. 01/834-6754), is better than ever. The menu undergoes seasonal changes, but you can count on good, wholesome food in the British tradition. The wine list is extensive, and the restaurant is widely praised for its moderate tabs on some excellent vintages. It's essential to reserve a table (many in-the-know locals call ahead and even order their wine so that it can be at the right temperature upon their arrival). Costing from £15 ($26.25) lunches in this highly unusual setting are served from noon to 3 p.m. Monday to Saturday. Tube: Pimlico. Bus: 88.

Top Curry Centre, Tandoori House, 3 Lupus St., S.W.1 (tel. 01/821-7572), has the colossal advantage of listing the hotness and strength of the curries graded from one to nine, so you need not suffer agonies if you prefer a mild dish. The bill will come to around £8.50 ($14.90) per person for a highly satisfying meal. Drinks are available, and you should certainly wash No. 9 curry down with lager unless you have an asbestos-lined palate. The center is open daily from noon to 3 p.m. and 6 to 11:30 p.m. Tube: Pimlico.

---

3. The City

When the English talk about "the City" (E.C.2, E.C.3), they don't mean London. The City is the British version of Wall Street. Not only is it an important financial and business square mile, but it contains much worth exploring.

Here are the buildings known all over the world: the Bank of England on Threadneedle Street (entrance hall open to the public); the Stock Exchange, where you can watch from a special gallery as fortunes are made and lost; and Lloyd's of London, on Leadenhall, one of the world's great insurance centers. Lloyd's will insure anything from a stamp collection to a giraffe's neck.

Typical English food—shepherd's pie, mixed grills, roast beef—is dished up in dozens of the old pubs of the City. Here you can eat along with the English, whether it be the man in the bowler worried about the value of his stocks, or a Cockney clerk who has stayed within the sound of the Bow Bells.

Many of the old pubs and wine bars date back to Elizabethan days and lay claim to having entertained literary celebrities. For the most part, the following recommendations have been selected not only because of their well-prepared and inexpensive food, but because the buildings themselves have interest. The pub might have been designed by Sir Christopher Wren, or Shakespeare might have performed in one of them . . . whatever.

Barbican Centre, Silk St., E.C.2 (tel. 01/638-4141), offers a choice of eating and drinking establishments in several price ranges. On Level 5, the Waterside Cafeteria is self-service, offering a range of hot meals, salads, sandwiches, pastries, tea, and coffee, along with wine and beer. It is open daily from 10 a.m. to 8 p.m. (on Sunday from noon to 8 p.m.), charging from £5 ($8.75) for a meal. On Level 7, Cut Above is a carvery, featuring roast joints along with an array of cold meats, fish, and salads. Charging £17 ($29.75) per person, it is open for lunch daily from noon to 3 p.m., for tea from 3:30 to 5 p.m., and for dinner from 5:45 p.m. until 30 minutes after the end of the last performance within Barbican Centre. From the restaurant, windows open onto St. Paul's Cathedral, St. Giles Cripplegate, and the Barbican Lake. On Level 6, you might also want to patronize Wine on Six, which has an extensive list of bottled and draft wines and beers, accompanied by a variety of cold meats, fish, and salads, along with specialty breads and cheese. Full meals cost from £7 ($12.25), and service is daily from noon to 2:30 p.m. and 5 to 8 p.m. If there is a concert or play in progress, Wine on Six remains open until the end of the concert's intermission. Tube: Moorgate.

Ye Olde Watling Restaurant, 29 Watling St., E.C.4 (tel. 01/248-6252), is rich in associations with Sir Christopher Wren. It was rebuilt after the Great Fire of London in 1666. In the intimate restaurant upstairs, meals are served Monday to Friday from noon to 2:30 p.m., under oak beams and on trestle tables. You can have a good choice of English food, with such traditional dishes as steak-and-kidney pie. Three or four hot dishes made on the premises daily are likely to include chicken-and-mushroom pie, moussaka, and chili con carne. Meals cost from £4 ($7). Freshly made sandwiches and homemade pork pies are served in the bar, which is filled with Wren memorabilia and is open from 11 a.m. to 9 p.m. Monday to Friday. Tube: Mansion House.

Café Burgundy, Cathedral Pl., E.C.4 (tel. 01/248-2550), stands close to St. Paul's (the nearest tube stop). It highlights the food and wines from the Burgundy region of France, featuring a fine selection reasonably priced. Plats du jour are featured. Guests have a choice of dining places, in either the mezzanine or ground floor–level restaurants or in the precinct-level wine bar. The café is open only Monday to Friday when workers from the City fill the place. The restaurant serves from noon to 3 p.m.; the Bar Burgundy is open from 11:30 a.m. to 3 p.m. for drinks and bar meals and from 3 to 5 p.m. for coffee and snacks, and from 5 to 8:30 p.m. for bar meals and drinks. The average cost for a meal here is £15 ($26.25), plus the cost of your drinks. Tube: St. Paul's.

Slender's Health Food Restaurant, 41 Cathedral Pl., E.C.4 (tel. 01/236-5974), is in a most convenient location as it is just across from the Underground station at St. Paul's. For an appetizer you might try one of their homemade soups, and for a main course, a selection of such dishes as lentil-and-egg pie or beans with chili and rice. The desserts, as the local office workers will testify, "are super," and likely to include plum crumble. Most diners enjoy the whole-food buns and scones which are freshly baked. Meals cost from £5.50 ($9.65), and the place is open only from 7:30 a.m. to 6:15 p.m. Monday to Friday.

Old King Lud, 78 Ludgate Hill, E.C.4 (tel. 01/236-6610), is a Victorian pub built in 1855 on the site of the Old Fleet Prison. The former dungeons are now the cellars of this old-world pub. It offers a selection of pâtés, ranging from venison to duck with orange. Both hot and cold dishes are dispensed, with light meals costing from £4 ($7), served at lunch only from Monday to Friday. The Old King has a new American food outlet, Pizza Hut, built into the public bar. Wine is sold by the glass, and you can also order good Marlow Bitter here. The decor is in varying shades of green, including the tufted banquettes. Pub hours are from 11:30 a.m. to 10 p.m. daily. Tube: Blackfriars.

WINE BARS

One of my favorites is **Bow Wine Vaults,** 10 Bow Churchyard, E.C.4 (tel. 01/248-1121), which has existed since long before the current wine bar fad. The atmosphere is staunchly masculine in the "Old Bar," but the clientele in the "New Bar" is fairly mixed. An assortment of table wines begins at £1.25 ($2.20) by the glass. Sandwiches, cheeses, and fruitcake are available in the Old Bar, varying salads and hot dishes in the New Bar. A bustling cellar restaurant completes the range of public services. The New Bar is open Monday to Friday from 11:30 a.m. to 3 p.m., and the Old Bar is open Monday to Friday from 11:30 a.m. to around 8 p.m., depending on business. The restaurant charges from £8 ($14) for a full meal, which is served at two different sittings Monday to Friday at 12:15 p.m. and again at 1:30 p.m. Tube: Mansion House or Bank.

Jamaica Wine House, St. Michael's Alley, off Cornhill, E.C.3 (tel. 01/626-

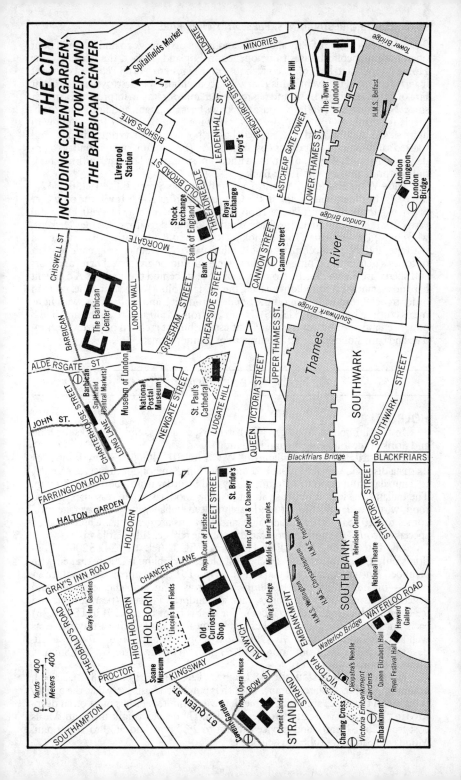

9496), lies in a tangle of City alleyways, and if you do manage to find it, you'll be at one of the first coffeehouses to be opened in England. In fact, the Jamaica Wine House is reputed to be the first coffeehouse in the Western world. Pepys used to visit it and mentioned the event in his *Diary*. The coffeehouse was destroyed in the Great Fire of 1666, rebuilt in 1674, and has remained, more or less, in its present form ever since. Nowadays the two-level house dispenses beer, ale, lager, and fine wines to appreciative drinkers. You can order a glass of wine from £1.10 ($1.95), along with light snacks such as pork pie, stuffed baked potatoes with various fillings, and toasted sandwiches. Light meals cost from £3.50 ($6.15). It is open Monday to Friday only from 11:30 a.m. to 8 p.m. without interruption. The Bank of England is only a stone's throw away. Tube: Bank.

Olde Wine Shades, 6 Martin Lane, off Cannon Street, E.C.4 (tel. 01/626-6876), is the oldest wine house in the City, dating from 1663. It was the only City tavern to survive the Great Fire of 1666, not to mention the blitz of 1940. Only 100 yards from the Monument, the Olde Wine Shades used to attract Charles Dickens, who enjoyed its fine wines. In the smoking room the old oil paintings have darkened with age, and the 19th-century satirical political cartoons remain enigmatic to most of today's generation. Some of the fine wines of Europe are served here, and port and sherry are drawn directly from an array of casks behind the counter. A candlelit bar and restaurant is found downstairs, but upstairs, along with your wine, you can order french bread with ham off the bone, Breton pâté, and sandwiches, with light meals costing from £7.50 ($13.15). Hours are from 11:30 a.m. to 3 p.m. and 5 to 8 p.m. Men must wear a jacket and tie. The establishment is closed on Saturday, Sunday, and bank holidays. Tube: Monument or Cannon Street.

4. Holborn and Bloomsbury

HOLBORN

In "legal London," you can join barristers, solicitors, and law clerks for food and drink at the following recommendations.

Spaghetti House, 20 Sicilian Ave., W.C.1 (tel. 01/405-5215), was known for its pasta dishes long before pasta became "the thing" in London. It serves Monday to Thursday from noon to 11 p.m., Friday and Saturday from noon to 11:30 p.m. The Italian-speaking waiters rush about, serving good, tasty, and reasonably priced food, with a wide selection of moderately priced Italian wines. The average meal comes to £10 ($17.50), a good value, and portions are generous. Children get a special welcome. In summer, you can dine on the terrace. Tube: Holborn.

My Old Dutch, 131 High Holborn, W.C.1 (tel. 01/242-5200), London's only Dutch restaurant, is a cheerful place, resembling a Dutch kitchen with scrubbed pine tables at which you can be served 101 different pancakes—all enormous—on huge Delft plates. Fillings and garnishes include cheese, meats, and vegetables, as well as sweet fillings, such as Pandora's Pleasure (pear, ginger, and ice cream with crème de cacao sauce). The cost is from £3 ($5.25) to £5 ($8.75) each, and one of these dishes makes a good meal. Tea and coffee are available, as well as wines and cocktails. My Old Dutch is open from noon to 10 p.m. Monday, to Thursday, and from noon to 11:30 p.m. on Friday, Saturday, and Sunday. Tube: Holborn.

North Sea Fish Restaurant, 7-8 Leigh St., W.C.1 (tel. 01/387-5892), is a real, honest-to-goodness fish restaurant. The fish is purchased fresh every day, the quality is high, and the prices are low. The menu is wisely limited. Fish is most often deep-fried in a batter, but you can also order it grilled. The decor is bright and clean. Meals cost from £6 ($10.50), and service is noon to 2:30 p.m. and 5:30 to 10:30 p.m. Monday to Saturday. Tube: Russell Square.

Cittie of Yorke, 22-23 High Holborn, W.C.1 (tel. 01/242-7670), stands near the Holborn Bars, the historic entrance to London marked by dragons holding the coat of arms of the City between their paws. Persons entering and leaving London were checked and paid tolls here. A pub has stood on this site since 1430. The present pub is named the Cittie of Yorke after a 16th-century hostelry later called the Staple Inn (now across on the other side of High Holborn). Its principal hall, said to have the longest bar counter in England, has handsome screenwork, comfortable little compartments, a long row of huge vats, and a high trussed roof. The place is popular with barristers and judges. Typical bar food is served along with fresh salads, grilled salmon, and steaks, meals costing £2 ($3) to £3 ($4.50). The pub is open from 11 a.m. to 11 p.m. Monday to Friday, from noon to 3 p.m. and 5:30 to 11:30 p.m. Saturday. It is closed Sunday. No meals are served on Saturday evening. Tube: Holborn.

BLOOMSBURY

The Big Mamma of a chain of spaghetti and pizza houses is the **Spaghetti House,** 15 Goodge St., W.1 (tel. 01/636-6582). Chianti bottles enhance an inviting, Italy-oriented atmosphere on floor after floor. A worthy main dish is veal escalope in butter, served with vegetables. The minestrone is flavorsome. For dessert, cassata siciliana makes a soothing selection. Expect to pay at least £9 ($15.75) for a complete meal. The Spaghetti House is open Monday to Saturday from noon to 11 p.m., and from 5:30 to 10:30 p.m. on Sunday. It's across Tottenham Court Road in the vicinity of Russell Square, which is the nearest tube stop.

British Museum Restaurant, Great Russell St., W.C.1 (tel. 01/636-1555), is obviously the best place for lunch if you're spending a day (or two or three) exploring the wonders of this world-renowned museum. One of several "museum restaurants" of London, this one is self-service style, and it offers most presentable and reasonably priced fare. Fresh, crisp salads are made daily, along with a selection of fish and cold meat dishes. A few hot specials (there's always one for vegetarians) are also made fresh daily. Meals cost from £5 ($8.75). Desserts include a selection of pastries and cakes. The restaurant is open, except on certain holidays, from 10:30 a.m. to 4:15 p.m. Monday to Saturday and 2:30 to 5:15 p.m. on Sunday. Tube: Holborn or Tottenham Court Road.

Museum Tavern, 49 Great Russell St., W.C.1 (tel. 01/242-8987), directly across the street from the British Museum, is a turn-of-the-century pub with all the trappings: cut velvet, oak paneling, and cut glass. Right in the center of the London University area, it is popular with writers and publishers. Very crowded at lunchtime, it is popular with researchers from the museum. It is said that Karl Marx wrote in the pub over a meal. Traditional English food is served. A hot-food meal costs from £4 ($7), a menu of cold food going for £3 ($5.25) and up. Beverages offered are several different real English ales, cold lagers, cider, Guinness, wines, and spirits. The tavern is open from 11 a.m. to 11 p.m. Monday to Saturday, and from noon to 3 p.m. and 7 to 10:30 p.m. Sunday. Food and coffee are served all day. Tube: Holborn or Tottenham Court Road.

---

5. Belgravia and Knightsbridge

BELGRAVIA

Belgravia (S.W.1), south of Hyde Park, is the so-called aristocratic quarter of London, challenging Mayfair for grandness. It reigned in glory along with Queen Victoria. But today's aristocrats are likely to be the top echelon in foreign embassies, along with a rising new-money class—or at least young fashion models or actresses clever enough to secure a most desirable flat here. Belgravia is near Buckingham Palace Gardens (how elegant can your address be?) and Brompton Road. Its center is Belgrave Square (take the Piccadilly Underground line to Hyde Park Corner), one of the more attractive plazas in London.

Antelope, 22 Eaton Terrace, S.W.1 (tel. 01/730-7781), is on the fringe of Belgravia, at the gateway to Chelsea. This eatery caters to a hodgepodge of clients. You can take lunch in a ground-floor bar that provides hot and cold pub food. On the second floor (or British first floor), food is served at a wine bar both morning and evening. The ground floor is devoted to drinks only at night. The food is principally English, with steak-and-kidney pie and jugged hare among the specialties. Meals are offered daily, except Sunday, from 11 a.m. to 3 p.m., costing from £10 ($17.50). Pub hours are Monday to Saturday from 11 a.m. to 11 p.m., and on Sunday from noon to 3 p.m. and 7:30 to 10:30 p.m. This is a base for English rugby aficionados (not to be confused with those who follow soccer). Tube: Sloane Square.

The Grenadier, Wilton Row, Belgrave Square, S.W.1 (tel. 01/235-3074), an oldtime pub on a cobblestone street, is one of the special pubs of London—associated with the "Iron Duke." But today it's filled with a sophisticated crowd of Belgravia flatmates and chic stable-dwellers. At the entrance to Wilton Row (in the vicinity of Belgrave Square), a special guard ("good evening, guv'nor") was once stationed to raise and lower a barrier for those arriving by carriage. The guard's booth is still there. A gentle ghost is said to haunt the premises, that of a Grenadier guard who was caught cheating at cards and died of the flogging given as punishment. Pub enthusiasts are fanatic about the Grenadier. If anyone tries to tear it down, he may meet his Waterloo.

You can lunch or dine as well as drink here. English meals are served in front of fireplaces in two of the small rooms behind the front bar. Lunch is available daily from noon to 2:30 p.m., and dinner is served from 6 to 9:45 p.m. Monday to Saturday and from 7 to 9:45 p.m. Sunday. A table d'hôte menu, costing £14 ($24.50), gives you a choice from among three appetizers and three main dishes, plus coffee. If you order à la carte, expect to spend from £12 ($21) to £16 ($28), depending on whether you include an appetizer and dessert. Reservations are required for dinner and Sunday lunch. Bar snacks are available during the same hours the restaurant serves. The bar is open from 11 a.m. to 3 p.m. and 5:30 to 11 p.m. Monday to Saturday, and from 11 a.m. to 3 p.m. and 7 to 10 p.m. Sunday. The Grenadier is known for its Bloody Marys, with a Bloody Mary bar being operated during lunchtime Saturday and Sunday. The pub is closed only on Christmas Day. Tube: Hyde Park Corner.

Motcomb's, 26 Motcomb St., S.W.1 (tel. 01/235-9170), opposite Sotheby's Belgravia, is one of the handsomest and most charming wine bars and restaurants in London. A complete range of food is served, and there is an excellent choice of wine as well, including several kinds sold by the glass. Specialties include what may be the best calves' liver and bacon in London, and salmon or trout grilled or poached to perfection. Dinners begin at £15 ($26.25). Motcomb's is open from noon to 3:30 p.m. and 7 p.m. to midnight Monday through Saturday. Tube: Knightsbridge.

KNIGHTSBRIDGE

Adjoining Belgravia is Knightsbridge (S.W.1), another top residential and shopping section of London, just south of Hyde Park. Knightsbridge is close in character to Belgravia. Much of this section, to the west of Sloane Street, is older, dating back (in architecture and layout) to the 18th century. This is where many Londoners go to shop, as several of the major department stores, such as Harrods, are here (take the Piccadilly Line to Knightsbridge to patronize any of the restaurants below).

Georgian Restaurant, Harrods Department Store, Brompton Rd., S.W.1 (tel. 01/730-1234, ext. 3467), lies on the top floor of this fabled emporium, under elaborate ceilings and belle-époque skylights. Breakfast, lunch, and afternoon tea are served. A member of a battalion of polite waitresses will bring you the first course of a fixed-price lunch, costing £14.25 ($24.95) per person. The second course is served from a buffet filled with cold meats and an array of fresh salads. Guests who want a hot meal can head for the carvery section, where a uniformed crew of chefs serves such dishes as Yorkshire pudding with roast beef, poultry, fish, and pork. Desserts are served tableside by your waitress. Harrods afternoon tea, costing £7.25 ($12.70) per person, is one of the most popular events. Breakfast is served from 9:30 to 11 a.m. and lunch from noon to 2:30. Teatime is 3:30 to 5:30 p.m., but guests start lining up before 3 p.m. Pastries are served from the "Grand Buffet," which shuts down at 5:15 p.m. Everything is closed on Sunday. Tube: Knightsbridge.

Bill Bentley's, 31 Beauchamp Pl., S.W.3 (tel. 01/589-5080), standing near Harrods, presents a varied list of reasonably priced wines, including a fine selection of Bordeaux. If you're in the neighborhood for lunch, you can enjoy a pub-style lunch, such as ham and salad. Hot main dishes are likely to include skate in black butter with capers and grilled lemon sole. Meals cost from £15 ($26.25). It's open from 11 a.m. to 11 p.m. Monday to Saturday. It's closed Sunday and bank holidays. Tube: Knightsbridge.

Chicago Rib Shack, 1 Raphael St., Knightsbridge, S.W.7 (tel. 01/581-5595), serves real American barbecued foods cooked in imported smoking ovens and marinated in a barbecue sauce containing 15 secret ingredients. The menu also includes their famous onion loaf, which *Harper's & Queen* described as "either a Brobding-nagian French fried onion or the Illinois equivalent of an onion bhaji." Visitors are encouraged to eat with their fingers, and bibs and hot towels are provided. A video is suspended in the bar showing American sports games. There is an overwhelming number of Victorian architectural antiques that have been salvaged from demolished buildings all over the country. The 45-foot-long ornate mahogany and mirrored bar was once part of a Glasgow pub, and eight massive stained-glass windows came from a chapel in Lancashire. The average tab comes to about £11 ($19.25) per head. The restaurant, which lies just 100 yards from Harrods, serves daily from 11:45 a.m. to 11:30 p.m. Tube: Knightsbridge.

Luba's Bistro, 6 Yeomans Row, S.W.3 (tel. 01/589-2950), is an oasis of moderately priced dining in tab-happy Knightsbridge. The food is good, and the chef believes in giving you enough of it. For openers, I'd suggest Luba's Russian borscht or else kapoostniak (braised cabbage with prunes and sour cream). Main courses include beef Stroganoff, chicken Kiev, hussar's steak, stuffed green pepper, and shashlik. A meal costs from £13 ($22.75). Bring your own wine. There is no corkage charge. There are two sittings a night, one at 7:30 p.m. and another at 9 p.m. (arrive on time). The place is closed Sunday. Tube: Knightsbridge.

---

6. Chelsea

In this area, comparable to the Left Bank of Paris or the more elegant parts of Greenwich Village, even the simplest stable has "glamour." Here the diplomats and wealthy-chic, the stars of stage and screen, and successful sculptors and painters now live alongside a decreasing number of poor and struggling artists. To reach the restaurants reviewed below, take the Circle or District Line to Sloane Square.

King's Road (S.W.3, named after Charles II) is the principal avenue, the main street of Chelsea, and activity is lively here both day and night. On Saturday morning, Chelsea boutiques blossom with London's flamboyantly attired. What were once stables and garages, built for elaborate town houses nearby, have been converted and practically rebuilt, so that you see little alleyways with two-story houses, all brightly painted.

In the Mauve Era, Chelsea became popular with artists. Oscar Wilde found refuge here—so did Henry James, Whistler, and many more. The Chelsea Embankment, an esplanade along the Thames, is also found here. Homes of writers, such as

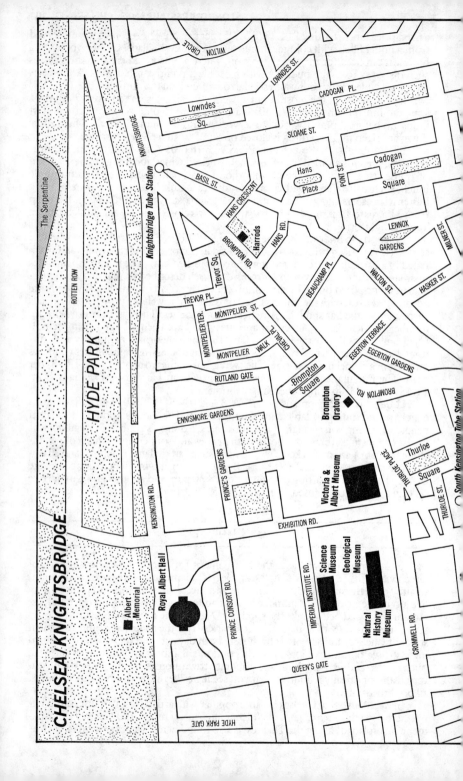

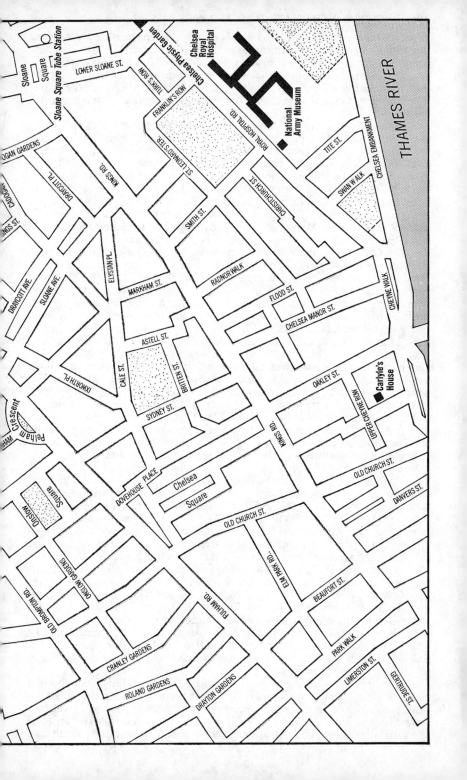

the one once occupied by George Eliot, line the street. The best-known and most interesting part of the Embankment, Cheyne Walk (pronounced Chain-y), contains some Georgian town houses. It's a good place to go for a stroll around dusk.

This district boasts some of the city's finest restaurants, but not the cheap ones. Still, most readers will probably want to go to Chelsea. If so, they'll find the following restaurant, pub, and wine bar recommendations offering good and reasonable meals.

Henry J. Bean's (But His Friends All Call Him Hank) Bar and Grill, 195 King's Rd., S.W.3 (tel. 01/352-9255), is another venture of that Chicago-born entrepreneur, Bob Payton of Chicago Pizza Pie Factory fame. Nearly opposite the Fire Station in Chelsea, it has brought renewed vitality to the restaurant scene in Chelsea. With a 250-foot garden, impossibly crowded on sunny days, it is open seven days a week: Monday to Saturday from 11:30 a.m. to 11:30 p.m., and on Sunday from noon to 10:30 p.m. Check the blackboard for Hank's daily specials, but know you can count on "chicken fried chicken," a smokehouse burger, nachos, and Henry J's own secret chili recipe. Meals costing from £8 ($14) are served against a backdrop of a late 1950s decor, American saloon style. Tube: Sloane Square.

The Chelsea Kitchen, 98 King's Rd., S.W.3 (tel. 01/589-1330), is the place for large portions of good, plain cooking at inexpensive prices. The minestrone is good-tasting, as is the coq au vin. Dinners are modestly priced at £5 ($9.75), and at lunch, you can eat for £3.50 ($6.15). The Kitchen is open from 8 a.m. to 11:45 p.m. Monday to Saturday and from noon to 11:30 p.m. on Sunday. In the evening, you are likely to hear classical tapes played as background music. Tube: Sloane Square.

King's Head & Eight Bells, 50 Cheyne Walk, S.W.3 (tel. 01/352-1820), a historic Thames-side pub in a fashionable residential area of London, is popular with stage and TV personalities as well as writers. The snackbar has been upgraded to Cordon Bleu standards at pub prices. The best English beers are served here, as well as a goodly selection of wines and liquors. A large plate of rare roast beef is a favorite selection, followed by a choice of salad from the salad bar—celery and sultana, rice, or beansprouts, for instance. Meals cost from £7 ($12.25). The pub is open Monday to Saturday from 11 a.m. to 3 p.m. and 5:30 to 11 p.m., and on Sunday from noon to 3 p.m. and 7 to 10:30 p.m. Food is served from 30 minutes after each opening until one hour before closing. It's a long walk from the Sloane Square tube stop.

One of the most-frequented of the Chelsea wine bars, **Blushes,** 52 King's Rd., S.W.3 (tel. 01/589-6640), stands across from a former duke of York's headquarters. Built in 1801, it is now the barracks of several London regiments of the Territorial Army. Full meals, including such dishes as Dover sole, freshly made salads, and steaks, cost from £10 ($17.50) per person. Many patrons visit just to drink, enjoying a glass of house wine from £1.50 ($2.65). It opens every day of the week in time for an early Chelsea breakfast, closing at 11:30 p.m. Its presentation changes throughout the day from a breakfast café to a restaurant to a wine bar. The lunch and dinner menu is available from noon to 11 p.m. A cocktail bar in the cellar is open only at night, from 6 to 11 p.m. Monday to Friday and from 1 to 11 p.m. on Saturday, and is closed on Sunday. Tube: Sloane Square.

Charco's Wine Bar, 1 Bray Pl., S.W.3 (tel. 01/584-0765), has an entrance on two streets in Chelsea, lying right off King's Road. A very bright crowd patronizes this establishment, enjoying the reasonably priced wines and the inexpensive food. A blackboard lists daily specials, all good, home-cooked dishes, costing from £12 ($21). Hours are from noon to 3 p.m. and 5:30 to 10:30 p.m. daily except Sunday. In summer, you can sit at one of the streetside tables and, in the evening, dine by candlelight. Tube: Sloane Square.

Ziani, 45 Radnor Walk, S.W.3 (tel. 01/351-5297), on a street of mews houses, is one of the finest but least known Italian restaurants in the Chelsea area. It is decorated in a garden and greenhouse style, brightly adorned with paintings. Meals cost from £15 ($26.25) and feature excellently prepared dishes. Roast quail with polenta is a particular favorite. This restaurant can get crowded, so make sure you call for a table. Hours are from 12:30 to 2:45 p.m. and 7 to 11:30 p.m. Monday to Saturday, and from 7 to 11 p.m. Sunday. Tube: Sloane Square.

EARL'S COURT

In an area filled with many B&B houses and not noted for restaurants, **Kramps Crêperie & Café Bar,** 6-8 Kenway Rd., S.W.5 (tel. 01/244-8759), is fully licensed and has a rustic French atmosphere. The music is mainly jazz at night, and the restaurant has a spacious, relaxed feel to it. Kramps stuffs its crêpes with all sorts of fresh goodies, ranging from the least expensive (ham, cheese, and egg) to the most expensive (fruits de mer). The dessert crêpes are excellently prepared, including some stuffed with pineapple and banana. Meals cost from £8 ($14), and are served daily, except Monday, from noon to 11 p.m. Kramps is closed Sunday, and it is closed Saturday for lunch. Tube: Earl's Court.

FULHAM

A typical Cockney delight is **Eel Pie and Mash Shop,** 140 Wandsworth Bridge Rd., S.W.6 (tel. 01/731-1232), outside of the East End and therefore more accessible to visitors. Here you can feast on jellied or stewed eels with mashed potatoes, on succulent homemade beef pie and mashed potatoes, or on "bangers and mash" (sausages and mashed potatoes). Meals cost from £2.50 ($4.40). Served in simple, pristine surroundings, it is something different, and you'll be sure to see some local color, for this sort of food is still much loved by Londoners. It's open from 11:45 a.m. to 6 p.m. on Tuesday and Wednesday, to 8 p.m. Thursday and Friday, and to 5 p.m. Saturday. It's closed Sunday and Monday. Your host is Mrs. Atkins. Tube: Fulham Broadway.

---

7. Kensington

Most smart shoppers in London patronize two busy streets: Kensington High, with its long string of specialty shops and department stores, and the abutting Kensington Church, with its antique shops and boutiques.

Twin Brothers, 51 Kensington Church St., W.8 (tel. 01/937-4152) offers good continental food in a cozy, relaxed atmosphere. Once only a small coffeeshop lying adjacent to the Carmelite Church, it is near the corner of Vicarage Gate. Here you might begin with Bismarck herring and go on to either chicken Kiev or Wiener Schnitzel. For dessert, try "Mother's apple cake." Every dish is freshly prepared for you. Only dinner is served, and it is offered daily, except Sunday, from 6:30 until the last orders go in at 11 p.m. Tube: Kensington High Street.

Maggie Jones, 6 Old Court Pl., off Kensington Church St., W.8 (tel. 01/937-1263), is a longtime favorite, with dining on three levels (I prefer the basement). It has plain pine furniture and candles stuck in bottles. You get British fare here with a vengeance. That means grilled saddle of lamb with rosemary, baked mackerel with gooseberries, or Maggie's fish pie. Dinners cost from £16 ($28), but a set lunch goes for only £8 ($14). Desserts, including a treacle tart, are called "puds." Lunch is from 12:30 to 2:30 p.m., Monday to Saturday and from 12:30 to 2:45 p.m. on Sunday, when the cost is £10.45 ($18.30). Dinner is from 7 to 11:30 p.m. Monday to Saturday and from 6:30 to 11 p.m. on Sunday. Tube: High Street Kensington.

Tumblers Wine Bar & Dining Rooms, 1 Kensington High St., W.8 (tel. 01/937-0393), occupies the white-tiled vaults of a bank from Victoria's day. Guests today come here to drink and dine in a candlelit atmosphere decorated with copper jugs, pewter tankards, and the like. The kitchen promises "fine English food prepared and served in the proper manner," and I see nothing to challenge that assertion. The menu is small but adequate, including Tumblers homemade pies, such as chicken and chestnut with a flaky pastry top or fishermen's pie with a potato topping. Meals cost from £10 ($17.50), and Tumblers is open Monday to Friday from 11:30 a.m. to 3 p.m. and 5:30 to 11 p.m., and on Saturday from 5:30 to 11 p.m. It is closed on Sunday. Tube: Kensington High Street.

Benedicts, 106 Kensington High St., W.8 (tel. 01/937-7580), stands across from the Kensington High Street tube. Climb to the second floor and enter a transplanted Irish world, with all sorts of odds and ends forming the decor. In a district filled with some high-priced restaurants nearby, Benedicts keeps its tabs reasonable, with meals costing from £12 ($21). Along with a good selection of wines, you can order country pâté to begin with, perhaps wild Irish smoked salmon, then follow with such main courses as beefsteak-and-ale pie or hot Gaelic pepper steak laced with whisky. Service is from noon to 3 p.m. and 5 to 10 p.m. daily, except Sunday.

Texas Lone Star Saloon, 154 Gloucester Rd., S.W.7 (tel. 01/370-5625), is "Tex-Mex," and that means enchiladas, hot chili, ribs, and burgers, everything washed down with beer or margaritas. Count on parting with £10 ($17.50) or more. Hours are noon to 11:30 p.m. Monday to Saturday and noon to 11:15 p.m. on Sunday. Tube: Gloucester Road.

SOUTH KENSINGTON

When you've grown weary of exploring this district's many museums, try a feast in one of the following recommendations.

Chanterelle, 119 Old Brompton Rd., S.W.7 (tel. 01/373-5522), used to be a part of the South Kensington Public Library. Now the smell is not of old books but of highly original English and continental cookery in a restrained setting of wood paneling. Chanterelle is open daily from noon to 2:30 p.m. and 7 to 11:30 p.m. A set lunch costs £8 ($14), and a set dinner goes for £13.50 ($23.65). After 10 p.m., a table d'hôte supper costs only £9.50 ($16.65). Main courses at dinner are likely to include filets of sole stuffed with scallops and served with a champagne sauce, roast saddle of hare, and filet of veal sautéed in sage. Wines are limited but well selected. Reservations are advised. Tube: South Kensington or Gloucester Road.

Victoria & Albert Museum Restaurant, Henry Cole Wing, Cromwell Rd., S.W.7 (tel. 01/589-6371), is a grade above your typical museum restaurant. On very busy days, the line is likely to move slowly in the cafeteria, as guests face temptations and decisions. The menu changes daily, but is likely to offer a good soup followed by many crisp salads, seafood, and fish and meat dishes. You can top off your meal with a selection of pastries and cakes. English wines are for sale, and you can eat here for around £5 ($8.75) and up, a remarkably good value. Service is daily from 10 a.m. to 5 p.m. (from 2:30 to 5:30 p.m. on Sunday). Tube: South Kensington.

Gilbert's, 2 Exhibition Rd., S.W.7 (tel. 01/589-8947), is a small restaurant that opened in 1988. The menu changes every two weeks, and the food is based on the products of the season, as much use is made of fresh ingredients. Virtually everything is prepared and cooked on the premises, including fudge with coffee and homemade rolls at dinner. The cuisine might be called "new British," using adaptations of mainly French dishes. The desserts are English, and the cheese selections are both French and English. The menu is normally limited to five choices per course, and there are often specials. At dinner there is a two- or three-course meal served at a fixed price, including bread, vegetables, and coffee, but not service. Meals range from £12 ($21) to £15 ($26.25). Lunch is cheaper, and many guests order only a main course. The wine list also changes frequently. Gilbert's is open 12:30 to 2 p.m. and 6:15 to 10:15 p.m., except for Sunday lunch, when hours are from 12:30 to 2:30 p.m. The restaurant is closed at lunchtime both Monday and Saturday. Tube: South Kensington.

Daquise, 20 Thurloe St., S.W.7 (tel. 01/589-6117), is a total anachronism, as it is a tea room sitting in the midst of the fast-food emporiums of South Kensington. Here you get typically Eastern European cuisine, including stuffed cabbage and other Slavic specialties. It has excellent pastries for dessert. Meals cost from £7

($12.25). Service is from noon to midnight, seven days a week. Tube: South Kensington.

---

8. West London

ST. MARYLEBONE

This area has quite a fine cross section of the best of what London has to offer in culinary treats.

Baker & Oven, 10 Paddington St., W.1 (tel. 01/935-5072), may be in an out-of-the-way neighborhood, but it's a big success—a little corner bakery, with a sales shop converted into a tavern with a genuine pub atmosphere. The very English food often pleases the most critical; the portions are large, the tabs moderate. With a bit of luck, you'll be given a bare wooden table in one of the brick cove-ceilinged nooks, the former ovens. The onion soup is a fine beginning, as is the country pâté. For the main course, there are several good choices, including roast Aylesbury duckling with stuffing and apple sauce, and jugged hare with red currant jelly. All main dishes include vegetables. For dessert, you can order a hot fruit pie and cream. Meals begin at £12 ($21), including wine. The restaurant is open Monday to Friday from noon to 3 p.m. and 6 to 11 p.m. On Saturday, it's open only in the evening. The same prices are charged for both lunch and dinner. The bar is open from 11 a.m. to 11 p.m. Monday to Saturday. Tube: Baker Street.

Light of India, 59 Park Rd., near Regent's Park, N.W.1 (tel. 01/723-6753), is often serving many homesick Indians. Happily, you can order varying strengths of curry, so have no fear about burning your throat if you're inexperienced. The traditional soup, of course, is mulligatawny. Warning: Unless you'd like a sneak preview of the heat of Hades, avoid anything labeled "vindaloo." Biryani, which is any dish prepared with rice and curry, comes with chicken, mutton, prawns, or even vegetables, and it is good for beginners. The restaurant also specializes in tandoori dishes cooked in a clay oven. Traditional charcoal instead of a gas fire is used. Meals cost from £9 ($15.75). The Light shines daily from noon to 3 p.m. and 6 p.m. to midnight. Tube: Baker Street.

Garfunkels, 57 Duke Street, W.1 (tel. 01/499-5000), is a coffeeshop operation with large glass walls that open onto the pavement, onto which the tables spill in summer. There is a large, well-stocked salad bar from which you help yourself. Typical fare includes roast chicken, chili con carne, and hamburgers. Meals cost from £6 ($10.50). There's also a children's menu for around £1.30 ($2.30). Garfunkels serves continuously from noon to 11 p.m. seven days a week. Tube: Bond Street. There are several branches of this operation around central London.

PADDINGTON

Many guests find themselves near Paddington Station, having booked into a B&B house on, say, Sussex Gardens or Norfolk Square. If so, it's best to go Oriental if you're seriously economizing.

Rasa Ria, 168 Sussex Gardens, W.2 (tel. 01/258-3997), stands in the midst of rows of B&B houses only two blocks from Paddington Station, the nearest tube stop. The cookery is a combination of Chinese dishes with several Singapore and Malaysian specialties, including laksa (spicy noodles in coconut milk). Try also gadogado, a Singapore salad bathed in spicy peanut sauce. You might follow with orange chicken or spicy prawns. Try the set menu at £12 ($21), although you can often come out for less by ordering à la carte. Lunch is Monday to Saturday from noon to 3 p.m., with dinner served from 6 to 11 p.m. On Sunday, hours are noon to 11 p.m.

The Mandarin, 33 Craven Rd., W.2 (tel. 01/723-8744), is a Bayswater budget favorite, and fortunately the food is good. A wide selection of Oriental dishes includes hors d'oeuvres (which the British call "starters"), fragrant crisp duck, and a number of vegetable dishes, such as creamed Chinese cabbage. The place is informal, functional, and often lively. Food is served from noon to 2:30 p.m. and 6 p.m. to midnight daily, with meals averaging around £10 ($17.50). However, the bargain is the set dinner at £7 ($12.25), although two must order it. Tube: Lancaster Gate.

BAYSWATER

All the children from a once far-flung empire seem to have come back to the mother country to open restaurants along Queensway and Westbourne Grove, known as streets of budget dining.

The most famous place on Queensway is **Hung Toa,** 59 Queensway, W.2 (tel. 01/727-6017). Because of its popularity, this restaurant could have raised its prices long ago, but it chose not to. Meals cost from £8 ($14). If you want a table, it's best to go at odd hours and not during the peak dining periods. This is easy to do, because this Cantonese eatery serves from noon to midnight daily. The kitchen is known for its superb roast duck, and "famous starters" include roast lobster with black bean sauce. There are many varieties of soups, such as different preparations of bird's-nest and shark's-fin. Service is often frantic, but hungry diners come here for the food, not the refinement. Tube: Bayswater or Queensway.

The Gandhi Cottage, 57 Westbourne Grove, W.2 (tel. 01/221-9396), the leading restaurant of Westbourne Grove, is known for its Indian and Mughlai cuisine. It serves daily from noon to 3 p.m. and 6 p.m. to midnight. "Some like it hot," others less so, and the chefs seem to understand. The restaurant offers a number of tandoori specialties as well as biryani dishes, the latter served with vegetable curry. Two chef's specialties are chicken makhani (mildly spiced and cooked in a clay oven in a special sauce) and nawabi lamb passanda (cooked in fresh cream with mixed ground nuts and yogurt). Meals cost from £10 ($17.50) to £17.50 ($30.60). Tube: Bayswater.

NOTTING HILL GATE/PORTOBELLO

Even if you make no purchases, you may want to spend time wandering up and down Portobello Road, which since the late 1940s has become the major source of antiques in London. Of course, its street market on Saturday—the most popular in the city—will be previewed later. Kensington Park Road runs parallel to Portobello.

Gate Diner, 184a Kensington Park Rd., W.11 (tel. 01/221-2649), a longtime favorite, is a bit like an American saloon with checkered tablecloths, movie posters, and old advertisements. If you're from the other side of the Atlantic, much of the fare tends to be familiar: spareribs, steaks, fried chicken, and bowls of chili. The salads tend to be huge. Or try the fresh fish of the day or a vegetarian dish of the day. You can finish the repast with a piece of Créole pecan pie. Meals cost from £12 ($21), unless you settle only for a big juicy hamburger. Service is from 11:30 a.m. to 11:30 p.m. daily. Tube: Notting Hill Gate or Ladbroke Grove.

9. East End

At least once you may want to plunge into the colorful East End. In restaurants it has a few potent drawing cards.

Bloom's, 90 Whitechapel High St., E.1 (tel. 01/247-6001), is overcrowded, with frantic service, and it continues to tempt with kosher delights supervised and inspected by a rabbi. Sunday lunch, however, is extremely busy, so try to schedule your visit at some other time. A chicken blintz might rest on your plate or borscht in your bowl. Main dishes include such specialties as boiled leg of fowl and salt beef (corned, to us). A good meal will cost around £12 ($21), but you can spend more.

Only full-service dinner patrons are seated. Hours are 11 a.m. to 9:30 p.m. Monday to Thursday and on Sunday. On Friday, it's open from 11 a.m. to 3:30 p.m. It is closed Friday evening and all day Saturday. Tube: Aldgate East.

Fox and Anchor, 115 Charterhouse St., E.C.1 (tel. 01/253-4838), is known for its real British breakfasts, the full house version costing £5.50 ($9.65) and served from 7 a.m. to 11 a.m. If you want a different meal, you can order toast and jam, filet, rump, or porterhouse steak, mushrooms, chips, tomatoes, and salad, costing about £12 ($21). With your food, you can order a glass of ale or a Black Velvet (champagne and Guinness). The pub is open from 6 a.m. to 3 p.m. Monday to Friday, serving lunch from noon to 2 p.m. You can order drinks any time during opening hours because of a special drinking license the establishment has. Charterhouse Street leads into a lovely tree-lined square where most of the buildings that survived the bombs in 1941 date from the 16th century. The pub has been serving the traders from the market since World War II. Tube: Farringdon.

Once frequented by Samuel Johnson, the **Olde Mitre** is hidden in Ely Court, E.C.1 (tel. 01/405-4751), a narrow little entryway linking Ely Place, which leads off Charterhouse Street at Holborn Circus, and Hatton Garden, home of London's diamond trade. Another entrance is beside 8 Hatton Garden. This tavern was first built in 1546 by the Bishop of Ely for his palace servants. The sign hanging outside the present building bears a drawing of a bishop's mitre, and the sign above the door bears the date. In good weather, you may be lucky enough to find a seat in the tiny courtyard between the pub and the Church of St. Etheldreda. Interesting relics in the pub include a preserved chunk of a cherry tree around which Queen Elizabeth I is said to have performed the maypole dance when the tree marked the dividing line between the part of the garden belonging to Sir Christopher Hatton and that which was the property of the bishop. A metal bar at the entrance of Ely Court was placed there to prevent horsemen from riding into this tiny space. Light bar meals are available in the tavern for £3 ($5.25) and up. Hours are 11 a.m. to 3 p.m. and 5:30 to 11 p.m. The tavern is closed Saturday and Sunday. Tube: Farringdon.

10. South of the Thames

The George, 77 Borough High St. (tel. 01/407-2056), across the bridge in Southwark, S.E.1, is a National Trust property, the last of the old galleried coaching inns of London. The inn was known to Charles Dickens, and some claim that Shakespeare and his troupe performed in an old inn that stood on the same ground. The George today is essentially late 17th century. You enter through a gateway into the Little Old Coffee Room. On the ground floor there are two bars and a wine bar where hot chili, sausages and mash, along with shepherd's pie and beans are served. There is a salad table, with some dozen different mixtures. Light meals here cost from £2.75 ($4.80). The restaurant upstairs serves meals Monday to Saturday from 6:30 to 9 p.m. Lunch is offered Monday to Friday only, from 12:30 to 2 p.m. From the à la carte menu, a three-course meal costs £12 ($21) to £15 ($26.75). Tube: London Bridge.

Royal Festival Hall Café, South Bank, S.E.1 (tel. 01/921-0810), is where you can get an inexpensive meal or snack in an unusual setting on the banks of the Thames. It's worth the five-minute trek over the bridge from the Embankment tube station to combine a meal with any of the activities at the Royal Festival Hall. The café is open daily from 10 a.m. to 8 p.m., and prices start at around £2.50 ($4.40) for a snack dish. Free lunchtime concerts are presented daily in the foyer upstairs, where the Festival Buffet, the coffee lounge, and the bar are situated. The coffee lounge serves cakes, pastries, and sandwiches from 10 a.m. to 10 p.m.

The Festival Buffet is known for vegetarian dishes and salads, but you can also have fish, ham, or pâté. The basic price is £3.75 ($6.55), each major addition costing around another £1.50 ($2.65). There is also a pasta bar where you have a choice of pasta with any of four different sauces, priced at £3.50 ($6.15). Hours for the buffet and pasta bar are daily from noon to 2:30 p.m. and 5:30 to 10:30 p.m. The main bar opposite the buffet is open daily from 11 a.m. to 11 p.m. The Review Restaurant on Level 3 offers the opportunity to sample the best in international cuisine with a predominantly French flavor at prices beginning at around £10 ($17.50) per person. The restaurant has a splendid view of London's skyline, overlooking the river.

From June to September, many free events take place here, indoors and outdoors as well as in the Jubilee Gardens adjacent to the Royal Festival Hall.

Goose and Firkin, 47 Borough Rd., S.E.1 (tel. 01/403-3590), brews its own beer, the product of owner-brewer David Bruce. David brews three special strengths: Goose at £1 ($1.75) for a pint; Borough Bitter at £1.12 ($1.95) a pint; and Dogbolter, £1.26 ($2.20) a pint. For special occasions, he produces a variety of strong ales with names such as Earthstopper, Kneetrambler, Gobstopper, and for Christmas, Slay Belles, all costing £1.70 ($3) and £2 ($3.50) a pint. Be warned: these latter brews are extremely potent. Food is also available in this lovely old London pub. A meal will cost from £2.50 ($4.40). The pub is managed by Niki and Alan Blunn, and the brewer is Pete Jamson. It is open seven days a week from 11:30 a.m. to 3 p.m. and 5:30 to 11 p.m. Most evenings, there is a pianist playing all the old numbers in a good old "knees up" style. Tube: Elephant and Castle.

---

11. Hampstead Heath

This residential suburb of London, beloved by Keats and Hogarth, is a favorite excursion spot for Londoners on the weekend. The Old Bull and Bush, made famous by Florrie Forde's legendary song, is long gone. (The pub bearing that name today is modern.) However, there are pubs up here with authentic historical pedigrees. Take the Northern Line of the Underground to the Hampstead Heath station, N.W.3.

Spaniards Inn, Spaniards Lane, N.W.3 (tel. 01/455-3276), is a Hampstead Heath landmark, site of the residence of the Spanish ambassador to the Court of James I. It's opposite the old tollhouse, a bottleneck in the road where people had to pay a toll to enter the country park of the Bishop of London. The notorious highwayman, Dick Turpin, didn't pay. He leaped over the gate on his horse when he was in flight from the law. The pub, opened by two Spanish brothers in 1630, was already a century old in Turpin's heyday. It still contains some antique benches, open fireplaces, and cozy nooks in the rooms with their low, beamed ceilings and oak paneling. Old muskets on the walls are mute survivors of the time of the Gordon Riots of 1780, when a mob stopped in for drinks on their way to burn nearby Kenwood House, property of Lord Mansfield. The innkeeper set up so many free drinks that when the Horse Guards arrived, they found many of the rioters *hors de combat* from too much libation and relieved them of their weapons. The pub serves traditional but above-average food. A light repast begins at £2.75 ($4.80). Hot dishes are served until half an hour before closing at lunchtime and until 9:30 p.m. Pub hours are from 11 a.m. to 11 p.m. Monday to Saturday, and from noon to 3 p.m. and 7 to 11:30 p.m. on Sunday. In summer, customers can sit at slat tables in a pleasant garden. The pub and garden were known to Byron, Dickens, Galsworthy, Shelley, and David Garrick. Tube: Hampstead or Golders Green.

Jack Straw's Castle, North End Way, N.W.3 (tel. 01/435-8374), is a weatherboard pub on the summit of the heath, about 443 feet above sea level. The nearby Whitestone Pond was used in World War II as an emergency water tank, and previously Shelley used to sail paper boats on the pond. The pub was rebuilt and enlarged in the 1960s on the site of the original. Jack Straw was one of the leaders of the peasants who revolted along with Wat Tyler in 1381 against what was, basically, a wage freeze. Prices were allowed to rise. The pub was created in Jack's old home, now a bustling place with a large L-shaped bar and quick-snack counter where there are cold salads, meats, and pies, plus three hot dishes with vegetables served every day. You can eat in the bar or on the large patio overlooking part of the heath. The up-stairs Carving Room, offering three courses for £12 ($21), is open from noon to 2:30 p.m. and 7 to 10:30 p.m. Monday to Friday, from 7 to 10:30 p.m. only on Saturday, and from noon to 2 p.m. and 7 to 10 p.m. on Sunday. Pub hours are 11 a.m. to 3 p.m. and 5:30 to 11 p.m. Monday to Saturday, and from noon to 2 p.m. and 7 to 10:30 p.m. on Sunday. After leaving the Underground station, the pub is a five-minute walk up the hill, where you can enjoy the good fresh air.

Manna, 4 Erskine Rd., N.W.3 (tel. 01/722-8028), offers a fine array of strictly vegetarian dishes to tempt even the most skeptical nonvegetarian. On its blackboard menu, you can check out the offerings for the day. They are likely to include hot garlic mushrooms, or lentil pâté, followed by such main dishes as stuffed pancakes or vegetable crumble. For dessert, try a lime mousse, chocolate and cashew tart, or meringues in brandy sauce. A meal will cost from £7 ($12.25) for two courses. Hours are 6:30 a.m. to 11:45 p.m. daily. The location is within a short walk of the Chalk Hill tube station. From Adelaide Road, cross the bridge at Regent's Park Road and go along King Henry's Road (Manna will be on the left at the corner of Erskine Road and Ainger Road).

---

12. Thames Dining

For a memorable experience, take a taxi, tube, or bus to Aldgate East and spend a hectic hour or so at **Petticoat Lane.** That's the street market where, on Sunday, even if you don't want to buy the goods, you can see the full wit and expertise of the Cockney street vendors. Look for the one who sells tea services, buy a toffee apple or a hot dog, and then go around the corner to **Club Row,** a street market for animals and birds.

A short walk will bring you down to the Tower of London and, right beside it, just below Tower Bridge, **St. Katharine's Dock.** After you've had a look around, you may be interested in dining or just having a snack to tide you over. Some places you'll see are overpriced and have become careless about the quality of their cuisine, while others still provide good food and good value.

At **Tower Thistle Hotel,** St. Katharine's Way, E.1 (tel. 01/481-2575), you can enjoy all you want of some of the most tempting roasts in the Commonwealth in the Carvery Restaurant in this modern hotel built overlooking the Thames. For example, you can select (rare, medium, or well done) from a standing rib of prime beef with Yorkshire pudding, horseradish sauce, and the juice; or from tender roast pork with "crackling" accompanied by a spiced bread dressing and apple sauce. Perhaps you'll prefer a selection of cold meats and salads from the buffet table. No one counts—even if you go back for seconds or thirds. Afterward, you can end the meal with a selection from the dessert trolley (especially recommended is the fresh fruit salad, ladled out with thick country cream poured over). You also receive a large cup of American-style coffee. Lunch costs £12.75 ($22.30), going up to £13.75 ($24.05) at dinner. Hours are daily from 12:15 to 2:30 p.m. and 6 to 10 p.m. Bus: 15.

Before or after dinner you might want to visit the Thames Bar. There is a small balcony outside for drinks in summer. Tube: Tower Hill.

Nearby is the **Dickens Inn by the Tower,** St. Katharine's Way, E.1 (tel. 01/488-9936). In a very carefully reconstructed 19th-century warehouse, it is a balco-nied pub/restaurant on three levels. Sitting on a wooden chair at an old table, you can enjoy such bar snacks as cockles, mussels, rollmops, and a ploughman's lunch. In the restaurant, the choice is seafood or traditional English meat dishes. Prices begin at £2.50 ($4.40) for one of the snacks, around £4 ($7) for the hot dish of the day accompanied by a vegetable. A three-course meal in the restaurant begins at around £15 ($26.25). The inn is open daily for lunch from 11:30 a.m. to 2:30 p.m. Hours for the pub are from 11 a.m. to 1 p.m. and 6:30 to 10:50 p.m. Monday to Saturday, and from noon to 3 p.m. and 7 to 10:30 p.m. Sunday. Tube: Tower Hill.

One of London's oldest riverside pubs, **The Prospect of Whitby,** 75 Wapping Wall, E.1 (tel. 01/481-1095), was founded originally in the days of the Tudors. The Prospect has many associations—it was visited by Dickens, Turner, and Whistler, each in search of local "colour." The pub is named after a ship, the *Prospect,* which sailed from its home port of Whitby and used to drop anchor outside the pub. Live music is presented Thursday to Sunday from 8:30 to 11 p.m. At the restaurant upstairs, you should reserve early and ask for the bow-window table with fine views over the Thames. Here, a meal will cost you from £14 ($24.50). In the bar, you can have snacks.

The street-level pub is open from 11:30 a.m. to 3 p.m. and 5:30 to 11 p.m. six days a week and from noon to 3 p.m. and 7 to 10:30 p.m. on Sunday. The upstairs restaurant's hours are noon to 2 p.m. and 7 to 10 p.m. daily. No lunch is served on Saturday and no dinner on Sunday evening. To get there, take the Metropolitan Line to Wapping station. When you emerge onto Wapping High Street, turn right and head down the road along the river. Wapping Wall will be on your right, running parallel to the Thames. It's about a five-minute walk.

CRUISE AND DINE

Explore the waterways of London while you dine and cruise along historic Regent's Canal aboard **My Fair Lady.** A three-course meal, is served, and you also have an open bar during the cruise. The dinner cruise boards Tuesday to Saturday at 7:30 p.m., sailing at 8 with a return at 11. The price is £16.95 ($29.65), including tax. It's also possible to take a Sunday lunch cruise, with a boarding at 12:30 p.m. Leaving at 1 p.m., the cruise takes 2½ hours, costing £12.75 ($22.30) for a menu of traditional English food. The location is at 250 Camden High St., N.W.1 (tel. 01/485-4433), 200 yards from Camden Town tube station (Northern Line).

R.S. (restaurant ship) **Hispaniola,** moored on the Thames at Victoria Embankment, Charing Cross, is a large and luxurious air-conditioned ship offering a splendid view of the heart of London from Big Ben to St. Paul's, armchair comfort at the tables, and two cocktail bars for other brands of comfort. The menu offers many meat and vegetarian dishes, and the cost is £15.50 ($27.15) for a set lunch, including dessert, with an average dinner going for £20 ($21), with the cover charge included. Lunch is served from noon to 2 p.m. Monday to Friday and on Sunday. Dinner is available seven days a week, from 6:30 to 10 p.m. Sunday and Monday, and 7 p.m. to midnight Tuesday to Saturday. For reservations, telephone 01/839-3011. Tube: Embankment.

---

13. For Fish and Chips

With the wealth of restaurants of all persuasions, snackbars, sandwich shops, fast-food take-out establishments, what have you, visitors from the United States are, by and large, likely to miss that most English of all products—fish and chips. True, the once ubiquitous fish-and-chips shops, also known as chippies, have become few in London today, and even those that remain are of such varying quality that it's difficult for a foreigner to be able to sample good chippie output.

Proper shops offer a selection of such deep-fried fresh fish, found by the proprietor at the New Billingsgate Market, as plaice, cod, haddock, skate, and rockfish.

This is served with potatoes Americans consider french fries, with vinegar and salt on the table or counter to be applied by the customer. The purpose of the vinegar is to offset the grease in which the fish and potatoes have been fried. For years, you were served this food in a cone made of printed newspaper, but today chippies must use paper without ink. However, the service is the same at the true dispensers of traditional fish and chips, and you can eat in the shop, usually at a communal table, or take your food outside, just so you eat it while it's hot. It's best to choose a fish and chips shop where a long queue of Londoners is to be seen at lunchtime awaiting what is unquestionably one of the earliest of the fast foods.

My favorite, the **Upper Street Fish Shop,** 324 Upper St., N.1 (tel. 01/359-1401), in Islington near the Camden Passage antiques center, is open from 5:30 to 10 p.m. Monday, from noon to 2 p.m. and 5:30 to 10 p.m. Tuesday to Friday, to 3 p.m. and 5:30 to 10 p.m. Saturday. Expect to spend about £4 ($7) for your fish and chips, something to drink, and perhaps a homey dessert such as jam roly-poly. Tube: Angel.

Geales, 2-4 Farmer St., W.8 (tel. 01/727-7969), is worth the investment in a subway ride to the western part of London if you're seeking some of the best fish and chips in the English capital, at prices around £8 ($14) for a meal. The fish is bought fresh daily, and it's not greasy as it is in most London chippies. Cod, hake, and plaice are the featured mainstays of the menu. This corner restaurant, at the end of a mews street, is run on informal lines and is open from noon to 3 p.m. and 6 to 11 p.m. Tuesday to Saturday. Tube: Notting Hill Gate.

Third in the trio of places for fish and chips that I think most worthy of recommendation is the **Sea Shell,** 49-51 Lisson Grove, N.W.8 (tel. 01/723-8703), one of the most popular places in London for fish and chips. The chips are more like Stateside french fries. Also, the fish here, although dipped in batter made with milk and egg, is fried in peanut oil. What with waitress service and other marks of progress, expect to pay at least £9 ($15.75) for a filling repast. Other fish dishes such as Dover sole are offered, and there's even a wine list. Service is from noon to 2 p.m. and 5:15 to 10:30 p.m. Tuesday to Saturday. Tube: Marylebone.

14. Time Out for Tea

During the 18th century, the English from every class became enamoured of a caffeine-rich brew finding its way into London from faraway colonies. The great craftsmen of England designed furniture, porcelain, and silver services for the elaborate ritual, and the schedules of aristocrats became increasingly centered around teatime as a mandatory obligation. Even Alexander Pope found it expedient to be witty publicly as he satirized teatime as something uniquely English.

The taking of tea is having a renaissance in the lives of the English. Viewed as a civilized pause in the day's activities, it is particularly appealing to people who didn't have time for lunch or who plan an early theater engagement. Some hotels feature orchestras and tea-dancing in afternoon ceremonies, usually lasting from 3:30 to 6:30 p.m.

For an experience in a tradition that could have sparked the American Revolution (remember the 1773 Tea Party in Boston?), try the old-fashioned atmosphere of **Richoux,** where waitresses wear period dresses with frilly aprons and good-quality pastries are wheeled around on a cart. For £3.50 ($6.15) per person you can order four hot scones with strawberry jam and whipped cream, or choose from a selection of pâtisserie. Of course, tea is obligatory. Always specify lemon or cream, and one lump or two.

There are three branches of Richoux in London. One stands opposite Harrods

Department Store in Knightsbridge, at 86 Brompton Rd., S.W.3 (tel. 01/584-8300), and it is open daily from 9 a.m. to 7 p.m. (Tube: Knightsbridge.) Another is at the bottom of Bond Street, 172 Piccadilly, W.1 (tel. 01/493-2204; tube: Green Park), and the last is at 41A South Audley St., W.1 (tel. 01/629-5228; tube: Hyde Park). The latter two are open daily from 8:30 a.m. to 11:30 p.m. The full menu is served all day long, seven days a week, at the three.

LONDON: WHAT TO SEE AND DO

1. SEEING THE SIGHTS

2. SHOPPING

3. LONDON AFTER DARK

4. TAKING THE TOURS

5. LONDON FOR CHILDREN

6. ONE-DAY TRIPS FROM LONDON

Dr. Johnson said: "When a man is tired of London, he is tired of life, for there is in London all that life can afford." "The Great Moralist" can say that again—even more so today.

Come along with me as I survey only a fraction of that life—ancient monuments, boutiques, debates in Parliament, art galleries, discos, Soho dives, museums, legitimate theaters, flea markets, and castles. Some of what we're about to see was known to Johnson and Boswell, even Shakespeare, but much of it is new.

1. Seeing the Sights

London is not a city to visit hurriedly. It is so vast, so stocked with treasures, that on a cursory visit a person will not only miss many of the highlights but will also fail to grasp the spirit of London and to absorb fully its special flavor, which is unique among cities. But faced with an infinite number of important places to visit and a time clock running out, the visitor will have to concentrate on a manageable selection.

I will lead off with a survey of what I consider the indispensable **Top Ten** sights of London. Try to see them even if you have to skip all the rest, saving them for next time.

1. THE TOWER OF LONDON

This ancient fortress and royal palace on the north bank of the Thames continues to pack 'em in because of its macabre associations with all the legendary figures who were either imprisoned or executed here, or both. James Street once wrote: "there are more spooks to the square foot than in any other building in the whole of haunted Britain. Headless bodies, bodiless heads, phantom soldiers, icy blasts, clanking chains—you name them, the Tower's got them."

Back in the days of the axman, London was "swinging." Ranking in interest are the colorful attending Yeoman Warders, the so-called Beefeaters in Tudor dress, who look as if they are on the payroll for gin advertisements (but don't like to be reminded of it).

Many visitors consider a visit to the Tower to be the highlight of their sightseeing in London, so schedule plenty of time for it. You don't have to stay as long as Sir Walter Raleigh (who was released after some 13 years), but give it an afternoon. Take either the Circle or District Line to Tower Hill station (the site is only a short walk away). Or on a sunny day, why not take a boat instead, leaving from Westminster Pier?

Admission to the Tower, including the Jewel House, is £4.50 ($7.90) for adults and £2 ($3.50) for children, except in February, when the Jewel House is closed for the annual cleaning and maintenance and prices are reduced to £3.50 ($6.15) for adults, £1.50 ($2.75) for children. Youngsters under five are admitted free. The Tower, closed on New Year's Day, Good Friday, the Christmas holidays, and on Sunday from November through February, opens at 9:30 a.m. Monday to Saturday all year and at 2 p.m. on Sunday from March to October. The last tickets are sold at 5 p.m. March to October and at 4 p.m. November to February, with actual closing being at 5:45 p.m. in summer, 4:30 p.m. in winter. The Tower Wharf, entered by the east or west gate, is open daily, except Christmas Day, from 7 a.m. Monday to Saturday and from 10 a.m. on Sunday. Closing times vary depending on the season, but closing is never earlier than 6:30 p.m.

Tours of approximately an hour in length are given by the Yeoman Warders at about 30-minute intervals, starting from the Middle Tower near the main entrance. The tours include the Chapel Royal of St. Peter ad Vincula. The last guided walk starts about 3:30 p.m. in summer, 2:30 p.m. in winter.

For further information about opening times and visiting privileges, telephone 01/709-0765, ext. 235.

Don't expect to find only one tower. The fortress is actually a compound, in which the oldest and finest structure is the **White Tower,** begun by William the Conqueror. Here you can view the Armouries, the present collection dating back to the reign of Henry VIII. A display of instruments of torture and execution is spread before you, recalling some of the most ghastly moments in the history of the Tower. At the Bloody Tower, the Little Princes (Edward V and the Duke of York) were allegedly murdered by their uncle, Richard III.

Through Traitor's Gate passed such ill-fated but romantic figures as Robert Devereux, a favorite of Elizabeth I, known as the second Earl of Essex. Elizabeth herself, then a princess, was once imprisoned briefly in Bell Tower. At Tower Green, Anne Boleyn and Katharine Howard, two wives of Henry VIII, lost their lives. The nine-day queen, Lady Jane Grey, also was executed here.

According to legend, the disappearance of the well-protected ravens at the Tower will presage the collapse of the British Empire (seen any around lately?).

To see the **Jewel House,** where the Crown Jewels are kept, go early in the day during summer, as long lines usually form by late morning. Get a Beefeater to tell you how Colonel Blood almost made off with the crown and regalia in the late 17th century. Of the three English crowns, the Imperial State Crown is the most important—in fact, it's probably the most famous crown on earth. Made for Victoria for her coronation in 1838, it is today worn by Queen Elizabeth when she opens Parliament. Studded with some 3000 jewels (principally diamonds), it contains the Black Prince's Ruby, worn by Henry V at Agincourt, the battle in 1415 when the English defeated the French. In addition, feast your eyes on the 530-carat Star of Africa, a cut diamond on the Royal Sceptre with Cross.

The Tower of London has an evening ceremony for locking up the Tower called

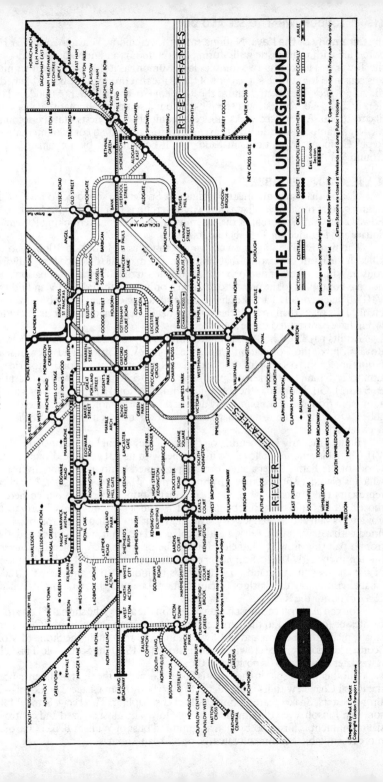

THE LONDON UNDERGROUND

Designed by Paul E Garbutt
Copyright London Transport Executive

the **Ceremony of the Keys.** Nothing stops the ceremony. During World War II, a bomb fell within the castle walls during the ceremony, and nobody flinched—but the Tower was locked up two minutes late. Rumor has it that the guard that night was censured for tardiness, the pilot of the plane that dropped the bomb blamed as the culprit. For free tickets, write to the Resident Governor, Tower of London, London EC3N 4AB, requesting a specific date but also giving alternative dates you'd like to attend. At least six weeks' notice is required. All requests must be accompanied by a stamped, self-addressed envelope *(British stamps only)* or two International Reply Coupons. With ticket in hand, you'll be admitted by a Yeoman Warder around 9:35 p.m.

2. WESTMINSTER ABBEY

No less than such an illustrious figure as St. Peter is supposed to have left his calling card at the abbey. What is known for certain is that in 1065 the Saxon king, Edward the Confessor, rebuilt the old minster on this spot overlooking Parliament Square and founded the Benedictine abbey.

The first English king crowned in the abbey was Harold, in 1066, who was killed at the Battle of Hastings that same year. The man who defeated him, Edward's cousin, William the Conqueror, was also crowned at the abbey; the coronation tradition has continued to the present day, broken only twice (by Edward V and Edward VIII). The essentially Early English Gothic structure existing today owes more to Henry III's plans than to any other sovereign, although many architects, including Wren, have contributed to the abbey.

Adults pay £2 ($3.50) and children 50p (90¢) to visit the Royal Chapels, the Royal Tombs, the Coronation Chair, the Henry VII Chapel, and the transepts. Hours are 9 a.m. to 4:45 p.m. (the last ticket is sold at 4 p.m.), Monday to Friday; 9 a.m. to 2:45 p.m. (last ticket at 2 p.m.) and 3:45 to 5:45 p.m. on Saturday (last ticket, 5 p.m.). On Wednesday the abbey, including the Royal Chapels, is open with free admission from 6 to 7:45 p.m. Only during this time is photography allowed in the abbey. On Sunday the Royal Chapels are closed, but the rest of the church is open between services.

Built in the early 16th century on the site of the ancient Lady Chapel, the Henry VII Chapel is among the loveliest in Europe, with its fan vaulting, Knights of the Order of the Bath banners, and Torrigiani-designed tomb of the king, in front of which is placed a 15th-century Vivarini painting, *Madonna and Child.* The chapel represents the flowering of the Perpendicular Gothic style. Also buried here are those feuding half sisters, Elizabeth I and Mary Tudor ("Bloody Mary"). Elizabeth I was always vain and adored jewelry. The effigy that lies on top of her tomb has been fitted with a new set of jewelry, a gilded collar and pendant, a modern copy derived from a painting now at Hatfield House. The originals were stolen by souvenir-hunters in the early 18th century. Her orb and sceptre were added earlier. In one end of the chapel you can stand on Cromwell's memorial stone and view the R.A.F. Chapel, containing the Battle of Britain memorial stained-glass window, unveiled in 1947 to honor the R.A.F.

You can also visit the most hallowed spot in the abbey, the shrine of Edward the Confessor (canonized in the 12th century). In the saint's chapel is the Coronation Chair, made at the command of Edward I in 1300 to contain the Stone of Scone. Scottish kings were once crowned on this stone (in 1950 the Scots stole it back, but it was later returned to its position in the abbey).

Another noted spot in the abbey is Poets' Corner, to the right of the entrance to the Royal Chapel, with its monuments to everybody from Chaucer on down—the Brontë sisters, Shakespeare, Tennyson, Dickens, Kipling, Thackeray, Samuel Johnson, Ben Jonson, even the American Longfellow. The most stylized and controversial monument is Sir Jacob Epstein's sculptured bust of William Blake. One of the more recent tablets commemorates the poet Dylan Thomas.

Statesmen and men of science, such as Benjamin Disraeli, Sir Isaac Newton, and Charles Darwin, are also either interred in the abbey or honored by monuments. Near the west door is the 1965 memorial to Sir Winston Churchill. In the vicinity of this memorial is the Tomb of the Unknown Soldier, symbol of British dead in World War I. Surprisingly, some of the most totally obscure personages are buried in the abbey precincts, including an abbey plumber.

Many visitors overlook such sights as the 13th-century **Chapter House** where Parliament used to meet. The Chapter House in the Great Cloister is open daily from 9:30 a.m. to 6 p.m. It shuts down at 3:30 p.m. off-season.

Even more fascinating is the **Abbey Museum** in the Norman undercroft (crypt), part of the monastic buildings erected between 1066 and 1100. The collection includes effigies—figures in wax, such as that of Nelson, and wood carvings of early English royalty. Along with the wax figures, the abbey's answer to Madame Tussaud, are ancient documents, seals, replicas of coronation regalia, old religious vestments (such as the cope worn at the coronation of Charles II), the sword of Henry V, and the famous Essex Ring that Elizabeth I is supposed to have given to her favorite earl. The museum is open daily from 10:30 a.m. to 4 p.m. Admission is £1.50 ($2.65) for adults, 40p (70¢) for children. This also provides visits to the Chapter House and the Pyx Chamber.

Guided tours of the abbey, costing £4 ($7) per person, operate Monday to Friday from 10 a.m. to the last tour at 3 p.m. On Saturday, tours are scheduled at 10 a.m., 11 a.m., and 12:30 p.m. Inquire at the west door for the meeting point.

For times of services and other information, phone the Chapter Office (tel. 01/222-5152).

Off the Cloisters, **College Garden** is the oldest garden in England, under cultivation for more than 900 years. Surrounded by high walls, flowering trees dot the lawns, and park benches provide comfort where you can hardly hear the roar of passing traffic. It is open on Thursday throughout the year, from 10 a.m. to 4 p.m. in winter, and to 6 p.m. in summer. In August and September, band concerts are held at lunchtime from 12:30 to 2 p.m. Admission is free. Tube: Westminster.

3. HOUSES OF PARLIAMENT

The spiritual opposite of the Tower, these are the stronghold of Britain's democracy, the assemblies that effectively trimmed the sails of royal power. Strangely enough, both Houses (Commons and Lords) are in the formerly royal Palace of Westminster, the king's residence until Henry VIII moved to Whitehall.

Although I can't assure you of the oratory of a Charles James Fox or a William Pitt the Elder, the debates are often lively and controversial in the House of Commons (seats are at a premium during crises). The chances of getting into the House of Lords when it's in session are generally better than they are of going to the more popular House of Commons, where even the queen isn't allowed. An old guard of the palace informs me that the peerage speak their minds more freely and are less likely to adhere to party line than their counterparts in the lower house.

The general public is admitted to the Strangers' Gallery in the House of Commons on "sitting days"—normally about 4:15 p.m. on Monday to Thursday and about 9:30 a.m. on Friday. You have to join a public queue outside the St. Stephen's entrance on the day in question. Often, there is considerable delay before the head of the public queue is admitted. You may speed matters up somewhat by applying at the American Embassy or the Canadian High Commission for a special pass, but this is too cumbersome for many people. Besides, the embassy has only four tickets for daily distribution, so probably you might as well stand in line. It is usually easier to get in after about 6 p.m. The head of the queue for the House of Lords is normally admitted to the Strangers' Gallery there after 2:40 p.m. Monday to Wednesday (often at 3 p.m. on Thursday).

The present House of Commons was built in 1840, but the chamber was bombed and destroyed by the German air force in 1941. The 320-foot tower that houses Big Ben, however, remained standing, and the celebrated clock continued to strike its chimes—the signature tune of Britain's wartime news broadcasts. "Big Ben," incidentally, was named after Sir Benjamin Hall, a cabinet minister distinguished only by his long-windedness.

Except for the Strangers' Galleries, the two Houses of Parliament and Westminster Palace are presently closed to the public.

Further information about the work of the House of Commons is available by phoning 01/219-4272 (House of Lords, 01/219-3107), or by accessing the Post Office Prestel Viewdata system, frame 5000.

In a fast-changing world, these details should be confirmed before planning a visit. Tube: Westminster.

4. THE BRITISH MUSEUM

Within its imposing citadel on Great Russell Street, W.C.1, in Bloomsbury (tel. 01/636-1555), the British Museum shelters one of the most catholic collections of art and artifacts in the world, containing countless treasures of ancient and modern civilizations. To storm this bastion in a day is a formidable task, but there are riches to see even on a cursory first visit, among them the Oriental collections (the finest assembly of Islamic pottery outside the Islamic world), the finest collection of Chinese porcelain in Europe, the best holdings of Indian sculpture outside India and Pakistan, and the Prehistoric and Romano-British collections, among many others. Basically, the overall storehouse splits into the national collections of antiquities; prints and drawings; coins, medals, and bank notes; and ethnography.

As you enter the front hall, you may want to head first to the Assyrian Transept on the ground floor, where you'll find the winged and human-headed bulls and lions that once guarded the gateways to the palaces of Assyrian kings. Nearby is the Black Obelisk of Shalmaneser III (858–824 B.C.), a tribute from Jehu, King of Israel. From here you can continue into the angular hall of Egyptian sculpture to see the Rosetta Stone, whose discovery led to the deciphering of the mysterious hieroglyphs, explained in a wall display behind the stone.

Also on the ground floor is the Duveen Gallery, housing the Elgin Marbles, consisting chiefly of sculptures from the Parthenon. The frieze shows a ceremonial procession that took place in Athens every four years. Of the 92 metopes from the Parthenon, 15 are housed today in the British Museum. These depict the to-the-death struggle between the handsome Lapiths and the grotesque, drunken Centaurs. The head of the horse from the chariot of Selene, goddess of the moon, is one of the pediment sculptures.

The classical sculpture galleries also hold a *Caryatid* from the Erechtheum, a temple started in 421 B.C. and dedicated to Athena and Poseidon. Displayed here, too, are sculptures from the Mausoleum at Halicarnassus (one of the Seven Wonders of the Ancient World) built for Maussollos, ruler of Caria, who died around 350 B.C. Look also for the blue and white Portland Vase, considered the finest example of ancient cameo carving, having been made in the first century B.C. or A.D.

The Department of Medieval and Later Antiquities has its galleries on the first floor (second floor to Americans), reached by the main staircase. Of its exhibitions, the Sutton Hoo Anglo-Saxon ship burial, discovered in Suffolk, is, in the words of an expert, "the richest treasure ever dug from English soil," containing gold jewelry, armor, weapons, bronze bowls and cauldrons, silverware, and the inevitable drinking horn of the Norse culture. No body was found, although the tomb is believed to be that of a king of East Anglia who died in the seventh century A.D. You'll also see the bulging-eyed Lewis chessmen, Romanesque carvings in Scandinavian style of the 12th century, and the Ilbert collection of clocks and watches.

The featured attractions of the upper floor are the Egyptian Galleries, especially the mummies. Egyptian Room 63 is extraordinary, looking like the props for *Cleo-*

patra, with cosmetics, domestic utensils, toys, tools, and other work. Some items of Sumerian art, unearthed from the Royal Cemetery at Ur (southern Iraq), lie in a room beyond: a queen's bull-headed harp (oldest ever discovered); a queen's sledge (oldest known example of a land vehicle); and a figure of a he-goat on its hind legs, crafted about 2500 B.C. In the Iranian room rests "The Treasure of the Oxus," a hoard of riches, perhaps a temple deposit, ranging in date from the sixth to the third century B.C., containing a unique collection of goldsmith's work, such as a nude youth, signet rings, a fish-shaped vase, and votive plaques.

If your visit to the museum makes you want to know more about this treasure trove, I recommend a book by Ms. M. L. Caygill of the museum director's office, *Treasures of the British Museum,* which gives a detailed account of the major treasures and summaries of departmental collections.

The museum is open Monday to Saturday from 10 a.m. to 5 p.m. and on Sunday from 2:30 to 6 p.m. (The galleries start to close ten minutes earlier.) It is closed Good Friday, December 24, 25, and 26, New Year's Day, and the first Monday in May. Admission to the entire museum is free. Tube: Holborn or Tottenham Court Road.

The British Library

Some of the treasures from the collections of the British Library (tel. 01/636-1544), one of the world's greatest libraries, are on display in the exhibition galleries in the east wing of the British Museum building. In the Grenville Library are displayed western illuminated manuscripts. Notable exhibits are the Benedictional (in Latin) of St. Ethelwold, Bishop of Winchester (963–984), the Luttrell Psalter, and the Harley Golden Gospels of about 800.

In the Manuscript Saloon are manuscripts of historical and literary interest. Items include two of the four surviving copies of King John's Magna Carta (1215) and the Lindisfarne Gospels (an outstanding example of the work of Northumbrian artists in the earliest period of English Christianity, written and illustrated about 698). Almost every major literary figure, including Charles Dickens, Jane Austen, Charlotte Brontë, and W. B. Yeats, is represented in the section given over to English literature. Also on display are historical autographs, including Nelson's last letter to Lady Hamilton and the journals of Captain Cook.

In the King's Library, so-called because this is where the library of King George III is housed, the history of books is illustrated by notable specimens of early printing, including the Diamond Sutra of 868, the first dated example of printing, as well as the Gutenberg Bible, the first book ever printed from movable type, dated 1455.

In the center of the gallery is an exhibition of fine bookbindings dating from the 16th century. Beneath Roubiliac's 1758 statue of Shakespeare is a case of documents relating to the Bard, including a mortgage bearing his signature and a copy of the First Folio of 1623. The library's unrivaled collection of philatelic items, including such exhibitions as the 1840 Great British Penny Black and the rare 1847 Post Office issues of Mauritius, are also to be seen.

The library regularly mounts special temporary exhibitions, usually in the Crawford room off the Manuscript Saloon. The hours of the British Library's exhibition galleries are the same as those of the museum. Admission free.

The Museum of Mankind

The Museum of Mankind, the Ethnography Department of the British Museum, is housed at 6 Burlington Gardens, W.1 (tel. 01/437-2224), where the galleries are open to the public during the same hours as those of the Bloomsbury museum. It has the world's largest collections of art and material culture from tribal societies. A selection of treasures from five continents is displayed, and a number of large exhibitions show the life, art, and technology of selected cultures. New exhibitions are mounted every year. There is no admission fee. Tube: Piccadilly Circus.

MADAME TUSSAUD'S

In 1770, an exhibition of life-size wax figures was opened in Paris by Dr. Curtius. He was soon joined by his niece, Strasbourg-born Marie Tussaud, who learned from him the secret of making lifelike replicas of the famous and the infamous. During the French Revolution, the head of almost every distinguished victim of the guillotine was molded by Madame Tussaud or her uncle.

After the death of Curtius, Madame Tussaud inherited the exhibition, and in 1802 she left France for England. For 33 years she toured the United Kingdom with her exhibition, and in 1835 she settled on Baker Street. The exhibition was such a success that it practically immortalized her in her day; she continued to make portraits until she was 81 (she died in 1850). The perennially popular waxworks are visited by some even before they check out Westminster Abbey or the Tower of London.

While some of the figures on display today come from molds taken by the incomparable Madame Tussaud, the exhibition continues to introduce new images of whoever is *au courant*. An enlarged Grand Hall continues to house years of royalty and old favorites such as Winston Churchill, as well as many of today's heads of state and political leaders. In the Chamber of Horrors, you can have the vicarious thrill of meeting such types as Dr. Crippen and walking through a Victorian street where special effects include the shadowy terror of the London of Jack the Ripper. The instruments and victims of death penalties contrast with present-day criminals portrayed within the confines of prison. You are invited to mingle with the more current stars in the Conservatory, as well as to see the Beatles relaxing.

"Super Stars" offers the latest technologies in sound, light, and special effects, combined with new figures in a celebration of success in the fields of film and sports. On the ground floor, you can relive the Battle of Trafalgar on the gun deck of Nelson's flagship, *Victory*.

Madame Tussaud's, air-conditioned throughout, is open daily, including Saturday and Sunday, year round (closed on Christmas Day only). Hours are 10 a.m. to 5:30 p.m. Monday to Friday and 9:30 a.m. to 5:30 p.m. Saturday and Sunday. Doors open earlier during the summer season. Admission for adults is £4.80 ($8.40) and £3.15 ($5.50) for children under 16. Prices are slightly lower in the off-season.

The **London Planetarium** is right next door, costing £2.65 ($4.65) for adults and £1.70 ($3) for children. A combined ticket, costing £6.10 ($10.70) for adults and £3.80 ($6.65) for children, will save you money. Children under 5 are not admitted to the Planetarium. For information, phone 01/935-6861. The entrance to Madame Tussaud's is on Marylebone Road. Tube: Baker Street.

6. TATE GALLERY

This building, beside the Thames on Millbank, S.W.1 (tel. 01/821-1313), houses the best collection of British paintings from the 16th century on, as well as England's finest collection of modern art, comprising the works of British artists born after 1860 together with foreign art from the impressionists onward. The Tate is open from 10 a.m. to 5:50 p.m. Monday to Saturday and on Sunday from 2 to 5:50 p.m. To reach it, take the tube to Pimlico or bus 88 or 77A. The number of paintings is staggering. If time permits, try to schedule at least two visits, the first to see the classic English works, the second to take in the modern collection. Since only a portion of the collections can be shown simultaneously, the works on display vary from time to time. However, the most time-pressed individual may not want to miss the following, which are almost invariably on view:

The first giant among English painters, William Hogarth (1697–1764), is well represented, particularly by his satirical *O the Roast Beef of Old England, Calais Gate*, with its distorted figures, such as the gluttonous priest. The ruby-eyed *Satan, Sin, and Death* remains one of his most enigmatic works.

Two other famous British painters of the 18th century are Sir Joshua Reynolds (1723–1792) and Thomas Gainsborough (1727–1788). Reynolds, the portrait painter, shines brightest when he's painting himself (two self-portraits hang side by side). Two other portraits, that of Francis and Suzanna Beckford, are typical of his work. His rival, Gainsborough, is noted for his portraits too, and also landscapes ("my real love"). His landscapes with gypsies are subdued and mysterious; *The View of Dedham* is more representative. One of Gainsborough's most celebrated portraits is of Edward Richard Gardiner, a handsome boy in blue (the more famous *Blue Boy* is in California). Two extremely fine Gainsborough portraits have recently been acquired: *Giovanna Baccelli* (1782), who was well known both as a dancer and as the mistress of the third Earl of Dorset, and *Sir Benjamin Truman,* the notable brewer.

In the art of J. M. W. Turner (1775–1851), the Tate possesses its greatest collection of the works of a single artist. Most of the paintings and watercolors exhibited here were willed to the nation by Turner. His studio at the time held 282 oils and more than 19,000 drawings, watercolors, and sketches. In 1987, a new wing at the Tate, called Clore Gallery, was opened so that the entire bequest of the artist can be seen. Of his paintings of stormy seas, none is more horrifying than *Shipwreck* (1805). In the Petworth series, he broke from realism (see his *Interior at Petworth*). His delicate impressionism is best conveyed in his sunset and sunrise pictures, with their vivid reds and yellows. Turner's vortex paintings, inspired by theories of Goethe, are *Light and Color—the Morning After the Deluge,* and *Shade and Darkness—the Evening of the Deluge.*

In a nation of landscape painters, John Constable (1776–1837) stands out. Some of his finest works include *Vale of Dedham* and *Flatford Mill, on the River Stour,* painted in 1817, both scenes from East Anglia.

American-born Sir Jacob Epstein became one of England's greatest sculptors, and some of his bronzes are owned and occasionally displayed by the Tate. Augustus John, who painted everybody from G. B. Shaw to Tallulah Bankhead, is also represented here with portraits and sketches.

The Tate owns some of the finest works of the Pre-Raphaelite period of the late 19th century. One of the best of the English artists of the 20th century, Sir Stanley Spencer (1891–1959), is represented by his two versions of *Resurrection* and a remarkable self-portrait (1913).

The Tate has many major paintings from both the 19th and 20th centuries, including Wyndham Lewis's portraits of Edith Sitwell and of Ezra Pound, and Paul Nash's *Voyages of the Moon.* But the sketches of William Blake (1757–1827) attract the most attention. Blake, of course, was the incomparable mystical poet and illustrator of such works as *The Book of Job, The Divine Comedy,* and *Paradise Lost.*

In the modern collections, the Tate contains Henri Matisse's *L'Escargot* and *The Inattentive Reader,* along with works by Salvador Dali, Marc Chagall, Amedeo Modigliani, Edvard Munch, Ben Nicholson (there is a large collection of his works), and Jean Dubuffet. The different periods of Picasso bloom in *Woman in a Chemise* (1905), *Three Dancers* (1925), *Nude Woman in a Red Armchair* (1932), and *Goat's Skull, Bottle and Candle* (1952).

Truly remarkable is the area devoted to the sculpture of Giacometti (1901–1966), and the paintings of two of England's most famous modern artists, Francis Bacon (especially gruesome is *Three Studies for Figures at the Base of a Crucifixion*) and Graham Sutherland (see his portrait of W. Somerset Maugham).

Rodin's *The Kiss* and Marino Marini's *Cavaliere,* both world-famous pieces of sculpture, are on show. In addition, sculptures by Henry Moore and Barbara Hepworth are displayed.

Downstairs is the internationally renowned, Rex Whistler–decorated restaurant and a coffeeshop.

7. NATIONAL GALLERY

On the north side of Trafalgar Square, W.C.2, in an impressive neoclassic building, the National Gallery (tel. 01/839-3321) houses one of the most comprehensive collections of Western paintings, representing all the major schools from the 13th to the 19th centuries. The largest part of the collection is devoted to the Italians, including the Sienese, Venetian, and Florentine masters.

Of the early Gothic works, the *Wilton Diptych* (French school, late 14th century) is the rarest treasure. It depicts Richard II being introduced to the Madonna and Child by such good contacts as John the Baptist and the Saxon king, Edward the Confessor.

A Florentine gem, a Virgin with grape-eating Bambino by Masaccio is displayed, as are notable works by Piero della Francesca, particularly his linear *The Baptism.*

Matter and spirit meet in the haunting netherworld of the *Virgin of the Rocks,* a famous Leonardo da Vinci painting. Also shown are two other giants of the Renaissance—Michelangelo (represented by an unfinished painting, *The Entombment*), and Raphael (*The Ansidei Madonna,* among others).

Among the Venetian masters of the 16th century, to whom color was paramount, the most notable works include a rare *Adoration of the Kings* by Giorgione; *Bacchus and Ariadne* by Titian; *The Origin of the Milky Way* by Tintoretto (a lush galaxy, with milk streaming from Juno's breasts), and *The Family Darius Before Alexander* by Veronese (one of the best paintings at the National). Surrounding are a number of satellite rooms, filled with works by major Italian masters of the 15th century—artists such as Andrea Mantegna of Padua (*Agony in the Garden*); his brother-in-law, Giovanni Bellini (his portrait of the Venetian doge, Leonardo Loredano, provided a change of pace from his many interpretations of Madonnas); and finally, Botticelli, represented by *Mars and Venus, Adoration of the Magi,* and *Portrait of a Young Man.*

The painters of northern Europe are well displayed; for example, Jan van Eyck's portrait of G. Arnolfini and his bride, and Pieter Brueghel the Elder's Bosch-influenced *Adoration,* with its unkingly kings and ghoul-like onlookers. The 17th-century pauper, Vermeer, is rich on canvas in *Young Woman at a Virginal,* a favorite theme of his. Fellow Delft-ite Pieter de Hooch comes on sublimely in *Patio in a House in Delft.*

One of the big drawing cards of the National is its collection of Rembrandts. Rembrandt, the son of a miller, became the greatest painter in the Netherlands in the 17th century. His *Self-Portrait at the Age of 34* shows him at the pinnacle of his life, and his *Self-Portrait at the Age of 63* is more deeply moving and revealing. For another Rembrandt study in old age, see his *Portrait of Margaretha Trip.* His *The Woman Taken in Adultery* shows the artist's human sympathy. Rembrandt's portrait of his mistress, Hendrickje Stoffels, is also displayed.

Part of the prolific output of Peter Paul Rubens is to be seen, notably his *Peace and War* and *The Rape of the Sabine Women.* A recent Rubens acquisition is *Samson and Delilah,* a little-known painting. It cost $5.4 million and has been described as the most important Rubens to come on the market for many years.

Five of the greatest of the homegrown artists—Constable, Turner, Reynolds, Gainsborough, and Hogarth—share their paintings with the Tate. But the National owns masterpieces by each of them. Constable's *Cornfield* is another scene of East Anglia, along with *Haywain,* a harmony of light and atmosphere. Completely different from Constable is the work of Turner, including his dreamy *Fighting Téméraire* and *Rain, Steam, and Speed.* In what is essentially a portrait gallery, you can see several works by Sir Joshua Reynolds, along with a Gainsborough masterpiece, *The Morning Walk,* an idealistic blending of portraiture with landscape. Finally, in a completely different brushstroke, Hogarth's *Marriage à la Mode* caricatures the marriages of convenience of the upper class of the 18th century.

The three giants of Spanish painting are represented in Velázquez's portrait of the sunken-faced Philip IV; El Greco's *Christ Driving the Traders from the Temple;* Goya's portrait of the Duke of Wellington (once stolen) and his mantilla-wearing *Dona Isabel de Porcel.*

Other rooms are devoted to 18th-century French painters such as Watteau and Fragonard; 19th-century French painters such as Delacroix and Ingres; the latter 19th-century French impressionists such as Manet, Monet, Renoir, and Degas; and post-impressionists such as Cézanne, Seurat, and Van Gogh.

The National Gallery is open Monday to Saturday from 10 a.m. to 6 p.m. and on Sunday from 2 to 6 p.m. It is closed January 1, Good Friday, the three-day Christmas holidays, and bank holidays. Admission is free. Tube: Charing Cross.

8. KENSINGTON PALACE

Home of the State Apartments, some of which were used by Queen Victoria, this is another of the major attractions of London, at the far western end of Kensington Gardens, W.8 (tel. 01/937-9561, ext. 2). The palace was acquired by asthma-suffering William III (William of Orange) in 1689, and was remodeled by Sir Christopher Wren. George II, who died in 1760, was the last king to use it as a royal residence.

The most interesting chamber to visit is Queen Victoria's bedroom. In this room, on the morning of June 20, 1837, she was aroused from her sleep with the news that she had ascended to the throne, following the death of her uncle, William IV. Thus the woman who was to become the symbol of the British Empire and the Empress of India began the longest reign in the history of England. In the anteroom are memorabilia from Victoria's childhood, such as a dollhouse and a collection of her toys.

A special attraction is the Court Dress Collection, which shows restored rooms from the 19th century, including Queen Victoria's birthroom and a series of room settings with the appropriate court dress of the day, from 1760 to 1950. However, it is a more modern dress that captures the attention of most visitors—the wedding dress worn by the Princess of Wales on July 29, 1981.

As you wander through the apartments, you can admire many fine paintings from the Royal Collection. The State Apartments are open Monday to Saturday from 9 a.m. to 5 p.m. and on Sunday from 1 to 5 p.m., throughout the year. They are closed New Year's Day, Good Friday, Christmas Eve, Christmas Day, and Boxing Day. Admission fees are as follows: adults pay £2.60 ($4.55) and children £1.30 ($2.30). You enter from the Broad Walk, and you can reach the building by taking the tube either to Queensway or Bayswater on the north side of the gardens, or High Street Kensington on the south side. You'll have to walk a bit from there, however.

The palace gardens, originally the private park of royalty, are also open to the public for daily strolls around Round Pond, near the heart of Kensington Gardens. The gardens adjoin Hyde Park. Also in Kensington Gardens is the Albert Memorial to Queen Victoria's consort. Facing Albert Hall, it reflects all the opulent overstatement of the Victorian era—it's fascinating, nonetheless.

9. ST. PAUL'S CATHEDRAL

During World War II, a newsreel footage reaching America showed the dome of St. Paul's Cathedral, St. Paul's Churchyard, E.C.1 (tel. 01/236-4128), lit by bombs exploding all around it. That it survived at all is miraculous, as it was hit twice in the early years of the Nazi bombardment of London. But St. Paul's is accustomed to calamity, having been burned down at least three times and destroyed once by invading Norsemen. It was in the Great Fire of 1666 that the old St. Paul's was razed, making way for a new Renaissance structure designed (after mishaps and rejections) by Sir Christopher Wren.

The masterpiece of this great architect was erected between 1675 and 1710. Its classical dome dominates the City's square mile. Inside, the cathedral is laid out like a Latin cross, containing few art treasures (Grinling Gibbons' choir stalls are an exception) and many monuments, including one to the "Iron Duke" and a memorial chapel to American military personnel who lost their lives in World War II while stationed in the United Kingdom. Encircling the dome is the Whispering Gallery, where discretion in speech is advised. In the crypt lie not only Wren but the Duke of Wellington and Lord Nelson, as well as Wren's Great Model and the Diocesan Treasury. It was in this cathedral on July 29, 1981, that Prince Charles married Lady Diana Spencer amid much pomp and ceremony.

The cathedral is open daily from 8 a.m. to 6 p.m. The crypt and galleries, including the Whispering Gallery, are open only from 10 a.m. to 4:15 p.m. Monday to Friday and from 11 a.m. on Saturday. Guided tours, lasting 1½ hours and including the crypt and other parts of St. Paul's not normally open to the public, take place daily at 11 and 11:30 a.m. and 2 and 2:30 p.m. when the cathedral is open (except Sunday) and cost £3.60 ($6.30) for adults and £1.60 ($3.80) for children.

St. Paul's is an Anglican cathedral with daily services held at 8 a.m. and at 5 p.m. On Sunday, services are at 10:30 and 11:30 a.m. and at 3:15 p.m. In addition, you can climb to the very top of the dome for a spectacular 360-degree view of all of London, costing £1 ($1.75) per person. Tube: St. Paul's.

10. VICTORIA AND ALBERT MUSEUM

When Queen Victoria asked that this museum be named after herself and her consort, she could not have selected a more fitting memorial. The Victoria and Albert is one of the finest museums in the world, devoted to fine and applied art of many nations and periods, including the Orient. In many respects it's one of the most difficult for viewing, as many of the most important exhibits are so small they can easily be overlooked. To reach the museum on Cromwell Road, S.W.7 (tel. 01/938-8500), take the tube to the South Kensington stop. The museum is open Monday to Saturday from 10 a.m. to 5:50 p.m. and on Sunday from 2:30 to 5:50 p.m.

I have space only to suggest some of its finest art. The early medieval art includes many treasures, such as the Eltenberg Reliquary (Rhenish, second half of the 12th century). In the shape of a domed, copper-gilt church, it is enriched with champlevé enamel and set with walrus-ivory carvings of Christ and the Apostles. Other exhibits in this same salon include the Early English Gloucester Candlestick; the Byzantine Veroli Casket, with its ivory panels based on Greek plays; and the Syon Cope, made in the early 14th century, an example of the highly valued embroidery produced in England at that time. The Gothic tapestries, including the Devonshire ones depicting hunting scenes, are displayed in another gallery.

An area devoted to Islamic art contains the Ardabil carpet from 16th-century Persia (320 knots per square inch).

Renaissance art in Italy includes such works as a Donatello marble relief, *The Ascension;* a small terracotta statue of the Madonna and Child by Antonio Rossellino; a marble group, *Samson and a Philistine,* by Giovanni Bologna; and a wax model of a slave by Michelangelo. The highlight of the 16th-century art from the continent is the marble group, *Neptune with Triton,* by Bernini.

The cartoons by Raphael, which are owned by the Queen, may also be seen. These cartoons, conceived as designs for tapestries for the Sistine Chapel, include scenes such as *The Sacrifice of Lystra* and *Paul Preaching at Athens.*

A most unusual, huge, and impressive exhibit is the Cast Rooms, with life-size plaster models of ancient and medieval statuary and architecture, made from molds formed over the originals.

Of the rooms devoted to English furniture and decorative art during the period from the 16th to the mid-18th century, the most outstanding exhibit is the Bed of Ware, big enough for eight. In the galleries of portrait miniatures, two of the rarest ones are both by Hans Holbein the Younger (one of Anne of Cleves, another of a Mrs. Pemberton). In the painting galleries are many works by Constable. His *Flatford Mill* represents a well-known scene from his native East Anglia.

No admission is charged, but they suggest a donation of £2 ($3.50) for adults, 50p (90¢) for children under 12.

A restaurant serving wholesome traditional English snacks and meals is open from 10 a.m. to 5 p.m. Monday to Saturday and from 2:30 to 5 p.m. Sunday. Two museum shops, with gifts, posters, cards, and books, are open from 10 a.m. to 5:30 p.m. Monday to Saturday and from 2:30 to 5:30 p.m. Sunday.

THE BEST OF THE REST

Now, for those with more time to get acquainted with London, we'll continue our exploration of a many-faceted city.

Royal London

From Trafalgar Square, you can stroll down the wide, tree-flanked avenue known as **The Mall.** It leads to **Buckingham Palace,** the heart of "Royal London" (English kings and queens have lived here since the days of Queen Victoria). Three parks—St. James's, Green, and the Buckingham Palace Gardens (private)—converge at the center of this area, where you'll find a memorial honoring Victoria.

London's most popular daily pageant, particularly with North American tourists, is the **Changing of the Queen's Guard** in the forecourt of Buckingham Palace (tube to St. James's Park or Green Park). The regiments of the Guard's Division, in their bearskins and red tunics, actually are five regiments in one, including the Scottish, Irish, and Welsh. The guards march to the palace from either the Wellington or Chelsea barracks, arriving around 11:30 a.m. for the half-hour ceremony. To get the full effect, go somewhat earlier. There is usually no ceremony when the weather is what the English call inclement. But remember that *your* idea of inclement may not be a weather-toughened Londoner's idea of inclement. These ceremonies are curtailed in winter, between October 1 and March 31. During those months the official schedule is that the Changing of the Guard takes place on even calendar days in October, December, and February, and on odd calendar days in November, January, and March.

Any and all of this information might change suddenly without notice, depending on circumstances, so you should phone 01/730-3488 for the most up-to-the-minute details. That way, you won't necessarily miss out on this most important ceremony, which every first- or even second-time visitor to London wants to see.

You can't visit the palace, of course, without an invitation, but you can inspect the **Queen's Gallery,** S.W.1 (entrance on Buckingham Palace Road; tel. 01/930-4832). The picture gallery may be visited from 10:30 a.m. to 5 p.m. Tuesday to Saturday and bank holidays, and from 2 to 5 p.m. Sunday. It is closed Monday, except bank holidays. Admission is £1.20 ($2.10) for adults, 60p ($1.05) for children. As is known, all the royal families of Europe have art collections, some including acquisitions from centuries ago. The English sovereign has one of the finest and has consented to share it with the public. Of course, I can't predict what exhibition you're likely to see, as they are changed yearly at the gallery. You may find a selection of incomparable works by Old Masters, and sometimes furniture and objets d'art. The queen's collection contains an unsurpassed range of royal portraits, from the well-known profile of Henry V through the late Plantagenets, the companion portraits of Elizabeth I as a girl and her brother, Edward VI, and the four fine Georgian pictures by Zoffany, to recent works including two portraits of Queen Alexandra from Sandringham and paintings of Queen Elizabeth II and other members of the present royal family. Tube: Green Park or St. James's.

You can get a close look at Queen Elizabeth's coronation carriage at the **Royal Mews,** on Buckingham Palace Road, S.W.1 (tel. 01/930-4832). Her Majesty's State Coach, built in 1761 to the designs of Sir William Chambers, contains emblematic and other paintings on the panels. Its doors were executed by Cipriani. It was formerly used by sovereigns when opening Parliament in person and on other state occasions. Queen Elizabeth used it upon her coronation in 1953 and in 1977 for her Silver Jubilee Procession. It is traditionally drawn by eight gray horses. Many other official carriages are housed here as well, including the Scottish and Irish state coaches. The Queen's carriage horses are also sheltered here. The Mews is open to the public on Wednesday and Thursday from 2 to 4 p.m. and charges an admission of £1 ($1.75) for adults, 50p (90¢) for children. It is closed during Ascot week in June. Tube: Green Park or St. James's.

Official London

Whitehall, S.W.1, the seat of the British government, grew up on the grounds of Whitehall Palace, which was turned into a royal residence by Henry VIII, who snatched it from its former occupant, Cardinal Wolsey. Beginning at Trafalgar Square, Whitehall extends south to Parliament (see "Houses of Parliament" and "Westminster Abbey," described earlier in this chapter). On this street, you'll find the Home Office, the Old Admiralty Building, and the Ministry of Defence.

Visitors today can see the **Cabinet War Rooms,** the bomb-proof bunker suite of rooms large and small, just as they were left by Winston Churchill in September 1945 at the end of World War II. Many objects were removed only for dusting, and the Imperial War Museum studied photographs to replace everything exactly as it was, including notepads, files, and typewriters—right down to pencils, pins, and paperclips. You can see the Map Room with its huge wall maps, the Atlantic map a mass of pinholes. Each hole represents at least one convoy. Next door is Churchill's bedroom-cum-office, reinforced with stout wood beams. It has a very basic bed and a desk with two BBC microphones on it for his broadcasts of those famous speeches that stirred the nation.

The Transatlantic Telephone Room, to give it its full title, is little more than a broom cupboard, but it had the Bell Telephone Company's special scrambler phone by the name of Sig-Saly. From here, Churchill and Roosevelt conferred. The scrambler equipment was actually too large to house in the bunker, so it was placed in the basement of Selfridges Department Store on Oxford Street. The actual telephone was still classified at the end of the war and was removed. Below ground level, it was impossible to know the world's weather conditions. Therefore a system of boards, rather like old railway-station boards, was used with laconic phrases such as "wet, very wet, hot and sunny, dry and dull."

The entrance to the War Rooms is by Clive Steps at the end of King Charles Street, S.W.1, off Whitehall near Big Ben (take the tube to Westminster). It is open Tuesday to Sunday from 10 a.m. to 5:50 p.m. (last admission at 5:15 p.m.). It is closed on Monday, New Year's Day, Good Friday, May bank holiday, and Christmas holidays. The rooms may be closed with short notice on state occasions. Admission is £2.80 ($4.90) for adults, £1.50 ($2.65) for children. For further information, telephone 01/930-6961.

At the **Cenotaph** (honoring the dead of the two world wars), turn down unpretentious Downing Street to the modest little town house at **No. 10,** flanked by two bobbies. Walpole was the first prime minister to live here, Churchill the most famous.

Nearby is the **Horse Guards Building,** Whitehall, S.W.1 (tel. 01/930-4466, ext. 2396), which is now the headquarters, Household Division and London District. There has been a guard change here since 1649, when the site was the entrance to the old Palace of Whitehall. You can watch the Queen's Lifeguards in the mounted guard-change ceremony at 11 a.m. (10 a.m. on Sunday). You can also see the smaller change of the guard hourly when mounted troopers are changed. At 4 p.m. you can watch the evening inspection when ten unmounted troopers and two mounted troopers assemble in the courtyard. As mentioned, the main guard change takes place at 11 a.m., when 12 mounted troopers arrive from the Knightsbridge Barracks. Photographers can get a good view of the London traffic halted for this troop to cross out of Hyde Park, past the Wellington Arch. They proceed down Constitution Hill and the Mall. If you are at Hyde Park Corner at 10:30 a.m., you can follow them. Tube: Westminster.

Across the street is Inigo Jones's **Banqueting House,** Palace of Whitehall, S.W.1 (tel. 01/930-4179), site of the execution of Charles I. William and Mary accepted the crown of England here, but they preferred to live at Kensington Palace. The Banqueting House was part of Whitehall Palace, which burned to the ground in 1698. The ceremonial hall escaped razing. Its most notable feature today is an allegorical ceiling painted by Peter Paul Rubens. The Banqueting House may be visited weekdays from 10 a.m. to 5 p.m. Tuesday to Saturday and on Sunday from 2 to 5 p.m. The admission fee is 80p ($1.40) for adults, and 40p (70¢) for children. Tube: Westminster.

Finally, you may want to stroll to Parliament Square for a view of **Big Ben,** the world's most famous timepiece, the very symbol of the heart and soul of England. Big Ben is actually the deepest and loudest bell, although it has become the common name for the clock tower on the Houses of Parliament. Opposite, in the gardens of Parliament Square, stands the statue of Churchill by Oscar Nemon.

Legal London

The smallest borough in London, bustling Holborn (pronounced Hoburn), W.C.1, is often referred to as Legal London, the home of the city's barristers, solicitors, and law clerks. It also embraces the university district of Bloomsbury. Holborn, which houses the ancient Inns of Court—Gray's Inn, Lincoln's Inn, Middle Temple, and Inner Temple—was severely damaged in World War II bombing raids. The razed buildings were replaced with modern offices, housing insurance brokers, realtors, whatever. But the borough still retains quadrangle pockets of its former days.

Going from the Victoria Embankment, Middle Temple Lane leads between Middle and Inner Temple Gardens in the area known as **The Temple,** E.C.4 (tel. 01/353-4366; tube: Temple), named after the medieval order of the Knights Templar (originally formed by the Crusaders in Jerusalem in the 12th century). It was in Temple Gardens that Henry II's barons are supposed to have picked the blooms of red and white roses and started the War of the Roses in 1430. Today only members of the Temples and their guests are allowed to enter the Inner Temple Gardens. The Middle Temple contains a Tudor hall completed in 1570 with a double hammerbeam roof. It is believed that Shakespeare's troupe played *Twelfth Night* here in 1602. A table on view is said to have come from timber from Sir Francis Drake's *The Golden Hind.* The hall may be visited from 10 a.m. to noon and 3 to 4:30 p.m. Monday to Saturday.

Within the precincts of the Inner Temple, E.C.4 (tube: Temple), is the **Temple Church,** one of three Norman "round churches" left in England. First completed in the 12th century, it has been restored. Look for the knightly effigies and the Norman door any time from 10 a.m. to 5 p.m. (4 p.m. in winter). Take note of the circle of grotesque portrait heads, including a goat in a mortar board. A caretaker can show you a "dungeon" one flight up. Continue north on Middle Temple Lane to about where The Strand becomes Fleet Street going east. Look for the memorial pillar called Temple Bar, marking the boundary of the City.

On to the north, across The Strand, stand the **Royal Courts of Justice,** W.C.2 (tel. 01/405-7641, ext. 3439; tube to Temple), which are open Monday to Friday from 10 a.m. to 4 p.m. You can go through the main doorway on The Strand and on through the building, which was completed in 1882 but designed in the style of the 13th century. This is the home of such courts as Admiralty, divorce, probate, chancery, appeals, and Queen's Bench. Leave the Royal Courts building by the rear door, and you'll be on Carey Street, not far from New Square. From there, you're in the near vicinity of **Lincoln's Inn,** W.C.2 (tube: Holborn), another of the famous Inns of Court, and **Lincoln's Inn Fields.**

Lincoln's Inn, founded in the 14th century, evokes colleges at Cambridge or Oxford. This ancient inn forms an important link in the architectural maze of London. Its chapel and gardens are open to the public between noon and 2:30 p.m., and they're well worth seeing. The chapel was rebuilt around 1620 by Inigo Jones. Cromwell lived here at one time. To the west of the inn lies the late 17th-century square, one of the few complete such areas left in London, called Lincoln's Inn Fields. It's a large square with a garden in the center and surrounded by buildings, including the Sir John Soane's Museum (see "The Best of the Museums" below). Near the south of the fields on Kingsway is the **Old Curiosity Shop,** immortalized by Charles Dickens.

If you proceed north on Chancery Lane to High Holborn, W.C.1, heading toward **Gray's Inn,** the fourth of the ancient Inns of Court still in operation, take a look at the old **Staple Inn,** near the Chancery Lane tube stop. This half-timbered edifice, and eight other former Inns of Chancery, are no longer in use in the legal world. Now lined with shops, it was built and rebuilt many times, originally having come into existence between 1545 and 1589. Dr. Johnson moved here in 1759, the year *Rasselas* was published.

Gray's Inn, on Gray's Inn Road north of High Holborn, is entered from Theobald's Road. As you enter, you'll see a late Georgian terrace lined with buildings that, like many of the other houses in the Inns, are combined residences and offices. Gray's has been restored after being heavily damaged by World War II bombings. Francis Bacon (not the modern artist) was the most eminent tenant who resided here in other days. The Inn contains a rebuilt Tudor Hall, but its greatest attraction is the plane tree–shaded lawn and handsome gardens, considered the best in the Inns. The 17th-century atmosphere exists today only in the square.

When Horace Rumpole, known to readers and TV audiences as *Rumpole of the Bailey,* leaves his chambers in one of the Temple Inns of Court to go to court, he usually heads not for the Royal Courts of Justice mentioned above, which are involved with civil cases, but to the **Central Criminal Court,** better known as **Old Bailey,** on the corner of Old Bailey and Newgate Street, E.C.4. To reach it, go east on Fleet Street, which along the way becomes Ludgate Hill. Cross Ludgate Circus and turn left to the Old Bailey, a domed structure with the figure of Justice standing atop it. It fronts on a small street called Old Bailey, from which the court gets its common appellation. The courthouse replaced the infamous Newgate Prison, once the scene of public hangings and other forms of public entertainment. Old Bailey has witnessed some great—and some dubious—moments in the history of British justice. The public is permitted to enter from 10:20 a.m. to 1 p.m. and 1:50 to 4 p.m. Monday to Friday. Entry is strictly on a first-arrival basis. Guests queue up outside (where, incidentally, the final public execution took place in the 1860s). Courts 1 to 4, 17, and 18 are entered from Newgate Street, the balance from Old Bailey (the street). No one under 14 is admitted, and persons from 14 to 17 must be accompanied by a responsible adult. No cameras or tape recorders are allowed. Tube: Temple, Chancery Lane, or St. Paul's.

The Best of the Museums

The present **Guildhall,** King Street in Cheapside (the City, E.C.2; tel. 01/606-3030; tube to Bank), was built in 1411. But the Civic Hall of the Corporation of London has had a rough time, notably in the Great Fire of 1666 and the 1940 blitz. The most famous tenants of the rebuilt Guildhall are *Gog and Magog,* two giants standing over nine feet high. The original effigies, burned in the London fire, were rebuilt only to be destroyed again in 1940. The present giants are third generation. Restoration has returned the Gothic grandeur to the hall—replete with a medieval porch entranceway; monuments to Wellington, Churchill, and Nelson; stained glass commemorating lord mayors and mayors; the standards of length; and shields honoring fishmongers, haberdashers, merchant tailors, ironmongers, skinners, and some of the major Livery Companies. The Guildhall may be visited Monday to Saturday, 10 a.m. to 5 p.m. and on Sunday, May to September only, from 10 a.m. to 5 p.m. Admission is free.

Sir John Soane's Museum, 13 Lincoln's Inn Fields, W.C.2 (tel. 01/405-2107), is the former home of an architect who lived from 1753 to 1837. Sir John, who rebuilt the Bank of England (not the present structure, however), was a "space-man" in a different era. With his multilevels, fool-the-eye mirrors, flying arches, and domes, Soane was a master of perspective, a genius of interior space (his picture gallery, for example, is filled with three times the number of paintings a room of similar dimensions would be likely to hold). That he could do all this and still not prove a demon to claustrophobia victims was proof of his remarkable talent. Even if you don't like Soane (he was reportedly a cranky fellow), you may still want to visit this museum to see William Hogarth's satirical series, *The Rake's Progress,* containing his much-reproduced *Orgy* and the less-successful satire on politics in the mid-18th century, *The Election.* Soane also filled his house with paintings (Watteau's *Les Noces,* Canaletto's large *Venetian Scene*), and classical sculpture. Finally, be sure to see the Egyptian sarcophagus found in a burial chamber in the Valley of the Kings. Soane turned his house over to his country for use as a museum. It is open Tuesday to Saturday from 10 a.m. to 5 p.m. Tube: Holborn or Chancery Lane.

Royal Academy of Arts, Piccadilly, W.1 (tel. 01/734-9052; 01/439-4996 for recorded information), was founded in 1768 and is the oldest established society in Great Britain devoted solely to the fine arts. The academy is made up of a self-supporting, self-governing body of artists, who conduct art schools, hold exhibitions of the work of living artists, and organize loan exhibits of the arts of past and present periods. A summer exhibition is held annually, with contemporary paintings, drawings, engravings, sculpture, and architecture on display. This summer show has been held without a break since 1769.

Occupying old Burlington House, which was built in Piccadilly in the 17th century, the Royal Academy had as its first president Sir Joshua Reynolds. The program of loan exhibition provides opportunities to see fine art examples on an international scale. The Royal Academy Shop and a restaurant are open during exhibition hours, usually 10 a.m. to 6 p.m. daily. The framing workshop is open from 10 a.m. to 5 p.m. Monday to Saturday. Admission is free. Burlington House is opposite Fortnum and Mason. Tube: Piccadilly Circus or Green Park. Buses 9, 14, 19, 22, and 38 stop outside.

Just across the Thames in Lambeth Road, S.E.1, is the **Imperial War Museum** (tel. 01/735-8922; tube to Lambeth North or Elephant and Castle). This large domed building, built around 1815, the former Bethlehem Royal Hospital for the Insane, or "Bedlam," houses the museum's collections relating to the two world wars and other military operations involving the British and the Commonwealth since 1914.

A wide range of weapons and equipment is on display, along with models, decorations, uniforms, posters, photographs, and paintings. You can see a Mark V tank, a Battle of Britain Spitfire, a German one-man submarine, and the rifle carried by Lawrence of Arabia, as well as the German surrender document, Hitler's political testament, and a German flying bomb. The museum is open seven days a week from 10 a.m. to 6 p.m. Admission is £2.50 ($4.40) for adults, £1.25 ($2.20) for children.

Apsley House, The Wellington Museum, 149 Piccadilly, Hyde Park Corner, W.1 (tel. 01/499-5676), takes us into the former town house of the Iron Duke, the British general (1769–1852) who defeated Napoleon at the Battle of Waterloo. Wellington's London residence was opened as a public museum in 1952. Once Wellington had to retreat behind the walls of Apsley House, even securing it in fear of a possible attack from Englishmen, who were outraged by his autocratic opposition as prime minister to reform. In the vestibule you'll find a colossal statue in marble of Napoleon by Canova—ironic, to say the least. Completely idealized, it was presented to the duke by King George IV. In addition to the famous *Waterseller of Seville* by Velázquez, the Wellington collection includes Coreggio's *Agony in the Garden,* Jan Steen's *The Egg Dance,* and Pieter de Hooch's *A Musical Party.* You can see the gallery where Wellington used to invite his officers for the annual Waterloo banquet (the banquets were originally held in the dining room). The house also contains a large porcelain and china collection—plus many Wellington medals, of course. Also displayed is a magnificent Sèvres porcelain Egyptian service, made originally for the Empress Josephine and given by Louis XVIII to Wellington. In addition, superb English silver and the extraordinary Portuguese centerpiece, a present from a grateful Portugal to its liberator, are exhibited. The residence was designed by Robert Adam and built in the late 18th century. The museum is open 11 a.m. to 5 p.m. Tuesday to Sunday. It is closed Monday, Christmas holidays, and New Year's Day. Admission is £2 ($3.50) for adults, £1 ($1.75) for children. Tube: Hyde Park Corner.

National Army Museum, Royal Hospital Road, S.W.3 (tel. 01/730-0717), in Chelsea, traces the history of the British land forces from 1485 to 1982, as well as the Indian Army and colonial land forces. (The Imperial War Museum above concerns itself with the world wars.) The army museum stands next door to Wren's Royal Hospital. The museum backers agreed to begin the collection at the year 1485, because that was the date of the formation of the Yeomen of the Guard. The saga of the forces of the East India Company is also traced, beginning in 1602 and going up to Indian independence in 1947. The gory and the glory—it's all here, everything from Florence Nightingale's lamp to the French Eagle captured in a cavalry charge at Waterloo, even the staff cloak wrapped round the dying Wolfe at Québec. Naturally, there are the "cases of the heroes," mementos of such outstanding men as the Dukes of Marlborough and Wellington. But the field soldier isn't neglected either. One gallery traces British military history from 1914 to 1982. The admission-free museum is open Monday to Saturday from 10 a.m. to 5:30 p.m. and on Sunday from 2 to 5:30 p.m. It is closed on New Year's Day, Good Friday, from December 24 to 26, and on the May bank holiday. Tube: Sloane Square.

In London's Barbican district near St. Paul's Cathedral, the **Museum of London,** 150 London Wall, E.C.2 (tel. 01/600-3699), allows visitors to trace the history of London from prehistoric times to the present through relics, costumes, household effects, maps, and models. Exhibits are arranged so that visitors can begin and end their chronological stroll through 250,000 years at the main entrance to the museum. You can see the death mask of Oliver Cromwell, but the pièce de résistance is the Lord Mayor's coach, built in 1757 and weighing three tons, still used each November in the Lord Mayor's Procession. This gilt-and-red horse-drawn vehicle is like a fairytale coach. Visitors can also see the Great Fire of London in living color and sound; a reconstructed Roman dining room with the kitchen and utensils; cell doors from Newgate Prison made famous by Charles Dickens; and perhaps most amazing of all, a shop display with pre–World War II prices on the items.

The museum, opened in 1976, overlooks London's Roman and medieval walls and, in all, has something from every era before and after, including little Victorian shops and re-creations of what life was like in the Iron Age. Anglo-Saxons, Vikings, Normans—they're all there, arranged on two floors around a central courtyard. With quick labels for museum sprinters, more extensive ones for those who want to study, and still deeper details for scholars, this museum, built at a cost of some $18 million, is an enriching experience for *everybody*.

At least an hour should be allowed for a full (but still quick) visit to the museum. Free lectures on London's past are given during lunch hours. These aren't given daily, but it's worth inquiring at the entrance hall. In addition, the museum holds special exhibitions. You can reach the museum by going up to the elevated pedestrian precinct at the corner of London Wall and Aldersgate, five minutes from St. Paul's. The museum also has a licensed restaurant, Milburns, overlooking a garden. It is open Tuesday to Saturday from 10 a.m. to 6 p.m., on Sunday from 2 to 6 p.m.; closed Monday. Admission is free. Tube: St. Paul's, Barbican, or Moorgate.

London Transport Museum, Covent Garden, W.C.2 (tel. 01/379-6344), is in a splendidly restored Victorian building that formerly housed the flower market.

Horse buses, motor buses, trams, trolley buses, railway vehicles, models, maps, posters, photographs, and audio-visual displays illustrate the fascinating story of the evolution of London's transport systems and how this has affected the growth of London. There are a number of unique working displays. You can "drive" a tube train, a tram, and a bus, and also operate full-size signaling equipment. The exhibits include a reconstruction of George Shillibeer's omnibus of 1829, a steam locomotive that ran on the world's first underground railway, and a coach from the first deep-level electric railway. The museum is open every day of the year, except the three-day Christmas holidays, from 10 a.m. to 6 p.m. Admission charges are £2.40 ($4.20) for adults and £1.10 ($1.95) for children. A family ticket for two adults and two children is £5.50 ($9.95).

The museum sells merchandise of London Transport, including maps of the London Underground system in their original size, books, souvenirs, photos, and reproductions of the famous London Transport poster collection in print and postcard form (see this chapter's "Shopping" section). Tube: Covent Garden.

Royal Air Force Museum, Grahame Park Way, Hendon, N.W.7 (tel. 01/205-2266), contains one of the world's finest collections of historic aircraft, illustrating all aspects of the history of the Royal Air Force and much of the history of aviation in general. The museum stands on ten acres of the former historic airfield at Hendon in North London, and its main Aircraft Hall occupies two hangars dating from World War I. From the museum's collection of more than 100 aircraft, some 60 machines are displayed, including the legendary Spitfire and Lancaster, plus German and American aircraft. On a site adjacent to the main building is the Battle of Britain Hall, containing a unique collection of British, German, and Italian aircraft that were engaged in the great air battle of 1940. The museum is a national memorial to the victorious forces and especially to "The Few." Machines include the Spitfire, Hurricane, Gladiator, Defiant, Blenheim, and Messerschmitt BF109. A central feature of the exhibition is a replica of the No. 11 Group Operations Room at RAF Uxbridge. Equipment, uniforms, medals, documents, relics, works of art, and other memorabilia of the period are included in the permanent memorial to the men, women, and machines involved in the air battle. Also in the same complex is the massive Bomber Command Hall, with its striking display of famous bomber aircraft, including the Lancaster, Wellington, B-17 Flying Fortress, Mosquito, and Vulcan.

Admission to the entire complex is £3 ($5.25) for adults, £1.50 ($2.65) for children. Hours are from 10 a.m. to 6 p.m. daily, except New Year's Day and from December 24 to December 26. The nearest Underground is Colindale on the Northern Line, and the nearest British Rail station is Mill Hill Broadway. Access by road is via the A41 (from the M1 at junction 4), the A1, and North Circular Road.

National Postal Museum, King Edward Building, King Edward Street, E.C.1 (tel. 01/239-5420), attracts philatelists from all over the world—and even vaguely kindred spirits. Actually part of the Post Office, it features permanent exhibitions of the stamps of Great Britain and the world and special displays of stamps and postal history, changing every few months, according to certain themes. For example, one exhibition featured "Crossing the Atlantic." The museum is open from 10 a.m. to 4:30 p.m. Monday to Thursday and to 4 p.m. on Friday. Admission is free. Tube: St. Paul's or Barbican.

Science Museum, Exhibition Road, S.W.7 (tel. 01/938-8000), traces the development of both science and industry and their influence in everyday life. The collections are among the largest, most comprehensive, and most significant anywhere. On display is Stephenson's original *Rocket,* the tiny locomotive that won a race against all competitors in the Rainhill Trials and became the world's prototype railroad engine. You can also see Whittle's original jet engine and the Gloster aircraft, the first jet-powered British plane. A cavalcade of antique cars from the Stanley steam car to the yellow Rolls-Royce can be seen, side by side with carriages and vintage bicycles and motorcycles. To aid the visitor's understanding of many scientific and technological principles, working model and video displays are here, including a hands-on gallery called the Launch Pad. A shopping concourse provides the opportunity of taking home a souvenir. The museum is open from 10 a.m. to 6 p.m. Monday to Saturday and from 11 a.m. to 6 p.m. Sunday. Admission is £2 ($3.50) for adults, £1 ($1.75) for children 5 to 15. Tube: South Kensington. Bus: 14.

The Greatest of the Galleries

National Portrait Gallery, St. Martin's Place, W.C.2 (tel. 01/930-1552; entrance around the corner from the National Gallery on Trafalgar Square), gives you a chance to outstare the stiff-necked greats and not-so-greats of English history. In a gallery of remarkable and unremarkable portraits, a few paintings tower over the rest, including Sir Joshua Reynolds's first portrait of Samuel Johnson ("a man of most dreadful appearance"). Among the best are Nicholas Hilliard's miniature of a most handsome Sir Walter Raleigh; a full-length Elizabeth I (painted to commemorate her visit to Sir Henry Lee at Ditchley in 1592), along with the Holbein cartoon of Henry VIII (sketched for a family portrait that hung, before it was burned, in the Privy Chamber in Whitehall Palace). You'll see a portrait of William Shakespeare with a gold earring. The artist is unknown, but the portrait bears the claim of being the most "authentic contemporary likeness" of its subject of any work yet known. The John Hayls portrait of Samuel Pepys adorns one wall. Whistler could not only paint a portrait, he could also be the subject of one. One of the most unusual portraits in the gallery—a group of the three Brontë sisters (Charlotte, Emily, Anne)— was painted by their brother, Branwell. A turbaned, idealized portrait of Lord Byron (painted from life by Thomas Phillips) is pleased with itself. Treat yourself to the likeness of the incomparable Aubrey Beardsley. For a finale, Princess Diana is on the Royal Landing. The gallery is open from 10 a.m. to 5 p.m. Monday to Friday, from 10 a.m. to 6 p.m. on Saturday, and from 2 to 6 p.m. on Sunday. Special exhibitions are held throughout the year. Admission to the gallery is free, except for special exhibitions. Tube: Charing Cross or Leicester Square.

The **Wallace Collection,** Manchester Square, off Wigmore Street, W.1 (tel. 01/935-0687), has an outstanding collection of works of art of all kinds that was bequeathed to the nation by Lady Wallace in 1897 and is still displayed in the house of its founders. There are important pictures by artists of all European schools, including Titian, Rubens, Van Dyck, Rembrandt, Hals, Velázquez, Murillo, Reynolds, Gainsborough, and Delacroix. Representing the art of France in the 18th century are paintings by Watteau, Boucher, and Fragonard, and sculpture, furniture, goldsmiths' work, and Sèvres porcelain. Valuable collections also are found of majolica and European and Oriental arms and armor. Frans Hals's *Laughing Cavalier* is the most famous painting in the collection, but Pieter de Hooch's *A Boy Bringing Pomegranates* and Antoine Watteau's *The Music Party* are also well known. Other notable works include Canaletto's views of Venice (especially *Bacino di San Marco*), Rembrandt's *Titus,* and Gainsborough's *Mrs. Robinson (Perdita).* Boucher's portrait of the Marquise de Pompadour is also worthy. The Wallace Collection may be viewed daily from 10 a.m. to 5 p.m. and on Sunday from 2 to 5 p.m. It is closed Christmas holidays, New Year's Day, Good Friday, and the first Monday in May. Tube: Bond Street.

The **Courtauld Institute Galleries,** Somerset House, The Strand, W.C.2 (tel. 01/580-1015), is the home of the art collection of London University, noted chiefly for its superb impressionist and post-impressionist works. It has eight works by Cézanne alone, including his *A Man with a Pipe.* Other notable works include Seurat's *Young Woman Powdering Herself,* Van Gogh's self-portrait (with ear bandaged), a nude by the great Modigliani, Gauguin's *Day-Dreaming,* Monet's *Fall at Argenteuil,* Toulouse-Lautrec's most delicious *Tête-à-Tête,* and Manet's *Bar at the Folies Bergère.* The galleries also feature classical works, including a *Virgin and Child* by Bernardino Luini, a Botticelli, a Giovanni Bellini, a Veronese, a triptych by the Master of Flémâlle, works by Pieter Brueghel the Elder, Massys, Parmigianino, 32 oils by Rubens, oil sketches by Tiepolo, three landscapes by Kokoschka, and wonderful Old Master drawings (especially those of Michelangelo and Rembrandt). The collection may be viewed Monday to Saturday from 10 a.m. to 5 p.m. and on Sunday from 2 to 5 p.m. Admission is £1.50 ($2.65) for adults, 50p (90¢) for children. Tube: Charing Cross.

Hayward Gallery, South Bank, S.E.1 (tel. 01/629-9495), presents a changing program of major exhibitions organized by the South Bank Centre. The gallery forms part of the South Banks Arts Centre, which also includes the Royal Festival Hall, the Queen Elizabeth Hall, the Purcell Room, the National Film Theatre, and the National Theatre. Admission to the gallery costs £2.50 ($4.40) to £4 ($7), with a one-day cheaper entry on Monday, and in the evening Tuesday and Wednesday between 6 and 8 p.m. Hours are Monday to Wednesday from 10 a.m. to 8 p.m., Thursday to Saturday from 10 a.m. to 6 p.m., and on Sunday from noon to 6 p.m. The gallery is closed between exhibitions, so check the listings before crossing the Thames. For information, phone 01/261-0127. Tube: Waterloo Station.

Homes of Famous Writers

Samuel Johnson's House: The Queen Anne house of the famed lexicographer is at 17 Gough Square, E.C.4 (tel. 01/353-3745). It'll cost you £1.50 ($2.65), and it's well worth it. Children pay £1 ($1.75). It was here that Dr. Johnson and his able copyists compiled his famous dictionary. The 17th-century building has been painstakingly restored (surely "Dear Tetty," if not Boswell, would approve). Although Johnson lived at Staple Inn in Holborn and at a number of other houses, the Gough Square house is the only one of his residences remaining in London. He occupied it from 1748 to 1759. It is open from 11 a.m. to 5:30 p.m. Monday to Saturday, May through September, closing half an hour earlier off-season. Take the tube to Blackfriars, then walk up New Bridge Street, turning left onto Fleet. Gough Square is a tiny, hidden square, north of the "street of ink."

Carlyle's House: 24 Cheyne Row, S.W.3 (tel. 01/352-7087), is in Chelsea (take bus 11, 19, 22, or 39). For nearly half a century, from 1834 to 1881, the handsome author of *The French Revolution* and other works, known as "the Sage of Chelsea," took up abode along with his letter-writing wife, in this modest 1708 terraced house, about three-quarters of a block from the Thames, near the Chelsea Embankment. Still standing and furnished essentially as it was in Carlyle's day, the house was described by his wife as being "of most antique physiognomy, quite to our humour; all wainscotted, carved and queer-looking, roomy, substantial, commodious, with closets to satisfy any Bluebeard." Now who could improve on that? The second floor contains the drawing room of Mrs. Carlyle. But the most interesting chamber is the not-so-soundproof "soundproof" study in the skylit attic. Filled with Carlyle memorabilia—his books, a letter from Disraeli, a writing chair, even his death mask —this is the cell where the author labored over his *Frederick the Great* manuscript. The Cheyne (pronounced Chainey) Row house is open daily from 11 a.m. to 5 p.m. from Easter Saturday to the end of October, except Monday and Tuesday. Admission is £1.60 ($2.80) for adults and half price for accompanied children. The nearest tube, Sloane Square, is a long way off.

Dickens's House: In Bloomsbury stands the house of the great English author Charles Dickens, accused in his time of "supping on the horrors" of Victoriana. Born in 1812 in what is now Portsmouth, Dickens is known to have lived at 48 Doughty St., W.C.1 (tel. 01/405-2127; tube to Russell Square), from 1837 to 1839. Unlike some of the London town houses of famous men (Wellington, Sloane), the Bloomsbury house is simple, the embodiment of middle-class restraint. The house contains an extensive library of Dickensiana, including manuscripts and letters second in importance only to the Forster Collection in the Victoria and Albert Museum. In his study are his desk and chair from the study at Gad's Hill Place, Rochester, on which he wrote his last two letters before he died. Also on display is the table from his Swiss chalet on which he wrote the last unfinished fragment of *The Mystery of Edwin Drood*. Dickens's drawing room on the first floor has been reconstructed, as have the still room, wash house, and wine cellar in the basement. The house is open daily, except Sunday and bank holidays, from 10 a.m. to 5 p.m. Admission is £1.50 ($2.65) for adults, 75p ($1.30) for children, and £3 ($5.25) for families.

Hampstead

Hampstead Heath, N.W.3, is hundreds of acres of wild and unfenced royal parkland about 4 miles north from the center of London, so elevated that on a clear day you can see St. Paul's Cathedral and even the hills of Kent south of the Thames. It is the scene of big one-day fairs in good weather, and it has for years drawn Londoners on such weekend pursuits as kite-flying, sunning, fishing in the ponds, swimming, and picnicking, and it is a favorite place for joggers. It was the common of Hampstead Manor in the time of King Charles II, a good ride out from London. Tube: Hampstead Heath.

Hampstead Village developed from the rural area around some of the substantial houses that were built in the area. From a village, a fashionable spa town developed in the 18th century, giving the name to Well Walk and other parts of the growing town. With the coming of the Underground in 1907, its attractions as a place to live, even for those who went frequently into the City, became widely known, with writers, artists, architects, musicians, and scientists coming to join earlier residents. The original village, on the side of a hill, still has pleasing features, such as the old roads, lanes, places, alleys, steps, rises, courts, and groves to be strolled through and enjoyed.

Good Regency and Georgian houses were built in this village, which is just 20 minutes by tube from Piccadilly Circus, with its palatable mix of history-rich pubs, toy shops, and chic boutiques, as seen along Flask Walk, a pedestrian mall.

Many eminent figures in the literary world have lived in Hampstead, and some still do, either full or part time: John Keats, D. H. Lawrence, Rabindranath Tagore, Percy Bysshe Shelley, Robert Louis Stevenson, Kingsley Amis, and John Le Carré, to name a few.

Keats's House: The darling of romantics, John Keats lived for only two years at Wentworth Place, Keats Grove, N.W.3 (tel. 01/435-2062; take the tube to Belsize Park or Hampstead, or bus 24 from Trafalgar Square). But for the poet, that was something like two-fifths of his creative life, as he died in Rome of tuberculosis at the age of 25 (in 1821). In Hampstead Keats wrote two of his most celebrated *Odes,* one in praise of a Grecian urn and one to a nightingale. In the garden stands an ancient mulberry tree that the poet must have known. His Regency house is well preserved and contains the manuscripts of his last sonnet ("Bright star, would I were steadfast as thou art"), a final letter to the mother of Fanny Brawne (his correspondence to his Hampstead neighbor, who nursed him while he was ill, forms part of his legend), and a portrait of him on his deathbed in a little house on the Spanish Steps in Rome. Wentworth Place is open from 2 to 6 p.m. Monday to Friday, 10 a.m. to 5 p.m. Saturday, and 2 to 5 p.m. Sunday and bank holidays April to October. From November to March, hours are from 1 to 5 p.m. Monday to Friday, 10 a.m. to 5 p.m. Saturday, and 2 to 5 p.m. Sunday. However, call to confirm hours, as they may be changed in the lifetime of this edition. The house is closed Christmas holidays, New Year's Day, Easter holidays, and May Day. Admission is free. Tube: Hampstead.

The **Iveagh Bequest, Kenwood House,** Hampstead Lane, N.W.3 (tel. 01/348-1286), on the rim of Hampstead Heath, handsome with its columned portico, was built as a gentleman's country home around the start of the 18th century. It became the seat of Lord Mansfield in 1754 and was enlarged and decorated by the famous Scottish architect Robert Adam starting in 1764. In 1927, it was given to the nation by Lord Iveagh, together with his collection of pictures. The Adam stamp is strongest in the restored oval library, painted in rose, blue, white, and gold. The rooms contain some fine neoclassical furniture, but the main attractions are the Old Masters and the work of British artists. You can see paintings by Rembrandt (*Self-Portrait in Old Age*), Vermeer, Turner, Hals, Cuyp, Crome, Gainsborough, Reynolds, Romney, Raeburn, Guardi, and Angelica Kauffmann, plus a portrait of the *Earl of Mansfield, Lord Chief Justice,* who made Kenwood such an important home. In the Coach House, where there is a cafeteria, stands a 19th-century family coach that carried 15 persons comfortably. The house is open daily from 10 a.m. to 6 p.m. Easter Saturday to September 30, and from 10 a.m. to 4 p.m. October 1 to Maundy Thursday. Admission is free. It is closed Christmas Eve, Christmas Day, and Good Friday.

On the south lawn, looking toward the lake, symphony concerts are held in summer, and chamber music concerts are presented in the Orangery. A charge is made for the concerts. Tube: Hampstead.

The Freud Museum, 20 Maresfield Gardens, N.W.3 (tel. 01/435-2002), is a spacious three-story red-brick house in which Sigmund Freud, father of psychoanalysis, lived, worked, and died after escaping with his family and possessions from Nazi-occupied Vienna. On view are rooms containing original furniture, letters, photographs, paintings, and personal effects of Freud and his daughter, Anna. A focal point of the museum is the study in which you can see the famous couch and large collection of Egyptian, Roman, and Oriental antiques. This domestic and working environment offers a unique perspective on the contribution that Freud made to the understanding of the human mind. The museum is developing as a research archive, educational resource, and cultural center. Temporary exhibitions, continuous guided tours, and an archive film program are available, plus a shop. Hours are from noon to 5 p.m. Wednesday to Sunday. Admission is £2 ($3.50). Tube: Finchley Road.

The Parks of London

London's parklands easily rate as the greatest, most wonderful system of "green lungs" of any large city on the globe. Not as rigidly artificial as the parks of Paris, those of London are maintained with a loving care and lavish artistry that puts their American equivalents to shame. Above all, they've been kept safe from land-hungry building firms and city councils, and they still offer patches of real countryside right in the heart of the metropolis. Maybe there's something to be said for inviolate "royal" property, after all. Because that's what most of London's parks are.

Largest of them—and one of the biggest in the world—is **Hyde Park,** W.2. With the adjoining Kensington Gardens, it covers 636 acres of central London with velvety lawns interspersed with ponds, flowerbeds, and trees. Hyde Park was once a favorite deer-hunting ground of Henry VIII. Running through the width is a 41-acre lake known as the Serpentine. Rotten Row, a 1½-mile sand track, is reserved for horseback riding and on Sunday attracts some skilled equestrians.

Kensington Gardens, W.2, blending with Hyde Park, border on the grounds of Kensington Palace. Kensington Gardens also contain the celebrated statue of Peter Pan, with the bronze rabbits that toddlers are always trying to kidnap. It also harbors Albert Memorial, that Victorian extravaganza.

East of Hyde Park, across Piccadilly, stretch **Green Park** and **St. James's Park,** S.W.1, forming an almost unbroken chain of landscaped beauty. This is an ideal area for picnics, and you'll find it hard to believe that this was once a festering piece of swamp near the leper hospital. There is a romantic lake, stocked with a variety of ducks and some surprising pelicans, descendants of the pair that the Russian ambassador presented to Charles II back in 1662.

Regent's Park, N.W.1, covers most of the district by that name north of Baker

Street and Marylebone Road. Designed by the 18th-century genius John Nash to surround a palace of the prince regent that never materialized, this is the most classically beautiful of London's parks. The core is a rose garden planted around a small lake alive with waterfowl and spanned by humped Japanese bridges. In early summer the rose perfume in the air is as heady as wine. Regent's Park also contains an Open Air Theatre and the London Zoo.

Landmark Churches

St. Martin-in-the-Fields, overlooking Trafalgar Square, W.C.2 (tel. 01/839-4342), is the Royal Parish Church, dear to the heart of many a Britisher, especially the homeless. The present classically inspired church, with its famous steeple, dates back to 1726; James Gibbs, a pupil of Wren's, was its architect. But the origins of the church go back to the 11th century. Among the congregation in years past was George I, who was actually a churchwarden, unique for an English sovereign. Because of St. Martin's position in the theater district, it has drawn many actors to its door—none more notable than Nell Gwynne, the mistress of Charles II. On her death in 1687, she was buried in the crypt. Throughout the war, many Londoners rode out an uneasy night in the crypt, while blitz bombs rained down overhead. One, in 1940, blasted out all the windows. The crypt now contains a pleasant restaurant, a bookshop, and a gallery. Tube: Charing Cross.

St. Etheldreda's, Britain's oldest Roman Catholic church, lies in Ely Place, Clerkenwell, E.C.1 (tel. 01/405-1061), leading off Charterhouse Street at Holborn Circus. Built in 1251, it was mentioned by the Bard in both *Richard II* and *Richard III*. It was one of the survivors of the Great Fire of 1666. The church was built and was the property of the Diocese of Ely in the days when many bishops had their episcopal houses in London rather than in the actual cathedral cities in which they held their sees. Until this century, the landlord of Ye Olde Mitre public house near Ely Place where the church stands had to obtain his license from the Justices of Cambridgeshire rather than in London, and even today the place is still a private road, with impressive iron gates and a lodge for the gatekeeper, all administered by six commissioners who are elected. St. Etheldreda, whose name is sometimes shortened to St. Audrey, was a 7th-century king's daughter who left her husband and turned to religion, establishing an abbey on the Isle of Ely. The name "St. Audrey" is the source of the word *tawdry*, from cheap trinkets sold at the annual fair honoring the saint. St. Etheldreda's is made up of a crypt and an upper church, catering to working people and visitors who come to pray. It has a distinguished musical tradition, with the 11 a.m. mass on Sunday sung in Latin. Other mass times are 9 a.m. and 6 p.m. on Sunday and 8 a.m. and 1 p.m. Monday to Friday. Lunches are served from noon to 2 p.m. Monday to Friday in The Pantry, with a varied choice of hot and cold dishes. Menus cost from £4 ($7).

Along the Thames

There is a row of fascinating attractions lying on, across, and alongside the River Thames. All of London's history and development is linked with this winding ribbon of water. The Thames connects the city with the sea, from which it drew its wealth and its power. For centuries the river was London's highway and main street.

Some of the bridges that span the Thames are household words. London Bridge, which, contrary to the nursery rhyme, has never "fallen down" but has been dismantled and shipped to the United States, ran from the Monument (a tall pillar commemorating the Great Fire of 1666) to Southwark Cathedral, parts of which date back to 1207.

Its neighbor to the east is the still-standing **Tower Bridge,** E.1 (tel. 01/407-0922), one of the city's most celebrated landmarks and possibly the most photographed and painted bridge on earth. Tower Bridge was built during 1886 to 1894 with two towers 800 feet apart, joined by footbridges that provide glass-covered walkways for the public who can enter the north tower, take the elevator to the walkway, cross the river to the south tower, and return to street level. It's a photographer's dream, with interesting views of the City of London and St. Paul's, the Tower of London, and in the distance, Big Ben and the Houses of Parliament. You can also visit the main engine room with its Victorian boiler and steam-pumping engines, which used to raise and lower the roadway across the river. Models show how the 1,000-ton arms of the bridge can be raised in 1½ minutes to allow ships passage upstream. Exhibitions trace the history and operation of this unique bridge. Nowadays, electric power is used to raise the bridge, usually once a day, much more often in summer. Admission to the exhibits is £2.50 ($4.40) for adults, £1 ($1.75) for children. It is open daily in summer from 10 a.m. to 6:30 p.m. (to 4:45 p.m. in winter). Tube: Tower Hill.

The piece of river between the site of the old London Bridge and the Tower Bridge marks the city end of the immense row of docks stretching 26 miles to the coast. Most of them are no longer in use, but they have long been known as the Port of London.

But the Thames meant more to London than a port. It was also her chief commercial thoroughfare and a royal highway, the only regal one in the days of winding cobblestone streets. Every royal procession was undertaken by barge—gorgeously painted and gilded vessels, which you can still see at the Maritime Museum at Greenwich. All important prisoners were delivered to the Tower by water—it eliminated the chance of an ambush by their friends in one of the narrow, crooked alleys surrounding the fortress. When Henry VIII had his country residence at Hampton Court, there was a constant stream of messenger boats shuttling between his other riverside palaces all the way to Greenwich. His illustrious daughter, Queen Elizabeth I, revved up the practice to such a degree that a contemporary chronicler complained he couldn't spit in the Thames for fear of hitting a royal craft. The royal boats and much of the commercial traffic disappeared when the streets were widened enough for horse coaches to maintain a decent pace.

Particular note should be taken of the striking removal of pollution from the Thames in the past decades. The river, so polluted in the 1950s that no marine life could exist in it, can now lay claim to being "the cleanest metropolitan estuary in the world," with many varieties of fish, even salmon, back as happy denizens of these waters.

The Thames Flood Barrier

Since its official opening in 1984, the engineering spectacle known as the Thames Flood Barrier has drawn increasing crowds to the site, at a point in the river known as Woolwich Reach in east London, where the Thames is a straight stretch about a third of a mile in width. For centuries, the Thames estuary has, from time to time, brought tidal surges that have on occasion caused disastrous flooding at Woolwich, Hammersmith, Whitehall, and Westminster, and elsewhere within the river's flood reaches. The flooding peril has increased during this century from a number of natural causes. These include the unstoppable rise of tide levels in the Thames, surge tides from the Atlantic, and the down-tilt of the country of some 12 inches a century. Also London is sinking at about that same rate into its clay foundations.

All this led to the construction, beginning in 1975, of a great barrier with huge piers linking mammoth rising sector gates, smaller rising sector gates, and falling radial gates, all of which when in use make a solid steel wall about the height of a five-story building, which completely dams the waters of the Thames, keeping the surge tides from passage up the estuary. The gates are operated every month or so to remove river silt and to ascertain that the operation is smooth.

London Launches offers trips to the barrier, operating from Westminster Pier. Four trips sail daily in summer at 10 and 11:15 a.m. and at 1:30 and 2:45 p.m. Except on the last trip, passengers can get off at the barrier pier, visit the Barrier Centre, and return by a later boat or by bus. An audio-visual show depicting the need for the barrier and its operation is presented at the center, where there are also a souvenir shop, a snackbar, and a cafeteria. Round-trip fare from Westminster Pier is £3.50 ($6.15) for adults, £2 ($3.50) for children. For further information, phone 01/854-1373.

London Docklands

What was a dilapidated wasteland, some eight square miles of property surrounded by water—and some 55 miles of waterfront acreage within a sailor's cry of London's major attractions—has been reclaimed as a leisure, residential, and commercial area.

Included in this complex are Wapping, the Isle of Dogs, the Surrey and Royal Docks, and more, all with Limehouse at its heart. The former urban wasteland of deserted warehouses and derelict wharves and the many facilities already completed can be visited by taking the Docklands Light Railway that links the Isle of Dogs and London Underground's Tower Hill station, via several local stations. To see the whole complex, take the railway at the Tower Gateway near Tower Bridge for a short journey through Wapping and the Isle of Dogs. You can get off at Island Gardens and then cross through the 100-year-old Greenwich Tunnel under the Thames to see the attractions of Greenwich described in section 6 of this chapter, "One-Day Trips from London."

A regular water bus service connects Greenwich with Charing Cross in a river voyage of about half an hour, and other tunnels are planned to link the Docklands with port points and motorways.

A visit to the **Exhibition Centre** on the Isle of Dogs gives an opportunity to see what the Docklands past, present, and future include. Already the area has provided space for overflow from the City of London's square mile, and it looks as though the growth and development is more than promising.

A shopping village at Tobacco Dock, a new home at Shadwell Basin for the Academy of St. Martin-in-the-Fields Orchestra, and the London Arena (largest man-made sport and leisure complex in the country) at the tip of the Isle of Dogs are being joined by luxury condominiums, offices, hotels, museums, and theaters. These and all the other amenities aimed at making the East End of London a shining star have been or soon will be completed.

---

2. Shopping

In London, "a nation of shopkeepers" displays an enormous variety of wares, and you can pick up values ranging from a still-functioning hurdy-gurdy to a replica of the Crown Jewels. For the best buys, search out the sensational clothing, as well as traditional and well-tailored men's and women's suits, small antiques and curios, woolens, tweeds, tartans, rare books, and Liberty silks, to name just a few.

Most stores are open from 9 a.m. to 5:30 p.m. Monday to Saturday, with late shopping until 8 p.m. on Thursday. In the East End, around Aldgate and Whitechapel, many shops are open on Sunday from 9 a.m. to 2 p.m. There are a few all-night stores, mostly in the Bayswater section.

Here's a brief survey of some of the attractive merchandise offered:

ANTIQUE MARKETS (FOR CURIOS):   Billed as the world's largest covered antique market, **Chelsea Antiques Market,** 245-253 King's Rd., S.W.3 (tel. 01/352-1720), is a gold mine where you can pan for some hidden little treasure. Sheltered inside a rambling old building, it offers endless browsing possibilities for the curio addict, stall after stall extending along a serpentine maze. In this ever-changing display you're likely to run across fur coats, Staffordshire dogs, shaving mugs, old books, prints, maps, paintings, Edwardian buckles and clasps, and much more. The market is open Monday to Saturday from 8 a.m. to 6 p.m. and is closed Sunday. Tube: Sloane Square.

Grays and **Grays in the Mews Antique Markets,** 58 Davies St. and 1-7 Davies Mews, W.1 (tel. 01/629-7034), just south of Oxford Street and opposite Bond Street Tube Station, are in a triangle formed by Davies Street, South Molton Lane, and Davies Mews. The two old buildings have been converted into walk-in stands with independent dealers. The term "antique" here covers items from oil paintings to, say, the 1894 edition of the *Encyclopaedia Britannica*. Also sold here are exquisite antique jewelry, silver, gold, antiquarian books, maps and prints, paintings and drawings, bronzes and ivories, arms and armor, Victorian and Edwardian toys, furniture, and other antique treasures. There is also a whole floor of repair workshops, an engraver, and a Bureau de Change.

Alfie's Antique Market, 13-25 Church St., N.W.8 (tel. 01/723-6066), is the biggest and one of the cheapest covered markets in London, and it's where many dealers come to buy. Alfie's is named after the father of Bennie Gray, the owner of Grays and Grays in the Mews Antique Markets and former owner of the Antique Hypermarket Kensington and Antiquarius. The market contains more than 370 stalls, showrooms, and workshops on 35,000 square feet of floor, plus an enormous, 70-unit basement area. Tube: Marylebone or Edgware Road.

Antiquarius, 131-141 King's Rd., S.W.3 (tel. 01/351-5353), echoes the artistic diversity of the street on which it is located. More than 200 stand-holders offer specialized and general antiques of all periods from ancient times to the 1950s. It's open Monday to Saturday from 10 a.m. to 6 p.m. Tube: Sloane Square. Bus 11, 19, or 22 will also take you there. Or you can travel on bus 137, alighting at Sloane Square.

ARTS AND CRAFTS: On a Sunday morning along **Bayswater Road,** for more than a mile, pictures, collages, and craft items are hung on the railings along the edge of Hyde Park and Kensington Gardens. If the weather is right, start at Marble Arch and walk and walk, shopping or just sightseeing as you go along. Along Piccadilly, you'll see much of the same thing by walking along the railings of Green Park on a Saturday afternoon.

The **Crafts Council,** 12 Waterloo Pl., S.W.1 (tel. 01/930-4811), is a public body that exists to promote crafts in England and Wales. It has galleries that offer a broad program of changing craft exhibitions from British domestic pottery to American traditional patchwork. Most exhibitions are free; otherwise concessions are available. Other facilities include a lively information center that can direct you to craft events throughout Britain, a slide library, and a book stall. (Note: The Crafts Council runs a quality craft shop at the Victoria and Albert Museum, South Kensington.) The galleries and information center are open Tuesday to Saturday from 10 a.m. to 5 p.m. and on Sunday from 2 to 5 p.m. Tube: Piccadilly Circus.

BEAUCHAMP PLACE: Of all the shopping streets of London, one has surfaced near the top. It's Beauchamp Place (pronounced Beecham), S.W.3, a block off Brompton Road, near Harrods department store. The *Herald Tribune* called it "a higgledy-piggledy of old-fashioned and trendy, quaint and with-it, expensive and cheap. It is deliciously unspecialized." Whatever you're looking for—a place to revamp your old alligator bag, reject china, collages, custom-tailored men's shirts—you should find it here. It's pure fun even if you don't buy anything.

BOOKS: For a wide choice of reading matter, go to **W. & G. Foyle, Ltd.,** 113-119 Charing Cross Rd., W.C.2 (tel. 01/439-8501), which claims to be the world's largest bookstore, with an impressive array of hardcovers and paperbacks, including travel maps. The shop includes records, videotapes, and sheet music. Tube: Leicester Square

Hatchards Ltd., 187-188 Piccadilly, W.1 (tel. 01/439-9921), is an old-fashioned-looking place on the south side of Piccadilly that is stuffed with books ranging from popular fiction and specialist reference books to paperbacks. There are shelves of guidebooks and atlases, cookbooks, and books of puzzles to occupy you on train and plane trips. Tube: Piccadilly Circus.

For history buffs, **History Bookshop,** 2 The Broadway, N.11 (tel. 01/368-8568), stands at the corner of Friern Barnet Road and MacDonald Road. Behind its 1890s facade, this is one of the largest repositories of secondhand books in London, containing some 80,000 volumes scattered over three floors. It specializes in military history. Catalogues are issued at regular intervals. It is open daily except Monday, Tuesday, and Wednesday from 9:30 a.m. to 5:30 p.m. Tube: Arnos Grove.

BRASS RUBBING: There is such a wealth of spectacular brasses in churches and cathedrals up and down the country that the pastime of brass rubbing is becoming more and more popular. The rubbing is made with a metallic wax on paper and can be done in about half an hour. The cost depends on the size. For a fee, materials are provided at the centers, which are in all parts of the country, including Stratford-upon-Avon, Oxford, York, Chester, Edinburgh, Coventry, and Chichester. It is wise to telephone ahead if you want to rub a particular brass.

The **London Brass Rubbing Centre,** formerly at St. James's Church in Piccadilly, is now at St. Martin-in-the-Fields Church, Trafalgar Square, W.C.2 (tel. 01/437-6023), in the big brick-vaulted 1730s crypt. The center has 70 exact copies of celebrated bronze portraits ready for use. Paper, rubbing materials, and instructions on how to begin are furnished. Classical music is played as visitors work at the task. The charges range from 50p (90¢) for a small copy to £12 ($21) for the largest, a life-size Crusader knight. It's open all year, except Christmas Day and Easter Thursday to Easter Sunday, from 10 a.m. to 6 p.m. Monday to Saturday and noon to 6 p.m. Sunday. A gift area is open, selling unusual historical goods, brass-rubbing kits for children, and much else. The center has a brasserie-style restaurant, bookshop, exhibition area, and original craft market. Free lunchtime concerts can be heard in the famous church. Tube: Embankment or Charing Cross.

The same company operates a brass-rubbing center at **All Hallows Church by the Tower,** Byward Street, E.C.3 (tel. 01/481-2928). Material and instructions are supplied. It is open on the same schedule and the prices are the same as given above. Next door to the Tower, this center is a quiet place to relax. The church is a fascinating place with a crypt museum, Roman remains, and traces of early London, including a Saxon wall pre-dating the Tower. Samuel Pepys, famed diarist, climbed the spire of this church to watch the raging fire of London in 1666. The center has a bookshop and a restaurant that is open from noon to 2 p.m. Monday to Friday. Tube: Tower Hill.

BRITISH DESIGN: Exhibitions in **The Design Centre,** 28 Haymarket, S.1.1 (tel. 01/839-8000), deal with topical design subjects of all kinds. There is an innovation center that provides a showcase for new ideas and prototypes to attract potential manufacturers and a related materials information center offering advice and information about materials. The Design Council Bookshop stocks a wide range of publications related to design, architecture, and crafts. In 1989, the Young Designers' Centre opened, providing the first permanent year-round national exhibition area dedicated to the work of design students and graduates. The Design Centre is open from 10 a.m. to 6 p.m. Monday and Tuesday, from 10 a.m. to 8 p.m. Wednesday to Saturday, and from 1 to 6 p.m. Sunday. Tube: Piccadilly Circus.

BURLINGTON ARCADE: A door west of the Royal Academy of Arts is the Burlington Arcade, W.1 (tel. 01/427-3568), which was built in 1819 by Lord George Cavendish. The bawdy Londoners of those days threw rubbish over the garden wall, particularly oyster shells, so he built the arcade as a deterrent—history's most expensive antigarbage campaign. The arcade is now an ancient monument protected by Her Majesty. You can wander at leisure through this holdover from Regency London, checking out each of its 38 shops for some antique or bric-a-brac. It's a concentrated bit of luxury. Who knows what might happen? Mary Ann Evans—alias George Eliot the novelist—met the journalist, George Lewes, in Jeff's Bookshop. They were lovers until he died in 1866. Charles Dickens commented on the arcade and its double row of shops, "like a Parisian passage," in his 1879 guide to London.

Pomp and ceremony may be departing, but if you linger in the arcade until 5:30 in the afternoon, you can watch the beadles, those ever-present attendants in their black-and-yellow livery and top hats, ceremoniously put in place the iron grills that block off the arcade until 9 the next morning, when they just as ceremoniously remove them, marking the start of a new business day. Also at 5:30 p.m., a hand-bell called the Burlington Bell is sounded, signaling the end of trading. It's run by one of the three beadles, the last of London's top-hatted policemen and Britain's oldest police force. They maintain the old Regency laws of courtesy. For fun, American tourists like to tease them with singing, running, and making merry. They are punished with "a polite telling off" (the origin of the phrase). Tube: Piccadilly Circus.

CARNABY STREET: You may be too young to remember Mary Quant, but she launched Carnaby Street back in the 1960s with her daring fashions that helped earn London the title of "swinging." Well, Carnaby Street is still here, and it's a vehicle-free pedestrian shopping mall today, displaying shop after shop of fashions for the young. And even Mary Quant (who has dozens and dozens of shops in Japan today) has returned with the **Mary Quant Colour Shop,** 21 Carnaby St., W.1 (tel. 01/494-3277), selling cosmetics, accessories, and some clothing, especially provocative swimwear. Even if you don't buy anything (highly unlikely), Carnaby Street still is good for an afternoon stroll. Tube: Oxford Circus.

CHILDREN: The largest specialist children's bookshop in Britain is the **Children's Book Centre Ltd.,** 237 Kensington High St., W.8 (tel. 01/937-7497). A feature of the shop is that fiction, both hardcover and paperback, is arranged according to age. The shop is open from 9:30 a.m. to 6 p.m. Monday to Saturday. Tube: High Street Kensington.

Hamleys of Regent Street, 188-196 Regent St., W.1 (tel. 01/734-3161), is an Ali Baba's cave of toys and games, ranging from electronic games and Star Wars robots on the ground floor to different toys on each of the other floors—table and card games, teddy bears, nursery animals, dolls, and outdoor games. The Hamleys train races around the walls. Tube: Oxford Circus.

CHINA: The firm of **Lawleys,** 154 Regent St., W.1 (tel. 01/734-3184), offers a wide range of English bone china, as well as crystal and giftware. They specialize in Royal Doulton, Minton, Royal Crown Derby, Wedgwood, and Aynsley china; crystal by Webb Corbett, Stuart, Waterford, Brierley, and Edinburgh; and Lladró figures. They also sell cutlery. Tube: Piccadilly Circus or Oxford Circus.

The legendary name of **Wedgwood** is in plentiful supply with its merchandise in London. Waterford Wedgwood has three large shops, all within a few hundred yards of Piccadilly Circus. There you can see a huge range of Wedgwood tableware, including Jasper, and Waterford crystal, along with giftware in bone china. Wedgwood porcelain figures are always popular, as are cameos in classical motifs (often dating from the 1700s). The shops are Waterford Wedgwood, 266 Regent St., W.1 (tel. 01/734-5656), Waterford Wedgwood, 158 Regent St., W.1 (tel. 01/734-7262), and Gered Wedgwood, 173-174 Piccadilly, W.1 (tel. 01/629-2614). Tube: Piccadilly Circus.

CHOCOLATES: The best chocolates in the world are arguably those made by **Charbonnel et Walker Ltd.,** 28 Old Bond St., W.1 (tel. 01/491-0939). They'll send messages of thanks or love, spelled out on the chocolates themselves. The staff at this bow-fronted shop on the corner of the Royal Arcade off Old Bond Street will help you choose from a variety of centers. A box is priced by weight. They have ready-made presentation boxes as well. Tube: Green Park.

Prestat, 14 Princes Arcade, S.W.1 (tel. 01/629-4838), is chocolate maker "to Her Majesty the Queen by appointment." Why not impress your friends by taking home a box of assorted Napoleon truffles or an assortment of connoisseur chocolates? Coffee or double mints and brandy cherries may tempt you. The boxes give Prestat products an extra touch of elegance. Tube: Bond Street.

COVENT GARDEN ENTERPRISES: In the Central Market Building, an impressive array of shops, pubs, and other attractions operates. For the shops listed below, take the tube to, of course, Covent Garden.

Contemporary Applied Arts, 43 Earlham St., W.C.2 (tel. 01/836-6993), is an association of Britain's best craftspeople that is pioneering in its energetic encouragement of contemporary artwork, both traditional and progressive. The galleries at the center are used to house a diverse retail display of members' work that includes glass, rugs, lights, ceramics for both use and decoration, fabric, clothing, papers, metalwork, and jewelry—all selected from the work of the most outstanding artisans currently producing in the country. There is also a program of special exhibitions that focus on innovations in the crafts. The center is open Monday to Saturday from 10 a.m. to 5:30 p.m.

The **General Store,** 111 Long Acre, W.C.2 (tel. 01/240-0331), offers thousands of ideas for gifts and souvenirs with prices of a few pence to several pounds. It is ideally situated in Covent Garden, and because of the entertainment nature of the area, the store offers extended trading hours: from 10 a.m. to 11:30 p.m. Monday to Saturday and 11 a.m. to 7 p.m. Sunday. The store also features The Green & Pleasant soup and salad restaurant.

The Market, Covent Garden, W.C.2 (tel. 01/836-9136), is a specialty shopping and catering center with 40 stalls selling antiques on Monday and craft goods Tuesday to Saturday. Shopping hours are from 10 a.m. to 7 p.m. Street entertainers perform daily.

The Bead Shop, 43 Neal St., W.C.2 (tel. 01/240-0931), specializes in loose beads and stones, providing the fittings, clasps, and strings to make necklaces and earrings.

Naturally British, 13 New Row, W.C.2 (tel. 01/240-0551), is owned and run by Jon Blake, who claims with total conviction that everything he sells is truly British—pottery, jewelry, knitwear, honey, toys, glass, woodwork, rocking horses, and wrought ironwork—products of Britain's Cottage Industry, fine for gifts.

The **Glasshouse,** 65 Long Acre, W.C.2 (tel. 01/836-9785), sells beautiful glass and also invites visitors into the workshops to see the craftspeople producing their wares. At street level, passersby can see glassblowers at work.

Penhaligon's, 41 Wellington St., W.C.2 (tel. 01/836-2150), established in 1870 as a Victorian perfumery, holds Royal Warrants to H.R.H. the Duke of Edinburgh and H.R.H. the Prince of Wales. It offers a large selection of perfumes, aftershaves, soaps, and bath oils for men and women. Perfect gifts include antique silver perfume bottles.

Behind the Warehouse off Neal Street runs a narrow road leading to **Neal's Yard,** a mews of warehouses that seems to retain some of the old London atmosphere. The open warehouses display such goods as vegetables, health foods, fresh-baked breads, cakes, sandwiches, and in an immaculate dairy, the largest variety of flavored cream cheeses you are likely to encounter.

The **Royal School of Needlework,** 5 King St., W.C.2 (tel. 01/240-3186), offers in kit form many of the almost-classic tapestry designs bequeathed to them by such designers as Burne-Jones and William Morris. The school also has a design stu-

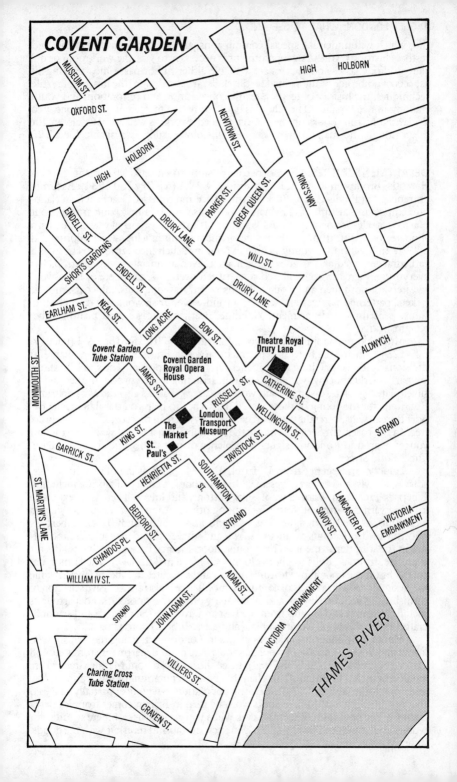

dio, which will undertake special commissions, and a workroom that repairs and restores historic textiles. An appointment is necessary to visit the workroom or design studio. Classes and courses are available either full or part time, covering all aspects of embroidery and related textile skills, art and design, the history of textile techniques, the history of textiles, textile conservation and restoration, and youth training in needle skills. The school is open from 10 a.m. to 5:30 p.m. Monday to Friday. Numerous books on the subject of needlework, as well as materials, are for sale through the mail-order service. A full-color catalog is available for £2.25 ($3.95).

DEPARTMENT STORES: The department store to end all department stores is **Harrods,** Brompton Road, at Knightsbridge, S.W.1 (tel. 01/730-1234). As firmly entrenched in English life as Buckingham Palace and the Ascot Races, it is an elaborate emporium, at times as fascinating as a museum. In a magazine article about Harrods, a salesperson was quoted as saying: "It's more of a sort of way of life than a shop, really." Aside from the fashion department (including high-level tailoring and a "Way In" section for young people), you'll find such incongruous sections as a cathedral-ceilinged and arcaded meat market, even a funeral service. Harrods has everything: men's custom-tailored suits, tweed overcoats, cashmere or lambswool sweaters for both men and women, handstitched traveling bags, raincoats, mohair jackets, patterned ski sweaters, scarves of hand-woven Irish wool, pewter reproductions, a perfumery department, "lifetime" leather suitcases, and pianos. Tube: Knightsbridge.

Much more economical, however, is **Selfridges,** 400 Oxford St., W.1 (tel. 01/629-1234), one of the biggest department stores in Europe, with more than 300 divisions, selling everything from artificial flowers to groceries. The specialty shops are particularly enticing, with good buys in Irish linen, Wedgwood, leather goods, silver-plated goblets, cashmere and woolen scarves. There's also the Miss Selfridge Boutique, for the young or those who'd like to be. To help you travel light, the Export Bureau will air-freight your purchases to anywhere in the world, completely tax free. In the basement Services Arcade the London Tourist Board will help you find your way around London's sights with plenty of maps, tips, and friendly advice. Tube: Bond Street.

Liberty, on Regent Street, W.1 (tel. 01/734-1234), is famous for its fabrics, scarves, shawls, and Liberty Presents. On one floor is a choice of fabrics, including Liberty's Tana lawn, Varuna wool, silks, cottons, and linens. There is an extensive knitting yarn department, featuring, among others, Anny Blatt, Emu, Argyll, and Velentino, as well as designer kits by Kaffe Fassett and Sandy Black. Liberty is known worldwide for its distinctive shawls and scarves, found in wool, silk, and cotton in the scarf department on the ground floor. Liberty Presents includes gifts for everyone, from rag dolls to photo albums, all made in Tana lawn. The fashion department on the floor above features dresses and separates in Liberty fabrics, while the designer room has labels of couture names. There is also an extensive selection of furnishing fabrics, bed linens, and table napery on another floor. Other departments include treasures and jewelry from the East and from Africa, modern and arts-and-crafts furniture, books, pictures, china, and glass. Tube: Oxford Circus.

Marks & Spencer has many branches in London, attracting the British, who know fine buys, especially in woolen goods. The main department store is at 458 Oxford St., W.1 (tel. 01/935-7954), three short blocks from Marble Arch. There are 268 branches in Britain. This chain has built a reputation for quality and value, and now clothes about 70% of the British population—wholly or partially! It is said that one in every four pairs of socks worn by men in Britain comes from Marks & Spencer. The prices are competitive even when you go as far as cashmere sweaters for women. All goods can be changed if you keep the tab and return it with the goods. Tube: Marble Arch.

Simpson's, 203 Piccadilly, W.1 (tel. 01/734-2002), opened in 1936 as the home of DAKS clothing, and it's been going strong ever since. It is known not only for men's wear, but women's fashions, cosmetics, perfume, jewelry, and lingerie. The clothes are of the highest quality and exude elegance and style, from casual weekend wear to a wide selection of evening dress. Tube: Piccadilly Circus.

DESIGNER CLOTHING (SECONDHAND): A London institution since it was first established in the 1940s, **Pandora,** 16-22 Cheval Pl., S.W.7 (tel. 01/589-5289), stands in fashionable Knightsbridge, a stone's throw from Harrods. It features dozens of hand-me-down designer dresses, and it is generally acknowledged that this store carries the finest such merchandise in London. Several times a week, chauffeurs will drive up with bundles packed by the anonymous gentry of England. These are likely to include dresses, jackets, suits, and gowns that the ladies wish to sell. Entire generations of London women have clothed themselves at this store. One woman, voted best dressed at Ascot several years ago, was wearing a secondhand dress acquired at Pandora's. Identities of the owners are strictly guarded. Pandora is especially popular with North American women, who can buy dresses to wear back home that have only been photographed in England. Prices are generally one third to one half of their retail value. Chanel, Yves St. Laurent, and Valentino are among the designers represented. Yes, Pandora is also the drag queen's emporium. Tube: Knightsbridge.

GROCERY STORE WITH ELEGANCE: Down the street from the Ritz, **Fortnum and Mason,** 181 Piccadilly, W.2 (tel. 01/734-8040), draws the carriage trade, the well-heeled dowager from Mayfair or Belgravia who comes seeking such tinned treasures as pâté de foie gras or a boar's head. She would never set foot in a regular grocery store, but Fortnum and Mason, with its swallow-tailed attendants, is no mere grocery store: it's a British tradition dating back to 1707. In fact, the establishment likes to think that Mr. Fortnum and Mr. Mason "created a union surpassed in its importance to the human race only by the meeting of Adam and Eve." Today this store exemplifies the elegance and style one would expect from an establishment with two Royal Warrants. Enter the doors and be transported to another world of deep red carpets, crystal chandeliers, spiraling wooden staircases, and unobtrusive tail-coated assistants.

The grocery department is renowned for its impressive selection of the finest foods from around the world—the best champagne, the most scrumptious Belgian chocolates, and succulent Scottish smoked salmon. You might choose one of their wicker baskets of exclusive foods to have shipped home, perhaps through their telephone and mail-order service. You can wander through the other four floors and consider the purchase of bone china and crystal cut glass, perhaps find the perfect present in the leather or stationery departments, or reflect on the changing history of furniture, paintings, and ornaments in the antiques department. For recommendations on the restaurant facilities here, see Chapter IV. Look for the Fortnum and Mason clock outside. Tube: Piccadilly Circus or Green Park.

IRISH WARES: Northern Ireland and the Republic of Ireland are united at the **Irish Shop,** 11 Duke St., W.1 (tel. 01/935-1366), by stocking so much stuff in such a small area. Directed by Gerard Collet and Anthony Tarrant, it is a useful place for those who missed buying souvenirs in Ireland. All products are genuine. Prices are reportedly as close to those you'd pay in Ireland as possible. Merchandise ranges from china to woolens, from tea-cozies to Celtic-design jewelry set with precious stones. Waterford and Galway crystal comes in all styles and types. Belleek china and Gaelic coffee glasses, single or in a set, are also featured. You can purchase handwoven tweed by the yard. A 45- by 45-inch Irish linen tablecloth, handembroidered, will be yours for £42 ($73.50) and up. As the jerseys are all hand-knitted, you have to rummage to find the exact one to suit your particular shape and size. Also offered are Donegal tweed jackets and suits for men and women. Duke Street is off Wigmore, a street running alongside Selfridges from Oxford Street. Tube: Bond Street or Marble Arch.

JEWELRY: A family firm, **Sanford Brothers Ltd.,** 3 Holborn Bars, Old Elizabethan Houses, E.C.1 (tel. 01/405-2352), has been in business since 1923. They sell anything in jewelry, both modern and Victorian, silver of all kinds, and a fine selection of clocks and watches. The old Elizabethan buildings are one of the sights of Old London. Tube: Chancery Lane.

London Diamond Centre, 10 Hanover St., W.1 (tel. 01/629-5511), offers organized tours of a permanent exhibition, showing how diamonds are mined, cut, polished, and made into exclusive jewelry, as well as a visit to the showroom where unmounted diamonds and ready-to-wear diamond jewelry, as well as other gem jewelry from costly to inexpensive, can be purchased or ordered to your requirements. Hours are from 9:30 a.m. to 5:30 p.m. Monday to Friday and from 9:30 a.m. to 1:30 p.m. Saturday. Admission is £3.45 ($6.05) per person, the fee including a souvenir brilliant-cut zirconium (not a diamond), which you can have mounted in a 9-karat gold setting of your choice at modest cost.

KING'S ROAD: The formerly village-like main street of Chelsea, although still the cutting edge for fashion trends, has undergone yet another metamorphosis—the trendies of the '70s who replaced the hippies of the '60s have been pushed aside by the punk scene. Numerous stores sporting American clothes have sprung up along its length.

King's Road, S.W.3, starts at Sloane Square (with Peter Jones's classy department store) and meanders on for a mile before losing its personality and dissolving into drabness at a sharp bend appropriately known as World's End. Along the way you'll see the tokens of Chelsea's former claims to fame—cozy pubs, smart nightclubs and discos, coffee bars, and cosmopolitan restaurants.

The leap of King's Road to the mod throne in the late '60s came with the advent of designer Mary Quant, who scored a bull's-eye on the English as well as the world fashion target. Ms. Quant is no longer here (she's back on Carnaby Street), but what seems like a myriad of others have taken her place. More and more, however, King's Road is becoming a lineup of markets and "multistores," large or small conglomerations of in- and outdoor stands, stalls, and booths fulfilling half a dozen different functions within one building or enclosure. They spring up so fast that it's impossible to keep them tabulated. Tube: Sloane Square.

MEN'S CLOTHING: A tailor-made British suit tends to be very, very expensive. A much cheaper alternative is to go to one of the **Burton** stores found all over Britain. There are some 66 branches in the Greater London area alone. The main store is at 214 Oxford St., W.1 (tel. 01/636-8040). Ready-made suits, where a man selects first his jacket, then the trousers to match in his size, range from a low of £90 ($157.50) to a high of £140 ($245). Tube: Oxford Circus.

NOTIONS: In business since 1740, **Floris,** 89 Jermyn St., S.W.1 (tel. 01/930-2885), has floor-to-ceiling mahogany cabinets lining the walls that are architectural curiosities. They were installed relatively late in the establishment's history—1851 —long after the shop had received its Royal Warrants as suppliers to the king and queen. The business was started by an 18th-century Minorcan entrepreneur, Juan Floris, who brought from his Mediterranean home a technique for extracting fragrances from local flowers. Fashionable residents of St. James's flocked to his shop, purchasing his soaps, perfumes, and grooming aids. Today, you can buy essences of flowers grown in English gardens, including stephanotis, rose geranium, lily of the valley, violet, Madagascar white jasmine, and carnation. Other items include cologne for men, badger-hair shaving brushes, ivory comb-and-brush sets, Chinese cloisonné, and combs made of wood. Open from 9:30 a.m. to 5:30 p.m. Monday to Friday, 9:30 a.m. to 4 p.m. Saturday. Tube: Piccadilly Circus.

OLD MAPS AND ENGRAVINGS: Antique maps, engravings, and atlases of all parts of the world are sold at **The Map House,** 54 Beauchamp Pl., S.W.3 (tel. 01/589-4325). The shop also has a vast selection of old prints of London and England, as well as engravings of flowers, birds, hunting scenes, lawyers, sports, and numerous other subjects. It's an ideal place to find an offbeat souvenir of your visit. The Map House is open from 9:45 a.m. to 5:45 p.m. Monday to Friday and from 10:30 a.m. to 5 p.m. on Saturday. Tube: Knightsbridge.

The **Record Office and History Library of the Greater London Council,** 40 Northampton Rd., E.C.1 (tel. 01/633-7193), in Clerkenwell, sells reproductions of old maps and prints of London. The office has archives, maps, history books, and photographs. Open Tuesday to Friday. Tube: Farringdon.

PHILATELY: A magnificent collection of postage stamps and allied material is at the **National Postal Museum,** King Edward Building, King Edward Street, E.C.1 (tel. 01/239-5420), open Monday to Thursday from 9:30 a.m. to 4:30 p.m. and to 4 p.m. on Friday. It also sells postcards illustrating the collection and has a distinctive Maltese Cross postmark first used on the Penny Black. A letter mailed from Heathrow Airport is franked at Hounslow with an attractive Concorde cancellation. In country areas, the post office provides a post bus service between many remote and otherwise isolated villages. Often passenger tickets are cancelled with a special stamp of collector interest; and postcards, depicting places of interest along the routes, are issued and mailed from these buses. Many of the narrow-gauge and privately owned railways in the country issue and cancel their own more specialized stamps. Among these are the Ravenglass and Eskdale, the Keighley and Worth Valley Light Railway, and the Bluebell Railway, along with the Romney, Hythe, and Dymchurch Railway. Tube: St. Paul's.

POSTERS: A fine collection of posters is offered at the **London Transport Museum Shop,** Covent Garden, W.C.2 (tel. 01/379-6344), open daily from 10 a.m. to 5:45 p.m., except the Christmas holidays. This unique shop carries a wide range of posters. The London Underground maps in their original size can be purchased here for £6 ($10.50), as well as massive pictorial posters as seen at tube stations (size: 40 inches by 60 inches) for £10 ($17.50). The shop also carries books, cards, T-shirts, and other souvenir items. Tube: Covent Garden.

PRINCES ARCADE: If you like "one-stop" shopping, you may be drawn to the Princes Arcade, which was opened by Edward VII when he was Prince of Wales in 1883. Between Jermyn Street and Piccadilly, in the heart of London, S.W.1, it has been restored. Wrought-iron lamps light your way as you search through some 20 bow-fronted shops, looking for that special curio (say, a 16th-century nightcap) or a pair of shoes made by people who have been satisfying royal tastes since 1847. A small sign hanging from a metal rod indicates what kind of merchandise a particular store sells. Tube: Piccadilly Circus.

SAINT CHRISTOPHER'S PLACE: One of London's most interesting and little-known (to the foreign visitor) shopping streets is Saint Christopher's Place, W.1. It lies just off Oxford Street—walk down Oxford from Selfridges toward Oxford Circus, ducking north along Gees Court across Barrett Street. There you will be surrounded by antique markets and good shops for women's clothing and accessories. The nearest tube is Bond Street.

SILVER: Looking for modern or antique items? The **London Silver Vaults,** Chancery Lane, W.C.2 (tel. 01/242-3844), were established in Victoria's day (1882) and soon became the largest silver vaults in the world. You can shop in vault after vault for that special treasure. The vaults are open Monday to Friday from 9 a.m. to 5:30 p.m. and on Saturday to 12:30 p.m. Tube: Chancery Lane.

SOUVENIRS: Charles Dickens enthusiasts can go to the **Old Curiosity Shop,** 13-14 Portsmouth St., off Lincoln's Inn Fields, W.C.2 (tel. 01/405-9891), used by Dickens as the abode of Little Nell. One of the original Tudor buildings still remaining in London and built in 1567, the shop crams every nook and cranny with general knickknackery, whatnots, and souvenirs, including Charles Dickens's first editions. A popular item is an unframed silhouette of a Dickens character. Horse brasses are also sold, as are Old Curiosity Shop bookmarks and ashtrays with Dickensian engravings. The shop is open every day of the week, including Sunday and holidays. Tube: Holborn.

STREET MARKETS: Street markets have played an important part in the life of London. They are recommended not only for bric-a-brac, but as a low-cost adventure. In fact, you don't have to buy a thing. But be warned, some of the stallkeepers are mighty convincing. Here are the best ones:

Portobello Road Market

This Saturday market is one of the city's most popular flea markets. Take the Notting Hill Gate tube to Portobello Road (W.11). Here you'll enter a hurly-burly world of stall after stall selling curios to tempt even the staunchest penny-pincher. Items include everything from the military uniforms worn by the Third Bavarian Lancers to English soul food. Some of the stallholders are antiquarians, with shops in fashionable Kensington, Belgravia, and Chelsea, and they know the price of everything. Feel free to bargain, however. A popular pastime is dropping in for a pint of ale at one of the Portobello pubs. The best time to visit is on a Saturday. The market is open Monday to Saturday from 7 a.m. to 6 p.m. and on Thursday until 1 p.m.

New Caledonian Market

Commonly known as the **Bermondsey Market** because of its location, this street market is on the corner of Long Lane and Bermondsey Street, S.E.1. At its extreme east end, it begins at Tower Bridge Road. This is one of Europe's outstanding street markets in size and quality of goods offered. The stalls are well known, and many dealers come into London from the country. The market gets under way on Friday at 7 a.m. The most serious bargain-hunters are the early birds. Antiques and other items are generally lower in price here than at Portobello Road and the other street markets, but bargains are gone by 9 a.m. The market closes at noon. It's best reached by taking the Underground to London Bridge station, then take bus 78 or walk down Bermondsey Street.

Petticoat Lane

On Sunday between 9 a.m. and 2 p.m. (go before noon), throngs of shoppers join the crowds on Petticoat Lane (also known as Middlesex Street, E.1). The lanes begin at Liverpool Street Station on the Bishopsgate side. Here you can buy clothing, food, antiques, and plenty of junk. Tube: Liverpool Street, Aldgate, or Aldgate East.

Camden Passage

This antique bric-a-brac market in Islington, N.1 (in back of the Angel), northeast of Bloomsbury, is open from 9 a.m. to 6 p.m. Monday to Saturday. The best time to visit is on Saturday market day. On all days, the emphasis is on books, prints, drawings, paintings, antiques, and similar items. Prices are not inexpensive, but there are bargains to be found if you look carefully through the more than 50 shops and 20 boutiques. Take the Northern Line tube to the Angel stop.

Jubilee Market

At Covent Garden Piazza, W.C.2, this is a small general market operating from 9 a.m. to 5 p.m. Monday to Saturday. Antiques are sold on Monday, crafts on Saturday, and various items on other days. Tube: Covent Garden.

Camden Lock

On Chalk Farm Road, Camden Lock, N.W. 6, is a five-minute walk from the Camden Town Underground station. It's a smaller and cozier version of Portobello. The stallkeepers sell old silver, jewelry, and other crafts, as well as unusual boots and shoes, even homemade cakes. This market is more out of the way than those previously recommended. Young women with spiky psychedelic hair stalk between the stalls, and you have the impression that sales are not vital to the stallkeepers but are more a perk in life, the cream on the trifle. It's well worth a visit just for the atmosphere. They are open all day Saturday and Sunday.

Leather Lane

Leather Lane, E.C.1 (tube: Chancery Lane), is open from 11 a.m. to 3 p.m., Monday to Saturday. It provides a bewildering array of clothes, furniture, and food, plus plenty of atmosphere. The lane is patronized mainly by local office workers, but also is colorful to the foreign visitor as well.

WOOLENS: One of the best and most obvious places in London for quality tweeds and woolens is **Scotch House,** 84 Regent St., S.W.1 (tel. 01/734-0203), with merchandise carefully crafted from the finest of Scotland's excellent woolen goods. Men's tweed blazers are a particular lure here, as well as woolens sold by the yard in patterns or plaids. There's also men's rainwear plus a good children's department for that tam o'shanter. The house stocks a full selection of sweaters and knitwear in cashmere and wool for both men and women. Tube: Piccadilly Circus.

Westaway & Westaway, near the British Museum at 62-65 Great Russell St., W.C.1 (tel. 01/405-0479), is a substitute for a shopping trip to Scotland. They stock an enormous range of kilts, scarves, waistcoats, capes, dressing gowns, and rugs in authentic clan tartans. What's more, they are knowledgeable on the subject of these minutely intricate clan symbols. They also sell superb—and untartaned—cashmere, camel-hair, and Shetland knitwear, along with Harris tweed jackets, Burberry raincoats, and cashmere overcoats for men. Another branch is at 92-93 Great Russell St., W.C.1. Tube: Tottenham Court Road.

---

3. London After Dark

London is crammed with nighttime entertainment. You'll have a wide choice of action—from the dives of Soho to elegant clubs. So much depends on your taste, pocketbook, and even the time of year. Nowhere else will you find such a panorama of legitimate theaters, operas, concerts, gambling clubs, discos, vaudeville at Victorian music halls, striptease joints, jazz clubs, folk music cafés, nightclubs, and ballrooms. For information about any of these events, ask a newsstand dealer for a copy of *Time Out* or *What's On in London,* containing listings of restaurants, theaters, and nightclubs.

THEATERS

The fame of the English theater has spread far and wide. In London, you'll have a chance to see it on its home ground. You may want to spend a classical evening with the National Theatre Company (formerly the Old Vic), or you may settle for a new play. You might even want to catch up on that Broadway musical you missed in New York, or be an advance talent scout for next year's big Stateside hit.

You can either purchase your ticket from the theater's box office (the most recommended method), or else from a ticket agent, such as the one at the reservations desk of American Express (with agent's fee charges, however). In a few theaters, you can reserve your spot in the gallery, the cheapest seats of all, but in some cases the inexpensive seats are sold only on the day of performance. This means that you'll have to buy your ticket earlier in the day, and—as you don't get a reserved seat—return about an hour before the performance and queue up for the best gallery seats. Occasionally you can enjoy a preshow staged by strolling performers called "buskers"—next year's Chaplins, or last year's (the theater has its peaks and valleys).

If you want to see two shows in one day, you'll find that Wednesday, Thursday, and Saturday are always crammed with matinee performances. Many West End theaters begin their evening performances at 7:30.

Students and senior citizens get a break at most theaters (subject to availability) by being granted a discount at the local box offices. Discounted tickets are sometimes offered for all comers, but only to long-running plays on their last legs or to new "dogs," which you may not want to see anyway. A really hot musical in its early life will almost never offer discounted tickets. Discounted tickets tend to be especially available for matinees.

Of London's many theaters, these are particularly outstanding:

The **National Theatre,** South Bank, S.E.1 (tel. 01/633-0880; for ticket information, 01/928-2252 or 01/928-8156), is a concrete cubist fortress, a three-theater complex that stands as a $32-million landmark beside the Waterloo Bridge on the south bank of the Thames. It was first suggested in 1848, and it took Parliament 101 years to pass a bill vowing government support. Flaring out like a fan, the most thrilling theater in this complex is the **Olivier,** named after Lord Laurence Olivier, its first director when the company was born in 1962. (Olivier was succeeded in 1973 by Sir Peter Hall, who created the Royal Shakespeare Company.) The Olivier Theatre bears a resemblance in miniature to an ancient Greek theater. It has an open stage and seats 1160. The **Cottesloe** is a simple box theater for 400 people. Finally, the 890-seat **Lyttelton** is a traditional proscenium arch house that doesn't have one bad seat for any theater-goer. In the foyers there are three bookshops, eight bars, a restaurant, and five self-service buffets (some open all day, except Sunday), and many outside terraces with river views. For everyone, with or without tickets for a play, there is live foyer music, free, before evening performances and Saturday matinees, and free exhibitions. The foyers are open 10 a.m. to 11 p.m., except Sunday. Also, guided theater tours are available daily, including backstage areas, for £2.50 ($4.40).

Tickets range from £6.50 ($11.40) to £14 ($24.50), and midweek matinees are £5 ($8.75). Some tickets are available on the day of the performance at £6.50 ($11.40) and £9 ($15.75). You can have a meal in the National Theatre Restaurant for around £13.50 ($23.65). Tube: Waterloo Station.

You may also be interested in the activities of the **National Film Theatre,** S.E.1 (tel. 01/928-3232), in the same South Bank complex. More than 2000 films a year from all over the world are shown here, including features, shorts, animation, and documentaries. A visitor can obtain daily membership at 40p (70¢). If booked in advance, tickets cost £3.25 ($5.70), or standby tickets can be obtained half an hour before a performance at £3 ($5.25). Tube: Waterloo Station.

MOMI, the Museum of the Moving Image, underneath Waterloo Bridge, S.E.1 (tel. 01/401-2636), is also part of the South Bank complex. Tracing the history of the development of cinema and television, MOMI takes the visitor on a journey from cinema's earliest experiments to modern animation, from Charlie Chaplin to the operation of a TV studio. There are artifacts to handle, buttons to push, and a cast of actors to tell visitors more. Admission is £3.25 ($5.70) for adults and £2.50

($4.40) for children. There is also a £10 ($17.50) family ticket. The museum is open from 10 a.m. to 8 p.m. Tuesday to Saturday and from 10 a.m. to 6 p.m. Sunday and bank holidays. It is closed Monday. Allow two hours for a visit. Tube: Waterloo Station.

The Old Vic, a 170-year-old theater on Waterloo Road, S.E.1 (tel. 01/928-2651, or the box office at 01/928-7616), underwent a mammoth facelift and modernization. The facade and much of the interior were restored in their original early 19th-century style, and most of the modernization was behind the scenes. The proscenium arch was moved back, and the stage trebled in size, and more seats and stage boxes added. It is air-conditioned and contains five bars. There are short seasons of varied plays, and several subscription offers have been introduced with reductions of up to 55% of regular prices. Otherwise, top prices vary, with the best stalls or dress circle seats going for about £15 ($26.25) a ticket. Tube: Waterloo Station.

The **Royal Shakespeare Company** has its famous theater in Stratford-upon-Avon and is also housed in the Barbican Centre, E.C.2 (tube to Barbican or Moorgate; tel. 01/638-8891 in London or 0789/295623 in Stratford-upon-Avon). This is the single theater group in Britain that most seriously concentrates on the theatrical works of the Bard, although it presents works by such relatively modern playwrights as Jean Genet. Plays run in repertoire and are presented two or three times a week each. The company also has three smaller theaters, where new and experimental plays are performed as well as classics: The Other Place and the new Swan Theatre, as well as the famous main (Memorial) theater in Stratford-upon-Avon, and The Pit at the Barbican Centre. Travel to Stratford from London's Euston Station is possible via the Shakespeare Connection, plus a theater/hotel/restaurant package available through the Shakespeare Stopover (tel. 0789/414999).

Royal Court Theatre, Sloane Square, S.W.1 (tel. 01/730-1745; take tube to Sloane Square), has been operated by the English Stage Company for more than 30 years. The emphasis is on new playwrights (John Osborne got his start here with the 1956 production of *Look Back in Anger*). Also on the premises is the Theatre Upstairs, the studio theater also devoted to the work of new playwrights. Prices of tickets are £5 ($8.75), £7 ($12.25), £9 ($15.75), and £12 ($21). At the Theatre Upstairs, the tickets go for £3 ($5.25) to £6 ($10.50). Shows are at 8 p.m. daily, 4 and 8 p.m. on Saturday downstairs; 7:30 p.m. daily and 3:30 and 7:30 p.m. on Saturday for the Theatre Upstairs; closed Monday.

The Young Vic, 66 The Cut, Waterloo, S.E.1 (tel. 01/928-6363), aims primarily at the 15 to 25 age group, but many older and younger people use the theater as well. The Young Vic's repertoire includes such authors as Shakespeare, Ben Jonson, Arthur Miller, and Harold Pinter, plus specially written new plays. Performances normally begin at 7:30 p.m. Seats cost £7.50 ($13.15), reduced to £3.75 ($6.55) for students and children. Tube: Waterloo Station.

Sadler's Wells Theatre, Rosebery Avenue, E.C.1 (box office tel. 01/278-8916), is on a site where a theater has stood since 1683, a short walk from Camden Passage. Resident companies—Sadler's Wells Royal Ballet and the new Sadler's Wells Opera (producing light opera, operetta, and fresh productions of that most English of theatrical institutions, the work of Gilbert and Sullivan)—are complemented by a program of British and foreign dance, opera, and ballet. Seats are offered at prices ranging from £4 ($7) to £20 ($35), the average being £16 ($28). Performances generally begin at 7:30 p.m. Reach the theater by the Angel tube or bus 19 or 38 from Piccadilly, Charing Cross, or Holborn.

Whitehall Theatre at the top of Whitehall, S.W.1 (tel. 01/930-7765), just off Trafalgar Square, has been restored to its original 1930s art deco glory. To the splendid auditorium has been added continental seating (620 seats) to allow greater comfort and more legroom for the audience. Air conditioning has been installed and the bar areas considerably enlarged. Tube: Charing Cross.

Many theaters will accept bookings by telephone if you give your name and credit-card number when you call. Then all you have to do is go along before the performance to collect your tickets, which will be sold at the theater price. All theater booking agencies charge a fee. Once confirmed, the booking will be charged to your account even if you don't use the tickets. Only cardholders can collect the tickets charged to their accounts.

OPEN-AIR ENTERTAINMENT

As the name indicates, **Regent's Park,** N.W.1 (tel. 01/486-2431), is an outdoor theater right in the center of Regent's Park. The setting is idyllic, and the longest theater bar in London provides both drink and food. Performances are given in June, July, and August only, evenings at 7:45, matinees on Wednesday, Thursday, and Saturday at 2:30 p.m. Presentations are mainly Shakespeare, usually in period costume. Both seating and acoustics are excellent. If it rains, you're given tickets for another performance. Prices are from £4.50 ($7.90) to £11 ($19.25). Tube: Baker Street.

The **Holland Park Open Air Theatre** is a charming stage in the park, W.8, close to the Commonwealth Institute. It really has the air of a court theater in some Renaissance palace yard, with the added attraction of a high-tensile fabric canopy covering the stage, seating stand, and bar area. There is a mixed program from June to August of dance, opera, and drama. Shows begin at 7:30 p.m. daily, Saturday matinees starting at 2:30 p.m. The Dutch Garden is floodlit until midnight, and there are two art galleries in the park open from 11 a.m. to 7 p.m. For program inquiries, phone 01/602-7856. Tube: Kensington High Street.

OPERA AND BALLET

The central shrine is the **Royal Opera House,** a classical building on Bow Street, W.C.2, actually the northeast corner of Covent Garden, which was London's first square, laid out by Inigo Jones as a residential piazza. Until a few years ago, the whole area was a thriving fruit and vegetable market, originally started by nuns selling surplus stocks from their convent garden. In the 16th century, the section became fashionable to live in and was soon to become one of the centers of London nightlife. The first theater was built on the present site in 1732. The existing opera house, one of the most beautiful theaters in Europe, was built in 1858 and is now the home of the Royal Opera and Royal Ballet, the leading international opera and ballet companies. Newspapers give full details of performances. The Opera House advance box office, at 48 Floral St., W.C.2 (tel. 01/240-1066), is open from 10 a.m. to 8 p.m. Monday to Saturday. Seat prices range from £1 ($1.75) to £37 ($64.75) for ballet, from £2.50 ($4.40) to £75 ($131.25) for opera. Tube: Covent Garden.

English National Opera, London Coliseum, St. Martin's Lane, W.C.2 (tel. 01/836-3161 for reservations, or 01/240-5258 for inquiries and credit-card booking), is one of the two national opera companies. It resides at the London Coliseum, London's largest and most splendid theater, built in 1904 as a variety theater and converted into an opera house in 1968. It performs a wide range of works, from great classics to operetta to world premieres, and every performance is in English. A repertory of 18 to 20 productions is presented five or six nights a week for 11 months of the year. Balcony tickets are available for as little as £2.50 ($4.40), but many visitors prefer the upper circle or dress circle at about £12.50 ($21.90) to £14 ($24.50). During the opera season, usually from August to June, about 100 cheap seats in the balcony are held for sale on the day of performance, from 10 a.m. Tube: Charing Cross or Leicester Square.

The **Barbican Centre,** The Barbican, E.C.2, is considered the largest art and exhibition center in Western Europe. It was created to make a perfect setting in which to enjoy good music and theater from comfortable, roomy seating. The theater is the London home of the Royal Shakespeare Company, already mentioned, which performs a wide range of works other than plays of the Bard. The Concert Hall is the permanent home of the London Symphony Orchestra and host to visiting orchestras and performers. As well as the art gallery, there are free foyer exhibitions and performances, including jazz at lunchtime Sunday. For quieter moments, the center has a rare and beautiful conservatory open to the public on Saturday, Sunday, and some other days. Hall seat prices range from £4 ($7) to £18.50 ($32.40). Theater matinee prices go from £5 ($8.75) to £13 ($22.75), and evening prices are from £6 ($10.50) to £15 ($26.25).

There are several bars, a self-service café with a lakeside terrace, and a restaurant (see my restaurant recommendations in Chapter IV). The following numbers will be useful: 01/638-8891 for the box office, 01/628-9760 or 01/628-2295 for 24-hour recorded information about the performances, and 01/638-4141, ext. 218, for general help from the information desk. Tube: Moorgate or Barbican. (Barbican tube is closed Sunday and public holidays.)

CONCERTS

In recent years the musical focal point in London has shifted to a superbly specialized complex of buildings on the South Bank side of Waterloo Bridge, S.E.1. This Cultural Centre—including pleasure gardens and the National Film Theatre —houses three of the most stylish, comfortable, and acoustically perfect concert structures in the world: the **Royal Festival Hall,** the **Queen Elizabeth Hall,** and the **Purcell Room.** Here, more than 1,200 performances a year are presented, and it's not all classical music. Included are ballet, jazz, popular classics, pop, and folk. The Royal Festival Hall is open from 10 a.m. every day and offers an extensive range of things to see and do. There are free exhibitions in the foyers and free lunchtime music from 12:30 to 2 p.m., plus guided tours of the building, and book, record, and gift shops. The Festival Buffet has a wide selection of food at reasonable prices, and there are several bars throughout the foyers. The office that prebooks with credit cards is open daily from 10 a.m. to 9 p.m. (tel. 01/928-8800). Tickets range from £4 ($7) to £20 ($35). Tube: Waterloo Station.

Royal Albert Hall, Kensington Gore, S.W.7 (tel. 01/589-8218), opened in 1871, dedicated to the memory of Queen Victoria's consort, Prince Albert. The building encircles one of the world's largest and finest auditoriums, with a seating capacity of 5500. Home since 1941 to the BBC Promenade Concerts, the famous eight-week annual festival of classical music, it is also a popular venue for light music by stars such as Frank Sinatra and Johnny Mathis, plus the latest in rock and pop. Sport and pageantry figure strongly. Boxing events are held here, as well as covered-court lawn tennis, with the Masters Doubles Championship being played here a month after the annual Royal British Legion Festival of Remembrance. A daily guided tour costs £2.50 ($4.40). Tube: South Kensington, High Street Kensington, or Knightsbridge.

At **Wigmore Hall,** 36 Wigmore St., W.1 (tel. 01/935-2141), you'll hear excellent recitals and concerts. At this intimate auditorium, there are regular series, master concerts by chamber music groups and instrumentalists, song recital series, Sunday morning coffee concerts, and concerts featuring special composers or themes throughout the year. In summer, Wigmore Summer Nights are featured. Many good seats are in the £4 ($7) range. A free list of the month's concerts is available from the hall. Tube: Bond Street or Oxford Circus.

GILBERT AND SULLIVAN EVENINGS

The English Heritage Singers present Gilbert and Sullivan programs at the **Mansion House at Grim's Dyke,** Old Redding, Harrow Weald, Middlesex, England HA3 6DH (tel. 01/954-4227), every other Sunday in winter and every Sunday the rest of the year. This is a dinner event, costing £25 ($43.75) per person. You arrive for cocktails in the Library Bar of the house where Gilbert once lived and where he and Sullivan worked on their charming operettas. A full Edwardian-style dinner is served at 8 p.m., with costumed performances of the most beloved of Gilbert and Sullivan songs both during and after the meal. You can request favorite melodies from the Gilbert and Sullivan works. The singers know them all.

MUSIC HALLS

The atmosphere of a Victorian music hall is recaptured at **The Cockney Club,** 18 Charing Cross Rd., W.C.2 (tel. 01/408-1001). At the whisky and gin reception, you'll have the cockles of your heart warmed and learn about "mother's ruin" (large gins). The lively waiters and waitresses join guests to sing along to the sounds of a honky-tonk piano. An East End meal, four courses of Cockney nosh, is served, along with unlimited beer and wine during dinner. Music for singing and dancing marks the evening. The show is divided into two parts, featuring cabaret with both production numbers and solo performances. The hall is open daily from 8 p.m., with dancing until midnight. The charge is £25 ($43.75) per person Sunday to Friday, £27 ($47.25) per person Saturday. Phone for reservations. Tube: Leicester Square.

The Water Rats, 328 Grays Inn Rd., W.C.1 (tel. 01/837-7269), perpetuates the world of Victorian music hall entertainment, and it's contained within a London pub famous since 1655. It is the headquarters of the Grand Order of Water Rats, a charitable organization of Britain's top variety performers. The cost of dinner and a music hall–type show is £17.50 ($30.63). If you want to go only for the show, the price is £8.50 ($14.90). It is open Monday to Saturday, with dinner served at 7:30 p.m. and the show presented at 9 p.m. On Sunday, dinner is at 7 p.m., with the show beginning at 8:30 p.m. Tube: Kings Cross.

The **Rheingold Club** thrives in a centuries-old wine cellar at Sedley Place, just off 361 Oxford St., W.1 (tel. 01/629-5343), and has a restaurant, two bars, and a good-size dance floor. The main attraction is a top-class band playing daily, except Sunday and bank holidays, from 9:30 p.m. to about 2 a.m. There is also an occasional cabaret, usually with big-time guest stars, but most of the entertainment is created by the patrons themselves. The Rheingold, founded in 1959, is the oldest and most successful "singles club" in London, existing long before the term had been coined. It is a safe place for men to take their wives or girlfriends, and single women are safe here. The club serves Viennese, German, and English food with a selection of German and French wines. The price of a three-course meal is about £8 ($14) per person, and membership for overseas visitors is available at the door at a charge of £5 ($8.75) for men and £4 ($7) for women. The club is open from 8 p.m. to 1:30 a.m. Monday and Tuesday; to 2 a.m. Wednesday, Thursday, and cabaret nights; and to 2:30 a.m. on Friday and Saturday. Take the tube to Bond Street station, use the main exit to Oxford Street, turn right, and turn right again to Sedley Place. It's only 40 yards from the station.

GAY NIGHTLIFE

The most reliable source of information on all gay clubs and activities is the **Gay Switchboard** (tel. 01/837-7324). The staff there runs a 24-hour service of information on places and activities catering openly to homosexual women and men.

For both men and women who aren't interested in bars or discos, the **London Lesbian & Gay Centre,** 67 Cowcross St., E.C.1 (tel. 01/608-1471), is the best bet. It is open Tuesday from 5:30 to 11 p.m.; Wednesday, Thursday, and Sunday from noon to 11 p.m.; Friday from noon to midnight; and Saturday from noon to 2 a.m. It is closed Monday. Entrance fee is 30p (55¢). Annual membership is £15 ($26.25), but you don't have to be a member to use the facilities. A women-only disco is held Saturday night and a mixed disco (called a tea dance) on Sunday night. Different courses, meetings, and activities take place in meeting rooms, and the café and bar area is open all the time. Tube: Farringdon.

Madame Jo Jo's, 8 Brewer St., W.1 (tel. 01/734-2473), is set side by side with some of Soho's more explicit girlie shows. Madame Jo Jo also presents "girls," but they are likely to be in drag. This is London's most popular transvestite show, with revues staged nightly at 12:15 a.m. and 1:15 a.m. The club itself, with its popular piano bar, is open Monday to Saturday from 10 p.m. to 3 a.m. Entrance ranges from

£6 ($10.50) to £8 ($14) per person, depending on the night of the week, and drinks cost around £3.50 ($6.15) each. Tube: Piccadilly Circus.

One club that welcomes overseas visitors, **The Heaven,** The Arches, Villiers Street, Charing Cross, W.C.2 (tel. 01/839-3852), is still considered the largest and most high-energy disco in Europe. It is a world of fantastic lasers, lights, and sounds. Unlike many other discos, which make Monday night gay night, Heaven makes every Monday straight night. Tuesday through Saturday is gay, although straight couples are welcomed and admitted as well. It is closed on Sunday. The entrance fee ranges from £2 ($3.50) to £5 ($8.75). Tube: Charing Cross Road.

NIGHTCLUBS

The night scene of London changes so rapidly that it's difficult to keep abreast of it. There are several general situations to keep in mind.

First, the English are strongly addicted to jazz, and there are several clubs ("dives") where you can fill up on a variety of jazz, whether it be the old-fashioned Louis Armstrong–type or progressive. Many a rendezvous for jazz enthusiasts is found in Soho, right off Shaftesbury Avenue. Few are licensed for alcohol, so you'll have to adjust in some cases to soft drinks as you get lost in rhythmic forces.

There are several kinds of nightclubs where you can eat or drink, be entertained or allowed to dance—even gamble. Most often these clubs are private. To avoid the unpopular early closing hour (11 p.m.) for licensed public establishments, the private club has come into existence (many stay open till 3 and 4 a.m.). In most cases the clubs welcome overseas visitors, granting them a temporary membership with proof of identity and perhaps a nominal charge. Many clubs offer dinner, a show, and dancing. Inquire before you commit yourself. No visitor to London should be afraid to ask about membership in a private club. After all, most of the clubs are in business to make money—and welcome foreign patronage. Following is my survey of a range of jazz and disco clubs that charge a low membership and a nominal entrance fee.

Comedy Store, 28a Leicester Square, W.C.2 (tel. 01/839-6665), is London's most visible showcase of rising and emerging comedic talent. Set in the heart of the city's nighttime district, it announces by means of a prerecorded message the various comedians and musicians who are scheduled to appear during the upcoming week. Even if the names of the performers are unfamiliar to you (highly likely), you will still enjoy the spontaneity of live comedy performed before a live British audience. Shows (subject to change) are currently performed Thursday at 9 p.m., Friday and Saturday at 8 p.m. and midnight, and Sunday at 8:30 p.m. No reservations are accepted in advance, and tickets are sold only for the day of that performance on the day of that performance. The club opens one hour prior to each show. There are two bars. Entrance ranges from £5 ($8.75) to £6 ($10.50). Tube: Leicester Square.

A unique theater restaurant in a unique setting, that's the **Talk of London** (tel. 01/408-1001), in the New London Theatre, an entertainment complex at Parker Street, off Drury Lane, W.C.2, the heart of the city's theaterland. The restaurant is ingeniously designed so that every guest gets "the best seat in the house." By using a circular layout and varying floor levels, everyone has an uninterrupted view of the show. The Talk of London offers a complete evening's entertainment from 8 p.m. to 1 a.m., a four-course dinner of your choice, dancing to an orchestra, and an international cabaret at 10:30 p.m. All this plus coffee, service, and VAT are included in the price of £23 ($40.25) Monday to Friday and £25 ($43.75) on Saturday. Drinks are extra. Phone for reservations, which are essential. Tube: Covent Garden or Holborn.

THE DISCOS

A firmly entrenched London institution, the disco is, nevertheless, as vulnerable as the Stone of Scone. Many of them open, enjoy a quick but fast-fading popularity, then close. Some possible favorites that may still be going strong upon your arrival include the following:

Samantha's, 3 New Burlington St., W.1 (tel. 01/734-6249), lies just off Regent Street and has been one of London's most popular discos for nearly 30 years. Actually, it's two separate discos on the same premises. At street level you can drink in the cocktail lounge or else order complete meals in Rocky's Restaurant, which is open from 6 p.m. to 6:30 a.m. The club itself is open from 9 p.m. to 3:30 a.m., except Sunday. Admission ranges from £4 ($7) to £7 ($12.25) per person. Tube: Oxford Circus.

Despite a move to a new address in 1988, **The Marquee,** 105 Charing Cross Rd., W.C.2 (tel. 01/437-6601), is still one of the best-known centers for rock music in Europe. Its reputation goes back to the 1950s. Since that time, many groups, such as The Rolling Stones, got their start at The Marquee. Admission ranges from £2 ($3.50) to £6 ($10.50), depending on who is playing at the time of your visit. Within a former movie theater, the club welcomes visitors on two different floors, the lower of which slopes toward the stage to permit everyone a view of the performers. It is open nightly at 7, with a relatively early closing of 11 p.m. Tube: Leicester Square.

Limelight, 136 Shaftesbury Ave., W.1 (tel. 01/434-1761), was originally built in the 1880s of beige sandstone by the Welsh Presbyterian Church. It was deconsecrated and subsequently sold in the early 1980s, reopening as a disco in 1986. You can dance beneath the soaring dome of the interior or sip iced vodka or champagne in the circular gallery high above the spectacle below you. You can also sample a French-inspired cuisine in what used to be the crypt. The average age of the clients in this unusual place is between 25 and 30 years old. Entrance fees range from £5 ($8.75) to £10 ($17.50), depending on the night of the week. A pint of lager costs £1.50 ($2.65). The music covers a broad range of electronically impulsed styles. Tube: Leicester Square.

Le Palais, 242 Shepherd's Bush Rd., W.6 (tel. 01/748-2812), was originally built in a working-class district of north London in the 1940s, welcoming British servicemen dancing to the Big Band sound. Then, on any given night, 2500 people could be crammed onto the dance floor, said to be the biggest in Britain. But the venue has radically changed. Today, it's a popular disco, with seven bars, two restaurants, and a wide array of electronic musical styles. If you show up on a Thursday, you might be joined by dozens of persons who—reached by a computer mail service —have their birthdays during that particular week. It is open Wednesday to Saturday from 9 p.m. to either 2 or 3 a.m., depending on the night of week. Admission ranges from £4 ($5.25) to £5 ($8.75). Tube: Hammersmith.

Camden Palace, la Camden High St., N.1 (tel. 01/387-0428), is housed inside what was originally a theater. It draws an over-18 crowd, who flock in various costumes and energy levels according to the night of the week. It is open nightly, except Sunday, from 9 p.m. to 2:30 a.m., offering a rotating style of music. It's best to phone in advance for the musical genre that appeals to your taste. Styles range from rhythm-and-blues to what young rock experts call "boilerhouse," "garage music," "acid funk," "hip-hop," and "twist and shout." There's also a restaurant if you get the munchies. Tube: Camden Town or Mornington Crescent.

Stringfellows, 16-19 Upper St. Martins Lane, W.C.2 (tel. 01/240-5534), is one of London's most elegant nighttime rendezvous spots, the creation of its owner and manager, Peter Stringfellow of Hippodrome fame. It is said to have $1 million worth of velvet and high-tech gloss and glitter. In theory, it's a members-only club, but—and only at the discretion of management—nonmembers may be admitted. It offers two lively bars, a first-class restaurant, and a theater. It's been called "an exquisite oasis of elegance," and its nightclub food "the best in London"—for a nightclub, that is. Dancing starts at 11 p.m., dinner at 8 p.m., and the fun continues until 3:30 a.m. daily, except Sunday. Prices start at £9 ($14) for entrance Monday to Thursday and at £15 ($26.25) Friday and Saturday; closed Sunday. Tube: Leicester Square or Covent Garden.

In the **Hippodrome,** at the Hippodrome Corner of Charing Cross Road and

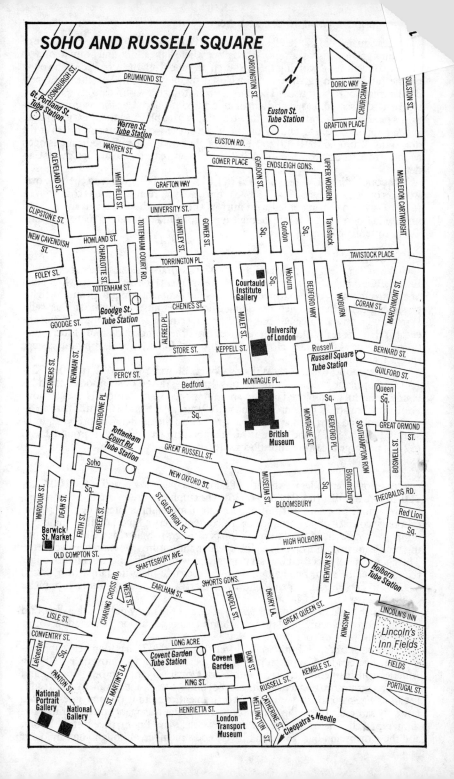

Leicester Square, W.C.2 (tel. 01/437-4311), Peter Stringfellow has created one of London's greatest discos, an enormous place where light and sound beam in on you from all directions. Revolving speakers even descend from the roof to deafen you in patches, and you can watch yourself on closed-circuit video. The Vari-lites are a spectacular treat not to be missed. There are six bars, together with a balcony restaurant, where food is served. Lasers and a hydraulically controlled stage for visiting international performers are only part of the attraction of this place. Monday is "gay night" at the Hippodrome. Depending on the night of the week, admission prices at the door range from £6 ($10.50) to £12 ($21) per person. The Hippodrome is open Monday to Saturday from 9 p.m. to 3:30 a.m. Tube: Leicester Square or Covent Garden.

Moonlighting, 17 Greek St., W.1 (tel. 01/734-6308), caters to a clientele over 21 years of age. Admission is £5 ($8.75), and once you're inside drinks cost from £1 ($1.75) at a trio of bars. Filled with mirrors and lights, this is a relatively new and untested London disco. It is open nightly, except Sunday, from 9 p.m. to 3:30 a.m. Tube: Tottenham Court Road.

EROTICISM IN SOHO

When it comes to taking it off, London is one of the breeziest, barest capitals of Europe. Soho reigns supreme in the nude department, the dives lining whole sides of the streets (many of the strippers work several joints, hustling back and forth between engagements—sometimes doing a little street hustling on the side as well). Wardour, Frith, and Greek Streets are especially strong on disrobing. Some of the cheaper dens are really bleak—far removed from the humor and camp of such nudity emporiums as the Crazy Horse Saloon in Paris. Other, more lavish houses stage spectacular numbers.

At **Raymond Revuebar,** Walker's Court, Brewer Street, W.1 (tel. 01/734-1593), proprietor Paul Raymond is considered the doyen of strip society, and his young beautiful hand-picked women are among the best in Europe. The stage show, Festival of Erotica, is presented Monday to Saturday at 8 and 10 p.m. There are licensed bars, and patrons may take their drinks into the theater. The price of admission is £15 ($26.25), and there is no membership fee. Whisky is around £1.50 ($2.65) per large measure. Tube: Piccadilly Circus.

JAZZ

A serious contender for the title of London's finest jazz center is the **100 Club,** 100 Oxford St., W.1 (tel. 01/636-0933). The emphasis here is strictly on the music, which begins each evening at 7:30 and lasts until midnight or later. The club's musical policy consists of jazz (traditional to contemporary), blues, rhythm-and-blues, jump-jive, whatever. Most of Britain's top performers play here, as well as many visiting musicians from Europe. The club's restaurant features a comprehensive menu. There's also a fully licensed bar, serving liquor, wine, and beer. The club no longer requires membership, but it imposes a door charge likely to range from £2.50 ($4.40) to £5 ($8.75), depending on which artist is appearing. Tube: Tottenham Court Road or Oxford Circus.

A much cheaper way to hear jazz is at one of the many pubs in the West End offering it on certain nights of the week. Some charge admission; others allow you to listen for the price of your drink.

Ronnie Scott's, 47 Frith St., W.1 (tel. 01/439-0747), has long held supremacy as the first citadel of modern jazz in Europe. Featured on almost every bill is an American instrumentalist, often with a top-notch singer. The best English and American groups are booked. In the heart of Soho, a ten-minute walk from Piccadilly Circus via Shaftesbury Avenue, it's worth an entire evening of your time. You can not only saturate yourself in the best of jazz but get reasonably priced drinks and dinners as well. There are three separate areas: the Main Room, the Upstairs Room, and the Downstairs Bar. You don't have to be a member, although you can join if you wish. The nightly entrance fee is £10 ($17.50), depending on who is appearing. If you have a student ID, you are granted considerable reductions on entrance fees.

Open Monday to Saturday, 8:30 p.m. to 3 a.m., the Main Room is built like an amphitheater with tiered tables, providing clear vision and good sound. You can either sit at the bar to watch the show or at the tables. The Downstairs Bar is more intimate—a pine-paneled rustic atmosphere, where you can meet and talk with the faithful habitués, usually some of the world's most talented musicians. The Upstairs Room is separate. It has a disco called the Tango and is open Monday to Thursday from 8:30 p.m. to 2 a.m. and from 8:30 p.m. to 3 a.m. on Friday and Saturday. Tube: Tottenham Court Road or Leicester Square.

The **Bull's Head,** 373 Lonsdale Rd., Barnes Bridge, S.W.13 (tel. 01/876-5241), has presented live modern jazz concerts every night of the week for more than 30 years. One of the oldest hostelries in the area, it was a staging post in the mid-19th century where travelers on their way to Hampton Court and beyond could eat, drink, and rest while the coach horses were changed. The place is known today for its jazz, performed by musicians from all over the world. It's said by many to be the best in town. Jazz concerts are presented on Sunday from noon to 2:30 p.m. and from 8:30 to 10:30 p.m. From Monday to Saturday, you can hear the music from 8:30 to 11 p.m. You can order good food at the Carvery in the Saloon Bar daily and dine in the 17th-century Stable Restaurant. The restaurant, in the original, restored stables, specializes in steaks, fish, and other traditional fare. It is open daily from 7 p.m. and on Sunday from noon. Meals cost from £4 ($7) up. To get there, take the tube to Hammersmith, then bus 9 the rest of the way.

In the Covent Garden area, the place where new bands are launched is the **Rock Garden,** 6-7 The Piazza, W.C.2 (tel. 01/240-3961), which offers live music every night of the week and at lunchtime Saturday and Sunday. Dire Straits, The Police, U2, Talking Heads, and T'Pau, to name a few, played here before they found fame. From noon to 3 p.m., three bands play on Saturday and top jazz musicians gather for a jam session on Sunday. The music venue is open from 7:30 p.m. to 3 a.m. every day. In the Rock Garden Restaurant, open from noon to midnight Sunday to Thursday and from noon to 1 a.m. Friday and Saturday, they serve a wide range of dishes, from swordfish to steak. A two-course meal costs around £10 ($17.50). In summer, you can dine al fresco in the heart of Covent Garden. Both the restaurant and music venue have licensed bars. Tube: Covent Garden. At night, buses run from neighboring Trafalgar Square.

FOR DANCING

A legendary setting is the **Café de Paris,** 3 Coventry St., off Piccadilly Circus, W.1 (tel. 01/437-2036). Once Robert Graves considered it a worthy subject for a book, and the Duke of Windsor came here to see Noël Coward perform. But those days are long gone. The place is almost unique in London in that it draws an older patronage who like to dance the way they did in the '50s. Admission ranges from £2 ($3.50) to £7 ($12.25), depending on what time you choose to enter. A half pint of lager costs £1.20 ($2.10) once you're inside. Hours are Monday and Thursday from 7:30 p.m. to 1 a.m., Friday and Saturday from 7:30 a.m. to 3 a.m., and Sunday from 7:30 p.m. to midnight. It is closed Tuesday and Wednesday. Afternoon tea dances draw a nostalgic crowd on Wednesday, Thursday, Saturday, and Sunday from 3 to 5:45 p.m. Tube: Piccadilly Circus or Leicester Square.

Empire, Leicester Square, W.C.1 (tel. 01/437-1446), was originally built in the 1880s, and it's been revamped and rebuilt so many times since then, going in and out of style, that today it is considered a virtual cultural monument. The bandstand is a leaping, revolving, and ever-changing spectrum of light. In the heart of London's entertainment district, the Empire features live bands of top caliber along with music played by DJs. It is closed on Sunday but open Monday to Saturday at 8 p.m., closing at either 2 a.m. or 3 a.m., depending on the night of the week. Live music begins at 10:30 p.m. nightly, except Monday. Admission ranges from £5

($8.75) to £8 ($14). There are six bars to quench your thirst between dances. Tube: Leicester Square.

VAUDEVILLE

Virtually extinct in America, the variety stage not only lives but flourishes in London. Streamlined and updated, it has dropped most of the corn and preserved all the excitement of the old vaudeville fare.

Top house in the field (not merely in London but in the world) is the **London Palladium,** Argyle Street, W.1 (tel. 01/437-7373), although it presents more than just vaudeville. It's hard to encapsulate the prestige of this establishment in a paragraph. Performers from Britain, Europe, and America consider that they have "arrived" when they've appeared here. Highlight of the season is the "Royal Command Performance" held before the queen, which includes an introduction of the artists to Her Majesty. It's amazing to watch hard-boiled showbiz champions moved close to tears after receiving the royal handshake.

Over the years, the Palladium has starred such aces as Frank Sinatra, Shirley MacLaine, Andy Williams, Perry Como, Julie Andrews, Tom Jones, Sammy Davis, Jr., and so on, like the Milky Way of stardom. Second-line program attractions are likely to include acts such as "Los Paraguayos" and the Ukrainian Cossack Ensemble. The prices are usually in the £8 ($14) to £17 ($29.75) range, and show times vary. Tube: Oxford Circus.

LONDON SPECTACLES

Take a trip back in time to where **Shakespeare's Feast,** 6 Hanover St., W.1 (tel. 01/408-1001), pays tribute to the Bard. Here, many of the most famous characters from Shakespeare's plays are re-created for a riotous night of fun, aided in no small part by jugglers, jesters, and magicians. There are even duelists. The costumed staff serves traditional honeyed wines, followed by a five-course banquet. The wine serving begins at 8 p.m. daily, and there is dancing until midnight. During dinner, guests enjoy unlimited wines and ale. The cost is £25 ($43.75) per person Sunday to Friday, rising to £27 ($47.25) on Saturday night. At the same address is the **Caledonian,** where guests enjoy an evening of Scottish hospitality. A "Tilt o' the Kilt" takes you to the land of the Highland fling. Kilts are supplied free to "men of courage," and whisky is served at 8 p.m. nightly, followed by dancing until midnight. In between there is the traditional ceremony of the haggis, as well as a five-course meal with unlimited wines. The cost is £25 ($43.75) per person Sunday to Friday, rising to £27 ($47.25) per person on Saturday night. Tube: Oxford Circus.

Beefeater Club by the Tower of London, St. Katharine's Yacht Marina, E.1 (tel. 01/408-1001), offers traditional feasting and continuous entertainment at the Court of Henry VIII in the historic vaults of Ivory House, surrounded on three sides by the Thames. British pageantry is re-created here, complete with jesters, knights, wenches, and royal entertainers. Traditional honeyed wine is served at 8 nightly, with dancing until 11:30 p.m. During a five-course medieval feast, guests are given unlimited wines and ale. The cost is £25 ($43.75) per person Sunday to Friday, rising to £27 ($47.25) per person on Saturday. Tube: Tower Hill.

GAMBLING

London was a gambling metropolis long before anyone ever heard of Monte Carlo and when Las Vegas was an anonymous sandpile in the desert. From the Regency period until halfway into the 19th century, Britain was more or less governed by gamblers. Lord Sandwich invented the snack named after him so he wouldn't have to leave the card table for a meal. Prime Minister Fox was so addicted that he frequently went to a cabinet meeting straight from the green baize table.

Queen Victoria's reign changed all that, as usual, by jumping to the other extreme. For more than a century, games of chance were so rigorously outlawed that no barmaid dared to keep a dice cup on the counter.

The pendulum swung again in 1960, when the present queen gave her Royal Assent to the new Betting and Gaming Act. According to this legislation, gambling was again permitted in "bona fide clubs" by members and their guests.

Since London's definition of a "club" is as loose as a rusty screw in a cardboard wall, this immediately gave rise to the current situation, which continues to startle, amaze, and bewilder foreign visitors. For the fact is that you come across gambling devices in the most unlikely spots, such as discos, social clubs, and cabaret restaurants—all of which may, by the haziest definition, qualify as "clubs."

The most legitimate gambling clubs offer pleasant trimmings in the shape of bars and restaurants, but their central theme is unequivocally the flirtation of Lady Luck. There are at least 25 of them in the West End alone, with many scattered through the suburbs. And the contrasts between them are much sharper than you find in the Nevada casinos.

Under the law, casinos are not allowed to advertise, and if they do, they are likely to lose their licenses. Their appearance in a travel guide is still considered "advertising"—hence I can't recommend specific clubs as in the past.

However, most hall porters can tell you where you can gamble in London. It is not illegal to gamble, just to advertise it. You'll be required to become a member of your chosen club, and you must wait 24 hours before you can play the tables, then strictly for cash. The most common games are roulette, blackjack, punto banco, and baccarat. Most casinos, as mentioned, have restaurants where you can expect a good standard of cuisine at a reasonable price.

---

4. Taking the Tours

In addition to the sites you can see in London by foot, or by utilizing the Underground, there are numerous attractions that can be reached via several coach tours. As an added bonus, there are dozens of fascinating trips that can be made on the Thames.

EASIEST WAY TO SEE LONDON

For the first-timer, the quickest and most economical way to bring the big city into focus is to take a two-hour, 20-mile circular tour of the West End and the City, the guided **London Transport Original Sightseeing Tour,** which passes virtually all the major places of interest in central London. Operated by London Transport, the city's official bus company, the journeys leave at frequent intervals daily from Piccadilly Circus (Haymarket), Victoria (Victoria Street), Marble Arch, and Baker Street. Departures are most frequent from 10 a.m. to 5 p.m. in July and August, with special late trips from Piccadilly Circus until 9 p.m. Some of the journeys are by open-top buses. Every bus has an experienced, qualified guide on board, and passengers are given a photographic album of celebrated and historical scenes. Tickets cost £6 ($10.50) for adults and £4 ($7) for children under 16 and are available from the driver. Tickets can also be purchased from London Regional Transport Travel Information Centres, where you can get a discount of £1 ($1.75) off each ticket. Locations of the travel information centers are given under "Transportation in Greater London," Chapter III of this book. In that section, you will also find information about **One-Day Off-Peak Travelcards,** which provide unlimited travel on red buses and the Underground.

LONDON'S WEST END AND THE CITY

If you prefer a more detailed look at the city's sights, **London Transport** offers highly regarded guided tours.

For a look at the West End, a three-hour tour is featured, passing Westminster Abbey (guided tour), the Houses of Parliament, Trafalgar Square, and Piccadilly Cir-

visit to the Changing of the Guard at Buckingham Palace or the Horse Guards
ie is also included. The cost is £10.50 ($18.40) for adults and £8.50 ($14.90)
children under 14.

London Transport's other popular three-hour tour is of the City, including
guided trips to the Tower of London and St. Paul's Cathedral. The fare for this one is
£15 ($26.25) for adults and £12 ($21) for children under 14, including admission
charges.

These two tours are combined to form the London Day Tour, which costs
£29.50 ($51.65) for adults, £24.50 ($42.90) for children under 14, including
lunch. The tour leaves at 10 a.m. The tours begin at Victoria Coach Station, at the
corner of Buckingham Palace Road and Elizabeth Street.

For details of London Transport's half- or full-day tours, phone 01/227-3456.

BOAT CRUISES ON THE THAMES

Touring boats operate in profusion on the Thames between April and September, with curtailed winter schedules, taking you various places within London, and
also to nearby towns along the Thames.

Main embarkation points are Westminster Pier, Charing Cross Pier, and Tower
Hill Pier, a system that enables you to take a "water taxi" to the Tower of London
and Westminster Abbey. Not only are the boats energy-saving, bringing you painlessly to your destination, but they permit you to sit back in comfort as you see London from the river.

Pleasure boats operate down the Thames from Westminster Pier to the Tower
of London and Greenwich and the Thames Barrier all year, departing every 20 minutes in summer, from 10 a.m. to 4 p.m., and every 30 minutes in winter. It takes 20
minutes to reach the Tower and 40 minutes to arrive at Greenwich. In summer, services operate upriver to Kew, Richmond, and Hampton Court from Westminster
Pier. There are departures every 30 minutes from 10:30 a.m. to 4 p.m. for the 1½-
hour journey to Kew and three departures daily for the 2½-hour Richmond trip.
The trip to Hampton Court is 3 to 5 hours each way. (For information on these and
other boat trips, call 01/730-4812).

The multitude of small companies operating boat services from Westminster
Pier have organized themselves into the **Westminster Passenger Service Association,** Westminster Pier, Victoria Embankment, S.W.1 (tel. 01/930-4721). Boats
leave the pier for cruises of varying length throughout the day and evening. Take the
Westminster tube to Westminster Pier.

CANAL BOATS TO LITTLE VENICE

When you get tired of fighting the London traffic, you might want to come
here and take a peaceful trip (1½ hours) aboard the traditionally painted narrow
boat *Jason* and her butty boat *Serpens*. Come for lunch along the most colorful part
of the Regent's Canal in the heart of London. The boat is moored in Blomfield
Road, just off Edgware Road in Maida Vale. Little Venice is the junction of two
canals and was given its name by Lord Byron.

To inquire about bookings, including the Boatman's Basket Luncheon Trip,
get in touch with **Jason's Trip,** Opp. No. 60 Blomfield Rd., Little Venice, W.9 (tel.
01/286-3428). Advance booking is essential during high season. If you come by
tube, take the Bakerloo Line to Warwick Avenue. Face the church, turn left, and walk
up Clifton Villas to the end and turn right (about two minutes). If you arrive early
you can browse around the shop, which sells many brightly colored, traditionally
painted canal wares.

On the trip you'll pass through the long Maida Hill tunnel under Edgware
Road, through Regent's Park, the Mosque, the Zoo, Lord Snowdon's Aviary, pass
the Pirate's Castle to Camden Lock and return to Little Venice. The season begins
Good Friday and lasts through September. During April and May, the boats run
daily at 12:30 and 2:30 p.m. In June, July, August, and September there are also

trips at 10:30 a.m. and 4:30 p.m. daily. Always telephone first. Refreshments are served on all trips: prebooked lunches on the 12:30 and 2:30 p.m. cruises, and a cream tea on the 4:30 p.m. voyage. The fare is £2.95 ($5.15) for adults, £1.75 ($3.05) for children.

Jenny Wren, 250 Camden High St., N.W.1 (tel. 01/485-4433), will take you through Camden Town to Little Venice and back. Along the way, you'll pass through a lock, London Zoo, Regent's Park, and Maida Hill Tunnel. The trip takes 1½ hours, costing £2.10 ($3.70) for adults and £1.10 ($1.95) for children. Departures are daily, except Saturday, at 11:30 a.m., 2 p.m., and 3:30 p.m. A three-hour mystery tour is conducted nightly from 7 to 10, with a stop at a canalside pub. Adults pay £3.50 ($6.15) for themselves and £2 ($3.50) for children. The boat lies a two-minute walk from Camden Town Underground station on the Northern Line.

ORGANIZED LONDON WALKS

Hunt for ghosts or walk in the steps of Jack the Ripper, the infamous East End murderer of prostitutes in the 1880s. Retrace the history of the city from the Romans to the Blitz. Visit glamorous Chelsea or elegant Mayfair. Investigate the London of Shakespeare, Dickens, and Sherlock Holmes, or taste the delights of an evening's drinking in four historic pubs. These and many other walks are included in the program of unusual and historical walks organized by **London Walks,** 10 Greenbrook Ave., Hadley Wood, Hertfordshire, England EN4 0LS (tel. 01/441-8906). Walks take place Saturday and Sunday throughout the year and also during the week from April to October. The cost is £3 ($5.25) for adults and £2.50 ($4.40) for students with ID cards; children under 14 go free. No reservations required. Get in touch with the above address for details.

Another small and enthusiastic company, a husband-and-wife team offering a vast variety of London walks, is **Discovering London.** It's operated by a Scot, Alex Cobban, a historian of some note whose guides are professionals. Mainly on Saturday and Sunday, but during the week as well, scheduled walks are planned, starting at easily found Underground stations: Dickens's London, Roman London, Ghosts of the City, the Inns of Court—Lawyers' London, and Jack the Ripper are examples. Mr. Cobban's knowledge of Sherlock Holmes is immense. No advance booking is necessary, and the walks cost £3 ($5.25) for adults; children under 16 go free, and students with ID cards are charged £2.75 ($4.80). Each walk takes about 1½ to 2 hours. Write, enclosing an International Reply Coupon, for a detailed schedule of the walks available during your stay in London. The address is Discovering London, 11 Pennyfields, Warley, Brentwood, Essex CM14 5JP (tel. 0277/213-704).

Londoner Pub Walks set out every Friday evening from the Temple Underground Station at 7:30 p.m. to discover places full of interest and history. By exploring away from the more regular tourist areas, the walks offer a chance to meet the local people and to discover what it is that makes the English pub a unique institution. Reservations are not necessary, but further details may be secured from Peter Westbrook, 3 Springfield Ave., London, N.10 (tel. 01/883-2656). The charge is £2.50 ($4.40), and you buy your own drinks.

---

5. London for Children

It's hard to draw a clear distinguishing line between junior and senior brands of entertainment in many areas. In London, it's almost impossible. The British Museum, for example, is definitely rated as an adult attraction. Yet I've watched group after group of kids stand absolutely spellbound in front of the Egyptian mummies, still completely absorbed long after their parents were champing at the bit to trot along.

The attractions to follow are *not* meant specifically for children. They are general and universal fun places to which you can take youngsters without having to worry about either their physical or moral safety. There's nothing to stop you from going to any of them minus a juvenile escort. It is even possible that you'll enjoy them more thoroughly than any kid around. Many of the interesting sights, such as the Royal Mews, where you can see the queen's horses and royal and state coaches, are described earlier in this chapter.

THE LONDON DUNGEON

The premises at 34 Tooley St., S.E.1 (tel. 01/403-0606), simulate a ghoulish atmosphere designed deliberately to chill the blood while reproducing faithfully the conditions that existed in the Middle Ages. Set under the arches of London Bridge Station, the dungeon is a series of tableaux, more grizzly than Madame Tussaud's, depicting life in medieval London. The rumble of trains overhead adds to the spine-chilling horror of the place. Bells toll, and there is constant melancholy chanting in the background. Dripping water and live rats (caged!) make for even more atmosphere. The heads of executed criminals were stuck on spikes for onlookers to observe through glasses hired for the occasion. The murder of Thomas à Becket in Canterbury Cathedral is also depicted. Naturally, there's a burning at the stake, as well as a torture chamber with racking, branding, and fingernail extraction. The Great Fire of London is brought to crackling life by a computer-controlled spectacular that re-creates Pudding Lane where the fire started.

If you survive, there is a souvenir shop selling certificates to testify that you have been through the works. The dungeon is open from 10 a.m. to 5:30 p.m. April through September and to 4:30 p.m. October through March, seven days a week. Admission is £3.50 ($6.15) for adults, £2 ($3.50) for children under 14. Tube: London Bridge Station.

BATTERSEA PARK

The park is a vast patch of woodland, lakes, and lawns on the south bank of the Thames, S.W.1, opposite Chelsea Embankment. It boasts just about everything that makes for happiness on a dry day: a tree-lined boulevard, fountains, and a children's zoo with baby animals. The nearest tube at Sloane Square is a long, long way away and on the north bank of the Thames (you'll have to cross Chelsea Bridge). Better ask at your hotel for a convenient bus route.

THEATERS FOR CHILDREN

At the Arts Theatre, Great Newport St., W.C.2, the **Unicorn Theatre** for children commissions several new plays each year as well as presenting dramatizations of classics such as *The Silver Sword* and *Pinocchio*. Each play is presented for a specific age range within the 4-to-12 age group, which is indicated on all publicity. Visiting children's theater companies perform at the Unicorn during the spring, and in the summer months, the Unicorn Summer Tour goes to parks and playgrounds in the London area. Performances are given Tuesday to Sunday at 2:30 p.m., costing from £2.50 ($4.40) to £5.50 ($9.65). For additional information, such as how to secure temporary memberships for foreigners, telephone 01/379-3280. To reserve tickets, call the box office (tel. 01/836-3334). Tube: Leicester Square.

The **Little Angel Marionette Theatre,** 14 Dagmar Passage, Cross Street, N.1 (tel. 01/226-1787), is especially constructed for and devoted to presentation of puppetry in all its forms. It is open to the general public, and 200 to 300 performances are given each year. The theater is the focal point of a loosely formed group of some 20 professional puppeteers who work here as occasion demands, presenting their own shows or helping with performances of the resident company. In the current repertory, there are 25 programs. These vary in style and content from *The Soldier's Tale*, using eight-foot-high figures, to *Wonder Island* and *Lancelot the Lion*, written especially for the humble glove puppet. Many of the plays, such as Hans Christian Andersen's *The Little Mermaid*, are performed with marionettes (string puppets), but whatever is being presented, you'll be enthralled with the exquisite lighting and skill with which the puppets are handled.

The theater is beautifully decorated and well equipped. There is a coffee bar in the foyer and a workshop adjacent where the settings and costumes, as well as the puppets, are made. To find out what's playing and to reserve your seats, call the number above. Performances are at 11 a.m. on Saturday, when the seats are £1.50 ($2.65) for children, £2.50 ($4.40) for adults, and at 3 p.m. on Saturday and Sunday, when the cost is £2.50 ($4.40) for children, £3.50 ($6.15) for adults. Take the tube to Angel Station, then walk up Upper Street to St. Mary's Church and down the footpath to the left of the church. You can go by car or taxi to Essex Road and then up to Dagmar Terrace.

LONDON ZOO

One of the greatest zoos in the world, the London Zoo is more than a century and a half old. Run by the Zoological Society of London, Regent's Park, N.W.1 (tel. 01/722-3333), with an equal measure of showmanship and scholarly know-how, this 36-acre garden houses some 8000 animals, including some of the rarest species on earth. One of the most fascinating exhibits is the Snowdon Aviary. Separate houses are reserved for some species: the insect house (incredible bird-eating spiders, a cross-sectioned ant colony), the reptile house (huge dragon-like monitor lizards and a fantastic 15-foot python), and other additions, such as the Sobell Pavilion for Apes and Monkeys and the Lion Terrace.

Designed for the largest collection of small mammals in the world, the Clore Pavilion has a basement called the Moonlight World, where special lighting effects simulate night for the nocturnal beasties, while rendering them clearly visible to onlookers. You can see all the night rovers in action—leaping bush babies, rare kiwis, a fierce Tasmanian devil, and giant Indian fruit bats with heads like prehistoric dogs.

Many families budget almost an entire day to spend with the animals, watching the sea lions being fed, enjoying an animal ride in summer, and meeting the baby elephants on their walks. The zoo is open daily from 9 a.m. in summer and from 10 a.m. in winter, until 6 p.m. or dusk, whichever is earlier. Last entrance is half an hour before closing. Admission is £4.30 ($7.55) for adults, £2.60 ($4.55) for children 4 to 15 (under 4 free). On the grounds are two fully licensed restaurants, one self-service and the other with waitresses. Take the tube to Baker Street or Camden Town, then take bus 74 (Camden Town is nearer and an easy ten-minute walk).

NATURAL HISTORY MUSEUM

This museum, on Cromwell Road, S.W.7 (tel. 01/938-9123), is the home of the national collections of living and fossil plants, animals, minerals, rocks, and meteorites, with lots of magnificent specimens on display. Exciting exhibitions designed to encourage people of all ages to enjoy learning about modern natural history include "Human Biology—An Exhibition of Ourselves," "Dinosaurs and Their Living Relatives," "Man's Place in Evolution," "British Natural History," and "Discovering Mammals." Admission is £2 ($3.50). The museum is open Monday to Saturday from 10 a.m. to 6 p.m. and on Sunday from 1 to 6 p.m. Tube: South Kensington.

BETHNAL GREEN MUSEUM OF CHILDHOOD

On Cambridge Heath Road, E.2 (tel. 01/980-2415), this establishment displays toys from the past century. The variety of dolls alone is staggering, some of them dressed in period costumes of such elaborateness that you don't even want to think of the price tags they must have carried. With the dolls go dollhouses, from simple cottages to miniature mansions, complete with fireplaces and grand pianos, plus carriages, furniture, kitchen utensils, and household pets. It might be wise to explain to your children beforehand that—no—none of them is for sale. In addition, the museum displays optical toys, toy theaters, marionettes, puppets, and a considerable exhibit of soldiers and battle toys of both world wars. There is also a display of children's clothing and furniture related to childhood. The museum is open Monday to Saturday, except Friday, from 10 a.m. to 6 p.m. and on Sunday from 2:30 p.m. Admission is free. Tube: Bethnal Green.

THE LONDON TOY AND MODEL MUSEUM

Two restored Victorian houses at 21-23 Craven Hill, W.2 (tel. 01/262-7905), off Bayswater Road, shelter one of the finest collections of commercially made toys and models on public display in Europe, with items by all the major toy and model manufacturers. The model and toy train collection is particularly comprehensive, tracing the development of the miniature train from the inception of railways in the early 19th century. There are several garden railway systems. including a child's ride-on train. The permanent collection details the rise of toys with the Industrial Revolution. There is a fine display of dolls, teddy bears, and a quarter-scale child's model of a Cadillac sports roadster made in 1916. A children's activity area within the museum also is an attraction. The museum has a café and a large recreational garden area. It's open Tuesday to Saturday from 10 a.m. to 5:30 p.m., Sunday from 11 a.m. to 5:30 p.m., and on bank holiday Monday. Admission is £2.20 ($3.85) for adults, 80p ($1.40) for children (free for children under 5 years of age). Tube: Lancaster Gate.

FUN ON HAMPSTEAD HEATH

This is the traditional playground of the Londoner, the 'Appy 'Ampstead of Cockney legend, the place dedicated "to the use of the public forever" by special Act of Parliament in 1872. Londoners might just possibly tolerate the conversion of, say, Hyde Park into housing estates or supermarkets, but they would certainly mount the barricades if Hampstead Heath were imperiled. This 800-acre expanse of high heath entirely surrounded by London is a chain of continuous park, wood, and grassland, bearing different names in different portions. It contains just about every known form of outdoor amusement, wiht the exception of deep-sea fishing and big-game hunting. There's something here for children and grownups alike, with activities to include the entire family. There are natual lakes for swimmers (who don't mind goosebumps), bridle paths for horseback riders, athletic tracks, hills for kite flying, and a special pond for model yachting.

At the shore of Kenwood Lake, in the northern section, is a concert platform devoted to symphony performances on summer evenings. In the northeast corner, in Waterlow Park, ballets, operas, and comedies are staged at the Grass Theatre in June and July.

History-minded youngsters and adults should stand for a moment on top of Parliament Hill on the south side. It was from that vantage point that the ancient British (Iceni tribe) Queen Boadicea and her daughters watched the burning of the Roman camp of Londinium, which her tribesmen put to the torch in A.D. 61. Tube: Hampstead or Belsize Park.

6. One-Day Trips from London

It would be sad to leave England without ever having ventured into her countryside, at least for a day. The English are the greatest excursion travelers in the world, forever dipping into their own rural areas to discover ancient abbeys, 17th-century village lanes, shady woods for picnic lunches, and stately mansions. From London, it's possible to avail yourself of countless tours—either by conducted coach, boat, or via a do-it-yourself method on bus or train. On many trips you can combine two or more methods of transportation; for example, you can go to Windsor by boat and return by coach or train.

Highly recommended are the previously described Green Line Coaches, operated by **Green Line Travel Ltd.** (see Chapter I, "Traveling Within England" section). For longer tours, say, to Stratford-upon-Avon, you will find the trains much more convenient. Often you can take advantage of the many bargain tickets outlined in Chapter I. For further information about trains to a specific location, go to the British Rail offices on Lower Regent Street.

The **London Regional Transport** system has conducted tours of places of interest in and around London. For example, a day tour (operating in summer) visits Windsor and Hampton Court Palace Monday to Saturday, departing Wilton Road Coach Station at 9:15 a.m. The return to Victoria Station is at 5:15 p.m. Adults pay £25 ($43.75) and children are charged £20 ($35). Operating all year, an afternoon tour visits Windsor and goes on a river cruise to Runnymede. Departures are from Wilton Road Coach Station on Tuesday, Wednesday, Friday, Saturday, and Sunday at 1 p.m., with a return to Victoria Station at 6:15 p.m. The price is £14 ($24.50) for adults and £12 ($21) for children. For details on the transport system's information and ticket centers, see "Transportation in Greater London," in section 1 of Chapter III.

HAMPTON COURT

On the north side of the Thames, 13 miles west of London in East Molesey, Surrey, this 16th-century palace of Cardinal Wolsey (tel. 01/930-0921) can teach us a lesson: Don't try to outdo your boss, particularly if he happens to be Henry VIII. The rich cardinal did just that. But the king had a lean and hungry eye. Wolsey, who eventually lost his fortune, power, and prestige, ended up giving his lavish palace to the Tudor monarch. In a stroke of one-upsmanship, Henry took over, outdoing the Wolsey embellishments. The Tudor additions included the Anne Boleyn gateway, with its 16th-century astronomical clock that even tells the high-water mark at London Bridge. From Clock Court, you can see one of Henry's major contributions, the aptly named Great Hall, with its hammer-beam ceiling. Also added by Henry were the tiltyard, a tennis court, and kitchens.

Hampton Court had quite a retinue to feed. Cooking was done in the Great Kitchen, which may be visited. Henry cavorted through the various apartments with his wives of the moment, from Anne Boleyn to Catherine Parr (the latter reversed things and lived to bury her erstwhile spouse). Charles I was imprisoned at one time and temporarily managed to escape his jailers.

Although the palace enjoyed prestige and pomp in Elizabethan days, it owes much of its present look to William and Mary of Orange, or rather to Sir Christopher Wren, who designed and had built the Northern or Lion Gates, intended to be the main entrance to the new parts of the palace. The fine wrought-iron screen at the south end of the south gardens was made by Jean Tijou around 1694 for William and Mary. You can parade through the apartments, filled with porcelain, furniture, paintings, and tapestries. The King's Dressing Room is graced with some of the best art, including Pieter Brueghel the Elder's macabre *Massacre of the Innocents*. Tintoretto and Titian deck the halls of the King's Drawing Room. Finally, be sure to inspect the Royal Chapel (Wolsey wouldn't recognize it). To confound yourself totally, you may want to get lost in the serpentine shrubbery Maze in the garden, also the work of Sir Christopher Wren.

The gardens, including the Great Vine, King's Privy Garden, Great Fountain Gardens, Tudor and Elizabethan Knot Gardens, Broad Walk, Tiltyard, and Wilderness, are open daily year-round from 7 a.m. until dusk, but not later than 9 p.m., and can be visited free. Cloisters, courtyards, and state apartments are open from 9:30 a.m. to 5 p.m. weekdays and from 2 to 7 p.m. Sunday, January 2 to March 31 and October 1 to December 31, with the same opening hours from April 1 to September 30 but closing at 6 p.m. The Great Kitchen and cellars, Tudor tennis courts, King's Private Apartments, Hampton Court Exhibition, and Mantegna Paintings gallery are open the same hours as the above, but only from April to September. The Maze is open daily from 10 a.m. to 5 p.m. March 1 to October 31. The year-round price for an all-inclusive ticket (except the Maze) costs £3.40 ($5.95) for adults and £1.70 ($3) for children. Tickets for the Maze cost an additional £1 ($1.75) for adults and 50p (90¢) for children. It is easiest to reach Hampton Court by frequent train service from Waterloo Station in London. You can also go by bus, but many prefer in summer to take a boat in either direction. From Easter until late September, Westminster Passenger Services, West Pier, Victoria Embankment, London, S.W.1 (tel. 01/930-4721) operates as many as four boats a day in either direction. The cost is £7 ($12.25) for adults round trip or £5.50 ($9.65) one way. Be warned: rides to Hampton Court from Central London are always slower than downstream rides back to the city. Also, depending on tides, a ride to Hampton Court could take from 2 to 4½ hours. Always ask about conditions of the river before booking a ticket, and plan your schedule accordingly.

KEW

Nine miles southwest of central London at Kew, near Richmond, are the **Royal Botanic Gardens,** better known as Kew Gardens (tel. 01/940-1171), among the best known in Europe, containing thousands of varieties of plants. But Kew is no mere pleasure garden—rather, it is essentially a vast scientific research center that happens to be beautiful. A pagoda, erected in 1761 and 1762, represents the flowering of chinoiserie. One of the oddities of Kew is a Douglas fir flagstaff more than 220 feet high. The classical Orangery, near the main gate on Kew Green, houses an exhibit telling the story of Kew, as well as a bookshop where guides to the gardens are available. The gardens cover a 300-acre site encompassing lakes, greenhouses, walks, garden pavilions, and museums, together with fine examples of the architecture of Sir William Chambers. At whatever season you visit Kew, there's always something to see: in spring, the daffodils and bluebells, through to the coldest months when the Heath Garden is at its best. Among the 50,000 plant species are notable collections of arum lilies, ferns, orchids, aquatic plants, cacti, mountain plants, palms, and tropical waterlilies. The gardens are open daily, except Christmas and New Year's Day, from 10 a.m. to either 4 or 5 p.m., depending on the season. The entrance fee has gone above the traditional "one penny" in effect for a couple of centuries and is now £1 ($1.75).

Much interest focuses on the red-brick **Kew Palace** (dubbed the Dutch House), a former residence of King George III and Queen Charlotte. It is reached by walking to the northern tip of the Broad Walk. Now a museum, it was built in 1631 and contains memorabilia of the reign of George III, along with a royal collection of furniture and paintings. It is open only from April to September, 11 a.m. to 5:30 p.m. daily. Admission is 80p ($1.40) for adults, 40p (70¢) for children.

At the gardens, **Queen Charlotte's Cottage** has been restored to its original splendor. Built in 1772, it is half-timbered and thatched. George III is believed to have been the architect. The house has been restored in great detail, including the original Hogarth prints that hung on the downstairs walls. The cottage is open from mid-April to mid-October from 11 a.m. to 5:30 p.m. on Saturday, Sunday, and bank holiday Mondays. Admission is 40p (70¢) for adults and 20p (35¢) for children.

The least expensive and most convenient way to visit the gardens is to take the District Line Underground to Kew. The most romantic way to come in summer is via a steamer from Westminster Bridge to Kew Pier.

London's living steam museum, **Kew Bridge Steam Museum,** Green Dragon Lane, Brentford, Middlesex (tel. 01/568-4757), houses what is probably the world's largest collection of steam-powered beam engines. These were used in the Victorian era and up to the 1940s to pump London's water, and one engine has a capacity of 700 gallons per stroke. There are six restored engines that are steamed on weekends, plus other unrestored engines, a steam railway, and a working forge. The museum has a tea room, plus free parking for cars. It's open and in steam from 11 a.m. to 5 p.m. on Saturday, Sunday, and Monday when it falls on a holiday. From

Monday to Friday, you can see it as a static exhibition during the same hours. Admission on steam days is £1.80 ($3.15) for adults, 90p ($1.60) for children, with a family price of £5 ($8.75). On other days, adults are charged £1 ($1.75) and children 50p (90¢), with the family rate being £2.75 ($4.80).

The museum is north of Kew Bridge, under the tower, a ten-minute walk from Kew Gardens. You can reach it by a Southern Region British Rail train from Waterloo Station to Kew Bridge Station; by buses 27, 65, 237, or 267 (7 on Sunday); or by Gunnersbury or South Ealing tube and thence by bus.

RUNNYMEDE

Two miles outside Windsor is the meadow on the south side of the Thames, in Surrey, where King John put his seal on the Magna Carta (Great Charter). John may have signed the document up the river on a little island, but that's being technical. Today Runnymede is also the site of the **John F. Kennedy Memorial,** one acre of English ground given to the United States by the people of Britain.

The Pagoda you can see from the road was placed there by the American Bar Association to acknowledge the fact that American law stems from the English system. The John F. Kennedy Memorial is a large block of white stone, hard to see from the road on the edge of the treeline.

GREENWICH

Greenwich Mean Time, of course, is the basis of standard time throughout most of the world, the zero point used in the reckoning of terrestrial longitudes since 1884. But Greenwich is also home of the Royal Naval College, the National Maritime Museum, and the Old Royal Observatory. In drydock at Greenwich Pier is the clipper ship **Cutty Sark,** as well as Sir Francis Chichester's **Gipsy Moth IV.**

About four miles from the City, Greenwich is reached by a number of methods, and part of the fun of making the jaunt is getting there. Ideally, you'll arrive by boat, as Henry VIII preferred to do on one of his hunting expeditions. In summer, launches leave at regular intervals from either the pier at Charing Cross, Tower Bridge, or Westminster. The boats leave daily for Greenwich about every half hour from 10 a.m. to 7 p.m. (times are approximate, depending on the tides). Bus 1 runs from Trafalgar Square to Greenwich; bus 188 goes from Euston through Waterloo to Greenwich. From Charing Cross station, the British Rail train takes 15 minutes to reach Greenwich, and there is now the new Docklands Light Railway, running from Tower Gateway to Island Gardens on the Isle of Dogs. A short walk under the Thames through a foot tunnel brings you out in Greenwich opposite the *Cutty Sark.*

Unquestionably, the *Cutty Sark*—last of the great clippers—holds the most interest, having been seen by millions. At the spot where the vessel is now berthed stood the Ship Inn of the 19th century (Victorians came here for whitebait dinners, as they did to the Trafalgar Tavern). Ordered built by Captain Jock Willis ("Old White Hat"), the clipper was launched in 1869 to sail the China tea trade route. It was named after the Witch Nannie in Robert Burns's *Tam o'Shanter* (note the figurehead). Yielding to the more efficient steamers, the *Cutty Sark* later was converted to a wool-clipper, plying the route between Australia and England. Before her retirement, she knew many owners, even different names, eventually coming to drydock at Cutty Sark Gardens, Greenwich Pier, S.E.10 (tel. 01/858-3445), in 1954. The vessel may be boarded, costing £1.30 ($2.30) for adults and 70p ($1.25) for children, from 10 a.m. to 6 p.m. Monday to Saturday, and from noon to 6 p.m. on Sunday. Closing time is 5 p.m. in winter. Of special interest is the completely refurbished lower hold, housing the largest collection of figureheads known.

A neighbor to the *Cutty Sark*—and also in drydock—is Sir Francis Chichester's *Gipsy Moth IV* (also tel. 01/858-3445), in which he circumnavigated the world in 1967. He single-handedly fought the elements in his vessel for 119 days. For 20p (35¢) for adults and 10p (20¢) for children, you can go aboard (same hours as the *Cutty Sark*). It's usually closed from October to April.

The **Royal Naval College** (tel. 01/858-2154) grew up on the site of the Tudor palace in which Henry VIII and Elizabeth I were born. William and Mary commissioned Wren to design the present buildings in 1695 to house naval pensioners, and these became the Royal Naval College in 1873. The buildings are a baroque masterpiece, in which the Painted Hall, by Thornhill (1708–1727), and the chapel are outstanding. Charging no admission, it is normally open to the public every day, except Thursday, Christmas, and Good Friday, from 2:30 p.m. until 5 p.m. (last entrance at 4:30 p.m.). However, it can be closed for security reasons.

The **National Maritime Museum** (tel. 01/858-4422), built around Inigo Jones's 17th-century Palladian Queen's House, portrays Britain's maritime heritage. Actual craft, marine paintings, ship models, and scientific instruments are displayed, including the full-dress uniform coat that Lord Nelson wore at the Battle of Trafalgar. In the west wing is a licensed restaurant. The museum is open from 10 a.m. to 6 p.m. in summer and from 10 a.m. to 5 p.m. in winter; from 2 to 6 p.m. on Sunday in summer, to 5 p.m. in winter. A combined ticket to the main buildings and the Old Royal Observatory (see below) costs £3 ($5.25) for adults, £1.50 ($2.65) for children. A £7.50 ($13.15) family ticket admits two adults and up to five children.

On the same visit, you can explore the **Old Royal Observatory** (tel. 01/858-4422). Sir Christopher Wren was the architect—after all, he was interested in astronomy before he became famous. The observatory overlooks Greenwich and the Maritime Museum from a park laid out to the design of Le Nôtre, the French landscaper. Here you can stand with one foot in the west, the other in the east, as the Greenwich Meridian line is well marked to divide the world into hemispheres. See also the big red time ball used in olden days by ships sailing down the river from London to set their timepieces by. There is a fascinating bewilderment of astronomical and navigational instruments, and time and travel become more realistic after a visit here. Other curiosities include the chronometer (or sea watch) used by Captain Cook when he made his Pacific explorations in the 1770s. The observatory is open all year Monday to Saturday from 10 a.m. to 6 p.m. (to 5 p.m. in winter), and on Sunday from 2 to 6 p.m. (to 5 p.m. in winter). It is closed December 24, 25, and 26, January 1, Good Friday, and May Day bank holiday.

Where to Eat and Drink

The **Cutty Sark Free House,** Ballast Quay, Lassell Street, S.E.10 (tel. 01/858-3146), has plenty of local color on its Thames-side perch. About a half mile from the railway station, this English riverside tavern will dispense drinks in an atmosphere in which you can eavesdrop on the conversation of oldtime salts. This riverside pub has lots of old beams, seats cut out of beer barrels, a flagstone floor, and real tradition. Bar snacks include everything from a ploughman's lunch to venison and vegetables. From the upstairs restaurant you'll have a view of the water. Naturally, fish such as trout, whitebait, and lemon sole are the main bill of fare. The street-level pub is open Monday to Saturday from 11 a.m. to 11 p.m., and on Sunday from noon to 3 p.m. and 7 to 10:30 p.m. The upstairs dining room, overlooking the Thames, serves meals "more or less" from 11:30 a.m. to 2:30 p.m. and 7 to 10 p.m. daily. Full meals, including the price of the popular Sunday lunch, is from £12 ($21) per person.

SYON PARK

Just nine miles from Piccadilly Circus, on 55 acres of the Duke of Northumberland's Thames-side estate, is one of the most beautiful spots in all of Great Britain. There's always something in bloom. Called "The Showplace of the Nation in a Great English Garden," Syon Park was opened to the public in 1968. A nation of green-thumbed gardens is dazzled here, and the park is also educational, showing amateurs how to get the most out of their small gardens. The vast flower-

and plant-studded acreage betrays the influence of "Capability" Brown, who laid out the grounds in the 18th century.

Particular highlights include a six-acre rose garden, a butterfly house, and the Great Conservatory, one of the earliest and most famous buildings of its type, built 1822–1827, housing everything from cacti to fuchsias. In it is also housed a walk-through aviary full of exotic and brilliantly colored birds. In the old dairy you will find an interesting seawater aquarium. There is a quarter-mile-long ornamental lake studded with waterlilies and silhouetted by cypresses and willows, even a huge gardening supermarket, and the Motor Museum, holding the Heritage Collection of British cars. With some 90 vehicles, from the earliest 1895 Wolseley to the present day, it has the largest collection of British cars anywhere.

Operated by the Gardening Center Limited, Syon was the site of the first botanical garden in England, created by the father of English botany, Dr. William Turner. Trees include a 200-year-old Chinese juniper, an Afghan ash, Indian bean trees, and a liquidambars.

On the grounds is **Syon House,** built in 1429, the original structure incorporated into the Duke of Northumberland's present home. The house was later remade to the specifications of the first Duke of Northumberland in 1762–1769. The battlemented facade is that of the original Tudor mansion, but the interior is from the 18th century, the design of Robert Adam. Basil Taylor said of the interior feeling: "You're almost in the middle of a jewel box." In the Middle Ages, Syon was a monastery, later suppressed by Henry VIII. Katharine Howard, the king's fifth wife, was imprisoned in the house before her scheduled beheading in 1542.

The house is open from Easter to the end of September from noon to 5 p.m. daily, except Friday and Saturday. The gardens are open all year, except for Christmas and Boxing Day. The gates open at 10 a.m. and close at dusk or 6 p.m. After October, the winter closing hour is 4 p.m. Admission to the gardens is £1.50 ($2.65) for adults and £1 ($1.75) for children. Admission to Syon House is £1.75 ($3.05) for adults, £1.25 ($2.20) for children. A combined ticket for house and gardens is £3 ($5.25) for adults, £2 ($3.50) for children. A separate ticket is required for entrance to the Motor Museum, costing £2 ($3.50) for adults, £1.25 ($2.20) for children. For more information, phone 01/560-0882.

THORPE PARK

One of Europe's leading family leisure parks, Thorpe Park, Staines Road, Chertsey, Surrey (tel. 0932/562633), lies only 21 miles from Central London on the A320 between Staines and Chertsey, with easy access from junctions 11 and 13 on the M25. The park has a "pay one price" system, meaning that after you pay the entrance fee of £7 ($12.25) for adults and £6.50 ($11.40) for children under 14, all rides, shows, attractions, and exhibits are free. Additional charges are made only for water sports, roller skate rental, and coin-operated amusements. Just a few of the favorite rides and shows are Treasure Island, Magic Mill, Phantom Fantasia, Thunder River, Space Station Zero, the Family Teacup ride, Cinema 180, Palladium Theatre, and Loggers Leap. Free transport is provided around the 500 acres by railway and water bus. Guests can picnic on the grounds or patronize one of the restaurants or fast-food areas, such as La Fontana, the French Café, Bavarian Festhalle, or the popular Mississippi Riverboat. The park is open from 10 a.m. to 6 p.m. daily from March 23 to October 29, except from July 22 to August 10, when it remains open until 8 p.m. To avoid the busiest times, Monday to Saturday are recommended for visits from April to July and in September. The nearest mainline station is Staines from Waterloo, and many bus services operate directly to Thorpe Park.

WINDSOR, OXFORD, AND THE HOME COUNTIES

1. WINDSOR

2. ASCOT

3. HENLEY-ON-THAMES

4. OXFORD

5. WOODSTOCK (BLENHEIM PALACE)

6. HERTFORDSHIRE

7. BUCKINGHAMSHIRE

8. BEDFORDSHIRE (WOBURN ABBEY)

Within easy reach of London, the Thames Valley and the Chilterns are a history-rich part of England, and they lie so close to the capital they can be easily reached by automobile or Green Line coach. You can explore here during the day and return in time to see a show in the West End.

Here are some of the most-visited historic sites in England: the former homes of Disraeli and Elizabeth I, the estate of the Duke of Bedford, and, of course, Windsor Castle, 22 miles from London, one of the most famous castles in Europe and the most popular day trip for those visitors venturing out of London for the first time.

Of course, your principal reason for coming to Oxfordshire, our second goal, is to explore the university city of Oxford, about an hour's drive from London. But Oxford is not the only attraction in the county, as you'll soon discover as you make your way through Henley-on-Thames. The shire is a land of great mansions, old churches of widely varying architectural styles, and rolling farmland.

In a sense, Oxfordshire is a kind of buffer zone between the easy living in the southern towns and the industrialized cities of the heartland. In the southeast are the chalky Chilterns, and in the west you'll be moving toward the wool towns of the Cotswolds. In fact, Burford, an unspoiled medieval town lying west of Oxford, is one of the traditional gateways to the Cotswolds (dealt with in a later chapter). The Upper Thames winds its way across the southern parts of the county.

The "Home Counties" are characterized by their river valleys and gentle hills. The beech-clad Chiltern Hills are at their most beautiful in spring and fall. This 40-mile chalk ridge extends in an arc from the Thames Valley to the old Roman city of

St. Albans in Hertfordshire. The whole region is popular for boating holidays, as it contains a 200-mile network of canals.

1. Windsor

A Green Line bus from London will deliver you in about an hour to Windsor, site of England's greatest castle and its most famous boys' school. Green Line buses 700, 702, and 704 leave from Eccleston Bridge behind Victoria Station (see "Buses in England," Chapter I, Section 2). Buses 700 and 702 are express service, but these can only be used at reduced rates after 9 a.m. For the return journey, you can either go straight back into London or stop off at Hampton Court on the way. Take bus 726 or 718 from Windsor. For further information, telephone 01/668-7261.

Windsor was called "Windlesore" by the ancient Britons, who derived the name from the winding shore—quite noticeable as you walk along the Thames here.

THE SIGHTS

Your bus will drop you near the Town Guildhall, to which Wren applied the finishing touches. It's only a short walk up Castle Hill to the following sights:

Windsor Castle

It was William the Conqueror who founded a castle on this spot, beginning a legend and a link with English sovereignty that has known many vicissitudes. King John cooled his heels at Windsor while waiting to put his signature on the Magna Carta at nearby Runnymede; Charles I was imprisoned here before losing his head; Queen Bess did some renovations; Victoria mourned her beloved Albert, who died at the castle in 1861; the royal family rode out much of World War II behind its sheltering walls. When Queen Elizabeth II is in residence, the Royal Standard flies. The State Apartments can be visited usually, except for about six weeks at Easter, all of June, and three weeks in December, when the court is at Windsor. At other times, the apartments are open during January, February, early March, November, and early December from 10:30 a.m. to 3 p.m. daily, except Sunday, and July to late October from 10:30 a.m. to 5 p.m. Monday to Saturday, and 1:30 to 5 p.m. on Sunday. Ticket sales cease about 30 minutes before closing, and last admissions are 15 minutes before closing time. The price of admission is £2 ($3.50) for adults, £1 ($1.75) for children. It is always advisable to check what is open before visiting by telephoning 0753/868286.

The apartments contain many works of art, porcelain, armor, furniture, three Verrio ceilings, and several Gibbons carvings from the 17th century. The world of Rubens adorns the King's Drawing Room, and in his relatively small dressing room is a Dürer, along with Rembrandt's portrait of his mother and Van Dyck's triple look at Charles I. Of the apartments, the Grand Reception Room, with its Gobelin tapestries, is the most spectacular.

The changing of the guard ceremony takes place at 11 a.m. daily, except Sunday from May to August. In winter, the guard is changed every 48 hours, except Sunday, so it's wise to phone in advance for information at the number listed above, extension 252. The Windsor changing of the guard is much more exciting than the London exercises. In Windsor, the guard marches through the town, stopping the traffic as it wheels into the castle to the tune of a full regimental band when the court is in residence. When the queen is not there, a fife-and-drum band is mustered.

Old Master Drawings

The royal family possesses a rare collection at Windsor of drawings by Old Masters, notably Leonardo da Vinci. One Leonardo sketch, for example, shows a cat in

20 different positions; another is a study of a horse; still a third is that of Saint Matthew, a warmup for the head used in *The Last Supper*. In addition, you'll find sketches by William Blake, Thomas Rowlandson, and 12 Holbeins (see in particular his sketch of Sir John Godsalve). The drawing exhibition may be visited at the same time as the State Apartments for an admission of 80p ($1.40) for adults and 40p (70¢) for children. It remains open, unlike the State Apartments, when the court is in residence.

Queen Mary's Dollhouse

Just about the greatest dollhouse in all the world is at Windsor. Presented to the late Queen Mary as a gift and later used to raise money for charity, the dollhouse is a remarkable achievement. It is a re-creation of what a great royal mansion of the 1920s looked like, complete with a fleet of cars, including a Rolls-Royce. The house is perfect for Tom Thumb and family and a retinue of servants. All is done with the most exacting detail—even the champagne bottles in the wine cellar contain vintage wine of that era. There's a toothbrush suitable for an ant. A minuscule electric iron really works. For late-night reading, you'll find volumes ranging from Hardy to Housman. In addition, you'll see a collection of dolls presented to the monarchy from nearly every nation of the Commonwealth. Queen Mary's Dollhouse may be viewed for an admission of 80p ($1.40) for adults, 40p (70¢) for children, even when the State Apartments are closed.

St. George's Chapel

A gem of the Perpendicular style, this chapel shares the distinction with Westminster Abbey of being a pantheon of English monarchs (Victoria is a notable exception). The present St. George's was founded in the late 15th century by Edward IV near the site of the original Chapel of the Order of the Garter (Edward III, 1348). You enter the nave first with its fan vaulting (a remarkable achievement in English architecture). The nave contains the tomb of George V and Queen Mary, designed by Sir William Reid Dick. Off the nave in the Urswick Chapel, the Princess Charlotte memorial provides an ironic touch. If she had survived childbirth in 1817, she—and not her cousin, Victoria—would have ruled the British Empire. In the aisle are the tombs of George VI and Edward IV. The Edward IV "Quire," with its imaginatively carved 15th-century choir stalls (crowned by lacy canopies and Knights of the Garter banners), evokes the pomp and pageantry of medieval days. In the center is a flat tomb, containing the vault of the beheaded Charles I, along with Henry VIII and one of his wives (no. 3, Jane Seymour). Finally, you may want to inspect the Prince Albert Memorial Chapel, reflecting the opulent tastes of the Victorian era. St. George's Chapel is usually open from 10:45 a.m. to 3:45 or 4 p.m. Monday to Saturday, and from 2 to 3:45 or 4 p.m. on Sunday. It is closed during services. Admission is £1.50 ($2.65) for adults, 60p ($1.05) for children. It's advisable to telephone to check opening hours if you're going to be there at a time not given as a regular opening time (tel. 0753/865538). It is closed in January and for a few days in mid-June.

Footnote: Queen Victoria died on January 22, 1901, and was buried beside her beloved Prince Albert in a mausoleum at **Frogmore** (a private estate), near Windsor (open only three days a year, in May). The Prince Consort died in December 1861.

The Royal Mews

Entered from St. Albans Street, the red-brick buildings of the Royal Mews and Burford House were built for Nell Gwynne in the 1670s. They were named for King Charles II's natural son by her, the Earl of Burford. When the child was 14 years old, he was created Duke of St. Albans, from which the street outside takes its name.

Housed in the mews is the exhibition of the Queen's Presents and Royal Carriages. Displayed are pictures of several members of the royal family, including those of Queen Elizabeth II as Colonel-in-Chief of the Coldstream Guards riding in the grounds of Buckingham Palace, the Duke of Edinburgh driving his horses through a water obstacle at Windsor, and the Queen Mother with Prince Edward, Viscount Linley, and Lady Sarah Armstrong-Jones in the Scottish State Coach. There is also a full-size stable with model horses showing stable kit, harnesses, and riding equipment. In the coach house is a magnificent display of coaches and carriages kept in mint condition and in frequent use. The exhibition of the Queen's Presents includes unique items of interest given to Her Majesty and the Duke of Edinburgh throughout her reign. There is also a collection of pencil drawings of the queen and family with horses and dogs.

The exhibition is open in November and December and from January to March from 10:30 a.m. to 3 p.m. Monday to Saturday. From April to October, hours are 10:30 a.m. to 5 p.m. From May to October, it is also open on Sunday, 10:30 a.m. to 3 p.m. Admission is £1 ($1.75) for adults, 50p (90¢) for children.

Royalty and Empire

The famous company founded by Madame Tussaud in 1802 has taken over part of the Windsor Town railway station to present an exhibition of "Queen Victoria's Diamond Jubilee 1837–1897." It's at the Windsor & Eton Central Railway Station on Thames Street (tel. 0753/857837). At one of the station platforms is a replica of *The Queen*, the engine used to draw the royal coaches, disembarking the life-size wax figures of guests arriving at Windsor for the Jubilee celebration. Seated in the Royal Waiting Room are Queen Victoria (in wax, of course) and her family. In one of the carriages, the Day Saloon, are Grand Duke Serge and the Grand Duchess Elizabeth (the queen's granddaughter) of Russia. The queen's faithful Indian servant, Hafiz Abdul Karim, the Munshi, waits in the anteroom. Among the famous guests portrayed are the Prince and Princess of Wales (Edward VII and Alexandra), the Empress Frederick of Prussia (Queen Victoria's eldest daughter), and the prime minister, Lord Salisbury.

The platform is busy with royal servants, a flower seller, a newsboy, an Italian with a barrel organ, and others who have come to see the arrival of the train. Drawn up on the ceremonial parade ground are the troops of the Coldstream Guards and the horse-drawn carriage that will take the party to the castle. With the sounds of military music in the background and the commands of the officers to their troops, you really feel you are present at Her Majesty Queen Victoria's arrival.

Afterward, at the end of the walkway through the Victorian Conservatory, you reach the 260-seat theater for a short audio-visual presentation, with life-size animated models giving further glimpses of life during Victoria's reign. The whole visit will only take 45 minutes. It is open daily, except Christmas, from 9:30 a.m. to 5:30 p.m. (4:30 p.m. in winter). Admission is £3.55 ($6.20) for adults, £2.55 ($4.45) for children.

Sunday Entertainment

There are often polo matches in **Windsor Great Park**—and at **Ham Common** —and you can often see Prince Charles playing and Prince Philip serving as umpire. The queen herself often watches. For more information, telephone 0753/860633.

Also, at the gates into the park are maps showing attractive paths for walking. You can circumnavigate Royal Lodge and walk through the Deer Park before enjoying a pint at one of the pubs outside the park (there's a pub at almost every gate).

The Town Itself

Windsor is largely a Victorian town, with lots of brick buildings and a few remnants of Georgian architecture. In and around the castle are two cobblestone streets —**Church and Market Streets**—with their antique shops, silversmiths, and pubs. One shop on Church Street is supposed to have been occupied by Nell Gwynne (she needed to be within beck and call of the king's private chambers). Church is also a good street on which to find low-cost tea room luncheons. After lunch or tea, you may want to stroll along the three-mile aptly named Long Walk.

Round Windsor Sightseeing Tour

A 35-minute tour of Windsor and the surrounding countryside is offered in an open-top, double-decker bus with commentary. The ten-mile drive starts from Windsor Castle and passes the Royal Mews, the Long Walk, the Royal Farms, Albert Bridge, Eton College, and the Theatre Royal. The departure point is Castle Hill, near the King Henry VIII Gateway to Windsor Castle. Adults pay £3 ($5.25) and children £2 ($3.50). Tickets, along with information about dates of operation and departure times, are available from **Windsorian Coaches,** 17 Alma Rd. (tel. 0753/856841).

Guided Tours

A 1½-hour guided tour of Windsor Castle and the town leaves from the **Tourist Information Centre** (tel. 0753/852010) in the Central Station, the one opposite the castle. The walking tour includes a look at the Long Walk, then the Guildhall and Market Cross House, along with the changing of the guard when possible. In the castle precincts you'll visit, the Cloisters and the Albert Memorial Chapel, finishing in the State Apartments, where no guiding is allowed. Subject to demand, the tours leave at 10:45 a.m. and 1:45 p.m. Monday to Saturday and at 1:45 p.m. on Sunday, costing adults £2 ($3.50) and children £1.50 ($2.65). All tours are accompanied by a licensed guide.

Boat Trips on the Thames

From an embarkation point on the Promenade, at Barry Avenue, there are regular boat departures for 35-minute trips to Boveney Lock. You pass the Windsor Horse Racecourse and cruise past Eton College's boathouses and the Brocas Meadows. On the return, you'll have a perfect view of Windsor Castle. The cost is £1.40 ($2.45) for adults, 70p ($1.25) for children. However, you can also take a two-hour trip through Boveney Lock and up past stately private riverside homes, The Bray Film Studios, Queens Eyot, and Monkey Island at a cost of £3.20 ($5.60) for adults, £1.60 ($2.80) for children. The boats carry light refreshments and have a licensed bar. There are toilets on board, and the decks are covered in case of that unexpected shower. However, your view of the river will be unimpaired. Tours are operated by **Windsor Boats,** Clewer Boathouse, Mill Lane, Windsor, Berkshire SL4 5JH (tel. 0753/862933).

WHERE TO EAT

Standing opposite the castle, the **Hideaway Bistro Grill,** 12 Thames St. (tel. 0753/842186), is operated by the prestigious Sir Christopher Wren's House Hotel. This is a far different place from their more formal restaurant, The Orangerie, which lies within the hotel itself. The Hideaway serves daily from 10 a.m. to 11 p.m., offering morning coffee, pastries, cakes, a wine and salad bar, cream teas, and informal candlelit dinners beginning at 6:30 p.m. It also features pre- and post-theater suppers. You can partake of the wine and salad bar for £4.50 ($7.90) to £5 ($8.75) or else try one of their fresh sandwiches (I'd suggest the "Covent Garden"). At night, dinners are priced from £12 ($21) and might begin with pâté of duckling and follow with a grill, perhaps stir-fry vegetables.

Dôme, 5 Thames St. (tel. 0753/864405), also across from the castle, is one of the most popular and sophisticated cafés in town. Sometimes live music is a feature, and its happy hour is perhaps its most engaging time of the day. It keeps long hours: daily from 9 a.m. to 11 p.m. (until 10:30 p.m. on Sunday), and serves food throughout the day. The selections run to such fare as light omelets, salmon mousse, or steak sandwiches. Look for the daily specials on a blackboard menu. Meals cost £5 ($8.75) and up.

The **William IV Hotel,** Thames Street, 100 yards from Eton Bridge (tel. 0753/851004), a lovely old place (circa 1500) with its armor, beams, and log fire, invites visitors in with its local atmosphere. Just outside is the chapter garden, where the Windsor martyrs were burned at the stake in 1544 for their religious beliefs. It was from this pub that they received their last cups of strong ale "in gratification of their last wish." The house built by Sir Christopher Wren for his own use is opposite the William IV, and the great architect of St. Paul's was reputedly a regular visitor to the old taproom, as were diarists Evelyn and Pepys. The present landlord is Ken Gardner, award-winning journalist and writer. Rub shoulders here with newspapermen and actors (nearby is the Theatre Royal), artists and river folk, and drink traditional ale. Food is home-cooked, and the portions are guaranteed to satisfy gargantuan appetites. You can sit at a sidewalk table in a pedestrian area by the Eton Bridge, gazing up at the castle while enjoying your lunch. At night, this is one of the busiest drinking spots in town. Pub hours for drinking are Monday to Saturday from 11 a.m. to 11 p.m., and on Sunday from noon to 3 p.m. and 7 to 10:30 p.m. Food service, however, is only from noon to 7 p.m. Monday to Saturday and noon to 3 p.m. on Sunday. Full meals cost from £4.50 ($7.90). The William IV lies at the bottom of Windsor Hill on the approach road to the bridge, which is open to pedestrians only. (In spite of its name, this place doesn't rent rooms.)

Country Kitchen, 3 King Edwards Court, Peascod Street (tel. 0753/868681). Walk from the castle gateway down Peascod Street to King Edwards Court for a good, home-cooked, whole-food meal in this light, airy, self-service restaurant above the shops. They make their own scones, tea bread, flans, cheesecake, and dessert. The soups, pâtés, and quiches are homemade, and only good vegetable oils, honey, lemon juice, herbs, and spices are used in the preparation of the main dishes. There's always a vegetarian dish, some low-fat, low-calorie ones, and 14 different salads. Hot dishes include chicken curry, lasagne, and chili con carne, and you can choose from the display of scrumptious desserts, including passion cake. They offer five different teas and herbs—decaffeinated if you wish—and fine house wines by the carafe or glass. You can eat here for £5 ($8.75) and up, plus the cost of your drink. On Sunday, a special two-course carvery lunch is offered for £5.95 ($10.40), with a selection from two or three roasts and five vegetables, or you can take the meat course and a selection of desserts. Everything is cooked on the premises here. Hours are from 10 a.m. to 5 p.m. Monday to Saturday and noon to 3 p.m. Sunday.

The **Drury House Restaurant,** 4 Church St. (tel. 0753/863734). The owner states with pride that all luncheons served in this wood-paneled 17th-century restaurant, dating from the days of Charles II, are home-cooked "and very English." A visit here could be included in a tour of Windsor Castle, as the entrance to the restaurant is only a stone's throw apart. A typical meal with soup, meat, vegetables, and dessert comes to about £6.50 ($11.40) per person. Owner Joan Hearne also serves a refreshing tea, including either homemade scones with jam and freshly whipped cream, or freshly made cream cakes, both offered with copious quantities of the obligatory tea. Drury House is open Tuesday to Sunday from 10 a.m. to 5:30 p.m.

Angelo's Wine Bar, 5 St. Leonards Rd. (tel. 0753/857600), is the unbeatable choice for good Italian wine and the savory cuisine of the Mediterranean (not the rubberlike pasta of many Italian restaurants in England). Try the minestrone, then follow with various Italian or international dishes. Meals are a good value, costing from £10 ($17.50), and are served daily, except Sunday, from noon to 2:30 p.m. and 5:30 to 11 p.m.

The Court Jester, Church Lane (tel. 0753/864257), is one of the town's most popular pubs, especially with young people in the evening when loud music plays. No evening meals are offered, but the traditional pub food during the day is priced at £2.50 ($4.40) and up. During the winter, there is a selection of hot dishes, while in summer an extensive buffet is offered. As well as a wide range of English ales, a traditional Sunday lunch is a feature of the week. Hours are from 11 a.m. to 2:30 p.m.

and 6 to 11 p.m. Monday to Saturday, and from noon to 3 p.m. and 7 to 10 p.m. Sunday.

WHERE TO STAY

You can get help at the **Tourist Information Centre,** Central Station, Thames Street (tel. 0753/852010), in the railway station at the top of the hill opposite the castle. Here you can book a bed ahead if you're touring or else find an accommodation in and around Windsor. This is a useful service, as many of the local guesthouses have no signs. There is also an information point in the Tourist Reception Centre at Windsor Coach Park.

Aurora Garden, 14 Bolton Ave., Windsor, Berkshire SL4 3JF (tel. 0753/868686), is a spacious Victorian house that has been successfully converted and modernized to receive paying guests. It's one of the most substantial places at which to stay in Windsor, charging more than your typical B&B, but making up for it in quality. The location is in the vicinity of Long Walk and Windsor Great Park. The hotel's most notable feature is its water garden, and umbrella-shaded tables are placed outside in summer. Each well-furnished unit—there are 14 in all—contains a private bath or shower, direct-dial phone, an alarm clock radio, and color TV. B&B rates are from £49 ($85.75) to £54 ($94.50) daily in a single and £60 ($105) to £65 ($113.75) in a double, with VAT included—a big splurge choice for Windsor.

Trinity Guest House, 18 Trinity Pl., Windsor, Berkshire SL4 3AT (tel. 9753/864186), offers one of the best values in town. B&B costs from £14 ($24.50) to £15 ($26.25) per person nightly, depending on the season. The guesthouse also accommodates families in its larger units. Because of its limited number of accommodations it can fill up quickly. The management is polite and courteous, and the rooms are pleasantly furnished. You'll be within walking distance of Windsor Castle.

Fairlight Lodge, 41 Frances Rd., Windsor, Berkshire SL4 3AQ (tel. 0753/861207), which was built in 1885 as the home of the mayor of Windsor, is highly rated among B&Bs inspected in Windsor. Located in a residential section only a few minutes' walk from the heart of Windsor and the castle, it offers comfortable bedrooms with private baths. Singles run £24 ($42) per night, doubles £39 ($68.25), and family rooms cost £49 ($85.75) per night. Accommodations have color TV and coffee-making facilities, and there is a place to park your car.

Alma House (not to be confused with Alma Lodge on the same street), 56 Alma Rd., Windsor, Berkshire SL4 3HA (tel. 0753/862983), drew praise from Helen Drew, a California reader, who proclaimed that in three years of "B & B'ing" in England she'd never found a more satisfactory place. The house is a well-built Victorian structure, about a five-minute walk from the castle. Many guests stay here and commute to Heathrow the following morning (depending on traffic, it's about a 20-minute ride). The hostess, Sally Shipp, is a wealth of information for travelers as well. She rents rooms for £13 ($22.75) to £16 ($28) daily in a single, £26 ($45.50) to £30 ($52.50) in a double. Two rooms contain private showers, and one is set aside for families.

For those who want to live across the river from Windsor town, **Christopher Hotel,** 110 High St., Eton, Windsor, Berkshire SL4 6AN (tel. 0753/852359), is the big splurge choice. At one time this was a noted coaching inn, and the former stable around the courtyard has been converted into modern bedrooms with showers, color TVs, radios, phones, trouser-presses, refrigerators, hairdryers, and other amenities. Singles range in price from £50 ($87.50) to £63 ($110.25) daily, with doubles costing from £65 ($113.75) to £80 ($140). Breakfast is extra. There are 35 rooms in all, 11 of which lie within the main building and 24 of which are in a annex across the courtyard. Also on the premises is a French restaurant, Grill Latour.

ETON

To visit Eton, home of what is arguably the most famous public school in the world (Americans would call it a private school), you can take a train from Paddington Station, go by car, or take the Green Line bus to Windsor. If you go by car, you can take the M4 motorway, leaving it at exit 5 to go straight to Eton. However, parking is likely to be a problem, so I advise turning off the M4 at exit 6 to Windsor. You can park there and take an easy stroll past Windsor Castle and across the Thames bridge. Follow Eton High Street to the college.

From Windsor Castle's ramparts, you can look down on the river and on the famous playing fields of Eton.

Eton College

Largest and best known of the public (private) schools of England, Eton College was founded by a teenage boy himself, Henry VI, in 1440. Some of England's greatest men, notably the Duke of Wellington, have played on the fields of Eton. Twenty prime ministers were educated at Eton, as well as such literary figures as George Orwell and Aldous Huxley. Even Ian Fleming, creator of James Bond, attended. The traditions of the school have had plenty of time to become firmly entrenched (ask a young gentleman in his Victorian black tails to explain the difference between a "wet bob" and a "dry bob"). If it's open, take a look at the Perpendicular chapel, with its 15th-century paintings and reconstructed fan vaulting. Visits to the school are possible from Easter to the end of September from 2 to 4:30 p.m. daily, with guided tours being given at 2:15 and 3:15 p.m. During the summer holidays, it is also open from 10:30 a.m. The guided tours of the school and museum (see below) cost £2.40 ($4.20) for adults, £1.80 ($3.15) for children. For information regarding visits, phone 0753/863593.

The Museum of Eton Life

The history of Eton College since its inception in 1440 is depicted in the museum situated in the vaulted wine cellars under College Hall, which were originally the storehouse for use of the college's masters. The displays, running from formal to extremely informal, include a turn-of-the-century boy's room, schoolbooks, sports trophies, canes that were used by senior boys to apply corporal punishment they felt needful to their juniors, and birch sticks used by masters for the same purpose. Also to be seen are letters written home by students describing day-to-day life at the school, as well as samples of the numerous magazines produced by students over the centuries, known as *ephemera* because of the changing condition of writers and ideas. Many of the items to be seen were provided by Old Etonians, with collections formerly scattered throughout the various buildings of the school also being included.

The museum schedule is based on the school year, with hours varying widely (see above). For information, contact The Custodian, Eton College (tel. 0753/863593).

For Meals

Eton Wine Bar, High Street (tel. 0753/854921), is owned and run by William and Michael Gilbey of the Gilbey's Gin family, even though no gin is served here. Just across the bridge from Windsor, it is a charming place, set among the antique shops with pinewood tables and old church pews and chairs. There is a small garden out back. Appetizers include borscht and a cheese-and-onion quiche. They also serve baked chicken with rosemary, Cornish smoked mackerel, cold roast beef, and salad. Each day several hot dishes are made, and desserts include pineapple and almond flan and damson crunch. Meals cost from £10 ($17.50) up. Wine can be ordered by the glass. Food is served from noon to 2:30 p.m. and 6 to 10:30 p.m. Monday to Thursday (to 11 p.m. Friday and Saturday). Sunday hours are from noon to 2 p.m. and 7 to 10 p.m.

Eton Buttery, 73 High St. (tel. 0753/854479), is just on the Eton side of the bridge from Windsor, a building among the boathouses of the college with magnificent views over the river and up toward the town and castle. Open seven days a week from 9:30 a.m. to 10:30 p.m., it is decorated with plain red brick walls, caneback chairs, and a mass of potted plants. This is an up-market self-service buffet owned by Doreen Stanton, who is also owner of The House on the Bridge restaurant opposite. Food is well displayed along spotless counters. There are waitresses to clear away and to bring you wine and drinks; otherwise you help yourself to a variety of quiches, cold sliced meats, and specialty salads and pâtés. There is also a hot roast of the day. Full meals cost from £12 ($21) per person.

NEARBY SIGHTS
Attractions of interest are in the surrounding area.

One of England's Great Gardens
Savill Garden, Wick Lane, Englefield Green (tel. 0753/860222), is in Windsor Great Park and is signposted from Windsor, Egham, and Ascot. Started in 1932, the garden is considered one of the finest of its type in the northern hemisphere. The display starts in spring with rhododendrons, camellias, and daffodils beneath the trees; then throughout the summer there are spectacular displays of flowers and shrubs, all presented in a natural state. It is open all year, except at Christmas, from 10 a.m. to 6 or 7 p.m., daily, and the admission is £1.80 ($3.15) for adults, free for accompanied children under 16.

Adjoining the Savill Garden are the **Valley Gardens,** full of shrubs and trees in a series of wooded natural valleys running down to Virginia water. It is open daily, for free, throughout the year.

Windsor Safari Park
Two miles southwest of Windsor Castle lies **Windsor Safari Park,** Winkfield Road (tel. 0752/869841), perhaps Britain's most exciting such park, with a killer whale/dolphin/sea lion show, plus shows of birds of prey, parrots, and a computer-animated Tiki show. There is also an exciting twin-track alpine toboggan run. You can see the tropical world of plants, alligators, butterflies, chimpanzees, and a host of other animals—tigers, lions, bears, wolves, baboons, and zebras, among others—in drive-through reserves. Open from 10 a.m. to dusk daily, except Christmas Day, the park has catering facilities, picnic areas, soft play centers, and adventure playgrounds. If you have a soft-top car or come on public transport, there is free safari bus service to take you through the reserves. The all-inclusive admission (for entrance and all shows and attractions) is £6.50 ($11.38) for adults, £5.50 ($9.65) for children. The park is 20 miles from London. Take the M4 motorway, leaving it at junction 6 and following the signs.

The Wellington Ducal Estate
If you'd like to make an interesting day trip in Berkshire, I suggest **Stratfield Saye House** (tel. 0256/882882), between Reading and Basingstoke on the A33. It has been the home of the dukes of Wellington since 1817 when the 17th-century house was bought for the Iron Duke to celebrate his victory over Napoleon at the Battle of Waterloo. Many memories of the first duke remain in the house, including his billiard table, battle spoils, and pictures. The funeral carriage that since 1860 had rested in St. Paul's Cathedral crypt is now in the ducal collection here. In the gardens is the grave of Copenhagen, the charger ridden to battle at Waterloo by the first duke. There are also extensive pleasure grounds together with a licensed restaurant and gift shop.

A short drive away is the **Wellington Country Park** (tel. 0734/326444) with the fascinating National Dairy Museum where you can see relics of 150 years of dairying. Other attractions include a riding school, nature trails, and boating and sailing on the lake. In addition, there are a miniature railway, the Thames Valley Time Trail, and a deer park.

The estate is open from 11:30 a.m. to 5 p.m. daily except Friday from May 1 to the last Sunday in September. Admission is £3 ($5.25) for adults and £1.50 ($2.65) for children. Wellington Country Park is open from 10 a.m. to 5 p.m. daily from March to September. Admission is £2 ($3.50) for adults, £1 ($1.75) for children. A combined ticket for the estate and park cost £4 ($7) for adults, £2 ($3.50) for children.

Mapledurham House

The Elizabethan mansion home of the Blount family (tel. 0734/723350) lies beside the river in the unspoiled village of Mapledurham, which can be reached by car from the A4074 Oxford-to-Reading road. A much more romantic way of reaching the old house is to take the boat, leaving the Promenade next to Caversham Bridge at 2:15 p.m. on Saturday, Sunday, and bank holidays from Easter to the end of September. The journey upstream takes about 40 minutes, and the boat leaves Mapledurham again at 5 p.m. for the journey back to Caversham.

This gives you plenty of time to walk through the house, viewing the Elizabethan ceilings and great oak staircase. You'll see portraits of the two beautiful sisters with whom the poet Alexander Pope, himself a frequent visitor, was in love. The family chapel, built in 1789, is a fine example of "modern Gothick."

Cream teas with homemade cakes are available at the house, and on the grounds is the last working watermill on the Thames. It still produces flour—100% wholemeal flour, which can be purchased. The house is open from 2:30 to 5 p.m. on Saturday, Sunday, and public holidays from Easter Sunday until the end of September. The mill is open from 1:30 to 5 p.m. on the same days in summer, and on Sunday from 2 to 4 p.m. in winter. Entrance to the house costs £2 ($3.50) for adults, £1 ($1.75) for children. To the mill, the charge is £1 ($1.75) for adults, 50p (90¢) for children.

The boat ride from Caversham costs £2.75 ($4.80) for adults, £1.95 ($3.40) for children for the round-trip. Further details about the boat can be obtained from **D&T Scenics Ltd.**, Pipers Island, Bridge Street, Caversham Bridge, Reading, Berkshire RG4 8AH (tel. 0734/481088).

2. Ascot

While following the Royal Buckhounds through Windsor Forest, Queen Anne decided to put a racecourse on Ascot Heath. The first race meeting at Ascot was inaugurated in 1711. Since then, the Ascot Racecourse has been a symbol of chic, as pictures of the Royal Family, including Queen Elizabeth II and Prince Philip, have been flashed around the world. Nowadays, instead of Queen Anne, you are likely to see Princess Anne, an avid horsewoman.

Ascot lies only 28 miles west of London, directly south of Windsor (take the A332). There is frequent rail service in London from Waterloo to Ascot Station, which lies about 10 minutes from the Racecourse.

Ascot Racecourse (tel. 0990/322211) is open throughout the year, except for March and August. There are three enclosures: Tattersalls is the largest, Silver Ring the least expensive, and the third is the Members Enclosure. Plenty of bars and restaurants exist to suit a wide range of pocketbooks. Tickets cost adults from £3 ($5.25) to £17 ($29.75); children under 16 are admitted free if accompanied by an adult. The highlight of the Ascot social season is Royal Week, in late June, but there is excellent racing on the third Saturday in July and the last Saturday in September, with nearly a million pounds in prize money.

FOOD AND LODGING

Should you like to stay here, there is a good, moderately priced hotel, **Highclere House Hotel,** Kings Road, Sunninghill, Ascot, Berkshire SL5 9AD (tel. 0990/

25220). Once an Edwardian private residence, this building has been refurbished, and now has a cozy bar and licensed restaurant. All bedrooms have tea- and coffee-making facilities, color TV, and direct-dial phones. Daily prices range from £30 ($52.50) in a single and £40 ($70) in a double Saturday and Sunday, and from £50 ($87.50) in a single and £60 ($105) in a double Monday to Friday. If you stay here, you'll be only a 12-minute drive from Windsor Castle.

More likely you'll be in Ascot for lunch. If so, I suggest the **Stag,** 63 High St. (tel. 0990/21622), where Ann McCarthy enjoys a local reputation for her good, hearty, and healthy cookery, like homemade whole-meal pasta. Whenever available, she uses organically grown vegetables. Some guests make a lunch just out of her stuffed potatoes. Meals cost from £6 ($10.50), but you can get by for less. Lunch is daily from noon to 2 p.m., dinner from 6 to 10 p.m.

---

3. Henley-on-Thames

At the eastern edge of Oxfordshire, only 35 miles from London, Henley-on-Thames is a small town and resort on the river at the foothills of the Chilterns. It is the headquarters of the Royal Regatta held annually in July, the number one event among European oarsmen. The regatta dates back to the first years of the reign of Victoria.

The Elizabethan buildings, the tea rooms, and the inns along its High Street live up to one's conception of what an English country town looks like—or should look like. Cardinal Wolsey is said to have ordered the building of the tower of the Perpendicular and Decorated parish church.

Life here is serene, and Henley-on-Thames makes for an excellent stopover en route to Oxford. However, readers on the most limited of budgets will find far less expensive lodgings in Oxford. The fashionable inns of Henley-on-Thames (Charles I slept here) are far from cheap. Warning: During the Royal Regatta rooms are difficult to secure, unless you've made reservations months in advance.

WHERE TO STAY

Lying off the A423, **Thamesmead House Hotel,** Remenham Lane, Remenham, Oxfordshire RG9 2LR (tel. 0491/574745), is a Tudoresque and Victorian-style house just over the bridge east of Henley-on-Thames near The Little Angel pub. Surrounded by a pretty garden, the house is of red brick with black and white timbers, and there is a parking area. The owner, Mrs. Maisie Vallance, has refurbished many bedrooms, adding showers and toilets. All rates include a full breakfast and VAT. Bathless singles cost £20 ($35) daily, and doubles are priced at £40 ($70) to £47.50 ($83.15), depending on the plumbing. Set lunches are offered for £6 ($10.50) and three-course dinners for £8.50 ($14.90). You can order an apéritif in the pleasant bar, and in winter you can enjoy log fires.

Flohr's Hotel and Restaurant, Northfield End, Henley-on-Thames, Oxfordshire RG9 2JG (tel. 0491/573412), is a 16th-century inn at the edge of town, yet within walking distance of the center and the river. The owners personally manage Flohr's and have kept its original charm, with oak beams and some period pieces, which offer modern comforts. All rooms have color TV and tea-and coffee-makers, and many have private showers and toilets. Singles cost from £30 ($52.50) daily, with doubles going for a splurgy £49 ($85.75) to £69 ($120.75). The restaurant boasts a creative continental menu, with many fish specialties.

WHERE TO EAT

Across the bridge on the London-Henley road (the A423) is a historic pub, **The Little Angel,** Remenham Lane, Remenham (tel. 0491/574165). It offers both pub meals and a charming dining room. Right on the highway, near the river, it serves ale brewed right in Henley and is also known for its fresh seafood. You can, in addition to fresh fish, get smoked salmon from Scotland, oysters and scallops, and many standard pub offerings. In fair weather, guests can enjoy tables placed outside, but in winter they are more likely to retreat to an intimate alcove, enjoying softly flickering candlelight. Your hosts, Paul and June Southwood, offer food daily from 10 a.m. to 2:30 p.m. and from 6 to 11 p.m. The setting is warm and welcoming, with old beamed ceilings. Meals cost from £8 ($14) in the bar, £15 ($26.25) in the restaurant.

Barnaby's Brasserie, 2 New St. (tel. 0491/572421), at the corner of Bell Street, is a half-timbered Tudor building, with a dark and warmly decorated traditional interior. From noon to 2 p.m. and from 7 to 10:30 p.m. (no lunch on Sunday), it offers a menu that is wide ranging, everything from barbecued back ribs to swordfish steak, from chili con carne to beef bourguignon. Count on spending from £9 ($15.75).

From Henley-on-Thames it is only a 24-mile drive to Oxford.

---

4. Oxford

A walk down the long sweep of The High, one of the most striking streets in England; a mug of cider in one of the old student pubs; the sound of a May Day dawn when choristers sing in Latin from Magdalen Tower; the Great Tom bell from Tom Tower, whose 101 peals traditionally signal the closing of the college gates; towers and spires rising majestically; the barges on the upper reaches of the Thames; nude swimming at Parson's Pleasure; the roar of a cannon launching the bumping races; a tiny, dusty bookstall where you can pick up a valuable first edition—all this is Oxford, 57 miles from London and home of one of the greatest universities in the world. An industrial city, the center of a large automobile business, as well as a university town, Oxford is better for sightseeing in summer. The students are wherever Oxford scholars go in the summer (allegedly they study more than they do at term time), and the many B&B houses—vacated by their gown-wearing boarders—will be happy to offer you an accommodation. But you'll be missing a great deal if you view Oxford without glimpsing its lifeblood.

However, at any time of the year you can enjoy a tour of the colleges, many of them representing a peak in England's architectural kingdom, as well as a valley of Victoriana. The Oxford Information Centre (see below) offers guided walking tours daily in summer and on Saturday in winter. Just don't mention the other place (Cambridge), and you shouldn't have any trouble.

The city predates the university; in fact, it was a Saxon town in the early part of the tenth century. And by the 12th century, Oxford was growing in reputation as a seat of learning at the expense of Paris. The first colleges were founded in the 13th century. The story of Oxford is filled with conflicts too complex and detailed to elaborate here. Suffice it to say that the relationship between town and gown wasn't as peaceful as it is today. Riots often flared, and both sides were guilty of abuses.

Nowadays the young people of Oxford take out their aggressiveness in sporting competitions, with the different colleges zealously competing in such games as cricket and soccer. However, all colleges unite into a powerful university when they face matches with their traditional rival, Cambridge.

Ultimately, the test of a great university lies in the persons it turns out. Oxford can name-drop a mouthful: Roger Bacon, Samuel Johnson, William Penn, John Wesley, Sir Walter Raleigh, Edward Gibbon, T. E. Lawrence, Sir Christopher Wren, John Donne, William Pitt, Matthew Arnold, Arnold Toynbee, Harold MacMillan, Graham Greene, A. E. Housman, and Lewis Carroll.

Many Americans arriving in Oxford ask, "Where's the campus?" If an Oxonian shows amusement when answering, it's understandable. Oxford University is, in fact, made up of 35 colleges. To tour all of these would be a formidable task. Besides, a few are of such interest they overshadow the rest.

PARK AND RIDE

Traffic and parking are a disaster in Oxford, and not just during rush hours. However, there are three large car parks on the north, south, and west of the city's ring road, all well marked. Car parking is free at all times, but at any time from 9:30 a.m. on, and all day on Saturday, you pay 60p ($1.05) for a bus ride into the city, getting off at St. Aldate's or Queen Street to see the city center. There is no service on Sunday, but then there's no need for it. The buses run every eight to ten minutes in each direction. The car parks are on the Woodstock road near the Peartree round-about, on the Botley road toward Faringdon, and on the Abingdon road in the southeast.

TOURS AND TOURIST SERVICES

A tourist reception center for Oxford is operated by **Guide Friday Ltd.,** at the railway station, Oxford. Their office dispenses free maps and brochures on the town and area and operates tours. Also available is a full range of tourist services, including accommodation references and car rental. In summer, the office is open daily from 9 a.m. to 6 p.m. In winter, hours are daily from 9 a.m. to 4 p.m. Guided tours of Oxford and the colleges leave from the railway station daily. In summer, aboard open-top double-decker buses, departures are every 15 minutes. The tour can be a 45-minute panoramic ride, or you can get off at any of the stops in the city. The ticket is valid all day. The tour price is £3 ($5.25).

THE SIGHTS

The best way to get a running commentary on the important sightseeing attractions is to go to the **Oxford Information Centre,** St. Aldate's Chambers, St. Aldate's, opposite the Town Hall, near Carfax (tel. 0865/726871). Walking tours through the city and the major colleges leave daily in the morning and afternoon. They last two hours and cost £2.40 ($4.20). The tour does not include New College or Christ Church. You can also get reservations for entertainment facilities, as well as for Stratford-upon-Avon and London West End theaters (tel. 0865/727855).

For a bird's-eye view of the city and colleges, climb **Carfax Tower.** This is the one with the clock and figures that strike the hours. Admission is 40p (70¢) for adults, 10p (20¢) for children. The tower is open from 10 a.m. to 6 p.m. Monday to Saturday and from 2 to 6 p.m. on Sunday from mid-March to late October. The rest of the year, hours are 10 a.m. to 4 p.m. Monday to Saturday and 1 to 4 p.m. on Sunday.

To help with an understanding of the university complex, **Heritage Projects Ltd.,** Broad Street (tel. 0865/728822), presents "The Oxford Story." It provides an insight into the structure of the colleges, with a look behind the portals at some of the architectural and historical features that might otherwise be missed. It also fills you in on the general background of the colleges and highlights the deeds of some of the famous personalities who have passed through its portals. The presentation is daily from 9 a.m. to 5 p.m., with an admission charge of £3 ($5.25) for adults and £1.50 ($2.65) for children.

At **Punt Station,** Cherwell Boathouse, Bardwell Road (tel. 0865/515978), you can rent a punt at a cost of £4 ($7) per hour, plus a £25 ($43.70) deposit. Similar charges are made on rentals at Magdalen Bridge Boathouse and at the Folly Bridge Boathouse. Hours are from 10 a.m. to 10 p.m. daily.

A Word of Warning

The main business of a university, is, of course, to educate—and unfortunately this function at Oxford has been severely interfered with by the number of visitors who have been disturbing the academic work of the university. So, with deep regret, visiting is now restricted to certain hours and small groups of six or fewer. In addition, there are areas where visitors are not allowed at all, but your tourist office will be happy to advise you when and where you may "take in" the sights of this great institution. Admission charges are levied at some places.

Christ Church

Begun by Cardinal Wolsey as Cardinal College in 1525, Christ Church, known as The House, was founded by Henry VIII in 1546. Facing St. Aldate's Street, Christ Church has the largest quadrangle of any college in Oxford.

Tom Tower houses Great Tom, the 18,000-pound bell referred to earlier. It rings at 9:05 nightly, signaling the closing of the college gates. The 101 times it peals originally signified the number of students at the time of the founding of the college. The student body number changed, but Oxford traditions live on forever.

In the 16th-century Great Hall, with its hammer-beam ceiling, are some interesting portraits, including works by those old reliables, Gainsborough and Reynolds. Prime ministers are pictured, as Christ Church was a virtual factory turning out actual and aspiring prime ministers: men such as Gladstone and George Canning. There is a separate picture gallery.

The cathedral, dating from the 12th century, was built over a period of centuries. (Incidentally, it is not only the college chapel but the cathedral of the diocese of Oxford.) The cathedral's most distinguishing features are its Norman pillars and the vaulting of the choir, dating from the 15th century. In the center of the Great Quadrangle is a statue of Mercury mounted in the center of a fish pond. The college and cathedral can be visited daily from 9:30 a.m. to noon, and 2 to 6 p.m. in summer (to 4:30 p.m. in winter). Entrance fee is £1 ($1.75).

Magdalen College

Pronounced "maud-len," this college was founded in 1458 by William of Waynflete, bishop of Winchester and later chancellor of England. Its alumni range all the way from Wolsey to Wilde. Opposite the botanic garden, the oldest in England, is the bell tower, where the choristers sing in Latin at dawn on May Day. The reflection of the 15th-century tower is cast in the waters of the Cherwell below. On a not-so-happy day, Charles I, his days numbered, watched the oncoming Roundheads. But the most celebrated incident in Magdalen's history was when some brave Fellows defied James II. Visit the 15th-century chapel, in spite of many of its latter-day trappings. The hall and other places of special interest are open when possible.

A favorite pastime is to take Addison's Walk through the water meadows. The stroll is so named after a former alumnus, Joseph Addison, the 18th-century writer and poet noted for his contributions to *The Spectator* and *The Tatler*. The grounds of Magdalen are the most extensive of any Oxford college, containing a deer park. You can visit Magdalen each day from 2 to 6:15 p.m.

Merton College

Founded in 1264, this college is among the trio of the most ancient at the university. It stands near Corpus Christi College on Merton Street, the sole survivor of Oxford's medieval cobbled streets. Merton College (tel. 0865/276310) is noted for its library, one of the oldest in England, having been built between 1371 and 1379. In keeping with tradition, some of its most valuable books were chained. Now only one book is so secured, to show what the custom was like. One of the treasures of the library is an astrolabe (astronomical instrument used for measuring the altitude of the sun and stars), thought to have belonged to Chaucer. You pay only 30p (55¢) to visit the ancient library, as well as the Max Beerbohm Room (named for the satirical English caricaturist who died in 1956). Both are open from 2 to 4 p.m. (to 4:30 p.m. March to October) Monday to Saturday, except between Christmas and the end of the second week in February and for a week at Easter. In addition, the college is open from 10 a.m. to noon on Saturday and Sunday only. You can also visit the chapel, dating from the 13th century, at these times.

University College

On the High, University College (tel. 0865/276602), is the oldest one at Oxford, tracing its history back to 1249 when money was donated by an ecclesiastic, William of Durham. More fanciful is the old claim that the real founder was Alfred the Great! Don't jump to any conclusions about the age of the buildings when you see the present Gothic-esque look. The original structures have all disappeared, and what remains today represents essentially the architecture of the 17th century, with subsequent additions in Victoria's day, as well as in more recent times. For example, the Goodhart Quadrangle was added as late as 1962. Its most famous alumnus, Shelley, was "sent down" for his part in collaborating on a pamphlet on atheism. However, all is forgiven today, as the romantic poet is honored by a memorial erected in 1894. The hall and chapel of University College can be visited during university vacations daily from 10 a.m. to noon and 2 to 4 p.m. (otherwise, 2 to 4 p.m.).

New College

New College was founded in 1379 by William of Wykeham, bishop of Winchester and later Lord Chancellor of England. The college at Winchester supplied a constant stream of candidates. The first quadrangle, dating from before the end of the 14th century, was the initial quadrangle to be built in Oxford, forming the architectural design for the other colleges. In the antechapel is Sir Jacob Epstein's remarkable modern sculpture of Lazarus and a fine El Greco painting of St. James. One of the treasures of the college is a crosier (pastoral staff of a bishop) belonging to the founding father. In the garden you can see the remains of the old city wall and the mound. The college (entered at New College Lane) can be visited daily from 2 to 5 p.m. at term time (otherwise, 11 a.m. to 5 p.m.).

Salter's River Thames Services

From mid-May until mid-September, Salter Brothers run daily passenger boat services on many reaches of the River Thames. Trips are to or from Oxford, Abingdon, Reading, Henley, Marlow, Cookham, Maidenhead, Windsor, Runnymede, and Staines. Combined outings from London can be made in conjunction with train or bus services. Full details can be obtained from **Salter Bros. Ltd.,** Folly Bridge, Oxford (tel. 0865/243421).

ACCOMMODATIONS

When the tourist rush is on, why tire yourself further? The **Oxford Information Centre,** St. Aldate's Chambers, St. Aldate's (tel. 0865/726871), operates a room-booking service for personal callers for a fee of £2 ($3.50) and a 7% refundable deposit. In addition, bed and breakfast accommodation can be arranged for visitors in most other areas of England for a £2 ($3.50) fee. If you'd like to seek lodgings on your own, you may try one of the following recommendations:

Bed and Breakfast

The **Old Parsonage Hotel,** 3 Banbury Rd., Oxford, Oxfordshire OX2 6NN (tel. 0865/310210), is so old it looks like an extension of one of the ancient colleges. Originally a 13th-century hospital named Bethleen, it was restored in the early 17th century. Today it's slated for designation as an ancient monument. Near St. Giles Church, it is set back from the street behind a low stone wall and sheltered by surrounding trees and shrubbery. However, most of the rooms are in a modern wing that is more institutional in character. The owners charge from £25 ($43.75) per person nightly for B&B in a single, £38 ($66.50) in a double or twin. With a

OXFORD

KEY TO NUMBERED SIGHTS:

1. Somerville College
2. Keble College
3. Mansfield College
4. Ruskin College
5. St. John's College
6. Trinity College
7. Wadham College
8. Manchester College
9. St. Catherine's College
10. Worcester College
11. Balliol College
12. New College
13. Nuffield College
14. St. Peter's College
15. Jesus College
16. Exeter College
17. Lincoln College
18. Brasenose College
19. Hertford College
20. All Souls College
21. Queen's College
22. Magdalen College
23. Oriel College
24. University College
25. Corpus Christi College
26. Christ Church College
27. St. Hilda's College

private shower, the price is £54 ($94.50) for two persons. A family room for three rents for £52 ($91) nightly, including a full English breakfast, VAT, and service. Some of the large front rooms, with leaded-glass windows, are set aside for tourists. You have breakfast in a pleasant modern dining room, overlooking the garden. A licensed restaurant and bar are on the premises. The cost of an average three-course meal is from £10 ($17.50).

Green Gables, 326 Abingdon Rd., Oxford, Oxfordshire OX1 4TE (tel. 0865/725870), was originally an Edwardian private residence before its transformation into a residence adapted to receive overnight visitors. The location is about a mile to the south of the university city, lying on the A4144. Trees screen the house from the main road. Mr. and Mrs. Jelfs rent eight comfortable bedrooms, three of which contain private baths. The charge for B&B is £15 ($26.25) daily in a bathless single, £34 ($59.50) to £38 ($66.50) in a double with bath, and £28 ($49) to £30 ($52.50) in a bathless double. Limited parking is available.

At **Cotswold House,** 363 Banbury Rd., Oxford, Oxfordshire OX2 7PL (tel. 0865/310558), Jim and Anne O'Kane operate a stone-built house that is one of the better B&Bs in the Oxford area. Large bedrooms with shower, toilet, refrigerator, TV, coffee-making equipment, and hairdryer range from £15 ($27.13) per person nightly. Traditional and vegetarian breakfasts and fresh fruit are always available, all with generous Irish helpings. There is ample off-street parking. The O'Kanes help with maps and give good touring advice. Cotswold House is about 1½ miles from the center, but it is much easier for motorists to use the ring road. Buses pass by about every five minutes.

Lonsdale Guest House, 312 Banbury Rd., Summertown, Oxford, Oxfordshire OX2 7PL (tel. 0865/54872), is another pleasant accommodation. This one is run by Roland and Christine Adams, who have established a gem of a little guesthouse. A comfortable bedroom, with hot and cold running water and free use of the corridor bath, plus an individually prepared breakfast, costs from £15 ($26.25) per person nightly (less for longer stays). A large family room has a private shower. All units have twin beds, lounge chairs, occasionally an antique chest of drawers, TV, innerspring mattresses, comforters of soft down, wall-to-wall carpeting, and central heating. A few units have their own showers. A full English breakfast is served. If you arrive at term time, you may think you're in a fraternity house. A heated indoor pool and several restaurants are about a two-minute walk from the house. You will also find tennis courts and a launderette.

At **St. Michael's Guest House,** 26 St. Michael's St., off Cornmarket, Oxford, Oxfordshire OX1 2EB (tel. 0865/242101), near Oxford Union, Mrs. Margaret Hoskins, the manager, welcomes guests in one of six comfortably furnished bathless rooms, each with color TV. With an English breakfast included in the price, charges are from £15 ($26.25) nightly in a single and £28 ($49) in a double. Part of the ancient medieval fortifications of Oxford run through the basement of this house.

Mr. and Mrs. R. J. Carter own the **Walton Guest House,** 169 Walton St., Oxford, Oxfordshire OX1 2HD (tel. 0865/52137), lying at the city end of Walton Street, 100 yards from the bus station and half a mile from the rail station. It overlooks the grounds of Worcester College. All the pleasantly furnished rooms have hot and cold running water, shaver points, central heating, tea- and coffee-makers, and TV. Terms are from £13 ($22.75) per person here, including a first-class English breakfast.

Belmont Guest House, 182 Woodstock Rd., Oxford, Oxfordshire OX2 7NG (tel. 0865/53698), is on a tree-lined avenue in the residential part of Oxford, about one mile from the city center. All rooms have central heating, hot and cold running water, and tea- and coffee-makers. A few have private showers. Most rooms can be used as either doubles, twins, or family rooms. The owners, Mr. and Mrs. J. Deadman, charge £13 ($19.25) per person nightly for B&B.

Willow Reaches Hotel, 1 Whytham St., Oxford, Oxfordshire OX1 4SU (tel.

0865/721545), lies on a cul-de-sac about a mile south from the center of Oxford. Attractively furnished bedrooms cost £19 ($33.25) to £22 ($38.50) daily in a single, £30 ($52.50) in a double. For a private bath, two persons pay from £36 ($63) to £39 ($68.25). A three-course table d'hôte dinner costs from £7.50 ($13.15) per person. Children are especially catered to, and there is a boating lake just for them nearby. Guests can relax in the garden or follow a special footpath to a nearby village for a pub meal or an early-morning constitutional.

Brown's Guest House, 281 Iffley Rd., Oxford, Oxfordshire OX4 4AQ (tel. 0865/246822), is a year-round guesthouse run by the Brown family. The half-dozen rooms are pleasantly furnished, with hot and cold running water, central heating, color TV, and beverage-making facilities. Guests are charged from £12 ($21) per person for B&B. There are adequate showers outside the rooms. Families are catered to, with special breakfasts if requested. The house is about a mile from the city center, with such nearby amenities as a post office, launderette, grocery store, drugstore, and bike rental shop.

Red Mullions Guest House, 23 London Rd., Oxford, Oxfordshire OX3 7RE (tel. 0865/64727), outside the center, is nevertheless convenient because of good bus connections. It lies near the ring road and a bus stop. Rooms are pleasantly and attractively furnished, all with private bath, color TV, and coffee-making equipment. The charge is £18 ($31.50) daily in a single, £30 ($52.50) to £38 ($66.50) in a double or twin, £45 ($78.75) in a room for three persons, and £55 ($96.25) in a room for four. A breakfast, for which your host, Mrs. Robinson, shops every day, is included.

At **Lakeside Guest House,** 118 Abingdon Rd., Oxford, Oxfordshire OX1 4PZ (tel. 0865/244725), proprietors Martin and Daniela Shirley run this Victorian house overlooking open fields and parklands that lead to the University Boat Houses. It is about five minutes from Christ Church College. The house has been remodeled and updated. Their facilities include a twin room with a bath, a double with bath, a family unit for four, and another family unit for three. The charge for B&B is £14 ($24.50) to £16 ($28) per person nightly, depending on the plumbing. There is hot and cold running water, tea- or coffee-making facilities, and color TV in all rooms. It is also centrally heated.

The **Galaxie Private Hotel,** 180 Banbury Rd., Oxford, Oxfordshire OX2 7BT (tel. 0865/515688), is owned by G. and M. Harries-Jones, whose rooms are spotlessly clean. A bus service on Banbury Road will take you the 1½ miles to the center of town. The location of this small family hotel is in Summertown, a choice suburb. All of the 33 bedrooms are equipped with reading lights, electric shaving points, hot and cold running water, central heating, and color TV. Many of the units have showers and toilets, for which you'll pay more, of course. For a bed and typical filling English breakfast, the cost per person daily for a single is from £20 ($35); a double is from £28 ($49). There is central heating, and parking space is available.

The **Pine Castle Hotel,** 290 Iffley Rd., Oxford, Oxfordshire OX4 1AE (tel. 0865/241497), is a comfortable Edwardian guesthouse operated by Peter and Marilyn Morris, with a host of amenities to make your stay enjoyable. The hotel has central heating, with tea- and coffee-making facilities and TV in all the rooms, plus a TV lounge if you prefer to watch in company. The Morrises can supply you with shoe-cleaning equipment, an iron, a hairdryer, current adapters, and an alarm clock as needed, and there are laundry, dry-cleaning, and post office outlets across the street. For B&B, charges are £13.50 ($23.65) to £16 ($28) per person per day, with furniture for small children available. They will also arrange tours of the city and university buildings. Their location is 1½ miles from the city center on a good bus route, convenient to a post office and a launderette. Evening meals can be arranged if you'd like to stay in.

Adams Guest House, 302 Banbury Rd., Oxford, Oxfordshire OX2 7ED (tel. 0865/56118), in Summertown, a suburb of Oxford, is operated by John Strange.

This is one of the best B&Bs in the Oxford area, offering comfortable and cozy rooms with hot and cold running water and TV. The B&B charge is from £13 ($22.75) per person, with some family rooms also available. Breakfast is served in a dining room decorated in an old-world style. Mr. Strange will provide touring tips.

River Hotel 17 Botley Rd., Oxford, Oxfordshire OX2 0AA (tel. 0865/243475), a well-run hotel opening onto a boat mooring on the Thames at Osney Bridge, lies to the west of the heart of Oxford but is still within walking distance. Owner-operated, the hotel offers more than two dozen bedrooms, a trio of which is set aside for families. The rooms are well furnished, with alarm clocks and direct-dial phones, and most of them offer a private bath or shower. The B&B rate in a single ranges from £30 ($52.50) to £35 ($61.25) daily, rising to £40 ($70) to £50 ($87.50) in a double. Guests can enjoy drinks in the lounge and bar overlooking the river, later ordering reasonably priced food in the aptly named River Restaurant.

Bravalla Guest House, 242 Iffley Rd., Oxford, Oxfordshire OX4 1SE (tel. 0865/241326), stands about a mile from the heart of Oxford and about half that distance from Magdalen College. It is small and well known, so reserve in advance in summer. Built in the late Victorian era, the house contains five pleasantly furnished bedrooms, two of which offer private baths or showers and two of which are suitable for families. Charges for two persons range from £24 ($42) to £34 ($59.50) a night for B&B. The Downes family members are your hosts.

Courtfield Private Hotel, 367 Iffley Rd., Oxford, Oxfordshire OX4 4DP (tel. 0865/242991), stands on a tree-lined street close to the center of Iffley Village, so it is most suitable for motorists who don't want to face the congested center. If you're not driving, you will find adequate public transportation. The house has been modernized with triple-glazed windows in the bedrooms, most of which contain a private bath or shower. B&B ranges from £16 ($28) to £20 ($35) daily in a single and £30 ($52.50) to £34 ($59.50) in a double.

On the Outskirts

Westwood Country Hotel, Hinksey Hill Top, Oxford, Oxfordshire OX1 5BG (tel. 0865/735408), is one of the most desirable of the moderately priced hotels on the outskirts of Oxford for those willing to pay a little more for its superior facilities. Family-run by the Parkers, it offers 26 well-furnished bedrooms (five for families), each with private bath or shower and such amenities as radio, color TV, intercom, beverage-making equipment, and video. Rates range from £32 ($56) daily in a single, rising to a range of £48 ($84) to £52 ($91) in a double. The hotel stands on 3 ½ acres of gardens and woodland. In winter, log fires invite you for a long, lingering session, and you can later enjoy the good home-cooked food after a drink in the cozy bar with a covered well. A Jacuzzi and small gym are also available to guests.

Tilbury Lodge Private Hotel, 5 Tilbury Lane, Eynsham Road, Botley, Oxford, Oxfordshire OX2 9NB (tel. 0865/862138), lies on a pleasant country lane about two miles from the center of Oxford, less than a mile from the railway station. However, you don't need a car to stay here, because Eddie Trafford has been known to pick up guests at the station. At the lodge, his wife, Eileen, welcomes guests, showing them to one of their well-furnished and comfortable rooms, all of which contain private baths. The B&B rate is from £20 ($35) daily in a single, £40 ($70) in a double. Children over 6 are made welcome. A bus that stops nearby takes visitors to the center of Oxford.

Highfield West Guest House, 188 Cumnor Hill, Oxford, Oxfordshire OX2 9PJ (tel. 0865/863007), stands three miles from the heart of Oxford on a good residential road, which is within easy access of the ring road surrounding Oxford. The little village of Cumnor, with its two country inns serving food and drink, is within walking distance. Tina and Robin Barrett offer B&B accommodations in single, double, twin, or family rooms, mostly with private bath, ranging from £15 ($26.25) to £18 ($31.50) per person nightly. A lounge is available for the use of guests, and in season visitors enjoy their heated outdoor pool. A bus into Oxford stops just outside their front yard, and there is also good local taxi service.

WHERE TO EAT

All Oxford undergraduates aren't the sons or daughters of wealthy dukes, as you'll soon discover when you see Oxford's numerous restaurants and cafés where you can get good food at reasonable prices. Here are my recommendations, which will be followed by my pub selections.

The **Cherwell Boathouse Restaurant,** Bardwell Road (tel. 0865/52746), is owned and run by Tony Verdin, with the help of a young crew. Two fixed menus are offered at each meal, and the cooks change the menu every two weeks to allow for the availability of fresh vegetables, fish, and meat. Appetizers include soups or fish or meat pâtés, followed by casseroles, pies, and hotpots. There is a very reasonable wine list. The restaurant is open every evening from 7:30 to 11:30 p.m. and for Sunday lunch from 12:30 to 2 p.m. For a table d'hôte dinner, the charge is from £12 ($21), and Sunday lunch is £9.25 ($16.20). It's recommended that you make a reservation. Children, if they don't order a full meal, are granted half price. In summer, the restaurant also does an all-day cold buffet on the terrace.

Munchy Munchy, 6 Park End St. (tel. 0865/245710), is known for its food of Southeast Asia, including Indonesian and Malaysian dishes. Some Oxford students, who frequent this location near the station, consider that this restaurant offers the best food value in the city. Dishes depend on what is available in the marketplace. Ethel Ow is adept at herbs and seasoning, and often uses fresh fruit inventively, as reflected by such dishes as scallops sautéed with ginger and lamb with passion-fruit sauce. Meals, costing from £7 ($12.25) to £10 ($17.50), are served Tuesday to Saturday from noon to 2:30 p.m. and from 5:30 to 10 p.m. It is closed on Sunday and for three weeks in August and another three weeks in December and January. The place is unlicensed, so you have to bring your own bottle. Sometimes, especially on Friday and Saturday, long lines form at the door.

Nosebag, 6-8 St. Michael's St. (tel. 0865/721033), one of the most popular places to eat among students at Oxford, is a self-service upstairs cafeteria on a side street off Cornmarket, opposite St. Michael's Church. But if you arrive at the busy main mealtimes, you'll probably have to queue (line up) on the stairs. At lunch you can get a homemade soup, followed by the dish of the day, perhaps a moussaka. Baked potato with a variety of fillings is a good accompaniment, as is the hot garlic bread. The menu increasingly leans to vegetarian dishes. Wine—white, red, or rosé —is available by the glass. A complete meal will cost from £5 ($8.75). The Nosebag is open Monday to Friday from 10 a.m. to 5:30 p.m., on Saturday from 9:30 a.m. to 6:30 p.m., and on Sunday from 10 a.m. to 6 p.m.

St. Aldate's Church Coffee House, 94 St. Aldate's (tel. 0865/245952), opened by the Archbishop of Canterbury in 1963, is almost opposite the entrance to Christ Church College, adjacent to St. Aldate's Church. An offbeat suggestion for eating, it is a bookshop/coffeehouse. Head for the back, where you'll find a large restaurant with counter service run by the church. All the food is homemade, including soups and salads from fresh produce daily. The generous meals are priced around £3.90 ($6.85). The coffeehouse is open from 10 a.m. to 5 p.m. daily, except Sunday.

Go Dutch, 18 Park End St. (tel. 0865/240686), opposite the railway station, evokes the Netherlands with crêpes served with savory fillings, such as bacon with apple or perhaps ham, corn, and green pepper. If you don't like the advertised stuffings, make up your own, perhaps with a few of the many sweet fillings. To go with your crêpe, order one of the crisp, fresh salads as a side dish. Count on spending from £5 ($8.75). Plenty of green plants have been placed about. The establishment is open from noon to 2:30 p.m. and 6 to 11 p.m. daily.

Browns, 5-9 Woodstock Rd. (tel. 0865/511995), is a big, bustling brasserie "à l'anglaise," popular with students who know of its quick snack meals. There is always a hamburger on the grill, and the staff will make you a hot pastrami on rye or perhaps a club sandwich. They also serve spaghetti with various sauces, salads, and such main dishes as fish pie topped with cheddar cheese pastry. You'll spend from £10 ($17.50) for a meal, less if you're snacking. Browns is open seven days a week, from 11 a.m. (from noon on Sunday) to 11:30 p.m. Sometimes you'll see long lines of students waiting to get in, as this is the most popular dining place in Oxford.

Maxwell's, 36-37 Queen St. (tel. 0865/242192), is a big, airy room that attracts homesick Americans with its cuisine. The Yankee theme is carried throughout the menu, which includes quarter-pound burgers, barbecued ribs, and T-bone steaks. Soda-fountain specials include malts, sundaes, and banana splits. Meals cost from £7 ($12.25). Maxwell's is open daily from noon to midnight. It's on a busy shopping street across from Marks & Spencer (you climb the stairs to its second-floor setting).

Opium Den, 79 George St. (tel. 0865/248680), attracts only those "addicts" who desire good Cantonese food at reasonable prices. Sizable dinners can be ordered in special fixed-price menus for one, two, three, or four diners. A typical dinner, plus an aromatic pot of Chinese tea, would bring the bill to £7.50 ($13.15). Budgeteers could select two courses at lunch from a wholesome variety of less expensive items for around £5 ($8.75). From Monday to Saturday, hours are noon to 2:30 p.m. and 6 p.m. to midnight. On Sunday, hours are 1 to 2:30 p.m. and 6 p.m. to midnight.

Raffles Tea Room, 90 High St. (tel. 0865/241855), a branch of a tea-room chain system, is located below the House of Tweed. It offers a variety of beverages, reminding me of a Parisian café, but the ambience is definitely English. Teatime can be an event, particularly if you order two scones with jam and cream, along with a pot of Ceylon or Earl Grey tea. There's a wide choice of cakes and eclairs, and hot dishes and cold salads that could be a satisfying lunch for around £4 ($7). An afternoon tea costs from £2 ($3.50). It is open from 9:30 a.m. to 5 p.m. Monday to Friday (from 10:30 a.m. to 4:30 p.m. on Sunday in summer). It is closed Saturday.

THE SPECIAL PUBS OF OXFORD

A short block from the High overlooking the northside of Christ Church College, the **Bear Inn,** Alfred Street (tel. 0865/244680), is an Oxford tradition. It's the village pub. Its swinging inn sign depicts the bear and ragged staff, old insignia of the Earls of Warwick, who were among the early patrons. Built in the 13th century, the inn has been known to many famous people who have lived and studied at Oxford. Over the years it's been mentioned time and time again in English literature.

The Bear has served a useful purpose in breaking down social barriers, bringing a wide variety of people together in a relaxed and friendly way. You might talk with a rajah from India, a university don, a titled gentleman—and the latest in a line of owners that goes back more than 700 years. Around the bar you'll see thousands of snipped portions of neckties, which have been labeled with their owners' names, the most famous of which is Lord Ismay, former head of NATO. For those of you who want to leave a bit of yourself, a thin strip of the bottom of your tie will be cut off (with your permission, of course) with a huge pair of ceremonial scissors. Then you, as the donor, will be given a free drink on the house. After this initiation, you may want to join in some of the informal songfests of the undergraduates. The shelves behind the bar are stacked and piled with items to nibble on: cheese, crisp rolls, cold meats, flans. Light meals cost from £3.50 ($6.05). Hours are daily from 11 a.m. to 2:30 p.m. and 5:30 to 11 p.m., and from noon to 3 p.m. and 7 to 10:30 p.m. Sunday.

The **Turf Tavern,** 4-5 Bath Place (tel. 0865/43235), a 13th-century tavern, is on a very narrow passage in the area of the Bodleian Library, off New College Lane. Thomas Hardy used the place for the setting of *Jude the Obscure.* It was "the local" of Burton and Taylor when they were in Oxford many years ago making a film, and today's star patrons include such names as Kris Kristofferson and John Hurt. At night, the old tower of New College and part of the old city wall are floodlit, enabling you, in warm weather, to enjoy an al fresco evening in a historical setting. In winter braziers are lighted in the courtyard and gardens, which adds a beautiful atmosphere. Inside the low-beamed hospice, you can order traditional English pub food. More impressive, however, is a table about eight feet long and four feet wide, covered with meats, fish, fowl, eggs, cheeses, bread puddings, sausages, cakes, and salads (all cold), and a selection of hors d'oeuvres, freshly prepared daily. You can fill your plate for about £5.50 ($9.65). Excellent local ales—try the Old Hooky—plus a range of country wines, are served all year, and a special punch is offered in winter to warm you through. Hours are from 11 a.m. to 11 p.m. Monday to Saturday, and from noon to 3 p.m. and 7 to 10:30 p.m. Sunday. It's reached via St. Helen's Passage between Holywell Street and New College Lane (you'll probably get lost, but any student worth his beer can direct you).

The **Trout Inn**, 195 Godstow Rd., near Wolvercote (tel. 0865/54485), lies on the outskirts of Oxford. Ask any former or present student of Oxford to name his or her most treasured pub, and the answer is likely to be the Trout. Hidden away from visitors and townspeople, the Trout is a private world where you can get ale and beer —and top-notch meals. Have your drink in one of the historic rooms, with their settles, brass, and old prints, or go out in sunny weather to sit on a stone wall. On the grounds are peacocks, ducks, swans, and herons that live in and around the river and an adjacent weir pool, joining with a shoal of chub fish in turning up for a free feast if you're handing out crumbs. Take an arched stone bridge, stone terraces, architecture with wildly pitched roofs and gables, add the Thames River, and you have the Trout. The Stable Bar, the original 12th-century part, complements the relatively new 16th-century bars of the Trout.

Daily specials are featured, and there is an excellent cold snack bar, with prices ranging from £1.50 ($2.65) to £4.85 ($8.50), the charge for a smoked salmon salad. Hot meals are served all day in the restaurant. You can dine well for £4.50 ($7.80) up to £8.15 ($14.25). Salads are served in summer and grills in winter. The Trout is open from 11 a.m. to 2:30 p.m. and 6 to 11 p.m. Monday to Saturday, and from noon to 2 p.m. and 7 to 10:30 p.m. Sunday. If you don't have a car, take bus 520 or 521 to Wolvercote, then walk to the pub. On your way there and back, look for the view of Oxford from the bridge.

A Shopping Note: An arcade of first-class shops and boutiques, the **Golden Cross** lies between Cornmarket Street and the Covered Market (or between High Street and Market Street). Parts of the arcade date from the 12th century. Many buildings remain from the medieval era, along with some 15th- and 17th-century structures. The market also has a reputation as the Covent Garden of Oxford, where live entertainment takes place on Saturday mornings in summer. In the arcade shops you'll find a wide selection of merchandise, including handmade Belgian chocolates, specialty gifts, clothing for both women and men, and luxury leather goods.

DIDCOT

A little town ten miles south of Oxford near the Berkshire border, east of the A34, Didcot is served by trains from Paddington Station in London. Didcot Parkway is a principal intercity station, with good connections to Oxford, Bristol, Reading, and the south coast. Didcot Halt is a typical small country station. It would be called a flag stop in the U.S.

For the railway buff, this place is paradise, the home of the **Didcot Railway Centre** (tel. 0235/817200). In the engine sheds are steam locomotives, and on "steaming days" you can roll gently along in a Great Western Railway train running on a recreation of Brunel's original broad-gauge Great Western track. In season, various other preserved railways in the country send visiting locomotives. The center is open Saturday, Sunday, and bank holidays from 11 a.m. to 5 p.m. March to mid-December, and daily from Easter to the beginning of September. Admission charges are £2 ($3.50) to £3.50 ($6.15), depending on the event.

---

5. Woodstock (Blenheim Palace)

The small country town of Woodstock, the birthplace of the Black Prince—ill-fated son of King Edward III—in 1330, lies on the edge of the Cotswolds. Some of the stone houses here were constructed when Woodstock was the site of a royal palace, which had suffered the ravages of time so that its remains were demolished when Blenheim Palace was built. Woodstock was once the seat of a flourishing glove industry.

Some 8 miles north of Oxford on the A34 road to Stratford-upon-Avon, Woodstock's main claim to fame today is—

BLENHEIM PALACE

This extravagant baroque palace regards itself as England's answer to Versailles. Blenheim is the home of the 11th Duke of Marlborough, a descendant of the first Duke of Marlborough (John Churchill), an on-again, off-again favorite of Queen Anne. In his day (1650–1722), the first duke became the supreme military figure in Europe. Fighting on the Danube near a village named Blenheim, Churchill defeated the forces of Louis XIV. The lavish palace of Blenheim was built for the duke as a gift from the queen. It was designed by Sir John Vanbrugh, who was also the architect of Castle Howard. Landscaping was carried out by Capability Brown.

The palace is loaded with riches: antiques, porcelain, oil paintings, tapestries, and chinoiserie. But many North Americans know Blenheim as the birthplace of Sir Winston Churchill. His birthroom forms part of the palace tour, as does the Churchill exhibition, four rooms of letters, books, photographs, and other Churchilliana. Today the former prime minister lies buried in Bladon Churchyard, near the palace.

Blenheim Palace is open every day from mid-March to October, from 10:30 a.m. to 5:30 p.m. The last admittance to the palace is at 4:30 p.m. Admission is £4.50 ($7.90) for adults, £2.20 ($3.85) for children.

In the park is the **Blenheim Butterfly and Plant Centre.** The complex contains a Butterfly House, containing tropical moths and butterflies in free flight in a virtually natural habitat; an Adventure Play Area; a Garden Cafe; a gift shop; and a shop for plants and gardening requirements.

The palace is at Woodstock, eight miles north of Oxford on the A34 road to Stratford-upon-Avon. From Oxford, there is a "Blenheim Palace and Historic Woodstock" open-top bus, which runs every 70 minutes from Beaumont Street. Tickets, which include the palace tour, can be purchased on the bus or, including rail travel, at any main-line railway station. For information, phone 0993/811325.

WHERE TO STAY

Much like a country house hotel, **The Kings Arms Hotel,** 19 Market Pl., Woodstock, Oxfordshire OX7 1ST (tel. 0993/811412), was one of the properties that Queen Elizabeth I gave to Woodstock when she came to the throne. The family-run hotel welcomes travelers on the A34 between Stratford-upon-Avon and the south. Go early to enjoy a drink in the bar, then later have a meal at Wheeler's St. James Restaurant, a branch of a well-known London seafood restaurant. Featuring the largest seafood menu in the area, they offer lunches for £9.50 ($16.65), dinners for £12 ($21). The bedrooms, 10 in all, are individually designed (one with a four-poster), each with private bath, direct-dial phone, hairdryer, coffee-making facilities, and color TV. Singles cost £40 ($70) daily, with doubles going for £54 ($94.50), including VAT and an English breakfast.

The **Marlborough Arms Hotel,** Oxford Street, Woodstock, Oxfordshire OX7 1TS (tel. 0993/811227), is a pleasant 16th-century coaching inn, with an arched alleyway leading to the courtyard. Bar snacks are ample and succulent, and there is a set lunch for £8.50 ($14.90), plus a dinner for £10 ($17.50). Bedrooms are simple and comfortable, containing color TV. The charge in a single is from £31 ($54.25) daily, rising to £41 ($71.75) in a double. This hostelry was called the George Inn in Sir Walter Scott's *Woodstock.*

WHERE TO EAT

Right in the heart of town, **Brothertons Brasserie,** 1 High St. (tel. 0993/811114), is your best bet. Carefully chosen raw materials form one of the reasons for the success of this place. It is open from 10:30 a.m. to 10:30 p.m., which makes it convenient for a visit regardless of how much time you spend at Blenheim Palace. Meals cost from £8 ($14), and are likely to feature such dishes as a selection of crûdités, smoked salmon, or game pie. There's always a vegetarian dish of the day, and families with small children are welcomed. Potted plants, pine chairs and tables, and gas mantles make for a simple but effective decor.

---

6. Hertfordshire

Like a giant jellyfish, the frontier of Greater London spills over into this country, once described by Charles Lamb as "hearty, homely, loving Hertfordshire." This fertile land lies northwest of London and supplies much of that city's food, in spite of encroachment by industry. Hertfordshire is sometimes called "the market basket of England."

Its most important attraction, which is usually visited on a day trip from London, follows.

HATFIELD HOUSE

One of the chief attractions of Hertfordshire, and one of the greatest of all English country houses, Hatfield House (tel. 07072/62823) is just 21 miles north of London. To build what is now the E-shaped Hatfield House, the old Tudor palace at Hatfield was mostly demolished. The Banqueting Hall, however, remains.

Hatfield was much a part of the lives of both Henry VIII and his daughter, Elizabeth I. In the old palace, built in the 15th century, Elizabeth romped and played as a child. Although Henry was married to her mother, Anne Boleyn, at the time of Elizabeth's birth, the marriage was later nullified (Anne lost her head and Elizabeth her legitimacy). Henry also used to stash away his oldest daughter, Mary Tudor, at Hatfield. But when Mary became Queen of England and set about earning the dubious distinction of "Bloody Mary," she found Elizabeth a problem. For a while she kept her in the Tower of London, but she eventually let her return to Hatfield (Elizabeth's loyalty to Catholicism was seriously doubted). In 1558, while at Hatfield, Elizabeth learned of her ascension to the throne of England.

The Jacobean house that exists today contains much antique furniture, tapestries, and paintings, as well as three much-reproduced portraits, including the famed ermine-and-rainbow portraits of Elizabeth I. The Great Hall is suitably medieval, complete with a minstrel's gallery. One of the rarest exhibits is a pair of silk stockings, said to have been worn by Elizabeth herself, the first lady in England to don such apparel. The park and the gardens are also worth exploring. The Riding School and Palace Stables contain an interesting vehicle exhibition with 40 vintage cars and the National (North) Collection of Model Soldiers.

Hatfield is usually open from March 25 to the second Sunday in October, Tuesday to Saturday from noon to 5 p.m., Sunday from 1:30 to 5 p.m., and bank holiday Mondays from 11 a.m. to 5 p.m. It is closed Monday and Good Friday. Admission is £3.20 ($5.60) for adults, £2.25 ($3.95) for children. The house is across from the station in Hatfield. From London, take the Green Line coach 794 or 797 or the fast trains from King's Cross. Luncheons or teas are available in the converted coach house in the Old Palace yard from 11 a.m. to 5:30 p.m. daily, except Monday.

Elizabethan banquets are staged on Tuesday, Thursday, Friday, and Saturday, with continuous entertainment from a group of Elizabethan players, minstrels, and jesters. Wine is included in the cost of the meal, but you must pay for your before-dinner drinks yourself. From London you can book an Evan Evans coach tour for an inclusive fee starting at £29.50 ($51.65), leaving from Russell Square or from 41 Tottenham Court Road. The coach returns to London after midnight. If you get there under your own steam, the cost is £19.50 ($31.15) on Tuesday, Thursday, and Friday, and £20.50 ($35.90) on Saturday. For reservations, phone 07072/62055.

The **Old Mill House Museum,** Mill Green, has displays of the history of the Hatfield area from the Stone Age to the present, including Mill Green Watermill. It's open Tuesday to Friday from 10 a.m. to 5 p.m., and Saturday, Sunday, and bank holidays from 2 to 5 p.m. Admission is free.

FOOD AND DRINK IN OLD HATFIELD

One of the finest restaurants in the Home Counties is the **Salisbury,** 15 The Broadway (tel. 07072/62220). Chef Graham Belcher creates individual yet highly disciplined dishes, like medallions of venison set on a sweet carrot and celeriac purée with a red wine sauce. His sauces are perfectly blended. Lunch menus cost £10.50 ($18.40) and £12.50 ($21.90), and dinners range from a two-course meal costing £19 ($33.25) to a filling five courses priced at £25 ($43.75). The restaurant is open daily from 12:30 to 2 p.m. and 7:30 to 9:30 p.m., except Sunday evening and all day Monday.

A fine place for light lunches and good lager is **Eight Bells,** a pub on Park Street (tel. 07072/66059). Dickens fans may like to know that this was the inn where Bill Sikes and his dog found temporary refuge after the brutal murder of Nancy. It's a rickety old corner inn with a central bar for drinks and dining nooks—in all, a forest of time-blackened beams, settles, and pewter tankards. A bowl of homemade soup is reasonably priced, and the cook's specialty is smoked mackerel filet. A light luncheon here will cost about £4 ($7) and dinners from £10 ($17.50). Food is served from noon to 2 p.m. and 6:30 to 10 p.m. daily. Pub hours are from 11 a.m. to 2:30 p.m. and 5:30 to 11 p.m. Monday to Saturday, and from noon to 3 p.m. and 7 to 10:30 p.m. Sunday.

HERTFORD

This old Saxon city is a country town, containing many fine examples of domestic architecture, some of which date from the 16th century. Hertford is reached via the A1 or A10 from London. Samuel Stone, founder of Hartford, Connecticut, was born here. The town's Norman castle has long been in ruins, and part of the still-standing keep dates from the 16th century.

For food and lodgings, try the **Salisbury Arms Hotel,** Fore Street, Hertford, Hertfordshire SQ14 1BZ (tel. 0992/583091), which has been called "always Hertford's principal inn." For 400 years it's been feeding and providing lodgings to wayfarers, or giving a hot grog to the coachman and a stable for his horses. The stables have long given way to a car park, but a sense of history still prevails. In the cellar is medieval masonry predating the 16th-century structure around it. Cromwell is said to have lodged here, and both Royalists and Roundheads have mounted the Jacobean staircase. Bedrooms now spill over into a modern extension. Singles cost £40.50 ($70.90) daily, with doubles or twins renting for £58 ($101.50). On Friday and Saturday, prices are lowered in a single to £29.50 ($51.65) per night, in a double to £45 ($78.75). Good wholesome English "fayre" is provided. At lunch, when most visitors stop by, the roast of the day goes for £5.50 ($9.65) with vegetables. There is, as well, a well-stocked wine cellar. Dinners are from £12 ($21).

ST. ALBANS

This cathedral city, just 21 miles northeast of London, dates back 2000 years. It was named after a Roman soldier, the first Christian martyr in England. Don't ask a resident to show you to the **Cathedral of St. Albans.** Here it's still known as "The Abbey," even though Henry VIII dissolved it as such in 1539. Construction on the cathedral was launched in 1077, making it one of the early Norman churches of England. The bricks, especially visible in the tower, came from the old Roman city of Verulamium at the foot of the hill. The nave and west front date from 1235.

The Chapter House, the first modern building beside a great medieval cathedral in the country, which also serves as a pilgrim/visitor center, was opened by the Queen in 1982.

The **Verulamium Museum** (tel. 0727/54659) at St. Michael's stands on the site of the Roman city. Here you'll view some of the finest Roman mosaics in Britain. Part of the Roman town wall, a hypocaust, and houses and shops are still visible. Visit in summer from 10 a.m. to 5:30 p.m. Monday to Saturday (on Sunday from 2 to 5:30 p.m.), and in winter from 10 a.m. to 4 p.m. Monday to Saturday (2 to 4 p.m. on Sunday), paying £1 ($1.75) for adults, 50p (90¢) for children.

The **Clock Tower** at Market Place (tel. 0727/53301) was built in 1402, standing 77 feet high, total of five floors. It is open from Easter to mid-September on Saturday and Sunday from 10:30 a.m. to 5 p.m.

From St. Albans you can see **Gorhambury House** (tel. 0727/54051), a classic-style mansion built in 1777, containing 16th-century enameled glass and historic portraits. It's open, May to September, only on Thursday (2 to 5 p.m.), charging adults £2 ($3.50) for admission; children pay £1 ($1.75). The location is 2½ miles west of St. Albans near the A4147.

On the outskirts, the **Mosquito Aircraft Museum,** the oldest aircraft museum in Britain, lies on the grounds of Salisbury Hall, just off the M25 London-to-St.-Albans road (turn off at junction 22) at London Colney, about five miles south of St. Albans. The museum is on the B556. The hall is no longer open to the public, but the museum can be visited from Easter Sunday to the end of October on Sunday and bank holidays from 10 a.m. to 5:30 p.m., and on Thursday from 2 to 5:30 p.m. from July to the end of September. Displayed is the prototype of the de Havilland "Mosquito" aircraft, which was designed and built at Salisbury Hall in World War II, plus 18 other aircraft of de Havilland origin, as well as memorabilia and relics. Admission is £1 ($1.75) for adults, 40p (80¢) for children. For more information, telephone 0727/22051.

Back in St. Albans, I offer the following recommendations for food and lodgings:

Melford House, 24 Woodstock Rd. North, St. Albans, Hertfordshire AL1 4QQ (tel. 0727/53642), is a 12-bedroom hotel-cum-guesthouse in the best residential area, where it is quiet and away from the busy town center, charging moderate prices for B&B: £20 ($35) to £34 ($59.50) in a single, £28 ($49) to £37 ($64.75) in a double, and £37 ($64.75) to £44 ($77) for three persons in a family room. The higher prices are for rooms with showers and toilets. Each unit is immaculately kept, with full central heating. There is a spacious residents' lounge with color TV. The house is licensed for beer and liquor, and there is a car park and a garden.

The best place in town for dining is **La Province,** 13 George St. (tel. 0727/52142), right in the heart of town, in the vicinity of the cathedral. Yet, for what it offers, it isn't expensive. Meals cost from £7 ($12.25) for a set lunch and from £14.50 ($25.40) for a table d'hôte dinner. Some of the fish dishes are excellent, as are the chicken Provençale and a pork filet with Calvados. Hours are from noon to

2:15 p.m. Tuesday to Saturday and until 3:30 p.m. Sunday. The restaurant is closed Sunday evening and all day Monday.

SHAW'S CORNER

In the village of Ayot St. Lawrence, three miles northwest of Welwyn, stands the home where George Bernard Shaw lived from 1906 to 1950. The house is practically as he left it at his death. In the hall, for example, his hats are still hanging, as if ready for him to don one. His personal mementos are in his study, drawing room, dining room, and writing hut. The kitchen and scullery are also open to view, as well as some first-floor rooms on some days. The house is open from 2 to 6 p.m. Wednesday to Saturday from April to the end of October, and from noon to 6 p.m. Sunday and bank holiday Mondays; closed Good Friday. Admission is £1.80 ($3.15) for adults, 90p ($1.60) for children. For more information, phone 0438/820307.

---

7. Buckinghamshire

This is a leafy county, lying north of the Thames and somewhat to the west of London. Its identifying marks are the wide Vale of Aylesbury, with its sprawling fields and tiny villages, and the long chalk range of the Chilterns. Going south from the range, you'll find what is left of a once-great beech forest.

CLIVEDEN

The former home of Nancy, Lady Astor, now a National Trust property, has been turned into a deluxe hotel, but the grounds and some of the sumptuously decorated rooms are on view to the public at certain times, so it's worth a visit, even if you can't afford to stay here. The garden features a rose garden, a magnificent box parterre, and an amphitheater where "Rule Britannia" was played for the first time. There are 375 acres of garden and woodland to explore. The house is open from the first of April to October, only on Thursday and Sunday from 3 to 6 p.m. The grounds are open March to December daily from 11 a.m. to 6 p.m. or sunset if earlier. Admission to the grounds is £2.40 ($4.20); to the house, 80p ($1.40). Children are admitted for half price. Cliveden is 20 miles west of London, lying two miles north of Taplow on the B476, off the A40.

AYLESBURY

The county town of Buckingham, Aylesbury has retained much of its ancient character, especially around the town center, with its narrow Tudor alleyways and several 17th-century houses. The parish church, **St. Mary's,** dates from the 13th century and has an unusual spirelet. A short walk from the church takes you to **Hickman's Almshouses** and the **Prebendal House,** both from the 17th century.

Less than 40 miles from London, Aylesbury is a market town, with both Wednesday and Saturday markets held in Friars Square, and its name has become synonymous with excellent ducks and ducklings.

Six miles northwest of Aylesbury on the Bicester road (A41), **Waddesdon Manor** contains an outstanding collection of French decorative art of the 17th and 18th centuries. Among the paintings are portraits by Reynolds, Gainsborough, and Romney. The manor was built in the late 19th century for Baron Ferdinand de Rothschild in the style of the French Renaissance. Now belonging to the National Trust, the manor stands in 150 acres of grounds with rare trees, an aviary, and a herd of Sika deer. Visiting times are from the end of March to the middle of October, from 1 to 5 p.m. Wednesday to Sunday. It costs £3 ($5.25) to enter the house, grounds, and aviary. For information, call the administrator, Aylesbury (tel. 0296/651282).

Back in Aylesbury, you can find big-splurge food and lodgings at the **Kings**

Head, Market Square, Aylesbury, Buckinghamshire HP20 1TA (tel. 0296/415158), a half-timbered hotel that was once a 15th-century coaching inn. It is one of the finest examples of Tudor architecture in Buckinghamshire. Its 24 bedrooms, about half of which have private baths, overlook a cobble courtyard. Depending on the plumbing, doubles cost from £38 ($66.50) to £48 ($84) daily, and singles go for £28 ($49) to £40 ($70), with an English breakfast included. The restaurant serves lunch daily from noon to 2 p.m. and dinner from 7 to 9 p.m., with meals costing from £8 ($14) to £11 ($19.25). Drinks are served in the cozy lounge bar in back, where you can see the chair used by Oliver Cromwell on his frequent visits to the inn. He slept in the Cromwell room upstairs, with its extra-large bed. Some of his weapons are also on display here.

BUCKINGHAM

This old market town on the River Ouse was once the county town of Buckingham. It has a fine 13th-century Chantry Chapel and some 18th-century houses.

For food and lodging, try the **White Hart,** Market Square, Buckingham, Buckinghamshire MK18 1NL (tel. 0280/815151), the best in town. This oldish market town hotel has 18th-century origins, but its plaster facade and portico are Victorian additions. In recent years, the hotel has been remodeled and equipped for modern comfort, its renovation bringing a workable efficiency to its interior. All of the hotel's 19 bedrooms contain a private bath or shower, with color TV and coffee-making facilities. Singles rent for £51 ($89.25) daily, and doubles or twins for £62 ($108.50), a worthy splurge choice considering the dearth of fine accommodations in the area. The hotel's dining room, the Georgian Room, has its own small dance floor, and there is a lounge bar as well. They also have Hathaways Kitchen, serving steaks and fish, with fresh salads and granary breads. Meals begin at £12 ($21).

JORDANS VILLAGE

A farm called **Old Jordans,** Jordans Lane, Jordans Village, near Beaconsfield, Buckinghamshire HP9 2SW (tel. 02407/4586), dates back to the Middle Ages. But its recorded history starts in the early 17th century, when one Thomas Russell, sitting tenant, bought the freehold, signing the deed with his thumbprint. The house was added to over the years, and in the mid-17th century William Penn, founder of Pennsylvania, and other well-known Dissenters stayed here and worshipped. Now the property of Quakers, the house is run as a guesthouse and conference center, with 30 simply furnished rooms available for overnight guests. Bathless rooms cost £20 ($35) daily in a single, £33.50 ($58.65) in a double. Rooms with bath rent for £30 ($52.50) in a single and £46.50 ($81.40) in a double. All tariffs include a full English breakfast. Lunch, served at 1 p.m., costs £5 ($8.75) Monday to Saturday, £6 ($10.50) on Sunday.

On the grounds is the Mayflower Barn, built almost undisputably of timbers from the ship *Mayflower* in which the first Pilgrims sailed to the New World. These days the beams ring to the strains of concert music and recitals performed by top-notch artists.

It's a very peaceful place, full of history and perhaps a little isolated from today's bustle. It is ideally situated midway between London and Oxford and makes a good first or last stop from Heathrow. Trains run frequently from Marylebone, London, to Seer Green Station three-quarters of a mile from Jordans Village. Taxis can usually be arranged to meet trains or buses if advance notice is given, or you may be able to find a taxi at Gerrards Cross or Beaconsfield.

MILTON'S COTTAGE

The modern residential town of Gerrards Cross is often called the Beverly Hills of England, as it attracts many wealthy persons who settle here in many beautiful homes. Surrounding this plush section are several tucked-away hamlets, including **Chalfont St. Giles,** where the poet Milton lived during the Great Plague in 1665.

He completed *Paradise Lost* here. In this 16th-century cottage are two museum rooms containing 93 rare books, including first editions of *Paradise Lost* and *Paradise Regained* and other works of Milton, with exhibits of interest to young and old. A beautiful cottage garden is a further attraction. The house is open from 10 a.m. to 1 p.m. and 2 to 6 p.m. Tuesday to Saturday and spring and summer bank holiday Mondays, and from 2 to 6 p.m. on Sunday from March 1 to October 31. Closed Monday and in November, December, January, and February. Admission is £1 ($1.75) for adults, 40p (70¢) for children. For information, write to Milton's Cottage, Dean Way, Chalfont St. Giles, Buckinghamshire HP8 4JH (tel. 02407/2313).

West of Gerrards Cross, the town of Beaconsfield, with its broad, tree-lined High Street, enjoys many associations with Disraeli. Visitors pass through here en route to—

HUGHENDEN MANOR

Outside High Wycombe, in Buckinghamshire, sits a country manor that gives us not only an insight into the age of Victoria but acquaints us with a remarkable man. In Benjamin Disraeli we meet one of the most enigmatic figures of 19th-century England. At age 21 Dizzy published anonymously his five-volume novel *Vivian Grey*. But it wasn't his shining hour. He went on to other things, marrying an older widow for her money. They developed, apparently, a most successful relationship. He entered politics and continued writing novels, his later ones meeting with more acclaim.

In 1848, Disraeli acquired Hughenden Manor, a country house that befitted his fast-rising political and social position. He served briefly as prime minister in 1868, but his political fame rests on his stewardship as prime minister during 1874–1880. He became Queen Victoria's friend, and in 1877 she paid him a rare honor by visiting him at Hughenden. In 1876, Disraeli became the Earl of Beaconsfield: he had arrived. Only his wife was dead, and he was to die in 1881. Instead of being buried at Westminster Abbey, he preferred the simple little graveyard of Hughenden Church.

Hughenden contains an odd assortment of memorabilia, including a lock of Disraeli's hair. The letters from Victoria, the autographed books, and especially a portrait of Lord Byron, known to Disraeli's father, are of interest.

If you're driving to Hughenden Manor on the way to Oxford, continue north of High Wycombe on the A4128 for about 1½ miles. If you're relying on public transportation from London, take coach 711 to High Wycombe, then board a Bee Line bus (High Wycombe-Aylesbury 323 or 324). The manor house and garden are open from 2 to 6 p.m. Wednesday to Saturday from Easter Saturday to October, from noon to 6 p.m. Sunday and bank holiday Mondays. It is open only on Saturday and Sunday from March 4 to March 19 from 2 to 6 p.m. It is closed from November to the end of March and on Good Friday. Admission is £2 ($3.50) for adults, £1 ($1.75) for children. For more information, phone 0494/32580.

WEST WYCOMBE

Snuggled in the Chiltern Hills 30 miles west of London, the village of West Wycombe still has an atmosphere of the early 18th century. The thatched roofs have been replaced with tiles, and some of the buildings have been removed or replaced, but the village is still two centuries removed from the present day.

In the mid-18th century, Sir Francis Dashwood began an ambitious building program at West Wycombe. His strong interest in architecture and design led Sir Francis to undertake a series of monuments and parks, which are still among the finest in the country today. He also sponsored the building of a road using the chalk quarries on the hill to aid in the support of the poverty-stricken villagers. The resulting caves are said to have been used by "The Knights of St. Francis of Wycombe," later known as "The Hellfire Club." The knights consisted of a number of illustrious men drawn from the social circle surrounding the Prince of Wales. Its members "gourmandized," swilling claret and enjoying the company of women "of a cheerful, lively disposition . . . who considered themselves lawful wives of the brethren during their stay."

A visit to West Wycombe wouldn't be complete without a tour of **West Wycombe Park,** seat of the Dashwood family, of both historical and architectural interest. Both George III and Ben Franklin stayed here, but not at the same time. The house is one of the best examples of Palladian-style architecture in England. The interior is lavishly decorated with paintings and antiques from the 18th century.

The caves, café, and gift shop are open from 1 to 6 p.m. Monday to Saturday from March to late May, and from 11 a.m. to 6 p.m. from late May to early September, as well as on Sunday and bank holidays from early April to late October. In winter, they are open from 1 to 5 p.m. only on Saturday and Sunday. The house and grounds are open from 2 to 6 p.m. Monday to Friday in June, with Sunday included in July and August. Admission to the caves is £2 ($3.50) for adults, £1 ($1.75) for children. To visit the house and grounds costs £2.60 ($4.55) for adults, £1.60 ($2.80) for children.

For information on the caves, house, and grounds, call the **West Wycombe Park Office,** West Wycombe (tel. 0494/24411).

Other sights at West Wycombe include the **Church of St. Lawrence,** perched atop West Wycombe Hill and topped by a huge golden ball. Parts of the church date from the 13th century; its richly decorated interior was copied from a third-century Syrian sun temple. The view from the church tower is worth the trek up the hill. Near the church stands the Dashwood Mausoleum, built in a style derived from Constantine's Arch in Rome.

During your tour, you may also wander freely through the village, stopping for lunch at one of the public houses. Four miles of nature trails also meander about the village, through woods and farmlands.

8. Bedfordshire (Woburn Abbey)

This county contains the fertile, rich Vale of Bedford, crossed by the River Ouse. Most visitors from London head here on a day trip to visit historic Woburn Abbey (previewed below). Others know of its county town—

BEDFORD

On the Ouse, Bedford contains many riverside parks and gardens but is better known for its associations with John Bunyan. On Mill Street stands the 1850 Bunyan Meeting Freechurch, encompassing the **Bunyan Museum** (tel. 0234/58870), erected on the site of a barn where Bunyan used to preach. Panels on the doors illustrate scenes from *Pilgrim's Progress.* The Bunyan Museum contains the surviving relics of Bunyan and a famous collection of the *Pilgrim's Progress* in 169 languages. It is open Tuesday to Saturday, April to September, from 2 to 4 p.m., charging an admission of 30p (55¢) for adults and 20p (35¢) for children.

About a mile south of Bedford lies Elstow, close to Bunyan's reputed birthplace. Here you can visit **Elstow Moot Hall,** a medieval timber-frame building originally used as a market hall and now managed as a museum containing a permanent display relating to the life of John Bunyan, which includes various editions of his work. It is open from 2 to 5 p.m. Tuesday to Saturday and bank holidays, from 2 to 5:30 p.m. Sunday from April to October. Admission is 35p (60¢) for adults, 20p (35¢) for children. For more information, phone 0234/228330.

The **Swiss Garden,** Old Warden, near Biggleswade, is an unusual romantic site dating from the early 19th century. It contains original buildings and features, together with many interesting plants and trees, some of great rarity. A lakeside picnic area in adjoining woodlands is open at all times. Hours for the garden are 2 to 6 p.m.

(last admission is at 5:15 p.m.) on Wednesday, Thursday, Saturday, Sunday, and bank holiday Mondays from April to October. The garden lies approximately 2½ miles west of Biggleswade adjoining the Biggleswade–Old Warden road about two miles west of the A1. For more information, telephone 0234/228330.

Food and Lodging

If you've decided to stay in Bedford for the night, the best place to head for food is the **Greek Villager Restaurant,** a tavern and kebab house at the Mews, St. Peters St. (tel. 0234/41798). It offers dining and dancing to live Greek music on Friday and Saturday. Bouzouki, guitars, and a belly dancer are featured, as well as Cypriot and Greek dancing. The restaurant is open six nights a week; until midnight Monday to Thursday, until 2 a.m. on Friday and Saturday (closed Sunday). A special feature of the chef is small portions of about 14 different Greek dishes served on separate plates at a cost of £10 ($17.50) per person. Otherwise, you get the usual Greek appetizers such as hummus and taramosalata, followed by such typical Greek dishes as moussaka and dolmades (stuffed vine leaves). Regular meals begin at £12 ($21).

Homeleigh Guest House, 26 de Pary's Ave., Bedford, Bedfordshire MK40 2TW (tel. 0234/59219), is near the center. A Victorian structure, with adequate car parking, it lies on a tree-lined street. A brother and sister, John and Janet Barnes, have renovated it and converted it into a place offering attractively furnished and pleasant rooms, many quite spacious. Only one room has a private bath, and that is more expensive, of course. Otherwise, if you don't mind sharing a bath, you'll find B&B rates costing from £16.50 ($22.90) daily in a single, rising to £28 ($49) in a double, including an English breakfast.

WOBURN ABBEY

Few persons visiting Bedfordshire miss the Georgian mansion of **Woburn Abbey,** the seat of the Dukes of Bedford for more than three centuries. The much-publicized 18th-century estate is about 42 miles from London outside of Woburn, which lies 13 miles southwest of Bedford. Its state apartments are rich in furniture, porcelain, tapestries, silver, and a valuable art collection, including paintings by Van Dyck, Holbein, Rembrandt, Gainsborough, and Reynolds. A series of paintings by Canaletto, showing his continuing views of Venice, grace the walls of the Canaletto Room, an intimate dining room. Of all the paintings, one of the most notable from a historical point of view is the *Armada Portrait* of Elizabeth I. Her hand rests on the globe, as Philip's invincible armada perishes in the background.

Queen Victoria and Prince Albert visited Woburn Abbey in 1841. Victoria slept in an opulently decorated bedroom. Victoria's Dressing Room contains a fine collection of 17th-century paintings from the Netherlands. Among the oddities and treasures at Woburn Abbey are a Grotto of Shells, a Sèvres dinner service (gift of Louis XV), and a chamber devoted to memorabilia of "The Flying Duchess." Wife of the 11th Duke of Bedford, she was a remarkable woman, who disappeared on a solo flight in 1937 (the same year as Amelia Earhart). The duchess was 72 years old at the time.

In the 1950s, the present Duke of Bedford opened Woburn Abbey to the public to pay off some $15 million in inheritance taxes. In 1974, he turned the estate over to his son and daughter-in-law, the Marquess and Marchioness of Tavistock, who reluctantly took on the business of running the 75-room mansion. And what a business it is, drawing hundreds of thousands of visitors a year and employing more than 300 persons to staff the shops and grounds.

Today Woburn Abbey is surrounded by the 3000-acre Deer Park that includes the famous Père David deer herd, originally from China and saved from extinction at Woburn. The Woburn Wild Animal Kingdom contains lions, tigers, giraffes, camels, monkeys, Prevalski horses, bongos, elephants, and other animals. What would Humphry Repton, the designer of the estate's park in the 19th century, say?

In January, February, and March, the park is open only on Saturday and Sunday from 10:30 a.m. to 3:40 p.m., and the abbey from 11 a.m. to 4:45 p.m. From April to October, the park hours are 10 a.m. to 4:45 p.m. daily (10 a.m. to 5:45 p.m. on Sunday), while the abbey is open from 11 a.m. to 5:45 p.m. daily and 11 a.m. to 6:15 p.m. on Sunday. The last admission to the abbey is 45 minutes before closing time. The charge to enter the park is £2 ($3.50) for a car and passengers, 50p (90¢) per person for cyclists and pedestrians. Admission to the abbey is £4 ($7) for adults, £1.50 ($2.65) for children 7 to 16. A family ticket, £9 ($15.75), admits two adults and two children, with reductions for more children.

The Deer Park admission does not apply to visitors purchasing the abbey entrance ticket as they enter the park. When not in use by the duke's family, visitors can see the private apartments at an additional charge of 30p (55¢) for adults, 10p (20¢) for children. For more information, phone 0525/290666.

Woburn Abbey is difficult to reach by public transportation from London, so you may prefer to take one of the organized tours.

A Pub at Woburn

Black Horse, Bedford Street (tel. 0525/290210), a former coaching inn, is the best-known pub in the area, serving good food. During the day you can order good-tasting pub food. In summer a cold buffet is featured, which can be enjoyed in a walled garden. A good luncheon goes from £3.50 ($6.15), and in the evening you can dine in the restaurant for around £10 ($17.50), including a half bottle of wine, which is also sold by the glass. Hours are from 11 a.m. to 2:30 p.m. daily and from 6 to 11 p.m. (on Sunday from noon to 3 p.m. and from 7 to 10:30 p.m.).

HISTORIC PLANES AND CARS

Should vintage airplanes and automobiles interest you, you can pay a visit to the **Shuttleworth Collection** at the Old Warden Aerodrome (tel. 076727/288). A classic grass aerodrome set in typically English countryside, it is the home of a unique selection of some 30 historic airplanes, maintained in a full flying status to illustrate the progress of aviation from a 1909 Bleriot XI to a 1941 Spitfire. An 1898 Panhard Levassor in which King Edward VII once drove to Ascot is just one of the fascinating vehicles. The collection can be visited daily from 10 a.m. to last admissions at 4 p.m. (at 3 p.m. November to March), closing one hour after last admissions. It is closed for a week at Christmas. Admission is £3 ($5.25) for adults, £1.50 ($2.65) for children 5 to 16. There are special charges for flying displays on the last Sundays of the months from April to September. The aerodrome is 2 miles west of the A1 roundabout at Biggleswade.

WHIPSNADE WILD ANIMAL PARK

This is the country breeding park of the Zoological Society of London (which also operates the London Zoo), where the animals roam free in large paddocks and certain species even wander among visitors. On the edge of the Chiltern escarpment in Bedfordshire, Whipsnade (tel. 0582/872171) lays claim to being the world's first open-air zoo. Many endangered species are here, including the cheetah, Père David deer, oryx, and Indian and white rhinos. There are also 12 species of crane, including the rare and beautiful red-naped or Manchurian crane. There is a lot of walking here to see everything in a single day, but the opportunities for photography are second to none. Exhibits include sea lions, a steam railway, a birds of prey show, a habitats exhibition, and a family center. Animals are in geographical groupings. Cars are admitted for £5 ($8.75), except from November 1 to February 28, when they are admitted free. In addition, you must pay £3.90 ($6.85) for adults and £2.40 ($4.20) for children. Children under the age of 4 are admitted free. The zoo is open daily from 10 a.m. to 6 p.m. or sunset, whichever is earlier. Take the train from St. Pancras to Luton, then a number 43 bus to Whipsnade Park.

VII

KENT, SURREY, AND SUSSEX

1. CANTERBURY

2. DOVER

3. ROYAL TUNBRIDGE WELLS

4. RICHMOND

5. HASLEMERE

6. RYE AND WINCHELSEA

7. HASTINGS AND ST. LEONARDS

8. BATTLE

9. ALFRISTON AND LEWES

10. BRIGHTON

11. ARUNDEL

12. CHICHESTER

Lying to the south and southeast of London are the shires (counties) of Kent, Surrey, and the Sussexes. Combined, they form a most fascinating part of England to explore—and are easy to reach, within commuting distance of the capital.

Of all the tourist centers, **Canterbury** in Kent is of foremost interest, but the old Cinque ports of **Rye** and **Winchelsea** in East Sussex are almost equally exciting, as is the resort of **Brighton and Hove** in a completely different way. In and around these major meccas are dozens of castles and vast estates, monuments, homes of famous men (Churchill, for example), cathedrals, yachting harbors, and little villages of thatched cottages.

The range of accommodations varies from an old-world smugglers' inn in the ancient seaport of Rye to a clean, comfortable Georgian guesthouse in the heart of medieval Canterbury. Regardless of the price range in which you travel, you'll discover some superb bargains throughout the counties of the South Coast.

In the fog-choked cities of north England, the great dream for retirement is to find a little rose-covered cottage in the south, where the living's easier. The South Coast is also a potent magnet for London's East Enders. Come with me as we examine the lure.

KENT

Fresh from his cherry orchard, the Kentish farmer heads for his snug spot by an inglenook, with its bright-burning fire, for his mellow glass of cherry brandy. The day's work is done. All's right with the world.

We're in what was once the ancient Anglo-Saxon kingdom of Kent, on the shirttails of London itself, yet far removed in spirit and scenery. Since the days of the Tudors, cherry blossoms have pinkened the fertile landscape. Not only orchards, but hops fields abound. The conically shaped oasthouses with kilns for drying the hops dot the rolling countryside. Both the hops and orchards have earned for Kent the title of the "garden of England." And in England the competition's rough for that distinction.

Kent suffered severe destruction in World War II, as it was the virtual alley over which the Luftwaffe flew in its blitz of London. After the fall of France, a German invasion was feared imminent. Shortly after becoming prime minister in 1940, Churchill sped to Dover, with his bowler, stogie, walking cane, and pin-striped suit. Once there, he inspected the coastal defense and gave encouragement to the men digging in to fight off the attack. But Hitler's "Sea Lion" (the code name for the invasion) turned out to be a paper tiger.

In spite of much devastation, Kent is filled with interesting old towns, mansions, and castles. The country is rich in Dickensian associations, and for that reason Kent is sometimes known as Dickens Country. His family once lived near the naval dockyard at Chatham.

ROCHESTER

In the cathedral city of Rochester, 30 miles from London, you can visit the **Charles Dickens Centre** and **Dickens Chalet** in Eastgate House, built in 1590. This center, on High Street in Rochester, is open seven days a week from 10 a.m. to 5 p.m. Admission is £1.60 ($2.80) for adults and £1 ($1.75) for children. The museum has tableaux depicting various scenes from Dickens's novels, including a Pickwickian Christmas scene, the fever-ridden graveyard of *Bleak House,* scenes from *The Old Curiosity Shop* and *Great Expectations,* along with scenes from *Oliver Twist* and *David Copperfield.* There is clever use of sound and light. Information is also available at the center on various other sights in Rochester associated with Dickens, including Eastgate House and, in the garden, the chalet transported from Gads Hill Place, where Dickens died, as well as the Guildhall Museum, Rochester Cathedral, and the mysterious "6 Poor Travellers' House." Pick up a brochure that includes a map featuring the various places and the novels with which each is associated. For further information, telephone 0634/44176.

At Broadstairs, the favorite seaside resort of the novelist—"our watering place"—the **Dickens House Museum** stands on the main seafront. This museum (tel. 0843/62853) was once the home of Mary Pearson Strong, on whom Dickens based much of the character of Betsey Trotwood, David Copperfield's aunt. It is open April to October daily from 2:30 to 5:30 p.m. Admission is 50p (90¢) for adults and 25p (45¢) for children.

At Broadstairs, you can also visit **Bleak House,** Fort Road (tel. 0843/62224), high up on the cliffs. At the peak of his fame, this mansion was occupied by Dickens and inspired the title of one of his greatest works, *Bleak House.* Here he entertained many men famous in art and literature, and he wrote the greater part of his novel *David Copperfield.* It is open seven days a week, Easter to November, from 10 a.m. to 6 p.m. From July through September it is open until 9 p.m. The property also contains a Maritime Museum and cellars once used by smugglers. Admission is £1.50 ($2.65) for adults and 85p ($1.50) for children under 12.

At Westerham, at the junction of the Edenbridge and Sevenoaks roads (the A25 and the B2026), an attraction especially for Canadian visitors is the square red-brick gabled home where James Wolfe, the English general who defeated the French in the battle for Québec, lived until he was 11 years old. Called **Québec House** (tel. 0959/62206), a National Trust property, it contains an exhibition about the capture of Québec and memorabilia associated with the military hero, who was born in Westerham (Kent) on January 2, 1727. The house may be visited daily, except Thursday and Saturday, from April to the end of October from 2 to 6 p.m. Admission is £1.40 ($2.45) for adults, 70p ($1.25) for children.

CHURCHILL'S HOME

For many years, Sir Winston lived at **Chartwell** (tel. 0732/866368), which lies 1½ miles south of Westerham in Kent. Churchill, a descendant of the first Duke of Marlborough, was born in grand style at Blenheim Palace on November 30, 1874. Chartwell doesn't pretend to be as grand a place as Blenheim, but it's been preserved as a memorial, administered by the National Trust. The rooms remain as Churchill left them, including maps, documents, photographs, pictures, and other personal mementos. In two rooms are displayed a selection of gifts that the prime minister received from people all over the world. There is also a selection of many of his well-known uniforms. Terraced gardens descend toward the lake with its celebrated black swans. In a garden studio are many of Churchill's paintings. Go if you want to see where a giant of a man lived and worked.

The house is open April to October from noon to 5 p.m. Tuesday, Wednesday, and Thursday, and from 11 a.m. to 5 p.m. Saturday and Sunday. In March and November, hours are 11 a.m. to 4 p.m. Wednesday, Saturday, and Sunday. The gardens and studio are not open in March and November, at which time admission to the house is only £1.80 ($3.15). Otherwise, you pay £3 ($5.25) to visit the house and garden, £1.20 ($2.10) to see the garden only, and 40p (70¢) for a visit to the studio. Children are charged half price. The restaurant offers light meals, salads, sandwiches, cakes, and a few hot dishes. It's open from 10:30 a.m. on the days the house is receiving visitors.

KNOLE

Begun in the mid-15th century by Thomas Bourchier, archbishop of Canterbury, Knole, Sevenoaks (tel. 0732/450608) is one of the largest private houses in England. It was an archbishop's palace from 1456 until the day Henry VIII's eye fell covetously upon it. He spent considerable sums of money on Knole, but there is little record of his spending much time there after extracting the gift from the reluctant Archbishop Cranmer. History records one visit only, in 1541. It was then a royal palace until Queen Elizabeth I granted it to Thomas Sackville, first Earl of Dorset, whose descendants have lived at Knole ever since. The building was given to the National Trust in 1946. The Great Hall and the Brown Gallery are Bourchier rooms, early 15th century, both much altered by Sackville, who made other additions in about 1603. The earl was also responsible for the Great Painted Staircase. The house covers seven acres and has 365 rooms, 52 staircases, and seven courts. The elaborate paneling and plasterwork provide a background for the 17th- and 18th-century tapestries and rugs, the Elizabethan and Jacobean furniture, and the family portraits. Knole, in the village of Sevenoaks, on the A225, is five miles north of Tonbridge and 25 miles south of London. Frequent train service is available from London (about every 30 minutes), and then you can take a taxi for the remaining 1½ miles to Knole.

Knole is open from Good Friday to the end of October, Wednesday to Saturday and bank holiday Monday from 11 a.m. to 5 p.m., on Sunday from 2 to 5 p.m. It is closed November to March. Last admission is an hour before closing. Guided tours for prebooked groups of 25 or more persons are given on Tuesday throughout the season (except after a bank holiday). Otherwise they are given only on Wednesday to

Friday in October (no reservations). The gardens are open May to September and may be visited on the first Wednesday of each month. Admission to the house is £2.50 ($4.40) for adults, £1.30 ($2.30) for children. On Friday (except Good Friday), extra rooms in Lord Sackville's private apartments are shown, costing £3 ($5.25) for adults, £1.50 ($2.65) for children. To visit the gardens only costs adults 50p (90¢), children 25p (45¢). The park is open daily to pedestrians, with cars being allowed to enter when the house is open.

IGHTHAM MOTE

A National Trust property, Ightham Mote, Ivy Hatch, Sevenoaks (tel. 0732/810378), is well worth a stop if you're in the area visiting other stately homes and castles. It was extensively remodeled in the early 16th century. The Tudor chapel with its painted ceiling, the timbered outer walls, and the ornate chimneys reflect that period. A stone bridge crosses the moat and leads into the central courtyard overlooked by the magnificent windows of the Great Hall. The rest of the house is built around the courtyard. From the Great Hall, a Jacobean staircase leads to the old chapel on the first floor, where you go through the solarium, with an oriel window, to the Tudor chapel.

Unlike many other ancient houses of England lived in by the same family for centuries, Ightham Mote passed from owner to owner, each family leaving its mark on the place. When the last private owner, an American who was responsible for a lot of the restoration, died, he bequeathed the house to the National Trust. It's open from 11 a.m. to 5 p.m. except Tuesday and Friday. Admission is £2.50 ($4.40) for adults, £1.50 ($2.65) for children.

SQUERRYES COURT

At Westerham, west of Sevenoaks on the A25, is Squerryes Court (tel. 0959/62345), a William and Mary period manor house built in 1681 and owned by the Warde family for 250 years. Besides a fine collection of paintings, tapestries, and furniture, in the Wolfe Room is a collection of pictures and relics of the family of General Wolfe. The general received his military commission on the grounds of the house at a spot marked by a cenotaph. The house and grounds are open from March to September (Sunday only during March). From April to September, you can visit on Wednesday, Saturday, Sunday, and bank holiday Monday from 2 to 6 p.m. Admission is £2.20 ($3.85) for adults, £1.20 ($2.10) for children.

DOWN HOUSE

North of the M25 motorway, Squerryes Court, and Chartwell, Down House, Luxted Road, Downe, Orpington (tel. 0689/59119), was the home of Charles Darwin for some 40 years. It was in this 18th-century house that he wrote *Origin of Species*. Visitors can see his memorial and museum containing articles including relics from the *Beagle* and other interesting items and pictures. Attractive gardens and the Sandwalk Wood are preserved. The house is open daily from 1 to 6 p.m., except Monday and Friday (open bank holidays). It is closed in February. Admission is £1.50 ($2.65) for adults, 30p (55¢) for children. The village of Downe is 5½ miles south of Bromley off the A233.

HEVER CASTLE

Built at the end of the 13th century, Hever Castle was then just a fortified farmhouse surrounded by a moat. A dwelling house was added within the fortifications some 200 years later by the Bullen family. In 1506, the property was inherited by Sir Thomas Bullen, father of Anne Boleyn. It was here that Henry VIII courted Anne for six years before she became his second wife and later mother of Elizabeth, who became Queen Elizabeth I of England. In 1538, Hever Castle was acquired by Henry VIII, who granted it to his proxy (fourth) wife, the "great Flanders mare," Anne of Cleves, when he discovered that this mail-order bride did not live up to her Holbein portrait. This luckier Anne did not seem to mind, however. She owned this comfortable castle for 17 years, supported by Henry with plenty of money.

In 1903, the castle was purchased by William Waldorf Astor, who spent five years restoring and redecorating it, as well as building the unique village of Tudor-style cottages connected to the castle, for use by his guests. Astor was responsible also for the construction of the spectacular Italian gardens with fountains, classical statuary, a maze, and an avenue of yew trees trimmed into fantastic shapes. He also had a 35-acre lake put in, through which the River Eden flows.

The castle and its grounds have been used as locations for a number of motion pictures. The forecourt and the gardens were used in filming *Anne of a Thousand Days* in 1969. More recently, Hever Castle was used in *Lady Jane.* Two permanent exhibitions here are "Henry VIII and Anne Boleyn at Hever Castle" and "The Astors of Hever."

The castle and grounds are open from Good Friday until the end of October. The gardens can be entered daily from 11 a.m. to 6 p.m. (last entry at 5 p.m.). The castle opens at noon. Admission is £3.70 ($6.50) for adults, £1.90 ($3.35) for children to both the castle and the gardens. To visit the gardens only, adults pay £2.50 ($4.40), children £1.50 ($2.65). For further information, call the Hever Castle Estate Office, Hever, near Edenbridge (tel. 0732/865224). The castle is three miles southeast of Edenbridge, midway between Sevenoaks and East Grinstead, 20 minutes from the M25 junction 6.

PENSHURST PLACE

A magnificent English Gothic mansion, Penshurst Place, at Penshurst, near Tonbridge (tel. 0892/870307), is one of the outstanding country houses in Britain. In 1338, Sir John de Pulteney, four times lord mayor of London, built the stone house whose Great Hall forms the heart of Penshurst still, after more than 600 years. The boy king, Edward VI, presented the house to Sir William Sidney, and it has remained in that family ever since. It was the birthplace, in 1554, of Sir Philip Sidney, the soldier-poet. In the first half of the 17th century, Penshurst was known as a center of literature, attracting such personages as Ben Jonson. Today it is the home of William Philip Sidney, the Viscount De L'Isle and Lady De L'Isle. Lord De L'Isle was in Winston Churchill's cabinet in the 1950s and was governor-general of Australia in the 1960s.

The Nether Gallery, below the Long Gallery that contains a suite of ebony and ivory furniture from Goa, houses the Sidney family collection of armor. Visitors can also see the splendid State Dining Room and Queen Elizabeth's Room. In the Stable Wing, there's an interesting Toy Museum. The place is open daily, except Monday, from April to the first Sunday in October. It is also open on Good Friday and all bank holiday Mondays. The gardens, home park, Venture Playground, nature trail, and countryside exhibition are open from 12:30 to 6 p.m., the house from 1 to last entry at 5 p.m. Admission to the house and grounds is £3 ($5.25) for adults, £1.60 ($2.80) for children. Penshurst Place is 33 miles from London and 6 miles west of Tonbridge.

SISSINGHURST CASTLE GARDEN

V. Sackville-West and her husband, Harold Nicolson, created the celebrated Sissinghurst Castle Garden, Sissinghurst, 2 miles northeast of Cranbrook (tel. 0580/712850), on view between the surviving parts of an Elizabethan mansion. The gardens are worth a visit at all seasons. There is a spring garden where bulb flowers flourish, a summer garden, and an autumn garden with flowering shrubs, as well as a large herb garden. The place is open Easter to mid-October, Tuesday to Friday from 1 to 6:30 p.m. and Saturday, Sunday, and Good Friday from 10 a.m. to 6:30 p.m. Admission is £3.50 ($6.15) for adults and £1.80 ($3.15) for children on Sunday, dropping to £3 ($5.25) for adults and £1.50 ($2.65) for children Tuesday to Saturday. Meals are available in the Granary Restaurant, open Good Friday to mid-

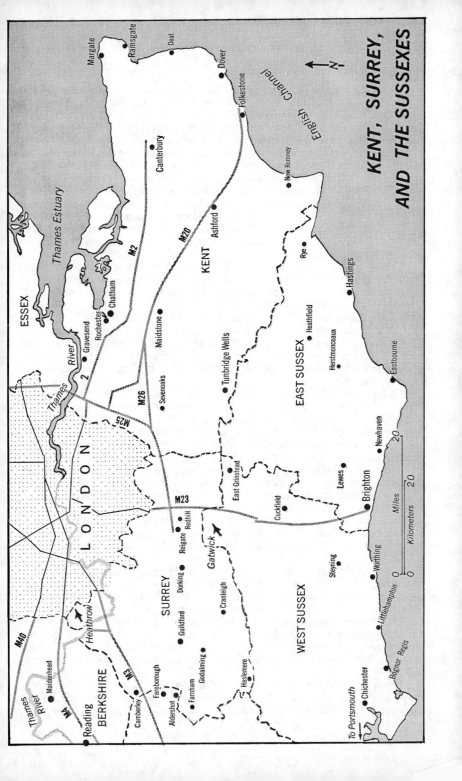

KENT, SURREY, AND THE SUSSEXES

October Tuesday to Friday from noon to 6 p.m., Saturday and Sunday from 10 a.m. to 6 p.m.

LEEDS CASTLE

Once described by Lord Conway as the loveliest castle in the world, Leeds Castle, Maidstone (tel. 0622/65400), dates from A.D. 857. Originally built of wood, it was rebuilt in 1119 in its present stone structure on two small islands in the middle of the lake, and it was an almost impregnable fortress before the invention of gunpowder. Henry VIII converted it to a royal palace.

The castle has strong links with America through the sixth Lord Fairfax who, as well as owning the castle, owned five million acres in Virginia and was a close friend and mentor of the young George Washington. The last private owner, the Honorable Lady Baillie, who lovingly restored the castle with a superb collection of fine art, furniture, and tapestries, bequeathed it to the Leeds Castle Foundation. Since then, royal apartments, known as *Les Chambres de la Reine* (the chambers of the queen), in the Gloriette, the oldest part of the castle, have been opened to the public. The Gloriette, the last stronghold against attack, dates from Norman and Plantagenet times, with later additions by Henry VIII.

Within the surrounding parkland, there is a wildwood garden and duckery where rare swans, geese, and ducks can be seen. The redesigned aviaries contain a superb collection of birds, including parakeets and cockatoos. Dogs are not allowed here, but dog lovers will enjoy the Great Danes of the castle and the Dog Collar Museum at the Gatehouse, with a unique collection of collars dating from the Middle Ages. A nine-hole golf course is open to the public. The Culpeper Garden is a delightful English country flower garden. Beyond are the castle greenhouses and the vineyard, recorded in the *Domesday Book* and now again producing Leeds Castle English white wine. There is also a recently opened maze with a beautiful underground grotto at its center.

In the summer, from April to October, Leeds Castle is open daily from 11 a.m. to 5 p.m. From November to March, it is open from noon to 4 p.m. Saturday and Sunday. It is closed on the first Saturday in July for the annual open-air concert and on a Saturday in early November for the grand fireworks display. Admission to the castle and grounds is £4.80 ($8.40) for adults and £3.30 ($5.80) for children. If you want to visit only the grounds, the charge is £3.80 ($6.65) for adults, £2.30 ($4.05) for children. Car parking is free, with a free ride on a tractor-trailer available for persons who cannot manage the half-mile or so walk from the car park to the castle.

Snacks, salads, cream teas, and hot meals are offered daily at a number of places on the estate, including Fairfax Hall, a restored 17th-century tithe barn with a self-service carvery restaurant and bar. There are special combined Sunday lunch/ entrance tickets available during the winter (these should be reserved in advance), but traditional roast beef lunches are always available for about £12 ($21) for three courses.

Kentish Evenings are presented in Fairfax Hall every Saturday throughout the year, starting at 7 p.m., with a sherry cocktail reception, then a guided tour of the castle. Guests feast on Kentish pâté, followed by broth and roast beef carved at the table, plus seasonal vegetables. The meal is rounded off by dessert, cheese, and coffee. A half bottle of wine is included in the overall price of £25.50 ($44.65) per person. During the meal, musicians play a selection of music suitable to the surroundings and the occasion. Advance reservations are required, made by calling the castle. Kentish Evenings finish at 12:30 a.m., and accommodation is available locally.

If you are not driving during your trip, British Rail and several London-based bus tour operators offer inclusive day excursions to Leeds Castle. The castle is four miles east of Maidstone at the junction of the A20 and the M20 London-Folkestone roads.

CHILHAM CASTLE GARDENS

In Chilham Village, 6 miles west of Canterbury, Chilham Castle Gardens (tel. 0227/730319), were originally laid out by Tradescant and later landscaped by Lancelot "Capability" Brown. On a former royal property, the gardens are visually magnificent, looking out over the Stour Valley. A Norman castle used as a hunting lodge once stood here. It was frequented by more than one royal personage until King Henry VIII sold it. The Jacobean castle, built between 1603 and 1616 by Sir Dudley Digges (whose descendant was governor-general of Virginia), was reputedly designed by Inigo Jones. It is one of the best examples extant of the architecture of its day and is built around a hexagonal open-ended courtyard. Medieval banquets are held in the Gothic Hall throughout the year at a cost of £23 ($40.25) per person.

The gardens are open daily from 11 a.m. to 6 p.m. mid-March to October (last entry at 5 p.m.). Admission is £2 ($3.50) for adults and £1 ($1.75) for children Tuesday, Wednesday, Thursday, and Saturday; £1.80 ($3.15) for adults and 90p ($1.60) for children Monday and Friday. On Sunday, with jousting included, the charge is £3 ($5.25) for adults and £1.50 ($2.65) for children. On bank holiday Sundays and Mondays, the prices are £4 ($7) for adults, £1.50 ($2.65) for children. Every afternoon except Monday and Friday there is a display of birds of prey from the Raptor Centre. You can also visit Petland and the old Norman castle keep.

The little village of Chilham has a lovely small square with a church at one end, the castle at the other, and a mass of half-timbered buildings interspersed with old red brick houses. It is on the A252 Canterbury-Maidstone road and the A28 Canterbury-Ashford road.

1. Canterbury

Under the arch of the ancient West Gate journeyed Chaucer's knight, friar, nun, squire, parson, merchant, miller, and others—filled with racy tales. Straight from the pages of *The Canterbury Tales,* they were bound for the shrine of Thomas à Becket, archbishop of Canterbury, who was slain by four knights of Henry II on December 29, 1170. (It is said that the king later walked barefoot from Harbledown to the tomb of his former friend, where he allowed himself to be flogged in penance.) The shrine was finally torn down in 1538 by Henry VIII, as a part of his campaign to destroy the monasteries and graven images. Canterbury, then, has been an attraction of long standing.

The medieval Kentish city, on the Stour River, is the mother city of England, its ecclesiastical capital. "Mother city" is an apt title, as Canterbury was known to have been inhabited centuries before the birth of Christ. Julius Caesar once went on a rampage near it. Although its most famous incident was the murder of Becket, the medieval city has witnessed other major moments in English history, including Bloody Mary's order that nearly 40 victims be burned at the stake. Richard the Lion Hearted came back this way from crusading, and Charles II passed through on the way to reclaim his crown.

Canterbury was once completely walled, and many traces of its old fortifications remain. In the 16th century, weavers—mostly Huguenots from northern France and the Low Countries—fled to Canterbury to escape religious persecution. They started a weaving industry that flourished until the expanding silk trade with India sent it into oblivion.

The old city is much easier to reach today than it was in Chaucer's time. Lying 56 miles from London, it is within a 1½-hour train ride from Victoria Station. The city center is closed to cars, but it's only a short walk from several car parks to the cathedral or walking-tour starting point.

From just below the Weavers House, boats leave for half-hour trips on the river with a commentary on the history of the buildings you pass. Umbrellas are provided to protect you against inclement weather. You can get more precise information from the **Tourist Office,** 34 St. Margaret's St. (tel. 0227/766567), a few doors away from St. Margaret's Church, from which Canterbury's Pilgrim's Way (see below) re-creates the Thomas à Becket pilgrimage of Chaucerian England.

Now as in the Middle Ages, the goal of the pilgrim remains:

CANTERBURY CATHEDRAL

The foundation of this splendid cathedral (tel. 0227/762862), dates back to the coming of Augustine, the first archbishop, from Rome in A.D. 597, but the earliest part of the present building is the great Romanesque crypt built circa 1100. The monastic choir erected on top of this at the same time was destroyed by fire in 1174, only four years after the murder of Thomas à Becket on a dark December evening in the northwest transept, still one of the most famous places of pilgrimage in Europe. The destroyed choir was replaced by a magnificent Early Gothic one immediately, which was first used for worship in 1185. The cathedral was the first great church in the Gothic style to be erected in England and set a fashion for the whole country. Its architects were the Frenchman, William of Sens, and "English" William who took Sens's place after the Frenchman was crippled in an accident in 1178 that later proved fatal.

This part of the church is noteworthy for its medieval tombs of royal personages such as King Henry IV and Edward the Black Prince, as well as numerous archbishops. To the later Middle Ages belongs the great 14th-century nave and the famous central "Bell Harry Tower." The cathedral stands in spacious precincts amid the remains of the buildings of the monastery—cloisters, chapter house, and Norman water tower, which have survived intact from the Dissolution in the time of King Henry VIII to the present day.

Becket's shrine was destroyed by the Tudor king, but the site of that tomb may be seen in Trinity Chapel, in the vicinity of the High Altar. Becket is said to have worked miracles. The cathedral contains some rare stained glass depicting those feats. Perhaps the most miraculous thing is that the windows escaped Henry VIII's agents of destruction and Hitler's bombs as well, having been removed as a precaution at the beginning of the war. The cathedral library was damaged by a German air raid in 1942, but the main body of the church was unharmed, although a large area of the town of Canterbury was flattened. The replacement windows of the cathedral were blown in, proving the wisdom of having the medieval glass safely stored away. East of the Trinity Chapel is "Becket's Crown," in which is a chapel dedicated to "Martyrs and Saints of Our Own Time." St. Augustine's Chair, one of the symbols of the authority of the archbishop of Canterbury, stands behind the high altar. The cathedral is open daily from 8:45 a.m. to 7 p.m. in summer (it closes at 5 p.m. in winter).

ROMAN PAVEMENT

This site is off High Street down Butchery Lane. It contains some fine mosaic pavement remains and treasures from excavations in the city. The Pavement is open daily from 10 a.m. to 1 p.m. and 2 to 4 p.m. (in winter, afternoons only). The entrance charge is 55p (95¢), which includes a ticket to the Westgate Towers Museum, which has the same hours. For information, call 0227/452747.

PILGRIM'S WAY

Re-creating the Thomas à Becket pilgrimage of Chaucerian England, **Canterbury Pilgrim's Way,** St. Margaret's Street (tel. 0227/454888), is open daily from 9 a.m. to 5 p.m., costing adults £3 ($5.25) and children £1.50 ($2.65). Visitors are taken on a tour through England of the Middle Ages, and they meet some of Chaucer's pilgrims, including the Wife of Bath. Audio-visual techniques bring these characters to life. Stories of jealousy, pride, avarice, romance, and certainly chivalry are recounted.

TOURS

Guided tours of Canterbury are organized by the **Guild of Guides,** Arnett House, Hawks Lane (tel. 0227/459779), costing £1.50 ($2.65), with three daily tours, each lasting 1½ hours, from April to October.

ACCOMMODATIONS

Before you can begin any serious exploring, you'll need to find a room. You have several possibilities within the city itself and on the outskirts, both budget guesthouses and splurge hotels.

Bed and Breakfast

Ebury Hotel, New Dover Road, Canterbury, Kent CT1 3DX (tel. 0227/768433), acclaimed as one of the finest B&B hotels in Canterbury, is a gabled Victorian house standing on the outskirts of the city. It is important to reserve here, as this owner-operated hotel is quite popular. Its rooms, 15 in all, each with private bath, are well furnished, roomy, and pleasantly decorated. B&B costs from £30 ($52.50) to £32 ($56) daily in a single, rising to £42 ($73.50) to £44 ($77) in a double. The hotel has an indoor swimming pool, as well as a spacious lounge and licensed restaurant serving good food made with fresh wholesome ingredients.

The **Georgian Guest House,** 69 Castle St., Canterbury, Kent CT1 2QF (tel. 0227/61111), is a venture of Mrs. Mary Kennett, who has restored and preserved the old architectural features, including a minstrels' gallery, of a 1502 building near the center of Canterbury. She has updated it with water basins, baths, and heating. The home is gracious and pleasant, furnished with antiques. Your timbered bedroom may have either a half-tester Victorian bed, or a slim four-poster, making sleeping here a retreat to Pickwickian days. The cost of a sleep in a treasured bed, with an abundant breakfast, is £12 ($21) daily in a single, £14 ($24.50) in a double. She rents out three singles, three doubles, and most interesting for families traveling with children, two family rooms suitable for three to four persons. The back drawing room is made from the old cellar kitchen overlooking the rear garden. Guests enjoy the restored Tudor exterior—wooden corbels, tile-hanging—at the back of the house and the garden. Mrs. Kennett is just the type for a stack of books beside a highbacked chair in front of the fireplace, ready for an evening's conversation on any subject. She's also considered one of England's authorities on Dr. Johnson.

Pilgrims Guest House, 18 The Friars, Canterbury, Kent CT1 2AS (tel. 0227/464531), dates back in part more than 300 years, and is just a three-minute walk from the cathedral. Comfort is assured by such items as innerspring mattresses, hot and cold running water in all the rooms, some with their own toilet and shower, enough corridor baths and toilets, and a central heating system. The charge for B&B is £15 ($26.25) to £20 ($35) daily in a single, £28 ($49) to £35 ($61.25) in a double. There's an adjoining concrete car park. Directly opposite is the Marlowe Theatre, which has many international personalities with top shows and plays.

Pointers, 1 London Rd., Canterbury, Kent CT2 8LR (tel. 0227/456846), is one of the city's finest guesthouses. This Georgian building stands across from St. Dunstan's Church. Owner-operated, it offers more than a dozen clean, comfortable rooms, several for single travelers and couples (double- or twin-bedded accommodations), as well as some family units. For the privilege of renting one, you pay from £22 ($38.50) per person daily, the tariff going up to £40 ($70) in a double. Bedroom amenities include private bath or shower, phone, radio, beverage-making equipment, and color TV. The location is about a 10-minute walk from the heart of Canterbury, and there is a private car park.

Ersham Lodge, 12 New Dover Rd., Canterbury, Kent CT1 3DX (tel. 0227/

463174), is a Tudor-style, 19th-century building at the edge of town. The owners, Mr. and Mrs. Pellay, run this pleasant lodge, and the whole place has been redecorated and is as fresh as a country morning in Kent. All rooms contain color TV, radio, telephone, and shower. Paying guests are accepted at a charge of £32 ($56) daily for B&B in a single room, £38 ($66.50) for two in a double. There are some rooms with private bath renting for £42 ($73.50) for two. The house is gracious in style—set back from the road and in the midst of many shade trees, with a back garden for children to play in. From the two-story living room, a winding staircase leads to the spacious and comfortably furnished corner bedrooms.

St. Stephens Guest House, 100 St. Stephens Rd., Canterbury, Kent CT2 7JL (tel. 0227/462167), is in a quiet part of the city, yet close to the main attractions. One of the most attractive buildings in Canterbury, St. Stephens is owned and managed by Robin and Valerie Quanstrom, who give visitors a warm welcome. The house, set in well-kept gardens and lawns, with its discreet extensions, has retained its character and yet offers modern accommodations for the guests. There are nine bedrooms, all with central heating, shaver points, and hot and cold water. The house can accommodate up to 16 guests. The cost is £12.50 ($21.90) daily in a single, £22 ($38.50) in a double, with a full English breakfast included. Dinner is offered during the high season at a charge of £5 ($8.75) for a set menu. Car parking is available at the rear.

Kingsmead House, 68 St. Stephens Rd., Canterbury, Kent CT2 7JF (tel. 0227/760132), is a lovely 17th-century house owned by Jan and John Clark, one of the most gracious and hospitable couples in Canterbury. The location of their timbered house is about six to eight minutes from the heart of Canterbury. They can accept only a half dozen guests, whom they put up in well-furnished rooms with private bath and central heating. The cost is from £17 ($29.75) per person nightly for B&B.

Ann's Hotel, 63 London Rd., Canterbury, Kent CT2 8LR (tel. 0227/68767), a family-owned B&B, stands on an artery leading out of town and has ample parking. You enter into a Victorian hallway, where Hayden and Liz Clements rent 19 bedrooms, each well furnished and comfortable, some with four-poster beds. A dozen of these have private baths, color TV, and coffee-making facilities. Singles without bath cost £16 ($28) daily, and doubles, also bathless, go for £26 ($45.50) to £28 ($49). With shower, two persons pay £35 ($61.25). VAT and service are included.

Yorke Lodge, 50 London Rd., Canterbury, Kent CT2 8LF (tel. 0227/451243), is a spacious, elegant Victorian B&B close to the city center and the cathedral. The bedrooms, all nonsmoking, have hot and cold water, and some have private baths. The charge is £14 ($24.50) per person daily for double occupancy. There is a sitting room opening onto a walled garden, plus a library/television room. Breakfasts are large and offer variety, and on some nights, home-cooked English meals are available.

Kingsbridge Villa, 15 Best Lane, Canterbury, Kent CT1 2BJ (tel. 0227/66415), is a bright, inviting guesthouse close to the cathedral. The owner rents a dozen rooms, some with private baths, at the rate of £15 ($26.25) to £20 ($35) daily in a single, £28 ($49) to £35 ($61.25) in a double. There's a small restaurant and bar in the basement, which is reached through the house or else by area steps past a medieval well where they once found a coin dating from A.D. 163. Clay pipes adorn the red brick walls, and there are comfortable settle seats around the bar.

Magnolia House, 36 St. Dunstan's Terrace, Canterbury, Kent CT2 8AX (tel. 0227/65121), is a quiet and pleasant Canterbury guesthouse run by owner-managers Ann and John Davies. A Georgian building, it stands within easy walking distance of the major points of sightseeing interest in this historic old city. Of the six rooms for rent, three have private baths. The B&B rate ranges from £12 ($21) to £20 ($35) per person daily. A reservation or call is important to secure accommodation. There is an interesting garden and limited off-street parking.

Alexandra House, 1 Roper Rd., Canterbury, Kent CT2 7EH (tel. 0227/

67011), is an 11-room guesthouse only a few minutes from the old city center and the cathedral. The house is centrally heated, and all rooms have TV, hot beverage facilities, and cold and hot water basins. Several also have shower units. B&B costs range from £12.50 ($21.90) per person daily in a single, the cost rising to £29 ($50.75) in a double. Evening meals can be arranged, costing from £6.50 ($11.40) for three courses, with coffee.

DINING IN CANTERBURY

Of special interest at **Queen Elizabeth's Restaurant,** 44-45 High St. (tel. 0227/464080), is the original room where Queen Elizabeth I entertained the Duke of Alençon, while she was trying to decide whether to marry him. The 16th-century interior, with its outstanding relief and wall paneling, recaptures the past admirably. The food is fresh and home-cooked—and very English as well, from the rich-tasting soups, such as cream of pea, to the roast pork with apple sauce and vegetables, to the deep-dish apple pie with heavy cream for dessert. A three-course meal costs from £5 ($8.75). If you go early enough, select the seat next to the window so you can look down the High Street. You can spot the restaurant easily by its gabled facade, which has plaster carving. Meals are served every day, except Sunday, from 9:30 a.m. to 6 p.m. English afternoon tea is a specialty.

George's Brasserie, 71-72 Castle St. (tel. 0227/65658), is an attractive establishment run by a brother and sister, Simon Day and Beverly Holmes, who pride themselves on the cleanliness of their restaurant and the quality of their food, made only of fresh ingredients. They serve everything from coffee and a croissant to gourmet meals. You can order from the fixed-price menu, costing from £6.50 ($11.40) for lunch, from £8.50 ($14.90) for dinner. On the à la carte listing, numerous appetizers are offered, including a fresh anchovy salad and George's terrines, all served with a basket of french bread. The selection of main dishes changes with the season, but it always includes fish and meat dishes and is served with new potatoes or french fries. George's is open Monday to Thursday from 10 a.m. to 10 p.m. and Friday and Saturday from 10 a.m. to 10:30 p.m., with last order time extended for theatergoers.

The **Mayflower Restaurant,** 59 Palace St. (tel. 0227/465038), stands on the corner of Palace and Sun Streets. There are very few good English home-cooking establishments in the whole city, and the Mayflower is one of them. This is also an area of the city where many of the Pilgrims who sailed for America on the *Speedwell* and *Mayflower* came from. On the first floor is the Pilgrims Bar. Meals are also served here. The downstairs restaurant is decorated in keeping with the old-world surroundings of the building, which dates back to 1601. The restaurant is open from 11 a.m. to 11 p.m. seven days a week, offering morning coffee, lunch, afternoon snacks, and dinner from 6 p.m. on. The Sunday lunch is traditional English, with roast beef, Yorkshire pudding, roast potatoes, and vegetables. There is an extensive à la carte menu, and the kitchen offers a chef's special every evening. The most expensive three-course dinner with wine and coffee costs around £15 ($26.25), and the cheapest full meal with wine and coffee goes for less than £7.50 ($13.15).

Alberrys Wine and Food Bar, 38 St. Margaret's St. (tel. 0227/452378), is fun—even the Victorian cartoons on its wine list claim that "Tomorrow morning you'll be able to perform great feats of strength if you drink plenty of wine tonight." Today, in the same area where slaves of the Romans once toiled (part of the exposed foundation was a section of a Roman amphitheater), live blues and pop music is performed from 9:30 p.m. to midnight every Thursday, free to customers. Alberry's offers an inexpensive and frequently changing repertoire of well-prepared food. Soup of the day, baked potato filled with chili con carne, followed by "Death by Chocolate," costs £5.50 ($9.65). Pizzas and quiches are available. Beer and mixed drinks are served, and wine is available by the glass. The place is open from noon to 2:30 p.m. and 5 p.m. to midnight Monday to Thursday, and from noon to midnight Friday and Saturday.

Cogan House, 53 St. Peter's St. (tel. 0227/472986), is a pleasantly inviting English brasserie, lying above a shop in the center of the city, about a block north of High Street. Climb a flight of steps to reach the second-floor dining room, housed in a building considered the oldest residence in the city, dating from 1170. Traditional English food, well prepared and served at attractive prices in generous portions, is the sustaining grace of this place. Desserts, especially their moist cakes, are also tempting. Food service is all day except Monday from 10:30 a.m. to 10:30 p.m. (Sunday from noon to 10:30 p.m.). Meals cost from £10 ($17.50).

Il Vaticano, 35 St. Margaret St. (tel. 0227/65333), is the best-known pasta parlor in Canterbury, bringing Italian flavor to wake up local tastebuds. All pasta is made on the premises, and you get a choice of sauces, including savory clam, carbonara, or a Pernod-spiked "fruits of the sea." The kitchen also does those three classics: lasagne, cannelloni, and ravioli. Meals cost from £8 ($14), and the restaurant is decorated in a simple but sophisticated trattoria style, with bentwood chairs, small marble-topped tables, and exposed brick. Open from 11 a.m. to 11 p.m. Monday to Saturday (from noon to 10 p.m. Sunday), it lies on a pedestrian street in the commercial center of the city.

ELHAM

If you should arrive in Canterbury during the peak season, you might be better off seeking accommodation in a little English village such as Elham, on the B2065 road in the beautiful Elham Valley ten miles south from Canterbury and nine miles northwest from Folkestone.

The **New Inn,** High Street, Elham, Canterbury, Kent CT4 6TD (tel. 030384/288), is an attractive traditional brick and tile building dating from 1820, its white walls, red doors, and black trim catching the eyes of passersby on the main street of the village. Locals congregate in the public pub. The separate lounge bar has a dining area where hot and cold meals are served for lunch and dinner. The B&B rooms rent for £26 ($45.50) daily for double occupancy, with a reduction of £8 ($14) if occupied as a single. All three rooms have private showers, toilets, handbasins, color TV, tea- and coffee-making facilities, and heaters.

KENT BATTLE OF BRITAIN MUSEUM

On a Battle of Britain airfield, this museum contains the most extensive collection of artifacts of this famous battle. It's at Hawkinge Airfield, Hawkinge, near Folkestone (tel. 030389/3140). On display are engines, pieces of downed aircraft, photographs, equipment, and letters from R.A.F. pilots. These exhibits are presented in once-abandoned airfield buildings. Hours are daily from 11 a.m. to 5 p.m. from May to September. From Easter to May 1 and October to November 1, the museum is open only on Sunday from 11 a.m. to 5 p.m. It is closed November to Easter. Admission is £1.50 ($2.65) for adults, 75p ($1.30) for children.

A RAILROAD RIDE

A few miles to the south is the **Romney, Hythe & Dymchurch Light Railway Co.,** New Romney Station, New Romney (tel. 0679/62353), the world's smallest public railway. There are 12 passenger locomotives, of which 11 are steam powered; more than 70 passenger coaches, most of which are fully enclosed; and a licensed observation saloon. The major difference between this and other tourist railways in Britain is its size. The locomotives are all one-third scale versions of British, German, and North American engines of the 1920s and 1930s. They run on narrow-gauge tracks for 13½ miles across Kent's historic Romney Marsh from Hythe to Dungeness Lighthouse, via New Romney and Dymchurch. Fares depend on the length of your journey, a round-trip over the entire line costing £5.40 ($9.45). Also, you can enjoy the freedom of the line for an entire day by buying a Day Rover Ticket, costing just over £8 ($14). Children are charged half of the adult rates. A round-trip takes about three hours, and shorter journeys can be made to suit your available time.

The railway operates a daily service from Easter to the end of September, with only Saturday and Sunday service in March and October. The railway is easily reached from the south coast along the A259 and from London by using the M20/A20. The closest mainline railway station is Folkestone Central. You can take a bus from Folkestone Bus Station to the RH&D station at Hythe. Telephone for train times.

To get to Hythe from Canterbury, leave on the Dover Road and follow the signs for Hythe.

LYMPNE CASTLE

Near Hythe stands the small, medieval Lympne Castle (tel. 0303/67571), built in the 14th century on land that was given to the church at Lympne in the 18th century. There is mention of a Saxon abbey on the site in the *Domesday Book* of 1085. Right on the edge of a cliff, the castle has magnificent views over the channel and across Romney Marsh to Fairlight. An ideal lookout against invasion, it has a Norman tower in the east and a medieval one to the west, with turret stairways leading to the main rooms, including the Great Hall.

Besides the building and its furnishings, there are exhibits of toys and dolls and full-size reproductions of church brasses, as well as a small period costume display. The castle is open daily from 10:30 a.m. to 6 p.m. June to September and bank holidays. Admission is £1.25 ($2.20) for adults, 30p (55¢) for children 5 to 14 years of age.

Port Lympne Zoo Park, Mansion, and Gardens (tel. 0303/264646), Lympne, near Hythe, has rare and endangered species among the animals housed in spacious enclosures in 270 acres of park and woodlands. Visitors can take a two-mile cross-country trek or a short main-drive walk to see the animals in their natural settings. Included are chimpanzees, wolves, Siberian and Indian tigers, Atlas lions, leopards, Siamang monkeys, wild horses, black and Sumatran rhinoceroses, sable and roan antelopes, elephants, wild dogs, honey badgers, small cats, and other rare and endangered species.

You can also visit the historic house built in Dutch colonial style, called "the most historic house built in the United Kingdom in this century." Features include the Rex Whistler tent room, the Moroccan patio, and the hexagonal library where the Treaty of Paris was signed. Owner John Aspinall's collection of wildlife paintings and other artworks are displayed in the galleries. The gardens have 15 acres of sculptured terracing, a remarkable Trojan stairway with 125 steps from which you can see across Romney Marsh to France on a clear day, a vineyard, a 125-foot-long herbaceous border, and striped, checkerboard, and clock gardens. Open from 10 a.m. to 5 p.m. (or dusk). Admission to the entire complex is £3.50 ($6.15) for adults, £2.50 ($4.40) for children 4 to 14.

---

2. Dover

One of the ancient Cinque ports, Dover is famed for its white cliffs. In Victoria's day it basked in popularity as a seaside resort, but today it is of importance mainly because it is a port for major cross-Channel car and passenger traffic between England and France (notably Calais). Sitting in the open jaws of the white cliffs, Dover was one of England's most vulnerable and easy-to-hit targets in World War II. It suffered repeated bombings that destroyed much of its harbor.

Hovering nearly 400 feet above the port is **Dover Castle** (tel. 0304/201623), one of the oldest and best known in England. Its keep was built at the command of Becket's fair-weather friend, Henry II, in the 12th century. You can visit the keep all year, generally daily from 9:30 a.m. to 6:30 p.m. in summer (it closes earlier off-season), for an admission of £2.50 ($4.40) for adults, £1.30 ($2.30) for children.

Admission to the castle grounds is free. The ancient castle was called back to active duty as late as World War II. The "Pharos" on the grounds is a lighthouse built by the Romans in the first half of the first century. The Romans landed at nearby Deal in 55 B.C. and 54 B.C. The first landing was not successful. The second in 54 B.C. was more so, but after six months they departed, and did not return until nearly 100 years later, A.D. 43, when they occupied the country and stayed 400 years.

The **Roman Painted House,** New Street (tel. 0304/203279), is a large section of a well-preserved Roman town house more than 1800 years old. It contains the oldest and best-preserved Roman wall paintings north of the Alps. There are many other Roman remains. It is open from April until the end of October, Tuesday to Sunday from 10 a.m. to 5 p.m., charging an admission of 80p ($1.40) for adults and 40p (70¢) for children.

ACCOMMODATIONS

Because Dover operates in a sellers' market, owing to the cross-Channel traffic, prices for lodgings tend to run high. But below you'll find some bargains.

Beaufort House, 18 Eastcliff, Marine Parade, Dover, Kent CT16 1LU (tel. 0304/216444), perhaps the finest of the small hotels of Dover, costs a little more than a typical B&B, but it's well worth it. There are 18 tastefully furnished accommodations, each with private bath or shower, color TV, direct-dial phone, beverage-making equipment, and hairdryers. The B&B rate ranges from £19 ($33.25) to £24 ($42) daily in a single, rising to £26 ($45.50) to £34 ($59.50) in a double. There is a licensed bar and restaurant on the premises.

St. Martins Guest House, 17 Castle Hill Rd., Dover, Kent CT16 1QW (tel. 0304/205938), stands a few blocks away from the cross-Channel ferries and the Hoverport, on the hillside leading to Dover Castle. The house, run by Mr. and Mrs. Morriss, is more than 130 years old, and is maintained and furnished to high standards, with full central heating. Bedrooms with double-glazed windows also contain color TV sets and facilities for making hot beverages. Most have private showers. B&B only is provided, from £9.50 ($16.65) to £14 ($24.50) per person daily. The house has a lovely guest lounge and a residential license. Ample parking is available.

The Morrisses now also operate the guesthouse next door to the St. Martins, **Ardmore Private Hotel,** 18 Castle Hill Rd., Dover, Kent CT16 1QW (tel. 0304/205895), in a 200-year-old building that has undergone extensive redecoration under the Morriss ownership, offering double or twin rooms and family rooms with private baths, color TV, tea- and coffee-making equipment, and double-glazed windows. Some have views of the harbor. The charge for a double or twin, including breakfast and tax, is £10 ($17.50) to £15 ($26.25) per person daily.

To the east of Dover stands **Wallett's Court,** West Cliffe, St. Margarets-at-Cliffe, Dover, Kent CT15 6EW (tel. 0304/852424), on about 3½ acres some three miles from Dover. A building has stood on this site for nearly 1000 years, and the present manor is a restored structure from the 17th century. B&B costs £30 ($52.50) daily in a single, from £35 ($61.25) in a double. All rooms contain private baths, and two accommodations are set aside for families. Thoughtful extras such as fresh flowers in the rooms make this an exceptional choice. Dinner is served, with a three-course meal, from 6:30 to 8:30 p.m. Monday to Friday, costing £12 ($21), a four-course repast on Saturday at 8:30 p.m. going for £15 ($26.25). All prices include VAT.

Beulah House, 94 Crabble Hill, London Road, Dover, Kent CT17 0SA (tel. 0304/824615), stands on the A256 (A2) road to London, and is run by its namesake, Beulah Abate, along with her husband, Donald. Their house is comfortably furnished, and their charge for B&B is from £14 ($24.50) per person nightly. What makes the house exceptionally appealing is its gardens in back, with sculptured yews and roses. They serve a bountiful breakfast as well.

Castle Guest House, 10 Castle Hill Rd., Dover, Kent CT16 1QW (tel. 0304/201656), is a small, clean B&B. Bedrooms are pleasantly furnished and well kept, each having a private shower (some with toilets), color TV, tea-maker, and central heating. The cost for a double or twin starts at £22 ($38.50) daily, at £34 ($59.50) for family rooms. A good hearty breakfast is provided, and if you're leaving early, the owners, Nona and Brian Howarth, will leave an overnight breakfast in your bedroom on request. There is a small car park for guests. Castle House was built about 1830 and is a listed building in the foothills of Dover Castle near the Roman Painted House.

Westbank Guest House, 239 Folkestone Rd., Dover, Kent CT17 9LL (tel. 0304/201061), one of the best B&B houses in the area, offers clean, comfortable, and well-appointed units, each with hot and cold running water, color TV, and tea- and coffee-makers. The tariff is from £11 ($19.25) per person daily, including a full English breakfast. If they're given a few hours notice, the hosts will provide an evening meal at £5 ($8.75) per person.

WHERE TO EAT

Finding a good place to eat in Dover is not easy. One of the most reliable establishments is **Britannia,** Townwall Street (tel. 0304/203248), across from the Dover Stagecoachotel, near the seafront. It has a box window, along with gilt and brass nautical accents on its black facade. A vast array of international favorites are featured on the menu, such as duck à l'orange. Naturally, Dover sole is on the menu (the chef grills it or prepares it verónique style). Meals cost from £8 ($14). The second-floor restaurant is open Monday to Saturday from noon to 2:30 p.m. and 7 to 10 p.m., and Sunday from noon to 2 p.m. and 7 to 10 p.m. A popular pub downstairs serves Monday to Saturday from 11 a.m. to 11 p.m., and Sunday from noon to 3 p.m. and 7 to 10:30 p.m.

Ristorante al Porto, 43 Townwall St. (tel. 0304/204615), brings a continental flair to Dover. One block from the landing dock of the ferryboats, this Italian-owned restaurant offers one of the largest menus in town, featuring such specialties as steak in black pepper, cream, and brandy sauce, along with cannelloni. Try the gelati misti (mixed ice cream) for dessert. Expect to pay from £10 ($17.50) for a meal here. However, an à la carte lunch goes for £4.75 ($8.30). Hours are from noon to 2:30 p.m. and 7 to 10:15 p.m.; closed Sunday.

On the Outskirts

Finglesham Grange, Finglesham, near Deal, Kent CT14 0NQ (tel. 0304/611314), is a country house of style, lying on the coast about 8 miles northeast of Dover. It stands in 4½ acres of grounds about a half mile from the village. The house, run by Mr. and Mrs. R. W. Styles, is within easy reach of the Channel ports, beaches, golf courses, and the Kentish countryside. B&B is offered to no more than six guests at a time, each of whom is charged £17.50 ($30.65) daily, with morning and afternoon tea and a good-night drink. Three spacious double rooms are offered, each with its own facilities. A lounge with TV and a billiard room are also for the use of guests. Evening meals can be served if arranged in advance. The Styleses are an accommodating and helpful couple, and their English breakfast has been called "super."

TWO CASTLES

Just south of Deal on the Strait of Dover lie **Walmer Castle and Gardens** (tel. 0304/364288) and **Deal Castle** (tel. 0304/372762), about a mile apart.

Walmer Castle and Gardens, about 6 miles north of Dover, was one of some 20 coastal forts built by Henry VIII to protect England from invasion from the continent. It is shaped like a Tudor rose, with a central three-story tower, and is surrounded by a moat, now dry. In the early 18th century, it became the official residence of the Lords Warden of the Cinque Ports, among them William Pitt the Younger and the Duke of Wellington, who died here in 1852. The duke's furnished rooms and possessions, including a uniform and his telescope, can be seen. Also preserved are rooms occupied by Queen Victoria and Prince Albert during visits. The magnificent formal gardens were laid out by Lady Hester Stanhope in 1805. A plaque at this location marks the spot where Julius Caesar is supposed to have landed in Britain in 55 B.C. The castle can be visited from 9:30 a.m. to 6:30 p.m. Tuesday to Saturday and 2 to 6:30 p.m. Sunday, mid-March to mid-October; from 9:30 a.m. to 4 p.m. Tuesday to Saturday and 2 to 4 p.m. Sunday, mid-October to mid-March. Admission is £1.60 ($2.80) for adults, 80p ($1.40) for children.

Just a mile north of Walmer Castle is Deal Castle, standing a mile south of the Deal town center. A defensive fort built about 1540, it is the most spectacular example of the low, squat forts constructed by Henry VIII. Its 119 gun positions made it the most powerful of his defense forts. Centered around a circular keep surrounded by two rings of semicircular bastions, the castle was protected by an outer moat. The entrance was approached by a drawbridge with a portcullis. The castle was damaged by bombs during World War II but has been restored to its early form. An exhibition on coastal defenses is in the basement. Hours are the same as those for Walmer Castle. Admission is £1.10 ($1.95) for adults and 55p (95¢) for children.

For our next and final stopover in Kent, we go inland—37 miles from London —to a once-fashionable resort:

---

3. Royal Tunbridge Wells

Dudley, Lord North, courtier to James I, is credited with the discovery in 1606 of the chalybeate spring that started it all. His accidental find led to the creation of a fashionable resort 36 miles south of London that reached its peak in the mid-18th century under the foppish leadership of "Beau" Nash. "Beau," or Richard, Nash (1674–1761) was a dandy of a style-setter in his day, the final arbiter of what to wear and what to say—even how to act (for example, he initiated the fashion of stockings and shoes, ending the reign of heavy boots).

Tunbridge Wells enjoyed a prime spa reputation from the days of Charles II through Victoria's time. Because so many monarchs had visited, Edward VII named it "Royal Tunbridge Wells" in 1909. Over the years, "the cure" was considered the answer for everything from too many days of wine and roses to failing sexual prowess.

The most remarkable feature of Royal Tunbridge Wells is its Pantiles, a colonnaded walkway for shoppers, tea-drinkers, and diners that was built near the wells. At the Assembly Hall, entertainment (opera and vaudeville) is presented.

Alas, there's nothing sadder in tourism than a resort that's seen its day: Royal Tunbridge Wells is more for Jane Austen than Jane Fonda. Still, it's worth a visit just for a fleeting glimpse at the good old days of the 18th century.

Canadians touring in the area may want to seek out the grave of the founder of their country's capital. Lieutenant Colonel John By of the Royal Engineers (1779–1836) died at Shernfold Park in Frant, East Sussex, near Royal Tunbridge Wells, and he is buried in the churchyard there. His principal claim to fame is that he built the Rideau Canal in Upper Canada and established what was later to be the capital of the Dominion of Canada, the city of Ottawa.

You can come to Royal Tunbridge Wells from London, via a fast express train service, taking about 40 minutes. The service is every 30 minutes. Many people have learned that because of the high cost of accommodations in London, it works out well for them to stay here and commute.

WHERE TO STAY

On the principal road between Eastbourne and Hastings, **Clarken Guest House,** 61 Frant Rd., Royal Tunbridge Wells, Kent TN2 5HL (tel. 0892/33397), is a spacious, comfortable home built in the 19th century. It lies about five minutes from the main station, where rail connections are made into London. It is almost the same distance to the Pantiles. Nine bedrooms are rented, two suitable for families, but only one accommodation has a private bath. The charges for B&B are from £12 ($21) to £18 ($31.50) daily in a single, rising to £24 ($42) to £36 ($63) in a double.

Grosvenor Guest House, 215 Upper Grosvenor Rd., Tunbridge Wells, Kent TN1 2EG (tel. 0892/32601), is one of the better B&B houses at the spa. That's because it's owned by Paul and Jackie Tripley, who are fine hosts, seeing that each guest is made comfortable. They charge from £12 ($21) daily for a good bed and a "very fattening" English breakfast. They rent out three double bedrooms and two family rooms, and the house has full central heating and hot and cold running water in all units. In addition, there is parking space for five cars. They offer evening meals at moderate prices.

House of Flowers, 80 Ravenswood Ave., Tunbridge Wells, Kent TN2 3SJ (tel. 0892/23069), takes its name not from the famous Broadway musical, but from a flower conservatory within the building. Near the heart of the old spa, it rents out a few rooms for paying guests, with a shared public bathroom. The charge, depending on the accommodation assigned, ranges from £10.50 ($18.40) daily in a single and from £21 ($36.75) in a double. A large English breakfast with homemade preserves is served.

For a real taste of English hospitality try **Birkfield,** 92 Ravenswood Ave., Tunbridge Wells, Kent TN2 3SJ (tel. 0892/31776), in a quiet residential area within walking distance of the town. Mrs. Anne Kibbey offers pleasant, comfortable rooms overlooking landscaped gardens. Her English breakfast will fortify you for the day. She charges £10 ($17.50) per person daily, single or double.

WHERE TO DINE

The second oldest house at the spa **Thackeray's House** was once inhabited by the novelist, William Makepeace Thackeray, author of *Vanity Fair.* This is the finest and most expensive restaurant at Tunbridge Wells. However, on the ground floor you can dine much less expensively at **Downstairs at Thackeray's,** 85 London Rd. (tel. 0892/37559), a cozy bistro with a patio. Members of the Conservative Club next door like to come here to enjoy the competently prepared food made with fresh ingredients delicately handled in the kitchen. The service is first class, and you can enjoy it daily from 12:30 to 2:30 p.m. and 7 to 11 p.m. It is closed on Sunday, however. You can often dine for around £10 ($17.50). A set lunch is a good value at £7 ($12.25). Reservations are needed.

Cheevers, 56 High St. (tel. 0892/45524), also bistro-like in style, is a bustling little brasserie offering professional and polite service. The cookery is very sound, as are the ingredients. The menu is wisely limited, and likely to include pheasant pot roast or a velvety mousse of crab wrapped in spinach. The wine list is reasonably priced. A set lunch costs £12 ($21), with dinner going for £16 ($28) and up. Service is daily, except Sunday and Monday, from noon to 2:30 p.m. and 7 to 10:30 p.m. You should always reserve a table.

Instead of leaving London for Kent, you might head directly south of the capital to inviting Surrey.

SURREY

This tiny county has for some time been in danger of being gobbled up by the growing boundaries of London and turned into a sprawling suburb, catching the overflow of a giant metropolis. But although it is densely populated in the area bordering the capital, Surrey still retains much unspoiled countryside, largely because its many heaths and commons form undesirable land for postwar suburbanite houses. Essentially, Surrey is a county of commuters (Alfred Lord Tennyson was among the first), since a worker in the city can practically travel to the remotest corner of Surrey from London in anywhere from 45 minutes to an hour.

Long before William the Conqueror marched his pillaging Normans across its chalky North Downs, Surrey was important to the Saxons. In fact, early Saxon kings were once crowned at what is now Kingston-on-Thames (their Coronation Stone is still preserved near the Guildhall).

---

4. Richmond

Want to spend an afternoon in a Thames river town? Richmond in Surrey is only a 30-minute ride from London and can be easily reached by the Underground trains, or by Green Line coaches 716 or 716a from Hyde Park Corner. The old town, popular in Victorian times, has good public rail links with London, and it offers the escape many seek from the rush and bustle of the metropolis. If you're feeling lighthearted, take the boat trip down the Thames. Turner himself, art materials in hand, came here for inspiration.

Richmond is only one mile from Kew and its botanical gardens. You may prefer a combined excursion to Kew Gardens and Richmond on the same day. One of the attractions of the Thames town is the 2500-acre **Richmond Park,** first staked out by Charles I in 1637. It is filled with photogenic deer and waterfowl. Richmond has long enjoyed associations with royalty, as Henry VIII's Richmond Palace stood here (an even earlier manor was razed). Queen Elizabeth I died in the old palace in 1603. Somebody's shortsightedness led to the palace's being carried away, and only a carriageway remains.

If you want to be like the English, you'll climb **Richmond Hill** for a view of the Thames considered by some to be one of the ten best views in the world. The scene reminded William Byrd of a similar view near his home on the James River in Virginia, inspiring him to name the city founded there in 1737, Richmond.

There are good shops and an excellent theater facing the green on which, in summertime, cricket matches are played. Many locals go boating on the river. Richmond Park has a public golf course, and you can rent a horse from one of the local stables. The Richmond Ice Skating Rink has been the nursery of many of England's skating champions. Wimbledon and the Tennis Championships are within easy reach, as is Hampton Court Palace.

At Petersham, the 13th-century St. Peter's Church is the burial place of Captain George Vancouver. The Queen Mother's parents, Lord and Lady Glamis, were married there. It also has some very old wooden box pews. At St. Anne's Church at Kew Green, the painters Gainsborough and Zoffany were buried.

From Richmond, you can take bus 65 or 71 to visit historic **Ham House** (disembark at the Fox and Duck Pub across from the grounds of the Ham Polo Club), eight miles from the heart of London. This historic house offers an amazing look into the lives of the aristocracy of 17th-century England. Unlike most such houses in Britain, this one has been maintained almost intact. Much of the house, especially the kitchen (modern for its time), was the work of Elizabeth Murray, Duchess of Maitland and Countess of Dysart. Her aim was to create the most sumptuous private residence in Restoration England, complete from ceilings depicting mythological scenes to elegant French upholstered pieces. One of the first private bathrooms in England was installed at Ham House. The house is open daily from 11 a.m. to 6 p.m., charging an admission of £2 ($3.50) for adults, £1 ($1.75) for children. In summer, you can order tea in the 17th-century garden. For more information, phone 01/940–1950.

WHERE TO EAT

Londoners often go down to Richmond for the day, browse through its art galleries, and then dine out. The best bargain follows.

Mrs. Beeton, 58 Hill Rise (tel. 01/940-9561), was presumably named after the famous English cookbook writer. Decked out in pine, the restaurant is low-key and decidedly informal, and most reasonable in price, charging from £6.50 ($11.40) per person for lunch, which is served from 10 a.m. to 5 p.m. Dinner is offered from 7 to 10 p.m., costing from £11 ($19.25). It's owned by a women's cooperative, and each day a particular member displays her culinary wares—so you never know what you're going to get. The place doesn't have a liquor license, but you are allowed to bring a bottle. After dinner you may want to visit the antique shop in the basement. Tube: Richmond.

5. Haslemere

A quiet town, Haslemere's attraction is that Early English musical instruments are made by hand here. An annual music festival (see below) is the town's main drawing card. Over the years the Dolmetsch family has been responsible for the acclaim that has come to this otherwise unheralded little Surrey town, lying in the midst of some of the shire's finest scenery. Haslemere is only an hour's train ride from Waterloo Station in London, about 42 miles away.

THE FESTIVAL

It isn't often that one can hear such exquisite music played so skillfully on the harpsichord, the recorder, the lute, or any of the instruments designed so painstakingly to interpret the music of earlier centuries. Throughout the year, the Dolmetsch family makes and repairs these instruments, welcoming visitors to their place on the edge of Haslemere. They rehearse constantly, preparing for the concerts that last eight days in July.

You can get specific information by writing to the **Haslemere Festival Office,** Jesses, Grayswood Road, Haslemere, Surrey GU27 2BS (or telephone 0428/2161 between 9 a.m. and 12:30 p.m. daily). During the festival, matinees begin at 3:15 p.m., evening performances at 7:30 p.m. For seats in the balcony, prices range from £4 ($7) to £6 ($10.50), with stall seats going from £2.50 ($4.40) to £5 ($8.75).

WHERE TO EAT

The best-known pub in town, **Crowns,** Weyhill (tel. 0428/3112), offers a wide range of ales and wines, complemented by an extensive range of creative home-cooked foods, such as peppered chicken and on Sunday the traditional roast. Vegetarians will find a wide and varied choice. The generously portioned meals cost from £3 ($5.25). In the lunch period, children are welcome. There is an English garden for summer drinks. Hours are from 11 a.m. to 2:30 p.m. and 6 to 11 p.m. Monday to Friday, from 11 a.m. to 11 p.m. Saturday, and noon to 3 p.m. and 7 to 10:30 p.m. Sunday.

If you're seeking more sophisticated dining, head for **Shrimptons Restaurant,** 2 Grove Cottage, Kingsley Green (tel. 0428/3539), where Mrs. B. S. Keeley runs one of the foremost restaurants in the area, certainly one of the oldest established, housed in a 17th-century building. The cuisine is a combination of classical continental and English cookery, using the best ingredients around, and offering unashamedly rich sauces. Mrs. Keeley proclaims, "We are wicked and proud of it." You face an à la carte menu and the day's specialty menu, which depends upon the catch of the day. They have daily deliveries of fish from the coast, and game, meat, and vegetables are delivered daily. Fresh double cream comes straight from the farm. Meals cost from £16 ($28). Hours are usually from 12:30 to 2 p.m. and 6:30 to 9:45 p.m., but closing times really depend upon their guests. Call for a table.

WHERE TO STAY

An attractive period house dating back some 300 years, **Houndless Water,** Bell Vale Lane, Haslemere, Surrey GU27 3DJ (tel. 0428/2591), should get your attention by its name alone. Here you get inexpensive living, English country style about 1¼ miles from the heart of town, lying off the A286. In one of the beauty spots of Surrey, you get comfortable rooms and a warm welcome, for which they charge £12 ($21) to £15 ($26.25) daily in a single and £20 ($35) to £30 ($52.50) in a double. It's best to book in here on half-board terms, ranging from £19 ($33.25) to £23 ($40.25) per person. It is closed in December.

GUILDFORD

The old and new meet in the county town on the Wey River, 40 minutes by train from Waterloo Station in London. Charles Dickens believed that its High Street, which slopes to the river, was one of the most beautiful in England. The Guildhall has an ornamental projecting clock that dates back to 1683.

Lying 2½ miles southwest of the city, **Loseley House** (tel. 0483/571881), a beautiful and historic Elizabethan mansion visited by Queen Elizabeth I, James I, and Queen Mary, has been featured on TV and in five films. Its works of art include paneling from Henry VIII's Nonesuch Palace, period furniture, a unique carved chalk chimney piece, magnificent ceilings, and cushions made by the first Queen Elizabeth. The mansion is open from the end of May to the end of September on Wednesday, Thursday, Friday, and Saturday from noon to 5 p.m., charging £2.80 ($4.90) for adults, £1.50 ($2.65) for children.

WHERE TO STAY

Back in Guildford, I suggest the following accommodations:

The **Carlton Hotel,** London Road, Guildford, Surrey GU1 2AF (tel. 0483/575158), just a three-minute walk to the London Road Station on the London (Waterloo) to Guildford line via Cobham. The tab here is £21 ($36.75) daily in a single, £17 ($29.75) per person in a double. If you require a private shower, a single is £28 ($49), and a double is £18 ($31.50) per person, including an English breakfast. You can spend the day visiting the London museums or theater and come home here to have an evening meal. All these prices include VAT and service. Bedrooms are centrally heated with hot and cold running water and have a radio and intercom. For an evening's relaxation, a saloon bar beckons.

Mrs. Linda Atkinson, 129 Stoke Rd., Guildford, Surrey GU1 1ET (tel. 0483/38260), is most reasonable for B&B, considering the warmth of the welcome and the quality of the rooms. Mrs. Atkinson includes VAT, service, and the use of ironing facilities in her charge of £13 ($22.75) per person daily. All rooms have TV, tea- and coffee-making facilities, central heating, and wash basins. Her breakfasts are plentiful and well prepared. Her house lies a ten-minute walk to the town center, opposite the scenic park with tennis courts and swimming pool.

WISLEY GARDEN

One of the great gardens of England and of the world, Wisley Garden in Wisley, near Ripley, off the M25, junction 10, on the A3, the main London-to-Portsmouth Road, is operated by the Royal Horticultural Society. Every season of the year, this 250-acre garden has a profusion of flowers and shrubbery, ranging from the New Alpine House with its delicate blossoms in spring to the old Walled Garden with formal flowerbeds in summer to the Heather Garden's colorful foliage in the fall and a riot of exotic plants in the glasshouses in winter. This garden is the site of a laboratory where botanists, plant pathologists, and entomologists experiment and assist amateur gardeners. All year, hours are 10 a.m. to 7 p.m. (or sunset if earlier) Monday to Saturday. It is closed Sunday. Admission is £2.50 ($4.40) for adults, £1 ($1.75) for children.

DORKING

This town, birthplace of Lord Laurence Olivier, lies on the Mole River, at the foot of the North Downs. Within easy reach are some of the most scenic spots in the shire, including Silent Pool, Box Hill, and Leith Hill. Three miles to the northwest and 1½ miles south of Great Bookham, off the Leatherhead-Guildford Road, stands **Polesden Lacey** (tel. 0372/58203), a former Regency villa containing the Greville collection of antiques, paintings, and tapestries. In the early part of this century it was enlarged to become a comfortable Edwardian country house when it was the home of a celebrated hostess, who frequently entertained royalty here. The 18th-century garden is filled with herbaceous borders, a rose garden, and beech walks, and in all the estate consists of 1000 acres. It's open in March and November on Saturday and Sunday from 1:30 to 4:30 p.m., and April to the end of October daily, except Monday and Tuesday, from 1:30 to 5:30 p.m. The charge to visit both the house and garden is £3.20 ($5.60) on Sunday and bank holidays, £2.50 ($4.40) on other open days. Children are admitted for half price. The garden is open daily all year from 11 a.m. to sunset. To visit just the garden, adults are charged £1.20 ($2.10), and children pay 60p ($1.05). A licensed restaurant on the grounds is open from 11 a.m. on the days the house can be visited.

Back in Dorking, you can find accommodations at the **Star and Garter Hotel,** Station Approach, Dorking, Surrey RH4 1TF (tel. 0306/882820). Bill and June Smith personally completed many of the renovations on what they call their "oldy worldly" establishment. It was originally built 150 years ago as the village's railroad inn. Today it is a popular pub and restaurant, serving such dishes as the traditional homemade steak-and-kidney pie. If you'd like such a pub-type accommodation, you'll find spacious and comfortable bedrooms, all with color TV and tea- and coffee-makers, renting for £20 ($35) daily in a single and from £34 ($59.50) in a double. Prices include breakfast, VAT, and service. None of the dozen rooms contains a private bath, but the public facilities are adequate. The snooker tables in the pub usually draw a lively crowd of onlookers.

THE SUSSEXES

If King Harold hadn't loved Sussex so much, the course of English history might have been quite different. Had the brave Saxon waited longer in the north, he could have marshaled more adequate reinforcements before striking out south to meet the Normans. But Duke William's soldiers were ravaging the countryside he knew so well, and Harold rushed down to counter them.

Harold's enthusiasm for Sussex is understandable. The landscape rises and falls like waves. The country is known for its downlands and tree-thickened weald, from which came the timber to build England's mighty fleet in days gone by. The shire lies south of London and Surrey, bordering Kent in the east, Hampshire in the west, and opening directly onto the sometimes sunny, resort-dotted English Channel.

Like the other sections in the vulnerable south of England, the Sussexes witnessed some of the most dramatic moments in the country's history, notably invasions. Apart from the Norman landing at Hastings, the most life-changing transfusion of plasma occurred in the 19th century, as middle-class Victorians flocked to the seashore, pumping new spirit into Eastbourne, Worthing, Brighton, and old Hastings itself. The cult of the saltwater worshippers has flourished to this day. Although Eastbourne and Worthing are much frequented by the English, I'd place them several fathoms below Brighton and Hastings, which are much more suitable if you're seeking a holiday by the sea.

Far more than the resorts, the old towns and villages of the Sussexes are intriguing, particularly Rye and Winchelsea, the ancient towns of the Cinque Ports Confederation. No Sussex village is lovelier than Alfriston (and the innkeepers know it too). Arundel is noted for its castle, and the cathedral city of Chichester is a mecca for theater buffs. Traditionally, and for purposes of government, Sussex is divided into East Sussex and West Sussex. I've adhered to that convenient designation.

I'll begin in East Sussex, where you'll find many of the inns and hotels within commuting distance of London.

---

6. Rye and Winchelsea

"Nothing more recent than a Cavalier's Cloak, Hat and Ruffles should be seen in the streets of Rye," exuded Louis Jennings. He's so right. This ancient town, formerly an island, was chartered back in 1229. Rye, 65 miles below London, near the English Channel, and neighboring Winchelsea were once part of the ancient Cinque Ports Confederation. Rye flourished as a smuggling center, its denizens sneaking in contraband from the marshes to stash away in little nooks (even John Wesley's firm chastisements couldn't stop an entrenched tradition).

But the sea receded from Rye, leaving it perched like a giant whale out of water, still carrying its mermaid-like veil of antiquity 2 miles from the Channel. Its narrow, cobblestone streets twist and turn like a labyrinth, with buildings jumbled along them whose sagging roofs and crooked chimneys indicate the town's medieval origins. The old town's entrance is Land Gate, where a single lane of traffic passes between massive, 40-foot-high stone towers. The parapet of the gate contains holes through which boiling oil used to be poured on unwelcome visitors, such as French raiding parties.

Attacked several times by French fleets, Rye was practically razed in 1377. But it rebuilt sufficiently, decking itself out in the Elizabethan style. Queen Elizabeth I, during her visit in 1573, bestowed upon the town the distinction of Royal Rye. This has long been considered a special place, having attracted any number of famous persons, including Charles Lamb (who considered the smugglers "honest thieves") and Henry James, who once lived in the **Lamb House**, West Street at the top of Mermaid Street, from 1898 to 1916. There are many James mementos in the Georgian house, which is set in a walled garden. It is open from 2 to 5:30 p.m. Wednesday and Saturday from the end of March to the end of October, charging an admission of £1 ($1.75).

Today the city has any number of specific buildings and sites of architectural interest, notably the 15th-century **St. Mary's Parish Church,** with its clock flanked by two gilded cherubs, known as the Quarter Boys from their striking of the bells on the quarter hour. If you're courageous, you can climb a set of wooden stairs and ladders to the bell tower of the church, from which an impressive view is afforded.

Rye Museum, 4 Church Square (tel. 0797/223254), is housed in the Ypres Tower, a fortification built circa 1250 by order of Henry III as a defense against French raiders. It's housed in an ancient building and contains collections of military objects, shipping artifacts, toys, Cinque Ports relics, Victoriana, inn lore, and pottery. From Easter to mid-October, its hours are Monday to Saturday from 10:30 a.m. to 1 p.m. and 2:15 to 5:30 p.m. (open at 11:30 p.m. Sunday). Admission is 75p ($1.30).

The sister Cinque port to Rye, Winchelsea too has witnessed its waters ebbing away. It traces its history back to Edward I and has experienced many dramatic moments, such as those from the sacking French. But today it is a staidly dignified residential town. In the words of a now-almost-forgotten 19th-century writer, Winchelsea is "a sunny dream of centuries ago." Its finest sight is a badly damaged 14th-century church, containing a number of remarkable tombs.

On the outskirts, you can visit the **Ellen Terry Memorial Museum,** Smallhythe Place, Tenterden (tel. 05806/2334), which for 30 years was the country house of Dame Ellen Terry, the English actress acclaimed for her Shakespearean roles, who had a long theatrical association with Sir Henry Irving. She died in the house in 1928. This timber-framed structure, of a type known as a "continuous-jetty house," was built in the first half of the 16th century. It is filled with Terry memorabilia. The house is on the B2082 near Tenterden, about 6 miles to the north of Rye. It's open April to October from 2 to 6 p.m., except Thursday and Friday. Admission is £1.40 ($2.45) for adults, 70p ($1.25) for children.

WHERE TO STAY IN RYE

A beautiful Georgian house, **Durrant House Hotel,** East Street, Rye, East Sussex TN31 7LA (tel. 0797/223182), is set on a quiet residential street in the old town at the end of Market Street. Over the years it has attracted many famous people, including John Wesley during his evangelical tours. In more recent times, the famous artist Paul Nash lived next door until his death in 1946. In fact, his celebrated view, as seen in his painting *View of the Rother,* can be enjoyed from the River Room of the hotel. Sir William Durrant, a friend of the Duke of Wellington, acquired the house, which is now named after him. In time, it was used as a relay station for carrier pigeons. These birds brought news of the victory at Waterloo. The hotel possesses much charm and is full of character. There is a cozy lounge with an arched brick fireplace, and across the hall is a residents bar. The hotel rents nine comfortably furnished bedrooms, seven of which contain private baths. Depending on the plumbing, singles range from £15 ($26.25) to £25 ($43.75) daily and doubles from £24 ($42) to £50 ($87.50), including an English breakfast.

Jeake's House, Mermaid Street, Rye, West Sussex TN31 7ET (tel. 0797/222828), is a hidden treasure, standing on the same street as the famous Mermaid Inn (see "Dining in Rye"). The American writer Conrad Aiken lived here for nearly a quarter of a century and was visited by such guests as T. S. Eliot, Henry James, the artist Paul Nash (who had a house nearby), and Radclyffe Hall (author of *The Well of Loneliness*). Today, the owners, Jenny and Francis Hadfield, lovingly take care of this five-floor house that was originally constructed by a Hugenot (for which it is named) in 1689. They are eager to share Aiken's collected letters and poems. After incorporating a former religious school next door, the Hadfields can now offer five double rooms, plus a single and a twin (four of these have a private bath or shower). Charges for B&B range from £15 ($26.25) to £18 ($31.50) per person nightly. The bedrooms have been handsomely styled with Laura Ashley prints, and the bathrooms have hand-painted tiles made at a Sussex factory. Breakfast is taken in a former galleried chapel, now elegantly converted.

Little Saltcote, 22 Military Rd., Rye, East Sussex, TN31 7NY (tel. 0797/223210), owned by Sally and Terry Osborne, is an attractive guesthouse, a five-minute walk from the town center, yet with a peaceful rural setting. The well-appointed rooms, complete with TV, central heating, razor points, and coffee- and tea-making facilities, cost from £12 ($21) per person nightly, including an English breakfast. Guests are provided with forecourt parking and may wander freely in the large garden.

Little Orchard House, West Street, Rye, East Sussex TN31 7ES (tel. 0797/223831), is among the most elegant and moderately priced accommodations in the old seaport. The Georgian house, built in the 18th century, was then the home of Rye's Mayor Thomas Proctor, who pursued his political life and engaged in smuggling at the same time. Others prominent in politics, if not in smuggling, also lived here through the years, even Prime Minister David Lloyd George 70 years ago. The house is tastefully furnished, using many antiques, and there is much Georgian paneling. A large open fireplace in the lounge-study has a blazing fire when it's needed, a big bouquet of dried flowers otherwise. From this room and the intimate breakfast room, you can see the old-style walled garden, with espaliered fruit trees. Bedrooms, all with color TV, hot drinks trays, and private baths, cost from £30 ($52.50) to £50 ($87.50) daily in a single, and from £50 ($87.50) to £56 ($98) in a double. Tariffs include a hearty Sussex breakfast.

Mizpah Guest House, 89 Military Rd., Rye, East Sussex TN31 7NY (tel. 0797/223657), offers reasonably priced accommodations in the heart of Rye, but the few rooms mean you must reserve or call ahead. Rooms have private showers, and two are reserved for families. It's best to take the half-board rate, costing from £17 ($29.75) per person nightly.

Cliff Farm, Military Road, Iden Lock, Rye, East Sussex TN31 7NY (tel. 07978/331), is a different way to live in Rye, providing you show up between March and November when Jeff and Pat Sullivin receive guests on their nearly 4½ acres of property. Because of the elevated position of the farm, you'll have good views of the area, particularly over Romney Marsh. Guests share the public bath, paying from £10 ($17.50) to £11 ($19.25) per person daily in a double. There's a sitting room where a log fire blazes when the weather is cool. Farm produce means a generous country breakfast, and you can see the farm animals as you stroll around. Cliff Farm is about two and a quarter miles from Rye. Fishing can be arranged.

DINING IN RYE

In an ancient vicarage converted into a tea room, **Fletcher's House,** Lion Street (near St. Mary's Church; tel. 0797/223101), serves morning coffee, hot or cold luncheons, and afternoon tea from 10 a.m. to 5 p.m. seven days a week. Daily specials are always featured. Meals start from as little as £2.50 ($4.40). The house is particularly noted for its Sussex cream teas, the scones for which are baked daily on the premises. John Fletcher, the Elizabethan dramatist and contemporary of Shakespeare, was born in the house in 1579, when his father was vicar of Rye. It still retains many of its original architectural features, such as the old hidden-away front door with its design of York and Tudor roses, and an impressive oaken room. Do look at the clock on that church. It contains animated figures.

Mermaid Inn, Mermaid Street (tel. 0797/223065), is the most famous of the old smugglers' inns of England—known to the band of cutthroats, the real-life Hawkhurst Gang, as well as to Russell Thorndike's fictional character, Dr. Syn. One of the present bedrooms, in fact, is called Dr. Syn's Bedchamber, and is connected by a staircase, set in the thickness of a wall, to the bar. The Mermaid had been open for 150 years when Elizabeth I visited Rye in 1573. The inn has 30 comfortable bedrooms, three four-posters, and central heating. The inn, the most charming tavern in Rye, serves good food daily—English with frills. For £9.50 ($16.65), you can have a table d'hôte luncheon. Luncheon is served from 12:30 to 2 p.m. At the dinner, from 7:30 to 9 p.m., your tab for four courses may average around £12 ($21). The dining room, with its linenfold paneling, Caen-stone fireplaces, and oakbeamed ceiling, makes for an ideal setting. Even if you're not dining at the Mermaid, drop in to the old Tudor pub, with its 16-foot-wide fireplace (look for a priest's hiding hole).

For a splurge, **Flushing Inn,** Market Street (tel. 0797/223292), is a family-run operation (since 1960), in a 16th-century inn on a cobblestone street. It has preserved the best of the past, including a wall-size fresco in the restaurant dating from 1544 and depicting a menagerie of birds and heraldic beasts. A rear dining room overlooks a carefully tended flower garden. A special feature is the Sea Food Lounge Bar, where sandwiches and plates of seafood are available from £5 ($8.75) to £9 ($15.75). In the main restaurant, luncheons are offered from £8.50 ($14.90), and dinners from £15 ($26.25). Besides these lunches and dinners, gastronomic evenings are held at regular intervals between October and April. For one of these specially prepared meals, including your apéritif, wine, and after-dinner brandy, you pay £33 ($57.75) per person. Fine Wine evenings cost £40 ($70) to £50 ($87.50) per person. Hours are from noon to 1:45 p.m. and 7:15 to 9 p.m. The inn is closed Monday night, all day Tuesday, and for two weeks after Christmas. The Flushing Inn has been run by the Mann family since 1960.

Durrant House Restaurant, East Street (tel. 0797/223182), in a hotel of the same name previously recommended, requires reservations, even from residents. They serve only dinner (except on Wednesday and Thursday) from 7 to 8:30 p.m. Guests peruse a fixed-price menu, costing £11.75 ($20.55) for five freshly prepared courses. While waiting for dinner, patrons of the restaurant enjoy a view of the rear garden. As befits a former seaport, the chef specializes in fresh fish. Only fresh vegetables are used, and desserts and ice creams are homemade. If you arrive early, have a drink in the Wellington Bar, which not only serves real ale but does light pub lunches from noon to 2 p.m. daily as well.

Swiss Patisserie and Tea Room, 50 Cinque Ports St. (tel. 0797/222830), is where expatriate Swiss-born Claude Auberson concocts creamy Swiss cakes, cream meringues, buns, and pastries. Everything is good and fattening, and it's to be washed down in a tiny tea room with coffee or Swiss-style hot chocolate. A cream tea goes for £1.70 ($3), and there is a selection of hot savory snacks baked daily on the premises. Hours are from 8 a.m. to 4:30 p.m. daily, except Tuesday, when it closes at 12:30 p.m. and all day Sunday.

FOOD AND LODGING IN WINCHELSEA

Sure to catch your eye is the **Strand House,** Winchelsea, East Sussex TN36 4JT (tel. 0797/226276), a weathered historic house and cottage set in a garden at the foot of a hill and separated from the sea by meadows in which sheep graze. The owners, Shane and Gary Redmond, are conscious of comforts, and their high standard includes complete baths in eight of the ten rooms, plus wall-to-wall carpeting, TV, hot beverage facilities, and central heating in all bedrooms. One of the rooms includes a four-poster bed. Reserved for the guests is a private dining room with a huge inglenook fireplace. There is ample parking for guests' cars within the hotel grounds. The house is open all year and charges from £11.25 ($19.70) to £17 ($29.75) per person daily for double occupancy. Singles cost from £15 ($26.25). All prices include a choice of a full English breakfast. The cottage can be hired on a self-catering basis for those wishing independence. The house is well over 500 years old and has irregular oak floors. The low, heavy oak ceiling beams have been taken from ships. It is believed that a tunnel near the house leads up to Winchelsea Town and is a relic of the days when smuggling was one of the main industries of the area. In World War II the wooded bank at the rear of the house was used to store rifles and ammunition in the event of a Nazi invasion (the meadow below was flooded to deter foot soldiers bent on invasion).

Manna Plat Restaurant, Mill Road (tel. 0797/226317), is a charming terracotta- and tile-covered stone cottage dating from 1750. It is open only from 11 a.m. to 5:30 p.m. daily, except Monday and Tuesday, for coffee or tea, light lunches, and drinks (fully licensed). Owner Denise Crispin serves only fresh homemade natural food from local produce and refuses to offer Coca-Cola. However, you can enjoy such dishes as homemade quiche, pork or fish pâtés, and tomatoes Provençal. Light lunches cost from £6 ($10.50).

7. Hastings and St. Leonards

The world has seen bigger battles, but few are as well remembered as the Battle of Hastings—1066. When William, Duke of Normandy, landed on the Sussex coast and lured King Harold (already fighting Vikings in Yorkshire) southward to defeat, the destiny of the English-speaking people was changed forever. It was D-Day in reverse. The actual battle occurred at what is now Battle Abbey (seven miles away), but the Norman duke used Hastings as his base of operation.

Hastings suffered other invasions, being razed by the French in the 14th century. But after that blow an old Tudor town grew up in the eastern sector, and it makes for a good stroll today. The more recent invasion threat—that of Hitler's armies—never came to pass. The "dragons' dentures" were put up across the countryside to bite into Nazi tanks.

Linked by a three-mile promenade along the sea, Hastings and St. Leonards were given a considerable boost in the 19th century by Queen Victoria, who visited several times. Neither town enjoys such royal patronage or prestigious-name guests today; rather, they do a thriving business with middle-class Midlands visitors who shun the wicked ways of the continent to bask in the highly unreliable English sun. Hastings and St. Leonards have the usual shops and English sea-resort amusements. Lying only 63 miles from London, the coastal resorts are serviced by fast trains from Victoria Station.

THE SIGHTS

This area has three major attractions of interest.

Hastings Castle

In ruins now, the first of the Norman castles to be built in England sprouted up on a western hill overlooking Hastings, circa 1067. Precious little is left to remind us of the days when proud knights, imbued with a spirit of pomp and spectacle, wore bonnets and girdles. The fortress was ordered torn down by King John in 1216, and later served as a church and monastery until it felt Henry VIII's ire. Owned by the Pelham dynasty from the latter 16th century to modern times, the ruins have been turned over to Hastings. From the mount, you'll have a good view of the coast and promenade. It is open from 10 a.m. to 5 p.m. daily from mid-March to the end of October. Admission is £1.30 ($2.30) for adults, 80p ($1.40) for children. A family ticket, for two adults and up to four children, costs £3.75 ($6.55).

The Hastings Embroidery

A commemorative work, the Hastings Embroidery, Town Hall, Queen's Road (tel. 0424/722026), was first exhibited in 1966. It is a remarkable achievement that traces 900 years of English history through needlework. Depicted are some of the nation's greatest moments (the Battle of Hastings, the coronation of William the Conqueror) and its legends (Robin Hood). In all, 27 panels, each nine feet wide (243 feet total), depicting 81 historic scenes, are exhibited at the Town Hall. The history of Britain comes alive—the murder of Thomas à Becket, King John signing the Magna Carta, the Black Plague, Chaucer's pilgrims going to Canterbury, the Battle of Agincourt with the victorious Henry V, the War of the Roses, the Little Princes in the Tower, Bloody Mary's reign, Drake's *Golden Hind*, the arrival of Philip's ill-fated Armada, Guy Fawkes's gunpowder plot, the sailing of the *Mayflower*, the disastrous plague of 1665 and the great London fire of the following year, Nelson at Trafalgar, the Battle of Waterloo, the Battle of Britain, and the D-Day landings at Normandy. In the center is a scale model of the battlefield at Battle, depicting William's one-inch men doing in Harold's small soldiers. The embroidery may be viewed from October to May, Monday to Friday from 11:30 a.m. to 3:30 p.m. From June to September, it is open Monday to Friday from 10 a.m. to 5 p.m. and on Saturday from 10 a.m. to 1 p.m. and 2 to 5 p.m. An admission of 75p ($1.30) is charged for adults and 40p (70¢) for children.

A Smugglers Adventure

You can descend into the underground haunts of smugglers in days of yore at **St. Clements Caves.** The caves cover four acres of passages, caverns, and secret chambers 60 feet below ground. You descend 140 feet down the monk's walk, a candlelit passage into the depths of the caves. There you'll find an exhibition of costumes, weapons, artifacts, and "tools of the trade" that tell the story of smuggling in the 18th century. More than 50 life-size figures are brought to life. It is open from mid-March until the end of October daily from 10 a.m. to 6 p.m., charging adults £1.80 ($3.15) and children £1.30 ($2.30).

BED AND BREAKFAST

One of the best guesthouses in the area is **Eagle House Hotel,** 12 Pevensey Rd., St. Leonards, East Sussex TV38 0JZ (tel. 0424/430535). This three-story mansion, originally built in 1860 as a palatial private home, lies in a residential section about a ten-minute walk from the beaches. There are 15 well-furnished bedrooms, 12 of which contain private bath, each with phone, color TV, central heating, and coffee-making facilities. Depending on the plumbing, singles rent for £21 ($36.75) to £25 ($43.75) daily and doubles for £28 ($49) to £35 ($61.25). It has a full residential and restaurant license.

Glastonbury Guest House, 45 Eversfield Pl., St. Leonards, East Sussex TN37 6DB (tel. 0424/422280), stands on the seafront adjoining the harbor. For a long time it has been receiving guests in its small number of rooms, some with private baths and color TV, and all with facilities for making hot drinks. It's one of the better values in town, offering a good, comfortable room and an English breakfast at a rate of £13 ($22.75) per person nightly.

Argyle, 32 Cambridge Gardens, Hastings, East Sussex TN34 1EN (tel. 0424/421294), enjoying a central location close to the oceanfront and the rail station, offers eight comfortably furnished bedrooms, three of which contain a private shower. The cost is from £12 ($21) daily in a single, rising to £21 ($36.75) in a double, which considering the amenities, makes this one of the best B&Bs for value at the resort. A trio of the accommodations is suitable for families, and a like number contain their own private shower and toilet. Breakfast is the only meal served.

Tamar Guest House, 7 Devonshire Rd., Hastings, East Sussex TN34 1NE (tel. 0424/434076), a favorite of readers, opens onto the cricket ground of Hastings, with a good view of the castle. The hotel is centrally located and convenient to the train station, where connections are made to London. In comfortably furnished bedrooms (none with private bath), guests pay £10.50 ($18.38) daily in a single, rising to £20 ($35) in a double.

WHERE TO DINE

Hastings is a fishing center, with a multitude of competitive small seafood restaurants along the street fronting the beach at the east side of the city (on the way to the old part of town).

Brant's, 45 High St., Old Town Hastings (tel. 0424/431896), a vegetarian restaurant run by Mr. and Mrs. Stevens, serves a wide variety of unusual salads with savory pies or quiches, cheese and vegetable pie, and homemade desserts, fruit pies, and other rich confections. All the food is prepared and cooked on the premises. A meal will cost around £4.50 ($7.90), and the establishment is open 10 a.m. to 4:30 p.m. (to 2 p.m. on Wednesday and 2 p.m. in winter). It closes for two weeks in April and two weeks in the fall.

If you have a car, you might leave Hastings and head for **Crossways,** corner of Waites Lane, at Fairlight, near Hastings (tel. 0424/812356), a country village restaurant about five miles away. It is known for its food, and many English residents in Sussex journey from miles around to enjoy the hospitality of Chris and Christine Rayner. They offer a three-course luncheon for a fixed price of £4.50 ($7.90) Monday to Saturday, £5 ($8.75) Sunday, from 12:30 to 2 p.m., and a three-course evening meal costing from £8.50 ($14.90) Wednesday to Saturday from 7:30 to 9:30 p.m., when reservations are requested. Vegetarian and lighter dishes are available. There's always a good dessert selection. Morning coffee and afternoon tea with homemade cakes are an additional attraction. It is closed Monday.

8. Battle

Nine miles from Hastings, in the heart of the Sussex countryside, is the old market town of Battle, famed in history as the setting for the Battle of Hastings in 1066. King Harold, last of the English kings, encircled by his housecarls, fought bravely, not only for his kingdom but for his life. In the battle Harold was killed by William, Duke of Normandy, and his body was dismembered. To commemorate the victory, William the Conqueror founded **Battle Abbey,** High Street (tel. 04246/3792), some of the stone for which was shipped from his own lands at Caen, in northern France.

During the dissolution of the monasteries in 1537 by King Henry VIII, the church of the abbey was largely destroyed. Some buildings and ruins, however, remain in what Tennyson called "O Garden, blossoming out of English blood." The principal building still standing is the Abbot's House, which is leased to a private school for girls and not open to the general public. Of architectural interest is the Gatehouse, with its octagonal towers, standing at the top of the Market Square. All of the north Precinct Mall is still standing, and one of the most interesting sights of the ruins is the ancient Dorter Range, where the monks once slept.

The town of Battle grew up around the abbey, but even though it has remained a medieval market town, many of the town's old half-timbered buildings regrettably have lost much of their original character because of stucco plastering carried out by past generations. The abbey is open from 10 a.m. to 6 p.m. daily in summer, and from 10 a.m. to 4 p.m. in winter. Admission is £1.50 ($2.65) for adults, 75p ($1.30) for children.

FOOD AND LODGING

Mainly French cuisine is offered at **La Vieille Auberge Hotel and Restaurant,** 27 High St., Battle, East Sussex TN33 0EA (tel. 04246/2255). It is housed in a structure rebuilt in 1688 using stones from the Battle Abbey kitchen, which was demolished in 1685. In the cozy restaurant is an inglenook fireplace where big logs are burned. Gourmet dishes with French provincial specialties are offered, as well as two fixed-price meals, all made with local products (fish, venison, and wild duck). The proprietors, Stephen and Kathy Dicky (Kathy is from Boston, Massachusetts), serve lunch daily from noon to 2 p.m. and dinner from 7 to 9 p.m. The fixed-price, three-course dinner goes for £12.50 ($21.90), the five-course repast costing £16.50 ($28.90). Expect to pay from £10 ($17.50) for an à la carte evening meal. There is a bar lounge, in addition to the comfortable bedrooms. Each of the units has individually controlled central heating, radio, direct-dial phone, and hot and cold running water. Most of the nine rooms contain private baths. The charge for B&B is £24 ($42) daily in a single, £29.50 ($51.65) to £55 ($96.25) in a double or twin, with service and VAT included.

Little Hemingfold, Telham, Battle, East Sussex TN33 0TT (tel. 04246/4338), lies 1½ miles from Battle off the A2100. Mrs. Benton and Mr. Barnes rent 13 well-furnished and comfortable bedrooms, some of which contain 19th-century antiques. The house abounds in art and objects, some a heritage from Ann Benton's celebrated sculptor father. Twelve of the bedrooms contain private baths. The B&B

rate (no advance bookings taken for that) is from £24 ($42) per person nightly, and stays of one night are not normally taken, but it's worth a call just in case. Normally guests book in for at least two nights in summer at a half-board cost of £72 ($126) per person. Four downstairs rooms have log-burning stoves, and one bedroom has a four-poster for which there is no extra charge. The house, reached by going down a steep road, is part 16th century and part early Victorian. At night some 20 guests gather around large Victorian tables for a sumptuous cuisine, much of the offerings grown locally on the farm.

Pilgrims Rest Restaurant, Battle Village Green, High Street (adjacent to Battle Abbey; tel. 04246/2314), is an early 15th-century, black-and-white timbered house, the preferred place for morning coffee, lunch, or afternoon tea while in town. You'll not only receive good portions of homemade food, but you'll encounter an authentic atmosphere. There is a good choice of appetizers, main courses, and desserts. A three-course meal could cost less than £6 ($10.50). There is also a light-meal menu. The restaurant is licensed. You may have your meal in the Long Room, the Great Hall, or in the garden with its view of the ancient stones of Battle Abbey Gateway, only 30 feet distant. For afternoon tea you can have a pot of tea, a Sussex cream tea, or something more substantial. Hours are daily from 10 a.m. to 6 p.m. from March to October.

Gateway Restaurant, 78 High St. (tel. 04246/2856), in a building originally constructed in the 17th century, offers dining costing from £4 ($7), although the price could go up to £12 ($21) for a more elaborate meal including one of the daily specials. Year-round hours for lunch and tea are from 10 a.m. to 5 p.m. daily (on Sunday from 11 a.m. to 5 p.m.). Dinner is served from 7 to 10:30 p.m. only on Thursday, Friday, Saturday, and Sunday.

Life at a 15th-Century Farmhouse

Kitchenham Farm, Bodiam, near Robertsbridge, East Sussex TN32 5UN (tel. 058085/357), is a 15th-century farmhouse owned and operated as a farm by Mrs. Daws and her family. Their house is typical of East Sussex: weather-boarded, with an interior boasting old beams, a fireplace with an inglenook, and a well-kept garden. The farm was originally called St. Christopher, because it was a resting place for pilgrims en route to Canterbury from Chichester. You'll be charged from £11 ($19.25) per person daily for B&B. Try to call before 6 p.m. Breakfast is prepared farm-style, including bacon, grilled tomatoes, freshly laid eggs, and homemade jam. The farm is on the Sussex border, half a mile from Bodiam Castle, built in 1386, the last military castle in Britain. That's only eight miles from Battle Abbey, the same distance from Rudyard Kipling's former home, and just 54 miles from London.

KIPLING'S HOME IN SUSSEX

Rudyard Kipling, the British writer famous for his stories about the days of empire in India, lived his last 34 years—1902 to 1936—at **Bateman's,** Burwash, Etchingham (tel. 0435/882302), a country house a half mile south of Burwash, on the A265, the Lewes-Etchingham road. The sandstone house, built in 1634, was bequeathed, together with its 300 acres of land and its contents, to the National Trust by Kipling's widow. East and West meet within the house, in Oriental rugs, antique bronzes, and other mementos the writer collected in India and elsewhere. Kipling's library is among the points of interest to be visited. The house is open from April to the end of October daily, except Thursday and Friday, from 11 a.m. to 6 p.m. (last admission at 5:30 p.m.). Admission to the house, a restored water mill, and the attractive garden is £2.50 ($4.40) for adults and £1.30 ($2.30) for children Monday to Friday, and £2.80 ($4.90) for adults and £1.40 ($2.45) for children Saturday, Sunday, and bank holidays.

9. Alfriston and Lewes

ALFRISTON

Nestled on the Cuckmere River, Alfriston is one of the most beautiful villages of England. Its High Street, with its old market cross, looks like one's fantasy of what an English village should be. Some of the old houses still have hidden chambers where smugglers stored their loot. Alfriston has several old inns.

During the day, Alfriston is likely to be overrun by coach tours (it's that lovely, and that popular). The village lies about 60 miles from London, northeast of Seaford on the English Channel, in the general vicinity of the resort of Eastbourne and the modern port of Newhaven.

You can visit **Drusilla's Zoo Park** (tel. 0323/870234), on the outskirts. This zoo has won awards. It is not large, but fascinating nonetheless with a flamingo lake, Japanese garden, and unusual breeds of some domestic animals, among other attractions. Children are especially delighted, as there is a playland covering more than one acre. An English Wine and Food Centre is also part of the complex. The park is open from late March until October daily from 11 a.m. to 5:30 p.m. (until dusk in winter), charging adults £2.50 ($4.38) and children the same.

Food and Lodging

Wingrove Inn, High Street, Alfriston, Polegate, East Sussex BN26 5TD (tel. 0323/870276), occupies a solid, early Victorian house with a balcony overlooking the village green. Sandra Calow offers three cozy bedrooms at prices—depending on size and plumbing (each unit has at least a shower, toilet, and sink)—that range from £25 ($43.75) to £30 ($52.50) a night, including a full English breakfast. Meals are also served to nonresidents, providing they phone in advance. Lunch is offered daily from noon to 2:30 p.m. and dinner from 7 to 9:30 p.m. A fixed-price Sunday lunch of roast beef and Yorkshire pudding goes for £10 ($17.50). À la carte lunches go for £6 ($10.50), with dinners costing £12 ($21) to £20 ($35) each. The menu changes with the availability of fresh produce and is made from English-inspired recipes. The dining room is paneled in light oak overlooking a garden. At night the tables are candlelit.

Riverdale Private Hotel, Seaford Road, Alfriston, Polegate, East Sussex BN26 5TR (tel. 0323/870397), is a family-run hotel with chimneys, bays, and gables, on the outskirts of the village, commanding views across the valley to the Downs. The owners, Rosalind and John Keble, supervise everything personally, making for a comfortable stay. Their well-furnished and carpeted bedrooms come with hot and cold running water, shaver sockets, color TV, beverage-making facilities, and some with private baths. Visitors are fascinated by the stained-glass front doors. Daily B&B terms are from £22 ($38.50) per person, inclusive of VAT and with a minimum two-night stay required. A good, filling four-course evening meal is available at an extra charge of £7 ($12.25).

Pleasant Rise Farm, Alfriston, near Polegate, East Sussex BN26 5TN (tel. 0323/870545), is an attractive farmhouse on 100 acres of beautiful farmland adjoining an old-world village. Delightful views are provided from quiet, comfortable rooms, some with private baths. Indoor and outdoor tennis and badminton courts and country walks add to the pleasure of a stay here. Mr. and Mrs. Savage are happy to advise on places to eat, sightseeing, and leisure activities. However, they rent only three or four bedrooms, depending on how many family members are in residence. The B&B charge is from £12.50 ($21.90) to £13.50 ($23.65) per person nightly.

George Inn, High Street, Alfriston, Polegate, East Sussex BN26 5SY (tel. 0323/870319), was first licensed as an inn in 1397, and in its time it's been a rendezvous for smugglers. Behind a facade with half-timbering and stone masonry, this is a long, low, and inviting inn, renting eight bedrooms, six of which contain private showers and toilets. The B&B rate begins at £26 ($45.50) daily in a single, rising to £40 ($70) in a double. However, the George is perhaps better known for good food, with a three-course dinner for £9.50 ($16.65) being one of the best values in town. If you're there for lunch, your meal will cost from £7.50 ($13.15). Food is served from noon to 2:15 p.m. and 6:30 to 9:30 p.m. daily. A garden is in back, but most guests head for the restaurant with its Windsor chairs and beamed ceiling.

LEWES

An ancient Sussex town, Lewes is worth exploring. Centered in the South Downs, Lewes lies 51 miles from London. Since the home of the Glyndebourne Opera is only five miles to the east, the accommodations of Lewes are often frequented by cultured guests.

The county town has many historical associations, listing such residents as Thomas Paine, who lived at Bull House, High Street, now a restaurant. The half-timbered **Anne of Cleves House,** so named because it formed part of that queen's divorce settlement from Henry VIII, is a Museum of Local History and is cared for by the Sussex Archaeological Society (tel. 0273/474610). Anne of Cleves never lived in the Anne of Cleves House, and there is no proof that she ever visited Lewes. The museum has a furnished bedroom and kitchen and displays of furniture, local history, the Wealden Iron Industry, and other local crafts. It is on Southover High Street and is open Monday to Saturday from mid-February to November from 10 a.m. to 5 p.m., and on Sunday, April to October, from 2 to 5 p.m. Admission is £1.10 ($1.95) for adults and 55p (95¢) for children.

Lewes, of course, grew up around its Norman castle. From the tower you can obtain a fine view of the countryside. To visit **Lewes Castle and Museum** (tel. 0273/474379), a joint ticket costs adults £1.30 ($2.30), and children pay 65p ($1.15). The castle and museum are open all year from 10 a.m. to 5:30 p.m. Monday to Saturday (also on Sunday, April to October, from 2 to 5:30 p.m.).

Where to Stay

Accommodations are difficult during the Glyndebourne Opera Festival, but adequate at other times.

Crown Hotel, High Street, Lewes, East Sussex BN7 2NA (tel. 0273/480670), will not please everybody, and it's not grand in any way, but many readers like it. It's a bit creaky, as it's one of the oldest bars in Lewes. Considerably refurbished, this is really a Georgian pub, renting 12 modest bedrooms, some with private baths and all containing TV, tea- and coffee-making facilities, and most with direct-dial phones. Bathless singles are priced at £22 ($38.50) daily, and singles with bath or shower cost £28 ($49) to £30 ($52.50). Doubles without bath rent for £30 ($52.50), doubles with bath or shower costing £35 ($61.25) to £38 ($66.50). It is run by Brian and Gillian Tolton. Opposite the War Memorial, the hotel stands at a traffic circle. Pub lunches are always available, and evening meals can be made up on request.

Felix Gallery, 2 Sun St., Lancaster Street, Lewes, East Sussex BN7 2QB (tel. 0273/472668), is one of the best buys, although it has only two rooms to rent. Completely up-to-date, this inviting cottage lies in a tranquil location a short walk from the heart of town and the already-previewed Lewes Castle. The rooms have color TV and hot-drink facilities. Rates for B&B are £13 ($22.75) to £14 ($24.50) daily in the single, depending on the season, and £26 ($45.50) to £28 ($49) in the twin-bedded room. Guests share the bath. Parking is available.

Where to Dine

Bull House, 92 High St. (tel. 0273/473936), at the West Gate in the oldest part of town, was a coaching inn in 1450, a knight's home in the 16th century, and the scene of a fight between the Cavaliers and Roundheads in the 17th century. Thomas Paine, who coined the name "United States of America," lived here from 1768 to 1774. The restaurant in this historic house specializes in a combination of both modern and old-fashioned British cuisine. Andrew Carter is the chef, and his wife, Jane, manages the dining room, which is decorated like the antique it is. Menu items include salmon, which the Carters smoke themselves on the premises, as well as filet steak flambéed with Drambuie and served with a green peppercorn sauce. Meals cost from £12 ($21) to £16 ($28) per person, with a fixed-price lunch going for £9.50 ($16.35). Lunch is daily from noon to 2 p.m. and dinner from 7 to 10 p.m. However it is closed for Sunday dinner and all day Monday. There is a car park opposite.

Ronnies Wine Bar, 197 High St. (tel. 0273/477879), is the most youth-oriented place in town, a popular wine bar decorated stylishly and attractively in a café-bistro style, with dark-wood chairs and circular tables. Jazz is featured on Sunday evening. Meals, costing from £2.50 ($4.40) to £6.35 ($11.10), are likely to offer special platters for vegetarians, lasagne verdi, roast beef salad, or chili con carne. Of the desserts none is better than the hot chocolate fudge cake. Hours are from 11 a.m. to 3 p.m. and 6 p.m. to 11 p.m. Monday to Saturday, and from 7 to 10:30 p.m. Sunday. Live music is presented every Thursday evening.

RODMELL

This small Downland village lies midway between Lewes and the port of Newhaven on the C7 road. The chief claim to fame here is **Monks House** (tel. 0273/479274), a National Trust property that was bought by Virginia and Leonard Woolf in 1919 and was their home until his death in 1969. Virginia wrote of the profusion of fruit and vegetables produced by the garden and of the open water meadows looking out on the downs. Much of the furniture of the house was decorated by Virginia's sister, Vanessa Bell, and the artist Duncan Grant. The house can be visited from 2 to 6 p.m. Wednesday and Saturday from May to the end of September, and from 2 to 5 p.m. Wednesday and Saturday in April and October. Last entry is half an hour before closing time. Admission is £1.20 ($2.10).

Rodmell also has a 12th-century church, a working farm, and a tiny Victorian village often visited.

THE BLUEBELL RAILWAY

This railway is at Sheffield Park Station, near Uckfield in East Sussex (tel. 082572/2370 Talking Timetable, 082572/3777 for information), on the A275 from Lewes to Danehill. It takes its name from the spring flowers that grow alongside the track, running from Sheffield Park to Horsted Keynes. A railway buff's delight, the steam locomotives date from 1872 to the 1950s and the end of steam in England. You can visit the locomotive sheds and works, plus a museum and a large buffet and bookshop. There's a carriage shed at Horsted Keynes. The Victorian room on the platform at Horsted Keynes offers refreshments while you wait for your train. The journey from Sheffield Park, climbing out of the Ouse Valley through lovely countryside, takes 15 minutes, costing adults £3 ($5.25) and children £1.50 ($2.65). There are several daily services from the end of May to the end of September. In spring and autumn, service is restricted mainly to Wednesday, Saturday, and Sunday. In December, January, and February trains operate on Sunday only.

10. Brighton

Back in 1753, when Dr. Russell propounded the seawater cure—even to the point of advocating the drinking of an oceanic cocktail—he launched a movement that was to change the life of the average Britisher, or at least his or her vacation plans. Brighton, 53 miles south of London, was one of the first of the great seaside resorts of Europe. The village on the sea from which the present town grew was named Brighthelmstone—so of course the English eventually shortened it to Brighton.

The original style-setter who was to shape so much of its destiny arrived in 1783, just turned 21; he was the then Prince of Wales, whose presence and patronage gave status to the seaside town.

Fashionable dandies from London, including Beau Brummell, turned up. The construction business boomed, as Brighton blossomed out with charming and attractive town houses, well-planned squares and crescents. From the prince regent's title came the voguish word "Regency," which was to characterize an era but more specifically refers to the period between 1811 and 1820. Under Victoria—and in spite of her cutting off the patronage of her presence—Brighton continued to flourish.

Alas, in this century, as the English began to discover more glamorous spots on the continent, Brighton lost much of its *joie de vivre*. It became more aptly tabbed as tatty, featuring the usual run of English seaside amusements ("Let's go down to Brighton, ducky"). Happily, that state of affairs has changed, owing largely to the huge numbers of Londoners moving in (some of whom have taken to commuting, as Brighton lies only one hour's—frequent-service—train ride from Victoria Station). It's London by the Sea. A beach east of the town has been opened for nude bathing, Britain's first venture into this sport. Introduction of real-life attractions of the flesh has certainly made passé such pictorial representations as were once the big draw shown on penny machines by the seafront. These, however, still clank and grind away in a museum, where you can take a trip back in time by means of an old penny purchased at the museum's kiosk.

The Lanes, a closely knit section of alleyways off North Street in Brighton (many of the present shops were formerly fishermen's cottages), were frequented in Victoria's day by style-setting curio and antique collectors. Many are still there, although sharing space with boutiques.

At **Hove,** once a separate town but now a part of the Greater Brighton complex, of special interest is the **Engineerium,** in a building that used to house a waterworks. Here you can see a little steam launch, models of engines and steam trucks, old motorbikes, and the Victorian waterworks kept in operative condition.

Still, the eternal attraction remains—

THE ROYAL PAVILION

Among the royal residences of Europe, the Pavilion at Brighton (tel. 0273/603005), a John Nash version of an Indian mogul's palace, is unique. Ornate and exotic, it has been subjected over the years to the most devastating wit of English satirists and pundits. But today we can examine it more objectively as one of the outstanding examples of the Orientalizing tendencies of the romantic movement in England.

Originally, the Pavilion was built in 1787 by Henry Holland. But it no more resembled its present look than a caterpillar does a butterfly. By the time Nash had transformed it from a simple classical villa into an Oriental fantasy, the prince regent had become King George IV. He and one of his mistresses, Lady Conyngham, lived in the place until 1827.

A decade before Victoria, then queen, arrived in Brighton. Although she was to bring Albert and the children on a number of occasions, the monarch and Brighton just didn't mix. The very air of the resort seemed too flippant for her, and the latter-day sea-bathing disciples of Dr. Russell trailed Victoria as if she were a stage actress. Further, the chinoiseries of the interior and the mogul domes and cupolas on the exterior didn't set too well with her firm tastes—even though the pavilion would have been a fitting abode for a woman who was to bear the title Empress of India.

By 1845 Victoria and Brighton had had it. She began packing, and the royal furniture was carted off. Its tenants gone, the Pavilion was in serious peril of being torn down. By a narrow vote, Brightonians agreed to purchase it. It is gradually being restored to its former splendor, enhanced in no small part by the return of much of its original furniture on loan by the present tenant at Buckingham Palace.

Of exceptional interest is the domed Banqueting Hall, with a chandelier of bronze dragons supporting lily-like glass globes. Around the room and on the central banqueting table, there is a spectacular collection of silver-gilt and gilt-bronze of the Regency period. In the Great Kitchen, with its old revolving spits, is a collection of Wellington's pots and pans, his *batterie de cuisine,* from his town house at Hyde Park Corner. In the State Apartments, particularly the domed Salon, dragons wink at you, serpents entwine, lacquered doors shine. The Music Room, with its scalloped ceiling, is a salon of water lilies, flying dragons, sunflowers, reptilian paintings, bamboo, silk, and satin. In the second-floor Gallery, look for Nash's views of the Pavilion in its elegant heyday. There is also an exhibition of Pavilion history, illustrating the damage caused by rainwater, frequent alterations, and the impressive program of repair and reclamation in progress.

Currently the Royal Pavilion is undergoing an extensive program of structural and decorative restoration. This inevitably results in occasional inconvenience to visitors, although the work is, in its own right, absolutely fascinating. The pavilion is open daily from 10 a.m. to 5 p.m. October to May and from 10 a.m. to 6 p.m. June to September. It is closed Christmas and Boxing Day. Admission is £2.30 ($4.05) for adults, £1.20 ($2.10) for children 5 to 15. A family ticket for one adult and up to four children costs £3.50 ($6.15), for two adults and up to four children £5.75 ($10.05).

SEEING BRIGHTON

A walking tour costs £1 ($1.75) for adults, 50p (90¢) for children. Tours are offered from March to December, but hours are subject to change. For times and places of departure, consult the **Tourist Information Centre,** Marlborough House, 54 Old Steine (tel. 0273/23755), by the Royal Albion Hotel and the bus terminal. You can also get help here if you have accommodations problems.

WHERE TO STAY IN BRIGHTON

Dozens of accommodations are to be found in all price ranges. I'll give you only a representative sampling in Brighton itself.

The **Adelaide Hotel,** 51 Regency Square, Brighton, East Sussex BN1 2FF (tel. 0273/205286), is a small hostelry in a beautifully restored Regency building that has been tastefully modernized and decorated without losing its early 19th-century ambience, which harmonizes with the amenities of today. All 12 units have complete bathrooms (some with showers), hairdryers, direct-dial phones, color TV, and facilities for making hot beverages. Singles, with breakfast and VAT, cost £27 ($47.25) daily, with doubles or twins going for £50 ($87.50) and family rooms for three persons for £60 ($105). The Adelaide is in the center of Brighton, just behind the West Pier.

The **Twenty-One Hotel,** 21 Charlotte St., Marine Parade, Brighton, East Sussex BN2 1AG (tel. 0273/686450), is perhaps the most sophisticated of the smaller hotels of Brighton, and it also serves some of the best food at the resort. But, regrettably, the dining room isn't open to nonresidents. Stuart Farquharson and Simon Ward rent only seven bedrooms in this early Victorian white-fronted house a block from the sea. Five of their attractive and well-furnished accommodations contain a private bath, and all of them offer color TV, direct-dial phone, radio, and coffee-making facilities. The basement-level garden suite opens directly onto an ivy-clad courtyard. All rooms are double, costing from £38 ($66.50) to £60 ($105), the latter the price of the garden suite. Tariffs include VAT, breakfast, and service. A superb menu dégustation of four courses costs £21.50 ($37.65) in the evening.

Le Fleming's Hotel, 12A Regency Square, Brighton, East Sussex BN1 2FG (tel. 0273/27539), one of the most highly acclaimed B&B hotels in the resort, is only a short walk from the seafront. It offers nine small, but handsomely furnished bedrooms, each with private bath, costing £30 ($52.50) daily in a single, rising to £40 ($70) in a double. A large English breakfast is also included. You'd better reserve in advance for this one, as it's worth it.

Marina House Hotel, 8 Charlotte St., Marine Parade, Brighton, East Sussex BN2 1AG (tel. 0273/605349), is one of the best accommodations in its price range at Brighton. This white-fronted town house sits about a block from the sea, near an interesting collection of antique shops. Built in the Regency style, it has 11 rooms, eight of which contain showers. Singles (all bathless) rent for £15 ($26.25) to £17 ($29.75) daily, two guests paying £29 ($50.75) to £33 ($57.75) with shower, £33 ($57.75) to £37 ($64.75) with full bath. Many of the accommodations have high ceilings and elaborate plasterwork. Visitors have free use of the elegant front parlor, and evening meals are available upon request. It is open all year.

Topps Hotel, 17 Regency Square, Brighton, East Sussex BN1 2FG (tel. 0273/729334), enjoys a diagonal view of the sea from its position beside the sloping lawn of Regency Square. The establishment contains 12 rooms, all with baths. Each accommodation is of a different shape and is furnished individually, sometimes with neo-Elizabethan pieces and early 19th-century moldings. Each contains a TV, radio, mini-bar, phone, and trousers-press. Closed during Christmas and the first week of January, the hotel charges £35 ($61.25) to £45 ($78.75) daily in a single and £65 ($113.75) to £75 ($131.25) in a double, with an English breakfast and VAT included. A small restaurant in the basement serves dinners to persons who reserve by noon.

The **Regency Hotel,** 28 Regency Square, Brighton, East Sussex BN1 2FH (tel. 0273/202690), is in a circa 1815 town house with bay windows, a carved door, and a canopied balcony facing south across the square toward the sea. Owners Mr. and Mrs. Simons have extensively renovated the establishment. The ground floor contains a high-ceilinged lounge with period furniture, Waterford chandeliers, and an original coal-burning fireplace. The 14 bedrooms, ten of which have private baths, rent for £26 ($45.50) to £34 ($59.50) daily in a single, £46 ($80.50) to £52 ($91) in a double with service, VAT, and a full English breakfast included. The higher up you go, the simpler the bedrooms become, but all of the hotel's accommodations have color TV, direct-dial phones, hairdryers, tea- and coffee-makers, radios, and central heating. Dinner is available by prior arrangement. There is an in-house bar.

Malvern Hotel, 33 Regency Square, Brighton, East Sussex BN1 2GG (tel. 0273/24302), only a stone's throw from the seafront, is an 1820 Regency building on this attractive square. The rooms are clean and brightly furnished, containing private showers and toilets, color TV, and tea- and coffee-making facilities. Singles rent for £26 ($45.50) daily and doubles for £44 ($77), all with a full English breakfast included. There's a small lounge bar with a residential license.

Rowland House, 21 St. George's Terrace, Kemp Town, Brighton, East Sussex BN2 1JJ (tel. 0273/603639), is open all year, has full central heating and units with shower, TV, room call, and courtesy coffee. It is a well-furnished house of ten bedrooms, located just behind the Royal Crescent on Marine Parade, 250 yards from the beach. No rooms are higher than the second floor. Rates are from £13 ($22.75) per person daily for a bed and full English breakfast.

Paskins Hotel, 19 Charlotte St., Brighton, East Sussex BN2 1AG (tel. 0273/601203), is a well-run small hotel only a short walk from the Palace Pier and Royal Pavilion. Michael Paskins offers 16 bedrooms with bath and four without bath. Tariffs depend on the plumbing and furnishings, and the most expensive units are fitted with four-poster beds. Doubles pay from £35 ($61.25) to £40 ($70) nightly, with a single costing only £17.50 ($30.65), with breakfast included.

Ascott House, 21 New Steine, Marine Parade, Brighton, East Sussex BN2 1PD (tel. 0273/688085), has sheltered many a satisfied reader. It enjoys a heartbeat location within a short walk of the Royal Pavilion. You'll also be near the pier and the famous Lanes, with their shops and boutiques. All the bedrooms have color TV, hot and cold running water, and central heating, and most contain private showers or full baths. Michael and Avril Strong charge from £14 ($24.50) to £21 ($36.75) per person daily. All of the front bedrooms have a sea view.

Trouville Private Hotel, 11 New Steine, Marine Parade, Brighton, East Sussex BN2 1PD (tel. 0273/697384), is a period town house tastefully restored and situated in a select square within walking distance of shops and restaurants. For a double room, including an English breakfast, prices range from £22 ($38.50) daily for a basic accommodation to £32 ($56) for a room with private bath.

DINING OUT IN BRIGHTON

Outside of London, in the south of England you'll find the best food and the widest choice of restaurants in the resort of Brighton. New restaurants of widely varying cuisine and standards are popping up all the time, and the foreign invasion isn't confined solely to Chinese and Indian. My sampling represents the best of the budget eating establishments.

Trogs, 125 King's Rd. (tel. 0273/26302), is a charming restaurant in the semi-basement of the Granville Hotel and under the same ownership. Its name is short for *troglodytes* (cave dwellers), but the little bistro eating place is far from cavelike, being a sunny place with a continental patio overlooking the sea. A fixed-price lunch costs £9.95 ($17.40), including VAT, and might offer such food as crêpes filled with creamed mushrooms (for vegetarians) or lamb noisette gingered and grilled. A three-course dinner, runs £16.95 ($29.65), plus service. A la carte meals cost from £16 ($28) up. Lunch is served from noon to 2:30 p.m. and dinner from 7 to 10:30 p.m.

Browns Restaurant and Coffee House, 3-4 Duke St. (tel. 0273/23501), is a rather 1930s place with plain tables and hoop-backed chairs. Dishes have interesting accompaniments. For example, spaghetti dishes are served with hot garlic bread and a salad; pies, including steak, mushroom, and Guinness, come with baked potatoes rather than the ubiquitous chips. A meal will cost around £8 ($14). The place is open from 11 a.m. to 11 p.m. Monday to Saturday and from noon to 11:30 p.m. on Sunday.

Food for Friends, 17A Prince Albert St., The Lanes (tel. 0273/202310), is a standout on "Restaurant Row" in Brighton. A vegetarian dining establishment, it seems to offer the freshest food and best value along this famed street, and it is so popular there may be a wait. But most patrons don't mind. Of course, in a vegetarian restaurant you expect homemade soups, fresh salads, and the like, but here you get many exotic varieties of vegetarian cookery, including dishes from India, Bali, or Mexico, depending on the night of the week. It is a self-service establishment, and meals cost from £6 ($10.50) and up. The cafeteria is open daily from 9 a.m. to 10 p.m. (until 11 p.m. on Friday and Saturday). On Sunday, its hours are from 11:30 a.m. to 10 p.m.

Cripes, 7 Victoria Rd. (tel. 0273/27878), really should be called "Crêpes," as it specializes in those delectable and savory offerings from Brittany. A corner establishment, rather cramped, it is old-fashioned in appearance, with oak tables and bentwood chairs, rather Edwardian. Those whole-meal buckwheat crêpes—called galettes here—are made to order for you, and you face many temptations as to fillings. Meals cost from £6 ($10.50), and service is daily from noon to 2:30 p.m. and 6 to 11:30 p.m.

Pinocchio Pizzeria Ristorante, 22 New Rd. (tel. 0273/677676), is a popular restaurant near the Theatre Royal and opposite the Royal Pavilion gardens in the center of the resort. It offers a large selection of pastas and pizzas with specialty Italian desserts. The restaurant is open from noon to 2:30 p.m. and 6 to 11:30 p.m., the average cost for a meal being around £6.50 ($11.40). Pinocchio's has a light, airy atmosphere together with a bright, efficient Italian staff.

Allanjohn's, 8 Church St. (tel. 0273/683087), is not a fish 'n' chips shop but a fascinating display of winkles, cockles, shrimp, crab, and lobster fresh from the sea to be eaten with brown bread and butter, salt, and vinegar. You can select a well-filled bowl of fresh crabmeat or a seafood plate with a salad. If you're lunching light, a smoked salmon sandwich will be prepared, or perhaps a crab sandwich. Hot food includes jumbo scampi, Chesapeake oysters, and shrimp royale, all served with salad and french fries. Meals cost from £6 ($10.50) up. John and Jackie Haslem, the hosts, keep the place open Monday to Thursday from 10 a.m. to 5:30 p.m., Friday from 9:30 a.m. to 6 p.m., Saturday from 9 a.m. to 6 p.m., and Sunday from 10:30 a.m. to 3 p.m.

STAYING AT HOVE

It may be small, but **Chatsworth Private Hotel,** 9 Salisbury Rd., Hove, East Sussex BN3 3AB (tel. 0273/737360), meets the tests of cleanliness, good food, sleep-producing beds, and a comfortable lounge with television—not to mention the Swiss-style personal services of Francis Gerber. The B&B rate is from £14 ($24.50) per person nightly. The bedrooms are large and suitably furnished, and there's a bathroom and toilet on every floor.

Hotel Brunswick, 69 Brunswick Pl., Hove, East Sussex BN3 1NE (tel. 0273/733326), originally built 200 years ago in a gray-stone Regency design, rises from a central position in the center of Hove. There are 27 bedrooms, about a third of which have private baths, some lying within a more modern wing that was originally built in the 1930s. An English breakfast is included in the price of £19 ($33.25) to £25 ($43.75) daily in a single, rising to £30 ($52.50) to £38 ($66.50) in a double. Each unit contains coffee-making facilities and a color TV.

---

11. Arundel

This small and beautiful town in West Sussex, only 58 miles from London and four miles from the English Channel, nestles at the foot of one of England's most spectacular castles. The town was once an Arun Riverport, its denizens enjoying the prosperity of considerable trade and commerce. The harbor traffic is gone, replaced by coaches filled with visitors who come in summer to hike through the vastness of—

ARUNDEL CASTLE

The seat of the present Duke of Norfolk, this baronial estate (tel. 0903/883136) is a much-restored mansion of considerable importance. Its legend is associated with some of the greatest families of England, the Fitzalans and the powerful Howards of Norfolk. But Arundel Castle traces its history back to King Alfred, while its keep goes back to the days before the Norman landing at Hastings.

Over the years, Arundel Castle suffered destruction, particularly during the Civil War, when Cromwell's troops stormed its walls, perhaps in retaliation for the 14th Earl of Arundel's (Thomas Howard's) sizable contribution to the aid of the faltering king. In the early 18th century, the castle virtually had to be rebuilt. In late Victorian times, it was remodeled and extensively restored again. Today it is filled, as you'd expect, with a good collection of antiques, along with an assortment of paintings by Old Masters such as Van Dyck and Reynolds.

The castle is open March 24 to the last Friday in October from 1 to 5 p.m. Sunday to Friday, opening at noon in June, July, August, and on bank holidays. Last admission is 4 p.m. It's closed Saturday. Admission is £3 ($5.25) for adults, £2 ($3.50) for children 5 to 15. Surrounding the castle is a 1100-acre park (scenic highlight: Swanbourne Lake).

OTHER SIGHTS

A delightful and intriguing family collection is in the **Arundel Toy and Military Museum** at "Doll's House," 23 High St. (tel. 0903/88310), with displays spanning many generations of old toys and games, small militaria, dolls, dollhouses, tin toys, musical toys, Britain's animals and soldiers, arks, boats, rocking horses, famous teddy bears, puppets, and crested military models. Housed in a Georgian cottage in the heart of historic Arundel, it is open most days from Easter to October (in winter on Saturday and Sunday only), or it may be seen at any time by arrangement. Admission is £1 ($1.75) for adults, 75p ($1.30) for children. The museum is opposite Treasure House Antiques Market.

Arundel Cathedral (the Cathedral of Our Lady and St. Philip Howard), London Road (tel. 0903/882297), stands at the highest point in town. A Roman Catholic cathedral, it was constructed for the 15th Duke of Norfolk by A. J. Hansom, who invented the Hansom taxi. However, it was not consecrated as a cathedral until 1965. The interior includes the shrine of St. Philip Howard, featuring Sussex wrought ironwork. Admission-free, it is open daily from 9 a.m. to 6 p.m. (it closes at dusk in winter). Donations are appreciated.

WHERE TO STAY

The best of the small hotels in town, **Dukes,** High Street, Arundel, West Sussex BN18 9AD (tel. 0903/883847), is big on amenities, charm, and character. Mike and Valerie Moore are the guiding light behind this little gem of a place, with six elegantly decorated rooms in the main building and two additional units in a Victorian cottage in the rear garden. Most of the accommodations have a TV, coffee-making facilities, and modern baths, while a few still retain their Regency detailing and ornate plasterwork. Depending on the plumbing, singles range from £20 ($35) to £35 ($61.25) daily, doubles costing £15 ($26.25) to £25 ($43.75) per person, with VAT and a full English breakfast included. The location is across a busy street from the crenellated fortifications surrounding the castle. The hotel's street-level restaurant is recommended separately.

Dating from the 17th century, **Arundel House,** 11 High St., Arundel, West Sussex BN18 9AD (tel. 0903/882136), is a guesthouse and licensed restaurant. Only seconds away from the castle entrance, it offers clean, comfortable rooms, with baths, color TV, and tea- and coffee-makers, costing from £12 ($21) per person nightly, including a full English breakfast. John and Christine Crowe are the resident owners. The house is open daily from 11 a.m. to 7 p.m. for morning coffee, hot meals, afternoon tea, and Sussex cream teas. A ham radio station (G4NHU) is available for persons with licenses.

The **Swan Hotel,** High Street, Arundel, West Sussex BN18 9AG (tel. 0903/882314), a Georgian inn on the River Arun, provides one of the best moderately priced accommodations in Arundel. Ken and Diana Rowsell offer comfortably furnished bedrooms, all with bath or shower, color TV, and equipment for making hot drinks. Most of the rooms are twins or doubles. The charge for a double with full English breakfast is £40 ($70) daily or £33 ($57.75) for single occupancy. You can enjoy drinks and bar snacks in the open bar space. The restaurant serves meals with the freshest of ingredients, and the service is polite and attentive. A fixed-price dinner is offered at £9 ($15.75).

Arden Guest House, 4 Queens Lane, Arundel, West Sussex BN18 9JN (tel. 0903/882544), has eight comfortably furnished rooms, some with private toilet and shower and all with hot and cold running water, color TV, and tea- and coffee-makers. Jeff and Carol Short, the proprietors, offer a warm welcome. They charge

£11 ($19.25) to £14 ($24.50) per person daily. A full English breakfast is included in the rates.

When the modern two-story house, **Portreeves Acre,** Causeway, Arundel, West Sussex BN18 9JJ (tel. 0903/883277), was built by a local architect within a stone's throw of the ancient castle, it caused much local comment. Today the glass-and-brick edifice is the property of Charles and Pat Rogers. The five double guest rooms, all with TV, are on the ground floor, which opens onto a view of the flowering acre in back. The property's boundary is bordered on one side by the River Arun, near which rabbits and flowering trees flourish. Each of the pleasant accommodations contains a private bath. The charge for B&B is £13 ($22.75) per person daily in low season, rising to £17 ($29.75) in summer.

WHERE TO EAT

Already recommended as a hotel, **Dukes,** High Street (tel. 0903/883847), is also one of the leading restaurant choices. Valerie and Michael Moore, the owners, invite guests into their elegant dining room on the street level. It is noted for its 17th-century ceiling, which was originally from a baroque Italian palace. Part of this ceiling was once installed in the home of Douglas Fairbanks, Jr. The ceiling is in gilt-carved walnut. Dinner is served Sunday to Thursday from 6 to 9 p.m. and until 10 p.m. on Friday and Saturday. The restaurant is closed on Sunday and Monday in low season. Typical dishes include steak au poivre, trout with almonds, and sole meunière. A la carte meals range from £8 ($14) to £20 ($35) per person.

If you're just passing through and are a bit rushed, **Partners,** High Street (tel. 0903/882018), may satisfy your needs. It is a sandwich bar and simple restaurant with a take-away service, lying across from the Swan Hotel. Light meals can be made up for £3 ($5.25). It is open daily from 9 a.m. to either 4:30 or 5:30 p.m., depending on the season.

On the Outskirts

George & Dragon, Houghton, about three miles north of Arundel (you turn off the A284 at Bury Hill onto the B2139; tel. 079881/559), is an old English pub known for excellent food. In 1651, Charles II, fleeing Cromwell's wrath after being crowned king at Scone in Scotland, stopped at the George & Dragon for food and drink before escaping to France. (He returned in 1660, after the death of Cromwell, to take the throne.) Originally a farmhouse, the inn is made up of two timber-and-flint cottages dating from the 13th century, with huge inglenook fireplaces and a shared chimney. An ancient spit in one of them was once used for preparing the roast joints of which the English are so fond. In winter, log fires blaze, making the pub toasty warm. The main bar and smaller apéritif bar, both with tapestry-covered seating and beamed ceilings, overlook the restaurant, where the cows dined back in the 17th century. The pub is open daily from 11 a.m. to 2:30 p.m. and 6 to 11 p.m. Food is served only from noon to 2 p.m. and 7 to 10 p.m., with lunch costing £6 ($10.50) to £7 ($12.25). Dinner is priced from £10 ($17.50) to £15 ($26.25). In summer, you can eat in the pleasant garden or on the terrace.

---

12. Chichester

According to one newspaper, Chichester might have been just a market town if the Chichester Festival Theatre had not been established in its midst. One of the oldest Roman cities in England, Chichester is in vogue, drawing a chic crowd from all over the world who come to see its theater's presentations.

Only a five-minute walk from the Chichester Cathedral and the old Market Cross, the 1400-seat theater, with its apron stage, stands on the edge of Oaklands Park. It opened in 1962 (first director: Lord Laurence Olivier), and its reputation has grown steadily, pumping new vigor and life into the former walled city. Of course, in some quarters there is still resentment, and occasionally you hear suggestions that the pounds could have been better spent on a municipal swimming pool. But others point to the success of the Chichester theater in having given fresh stimulus to the living theater in England.

THE FESTIVAL THEATRE

Booking opens in March, and the season runs from the middle of April until late September. The price of seats ranges from £6.50 ($11.38) to £14 ($24.50) for the finest tickets in the house. A limited number of seats go on sale at the box office on the day of each performance, sold on a first-come, first-served basis. Reservations made over the phone will be held for a maximum of four days (call 0243/781312). It's better to mail inquiries and checks to the box office, **Chichester Festival Theatre,** Oaklands Park, Chichester, West Sussex PO19. Matinee performances begin at 2:30 p.m., evening shows at 7:30 p.m., except "First Nights," which are at 7 p.m.

How to get there: If you would like to come down from London, 62 miles away, for a matinee, catch the 11:21 a.m. train from Victoria Station, which will deliver you to Chichester by 1:01 p.m., in plenty of time. For an evening performance, board the 4:21 p.m. train from Victoria Station, arriving at 6:06 p.m. Regrettably, there is no direct late train back to London after the show. Visitors who must return can make a connection via Brighton, arriving at Victoria Station shortly after midnight.

WHERE TO STAY

Tracing its origins to the 18th century, **Bedford Hotel,** Southgate, Chichester, West Sussex PO19 1DP (tel. 0243/785766), offers 28 comfortable and quiet rooms. Accommodations contain color TV and hot and cold running water, and some also have private showers and toilets. The charge of £19 ($33.25) to £24 ($42) per person daily in a double, £23.50 ($41.15) to £37 ($64.75) in a single also includes a full English breakfast. In summer advance reservations are strongly advised. This is one of the best all-around budget accommodations in Chichester.

Rawmere, Rew Lane, Summersdale, Chichester, West Sussex PO19 4QH (tel. 0243/527152), on the northern periphery a mile from the heart of the city, enjoys a tranquil and bucolic setting. Nonsmokers only are welcome, and two or more night stays are preferred. Pleasantly furnished accommodations rent for £15 ($26.25) per person daily for bed and breakfast. The double room has a private bath. Gatwick Airport is only an hour's journey away, and Brighton and Portsmouth are both easily accessible.

Mrs. Trenchard, Abbotsford, Summersdale Road at Broadway, Chichester, West Sussex PO19 4PW (tel. 0243/527307), is a "villa style" Victorian house built in 1895 to house two doctors at a local hospital. Adorned with wrought-iron accents and ringed with a pleasant garden, the house has a big bay window, a porch, and two bedrooms to rent, both sharing a bath at the end of the hall. Mrs. Trenchard, a retired teacher of art and art history, charges £11 ($19.25) per person daily, based on double occupancy, with breakfast included.

Whyke House, 13 Whyke Lane, Chichester, West Sussex PO19 2JR (tel. 0243/788767), a short distance from the heart of Chichester, has a relaxed atmosphere and makes a good base not only for seeing a production at the theater but for exploring such attractions in the environs as Fishbourne Palace and Old Bosham. Rooms are tidily decorated, warm, and comfortable. Reservations are important, as there are only three rooms for rent, one suited for families (none has a private bath, however). Charges range from £11.50 ($20.15) to £13.50 ($23.65) daily in a single and £22 ($38.50) to £26 ($45.50) in a double. Limited parking is available.

WHERE TO EAT

Snacks and light meals are served at the **Roussillon Coffee Shop,** Dolphin & Anchor, West Street (tel. 0243/785121), from 10 a.m. to 10 p.m. daily. A complete hot meal is likely to cost from £8 ($14). Children under 14 may choose from the main menu at half price.

The Noble Rot Brasserie and Wine Bar, Little London, off East Street (tel. 0243/779922), consists of three 200-year-old wine cellars within the city walls, converted into one of the most popular and lively before- and after-theater restaurants in West Sussex. The interior is covered with posters of famous theatrical productions from all over the world, and the atmosphere is decidedly continental. Meals, costing from £11 ($19.25), might include roast duck in orange sauce, veal dijonnaise, or a variety of locally produced steaks. At lunchtime, a special inclusive buffet menu is available, costing £4.50 ($7.90). The Noble Rot is open from 11 a.m. to 11 p.m. seven days a week. To reach it, you descend a flight of exterior steps from Little London and step back in time to the 1780s.

Nicodemus, 14 St. Pancras (tel. 0243/787521), in a 19th-century house not far removed from the center of town, has an Old English decor with a partially beamed ceiling. It offers what is reputed to be the best Italian cuisine in the area in the trattoria tradition. Try the cannelloni Nicodemus (with a minced lamb and spinach filling). You can also order various kinds of pasta with savory sauces or perhaps a pizza. Full meals without wine cost from £7 ($12.25) to £13 ($22.75) and are served from noon to 2 p.m. and 7 to 10 p.m. The restaurant is closed all day Sunday and on Monday at lunch.

Clinchs Salad House, 14 Southgate (tel. 0243/788822), the outstanding vegetarian restaurant in the area, is often frequented by health-conscious diners who aren't necessarily vegetarian. They know they get good food value here, and they can do so from 8 a.m. (go for breakfast if you wish) until 5:30 p.m. daily, except Sunday. The salads are always freshly made of quality ingredients, and there are always several hot dishes of the day, usually "vegetable bakes." Meals cost from £5 ($12.25), and children are not only welcomed, they are especially welcomed. You can wash it all down with an herbal tea.

On the Outskirts

The Hunters Inn, Lavant, Chichester, West Sussex PO18 0DA (tel. 0243/527329), two miles north of Chichester, dates back to the early 16th century, and its present facade was added in the 18th century by the Duke of Richmond. In the 1940s, it was the center for the Goodwood motor-racing fraternity, and now with extensive modernization it is an inn where you can find pleasant rooms and excellent meals, featuring fresh fish dishes. The bedrooms overlook the garden and are nicely appointed with hot and cold running water, and the charge, including VAT, service, and a complete English breakfast, is £15 ($26.25) to £20 ($35) daily in a single, from £35 ($61.25) in a double. There are only six bedrooms with private baths.

The chef and patron, Allan Hope-Kirk, has two restaurants, a small à la carte dining room with an English and French cuisine, and the "Light Bite" bar, serving everything from sandwiches to steaks at reasonable prices, but still with waiter service. The bars, both the public bar and the lounge bar, serve no fewer than 40 different beers and lagers. In winter an open fireplace provides cheer and warmth. The more formal à la carte restaurant is open daily from noon to 1:30 p.m. and 7 to 9:30 p.m.

WEALD AND DOWNLAND OPEN AIR MUSEUM

This museum stands on a 40-acre site at Singleton, six miles north of the cathedral city of Chichester on the A286 (London road). In a beautiful downland setting, rescued historic buildings dating from the Middle Ages to the 19th century are being reassembled. The museum is open every day from 11 a.m. to 6 p.m., April 1 to October 31. From March to November, it is open only on Wednesday and Sunday from 11 a.m. to 5 p.m. Admission is £2.50 ($4.40) for adults, £1.25 ($2.20) for children. Still developing, the museum shows the history of traditional buildings in southeast England. Exhibits include a Tudor market hall; timber-framed medieval houses dating from the 14th to the 16th centuries with wattle-and-daub walls; a working water mill producing stone-ground flour; a blacksmith's forge; plumbers' and carpenters' workshops; a toll cottage; a 17th-century treadwheel; agricultural buildings, including thatched barns and an 18th-century granary; a charcoal burner's camp; and a 19th-century village school. For further information, telephone 024363/348.

FISHBOURNE

A trip well worth the taking and just a few miles away from Chichester is to the largest Roman palace yet discovered. It's called the **Fishbourne Roman Palace and Museum,** Salthill Road (tel. 0243/785859). Built in A.D. 75, it is architecturally pure Italian, and you will be amazed to discover it has an underground heating system. Mosaic floors survive, and the first-century garden has been replanted. There is good parking and a cafeteria on the premises that serves coffee and sandwiches. Admission is £1.80 ($3.15) for adults, £1 ($1.75) for children.

OLD BOSHAM

A few miles west from Fishbourne is Bosham, one of the most charming villages in West Sussex. It was the site of the first establishment of Christianity on the Sussex coast. The Danish King Canute made it one of the seats of his North Sea empire, and it was the site of a manor (now gone) of the last of England's Saxon kings, Harold, who sailed from here to France on a journey that finally culminated in the invasion of England by William the Conqueror in 1066. Bosham's little church was depicted in the Bayeux Tapestry. Near the harbor, it is reached by a narrow lane. Its graveyard overlooks the boats. A daughter of King Canute is buried inside. The church is filled with ship models and relics, showing the villagers' link to the sea. Bosham is principally a sailing resort, linked by good bus service to Chichester.

If you're seeking rooms, try the flippantly named **Hatpins,** Bosham Lane, Bosham, near Chichester, West Sussex PO18 8HL (tel. 0243/572644), one of the most delightful accommodations in the area. Run by Mr. and Mrs. Waller, it is far superior to your typical B&B, but there are only two bedrooms, with adjoining baths. Guests can enjoy breakfast in an attractive conservatory, but that is the only meal served. Reservations are a must.

VIII

HAMPSHIRE AND DORSET

1. **PORTSMOUTH AND SOUTHSEA**
2. **SOUTHAMPTON**
3. **NEW FOREST**
4. **ISLE OF WIGHT**
5. **WINCHESTER**
6. **BOURNEMOUTH**
7. **SHAFTESBURY**
8. **WAREHAM**
9. **DORCHESTER**
10. **BRIDPORT**
11. **CHIDEOCK**
12. **CHARMOUTH**
13. **LYME REGIS**
14. **DONYATT**
15. **SHERBORNE**

The images of the countryside seem to be conjured from Burke's *Landed Gentry:* stone farmhouses; fireplaces where stacks of logs burn gaily; wicker baskets of apples, freshly brought in from the orchard, waiting to be transformed into home-made apple butter; chickens stuffed with dressing and roasted with strips of bacon on top to keep them tender and juicy; milk that doesn't come from bottles; and mellowed village houses, now run as hotels. Beyond the pear trees, on the crest of a hill, are the ruins of a Roman camp. And a village pub, with two rows of kegs filled with varieties of cider, is where the hunt gathers.

You're in Hampshire and Dorset, two shires guarded zealously by the English, who protect their special rural treasures. Everybody knows of Southampton and Bournemouth (Dorset), but less known is the undulating countryside lying inland. Your car will take you through endless lanes, revealing tiny villages and thatched cottages untouched by the industrial invasion.

HAMPSHIRE

This is Jane Austen country—firmly middle class, largely agricultural, its inhabitants doggedly convinced that Hampshire is the greatest spot on earth. The English writer left six novels of manners, including *Pride and Prejudice* and *Sense and Sensibility,* which earned her a room at the top among 19th-century English novelists. Her books provided a keen insight into the solid middle-class English who were to build such a powerful empire. Although the details of the life she described have now largely faded ("at five o'clock the two ladies retired to dress, and at half-past six Elizabeth was summoned to dinner"), much of the mood and spirit of Hampshire depicted in her books remains.

Born in 1775, Miss Austen was the daughter of the Oxford-educated rector, the Reverend Mr. George Austen, a typical Hampshire country gentleman, who had much charm but little money. In keeping with a custom of the time, the Austens gave their second son, Edward, to a wealthy, childless family connection, Thomas Knight, whose heir the young man became. It was Edward who gave to his mother and sisters **Chawton Cottage,** at Chawton near Alton (tel. 0420/83262), where visitors can see the surroundings in which the novelist spent the last 7½ years of her life, her period of greatest creation. In the unpretentious but pleasant cottage, you can see the table on which Jane Austen penned new versions of three of her books and wrote three more including *Emma* (named for her "handsome, clever, and rich" heroine, Emma Woodhouse). You can also see the rector's George III mahogany bookcase and a silhouette likeness of the Reverend Austen presenting his son to the Knights. It was in this cottage that Jane Austen became ill in 1817 of what would have been diagnosed by the middle of the 19th century as Addison's disease.

There is an attractive garden in which visitors are invited to have picnics and an old bakehouse with Miss Austen's donkey cart. About two miles from the station, the home is open daily including Sunday from 11 a.m. to 4:30 p.m. April to October. Admission is £1 ($1.75) for adults, 50p (90¢) for children under 14. It is closed Monday and Tuesday in November, December, and March. In January and February it is open only on Saturday and Sunday. It is closed Christmas Day and Boxing Day.

Hampshire embraces the **New Forest** (don't expect anything in England labeled "new" to be new), the **South Downs,** the **Isle of Wight** (Victoria's favorite retreat), the passenger port and gateway city of **Southampton,** and the naval city of **Portsmouth.**

Going west from Southampton, you'll come to the New Forest, more than 90,000 acres selfishly preserved by William the Conqueror as a private hunting ground (poachers met with the death penalty). William lost two of his sons in the New Forest, one killed by an animal, the other by an arrow. Today it is a vast and unspoiled woodland and heath ideal for walking and exploring.

1. Portsmouth and Southsea

Virginia, New Hampshire, and Ohio may have their Portsmouths, but the daddy of them all is the old port and naval base on the Hampshire coast, about 70 miles south of London. German bombers in World War II virtually leveled the city, destroying or hitting about nine-tenths of its buildings. But the seaport has recovered admirably.

Its maritime associations are famous. From Sally Port, the most interesting district of the Old Town, "naval heroes innumerable have embarked to fight their

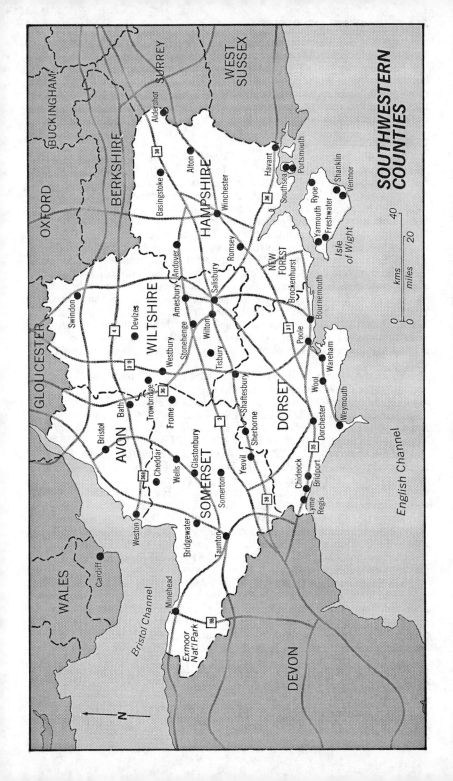

SOUTHWESTERN COUNTIES

country's battles." That was certainly true on June 6, 1944, when Allied troops set forth to invade occupied France.

Southsea, adjoining Portsmouth, is a popular seaside resort with fine sands, beautiful gardens, bright lights, and a host of holiday attractions. Many historic monuments can be seen along the stretches of open space, where you can walk on the Clarence Esplanade and look out on the Solent, viewing the busy shipping activities of Portsmouth harbor.

THE SIGHTS

Some 400 years before D-Day, an English navy ship didn't fare as well. The **Mary Rose,** flagship of the fleet of King Henry VIII, sank in the Solent in 1545 in full view of the king. In 1982 a descendant of that monarch, and heir to the throne, Charles, Prince of Wales, watched the *Mary Rose* break the water's surface after almost four centuries spent lying on the sea bottom, not exactly shipshape and Bristol fashion but surprisingly well preserved nonetheless. Now the remains are on view, but the hull must be kept permanently wet. The hull and the more than 10,000 discoveries brought up by the divers constitute one of the major archeological discoveries of England in many years. Among the artifacts on permanent exhibit are almost the complete equipment of the ship's barber, with surgeon's cabin saws, knives, ointments, and plaster all ready for use; longbows and arrows, some still in shooting order; carpenters' tools; leather jackets; and some fine lace and silk. Close beside the dock where the hull lies is the *Mary Rose* Exhibition in Boathouse No. 5. The artifacts rescued from the ship are stored there. It contains an audio-visual theater and a spectacular two-deck reconstruction of a segment of the ship, including the original guns. A display with sound effects recalls the sinking of the vessel.

To see the *Mary Rose* Ship Hall and Exhibition (tel. 0705/750521), use the entrance to the Portsmouth Naval Base through the Victory Gate (as for H.M.S. *Victory*), and follow the signs. It is open every day from 10:30 a.m. to 5:30 p.m. (closed Christmas Day). Admission is £2.80 ($4.90) for adults, £1.80 ($3.15) for children, and £7.50 ($13.15) for a family ticket. For information, write to the *Mary Rose* Trust, College Road, H.M. Naval Base, Portsmouth, Hampshire PO1 3LX.

Of major interest is Lord Nelson's flagship, **H.M.S. Victory,** a 104-gun, first-rate ship of the line, now at No. 2 Dry Dock in Portsmouth (tel. 0705/826682). Although she first saw action in 1778, her fame was earned on October 21, 1805, in the Battle of Trafalgar, when the British scored a victory over the combined Spanish and French fleets. It was in this battle that Lord Nelson lost his life. The flagship, after being taken to Gibraltar for repairs, returned to Portsmouth with Nelson's body on board (he was later buried at St. Paul's in London). It is open from 10:30 a.m. to 5 p.m. Monday to Saturday and from 1 to 5 p.m. Sunday; closed Christmas Day. Admission is £2.80 ($4.90) for adults, £1 ($1.75) for children, and £4.60 ($8.05) for a family of four.

The **Royal Naval Museum** (tel. 0705/733060) stands next to Nelson's flagship, H.M.S. *Victory,* and the *Mary Rose* in the heart of Portsmouth's historic naval dockyard. The only museum in Britain devoted exclusively to the general history of the Royal Navy, it contains relics of Nelson and his associates, together with unique collections of ship models, naval ceramics, figureheads, medals, uniforms, weapons, and other naval memorabilia. Special displays feature "The Rise of the Royal Navy" and "H.M.S. *Victory* and the Campaign of Trafalgar." The museum is open daily from 10:30 a.m. to 5 p.m. (with some seasonal variations). An admission charge of £1 ($1.75) for adults, 75p ($1.30) for children is levied. There is a buffet and a souvenir shop in the museum complex.

Portsmouth was the birthplace of Charles Dickens, and the small terrace house dated 1805 in which the future famous novelist made his appearance in the world on

February 7, 1812, and lived for a short time, has been restored and furnished to illustrate the middle-class taste of the early 19th century. Called the **Charles Dickens' Birthplace Museum,** it is at 393 Old Commercial Rd., Mile End (tel. 0705/827261). It is open daily from 10:30 a.m. to 5:30 p.m. (closed November to the end of February). Admission is 60p ($1.05) for adults, 30p (55¢) for children. Family tickets (four persons) are available for £1.50 ($2.65). Last tickets are sold at 5 p.m.

On the Southsea front, you can see a number of naval monuments, including the big anchor from Nelson's ship, *Victory;* a commemoration of the officers and men of H.M.S. *Shannon* for heroism in the Indian Mutiny; an obelisk with a naval crown in memory of the crew of H.M.S. *Chesapeake;* and a massive column, the Royal Naval memorial honoring those lost at sea in the two world wars, as well as a shaft dedicated to men killed in the Crimean War. There are also commemorations of persons who fell victim to yellow fever in Queen Victoria's service in Sierra Leone and Jamaica. The Southsea Common, between the coast and houses of the area, known in the 13th century as Froddington Heath and used for army bivouacs, is a picnic and play area today. Peaceful walks can be taken along Ladies' Mile if you want to be away from the Common's tennis courts, skateboard and roller-skating rinks, and other activities.

Southsea Castle, built in 1545 as part of the coastal defenses ordered by King Henry VIII, and the D-Day Museum (see below), devoted to the Normandy landings 399 years later, are next door to each other on the Clarence Esplanade of Southsea. The castle, a fortress built of stones from Beaulieu Abbey, houses a museum with displays tracing the development of Portsmouth as a military stronghold, as well as naval history and the archeology of the area. The castle is open daily from 10:30 a.m. to 5:30 p.m., except on Christmas Eve, Christmas Day, and Boxing Day. Admission is 50p (90¢) for adults, 25p (45¢) for children.

The **D-Day Museum** contains the Overlord Embroidery, showing the complete story of Operation Overlord, as the D-Day action was designated, including the men and the machines that were featured in the invasion operation. The appliquéed embroidery, believed to be the largest of its kind (272 feet long and three feet high), was designed by Sandra Lawrence and took 20 women of the Royal School of Needlework five years to complete. There is a special audio-visual program with displays, including reconstructions of various stages of the mission with models and maps. You'll see a Sherman tank in working order, Jeeps, field guns, and even a DUKW (popularly called a Duck), that incredibly useful amphibious truck that operated on land and sea. The museum is open seven days a week from 10:30 a.m. to 5:30 p.m., except during the three-day Christmas holiday. Admission is £2 ($3.50) for adults, £1.20 ($2.10) for children, and £5.20 ($9.10) for families of up to two adults and two children. For information on both Southsea Castle and the D-Day Museum, phone the Visitors Services Organiser at the City Museums office (tel. 0705/827261).

On the northern side of Portsmouth Harbour on a spit of land are the remains of **Portchester Castle** (tel. 0705/378291), built in the late 12th century by King Henry II, plus a Norman church. The castle remains are set inside the impressive walls of a third-century Roman fort built as a defense against Saxon pirates when this was the northwest frontier of the declining Roman Empire. By the end of the 14th century, Richard II had modernized the castle, making it a secure small palace. Among the ruins are the hall, kitchen, and great chamber of this palace. Portchester was popular with medieval kings who stayed here when they visited Portsmouth. The last official use of the castle was as a prison for French seamen during the Napoleonic wars. It is open from 10 a.m. to 6 p.m. daily, except Monday from Good Friday to the end of September, charging an admission of £1.10 ($1.95) for adults and 55p (95¢) for children.

Cross Portsmouth Harbour by one of the ferries that bustle back and forth all day to Gosport. Some departures go directly from the station pontoon to H.M.S. *Alliance* for a visit to the **Royal Navy Submarine Museum** (tel. 0705/529217). The museum traces the story of underwater warfare and life below the seas from the earliest days to the present nuclear age, and contains excellent models, dioramas, medals, and displays from all ages. There is also as much about submariners themselves as about the steel tubes in which they make their homes, and although the museum focuses on British boats, it includes much of international interest. The principal exhibit is H.M.S. *Alliance,* and after a brief audio-visual presentation, visitors are guided through the boat by ex-submariners, experiencing the true feeling of life on board in the artificial world beneath the sea. Midget submarines, both British and others, including an X-craft, can be seen outside the museum. Also on display is H.M. *Torpedo Boat No. 1,* better known as *Holland I,* launched in 1901, which sank under tow to the breaker's yard in 1913 and was salvaged in 1982. Admission to the museum is £2 ($3.50) for adults, £1.20 ($2.10) for children.

Overnighting in Portsmouth? If so, I have the following recommendations.

LIVING IN OLD PORTSMOUTH

A charming small house, **Fortitude Cottage,** 51 Broad St., Old Portsmouth, Hampshire PO1 2JD (tel. 0705/823748), is on Camber inner harbor. It is a narrow, four-story structure, with a steep staircase, almost in Dutch fashion, that leads to the compact home of Carol Harbeck. There are several rooms available, and the charge is £12.50 ($21.90) nightly for B&B. Mrs. Harbeck has demonstrated her excellent taste in the designing and furnishing of the home. It is airy, colorful, modern, yet not too extreme, and the views from the rooms are good. Her breakfasts are on a "what you want" basis.

Keppel's Head Hotel, The Hard, Portsmouth, Hampshire PO1 3DT (tel. 0705/833231), is an impressive Victorian brick monument facing the train, bus, and ferry stations and overlooking the Solent. A prestigious hotel for generations, it has 27 comfortable, well-furnished bedrooms, all with private baths or showers, color TV, radios, phones, and facilities for making tea or coffee. Singles rent for £56 ($98) and doubles for £65 ($113.75) per night, including a full English breakfast and VAT. Dinners in the 19th-century-style restaurant of this Trusthouse Forte Hotel cost from £12 ($18), and there's an inviting bar.

LIVING IN SOUTHSEA

Southsea abounds with moderately priced small hotels or B&B houses. One of the best is the **Bristol Hotel,** 55 Clarence Parade, Southsea, Hampshire PO5 2HX (tel. 0705/821815). This family-run hotel is small and inviting, occupying half of a twin-gabled Victorian house whose windows overlook a seaside park. It's run by Edward and Jean Fry (he spent 25 years in the Royal Navy before opening this place). They offer a total of 13 modernized rooms, nine of which have their own private bath. A single without bath costs from £15.50 ($27.15) daily, going up to £23 ($40.25) with shower and toilet. Two persons pay £31 ($54.25) in a bathless room, £38 ($66.50) in a room with shower and toilet. A full English breakfast and VAT are included in all the tariffs.

WHERE TO EAT

Head up Broad Street to the **Lone Yachtsman** (tel. 0705/24293), a revamped pub that is the center of much of the local life of Old Portsmouth. Decorated in a nautical theme, it commands a view of the harbor from its perch on the end of a promontory. You can drink in both the Sir Alec Rose bar (popular with yacht people) or dine at the Lively Lady (hot luncheons and evening meals seven days a week from noon to 2:30 p.m. and 7:30 to 10:30 p.m.). Among the usual entrees are such tempting items as soup of the day and steak, kidney, and mushroom pie. A set lunch costs £5 ($8.75). The Dover sole, depending on size, is excellent, as are many other seafood dishes. A tradition is the hot fruit pie, served with thick cream. Dinners cost from £10 ($17.50).

If you're staying at one of the B&Bs, a good place to eat is **Country Kitchen,** 59 Marmion Rd. (tel. 0705/811425). Self-service, it is open daily except Sunday from 9 a.m. to 5 p.m., charging from £5 ($8.75) and up for a complete vegetarian meal. The fare runs to homemade soups, fresh crisp salads, and special hot dishes of the day, followed by tea and cake. The kitchen is unlicensed.

For dining in the evening, consider **Rosie's Vineyard,** 87 Elm Grove (tel. 0705/755944), which is like a little place you might find on the continent. It is open only for dinner daily from 7 to 10:30 p.m. (sometimes later in summer). It also serves a much-frequented Sunday lunch from noon to 2 p.m. In summer guests prefer a table in the pergola garden. The cookery is accomplished and often imaginative, and items change based on the season. Look for the daily specials. Count on spending from £10 ($17.50). It's best to call and reserve a table here.

Between Portsmouth and Southampton lies an increasingly popular attraction in this part of the country—

BROADLANDS

The home of Earl Mountbatten of Burma until his assassination in 1979, Broadlands, Romsey (tel. 0794/516878), lies on the A31, 72 miles southwest of London. Lord Mountbatten lent the house to the then Princess Elizabeth and Prince Philip, Mountbatten's nephew, as a honeymoon haven in 1947, and in 1981, Prince Charles and Princess Diana spent the first nights of their honeymoon here. Broadlands is owned by Lord Romsey, Lord Mountbatten's eldest grandson, who has created a fine exhibition and audio-visual show depicting the highlights of the brilliant career of his grandfather as a soldier and statesman, who has been called "the last war hero."

The house, originally linked to Romsey Abbey, was purchased by Lord Palmerston in 1736. It was later transformed into an elegant Palladian mansion by Capability Brown and Henry Holland. Brown landscaped the parkland and grounds, making the river (the Test) the main object of pleasure. The house, the Mountbatten Exhibition, and the Riverside lawns are open daily from 10 a.m. to 4 p.m. from March 23 to October 1; closed Monday, except in August, September, and on bank holidays. Admission is £3.95 ($6.90) for adults, £2.25 ($3.95) for children.

---

2. Southampton

To many North Americans, England's premier passenger port, home base for the Cunard's *Queen Elizabeth 2,* is the gateway to Britain. Southampton is changed today, a city of wide boulevards, parks, and shopping centers. It was rebuilt after German bomb damage, which destroyed hundreds of its old buildings.

In World War II, some 3½ million men embarked from here (in World War I, more than twice that number passed through Southampton). Its supremacy as a port has long been recognized and dates from Saxon times, when the Danish conqueror, Canute, was proclaimed king here in 1017.

Southampton was of special importance to the Normans, keeping them in touch with their homeland. And it shares the dubious distinction of having "imported" the bubonic plague in the mid-14th century that wiped out a quarter of the English population. On the Western Esplanade is a memorial tower to the Pilgrims, who set out on their voyage to the New World from Southampton on August 15, 1620. Both the *Mayflower* and the *Speedwell* sailed from here but were forced by storm damages to put in at Plymouth, where the *Speedwell* was abandoned. The memorial is a tall column with an iron basket on top of the type used as a beacon before lighthouses.

If you're waiting in Southampton between boats, you may want to use the time to explore some of the major sights of Hampshire that lie on the periphery of the port—the New Forest, Winchester, the Isle of Wight, and Bournemouth in neighboring Dorset.

Finding an accommodation directly in Southampton isn't as important as it used to be. Very few ships now arrive, and the places to stay just outside the city are, in the main, superior to what one finds directly in the heartland. For accommodations in the area, refer to the "New Forest" section. However, I'll provide some budget accommodation listings for those who for transportation or other reasons may want to stay within the city center.

WHERE TO STAY

One of the most substantial of the moderately priced inns in the center is **The Star Hotel,** 26 High St., Southampton, Hampshire SO9 4ZA (tel. 0703/339939). Its origins are uncertain (it may date from 1601), and it was a fashionable rendezvous in Georgian times. The Victoria Room at the Star commemorates the visit of little Princess Victoria in 1831 at the age of 12. The Star has kept abreast of the times, and today it rents 45 centrally heated and comfortably furnished bedrooms, with radio, phone, hot and cold running water, and (in many cases) private baths. Depending on the plumbing, singles rent for £28 ($49) to £39 ($68.25) daily, doubles or twins from £49 ($85.75) to £59 ($103.25). However, if you can stay on a Friday, Saturday, or Sunday night for at least two nights, you get substantial reductions, except in September. Tariffs include a full English breakfast and VAT. There's an informal but popular pub facing the street, plus an inexpensive restaurant on the premises.

Hunters Lodge Hotel, 25 Landguard Rd., Shirley, Southampton, Hampshire SO1 5DL (tel. 0703/227919), is one of the best of the small hotels of Southampton, lying only a short distance from the center. The late Victorian building has outstanding gardens. Of the 16 accommodations decorated in a floral motif, half are equipped with private baths or showers. Rates are based on the plumbing: from £17 ($29.75) to £27 ($47.25) daily in a single, rising to £35 ($61.25) to £38 ($66.50) in a double. An evening meal is served from 6:30 p.m. The hotel takes a long holiday over Christmas, but otherwise remains open all year.

Banister House Hotel, 11 Brighton Rd., Southampton, Hampshire SO1 2JJ (tel. 0703/221279), a privately run hotel that manages to be comfortable while still charging bargain rates, is one of the best B&Bs in the area. Seven of its bedrooms contain private showers for which you pay more. Singles, depending on the plumbing, range from £18.50 ($32.40) to £23.50 ($41.15) daily, with doubles costing £27 ($47.25) to £31 ($54.25). Half-board terms are also quoted if you'd like to eat in, enjoying home-cooked meals.

Rosida Garden Hotel, 25-27 Hill Lane, Southampton, Hampshire SO1 5AB (tel. 0703/228501), in the heart of town, is a hotel with a respect for the sensitivity of the needs of today's travelers. It is not only geared to accommodate visitors in a wheelchair, but conversely, it has facilities for the athletic, including a heated swimming pool outdoors and a small workout room. Set in about two acres of grounds, including a small body of water, the hotel was renovated in the mid-1980s and is still well maintained. Guests enjoy a sun terrace in summer. All 29 bedrooms are comfortably appointed, and each has a private bath. For this, you'll pay more than in a typical B&B, but many visitors to Southampton find the investment worth the price of £35 ($61.25) to £38 ($66.50) daily in a single and £45 ($78.75) to £50 ($87.50) in a double.

The Linden, 51-53 The Polygon, Southampton, Hampshire SO1 2BP (tel. 0703/225653), sits behind a forest green facade and under an elaborate twin-gabled roof. This turn-of-the-century building is operated by Patricia and David Hutchins, who rent 13 comfortably furnished bedrooms for £11 ($19.25) per person nightly. None of the accommodations has a private bath, but each is equipped with hot and cold running water. Only breakfast is served.

WHERE TO EAT

Southampton isn't distinguished for its gastronomy. However, some of the best meals are found at **Pearl Harbour,** 86A Above Bar St. (tel. 0703/225248), the finest Cantonese restaurant in the area. It's far superior to most Chinese restaurants you encounter on the southern coast. Concentrate on the fish specialties, such as braised lobster, for the finest dining sensations. Set menus begin at £7.50 ($13.15) and are served daily from noon to midnight. A set lunch is priced at only £4 ($7). The restaurant lies on the second floor of a building right in the heart of town.

La Margherita, 4 Commercial Rd. (tel. 0703/333390), popular with young people and families, offers pizza and pasta. Open daily, except Sunday, from noon to 2 p.m. and 6:30 to 11:15 p.m., it offers meals from £6 ($10.50) and up. If you don't want pizza or pasta, you can order veal, poultry, beef, or fish main dishes as well. You can also ask for wine by the glass, followed by a strong espresso.

The **Red Lion,** High Street (tel. 0703/333595), is one of the few architectural jewels to have survived World War II. This pub has its roots in the 13th century (as a Norman cellar), but its high-ceilinged and raftered "Henry V Court Room" is in the Tudor style. The room was the scene of the trial of the Earl of Cambridge and his accomplices, Thomas Grey and Lord Scrope, who were condemned to death for treason in plotting against the life of the king in 1415. The Court Room is adorned with coats of arms of the noblemen who served as peers of the condemned trio. The Red Lion is a fascinating place at which to stop in for a drink and a chat. Pub lunches, served from 11:30 a.m. to 9:30 p.m. daily cost from £4 ($7). The Red Lion is open daily from 11 a.m. to 11 p.m.

---

3. New Forest

The New Forest came into the limelight in the times of Henry VIII, who loved to hunt here, as venison abounded. Also, with his enthusiasm for building up the British naval fleet, he saw his opportunity to supply oak and other hard timbers to the boatyards at Buckler's Hard on the Beaulieu River for the building of stout-hearted men-o'-war. Today you can visit the old shipyards and the museum with its fine models of men-o'-war, pictures of the old yard, and dioramas showing the building of these ships, their construction, and their launching. It took 2000 trees to build one man-o'-war.

Stretching for about 92,000 acres, New Forest is a large tract 14 miles wide and 20 miles long. William the Conqueror laid out the limits of this then-private hunting preserve. Those who hunted without a license faced the executioner if they were caught, and those who hunted but missed had their hands severed.

Nowadays New Forest is one of those places traversed by motorists bound for the southwest. However, I'd suggest you stop a moment and relax.

This used to be a forest, but now the groves of oak trees are separated by wide tracts of common land that is grazed by ponies and cows, hummocked with heather and gorse, and frequented by rabbits. Away from the main arterial roads, where signs warn of wild ponies and deer, there is a private world of peace and quiet.

BEAULIEU ABBEY–PALACE HOUSE

This stately home is in the New Forest (tel. 590/612345). The abbey and house, as well as the National Motor Museum, are on the property of Lord Montagu of Beaulieu, at Beaulieu, five miles southeast of Lyndhurst and 14 miles south of Southampton. A Cistercian abbey was founded on this spot in 1204, and the ruins can be explored today. The Palace House was the great gatehouse of the abbey before it was converted into a private residence in 1538. The house is surrounded by gardens.

In the grounds, the **National Motor Museum,** one of the best and most comprehensive motor museums in the world, with more than 250 vehicles, is open to the public. It traces the story of motoring from 1895 to the present. Famous autos include four land-speed record-holders, among them Donald Campbell's *Bluebird.* The museum was built around Lord Montagu's family collection of vintage cars. A special feature is called "Wheels." In a darkened environment, visitors can travel in specially designed "pods," each of which carries up to two adults and one child, along a silent electric track. They move at a predetermined but variable speed, and each pod is capable of rotating almost 360°. This provides a means by which the visitor is dramatically introduced to a variety of displays, spanning 100 years of motor development. Sound and visual effects are integrated into individual displays. In one sequence, visitors experience the smell, noise, and visual thrill of being involved in a Grand Prix race.

All facilities are open daily from 10 a.m. to 6 p.m. Easter to September, and from 10 a.m. to 5 p.m. October to Easter. The facilities are closed Christmas Day. Admission to the motor museum, palace and gardens, abbey ruins, and exhibition of monastic life costs £5.25 ($9.20) for adults, £3.50 ($6.15) for children. For further information, contact the Visitor Reception Manager, John Montagu Building, at the number above.

BUCKLER'S HARD

This historic 18th-century village on the banks of the River Beaulieu is where ships for Nelson's fleet were built, including the admiral's favorite, *Agamemnon,* as well as *Eurylus* and *Swiftsure.* The **Maritime Museum** (tel. 059063/203) reflects the shipbuilding history of the village. Its displays include shipbuilding at Buckler's Hard; Henry Adams, master shipbuilder; Nelson's favorite ship; Buckler's Hard and Trafalgar; and models of Sir Francis Chichester's yachts and items of his equipment. The cottage exhibits are a re-creation of 18th-century life in Buckler's Hard. Here you can stroll through the New Inn of 1793 and a shipwright's cottage of the same period or look in on the family of a poor laborer at home. All these displays include village residents and visitors of the late 18th century.

The museum is open daily from 10 a.m. to 6 p.m. Easter to May, 10 a.m. to 9 p.m. June to September, and 10 a.m. to 4:30 p.m. September to Easter. Admission is £1.85 ($3.25) for adults, £1.10 ($1.95) for children. The walk back to Beaulieu, 2½ miles along the riverbank, is well marked through the woodlands. During the summer, you can take a half-hour cruise on the River Beaulieu in the present *Swiftsure,* an all-weather catamaran cruiser.

FOOD AND LODGING

My recommendations for food and lodging in the New Forest include a few places for overnighting.

Whitley Ridge, Beaulieu Road, Brockenhurst, Hampshire SO42 7TA (tel. 0590/22354), is a Georgian country house built as a royal hunting lodge around the 18th century. The addition of an extension in Victorian times created a large and elegant home. It stands in nearly five acres of secluded grounds in the heart of the New Forest. The hotel of today has 12 comfortable bedrooms, all with baths or showers, toilets, TV, phones, and coffee-making equipment. Charges are from £59 ($103.25) daily for double occupancy of a twin- or double-bedded room, or from £40 ($70) used as a single. A full English breakfast and VAT are included. The hotel is known for its food and wines, offering different meals ranging from unusual and imaginative dishes to classic cuisine. A table d'hôte dinner, costing £12.50 ($21.90), is served from 7:30 to 8:30 p.m. daily. A comfortable and intimate bar is inviting, and there are two well-furnished lounges.

Grove House, Newtown Minstead, near Lyndhurst, Hampshire SO43 7GG (tel. 0703/813211), is owned and run by Marion Dixon, who offers accommodations in her own family's home. She has a comfortable family room to accommodate from two to four persons, facing south and west and going for £11 ($19.25) per person per night, including a large breakfast. An evening meal can be arranged from £7 ($12.25) per person. This pleasant farmhouse lies at the rural end of the village, with the New Forest a quarter mile away up a country lane.

Lyndhurst House, 35 Romsey Rd., Lyndhurst, Hampshire SO43 7AA (tel. 042128/2230), is a solid, turn-of-the-century house opposite Pat's Garage in the town. It's the home of Sydney and Yvonne Renouf, who rent several rooms in their main house, plus three more in a chalet behind, at a cost of £10 ($17.50) per person nightly. The house is close to the New Forest and to shops.

Caters Cottage, Latchmoor, Brockenhurst, Hampshire SO42 7UP (tel. 0590/23225), charges reasonable prices in a village filled not only with thatched cottages but an array of expensive upmarket hotels. It enjoys its own patch of the forest, and has a lot of character. The only problem is, it offers only a handful of rooms, each comfortably and attractively decorated. The bath is shared. B&B costs from £13 ($22.75) daily in a single and £24 ($42) in a double.

Bay Tree House, 1 Clough Lane, Burley, near Ringwood, Hampshire BH24 4AE (tel. 04253/3215), is a small guesthouse renting both a single and a family room. Guests share the one bath. Open all year, except in December, it charges from £12 ($21) daily in a single and £22 ($38.50) in a double. Reservations are a must.

Old Well Restaurant and Guesthouse, Copythorne, Hampshire SO4 2PE (tel. 0703/812321), is on the A31 in the hamlet of Copythorne, ten miles north of Southampton. Pat and Laurie Martin's family used to own the village grocery store, and they are true forest folk. In 1960, they bought the Old Well, which serves only morning coffee and lunch in its restaurant, open from 8:30 a.m. to 2:30 p.m. daily, except Monday. A three-course lunch costs £5.50 ($9.65). On Sunday they always have a traditional roast joint for lunch. If you decide to stay over, they have five rooms to rent, costing £12.50 ($21.90) to £14.50 ($25.40) per person daily, with a large and wholesome breakfast included.

The Vicarage, Church Corner, Burley, near Ringwood, Hampshire BA24 4AP (tel. 04253/2303), is a quiet house set in an informal and secluded garden in a clearing in the New Forest, opposite the church in the village of Burley. The village lies between the A31 and the A35 main roads near Ringwood, and it is a good center for seeing the forest and coastal resorts. The house is run by Mrs. Alan Clarkson, the vicar's wife, who can accommodate up to six people at £10 ($17.50) to £12 ($21) per person nightly. The units are pleasant and comfortable, and a home-like atmosphere prevails. Smoking is discouraged.

Jack in the Basket, 7 St. Thomas St., Lymington, Hampshire SO41 9NA (tel. 0590/73447), in a building dating back to the 17th century, consists of a restaurant and three bedrooms. The rooms rent for £15 ($26.25) in a single, £25 ($43.75) in a bathless double, and £30 ($52.50) in a double with bath for bed and breakfast. The restaurant, respected for its home-cooked food served in a pleasant and friendly atmosphere, is open from 9 a.m. to 5 p.m., except on market day, Saturday, when they open early for breakfast. The establishment is at the top end of Lymington High Street with a large, free car park behind.

4. Isle of Wight

Four miles across the Solent from the South Coast towns of Southampton, Lymington, and Portsmouth, the Isle of Wight is known for its sandy beaches and its ports, favored by the yachting set. The island, which long attracted such literary figures as Alfred Tennyson and Charles Dickens, is compact in size, measuring 23 miles from east to west, 13 miles from north to south. You can take regular ferry-boats over. Hydrofoils cross the Solent in just 20 minutes from Southampton.

The price of a round-trip ticket on the ferry from Southampton to Cowes is from £3.40 ($5.95) to £4.30 ($7.55) per passenger. Taking a car over for the day costs from £17 ($29.75) to £25 ($43.75), depending on the size of the vehicle.

The ferry from Lymington to Yarmouth for a day round-trip costs £3.40 ($5.95) for adults, £1.85 ($3.25) for children. Transport of an average car, round-trip, is £26 ($45.50).

The more usual way of reaching the island from London is by ferry from Portsmouth Harbour or by Hovercraft from Southsea, both of which take you to Ryde, the railhead for the island's communications system. Arriving in Yarmouth via Lymington, however, is something else—a busy little harbor providing a mooring for yachts and also for one of the lifeboats of the Solent area.

Visitors who'd like to explore the Isle of Wight for the day can take an **Around the Island Rover** ticket, which may be purchased on the bus. This enables anyone to board and leave the buses at any stop on the island. The price is £4 ($7) for adults per day and £2 ($3.50) for children. It also gives passage on the island's only railway, running from the dock at Ryde to the center of Shanklin, a distance of 12 miles. For further information, phone 0938/523821.

Long a favorite of British royalty, the island has as its major attraction **Osborne House** (tel. 0983/200022), Queen Victoria's most cherished residence, lying a mile southeast of East Cowes. Prince Albert, with his characteristic thoroughness, contributed to many aspects of the design of the Italian-inspired mansion, which stands in lush gardens right outside the village of Whippingham, with its much-visited church. The rooms have remained as Victoria knew them, right down to the French piano she used to play and with all the cozy clutter of her sitting room. Grief-stricken at the death of Albert in 1861, she asked that Osborne House remain as it was, and so it mainly has been kept. Even the turquoise scent bottles he gave her, decorated with cupids and cherubs, are still in place. It was in her bedroom in Osborne House that Victoria died on January 22, 1901. In the gardens are the Swiss Cottage where the royal children played and the queen's bathing machine. The house is open to the public from Easter to the end of October from 10 a.m. to 5 p.m. daily. Admission is £3 ($5.25) for adults, £1.50 ($2.65) for children.

A completely different attraction, **Carisbrooke Castle** (tel. 0983/522107) is where Charles I was imprisoned by the Roundheads in 1647. This fine medieval castle is in the center of the island, 1½ miles southwest of Newport. Everybody heads for the Well House, concealed inside a 16th-century stone building. Donkeys take turns treading a large wooden wheel connected to a rope, which hauls up buckets of water. The castle is open Monday to Saturday, mid-March until mid-October, from 10 a.m. to 6 p.m. (to 4 p.m. from mid-October to mid-March). However, Sunday hours are different. From mid-March until March 31 and from October 1 to mid-October it is open on Sunday from 2 to 6 p.m. From April 1 to September 30 it is open on Sunday from 10 a.m. to 6 p.m., and from mid-October to mid-March, Sunday hours are from 2 to 4 p.m. Admission is £2.20 ($3.85) for adults, £1.10 ($1.95) for children.

You have a choice of several bases on the Isle of Wight unless you're what the English call a "day-tripper."

Cowes is the premier port for yachting in Britain. Henry VIII ordered the castle built there, but it is now the headquarters of the Royal Yacht Squadron. The seafront, the Prince's Green, and the high cliff road are worth exploring. Hovercraft are built in the town, and it is also the home and birthplace of the well-known maritime photographer, Beken of Cowes.

Along the southeast coast are the twin resorts of **Sandown,** with its pier complex and theater, and **Shanklin,** at the southern end of Sandown Bay, which has held the British annual sunshine record more times than any other resort. Keats once lived in Shanklin's Old Village.

Farther along the coast, **Ventnor** is called the "Madeira of England," because it arises from the sea in a series of steep hills.

On the west coast, the sand cliffs of **Alum Bay** are a blend of many different colors, a total of 21 claimed. The Needles, three giant chalk rocks, and the Needles Lighthouse are further features of interest at this end of the island. If you want to stay at the western end of Wight, refer to my recommendations under "Totland Bay" and "Freshwater Bay."

Newport is the capital, a bustling market town lying in the heart of the island.

RYDE

A good anchor for the Isle of Wight is the **Seaward Guest House,** 14-16 George St., Ryde, Isle of Wight PO33 2EW (tel. Ryde 63168), as Ryde is a good center for exploring the island. Many tour buses leave from here, as well as the train from the ferry docks at Ryde. Harold and Margaret Gath, a helpful couple, receive guests into their century-old home, charging from £10.50 ($18.40) per person nightly for B&B, including a four-course breakfast. A four-course evening dinner will also be served for another £4.25 ($7.45). Everything is well kept in their pleasant home, and Mr. Gath works with the tourist board. Even if they can't accommodate you in their busy season, they'll have suggestions where you can find a room.

The Dorset Hotel, 31 Dover St., Ryde, Isle of Wight PO33 2BW (tel. 0983/64327), was originally built late in the 19th century to accommodate the government officials who accompanied Queen Victoria on her summer visits. Today, the site of so many hopes and ambitions is presided over by a charming Welsh-born owner, Joseph Randall Griffiths (J. R. to his friends). The house offers 25 bedrooms, 7 of which have a private bath or shower. An outdoor heated swimming pool is open throughout the year. Per-person rates, single or double occupancy, cost £14 ($24.50) daily, with VAT and breakfast included. Rooms with private facilities rent for another £2 ($3.50) per person nightly.

Holmsdale Guest House, 13 Dover St., Ryde, Isle of Wight PO33 2AQ (tel. 0983/614805), is set within a ten-minute walk of the main shopping district, within a five-minute walk of the ferryboat terminal, and within 200 yards of the beach. The owners, Ted and Jean Taylor, charge from £12.50 ($21.90) to £16.50 ($28.90) daily for B&B, with singles costing a daily supplement of £3 ($5.25). The price variation is a function of the season, not of the accommodation. Each room has a bath or shower and all but one has a toilet. There are only four rooms, each with color TV and beverage-making equipment.

SHANKLIN

A comfortable choice is **Apse Manor Country House,** Apse Manor Road, Shanklin, Isle of Wight, PO37 7NP (tel. 0983/866651). This is a superb 16th-century manor house situated in an acre of secluded gardens surrounded by woods and open country, yet only three minutes from Shanklin with all its amenities and safe sandy beaches. All five units are comfortably furnished and have baths, color TV, tea and coffee-making facilities, and views of the grounds. The cooking is done under the personal supervision of Mrs. P. Boynton, proprietor, with a liberal and varied menu using fresh garden produce where possible. Bed, breakfast, and evening dinner cost from £26 ($45.50) per person per day.

VENTNOR

Perhaps one of the nicest places to stay on the Isle of Wight is **Madeira Hall,** Trinity Road, Ventnor, Isle of Wight PO38 1NS (tel. 0983/852624). In an estate garden of lawns, tall trees, and flowering shrubs stands this stone manor house, with mullioned windows, gables, and bay windows. It has housed interesting people, such as Lord Macaulay, who wrote some of his well-known essays here. And there are associations with Charles Dickens and some of his characters. On the grounds is a heated swimming pool and an 18-hole putting course. All bedrooms have color TV and facilities for making hot beverages. Most have private baths or showers. The owners charge from £17.50 ($30.65) daily in a single, the cost going up to £40 ($70) in a double. The establishment is open from mid-March to October.

FRESHWATER BAY

Some 300 yards from the beach and caves at Freshwater Bay, **Blenheim House,** Gate Lane, Freshwater Bay, Isle of Wight PO40 9QD (tel. 0983/752858), is a twin-gabled, brick-fronted house laden with gingerbread. Built in 1894 as a private house, it offers eight well-furnished bedrooms, most of which contain private showers, toilets, and color TV with full central heating. Hazel and Jon Shakeshaft, the owners, charge from £21.50 ($37.65) per person for half board, including VAT and service. In back is a heated swimming pool. Good meals are served in the dining room, with French windows opening onto the patio and lawn. Fresh local produce is used whenever possible.

TOTLAND BAY

A pleasant stay will be yours at **Littledene Lodge Hotel,** Granville Road, Totland Bay, Isle of Wight PO39 0AX (tel. 0983/752411). Owned and managed by Mrs. Maureen Wright, the hotel is small enough that you receive plenty of personal attention. Each of the nicely furnished rooms has facilities for comfort. Some have private bath. There is a TV lounge for the use of residents, and the hotel is centrally heated. Maureen is proud of her reputation for good, well-presented food served in the spacious bar/dining room. The charge is £18 ($31.50) per person per day for B&B and dinner, while B&B only costs from £12.50 ($21.90) per day. Children are welcome.

WOOTTEN

One of the best restaurants on the island, worth a special trip, is **Lugleys,** Staplers Road, Wootten Common, Wootten, Isle of Wight PO33 4RW (tel. 0983/882202), on the main road running from Newport to Ryde, four miles from either town. There are only 16 table settings within the Victorian-inspired dining room of Angela Hewitt, who offers a variety of seasonal dishes throughout the year. Typical menu items include grilled spring lamb served with Welsh lava bread and orange sauce, seasonal local produce, and hormone-free, naturally raised beefsteak. Reservations are requested for full meals costing from £20 ($35) and worth the splurge. Only dinner is served nightly, except Sunday, from 7 to 9:30. B&B is offered for £18 ($31.50) per person daily.

---

5. Winchester

The most historical city in all of Hampshire, Winchester is big on legends. It's even associated with King Arthur and the Knights of the Round Table. In the Great Hall, the remains of Winchester Castle, a round oak table, with space for King Arthur and his 24 knights, hangs on the wall. But all that spells undocumented romance. What is actually known is that when the Saxons ruled the ancient kingdom of Wessex, Winchester was the capital.

The city is also linked with King Alfred, who is honored today by a statue and is believed to have been crowned there. The Danish conqueror, Canute, came this way too, as did the king he ousted, Ethelred (Canute got his wife, Emma, in the bargain). The city is the seat of the well-known Winchester College, whose founding father was the bishop of Winchester, William of Wykeham. Established in 1382, it lays claim to being the oldest public (private) school in England.

Traditions are strong in Winchester. It is said (although I've never confirmed the assertion) that if you go to St. Cross Hospital, now an almshouse, dating from the 12th century, you'll get ye olde pilgrim's dole of ale and bread (and if there's no bread, you can eat cake). Winchester, 65 miles from London, is essentially a market town, on the downs by the Itchen River.

WINCHESTER CATHEDRAL

For centuries Winchester Cathedral (tel. 0962/53137) has been one of the great mother churches of England. The present building, the longest cathedral in Britain, dates from 1079, and its Norman heritage is still in evidence. Early in this century, when parts of the cathedral were breaking away and sinking into the log raft and peat bed on which it had been built in the 13th century, a diver, William Walker, worked in darkness for several years in the water below to build a brick and concrete base to support the massive structure. When a Saxon church stood on this spot, St. Swithun, bishop of Winchester and tutor to young King Alfred, suggested modestly that he be buried outside. When he was later buried inside, it rained for 40 days. The legend lives on; just ask a resident of Winchester what will happen if it rains on St. Swithun's Day, July 15.

Of the present building, the nave with its two aisles is most impressive, as are the chantries, the reredos (late 15th century), and the elaborately carved choir stalls. Of the chantries, that of William of Wykeham, founder of Winchester College, is perhaps the most visited (it's found in the south aisle of the Nave). The cathedral also contains a number of tombs, notably those of novelist Jane Austen and Izaak Walton (exponent of the merits of the pastoral life—*The Compleat Angler*). The latter's tomb is to be found in the Prior Silkestede's Chapel in the South Transept. Miss Austen's grave is marked with a commemorative plaque. Winchester Cathedral contains in chests the bones of many of the Saxon kings, and the remains of the Viking conqueror, Canute, and his wife, Emma, are in the presbytery. The son of William the Conqueror, William Rufus (who reigned as William II in 1087), is also believed to have been buried at the cathedral. There are free guided tours Monday to Saturday at 11 a.m. and 3 p.m. from April to the end of October.

The Crypt is flooded for a large part of the year, and at such times is closed to the public. When it's not flooded, there are regular tours at 10:30 a.m. and 2:30 p.m. daily except Sunday. The Library, in which is displayed the *Winchester Bible* and other ancient manuscripts, is open for limited hours throughout the summer (except Monday morning and Sunday) and on Wednesday and Saturday for the rest of the year (except January, when it's open only on Saturday). The Treasury is open during the summer season from 11 a.m. to 5 p.m. It is small and does not require a guide. No admission fee is charged, but a donation of £1 ($1.75) for the upkeep of the cathedral is suggested. A Triforium Gallery museum and Library ticket costs £1 ($1.75).

WHERE TO STAY

One of the best places is **Harestock Lodge,** Harestock Road, Winchester, Hampshire SO22 6NX (tel. 0962/881870), a lovely country residence constructed in 1885 on the northern perimeter of the city (between the A32 Andover road and the A272 Stockbridge highway). Accommodations are well appointed and maintained, of which nine have private baths. The B&B rate in a single ranges from £20 ($35.90) to £27 ($47.25) daily, going up to £33 ($57.75) to £41 ($71.75) in a double. Extra amenities in the rooms include radio and phone, whereas special features of the hotel include an outdoor swimming pool and an indoor spa pool. Sound British cooking is featured in the restaurant. The location is about two miles north of the city, and motorists will find ample parking.

Originally built in 1897, **Florum House,** 47 St. Cross Rd., Winchester, Hampshire SO23 9PS (tel. 0962/840427), is a brick-fronted Victorian house whose private gardens ring it in front and back. It is set about a half mile south of the city center. The six bedrooms, each comfortably furnished with color TV, a shower, and beverage-making equipment, cost £25 ($43.75) daily for a single and £32 ($56) for a double. A cozy triple, suitable for families, is priced at £36 ($63). A full English breakfast is included in the price.

Aquarius Bed & Breakfast, 31 Hyde St., Winchester, Hampshire SO23 7DX (tel. 0962/54729), is set within a stucco-covered Victorian town house lying within a ten-minute walk of the cathedral and a five-minute walk from the rail and coach stations. Mrs. Maureen Hennessy rents three bedrooms at a cost of £15 ($26.25) per person daily, including a hearty five-course breakfast. Only one of these accommodations contains a private bath, but two of them are large enough for a small family.

Brentwood, 178 Stockbridge Rd., Winchester, Hampshire SO22 6RW (tel. 0962/53536), a turn-of-the-century, red-brick semidetached house, has a pleasant garden out back, and the location is on a main road between Winchester and Stockbridge, within a ten-minute walk of the cathedral and a five-minute walk of the rail station. With a full English breakfast included, singles cost £15 ($26.25) daily, with doubles going for £22 ($38.50). A family room, suitable for four occupants, rents for £34 ($59.40). None of the three bedrooms has a private bath, and no meals other than breakfast are served. Mrs. Wright, the owner, will direct guests to the Roebuck Buck just across the road, where a meal costs from £4 ($7) to £7 ($12.25).

Ann Farrell, 5 Ranelagh Rd., St. Cross, Winchester, Hampshire SO23 9TA, (tel. 0962/69555), offers one of the best values. Near the heart of the city, the house has only three rooms to rent, which contain hot and cold running water. A bathroom and shower are for exclusive use of guests. This is a Victorian house furnished in that period but with comfort. Rates are from £11 ($19.25) daily in a single, £22 ($38.50) in a double.

You might also try **Mrs. Lawrence,** 67 St. Cross Rd., Winchester, Hampshire SO23 9RE (tel. 0962/63002), who will house you in comfort, giving you a complete English breakfast for £21 ($36.75) to £23 ($40.25) nightly. One room is rented to families. The location is near the heart of the city.

FOOD AND DRINK

Just by the cathedral, the **Wessex Hotel,** Paternoster Row (tel. 0962/61611), has a bright coffeeshop, with a separate entrance from the street, where hot and cold snacks are available all day. A typical meal of soup, breaded plaice with fried potatoes, apple pie and cream, plus coffee, will cost about £7.25 ($12.70). They also do a traditional afternoon tea. From noon to 2 p.m. the cocktail bar in the hotel has a table where you can help yourself to a selection of English cheeses and pâté, pickles, and salad ingredients. The chef's homemade soup and freshly baked rolls are also offered. In the elegant Walton Restaurant, overlooking the cathedral, a full three-course lunch costs £9.65 ($16.90), and a four-course dinner costs £13.50 ($23.65). The best time to go for dinner is from 7 to 9 p.m.

Minstrels, 2 Little Minster St. (tel. 0962/67212), serves a variety of functions: it's ideal for morning coffee and a pâtisserie, quick and reasonably priced lunches, and afternoon teas extending to light suppers suitable for family and friends. The menu is limited, simple fare such as homemade soup, and fisherman's pie. Continental dishes, however, also appear, and they cater to vegetarians. Expect to spend no more than £5 ($8.75), unless you're ravenously hungry. A hot menu is available all day, and there is take-away service. Hours are Monday to Saturday from 9:30 a.m. to 5:30 p.m. and Sunday from 11:30 a.m. to 5 p.m.

Raffles Tea Room, 12 The Square (tel. 0962/61736), is above the House of Tweed shop. It's a traditional English tea room, offering morning coffee with pastries or toasted buns, as well as light lunches, including sandwiches, salads, chicken pie, and quiche, costing around £4 ($7). Afternoon teas are a specialty. You can have warm scones with strawberry jam and clotted cream, plus a choice of five blends of tea, all costing less than £3 ($5.25). The place is open from 9:30 a.m. to 5 p.m. Monday to Saturday.

The Pick of the Pubs

Instead of lunching at one of the above restaurants, you may want to drop in at the **Royal Oak Pub,** Royal Oak Passage (tel. 0962/61136), which is to be found in a passageway next to the God Begot House in the High Street. This pub reputedly has the oldest bar in England. Luncheons are served at the bar daily from noon to 2 p.m. Various hot dishes and snacks are available. Expect to pay from £5 ($8.75) for a full meal. A traditional Sunday lunch is served from noon to 1:30 p.m., costing £6.50 ($11.40). Neil and Chris Pawley, the publicans, offer live jazz on Sunday. Admission is free. This is a busy pub with plenty of atmosphere, where the hosts and staff enjoy serving good food and drink. Hours are daily from 11 a.m. to 2:30 p.m. and 6 to 11 p.m.

Olde Market Inn, 34 The Square (at Market Street; tel. 0962/52585), is ideal for those who enjoy a local pub. It sits opposite the cathedral in the oldest, most historic district of Winchester. It's mellowed enough to have timbers galore, cozy nooks, and comfortable chairs. A selection of hot and cold bar snacks is available at lunchtime, including home-cooked steak-and-kidney pie, cottage pie, and chicken-and-mushroom pie. Prices begin at £2 ($3.50). The place is open Monday to Saturday from 11:30 a.m. to 3 p.m. and 5:30 to 11 p.m., and on Sunday from noon to 3 p.m. and 7 to 10:30 p.m.

DORSET

This is Thomas Hardy country. You may long ago have read *Jude the Obscure* or *Tess of the D'Urbervilles,* and know that Dorset is the Wessex of Hardy novels. Some of the towns and villages, although altered considerably, are still recognizable from his descriptions—however, he changed the names to protect the innocent. Poole, for example, became Havenpool; Weymouth converted to Budmouth. The last of the great Victorians, as he was called, died in 1928 at the age of 88. His tomb rests in a position of honor in Westminster Abbey, but his heart was buried in his beloved Dorsetshire.

One of England's smallest shires, Dorset stretches all the way from the Victorian seaside resort of Bournemouth in the east to Lyme Regis in the west (known to Jane Austen, who couldn't find where all the action was). Dorset is a southwestern county, bordering the English Channel. It's big on cows, and Dorset butter is served at many an afternoon tea. Mainly, it is a land of farms and pastures, with plenty of sand heaths and chalky downs.

The most prominent tourist center of Dorset is the Victorian seaside resort of Bournemouth. If you don't anchor there, you might also try a number of Dorset's other seaports, villages, and country towns. For the most part, I've hugged closely to the impressive coastline.

Incidentally, Dorset, as the vacation-wise Britisher might tell you if he or she wanted to divulge a secret, is a friend of the budget traveler.

6. Bournemouth

The South Coast resort at the doorstep of the New Forest didn't just happen: it was carefully planned and manicured, a true city in a garden. Flower-filled, park-dotted Bournemouth contains great globs of architecture inherited from those arbiters of taste, Victoria and her mischievous boy, Edward. Its most distinguishing feature is its Chines (shrub-filled narrow steep-sided ravines) along the zigzag coastline.

The walking English strike out at, say, Hengistbury Head, making their way past sandy beaches and both the Boscombe and Bournemouth Piers, finally reaching Alum Chine—a distance of six miles away, but a traffic-free walk to remember.

It is estimated that of the nearly 12,000 acres that Bournemouth claims for its own, about one-sixth is turned over to green parks, stage-setting-type waters, and even flowerbeds, such as the Pavilion Rock Garden, through which amblers pass both day and night. The total effect, especially in spring, tends to be dramatic and helps explain Bournemouth's long-established popularity with the garden-loving English. Bournemouth was discovered back in Victoria's day, when sea-bathing became a firmly entrenched institution, often practiced with great ritual. Many of the comparatively elegant villas that exist today (now largely B&B houses and hotels) once privately housed eminent Victorians.

Bournemouth, which along with Poole and Christchurch forms the largest urban area in the south of England, is not as sophisticated as Brighton. Increasingly, it is retirement acres for widowed or spinster English ladies who have found their place in the sun by playing the wicked game of Bingo. Increasingly, too, Bournemouth and its neighbors have a floating population of some 20,000 students attending one of its schools or colleges and in their off-hours exploring places written about or painted by such poets and artists as Shelley, Beardsley, and Turner.

The resort's amusements are wide and varied. At the Pavilion Theatre, for example, you can see West End–type productions from London; the Bournemouth Symphony Orchestra is justly famous in Europe; and there's the usual run of golf courses, band concerts, variety shows, and dancing.

Bournemouth is about 104 miles from London, easily reached in about an hour and 40 minutes on an express train from Waterloo Station in London. It makes a good base for exploring a history-rich part of England. On its outskirts are the New Forest, Salisbury, Winchester, and the Isle of Wight (an island that lies 15 miles away, the former seaside retreat of Victoria).

WHERE TO STAY

One of the most dramatically situated hotels in Bournemouth is the aptly n-amed **Cliff House,** 113 Alumhurst Rd., Alum Chine, Bournemouth, Dorset BH4 8HS (tel. 0202/763003). This white-painted house, operated by the Clark family, is also one of the best B&Bs at the resort. The hotel faces the sea, and you can walk along the promenade to the pier, shops, and amusements. The interior of this gabled house has a modernized decor, and each accommodation has a sea view. All but one of the units offers a private bath or shower and a toilet. B&B costs £16.50 ($28.90) per person daily. For bed, breakfast, and dinner, the price is £23.50 ($41.15) per person daily. The hotel shuts down in October.

Hinton Firs Hotel, Manor Road, East Cliff, Bournemouth, Dorset BH1 3HB (tel. 0202/25409), near the sea, is a turn-of-the-century country house enjoying a tranquil setting in a pine grove. It is a substantial and inviting hotel. The Waters family, owners of Hinton Firs for 40 years, rent 52 bedrooms, all with color TV, direct-dial phones, and tea- and coffee-making equipment. The furnishings are modern, as the hotel has been considerably upgraded in recent years. It's best to take the half-board rate of £25 ($43.75) to £36 ($63) per person daily for double occupancy, depending on the season and the plumbing. Singles pay an extra £5 ($8.75) per day. There's a comfortable array of tastefully decorated public rooms, including a bar, TV lounge, and a dining room, as well as a garden. An indoor swimming pool is complete with spa pool and underwater swim jet, and the outdoor swimming pool is heated seasonally. The hotel also has a sauna, a solarium, an elevator, and car parking.

Chilterns Hotel, 44 Westby Rd., Boscombe, Bournemouth, Dorset BH5 1HD (tel. 0202/36539), stands on the seaside of Christchurch Road. The setting is that of a turn-of-the-century street lined with B&Bs, of which this one is the most outstanding. There are 19 comfortably furnished bedrooms, five of which have full private baths. The B&B rate ranges from £9.50 ($16.65) to £13 ($22.75) per person daily, and evening meals can be served, but only to residents. The hotel has a sunny lounge with color TV, along with a bar.

Blinkbonnie Heights Hotel, 26 Clifton Rd., Southbourne, Bournemouth, Dorset BH6 3PA (tel. 0202/426512), is set in the resort of Southbourne, four miles to the east of the center of Bournemouth. In a quiet residential neighborh⌐d, this family-run hotel offers 12 comfortably furnished bedrooms. Bathless rooms cost from £10 ($17.50) to £13.50 ($23.65) per person daily, according to the season, with breakfast and VAT included. However, there is a £2.50 ($4.40) per person daily surcharge in accommodations with private baths. Residents can also arrange for an evening meal.

Park View Hotel, 27 Spencer Rd., Bournemouth, Dorset BH1 3TE (tel. 0202/28955), stands on a hillside, away from the bustle of Bournemouth center, with an impressive view of the resort. Anita and Mitch Stanley and family welcome guests at a cost of £10 ($17.50) per person. Rooms come with hot and cold running water and are comfortably furnished. Dinner is an extra £4 ($7) per person. Parking is available in the forecourt.

Belgravia Hotel, 56 Christchurch Rd., East Cliff, Bournemouth, Dorset BH1 3PF (tel. 0202/290857), is a gracious brick mansion in a posh section of the resort, set in its own garden, the pride of the owners. For from £10.35 ($18.10) to £16.10 ($28.20) per person daily, you can stay here and have B&B. Dinner is available on request at £7 ($12.25) per person. The Belgravia is a five-minute walk along a zigzag path to the water. The bedrooms are sun-filled and roomy. The beds have innersprings, and the rooms contain built-in wardrobes, bedside lamps, and armchairs. Reservations of only a night or two are almost impossible to get during the summer season (when the one-weekers are given priority, of course).

Sunnydene, 11 Spencer Rd., Bournemouth, Dorset BH1 3TE (tel. 0202/22281), is a substantial gabled house on a tree-lined road between the Central Station and Bournemouth Bay. This comfortable turn-of-the-century private hotel has recently made many additions, including a cozy licensed bar and an enlarged dining room. Winter visitors also enjoy central heating. All bedrooms are carpeted and have hot and cold running water, and many contain private baths. The cost for B&B is from £12 ($21) per person daily. An excellent evening meal of four courses, with some choice of menu, will cost an extra £6.50 ($11.40) per person. The hotel is open all year, and daily accommodation is usually readily available during all months except July and August.

WHERE TO DINE

A restaurant that lives up to its name in food and decor is **Old England,** 74 Poole Rd., Westbourne (tel. 0202/766475). The decor is darkly Old English, with semiprivate booths that are much in demand. Dishes tend to run to such plates as roast Hampshire pork, roast fresh Dorset chicken, and Scottish beef. For dessert, you might try a fruit pie with custard or cream. Meals cost from £10 ($17.50) to £15 ($26.25), depending on what you order. Hours are daily from 11:45 a.m. to 2:30 p.m. and from 6 or 6:30 p.m. to 10 or 11 p.m., depending on the season (there are longer opening hours in summer).

Coriander, 14 Richmond Hill (tel. 0202/22202), is a Mexican restaurant that brings South-of-the-Border flair to staid Bournemouth. You get the usual range of Mexican specialties, but are also given some well-prepared vegetarian dishes made with fresh ingredients. Meals, costing from £6 ($13.15), are served from noon to 2:30 p.m. and 6 to 11 p.m. It is closed for lunch on Sunday.

The **Salad Centre,** Post Office Road (tel. 0202/21720), is for devotees of vegetarian and "whole-food." There is always a large selection of salads, and you can also count on a fresh soup every day. Various quiches are presented, as are vegetable flans. There is no fixed menu, however, and the center is more or less cafeteria-style. Meals begin at £3.50 ($6.15), and hours are Monday to Saturday from 9 a.m. to 4 p.m. The center is run by Mrs. Doreen Fisher, who provides a warm welcome.

ON THE OUTSKIRTS

Dating back to 1673, the **Fisherman's Haunt Hotel,** Winkton, Christchurch, Dorset BH23 7AS (tel. 0202/484071), is a wistaria-covered country house run by James Bochan, of Ukrainian origin, who came to England with the Polish forces in 1943. He welcomes guests all year, charging £21 ($36.75) daily for bathless singles, going up to £41 ($71.75) in a bathless double. Doubles with private baths and toilets cost £44 ($77), those with four-poster beds going for £48 ($84). Authentic regional British dishes are the fare of the dining room, which overlooks the River Avon. Open from noon, the restaurant at Fisherman's Haunt Hotel offers a set luncheon for £7 ($12.25). Dinners are served from 7 to 10 p.m. A special feature of the restaurant is the traditional Sunday midday meal. If you do stay over, you will be served a full English breakfast. All bedrooms have full central heating and tea- or coffee-making facilities. Bedroom windows afford views of the garden, the river, and the meadows. The hotel lies only seven miles from Bournemouth and a mile and a half from Christchurch.

KINGSTON LACY

An imposing 17th-century mansion, Kingston Lacy at Wimborne Minster, on the B3082 Wimborne-Blandford road 1 ½ miles west of Wimborne, was the home for more than 300 years of the Bankes family, who had as guests such distinguished persons as King Edward VII, Kaiser Wilhelm, Thomas Hardy, King George V, and the Duke of Wellington. The house contains a magnificent collection of artwork, tapestries, and furnishings brought from abroad by Sir Charles Barry (designer of the House of Commons) at the request of William Bankes, a friend of Lord Byron. The present house was built to replace Corfe Castle, the Bankes family's home that was destroyed in the Civil War. During her husband's absence in pursuit of duties as chief justice to King Charles I, Lady Bankes led the defense of the castle, withstanding two sieges before being forced to surrender to Cromwell's forces in 1646 through actions of a treacherous follower. The keys of Corfe Castle hang in the library of Kingston Lacy. The house, set in 250 acres of wooded park, is open from 1 to 5 p.m. daily, except Thursday and Friday, from April to the end of October. The park is open from noon to 6 p.m. Admission to the house and garden is £3.50 ($6.15) for adults, £1.75 ($3.05) for children. The park and garden can be visited for £1 ($1.75) for adults, 50p (90¢) for children.

7. Shaftesbury

The origins of this typical Dorsetshire market town date back to the ninth century, when King Alfred founded the abbey and made his daughter the first abbess. King Edward the Martyr was buried here, and King Canute died in the abbey but was buried in Winchester. Little now remains of the abbey, but the ruins are beautifully laid out. The museum adjoining St. Peter's Church at the top of Gold Hill gives a good idea of what the ancient Saxon hilltop town was like.

Today, ancient cottages and hostelries cling to the steep cobblestone streets, thatch roofs frown above tiny-pane windows, and modern stores vie with the street market in the High Street and the cattle market off Christy's Lane.

The town, right on the A30 from London, is an excellent center from which to visit the Hardy Country (it appears as Chaston in *Jude the Obscure*), Stourhead Gardens, and Longleat House.

FOOD AND LODGING

About a half mile from Shaftesbury, **The Old Rectory,** St. James, Shaftesbury, Dorset SP7 8HG (tel. 0747/52003), offers one of the most moderately priced accommodations in the area. A Georgian building, it stands on attractive grounds and offers well-furnished rooms with private bath for £20 ($35) per person daily, double occupancy. The hostess is a Cordon Bleu cook, serving excellent meals costing from £12 ($21) per person.

You might also consider **Vale Mount,** 17A Salisbury St., Shaftesbury, Dorset SP7 8EL (tel. 0747/2991), which lies about two minutes from the heart of town. A comfortable, pleasantly furnished house, it is a very good bargain at £10 ($17.50) in a single and £20 ($35) in a double. Baths are shared.

Gullivers Farm, East Orchard, near Shaftesbury, Dorset SP7 0LQ (tel. 0747/811331), on the outskirts, is a delightful house set in lovely grounds with a swimming pool. Commander and Mrs. Ian Ashton-Johnson offer a twin room and a single with a shared bathroom. However, each unit has hot and cold running water. Charges are £17 ($29.75) per person daily for B&B. Mrs. Ashton-Johnson is an excellent cook, so you may want to arrange for dinner, costing £12 ($21).

---

8. Wareham

On the Frome River, this historic little town is about a mile west of Poole Harbour. Many find it a good center for touring the South Dorset coast and the Purbeck Hills. It contains remains of early British and Roman town walls, and the Saxon church of St. Martin has an effigy of Lawrence of Arabia (T. E. Lawrence).

Lawrence died in a motorcycle crash in 1935, and his former home, **Clouds Hill** (no phone), near Wool, lies seven miles to the northwest of Wareham near Wareham Forest, one mile north of Bovington Camp. The house is open Wednesday, Friday, and Sunday from 2 to 5 p.m. from April to the end of September. It is open only on Sunday, from 1 to 4 p.m., the remainder of the year. Admission is £1.50 ($2.65) for either an adult or child, and no photography is allowed.

The sleepy hamlet of Wool is 19 miles west of Bournemouth on the River Frome. One of the most charming places in East Dorset, it has thatched cottages on either side of the road. It lies west of Wareham just off the A352 on the B3071 road leading to the channel.

FOOD AND LODGING

A riverside country restaurant, **The Old Granary,** The Quay, Wareham, Dorset, BH20 4LP (tel. 0929/552010), is near a double-arched bridge. You dine either inside or on a terrace overlooking the boats and swans. The interior dining room has a charm of its own, with bentwood chairs, saffron cloths, a wine rack, a natural wood sideboard, and a collection of locally painted watercolors. A gracious and informal atmosphere prevails. The secret behind the success of the Old Granary is its fine cuisine; the owners, Mr. and Mrs. Derek Sturton, try hard to stick to natural country foods. A four-course table d'hôte menu costs £12 ($21), and you can also order à la carte. The restaurant is open every day and serves food from noon to 2 p.m. and 6:30 to 9:30 p.m. If you wish to overnight here, the charge per person is £18 ($31.50) daily without bath, £22 ($38.50) with bath, including a full English breakfast and VAT. Children are not accepted overnight.

9. Dorchester

Thomas Hardy, in his 1886 Victorian novel *The Mayor of Casterbridge,* gave it literary fame, but Dorchester was known to the Romans. In fact, its Maumbury Rings, south of the town, are considered the best example of a Roman amphitheater in Britain, having once resounded with the shouts of 12,000 spectators screaming for gladiator blood. Dorchester, the county town, was the setting of another blood letting, the Bloody Assize of 1685, when Judge Jeffreys, suffering from "the stone," dispensed the ultimate in justice to the poor wretches condemned for supporting the Duke of Monmouth's ill-fated attempt to become the English monarch.

But it is mostly through Hardy that the world knows Dorchester. Many of his major scenes of love and intrigue took place on the periphery of Dorchester. The land was well-known to Hardy, since he was born in 1840 at **Higher Bockhampton,** three miles northeast of Dorchester, off the A35. His home, now a National Trust property, may be visited by the public daily from March to October, from 11 a.m. to 6 p.m. or dusk, whichever is earlier. But to go inside, you must make an appointment with the tenant. You may write in advance to **Hardy's Cottage,** Higher Bockhampton, Dorchester, Dorset DT1, or telephone 0305/62366. You approach the cottage on foot, a seven-minute walk after parking your vehicle in the space provided in the wood. The admission is £1.50 ($2.65). Within easy reach of the cottage is **Rainbarrow,** mentioned by Hardy in *Return of the Native.*

You may also want to browse around the **Dorset County Museum,** High West Street (next to St. Peter's Church; tel. 0305/62735), with memorabilia of Thomas Hardy and other famous inhabitants of Dorset. In addition, you'll find prehistoric and Roman relics, plus natural history exhibits and others pertaining to the geology of the region. There is also a rural craft section of bygones. Displays and finds from Maiden Castle, Britain's largest Iron Age hill fort, can be seen, plus galleries on the geology and natural history of Dorset. The museum is open Monday to Saturday from 10 a.m. to 1 p.m. and 2 to 5 p.m. Admission is £1.20 ($2.10) for adults, 60p ($1.05) for children 5 to 16 years of age (children under 5 free).

Five miles east of Dorchester, on the Dorchester-Bournemouth road (A35), one mile east of Puddletown, stands **Athelhampton** (tel. 0305/848363), one of England's great medieval houses, considered the most beautiful and historic in the south. It was begun in the reign of Edward IV on the legendary site of King Athelstan's palace. It was Thomas Hardy's Athelhall. A family home for more than 500 years, it is noted for its 15th-century Great Hall, its Tudor Great Chamber, its State Bedroom, and King's Room. The house stands on ten acres of formal and landscaped gardens, with a 15th-century dovecote, river gardens, fish ponds, fountains, and rare trees. It is open to the public on Wednesday, Thursday, Sunday, and bank holidays, from the Wednesday before Easter to the second Sunday in October, 2 to 6 p.m. In August it is also open on Monday and Tuesday. Admission is £1.25 ($2.20) to the garden and another £1.25 to the house.

WHERE TO STAY

Built on medieval foundations, the **Wessex Hotel,** High West Street, Dorchester, Dorset DT1 1UP (tel. 0305/62660), is a listed Georgian structure, once the home of Lord Ilchester. In the town center, the hotel offers 20 bedrooms with baths or showers, ranging from £24 ($42) for a single and £38 ($66.50) for a double or twin, including a full English breakfast and VAT. The Wessex has a busy licensed restaurant and a good wine list.

East Linton, 7 Damers Rd., Dorchester, Dorset DT1 2JX (tel. 0305/64547), is one of the best B&B houses in the town. A short walk from the heart of town, it is a Victorian building that has not been ruined by modernization. It is comfortable and pleasantly furnished, and one room is set aside for families. Guests are welcomed from Easter to the end of September and are charged from £10 ($17.50) per person for B&B. Guests must share a bath, and the rate includes a full English breakfast.

WHERE TO EAT

Opposite the County Museum, **Judge Jeffreys' Restaurant,** 6 High West St. (tel. 0305/64369), built as a house in 1398, is an attractive stopover on your cross-country jaunt. It had the dubious distinction of lodging that "cantankerous alcoholic," Judge Jeffreys, during the Bloody Assizes. The place has an Old English atmosphere of massive oak beams, a spiral staircase, stone-mullioned windows, and paneled rooms, along with Tudor fireplaces. It is open Monday to Saturday from 9:30 a.m. to 5:30 p.m., serving morning coffee, lunches, and traditional afternoon teas. Lunches cost from £5 ($8.75). It is also open in the evening from 7 to 9 p.m., offering an extensive à la carte menu, with meals beginning at £9 ($15.75).

At **The Horse with the Red Umbrella,** 10 High West St. (tel. 0305/62019), the window of this shop/coffeehouse is filled with bakewell tarts, and other baked goods, and inside you will find neat tables and chairs where you can watch the passing locals and enjoy quiche and various toasted snacks. It is cheap and good. In winter they also have stuffed baked potatoes. Meals cost from £4 ($7). It's open from 8:30 a.m. to 5:30 p.m. Monday to Saturday.

Potter In, 19 Durngate St. (tel. 0305/68649), is a cheerful little place really known only to the local people who flock in for the whole-meal scones, home-baked rolls, flapjacks, and a spicy, moist carrot cake that is worth stopping in for. Two specials are offered at lunch, served noon to 2 p.m., which may be roast chicken and vegetables or a filling vegetable casserole. A meal costs from £5 ($8.75) up. The establishment is open from 10 a.m. to 5 p.m. daily, except Sunday.

On the Outskirts

At **Brace of Pheasants,** Plush (tel. 03004/357), Jane and Geoffrey Knights run a charming thatched country restaurant and inn that has beautiful views through its little dormer windows, opening onto a rural setting. To reach it, take the B3143 out of Dorchester to Piddletrenthide, turning off at the sign to Plush. The inn is on your left. Geoffrey does the cooking, with an emphasis on traditional country dishes and game specialties. The restaurant and bar have old paintings, antique tables, and are warmed by an open fire. The Brace serves bar meals, lunches, and dinners. It also has a covered patio in the garden that is inviting in summer. The variety of food offered in this inn is enormous, including at least eight appetizers and ten main courses, along with a large selection of desserts. The cost is about £10 ($17.50) per person, including VAT. It's open daily from 11 a.m. to 2:30 p.m. and 7 to 11 p.m. Reservations are advised.

Yarlbury Cottage, Lower Bockhampton, near Dorchester (tel. 0305/62382), is a thatch-roofed cottage with inglenook and beamed ceilings in a small country village in the heart of Hardy country and, in fact, within walking distance of Thomas Hardy's cottage and of Stinsford Church, where his heart is buried.

The restaurant, particularly popular with locals and visitors alike in summer at lunchtime, has good food and a warm atmosphere. You might choose from cold dishes such as roast beef, fresh salmon, or ham, although a hot dish of the day and a ploughman's lunch are also offered. The à la carte menu in the evening is short but special. A specialty is the English lamb. Good sauces and lightly cooked fresh vegetables are important. Lunches cost from £5 ($8.75) and dinners from £10 ($17.50). Reservations are required for dinner. The restaurant is open all year, but hours are shortened in winter, so check first. In summer, it's best to go from noon to 2 p.m. and 7 to 9 p.m. daily.

FLEET AIR ARM MUSEUM AND CONCORDE EXHIBITION

This museum at the Royal Naval Air Station, Yeovilton in Somerset (tel. 0935/840565), contains the largest collection of historic military aircraft in Europe, including the Concorde 002. It also displays scale models and other memorabilia associated with the RN Air Service and the Fleet Air Arm. Flying displays from the airfield can be viewed from the car park area. Special exhibitions include the Falkland Islands conflict and the Japanese Kamikaze suicide bombers of World War II. Hours are from 10 a.m. to 5:30 p.m. daily from March to October, and from 10 a.m. to 4:30 p.m. from November to February. Admission is £3 ($5.25) for adults, £1.50 ($2.65) for children. There are a tea room and a picnic area. From Dorchester, we continue west 15 miles to:

10. Bridport

In Thomas Hardy's fictional Wessex terrain, Bridport was Port Bredy. The town lies inland, although there is a harbor one mile away at the holiday resort of West Bay, near the end of Chesil Beach. Ropes and fishing nets are Bridport specialties. Many a man dangled from the end of a Bridport dagger—that is, a rope—especially when some homegrown rebels were carted off to Dorchester to face Hanging Judge Jeffreys.

An interesting excursion from Bridport is to visit **Parnham** at Beaminster (tel. 0308/862204). One of the loveliest houses in Dorset, it stands in a wooded valley beside the River Brit. Since Tudor times it has been surrounded by sweeping lawns and magnificent trees, along with terraces and falling water. In 1976 John Makepeace, internationally known designer and furniture-maker, bought Parnham, made it his home, and set up his workshop in the former stables. Here his team of artisans make the unique pieces of exquisite commissioned furniture Makepeace designs and on which his reputation is based. The well-restored rooms of the great house display recently completed pieces from the workshop, and there are monthly exhibitions by Britain's leading contemporary artists, designers, and artisans. The ornate plastered ceilings, paneled walls, and stone fireplaces are a splendid setting for the best of 20th-century design and craftsmanship.

Light lunches and teas with homemade cakes and local clotted cream are served in the 17th-century licensed buttery. The house, gardens, exhibitions, and workshop are open from 10 a.m. to 5 p.m. on Wednesday, Sunday, and bank holidays from Easter to October. Admission is £2.50 ($4.40) for adults and £1.20 ($2.10) for children. Parnham is on the A3066, five miles north of Bridport.

FOOD AND LODGING

A 16th-century coaching inn, the **Bull Hotel,** 34 East St., Bridport, Dorset DT6 3LF (tel. 0308/22878), now houses wayfarers in one of its 22 bedrooms, which come with a variety of plumbing options. Each is comfortable, neat, and clean. With an English breakfast included, singles are priced from £16.50 ($28.90) to £29 ($50.75) daily, with doubles costing from £31 ($54.25) to £40 ($70). In 1939, George VI stopped here, and you may want to follow in his footsteps. Nonresidents can patronize its restaurant, the Dorset Room, where fixed-price lunches cost £7 ($12.25) and are served daily from noon to 2 p.m. A set dinner is offered for £8.50 ($14.90), and is served from 7:15 to 9:15 p.m. You can also order à la carte, enjoying such dishes as steak au poivre, grilled salmon, and lobster thermidor.

A good bet for the budget is **Britmead House,** 154 West Bay Rd., Bridport, Dorset DT6 4EG (tel. 0308/22941), which lies south of the A35 between Bridport and the harbor at West Bay. You get personal attention here and good clean rooms, most of which contain a full private bath along with such amenities as beverage-making equipment, hairdryers, a mini-bar, and color TV. Six bedrooms are rented at a cost ranging from £17.50 ($30.63) to £24.50 ($42.90) daily in a single, rising to £28 ($49) to £36 ($63) in a double. The house also has a good restaurant that makes extensive use of locally caught seafood and produce.

Eype's Mouth Country Hotel, Eype, Bridport, Dorset DT6 6AL (tel. 0308/ 23300), lies 1 ½ miles west of Bridport and a mile south of the A35 Bridport–Lyme Regis road. It is a gracious country house a five-minute walk from the beach. All 18 bedrooms have private baths, color TV, phones, and tea- and coffee-makers. The hotel is centrally heated. The charge for B&B in a double or twin is £38.50 ($67.40) nightly, a single going for £30 ($52.50). The hotel, owned by Mr. and Mrs. Rawlings, has a fine restaurant, providing meals for nonresidents as well as hotel guests. The Captain's Bar is an old-world cellar bar where beer and food are available. It leads off onto a pretty garden patio overlooking the sea.

11. Chideock

A model village of West Dorset, Chideock is bathed in charm. In this main-road hamlet of thatched houses, a mellowed stone is used for most of the buildings. A dairy farm is found in the village itself. About a mile from the coast, it's a gem of a place for overnight stopovers or even longer stays. The beautiful countryside, with its rolling hills, makes excursions a temptation.

The Duke and Duchess of York live at Chideock Manor, a handsome old stone structure. Perhaps you'll see Fergie somewhere around the village or countryside.

FOOD AND LODGING

At the edge of the village, **Betchworth House,** Chideock, Dorset DT6 6JW (tel. 0297/89478), is a 17th-century guesthouse on the main road. Owned by Mr. and Mrs. David Scott, it purveys accommodations that are immaculate, homey, and a good bargain—£12 ($21) to £16 ($28) per person daily for B&B. The house is open all year. There's a large free car park just opposite the house, and a walled garden in back of the building where you can sit and enjoy the peace among the flowers.

The 15th-century **Chideock House Hotel,** Chideock, Dorset DT6 6JN (tel. 0297/89242), perhaps the prettiest thatched house in Chideock, is set near the road, with a protective stone wall and a rear garden of flowers, shrubs, and fruit trees. A driveway through the gardens leads to a large car park in the rear. You go directly into the beamed lounge, with its two fireplaces, one an Adam fireplace with a wood-burning blaze on cool days. Most of the bedrooms have private baths, and all have TV and coffee-making equipment. You can stay here on a B&B basis at a cost beginning at £18 ($31.50) per person daily. The cuisine is a local favorite with the best dessert table in town and offers a good table d'hôte or à la carte menu, served from 7 to 9 p.m. daily. The house quartered the Roundheads in 1645, and the ghosts of the village martyrs are still said to haunt it, as their trial was held at the hotel. Resident owners are Derek and Jenny Hammond.

The Thatch Cottage, Chideock, Dorset DT6 6JE (tel. 0297/89794), is essentially a summer resort, but there are those who welcome the idea of staying winter weekends, snugly sitting in front of the fireplace after enjoying good home cooking. The owner of this 17th-century cottage, Philip Hughes, accepts paying guests all year. A table d'hôte dinner at £8 ($14) is featured. Fresh local produce is a specialty. Most of the year, the charge is £12.50 ($21.90) per person daily for B&B. With dinner, the rate becomes £19 ($33.25) per person. If you want to walk to the beach, you can ask your host to pack a picnic lunch. It's best to make Chideock your center for a week, exploring the many sights in the area on day trips. Reservations are necessary from June to September.

Dating from 1685, the **George Inn** (tel. 0297/89414) is the oldest establishment in the village, right on the A35. The owners, Mike and Marilyn Tuck, extend a warm welcome to all and offer food either in the bar or dining room. Three-course meals can be obtained for prices from £8 ($14), featuring daily specials such as venison in wine sauce and veal à la crème. The George Inn is fully licensed, with facilities for children, a game room, and a well-kept beer garden. The pub serves food from noon to 2 p.m. and 6:30 to 10 p.m. daily. À la carte three-course meals cost from £4 ($7) to £6 ($10.50).

---

12. Charmouth

On Lyme Bay, Charmouth is still another winner. A village of Georgian houses and thatched cottages, Charmouth contains some of the most dramatic coastal scenery in West Dorset. The village lies to the west of Golden Cap, which is—according to the adventurers who measure such things—the highest cliff along the coast of southern England.

Catherine of Aragon, the first of Henry VIII's six wives and the daughter of Ferdinand and Isabella of Spain, stayed in **Queen's Armes Hotel,** Charmouth, Dorset DT6 6QF (tel. 0297/60339), near the sea. A small medieval house, it also figured in the flight of the defeated King Charles, the Roundheads in hot pursuit. Since the Queen's Armes is right on the road, you may not suspect its inner charm: a rear flower garden, oak beams, a dining room with dark oak tables and Windsor chairs, and the living room with its Regency armchairs and antiques. Out of 11 rooms, ten have private baths, and all have color TV. B&B costs £20 ($35) to £23.50 ($41.15) per person daily, depending on the season (prices are higher during Christmas week). For an additional £12.50 ($21.90) per person, you can have dinner. The hotel specializes in well-prepared English fare, with some continental dishes, and there's a vegetarian menu.

Newlands House, Stonebarrow Lane, Charmouth, Dorset DT6 6RA (tel. 0297/60212), lies on the periphery of the village, within walking distance of the beach. Originally a 16th-century farmhouse, it is set in 1½ acres of grounds at the foot of Stonebarrow Hill, which is part of the National Trust Golden Cup Estate. It draws favorable reports from readers for its comfortable and well-furnished bedrooms, all centrally heated and equipped with color TV and tea- and coffee-making facilities, as well as private baths. The rate for B&B ranges from £14.25 ($24.95) to £16.25 ($28.45) per person nightly, depending on the accommodation assigned. It's also possible to take half board, costing from £21.75 ($38.05) to £23.75 ($41.55) per person nightly.

---

13. Lyme Regis

On Lyme Bay near the Devonshire border, the resort of Lyme Regis is one of the most attractive centers along the South Coast. For those who shun such big commercial holiday centers as Torquay or Bournemouth, Lyme Regis may be ideal—the true English coastal town, with a highly praised mild climate. Sea gulls fly overhead; the streets are steep and winding; walks along Cobb Beach are brisk and stimulating; the views, particularly of the craft in the harbor, are photogenic. Following Lyme Regis's career as a major seaport (the Duke of Monmouth landed here to begin his unsuccessful attempt to become king), one finds it was a small spa for a while, catering to such visitors as Jane Austen, who was also fond of nearby Charmouth.

The stone breakwater, the Cobb, was immortalized in the book and film *The French Lieutenant's Woman.* As you walk on the Cobb—and everybody does—the waves crash around you, and as a backdrop you have the Dorset cliffs, which seem to tumble into the sea. The actors stayed in the town's two main hotels, and John Fowles, the book's author, is a resident of Lyme Regis.

The town also boasts the 1979–1981 world champion and best-dressed town crier. Richard Fox is just maintaining a tradition that has been handed down for

1000 years in Lyme Regis when he announces the local news. He'll also take visitors on a two-hour tour of the resort on Tuesday and Thursday at 3 p.m. to see the Cobb, the harbor from which ships sailed to fight the Spanish Armada. The walks head up old Broad Street. Mr. Fox can be reached at Flat 2, 22a Broad St. Lr. (tel. 02974/3568).

The surrounding area is a fascinating place for fossilism. Mary Anning discovered in 1810 at the age of 11 one of the first articulated ichthyosaur skeletons. She went on to become one of the first professional fossilists in the country. Books telling of walks in the area and the regions where the fossils can be seen are available at the local information bureau in the Guildhall on Bridge Street (tel. 02974/2138).

WHERE TO STAY

Some 100 yards from the sea, the **Three Cups Hotel,** Broad Street, Lyme Regis, Dorset DT7 3QE (tel. 02974/2732), is on the main street close to the shops. About 200 years old, it boasts a handsome columned entrance with a Regency bow window above, which was used in the film *The French Lieutenant's Woman.* Inside the hotel, the rooms are light and airy, some with sea views, with features such as stained-glass windows and sloping corridors giving added character. There are 20 bedrooms, seven of which have private baths. All have hot and cold running water, tea- and coffee-makers, radios, and TV. From April to October, accommodations cost from £18.50 ($32.40) to £19.75 ($34.55) per person daily. Off-season, prices are reduced to £14.50 ($25.40) per person. Breakfast is included in the tariffs, and there is a daily surcharge of £8.50 ($14.90) per room for a unit with private bath or shower. The hotel has a restaurant serving à la carte meals daily from noon to 2 p.m. and 6:30 to 9 p.m., costing from £12 ($21).

The White House, 47 Silver St., Lyme Regis, Dorset DT7 3HR (tel. 02974/3420), is a small, centrally heated guesthouse run by John and Ann Edmondson. It is only a few minutes' walk from the harbor and the center of town. The house is attractively furnished and well maintained, offering B&B from £11.50 ($20.15) per person daily. Of the house's seven rooms, five are doubles and two have twin beds. Four have private shower, toilet, and basin, while one has a basin and shower and two have basins only. All units have tea- and coffee-making facilities, color TV, and digital clock radios. A large lounge is set aside for residents. The White House is fully licensed and has a private car park.

Norman House, Coombe Street, Lyme Regis, Dorset DT7 3PP (tel. 02974/3191), is one of the best B&Bs in the area. Built in the 1500s, it opens onto a historic narrow street at the foot of Lyme Regis, a short walk from the Guildhall, the sea wall fronting the Channel, and the local museum. Readers James and Nancy Heldman, who found this place for me, write: "The owner, Mrs. Franklin, is gracious and cultivated, a warm lady who goes out of her way to make her guests feel that they are visiting her." She rents one double (with private bath), plus four other doubles and a single with a shared bath. The rate is from £9.50 ($16.65) per person daily for B&B.

WHERE TO EAT

Down by the Cobb, the **Cobb Arms,** Marine Parade (tel. 02974/3242), is a pub right on the harborside where you can order bar snacks such as braised beef with vegetables. There are grill dishes to order as well. As you eat, you can look over the harbor in much the same way the French lieutenant's woman did. It was in this pub that members of the cast were dressed and made up for their parts in the film. In summer, hot food is served only from noon to 3 p.m. and 7 to 9:30 or 10 p.m. daily. During the afternoon, sandwiches can be ordered from the menu. In winter only, lunch is served daily from noon to 2 or 2:30 p.m., depending on business. Meals cost from £4 ($7) to £8 ($14).

Next to the inn is the Lifeboat Station, with its boat ever ready to put to sea to rescue sailors in distress.

---

14. Donyatt

After Lyme Regis, you may want to journey to Donyatt, a village near Ilminster. Just outside the village, between the A303 and the A30 London–West Country roads, stands **Thatchers Pond** (tel. 04605/3210), a 15th-century thatched hamstone (a local rock) farmhouse. There is a vast cold table here for lunch and dinner daily, except Monday. The house is warm and welcoming, with old clocks, guns, and swords adorning the walls of the flagstoned hall and carpeted dining room. Meals are served from a vast table laden with fresh lobster, salmon, crab, prawns, cold roast beef, ham, tongue, homemade pâté, quiches, and mousse. After your choice from the buffet, you are invited to help yourself from a selection of 25 different salads. The main course is large enough, but if you're a gourmand, you can choose from a range of appetizers. The dessert trolley or the cheese board will supply the finish to your meal. The bar offers beers, wines, spirits, liqueurs, coffee, and tea. Lunch from the buffet costs £9 ($15.25), and dinner goes for £12 ($21). Thatchers is open from noon to 2 p.m. and 7 to 9 p.m. It closes Saturday at lunch, Sunday evening, and all day Monday.

---

15. Sherborne

A little gem of a town with well-preserved medieval, Tudor, Stuart, and Georgian buildings, Sherborne is in the heart of Dorset in a setting of wooded hills, valleys, and chalk downs. It was here that Sir Walter Raleigh lived before the vicissitudes of power dislodged him forever.

Sherborne Old Castle (tel. 093581/2730), a half mile east of the town, was built in the early 12th century by the powerful Bishop Roger de Caen, but it was soon seized by the Crown about the time of the death of King Henry I in 1135 and the troubled accession to the throne of Stephen. The castle was given to Sir Walter Raleigh by Queen Elizabeth. The gallant knight built Sherborne Lodge on the grounds. The buildings were mostly destroyed in the Civil War, but you can still see a gatehouse, some graceful arcades, and decorative windows. The castle ruins can be visited from 10 a.m. to 6 p.m. daily from Good Friday to September 30. From November 1 to Maundy Thursday, hours are from 10 a.m. to 4 p.m.; closed Monday, three days at Christmas, and New Year's Day.

Sherborne Castle (tel. 0935/813182) was built by Sir Walter Raleigh in 1594, when he decided that it would not be feasible to restore the old castle to suit him. His new home was an Elizabethan residence, a square mansion, which later owners gussied up with four Jacobean wings to make it more palatial. After King James I had Raleigh imprisoned in the Tower of London, the monarch gave the castle to a favorite Scot, Robert Carr, so that the Raleighs were banished from their home. It became the property of Sir John Digby, first Earl of Bristol, in 1617 and has been the Digby family home ever since. The mansion was enlarged by Sir John in 1625, and in the 18th century, the formal Elizabethan gardens and fountains of the Raleighs were altered by Capability Brown, who created a serpentine lake between the two castles. The 20 acres of lawns and pleasure grounds around the 50-acre lake are open to the public. In the house are fine furniture, china, and paintings by Gainsborough, Lely, Reynolds, Kneller, and Van Dyck, among other artists. Easter Saturday to the end of September, the house is open on Thursday, Saturday, Sunday, and bank holiday Mondays from 2 to 6 p.m. Admission to the castle is £2.70 ($4.75) for adults, £1.35 ($2.35) for children; to the grounds only, £1 ($1.75) for adults, 50p (90¢) for children.

Sherborne Abbey is worth visiting to see the splendid fan vaulting of the roof, as well as the many monuments, including Purbeck marble effigies of medieval abbots and the Elizabethan four-posters and canopied Renaissance tombs. A baroque statue of the Earl of Bristol, standing between his two wives, was carved in 1698. The church is open daily until dusk. Many of the abbey's medieval monastic buildings are still in existence, used today to house a school. This British public school was the setting of a novel by Alec Waugh, *The Loom of Youth*.

FOOD AND LODGING

Once one of the shire's mellow old tollhouses, **Farthing Gate,** Holnest, near Sherborne, Dorset DT9 5PX (tel. 096321/479), lies in the hamlet of Holnest, four miles north of Sherborne, midway between Sherborne and Dorchester. Originally built in the 16th century of foot-thick stone walls, it was used to collect one farthing from passengers as toll for use of the highway. Today, it has been turned into a pleasant guesthouse with a garden and a glassed-in conservatory. The owners, the Veall family, rent two double bedrooms, each comfortably and attractively furnished, from April to October. Accommodations are bathless, costing from £20 ($35) to £22 ($38.50) for two nightly, with breakfast included.

A more substantial hotel is **Half Moon,** Half Moon Street, Sherborne, Dorset DT9 3LN (tel. 0935/812017), centrally located in Sherborne, in a red-brick 17th-century building opposite the abbey. It rents 15 well-furnished and comfortable bedrooms, all with private baths, for £40 ($70) daily in a single, £50 ($87.50) in a double, and £60 ($105) in a quad or family room. Discounts of around £10 ($17.50) per room are offered for stays on Friday, Saturday, and Sunday nights. The carvery restaurant serves daily from noon to 2 p.m. and 6 to 10 p.m., offering one of the best food values in town at a cost of £6.25 ($10.95) for a meal.

IX

DEVON

1. EXETER

2. DARTMOOR

3. CHAGFORD

4. TORBAY (TORQUAY)

5. TOTNES

6. DARTMOUTH

7. SALCOMBE

8. PLYMOUTH

9. CLOVELLY

10. COMBE MARTIN AND LYNTON-LYNMOUTH

The great patchwork-quilt area of the southwest of England, part of the "West Countree," abounds with cliffside farms, rolling hills, foreboding moors, semitropical plants, and fishing villages—all of which combine to provide some of the finest scenery in England. The British from other parts of the country approach the sunny counties of Devon and Cornwall (see next chapter) with the same kind of excitement one would normally reserve for hopping over to the continent. Especially along the coastline, the British Riviera, many of the names of the little seaports, villages, and resorts have become synonymous with holidays in the sun: Torquay, Clovelly, Lynton-Lynmouth.

It's easy to involve yourself in the West Country life, as lived by the British vacationers. Perhaps you'll go pony-trekking across moor and woodland, past streams and sheep-grazing fields, stopping off at local pubs to soak up atmosphere and mugs of ale. Chances are your oddly shaped bedroom will be in a barton (farm) mentioned in the *Domesday Book* or in a thatch-roofed cottage neither straight, level, nor true.

Fishermen may catch their lunch (salmon and trout in such rivers as the Dart), then take it back to the kitchen of their guesthouse to be grilled. Life is often most informal. Your hosts, many being of farming stock themselves, don't like to muck about putting on airs for tourists. In the morning, your landlady might be out picking string beans for your dinner. Later she'll bring up pails from the milk house, and you can watch her create her own version of clotted Devonshire cream cooked on the back of the stove. For dessert that night, you'll get a country portion heaped on your freshly picked gooseberries.

When a Devonian invites you to walk down the primrose path, he or she means just that. The primrose is practically the shire flower of this most beautiful of counties. Devon is a land of jagged coasts—the red cliffs in the south facing the English Channel, the gray cliffs in the north opening onto the Bristol Channel. Sandwiched between them is some of the most widely varied scenery in England, ranging from heartlands and wooded valleys to buzzard-haunted combes. Aside from the shores, a great many of the scenic splashes appear in the two national parks, **Dartmoor** in the south, **Exmoor** in the north.

A SPECIAL BUS TICKET

The two main bus companies of Devon and Cornwall combine to offer a **Key West ticket,** granting unlimited travel anywhere on the two networks for any seven consecutive days at a cost of £15 ($26.25) for adults and £10 ($17.50) for children under 14. You can plan your journeys from the maps and timetables available at any Western National/Devon General offices when you purchase your ticket. Further information may be obtained from Devon General Ltd., Belgrave Road, Exeter, Devon EX1 2LB (tel. 0392/439333).

SOUTH DEVON

It can be the lazy life in South Devon, as you recline in an orchard, enjoying the view of the coast from which native sons Raleigh and Drake set sail. Almost every little hamlet, on some level, is geared to accommodate visitors, who flock here in great numbers from early spring to late fall. There is much to see and explore. Mainly the tranquil life prevails.

1. Exeter

The county town of Devonshire on the banks of the Exe River, Exeter was a Roman city founded in the first century A.D. Two centuries later it was encircled by a mighty stone wall, traces of which remain today. Conquerors and would-be conquerors, especially the Vikings, stormed the fortress in the centuries ensuing. None was more notable than William the Conqueror. Irked at Exeter's refusal to capitulate (and perhaps at the sheltering of Gytha, mother of the slain Harold), the Norman duke brought Exeter to its knees in short order.

Under the Tudors the city grew and prospered. The cocky Sir Walter Raleigh and Sir Francis Drake cut striking figures strolling through Exeter's medieval and Elizabethan streets. Regrettably, in May of 1942 the skies over Exeter were suddenly filled with German bombers. When their merciless task was over, Exeter was in flames. One of the most beautiful and historic cities of England was a mere shell of its former self. Exeter grew back, of course, but the new, impersonal-looking shops and offices couldn't replace the Georgian crescents, or the black-and-white timbered buildings with their plastered walls. Fortunately, much was spared, including the major architectural treasure—

EXETER CATHEDRAL

Owing its present look to the Decorated style of the 13th and 14th centuries, the Exeter Cathedral of St. Peter (tel. 0392/55573) actually goes back to Saxon times. Even Canute, the Viking conqueror, got in on the act of rebuilding around 1017. The Norman cathedral of Bishop Warelwast came into being in the early 12th century, and the north and south towers serve as reminders of that period. The remarkable feature of the present Gothic building is the interior, with its tierceron vaulting stretching out for some 300 feet. The cathedral did suffer damage in the 1942 German bombings, which destroyed its St. James's Chapel (subsequently restored). But most of the treasures remain intact, including the rows of sculpture along the west front, the 14th-century Minstrels' Gallery, and the bishop's throne. The cathedral asks that visitors contribute at least £1 ($1.75) toward its upkeep for the future.

EXETER MARITIME MUSEUM

At the Quay (tel. 0392/58075), the maritime museum has a collection of more than 160 small craft, many of which are on display, and it shelters the world's largest collection of English and foreign craft from the Congo to Corfu. The larger boats afloat in the canal basin can be boarded. There are canoes and boats that have been rowed across the Atlantic, and you can go aboard the oldest working steamboat or even picnic on a Hong Kong junk or an Arab dhow. This is an active museum, and the ISCA members who maintain the boats sail some of them during the summer months. Five colorful Portuguese chatas are available for rent at the museum from May to September, each carrying a maximum of six passengers. The boats are rowed along the three miles of navigable water on the historic canal at a charge of £2 ($3.50) per hour. The museum is open every day of the year, except Christmas and Boxing Day, from 10 a.m. to 5 p.m. October to June, and from 10 a.m. to 6 p.m. July to September. Adults pay an admission of £3 ($5.25), and children, £1.75 ($3.05).

Note: Occasionally, individual boats for special events or sailing may not be on display.

OTHER ATTRACTIONS

Much of the old remains. The **Exeter Guildhall,** a colonnaded building on the High Street (tel. 0392/265500), is regarded as the oldest municipal building in the kingdom. The earliest reference to the Guildhall is contained in a deed of 1160. The Tudor front that straddles the pavement was added in 1593. Inside is a fine display of silver in the gallery. It contains a number of paintings as well, including one of Henrietta Anne, daughter of Charles I (she was born in Exeter in 1644). The ancient hall is paneled in oak. The Guildhall is open throughout the year, Monday to Saturday from 10 a.m. to 5:30 p.m., when civic functions permit, and admission is free.

Just off "The High" is a green historic oasis. At the top of Castle Street stands an impressive Norman Gate House from William the Conqueror's Castle. Although only the house and walls survive, the view from here and the surrounding gardens is spectacular. Just by the Gate House is a charming Regency villa, adapted from an earlier house and now the **Rougemont House Museum of Costume and Lace,** Castle Street (tel. 0392/265858), which is open daily from 10 a.m. to 5:30 p.m. The museum features costumes displayed in period rooms (these change twice a year), along with one of the largest lace collections in Europe. It charges £1.70 ($3) for adults and 70p ($1.25) for children.

On the way to the Quay you will pass the Underground Passages, the subterranean water-supply channels of medieval times. **St. Nicholas Priory,** The Mint, off Fore Street (tel. 0392/265858), is open Tuesday to Saturday from 10 a.m. to 5:30 p.m., charging adults 60p ($1.05) and children 30p (55¢). This is the guest wing of a Benedictine priory founded in 1070. You'll see fine plaster ceilings and period furniture.

On the Outskirts

Powderham Castle, Powderham (tel. 0626/890243), lies eight miles south of Exeter off the A379 Dawlish road. A castle here was built in the late 14th century by Sir Philip Courtenay, sixth son of the second Earl of Devon, and his wife, Margaret, granddaughter of Edward I. Their magnificent tomb is in the South Transept of Exeter Cathedral. The castle suffered damage during the Civil War and was restored and altered in the 18th and 19th centuries, but its towers and battlements are still pure 14th century. The castle contains much fine furniture, including a remarkable clock that plays full tunes at 4, 8, and 12 o'clock, some 17th-century tapestries, and a chair used by William III for his first Council of State at Newton Abbot. The staircase hall contains some remarkable plasterwork set in bold relief against a brilliant turquoise background more than two centuries old, as well as a detailed pedigree of the Courtenay family, a document more than 12 feet high. The chapel dates from the 15th century, with hand-hewn roof timbers and carved pew ends. Powderham Castle is a private house lived in by Lord and Lady Courtenay and family. From the Sunday of the late spring bank holiday to the second Thursday in September, the castle is open daily from 2 to 5:30 p.m., except Friday and Saturday, when it's closed. Admission is £2.75 ($4.80) for adults, £1.75 ($3.05) for children 8 to 16.

WHERE TO STAY

On the outskirts of the town, the **Lea-Dene,** 34 Alphington Rd. (A377), St. Thomas, Exeter, Devon EX2 8HN (tel. 0392/57257), is a semidetached Edwardian house with gardens. Mr. and Mrs. Rogers offer a lot of extras, including a large free car park mainly behind the house, a double garage, a choice of evening meals, family rooms (with cots and highchairs), full central heating, a public phone, a color TV lounge (the units also have private color TV sets), and free baths and showers. They'll also provide a babysitting service, and will even arrange for special diets if given advance notice. Each bedroom is carpeted and well furnished, and rates are from £12 ($21) to £15 ($26.25) per person daily for B&B. Regular bus service into the center of town goes right by the front door.

Trenance House Hotel, 1 Queen's Crescent, York Road, Exeter, Devon EX4 6AY (tel. 0392/73277), is one of the best B&Bs in town, lying just three minutes from the heart of town in the vicinity of the coach station. The resident owners, the Breading family, welcome guests to their 14 comfortably furnished bedrooms, some of which contain a private bath or shower. Singles pay from £14 ($24.50) to £15 ($26.25) daily, depending on the plumbing, and doubles cost from £22 ($38.50) to £25 ($43.75) on the same basis.

Sylvania House, 64 Pennsylvania Rd., Exeter, Devon EX4 6DF (tel. 0392/ 75583), is a spacious Edwardian house that was designed by a sea captain for his retirement. Many of the original characteristics have been preserved in its conversion to a comfortable hotel. All rooms are large and most have private baths. Each unit is well furnished and has color TV and beverage-making facilities. The charge is £11 ($19.25) per person daily for double occupancy of a bathless room, £14 ($24.50) for a room with private bath. A full English breakfast is included. The establishment is about ten minutes from the center of Exeter, lying in a tranquil residential area in the vicinity of the university.

Claremont, 36 Wonford Rd., Exeter, Devon EX2 4LD (tel. 0392/74699), is a Regency-style town house (circa 1840), which lies within a quiet residential part of the city, yet is within easy access to the heart. All its bedrooms are well kept, and each has hot and cold running water (some have a private bath or shower), as well as beverage-making equipment. B&B costs from £14 ($24.50) to £16 ($28) daily in a single, rising to £22 ($38.50) to £24 ($42) in a double, including breakfast. Geoff and Jacqui Self, who run the property, welcome both British and foreign visitors and assist them in many ways, such as by storing luggage for them until their return.

Trees, 2 Queen's Crescent, York Road, Exeter, Devon EX4 6AY (tel. 0392/ 59531), is a "mini-hotel" run by Dick and Bridget Bigwood, about a five-minute walk from the city center, near the bus station. There are 12 bedrooms, all with washbasins, shaver points, and TV. The B&B rate is £12 ($21) daily in a single, £21

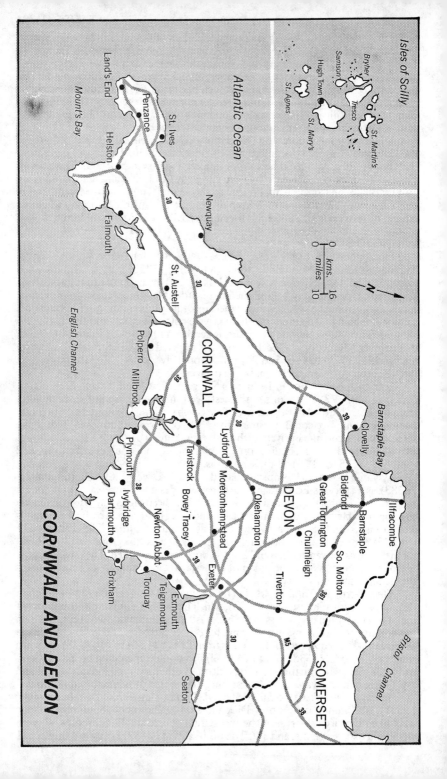

CORNWALL AND DEVON

($36.75) in a double, and £28 ($49) in a twin-bedded room, the latter with private bath. The Bigwoods welcome their guests with a smile and a pot of tea.

If you're driving, your best bet might be the **Lord Haldon Hotel,** Dunchideock, near Exeter, Devon EX6 7YF (tel. 0392/832483), which was constructed in 1735 as the seat of the Lords of Haldon. A major part of the original structure was destroyed in this century, but the remaining wing has been converted into a country-house hotel that still retains an archway created by 18th-century architect Sir Robert Adam. All 26 rooms have private baths or showers, TV, tea- and coffee-makers, and direct-dial phones. The views from the majority of the rooms are of the countryside. The B&B rate is from £22 ($38.50) daily in a single and from £44 ($77) in a double. There are four rooms with four-poster beds as well as executive suites. The best rate is for half board, from £29 ($50.75) per person daily. The meals are reliable, using fresh local produce in traditional British dishes.

Gipsy Hill, Gipsy Hill Lane, via Pinn Lane, Pinhoe, Exeter, Devon EX1 3RN (tel. 0392/65252), is a late Victorian country-house hotel standing in beautiful gardens close to the heart of the city and the airport (it is also suitable for motorists and within easy reach of M5 junction 30). Family operated, this brick house has been modernized and offers 20 well-appointed bedrooms, each with private bath. For such amenities, you expect to pay more than typical B&B prices: from £38 ($66.50) in a single and from £49 ($85.75) in a double. A couple of rooms have four-poster beds, and these are highly desired. A restaurant on the premises serves both British and continental dishes.

WHERE TO EAT

A short walk from the cathedral, **Ship Inn,** Martin's Lane (tel. 0392/72040), was often visited by Sir Francis Drake, Sir Walter Raleigh, and Sir John Hawkins. Of it Drake wrote: "Next to mine own shippe, I do most love that old 'Shippe' in Exon, a tavern in Fyssh Street, as the people call it, or as the clergie will have it, St. Martin's Lane." The pub still provides tankards of ale, lager, and stout and is still loved by both young and old. A large selection of snacks is offered in the bar every day, while the restaurant upstairs provides more substantial English fare. Main courses, including vegetables, roll, and butter, will cost from £6 ($10.50) to £10 ($17.50). Portions are large, as in Elizabethan times. The restaurant is open from noon to 2 p.m. Monday to Saturday and from 6:30 to 10 p.m. Monday to Thursday, and 6:30 to 10:30 p.m. Friday and Saturday. It is closed Sunday and bank holidays. The bar is open from 11 a.m. to 2:30 p.m. and 5 to 11 p.m. Monday to Saturday, and from noon to 2 p.m. and 7 to 10:30 p.m. Sunday.

The **Port Royal Inn,** The Quay (tel. 0392/72360), stands close to the Maritime Museum, along the edge of the River Exe, a two-minute walk from the quay. In fair weather, tables are placed outside overlooking the river. This is a real ale house, also known for its ports and sherries. With such a name, the pub reminds one of smugglers in the Caribbean, intrepid explorers, and famous navigators. The bar food offered will revive the inner person in a more modern way. Salads are tempting, and you can also order a ploughman's lunch or pâté and toast. Sandwiches made from granary bread are filled with meat or cheese. There are also mini-loaves of white or granary bread filled with salad, cheese, or meat. Each day they provide two or three hot specials such as seafood, roast chicken, and roast lamb. There are also desserts and coffee with cream, and the pub serves real ales from various breweries. All food is ordered at the pub but will be delivered to your table by a waitress. Meals cost from £6 ($10.50). Lunch is served daily from 11 a.m. to 2:30 p.m. and dinner from 6 to 10 p.m. The inn is open seven days a week.

At **Coolings Wine Bar,** 11 Gandy St. (tel. 0392/434183), the family who runs this place welcomes guests as friends, even if they don't know you. It's a little hideaway that is both unpretentious and enjoyable. The beams overhead are familiar enough, and the bright tables create an English version of a bistro. You're also allowed to dine below in the cellar, which is most atmospheric Everything tastes fresh here. Try the daily specials, or, at the serve-yourself counter, you can make up your own smörgåsbord-inspired plate. Expect to spend from £6 ($10.50) up. Hours are from 11 a.m. to 11 p.m. Monday to Saturday, and from noon to 3 p.m. and 7 to 10:30 p.m. Sunday.

LIVING ON THE OUTSKIRTS

Perhaps the finest way to enjoy the cathedral city of Exeter, especially if you have a car, is to live on the outskirts, from 10 to 19 miles from the heart of the city.

At Whimple

Nine miles from Sidmouth, which lies on the South Devon coast, and ten miles from Exeter, **Down House,** Whimple, Devon EX5 2QR (tel. 0404/822860), is an ideal base for touring in Devon. Alan and Vicky Jiggins welcome visitors to their gracious Edwardian gentleman's farmhouse set in five acres of garden and paddocks. Guests can relax in the elegant lounge or on the terrace and enjoy the fine cuisine in which garden fruit and vegetables and local eggs are used. B&B costs from £10 ($17.50) to £14 ($24.50) per person daily, with an evening meal served from £7($12.25).

At Bickleigh

In the Exe Valley, four miles south of Tiverton and nine miles north of Exeter, lies a hamlet with a river, an arched stone bridge, a mill pond, and thatch-roofed cottages—a cliché of English charm, one of the finest spots in all of Devon.

Bickleigh Cottage Country Hotel, Bickleigh Bridge, Bickleigh, Devon EX16 8RJ (tel. 08845/230), is a thatched, 17th-century guesthouse with a riverside garden leading down to the much-photographed Bickleigh Bridge. Add to this image swans and ducks gliding by to get your leftover crumbs from tea on the lawn. Mr. and Mrs. Stuart Cochrane, the owners, charge from £11.50 ($20.15) to £14 ($24.50) per person nightly for B&B. In a room with a private bath, the rate is from £14.50 ($25.40) per person nightly. Meals are good and nourishing. The raspberries and gooseberries come fresh from the garden, topped with generous portions of Devonshire cream. Dinner is priced from £7.50 ($13.15). Inside, the rooms are cozy, with oak beams and old fireplaces. The no. 354 bus runs between Exeter and Tiverton, if you don't have a car.

Trout, Bickleigh, near Tiverton, Devon EX16 8RJ (tel. 08845/339), on the main Tiverton-Exeter road, the A396, four miles south of Tiverton, is a former 17th-century coaching inn transformed into a pub and a restaurant. The thatch roof is long and low, and there are tiny leaded windows. Former stables have been converted into rooms for dining. One of the favored rooms contains an old fireplace, made from the original bridge stone. A sign indicates that the inn was built in 1630 as a trout hatchery. All year round they have hot and cold bar snacks, home-baked ham, homemade pies, and a selection of salads. The restaurant is open daily in summer for lunch from noon to 2 p.m. and for dinner from 7 to 9:30 p.m. (in winter for dinner only, from 7 to 9 p.m.). A buffet lunch, available all year, goes for £6 ($10.50). There are four double and twin rooms with private baths. They overlook the river. The bedrooms have easy chairs. Bed, a full English breakfast, and VAT cost £17.50 ($30.65) per person daily.

---

2. Dartmoor

Antiquity-rich Dartmoor lies in the southern part of the shire. The **Tors,** huge rock formations of this granite mass, sometimes soar to a height of 2000 feet. The national park is a patchwork quilt of mood changes: gorse and purple heather, gorges with rushing water—a foreboding landscape for the experienced walker only. Look for the beautiful Dartmoor pony.

Accommodation information is available from the Dartmoor Tourist Association, 8 Fitzford Cottages, Tavistock (tel. 0252/3501). Local information centers will also provide a list of accommodations.

Some 13 miles west from Exeter, the peaceful little town of **Moreton Hampstead,** perched on the edge of Dartmoor, makes a good center. Moreton Hampstead contains much that is old, including a market cross and several 17th-century colonnaded almshouses.

The heavily visited Dartmoor village of **Widecombe-in-the-Moor** is only seven miles from Moreton Hampstead. The fame of the village of Widecombe-in-the-Moor stems from an old folk song about Tom Pearce and his gray mare, listing the men who were supposed to be on their way to Widecombe Fair when they met with disaster: Bill Brewer, Jan Stewer, Peter Gurney, Peter Davy, Daniel Whiddon, Harry Hawke, and Old Uncle Tom Cobley. Widecombe also has a parish church worth visiting. Called the **Cathedral of the Moor,** with a roster of vicars beginning in 1253, this house of worship in a green valley is surrounded by legends. When the building was restored, a wall-plate was found bearing the badge of Richard II (1377–1399), the figure of a white hart.

The **National Park Authority** operates a summer bus service throughout the moor. Services have such inviting names as the Pony Express and the Transmoor Link and are an ideal way to get onto the moor to hike the 500 miles of foot- and bridgepaths. The country is rough, and on the high moor you should always make sure you have good maps, a compass, and suitable clothing and shoes. Don't be put off, however. Unless you are a professional hiker, it is unlikely that you will go very far from the well-trodden paths. The park authority also runs guided walks from selected starting points.

Information on the bus links between various villages and towns on Dartmoor is available from Plymouth CityBus, Milehouse, Plymouth (tel. 0752/264888), and from Devon General, Exeter Bus Station, Paris Street, Exeter (tel. 0392/219911).

There are also guided walking tours of varying difficulty, ranging from 1½ hours up to six hours for a trek of some 9 to 12 miles. All you have to do is turn up suitably clad at your selected starting point, and there you are. Details are available from the Dartmoor National Park Information Centres or from the **Dartmoor National Park Authority,** Parke, Haytor Road, Bovey Tracey, Newton Abbot, Devon TQ13 9JQ (tel. 0626/832093). The charge for walks is 70p ($1.25) to £2 ($3.50).

Throughout the area are stables where you can arrange for a day's trek on horseback across the moors. For horse-riding on Dartmoor, there are too many establishments to list. All are licensed, and you are accompanied by an experienced rider/guide. The moor can be dangerous, with sudden fogs descending without warning on treacherous marshlands. All horse-rental stables are listed in a useful free publication, the *Dartmoor Visitor,* obtainable from tourist and visitor centers or by mail. Send an International Reply Coupon to the Dartmoor National Park Authority (address above). Prices are around £3 ($5.25) per hour, £8 ($14) for a half day, and £14 ($24.50) for a full day.

The **Museum of Dartmoor Life,** The Dartmoor Centre, West Street, Okehampton (tel. 0837/53020), owes its existence, with the market town of Okehampton, to the Norman castle built by Baldwin de Bryonis, sheriff of Devon, under orders from his uncle, William the Conqueror, in 1068, just two years after the Conquest. The Courtenay family lived there for many generations until Henry VIII beheaded one of them and dismantled the castle in 1538. The museum is a number of authentic buildings grouped around a courtyard. These include two 19th-century cottages, an agricultural mill, and a printer's workshop. They display farm machinery and some old vehicles: a Devon box wagon of 1875, a 1922 Bullnose Morris motorcar, and a 1937 motorcycle. There is a reconstructed waterwheel, a blacksmithy, a wheelwright's shop, a cider press, domestic items, minerals, industrial equipment, and a courtyard featuring working craft studios, Victorian tea rooms, and a tourist information center. The museum is open March to December from 10 a.m. to 5 p.m. Monday to Saturday (and on Sunday in July and August). Admission is 50p (90¢) for adults, 30p (55¢) for children.

FOOD AND LODGING

Near the heart of Postbridge, **Lydgate House Hotel,** Postbridge, Devon PL20 6TJ (tel. 0822/88209), began life as a squatter's cottage in the early 1700s, but what you'll see today is a mid-Victorian enlargement. The Dart River runs through the grounds, which cover 38 acres. Mr. and Mrs. Beale give guests a warm welcome, providing a comfortable accommodation and English food. Log fires burn on cold nights, but there is also central heating. The breakfasts are generous, as are the dinners. Big windows allow views of the river. In a snug bar, before-dinner drinks are served. Dinner is served nightly at 7:30, a five-course table d'hôte costing £9 ($15.75). Rooms with bath and breakfast rent for £18 ($31.50) per person nightly, or else £27 ($47.25) per person with half board included. Single occupants of a double room pay a £5 ($8.75) surcharge, and rooms without bath qualify for a £2 ($3.50) per person daily discount. From Exeter, take the A38 Plymouth road to Peartree Cross (signposted Ashburton to Dartmoor), follow the B3357 to Two Bridges, and turn right onto the B3212.

Old Walls Farm, Ponsworthy, near Widecombe-in-the-Moor and Newton Abbot, Devon TQ13 7PN (tel. 03643/222), is a substantial, stone-colored plastered country home set remotely on a working farm and reached by narrow lanes. Here you are comfortably in the heart of the moors, and in the safe, knowing hands of owner Bill Fursdon, an expert on the area. He is a genial, white-haired man with a gracious smile who is by avocation a naturalist. He'll take you on a short walk around his farm, showing you his collection of cows, Jack Russell terriers, ducks, a pet goat (its milk is served at breakfast, but it's strictly optional), and a beautiful little river, which gives electric power to the house. He'll make handmade maps, pinpointing the places of interest within driving distance. His house is a living tribute to a fast-disappearing era. He is assisted by his wife, Elizabeth, who plays the organ on Sunday at the village church, and their son, who lives in a separate home close by. Guests relax around a stone fireplace in the drawing room, or on a sunny day enjoy a crescent-shaped, all-glass sun room. From the latter, the view of the moorland is exceptional. The living room has an old grand piano, a Victorian card table, a soft sofa, and armchairs placed in a curving bay recess. The B&B rate is £16 ($28) per person nightly. Breakfast is a special event in the dining room, and you can have as much food as you want.

Old Walls Farm is reached from the A38 dual carriageway between Exeter and Plymouth. Turn right past Ashburton onto the B3357, then right at Poundsgate onto the Ponsworthy-Widecombe road. Go through the hamlet of Ponsworthy, passing the all-purpose post office and store, and look for the B&B sign on the left about 600 yards on.

Leusdon Lodge, Leusdon-Lower Town, Poundsgate, Dartmoor, Devon TQ13 7PE (tel. 03643/304), is a 150-year-old granite country house set in Dartmoor National Park overlooking the Dart Valley. Most of the nine bedrooms have private baths, and there is a family room. Half board in a bathless room (with a handbasin) costs £24 ($42) per person daily. In a room with bath, the price goes up to £26 ($45.50) per person for half board. Traditional English food and a hearty English breakfast are served in the dining room, with hand-carved paneled walls and an ornate fireplace, where logs blaze on winter nights. There is also a cozy bar. Leisure pursuits include horseback riding, canoeing, fishing, and walking the moors. The kitchen will prepare a picnic lunch for guests who participate in outdoor activities.

Lydford House Hotel, Lydford, near Okehampton, Devon EX20 4AU (tel. 082282/347), is a family-run country-house hotel, standing in some eight acres of gardens and pastureland on the outskirts of Lydford, just on the edge of Dartmoor. It was built in 1880 for the Dartmoor artist William Widgery, and several of his paintings hang in the residents' lounge. Owners Ron and Ann Boulter offer varied and interesting menus, all of which feature home-cooking using local produce. The rates are £21 ($36.75) per person per night for a room with private bath, shower, toilet, color TV, tea- and coffee-making facilities, and a full English breakfast, while a table d'hôte dinner costs £9 ($15.75). All prices include taxes. The hotel is seven miles south of Okehampton, just off the A386, and it's on your right as you approach the hamlet of Lydford. Lydford House has its own riding stables in the hotel grounds under the personal supervision of daughter Claire Boulter, BHSAI. Superb riding on Dartmoor is available.

The Old Inn, Widecombe-in-the-Moor (tel. 03642/207), is a real traditional old country inn run by the Boults. There are the usual "olde world" bars, such as the Old Grey Mare Lounge, the Cobley Room, and the public bar, each well patronized by the local farming community. Traditional English country fare is always available, but you can also order superb steaks and many international dishes, including Mexican beef, beef bourguignon, and moussaka. A two-course meal will cost around £6 ($10.50). Hours are Monday to Saturday 11 a.m. to 2:30 p.m. and 6 to 11 p.m., and Sunday noon to 3 p.m. and 7 to 10:30 p.m.

Ring of Bells, North Bovey, Devon TO13 8QY (tel. 0647/40375), is a 13th-century inn in the moorland village, set just off the village green. Here you can sleep in a four-poster bed surrounded by three-foot-thick walls supported by time-blackened beams and have meals in the pub, costing from £3.50 ($6.15). Tony and Brenda Rix, the proprietors, offer B&B for £17.50 ($30.65) per person daily. Meals in the restaurant cost from £7.50 ($13.15). There's ample free parking, and a swimming pool is available during the summer. North Bovey is 1½ miles from Moretonhampstead.

The **White Hart Hotel,** The Square, Moretonhampstead, Newton Abbot, Devon TQ13 8NF (tel. 0647/40406), is a 300-year-old inn, a Georgian posting house on the main street, with a white hart on the portico over the front door. All rooms have bath, tea- and coffee-making facilities, TV, and central heating. They vary in size, and some have beamed ceilings. Meals are taken in the polished dining room graced by a carved sideboard, antique grandfather clock, and magnificent silver candelabra. You may enjoy a drink or snack in the cheerful oak-beamed bar, sharing the warmth of the log fire with the locals. A three-course meal will cost about £11.50 ($20.15), or you can choose the tourist menu for £9.75 ($17.05). Dinner is served from 7 to 9 p.m. daily. "Mine host" is Peter Morgan, hotelier in Devon for some three decades. Overnight rates are £19.50 ($34.15) per person for a room with bath, an English breakfast, and VAT. A special two-day bargain rate is offered for £62 ($108.50) per person and includes dinner, B&B, bath, and VAT.

3. Chagford

Six hundred feet above sea level, Chagford is an ancient Stannary Town. With the moors all around it, it is a good base for your exploration of the region of North Dartmoor. It is approximately 20 miles from Exeter, Torquay, and Plymouth. Chagford overlooks the Teign River in its deep valley, and is itself overlooked by the high granite tors. There's good fishing in the Teign (ask at your hotel). From Chagford, the most popular excursion is to **Postbridge,** six miles to the southwest, a village with a prehistoric clapper bridge.

Near Chagford stands **Castle Drogo,** in the hamlet of Drewsteignton (tel. 06473/3306). This massive granite castle was designed and built by Sir Edwin Lutyens and the castle's owner, Julius Drewe, in the early 20th century. It stands high above the River Teign, with gorgeous views over the moors. The family can trace its origins back to the Norman Conquest. Julius Drewe wanted to create a home worthy of his noble ancestors. He found the bleak site high above the moors. Between them, he and Lutyens created a splendid modern castle. The tour includes the elegant library, the drawing room, the dining room with fine paintings and mirrors, and a simple chapel, along with a vault-roofed gun room. There is a restaurant open daily from 11 a.m. to 5:30 p.m. The castle is open from April until the end of October from 11 a.m. to 5:30 p.m., charging an admission of £2.80 ($4.90) for adults. If you wish to visit only the grounds, the fee is £1.30 ($2.30). Children are admitted for half price.

FOOD AND LODGING

There are several good possibilities in the area.

Three Crowns Hotel, High Street, Chagford, Devon TQ13 8AJ (tel. 06473/ 3444), is a granite inn of the 13th century built to withstand the rigors of the climate, with open fireplaces, roaring log fires, and firelight dancing on old oak beams. Much of the furniture is of the period. The old manor house has modern conveniences, central heating, hot water, and bathrooms. Elizabeth and John Giles charge from £20 ($35) to £25 ($43.75) per person daily for B&B, the latter price for a room with bath and toilet. The bar snacks are very good and are served at lunch and in the evening too. They also do a set dinner from £12.50 ($21.90). Some specialty dishes include coq au vin and escalope of Devon veal. There are desserts and a good selection of cheese assortments to finish off with.

Glendarah House, Chagford, Devon TO13 8BZ (tel. 06473/3270), is a clean, comfortable guesthouse run by Edward and Marian Willett. The house is on the edge of Chagford and makes a good base for exploring Dartmoor National Park. The Willetts offer good accommodations, with color TV in the residents' lounge and a licensed bar featuring a range of local wines. The two baths in the house contain showers. There is also a cottage suite with a four-poster bed, a complete bath, exposed oak beams, and color TV. It is in converted stables, only a short distance from the house. Mrs. Willett provides ample breakfasts and an excellent four-course dinner every night. The B&B rate is £12 ($21) per person daily, and dinner, bed, and breakfast goes for £19.50 ($34.15) per person.

Claremont Guest House, Mill Street, Chagford, Devon TQ13 8AW (tel. 06473/3304), is a family-run place with a warm welcome and home cooking. The well-appointed rooms rented by Mr. and Mrs. A. P. May have color TV, two have private baths, and prices range from £13 ($22.75) to £16 ($28) per person daily for B&B, with an evening meal costing from £8 ($15.75). They'll pack lunches for your excursions into neighboring Dartmoor National Park if you request it. The house has a comfortable guest lounge and bar.

Bly House, Chagford, Devon TQ13 8BW (tel. 06473/2404), is a country-house hotel converted from a former rectory. A short walk from the village of Chagford, it is set in five acres of grounds with sweeping lawns. The house is elegantly furnished with antiques, and some bedrooms have four-poster beds. Mr. and Mrs. G. B. Thompson welcome you to occupy one of their seven doubles, all with private baths, color TV, and tea- and coffee-makers. B&B costs from £15 ($26.25) per person daily. Small children are not accepted. The hotel isn't licensed, but guests can bring their own liquor, perhaps enjoying it in front of the log fire in the comfortable lounge when the weather is cool, although the house is centrally heated. Breakfast is the only meal served, but there are six good pub restaurants in the village.

A VISIT TO AN ABBEY

Of interest to visitors is **Sir Francis Drake's House,** Buckland Abbey, Yelverton (tel. 0822/853607), originally a Cistercian monastery, founded in 1278. It was dissolved in 1539 and became the country seat of Sir Richard Grenville and later Sir Francis Drake (two great sailors). It remained in the Drake family until 1946, when the abbey and grounds were given to the National Trust. The abbey is now a museum, housing exhibits, including Drake's drum, banners, and other artifacts. (You probably won't get a chance to beat Drake's drum, but if you do, remember the words of Henry Newbold's poem: "Drake shall quit the port of heaven and come to England's aid once more.") The abbey lies three miles west of Yelverton off the A386. It is open daily from 11 a.m. to 6 p.m. from April to the end of October. The rest of the year, it is open only on Wednesday, Saturday, and Sunday from 2 to 5 p.m. Admission is £2.80 ($4.90) for adults, £1.40 ($2.45) for children. Light snacks are available when the abbey is open daily.

The largest collection of hotels on the Devon coastline is found in:

4. Torbay (Torquay)

In 1968, the towns of Torquay, Paignton, and Brixham combined to form the County Borough of Torbay, as part of an overall plan to turn the area into one of the super three-in-one resorts of Europe. Escapees from the factories of the Midlands find it easier to bask in the home-grown Devonshire sunshine than to make the pilgrimage to Rimini or the Costa del Sol.

Torquay, set against a backdrop of the red cliffs of Devon, contains 11 miles of coastline, with many sheltered pebbly coves and sandy beaches. With its parks and gardens (including numerous subtropical plants and palm trees), it isn't hard to envision it as a Mediterranean-type resort (and its retired residents are fond of making this comparison, especially in postcards sent back to their cousins in Manchester). At night, concerts, productions from the West End (the D'Oyly Carte Opera appears occasionally at the Princess Theatre), vaudeville shows, and ballroom dancing keep the holiday-makers (and many honeymooners) regally entertained.

If you suddenly long for an old Devonshire village, you can always ride the short distance inland to **Cockington,** still in the same borough, which contains thatched cottages, an old mill, a forge, and a 12th-century church. Furthermore, if you want to visit one of the great homes of England, you can call on **Oldway,** in the heart of Paignton (tel. 0803/296244). Started by the founder of the Singer sewing-machine dynasty, Isaac Merritt Singer, and completed the year after he died (1875), the neoclassic mansion is surrounded by about 20 acres of grounds and Italian-style gardens. Inside, if you get the feeling you're at Versailles, you're almost right, as many of the rooms were copied. Open all year, Oldway can be visited Monday to Saturday from 9 a.m. to 1 p.m. and 2 to 5:15 p.m. From May to September, it is also open from 2:30 to 5 p.m. Saturday and Sunday. Admission is free. The gardens are always open.

BED AND BREAKFAST

For B&B accommodations, I've focused on one of the choicest hotel and residential districts of Torquay. The prices, especially the weekly partial-board terms, are moderate.

Glenorleigh, 26 Cleveland Rd., Torquay, Devon TQ2 5BE (tel. 0803/292135), known in many circles as the "best B&B in Torquay," is a worthy choice if you can get in. The bedrooms, 16 in all, have been tastefully modernized, and they are well maintained. The B&B rate ranges from £15 ($26.25) to £16 ($28) per person nightly, with half-board terms going from £16 ($28) to £21 ($36.75) per person. In summer, many guests are booked in for the week, so you'll have to call and see if they have space for any short-time visitors. The hotel has a solarium and a game room.

Cranborne Hotel, 58 Belgrave Rd., Torquay, Devon TQ2 5HY (tel. 0803/294100), is small but select, a family-run enterprise where guests get a personal welcome and warm hospitality from Mr. and Mrs. Dawkins, who rent a total of 14 comfortably furnished bedrooms, nine of which have private baths. All have color TV and tea- and coffee-makers. The B&B rate ranges from £10 ($17.50) to £15 ($26.25) per person nightly, with half board costing from £14.50 ($25.40) to £19 ($33.25) per person. Guests mix informally either in a lounge reserved for them or on the patio. It is closed in December.

Craig Court Hotel, 10 Ash Hill Rd., Castle Circus, Torquay, Devon TQ1 3HZ (tel. 0803/294400), gives guests a relaxing break in a large Victorian mansion facing a southern exposure, lying a short walk from the heart of town. It offers excellent value in its discreetly modernized bedrooms, 10 in all, many with private facilities. The owners, Joyce and David Anning, charge from £11 ($19.25) to £16.50 ($28.90) per person daily for B&B, from £17 ($29.75) to £22.50 ($39.40) per person for half board. In addition to enjoying the good, wholesome food served here, guests can also make use of a well-appointed lounge or an intimate bar opening onto the grounds (there is a model railway in the garden). To reach the hotel, take St. Marychurch Road (signposted St. Marychurch, Babbacombe) from Castle Circus (Town Hall). The first turn on the right is Ash Hill Road, and the hotel is 200 yards from the turn on the right-hand side.

Kelvin House, 46 Bampfylde Rd., Torquay, Devon TQ2 5AY (tel. 0803/ 297313), is a Victorian villa within walking distance of the sea, the English Riviera Leisure and Conference Centre, and the center of town. Sunny rooms are extra clean, sufficiently comfortable, and moderately priced from £10 ($17.50) per person daily for B&B. The price for half board is from £14 ($24.50) per person. There's no skimping, since the bedrooms have innerspring mattresses and basins with hot and cold running water. Some have private showers and color TV. In addition, the resident owners, Mr. and Mrs. Geoff Kirkby, have provided a lounge for television and a pleasant bar for that after-dinner English pint.

Colindale, 20 Rathmore Rd., Torquay, Devon TQ2 6NY (tel. 0803/293947), is a good choice. And it's about as central as you'd want, opening onto King's Garden, as well as lying within a five-minute walk of Corbyn Beach, and three minutes from the railway station. The B&B rate, set by Mr. and Mrs. A. C. Martin, is from £12 ($21) per person daily in high season. But the best arrangement in one of their nine well-kept double rooms is to take the weekly half-board rate of £98 ($171.50) per person. The hotel has a cocktail bar and a resident's lounge and dining room. Colindale is one of a row of attached brick Victorian houses, with gables and chimneys. It's set back from the road, with a parking court in front.

Blue Haze Hotel, Seaway Lane, Torquay, Devon TQ2 6PS (tel. 0803/ 607186), is an elegant Victorian house with a large garden, set in a residential area 500 yards from the beaches. There are ten spacious bedrooms, all with private baths, color TV, refrigerators, tea- and coffee-makers, and hairdryers. Rates for B&B are £17 ($29.75) to £21 ($36.75) per person per day. Half board costs £25 ($43.75) to £29 ($50.75) per person. The higher prices are charged in summer. The hosts, Doug and Hazel Newton, serve four-course, home-cooked meals in their licensed hotel. There is a large private car park.

Fairmont House Hotel, Herbert Road, Chelston, Torquay, Devon TQ2 6RW (tel. 0803/605446), a Victorian building that has been well preserved with stained glass, marble fireplaces, and other adornments of that grand age, lies in a tranquil residential area of the resort, about a mile from the harbor. Each of its seven rooms is comfortably furnished, with such amenities as private baths or showers. The hotel receives guests from mid-February to mid-November, charging them from £14 ($24.50) to £18 ($31.50) daily in a single, the tariff rising to £28 ($49) to £36 ($63) in a double. Good, sound British cooking is the rule here, and after a meal guests can relax in the public rooms, especially a conservatory bar lounge. Bar lunches are available at noon.

Cresta Hotel, St. Agnes Lane, Torquay, Devon TQ2 6QD (tel. 0803/ 607241), is a family hotel full of character, standing in a secluded position close to the waterfront and the train terminal. The hosts, John and Lucy Macmillan, are helpful, offering ten comfortably furnished rooms, some with sea views. Five of the units are usually set aside for families, most have showers, and some also have toilets. Free TV and tea- and coffee-makers are available on request. In high season, the charge is from £14 ($24.50) per person nightly for B&B, but most guests prefer the half-board rate of £19 ($33.25) per person, which includes a traditional roast for a four-course evening meal with tea or coffee in addition to bed and breakfast.

WHERE TO DINE

Imbued with a continental flair, **Old Vienna,** 6 Lisburne Square (tel. 0803/295861), owned by Linz-born Werner Rott, offers a modernized, stylized, Austrian-inspired cuisine adapted for British tastes. It is housed within an early Victorian town house with an open fireplace and pinewood paneling. Ample portions and a free glass of schnapps complete any meal here. The menu changes three times a year, but it is likely to offer paprikaschnitzel and tafelspitz, the famed boiled beef dish of Old Vienna. No lunch is offered, but dinner is served nightly, except Monday, from 7 to 10:30, with full meals costing from £18 ($31.50) per person. A worthy splurge.

Within a Regency terrace of structures, **Capers Restaurant,** 7 Lisburne Square (tel. 0803/291177), specializes in fish, although there are always two or three meat dishes on the menu. In this attractive, cozy restaurant on Lisburne Square, lying slightly outside the heart of Torquay, the chef-owner, Ian Cawley, makes everything himself (except the wines), using herbs and many vegetables grown under his supervision. "The menu is just ideas," Mr. Cawley says. "I can always cook things in different ways because it is all cooked to order." Capers is open from 7 to 11 p.m. Tuesday to Saturday, with dinners costing around £18 ($31.50).

Within a residential suburb about two miles north of Torquay, **Harvey's of Wellswood,** 35 Ilsham Rd., Wellswood (tel. 0803/293025), enjoys a lot of local popularity. Most guests opt for a before-meal drink beside a gas fire, where the owner claims that more than 600 bottles of whisky are displayed and served. Lunch is noon to 2 p.m. and dinner 7 to 10 p.m. daily, except Sunday and Monday. A fixed-price lunch goes for £6.95 ($12.15), with a set dinner costing £10.95 ($19.15). You can also order à la carte for £12 ($21). Menu items include such dishes as steak Diane and roast mushrooms with garlic. Owner Brian Liversedge, a crusty, engaging Yorkshireman, naturally serves roast beef with Yorkshire pudding.

---

5. Totnes

One of the oldest towns in the West Countree, the ancient Borough of Totnes rests quietly in the past, seemingly content to let the Torbay area remain in the vanguard of the building boom. On the River Dart, 12 miles upstream from Dartmouth, Totnes is so totally removed in character from Torquay that the two towns could be in different countries. Totnes shelters a number of historic buildings, notably the ruins of a Norman castle, the ancient Guildhall, and the 15th-century church of St. Mary, made of red sandstone. In the Middle Ages, the old cloth town was encircled by walls, and the North Gate serves as a reminder of that period.

FOOD AND LODGING IN THE ENVIRONS

In and around the ancient Elizabethan town is some of South Devon's most beautiful scenery, with valleys and hamlets, such as Harberton and Dartington, that are especially pleasing, and each motorist approaches the area with the freshness of a personal discovery.

FOOD AND LODGING IN TOTNES

For the budget, the best place to stay is **Old Forge,** Seymour Place, Totnes, Devon TQ9 5AY (tel. 0803/862174), which is a restored former blacksmith's and wheelwright's workshop dating back six centuries. The owner of Old Forge, Mr. Allnut, still carries on this ancient tradition. Part of the present-day Old Forge is said to have incorporated the Totnes jail. Near the River Dart, B&B accommodations are provided in eight attractively decorated bedrooms, four of which are ideal for families. Four private bathrooms have been installed (otherwise guests share the one public facility). B&B charges in a single go from £25 ($43.75) to £32 ($56) nightly, rising to a range of £28 ($49) to £35 ($61.25) in a double, the tariffs depending on the plumbing.

For meals, consider **Willow,** 87 High St. (tel. 0803/862605), right in the center of town. Using quality ingredients prepared with care, this is a self-service wholefood vegetarian place. In summer, this bright, welcoming establishment is open daily from 9 a.m. to 5 p.m., except Sunday, and it also serves dinner nightly, except Sunday and Monday, from 6:30 to 10 p.m. In winter, it opens an hour later in the morning and serves dinner only on certain nights of the week (so call first). Meals cost from £5 ($8.75) and are likely to include such dishes as an herb-flavored tofu dip with pita bread or couscous with peanut sauce.

Farmhouses on the Outskirts

Ford Farm House, Harberton, near Totnes, Devon TQ9 7SJ (tel. 0803/863539), is a 17th-century house in a rural village of South Devon. Near the moors, the house is capably managed by Mike and Sheila Edwards, who rent a single and a twin-bedded room with hot and cold water basins, plus a double with a private shower and toilet. B&B rates are from £15 ($26.25) daily in a single, £29 ($50.75) in a twin, and £33 ($57.75) in a double with bath. Tariffs include VAT and service. Sheila's culinary skills, sharpened by Cordon Bleu training, turn out tasty dinners by arrangement, costing £8.50 ($14.90).

About ten minutes' walk from Totnes, in a secluded valley with magnificent views of Dartmoor National Park, **Broomborough House Farm,** Broomborough Drive, Higher Plymouth Road, Totnes, Devon TQ9 5LU (tel. 0803/863134), is listed as an elegant gabled mansion. It was designed by Sir George Gilbert Scott, who also designed the Albert Memorial and other structures of architectural heritage in London. The house has central heating, spacious lounges, and the three bedrooms have tea- and coffee-making facilities and electric blankets. Bob and Joan Veale, who operate the house along with their 600-acre farm, charge £13.50 ($23.65) per person daily for B&B. An evening meal costs £7.80 ($13.65).

At Dartington

For such a small hamlet, Dartington attracts a surprising number of international visitors, mainly because of **Dartington Hall** (tel. 0803/862271), an experimental Anglo-American alliance dating back to 1925. A Yorkshire man and his American-born wife (one of the Whitneys), Leonard and Dorothy Elmhurst, poured energy, courage, imagination, and money into the theory that such a village could be self-sufficient. They used historic Dartington Hall, built in the late 14th century and restored by them after 1925, as their center. In the surrounding acres of undulating hills and streams, several village industries were created: housing construction, advanced farming, milling of cloth, and an experimental school. One famous activity here is the College of Arts, in which students live and work in a series of modern buildings erected since the formation of the college in 1961. The Summer School of Music spends the month of August here, occupying the school and college buildings and giving numerous concerts. During the day, visitors are welcome to tour the extensive grounds and can make purchases of handmade crafts in the Cider Press Centre, a complex designed to provide a showcase for the work of leading British craftspeople. You'll find a craft gallery and shop, a print gallery, souvenir shop, toy shop, and a Cranks health food restaurant. One of the shops sells Dartington glass "seconds," along with many interesting souvenirs. The center is open from 9:30 a.m. to 5:30 p.m. Monday to Saturday (also on Sunday in summer). Admission is by donation.

Cranks Health Food Restaurant, Dartington Cider Press Centre, Shinners Bridge (tel. 0803/862388), owes its concept to its parent restaurant in London, where it instantly became the leading health-food restaurant. Now, here at the creative craft center of Dartington in an old Devonshire farmstead, it has found new dimensions. The center, with its handmade chairs, tables, and pottery, displays the work of various craftspeople. It's strictly self-service, and there's a buffet featuring salads. They use compost-grown vegetables when available, and serve freshly made vegetable soup, also live yogurts and freshly extracted fruit and vegetable juices. The Devonshire cream teas with Cranks's newly baked whole-meal scones are popular. The restaurant is open Monday to Saturday from 10 a.m. to 5 p.m. Meals begin at £6 ($10.50).

The **Cott Inn,** Dartington, near Totnes, Devon TQ9 6HE (tel. 0803/863777), on the old Ashburton-Totnes turnpike, is the second-oldest inn in England, built in 1320. It is a low rambling two-story building of stone, cob, and plaster, with a thatch roof and walls three feet thick. The owners, Steve and Gill Culverhouse, charge £19.50 ($34.15) per person daily, including VAT, for a full English or a continental breakfast and occupancy of one of their low-ceilinged old beamed rooms upstairs, where modern conveniences, including hot and cold running water, have been installed. The inn is a gathering place for the people of Dartington, and here you'll feel the pulse of English country life. In winter, log fires keep the lounge and bar snug. You'll surely be intrigued with the tavern, perhaps wanting to take a meal there. A buffet is laid out at lunchtime, priced according to your choice of dish. The evenings see the presentation of an à la carte featuring local produce prepared in interesting ways. Scallops, duck, steak, or fresh salmon may be available. Even if you're not staying over, at least drop in at the pub (seven beers are on draft). Hours are daily from 11 a.m. to 2:30 p.m. and 6 to 11 p.m.

---

6. Dartmouth

At the mouth of the Dart River, this ancient seaport is the home of the Royal Naval College. Traditionally linked to England's maritime greatness, Dartmouth sent out the young midshipmen who saw to it that "Britannia ruled the waves." You can take a river steamer up the Dart to Totnes (book at the kiosk at the harbor). The scenery along the way is breathtaking, as the Dart is Devon's most beautiful river.

Dartmouth's 15th-century castle was built during the reign of Edward IV. The town's most noted architectural feature is the Butterwalk, lying below Tudor houses. The Flemish influence in some of the houses is pronounced.

WHERE TO STAY

A small guesthouse, **Ridgeway Cottage,** 27 Ridge Hill, Dartmouth, Devon TQ6 9PE (tel. 08043/2799), owned by Mrs. Elizabeth Crotty, has one twin-bedded room facing the river and one single room fronting the Naval College. Both rooms have the exclusive use of the bathroom and shower, with a separate toilet. For B&B, according to season and length of stay, the cost goes from £10 ($17.50) to £12 ($21) per person per day.

Victoria Hotel, Victoria Road, Dartmouth, Devon TQ6 9DX (tel. 08043/2572), is a small, family-run hotel in the center of Dartmouth, only 150 yards from the harbor. The characteristic cottage-style bedrooms are tastefully furnished, and with private baths rent for £18 ($31.50) per person daily, with bathless rooms costing £15 ($26.25) per person. Tariffs include a full English breakfast, VAT, and service. Bar snacks are available from the spacious bar/lounge area, and an evening meal can be ordered in the restaurant.

The Captain's House, 18 Clarence St., Dartmouth, Devon TQ6 9NW (tel. 08043/2133), run by Ann and Nigel Jestico, is a 200-year-old Georgian house near the waterfront. This well-run, clean, and inviting house has central heating, and all the bedrooms have private baths, color TV, radios, and tea- and coffee-makers. You get excellent hospitality and good beds, B&B costing £12 ($21) to £13 ($22.75) per person daily, the higher rates for the high summer season.

WHERE TO EAT

Behind a former Victorian storefront, C. M. and F. A. Brendon Copp operate **Cranfords Restaurant,** 29 Fairfax Pl. (tel. 08043/2328), a typical English tea shop with cakes displayed for sale in the windows. Inside, it has wheelback chairs placed around dark mahogany tables. In summer, when business warrants, lunch overflows to a paneled dining room upstairs. Fully licensed for drinks, the place offers steak, a selection of fish, salads, and an array of freshly made desserts. They also offer scones and Devonshire cream with jam for tea, going for £1.80 ($3.15). Lunch starts at £4.50 ($7.90), and dinner costs from £4.50 ($7.90) to £12 ($21). In summer, Cranfords is open daily from 9:30 a.m. to 8 p.m., and in winter hours are from 10 a.m. to 5:30 p.m. daily.

An alternative possibility is the **Scarlet Geranium,** 10 Fairfax Place (tel. 08043/2491), a charming old restaurant off the Quay. Built originally in 1333, it was once known as the Albion Inn. Try it for morning coffee or a three-course table d'hôte luncheon (noon to 2:30 p.m.) for £4.50 ($7.90), which features such temptations as roast leg of lamb or baked Wiltshire ham. When available, you can order the locally caught and dressed crab or fresh-caught salmon. The Scarlet Geranium blossoms at night, too, with dinner costing from £8 ($14), served from 7 to 9:30 p.m. A licensed bar is on the premises. It is open daily.

Billy Budd's, 7 Foss St. (tel. 08043/4842), might suggest a Melville story to some, but if you ask a resident of Dartmouth, he or she will surely direct you to this local favorite. Once there, you are treated to viands from the kitchen of Keith Belt, such as very fresh fish, locally fattened lamb, salmon from the Dart River, and thick cream from Devonshire cows. The dishes are imaginative, with quality seasonal ingredients and a marvelous lack of pretense. The natural flavor in each dish is allowed to surface. For what you get, the prices are very reasonable, with lunches costing from £6 ($10.50) and dinners going for £15 ($26.25) and up. Service is noon to 2 p.m. and 7:30 to 10 p.m. Wednesday to Saturday. Only lunch is served on Tuesday. Of course, it's necessary to reserve a table.

---

7. Salcombe

At the tip of the southernmost part of Devon lies an estuary dominated today by the seaside resort of Salcombe. This is a place that became memorable to many Americans in military service during World War II. The names of East Portlemouth, Strete Slapton, Torcross, even Kingsbridge are little known to many travelers, unless they happen to be boating people, but those names and that of Salcombe were the center of a world at war when the Salcombe estuary, known in ages past simply as the Haven, was selected as being an ideal point from which to launch many of the craft involved in the invasion of Normandy. The area around Slapton, on the East Coast of the English Channel a few miles from the main estuary, was found to be quite similar to the Normandy coastal point that would be called Omaha Beach.

At Salcombe, on the western side of the mouth of the estuary, a waterfront square is called **Normandy Way,** commemorating the U.S. Navy's part in the splendid Allied D-Day effort, and at **Slapton Cellars** there is a **monument** presented by the U.S. Army to the people of the area, known as the South Hams, for their generosity in leaving their homes and property to provide a battle practice area in preparation for the assault in June 1944.

Salcombe today is a beautiful and peaceful seaside resort, with fine beaches, a harbor that is almost completely landlocked, a good deep-water port, excellent fishing facilities, and coastal walking paths in National Park coastal countryside.

The old market town of Kingsbridge is about five miles from Salcombe, at the head of the estuary. Market day here is Tuesday, and tourists and country people alike crowd the market precincts. The A381 road runs between Salcombe and Kingsbridge, and in summer they are connected by a ferry service.

Salcombe's two principal beaches, North Sands and South Sands, can be reached by road. They have car parks and full catering facilities. On the eastern side of the estuary across from Salcombe, a series of beaches is popular, partly because of their safety for children. These can be reached by car or boat, the area being served by the East Portlemouth passenger ferry.

Salcombe is accessible via the A391 south from Totnes, going through Kingsbridge. It is some 25 miles east of Plymouth and can be reached by train from London to Plymouth and then by public bus to Salcombe.

Overbecks Museum and Garden, Sharpitor, Salcombe (tel. 054884/2893), is a National Trust property 1½ miles southwest of Salcombe. The six acres of gardens have rare and tender plants and beautiful views over Salcombe estuary. Part of the house contains a museum of local interest, with emphasis on items that appeal to children. The gardens are open daily all year. The museum is open from the end of March to October from 11 a.m. to 5 p.m. daily. Admission to the museum and garden is £1.70 ($3) for adults, half price for children. Admission to the gardens only is £1 ($1.75). There is a gift shop, and you can picnic in the grounds if you wish. Signs point the way to this site from both Malborough to the north and from Salcombe.

FOOD AND LODGING

One of the best bargains at the resort is **Charborough House Hotel,** Devon Road, Salcombe, Devon TQ8 8HB (tel. 054884/2260), a gabled house lying near the center of town and the harbor, convenient to ferryboat connections and stores. The rooms are comfortably furnished, and nearly all contain private baths or showers. B&B costs from £24 ($42) daily in a single, rising to £37 ($64.75) in a double. The food is good, the kitchen turning out both British and continental dishes and whenever possible using fresh produce. Dinner costs from £11 ($19.25). The hotel is closed from the middle of October until the middle of January.

Trennels Private Hotel, Herbert Road, Salcombe, Devon TQ8 8HR (tel. 054884/2500), is one of the outstanding small hotels of the area, attracting those who enjoy natural beauty, part of the surroundings being under the protection of the National Trust. Cliff walking is a popular pastime here, and later guests return to the comforts of this stone-built, homelike place, enjoying its views over the Salcombe estuary. The B&B rate ranges from £14.50 ($25.40) to £16.50 ($28.90) daily in a single, rising to £28 ($49) to £32 ($56) in a double, the higher rates being charged for private bath. Good home cooking, British-style, is also available here, and an evening meal is served at 7:30 p.m. for those who request in advance.

8. Plymouth

The historic seaport is more romantic in legend than in reality. But this was not always so. In World War II, the blitzed area of Greater Plymouth lost at least 75,000 buildings. The heart of present-day Plymouth, including the municipal civic center on the Royal Parade, has been entirely rebuilt, and the way it was done became the subject of controversy.

For the old you must go to the Elizabethan section, known as the **Barbican,** and walk along the quay in the footsteps of Sir Francis Drake (once the mayor of Plymouth) and other Elizabethan seafarers, such as Sir John Hawkins, English naval commander and slave trader. It was from here in 1577 that Drake set sail on his round-the-world voyage. An even more famous sailing took place in 1620, when the Pilgrims left their final port in England for the New World. That fact is commemorated by a plaque at the harbor.

Legend has it that while playing bowls on Plymouth Hoe (Celtic for "high place"), Drake was told that the Spanish Armada had entered the sound and, in a masterful display of confidence, he finished the game before going into battle. A local historian questions the location of the bowls game, if indeed it happened, starring Sir Francis. I am told that the Hoe in the 16th century was only gorse-covered scrubland outside tiny Plymouth and that it is more likely that the officers of the Royal Navy would have been bowling (then played on a shorter green than today) while awaiting the Armada arrival at the Minerva Inn, Looe Street, 20 yards from the house where Sir Francis lived, and about two minutes' walk from the Barbican.

Of special interest to visitors from the U.S. is the final departure-point of the Pilgrims in 1620, the already-mentioned Barbican. The two ships, *Mayflower* and *Speedwell,* that sailed from Southampton in August of that year put into Plymouth after they suffered storm damage. Here the *Speedwell* was abandoned as unseaworthy, and the *Mayflower* made the trip to the New World alone. The Memorial Gateway to the Waterside on the Barbican marks the place, tradition says, whence the Pilgrims' ship sailed.

Here too is the **Black Friars Refectory Room,** dating from 1536, in Southside Street. The building is a national monument and one of Plymouth's oldest surviving buildings. It's now owned by Plymouth Gin Distillery, which welcomes visitors Monday to Friday to see the small exhibition of the history of the building. It was here that the Pilgrims met prior to setting sail for the New World.

Prysten House, Finewell Street (tel. 0752/661414), is another place with a strong U.S. connection. Built in 1490 as a town house close to St. Andrew's Church, it is now a church house and working museum. Rebuilt in the 1930s with American help, it contains a model of Plymouth in 1620 and tapestries depicting the colonization of America. At the entrance is the gravestone of the captain of the U.S. brig *Argus,* who died on August 15, 1813, after a battle in the English Channel. The house is open from 10 a.m. to 4 p.m. Monday to Saturday, April to October. Admission is 50p (90¢) for adults, 25p (55¢) for children.

The Barbican is a mass of narrow streets, old houses, and quayside shops selling antiques, brasswork, old prints, and books. Fishing boats still unload their catch at the wharves, and passenger-carrying ferryboats run short harbor cruises. A trip includes a visit to Drake's Island in the Sound, the dockyards, and naval vessels, plus a view of the Hoe from seaside.

Plymouth Harbour costs £2 ($3.50) for adults, £1 ($1.75) for children. Departures are from February through November, with cruises leaving every half hour from 10 a.m. to 4 p.m. daily. These **Plymouth Boat Cruises** are booked at the Phoenix Wharf, the Barbican (tel. 0752/822202).

The **Barbican Craft Centre,** White Lane (tel. 0752/662338), in the Barbican, has workshops and showrooms where you can watch and talk to people engaged in crafts. You'll see such sights as a potter throwing a special design or a glassblower fashioning a particular glass. Woodcarvers, leather workers, and weavers are also busy, and you can buy their products at reasonable prices, even commissioning your own design if you're lucky.

A major base for the British navy, Plymouth makes for an interesting stopover.

BED AND BREAKFAST

Present-day pilgrims from the New World who didn't strike it rich are advised to head for Smeaton Terrace, in one of the most colorful parts of Plymouth, West Hoe. Here they'll find a number of inexpensive B&B houses on a peaceful street near the water. My recommendations for overnighting follow.

The **Imperial Hotel,** 3 Windsor Villas, Lockyer Street, The Hoe, Plymouth, Devon PL1 2OD (tel. 0752/227311), owned by Alan and Prue Jones, is an attractive and tastefully decorated Victorian hotel on Plymouth Hoe, with 23 bedrooms, 16 with private bath. It offers a homelike atmosphere. Alan (Lieutenant-Commander Royal Navy Reserve, retired) was in the merchant navy for 13 years and is a former chairman of the Personal Service Hotel Group and a director of the Marketing Bureau in Plymouth. With their experience, Alan and Prue are more than able to help and advise overseas visitors with limited time on where to go and what to see, including the place where the Pilgrims embarked for the New World. Rates depend on the plumbing. Singles cost from £20 ($35) to £27 ($47.25) daily, with doubles going for £17.50 ($30.65) to £19.75 ($34.55) per person. Ground-floor rooms are available, and there is ample parking space on the premises.

The **Wiltun,** 39 Grand Parade, West Hoe, Plymouth, Devon PL1 3DQ (tel. 0752/667072), is set on Plymouth's historic foreshore overlooking Drake's Island and Plymouth Sound. This Victorian house has many modern facilities, but retains several of the architectural features of the 1850s. Family rooms are available. There's a private lawn to relax on and watch the ships go by. The charge is from £12.50 ($21.90) per person per day, including a large English breakfast. The well-prepared evening meal goes for £6 ($10.50), including VAT.

Georgian House, 51 Citadel Rd., The Hoe, Plymouth, Devon PL1 3AU (tel. 0752/663237), is one of the finest guesthouses in Plymouth. This Georgian town house also includes the fully licensed Fourposter Restaurant. Each of the 12 rooms is well maintained and comfortably furnished, containing a private bath or shower, direct-dial phone, trouser-press, beverage-making equipment, and hairdryers, along with color TV. B&B charges are from £25 ($43.75) daily in a single, rising to £36 ($63) in a double. British and international dishes are served in the candlelit restaurant, costing from £10 ($17.50) for a meal. You might precede your meal with a drink in the cocktail bar. The location is about five minutes from the ferry terminal.

Invicta Hotel, 11-12 Osborne Pl., Lockyer Street, The Hoe, Plymouth, Devon PL1 2PU (tel. 0752/664997), is a Victorian building now converted to a hotel, standing at the entrance to Plymouth Hoe. Family operated, it is convenient not only to the heart of Plymouth but to the ferries departing for Brittany on the French coast. This modernized hotel offers nearly two dozen bedrooms, most with private bath or shower, all with hot and cold running water, beverage-making equipment, and color TV. Bedrooms are comfortably and pleasantly furnished. The single B&B rate ranges from £21 ($36.75) to £23 ($40.25) daily, with doubles costing from £29 ($50.75) to £35 ($61.25). The Invicta also has a restaurant serving grills for the most part.

St. Rita Hotel, 76 Alma Rd., Plymouth, Devon PL3 4HD (tel. 0752/667024), is close to the Plymouth railway station in a row of blue-painted Victorian houses on the main bus route to the city center, approximately one mile away. There are 15 clean, comfortable rooms, each with a wardrobe and chest. The tariff varies with the room, but averages £13 ($22.75) per person nightly, including breakfast. The accommodations at the back are quieter. Evening meals are offered only from October to May. However, you have to have something to eat if you want to drink because of license requirements. There is good parking at the rear of the hotel.

Camelot Hotel, Elliott Street, The Hoe, Plymouth, Devon PL1 2PP (tel.

0752/221255), stands on a small road just off the grassy expanse of the Hoe. It is a neat, tall house with a pleasant small bar and restaurant, with set-menu meals and a short à la carte menu in the evening. There is a lounge with color TV and video, or else you can watch from your own set in your bedroom. Accommodations go for £28 ($49) daily in a single with bath. Two persons can stay here for £40 ($70) in a room with private bath. These tariffs include a full English breakfast, service, and VAT. There are facilities for laundry and dry cleaning nearby.

Osmond Guest House, 42 Pier St., Plymouth, Devon PL1 3BT (tel. 0752/229705), well known and quite popular, has only six bedrooms, but if you plan far enough ahead you might get in. Half of the accommodations are suitable for families. No private baths are offered, but personal attention is excellent. The price is right too: from £11 ($19.25) to £12 ($21) daily in a single, rising to £19 ($33.35) to £21 ($36.75) in a double. An evening meal can be taken here if ordered in advance.

Hoe Guest House, 20 Grand Parade, West Hoe, Plymouth, Devon PL1 3DF (tel. 0752/665274), was built in Edwardian days, perhaps because of its location with a view of Plymouth Sound and of Drake's Island. The guesthouse is small, only six bedrooms to rent and three baths to share, but each unit is comfortably appointed and well maintained. The B&B charges are reasonably priced, ranging from £12 ($21) to £15 ($26.25) daily, rising to £21 ($36.75) to £29 ($50.75) in a double. You can walk to the Barbican and the center of Plymouth from this guesthouse where only breakfast is served.

Hosteria Romana, 58 Southside St., Blackfriars Yard, Plymouth, Devon PL1 2LA (tel. 0752/668827), is contained within an old building, possibly dating from the 17th century. It was originally constructed as a malthouse and is one of the few hotels set directly on the Barbican. The hotel contains a good Italian restaurant (see below), and about a dozen simply furnished but clean and comfortable bedrooms, each with private shower or toilet. With breakfast included, singles cost £22 ($38.50) daily, with doubles going for £30 ($52.50) to £35 ($61.25).

WHERE TO DINE

If you're pressed for time and are only passing through, try at least to visit the Barbican—perhaps for a meal. A good dining choice is the **Green Lanterns,** 31 New St., The Barbican (tel. 0752/660852). A 16th-century eating house on a Tudor street, the Green Lanterns lies 200 yards from the Mayflower Steps, about as close to the Pilgrims as you can get. Even to this day, it's a good restaurant. At lunchtime, an extensive menu of reasonably priced dishes is served from £5 ($8.75) up, including such items as farmhouse pâté, harvest home pie, beef in a blanket, and Lancashire hotpot. All courses at both lunch and dinner are served with fresh vegetables of the day. Some unusual dishes are on the dinner menu, such as roast "gliny" (guinea fowl roasted with wine-flavored gravy), cider-baked rabbit, jugged steak (a casserole of chuck steak and celery flavored with spices, red currant jelly, and port wine), and chicken pepper pot (from an 18th-century recipe). Devonshire bass is good if it's available, or you might choose sole with herbs or one of the lamb dishes. Desserts include several tempting hot and cold selections, many served with Devon clotted cream. Expect to spend from £12 ($21) for a full dinner. Family owned, the Green Lanterns is run by Sally M. Russell and Kenneth Pappin, who are fully aware that voyaging strangers like the Elizabethan atmosphere, traditional English fare, and personal service. The restaurant is near the municipally owned Elizabethan House. Lunch is served from 11:45 a.m. to 2:15 p.m. and dinner from 6:30 to 10:45 p.m. daily, except Sunday. Reservations for dinner are advised.

The Ship Tavern, The Barbican (tel. 0752/667604), is a stone-fronted building facing the marina. Its tables are placed to offer a view over the harbor. You pass through a pub and take a flight of stairs one floor above street level, where a well stocked salad bar and a carvery await you. The carvery presents at least three roast joints, and you're allowed to eat as much as you want. Adults pay £6.95 ($12.15) for the privilege, children £4.25 ($7.45). The first course is from a help-yourself buffet, and a chef carves your selection of meats for your second course. Desserts are extra. This is one of the best food values in Plymouth, and it's available daily from noon to 2 p.m. and 6:30 to 10:30 p.m.

The **Queen Anne Eating House,** 2 White Lane, The Barbican (tel. 0752/262101) stands next to the previously recommended Barbican Craft Centre. It's a bow-fronted, white-painted establishment open daily from 10:30 a.m. to 9:30 p.m., during which time you can order fresh coffee, tea, and other beverages. From noon till closing time, you can also order good wholesome food such as roast beef and Yorkshire pudding, steak-and-kidney pie, roast chicken, fish and chips, and other hot meals. For an appetizer, I suggest the homemade pâté. Salads are available on request. Service is fast and polite, but the homemade 8½-inch pizzas take about 15 minutes, costing from £2.60 ($4.55) to £4.80 ($8.40). Full meals, with the house wine or cooled lager, go for £3.50 ($6.15) to £6.75 ($11.80). There's a special Kiddies Corner on the menu, with meals costing from £1.15 ($2). If you're not looking for a full meal, try the Devonshire cream tea. It's served any time of the day for £1.65 ($2.90), and the homemade scones are half white and half whole-wheat flour. White wood tables and chairs, along with white-paneled walls, make this a bright place.

The **Ganges** (Indian Tandoori Restaurant), 146 Vauxhall St. (tel. 0752/667810), provides a good change of pace from English cookery. Part of a chain that has other locations in the West Country, it is decorated with touches of the East. You can dine in air-conditioned, candlelit comfort, while enjoying an array of spicy dishes. One of the chef's specialties is a whole tandoori chicken superbly spiced and flavored. You can also order the usual array of curries and biryanis. Vegetarians will also find sustenance here as well. Service is daily from 5:30 to 11:45 p.m., with meals costing from £10 ($17.50).

Hosteria Romana, 58 Southside St., Blackfriars Yard (tel. 0752/668827), was established in the mid-1980s by a hard-working community of Italians. This pleasant trattoria offers some of the most authentic food in Plymouth, with recipes inspired by the kitchens of Genoa, Rome, and Venice. Full meals cost from £18 ($31.50) and include an array of grilled meats, pastas, and other Italian dishes. Service is daily, except Sunday, from noon to 2:30 p.m. and 7 to 11 p.m.

Most tourists at this point will want to continue their trip into Cornwall. However, if you're entering Devon from Somerset, you may first want to explore:

NORTH DEVON

"Lorna, Lorna . . . Lorna Doone, my lifelong darling," is the wailing cry you're likely to imagine from your farmhouse bed in North Devon. A wildness seems to enter the air at night on the edge of the moody Doone Valley. Much of the district is already known to those who have read Victorian novelist R. D. Blackmore's romance of the West Country, *Lorna Doone.*

The coastline is mysterious. Pirates and smugglers used to find havens here in crooked creeks and rocky coves. The ocean crashes against the rocks, and the meadows approach so close to the cliff's edge that you wonder why they don't go spilling into the sea, sheep and all. The heatherclad uplands of Exmoor spill over into North Devon from Somerset, a perfect setting for an English mystery thriller. Favorite bases are Clovelly, the twin resorts of Lynton and Lynmouth, and Combe Martin. Our first stopover is the best:

9. Clovelly

This is the most charming of all Devon villages and is one of the main attractions of the West Country. Starting at a great height, the village cascades down the mountainside, with its narrow, cobblestone High which makes travel by car impossible (you park your car at the top and make the trip by foot). Supplies are carried down by donkeys. Every yard of the way provides views of tiny cottages, with their terraces of flowers, lining the main street. The village fleet is sheltered at the stone quay at the bottom.

If you don't want to climb back up the slippery incline, go to the rear of the Red Lion Inn and "queue up" for a Land Rover. In summer the line is often long, but considering the alternative, it's worth the wait. Two Land Rovers make continuous round-trips, costing 40p (70¢) per person each way.

Tip: To avoid the flock of tourists, stay out of Clovelly from around 11 in the morning till teatime. After tea, settle in your room and have dinner, perhaps spend the night in peace and contentment. The next morning after breakfast, you might walk around the village or go for a swim in the harbor, then visit the nearby villages during the middle of the day when the congestion sets in. Bideford, incidentally, is 11 miles away.

Be forewarned: It's not easy to get a room in Clovelly. Advance reservations, with a deposit, are imperative during the peak summer months. However, you can telephone in advance and *possibly* get a bed.

WHERE TO STAY

At the bottom of the steep cobble street, right on the stone seawall of the little harbor, the **Red Lion,** The Quay, Clovelly, near Bideford, Devon EX39 5TF (tel. 02373/237), may well occupy the jewel position of the village. Rising three stories with gables and a courtyard, it is actually an unspoiled country inn, where life centers around an antique pub and village inhabitants, including sea captains, gather to satisfy their thirsts over pints of ale. Most of the bedrooms look directly onto the sea, and all of them contain hot and cold running water and adequate furnishings. The cost is from £14.50 ($25.40) per person nightly, including breakfast. Other meals are available in the sea-view dining room. Dinner goes for £10 ($17.50), with a choice of four main dishes, two of which are always fresh local fish, then a selection from the dessert trolley. The manager suggests that the Red Lion is not suitable for children under 7 years of age.

Bed and Breakfast in Higher Clovelly

Overflow lodgings in summer are available in the tiny hamlet of Higher Clovelly, lying above the main village. Although Higher Clovelly has none of the charm of Clovelly, you don't have to face the problem of carting luggage down that steep cobblestone street. To get you started on your search for a room here, I'd recommend—

Jonquil House, Burscott Road, Higher Clovelly, near Bideford, Devon EX29 5RR (tel. 02373/346), is operated by Mrs. Grace Kelly, who welcomes guests warmly into the inviting atmosphere of the house, set just off the main road into Clovelly. The Jonquil offers views over the adjoining farmland. All rooms are centrally heated and have washbasins. B&B costs from £8 ($14) per person daily. The lounge/dining room has a color TV, and the bathroom is equipped with a shower.

The Four Poster, 5 Underdown, Clovelly, Bideford, Devon EX39 5TA (tel. 02373/748), is the most romantically named accommodation in the upper or lower villages. It's also one of the most reasonable in price, charging from £9 ($15.75) per person nightly for a good Devonshire breakfast and a comfortable bed. The price also includes a "wake-up" pot of tea and crackers served early in the morning if you like to get up early. A four-course evening meal is available, costing £9 ($15.75), with wine, if you order before 5 p.m. Mr. and Mrs. T. W. L. Clark are among the most accommodating hosts in Clovelly. Mr. Clark, a retired military man, is a fount of information on local, regional, and nationwide attractions. He also makes all his own wine, beer, and cider. The immaculately kept stone house was built originally for use of the Coast Guard. It is adjacent to the Visitors Centre on Clovelly Main Car Park.

10. Combe Martin and Lynton-Lynmouth

COMBE MARTIN

One of the best bases for excursions into Exmoor, Combe Martin is a lovely village, lying in a valley or combe. Cliffs, ideal for rambles, soar on both sides. After you've traversed its High Street, you've about seen the village. Its old church is built in the Early English and Perpendicular styles. The English like to sunbathe and swim nearby in the sheltered little coves with their pebblestone beaches. Combe Martin lies six miles from Ilfracombe.

Staying over? I suggest the following accommodations:

Where to Stay

Saffron House, King Street, Combe Martin, Devon EX34 0BX (tel. 027188/ 3521), is an old farmhouse successfully adapted into a popular small licensed family hotel offering all-year accommodation with the benefit of full central heating for those early and late holidays. The hotel, which is set back from the road, is just a short walk away from the beach and harbor and commands extensive views of the village and surrounding countryside, as well as the famous "Hangman Hill." The owners, Sharon and Martin Hall, are sincerely interested in your comfort, being well traveled themselves, and from the moment of your reception you know that you are going to have an enjoyable stay. The guest rooms vary in size and are clean and comfortable. You will find two lounges, a private heated swimming pool, a garden, and a sun terrace. B&B rates are from £12 ($21) to £14 ($24.50) per person daily, including VAT, with reductions for children. Some rooms have private baths. The Halls will point out the areas of interest and, if not too busy, will accompany you on a walk through the cliff paths.

The London Inn, Leigh Road, Combe Martin, Devon EX34 0NA (tel. 027188/3409), is a roadside inn standing fresh and prim at the upper part of the village road. The owners, Mr. and Mrs. A. W. Gurr, charge from £12 ($21) per person daily for B&B, based on double occupancy. The lounge tavern, heavy beams and all, is the meeting place for the nearby villagers, as well as residents. All are warmed by its old features—four settles, a stone fireplace with logs on a raised hearth, a copper hood, and shelves of pewter and copper steins and mugs. The residents' lounge is comfortably furnished, as are the pleasantly decorated bedrooms. The emphasis is on comfort, good food, and cleanliness. On the rear lawn, you can sit quietly, listening to the movement of the nearby trout stream at the bottom of the garden, later enjoying music and dancing in the bar.

Twelve miles to the east is still another good base for exploring Exmoor—

LYNTON-LYNMOUTH

The north coast of Devon is set off dramatically in Lynton, a village some 500 feet high. It is a good center for exploring the Doone Valley and that part of Exmoor that overflows into the shire from neighboring Somerset. The Valley of Rocks, west of Lynton, offers the most spectacular scenery

The town is joined by a cliff railway to its sister, Lynmouth, about 500 feet lower. The East Lyn and West Lyn Rivers meet in Lynmouth, a popular resort with the British. For a panoramic view of the rugged coastline, you can walk on a path halfway between the towns that runs along the cliff. From Lynton, or rather from Hollerday Hill, you can look out onto Lynmouth Bay, Countisbury Foreland, and Woody Bays in the west. This area offers the same kind of scenic excitement that Big Sur does in California.

Where to Stay

Countisbury Lodge, Countisbury Hill, Lynmouth, Lynton, Devon EX35 6NB (tel. 0589/52388), is a former Victorian vicarage overlooking Lynmouth and the West Lyn River. The hosts, Margaret and John Hollinshead, are enthusiastic innkeepers. Their basic tariff is from £13 ($22.75) per person daily for bed and a full English breakfast. Dinner at £8 ($14) includes VAT. The lodge offers eight double rooms, some with twin beds, some with double beds. Most rooms contain private baths or showers. The lodge has a unique bar, which was built into the rock face of Countisbury Hill.

Sandrock, Longmead, Lynton, Devon EX35 6DH (tel. 0598/53307), is a substantial, three-story house on the edge of Lynton, one of the best economy oases in North Devon. The house is on the lower part of a hill beside the road, with most of its bedrooms opening onto views. You can see the beginning peaks of the Valley of Rocks. Fortunately, it's a hotel with many windows, and the rooms are sunny and bright. The bedrooms, generally quite large, are interestingly shaped; the third floor has dormer windows, which make the rooms even cozier. Each accommodation has its own water basin; the beds have innerspring mattresses, and there are plenty of bathrooms in which you can soak after those long walks. The high-season rate for your B&B and evening dinner ranges from £26 ($45.50) to £27 ($47.25) per person daily, depending on the plumbing. The owners, Mr. and Mrs. Harrison, manage everything at the Sandrock, and they do it well, taking a personal interest in the welfare of their guests. Their baked goods are a delight, especially the deep-dish apple and rhubarb pies, which are tasty, tart, and sweet at the same time. In the Anglers' Bar, foreign visitors meet the Lynton locals after dinner.

Gordon House Hotel, 31 Lee Rd., Lynton, Devon EX35 6BS (tel. 0598/53203), is an old hotel with much warmth and character. From March to November, guests are received in its comfortably furnished and well-maintained bedrooms. Each of the seven bedrooms contains a private bath or shower, and B&B charges are from £15 ($26.25) daily in a single, going up to £30 ($52.50) in a double. Since the small hotel is noted for its good, wholesome food, you may also request an evening meal, provided you don't mind dining by 7 p.m. This hotel was built in Victoria's day, and it has been rejuvenated in keeping with its old antique charm.

Hazeldene, Lee Road, Lynton, Devon EX35 6BP (tel. 0598/52364), is a Victorian home with a good deal of charm. Many consider it among the best of the small B&B hotels in this popular summer resort. Except for a Christmas break, guests are received all year at this nine-bedroom establishment, each with private bath or shower. Bedrooms are kept sparkling clean and are a pleasure to return to after a day of walking along the coast. Derek and Hazel Blight charge from £12.50 ($21.90) to £16 ($28) daily in a single, the tariff going up to £24 ($42) to £31 ($54.25) in a double. Accommodations also include piped video, beverage-making equipment, and color TV. You can enjoy a drink in a cozy bar and later a meal in the candlelit dining room.

Bonnicott Hotel, Watersmeet Road, Lynmouth, Lynton, Devon EX35 6EP (tel. 0598/53346), was built 170 years ago as a rectory. John and Brenda Farrow, who now own and run it as a private hotel, are most helpful. Each of their nine bedrooms is attractively decorated, most with private showers and views over Lynmouth Bay or the Lyn Valley. On cooler days a log fire burns in the lounge and bar. John and Brenda, who used to own a pub in London, offer good food, specialties being local fish and Scotch steak, served in the Bonnicott Grill. Half board and a room costs from £25 ($43.75) per person per day. Special diets and vegetarian meals can be provided. John is glad to advise on walks, fishing, and riding, and to give details about the real-life locations of scenes from the novel *Lorna Doone*.

Denes Guest House, Longmead, Lynton, Devon EX35 6DQ (tel. 0598/53573), is a tastefully decorated accommodation operated by Mr. and Mrs. Gay, who accept only nonsmokers. The seven immaculate rooms are spacious, with hot and cold running water. B&B costs from £11 ($22.75) per person daily, plus another £7 ($12.25) if you want dinner. Tasty and filling meals are served in a cheerful dining room. Special rates are quoted for children.

Where to Dine (Lynton)

Greenhouse Restaurant, Lee Road (tel. 0598/53358), was originally the greenhouse on the grounds of an old hotel. The facade is green and cream colored, and inside, all is blue. Many of the overhead windows and skylights of the building have been replaced with solid walls and ceilings for the sake of practicality, but the effect is still that of a greenhouse. The restaurant is owned by Jill and John Hodgkinson, who bake their own bread and pastries on the premises daily. There is a wide range of dishes, all homemade, including steak-and-kidney pie, quiche Lorraine, lasagne, Cornish pasties, and dishes such as local trout and steaks. A three-course meal with drinks costs around £10 ($17.50). Vegetarian menus are also offered. Cooked meals, morning coffees, and afternoon teas are available daily from 10:30 a.m. to 8 p.m. in summer and from 10:30 a.m. to 5:30 p.m. in winter.

CORNWALL

1. LOOE

2. POLPERRO

3. FOWEY

4. TRURO

5. ST. MAWES

6. FALMOUTH

7. PENZANCE

8. THE ISLES OF SCILLY

9. NEWLYN, MOUSEHOLE, AND LAND'S END

10. ST. IVES

11. PORT ISAAC

12. TINTAGEL

13. BOLVENTOR

The ancient duchy of Cornwall is the extreme southwestern part of England—often called the "toe." But Cornwall is one toe that's always wanted to dance away from the foot. Even though a peninsula, it is a virtual island—if not geographically, then spiritually. Encircled by coastline, it abounds with rugged cliffs, hidden bays with fishing villages, sandy beaches, sheltered coves, and secluded creeks where the age-old art of smuggling was once practiced with consummate skill. Many of the hillside-clinging cottages in some of the little seaports are reminiscent of towns along the Mediterranean, although Cornwall retains its own distinctive flavor.

The true Cornish people are generally darker and shorter than the denizens with whom they share the country. These characteristics reflect their pre-Celtic and Celtic origins, which still lives on in superstition, folklore, and fairy tales. King Arthur, of course, is the most vital legend of all. When Cornish folk speak of King Arthur and his Knights of the Round Table, they're not just handing out a line for the tourist. To them, Arthur and his knights really existed, romping around Tintagel Castle, now in ruins—Norman ruins, that is—lying 300 feet above the sea, 19 miles from Bude.

This ancient land had its own language up until about 250 years ago. And some of the old words ("pol" for pool, "tre" for house) still survive. As you move into the backwoods, you'll encounter a dialect more easily understood by the Welsh than by those who speak the queen's English.

The Cornish, like the Welsh, are great miners (tin and copper), and they're fond of the tall tale. Sometimes it's difficult to tell when they're serious. One resident, for example, told me that he and his wife had been out walking in the woods near twilight but had lost their way. He claimed that the former owner of the estate (in Victoria's day) appeared suddenly in a dog-carriage and guided them back to where they'd taken the wrong turn. If this really happened I wouldn't be surprised, at least not in Cornwall.

Traditionally, the typical oldtimer in Cornwall is a person involved in a vendetta. I heard of one rich and wicked moneylender in Victorian times who wanted to live in total seclusion, but was frustrated in this ambition by two spinster sisters who kept a neighboring farm. So he bought a public chiming clock from Looe, placed it in the tower over the house, and set the quarter-only chimes going only at night—until he finally drove the good ladies out. The Cornish, they are a colorful lot.

The English come here for their holidays in the sun. I suggest anchoring at one of the smaller fishing villages, such as East and West Looe, Polperro, Mousehole, or Portloe, where you'll experience firsthand the charm of the duchy. Many of the villages, such as St. Ives, are artists' colonies. In some of the pubs and restaurants frequented by painters, a camaraderie prevails, especially in the nontourist months. Recently, for instance, at one of the artists' hangouts, three young men who had finished dining brought out their guitars and spontaneously launched into folk songs for the rest of the evening. Detecting the accent of some visiting Americans, they sang (with appallingly perfect accents) several country music favorites, although it was their repertoire from Ireland and Wales that cast the greater spell. Living here with these artists is like going back 40 years, experiencing dependence upon yourself and your associates for entertainment. By all means, cross over the Tamar from Devon and see what Cornwall is up to.

Except for St. Ives and Port Isaac, most of my recommendations lie on the Southern Coast, the so-called Cornish Riviera, which strikes many foreign visitors as being the most intriguing. However, the North Coast is not without its own peculiar charm.

1. Looe

After your visit to Plymouth about 15 miles away, you can either take the Tamar Suspension Bridge to Cornwall or cross by ferry from Plymouth. You'll soon arrive in the ancient twin towns of East and West Looe, connected by a seven-arched stone bridge that spans the river. In the jaws of shrub-dotted cliffs, the fishing villages present a stark contrast to Plymouth. Houses scale the hills, stacked one on top of the other in terrace fashion.

In both fishing villages you can find good accommodations and meet interesting people. Fishing and sailing are two of the major sports, and the sandy coves, as well as East Looe Beach, make choice spots for sea bathing, as uniquely practiced by the British. Beyond the towns are cliff paths and downs worth a ramble.

In these villages are several levels of life, the most traditional of which is that followed by the Cornish villagers, many of whom are fishermen (go down to the harbor and watch the pilchard boats come in). Then there is a sophisticated group whose members enjoy the atmosphere. A large transient group, representative of no special class, trips down for a week or so, mostly in the summer months. But all year you can watch the artists and craftspeople who live and work here.

Looe is noted for its shark-angling, but you may prefer simply walking the narrow, medieval streets of East Looe, with its harbor and 17th-century Guildhall.

WHERE TO STAY

Spaces and prices are at a premium in Looe, as they are in all of Cornwall in July and August.

Klymiarven Hotel, Barbican Hill, East Looe, Cornwall PL13 1BH (tel. 05036/2333), is set in two acres of woodland and terraced gardens, with a view of the harbor. The terrace overlooks a heated swimming pool. Guests enjoy the use of comfortable lounges and two bars. One of the best accommodations in the Looe area, it is run by Rosemary and Greg Symons. Their bedrooms are tastefully furnished, and most of them contain private baths or showers, each with color TV and beverage-making equipment. With a full English breakfast, charges are from £16 ($28) per person off-season, rising to £22 ($38.50) in peak season. The 400-year-old cellar bar has a lot of character, with a smuggler's passage, flagstone floors, and old timber beams. The cuisine in the candlelit restaurant is first-rate, offering both a table d'hôte and an à la carte menu. Fresh produce is used.

Pixies Hotel, Shutta, East Looe, Cornwall PL13 1JD (tel. 05036/2726), is one of the most acclaimed little guesthomes in the area. Set on about 1½ acres of land with panoramic views, it is a desirable oasis. The bedrooms are well kept and comfortable, and the breakfast is substantial. Seven bedrooms are rented, only three of which have a private bath or shower. Other guests share the one public facility. B&B terms range from £11.50 ($20.15) to £17 ($29.75) daily in a single, rising to £22 ($38.50) to £33 ($57.75) in a double, depending on the plumbing. The cooking is solid and reliable, so you may want to make arrangements for an evening meal.

Kantara Guest House, 7 Trelawney Terrace, Looe, Cornwall PL13 2AG (tel. 05036/2093), is one of the best bargains of Looe, a comfortably appointed guesthouse looking out over the river. It lies about an eight-minute leisurely stroll from the water and the heart of the resort. Standing across from the spacious car park, it offers only six rooms, three of which are usually occupied by families. The two bathrooms are shared. From April to October, guests are received and charged from £10 ($17.50) daily in a single and from £17 ($29.75) in a double.

Sea Haze Guest House, Polperro Road, Looe, Cornwall PL13 2JS (tel. 05036/2708), is immaculately kept, opening onto scenic vistas of the surrounding area. It lies on the road between Looe and Polperro. You get a lot of service and always a polite welcome at this Cornish spot of hospitality. Bedrooms are pleasantly furnished and comfortable, and the two public baths must be shared. With a Cornish breakfast included, the B&B rate, depending on the time of year, ranges from £12 ($21) to £18 ($31.50) daily in a single and from £17 ($29.75) to £30 ($52.50) in a double. Guests are accepted from April to October.

Jesmond Guest House, Hannafore Road, Looe, Cornwall PL13 2DQ (tel. 05036/4156), has one of the best locations in town, lying only three minutes from the water. It is also the finest bargain if you take the daily half-board terms, ranging from £11.50 ($20.15) to £13.50 ($23.65) per person nightly. The hotel, operated by Carol Brown and Christopher Webb, has only six bedrooms, one of which has a private bath. The kitchen caters to vegetarians, and the house is licensed.

Lodgings on the Outskirts

Coombe Farm, Widegates, Cornwall PL13 1QN (tel. 05034/233), about 3½ miles from Looe, is an eight-bedroom country house nestling in 10½ acres of lawns, meadows, woods, streams, and ponds, with views down a wooded valley to the sea. Alexander and Sally Low have furnished the centrally heated house with antiques, paintings, and other interesting objects. Open log fires blaze in the dining room and lounge in cool weather. The bedrooms, all with fine views of the countryside, have hot and cold water basins. For half board, the charges are £21 ($36.75) to £25 ($43.75) per person daily, depending on the season. Dinner, served in the candlelit dining room with views toward the sea, includes traditional English and Cornish dishes. The Lows invite guests to use the heated outdoor swimming pool in summer.

Just 1½ miles out of Looe on the east side is **Tregoad Farm Hotel,** St. Martins-by-Looe, Looe, Cornwall PL13 1PB (tel. 05036/2718), a lovely old Georgian farmhouse owned by Kenneth Hembrow and his wife, Joyce. Set atop a hill, the house overlooks the sea, and you can sit in bed and watch the Looe fishermen in the bay. Joyce does the cooking and produces large, nourishing breakfasts and five-course dinners, as well as packed lunches. The charge for B&B is £12 ($21) to £15 ($26.25) daily in a single, £20 ($35) to £26 ($45.50) in a double. Half board costs £15 ($26.25) to £17 ($29.75) per person daily, according to the season. There are tea- and coffee-making facilities in the rooms and color TV in the residents' lounge. The hotel is open from early April to the end of October.

The **Slate House,** Bucklawren, St. Martins-by-Looe, near Looe, Cornwall PL13 1NZ (tel. 05034/418), is a traditional old farmhouse that is beautifully kept by John and Betty-Ann Baynes-Reid. Arriving on a cool day in early autumn, you'll find a log fire burning. After a walk in the garden, you'll be ready for an evening meal before retiring to a comfortable room, costing from £10 ($17.50) to £11.50 ($20.15) per person daily for B&B, depending on the season. One reader found this place has "more than a touch of class."

WHERE TO EAT

Looe, both east and west, is another one of those gastronomic wastelands that one encounters in England, surprisingly in major tourist centers. An exception or two to that is previewed below.

Flower Pot, Lower Market Street, East Looe (tel. 05036/2314), has won the praise of many a reader. An old structure, typical of the port, it lies in the vicinity of the quay. From noon to 2 p.m. and 7 to 10 p.m. daily, it offers a good menu. The kitchen specializes in the fresh fish of the area, including, on occasion, sardines. The daily offerings are based on the shopping for seasonal produce. The repertoire is a sensible mix of dishes, and a widely diversified clientele, more noticeable in summer, likes the food. Nearly everyone finds the prices compatible: from £3.50 ($6.15) for lunch, with dinners costing from £10 ($17.50). You can buy wine by the glass should you not want a whole bottle.

On the outskirts, the **Talland Bay Hotel,** Talland Bay, Talland-by-Looe (tel. 0503/72667), lies four miles southwest of Looe by A387. An old country house set on 2½ acres, it serves the best food in the area. Yet a Sunday lunch with perfectly done roasts costs only £6.45 ($11.30), a set dinner going for £11.50 ($20.15). Meals are served daily from 12:30 to 2 p.m. and 7 to 9 p.m. A cold but enticing buffet of goodies is presented for lunch. Cornish seafood, of course, is the most preferred bill of fare, especially the locally caught crab and scallops.

If you wish, you can strike out from Looe on the cliff walk—a distance of 4½ miles—to Polperro. The less adventurous will drive.

2. Polperro

This ancient fishing village is reached by a steep descent from the top of a hill. Motorists in summer are forbidden to take their cars down unless they are booked in a hotel. Why? Because otherwise they'd create too much of a traffic bottleneck in July and August. The British have long been aware of the particular charm of this Cornish village.

At one time it was estimated that nearly every man, woman, and child in the village spent time salting down pilchards for the winter, or else was engaged in the art of smuggling. Today, tourists have replaced the contraband.

You'd have to search every cove and bay in Cornwall to come up with a village as handsomely mellowed as Polperro, which looks almost as if it had been removed intact from the 17th century. The village is tucked in between some cliffs. Its houses —really no more than fishermen's cottages—are bathed in pastel-wash. A small river, actually a stream called the Pol, splits its way through Polperro. The heart of the village is its much-photographed, much-painted fishing harbor, where the pilchard boats, loaded to the gunnels, used to dock.

ACCOMMODATIONS

In and around Polperro, you'll find a number of quite good and colorful cottages and houses that receive paying guests.

Landaviddy Manor, Polperro, Cornwall PL13 2RT (tel. 0503/72210), is a 200-year-old manor house built of gray Cornish stone on a secluded ledge on a hill above the village on the west side of Polperro. The manor stands in a peaceful and attractive setting, commanding a view of Polperro Bay and the coast. It adjoins National Trust land, giving access to cliff paths and coves along the coast. The Cornish moors and Dartmoor are easily accessible, as are numerous beaches nearby. Landaviddy retains its old character, yet all its bedrooms have hot and cold running water and innerspring mattresses. Some have private facilities. There is central heating as well, plus a comfortable lounge with TV, a cozy bar, and a licensed dining room. The owners, Sylvia and Derek Richards, charge £15 ($26.25) to £23.50 ($41.15) per person daily, depending on the room and its facilities. The higher price is for a four-poster bedroom with sea/country views and a shower and toilet. Reservations are required. Dinner of three courses and coffee is £10.50 ($18.40) per person. All prices include VAT.

The Old Vicarage, The Coombes, Polperro, Cornwall PL13 2RG (tel. 0503/72157), is a licensed, year-round guest hotel that is ideally located, lying right in the heart of town in the center of resort life. You are well taken care of here in one of the hotel's 14 bedrooms, five of which contain a full private bath. The best bargain is the half-board rate, costing from £12 ($21) to £15 ($26.25) per person nightly. Guests meet fellow guests in the sitting room or can enjoy a drink in the bar. Several cars can be accommodated in a private zone as well.

New House, Talland Hill, Polperro, Cornwall PL13 2RX (tel. 0503/72206), is a substantial guesthouse in a dramatic position overlooking the harbor and out toward the Eddystone light. Ken and Polly Perkins welcome guests warmly to their immaculate house. For a double room with a private bath and balcony, the charge for B&B is £26 ($45.50) daily, bathless twin-bedded and doubles costing £20 ($35) for B&B. Among the attractions are a pleasant lounge with color TV and a lovely garden for the use of guests. With only four units for rent, it is important to reserve your room in advance.

On the outskirts, **Allhays Country House Hotel,** Talland Bay, Looe, Cornwall PL13 2JB (tel. 0503/72434), stands at the edge of a narrow lane. It is a large country house filled with character, with white stucco walls, cozy nooks, comfortable furniture, and imposing stone fireplaces. Lynda and Brian Spring, urban refugees from London, purchased the place in 1985 and have considerably upgraded it. The house was built in the 1930s. They rent seven attractively furnished bedrooms, most of which contain private baths or showers, including the master bedroom with a fine brass four-poster bed, plus the Carriage House, recently converted to a luxury bedroom with a Victorian-style bath. The cost ranges from £25 ($43.75) to £37.50 ($65.65) per person daily for half board. The good-tasting English food is served in an Edwardian conservatory. Dishes are likely to include duck with orange and lemon sauce or chicken in cider and honey. The house is surrounded by nearly two acres of gardens and grounds, with a greenhouse for growing flowers and grapes. From many of the bedroom windows, you'll have views of the Channel. The hotel lies 2½ miles east of Looe, 2½ miles west of Polperro.

WHERE TO EAT

Good English cookery is offered at **The Kitchen,** Fish na Bridge (tel. 0503/72780), a pink cottage about halfway down to the harbor from the car park. Once a wagon-builder's shop, it is now a restaurant, run by Vanessa and Ian Bateson. Everything is homemade from the best fresh ingredients available. Ian is the chef, except Vanessa makes all the homemade desserts herself, and bakes the bread. Reservations are essential. The menu changes seasonally and is biased toward local fresh fish. Typical dishes include crab in phyllo pastry, seafood Provençal, and roasted garlic monkfish. Lunch is from 12:30 to 2:30 p.m. daily, two courses costing from £6 ($10.50). Dinner, nightly in summer from 7 to 9:30, costs from £9.50 ($16.35), although you can order a house menu at £12 ($21) and a vegetarian menu at £8 ($14). In winter, service is offered only on Friday and Saturday.

The **Captain's Cabin,** Lansallos Street (tel. 0503/72292), in one of the mellow old structures of town, a 16th-century fisherman's cottage, invites you to dine among antiques and brass in the beamed, low-ceilinged dining room. The owner, Lesley Jacobs, and her staff offer a comprehensive cuisine. The chef has a fine reputation for his local fish dishes, from among which you might choose crab mornay, lobster thermidor, or grilled lemon sole. The wide variety of fresh local fish is brought in daily by the fishermen of Polperro. At lunchtime, 11:30 a.m. to 2:30 p.m., you can order à la carte meals for around £6 ($10.50), or special snacks and sandwiches such as fresh crab and salad. At dinner there are à la carte listings and chef's specials, as well as two set meals: three courses for around £7.95 ($13.90), and four courses for £10.95 ($19.15) to £12.95 ($22.65). Dinner is served from 7 to 11 p.m. The Cabin is open daily all year, including holidays.

Nelsons Restaurant, Saxon Bridge (tel. 0503/72366), is owned and run by the Nelson family, not only Peter and Betty but Tony as well. Peter and Tony do the cooking, and Betty takes care of everything up front. They always have at least three soups—fish, crab, lobster, vegetable, meat. Each pot is homemade. Before your main course rests on your plate, it was probably swimming. However, you can also order home-cooked ham or beef, served with vegetable and a salad. A three-course menu goes for £10.50 ($18.40), and you can also order à la carte. For dessert, try one of their homemade ice creams using fresh fruit. They also offer many classic flans and pies. Hours are from noon to 2 p.m. and 7 to 9:30 p.m., except at lunchtime on Saturday and all day Monday. The place is richly decorated in reds with nautical trappings.

Crump's Bistro, Crumplehorn (tel. 0503/72312) always gives you a warm welcome. It used to be hard to find an inexpensive place to eat in Polperro until this family-owned and -run bistro and wine bar opened in a farmhouse with heavy beams that is well on its way to three centuries of life. Most visitors seem to pass through this pleasant little place for lunch, enjoying fairly light fare such as quiches and good-tasting, crisp salads. You can also get a pizza. Expect to escape for around £5 ($7.50). If you're lucky enough to get to spend at least one night of your life in Polperro, you can partake of more substantial fare, ordering from a set menu. Lunches cost from £5 ($8.75) and dinners from £8 ($14). Hours are from 11 a.m. to 5 p.m. and 7 to 9:30 p.m. daily.

THE VILLAGE PUB

Near the harbor, the **Three Pilchards** (tel. 0503/72233) is where the locals and sophisticates alike go for their pints of beer and social activity. It's a large L-shaped room with a fireplace that burns brightly at night. Black oak is used almost everywhere. Why don't you sit in the window-seat and listen to the talk of the villagers? That isn't really as rude as it sounds, as you may not be able to understand a word of their thick Cornish dialect. Food is served continuously during opening hours in the form of bar snacks that are rather substantial platters, everything from a Polperro fish bake to "drunken pig" cooked in cider. Plates begin at £3.50 ($6.15). The pub is open from 11 a.m. to 11 p.m. Monday to Saturday, and from noon to 3 p.m. and 7 to 10:30 p.m. Sunday.

3. Fowey

Called the Dartmouth of Cornwall, Fowey is an old town of historical interest, one of the most ancient seaports in the West Country. Once the Fowey Gallants sailed the seas and were considered invincible when raiding French coastal towns. At the time of the Armada, Fowey sent more ships than London. With its narrow streets and whitewashed houses, the town has remained unspoiled over the years, enjoying a sheltered position on a deep-water channel. Its creeks and estuary attract sailors and fishermen. If you climb to St. Catherine's Point, you'll be rewarded with a view of the harbor. There are sandy beaches and coves to explore here, as well as an 18-hole golf course within easy reach of Carlyon Bay.

FOOD AND LODGING

Right in the heart of town, opening onto a quay, the **King of Prussia,** Town Quay, Fowey, Cornwall PL23 1AT (tel. 072683/2450), is a modest hotel and busy public house operated by Andy and Lesley McCartney. It's named after a local character who was a famous smuggler. Aside from having a rather formal appearance and a central exterior staircase, it is quite informal. It is the best low-priced hotel in Fowey. The charge is £12.50 ($21.90) per person daily for B&B in a bathless room. A room with private bath costs £35 ($61.25) for double occupancy. Prices increase slightly in July and August. Each room has hot and cold running water, color TV, and a river view. Everything is well kept. A small restaurant is open in summer, and in a bar overlooking the river, a variety of snacks is available at lunchtime and in the evening. You can also order Cornish ale "from the wood" (that is, from traditional wooden barrels).

Riverside, Passage Street, Fowey, Cornwall PL23 1DE (tel. 072683/2275), is the all-purpose ferry-landing hotel of Fowey, run under the watchful eye of Mr. and Mrs. H. L. Elliott, the owners. Directly on the water as well as the main street at Fowey, the hotel is at the little car-ferry station where regular crossings leave for Bodinnick. The establishment has an individualistic decor. Most have views of the river, and from your window you can observe the passing river craft and ferries. All 14 of the hotel's bedrooms have hot and cold running water, but only six are equipped with private baths or showers. Rates are based on the time of the year, the plumbing, and the view. Bed and a full English breakfast costs from £17 ($29.75) to £23 ($38.50) per person daily. For stays of more than two nights, a half-board rate of £27 ($47.25) to £33 ($57.75) per person nightly will be quoted. The chef specializes in hot and cold salmon and lobster dishes; the produce caught locally is fresh and tasty.

At Bodinnick-by-Fowey

At **The Old Ferry Inn,** Bodinnick-by-Fowey, Cornwall PL23 1LX (tel. 072687/237), it's hard to believe that this warm fresh comfortable place has been standing here overlooking the Fowey Estuary for four centuries. The inn is easily reached by car-ferry from Fowey. Charming and spotless, it's filled with antiques, mostly 18th century, and paintings. Six comfortably furnished bedrooms are rented in the older section, plus another seven in a modern addition. Five contain private bath. The charge, depending on the plumbing, ranges from £22.50 ($39.40) per person daily. Dinner in the atmospheric restaurant is another £15 ($26.25) per person. In the pub you can enjoy nautical prints and seagoing paraphernalia while sampling the good ale and drink.

4. Truro

This ancient town on the Truro River is the only cathedral city in Cornwall. As such, it is the ecclesiastical center of Cornwall. The Cathedral Church of St. Mary was begun in 1880 in the Early English style (the spires are in the Norman Gothic design). The town is within 8 to 20 miles of the Cornish beaches. It can be used as a base to explore the countryside, ranging from bleak Bodmin Moor to fertile farmland and the Winter Roseland of the Falmouth Estuary.

Trelissick Garden (tel. 0872/862090) lies on both sides of the B3289 south of Truro, overlooking King Harry Passage. The entrance is just off the King Harry Ferry up the hill and beyond the circular tower. In this beautiful wooded park with peaceful walks through the well-tended trees and shrubs, the rhododendrons are a splash of color in early summer. Upon arrival, you pick up a map and set out on a woodland walk that will take you through the plantations to the banks of Lamouth Creek and all along the edge of the River Fal and Channals Creek before you return to the center of the garden, about a one-hour stroll. Then you can visit the gardens where the vegetation is more controlled and see the special plant section where experiments on acclimatization are made.

The restaurant here (tel. 0872/863486) is open daily at 11 a.m. for coffee and from 12:15 to 2:15 p.m. for lunch, with afternoon teas served until 6 p.m. The emphasis is on wholesome, fresh food, such as homemade soup and Cornish ice creams and clotted cream. A lunch costs £6 ($10.50) Monday to Saturday, £8.25 ($14.45) for a three-course meal on Sunday, which includes a roast and coffee. You can also have sherry Cornish cider or one of the various lagers.

The garden is open April to October from 11 a.m. to 6 p.m. Monday to Saturday, 1 to 6 p.m. (or to sunset if earlier) on Sunday. Entry to the park and woodland walk is free. To visit the gardens costs adults £1.80 ($3.15), and children pay 90p ($1.60).

WHERE TO STAY

At a seven-room guest house, **Colthrop,** 46 Tregolls Rd., Truro, Cornwall TR1 1LA (tel. 0872/72920), you get a hearty welcome and a good bed and a large Cornish breakfast the next morning. That way, you can take the bargain half-board rate, costing from £10 ($17.50) to £12.50 ($21.90) per person nightly. Six of the rooms have a private shower, and one accommodation is reserved for families.

Outside of town, you might try **Greatwood,** Allet, near Shortlanesend, Truro, Cornwall TR4 9DW (tel. 0872/76581), which stands on about six acres of land. It attracts seekers of tranquility to its precincts, where guests are housed comfortably. Three rooms are reserved for families, and the public bath is shared. The rate is among the best in the area: only £9.75 ($17.05) per person daily for B&B, and from £13.50 ($23.65) to £15.50 ($27.15) per person for bed, a Cornish breakfast, and a farm-style dinner. The guesthouse is closed in November and December.

At Tresillian

About three miles from Truro, the village of Tresillian lies along the River Fal. In the heart of the village, David Cocks has opened a guesthouse, **The Granary,** Tresillian, near Truro, Cornwall TR2 4BN (tel. 087252/279), with six bedrooms, all with hot and cold running water, and one with a private bath. He offers B&B for £9 ($15.75) to £10.50 ($18.40) per person daily, with evening meals available by arrangement, costing £4.50 ($7.90). David learned the basics of successful guesthouse operation from his parents, who run Colthrop in Truro, recommended above.

5. St. Mawes

Overlooking the mouth of the Fal River, St. Mawes is often compared to a port on the Riviera. Because it's sheltered from the northern winds, subtropical plants are found here. From the town quay, you can take a boat to Frenchman's Creek, Helford River, and other places. Mostly, St. Mawes is noted for its sailing, boating, fishing, and yachting. A half dozen sandy coves lie within 15 minutes by car from the port. The town, built on the Roseland Peninsula, makes for interesting walks, with its color-washed cottages and sheltered harbor. On Castle Point, Henry VIII ordered the construction of St. Mawes Castle. Falmouth, across the water, is only two miles away.

FOOD AND LODGING

A little gem along the waterfront, **St. Mawes Hotel,** The Seafront, St. Mawes, Cornwall TR2 5DW (tel. 0326/270266), was built as a hotel in the 17th century in an architectural style known as "William and Mary." Several historians have mentioned the hotel in accounts of long ago. Clifford and Juliet Burrows run the kind of place that people in the cold north dream of for their holiday on the Cornish Riviera. In spite of the antiquity of the place, everything is kept up-to-date. The Burrowses offer only seven bedrooms, and these are grabbed up quickly in July and August by those who have made reservations in advance. Rooms at this family-owned small hotel of character cost £30 ($52.50) per person daily based on double occupancy (there are no single rooms). Each well-furnished accommodation contains a private bath. Even if you don't stay here, you can visit for a meal, enjoying British and continental dishes, with dinners costing from £13 ($22.75). As befits its location on the sea, the kitchen specializes in fresh fish, including lobster and crab. The hotel is closed November to January.

Georgian House, 5 Grove Hill, St. Mawes, Cornwall TR2 5BJ (tel. 0326/270707), is one of the best B&Bs in the area, lying smack in the center behind a red-brick facade built in the Georgian style in the early 19th century. It opens onto views of the water and is close to the terminal where, if you wish, you can board a ferry for Falmouth (which will be previewed later). Open March to October, the house has three bedrooms to rent, none with private bath. The cost for B&B is from £12.50 ($21.90) per person nightly, with breakfast included.

Opposite the Catholic Church, **Braganza,** Grove Hill, St. Mawes, Cornwall TR2 5BJ (tel. 0326/270281), is a Regency house, furnished with antiques and furniture of the period. It offers three twin-bedded rooms with private bath and two without. All are centrally heated. There is a perfect Regency staircase. The house has a lounge with TV, and bedrooms have tea- and coffee-makers. Charges range from £16 ($28) to £20 ($35) per person daily and include an English breakfast and VAT. There is ample parking space. The house, operated by the owner, Mrs. Zofia Moseley, has an extensive garden overlooking the harbor of St. Mawes, where yacht racing takes place twice a week in the summer. Lord Byron, who stayed in Falmouth in 1809, may have visited this house, for he mentions its name in one of his poems. It's said that his limping step can be heard at the Braganza on windy nights.

Green Lanterns, Marine Parade, St. Mawes, Cornwall TR2 5DW (tel. 0326/270502), was originally built in 1900 but since then its stone exterior has been painted white. It is one of the better guesthouses in the area, run by the Brown family. Each of its eight comfortable bedrooms contains a private bath, costing from £21 ($36.75) per person daily for B&B. Each accommodation has a TV and beverage-making equipment. Dinner is offered to both residents and nonresidents daily from 7 to 9:30 p.m., costing from £13.50 ($23.65) to £15 ($26.25), depending on the menu that night.

PORTLOE

If you really want to get away from it all and go to that hidden-away Cornish fishing village, then Portloe may be for you. On the slope of a hill opening onto Veryan Bay, it is reached by a road suitable for cars.

Portloe might be an ideal stopover on the South Cornish Coast if you're traveling to the West Country in July and August, which are the months when the popular tourist centers, such as Looe and St. Ives, are overrun with sightseers. Here, in Portloe, the living's more relaxed.

The **Lugger Hotel,** Portloe, Cornwall TR2 5RD (tel. 0872/501322), is a 17th-century establishment at the top of the harbor slip, with a bay and boats as part of the scene. It is believed to have been a smugglers' hideaway in its early days, but today the Powell family runs it as a modernized, sparkling-clean hotel on the water's edge. The 20 bedrooms all have private baths or showers and toilets, color TV, radios, central heating, tea- and coffee-makers, and direct-dial phones. The charges are from £39.50 ($69.15) to £44 ($77) per person daily for a bed, an English breakfast, dinner, and VAT. Accommodations in the main building and the 19th-century bedroom wing are traditionally furnished in Tudor or Victorian style. The restaurant, which is open to nonresidents for dinner, has a panoramic view of the cove. A cocktail bar occupies the original inn parlor, and the hotel also has lounges, a sauna, and a solarium. Guests are allowed reduced greens fees at nearby Truro Golf Club. The hotel is open from mid-March to early November, with room rates reduced for stays of more than two days.

---

6. Falmouth

A lot of cutthroat smugglers used to live in the area. In fact, when John Killigrew, a leading citizen, started to build a lighthouse on Lizard Head, they protested that the beacon in the night would deprive them of their livelihood and "take awaye God's Grace from us." Falmouth, 26 miles from Penzance, is today a favorite base for the yachting set, which considers it one of the most beautiful harbors in Europe. On a small peninsula, Falmouth's old section overlooks the landlocked inner harbor. The newer part, the center for most of the hotels, faces the bay and commands a panoramic sweep from St. Anthony's Lighthouse to Pendennis Castle. Warmed in winter by the Gulf Stream, Falmouth has become an all-year resort. Built on a promontory overlooking the fjord-like estuary of the Fal, it was once occupied in part by the captains of old mail-carrying packet ships. Many find it a good center for touring the rugged Cornish coastline. It's possible, for example, to take a ferry from Falmouth to St. Mawes, a 20-minute ride.

Pendennis Castle was once part of Henry VIII's coastal defense system. It dates from 1544, when the central circular keep with semicircular bastions enclosed by a curtain wall was completed on the site of a prehistoric fortress. Since Tudor days it has protected the entrance to Falmouth Harbour. During the Civil War it suffered siege. Henrietta Maria, wife of Charles I, found shelter here as she fled to France. The castle was besieged in 1646 by Parliamentary forces into surrender, but because of the bravery of the governor, his soldiers and citizens were allowed to march out with drums beating, colors flying, and trumpets sounding.

Nowadays it is a more peaceful place, besieged only by tourists and sightseers. It is host to the Youth Hostels Association, who run a hostel in the old barrack block. The castle is open daily from Good Friday until the end of September from 10 a.m. to 6 p.m. Off-season hours are from 10 a.m. to 4 p.m. Admission is £1.30 ($2.30) for adults, 65p ($1.15) for children. For information, phone 0326/316594.

During most of the year, sightseeing craft ply up and down the River Fal from the Prince of Wales Pier in Falmouth to the Town Quay in Truro. There are also morning and afternoon cruises to view the docks and the castle, St. Just, as well as romantic creeks, stately riverside mansions, and smugglers' cottages.

WHERE TO STAY

One of the finest of the small hotels, **Tresillian House,** 3 Stracey Rd., Falmouth, Cornwall TR11 4DW (tel. 0326/312425), is family owned and operated, lying in a tranquil district close to the center of town and the harbor. Mr. and Mrs. Brown rent a dozen well-furnished and tastefully decorated bedrooms, each with private bath or shower. Amenities include such extras as hairdryers, color TV, and phones, as well as beverage-making equipment. B&B rates range from £17 ($29.75) to £18.50 ($32.40) daily in a single, going up to £33 ($57.75) to £36 ($63) in a double. Guests are received from March to October. The cuisine is excellent, and you may consider taking all your meals here. You can order bar lunches, afternoon tea, and a dinner costing about £9 ($15.75), which has been specially prepared by Mrs. Brown herself. The fare is British. The hotel is fully licensed for drinks.

A family-run establishment, the **Tudor Court Hotel,** 55 Melvill Rd., Falmouth, Cornwall TR11 4BR (tel. 0326/312807), is within a few minutes' walk of the beaches and the town center. Ron and Kay Swadé, assisted by their sons David and Robert, see to all your requirements. Most rooms have private baths or showers, and all contain color TV, tea- and coffee-makers, full central heating, and all are comfortably furnished. The cost for a bed, full English breakfast, and four-course dinner is from £19.50 ($32.40) per person daily. There is a separate lounge/dining room, and a small bar is entered from the lounge. You can order at extra cost such things as bar meals, packed lunches, and sandwiches.

Harbour Hotel, 1 Harbour Terrace, Falmouth, Cornwall TR11 2AN (tel. 0326/311344), is a small, family-run establishment operated by Colin and June Larkin. It gives personal service and has a homelike atmosphere. The cost of one of the six bedrooms is from £11.50 ($20.15) per person daily for B&B. Some rooms have a toilet and shower. Half board costs from £16 ($28) to £17.50 ($30.65) per person. The hotel has central heating throughout, and each unit has tea- or coffee-making facilities. The hotel has views overlooking Falmouth Inner Harbour and 4½ miles beyond. There is also a licensed bar.

Beach Walk House, 39 Castle Dr., Falmouth, Cornwall TR11 4NF (tel. 0326/319841), was originally built in the 1870s as a cottage for members of the British Coast Guard and their families. This pleasant ocean-fronting house contains four guest bedrooms, each with private bath and color TV. Set on the south coast of Falmouth (the more tranquil side), the establishment is owned and operated by Mr. and Mrs. A. G. Clarke, who keep the place neat and clean. Behind a facade of pebble-studded stucco, you will find good views of the coastline (on a clear day you can see all the way to Lizard's Point). Only breakfast is served, and it's included in the price of £12 ($21) per person nightly. Unlike many of its neighbors, the Beach Walk is open all year.

WHERE TO EAT

Overlooking the harbor, **Secrets,** 6 Arwenack St. (tel. 0326/318585), is run with dedication by its hard-working owners. In summer they fill up with visitors, but in winter they cater mainly to their reliable friends, the local residents who know they can get some of the best and most reasonably priced food in town here. No one puts on airs. The menu is straightforward, using fresh ingredients. Try, for example, the Cornish fishermen's pie or one of the posted (changing daily) specials. Crêpes and quiche, along with fresh salads, are regularly featured. In summer, hours are from 10 a.m. to 4:30 p.m. (they do a brisk afternoon tea business) and 7 to 10 p.m. In winter, they are open only from 11 a.m. to 2:30 p.m., and they serve dinner at that time only on Friday and Saturday from 7 to 10 p.m. They are also closed on Sunday in winter. Meals cost from £6 ($10.50).

The **Cornish Kitchen Café and Bistro,** 28 Arwenack St. (tel. 0326/316509), is a small eating place backing up to the water. Michael McDonald and Connie own the establishment. At lunch, you can order a hot soup and crusty bread, or perhaps shrimp and mussels, and certainly fried scampi (shrimp) and chips. My crab sandwich bulged, and I could also have ordered the local crab salad. A simple lunch costs from £4 ($7). In the evening, Connie cooks excellent dishes, especially crab soup and French onion soup. Main courses include local lemon sole grilled with prawns, monkfish, giant prawn kebabs, and pan-fried chicken with bacon, sage, and wine sauce. They also serve Falmouth Bay lobster and local oysters and clams in the evening. A three-course meal with a glass of wine costs about £8 ($16). Hours are daily from 11 a.m. to 2 p.m. and 6 to 10:30 p.m.

POLDARK MINE

Three miles north of Helston on the B3297 is the **Poldark Mine and Heritage Complex,** Wendron (tel. 0326/573173). As you have driven around Cornwall, the old workings of the tin mines will have been evident everywhere. Here you have the chance to visit a mine and walk through the old works, which extend for several miles beneath the surface. Recent extension of the area open to the public into newly discovered caverns has made the tour of the mine last more than an hour. There are extensive Heritage Museums depicting the living conditions of the 18th-century mining community and the history of tin. One museum houses the famous Holman collection, and another features the largest collection of flatirons in Europe and perhaps the world. Amid prize-winning gardens are restaurants, Cornish craft shops, picnic areas, and children's play areas. The Mine and Heritage Complex is open from 10 a.m. to 6 p.m. daily April to October (to 8 p.m. in August). The last mine tour is one hour before closing. Admission to the mine is £3.30 ($5.80) for adults, £2 ($3.50) for children.

The mine and surrounding area are of particular interest to readers and television viewers of the *Poldark* series, filmed from novels by Winston Graham.

A SIDE TRIP TO LIZARD

The most southerly point of England is Lizard, an unremarkable spot with jagged rocks reaching out into the sea where cormorants and gulls fish.

Right on the point, beneath the lighthouse, is the workshop of a man who must surely have one of the most perfect one-man cottage industries in the country. Mr. Casley runs **Lizard Point Serpentine Works** (tel. 0326/290706) in one of the small shacks by the car park. There he turns, polishes, and fashions into pots, vases, ashtrays, and dishes the serpentine stone found only in this part of the country. The veins in the stone can be green, gray, or sometimes red.

Ornamental barometers and clocks are costly, but these are absolutely genuine souvenirs made by a man who is entirely at peace with himself and the country he lives in. His two sons assist with the quarrying of the stone, which comes from under Coonhilly Down close by, the site of the country's largest radio-receiving and space-tracking station. Mr. Casley's son, another blue-eyed Cornishman, is fast learning the trade, so there is every hope that in 50 years there will still be someone whistling happily in the tiny workshop at the tip of Lizard.

Mrs. Ingrid Sowden, Villa Clare, Lizard Point near Helston, Cornwall TR12 7NU (tel. 0326/290300), must be the owner of the most southerly bedroom in England. Her home is definitely the most southerly house in the country, built on solid granite with a terraced garden. It opens onto fantastic views over the sea and the cliff edge from the garden fence some 170 feet above sea level. Despite this, the house is frequently showered with spray from the breakers below during storms. Mrs. Sowden, who settled here from Germany some 30 years ago, charges £9 ($15.75) per person daily for B&B. If she can't take you in, she'll recommend one of her friends in the village. If given advance notice, she will also prepare a four-course evening meal for £4 ($7).

7. Penzance

This little Gilbert and Sullivan harbor town is the end of the line for the Cornish Riviera Express. A full 280 miles southwest from London, it is noted for its equable climate (it's one of the first towns in England to blossom out with spring flowers), and summer throngs descend for fishing, sailing, and swimming. Overlooking Mount's Bay, Penzance is graced in places with subtropical plants, as well as palm trees.

The harbor is used to activity of one sort or another. *The Pirates of Penzance* were not entirely fictional. The town was raided by Barbary pirates, destroyed in part by Cromwell's troops, sacked and burnt by the Spaniards, and bombed by the Germans. In spite of its turbulent past, it offers tranquil resort living today.

The most westerly town in England, Penzance makes a good base for exploring Land's End, the Lizard Peninsula, St. Michael's Mount, the old fishing ports and artists' colonies of St. Ives, Newlyn, Mousehole, and the Isles of Scilly.

THE SIGHTS

Three miles east of Penzance, **St. Michael's Mount** is reached at low tide by a causeway. Rising about 250 feet from the sea, St. Michael's Mount is topped by a partially medieval, partially 17th-century castle. At high tide the mount becomes an island, reachable only by motor launch from Marazion. A Benedictine monastery, the gift of Edward the Confessor, stood on this spot in the 11th century. The castle, with its collections of armor and antique furniture, is open from 10:30 a.m. to 5:45 p.m. Monday to Friday from the end of March to the end of October. Admission is £2.50 ($4.40) for adults, £1.25 ($2.20) for children. From Penzance take bus 20, 21, or 22, then get off at Marazion, the town opposite St. Michael's Mount. To avoid disappointment, it's a good idea to telephone the office of St. Michael's Mount (tel. 0736/710507) to learn the state of the tides, especially during the winter months, when a regular ferry service does not operate. After a longish walk over the causeway, be warned that there is quite a hard climb up cobbled streets to reach the castle. You must wear sensible shoes.

The **Minack Theatre** in Porthcurno, nine miles from Penzance, is unique. It's carved out of the Cornish cliff face with the Atlantic as its impressive backdrop and was built almost entirely by one woman, Rowena Cade. In tiered seating, similar to that of the theaters of Ancient Greece, 550 persons can watch the show and the rocky coast beyond the stage. The theater's season of plays and musical shows begins at the end of May and continues until mid September. There is an exhibition hall that houses a permanent record of the life and work of Rowena Cade. This exhibition center is open from Easter to October 31 and includes a chance to visit the theater outside of performance times. Seats cost around £3 ($5.25) and may be purchased at the box office. The price includes a free visit to the exhibition center. When no performance is on, admission to the center and to see the theater is £1 ($1.75). For details, phone 0736/810471 during the season. To reach Minack, leave Penzance on the A30 heading toward Land's End. After three miles, bear left onto the B3283 and follow signposts to Porthcurno.

WHERE TO STAY

On a quiet street, **Alexandra Hotel,** Alexandra Terrace, Penzance, Cornwall TR18 4NX (tel. 0736/62644), is interconnected on two levels with an adjacent hotel, the **Southern Comfort.** These properties contain a total of 33 pleasant bedrooms. All but two of them have private baths. Both were originally built as 19th-century town houses lying within a ten-minute walk of the center of Penzance. Depending on the season, per person rates range from £16 ($28) to £19 ($33.25) daily for B&B. Single occupancy costs another £8 ($14) to £9 ($15.75) daily, and bathless rooms rent for about £2 ($3.50) less. A four-course fixed-price dinner goes from £8 ($14) per person, and the hotel is licensed to serve drinks from its bar.

Directly on the sidewalk, **Mincarlo,** Chapel Street, Penzance, Cornwall TR18 4AE (tel. 0736/62848), is a guesthouse owned by Mrs. Welsh. It is near the Admiral Benbow restaurant. Mrs. Welsh tends to the large house herself, serving hearty Cornish breakfasts in her dining room, which is filled with antiques. Bright of spirit and most hospitable, she charges from £8 ($14) per person daily for B&B. In one room, a four-poster was installed by popular demand. Mincarlo is neat and adequate.

Richmond Lodge, 61 Morrab Rd., Penzance, Cornwall TR18 4EX (tel. 0736/65560), is a comfortable early Victorian house with a nautical flavor lying a few steps from Market Jew Street (the main street) and within an easy walk of the Promenade along the sea wall. The Morrab Gardens are across the street. The host-owners, Jean and Pat Eady, have warm courtesy, down-to-earth friendliness, and an unrehearsed charm. A Cornish woman, Mrs. Eady provides faultless service in this clean bright homelike place with full central heating to keep out the chill and a fully licensed bar for the occasional toddy. Some bedrooms have private baths. The tariff for B&B is £10 ($17.50) per person daily, plus a £2 supplement for such rooms as those with four-poster beds and private baths. Dinner can be ordered daily at £5.50 ($9.65).

Kimberley House, 10 Morrab Rd., Penzance, Cornwall TR18 4EZ (tel. 0736/62727), lies between the Promenade and the center of town, opposite Penlee Park and near the Morrab Gardens. Avril and Rex Mudway have run this house since his retirement after a long seagoing career. They are gracious to their guests, not only providing good food and accommodations but offering tips about what to see in the area. B&B costs £11 ($19.25) per person, and a rather large dinner goes for £6 ($10.50).

Carnson House Hotel, East Terrace, Penzance, Cornwall TR18 4TD (tel. 0736/65589), is personally run by Trisha and Richard Hilder, two friendly owners. Close to the harbor, town center, station, and beach, their house is convenient for train, coach, and bus travelers. They charge from £11 ($19.25) per person daily for B&B, plus another £6.25 ($10.95) for dinner. All bedrooms have tea- and coffee-makers and some have private showers and toilets. There is a comfortable TV lounge for the use of guests, and the house is licensed to serve alcoholic beverages. The Hilders provide a tourist information service on local "things to do." They are also ticket agents for local bus and coach tours as well as steamer trips to the Isles of Scilly.

Sea & Horses Hotel, Alexandra Terrace, Penzance, Cornwall TR18 4NX (tel. 0736/61961), was originally built in 1830 as a "gentleman's private house." Its solid granite exterior rises from a spot only 150 yards from the sea. You'll find it on the western outskirts of town, within easy walking distance of the center. Alec Mansfield, the owner, charges from £15 ($26.25) per person nightly for B&B. Each of his 11 comfortable bedrooms contains a private bath and beverage-making equipment. Four-course fixed-priced dinners can also be ordered here for £7.50 ($13.15).

Tremont Hotel, Alexandra Road, Penzance, Cornwall TR18 4LZ (tel. 0736/62614), is a pleasant guesthouse on a tree-lined street just up from the Promenade and the seafront. Mrs. Maureen Pengelly runs this stone-built house with its scrupulously clean bedrooms and comfortable furnishings. Guests are housed in single, double, or twin-bedded rooms, some with bath but all with color TV and full central heating. Some rooms are suitable for families. Charges are from £11 ($19.25) per person nightly for B&B, plus another £6 ($10.50) for a well-prepared dinner, which you should arrange in advance.

On the Outskirts

Higher Trevorian Hotel, St. Buryan, Penzance, Cornwall TR19 6EA (tel. 0736/810348), is a small secluded informal hotel ideally situated for exploring "Poldark Country," with all the beaches, coves, cliffs, harbors, and streams visited in novels and pictured in the "Poldark" TV series. Vivian and Paul Trimble receive B&B guests in their hotel in a section between Penzance and Land's End, just a quarter mile from the village of St. Buryan. The nine bedrooms, some with private baths, are rented for £11.50 ($20.15) per person daily. Dinner is served for £7 ($12.25). Home-cooked food is served, making use of much local produce. Guests can relax in the TV lounge or in the Grapevine Bar. There's plenty of free parking.

WHERE TO EAT

A second-floor dining room, **Olive Branch Vegetarian Restaurant,** 3a The Terrace, Market Jew Street (tel. 0736/62438), is over a store that was the birthplace of Humphrey Davy. A plaque commemorates that event, and a statue of Davy stands on the square. Try for a chair with a view overlooking St. Michael's Mount. You might begin with a homemade vegetable soup, then follow with a "bean burger" or else parsnip-and-cashew patties. Snacks or sandwiches are made to order. Meals cost from £6 ($10.50). Throughout the year, lunch is served daily from 10 a.m. to 2:30 p.m. Dinner is offered from 5 to 8 p.m. nightly in summer, but only on Tuesday, Thursday, and Friday in winter.

Turk's Head, Chapel Street (tel. 0736/63093), is reputed to be the oldest inn in Penzance, dating from 1233. It serves the finest food of any pub in town, far superior to its chief rival, the nearby Admiral Benbow. In summer, drinkers overflow into the garden. Inside, the inn is decorated in a mellow old style, as befits its age, with flatirons and other artifacts hanging from its time-worn beams. Meals, costing from £6 ($10.50), include fishermen's pie, T-bone steaks, and chicken curry. Food is served from 11 a.m. to 2:30 p.m. and 5:30 to 10 p.m. Monday to Saturday, and from noon to 2:30 p.m. and 7 to 10 p.m. Sunday. The bars are open from 11 a.m. to 11 p.m. Monday to Saturday, and from noon to 3 p.m. and 7 to 10:30 p.m. Sunday.

On the outskirts, **Enzo Restaurant,** Newbridge (tel. 0736/63777), serves the best Italian food in the area. Family owned by two Scottish-born immigrants to Cornwall, Anne and Bill Blows, it charges from £7 ($12.25) to £15 ($26.25) for a full meal. You might have a predinner drink in the bar before selecting a seat in either a beamed and old-fashioned dining room or within a glass-walled, greenhouse-like conservatory. Within the conservatory, diners enjoy a "cuisine as theater" view of the family preparing pastas and grilled fish. Specialties include spaghetti with clam sauce, pollo Vesuviano (chicken with tomatoes, mozzarella, and herbs), and an array of veal and beef dishes. Only dinner is served nightly from 7 to 9:30. The establishment is closed Tuesday in winter, and Sunday lunch is also offered from 12:30 to 2 p.m.

8. The Isles of Scilly

Perhaps the most interesting and scenic excursion from Penzance is a day trip to the Isles of Scilly, which lie off the Cornish coast about 27 miles west-southwest of Land's End. There are five inhabited and more than 100 uninhabited islands in the group, some consisting of merely a few square miles and others, such as St. Mary's, the largest, encompassing some 30 square miles. Two of these islands attract tourists, St. Mary's and Tresco.

These islands were known to the early Greeks and the Romans, and in Celtic legend they were inhabited entirely by holy men. There are more ancient burial mounds in the islands than anywhere else in southern England, and artifacts found establish clearly that people lived here more than 4000 years ago.

Today there is little left of this long history to show the visitor. Now these are islands of peace and beauty, where early flowers are the main export and tourism the main industry.

St. Mary's is the capital, containing about seven-eighths of the total population of all the islands, and it is here that the ship from the mainland docks at Hugh Town. However, for the day visitor, I recommend the helicopter flight from Penzance to **Tresco,** the neighboring island.

HOW TO GET THERE

Daily departures are made by the **Isles of Scilly Steamship Company,** Quay Street, Penzance (tel. 0736/62009), from March to October, except Sunday. The trip from Penzance to Hugh Town, St. Mary's, takes about three hours. Steamships leave Penzance daily at 9:15 a.m. and return from Scilly at 4:45 p.m. In winter there is restricted service. Rates start with a walk-on single same-day round-trip fare of £22 ($38.50) for adults, £10 ($17.50) for children. To visit the other islands, go first to St. Mary's by steamship and take the small interisland boat. For information on interisland launches, phone Kathy Stedeford at 0720/22886.

British International Helicopters, at the Penzance Airport (tel. 0736/63871), operates a year-round helicopter service between Penzance and St. Mary's or Tresco. Flight time is 20 minutes. The standard fare from Penzance to either of the islands is £24 ($42) each way. Flights start at 7:50 a.m. in high season, July to September, and at 8:45 at other times. They continue regularly throughout the day, with the last flight back to Penzance at 6:15 p.m. in high season, 4:10 p.m. otherwise. For people arriving in Penzance on the train, there is bus service between the railway station and the heliport. The cost is £1 ($1.75) each way; the travel time, only five minutes.

British Rail runs express trains from Paddington Station, London, to Penzance. BritRail Passes can be used. Travel time is about five hours. There are special offers on the Night Riviera Express.

For those who wish to travel to Penzance by road, there is good express bus service. The Rapide costs from around £23.50 ($41.15) round-trip for the journey from London, about eight hours each way. The buses are fitted with toilets and have reclining seats and a hostess who dispenses coffee, tea, and sandwiches. These buses are run by **National Express** from Victoria Coach Station, 172 Buckingham Palace Rd., London, S.W.1 (tel. 01/730-0202).

WHERE TO STAY ON TRESCO

You are welcomed to the **New Inn,** Tresco, Isles of Scilly, Cornwall TR24 0PU (tel. 0720/22844) by Chris and Lesley Hopkins. Their pub, built of stone, has an outdoor area for those who wish to picnic and drink a glass of ale. The bar is a meeting place for tourists and locals alike. Lunch snacks are available, a bar meal costing £6 ($10.50) for two courses. Dinners are £13 ($22.75) to £15 ($26.25). The pictures in the bar are worth a look. They show many of the ships that sank around the islands in the past, as well as some of the gigs used in pilotage, rescue, smuggling, and pillage. The inn has 12 rooms, all twins and doubles with private baths. Here, too, there is a wide range of prices. Accommodation prices start from £15 ($26.25) per person daily for B&B until mid-April, after which a dinner, bed, and breakfast tariff applies until mid-October. The prices range from £30 ($52.50) to £40.50 ($70.90) during that time. The inn has a heated outdoor swimming pool.

Tremellyn Guest House, Church Road, St. Mary's, Isles of Scilly, Cornwall TR21 0NA (tel. 0720/22656), is a Victorian house on a hill behind Hugh Town with sheltered gardens and a beautiful view of the islands. Colin and Liz Ridsdale run a trim ship, offering comfortable rooms with hot and cold water, TV, and tea- and coffee-makers. B&B costs from £18 ($31.50) per person nightly, and dinner is another £9 ($15.75). Boating, sailing, cycling, golf, tennis, and squash can be arranged if you wish.

At **Mincarlo Guest House,** Hugh Town, St. Mary's, Isles of Scilly, Cornwall TR21 0JN (tel. 0720/22513), the Duncan family has owned this lovely house right on the edge of the harbor for 40 years. Colin and Jill Duncan charge £12 ($21) per person daily for B&B, or from £18 ($31.50) per person for half board, plus VAT.

The cozy house has a variety of accommodations, some with showers and toilets. Many overlook the harbor, only a five-minute walk away. Colin prepares and cooks the evening meal, featuring a selection of local produce, fish, and shellfish.

Evergreen Cottage Guest House, The Parade, Hugh Town, St. Mary's, Isles of Scilly, Cornwall TR21 0LP (tel. 0720/22711), is one of the island's oldest cottages. Originally the home of sea captains and once a smithy, Evergreen is modernized to provide comfortable, adequate facilities. This cottage retains much character, having maritime artifacts and also one of the rarest long-case clocks in Britain. B&B is provided at a cost of £12 ($21) to £13 ($22.75) per person daily. Tony and Primrose Theelke are the resident proprietors.

WHAT TO SEE AND DO ON TRESCO

No cars or motorbikes are allowed on the island, but walking or bicycling is pleasant. Bikes can be rented for £3 ($4.50) per day. The hotels use a special wagon towed by a farm tractor to transport guests and luggage from the harbor.

The phone number for information to do with Tresco is 0720/22849. Call it to find out about boat schedules, possible changes in hours and prices at the abbey, and other matters.

The **Abbey Gardens** and **Valhalla,** mentioned above, are the most outstanding features of Tresco. Here you can enjoy a day's walk through the 735 acres, mostly occupied by the celebrated Abbey Gardens. These gardens were started by Augustus Smith in the mid-1830s. When he began work, the area was a barren hillside, a fact visitors find hard to believe.

The gardens are a collector's dream, with more than 5000 species of plants from some 100 different countries. The old abbey, or priory, in ruins now, is said to have been founded by Benedictine monks in the 11th century, although some historians date it from A.D. 964. Of special interest in the gardens is Valhalla, a collection of nearly 60 figureheads from ships wrecked around the islands. There is a rather eerie atmosphere surrounding these gaily painted figures from the past, each one a ghost with a different story to tell. Hours are from 10 a.m. to 4 p.m. daily. Admission is £2.50 ($4.40).

After a visit to the gardens, walk through the fields, along paths, and across dunes thick with heather. Flowers, birds, shells, and fish are so abundant that Tresco is a naturalist's dream and a walker's paradise. Birds are so unafraid that they land within a foot or so of you and feed happily.

WHERE TO STAY ON ST. MARY'S

The only hotel in the islands that is actually set at the water's edge is the **Atlantic Hotel,** Hugh Town, St. Mary's, Isles of Scilly, Cornwall TR21 0PL (tel. 0720/22417). From your seat in the restaurant, you can feel you're almost in the midst of the fishing boats bobbing about. The inn is old and rambling, with different sizes of bedrooms, 24 in all, many with views over the water and several with private bath and toilet. They rent for £29 ($50.75) daily in a single, £38 ($66.50) in a double for a comfortable room, a large breakfast, and a four-course dinner. The Shipwreck Bar and Cocktail Bar lead directly onto a patio from which you can climb down to the beach at low tide. The restaurant has a good choice for each course on its four-course table d'hôte, including grilled Cornish mackerel or freshly caught John Dory, a local fish. The hotel is open from April to October.

Lyonnesse Guest House, The Strand, St. Mary's, Isles of Scilly, Cornwall TR21 0PS (tel. 0720/22458), is another large family home in the quieter part of Hugh Town, but close to shops and the harbor. Derek and Melanie Woodcock are both young islanders who take pride in telling their guests about the Scillies. There is a large lounge, and the house is well appointed, the front rooms and lounge having views of the harbor and islands. All units have heating, hot and cold water basins, and shaver points. The daily half-board rate is £18.50 ($32.40) per person.

Crebinich House, Church Street, St. Mary's, Isles of Scilly, Cornwall TR21 0JT (tel. 0720/22968), is named after one of the massive offshore rocks that in the 19th century caused a major shipwreck. It is owned and operated by two refugees from the urban landscape of London, Lesley and Phillip Jones. The house was originally built of granite blocks in 1760, although modern additions have significantly expanded it in the rear. A "listed" building, its facade can't be altered. The house lies in the center of the village. There are no sea views, but the water is reachable in two directions after a 50-yard walk. The Jones couple rents six prettily furnished bedrooms filled with floral-patterned Sanderson (a fashionable manufacturer) fabrics. None of these accommodations has a private bath, and they are rented from March to October. The per-person B&B rate ranges from £21.50 ($37.65) to £23.50 ($41.15) daily, with VAT. Dinners for residents only are prepared by Lesley herself.

WHERE TO EAT ON ST. MARY'S

If fish is your dish, go to the **Galley Restaurant,** Parade, Hugh Town (tel. 0720/22602), a small, two-floor establishment run by Peter Thompson. On the street level, he sells take-away fish and chips, plus raw fish to be cooked at home. The upstairs restaurant is a light, wood-paneled room with pinewood tables and wheelback chairs, serving fresh local fish such as cod, plaice, and crab. A specialty is the chef's tasty fish pie. Unusual dishes to order include megrim (a local sole), "skate wings," and John Dory. Meals cost from £5 ($8.75). The restaurant is open daily, except Sunday, from noon to 1:30 p.m. and 6 to 8:30 p.m.

WHAT TO DO AND SEE ON ST. MARY'S

Expert diver Mark Groves, who runs **Underwater Island Safaris,** "Nowhere," Old Town, St. Mary's (tel. 0720/22732), has worked as a diver in both the Caribbean and the Red Sea. He can entertain both the experienced and the inexperienced diver. A diving safari costs from £20 ($35) for three hours of instruction and diving, including gear rental. Diving for qualified persons takes place on many of the historic wrecks and beautiful drop-offs. Waterskiing is also available.

The **Isles of Scilly Museum,** St. Mary's (tel. 0720/22337), is open daily in summer from 10 a.m. to noon, 1:30 to 4:30 p.m., and 7 to 9 p.m. In winter, it is open on Wednesday from 2 to 4 p.m. Admission is 40p (70¢). The museum shows the history of the islands from 1500 B.C. with artifacts from wrecked ships, drawings, and relics discovered in the Scillies.

Cars are available but hardly necessary. The Island Bus Service has a basic charge of 50p (90¢) from one island point to another. However, visitors can circumnavigate the island for esthetic purposes, paying £1 ($1.75) for the privilege. Children are charged half fare.

Bicycles are one of the most practical means of transport. **Buccabu Bicycle Rentals,** The Strand, St. Mary's (tel. 0720/22289), is the major rental agency. The cost, depending on the type of bicycle you want, ranges from £3.40 ($5.95) to £10 ($17.50) per day, the latter the price for a tandem bike.

The **Tourist Information Office** at Town Hall on St. Mary's offers friendly service (tel. 0720/22536).

WHERE TO SHOP ON ST. MARY'S

For a perfect and useful souvenir of the Scillies, visit the **Glassblowers** (tel. 0720/22900) and watch crystal glass blown from a furnace and made into goblets, vases, cream jugs, and ornaments. Then visit the Crystal Glass Shop and browse around. David Langsworthy is the designer and craftsman, and each piece is stamped and hand-engraved by the glassmaker.

The **Man of War** (tel. 0720/22563), is a nautical antique shop where you can buy ancient coins recovered from vessels around the island. They are made into pendants and cuff links or just mounted.

FOOD AND LODGING AT ST. AGNES

When you visit the Isles of Scilly, it is worth considering a stay at **Coastguards,** St. Agnes, Isles of Scilly, Cornwall TR22 0PL (tel. 0720/22473), the home of Danny and Wendy Hick. They have two double rooms, one with two beds, and charge £18 ($31.50) per person per day for bed, breakfast, and an evening meal. There are tea- and coffee-makers in the rooms. The house is the middle one of three and has excellent sea views. There is no choice on the daily menu, but special diets are catered to if advance notice is given. Mr. Hick is a model shipwright who sells his fine works through agents in London and New England, as well as doing work on private commissions.

The Turks Head (tel. 0720/22434) offers bar lunches, including homemade soups and Cornish pasties. Meals cost from £2.50 ($4.40). Only lunch is served daily from 11:30 a.m. to 2:30 p.m. The place is known throughout the islands.

Now we turn to the outlying district of Penzance, heading south to Newlyn and Mousehole.

9. Newlyn, Mousehole, and Land's End

NEWLYN

From Penzance, a promenade leads to Newlyn, a mile away, another fishing village of infinite charm on Mount's Bay. In fact, its much-painted harbor seems clogged with more fishing craft than that of Penzance. Stanhope Forbes, now dead, founded an art school in Newlyn, and in the past few years the village has gained an increasing reputation for its artists' colony, attracting both the serious painter and the Sunday sketcher. From Penzance, the old fishermen's cottages and crooked lanes of Newlyn are reached by bus. For a dining or overnighting recommendation, try the following:

Panorama Guest House, Chywoone Hill, Newlyn, Cornwall TR18 5AR (tel. 0736/68498), is run by Harry and Teresa Shead, who extend a warm welcome to their guests, taking care of them comfortably in a small collection of rooms. Some units contain private baths and have sea views. All have central heating, color TV, tea- and coffee-makers, and hot and cold running water. B&B rates run from £13 ($22.75) per person per night, with dinner costing £8 ($14). There is space to park your car, and use of a gymnasium with heated indoor swimming pool is available. Guests relax in Harry's Bar.

Smugglers Hotel and Restaurant, Fore Street, Newlyn, Cornwall TR18 5JR (tel. 0736/64207), was chosen by the English Tourist Board to represent the "best of Cornish accommodation" in one of their campaigns. The choice was appropriate. It has a crooked beamed front, irregular windows, and an uneven roof. Most of the 12 accommodations open onto lovely views over the fishing boats in the harbor and across Mount's Bay. All have hot and cold running water, and many have private bath. Depending on the plumbing, singles rent for £18 ($31.50) to £22 ($38.50) daily and doubles for £16 ($28) to £18 ($31.50) per person nightly, including a continental or English breakfast. The Cellar Bar epitomizes the old inn's atmosphere and age. Here David Reeve, owner and manager, presides over the bar and generates conversation, dispensing drink and cheer in equal quantities. The restaurant enjoys a good local reputation, and you can sample some of the inn's specialties, including a duck à l'orange, pork marsala, or beef bourguignon. Dinners, nightly from 7 to 10:30, cost from £12 ($21). No lunch is served.

MOUSEHOLE

Still another Cornish fishing village, Mousehole lies three miles south of Penzance (take bus 9) and two miles from our last stopover in Newlyn. The hordes of tourists who flock here haven't changed it drastically—the gulls still squawk, the cottages still huddle close to the harbor wall (although they look as if they were built more to be photographed than lived in), the fishermen still bring in the day's catch, the salts sit around smoking tobacco, talking about the good old days, and the lanes are as narrow as ever. About the most exciting thing that's occurred was the arrival in the late 16th century of the Spanish galleons, whose ungallant sailors sacked and burnt the village. In a sheltered cove off Mount's Bay, Mousehole (pronounced mou-sel) today has developed the nucleus of an artists' colony. For rooms and meals, try the following recommendations, all within the village:

Food and Lodging

Renovelle, 6 The Parade, Mousehole, Cornwall TR19 6PN (tel. 0736/731258), is a pretty little villa, all fresh blue and white, at the edge of the village. It's aptly perched right beside the sea, on a cliff, which makes the view memorable. Mrs. Stella Bartlett, the owner, has made it charming and comfortable. Her guests keep returning year after year and pay a B&B rate of £10.50 ($18.40) per person nightly. Each bedroom is comfy, equipped with a water basin and shower, and they have good views of the sea. It's a pleasure to have breakfast set before you in the sunny little dining room.

At **Dolphins,** The Parade, Mousehole, Cornwall TR19 6PT (tel. 0736/731828), a steep drive up to this house is rewarded with peace and quiet, plus a view over Mount's Bay with the harbor and fishing boats below. Guests can relax and sunbathe in the sunny garden, later enjoying the comfortable lounge before retreating to one of the well-furnished bedrooms (the doubles have private bath or shower). Tea- and coffee-makers are in all the units, and the two bedrooms overlooking the sea have color TV. A good breakfast is provided. The B&B charge is from £10 ($17.50) to £14 ($24.50) per person daily. Dolphins is run by Yvonne Lodge, who for many years was a naval nursing officer. Her whole place is neat and trim, and there's a private car park. Ask directions as you enter Mousehole.

Pam's Pantry, Mill Lane (tel. 0736/731532), is a small and cheerful café and kitchen that is open daily from 9 a.m. to 6 p.m. Some of the dishes here feature fish caught locally. You can order crab salad, a summer favorite, or smoked mackerel. To complete the meal, a homemade apple pie with Cornish clotted cream is served. The cost of a meal is £8 ($14).

On the Outskirts

Raginnis Farm, Mousehole, Cornwall TR19 6NJ is owned and run by the Harvey brothers. It is a 100-odd–acre tract of dairyland with a 70-strong Friesian herd. You get good local produce and views over the countryside to the far-off sea. The brothers' wives offer B&B. Tanya, wife of Robert, houses guests in her lovely thatched home, Thatch Cottage, Raginnis Farm, Mousehole (tel. 0736/731333), charging £9 ($15.75) per person per night. The early 18th-century place is not large enough to accommodate visitors with children. Doubles are offered with private showers and toilets. An evening meal can be supplied. Also at Raginnis Farm (tel. 0736/731523), Penny Harvey has children of her own and more space to welcome guests with families. She charges the same price.

LAND'S END

Craggy Land's End, where England comes to an end, is where you'll find the last of everything. It lies nine miles west of Penzance and is reached by bus 1 or 1B. America's coast is 3291 miles away to the west of the rugged rocks that tumble into the sea beneath Land's End.

Publicity says that "everyone should stand here, at least once." Given the romantic conception that this is the piece of England closest to America and the most distant point you can go on mainland England, this is so. It must still retain some of its mystique even if Big Business has now opened the Land's End Heritage Museum, the Man and the Sea Exhibition, and the Worzel Gummidge Exhibition, not to mention a Video Theatre with continuous performances and the First and Last Craft Workshop from which to buy your first and "last" souvenirs. Better to ignore the commercial aspect and enjoy the cliff walks and spectacular views.

Food and Lodging

To reach **Old Success Inn,** Sennen Cove, Land's End, Cornwall TR19 7DG (tel. 073637/232), turn right and follow the road down to Sennen Cove just before you reach Land's End. The Old Success lies at the bottom, facing the sea and wide sandy beaches. Surfing rollers come in from the Atlantic almost to the foot of the sea wall beneath the 17th-century fishermen's inn. Over the years it has been extended and modernized, now offering bright, clean rooms, many with private bath and all with radio, tea- and coffee-maker, electric heater, and washbasin. Half board costs from £24 ($42) to £26.50 ($46.40) per person nightly. Downstairs, the inn has a lounge with color TV and panoramic views over the Atlantic, a cozy lounge bar, and Charlie's Bar where the locals and fishermen join the residents of the evening. Frank Carroll, resident manager, and his staff provide a varied dinner menu in the Seine Room, the house restaurant, for £9 ($15.75) and up. Hours are from 11:30 a.m. to 2:30 p.m. and 6:30 to 10 p.m. daily.

10. St. Ives

This North Coast fishing village, with its sandy beaches, is England's most famous art colony. Only 20 miles from Land's End and ten from Penzance it is a village of narrow streets and well-kept cottages. The artists settled in many years ago and have integrated with the fishermen and their families.

The art colony was established long enough ago to have developed several schools or splits, and they almost never overlap, except in pubs where the artists hang out, at an occasional café, and where classes are held. The old battle continues between the followers of the representational and the devotees of the abstract in art, with each group recruiting young artists all the time. In addition, there are the potters, weavers, and other artisans, all doing things creatively and exhibiting and selling in this area. There are several galleries to visit, with such names as the Sail Loft.

A word of warning: St. Ives becomes virtually impossible to visit in August, when you're likely to be trampled underfoot by busloads of tourists, mostly the British themselves. However, in spring and early fall, the pace is much more relaxed, and a visitor can have the true experience of the art colony.

PARK AND RIDE

During the summer months, many of the streets in the center of town are closed to vehicles. You may want to leave your car in the **Lelant Saltings Car Park,** three miles from St. Ives on the A3074, and take the regular train service into town, an 11-minute journey. Departures are every half hour. It's free to all car passengers and drivers, and the car-park charge is £2 ($3.50) a day. Or you can use the large **Trenwith Car Park,** close to the town center, for 35p (60¢) and then walk down to the shops and harbor or take a bus, costing 30p (55¢) for adults and 15p (25¢) for children.

WHERE TO STAY

Avoid the snug suburban houses built on the edge of St. Ives and go instead to the end of the peninsula, or "island" as it's called (it's not one actually). In these winding streets, you'll find the studios of the working artists, the fishermen, and the unusual places set aside to show and sell works of art. And you'll also find here a number of B&B guesthouses and cottages. For the most part, they are easy to find; simply look for B&B signs as you walk along the narrow streets.

Hollies Hotel, Talland Road, St. Ives, Cornwall TR26 2DF (tel. 0736/796605), derives much of its charm from its ownership by an Anglo-American couple, who seem to enjoy what they are doing. John and Beverley Dowland originally met in her home state of Arkansas, and after they married they returned to his hometown in Cornwall. Today they operate a nine-room hotel lying about a five-minute walk from the beach. The house, built of dark gray granite with a dark slate roof, lies within a row of about a dozen similar semidetached homes, each constructed about a century ago. Depending on the season, per-person rates, based on double occupancy, range from £13 ($22.75) to £17.50 ($30.65) daily. A fixed-price three-course meal goes for £6 ($10.50). The hotel is fully licensed to serve drinks to its residents and members of the community.

Blue Hayes Guest House, Trelyon Avenue, St. Ives, Cornwall TR26 2AD (tel. 0736/797129), is set within a pleasant garden on land that rolls smoothly down to the sea. This solid, Edwardian-style home was originally constructed in 1922 behind a gray stucco facade beneath a gray slate roof. Today the warm and cozy house contains nine bedrooms to rent, only five of which offer a private bath or shower. Depending on the facilities, per-person rates for B&B cost from £14 ($24.50) to £17.50 ($30.65) daily, with VAT included. The charming hosts, Jan and John Shearn, prepare a three-course evening meal for residents only at a cost of £7 ($12.25). Open only from Easter to late October, the guesthouse lies within a ten-minute walk of both the beach and the heart of St. Ives.

Craigmeor, Beach Road, St. Ives, Cornwall TR26 1JY (tel. 0736/796611), is owned and operated by Lancashire-born Mrs. Ada Taylor. Her place lies between the road and the beach, about a five-minute walk from the center of St. Ives. The footpath that rings the coast of Cornwall and which is popular with backpackers and hikers lies only a few paces from her house. Mrs. Taylor owns the right half of a semidetached building, which was constructed right after World War II. She offers five rooms to rent, none with private bath, although each has fitted carpets, flowery curtains, and hot and cold running water. With breakfast included, her overnight charges are from £11 ($19.25) per person. The house is open only from March to October and has a rigid ban against smoking. The house affords a good view of Porthmeor Beach, which is known throughout Cornwall as a good place for surfers.

Kandahar, 11 The Warren, St. Ives, Cornwall TR26 3AA (tel. 0736/796183), enjoys a waterfront location so that its rooms open onto the harbor and the bay. It's also near the town center and some 600 feet from the British Rail and bus terminals. Centrally heated rooms are pleasantly furnished, and the hotel is attractively decorated. The resident proprietors, Derek and Diana Mason, have provided all rooms with color TV and tea and coffee-makers. Two rooms have private showers and toilets. Tariffs, including a full English breakfast, are from £12 ($21) to £15 ($26.25) daily in a single, and from £22 ($38.50) to £30 ($52.50) in a double.

Dean Court Hotel, Trelyon Avenue, St. Ives, Cornwall TR26 2AD (tel. 0736/796023), opens onto the harbor and beach, and naturally the most desirable accommodations are those that have views over the water. Each of the 12 bedrooms has a private bath. A family-run place open from May to October, the hotel takes guests for B&B for £23 ($40.25) daily in a single, going up to £55 ($96.25) in a double. Meals, served by arrangement, cost from £9 ($15.75). You get good food and good hospitality here.

Primrose Valley Hotel, Primrose Valley, St. Ives, Cornwall TR26 2ED (tel. 0736/794939), lies on a private road in the vicinity of Porthminster Beach. It is a most desirable accommodation, offering pleasantly furnished and comfortable bedrooms. Family run, it quotes half-board terms ranging from £17.35 ($30.35) to £26.35 ($46.10) per person nightly, which is a very good value for the area. Children are welcome, the food is good, and there is plenty of parking.

Hobblers Guest House and Restaurant, The Wharf, St. Ives, Cornwall TR26

1LR (tel. 0736/796439), is right on the harborside, a black and white building next to a shellfish shop. Paul Folkes has only three rooms to rent at £12.50 ($21.90) per person nightly. None of these has a private bath. His main interest is in his restaurant, which is recommended separately. Because it's bull's-eye center, it may be hard to get a room here in high season. The house was built in the 17th century as a pilot's house. The hotel is closed from November to two weeks before Easter.

Trecarrell Hotel, Carthew Terrace, St. Ives, Cornwall TR26 1EB (tel. 0736/ 795707), is housed in a 140-year-old building in a quiet quarter of St. Ives. The restaurant, bar, and kitchen are under the close personal supervision of the proprietors, the Bayfields, who take pride in their table. The best local produce and meats are used, along with fish caught fresh from the Atlantic Ocean. They make many "Olde English" dishes and offer specialties. The hotel is centrally heated throughout and is small, with 16 guest rooms in all. But each room is individually decorated, and many have private bathroom or shower. A double in high season costs £41 ($71.75) to £45 ($78.75) per person daily for double occupancy of a room with bath, including dinner, bed, and breakfast. The bar is well stocked with beers, liqueurs, and liquors, and a wide range of table wines is available. The Trecarrell offers excellent service and good food.

Pondarosa, 10 Porthminster Terrace, St. Ives, Cornwall TR26 2DQ (tel. 0736/795875), offers good value for the money and a prominent location near the harbor and beach. An Edwardian house, it offers a selection of single, double, and family rooms, some with private bath. All of them have such amenities as hot and cold running water, beverage-making equipment, and central heating. The rate for B&B ranges from £10.50 ($18.40) to £11 ($19.25) per person nightly. Sylvia Richards, the owner, will also prepare an evening meal of good quality if notified in advance. There's a private car park adjoining the house.

Woodcote Hotel, The Saltings, Lelant, St. Ives, Cornwall TR26 3DL (tel. 0736/753147), was originally built in 1920 on a peninsula jutting out from the Cornish coast. Constructed in the mock-Tudor style, it became the first vegetarian hotel in Britain. Still going strong, it features a small copse of trees in back and sweeping views of the tidal estuary of the Hayle. The hotel lies 3½ miles south of St. Ives in the hamlet of Lelant. The beach is about a ten-minute walk from the hotel. John and Pamela Barrett offer eight bedrooms, four with private bath. Depending on the plumbing, the half-board rate ranges from £17 ($29.75) to £21 ($36.75) per person daily. If there is space, nonresidents can dine here (see below).

WHERE TO EAT

At this previously recommended guesthouse, **Hobblers Restaurant,** The Wharf (tel. 0736/796439), serves meals daily from either 5:30 or 6 p.m. until the last orders are accepted at either 10 or 11:30 p.m. (hours depending on business and the season). At about £11 ($22.75) per person, you get some of the finest seafood in St. Ives. Dishes are likely to include scallops, halibut, scampi, and plaice, along with mussels and a cream-of-lobster bisque to begin with. If you don't want fish, you might settle happily for the chicken Kiev or a filet steak. Of course, the dishes come with "chips" and peas. The paneled rooms are decorated with pictures of ships and seascapes. It's cramped, nautical, and intimate. The restaurant is closed from November to two weeks before Easter.

The Sloop Inn, The Wharf (tel. 0736/796584), is one of the most popular pubs—perhaps *the* most popular—in St. Ives. Most people come here to drink (and they often do a lot of that), whereas the food is in the bar snack or bar platter category. That means plates of chicken, sausage, and the ubiquitous scampi. The pub is open Monday to Saturday from 11 a.m. to 11 p.m., and on Sunday from noon to 3 p.m. and 7 to 10:30 p.m. A pint of draft lager goes for £1.10 ($1.95).

The Balancing Eel, Black Lane (tel. 0736/796792), is almost a traditional fish and chips shop where you line up at the take-out counter and receive your supper wrapped—not in newspaper these days, pity!—or take it upstairs to eat in the restaurant. A bag of sole and chips is £1.75 ($3.05). There are the usual bottles on the counter—vinegar, catsup, chutney, and pickled onions. It's open from noon to 2 p.m. and 5:30 to 8 p.m. daily, except Sunday. It's close to the Wharf Post Office and Chy-an-Chy Street.

The **Pudding Bag Restaurant,** in the Sloop Craft Market in St. Ives (tel. 0736/797214), is open daily from 10 a.m. to 10 p.m. A long, narrow cafeteria opens into a seating area, where gargantuan Cornish pasties are served. In one of the steak pies, the meat alone weighs a quarter pound. You're served vegetables too. There's always a soup and the inevitable mixed grill. A good and filling meal can be ordered here at a cost of £4.50 ($7.90), including a beer and coffee. If you don't enter through the Craft Market, you can go to the entrance on Back Road West.

Woodcote Hotel, The Saltings, Lelant (tel. 0736/753147), previously recommended as the first vegetarian hotel ever built in Britain, accepts fill-in bookings from nonresidents if there is space. One must phone for a reservation. Dinner is served from 6:30 to 7:30 nightly, costing from £7 ($12.25) for a fixed-price vegetarian meal. Typical dishes include leek-and-potato soup, savory pancakes filled with mushrooms, spinach, and cheese sauce, and fresh bilberries with coconut for dessert. The kitchen uses eggs but no fish. This is an unusual choice for St. Ives if such fare appeals to you.

BARBARA HEPWORTH MUSEUM

At Trewyn Studio and Garden on Barnoon Hill (tel. 0736/796226), the former home of Dame Barbara Hepworth contains a museum of sculpture by the artist from 1929 until her death in 1975, together with photographs, letters, and other papers documenting her life and background. The garden also contains sculpture, and is well worth a visit. The museum is open daily from 10 a.m. to 5:30 p.m. in summer, and to 4:30 p.m. in winter. Admission is 50p (90¢) for adults, 25p (45¢) for children. There is limited parking some 200 yards away.

11. Port Isaac

The most unspoiled fishing village on the north Cornish coastline is Port Isaac, nine miles from Wadebridge. This Atlantic coastal resort retains its original character, in spite of the intrusions of large numbers of summer visitors. You can wander through its winding, narrow lanes, gazing at the whitewashed fishermen's cottages with their rainbow trims.

WHERE TO STAY

Considered the most desirable accommodation in Port Isaac, **Castle Rock Hotel,** Port Isaac, Cornwall PL29 35B (tel. 0208/880300), is a carefully cared-for pink house with a magnificent view over the coast to as far away as Tintagel. It is run by Brian and Margaret Firth, who offer 19 attractively furnished bedrooms, most of which contain private bathrooms. They charge from £27.50 ($21.90) to £34.50 ($60.40) per person daily for half board. B&B costs from £17 ($29.75) to £24 ($42) per person. Guests meet each other at the well-stocked bar before going into the dining room, where home-cooked meals (Mrs. Firth is a Cordon Bleu cook) are served, using, whenever possible, local produce. The good food served here is part of the Castle Rock's attraction, along with that view.

Rogues Retreat, Roscarrock Hill, Port Isaac, Cornwall PL29 3RG (tel. 0208/880566), is a licensed guesthouse run by Frank and Jill Gadman, who are marvelous hosts even though this is their first venture at innkeeping (perhaps that's why they're so good). They rent seven comfortable bedrooms, with hot and cold running water and coffee- or tea-making facilities. Their charge of £8.50 ($14.90) per person nightly in low season, £9.50 ($16.65) in high season is most reasonable. Reductions are granted off-season. The guesthouse has scenic views over the fishing village and harbor. It lies adjacent to a National Trust footpath where walkers can enjoy the scenery of the coast and deserted coves. An evening meal with a selection of fine wines is served from 7 p.m. in a cozy dining room. Table settings are color-coordinated in royal blue and white. An evening meal costs £5.50 ($9.65). Unusual for Port Isaac, they have private parking.

The Old School, Port Isaac, Cornwall PL29 3RB (tel. 020880/721), dates from 1875, a sentinel on a clifftop overlooking the harbor and out to sea over a pier built in the reign of Henry VIII. Sportsmen are drawn to the hotel, taking part in shark and deep-sea fishing, sailing, windsurfing, and waterskiing. Even if you're not interested in that, you'll surely enjoy the harbor view and a day or two's rest in comfortable bedrooms with bath. A night will cost from £9.50 ($16.65) per person in low season in a bathless double up to £20.50 ($21.90) per person in high season in a twin or double with bath or shower. Some of the suites have half-tester beds. Breakfast, included in the price, is eaten in the Refectory, a long room with tall windows and tables with settle benches. A three- or four-course dinner costs from £7.50 ($13.15). Mike and Alicia Warner, the owners, go out of their way to make guests comfortable.

WHERE TO EAT

In the center of the village, **Harbour Seafood Restaurant,** Fore Street (tel. 0208/880237), has special fame, since it was featured several times on British television and once in scenes from a Sherlock Holmes thriller, *The Devil's Foot*. This unique restaurant is designated as a building of architectural and historic interest and is one of several on this treacherous stretch of coast that used the timber of wrecked ships in its construction. It is open only in summer, April to October, from 10:30 a.m. until the last order goes in, usually around 9:30 p.m. Service is daily. Full meals cost from £10 ($17.50) and are likely to include locally caught fish, crab, and lobster.

The **Golden Lion,** Fore Street (tel. 0208/880336), is perhaps the most handsomely positioned pub in the old fishing village, with a view of the harbor from a drinking patio. Mr. and Mrs. Spry, the owners, offer good drinks, snacks, and crab sandwiches. Light meals cost from £5 ($8.75). Hours are from 11 a.m. to 11 p.m. Monday to Saturday in summer, and from noon to 3 p.m. and 7 to 10:30 p.m. Sunday. Winter hours are daily from 11 a.m. to 3 p.m. and 6 to 11 p.m.

---

12. Tintagel

On a wild stretch of the Atlantic coast, Tintagel is forever linked with the legends of King Arthur, Lancelot, and Merlin. The 13th-century ruins of Tintagel Castle (tel. 0840/770328), popularly known as King Arthur's Castle, stand 300 feet above the sea on a rocky promontory. It is open from 10 a.m. to 6 p.m. daily from Good Friday to September 30. Hours off-season are from 10 a.m. to 4 p.m.; closed Monday. Admission is £1.30 ($2.30) for adults, 65p ($1.15) for children. The colorful writing of Lord Tennyson in *Idylls of the King* greatly increased the interest in Tintagel, as did the writings of Geoffrey of Monmouth. The ruins, which date from Geoffrey's time, are what remains of a castle built on the foundations of a Celtic monastery from the sixth century, a long, steep, tortuous walk from the car park.

The **Old Post Office** at Tintagel is a National Trust property. It was once a 14th-century manor, but since the 19th century it has had connections with the post office. In the village center, it has a genuine Victorian post room which is open, April to October, daily from 11 a.m. to last admission at 5:45 p.m. or sunset if that is earlier. Admission is £1 ($1.75) for adults, 50p (90¢) for children.

In summer, many visitors make the ascent to Arthur's lair, 100 rock-cut steps. You can also visit Merlin's Cave.

If you become excited by legends of Knights of the Round Table, you can even go to **Camelford,** just five miles inland from Tintagel. The market hall there dates from 1790, but more interestingly, the town claims to be Camelot.

FOOD AND LODGING

A family-run hotel, **Trenowan Hotel,** Treknow, near Tintagel, Cornwall PL34 0EJ (tel. 0840/770255), provides personal service and home-style cookery. Built in the late Victorian style as identical twin houses, it is now owned by Barbara and George Bond, who welcome guests and are helpful in telling them of nearby attractions. They rent a total of nine comfortably furnished rooms, most with TV, video, tea- and coffee-makers, and private shower and toilet. B&B costs £11.50 ($20.15) per person daily, and the half-board rate is £18 ($31.50) per person. Mrs. Bond is a "proper English cook," using fresh vegetables grown by her husband. Their quiet retreat stands on its own grounds overlooking the coast near Trebarwith Sands. They are open year round.

Pennallick Hotel, Treknow, near Tintagel, Cornwall PL34 0EJ (tel. 0840/ 770296), is another small, family-run hotel, where the living is relaxed and home-like. Edna and Jim Russell welcome you to their house overlooking spectacular cliffs and coastline, with cliff walks to secluded beaches and coves. The hotel is only one mile from historic Tintagel. Their eight bedrooms all have hot and cold running water, and doubles units contain showers as well as TV and tea- and coffee-makers. The charge in peak summer months is £21 ($36.75) per person daily for half board. Off-season bargain breaks are offered in autumn. The hotel has a lounge and a small licensed bar.

Belvoir House, Tregatta, Tintagel, Cornwall PL34 0DY (tel. 0840/770265), was formed by combining two Cornish cottages with an old smithy. Joyce Martin welcomes guests into her delightful accommodation, all but one with a private bath, charging them from £10.50 ($18.40) per person nightly for B&B. For another £6 ($10.50) per person, an evening dinner can be arranged. My favorite section is the old smithy, which now has a double bedroom with a bath and toilet. Other rooms are comfortably and tastefully furnished. Guests enjoy both a sun lounge and a TV lounge, and the hotel has a residential license. It's especially pleasant in chilly weather with a log fire in the lounge.

A FARMHOUSE NEAR BUDE

A 250-year-old farmhouse, **Forda Farm,** Morwenstow, near Bude, Cornwall EX23 9HT (tel. 028883/275), is nestled in a wooded coombe about 1½ miles from the sea. Ruth Manfield likes to keep guests to a minimum so "they will feel more like a friend of the family than a paying guest." Guests, no more than four or five at a time, gather around the table at night, as the farm is noted for its excellent cuisine, using wholesome foods, including their own dairy products and home-grown vegetables. Breakfast is in the traditional Cornish style, and a picnic lunch will be provided if you want to go touring during the day. Daily rates for B&B are £10 ($17.50) per person. For bed, breakfast, early-morning tea, and a table d'hôte dinner, the charge is from £22 ($38.50) per person, plus another £2.50 ($4.40) for a packed lunch. You can also go on guided tours at £6 ($10.50) per person. Readers Dr. and Mrs. William Douglas write: "We arrived in time for haying and milking. We pitched in with the family and later shared a warm evening and a wonderful meal together. One can walk through lovely meadows overlooking the sea to Ireland and share from the local inhabitants the charm of one of the loveliest parts of England."

---

13. Bolventor

This village in central Cornwall, near Launceston, was visited by the late Daphne du Maurier, as it was the setting for her novel *Jamaica Inn* (see below). The inn is named for the Caribbean island where the onetime owner of the inn had become prosperous from sugar on his plantation. Opposite the inn, a small road leads to Dozmary Pool, where the "waves wap and the winds wan" and into which Sir Bedivere threw Excalibur at King Arthur's behest.

Jamaica Inn, Bolventor, Launceston, Cornwall PL15 7TS (tel. 056686/250), is a long, low building beside the main road across Bodmin Moor, an ideal spot on the desolate moor for a smuggler's den in other times. Busy throughout most of the day with passing trade, it has welcoming bars where food and soft drinks are dispensed along with local beer and cider. Bedrooms with private bath rent for £35 ($61.25) daily for double occupancy, with singles going for £20 ($35). There is a restaurant with waitress service open in the evening and a potters museum in the courtyard. The bar is open from 11 a.m. to 11 p.m., with a food bar serving from 9:30 a.m. to 10 p.m.

XI

WILTSHIRE, SOMERSET, AND AVON

1. SALISBURY

2. CASTLE COMBE

3. EXMOOR NATIONAL PARK

4. DUNSTER

5. GLASTONBURY

6. WELLS

7. THE CAVES OF MENDIP

8. BATH

9. BRISTOL

For our final look at the West Countree, we move now into Wiltshire, Somerset, and Avon, the most antiquity-rich shires of England. When we reach this area of woodland and pastoral scenes, London seems far removed from the bucolic life here.

On cold, windswept nights in unrecorded times, the Druids used to steal across these plains armed with twigs. Sheltered by boulders, they'd burn their sloe with rosemary to ward off the danger of witchcraft.

Most people seem to agree that the West Country, a loose geographical term, begins at Salisbury, with its Early English cathedral. Nearby is Stonehenge, England's oldest prehistoric monument. Both Stonehenge and Salisbury are in Wiltshire.

Somerset is even more varied, the diet richer not only in historical cities but in wild scenic grandeur, especially in Exmoor. The legendary burial place of King Arthur at Glastonbury and the cathedral city of Wells also await you on your visit to Somerset. The old Roman city of Bath is the main target in the county of Avon.

WILTSHIRE

When you cross into Wiltshire, you'll be entering a county of chalky, grassy uplands and rolling plains. Most of the shire is agricultural, and a large part is devoted to pastureland. Wiltshire produces an abundance of England's dairy products, and is noted for its sheep raising. In this western shire, you'll traverse the Salisbury Plain, the Vale of Pewsey, and the Marlborough Downs (the last gobbling up the greater part of the land mass). Unquestionably, the crowning achievement of Wiltshire is:

1. Salisbury

Long before you've made the 83-mile trek from London, the spire of Salisbury Cathedral comes into view, just as John Constable painted it so many times. The 404-foot pinnacle of the Early English and Gothic cathedral is the tallest in England. But Salisbury is also a fine base for touring such prehistoric sights as Stonehenge.

Market days are generally Tuesday and Saturday. There is a general market in the Market Place, where stalls sell anything from meat by auction to clothes and household goods, plants, and sweets.

THE SIGHTS

Salisbury, or New Sarum, lies in the valley of the Avon River. Filled with Tudor-style inns and tea rooms, it is known to readers of Thomas Hardy as Melchester and to the Victorian fans of Anthony Trollope as Barchester.

Salisbury Cathedral

You can search all of England, but you'll find no purer example of the Early English, or Pointed, style than Salisbury Cathedral. Its graceful spire has already been mentioned, but the ecclesiastical building doesn't depend totally on the tower for its appeal. Construction began on the structure as early as 1220, then took 38 years to complete, which was jet-age speed in those days (it was customary to drag out cathedral building for three centuries at least). The spire was to soar at the end of the 13th century. Despite an ill-conceived attempt at revamping in the 18th century, the architectural harmony of the cathedral was retained.

The cathedral's Chapter House (note the fine sculptures) is especially attractive, dating from the 13th century. It also contains one of the four copies of the Magna Carta, together with treasures from the Diocese of Salisbury and manuscripts and artifacts belonging to the cathedral. There is a charge of 25p (45¢) to visit the Chapter House. The Cloisters enhance the beauty of the cathedral. The Close, with at least 75 buildings in its compound (some from the early 18th century, although others predate that), is exceptionally large, setting off the cathedral most fittingly. An interesting clock in the North Transept is considered the oldest working mechanism in Europe. A voluntary contribution of 75p ($1.30) is asked to enter the cathedral.

The cathedral has a good **Brass Rubbing Centre** where you can choose from a selection of exact replicas molded perfectly from the original brasses. The small charge made for each rubbing includes the cost of materials and a donation to the church from which it comes. The center is open at the cathedral from early June to early September, Monday to Saturday from 10 a.m. to 5 p.m., and from 2 to 5 p.m. on Sunday.

One of the most distinguished houses in Cathedral Close is **Mompesson House and Garden,** built by Charles Mompesson in 1701. It was the home of the

Townsend family for more than a century, and is well known for its fine plasterwork ceilings and paneling. There is also a magnificent collection of 18th-century drinking glasses. It is open April to October daily, except Thursday and Friday, from 12:30 to 6 p.m. or dusk, charging an admission of £1.50 ($2.65) for adults, 75p ($1.30) for children.

Also in the Close is the **Regimental Museum** of the Duke of Edinburgh's Royal Regiment (Berkshire and Wiltshire), The Wardrobe, 58 The Close (tel. 0722/336222, ext. 2683), in an elegant house, the origins of which date from 1254. One of the finest military museums in the country, it has exhibits telling the story of nearly 250 years of this famous regiment, including uniforms, pictures, weapons, and other militaria. Admission is £1.10 ($1.95) for adults, 50p (90¢) for children. It is open from 10 a.m. to 4:30 p.m. Monday to Friday from February to the end of November. It is also open on Sunday from April to October and on Saturday in July and August.

TOURS

Leisurely guided walks through the city and car tours of the surrounding countryside, including Stonehenge and Avebury and even farther afield, are run by **Wessexplore.** Telephone Don Cross at 0722/26304 for information. Regular guided walks of about 1½ hours' duration take you through the city, visiting St. Thomas's Church and the Cathedral Close. The starting point is the **Tourist Information Bureau** in Fish Row. Departures are daily at 8:30 a.m. May to September. The cost is 90p ($1.60) for adults 40p (70¢) for children. An entire family can go for a guided walk for £1.60 ($2.80).

A tourist reception center for Salisbury is operated by **Guide Friday Ltd.,** at the Railway Station. Their office dispenses free maps and brochures on the town and area and conducts tours. Also available is a full range of tourist services, including accommodation references and car rental. In summer, the office is open daily from 9 a.m. to 6 p.m. In winter, hours are daily from 9 a.m. to 4 p.m. Guided tours of the city leave from the Railway Station daily—in summer, aboard open-top double-decker buses leaving every 15 minutes. The tour can be a 45-minute panoramic ride, or you can get off at any of the stops in the city. The ticket, costing £3.50 ($6.15), is valid all day.

WHERE TO STAY

Originally built of brick and stucco in the 14th century, **Old Bell**, 2 St. Ann St., Salisbury, Wiltshire SP1 2DN (tel. 0722/27958), might be the oldest hostelry in Salisbury. It sits opposite St. Ann's Gate, just a few paces from the cathedral, at the corner of Exeter Street. Most residents of Salisbury know it for its low-beamed and rustically elegant pub, where lunches are served daily from noon to 2 p.m., often within range of a blazing fireplace in winter. A hot dish of the day, preceded by homemade soup and followed by a "sweet," might cost from £6 ($10.50) per person. The Old Bell also offers seven bedrooms, each with a private bath. Some are half timbered, and each has been carefully decorated to reflect touches of elegance. For this, of course, you pay more than at a typical B&B, but many readers prefer the extra luxuries here. With a continental breakfast included, doubles range from £45 ($78.75) to £50 ($87.50) nightly, depending on the room assignment. The more expensive rooms contain four-poster beds.

White Lodge, 68 London Rd., Salisbury, Wiltshire SP1 3EX (tel. 0722/27991), is the residence of Canada-born Barbara Smith, who receives guests in her attractive brick-gabled house, charging £14 ($24.50) daily for a single, £12 ($21) per person for a double for B&B. The rooms are pleasant and the breakfasts personalized. The entrance to White Lodge is, in reality, a greenhouse, with lots of potted geraniums and trailing vines. The place is opposite St. Mark's Church, on the A30 at the edge of the city coming in from London.

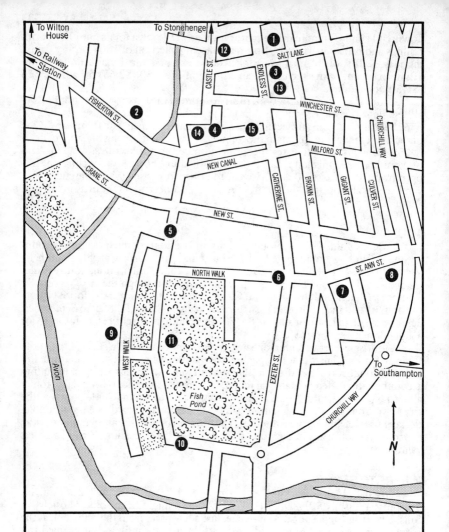

SALISBURY

	meters	
0		250
0	feet	750

KEY TO NUMBERED SIGHTS:

1. Shoemakers' Hall
2. Theatre
3. Bus Station
4. St. Thomas' Church
5. North Gate
6. St. Ann's Gate
7. Museum
8. Joiners' Hall
9. King's House
10. Harnham Gate
11. Salisbury Cathedral
12. Post Office
13. Tourist Information Centre
14. Market Place
15. Guildhall

Glen Lyn Guest House, 6 Bellamy Lane, Milfort Hill, Salisbury, Wiltshire SP1 2SP (tel. 0722/27880), is a large, comfortably furnished Victorian house in a quiet cul-de-sac a few minutes' walk from the city center. Tony and Jean Poat, the proprietors, rent seven rooms, four of which have private baths. All the units have central heating, tea- and coffee-makers, shaver points, and color TV. The charge is £13 ($22.75) per person daily for bathless rooms, £15 ($26.25) per person in rooms with bath. All tariffs include a full English breakfast.

Stratford Lodge, 4 Park Lane, Castle Road, Salisbury, Wiltshire SP1 3NP (tel. 0722/25177), is run by Jill Bayly, who welcomes you at her B&B, charging from £16 ($28) per person nightly. Her lodge stands in a residential area across from Victoria Park. The house is attractively furnished with pictures and antiques, and all bedrooms have their own bath or shower. Whenever possible, home produce is offered, and the cookery is just fine—so good, in fact, that you should stay for dinner at £10 ($17.50) per person.

Hayburn Wyke Guest House, 72 Castle Rd., Salisbury, Wiltshire SP1 3RL (tel. 0722/412627), next to Victoria Park and a half mile from the cathedral, is a handsomely decorated Victorian house where you will receive a warm welcome from Dawn and Alan Curnow. They offer six pleasantly furnished bedrooms with hot and cold running water, TV, and tea- and coffee-makers. Two of the units have private baths. The charge, including a full English breakfast, is £11 ($19.25) per person daily.

In the vicinity, **Treetops Guest House,** 99 Castle Rd., Salisbury, Wiltshire SP1 3RP (tel. 0722/22286), is a spacious house across from Victoria Park. From April to October it receives paying guests, charging them from £24 ($42) daily in a double. Rooms are pleasantly and comfortably decorated, and guests share the one public bath.

Richburn Guest House, 23-25 Estcourt Rd., Salisbury, Wiltshire SO1 3AP, is one of the better bargains in Salisbury. A spacious Victorian home, it has been converted to receive paying guests and is run by Sandra and David Loader. The rate, including a good Wiltshire breakfast and VAT, ranges from £12 ($21) to £13 ($22.75) daily in a single and from £20 ($35) to £28 ($49) in a double. A trio of family rooms is available, as is a large TV lounge. The location is convenient to the monumental heart of Salisbury, and there is a place to park your car.

Wyndham Park Lodge, 51 Wyndham Rd., Salisbury, Wiltshire SP1 3AB (tel. 0722/28851), is an attractively decorated Victorian house run by Mr. and Mrs. Legg, who have been most helpful to readers. Their rooms are comfortable, and each one has a private bath. Since only three rooms are available to rent, it's best to reserve. B&B ranges from £13 ($22.75) to £17 ($29.75) daily for a single and £25 ($43.75) to £33 ($57.75) for a double. The house lies within an easy walk of the heart of Salisbury and its magnificent cathedral.

On the Outskirts

Mill House, Berwick St. James, Salisbury, Wiltshire SP3 4TS (tel. 0722/790331), was built in 1785 and was added to and modernized in 1960. Standing in a lovely garden through which the River Till runs, the house is the pride of Mrs. Diana Gifford-Mead, who accepts paying guests into her six bedrooms, three of which have hot and cold water basins and one a complete bath. Depending on your room assignment, B&B rates range from a low of £16 ($28) per person daily to a high of £20 ($35). You must walk over a bridge from the barns and garage to the house. The old mill with two large wheels is about 100 yards up the river from the bridge. The 12 acres in which the mill stands is a nature reserve where you can see birds and wildflowers that have been destroyed elsewhere. Water for the farm is pumped by the mill. The pretty village of Berwick St. James, near Salisbury, has a population of about 150, a church, a pub, and a village shop. A short distance northwest of Salisbury on the A36, you turn right onto the B3083.

Nuholme, Ashfield Road, Salisbury, Wiltshire SP2 7EW (tel. 0722/336592), is a fine B&B establishment in a large row house just a few minutes from the train station. The warm and hospitable proprietor, Mrs. G. Spiller, rents three comfortably furnished rooms at a cost of £9 ($15.75) per person nightly. For that, you get a good home-cooked breakfast. From Salisbury, follow the A30 road until you run into Wilton Road (still the A30). Ashfield Road turns off opposite the Horse and Groom Inn.

Cross Keys Hotel, Shaftesbury Road, Fovant, Salisbury, Wiltshire SP3 5JH (tel. 072270/284), is ideal if you're motoring. A stone building, it dates from the late 15th century and is said to have been frequented by the notorious highwayman Jack Rattenbury. Pauline Story not only does B&B at £12.50 ($21.90) per person daily, but she prepares excellent English fare, including pheasant on occasion, along with venison, local trout, and honey roast duck. Cottage pie is regularly featured, and you can always get a steak. Usually there is a choice of a dozen main courses, along with about seven appetizers and the equivalent number of desserts. For a typical meal, expect to spend from £8 ($14). Hours are 8 a.m. to 9:30 p.m. every day; however, alcoholic beverages can only be served during regular licensing hours, in the stone stable bar.

Holmhurst, Downtown Road, Salisbury, Wiltshire SP2 8AR (tel. 0722/23164), lies on the A338 Ringwood-Bournemouth road. Mr. and Mrs. Curley invite you to share their home, giving you a good clean well-furnished accommodation, along with an excellent breakfast, all for a cost of £12 ($21) per person nightly. Most rooms have private showers and toilets.

Staying Near Stonehenge

Fair Lawn Hotel, 42 High St., Amesbury, Wiltshire SP4 7DJ (tel. 0980/22103), 13 miles north of Salisbury, is ideally located for an in-depth visit to the archeological sites on Salisbury Plain. It is only two miles from Stonehenge and one mile from Woodhenge and Durrington Walls, a short distance outside Amesbury. The hotel, owned by Paul and Doreen Banks, is a Georgian building well into its third century. B&B costs from £12 ($21) daily in a single and £24 ($42) to £36 ($63) in a double, the latter price for a room with a private shower. All tariffs include VAT and a full English breakfast. The rooms are clean and sunny. The hotel also has a cocktail lounge and restaurant serving a three-course dinner for around £11 ($19.25), depending on the main course you choose. Food is served from noon to 2 p.m. and 6:30 to 10 p.m. daily. Gerald Hawkins, author of *Stonehenge Decoded*, stayed at the Fair Lawn when he visited the area.

WHERE TO DINE

The best all-around tea room and pâtisserie in Salisbury is that of **Michael J. R. Snell,** 8 St. Thomas's Square (tel. 0722/336037). His specialty is tea and coffee along with handmade chocolates. Trained in Switzerland, Mr. Snell is a considerate owner-manager. He keeps his place open Monday to Saturday from 9 a.m. to 5:30 p.m. In fair weather, the atmosphere becomes quite continental, with umbrella-shaded tables placed out on the square. In the afternoon, you can enjoy a Wiltshire clotted cream tea with scones. Among the dessert specialties, I'd make a detour for a slice of his forêt noire gâteau, a Black Forest cake. Try also his black cherry cheesecake for the same price. A reasonable luncheon menu, which is likely to include everything from local smoked trout to pizza flan, is offered until 2:30 p.m., costing from £3.50 ($6.15) per person. Each main dish is served with a choice of salads. Coffee is roasted right on the premises, and you can see the coffee-roasting room by the river. Children's portions are also available.

Old House Restaurant, 47 New St. (tel. 0722/334651), is in an early 15th-century building. Denise Maidment, the "governor," offers a table d'hôte menu for both lunch and dinner for £10.50 ($18.40). Food is served from noon to 2 p.m. and 7 to 9:30 p.m. daily, except that no dinner is available Sunday and Monday.

Red Lion Hotel, Milford Street (tel. 0722/23334), is too stately to roar. But since the 1300s it's been putting up wayfarers who rumbled in stagecoaches from London across the Salisbury Plain to the West Countree. Cross under its arch into a courtyard with a hanging and much-photographed creeper, a red lion, and a half-timbered facade, and you'll be transplanted back to the good old days. An à la carte luncheon costs from £6.50 ($11.40). The recommendable dinner ranges from £12 ($21) for a three-course meal. House specialties include jugged hare with red currant jelly, roast venison, steak-and-kidney pie, and roast beef with horseradish sauce. Meals are served daily from 12:30 to 1:45 p.m. and 7 to 9 p.m.

The New Inn, 41-43 New St., Salisbury, Wiltshire SP1 2PH (tel. 0722/27679), isn't all that new: In the old part of the city with an attractive walled garden adjoining the Cathedral Close, it is a charming 15th-century "listed" inn enjoying an international reputation for the quality and excellence of its traditional English ales, fine wines, and freshly prepared home-cooked food, personally created and well presented by J. F. Spicer and partners. It is open all day for refreshments, including afternoon tea. Hours are from 11 a.m. to 3 p.m. and 6 to 10:30 p.m. Monday to Saturday, and from noon to 3 p.m. and 7 to 10:30 p.m. Sunday. Tastefully restored rooms are rented to nonsmokers only. All have private baths, color TV, and four-poster or brass beds. The tariff for accommodation costs £39 ($68.25) to £49 ($85.75) for a double.

Harper's Restaurant, 7-9 Ox Row, the Market Square (tel. 0722/333118), is run by its chef-patron, Adrian Harper, who prides himself on specializing in "real food," homemade and wholesome. The pleasantly decorated restaurant offers such à la carte selections as quiche maison garnished with salad, Harper's pâté with whole-meal toast, and keftedakia (lamb meatballs with a yogurt, mint, chili, and garlic dip) among the appetizers. Main dishes include sirloin and filet steaks, noisettes of lamb with apricot sauce, the captain's pie (cod in a creamy sauce topped with potato), and vegetarian food. Luscious desserts complete the menu. Expect to pay from £10 ($17.50) for an à la carte meal. Fixed-price menus are also offered, costing £5.50 ($9.65) at lunch and £9.50 ($16.65). Special menus for children, costing £2.25 ($3.95), include fish fingers, beefburgers, or sausage, all with french fries, beans, and ice cream. Harper's is open from noon to 2 p.m. and 6:30 to 10 p.m. Monday to Saturday. It's best to reserve a table.

Raffles Tea Room, Mitre House, 37 High St. (tel. 0722/333705), lies above the House of Tweed, offering convenient refreshment for visitors or shoppers. Light meals are served, including homemade soups, cakes, and lunch dishes. A refreshing English tea at Raffles includes two scones with jam and cream and, naturally, a large pot of Earl Grey or Ceylon tea. Raffles is open daily from 9:30 a.m. to 5 p.m. Monday to Saturday, and from 10:30 a.m. to 4:30 p.m. Sunday.

Mo's, 62 Milford St. (tel. 0722/331377), one of the most popular low-cost spots in Salisbury, is at its most bustling in the evening. It serves the type of food you are familiar with, and that means steaks, barbecue spareribs, chili con carne, and burgers American style (try the one with mozzarella on a sesame bun). Of course, British food isn't neglected either, and you'll find steak-and-kidney pie and other such fare on the menu. Vegetarians are also catered to, with a selection of offerings. Meals costing from £4 ($7), are served from noon to 2:30 p.m. and 5:30 to 11 p.m. (on Friday until midnight, and 6 to 10:30 p.m. on Sunday). It is closed for Sunday lunch.

Mainly Salads, 18 Fisherton St. (tel. 0722/22134), is a self-service vegetarian restaurant. Fresh, crisp salads, including slices of red pepper with peanuts, or leek, lentil, and mushrooms, are on display on a long counter. What makes the place—run by June and Ron Ceresa—interesting are these imaginative salad combinations, which are not your typical potato salad and cole slaw variety. You might also try their curried nut loaf and for dessert, if featured, a Dutch apple pie. The place can get exceptionally busy during the lunch break, but it remains open daily, except Sunday, from 10 a.m. to 5 p.m., charging £3.50 ($6.15) and up for a meal. It is unlicensed. You might also try it for morning coffee or afternoon tea.

SIDE TRIPS FROM SALISBURY

In this area rich in reminders of England's heritage, traces have been found of human occupation long beyond the dawn of history. Neolithic man, Iron Age inhabitants, Romans, Saxons, Danes, Normans, and English people of today have all left their mark on the land and their artifacts can be visited during your stay at Salisbury.

Old Sarum

About 2 miles north of Salisbury off the A345 is Old Sarum (tel. 0722/335398), the remains of what is believed to have been an Iron Age fortification. The earthworks were known to the Romans as Sorbiodunum, and later to the Saxons. The Normans, in fact, built a cathedral and a castle in what was then a walled town of the Middle Ages. Parts of the old cathedral were disassembled to erect the cathedral at New Sarum. It is open daily from 10 a.m. to 6 p.m. from Good Friday to the end of September; from 10 a.m. to 4 p.m. off-season. It is closed Monday. Admission is 80p ($1.40) for adults and 40p (70¢) for children.

Old Wardour Castle

The ruined 14th-century English Heritage castle (tel. 0747/870487) stands in a lakeside setting in the landscaped grounds of New Wardour Castle, a 1770 Palladian mansion that now houses a girls' school. The old castle, built in 1392 by Lord Lovel, was acquired in 1547 by the Arundell family and modernized in 1578. After being besieged during the Civil War, however, it was abandoned. Today it houses displays on the war sieges and the landscape, as well as an architectural exhibition. It lies 1½ miles north of the A30 going west out of Salisbury, 2 miles southwest of Tisbury. From April to September, it is open from 9:30 a.m. to 6:30 p.m. Monday to Saturday, and 2 to 6:30 p.m. on Sunday. In the winter season, it is open weekends only, from 9:30 a.m. to 4 p.m. on Saturday and 2 to 4 p.m. on Sunday. Admission is 80p ($1.40) for adults, 60p ($1.05) for children.

Wilton House

In the small borough of Wilton, less than three miles to the west of Salisbury, is one of England's great country estates, Wilton House (tel. 0722/743115), the home of the Earl of Pembroke. The stately house in the midst of 20 acres of grounds dates from the 16th century but has seen modifications over the years, some as late as Victoria's day. It is noted for its 17th-century State Rooms by Inigo Jones. Many famous personages have either lived at or visited Wilton. It is believed that Shakespeare's troupe entertained here. Plans for the D-Day landings at Normandy were laid out here in the utmost secrecy by Eisenhower and his advisers, with only the silent Van Dycks in the Double Cube Room as witnesses. The house is filled with beautifully maintained furnishings, especially a collection of Chippendale. Wilton House displays some of the finest paintings in England, including works by Rembrandt, Rubens, Reynolds, and the already-mentioned Van Dyck.

The estate lies in the midst of gardens and grounds, with cedars of Lebanon, the oldest of which were planted in 1630. The Palladian Bridge was built in 1737. Wilton House may be visited Tuesday through Saturday and bank holidays from 11 a.m. to 6 p.m., and on Sunday from 1 to 6 p.m. from Easter weekend to mid-October. Guided tours are conducted daily, except Sunday and special days. Admission to the house and grounds only is £2.40 ($4.20) for adults, £2 ($3.50) for children under 16. An inclusive ticket to the house, grounds, and exhibitions costs £3.40 ($5.95) for adults, £2.50 ($4.40) for children.

The excellent, fully licensed self-service restaurant is open during house hours and offers homemade cooking. Hot dishes can be had by ordering ahead. Don't miss a Wilton House cream tea. There is an Adventure Playground for children, plus an exhibition of 7000 model soldiers and "The Pembroke Palace" dollhouse. You can also visit "Wiltshire in Miniature," a model railway in the 14th-century abbey building, and a historical tableau of dolls and toys through the ages.

Stonehenge

Two miles west of Amesbury on the junction of A303 and A344/A360 and about nine miles north of Salisbury is the renowned Stonehenge, believed to be anywhere from 3500 to 5000 years old. This huge circle of lintels and megalithic pillars is the most important prehistoric monument in Britain.

Some North Americans have expressed their disappointment after seeing the concentric circles of stones. Admittedly, they are not the pyramids, and some imagination has to be brought to bear on them. But pyramids or not, they represent an amazing engineering feat. Many of the boulders, the bluestones in particular, were moved many miles, perhaps from southern Wales, to this site by the ancients. If you're fanciful, you can always credit Merlin with delivering them on clouds from Ireland.

The widely held view of the 18th- and 19th-century romantics that Stonehenge was the work of the Druids is without foundation. The boulders, many weighing into the tons, are believed to have predated the arrival in Britain of that Celtic cult. Recent excavations continue to bring new evidence to bear on the origin and purpose of Stonehenge. The prehistoric site was a subject of controversy following the publication of *Stonehenge Decoded* by Gerald S. Hawkins and John B. White, which maintained that Stonehenge was in fact an astronomical observatory—that is, a Neolithic computing machine capable of predicting eclipses.

Others who discount Hawkins's decoding would prefer to adopt Henry James's approach to Stonehenge, which regards it as "lonely in history," its origin and purposes (burial ground, sun-worshipping site, human sacrificial temple?) the secret of the silent, mysterious Salisbury Plain.

Admission is £1.60 ($2.80) for adults, 80p ($1.40) for children. From Good Friday to September 30, hours are daily from 10 a.m. to 6 p.m. From October to Maundy Thursday, hours are daily from 10 a.m. to 4 p.m. Your ticket permits you to go inside the fence surrounding the site to protect the stones from vandals and souvenir hunters. You can go all the way up to a short rope barrier about 50 feet from the stones. If you don't have a car, you can take a bus from the Salisbury train station. There are also organized bus tours out of Salisbury.

Nether Wallop

On a country road between the A343 and the A30 east of Salisbury is the little village of Nether Wallop (not to be confused with Over Wallop or Middle Wallop in the same vicinity). Aficionados of television films about Agatha Christie's *Miss Marple* will be interested in this village, used as Miss Christie's fictitious St. Mary Mead, home of Miss Marple. Visitors to Nether Wallop easily identify the sites in many of the TV movies.

The village is about 12 miles from Stonehenge and about equidistant between Salisbury and Winchester. A stream winds through the valley in which Nether Wallop nestles, and there are many thatch cottages and a ninth-century church with medieval wall paintings.

You can stay in this inviting village at **Broadgate Farm,** Nether Wallop, Stockbridge, Hampshire SO20 8HA (tel. 0264/781439), a beautiful Georgian farmhouse with a walled garden, right in the center of Nether Wallop. Susan and Richard Osmond offer two spacious bedrooms and a good English breakfast for £14 ($24.50) per person daily. The house has full central heating, a dining room, and a well-furnished lounge. Richard's family has farmed in Nether Wallop since 1622, and the Osmonds still run the farm, with a pedigree herd of Friesian cows, 300 sheep, and grain crops.

Longleat House

Between Bath and Salisbury, Longleat House (tel. 09853/551) lies four miles southwest of Warminster, 4½ miles southeast of Frome on the A362. The first view of this magnificent Elizabethan house, built in the early Renaissance style, is romantic enough, but the wealth of paintings and furnishings within its lofty rooms is enough to dazzle. The Venetian ceilings were added in Queen Victoria's time by the fourth Marquess of Bath.

A tour of the house, from the Elizabethan Great Hall, through libraries, the State Rooms, and the Grand Staircase, is awe-inspiring in its variety and splendor. The State Dining Room is full of silver and plate, and fine tapestries and paintings adorn the walls in rich profusion. The Victorian kitchens are open during the summer months, offering a glimpse of life below the stairs in a well-ordered country home. Various exhibitions are mounted in the Stable Yard, and the Safari Park contains a vast array of animals in open parklands, including Britain's only white tiger. During the summer months, a program of outside events is arranged on weekends.

A maze, believed to be the largest in the world, was added to the attractions by Lord Weymouth, son of the marquess. It has more than 1½ miles of paths among yew trees. The first part is comparatively easy, but the second part is very complicated, with bridges adding to the confusion. It knocks the Hampton Court maze into a cocked hat, as the British say. The house also contains more than 39,000 magnificent books and rare manuscripts, some of which are on display to the public.

The house is open daily all year, except Christmas Day. The Safari Park closes November through mid March. Admission to the house is £3 ($5.25) for adults, £1 ($1.75) for children. The Safari Park costs £3.80 ($6.65) for adults, £2.50 ($4.40) for children. There are many attractions within the grounds, including a 15-inch–gauge railway ride, safari boats, a pets' corner, a doll's house, and a Dr. Who exhibition. Lord Weymouth has added an Adventure Castle for children.

For travelers who may wish to stay in the Longleat area, there is the **Bath Arms,** Horningsham, Warminster, Wiltshire BA12 7NN (tel. 09853/308), an old gray stone house that lies just beyond the main gatehouse of Longleat House. It is set among fine trees, among them more Glastonbury cockspur plants (the thorn tree that legend says was planted by Joseph of Arimathea) than you find at Glastonbury. The place has been an inn for more than 200 years, owned by the big house and leased to a succession of tenant landlords. Today the Lovatt family—Joe and his wife, Beryl, assisted by son Paul—are the landlords who operate the inn in a personal way, providing a warm welcome to passersby and overnight guests. They have seven well-furnished bedrooms with baths and TVs, which go for £29.50 ($51.75) daily in a single, £41 ($71.75) in a double, including a large English breakfast. There is a cheerful bar that serves the local citizenry as well as guests, and a dining room where Beryl enjoys a reputation for her country food, homemade meat and fish pies, and international dishes, interspersed with seasonal specialties. A three-course Sunday lunch at £6.95 ($12.15) is likely to include roast venison from the estate. Regular meals begin at £13 ($22.75) per person.

Stourhead

After Longleat, drive six miles south down the A3092 to Stourton, a village just off the A3092 and three miles northwest of Mere (A303). Stourhead (tel. 0747/840348), a Palladian house, was built in the 18th century by the banking family of Hoare. On the site of an old Gothic house called Stourton, the present mansion was designed by Colen Campbell, the renowned early 19th-century architect. The furniture is mostly the work of Thomas Chippendale the Younger. Stourhead's landscaping, however, is the most outstanding thing about the property, which now belongs to the National Trust. The pleasure grounds became known as *le jardin anglais,* in that they blended art and nature. Set around an artificial lake, the grounds are decorated with temples, bridges, islands, and grottoes, as well as statuary. The house is open from March 25 to November 5. Hours are 2 to 6 p.m. from March 25 to April 1 and October 1 to November 5, Saturday to Wednesday, plus Thursday from May to the end of September. It is closed Friday. Last admission is at 5:30 p.m. Admission is £2.50 ($4.40) for adults and £1.30 ($2.30) for children 5 to 16. The gardens are open daily from 8 a.m. to 7 p.m. (until dusk if earlier) all year. Admission to the gardens is £2 ($3.50) for adults and £1 ($1.75) for children. In May and June, adults are charged £2.50 ($4.40), and children pay £1.30 ($2.30). From November to February, admission is £1.50 ($2.65) for adults, 70p ($1.25) for children.

Avebury

One of the largest prehistoric sites in Europe, Avebury lies about six miles west of Marlborough on the Kennet River. It is gaining in popularity with visitors now that the British have had to rope off the circle at Stonehenge. Explorers are able to walk the 28-acre site at Avebury, winding in and out of the circle of more than 100 stones, some weighing up to 50 tons. They are made of sarsen, a sandstone found in Wiltshire. Inside this large circle are two smaller ones, each with about 30 stones standing upright. Native Neolithic tribes are believed to have built these circles. The village of Avebury, taken over by the National Trust, bisects the prehistoric monument and is worth exploring.

Dating from before the Conquest, **Avebury Manor** (tel. 06723/203) was built on the site of a Benedictine cell. An early Elizabethan manor house, it stands beside the great stone circle of Avebury. Original oak-paneled rooms and plasterwork ceilings, fine oak furniture, and early paintings fill the house. The manor is steeped in history. The attic and anterooms have been chosen to take you back in time. There you will see wax figures of the notorious William Sharington, the staunch Royalist Sir John Stawell, and Sir Richard Holford, all once owners of the house. Additional attractions include Sir John Stawell's armory, supplied by the Tower of London. Replica jewelry and dress of the Elizabethan period, artifacts of torture, and exhibitions of Civil War arms are displayed. Within the grounds, visitors can see an Elizabethan market square full of craft workshops, music-making minstrels, jugglers, strolling players, lords and ladies, and jesters. There is also an adventure playground, plus falconry demonstrations. Surrounding gardens and parkland are equally intriguing. The manor is open from 11:30 a.m. to 6 p.m. Monday to Saturday and 1:30 to 6 p.m. Sunday from March 24 to October 8. Admission is £3.50 ($6.15) for adults, £2.50 ($4.40) for children 4 to 14. The manor lies 1½ miles from the A4 London-to-Bath road, 9 miles from junction 15 (the Swindon exit) on the M4, and 6 miles from Marlborough.

The **Avebury Museum** (tel. 0672/3250), founded by Alexander Keiller, houses one of Britain's most important archeological collections. It began with Keiller's material from excavations at Windmill Hill and Avebury, and it now includes artifacts from other prehistoric digs at West Kennet, Long Barrow, Silbury Hill, West Kennet Avenue, and the Sanctuary. It is open from 10 a.m. to 6 p.m. from Good Friday to the end of September, and from 10 a.m. to 4 p.m. off-season. It is closed Monday. Admission is 80p ($1.40) for adults and 40p (70¢) for children.

The **Great Barn Museum of Wiltshire Folk Life** (tel. 06723/555), housed in a 17th-century thatched barn, contains displays on cheese making, blacksmithing, thatching, sheep and shepherds, the work of the wheelwright and other rural crafts, as well as local geology and domestic life of the last three centuries. From mid-March to the end of October, it is open daily from 10 a.m. to 5:30 p.m. The remainder of the year, it is open on Saturday from 1 to 4:30 p.m. and on Sunday from 11 a.m. to 4:30 p.m. Admission is 95p ($1.65) for adults, 50p (90¢) for children, and £2.25 ($3.95) for a family ticket.

After sightseeing—and still in the same vicinity—you may be ready for a bite to eat.

Stones Restaurant, High Street (tel. 06723/514), has made an impact on the palates in the area since its opening in 1984 by Dr. Hilary Howard and Michael

Pitts. They specialize in freshly made original high-quality food (no additives), served in attractive surroundings at reasonable prices. You can have a meal for around £5 ($8.75), including drinks. A wide range of cakes, desserts, and cold savories is available throughout the day, supplemented at lunchtime by a full hot-food menu that can be accompanied by the local prize-winning ale, Wadworth's 6X. Other drinks are available, including coffee, tea by the pot, fruit juices, and bottled beer. There is an exceptional range of handmade unpasteurized English and Welsh cheeses. In summer, queues get long at lunchtime, so it's best to arrive early (lunch starts at noon), and to avoid Sunday lunchtime entirely. Cream teas here are famous, with Stones's own scones and jam plus clotted cream brought from Cornwall. Stones is open April to mid-October from 10 a.m. to 6 p.m. seven days a week.

Afterward, you can drop in for a drink at the **Red Lion** (tel. 06723/266), a typical English country inn complete with thatch roof and Tudor half-timbering. It even has its own resident ghost, Florrie, supposed to have been killed by her husband when he returned from the wars and discovered she had been unfaithful. Parts of the building are from the 1600s, but there isn't any record as to just how long Florrie has been on hand. The inn is open daily from 11 a.m. to 2:30 p.m. and 6 to 11 p.m. Food is served from noon to 2 p.m. and 7 to 10 p.m.

On the A350 Blandford road, 20 miles from Warminster, stands **Milestones,** Compton Abbas, near Shaftesbury in Dorset (tel. 0747/811360), a 17th-century tea room right next to the church, with gorgeous views over the Dorset hills. This spotless little place is presided over by two delightful women who serve real farmhouse teas or a ploughman's lunch. Fresh sandwiches are also offered. Light meals and teas cost from £2 ($3.50). This is really the ideal English tea room, and the women who run it are charming. Their place is open from 10 a.m. to 5:30 p.m., except Thursday and November to March.

Lacock

Lacock is a National Trust village with an abbey dating from 1232 and the famous **Fox Talbot Museum** (tel. 024973/459), tracing the history of photography. It's open daily from 11 a.m. to 6 p.m. March to October except Good Friday. Admission is £1.50 ($2.65) for adults, 70p ($1.25) for children. Lacock is a good base for exploring Bath, Castle Combe, and Longleat.

Your best accommodations bet is **The Old Rectory,** Cantax Hill, Lacock, near Chippenham, Wiltshire SN15 2JZ (tel. 024973/335). Mrs. Margaret Addison welcomes visitors to her old house built in 1866. The house stands in its own grounds of eight acres, with ample car parking space just off the A350 Chippenham-Melksham road. In comfortably furnished rooms, all with private baths, color TV, and beverage-making facilities, B&B is £13 ($22.75) daily per person. A TV lounge is offered for use of guests.

---

2. Castle Combe

Once voted Britain's prettiest village, Castle Combe was used for location shots for the film *Dr. Dolittle.* About ten miles from Bath, this little Cotswold village is filled with shops selling souvenirs and antiques. The village cottages are often set beside a trout stream and are made of stone with moss-laden roofs. The church is unremarkable, except for its 15th-century tower. An old market cross and a triple-arched bridge are much photographed.

No accommodation but plenty of local color is offered at the **White Hart,** on the main road through the village (tel. 0249/782295). It's a white-painted pub built of Cotswold stone and covered with a stone tile roof. Dating from either the 13th or 14th century, it has low ceilings (and in the cellars are Norman arches). The main bar is divided into two parts, with a cold buffet counter for meals. The garden is also open to visitors, and the parlor bar admits children. Home-cooked ham or beef, with cole slaw and bread and butter, is offered. In winter, hot soups, chili, hot pasties, and toasted sandwiches are available. Bar meals cost from £4 ($7) at both lunch and dinner. Bitter beer from traditional wooden barrels is popular with the locals. This is one of the few traditional English pubs in the Cotswolds recommended for nightlife. It's open from 11:30 a.m. to 2:30 p.m. and 6 to 11 p.m. Monday to Saturday, and from noon to 3 p.m. and 7 to 10:30 p.m. Sunday.

You can stop for B&B at a place with a similar name, the **White Hart Inn,** Fort, near Chippenham, Wiltshire SN14 8RP (tel. 0249/782213), a short distance south of Castle Combe on the A420 west of Chippenham. Here Bill and Jane Futcher cater to the local population that is swelled during the summer months by passing tourists. The inn is a lovely old 16th-century building with gardens running down to the river. They have added a heated swimming pool to the amenities, but the bars remain low-ceilinged with blackened beams and open fires. Various local souls help in the bars and in the dining room, where residents can dine for £12 ($21) from a menu including braised venison (caught, matured, and marinated locally in port wine). If this is not enough, food offered in the old buttery can be anything from chicken casserole in cider to home-cooked ham or excellent steak-and-kidney pies made to order. Bedrooms, some with four-poster beds, contain private baths. Singles begin at £35 ($61.25) daily and doubles at £49 ($85.75), including an enormous breakfast with lots of coffee.

GRITTLETON

Just three miles from Castle Combe, **Neeld Arms Inn,** Grittleton, Wiltshire SN14 6AP (tel. 0249/782470), is a charming 17th-century inn. The unspoiled village of Grittleton, in Beaufort hunt country, is built of the golden stone of Wiltshire. The inn is included on a map of 1760, but one section has been dated from the previous century. The family of Joan Wheatcroft, headed by her son-in-law, Paul Gallant, and her daughter Alison, make guests feel welcome when they stay overnight or just stop in the pub, as many locals do, for a drink and perhaps a snack. There are four bedrooms to rent, one with a private bath and one with a shower and washbasin. Prices are from £15 ($26.25) per person daily for a bed and a full English breakfast. There is a dining area on each side of the bar where you can eat well from a large selection of dishes such as filet steak, chicken Kiev, boeuf en croûte, trout with almonds, and steak in wine and herbs. Otherwise, you can choose from a separate bar menu that includes a ploughman's lunch, lasagne with salad, and steak-and-mushroom pie. To complement the food there is an extensive wine list and a choice of real country ales. Meals costing from £5 ($8.75) are served daily from noon to 2 p.m. and 7 to 9:30 p.m.

In the mid-1600s, an inn at Grittleton, the King's Arms, was closed down by Oliver Cromwell during the Civil War. For his forays in this area, Cromwell made his headquarters at nearby Fosscote Farm. The Neeld Arms Inn is a good base for visiting a number of interesting little towns and hamlets in Wiltshire, among them Lacock, only six miles away.

SOMERSET

When writing about Somerset, it's difficult to avoid sounding like the editor of *The Countryside Companion,* waxing poetic over hills and valleys, dale and field. In scenery, the western shire embraces some of nature's most masterly touches in England. Mendip's limestone hills undulate across the countryside (ever had a potholing holiday?). The irresistible Quantocks are the pride of the west, especially lovely in spring and fall. Here, too, is the heather-clad **Exmoor National Park,** a wooded area abounding in red deer and wild ponies, much of its moorland 1200 feet above sea level. Somerset opens onto the Bristol Channel, with Minehead being the chief resort.

Somerset is rich in legend and history and is particularly fanciful about its associations with King Arthur and Queen Guinevere, along with Camelot and Alfred the Great. Its villages are noted for the tall towers of their parish churches.

A quiet, unspoiled life holds forth in Somerset. You're likely to end up in a vine-covered old inn, talking with the regulars about stag hounds. Or you may anchor at a large estate that stands in a woodland setting surrounded by bridle paths and sheep walks (Somerset was once a great wool center). Maybe you'll settle down in a 16th-century thatched stone farmhouse set in the midst of orchards in a vale. Somerset is reputed (and I heartily concur) to have the best cider anywhere. When you lounge under a shady Somerset apple tree, downing a tankard of refreshingly chilled golden cider, everything you've drunk in the past tastes like apple juice.

My notes on Somerset, accumulated over many a year, would easily fill a book. But space and limited schedule being what they are, I confined the following comments in the main to the shire's two most interesting towns, Wells and Glastonbury. Still, I'll throw in a few farmhouse recommendations off the beaten path for those who want rural atmosphere.

---

3. Exmoor National Park

The far west of Somerset forms most of the Exmoor National Park. In addition to the heather-clad moor, the park includes the wooded valleys of the Rivers Exe and Barle, the Brendon Hills, and the sweeping stretch of coast from Minehead to the boundary of Devon. This is more of the land of Blackmore's *Lorna Doone*. You can walk up Badgworthy Water from Malmsmead to Doone Valley, divided by the Somerset-Devon line, or visit tiny Oare Church and see the window through which Carver Doone shot Lorna at her wedding. The moors, which rise to 1707 feet at Dunkery Beacon, are inviting to walkers and pony trekkers, with ponies and wild deer roaming freely.

Visit England's smallest complete church at Culbone and the centuries-old clapper bridge over the River Barle at Tarr Steps. Some of England's prettiest villages are within the national park, and some lie along its borders. Selworthy, an idyllic little town, is in Exmoor, as is Allerford, with its packhorse bridge and its walnut tree, both of them owned and preserved by the National Trust.

Minehead, a fine resort, is just outside the park's northeastern boundary, but in some ways the little villages that have that town as a focal point have more charm.

For places to stay in Exmoor National Park, I suggest a trio of villages in the heart of the park, all to the southwest of Minehead.

WITHYPOOL

In this charming little village on the River Barle, **Westerclose Country House Hotel,** Withypool, Somerset JA24 7QR (tel. 064383/302), was built as a hunting lodge more than 60 years ago. Now a hotel, it is surrounded by unspoiled country-side and stands in nine acres of gardens and paddocks in the middle of Exmoor National Park, within sight of the village of Withypool. It was built in the Edwardian age, with polished oak floors, several fireplaces, and a scattering of four-poster beds. Some of the 11 bedrooms are contained within the main house, while others lie in a cozy annex at the far edge of the stable yard. All the accommodations have private baths, color TV, and tea- and coffee-makers. John and Judith Kelly, the owners, charge £19 ($33.25) daily in a single, from £38 ($66.50) to £44 ($77) in doubles. Dinner costs from £11 ($19.25). Traditional English and classic French dishes are served, with à la carte and fixed-price dinners prepared using local products. Coffee and tea are served on the south-facing terrace and lawn in summer. To reach Withypool, take the A361 Taunton-Barnstaple road at Bampton and then the B3222 road through Exebridge to Dulverton. From Dulverton, the B3223 Lynton road goes across the moor, where after about seven miles you'll see the signs for the village.

EXFORD

On the River Exe, at the junction of the B3224 and B2223 roads a short distance north of Withypool, lies **Edgcott House,** Exford, Somerset TA24 7QG (tel. 064383/495), a large old country house with a sheltered garden, close to the village of Exford. It offers comfortable bedrooms, some with private baths, and a warm lounge with an open fire in cool weather. A typical country atmosphere prevails. Enormous breakfasts are served, and dinners can be prearranged. Your hostess, Mrs. Lamble, is a friendly person and a good cook. She charges from £12 ($21) per person nightly for B&B and from £19.50 ($34.15) per person for half board.

SIMONSBATH

Another village in the heart of Exmoor National Park, Simonsbath is about six miles to the west of Exford on the B3223 road. Open March to October, **Emmett's Grange,** Simonsbath, near Minehead, Somerset TA24 7LD (tel. 064383/282), is run by Mr. and Mrs. A. R. Brown. Their farm, built in 1844 but offering the facilities of a modern home, lies 2½ miles from Simonsbath on the South Molton road (it is signposted). This 1200-acre beef-and-sheep hill farm offers rooms with and without private bath. A bed and a full breakfast costs from £13.50 ($23.63) to £16 ($28) per person nightly, increasing to £23.50 ($41.13) to £26 ($45.50) for half board. A good selection of drinks, including wines and local cider, are served. The place is known for its country food.

---

4. Dunster

The village of Dunster lies in Somerset near the eastern edge of Exmoor National Park, three miles southeast of Minehead, just off the A39. It grew up around the original Dunster Castle, constructed as a fortress for the de Mohun family, whose progenitor came to England with William the Conqueror. The village, about four miles from the Cistercian monastery at Cleeve, has an ancient priory church and dovecote, a 17th-century gabled Yarn Market, and little cobbled streets along which whitewashed cottages gleam proudly.

DUNSTER CASTLE

On a tor (high hill) from which you can see the Bristol Channel, Dunster Castle (tel. 0643/821314) stands on the site of a Norman castle granted to William de Mohun of Normandy by William the Conqueror shortly after the conquest of England. The 13th-century gateway built by the de Mohuns is all that remains of the original fortress. In 1376, the castle and its lands were bought by Lady Elizabeth Luttrell and belonged to her family until given to the National Trust in 1976, together with 30 acres of surrounding parkland. The first castle was largely demolished during the Civil War, and the present Dunster Castle is a Jacobean house built in the lower ward of the original fortifications in 1620, then rebuilt by Salvin in 1870 to look like a castle. Terraced walks and gardens command good views of Exmoor and the Quantock Hills.

Outstanding among the contents within are the 17th-century panels of embossed, painted, and gilded leather depicting the story of Antony and Cleopatra, and a remarkable allegorical 16th-century portrait of Sir John Luttrell, showing him wading naked through the sea with a female figure of Peace and a wrecked ship in the background. The 17th-century plasterwork ceilings of the dining room and staircase and the finely carved staircase balustrade of cavorting huntsmen, hounds, and stags are also particularly noteworthy. The castle and grounds can be visited from April to the end of September every day, except Friday and Saturday, from 11 a.m. to 5 p.m. (last admission at 4:30 p.m.). In October, it is open daily, except Friday and Saturday, from 2 to 4 p.m. (last admission at 3:30 p.m.). Admission to both the castle and grounds is £3 ($5.25) for adults, £1.50 ($2.65) for children. To the grounds only, admission is £1.50 ($2.65) for adults, 50p (90¢) for children.

COMBE SYDENHAM HALL

Between Dunster and Taunton, on the B3188 just south of Monksilver, you can visit Combe Sydenham Hall (tel. 0984/56284), which was the home of Elizabeth Sydenham, wife of Sir Francis Drake. It stands on the ruins of monastic buildings that were associated with nearby Cleeve Abbey. At the hall, you can see a cannonball that legend says halted the wedding of Lady Elizabeth to a rival suitor in 1585. The gardens include Lady Elizabeth's Walk, which circles around ponds originally laid out when the knight was courting his bride-to-be. The valley ponds are fed by springwater full of rainbow trout (ask about the fly fishing and tuition). Woodland walks are possible to Long Meadow with its host of wildflowers. Also to be seen are a deserted hamlet whose population reputedly was wiped out by the Black Death and a historic corn mill, presently being restored. In the hall's tea room, smoked trout and pâté are produced on oak chips, as in days of yore, and there are a shop and car park. The hall is open from 11 a.m. to 4 p.m. in July, August, and September, and from 11 a.m. to 3 p.m. in April, May, June, and October, except on Saturday and Sunday. The country park hours are from 11 a.m. to 6 p.m. in July, August, and September, and from 11 a.m. to 5 p.m. in April, May, June, and October, except on Saturday. Admission is £2.20 ($3.85) for adults, £1.50 ($2.65) for children.

Combe Sydenham is five miles south of Watchet on the B3188 road between Monksilver and Elsworthy. Incidentally, it was from Watchet, a few miles east of Minehead along the coast, that Coleridge's Ancient Mariner sailed.

COLERIDGE COTTAGE

Across the Quantock Hills to the east of the area just previewed, the hamlet of Nether Stowey lies on the A39 at the northern edge of Quantock Forest. Here you can visit Coleridge Cottage (tel. 0278/732662), home of Samuel Taylor Coleridge when he wrote *The Rime of the Ancient Mariner*. During his 1797–1800 sojourn here, he and his friends, William Wordsworth and sister Dorothy, enjoyed exploring the Quantock woods. The cottage, at the west end of Nether Stowey on the south side of the A39 and eight miles west of Bridgwater, has its parlor and reading room open to visitors from April to the end of September from 2 to 5 p.m. Tuesday to Thursday and on Sunday. Admission to the National Trust property is £1 ($1.75).

FOOD AND LODGING

Acceptable as both a B&B and a low-cost restaurant, **The Yarn Market,** 25-27 High St., Dunster, Minehead, Somerset TA24 6SF (tel. 0643/821425), lies behind a white-painted facade of the tallest building on "The High." Originally built as a warehouse, it overlooks both the half-timbered facade of the town's 16th-century Yarn Market as well as more distant views of Dunster Castle. Each of four comfortably furnished bedrooms contains a private bath, costing £20 ($35) per person nightly, including a copious breakfast and VAT. The tariff goes down to £15 ($26.25) per person nightly after the first night (this is to encourage longer stays). The ground floor contains an unpretentious café and restaurant, which is open daily from 10 a.m. to 5:30 p.m. (until 9:30 p.m. in summer). It serves a £6.50 ($11.40) table d'hôte dinner, with à la carte lunches going for £3 ($5.25) each. The menu lists such daily specials as steak-and-kidney pie.

Bilbrook Lawns, Bilbrook, Dunster, Somerset TA24 6HE (tel. 0984/

40331), is owned by the Whymark family. Their white-fronted Georgian house lies within an extensive garden 1½ miles east of the center of Dunster. A brook runs through the garden, and much of the building's front is covered with the kind of veranda where summer nights can happily be spent reading a book or talking quietly. The location is about a mile from the sea. Except in November, the establishment rents seven bedrooms. Tariffs depend on the plumbing, and range from £16 ($28) to £18 ($31.50) per person, single or double occupancy, with breakfast and VAT included. A fixed-price three-course dinner can be arranged for £8 ($14) per person.

5. Glastonbury

The goal of the medieval pilgrim, **Glastonbury Abbey** (tel. 0458/32267), once one of the wealthiest and most prestigious monasteries in England, is no more than a ruined sanctuary today. But it provides Glastonbury's claim to historical greatness, an assertion augmented by legendary links to such figures as Joseph of Arimathea, King Arthur, Queen Guinevere, and St. Patrick.

It is said that Joseph of Arimathea journeyed to what was then the Isle of Avalon with the Holy Grail in his possession. According to tradition, he buried the chalice at the foot of the conically shaped Glastonbury Tor, and a stream of blood burst forth. (You can scale this more than 500-foot-high hill today. A 15th-century tower rests atop it.)

At one point, the early saint is said to have leaned against his staff, which immediately was transformed into a fully blossoming tree. A cutting alleged to have survived from the Holy Thorn can be seen on the abbey grounds today. It blooms at Christmastime and in the early summer. Some historians have traced this particular story back to Tudor times.

Joseph, so it goes, erected a church of wattle (reeds and branches) in Glastonbury. In fact, excavations have shown that the town may have had the oldest church in England.

The most famous link, fanned for Arthurian fans in the Victorian era by Alfred Lord Tennyson, concerns the burial of King Arthur and Queen Guinevere on the abbey grounds. In 1191, the monks dug up the skeletons of two bodies on the south side of the Lady Chapel, said to be that of the king and his queen. In 1278, in the presence of Edward I, the bodies were removed and transferred to a black marble tomb in the choir. Both their alleged burial spot and their shrine are marked today.

A large Benedictine Abbey of St. Mary grew out of the early wattle church. St. Dunstan, who was born nearby, was the abbot in the tenth century, later becoming archbishop of Canterbury. At its most powerful stage in English history, Edmund, Edgar, and Edmund (Ironside)—three early English kings—were buried at the abbey.

In 1184, a fire of unknown origin swept over the abbey, destroying most of it, along with what must have been vast treasures. It was eventually rebuilt after much difficulty, only to be dissolved by Henry VIII. Its last abbot, Richard Whiting, was hanged by the neck at Glastonbury Tor. For years after, the abbey, like the Roman Forum, was used as a stone quarry.

The modern-day pilgrim to Glastonbury can visit the ruins of the Lady Chapel, which is linked by an early English "Galilee" to the nave of the abbey. The best-preserved building on the grounds is a 14th-century octagonal Abbot's Kitchen, where oxen were once roasted whole to feed the wealthier of the pilgrims (that is, the biggest donors). You can visit the ruins from 9:30 a.m. till dusk, for £1 ($1.75) for adults, 50p (90¢) for children under 16.

Glastonbury may be one of the oldest inhabited sites in Britain. Excavations have revealed Iron Age lakeside villages on its periphery. Some of the discoveries dug up may be viewed in a little museum in the High Street.

After the destruction of its once-great abbey, the town lost prestige. It is a market town today. The ancient gatehouse entry to the abbey, by the way, is a museum, its principal exhibit a scale model of the abbey and its community buildings as they stood in 1539, at the time of the dissolution. The above fees include entry to the abbey museum.

SOMERSET RURAL LIFE MUSEUM

The history of the Somerset countryside over the last 100 or so years is explained in a museum, Abbey Farm, Chilkwell Street (tel. 0458/32903). The main part of the exhibition is Abbey Barn, the home barn of the abbey, built in 1370. The magnificent timbered roof, the stone tiles, and the sculpture outside, including a head of Edward III, make it special. There are also a Victorian farmhouse and various other exhibits illustrating farming in Somerset during the "horse age" and domestic and social life in Victorian times. In summer they have demonstrations of buttermaking, weaving, basketwork, anything that has reference to the rural life of the country, now rapidly disappearing with the invention of the engine, the freezer, and the instant meal. The museum is open daily from 10 a.m. to 5 p.m. (2 to 6:30 p.m. on Saturday and Sunday; 2:30 to 5 p.m. in winter). Admission is 70p ($1.25) for adults, 20p (35¢) for children. There is a museum shop.

ACCOMMODATIONS

Although I'll document some exceptional places to stay in the area, you might need emergency assistance if you arrive when all the rooms listed are taken. In that case, there is a nonprofit **Tourist Information Centre** run by volunteers. The center (tel. 0458/32954) is entered from Northload Street. Look for a narrow passage at the end of which is a terrace of flower-bedecked old brick cottages (the tourist office is in the first cottage). It is open Easter to late October from 9:30 a.m. to 5 p.m. daily, plus 10 a.m. to 4 p.m. on Sunday in summer, and can deal with accommodations inquiries.

Tor Down, Ashwell Lane, Glastonbury, Somerset BA6 4BG (tel. 0458/32287), is a late Victorian, red-brick, very comfortable house "just beneath the Tor." It requires a three-quarter-mile or a brisk 15-minute downhill walk to reach the center of Glastonbury. Ms. Parfitt welcomes you into her home, which is well cared for and centrally heated. There's an expansive view from the Tor of the Isle of Avalon. She charges only £11 ($19.25) per person daily, based on double occupancy. A pair of small but cramped singles rent for £15 ($26.25) each. None of these accommodations has a private bath. A copious breakfast, suitable for the most vigorous hill-climbers, is included. Ms. Parfitt will pack lunches if asked. Guests gather in the parlor in the evening for tea and crackers (called "biscuits" here).

Little Orchard, Ashwell Lane, Glastonbury, Somerset BA6 8BG (tel. 0458/31620), on the A361 Glastonbury-to-Shepton Mallet road, is a Tyrolean-type brick structure at the foot of Glastonbury Tor, with striking views over the Vale of Avalon. Rodney and Dinah Gifford rent centrally heated bedrooms with hot and cold water basins accommodating up to ten guests. Rates are £9 ($15.75) per person daily for B&B, with a full English breakfast served. The house has a fire certificate, and there is a color TV lounge. In summer, guests can enjoy the sun patio and large garden. Note the attractive stained-glass window in the staircase.

Market House Inn, Magdalene Street, Glastonbury, Somerset BA6 9EW (tel. 0458/32220), is a two-story building with Georgian detailing behind a red-brick facade. It enjoys a superb location across from the ruined abbey in an 18th-century building. Christine and Leslie Moore operate not only this small inn but also run a popular restaurant, beer garden, and skittle alley. They charge £15 ($26.25) per person daily for a double and £20 ($25) for a single. All rooms have color TV and tea-and coffee-makers. Prices include a full English breakfast. However, they offer only five rooms, and in summer these tend to go quickly. There are two areas for eating and drinking. Both are cozy, rustic, and pleasantly old-fashioned. The bars are open daily from 11 a.m. to 11 p.m., and meals are served from noon to 7 p.m. Monday to Saturday and noon to 3 p.m. Sunday. The extensive menu includes homemade specialty dishes fresh daily.

Berewall Farm Country Guest House, Cinnamon Lane, Glastonbury, Somerset BA6 8LL (tel. 0458/31451), is operated by Mrs. Nurse on the periphery of Glastonbury. From this piece of property, a panoramic sweep of Glastonbury Tor unfolds. Here is good, country living on a dairy with almost 150 acres. Her rooms are attractive and comfortable, with many amenities. In fact, all nine rooms contain full private baths and color TV. With an English or continental breakfast included, the charge is £16.50 ($28.90) per person daily in a double, £17.50 ($30.65) in a single. Some family rooms are available. Because of the good hearty farmhouse cooking, you'll want to stick around for dinner.

Woodlands, 52 Bove Town, Glastonbury, Somerset BA6 8JE (tel. 0458/32119), is an attractive and cozy residence lying within easy access to the ruins of Glastonbury Abbey. Guests receive a warm welcome and are housed in one of three twin-bedded rooms, the occupants of which share a well-maintained public bath. The charge for B&B ranges from £26 ($45.50) to £32 ($56) for two persons daily, these tariffs including a continental breakfast. The property has a garden, and the owners maintain animals and poultry. Woodlands, like the previous recommendation, also opens onto a view of Glastonbury Tor. There is parking.

St. Edmunds House, 26 Wells Rd., Glastonbury, Somerset BA6 9BS (tel. 0458/33862), is a spacious Victorian house standing in its enclosed garden within an easy walk of the ruins of Glastonbury Abbey and High Street. Rooms are simply but comfortably furnished, each containing hot and cold running water and tea-making equipment. Doreen and Trevor Butler charge from £11 ($19.25) per person nightly for a bed and a full English breakfast. An evening meal is available by prior arrangement.

WHERE TO EAT

For centuries, pilgrims have been welcomed at **The George & Pilgrims,** High Street (tel. 0458/31146), one of the few pre-Reformation hostelries still left in England. The inn has a facade that looks like a medieval castle, with stone-mullioned windows with leaded glass. Its rooms are over our budget; however, in its downstairs section it serves some of the most reasonably priced food in town. You may be drawn to the old kitchen, which is now the Pilgrims' Bar, with its old oak beams. Lunches cost from £9.50 ($16.65) and dinners from £14.50 ($25.40). You can also order bar lunches in the pub for £2 ($3.50) and up. Food is served from noon to 2:30 p.m. and 6 to 9:30. However, the pub remains open until 11 p.m. daily, and until 10:30 p.m. on Sunday.

The vegetarian side of you will be satisfied by the whole-food served at **Rainbow's End Café,** 17A High St. (tel. 0458/33896). This is one of the town's most charming cafés, where changing art exhibitions are held. You get good food, reasonably priced, in attractive surroundings. In summer, food is served on a patio when the weather's not acting up. Daily specials are posted, meals costing from £5 ($8.75). Hours are Monday to Thursday (Saturday too) from 10 a.m. to 4:30 p.m., and on Tuesday from 9:30 a.m. to 4:30 p.m. It is closed on Wednesday, but lunch is offered on Sunday from noon to 2 p.m. For the decor, you get Laura Ashley prints and stripped pine.

LIVING IN THE ENVIRONS

About two miles from Glastonbury, **Cradlebridge Farm,** Cradlebridge, Glastonbury, Somerset BA16 9SD (tel. 0458/31827), is a secluded farmhouse where you can get not only B&B, but an evening meal as well. In this unsophisticated atmosphere, Mr. and Mrs. Henry Tinney will go out of their way to make you comfortable and will prepare old-fashioned meals. They have three doubles and one single. The charge is from £12 ($21) to £15 ($26.25) per person per night, with a

£2.50 ($4.40) supplement for a single person booking a double room. Some units have their own TV and tea- and coffee-makers, and each bedroom has its own private bath. You reach the farm by taking the A39 road from Glastonbury. Turn at the second right after passing the Morlands Shoe Factory, then take the first left, and Cradlebridge Farm will be at the end of the road.

For a deeply rural setting, head five miles south of Glastonbury to **The Vicarage,** Compton Dundon, Somerset TA11 6PE (tel. 0458/72324). Run by Joy Adams, it was built of local stone in 1867 on the site of a medieval manor and next to a medieval church. A well in the vicarage cellar is part of the ancient house. There are two double bedrooms, one with private bath. Both units have views over the unspoiled hills where deer can sometimes be seen. In the house are some interesting antiques, including a grandfather clock and a Welsh dresser. In addition to central heating, log fires burn on cooler days. Charges are £15 ($26.25) daily in a single, £25 ($43.75) to £28 ($49) in a double, depending on the plumbing, the rates including an English breakfast and an evening drink. The two-acre garden surrounding the property includes a Somerset orchard.

An attractive stone house set back from the road, the **Hayvatt Manor Guest House,** Hayvatt, Somerset BA6 8LF (tel. 0458/32330), has true English gardens, even a hothouse where grapes are grown for making wine. The manor house is three miles from Glastonbury via the Shepton Mallet road, close to the foot of Glastonbury Tor and the abbey ruins. The owners, Mr. and Mrs. E. N. Collins, quickly become Norman and Molly, they are so hospitable. They have three doubles and one single room, for which they charge from £12 ($21) per person for B&B, plus £6 ($10.50) for an evening dinner of three courses and coffee. They grow their own vegetables and fruits for their meals.

---

6. Wells

In Wells, we meet the Middle Ages. At the south of the Mendip Hills, the cathedral town is a medieval gem. It lies only 21 miles from Bath but 123 from London. Wells was a vital link in the Saxon kingdom of Wessex—that is, it was important in England long before the arrival of William the Conqueror. Once the seat of a bishopric, it was eventually toppled from its ecclesiastical hierarchy by the rival city of Bath. But the subsequent loss of prestige has paid off handsomely in Wells today. After experiencing the pinnacle of prestige, it fell into a slumber, and for that reason much of its old look remains. Wells was named after wells in the town, which were often visited by pilgrims to Glastonbury in the hope that their gout could be eased by the supposedly curative waters. The crowning achievement of the town is:

WELLS CATHEDRAL

Begun in the 12th century, Wells Cathedral is a well-preserved, mellow example of the Early English style of architecture. The medieval sculpture (six tiers of hundreds of statues recently restored) of its west front is without peer in England. The western facade was completed in and around the mid-13th century. The central tower was erected in the 14th century, with its attractive fan vaulting attached later. The inverted arches were added to strengthen the top-heavy structure.

Much of the stained glass dates from the 14th century. The fan-vaulted Lady Chapel, also from the 14th century, is in the Decorated style. To the north is the vaulted Chapter House, built in the late 13th century. Look also for a medieval astronomical clock in the North Transept. There is no charge to enter the cathedral. However, visitors are asked to make voluntary donations of at least £1 ($1.75) for adults, 50p (90¢) for children. For information, telephone the cathedral offices (tel. 0749/74483).

After a visit to the cathedral, walk along its cloisters to the moated Bishop's Palace of the Middle Ages. In the moat, the swans ring a bell when they're hungry. The Great Hall, built in the 13th century, is now in ruins. The street known as the Vicars' Close is one of the most beautifully preserved streets in England.

WHERE TO STAY

You may want to base at Wells, as its budget establishments are easier on the purse than equivalent lodgings at Bath.

Ancient Gate House Hotel, Sadler Street, Wells, Somerset BA5 2RR (tel. 0749/72029), is run by Francesco Rossi, known as Franco to everyone. Its front is on Sadler Street, and the back overlooks the cathedral and the lovely open lawn in front of the cathedral's west door. There are 11 rooms, three in the front. Two of these have showers and one a full bath. These doubles are £39.50 ($69.15) daily for B&B. Other rooms cost £35.50 ($62.15) in a double, £19 ($33.25) in a single, with a full English breakfast and VAT included. Six rooms have four-poster beds.

Franco also runs the Rugantino Restaurant attached to the hotel, where pastas and Italian dishes are a specialty. Popular dishes are scaloppine rustica (breadcrumbed veal escalope topped with tomato sauce and grated cheese and glazed) and tournedo au champignons (filet steak, shallow-fried with button mushrooms, shallots, brandy, and espagnole sauce). There's also a list of interesting appetizers. Vegetarian dishes and fresh vegetables are offered, including some imported items. A set dinner costs around £9.50 ($16.65), including VAT.

Sherston Inn, Priory Road, Wells, Somerset BA5 1SU (tel. 0749/73743), is a pleasant pub on the edge of town on the road to Glastonbury, with a car park and beer garden. Part of the building is from the 17th century. Roy and Sheila Hampshire rent four modest but clean bedrooms, none with private bath. With breakfast included, charges are from £12 ($21) daily in a single, rising to £23 ($40.25) in a double or twin. Bar meals are served in the cozy Moat Bar or the more spacious Knights Bar, offering such dishes as chicken cooked with cheddar-cheese-and-chestnut filling in a cider and cream sauce. Daily home-cooked specials and the Sunday roast beef lunch are especially popular. Meals are served seven days a week from 11:30 a.m. to 2 p.m. and 6 to 10 p.m. They cost from £5.50 ($9.65).

Bekynton House, 7 St. Thomas St., Wells, Somerset BA5 2UU (tel. 0749/7222), is a family-run guesthouse where you get a much more attractive price than at the higher-priced inns in the center of Wells, about a five-minute walk away. The nine rooms include some for families, some with private showers and toilets. All are clean and comfortable, renting from £13 ($22.75) to £16 ($28) per person daily for B&B. Evening meals can be arranged in the pleasant dining room, although several good restaurants are not far away. The Bekynton has a car park where guests can leave their cars and walk to sights in Wells, where parking space is scarce.

Tor Guest House, 20 Tor St., Wells, Somerset BA5 2US (tel. 0749/72322), is where Adrian and Letitia Trowell and their family welcome you to their 1610 home. From the front rooms, there is a view of the Bishop's Palace and the east face of the cathedral, which are reached by a three-minute walk along the palace moat. Tor house has a Queen Anne shell front porch, and in the front garden is a magnolia tree said to be the oldest in Europe. The Trowells rent nine attractively furnished, centrally heated rooms, two of which have private showers and toilets. They charge from £12 ($21) per person daily for B&B and from £19 ($33.25) per person for dinner, bed, and breakfast. Rates include VAT and service. The house has its own large car park.

Only about a 15-minute walk from the center of Wells, **The Coach House,** Stoberry Park, Wells, Somerset BA5 3AA (tel. 0749/76535), stands in six acres of secluded grounds on the southern slope of the Mendip Hills. From College Road, you follow a quarter-mile drive through parkland dotted with ancient trees to the spacious, immaculate guesthouse run by Ian and Fay Poynter. They offer B&B from £14 ($24.50) per person daily. Half board, recommendable because of the quality of the meals served, costs from £23 ($40.25) to £27 ($47.25) per person. However, meals must be booked in advance. From this pastoral setting, you can enjoy views over the city of Wells and the cathedral as well as Glastonbury in the distance.

WHERE TO EAT

The former city jail, the **City Arms,** 69 High St. (tel. 0749/73916), is now a pub with a pretty, open courtyard furnished with tables, chairs, and umbrellas. In summer, it's a mass of flowers, and there is an old vine growing in the corner. It is open daily, except Sunday, from 10:30 a.m. to 2:30 p.m. for drinks and coffee and from 6 to 11 p.m. for drinks. Meals are served daily, except Sunday, from noon to 2 p.m. and 7 to 10 p.m. Full meals cost from £8 ($14), and are likely to include a homemade soup of the day, fresh salmon, steaks, lamb in burgundy sauce, and Somerset Stroganoff (pork filet with white wine, cider, and sour cream).

Penn Bar and Eating House, Crown Hotel, Market Place (tel. 0749/73457), has a sign outside that says that William Penn, founder of Pennsylvania, preached to a vast congregation from a window of the inn in 1685. Appetizers in the cozy dining room include pâté, butterfly prawns, and other good dishes, along with such main courses as escalope of salmon, trout, Scottish steaks, English lamb, and salads. The chef always has a special dish of the day, which might be curry, and there's the inevitable steak-and-kidney pie so beloved by the English. A set three-course dinner is presented for £14.50 ($25.40). Sunday lunch is £8.50 ($14.90), and a hot buffet lunch on Monday to Friday costs £8.95 ($15.65). Hours are from 10 a.m. to 9 p.m. daily.

ON THE OUTSKIRTS

On the slopes of the Mendips lies **Manor Farm,** Old Bristol Road, Upper Milton, near Wells, Somerset BA5 3AH (tel. 0749/73394). An Elizabethan manor house of stone, it is supported by the proceeds of 130 acres of farmland. Its owner, Mrs. Janet Gould, has renovated three corner rooms with the best views ("clear to the Bristol Channel on a day that's not misty"), and has made them comfortably suitable for B&B guests. And she transformed the attic room into a vivid bathroom. Mrs. Gould charges £10 ($17.50) per person daily for B&B. The full breakfast includes about five choices as a main course. Summer days and evenings are often spent on a flagstoned terrace, overlooking the meadow and enjoying the pale roses climbing over the stone walls. The manor lies about a mile from Wells. Take the A39 north out of Wells and turn left at the second turning after the mini-roundabout at the edge of the city, then turn right up Old Bristol Road.

Crapnell Farm, Dinder, near Wells, Somerset BA5 3HG (tel. 0749/2683), is a 16th-century farmhouse on the south side of the Mendip Hills, three miles from Wells. The proprietor, Mrs. Pamela Keen, offers B&B from £10 ($17.50) per person daily. All bedrooms have hot and cold water basins and beverage-making facilities, and there is a guest lounge where you can watch color TV. A large snooker room and a swimming pool add to the enjoyment of a stay here. The food is traditional farmhouse cooking, using produce from the farm, freshly prepared and cooked. Evening meals, costing £8 ($14), are sometimes available.

Long House, Pilton, near Shepton Mallet, Somerset BA4 4BP (tel. 074989/283), is a 17th-century building run by Paul Foss and Eric Swainsbury. Guests coming here for the first time, particularly Americans, comment on the comfortable beds, "the best coffee in England," the plentiful towels, and the excellent food. Paul, an experienced chef, shuns instant or so-called convenience foods. They treat their guests as they would wish to be treated—that is, with an easy graciousness. Bedrooms are attractively furnished, and most of the units have private bathrooms with showers. For half board the rate for a room with a private bath ranges from £13.50 ($23.65) to £16.50 ($28.90) per person nightly. Full board is £19.50 ($34.15) to £24 ($42) per person. Guests are encouraged to stay at least three nights, using Long House as a base for touring sights nearby. Facilities at Long House include a comfortably furnished lounge and dining room that's like that of a private home, plus a well-stocked bar. There your hosts are likely to talk to you about everything from architecture to zoology. As a word of warning, I caution that there are two Piltons in Somerset, and this has led to some confusion.

Burcott Mill, Burcott, near Wells, Somerset BA5 1NJ (tel. 0749/73118), was originally built in the 19th century as a stone-sided mill set beside the River Axe about two miles from Wells. Within the building, the owners rent six bedrooms, three of which contain a private bath. Per-person rates, single or double occupancy, range from £11 ($19.25) to £13 ($22.75) daily. If you make arrangements in advance, an evening meal will be prepared for you for £6 ($10.50).

---

7. The Caves of Mendip

The Caves of Mendip are two exciting natural sightseeing attractions in Somerset—the great caves of Cheddar and Wookey Hole, both easily reached by heading west out of Wells.

THE CAVES

After leaving Wells, you'll first come to **Wookey Hole** (tel. 0749/72243), less than two miles away, the source of the Axe River. In the first chamber of the caves, you can see, as legend has it, the Witch of Wookey turned to stone. These caves were believed to have been inhabited by prehistoric man at least 60,000 years ago. Even in those days there was a housing problem, with hyenas moving in and upsetting real-estate values. A tunnel opened in 1975 leads to chambers unknown to early man and previously accessible only to divers.

In 1973, Madame Tussaud's bought the ravine and joined the celebrated caves and old paper mill into one remarkable sequence. Leaving the caves, you follow a canal path to the mill, where paper has been made by hand since the 17th century. Here you can watch the best-quality paper being made by skilled workers according to the traditions of their ancient craft. Also in the mill is housed a "Fairground by Night" exhibition, an extraordinary and colorful assembly of relics from the world's fairgrounds, and Madame Tussaud's Cabinet of Curiosities, a re-creation of her traveling exhibitions. Visit the seaside at the Edwardian Penny Pier Arcade (still using "old pennies"). Adults pay £3.70 ($6.50), children under 17 being charged £2.60 ($4.55) for a guided tour lasting about two hours. Free parking is provided, and visitors can use a cafeteria and picnic area. Wookey Hole is open every day from 9:30 a.m. to 5:30 p.m. in summer, and from 10:30 a.m. to 4:30 p.m. in winter.

A short distance from Bath, Bristol, and Wells is the village of **Cheddar,** birthplace of Cheddar cheese. It lies at the foot of Cheddar Gorge. A climb up the 274 steps of Jacob's Ladder offers views of the Mendip Hills and over Somerset. On a clear day, you may even see as far as Wales. Within the gorge are the **Cheddar Showcaves,** with impressive formations and a museum displaying prehistoric artifacts dating from when the caves were the home of Cheddar Man, whose skeleton is also on display. The caves are open all year, except Christmas Eve and Christmas Day. Hours are from 10 a.m. to 5:30 p.m. Easter to the end of September, and from 10:30 a.m. to 4:30 p.m. the remainder of the year. Admission to all attractions is £3.10 ($5.45) for adults, £1.70 ($3) for children. If you are more than 12 years of age, and you are fit and bold, you can take one of the Adventure Caving Expeditions. It costs £4.25 ($7.45) per person and takes you beyond the showcase on a tour of discovery lasting 1½ hours. Overalls, helmets, and lamps are supplied.

THE CHEESE TOUR

Still making Cheddar in the traditional way is the **Chewton Cheese Dairy,** Priory Farm, Chewton Mendip (tel. 076121/666). The dairy is owned by Lord Chewton, and visitors are welcome to watch through the viewing window in the restaurant as the cheese-making process is carried out every morning. The best time to visit the dairy is between noon and 2:30 p.m. You can purchase a "truckle" (or wheel) of mature Cheddar to send home. A six-pound wheel costs about £29 ($50.75), including shipping. The restaurant offers coffee, snacks, farmhouse lunches, and cream teas.

WHERE TO STAY

In and around this area you'll find some interesting accommodations, as typified by the **George Hotel,** Church Street, Wedmore, Somerset BS28 4AB (tel. 0934/712124), which lies three miles south of the Cheddar Gorge in the modest village of Wedmore. Here, King Alfred made peace with the Danes and their ruler, Guthrum, in A.D. 878, forcing him to be baptized. Faced with such antiquity, nothing but an old-world coaching inn will do. The George, part of which dates back to the 1350s, has for centuries been giving strangers a refreshing pint of ale and a restful night's sleep in one of the nine upstairs bedrooms, only one with a private shower. The charge is from £14 ($24.50) per person daily, single or double occupancy. There is no set lunch, but you can compose a two-courser of bar snacks for £3 ($5.25) to £4.50 ($7.90). In the evening, you're presented with an à la carte menu and are likely to spend from £10 ($17.50). Many ancient artifacts hang from the beams in the cellar bar, and you can play skittles in the alley adjoining. Everywhere there is a sense of living in the past. It was in 1926 that the custom of holding "court leet of Wedmore" (a special type of manorial court) was abandoned, but the inn still functions as the center of village life. Kenneth and Valerie James, who own and manage the inn, are aware of this heritage—and its responsibilities.

In Cheddar, the best base is the **Gordons Hotel,** Cliff Street, Cheddar Gorge, Cheddar, Somerset BS27 3PT (tel. 0934/742497), which lies at the foot of Cheddar Gorge. Mr. and Mrs. J. P. Barker welcome visitors to their licensed hotel, offering 14 bedrooms, some with bathrooms and all with hot and cold running water, TV, tea-makers, and views of the Mendip Hills. For B&B, they charge from £12 ($21) daily. There is a comfortable lounge with color TV, plus a well-stocked bar where not only drinks but bar snacks are sold. The beamed restaurant, definitely "olde worlde," offers game when available. Dinner ranges from £6 ($10.50) to £10 ($17.50) for three courses. Outside is a garden with lawns and a heated swimming pool, and there's plenty of room for children to play.

A Farm Near Bridgwater

Pear Tree Guest House, 16 Manor Rd., Catcott, near Bridgwater, Somerset TA7 9HF (tel. 0278/722390), is a 300-year-old converted farmhouse standing in a history-rich part of England. Chris and Jan Hill, the owners, offer comfortable accommodation. All rooms have hot and cold running water and tea- and coffeemakers. B&B costs £11.50 ($20.15) per person daily, with half board priced at £16.75 ($29.30) per person.

The village of Catcott, on the slopes of the Polden Hills halfway between Glastonbury and Bridgwater on the A39, was the camping ground of the Danes in A.D. 610. It has a 13th-century church and tarry house, once used by the pilgrims on their way to Glastonbury, seven miles away. On the crest of the hill, you can look down on the battleground of Sedgemoor (1685), location of the last major battle on English soil, between supporters of James II and forces loyal to the Duke of Monmouth.

AVON

Avon is the name that has been given to the area around the old port of Bristol, an area that used to be in Somerset.

8. Bath

Victoria didn't start everything. In 1702, Queen Anne made the 115-mile trek from London to the mineral springs at Bath, thereby launching a fad that was to make the city the most celebrated spa in England. Of course, Victoria hiked up too, in due time, to sample a medicinal cocktail (which you can still do today), but Bath by then had passed its zenith.

The most famous personage connected with Bath's scaling the pinnacle of fashion was the 18th-century dandy, Beau Nash. Dressed in embroidered white, he was the final arbiter of taste and manners (as one example, he made dueling déclassé). The master of ceremonies of Bath, he cut a striking figure as he made his way across the city, with all the plumage of a bird of paradise. Dispensing (at a price) trinkets to the courtiers and aspirant gentlemen of his day, Beau was carted around in a liveried carriage.

Nash was given the proper setting for his considerable social talents by 18th-century architects John Wood the Elder and his son. These architects designed a city of stone from the nearby hills, a feat so substantial and lasting that Bath today is the most harmoniously laid out city in England.

This Georgian city on a bend of the Avon River has, throughout history, attracted a following among leading political and literary figures, among them Dickens, Thackeray, Lord Nelson, and William Pitt. Canadians may know that General Wolfe lived on Trim Street, and Australians may want to visit the house at 19 Bennett Street where their founding father, Admiral Philip, lived. Henry Fielding came this way, observing in *Tom Jones* that the ladies of Bath "endeavor to appear as ugly as possible in the morning, in order to set off that beauty which they intend to show you in the evening."

Bath has had two lives. Long before its Queen Anne, Georgian, and Victorian popularity, it was known to the Romans as Aquae Sulis. The foreign legions founded their baths (which may be visited today) here, so they might ease their plight of rheumatism in the curative mineral springs.

That Bath retains its handsome look today is the result of remarkable restoration and careful planning. The city suffered devastating destruction from the infamous Baedeker air raids of 1942, when Luftwaffe pilots seemed more bent on bombing historical buildings, such as the Assembly Rooms, than in hitting any military target.

The major sights today are the rebuilt Assembly Rooms, the abbey, and the Pump Room and Roman Baths. But if you're intrigued by architecture and city planning, you may want to visit some of the buildings, crescents, and squares. The North Parade, where Goldsmith lived, and the South Parade, where Fanny Burney (English novelist and diarist) once resided, represent harmony, the work of John Wood the Elder. The younger Wood, on the other hand, designed the Royal Crescent, an elegant half-moon row of town houses copied by Astor architects for their colonnade in New York City in the 1830s. Queen Square is one of the most beautiful (Jane Austen and Wordsworth used to live here, but hardly together), showing off quite well the work of Wood the Elder. And don't miss his Circus, built in 1754, as well as the shop-flanked Pulteney Bridge designed by Robert Adam and compared aptly to the Ponte Vecchio of Florence.

THE SIGHTS

Since Bath suffers from a proliferation of one-way streets and traffic congestion, it is best to park in the heart of the city and explore its wonders on foot.

Bath Abbey

Built on the site of a much larger Norman cathedral, the present-day abbey is a fine example of the late Perpendicular style. When Queen Elizabeth I came to Bath in 1574, she ordered that a national fund be set up to restore the abbey. The west front is the sculptural embodiment of a Jacob's Ladder dream of a 15th-century bishop. When you go inside and see its many windows, you'll understand why the abbey is called the "Lantern of the West." Note the superb fan vaulting, achieving at times a scalloped effect. Beau Nash was buried in the nave and is honored by a simple monument totally out of keeping with his flamboyant character.

Pump Room and Roman Baths

Founded in A.D. 75 by the Romans, the baths were dedicated to the goddess Sulis Minerva. In their day they were an engineering feat, and even today are considered among the finest Roman remains in the country. They are still fed by the only hot spring water in Britain. After centuries of decay, the baths were rediscovered in Victoria's reign, and the site of the Temple of Sulis Minerva has been excavated and is open to view. The museum connected to the baths contains many interesting objects from Victorian and recent digs (look for the head of Minerva). Coffee, lunch, and tea, usually with music from the Pump Room Trio, can be enjoyed in the 18th-century Pump Room, overlooking the hot springs. There's a drinking fountain serving hot mineral water. The Pump Room, Roman baths, excavations, and museum are open daily in summer from 9 a.m. to 6 p.m. In winter, hours are 9 a.m. to 5 p.m., and on Sunday from 10 a.m. to 5 p.m. Admission is £2.70 ($4.75) for adults, £1.40 ($2.45) for children. For more information, phone 0225/461111 Monday to Friday.

Bath International Festival

Bath's graceful Georgian architecture provides the setting for one of Europe's most prestigious international festivals of music and the arts. For 17 days in late May and early June each year, the city is filled with more than 1000 performers. The festival is built around a base of classical music, jazz, and the contemporary visual arts, with orchestras, soloists, and artists from all over the world. In addition to the main music and art program, there is all the best in films, talks, tours, and the festival fringe. Ticket prices are £3 ($5.25) for lunchtime recitals and range from £3 ($5.25) to £20 ($35) for evening concerts and operas. Full details can be obtained from Bath Festival, 1 Pierrepont Pl., Bath BA1 1JY (tel. 0225/462231). In the U.S., full details and tickets are available from Keith Prowse, 234 W. 44th St., New York, NY 10036 (tel. 212/398-1430).

The Theatre Royal

The Theatre Royal, Saw Close, has been restored and refurbished with plush red-velvet seats, red carpets, and a painted proscenium arch and ceiling, and it is now regarded as the most beautiful theater in Britain. It is a 1000-seat theater with a small pit and grand circles rising to the upper circle. Beneath the theater, reached from the back of the stalls or by a side door, are the theater vaults. There you will find a bar in one of the curved vaults with stone walls. In the next vault is the Brasserie, and a Japanese restaurant is beside the stage door.

The theater advertises a sophisticated list of forthcoming events with a repertoire that includes, among other offerings, West End shows. The box office (tel. 0225/448844) is open from 9:30 a.m. to 8 p.m. Monday to Saturday.

A Georgian House

No. 1 Royal Crescent (tel. 0225/28126) gives you the chance to see inside a Bath town house that has been redecorated and furnished by the Bath Preservation Trust so that it appears as it might have toward the end of the 18th century. The house is in a splendid position at one end of Bath's most magnificent crescent. It is open to the public from March to the end of October from 11 a.m. to 5 p.m. Tuesday to Saturday, and from November to Christmas from 11 a.m. to 3 p.m. Saturday and Sunday. Last admissions are 30 minutes before closing. It is closed Monday, except bank holidays and during the Bath Festival. Admission is £1.50 ($2.65) for adults, £1 ($1.75) for children.

The American Museum

Some 2½ miles outside Bath you get a glimpse of life as lived by a diversified segment of American settlers until Lincoln's day. This was the first American museum established outside the United States. In a Greek Revival house designed by a Georgian architect, **Claverton Manor,** the museum (tel. 0225/60503), sits proudly in its own extensive grounds high above the Avon valley. Among the authentic exhibits—shipped over from the States—are a New Mexico room, a Conestoga wagon, an early American beehive oven (ever had gingerbread baked from the recipe of George Washington's mother?), the dining room of a New York town house of the early 19th century, and (on the grounds) a copy of Washington's flower garden at Mount Vernon. You can visit the museum from the end of March to the end of October daily, except Monday, from 2 to 5 p.m. There is an American arboretum on the grounds. Admission to the house and gardens is £3 ($5.25) for adults, £2.50 ($4.40) for children.

Walking Tours

A good look at Bath is provided by the **Mayor's Corps of Honorary Guides** in the free walking tours of the city. The guides are all unpaid volunteers acting in an honorary capacity to point out the beauties of their city. They don't accept tips. Tours, lasting about two hours, leave from the abbey churchyard outside the Pump Room. Visitors see the historical and architectural features of the city but are not shown into any buildings. From May to October, tours are offered at 10:30 a.m. Sunday to Friday, at 2:30 p.m. on Sunday and Wednesday, and at 7 p.m. on Tuesday and Friday, except in October. Saturday tours are at 6 p.m., except in October. From November to April, the walks are Sunday to Friday at 10:30 a.m. and on Sunday at 2:30 p.m. The tours are arranged by the guides corps in conjunction with the Bath City Council (tel. 0225/461111, ext. 2785).

Tours and Tourist Services

A tourist reception center for Bath is operated by **Guide Friday Ltd.** in the Railway Station (tel. 0225/444102). Their office dispenses free maps and brochures on the town and area and provides tours. Also available is a full range of tourist services, including accommodation references and car rental. In summer, the office is open daily from 9 a.m. to 6 p.m. In winter, hours are from 9 a.m. to 4 p.m. daily. Guided tours of Bath leave the Railway Station daily. In summer, open-top double-decker buses depart every 15 minutes. The tour can be a one-hour panoramic ride, or you can get off at any of the stops in the city. The ticket, costing £3 ($5.25), is valid all day.

WHERE TO STAY

One of Bath's most upmarket B&Bs and a real delight, **Holly Lodge,** 8 Upper Oldfield Park, Bath, Avon BA2 3JZ (tel. 0225/24042), is a choice piece of real estate. In 1880, the country's biggest landowner built a mansion on a hilltop near the center of his acreage. But a century later it had decayed into a derelict hovel inhabited by squatters. In 1986, partners Carrolle Sellick and George Hall lavished time and money on it, restoring the beige stone exterior made of Bath Ashler stone and turning the one acre that remained around the house into a pleasant park and garden. Capped with a turret offering wide-scope views of the surrounding landscape, the establishment lies within a ten-minute walk from the center of town. Within it, you'll find the original Victorian marble fireplaces, clusters of antiques, richly detailed cove moldings, and ceilings rising loftily to as much as 15 feet. Six carefully decorated bedrooms, sometimes with brass beds and Laura Ashley fabrics, rent for £35 ($61.25) daily, rising to £50 ($87.50) to £55 ($96.25) in a double, and they are well worth the splurge. Each accommodation contains a private bath, color TV, and beverage-making equipment. Smokers are forbidden. Breakfast is served in a room filled with white wicker chairs with French-windowed doors overlooking a view of Bath.

Sydney Gardens Hotel, Sydney Road, Bath, Avon BA2 6NT (tel. 0225/64818), is reminiscent of the letters of Jane Austen, who wrote to friends about the long walks she enjoyed in Sydney Gardens, a public park just outside the city center. In 1856, an Italianate Victorian villa was constructed here of gray stone on a lot immediately adjacent to the gardens. Today Stanley and Diane Smithson maintain six rooms to rent, each of which has a private bath and comes with a good breakfast included in the price. Single rooms cost £45 ($78.75) daily, doubles £55 ($96.25). No meals other than breakfast are served, since the center of town with its many dining spots lies within a ten-minute walk. There's also a footpath running beside a canal for an additional pedestrian adventure.

Paradise House Hotel, 88 Holloway, Bath, Avon BA2 4PX (tel. 0225/317723), stands in its own half-acre garden on a quiet cul-de-sac within a ten-minute walk of the center of the city. Built around 1730 of blocks of local beige stone, it contains nine carefully decorated bedrooms, only seven of which offer a private bath. Breakfast is included in the rates of £34 ($59.50) to £48 ($84) daily in a double, depending on the plumbing. Reductions of £7 ($12.25) are made in each category for single occupancy. Each well-decorated accommodation contains a TV, radio, and beverage-making equipment.

Haydon House, 9 Bloomfield Park, Bath, Avon BA2 2BY (tel. 0225/427351), was originally built of honey-colored stone at the beginning of the Edwardian age. It lies in a pleasant garden one mile south of the city center of Bath. Today it is the domain of Gordon and Magdalene Ashman (he is a former commander in the Royal Navy). They are justifiably known for their "Bloomfield Breakfasts," which incorporate such fare as whisky porridge and other country-inspired recipes. Guests relax in the chintz- and antique-filled lounge, with a fireplace that was removed from a house in Bath where Haile Selassie was sheltered from the Italian invasion of Ethiopia during World War II. When the house was demolished, Haydon House got the mantelpiece. Rooms are comfortably and attractively furnished, and two of the four have private baths. Rates range from £38 ($66.50) to £45 ($78.75) daily for two persons, with VAT and breakfast included.

Somerset House, 35 Bathwick Hill, Bath, Avon BA2 6DL (tel. 0225/66451), is contained within a stone-built Georgian house, which is really a lot like a big country home in the middle of the city. In fact, it was constructed as a private home in 1827. Within its garden grows one of the oldest and largest Judas trees in Britain. It is probably 350 years old. This form of redbud was common to the American Carolinas. The house has its own walled garden, but many of the vegetables served at Somerset are grown by its owner, Malcolm Seymour, on a separate plot of land within a five-minute walk of the house. Malcolm and his wife, Jean, are "keen gardeners." Food is served in what was originally built as a butler's pantry. Nonresidents who call in advance are welcome. Somerset House is fully licensed. Meals cost from £12.50 ($21.90). Specialties are inspired by the West Country and tend to use a lot of pork (usually cooked with apples and cider) and some dishes that rely on the use of brandy and liquor. The hotel offers nine desirable bedrooms, each with private bath. The tariff of £33 ($57.75) per person nightly, single or double occupancy, includes bed, breakfast, and dinner. The house lies within the district of Bathwick, a residential neighborhood within a 12-minute walk of the center of Bath.

Brompton House Hotel, St. John's Rd., Bathwick, Bath, Avon BA2 6PT (tel. 0225/20972), is an elegant Georgian rectory set in tranquil grounds within an easy commute of the heart of the city. This residence was formerly the Old Rectory for St. Mary's Church back in the days when Bathwick was merely a village. When it was constructed in 1777, it was built on the site of a manor farm from the 16th century. Its Victorian owners added a wing. Today, the small hotel is well recommended, and its owners, Edward and Ida Mills, are helpful, seeing to your comfort. They rent singles without bath for £18.50 ($32.38) nightly. Doubles with private bath or shower cost from £36 ($63) to £38 ($66.50). You can enjoy, included in the price, a traditional English breakfast or a whole-food breakfast.

Grove Lodge Guest House, 11 Lambridge, London Road, Bath, Avon BA1 6BJ (tel. 0225/310860), is a typical Georgian home dating from 1787, with well-furnished and spacious rooms, most with large windows overlooking a stone terrace, attractive garden, and the surrounding wooded hills. Just a few minutes from the city center, the lodge is serviced by frequent buses at the front gate. A warm welcome and personal attention are guaranteed by the owners, Roy and Rosalie Burridge. There is a selection of single, twin, and double rooms, as well as large family rooms sleeping three or four persons. All units are equipped with color TV and hot and cold running water. There are ample shared bathroom and shower facilities. Drinks of all kinds are served until 10:30 p.m. The basic cost of a room, including a full breakfast and VAT, is £16 ($28) per person daily, but reductions are available for the larger rooms shared by three or more persons.

Chesterfield Hotel, 11 Great Pulteney St., Bath, Avon BA2 4BR (tel. 0225/460953), stands on a street laid out by Thomas Baldwin in 1798. It leads to the Pulteney Bridge, with its shops on either side, built over the River Avon. The hotel is within a few minutes' walk of the center of Bath. It is a "listed" Georgian building, centrally heated, and has 28 bedrooms, with views from both front and back. All units are comfortably furnished, some with four-poster beds and antiques. Many units have private bathrooms, and color TVs are installed in the lounge and all principal bedrooms. Depending on the plumbing, singles range from £19 ($33.25) to £27.50 ($48.15) daily, and doubles cost £34 ($59.50) to £48 ($84). A room with a four-poster bed costs from £50 ($87.50) nightly. Breakfast is typically English, ample and well prepared. Garage parking is limited.

Highways House, 143 Wells Rd., Bath, Avon BA2 3AL (tel. 0225/21238), is an elegant Victorian family home within minutes of the historic center. There is private, off-street parking for guests, a rare facility within a city built when the sedan chair and coach and horses reigned supreme. Highways is the home of David and Davina James and their family. They offer seven rooms, all with private showers and/or toilets, as well as beverage-making facilities. Prices are £24 ($42) daily in a single, £34 ($59.50) to £38 ($66.50) in a double or twin, including service, VAT, and a full English breakfast. The hosts know a lot about Bath and its environs and always show a willingness to help guests in their planning. Their ironing facilities may come in handy in an emergency, and drinks and snacks can be arranged. Ice is always available here.

Millers Hotel, 69 Great Pulteney St., Bath, Avon BA2 4DL (tel. 0225/65798), stands on a residential street of Georgian buildings, close to the heart of the city. Run by M. J. Miller, it offers 14 colorful, relaxing rooms, six of which have private baths. The hotel is centrally heated, and each unit can be controlled to a desired temperature. A single rents for £20 ($35) to £22 ($38.50) daily, and a double or twin goes for £30 ($52.50) to £34 ($59.50) if bathless. With bath or shower, a double or twin costs from £38 ($66.50) to £44 ($77). Single accommodations house three persons at ranges of £38 ($66.50) to £50 ($86.60), while four persons can rent a room for £48 ($84) to £60 ($105). All these tariffs include a full English breakfast and VAT. There is a comfortable dining room with an adjoining licensed lounge bar. The hotel is well managed.

Oldfields, 102 Wells Rd., Bath, Avon BA2 3AL (tel. 0225/317984), is a traditional bed and breakfast accommodation, occupying two semidetached Victorian houses dating from 1875. Anthony and Nicole O'Flaherty joined their family home to the one next door, restoring the facilities so that now they offer comfortably appointed rooms with color TV and beverage-making facilities. Eight of the units have private showers and toilets. The rates begin at £14.75 ($25.80) per person daily in a bathless room, rising to £22 ($38.50) per person if you want private plumbing. A full English breakfast and VAT are included in the tariffs. The house has a spacious lounge with decorated plaster ceilings and tall windows with lace curtains. Fine views of the hills and the city are part of the attraction. Parking is available at Oldfields, which lies about a 12-minute walk from the heart of Bath.

Dorian House, 1 Upper Oldfield Park, Bath, Avon BA2 3JX (tel. 0225/26336), is a restored 100-year-old Victorian residence owned by Ian and Doreen Bennetts, who enjoy sharing their home with guests and are always on hand to suggest what to see in Bath. On the southern slopes, the house is only a ten-minute walk from the city center. Dorian House is furnished with antiques and many period pieces. The bedrooms have good views. Some have canopied beds, and all have tea- and coffee-makers. Most have private baths or showers. Tariffs, including a full English breakfast, VAT, and service, are £19 ($33.25) daily in bathless singles, £25 ($43.75) in singles with bath or shower. Doubles are £29 ($50.75) without bath, £34 ($59.50) with bath.

Harington's Hotel and Restaurant, 8-10 Queen St., Bath, Avon BA1 2HH (tel. 0225/61728), is known primarily as a place to eat, but the proprietors, Anthony and Sally Dodge, also offer comfortable overnight accommodations consisting of rooms with water basins, color TV, radio intercoms, and tea- and coffee-makers. Some units have private showers and toilets. Charges are £30 ($52.50) to £36 ($63) daily for a double or twin, £40 ($70) to £46 ($80.50) for a family room. Harington's consists of several 19th-century buildings on the corner of Harington Place and Queen Street, on land owned by the Harington family after the Dissolution of the Monasteries. Sir John Harington was a godson of Queen Elizabeth I, and his main claim to fame is his invention of the water closet (flush toilet). Harington's is on an attractive cobbled street within easy walking distance of the major points of interest in Bath.

Orchard House, Warminster Road, Bathampton, Bath, Avon BA2 6XG (tel. 0225/66115), provides excellent B&B, and all rooms have baths and showers, tea- and coffee-making facilities, color TV, radio, central heating, and double glazing. Built in 1984, the hotel has an à la carte restaurant, a sauna, solarium, and spa in a special health facility. A double room costs from £25 ($43.25) per person per night. A large traditional English breakfast is served, and the place is kept neat and clean. The owners, Keith and Barbara Reynolds, make guests feel welcome and comfortable. You can reach the place on the A36, just five minutes' drive from the heart of Bath. It's conveniently situated on a local bus route. In semirural surroundings, this is a peaceful and tranquil choice, and there is off-street parking.

Arden Hotel, 73 Great Pulteney St., Bath, Avon BA2 4DL (tel. 0225/466601), is owned by Eric and Jacqueline Newbigin, whose aim is to run a pleasant small hotel. A Georgian building, the hotel is licensed and has ten bedrooms, all with private baths, color TV, and tea- and coffee-makers. The price in a single is £22 ($38.50) daily, and a double or twin goes for £25 ($43.75). The hotel has recently been entirely refurbished. Guests can enjoy a drink in the bar. The establishment stands in one of Bath's most famous streets, a few minutes' walk from the major sights.

Cheriton House, 9 Upper Oldfield Park, Bath, Avon BA2 3JX (tel. 0225/29862), is a rather elegant late Victorian home that has been converted to receive paying guests. Many of the early architectural adornments, including the original fireplaces, are still here to please the modern visitor. Mike and Jo Babbage, the owners, work hard to make their guests comfortable, and they are most accommodating. They maintain their small house spotlessly clean. All year, they rent six pleasantly furnished doubles or twins, each with private bath or shower, charging from £17 ($29.75) to £21 ($36.75) per person nightly for B&B. This is really a house for adults, not young children. Only breakfast is served.

Tasburgh Hotel, Warminster Road, Bathampton, Bath, Avon BA2 6SH (tel. 0225/25096), is a spacious Victorian country house built in 1890. Set in pleasant gardens, the red-brick structure has a lounge and a residential license. Most rooms have private baths, and all contain TV, washbasins, and beverage-making facilities. For B&B, singles cost from £20 ($35) daily, doubles from £32 ($56) and family rooms for three from £38 ($66.50) to £58 ($101.50), VAT included. The Avon and Kennet Canal runs along the rear of the property, and guests enjoy summer walks on the towpath. Audrey B. Archer is the gracious hostess.

WHERE TO DINE

An excellent choice is **Harington's Hotel and Restaurant,** Queen Street (tel. 0225/61728), recommended above for lodgings. This is the kind of dining establishment known to locals who have resided in the city for some time. It's hidden from the casual visitor on a narrow cobble street in the heart of Bath. The protruding bay window lets in the sun, and you can sit in the front and watch the passing parade. The fully licensed restaurant offers English and French cuisine, the house specialties including Harington's Dover sole and chateaubriand. Other fish dishes are seafood pancakes (crêpes), grilled pink trout, and smoked haddock en papillotte. Of course, they serve steaks, chops, and ham. Lunches are offered, costing from £3.50 ($6.15). For dinner from the à la carte menu, you'll pay from £8 ($14). The restaurant is open for lunch from noon to 2 p.m. and for dinner from 6:30 to 10:30 p.m.

Evans Fish Restaurant, 7-8 Abbeygate St. (tel. 0225/463981), only a three-minute walk from the abbey, features superb fish dinners at moderate cost. Created by Mrs. Harriet Evans in 1908, it is a family restaurant where you can have a three-course luncheon for as little as £5 ($8.75). The set meal might include the soup of the day, fried filet of fish with chips, and a choice of desserts. Mrs. Hunt carries on today in the fine traditions established by the Evans family. Only the freshest of fish is served in this restaurant, but—just so it won't smell fishy—the staff comes in extra early on Monday morning, when every square inch is scrubbed clean. The lower floor has a self-service section for quickies. On the second floor is an Abbey Room catering to families. The preferred dining spot is the Georgian Room—so named after its unspoiled arched windows and fireplace. You can order a number of crisply fried fish specialties, such as deep-fried scampi with chips, and many other main-dish fish courses from the take-out section. Sit-down dinners cost from £7.50 ($13.15). The restaurant is open Monday to Saturday from 11:30 a.m. to 2:30 p.m., reopening from 6 to 8:30 p.m. in summer. Self-service and take-out counters are open Monday to Saturday from 11:30 a.m. to 8:30 p.m.

Theater Vaults Restaurant, Saw Close (tel. 0225/465074), required an imaginative entrepreneur to convert the stone vaults beneath the Theatre Royal into an engagingly decorated brasserie. Its late closing makes it a favorite of an after-theater crowd. However, daytime people can drop in to enjoy morning coffee, drinks, or lunch. Menu specialties include homemade game terrines and soups, fresh fish of the day, juicy steaks, and regional dishes prepared by the French chef. Meals cost from £6.50 ($11.40) for two courses. The restaurant is open daily, except Sunday, from 10 a.m. to 12:30 p.m. for coffee, 12:30 to 2:30 p.m. for lunch, and 6 to 11 p.m. for dinner and drinks.

Binks Restaurant (downstairs) **and Coffeeshop** (upstairs), Abbey Churchyard (tel. 0225/66563), stands across the pavement from the Roman Baths and the abbey. Inside, the bakers start early in the morning preparing fresh croissants and *pain au chocolat* for breakfast, together with the renowned Bath buns made from a recipe handed down from a Dr. Oliver to his coachman. Bread, cakes, and ice cream are sold in the coffeeshop, according to the season. Also served are early morning breakfast, light lunches, traditional cream teas, and early evening meals. The restaurant provides a variety of meals, from pies to salads, gâteaux to lemon meringue, all at reasonable prices. A three-course meal will average £6.50 ($11.40). The restaurant is open daily from 8 a.m. to 10:30 p.m.

The Walrus & the Carpenter, 28 Barton St. (tel. 0225/314864), is a French bistro–style place lying a block from the Theatre Royal, off Queens Square. An appealing choice and youth oriented, it offers a wide array of well-prepared dishes at attractive prices. You pay £7.50 ($13.15) for a full meal. You get not only steaks and fresh, crisp salads, but beef burgers and vegetarian specialties as well. Hours are daily, except Sunday at lunch, from noon to 2 p.m. and 6 to 11 p.m.

The Pump Room (tel. 0225/444477) was already previewed as a sightseeing attraction. Now run by Milburns Restaurants, it is a tradition in Bath, having once been patronized by the likes of Beau Nash and Jane Austen and her mother. It is open daily in winter from 9 a.m. to 5:30 p.m. and in summer from 9 a.m. to 7 p.m. This place has been going since the 18th century, and the newest Pump Room Restaurant opened in 1988. Guests often enjoy music from a Pump Room trio while they drink or eat. Some visitors arrive for breakfast, when they can enjoy such typical dishes as kedgeree, Cobb's original Bath bun and butter, or plain scones served with clotted cream and strawberry jam. Hot dishes are served from 11:30 a.m. to 2:30 p.m., including, for example, venison pasties and Cumberland sauce, or rabbit and carrot stew with parsley dumplings. Meals cost from £7 ($12.25). The famous afternoon Pump Room tea is a favorite, even among the locals, who enjoy their Grey, Darjeeling, or whatever along with sandwiches, scones, cakes, and pastries for £4.70 ($8.25).

Clarets Restaurant and Wine Bar, 7a Kingsmead Square (tel. 0225/66688), near the Theatre Royal, is a cellar with whitewashed walls beneath one of Bath's Georgian houses. The chefs here have a certain culinary expertise, making Clarets one of Bath's most popularly priced eating and meeting places. The menu changes frequently and is an imaginative and varied list of items. In season, tables are placed in the square for persons wishing to eat al fresco. Restaurant bookings are recommended. It is open daily, except Sunday. Hours are from noon to 2 p.m., when lunches go for £5 ($8.75) and up, with dinners served from 5:30 to either 10:30 or 11 p.m. in a price range of £12 ($21).

Sally Lunn's House, 4 North Parade Passage (tel. 0225/61634), is a tiny gabled licensed coffeehouse and restaurant, with a Georgian bow window set in the "new" stone facade put up around 1720. Original Tudor fireplaces and secret cupboards are inside. The house is a landmark in Bath, the present wood-frame building dating from about 1482 being the oldest in the city. If that was not enough, it is built on the site of the monastery kitchen that dated from around 1150, which itself was constructed on the site of a Roman mansion erected in about A.D. 200. Visitors to Bath have been eating here for more than 1700 years. Sally Lunn, the person, is a legend in Bath. She came from France during the 1680s, and her baking became so popular and her buns, based on the French brioche, so well known, that locals and visitors named the house and the bun after her. Today the cellar bakery where she worked and recent excavations showing the earlier buildings are a museum, open mornings only.

On the ground and first floors, the Sally Lunn buns are served sweet or savory, fresh from the modern bakery on the third floor. Excellent coffee and toasted Sally Lunn buns with "lashings" of butter, whole fruit strawberry jam, and real clotted cream is everybody's favorite and is described by the owners, Mike and Angela Overton, as "heaven on a plate." You can have a bun served with various salads, chili, curry, traditional Welsh rarebit (a cooked cheese dish), or many other ways. The all-day menu is easy for travelers. Light meals cost less than £5 ($8.75). The place is easy to find—near the abbey between Abbey Green and the Fernley Hotel. Hours are daily from 10 a.m. to 6 p.m.

A Favorite Pub

Crystal Palace, Abbey Green (tel. 0225/23944), is reached via Church Street, around the corner from Bath Abbey. On a small square, it is one of the few places in England where you can order Thomas Hardy ale, an expensive drink with the highest alcohol content of any beer in the world. In summer, they place tables outside. In cooler weather, guests retreat inside, enjoying the dark beams and the paneled fireplace. Come here for both food and drink, including sandwiches, baked potatoes, or a ploughman's lunch, along with traditional English fare, such as steak-and-kidney pie. Meals cost from £5 ($8.75). Hours are from 11 a.m. to 2:30 p.m. and 6 to 11 p.m. Monday to Thursday, from 11 a.m. to 11 p.m. Friday and Saturday, and from noon to 3 p.m. and 7 to 10:30 p.m. Sunday.

ON THE OUTSKIRTS

A high-grade accommodation in a converted barn and stables, the **Wheelwrights Arms,** Monkton Combe, Bath, Avon BA2 7HD (tel. 022122/2287), lies in the beautiful Midford Valley, three miles south of Bath. This unique place of character is run by Ric and Monica Gillespie as a "free house," but it was once a pub, which was in competition with the local monastery that brewed its own ale. The pub was refurbished and became the Wheelwrights Arms, a charming hostelry. Homemade snacks, luncheons, and steak dinners, costing from £8 ($14), are served in the bar. Warmed by a huge log fire in winter, it is here that the locals play darts, cribbage, and bar cricket. You have a choice of four real ales. The eight bedrooms are equipped with showers, toilets, washbasins, color TV, direct-dial phones, and tea- and coffeemakers. Rates are £36 ($63) daily in a single, £42 ($73.50) in a double. To reach the place, take the A36 out of Bath in the direction of Warminster, turning off toward Monkton Combe.

Fern Cottage Hotel, 9 Northend, Batheaston, near Bath, Avon BA1 7EE (tel. 0225/858190), lies at the end of St. Catherines, the most southerly of the Cotswold valleys. The hotel, in a quiet spot with plenty of car parking, has modern amenities, but its furnishings and decor are in keeping with its age, some 250 years. All five rooms have hot and cold running water basins, TV, and facilities for making tea or coffee. Some have private bathrooms. Prices range from £30 ($52.50) to £45 ($78.75) daily in a double, depending on the plumbing and the room placement, with VAT and breakfast. The hotel has a TV lounge, a dining room where evening meals are available, and a bar lit with the original gaslights installed in Fern Cottage around 1890. Some three miles southeast of Bath, this pleasant establishment nestles at the foot of Little Solsbury Iron Age Hill Fort (the location of Bath before the Romans). To find the hotel, take the A4 from Bath toward Chippenham. In Batheaston, the turning to Northend is second on the left. Fern Cottage is about 400 yards along from the turn, on the left opposite School Lane.

---

9. Bristol

Bristol, the largest city in the West Country, is a good center for touring western Britain. Its location is ten miles west of Bath, just across the Bristol Channel from Wales, 20 miles from the Cotswolds, and 30 miles from Stonehenge. This historic inland port is linked to the sea by seven miles of the navigable Avon River. Bristol has long been rich in seafaring traditions and has many links with the early colonization of America. In fact, some claim that the new continent was named after a Bristol town clerk, Richard Ameryke. In 1497, John Cabot sailed from Bristol, which led to the discovery of the northern half of the New World.

THE SIGHTS

In Bristol, the world's first iron steamship and luxury liner basks in her 1843 glory. She's the 3000-ton **S.S. *Great Britain*** and was created by Isambard Brunel, a Victorian engineer. Visitors can go aboard this "floating palace" at Great Western Dock, Gas Ferry Road, off Cumberland Road (tel. 0272/260680). She is open daily in summer from 10 a.m. to 6 p.m. (until 5 p.m. in winter). Admission is £1.70 ($3) for adults, 80p ($1.40) for children.

At the age of 25 in 1831, Brunel began a Bristol landmark, a suspension bridge over the 250-foot-deep Avon Gorge at Clifton.

Bristol Cathedral, College Green (tel. 0272/264879), was begun in the 12th century and was once an Augustinian abbey. The central tower was added in 1466. The Chapter House and Gatehouse are good examples of late Norman architecture, and the choir is magnificent. The cathedral's interior was singled out for praise by Sir John Betjeman, the late poet laureate.

Another church, **St. Mary Redcliffe,** 10 Redcliffe Parade West (tel. 0272/291962), was called "the fairest, the goodliest, and most famous parish church in England" by such an authority as Elizabeth I. Built in the 14th century, it has been carefully restored. One of the chapels is called "The American Chapel," where the kneelers show the emblems of all the states of the U.S.A. The tomb and armor of Admiral Sir William Penn, father of the founder of Pennsylvania, are in the church.

Cobbled King Street is known for its **Theatre Royal,** built in 1776 and now the oldest working playhouse in the United Kingdom. It is the home of the Bristol Old Vic company. Backstage tours leave the foyer at noon every Friday and Saturday. Phone 0272/250250, box office, or 0272/277466, administration.

Guided walking tours are conducted in summer, and these last about 1½ hours, leaving from Neptune's statue. The tour departs daily at 11 a.m. and 2:30 p.m. On Sunday, guided tours are also conducted through Clifton, a suburb of Bristol that has more Georgian houses than the just-previewed Bath.

Additional information on special walks is provided by **Bristol Tourist Information,** 14 Narrow Quay (tel. 0272/260767).

LODGINGS

Instead of finding lodgings in the center of Bristol, many visitors prefer to seek out accommodations in the leafy Georgian suburb of Clifton, near the famous suspension bridge already mentioned.

There you'll find **Oakfield Hotel,** Oakfield Road, Clifton, Bristol, Avon BS8 2BG (tel. 0272/735556), an impressive guesthouse that would be called a town house in New York and that has an Italian facade. It's on a quiet street, and everything is kept spic-and-span under the watchful eye of Mrs. D. L. Hurley. Every pleasantly furnished bedroom has hot and cold running water and central heating. The charge is £17.25 ($30.20) per person daily for B&B in a single, and £12.65 ($22.15) per person in a double. For another £5 ($7.50), you can enjoy a good dinner.

The **Glenroy Hotel,** Victoria Square, Clifton, Bristol, Avon BS8 4EW (tel. 0272/739058), stands across from a park in a gracious Regency neighborhood. Built of honey-colored limestone, the house has lawns and flowering shrubs. There's a big bow-windowed breakfast room, along with an adjacent bar lounge. You can still see many of the elaborate ceiling and cove moldings from the house's original construction. In Clifton, the hotel is within walking distance of the suspension bridge. Jean and Mike Winyard, the owners, rent some 40 comfortably furnished bedrooms, most of which have private baths. Each accommodation has color TV, phone, a radio, and coffee-making equipment. In one of two buildings, you'll be assigned a single costing from £24 ($42) to £30 ($52.50) daily, a twin or double from £34 ($59.50) to £42 ($73.50). The hotel is considered one of the finest B&Bs in the Clifton/Bristol area.

Westbury Park Hotel, 37 Westbury Rd., Bristol, Avon BS9 3AU (tel. 0272/620465), is a small, privately owned and run hotel on the A4018, one of Bristol's main arteries linking the city center with the M4 and M5 motorways. The hotel stands about three miles from Exit 17 on the M5 and about two miles from the city center. After a two-minute walk, you'll be at the Durdham Downs, which are acres of open park stretching from the Avon Gorge to Brunel's suspension bridge. Tim and

Anne Marie Pearce, the owners, maintain a personal style of service and a high standard of innkeeping. The hotel is an elegant Victorian house with a comfortable drawing room, a pretty sitting room where drinks are served, and well-appointed bedrooms with color TV. In a bathless single, B&B costs £19.50 ($34.15) daily, a single with bath going for £27 ($47.25). Doubles cost £29 ($50.75) bathless, £35 ($61.25) with bath. VAT and a good English breakfast are included. Only fresh food, including vegetables, is used in the kitchen, and interesting dishes are prepared for lunch and dinner daily. The table d'hôte dinner menu is £9.75 ($17.05). Sunday lunch is a traditional affair with English lamb and local pork costing £7.50 ($13.15).

Alandale Hotel, Tyndall's Park Road, Clifton, Bristol, Avon BS8 1PG (tel. 0272/735407), is an elegant early Victorian house that retains a wealth of its original features, including a marble fireplace and ornate plasterwork. Note the fine staircase in the imposing entrance hall. The hotel is under the supervision of Mr. Johnson, who still observes the old traditions of personal service. For example, afternoon tea is served, as are sandwiches, drinks, and snacks in the lounge (up until 11:15 p.m.). A continental breakfast is available in your bedroom until 10 a.m., unless you'd prefer the full English breakfast in the dining room. Terms are from £17 ($29.75) per person nightly in a twin-bedded unit, including VAT. All the bedrooms have direct-dial phones and tea- and coffee-makers.

Washington Hotel, 11-15 St. Paul's Rd., Clifton, Bristol, Avon BS8 1LX (tel. 0272/733980), is on a quiet street just north of the city center, with space for cars to park. Of the 43 bedrooms, 29 have private baths and all contain TV, radios, tea- and coffee-makers, hairdryers, and phones. They have been refurbished to a high standard. Depending on the plumbing, singles rent for £21 ($36.75) to £34.50 ($60.40) daily, and doubles go for £32 ($56) to £46.50 ($81.40).

Clifton Hotel, St. Paul's Road, Clifton, Bristol, Avon BS8 1LX (tel. 0272/736882), has been improved greatly. On a peaceful street near the University of Bristol, it offers attractively furnished rooms that contain color TV, tea- or coffee-making facilities, and often a private bath or shower. Doubles range in price from £34.50 ($60.40) to £48.50 ($84.90) daily, and singles cost from £23 ($40.25) to £34.50 ($60.40). The hotel has an intriguing vaulted bar converted from the old cellars and a fully licensed 1930s-style restaurant with an excellent chef providing good cooking.

Orchard House, Bristol Road, Chew Stoke, Avon BS18 8UB (tel. 0272/333143), is a 200-year-old Georgian house with stucco-covered stonework lying about eight miles south of Bristol. It is run by Ann and Derek Hollomon, who offer comfortable and immaculately clean bedrooms, five in all, one with a private shower. Overnight rates for B&B range from £12.50 ($21.90) to £13.50 ($23.65) per person, with breakfast and VAT included. Single occupants pay no surcharge. Evening meals with the family cost from £6 ($10.50) to £8 ($14) per person, but notice must be given in advance. Local produce is used, and house wines are served. Chew Stoke is a good center for touring the area, and there is a nearby lake for trout fishing.

WHERE TO EAT

Right in the heart of town, **Guild Restaurant,** 68-70 Park St. (tel. 0272/291874), forms a section of the Bristol Guild Shop. While traffic in the distance roars down Park Street, you dine here in a secluded atmosphere of style and comfort. A covered terrace opens in fine weather onto a secluded garden. The restaurant is open from 9:30 a.m. (drop in for coffee) to 5 p.m. Monday to Friday; however, it shuts down at 4:30 p.m. on Saturday and is closed all day on Sunday. Soups at lunch are hearty and homemade, although you might prefer one of the pâtés or quiches to launch your repast. Salads are outstanding here, and casseroles are hot, tasty, and filling. Many of the dishes are inspired by the continental kitchen. Expect to spend from £7.50 ($13.15) for a complete meal.

Henry J. Bean's, St. Augustine Parade (tel. 0272/298391), has invaded Bristol. Henry J. Bean's ("but all his friends all call him Hank") already took London by storm, as our preview of Chelsea dining revealed. Now it is looking for other sites in the U.K., and Bristol seemed ideal for Hank's daily specials, which always include "chicken fried chicken," a smokehouse burger, nachos, and Henry J's own secret chili recipe. Meals cost from £9 ($15.75) and are served daily from 11:30 a.m. to 10 p.m. (a little later on Friday and Saturday).

Cherries Vegetarian Bistro, 122 St. Michael's Hill (tel. 0272/293675), is an informal bistro that is reputed to serve the finest vegetarian dishes in town. Look for the blackboard specials, which are more limited at lunch but fuller of scope in the evening. You don't get bland, insipid vegetarian fare but rather tasty, flavorsome dishes made with fresh, wholesome ingredients. Vegetables are concocted into a different soup every day, followed by crêpes stuffed with vegetables, then a wide range of succulent desserts, including perhaps a baked banana concoction. Meals are reasonable in price, costing from £8 ($14). Service is daily, except Sunday, from noon to 2:30 p.m. and 7 to 11:30 p.m.

Flipper, at 6 St. James Barton (tel. 0272/290260), at the Bristol city center, is said to serve the best fish 'n' chips in town. If you want to take out your dinner, it'll cost only £1.50 ($2.65), a little more if you prefer to sit down and eat it on the premises. Good-tasting cod or halibut, served with crisp chips, is freshly prepared daily from 7:30 a.m. to 6:30 p.m.

Behind a Georgian facade, **51 Park Street** (tel. 0272/268016) caters to a wide range of tastes. Open seven days a week from 11 a.m. to 11 p.m., the place has a simple, clean, and stylish ambience. The variety of food is such that you can have a snack or a three-course meal, depending on your needs, at any time. The food is fresh and continental in outlook. The service is fast but polite, and above all, the menu is a good value for the money. The average price for a meal is £7 ($12.25), VAT and service included.

A Local Pub

Fleece and Firkin, St. Thomas Lane (tel. 0272/277150), is Bristol's only pub/brewery, a good place for the real ale aficionado, as the whole place is dedicated to the brewing and serving of ales. A huge converted wool warehouse has a long bar with the traditional brass rail, as well as tables and chairs for the more sedentary. At lunchtime daily they also serve substantial bar food, with meals costing from £3.50 ($6.15). Baked potatoes with various fillings and large bread baps stuffed with cheese, ham, or beef are featured, all served with a salad. Evenings are the real drinking time, with a young crowd listening to live music. No food is served in the evening. The pub is open from 11 a.m. to 3 p.m. and 5 to 11 p.m. Monday to Friday, from 11 a.m. to 3 p.m. and 7 to 11 p.m. Saturday, and from noon to 3 p.m. and 7 to 10:30 p.m. Sunday.

XII

THE COTSWOLDS

1. WOTTON-UNDER-EDGE

2. TETBURY

3. MALMESBURY

4. CIRENCESTER AND PAINSWICK

5. CHELTENHAM

6. SUDELEY CASTLE

7. BIBURY

8. BURFORD AND MINSTER LOVELL

9. SHIPTON-UNDER-WYCHWOOD

10. CHIPPING NORTON

11. BOURTON-ON-THE-WATER

12. STOW-ON-THE-WOLD AND LOWER SWELL

13. MORETON-IN-MARSH

14. BROADWAY

15. CHIPPING CAMPDEN

The Cotswolds, a once-great wool center of the 13th century, lie mainly in the county of Gloucestershire, with parts dipping into Oxfordshire, Warwickshire, and Worcestershire. If possible, try to explore the area by car. That way you can spend hours surveying the land of winding goat paths, rolling hills, and sleepy hamlets with names such as Stow-on-the-Wold, Wotton-under-Edge, Moreton-in-Marsh, Old Sodbury, Chipping Campden, Shipton-under-Wychwood, Upper and Lower Swell, and Upper and Lower Slaughter (often called the Slaughters). These most beautiful of English villages keep popping up on book jackets and calendars.

Cotswold lambs used to produce so much wool that they made their owners rich, wealth they invested in some of the finest domestic architecture in Europe, made out of the honey brown Cotswold stone. The wool-rich gentry didn't neglect their church contributions either. Often the simplest of villages will have a church that in style and architectural detail seems to rank far beyond the means of the hamlet.

"Come on in through the kitchen" is all you need hear to know that you've found a homelike place where naturalness and friendliness prevail. Many readers will want to seek out comfortable (even though un-chic) accommodations in little stone inns that exist in the midst of the well-known and sophisticated hotels that advertise heavily. Perhaps you'll be served tea in front of a two-way fireplace, its walls made of natural Cotswold stone. Taking your long pieces of thick toasted bread saturated with fresh butter, you'll find the flavor so good you won't resist putting on more chunky cherry jam.

Or maybe you'll go down a narrow lane to a stately Elizabethan stone manor, with thick walls and a moss-covered slate roof. Perhaps you'll arrive at haying time and watch the men at work in the fields beyond, as well as the cows and goats milked to produce the rich double cheese you'll be served later. Your dinner that night? Naturally, a roast leg of Cotswold lamb. If you arrive at a different season, you can enjoy the warmth and crackle of the logs on the fire in the drawing room.

Or you may want to settle down in and around Cheltenham, where the view from your bedroom window of the Severn Valley to the Malvern Hills to the Welsh mountains is so spectacular that old King George III came for a look. The open stretches of common, woodlands, fields, and country lanes provide the right setting for picnics. Life inside your guesthouse may be devoted to comfort and good eating —baskets of fresh eggs, Guernsey milk, cream, poultry, and a variety of vegetables from the garden.

If your tastes are slightly more expensive, you may seek out a classical Cotswold manor (and there are dozens of them) featuring creamy fieldstone, high-pitched roofs, large and small gables, towering chimneys, stone-mullioned windows, a drawing room with antique furnishings, a great lounge hall, an ancient staircase, and flagstone floors. Such Cotswold estates represent England at its best, with clipped hedges, rose gardens, terraces, stone steps, sweeping lawns, age-old trees, and spring flowers. You can revel in a fast-disappearing English country life, perhaps rent or borrow a pink coat (actually, it's red), and go on a genuine hunt, chasing a sly fox.

After leaving Bristol (our last stopover), we will head north, with Stratford-upon-Avon as our eventual goal. However, along the way, I've picked out what I consider the most rewarding Cotswold villages. Perhaps you'll find others equally enchanting on your own.

The adventure begins in:

---

1. Wotton-under-Edge

At the western edge of the Cotswolds, in Gloucestershire, Wotton-under-Edge is in the rural triangle of Bath (23 miles), Bristol (20 miles), and Gloucester (20 miles). Many of its old buildings indicate its former prosperity as a thriving wool town. One of its obscure claims to fame is that it was the home of Sir Isaac Pitman, who invented shorthand. Its grammar school is one of the oldest in England, founded in 1384 and once attended by Dr. Edward Jenner, the discoverer of the vaccine against smallpox.

FOOD AND LODGING

In the heart of the village, the **Falcon,** Church Street, Wotton-under-Edge, Gloucestershire GL12 7HB (tel. 0453/842138), is a typical plastered Cotswold stone inn, with attractively priced accommodation rates. B&B costs £13 ($22.75) daily in a single, £20 ($35) in a double, including VAT and service. The owner is Tony Stephenson, who watches after the needs of guests very well. He runs the 17th-century coaching house capably and provides bar meals and snacks as well as evening meals upon request.

2. Tetbury

In the rolling Cotswolds, Tetbury was never in the mainstream of tourism (like Oxford or Stratford-upon-Avon). However, ever since an attractive man and his lovely bride moved there and took the Macmillan place, a Georgian building on nearly 350 acres, it is now drawing crowds from all over the world.

Charles and Diana will, of course, doubtless one day be King and Queen of England. Their nine-bedroom mansion, Highgrove, lies just outside the town on the way to Westonbirt Arboretum. The house cannot be seen from the road, but you might see the Princess of Wales shopping in the village.

Princess Anne, an avid horsewoman, also lives in the vicinity.

The town has a 17th-century Market Hall and lots of antique shops along with trendy boutiques (one is called "Diana's").

FOOD AND LODGING

One of the most agreeable stopovers in this small market town is at the **Priory Inn and Restaurant,** London Road, Tetbury, Gloucestershire GL8 8JJ (tel. 0666/52251). This old Cotswold inn has many winning attributes, including well-furnished and comfortable bedrooms. None of these has a private bath, but all are inviting. In high-priced Tetbury, the overnight B&B charges are a relief at £18.50 ($32.40) to £19.50 ($34.15) in a single, rising to £32.50 ($56.90) to £35 ($61.25) in a double. The inn also serves a reliable cuisine, and evening meals are offered from 7 to 10 p.m. There is generous parking as well.

The Crown Inn, Gumstool Hill, Tetbury, Gloucestershire GL8 8DG (tel. 0666/52469), one of the best bargains in this very expensively priced Cotswold town, is a stone-built structure with three gables. A pub is downstairs, serving fine wines and good beer and ale, which in fair weather can be enjoyed in a garden. Bar snacks are available, and you can also order full dinners costing from £9 ($10.50). Rooms are small but comfortable, often with beamed ceilings. Singles rent from £19 ($33.25) daily, doubles from £29 ($50.75). Units contain hot and cold running water, and there is central heating.

On the outskirts, **The Hare & Hounds Hotel,** Westonbirt, Tetbury, Gloucestershire GL8 8QL (tel. 066688/233), lies 2½ miles southwest of Tetbury on the A433. One of the more substantial buildings in the area, it has stone-mullioned windows and gables and is set in its own ten acres of private grounds with two hard tennis courts. Originally a farmhouse in the 19th century, the Hare & Hounds was turned into a Victorian inn, and the lounge and country bars remain from those days. However, the main hotel building was added as late as 1928, but it was constructed so faithfully in the original stone that it looks much older. This traditional country hotel, often favored as a site of conferences, is run by the Price brothers, and they do a good job welcoming and entertaining guests, making the place a worthy splurge choice. All of the 26 well-furnished bedrooms have private baths and are comfortable, with many amenities. The cost ranges from £42 ($73.50) daily in a single to £65 ($113.75) in a double. Under a hammerbeam ceiling, the restaurant serves a combination of British and continental dishes, with seasonal specialties. A four-course table d'hôte dinner goes for £13 ($22.75).

3. Malmesbury

At the southern tip of the Cotswolds, the old hill town of Malmesbury in the county of Wiltshire is moated by the Avon River. In the center of England's Middle West, it makes a good base for touring the Cotswolds. Cirencester is just 12 miles away; Bibury, 19 miles; and Cheltenham, 28 miles. Malmesbury is a market town, with a fine market cross. Its historical fame is reflected by the Norman abbey built there on the site of King Athelstan's grave. You can walk around the ruins and go through the cloister gardens.

Malmesbury is considered the oldest "borough" in England, as it was granted its charter by Alfred the Great in 880. In 1980, it celebrated its 1100th anniversary. Some 400 years ago the Washington family lived there, leaving their star-and-stripe coat-of-arms on the church wall. In addition, Nancy Hanks, Abraham Lincoln's mother, came from Malmesbury. The town still has members of the family, noted for their lean features and tallness. The Penns of Pennsylvania also originally came from Malmesbury.

FOOD AND LODGING

A Cotswold cottage in a tranquil setting, **The Chestnuts,** Cleverton, near Chippenham, Wiltshire SN15 5BT (tel. 06662/3472), lies about 3¼ miles to the east of Malmesbury. Mrs. Sandra McDowell rents two comfortable rooms, each with color TV, a radio, and beverage-making facilities in the centrally heated house. Half board costs £28.50 ($49.90) daily in a single, £24.50 ($42.90) per person in a double and includes a traditional English breakfast and a choice of dinner, with good English cookery. Log fires and two acres of land in the heart of the country make staying here a worthwhile experience.

Apostle Spoon, 6 Market Cross (tel. 0666/823129), nestling between the abbey and the original market cross, was built in the 14th century as the abbey hospice. It was named after the Apostle's spoon, an old spoon emblazoned with the likeness of the head of one of the Apostles found at the bottom of a well that was incorporated into the bar. The building is reputed to be one of the oldest houses in one of the oldest boroughs in England. You get good English food here, and many visit just for a cream tea costing from £1.75 ($3.05). A Sunday lunch requires advance reservations and is an important event in town, costing £5 ($8.75). Lunches cost from £4 ($7), with dinners going for £11 ($19.25) and up. Hours are Tuesday to Saturday from 10 a.m. to 9:30 p.m. and Sunday from 10 a.m. to 6 p.m. (closed Monday).

---

4. Cirencester and Painswick

CIRENCESTER

Don't worry about how to pronounce the name of the town. Even the English are in disagreement. Just say "siren-cess-ter" and you won't be too far wrong. Cirencester is often considered the unofficial capital of the Cotswolds, probably a throwback to its reputation in the Middle Ages, when it flourished as the center of the great Cotswold wool industry.

In Roman Britain, five roads converged on Cirencester, which was called Corinium in those days. In size, it ranked second only to London. Today it is chiefly a market town, a good base for touring, as it lies 34 miles from Bath, 16 from the former Regency spa at Cheltenham, 17 from Gloucester, 36 from Oxford, and 38 from Stratford-upon-Avon. The trip from London is 89 miles.

Corinium Museum

On Park Street, the museum houses the archeological remains left from the Roman occupation of Cirencester. The mosaic pavements found on Dyer Street in Cirencester in 1849 are the most important exhibit. And the provincial Roman sculpture (Minerva, Mercury), the pottery, and the bits and pieces salvaged from long-decayed buildings provide a remote link with the high level of civilization that once flourished here. The museum has been completely redeveloped and modernized. It's open from 10 a.m. to 5:30 p.m. Monday to Saturday, and from 2 to 5:30 p.m. on Sunday. Admission is 60p ($1.05) for adults; for children 30p (55¢). For information, telephone 0285/655561.

Cirencester Lock-Up

The restored 19th-century two-cell jail, or lock-up as it was called in its heyday, on Trinity Road (tel. 0285/65561), is open daily by arrangement so visitors can see interpretive displays, including one on architectural conservation in the Cotswolds. Details of the exhibits here may be acquired at the Corinium Museum.

Cirencester Parish Church

Dating back to Norman times and Henry I, the Church of John the Baptist overlooks the Market Square. (Actually, a church may have stood on this spot in Saxon times.) In size, the Cirencester church appears to be a cathedral, not a mere parish church. It is in fact one of the largest parish churches in the country. The present building represents a variety of styles, largely Perpendicular, including its early 15th-century tower. Among the treasures inside are a 15th-century pulpit and a silver-gilt cup given to Queen Anne Boleyn two years before her execution.

Where to Stay

La Ronde Hotel, 52-54 Ashcroft Rd., Cirencester, Gloucestershire GL7 1QX (tel. 0285/654611), is a licensed small hotel run by the Shales family. It stands in the town center within walking distance of Cirencester Park, the abbey grounds, Corinium Museum, and the parish church. Accommodations are comfortable and centrally heated, with either baths or showers, color TV, and tea- and coffee-makers. Singles rent for £32.50 ($56.90) daily. Doubles or twins cost £19.25 ($33.70) per person, and family rooms go from £15 ($26.25) per person. Tariffs include a full English breakfast and taxes. There is a cozy bar and an intimate restaurant with an open fire, where you can choose from a varied menu and a good wine list. Bar lunches are available on request. La Ronde serves as a touring base for the Cotswolds, and the Shales family can provide a printed leaflet detailing 14 different tours of the surrounding area.

Wimbourne Guest House, 91 Victoria Rd., Cirencester, Gloucestershire GL7 1ES (tel. 0285/653890), is a Cotswold stone house built in the Victorian era (1886). It is near the town center and marketplace, which is dominated by the parish church. Nearby lie Cirencester Park, with 3000 acres of beautifully wooded parkland, the abbey grounds, and the Corinium Museum. A welcoming atmosphere is provided by the owners, Dianne and Marshall Clarke. All the bedrooms have private baths, color TV, beverage-making facilities, clock radio–alarms, and are centrally heated. Rates are £11 ($19.25) to £14 ($24.50) per person daily for B&B, with an evening meal costing £7.50 ($13.15). There's a free car park.

Raydon House Hotel, 3 The Avenue, Cirencester, Gloucestershire GL7 1EH (tel. 0285/653485), is a Victorian mansion only five minutes from the town center in a peaceful residential area adjoining an attractive garden complex. Of the 11 bedrooms, seven have private baths or showers. B&B costs £18 ($31.50) to £21 ($36.75) daily in a single, £40 ($70) in a double. A full English breakfast is included in the rates. All the units have tea- and coffee-making equipment. The hotel has an excellent restaurant and bar. If you are driving, there is space for your car in the parking area. From Market Place, drive along Cricklade Street and Watermoor Road, turning left on The Avenue.

Warwick Cottage Guest House, 75 Victoria Rd., Cirencester, Gloucestershire GL7 1ES (tel. 0285/656279), is an attractive Victorian town house owned and run by Pat and Dave Gutsell. Within easy walking distance of the town center, the house enjoys full central heating. The four bedrooms have hot and cold running water, color TV, radios, and tea- and coffee-makers. Two of them contain private baths. Rates are from £11 ($19.25) to £13 ($28.50) per person per night for B&B. A range of snack meals is available, and a two-, three-, or four-course dinner costs from £5.50 ($9.65) to £7 ($12.25). Pat and Dave can also provide such amenities as babysitting, hairdressing for women, and transportation to and from the bus and train stations. Car parking is available at the rear of the house.

Where to Dine

Cottage of Content, 117 Cricklade St. (tel. 0285/652071), is a delightful little restaurant owned and run by Mr. and Mrs. Pugh, who cook, serve, and even do the washing up. Serving only in the evening, they have a variety of succulent T-bone steaks, all served with fresh vegetable, salads in season, and a dessert. Meals begin at £10 ($17.50). They are open daily (except Sunday, Monday, and bank holidays) from 7:30 to 9:30 p.m. (to 10:30 p.m. Saturday).

At **Shepherds Wine Bar,** Fleece Hotel, Market Place (tel. 0285/658507), its half-timbered facade hints at its origins as an Elizabethan coaching inn. Inside, a handful of open fireplaces warm the beamed interior whenever it's chilly. This establishment has an attractive and more upmarket restaurant, but it also presents a congenial wine bar where local residents shuffle through a layer of sawdust. Under a low ceiling, the decor consists of dividing curtains and wood panels. Hours are daily from 10:30 a.m. to 2:30 p.m. and 7 to 11 p.m., and meals cost from £6 ($10.50). Try one of their usually reliable daily specials, and to finish, one of their selections of English cheese. The location is across the courtyard from the hotel.

Crown, 17 West Market Pl. (tel. 0285/653206), is the best-loved pub in town. A coaching inn since the 14th century, it stands opposite the lovely parish church. Many of its original architectural features have been preserved, and the old beams tell a story of long ago. The setting is one of log fires, country chairs, cushioned pews, and plain stonework. The Crown serves pub food that is far above such offerings usually found elsewhere. Daily specials are written on a blackboard and might include homemade eggplant casserole, grilled sausages, and black pudding with scrambled eggs. Meals cost from £6 ($10.50). Food is served daily from noon to 2:15 p.m. and 7 to 10 p.m. The pub is open from 11:30 a.m. to 2:30 p.m. and 6 to 11 p.m. Monday to Saturday, and from noon to 3 p.m. and 7 to 10:30 p.m. Sunday.

PAINSWICK

The sleepy little town of Painswick, four miles northeast of Stroud, is considered a model village. All its houses, although erected at different periods, blend harmoniously because the former villagers used only Cotswold stone as their building material. The one distinctive feature on the Painswick skyline is the spire of its 15th-century parish church. The church is linked with the legend of 99 yew trees, as well as its annual Clipping Feast (when the congregation joins hands and circles around the church as if it were a Maypole, singing hymns as they do). Ancient tombstones dot the churchyard.

Where to Stay

Falcon Hotel, New Street, Painswick, Gloucestershire GL6 6YB (tel. 0452/812189), is a limestone Georgian-era building across from the village churchyard. Originally built in 1554, then reconstructed in 1711, the hotel is owned by the Kimber family, who have 12 rooms, all of which contain private baths or showers and are comfortably furnished. Each unit has hot and cold running water, tea-making equipment, and shaver points. A single costs from £25 ($43.75) daily, a double or twin-bedded unit £38 ($66.50). Special reduced rates are sometimes quoted on Friday and Saturday nights. Guests enjoy use of a cocktail lounge (very English with flowery wallpaper) and twin limestone fireplaces illuminate the dining room. Even if you're not staying at the hotel, you may want to consider a meal here at a cost of £12 ($21). Dishes include tournedos Rossini, roast lamb with mint sauce, and cuts from the Kimbers' own Aberdeen Angus beef. Meals are served daily from noon to 2 p.m. and 7:15 to 10 p.m. The dining room is closed on Sunday night.

Where to Eat

Painswick Hotel, Kemps Lane (tel. 0452/812160), at the rear of the Painswick church, is recommended in our companion guide, *Frommer's England & Scotland,* as the most prestigious place to stay in this most delightful of Cotswold villages. But even if its rooms are over our budget for this guide, it nevertheless offers one of the finest and most reasonably priced luncheon buffets in the area, at a cost of only £3.75 ($6.55). Service is daily, except Sunday, from 12:30 to 2 p.m. You face a selection of freshly prepared salads, along with cold cuts and potatoes boiled in their skins, as well as a hot dish of the day.

---

5. Cheltenham

In a sheltered area between the Cotswolds and the Severn Vale, a mineral spring was discovered by chance. An interesting legend is that the people of this Cotswold stone village noticed pigeons drinking from a spring and observed how healthy they were. As a result of this story, the pigeon has been incorporated into the town's crest.

Always seeking a new spa, George III arrived in 1788 and launched the town. In trouble because of a liver disorder, the Duke of Wellington also is responsible for fanning its praise. Lord Byron came this way too, proposing marriage to Miss Millbanke.

Some 100 miles from London, Cheltenham is one of England's most fashionable spas. Its architecture is mainly Regency, with lots of ironwork, balconies, and verandas. Attractive parks and open spaces of greenery make the town inviting.

The main street, the Promenade, has been called "the most beautiful thoroughfare in Britain." Rather similar to the Promenade are such thoroughfares as Lansdowne Place and Montpellier Parade. The design for the dome of the Rotunda was based on the Pantheon in Rome. Montpellier Walk, with its shops separated by caryatids, is one of the most interesting shopping centers in England.

Guided walking tours of Cheltenham leave from the **Tourist Information Centre,** Promenade (tel. 0242/522878). However, an advance notice of at least two days is required.

WHERE TO STAY

In the heart of Cheltenham, **Carr's Hotel,** 42 Clarence St., Cheltenham, Gloucestershire GL50 3PL (tel. 0242/524003), is a Georgian hotel run by Chris and June Douglas. Carr's is close to the National Coach Station and the local bus station. It is opposite the art gallery, museum, and library. The Douglases create an inviting atmosphere in their 15-bedroom hotel. Some units include showers and toilets. Singles cost £17 ($29.75) to £22 ($38.50) daily, doubles and twins going for £26 ($45.50) to £34 ($59.50). Special rates are quoted for family rooms. There is an extensive menu for a traditional English breakfast, included in the room prices.

Cleevelands House Hotel, 38 Evesham Rd., Cheltenham, Gloucestershire GL52 2AH (tel. 0242/518898), in a quiet area near the heart of the spa, has many winning features. A Regency town house, it opens onto Pittville Park with its aviary and small lake. The bedrooms are kept to a high standard, but the prices are most reasonable for what is offered. The owners rent 14 bedrooms, eight with private bath. Depending on the plumbing, overnight B&B charges range from £17 ($29.75) to £22 ($38.50), with doubles costing £29 ($50.75) to £36 ($63). The small hotel has a licensed restaurant and will serve you an evening meal if you desire.

Beaumont House Hotel, 56 Shurdington Rd., Cheltenham, Gloucestershire GL53 0JE (tel. 0242/245986), is a detached Victorian-era building in its own gardens, giving you a tranquil location where you are yet only minutes from the center of this old spa town. The house has been tastefully converted to receive paying guests, which it accepts all year. The 18 comfortable bedrooms contain private baths or showers for the most part, and tariffs for B&B depend on the plumbing and room assignment. Overnight charges go from £13 ($22.75) to £23 ($40.25) in a single, rising to £29 ($50.75) to £41 ($71.75) in a double. The accommodations have a number of amenities, including TV and beverage-making equipment. Good British fare is also served in the dining room, where you may want to reserve for dinner.

North Hall Hotel, Pittville Circus Road, Cheltenham, Gloucestershire GL52 2PZ (tel. 0242/520584), is a substantial and attractive 19-bedroom house, which lies close to the center of town as well as the race course and Pittville Park. There's free parking in the private forecourt. The house is nicely appointed, with full central heating. Rooms, 12 with private baths, are well furnished and comfortable, containing color TV, beverage-making facilities, central heating, hot and cold running water, and razor plugs. In a double, the rate is £36.80 ($64.40) daily, dropping to £14.45 ($25.30) in a single. Children are granted reductions. There's a lounge and a dining room that serves good but simple English-style food, such as roast chicken with savory stuffing or roast beef with horseradish sauce, a complete meal costing from £7.50 ($13.15).

Lawn Hotel, 5 Pittville Lawn, Cheltenham, Gloucestershire GL52 2BE (tel. 0242/526638), is a well-maintained Regency house built within the iron gates leading to Pittville Gardens and Pump Room. The house is one of 300 constructed around the same town, as well as one of the few in the neighborhood that are still single units. Joan and Ron Wakeman rent nine rooms to guests, each of whom pays £13 ($22.75) daily for B&B or £20 ($35) for half board. The rooms have tea- and coffee-making facilities and color TV. In addition to an evening meal, a variety of snacks is available and afternoon tea is served. The Wakemans keep a bulletin board and information counter with details of nearby cultural events. The house is a five-minute walk from the town center and bus station.

DINING IN CHELTENHAM

An imposing Regency building, **Montpelier Wine Bar and Bistro,** Bayshill Lodge, Montpelier Street (tel. 0242/527774), was converted from an old established shop to a cellar bistro and a first-floor wine bar. Very busy at lunchtime but worth the effort to get in, it offers a choice of some 12 wines by the glass. Then you can select a hot meal from the blackboard menu. A hot soup is always featured among the various appetizers, then cold meats and salad, hot meat pies, smoked fish, lasagne, interesting salads, and a good selection of desserts. You'll pay from £6 ($10.50) for a satisfying meal either in the cellar or, in good weather, on the terrace. Hours are 11 a.m. to 11 p.m. Monday to Saturday, and noon to 2:30 p.m. and 7 to 10:30 p.m. on Sunday. Hot food is served from noon to 10 p.m. On Sunday, hot food selections are limited but snacks and salads are available anyway.

At **Forrest Wine Bar,** 1 Imperial Lane (tel. 0242/238001), wines are sold by the glass, which you can sip while admiring the lofty ceilings of this room, a former bakery. With meals costing from £6 ($10.50), the kitchen offers such dishes as seafood shell with prawns and dill, Mexican enchiladas, a mignon of pork on toast with mushroom sauce, and an array of freshly made salads. The wine bar is open from noon to 2:15 p.m. and 6 to 11 p.m. daily, except Sunday.

The Retreat, 10 Suffolk Parade (tel. 0242/235436), is a centrally located and often crowded oasis popular with young people, who come here for fine wine and reasonably priced, freshly prepared food. Its most distinctive feature is its plant-filled garden courtyard. Frankly, lunch can get a little rushed, but the atmosphere is more mellow in the evening. Meals cost from £6 ($10.50) and are likely to include an array of fresh salads, with healthy ingredients often blended into a medley of imaginative combinations. The bread also carries out the health theme, as it's most often granary or pita. A typical daily special might include spinach-with-cream-cheese strudel with a fresh tomato and basil sauce, served with a choice of two salads. It is open daily, except Sunday, from noon to 2:30 p.m. (until 3:30 p.m. on Saturday) and 6 to 8:30 p.m. The bar associated with the place, however, is open from 5 to 11 p.m. daily, except Sunday.

Below Stairs Restaurant, 103 Promenade (tel. 0242/234599), in the heart of the spa, is, as suggested by its name, below street level. You can enter from the Promenade through a basement doorway. But this is no dank, Dickensian cellar: it's one of the best and most rewarding targets for food and drink in Cheltenham. The international menu caters to local and foreign tastes alike. For example, crêpes filled with ratatouille is a good selection, and you'll nearly always do well to order one of the fresh fish dishes, most likely rushed in from the seacoast of southern England. Game is a seasonal feature. Set lunches cost from around £6 ($10.50), with dinners going for £10 ($17.50), but a lot depends on your appetite and what you order. Lunch is from noon to 3 p.m. Monday to Saturday, dinner from 6 p.m. to midnight Thursday through Saturday only.

---

6. Sudeley Castle

Sudeley is a 15th-century castle in the Cotswolds village of Winchcombe, six miles northeast of Cheltenham. The history of the castle dates back to Saxon times, when the village was the capital of the Mercian kings.

One of England's finer stately homes, Sudeley Castle attracts visitors from all over the world. There are works of art here by Constable, Turner, Rubens, Van Dyck, and many others. The gardens are formal and surrounded by rolling farms and parkland. The Queen's Garden (replanted with old-fashioned roses) dates from the time when Katherine Parr, sixth wife of Henry VIII, lived and died at Sudeley. There are several permanent exhibitions, some magnificent furniture and glass, and many relics from the castle's past. Waterfowl are to be found on the Moat Pond, and peacocks strut around the grounds.

In an area to the right of the keep as you enter the castle are workshops for talented local artisans, who use traditional skills to produce stained glass, textiles, wood and leather articles, and marbled paper, among other items. There is also a design exhibition illustrating the use of craftsmanship in country houses.

The castle is open daily from noon to 5 p.m. from Easter to the end of October. The grounds are open from 11 a.m. Admission to the castle, exhibitions, and grounds is £3.25 ($5.70) for adults, £1.74 ($3.05) for children. A family ticket for two adults and two children costs £8 ($14). For more information, phone 0242/602308.

The present owner of Sudeley Castle, Lady Ashcombe, an American by birth, has lived here for more than 25 years.

If you'd like to stay near the castle, **Isbourne House,** Castle Street, Wichcombe, Cheltenham, Gloucestershire GL54 5JA (tel. 0242/602281), is an excellent choice. Edward Saunders and his friend and colleague, Dick Whittamore, receive guests in a part Georgian, part Elizabethan Cotswold stone house surrounded by a well-kept garden, stone walls, and wrought-iron gates. They operate an extremely high standard B&B, providing a full-platter English breakfast in the morning. Charges are from £32 ($56) to £40 ($70) daily in a double, depending on whether you have a room with complete bath or with just a shower. On 24 hours notice, elegant dinners can be provided. Sometimes guests can be introduced to country pastimes such as horse, country, or lurcher shows or fox hunting English-style.

7. Bibury

Bibury, on the A433 road from Burford to Cirencester, is one of the loveliest spots in the Cotswolds. In fact, the utopian romancer of Victoria's day, poet William Morris, called it England's "most beautiful village." On the banks of the Coln River, Bibury is noted for **Arlington Row,** a gabled group of 15th-century cottages, its biggest and most-photographed drawing card. The row is protected by the National Trust.

Arlington Mill Museum (tel. 028574/368) dates from the *Domesday* survey and was in use until the outbreak of World War I. There are four floors in the mill and three in the cottage, with 16 exhibition rooms. It contains a collection of 19th-century mill machinery, along with agricultural and domestic bygones, Victorian costumes, toys, and furniture, and changing exhibitions of contemporary art. The mill is open daily from 10:30 a.m. to 7 p.m. (or dusk if earlier) from mid-March to October, and on Saturday and Sunday from November to February. Admission is £1.50 ($2.65) for adults and 70p ($1.25) for children.

FOOD AND LODGING

If you want to stay in this famed village, you will have to pay big-splurge prices at the inns previewed below.

Bibury Court Hotel, Bibury, Gloucestershire GL5 5NT (tel. 0285/74337), is a Jacobean manor house built by Sir Thomas Sackville in 1633 (parts of it date from Tudor times). Its eight acres of grounds are approached through a large gateway, the lawn extending to the encircling Coln River. The structure is built of Cotswold stone, with many gables, huge chimneys, leaded-glass, stone-mullioned windows, and a formal gravel entryway. Inside there are many country manor furnishings and antiques, as well as an open stone log-burning fireplace. In rooms with bath, the rent is from £36 ($63) daily in a single, £48 ($84) to £56 ($98) in a double. Many of the rooms have four-poster beds, original oak paneling, and antiques. Meals are an event in the stately dining room, where dinners are priced from £14 ($24.50). Lunchtime bar meals cost from £4 ($7). After tea and biscuits in the drawing room, walk across the lawn along the river, where you'll find a doorway leading to a little church. On your return, head for one of the coaching houses that has been converted into a drinking lounge, a restful place for a glass of stout.

The Swan Hotel, Bibury, Gloucestershire GL7 5NW (tel. 0285/74204), is a scene-stealer. Before you cross over the arched stone bridge spanning the Coln, pause and look at the vine-covered facade. Yes, it's the same view that has appeared on many a calendar. The former coaching inn will bed you down for the night in one of its handsomely appointed chambers, all with bath or shower, costing £35 ($61.25) daily in a single, £62.50 ($109.40) in a double nightly for B&B. A traditional English breakfast and VAT are included. All the rooms have been modernized, and there are many comforts. The special feature of the Swan is the small stretch of trout stream reserved for guests. The restaurant serves an English and French cuisine, with lunches costing from £11.50 ($20.15) and dinners from £15.25 ($26.70).

8. Burford and Minster Lovell

BURFORD

In Oxfordshire, Burford is the gateway to the Cotswolds. This unspoiled medieval town built of Cotswold stone lies 19 miles to the west of Oxford, 31 miles from Stratford-upon-Avon, 14 miles from Blenheim Palace, and 75 miles from London.

Its fame rests largely on its early Norman church (c. 1116) and its High Street lined with coaching inns. Oliver Cromwell passed this way, as (in a happier day) did Charles II and his mistress, Nell Gwynne. Burford was one of the last of the great wool centers, the industry bleating out its last breath as late as Victoria's day. You may want to photograph the bridge across the Windrush River where Queen Elizabeth I once stood. Burford is definitely equipped for tourists, as the antique shops along the High will testify.

Food and Lodging

The Bull, High Street, Burford, Oxfordshire OX8 4RH (tel. 099382/2220), today a 14-bedroom three-star hotel in the Cotswolds, has a long history, as it is the oldest hotel in Burford. The building—or at least its core—dates from around 1475, but it may be older than that. Establishment of a rest house for Burford Priory was authorized by Papal Bull (hence the name) sometime before 1403. The priory was given by Henry VIII to his barber-surgeon in 1544 after the monasteries were dissolved, and from 1603, when John Silvester became inn holder, the history of the Bull can be traced. Such visitors as the king's troops in the battle with Cromwell's Parliament Dragoons, Cromwell himself, and later King Charles II and Nell Gwynne have been lodged here. During the 18th century, the Bull was an important stop on the road, with 40 coaches passing through Burford each day. The hotel is distinguished by its brick-and-stone front dating from 1658, when the "new" additions increased the size of the hostelry. Today, old-world charm blends with modern comfort. Ten of the bedrooms have private baths, and all have central heating. Depending on the plumbing, singles cost £29 ($50.75) to £36 ($63) daily for B&B, and doubles or twins go for £46 ($80.50) to £61 ($106.75). Even if you don't stay here, drop in for a drink in the pub or for a good meal.

The Winter's Tale, Burford, Oxfordshire OX8 4PH (tel. 099382/3176), might attract you by its old-fashioned name alone. It is an early 19th-century stone-built inn on its own grounds at the edge of Burford. Joy Lindsay rents ten comfortably and attractively furnished bedrooms, half of which contain a private bath or shower. These double rooms cost from £26 ($45.50) to £35 ($61.25) daily, depending on the plumbing. Clients get to meet each other in the cozy bar, and in winter log fires burn. The hotel also serves meals, with lunches costing from £7 ($12.25) and dinners from £9 ($15.75).

Andrews Hotel, High Street, Burford, Oxfordshire OX8 4RJ (tel. 099382/3151), is one of the best B&Bs in town. It is a 15th-century Cotswold stone-and-timber village residence, with baths added to the bedrooms. The units are attractive and comfortable. All have color TV and direct-dial phones. The charge for doubles is from £36.75 ($64.30) daily, £28.75 ($50.30) for singles. VAT is included in the prices.

The Boltons, 9 Windrush Close, Burford, Oxfordshire OX8 4SL (tel. 099382/2051), is Mrs. E. Barrett's three-bedroom guesthouse made of Cotswold stone with a natural state roof. From many of the windows, you can look out over gardens, green fields, hills, and sheep. The units are kept clean and neat. Doubles rent for £20 ($35) daily. Mrs. Barrett is a hostess whose warmth, added to that of a cup of tea in the pleasant living room, takes the chill off a cool Cotswold day. She maintains a "home away from home" atmosphere.

MINSTER LOVELL

From Oxford along the A40, you pass through Witney. Soon after, you turn right at the Minster Lovell signpost, about a half mile off the highway between Witney and Burford. Long since passed by the main road, the village is visited because of **Minster Lovell Hall and Dovecot** (tel. 0993/775315). In ruins, the hall dates from the 1400s. The medieval dovecot with nesting boxes survives. An early Lovell is said to have hidden in the moated manor house and subsequently starved to death after a battle in the area. The hall and dovecot can be visited daily from 10 a.m. to 6 p.m. from Good Friday to the end of September, and from 10 a.m. to 4 p.m. off-season; closed Monday. Admission is 80p ($1.40) for adults, 40p (70¢) for children.

It was in the village that the legend of the mistletoe bough originated by the Windrush River. Minster Lovell is mainly built of Cotswold stone, with thatch or stone-slate roofs. It's rather a pity that there is a forest of TV aerials, but the place is still attractive to photographers.

Where to Stay

Mrs. Brown, Hill Grove Farm, Crawley Road, Minster Lovell, Oxfordshire OX8 5NA (tel. 0993/703120), accepts paying guests with a warm welcome at her stone farmhouse set on about 300 acres 1½ miles east of Minster Lovell in the direction of the village of Crawley. This family-run place has views over the Windrush Valley, which is traversed by a river. Mrs. Brown accepts a handful of guests for £24 ($42) to £26 ($45.50) daily in a double or twin-bedded room, including a country breakfast.

9. Shipton-under-Wychwood

Taking the A361 road en route from Burford to Chipping Norton, you arrive after a turnoff at the little village of Shipton-under-Wychwood, in Oxfordshire. It's about four miles north of Burford, but don't blink—you'll pass it right by. The monks of Bruern Abbey used to run a hospice in the village.

FOOD AND LODGING

A small Cotswold stone inn, **The Lamb,** High Street, Shipton-under-Wychwood, Oxfordshire OX7 6DQ (tel. 0993/830465) is perfect if you're seeking a simple village stopover serving an excellent cuisine. It's owned by Hugh and Lynne Wainwright, who give a cordial welcome. Singles are priced from £25 ($43.75) daily, twins or doubles going for £40 ($70), breakfast and VAT included. The inn is in the country style, and each accommodation has a private bath. Main dishes in the dining room are based on the season and the day's marketing. They are likely to include roast pheasant, grilled trout with almonds, and duck cooked in various ways. A set menu is £13.50 ($23.65). A Sunday roast beef or lamb lunch is traditionally offered with all the trimmings for £7.50 ($13.15). The restaurant is closed on Sunday evening.

10. Chipping Norton

Just inside the Oxfordshire border, Chipping Norton is another gateway to the Cotswolds. Since the days of Henry IV it has been an important market town. Its main street is a curiosity in that it follows along a slope, making one side terraced over the lower part. The highest town in Oxfordshire at 650 feet, Chipping Norton was long noted for its tweed mills. Seek out its Guildhall, its church, and its handsome almshouses. If you're touring, you can search for the nearby Rollright Stones, more than 75 stones forming a prehistoric circle 100 feet in diameter, the Stonehenge of the Cotswolds. Chipping Norton lies 11 miles from Stratford-upon-Avon.

WHERE TO STAY

Originally a coaching inn, **The Crown & Cushion,** 23 High St., Chipping Norton, Oxfordshire OX7 5AD (tel. 0608/2533), dates from 1497. All 18 bedrooms are centrally heated and have private baths, color TV, and tea- and coffee-makers.

Some have phones and four-poster beds. They rent for £27 ($47.25) to £34 ($59.50) daily in a single, £40 ($70) to £55 ($96.25) in a double, a full English breakfast and VAT included. Only fresh food is used in the cuisine, with à la carte or table d'hôte meals being served in the comfortable dining room or, in winter, in the cozy lounge bar, with its oak beams and open log fire. An outdoor beer garden at the hotel is a lure for summer visitors.

Hill View Guest House, 1 London Rd., Chipping Norton, Oxfordshire OX7 5AR (tel. 0608/2682), is the domain of Elizabeth and Roy Horobin, a welcoming couple. They charge £12 ($21) per person daily for B&B in rooms with facilities for making hot beverages. The big English breakfast they serve will keep you going for your excursions into the country round about. It's only about a 3½-mile walk to the Rollright Stones.

WHERE TO EAT

For good food at reasonable prices, try **Nutters,** 10 New St. (tel. 0608/41995). The owner, Elizabeth Arnold, sees that everything is homemade with fresh ingredients—no additives, artificial colorings, or flavorings are used. Menus are low in salt, fat, and sugar, but high in fiber. A bright, refreshing stopover, with a small garden in back, it offers the best food in town for the price. However, it serves only from 10 a.m. to 6 p.m. Tuesday to Saturday, with meals costing from £5 ($8.75). If you go early for morning coffee, try one of their potato scones. Main dishes are likely to include beef in red wine, vegetable lasagne, or cheese cauliflower. You order what you want at a counter, then carry your tray to one of the tables.

AN OLD INN AT BLEDINGTON

On the B4450 across country from Chipping Norton to Stow-on-the-Wold in the heart of the Cotswolds nestles the **Kings Head Inn & Restaurant,** The Green, Bledington, near Kingham, Oxfordshire OX7 6HD (tel. 060871/365). This 15th-century inn, occupying a beautiful position right on the village green complete with brook and ducks, has been catering to travelers since time immemorial. If you are just passing through, you can stop for real ale, to be quaffed in the beer garden or in the low-ceilinged, timbered bars with inglenook fireplaces. Hot and cold buffet-bar "fayre" is available at lunchtime, with hot bar food and a full à la carte menu served in the evening. Prices are from £3.50 ($6.15) to £8 ($14). You can also spend the night in one of the lovely double bedrooms here, all with private baths, color TV, and beverage-making facilities. The cost of £39 ($68.25) per night in a double includes a full breakfast. The bar here is noted for its King Henry punch and a selection of malt whiskies.

---

11. Bourton-on-the-Water

In this most scenic Cotswold village, you can be like Gulliver, voyaging first to Brobdingnag, then to Lilliput. Brobdingnag is Bourton-on-the-Water, lying 85 miles from London, on the banks of the tiny Windrush River. Its mellow stone houses, its village greens on the banks of the water, and its bridges have earned it the title of the Venice of the Cotswolds. But such a farfetched label as that tends to obscure its true charm.

To see Lilliput, you have to visit the **Old New Inn** (tel. 0451/20467). In the garden is a near-perfect and most realistic model village. It is open daily from 9:30 a.m. till dusk, and costs 90p ($1.60) for adults, 80p ($1.40) for children.

Among the attractions in the area, **Birdland** (tel. 0451/20689) is a handsomely designed garden set on about five acres. Exotic birds and flowers include the most varied and largest collection of penguins in any zoo, with underwater viewing and a tropical house. In the latter are hummingbirds. Many of the birds are at liberty for the first time in the world. Hours are March to November from 10:30 a.m. to 5 p.m.; otherwise, from 10:30 a.m. to 4 p.m. Admission is £1.75 ($3.05) for adults and £1 ($1.75) for children to 14 years.

If you're coming to the Cotswolds by train from London, you'll find the nearest rail station is Moreton-in-Marsh, eight miles away. However, buses make connections with the trains.

WHERE TO STAY

Built of sturdy Cotswold stone, **Brookside Hotel,** Riverside, Bourton-on-the-Water, Cheltenham, Gloucestershire GL54 2AH (tel. 0451/20371), was originally a 17th-century manor house in the center of the village, standing on the banks of the River Windrush. All of its original character has been retained, and it has the atmosphere of a country home. Even the dining room, with its dark polished wood, time-blackened Windsor chairs, and bright and cheery fabrics, is an ideal setting. Every bedroom is centrally heated, with emphasis on comfort and simplicity rather than sophistication. All rooms have hot and cold running water, radio, and intercom, and some of the larger rooms have a private bathroom. Depending on the plumbing, B&B costs from £22 ($38.50) per person nightly, single or double occupancy. VAT is included. You can have a typical dinner in the dining room for £9 ($15.75), or, if you wish, bar snacks are available.

Duke of Wellington Inn, Sherbourne Street, Bourton-on-the-Water, Cheltenham, Gloucestershire GL54 2BY (tel. 0451/20539), provides comfortable accommodations in a centuries-old former coaching inn. Heavily beamed ceilings and stone walls give a warm Old English atmosphere. Guests in the three bedrooms (who share two public bathrooms) pay from £31 ($54.25) to £33 ($57.75) per night in a double room. Bar snacks are available in the bistro, or you can also have evening meals. Car parking is available. You can relax with fellow guests in the residents' TV lounge.

Chester House Hotel & Motel, Victoria Street, Bourton-on-the-Water, Cheltenham, Gloucestershire GL54 2BU (tel. 0451/20286), is a weathered, 300-year-old Cotswold stone house built on the banks of the Windrush River. Owned and managed by Mr. J. Davies, the hotel is a convenient place to stay. All rooms have baths or showers, TV, and phones. The charge is from £22 ($38.50) per person daily.

Little Rissington Manor, near Bourton-on-the-Water, Cheltenham, Gloucestershire GL54 2NB (tel. 0451/21078), is a 19th-century Victorian manor house set on 11 acres of ground, which include a tennis court, croquet lawn, and swimming pool. To reach it, leave Bourton-on-the-Water on the Little Rissington Road, passing the Great Rissington turning and continuing for some 400 yards uphill. Then turn right through the white gates next to the lodge and follow the gravel drive. Once there, Mrs. Annabel Kirkpatrick will welcome you to one of her comfortably furnished bedrooms. She can accommodate only eight guests, so you should reserve. She has a twin-bedded room with private bath, one family or double room with bath, and one double and single to share a bath. Prices are from £16 ($28) daily in a single, rising to £32 ($56) in a double. Guests are accepted from March to September.

WHERE TO EAT

Previously mentioned, the **Old New Inn,** High Street (tel. 0451/20467), with its popular wine garden, is one of the best places for food in Bourton-on-the-Water. You can dine here on different price levels. Local residents know of its good, fresh, and reasonably priced bar snacks (which can easily be turned into a full meal), or else you can partake of more formal dinners in the evening. At lunchtime, guests not only enjoy the snacks but can play darts or chat with the villagers. Lunch from noon to 2:30 p.m. daily costs from £5 ($8.75). At night you can order from 6 to 8:30 p.m., enjoying good English cookery, with meals costing from £12 ($21).

Previously recommended, the **Chester House Restaurant,** Chester House Hotel and Motel, Victoria Street (tel. 0451/21522), is another good place to go for food. Part of this popular motel that was constructed around what had been a stable for horses, the dining room serves good-tasting food daily from noon to 2 p.m. and 7 to 9:30 p.m. In off-season, no lunches are offered. The chef relies on quality ingredients in turning out a selection of English and continental dishes, with lunches costing from £7.95 ($13.90), dinners from £11.75 ($20.55).

COTSWOLD COUNTRY MUSEUM

Opened in 1981, the **Cotswold Countryside Collection,** Fosseway, Northleach, Cheltenham (Cotswold District Council; tel. 0451/60715), is a museum of rural life displays. You can see the Lloyd-Baker collection of agricultural history, including wagons, horse-drawn implements, and tools, as well as a "seasons of the year" display. A Cotswold gallery records the social history of the area. "Below Stairs" is an exhibition of laundry, dairy, and kitchen. The museum's home was once the Northleach House of Correction, and its history is displayed in the reconstructed cellblock and courtroom. The museum is open daily from 10 a.m. to 5:30 p.m. (from 2 to 5:30 p.m. on Sunday). Admission is 75p ($1.30) for adults, 45p (80¢) for children. Northleach lies off the A40 between Burford and Cheltenham.

A VISIT TO THE "SLAUGHTERS"

Midway between Bourton-on-the-Water and Stow-on-the-Wold are the twin villages of **Upper and Lower Slaughter.** Don't be put off by the names, because these are two of the prettiest villages in the Cotswolds. Actually the name "Slaughter" was a corruption of "de Sclotre," the name of original Norman landowner.

The houses are constructed of honey-colored Cotswold stone, and a stream meanders right through the street, providing a home for the ducks that wander freely about, begging scraps from kindly visitors.

12. Stow-on-the-Wold and Lower Swell

STOW-ON-THE-WOLD

This is an unspoiled Cotswold market town, in spite of the busloads of tourists who stop off en route to Broadway and Chipping Campden nine to ten miles away. The town is the loftiest in the Cotswolds, built on a wold (rolling hills) about 800 feet above sea level. In its open market square, you can still see the stocks where offenders in days gone by were jeered at and punished by the townspeople throwing rotten eggs. The final battle between the Roundheads and the Royalists took place in Stow-on-the-Wold. The town, which is really like a village, is used by many for exploring not only the Cotswold wool towns, but Stratford-upon-Avon 21 miles away. The nearest rail station is at Moreton-in-Marsh, four miles away.

Where to Stay

The White Hart, The Square, Stow-on-the-Wold, Gloucestershire GL54 1AF (tel. 0451/30674), is a limestone-fronted building on the main square of town. You register at the bar of the street-level pub, which is laden with brass accents and open fireplaces. Since 1698, this has been a thriving coaching inn, welcoming wayfarers from all over the world. There is a healthy respect for the traditional around here, and the place has a mellow old atmosphere of uneven floors and low doorways. The innkeeper offers only seven bedrooms, one with private bath. All have color TV and coffee-making equipment. Half-board rates (the most economical way of staying here) range from £17.50 ($30.65) to £29.50 ($51.65) per person daily. The food, especially the steaks, are good tasting, and you can also order such dishes as steak-and-kidney pie and grilled local trout.

The Old Stocks Hotel, The Square, Stow-on-the-Wold, Gloucestershire GL54 1AF (tel. 0451/30666), in spite of its ominous name is one of the most inviting inns of Stow-on-the-Wold. Alan and Caroline Rose run this mellow limestone-fronted inn overlooking the marketplace that has been the scene of so much violence and bloodshed, although all is peaceful today, except for the hordes of tourists who pass through. The hotel is made up of a trio of buildings from the 1500s and 1600s, which were constructed in part with natural stone and oak timbers from sailing vessels. The bedrooms, a total of 17, all with private bath, are tastefully decorated with many amenities. The charge is £23.50 ($41.15) per person nightly for a bed and a full English breakfast. Even if you're not staying here, you may want to order a three-course special-value menu for £6.95 ($12.15) or a comprehensive table d'hôte dinner costing £11.95 ($20.90). In winter you can warm yourself by a log fire, retreating to a walled garden in summer.

Limes, Tewkesbury Road, Stow-on-the-Wold, Gloucestershire GL54 1EN (tel. 0451/30034), is a Georgian building of character that lies about a five-minute walk from the heart of this famed Cotswold village. It has a lovely garden, and in chilly weather log fires make it warm and inviting. Bedrooms are pleasantly and comfortably furnished, all with washbasins. One room with an early Victorian four-poster bed has a private shower. Two persons pay £23 ($40.25) daily in a room without bath, £29 ($50.75) in a room with a four-poster bed and a shower, and £32 ($56) for a spacious accommodation with TV and a private bath. The owners, Mr. and Mrs. Keyte, personally supervise the operation of the Limes.

West View, Fosseway, Stow-on-the-Wold, Gloucestershire GL54 1DW (tel. 0451/30492), is run by Nancy White, who charges from £9.50 ($16.65) to £10 ($17.50) daily for a comfortable bed and a good English breakfast. The shared bathroom has a shower with plenty of hot and cold running water. Mrs. White has furnished the place attractively, in part with antiques. She is most gracious as a hostess, serving a large breakfast. The location is about a block from the center of Stow.

South Hill Farm House, Fosseway, Stow-on-the-Wold, Gloucestershire GL54 1JU (tel. 0451/31219), a Victorian farmhouse built in Cotswold stone, lies a quarter mile from Stow, set in large grounds with ample parking. Shaun and Gaye Kenneally offer a high standard of traditional B&B accommodation and service. Some rooms have private baths or showers. All are centrally heated, and there is a lounge and TV area for the use of guests. The tariff is from £12 ($21) per person nightly

Where to Eat

St. Edwards, The Square (tel. 0451/30351), is a little tea room that's easy to spot, as it opens onto the market square. It has a formal facade with fluted stone pilasters. Inside, you can have morning coffee, lunches, or afternoon tea, while sitting on Windsor chairs in front of an open fireplace. Lunch costs £6 ($10.50) for three courses. A typical one, prepared with care, might include homemade soup, a steak "pastie," apple pie with fresh cream, and coffee. The set afternoon tea is £3 ($5.25) and includes freshly baked muffins and cake. The tea room is open from 9 a.m. to 6 p.m. in summer, and from 9 a.m. to 5:30 p.m. in winter.

Prince of India, Park St. (tel. 0451/31198), has awakened the tastebuds of Stow-on-the-Wold with spices skillfully used in a wide range of dishes. If you have an asbestos palate, try the meat vindaloo, but you can also order less tongue-wilting fare, including tandoori chicken or hot and sour prawns Madras. Leavened bread is served, and there are many vegetarian dishes. A savory beginning is the lentil soup. Meals cost from £8 ($14) and are served from noon to 3 p.m. and 6 to 11:30 p.m. seven days a week.

LOWER SWELL

Near Stow-on-the-Wold, Lower Swell is a twin. Both it and Upper Swell, its sister, are small villages of the Cotswolds. The hamlets are not to be confused with Upper and Lower Slaughter.

Where to Stay and Eat

Old Farmhouse Hotel, Lower Swell, Stow-on-the-Wold, Cheltenham, Gloucestershire GL54 1LF (tel. 0451/30232), is a small, intimate 16th-century hotel in the heart of the Cotswolds, one mile west of Stow-on-the-Wold. It was converted from a 16th-century farmhouse. The hotel has been completely refurbished and the original fireplaces restored, once again blazing with log fires. The relaxed, friendly atmosphere, together with excellent food and wine, has made this a popular stop for visitors, so reserving a room before arrival is strongly recommended. Rollo and Rosemary Belsham have 13 bedrooms to rent, all with color TV and 11 with private bath. Two accommodations under the eaves share a bath. All the units are different because of the building's farmhouse origin, so there are two price levels for B&B with private bath (according to room quality), plus a third for the two four-poster bedrooms. All prices include a cooked English breakfast. The B&B rate in a double or twin-bedded room ranges from £39 ($68.25) daily with a shared bath up to £60 ($105) with a four-poster bed and a private bath. Dinner is served daily from 7 p.m., with last orders taken at 9 p.m. The table d'hôte menu is changed daily, costing £10.50 ($18.40). The hotel has a secluded walled garden and ample private parking. It is closed from Christmas to mid-January.

13. Moreton-in-Marsh

Connected by rail to Paddington Station in London (83 miles away), Moreton-in-Marsh is an important center for British Rail passengers headed for the Cotswolds because it is so near many villages of interest—Bourton-on-the-Water (eight miles), Stow-on-the-Wold (four miles), Broadway (eight miles), Chipping Campden (seven miles), Stratford-upon-Avon (17 miles away).

Each of the stone Cotswold towns has its distinctive characteristics. In Moreton-in-Marsh, look for a 17th-century Market Hall, an old Curfew Tower, and then walk down the High, where Roman legions trudged centuries ago. The town once lay on the ancient Fosse Way. Incidentally, if you base here, don't take the name "Moreton-in-Marsh" too literally. "Marsh" derives from an old word meaning "border."

WHERE TO STAY

Set on the main street of town, **Moreton House,** High Street, Moreton-in-Marsh, Gloucestershire GL56 0LQ (tel. 0608/50747), is perhaps the most desirable budget accommodation in the center of this popular Cotswold village. A mellow old house that has a Tudor facade of honey-colored sandstone, it has a very correct and attractive tea room on its street level. You register at a small reception desk inside this room. There are 12 attractively furnished and comfortable bedrooms upstairs, five of which contain private baths or showers. A bathless single rents for £16 ($28) nightly, and doubles cost from £28 ($49) to £35 ($61.25), depending on the plumbing. Tariffs include an English breakfast. Dinner will be served if arranged in advance at this family-run place.

Treetops, London Road, Moreton-in-Marsh, Gloucestershire GL56 0HE (tel. 0608/51036), originated in 1983, when a former nurse and her husband manifested their dream of designing and building their own house. Using practical skills gathered through previous years of planning, they physically assembled most of the house themselves, including the honey-colored facade of Cotswold stone blocks. Today three bedrooms, each of which shares a communal bath, are available for overnight guests. With breakfast included, charges are from £15 ($26.25) daily in a single, rising to £20 ($35) in a double. Brian and Elizabeth Dean are your hosts. Their house stands amid fir and beech trees in almost an acre of garden, about a five-minute stroll from the heart of Moreton-in-Marsh. A sign leads several hundred yards down a driveway funneling into the main A44 road heading south.

Blue Cedar House, Stow Road, Moreton-in-Marsh, Gloucestershire GL56 0DW (tel. 0608/50299), is named after an enormous tree growing in the front yard. This pleasant brown-brick house was erected in 1952 on the edge of the village center. It is owned and operated by Sandra and Graham Billinger, who rent four bedrooms, two with private shower. The cost ranges from £10 ($17.50) to £11.50 ($20.15) per person daily. The house stands on a half acre of land with a fish pond, and it is within a ten-minute walk from the rail station.

A Farmhouse in Dorn

A mile north of Moreton-in-Marsh, just off the A429, **New Farm,** Dorn, Moreton-in-Marsh, Gloucestershire GL56 9NS (tel. 0608/50782), is mainly a dairy farm of about 250 acres and 90 Friesian milk cows. The farmhouse, built about 300 years ago of Cotswold stone, is where Catherine Righton accepts B&B guests in three bedrooms, two with hot and cold running water and one a family room with a private bath. She charges £12 ($21) per person per night for a bed and a full English breakfast served with fresh hot crispy bread. Mrs. Righton accepts guests from Easter to mid-October.

WHERE TO EAT

In the center of the village, **Market House,** 4 High St. (tel. 0608/50767), is an ideal choice for morning coffee, a good-tasting lunch, afternoon tea, or a reasonably priced and well-prepared dinner. In this cozy tea-room atmosphere, you can enjoy grills or such main dishes as chicken Kiev or fried plaice (perhaps haddock or cod), followed by a piece of moist cake or some other dessert. Sandwiches and fresh salads are also served, with meals costing from £5 ($8.75). In summer, hours are from 9 a.m. to 8 p.m. Monday to Saturday and from 10 a.m. to 5:30 p.m. Sunday. In winter, hours are from 9 a.m. to 5 p.m. Monday to Saturday, 11 a.m. to 5 p.m. Sunday.

---

14. Broadway

This is the best-known Cotswold village. Its wide and beautiful High Street is flanked with honey-colored stone buildings, remarkable for the harmony of their style and design. Overlooking the Vale of Evesham, Broadway, a major stopover for bus tours, is mobbed in summer. That it retains its charm in spite of the invasion is a credit to its character.

Broadway lies near Evesham at the southern tip of Hereford and Worcester. Many of the prime attractions of the Cotswolds as well as the Shakespeare Country lie within easy reach of Broadway: Stratford-upon-Avon is only 15 miles away. The nearest rail stations are at Evesham and Moreton-in-Marsh.

For lodgings, Broadway has the dubious distinction of sheltering some of the most expensive inns in the Cotswolds. The guesthouses can also command a good price—and get it.

BED AND BREAKFAST

In the heart of an expensive village, **Olive Branch Guest House,** 78-80 High St., Broadway, Hereford & Worcester WR12 7AJ (tel. 0386/853440), is a budget oasis. You can get an English breakfast and a comfortable bed as the guest of Peter and Sylvia Riley. They have nine bedrooms, with a wide range of plumbing options, for which they charge from £13.50 ($23.65) to £16.50 ($28.90) per person daily, with VAT and breakfast included. Behind the house is a large walled English garden and car park. The house, dating back to the 17th century, retains its old Cotswold architectural features. Guests are allowed a discount in the owners' attached antique shop.

Half Way Guest House, 89 High St., Broadway, Hereford & Worcester WR12 7AL (tel. 0386/852237), is a little treasure in this picture-postcard village. True to its name, it lies halfway between the village green and the edge of town. Formerly a coaching inn built in 1600, it has a carriage passageway to a rear courtyard. It is now a first-rate guesthouse, owned by the salty and dynamic Mrs. Brodie, who used to operate one of Broadway's fine antique shops. She is assisted by her daughter, Gillian, and they rent six bedrooms. They charge from £25 ($43.75) daily in a single and £17 ($29.75) to £20 ($35) per person for double occupancy. An English breakfast is included. In the olden days, you'd have come out for less, as an old inn sign they display will testify—"4 pence a night for bed, 6 pence with pot luck. No more than five to sleep in one bed." For the antique-lover, the house is sheer heaven, as Mrs. Brodie brought with her an excellent collection of furniture and bric-a-brac, enough to make each bedroom as well as the living room special and tasteful. Even the bathroom, opening onto the rose garden, has a gilt cherub and a Cromwellian chair.

Milestone House, 122 High St., Broadway, Hereford & Worcester WR12 7AJ (tel. 0386/853432), is the kind of place to be found only in England. Luigi and Pauline Bellorini have created a homelike atmosphere in this little private hotel. Once an inn known as the Fox & Dog, it now receives B&B guests. The rooms have soft, downy beds and are immaculately kept. Nor have modern comforts been neglected; there is central heating and plenty of hot and cold running water. Single rooms cost from £22.50 ($39.40) daily for B&B, £32.50 ($56.90) for half board. Double or twin units rent for £20 ($35) per person for B&B, £30 ($52.50) for dinner, bed, and breakfast. Most of the rooms have private baths or showers, and a full English breakfast is prepared. Dinner is served daily in a lovely old beamed dining room from 7:30 to 9:30 p.m. The menu is a mix of traditional English and Italian, as you might guess, since Luigi is Italian and Pauline is English.

Whiteacres, Station Road, Broadway, Hereford & Worcester WR12 7DE (tel. 0386/852320), is one of the best B&Bs in this high-priced town. In their Victorian house, Helen and Alan Richardson rent three comfortably furnished doubles, plus another unit with twin beds, each equipped with private showers and toilets. A single costs from £18 ($31.50) daily, while a double goes for £28 ($49). Guests gather in the lounge to have afternoon tea with Mr. and Mrs. Richardson.

Pathlow House, 82 High St., Broadway, Hereford & Worcester WR12 7AJ (tel. 0386/853444), places you right in the heart of the action of this model village of the Cotswolds. From spring through autumn, guests from around the world are received at this house of character, which rents out doubles (two on the ground floor), a twin, and a family room. Guests share three bathrooms.

There is also a small cottage in the courtyard containing one double and one twin with shared shower and toilet. The rate for B&B is from £25 ($43.75) daily for a double, which is quite reasonable considering the heartbeat location of the property. The house is centrally heated, and all bedrooms have TV and beverage-making facilities. The house, run by Des and Iris Porter, has parking in the rear.

East Bank, Station Drive, Broadway, Hereford & Worcester WR12 7DF (tel. 0386/852659), is a bargain for Broadway. The stone house where Anne and Ken Evans receive B&B guests is in a tranquil location, about a 12-minute walk from the center of the village, with unlimited parking on the grounds of the house or on the approach drive. The comfortable rooms, all with private baths, cost £17 ($29.75) to £20 ($35) for single occupancy of a double unit, £22 ($38.50) to £30 ($52.50) for a double or twin-bedded accommodation, and £30 ($52.50) to £40 ($70) for a family room. The house is centrally heated, but in addition a log fire blazes in the guest lounge during cooler weather. With prior notice, a selection of evening meals can be provided, costing £8 ($14) to £10 ($17.50) each.

The **Crown and Trumpet,** Church Street, Broadway, Hereford & Worcester WR12 7AE (tel. 0386/853202), might be ideal if you're seeking an old English inn with pub action that also rents out a few rooms. The B&B rate is £14.50 ($25.40) per person daily in a double. It's far more economical, however, to take the half-board rate, costing £17 ($29.75) per person. There are no private baths. Good English "fayre" is served, and the location is right near the old village green of Broadway.

Mill Hay, Snowshill Road, Broadway, Hereford & Worcester WR12 7LB (tel. 0386/852498), the home of the owner of Broadway Tower and Country Park, accepts a small number of B&B guests in this Queen Anne country house in a secluded position in the village. In a garden setting, the house has a spacious lounge where guests watch color TV. All the bedrooms, which vary in position and furnishings, have hot and cold water basins and tea- and coffee-making equipment, and some have private baths. For B&B, the price in rooms with queen- or king-size beds, one with a four-poster, is £50 ($87.50) daily for two people. Others rent for £25 ($43.75) in a four-poster single room to £40 ($70) for a couple in a large twin unit. The house is centrally heated. Smoking is prohibited in the bedrooms. The house is closed from mid-January until March.

WHERE TO DINE

With black-and-white timbered walls, **Goblets Wine Bar,** High Street (tel. 0386/852255), is a 17th-century inn built of Cotswold stone. It is filled with antiques that are much enjoyed by the people of Broadway themselves, who frequent the place along with tourists. Additions to the menu, which is changed every six weeks, are marked on the blackboard, and orders should be placed at the bar. The menu is limited but tasty. It begins with such appetizers as taramosalata and goes on to such daily specials as chicken marengo or duckling in orange sauce. About four desserts appear daily, including, for example, a hot gingerbread pudding. The coffee is well made, and the welcome is warm. Meals cost from £6 ($10.50). It is open from noon to 2:30 p.m. and 6 to 9:30 p.m. daily (to 10 p.m. Friday and Saturday). The location is next to the Lygon Arms.

The Coach House Restaurant, The Green (tel. 0386/853555), is set on the main square of this celebrated village behind a facade of honey-colored Cotswold stone. The dining room is very, very old English in style, filled with ceiling beams and alcoves. The kitchen turns out such time-tested dishes as steak-and-kidney pie (or chicken pie), plaice stuffed with prawns and mushrooms, and gammon (ham) steak. You can also order that famous dish, beef Wellington. In winter the establishment is open daily, except Monday, from 9 a.m. to 6 p.m., and in summer dinners are also served nightly (again, except Monday) from 6 to 9 p.m.

---

15. Chipping Campden

The English, regardless of how often they visit the Cotswolds, are attracted in great numbers to this town, once a great wool center. It's neither too large nor too small. Off the main road, it's easily accessible to major points of interest, and double-decker buses frequently run through here on their way to Oxford (36 miles away) or Stratford-upon-Avon (12 miles away).

On the northern edge of the Cotswolds above the Vale of Evesham, Campden, a Saxon settlement, was recorded in the *Domesday Book*. In medieval times, rich merchants built homes of Cotswold stone along its model High Street, described by the historian G. M. Trevelyan as "the most beautiful village street now left in the island." The houses have been so well preserved that Chipping Campden to this day remains a gem of the Middle Ages. Its church dates from the 15th century, and its old Market Hall is the loveliest in the Cotswolds. Look also for its almshouses. They and the Market Hall were built by a great wool merchant, Sir Baptist Hicks, whose tomb is in the church.

WHERE TO STAY

The best bet in our price range is **Seymour House Hotel & Restaurant,** High Street, Chipping Campden, Gloucestershire GL55 6AH (tel. 0386/840429). Its well-established premises are composed of four interconnected buildings, two of which date from the 15th century. The decor today, including the facade, is basically Georgian. A fireplace is likely to be burning in the lobby if the day is cold. The hotel welcomes nonresidents to its Italian-inspired restaurant, where a single large vine twines itself among the rafters beneath a roof pierced with skylights. Full meals cost from £15 ($26.25) and are served daily from 7:30 to 9:30 p.m. The menu might offer tagliatelle with mint and fresh cream, pan-fried filets of trout coated with anchovy butter, and a suprême of chicken filled with bel paese cheese, wrapped in bacon, and roasted with marsala. The hotel is owned and operated by the same company that caters to the Royal Shakespeare Theatre in Stratford-upon-Avon. It maintains 15 cozy bedrooms, eight of which have their own private baths. With an English breakfast included, rooms with bath cost £23 ($40.25) per person daily. Bathless rooms rent for £20 ($35) per person. Some accommodations overlook the calm of the hotel's walled garden in back, and these units are quieter.

Sandalwood House, Back-Ends, Chipping Campden, Gloucestershire GL55 6AU (tel. 0386/840091), offers comfortable accommodation and a warm welcome to nonsmokers. Peacefully situated in a garden with ample safe parking in its own driveway, the house is a five-minute walk from the center of town. The two lockable rooms, one twin and one family room suitable for three persons, are spotless, large, and airy, with comfortable beds, washbasins, and tea- and coffee-makers. The bathroom has a tub and shower. The price is right for such a popular area: £15 ($26.25) per person daily for B&B. Diana Bendall, the hostess, has two dining rooms where you have a choice of dishes from a breakfast menu. There is a cozy lounge where Di serves hot drinks every evening at 9:30 p.m.

Sparlings, Leysbourne, Chipping Campden, Gloucestershire GL55 6HL (tel. 0386/840505), stands at the far north end of Chipping Campden's High Street. It is a restored 18th-century Cotswold-stone town house, named after two well-known ladies who used to live there. The house has exposed beams, stone walls, and some flagstone floors, as well as two double bedrooms to rent, each with their own bath. Graeme Black charges from £31 ($54.25) to £33 ($57.75) for two persons nightly. Unrestricted parking for cars is available on a service road, and bikes are secure at the rear of the property.

The Dragon House, High Street, Chipping Campden, Gloucestershire GL55 6AT (tel. 0386/840734), stands close to the Market Place. It is run by a pleasant Yorkshire proprietor, Mrs. Valerie James, who serves you tea in the evening as well as an excellent and plentiful breakfast the next morning. Rooms are attractively decorated and quite comfortable, costing from £11 ($19.25) per person daily for a bed and filling breakfast, quite a bargain for high-priced Chipping Campden. A separate house out in the back yard contains two double bedrooms and one modern bath. There's also a living/dining room area with TV.

Trinder House, High Street, Chipping Campden, Gloucestershire GL55 6AG (tel. 0386/840869), is where Mrs. Dorothy Hart rents two rooms at a rate of £10 ($17.50) per person daily for B&B. She is helpful and courteous and runs her house like a real home. The front door is an often-open stable door with hanging flowers framing the woodwork. Rooms are comfortable and pleasantly furnished.

On the outskirts, **Holly Mount,** High Street, Mickleton, Chipping Campden, Gloucestershire GL55 6SL (tel. 0386/438243), lies three miles from Chipping

Campden in a village called "the northern gateway to the Cotswolds." Patrick Green has taken a former farmhouse dating from the early 19th century and converted it to provide three double rooms, each with private shower and toilet and such amenities as TV and beverage-making equipment. The beds are queen-size in the "Pink or Peach Room" and king- or twin-size in the "Blue Room." All rooms are tastefully decorated in the style of the period of the origin of the house. The price for B&B is from £14.50 ($25.40) per person daily. For your evening meal you will be directed to two local pubs within walking distance of Holly Mount, but breakfast is served on the premises in a conservatory.

The Malt House, Broad Campden, Chipping Campden, Gloucestershire GL55 6UU (tel. 0386/840295), lies in the satellite hamlet of Broad Campden, one mile west of Chipping Campden. It was purchased by Ms. Pat Robinson, who transformed it into a B&B with oak beams, diamond-patterned leaded windows, and stone mullions. It was originally built 400 to 500 years ago as a pleasant cottage within 4½ acres of gardens. Today, it provides a highly acclaimed accommodation. Ms. Robinson rents only five bedrooms, each tastefully furnished and well maintained. There is only one small single—bathless—costing £18 ($31.50) daily. Doubles, depending on the plumbing, cost from £55 ($96.25) to £65 ($113.75) nightly, with an English breakfast and VAT included. If you order it at breakfast, a four-course dinner can be prepared for £6.50 ($11.40) per person.

WHERE TO EAT

A full restaurant and pub are in the **Kings Arms,** The Square (tel. 0386/840256), as well as hotel accommodations. Even if you don't stay here, try to visit for the best bar snacks in Chipping Campden. You're likely to be tempted with artichokes and Stilton dressing, baked eggs, crab with Gruyère cheese and cream, fresh filet of mackerel with a mustard cream sauce, and taramosalata with hot toast, these items vying with the more prosaic soups and pâtés, all in the £1.20 ($2.10) to £6 ($10.50) range. Bar lunches are served from noon to 2 p.m., dinners from 6 to 10:30 p.m. In the formal dining room, you can order a complete evening meal for £14.50 ($25.40) per person. Main dishes include such continental fare as roast duck in a piquant orange sauce, beef Stroganoff, and filet of pork Calvados.

Greenstocks, Cotswold House Hotel, The Square (tel. 0386/840330), serves good and moderately priced food daily from 9:30 a.m. to 10:30 p.m. Conceivably, you can eat everything from breakfast to a late dinner here, thus avoiding the sometimes draconian English opening and closing hours. Mr. and Mrs. Greenstock, who own and run Chipping Campden's most elegant hostelry, oversee a staff that will serve you such dishes as an individual steak-and-Guinness pie or even a T-bone steak. They are noted for their desserts, which the English call "puddings." Try the treacle tart. Meals cost from £6 ($10.50).

The **Badger Bistro and Wine Bar,** High Street (tel. 0386/840520), is a very attractive little Cotswold shop with a bar and tables all made of pinewood. A comfortable, cheerful place, it offers such items as grilled local trout, chicken fricassee hunter style, and whole-food lasagne and salad. In fair weather, tables are placed in the garden. Colin and Diane Clark, who run the Badger, serve food daily, except Thursday from 11 a.m. to 2:30 p.m. and 7 to 11 p.m. Meals cost from £6 ($10.50) up.

Island House/Bagatelle French Restaurant, High Street Chipping Campden, Gloucestershire GL55 6AT (tel. 0386/840598), is one of the best restaurants in town, situated in a Cotswold stone building dating from 1673. There is a dining room on the ground floor with an open fireplace, plus a cellar restaurant with a small bar. Excellently prepared continental meals are served, and the menu is likely to offer such dishes as chicken medallions wrapped in cabbage (served with a white wine and truffle sauce), grilled scallops of monkfish with basil and garlic sauce, and tournedos with a red pepper and white wine sauce. Menus start at £7.50 ($13.15) per person, going up. Dinner is served nightly from 7 to 9:30 p.m. The house also rents two bedrooms, each fitted with carpeting, central heating, and a shower. The charge is £28 ($49) for two persons, including a continental or full English breakfast.

Bantam Tea Rooms, High Street (tel. 0386/840386), lying opposite the historic Market Hall, is a lovely, bow-windowed, 17th-century stone house where old-fashioned English afternoon teas are served. Tea can be just a pot of the brew and a tea cake, or you can indulge in homemade scones, crumpets, sandwiches, and homemade pastries and cakes. Lunches are served, with a selection of local ham and salad, chicken pie, pâtés, omelets, and salads. Cream teas cost from £1.90 ($3.35), and full meals, served only from noon to 2:30 p.m., start at £6 ($10.50). Hours are from 9:30 a.m. to 5:15 p.m. Monday to Saturday and 3 to 5:15 p.m. Sunday. It is closed Monday from mid-June to mid-September, when it remains open every day.

XIII

STRATFORD AND THE HEART OF ENGLAND

1. STRATFORD-UPON-AVON

2. WARWICK

3. KENILWORTH CASTLE

4. COVENTRY

5. HEREFORD AND WORCESTER

So close to London, so rich in fascination, the Shakespeare Country in the heart of England is that district most visited by North Americans (other than London, of course). Many who don't recognize the county name, Warwickshire, know its foremost tourist town, Stratford-upon-Avon, the birthplace of England's greatest writer.

The county and its neighboring shires form a land of industrial cities, green fields, and market towns dotted with buildings, some of which have changed little since Shakespeare's time. Here are many of the places that have magic for overseas visitors, not only Stratford-upon-Avon, but also Warwick and Kenilworth Castles, as well as Coventry Cathedral.

Those who have time to penetrate deeper into the area will find elegant spa towns, such as Great Malvern, and historic cathedral cities, such as Hereford and Worcester. Scenery ranges from untamed borderlands to gentle plains, which give way in the north to wooded areas and meres.

1. Stratford-upon-Avon

The magnitude of traffic to this market town on the Avon River, the oldest and most attractive in Warwickshire, is one of the phenomena of tourism. Actor David Garrick really got the shrine launched in 1769 when he organized the first of the Bard's birthday celebrations. It is no secret by now, of course, that William Shakespeare was born in Stratford-upon-Avon.

Surprisingly little is known about his early life, as the frankest of his biographers concede. Perhaps because documentation is so lacking about the writer, much useless conjecture has arisen (did Elizabeth I really write the plays?). But the view that Francis Bacon authored Shakespeare's body of work would certainly stir up *The Tempest* if suggested seriously to the innkeepers of Stratford-upon-Avon. Admittedly, however, some of the stories and legends connected with Shakespeare's days in

Stratford are largely fanciful, invented belatedly to amuse and entertain the vast number of literary fans making the pilgrimage.

Today's magnet, in addition to Shakespeare's Birthplace, is the Royal Shakespeare Theatre, where Britain's foremost actors perform during a long season that lasts from Easter until late January. Stratford-upon-Avon is also a good center for trips to Warwick Castle, Kenilworth Castle, Sulgrave Manor (ancestral home of George Washington), Compton Wynyates, and Coventry Cathedral. The market town lies 92 miles from London, 40 from Oxford, and eight from Warwick.

THE SIGHTS

In addition to all the attractions on the periphery of Stratford, there are many Elizabethan and Jacobean buildings in this colorful town, many of them administered by the Shakespeare Birthplace Trust Properties. One ticket, costing £5 ($8.75) for adults, £2 ($3.50) for children, will permit you to visit the five most important sights. You should pick up the ticket if you're planning to do much sightseeing (obtainable at your first stopover at any one of the Trust properties). The properties are open all year, except Good Friday morning, December 24 to December 25, and the morning of January 1. From April to September, hours are from 9 a.m. to 6 p.m. Monday to Saturday, and from 10 a.m. to 6 p.m. Sunday. October opening times are the same, with closing at 5 p.m. From November to March, hours are from 9 a.m. to 4:30 p.m. Monday to Saturday. On Sunday in winter, only Shakespeare's Birthplace and Anne Hathaway's Cottage are open, hours being from 1:30 to 4:30 p.m. The other three properties (Mary Arden's House, Hall's Croft, and New Place/Nash's House) are closed on Sunday in winter. Last admissions all year are 20 minutes before closing time.

For further information concerning the Trust's activities, send a stamped (English postage, please), self-addressed envelope to the Director, the Shakespeare Centre, Henley Street, Stratford-upon-Avon, Warwickshire CV37 6QW (tel. 0789/204016).

Shakespeare's Birthplace

On Henley Street, the son of a Glover and Whittawer was born on St. George's day (April 23) in 1564 and died 52 years later on the same day. Filled with Shakespeare memorabilia, including a portrait, and furnishings of the writer's time, the Trust property is a half-timbered structure dating from the early years of the 16th century. The house was finally bought by public donors in 1847 and preserved as a national shrine. You can visit the oak-beamed living room, the bedroom where Shakespeare was born, a fully equipped kitchen of the period (look for the "babyminder"), and a Shakespeare Museum illustrating his life and times. Later, you can walk through the garden out back. It is estimated that some 660,000 visitors pass through the house annually. If visited separately, admission is £1.70 ($3) for adults, 70p ($1.25) for children. Next door to the birthplace is the modern Shakespeare Centre, built to commemorate the 400th anniversary of the Bard's birth. It serves both as the administrative headquarters of the Birthplace Trust and as a library and study center. An extension to the original center, opened in 1981, includes a Visitors' Centre providing reception facilities for all those coming to the birthplace.

Anne Hathaway's Cottage

One mile from Stratford in the hamlet of Shottery is the thatch, wattle, and daub cottage where Anne Hathaway lived before her marriage to the poet. In sheer charm it is the most interesting and most photographed, it would seem, of the Trust properties. The Hathaways were yeoman farmers, and aside from its historical interest, the cottage provides an insight into the life of a family of Shakespeare's day. If the poet came a-courtin', he must have been treated as a mere teenager, as he married

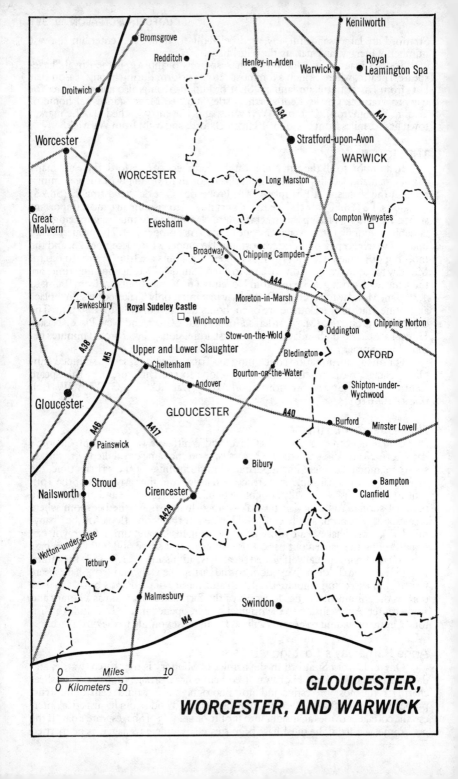

GLOUCESTER, WORCESTER, AND WARWICK

Miss Hathaway when he was only 18 years old and she much older. Much of the original furnishings, including the courting settle, and utensils are preserved inside the house, which was occupied by descendants of Shakespeare's wife until 1892. After a visit through the house, you'll want to linger in the garden and orchard. You can either walk across the meadow to Shottery from Evesham Place in Stratford (pathway marked), or take a bus from Bridge Street. The admission is £1.60 ($2.80) for adults, 60p ($1.05) for children.

New Place/Nash's House

This site is on Chapel Street, where Shakespeare retired in 1610, a prosperous man by the standards of his day. He died there six years later at the age of 52. Regrettably, only the site of his former home remains today, as the house was torn down. You enter the gardens through Nash's House (Thomas Nash married Elizabeth Hall, a granddaughter of the poet). Nash's House has 16th-century period rooms and an exhibition illustrating the archeology and later history of Stratford. The heavily visited Knott Garden adjoins the site and represents the style of a fashionable Elizabethan garden. New Place has its own Great Garden, which once belonged to Shakespeare. Here the Bard planted a mulberry tree, so popular with latter-day visitors to Stratford that the cantankerous owner of the garden chopped it down. The mulberry tree that grows there today is said to have been planted from a cutting of the original tree. The admission is £1.10 ($1.95) for adults, 50p (90¢) for children.

Mary Arden's House and the Shakespeare Countryside Museum

This Tudor farmstead, with its old stone dovecote and various outbuildings, was the girlhood home of Shakespeare's mother. It is situated at Wilmcote, three miles from Stratford. The house contains rare pieces of country furniture and domestic utensils. The barns, stable, cowshed, and farmyard are used to display an extensive collection of farming implements and other bygones illustrating life and work in the local countryside from Shakespeare's time to the present century.

Visitors also see the neighboring Glebe Farm whose interior evokes farm life in late Victorian and Edwardian times. A working smithy and displays of country crafts are added attractions. Light refreshments are available, and there is a picnic area. Admission is £1.60 ($2.80) for adults, 70p ($1.25) for children.

Hall's Croft

This house is in Old Town, Stratford-upon-Avon, not far from the parish church, Holy Trinity. It was here that Shakespeare's daughter Susanna lived with her husband, Dr. John Hall. Apart from that association, Hall's Croft is a Tudor house of outstanding character with a particularly beautiful walled garden. Dr. Hall was widely respected and built up a large medical practice in the area. Exhibits illustrating the theory and practice of medicine in Dr. Hall's time are on view in the house, which is furnished in the style of a middle-class Tudor home. The admission is £1.10 ($1.95) for adults, 50p (90¢) for children. Visitors to the house are welcome to use the adjoining Hall's Croft Club, which serves morning coffee, lunch, and afternoon tea.

Other interesting sights not administered by the Trust foundation include the following:

Holy Trinity Church

In an attractive setting near the Avon, the parish church of Stratford-upon-Avon is distinguished mainly because Shakespeare was buried in the chancel ("and curst be he who moves my bones"). The Parish Register records his baptism and burial (copies of the originals, of course). No charge is made for entry into the church, described as "one of the most beautiful parish churches in the world," but visitors wishing to view Shakespeare's tomb are asked to donate a small sum, at least 40p (70¢), toward the restoration fund. Hours are from 8:30 a.m. to 6 p.m. Monday to Saturday and from noon to 5 p.m. Sunday from April to October 31, and from 8:30 a.m. to 4 p.m. Monday to Saturday and 2 to 5 p.m. Sunday from November to March 31.

Harvard House

Not just of interest to Harvard students and alumni, Harvard House on High Street (tel. 0789/204507) is a fine example of an Elizabethan town house. Rebuilt in 1596, it was once the home of Katherine Rogers, mother of John Harvard, founder of Harvard University. In 1909, the house was purchased by a Chicago millionaire, Edward Morris, who presented it as a gift to the American university. With a profusion of carving, it is the most ornate house in Stratford. Its rooms are filled with period furniture, and the floors, made of the local flagstone, are authentic. Look for the Bible Chair, used for hiding the Bible during the days of Tudor persecution. Harvard House, charging admission of £1 ($1.75) for adults, 50p (90¢) for students and children, is open April through September from 9 a.m. to 1 p.m. and 2 to 6 p.m. on weekdays, and 2 to 6 p.m. on Sunday.

A Motor Museum

Stratford-upon-Avon Motor Museum, 1 Shakespeare St. (tel. 0789/69413), just around the corner from Shakespeare's birthplace, is a small but interesting museum started in 1974 by Bill Meredith-Owens, internationally known motor rally driver. The Roaring '20s era is portrayed and consists of many Rolls-Royces (some specially built for the maharajas of India), Bugattis, early Jaguars, and many others. They also have a reconstructed garage of the '20s and a specialty bookshop where maintenance books on the old models and vintage cars are for sale, as well as a collection of car badges (not for sale). Admission is £2 ($3.50) for adults, £1 ($1.75) for children. The museum is open daily from 9 a.m. to 6 p.m. April to October, and from 10 a.m. to 4 p.m. November to March. It is closed Christmas Day.

A Brass-Rubbing Center

At the **Royal Shakespeare Theatre Summer House,** Avonbank Gardens (tel. 0789/297671), which is open seven days a week from 10 a.m. to 6 p.m. in summer, you can explore brass rubbing. Admission is free. Medieval and Tudor brasses illustrate the knights and ladies, scholars, merchants, and priests of a bygone era. The Stratford collection contains a large assortment of exact replicas of brasses. The charge made for the rubbings includes the special paper and wax required and any instruction you might need.

GETTING THERE

A service allowing you to spend the entire day in Stratford and Shakespeare's Country is the **Shakespeare Connection "Road and Rail Link,"** leaving from London's Euston Station Monday to Friday at 8:40, 10:10, and 10:40 a.m. and at 12:40, 4:40, and 5:10 p.m.; on Saturday at 8:40 and 10:40 a.m. and 12:40, 4:40, and 5:10 p.m.; and on Sunday at 9:40 a.m. and 6:10 p.m. (the 8:40 a.m. Monday to Friday and 12:40 p.m. Monday to Saturday trains do not operate in winter). This is a safe, sure way for you to attend the Royal Shakespeare Theatre and return to London on the same day. If you only want to attend the evening performance at the theater, again the Shakespeare Connection is your best bet, trains leaving London at 4:40 or 5:10 p.m. Monday to Saturday. Returns to London are timed to fit theater performances, with departure at 11:15 p.m. from either the Guide Friday Ltd. office at the Civic Hall, 14 Rother St., or just opposite the theater. The service is the fastest way of reaching Stratford from London, journey time averaging two hours. It is operated by **British Rail** and **Guide Friday** (tel. 0789/294466). Prices are £17.75 ($31.05) for a one-way fare, £19.75 ($34.55) for a round-trip ticket valid for three months. Ask for a Shakespeare Connection ticket at London's Euston Station or at any British Rail London Travel Centre. BritRail pass holders using the service simply pay the bus fare to Stratford-upon-Avon from Coventry, £4 ($7) one way, £5.50 ($9.65) for a round-trip ticket.

TOURS AND TOURIST SERVICES

A tourist reception center for Stratford-upon-Avon and Shakespeare's Country is operated by **Guide Friday Ltd.,** the Civic Hall, 14 Rother St. (tel. 0789/294466). The center dispenses free maps and brochures on the town and area and operates tours. Also available is a full range of tourist services, including accommodation booking, car rental, and theater tickets. In summer, the center is open daily from 9 a.m. to 7 p.m. In winter, hours are from 9 a.m. to 5:30 p.m. Monday to Friday, from 9 a.m. to 4 p.m. Saturday, and from 9:30 a.m. to 4 p.m. Sunday.

Guided tours of Stratford-upon-Avon leave the Guide Friday Tourism Centre daily. In summer, aboard open-top double-decker buses, departures are every 15 minutes from 9:30 a.m. to 5:30 p.m. The tour can be a one-hour panoramic ride, or you can get off at any or all of the Shakespeare's Birthplace Trust properties. Anne Hathaway's Cottage and Mary Arden's House are the two logical stops to make outside the town. Tour tickets are valid all day for you to hop on and off the buses. The price for these tours is £3.50 ($6.15) per person. Tours are also offered to Warwick Castle, Kenilworth Castle, and Charlecote Park, costing £6.50 ($11.40) per person; to Cotswold Country Villages for £9 ($15.75) per person; to Cotswold Country Pubs for £6.50 ($11.40) per person; and to Blenheim Palace and Bladon (the Churchill Story tour) for £9 ($15.75) per person. Tour prices do not include entrance fees at the stops made.

ATTENDING THE THEATER

On the banks of the Avon, **Royal Shakespeare Theatre** (tel. 0789/295623), is the number one theater for Shakespearean productions. The season runs for ten months from late March to late January, with a winter program in February. The present theater was opened in 1932, after the old Shakespeare Memorial Theatre, erected in Victoria's day, burned down in 1926. The theater employs the finest actors and actresses on the British stage. In an average season, six Shakespearean plays are staged.

Usually, you'll need reservations: there are two successive booking periods, each one opening about two months in advance. You can best pick these up from a North American or an English travel agent. If you wait until your arrival in Stratford, it may be too late to get a good seat. Tickets can be booked through New York agents Edwards and Edwards or Keith Prowse or direct with the theater box office with payment by major credit card. There are eight lines in, and the number to call is listed above. The price of seats generally ranges from £4.50 ($7.90) to £22 ($38.50). A small number of tickets are always kept back for sale on the day of a performance. You can phone from anywhere and make a credit card reservation, picking up your ticket on the day it is to be used, but there is no cancellation once your reservation is made.

In the Victorian Wing of the old Memorial Theatre, spared by the fire of 1926, is the **Swan Theatre,** opened in 1986 and built in the style of an Elizabethan playhouse. Here the Royal Shakespeare Company presents plays by Shakespeare and his contemporaries, as well as those by Restoration and later writers. For information about performances, phone the box office number for the Royal Shakespeare, 0789/295623. This building also houses the company's **Collection,** an exhibition of stagecraft from medieval mummers to the present day, with costumes and props from Royal Shakespeare Company productions. Backstage/RSC Collection tours are available. The Collection is open April to January from 9 a.m. to 6 p.m. Monday to Saturday, and from noon to 5 p.m. Sunday. Admission is £1.50 ($2.65) for adults, £1 ($1.75) for children.

The company has a third theater in Stratford, **The Other Place,** seating just over 100 persons, where new plays are presented.

CAUGHT WITHOUT A ROOM?

During the long theater season, the hotels in Stratford-upon-Avon are jam-packed, and you may run into difficulty if you arrive without a reservation. However, you can go to the **Tourist Information Centre** (tel. 0789/293127) from 9 a.m. to 5:30 p.m. mid-March to the end of October, Monday to Saturday (from 2 to 5 p.m. on Sunday); November to mid-March, Monday to Saturday from 10:30 a.m. to 4:30 p.m. Personal callers are charged 95p ($1.65) per room. A staff person who is experienced in finding accommodation for travelers in all budget categories will get on the telephone and try to book a room for you in the price range you are seeking.

It is also possible to reserve accommodations if you write well enough in advance. By writing to the Information Centre, you'll be spared having to get in touch with several hotels on your own and running the risk of getting turned down. If you do write, specify the price range and the number of beds required. The Centre often gets vague letters, and the staff doesn't know whether to book you into a private suite at the Shakespeare Hotel or else lend you a cot to put in front of the Royal Shakespeare Theatre. For this postal "book-a-bed-ahead" service, the charge is £2.50 ($4.40), payable in pounds sterling only. The complete address is **The Information Centre,** Judith Shakespeare's House, 1 High St., Stratford-upon-Avon, Warwickshire CV37 6AU.

BED AND BREAKFAST

A Victorian family house, the **Marlyn Hotel,** 3 Chestnut Walk, Stratford-upon-Avon, Warwickshire CV37 6HG (tel. 0789/293752), has been welcoming B&B guests since 1890. It is pleasantly and conveniently situated near Hall's Croft, the former home of Shakespeare's daughter, and is within a five-minute walk of the town center and the Royal Shakespeare Theatre. The hotel is centrally heated throughout, each bedroom contains tea- and coffee-making facilities, and there is a small lounge with TV. If you don't want to pack your Shakespeare, don't worry. A copy of the complete works of the Bard is available for reference in every bedroom. Free and unrestricted parking is available under the chestnut trees opposite the hotel. The Marlyn has been owned and managed since 1973 by the Allen family, and Mrs. Mary Allen endeavors to provide guests with comfortable accommodation throughout their stay. Daily rates are £13 ($22.75) per person for bed and an English breakfast, inclusive of tax.

Midway Guest House, 182 Evesham Rd., Stratford-upon-Avon, Warwickshire CV37 9BP (tel. 0789/204154), is the domain of Janet and Keith Cornwell. All their bedrooms contain a private bath or shower with toilet, along with carpeting and up-to-date furnishings and equipment. Amenities include such items as beverage-making equipment, hairdryers (on request), and central heating. Charges are from £11 ($19.25) per person nightly for B&B.

Penny Acres, 183 Evesham Rd., Stratford-upon-Avon, Warwickshire CV37 9BP (tel. 0789/299652), one of the brightest and cheeriest places on this road, is owned by Mr. and Mrs. Calcutt, who can accommodate six guests in comfortable and tastefully decorated rooms. Singles, which are hard to find in Stratford-upon-Avon, rent for £10 ($17.50) daily and doubles from £10.50 ($18.40) per person, depending on the season. These prices include a full English breakfast. Tea- and coffee-makers are provided, and there is color TV in the double rooms.

Lemarquand, 186 Evesham Rd., Stratford-upon-Avon, Warwickshire CV37 9BS (tel. 0789/204164), is run by Anne Cross, who offers three bedrooms—two doubles and one twin—each comfortably equipped and containing hot and cold running water. The shared bathroom has a shower much appreciated by her American visitors. Rates of £10.50 ($18.40) to £11 ($19.25) per person nightly include a full English breakfast and pots of tea. She gives good service, and her location is close to the theater and town center.

Ashburton House, 27 Evesham Pl., Stratford-upon-Avon, Warwickshire

CV37 6HT (tel. 0789/292444), is a guesthouse with a restaurant license and is one of the better selections in Stratford. Evening dinners, particularly pretheater ones, are a specialty, but must be booked in advance. Rooms are handsomely furnished and well equipped with color TV and tea- and coffee-makers in all units and private showers in two units. The establishment is centrally heated, and hot water is available for baths and showers at all times. Hosts are Steve and Bridget Downer, who are delighted to receive foreign visitors, charging from £13 ($22.75) per person daily for bed and a full-menu breakfast. Dinners are optional and cost £12 ($21) for the four-course pretheater repast served at 6 p.m., in good time before the eight-minute walk to the Royal Shakespeare Theatre. Advance reservations by letter with a £5 ($8.75) deposit are strongly recommended. All charges are inclusive of service charge and tax.

Aidan Guest House, 11 Evesham Pl., Stratford-upon-Avon, Warwickshire CV37 6HT (tel. 0789/292824), is a large Victorian family house belonging to Kari and Barry Coupe. It has retained some of the best features and character of its architectural period. Close to the town center, the house lies within a five-minute walk of the theater and railway station. All rooms have central heating as well as hot and cold running water and beverage-making facilities. Some units have private showers. The place is particularly recommended for parents traveling with small children, as babysitting can be arranged. Children's cots are also available. Charges are from £11 ($19.25) per person nightly, including breakfast, service, and taxes. The Coupes keep their place impeccably clean and have tastefully furnished it.

The Hollies, 16 Evesham Pl., Stratford-upon-Avon Warwickshire CV37 6HT (tel. 0789/66857), is a welcoming B&B establishment run by a mother and daughter, Mrs. Mavis Morgan and Mrs. L. Burton. Their guesthouse is in a renovated three-story building that was once a school, although it looks like a stately old home. The bedrooms have plenty of wardrobe and breathing space, and beds have good, firm mattresses. The rate for rooms and plentiful breakfast served in a sunny dining room decorated with hand-cut crystal ranges from £12 ($21) to £16 ($28) per person, the latter price for a private bath. Babysitting can be arranged.

Grosvenor Villa, 9 Evesham Pl., Stratford-upon-Avon, Warwickshire CV37 6HT (tel. 0789/66192), owned and run by Marion Davies, was built in 1884 of red brick and white stucco. Eight spotless rooms are available, costing £13 ($22.75) nightly in a bathless single, and from £12 ($21) to £17 ($29.75) per person in a double, depending on the plumbing. VAT and breakfast are included in the rates. There is a comfortable lounge with color television and a small licensed bar. On the second floor, hot tea, coffee, and soups are available. Each room has a washbasin and hot running water, and there are several bathrooms. There's parking for six cars. The house is on the main road toward Evesham, and is only a few minutes from Market Place and about eight minutes from the theater.

Twelfth Night, Evesham Place, Stratford-upon-Avon, Warwickshire CV37 6HT (tel. 0789/414595), is aptly named. In fact, when the Royal Shakespeare Theatre accommodated actors here for nearly a quarter of a century, many of them had appeared in productions of *Twelfth Night*. A Victorian house, the place has now been restored and vastly improved, until it is today rated as one of the finest guest accommodations in Stratford. Nonsmokers are invited to occupy one of its seven bedrooms, five of which contain a private shower. The B&B rate in a single is from £16 ($28) to £17 ($29.75) daily, with doubles costing from £31 ($54.25) to £35 ($61.25).

Sequoia House, 51-53 Shipston Rd., Stratford-upon-Avon, Warwickshire CV37 7LN (tel. 0789/68852), is a privately run hotel with its own beautiful garden, and it is centrally located if you're visiting the major Shakespeare properties of the National Trust. It also lies within an easy walking distance of the theater if you're planning to see one of the Bard's plays that night. In fact, the hotel is just across the Avon River opposite the theater. The house has been vastly improved after a rejuvenation. Today it offers 21 well-furnished and comfortable bedrooms, many with private bath or shower, but all with color TV, beverage-making equipment, and hot and cold running water, as well as direct-dial phone. B&B charges range from £26 ($45.50) to £38 ($66.50) daily in a single, rising to £30 ($52.50) to £44 ($77) in a double. The more expensive tariffs are for private baths, of course. Guests gather in a pleasant lounge that has a licensed bar and an open Victorian fireplace.

Ravenhurst Hotel, 2 Broad Walk, Stratford-upon-Avon, Warwickshire CV37 6HS (tel. 0789/292515), is a seven-bedroom Victorian town house in a quiet street of the Old Town, in easy reach of the historic town center. Richard and Brenda Workman invite guests to enjoy the comfortable rooms, all of which have color TV and beverage-making facilities. Some units have private baths. Bed and a full English breakfast are priced from £10 ($17.50) to £16 ($28) per person daily. The Workmans are Stratfordians whose extensive local knowledge can add to the pleasure of your visit.

At **Parkfield Guest House,** 3 Broad Walk, Stratford-upon-Avon, Warwickshire CV37 6HS (tel. 0789/293313), Pauline Rush is the hostess with the mostest, having drawn more reader recommendations than any other place in Stratford-upon-Avon. She runs an immaculately kept and conveniently located guesthouse, charging £11 ($19.25) per person nightly. Rooms are well furnished with adequate facilities, such as color TV and tea- and coffee-makers. Some units have full private baths. Rates include a superb English breakfast, better than in most guesthouses. Mrs. Rush, if possible, will help guests obtain theater tickets.

Newlands, 7 Broad Walk, Stratford-upon-Avon, Warwickshire CV37 6HS (tel. 0789/298449), is where Sue and Rex Boston welcome B&B guests to their one single and two double rooms, which have hot and cold water basins, color TV, tea- and coffee-making facilities, and central heating. A full English breakfast is included in the prices that range from £10 ($17.50) to £11 ($19.25) per person nightly, depending on the season.

The Croft, 49 Shipston Rd., Stratford-upon-Avon, Warwickshire CV37 7LN (tel. 0789/293419), is a B&B traditionally run guesthouse that has been in business many years and is kept up-to-date. A visitor's book testifies to all those who have been pleased. The Croft stands on the A34 only five minutes from the center of town and the Memorial Theatre. Fully modernized, the house has central heating, color TV, and tea- and coffee-makers in all the rooms. Some units have private baths. Kevin and Jeanne Hallworth welcome you to their home and offer a full English breakfast as well as comfortable accommodation. A single room costs £14.50 ($25.40) nightly, and doubles or twins range from £11 ($19.25) to £17 ($29.75) per person for B&B. There are special rates for families of three to five persons.

Craig House Guest House, 67-69 Shipston Rd., Stratford-upon-Avon, Warwickshire CV37 7LN (tel. 0789/296573), is a family-run place under the management of its owners, Terry and Margarita Palmer. There is a comfortable guest lounge with TV. The Palmers rent 12 bedrooms, five of which contain private showers and toilets. The cost ranges from £12.50 ($21.90) to £16.50 ($28.90) per person nightly, including breakfast and tax. The house lies across the old Clopton Bridge from Stratford, a span that was there in Shakespeare's time. The theater is no more than ten minutes' walk from the guesthouse if you use the old tramway bridge across the river.

Salamander Guest House, 40 Grove Rd., Stratford-upon-Avon, Warwickshire CV37 6PB (tel. 0789/205728), one of the better guesthouses of Stratford-upon-Avon, is well maintained and homelike, fronting a woodsy park. Maurice and Ninon Croft rent eight comfortably furnished rooms, including one for families, and the two public bathrooms are shared. The B&B rate in a single is from £10 ($17.50) daily and from £21 ($36.75) in a double. Evening meals, prepared by Maurice, who is a qualified chef, can be ordered, costing from £5 ($8.75) per person for three courses. Serving is timed so that patrons can get to the theater for the evening performances. The house is about a five-minute walk from the center of town.

Courtland Hotel, 12 Guild St., Stratford-upon-Avon, Warwickshire CV37 6RE (tel. 0789/292401) is a large, comfortable Georgian house with some antique furniture. The owner, Mrs. Bridget Johnson, gives her personal attention. The location is in the town center, one minute from the bus station, a five-minute walk from the rail station, and three minutes from the theater. Rooms, each with color TV and hot and cold running water, are reasonable in price. With shared bathrooms, singles rent from £12 ($21) to £13.50 ($23.65) nightly, with doubles or twins costing £24 ($42) to £26 ($45.50). A family room costs from £34 ($59.50) to £36 ($63). Three double rooms have private baths, and these rent for £30 ($52.50) to £38 ($66.50) nightly. English and continental breakfasts are served (the preserves are home-made). Some special diets are available on request.

Hunters Moon, 150 Alcester Rd., Stratford-upon-Avon, Warwickshire CV37 9DR (tel. 0789/292888), is a family-run guesthouse on the fringe of Stratford and near Anne Hathaway's Cottage. The owner, John Monk, has operated the place for more than 32 years and has an interest in another house a few doors along, so you may be lodged there. Both of the houses have been completely modernized and extended. Most rooms have showers, toilets, color TV, dual-voltage shaver points, hairdryers, and tea- and coffee-makers. At Hunters Moon, most of the units have orthopedic beds. Between the two guest accommodations, the Hunters Moon complex can receive 40 persons. There is a good selection of rooms, the price being £13.50 ($23.65) per person per night, including a full English breakfast. There is a self-contained cedar chalet with private plumbing on the grounds at the rear of the main house in a well-maintained setting.

Moonraker House, 40 Alcester Rd., Stratford-upon-Avon, Warwickshire CV37 2RD (tel. 0789/67115), is a pleasant B&B where hardworking, competent Mike Spencer receives guests in rooms with showers, toilets, color TV, hairdryers, and beverage-making facilities. He charges from £26 ($45.50) daily for two persons. A luxury suite with a bedroom, lounge, and kitchenette is more expensive, of course. Among amenities are four-poster beds, a nonsmoking lounge area, and garden patios. The house is five minutes by car from the heart of town.

Victoria Spa, Bishopton Lane, Stratford-upon-Avon, Warwickshire CV37 9QY (tel. 0789/67985), is a large house dating from 1837 and lying 1½ miles from the center of town. The lodge actually was a spa in its early days and once had Queen Victoria's eldest daughter, Princess Vicky, as a guest. Paul and Dreen Tozer are accommodating hosts. Their bedrooms are tastefully decorated with Laura Ashley wallpaper and matching bedspreads, as well as tea- and coffee-makers. Most of their units contain private baths, for which you pay more, of course. B&B ranges from £15 ($26.25) to £17.50 ($30.65) per person nightly. A full English breakfast is served in a cheerful and antique-filled room.

A Town House Complex

Lysander Court, Riverside, Stratford-upon-Avon, Warwickshire CV37 6BA (tel. 0789/414999 for information and reservations), is a new concept in "home from home" accommodations. Six Elizabethan-style town houses grouped around a charming and private courtyard are luxuriously furnished and can house two to six persons. Each has a pleasant lounge, kitchen and dining area, bathroom, toilet, three bedrooms, color TV, metered telephone, and car parking. Linen and toiletries are provided, and full service is supplied if required. A full English breakfast is included in the rates of £19 ($33.25) to £32 ($56) per person per night, depending on the number accommodated. Right in the heart of Stratford, Lysander Court is within easy walking distance of the theater, shops, and other attractions.

WHERE TO EAT

In the best position in town, the **Box Tree Restaurant,** Royal Shakespeare Theatre, Waterside (tel. 0789/414999), is in the theater, with walls of glass providing an unobstructed view of the Avon and its swans. The meals and service are worthy of its unique position. The restaurant is open on matinee days from noon to 2 p.m., when a three-course table d'hôte luncheon costs £10.75 ($18.80). Evening hours are 5:45 p.m. to midnight, a three-course pretheater dinner being featured. During intermission, there is a snack feast of smoked salmon and champagne. After each evening's performance, you can dine by flickering candlelight. Classical French, Italian, and English cuisine is served. Dinner and supper are à la carte and cost from £15.75 ($27.55) to £20 ($35) per person. Be sure to book your table in advance, especially on the days of performances (there's a special phone for reservations in the theater lobby).

Also overlooking the Avon, the **River Terrace Restaurant** in the theater is open to the general public as well as to playgoers. A coffeeshop and licensed restaurant serves typical English and pasta dishes, morning coffee, and afternoon teas, which are offered on a self-service basis. Meals cost from £4 ($7) to £8.50 ($14.90). It is open from 10:30 a.m. to 9:30 p.m. Sunday hours are from 11 a.m. to 5 p.m. The restaurant has the same phone as the Box Tree (above).

Bobby Brown's, 12 Sheep St. (tel. 0789/292554), is a black and white timbered building with a high gabled wing dating from the early 16th century. It's steeped in associations with the days of Shakespeare. On the second floor, a maze of three rooms is filled with antique oak tables, Windsor chairs, and settles. The whole place has a certain medieval charm. Closing time is Sunday evening in winter. Other than that, hours are daily from noon to 2:30 p.m., when à la carte lunches cost from £7 ($12.25). A snack menu is offered from noon to 6 p.m. From 6 to 7 p.m., a pretheater dinner is served, costing £7.95 ($13.90) for three courses. From 7 to 11 p.m., you can dine à la carte from £11 ($19.25) per person, enjoying steaks, lasagne, meat pies, and the like.

Thatch Restaurant, Cottage Lane, Shottery (tel. 0789/293122), is two doors from Anne Hathaway's Cottage and two miles from Stratford-upon-Avon. Almost hidden by the entrance to the big coach park, this tea room provides a relaxed meal away from the hurly-burly of the town of Stratford. Apart from morning coffee and afternoon cream teas, the Thatch offers meals for £6.50 ($11.40) to £9 ($15.75). Wine, liquor, or beer is available to have with your meal. You might like to sit outside on the covered patio and watch the visitors lining up to see Anne Hathaway's house, or just listen to the chirping of the birds. The food is good, the prices reasonable, and the atmosphere pleasant. Hours are 9:30 a.m. to 5:30 p.m. daily; it is closed from October to Easter.

Hathaway Tea Rooms, 19 High St. (tel. 0789/292404), is housed in a mellowed 380-year-old building, timbered and rickety as its across-the-street neighbor, Harvard House. You pass through a bakery shop up to the second floor, into a forest of olden beams. Sitting at the English tables and chairs you can order wholesome food made from time-tested recipes. The soup of the day is homemade. Usually, you have a choice of six main dishes, such as roast beef with Yorkshire pudding or steak-and-kidney pie. The classic steaming hot fruit pies round off most meals. Hathaway is recommended as a luncheon stop, with meals costing from £6.50 ($11.40). You might also want to visit it for afternoon cream tea from 3 to 5 p.m., costing £2.50 ($4.40) or for a high tea (which is cream tea with sandwiches) costing £4 ($7). Hours are from 9 a.m. to either 5:30 or 6 p.m. Monday to Saturday, and from 11 a.m. to 5:30 p.m. Sunday.

The **Black Swan,** Waterside Street (tel. 0789/297312), is affectionately known as "The Dirty Duck." By whatever bird it's called, it's been popular since the 18th century as a favorite hangout of Stratford players. Autographed photographs of its patrons, such as Lord Laurence Olivier, line the wall. The front lounge and bar crackle with intense conversation. The choices change daily, and in the bar you'll find good value and quick service, everything washed down with mellow beer. In the Dirty Duck Grill Room, typical English grills, among other dishes, are featured.

You're faced with a dozen appetizers, most of which would make a meal in themselves. Main dishes include braised kidneys. Meals cost from £12 ($21). Hours are from 11 a.m. to 3 p.m. and 5:30 to 11 p.m. Monday to Saturday, and from noon to 3 p.m. and 7 to 10:30 p.m. Sunday.

The **Horseshoe Buttery and Restaurant,** 33-34 Greenhill St., Stratford-upon-Avon, Warwickshire CV37 6LF (tel. 0789/292246), is a family-run business offering good old-fashioned straightforward English cookery at reasonable prices. Centrally situated opposite the Safeway store, the café is open daily from 7:30 a.m. to 9 p.m., serving grills, snacks, salads, sandwiches, burgers, and pizzas. In the restaurant, open from noon to 2:30 p.m. and 5 to 9 p.m. daily, the fare runs to steaks, chops, cutlets, scampi, fish, chicken, and salads. A two- or three-course luncheon is served daily for £4.50 ($7.90). The best dish to order is a homemade steak-and-kidney pie, or a roast joint, each served with fresh vegetables and creamed or boiled potatoes. Because of their 50% patronage by Americans or Canadians, ice water is always available. But you can also order iced lagers, beer, ales, and wines by the glass. The owner rents six bedrooms priced at £15 ($26.25) per person nightly, based on double or single occupancy. Rooms are attractively furnished and have color TV and private showers.

Marlowe's Restaurant, Marlowe's Alley, 17-18 High St. (tel. 0789/ 204999), is made up of the Elizabethan Room, a 16th-century oak-paneled dining room, and the Loose Box Restaurant (see below), once the hayloft of this ancient house. Meals in the Elizabethan Room start from around £10 ($17.50). The garden patio overflows with flowers, and the owners, George and Judy Kruszynskyj, invite you to have a drink or even an al fresco meal here. Hours are from pretheater to 10:30 p.m. Monday to Friday, and to 11 p.m. Saturday. A traditional Sunday lunch is served from noon to 2:30 p.m., and it is also open Sunday evening from 7 to 9:30.

The Loose Box Restaurant, in the former hayloft, serves meals starting at £3 ($5.25), specializing in lunch snacks and evening bistro-style dining. Hours are from 6 to 10 p.m. Monday to Saturday; closed Sunday.

Slug & Lettuce, 38 Guild St. (tel. 0789/299700), is a brick building with a cozy pub atmosphere of wood tables along with good food and ale. In fair weather, tables open onto Garden Patio on Union Street. Standing on a busy highway, it draws a lot of local business as well as tourists. The menu is robust, prepared from fresh ingredients, and you get excellent value here, with meals costing from £8 ($14). You might begin with a hearty soup or a fresh, crisp salad before going on to one of the specials, which change daily. For example, you might try pork chops cooked with apples and flavored with Calvados, or fresh mussels in garlic butter. Hours are from noon to 10 p.m. Monday to Saturday, and from noon to 2:15 p.m. and 7 to 9:30 p.m. Sunday.

Pinocchio, 6 Union St. (tel. 0789/69106), standing next to the previously recommended Slug & Lettuce, is a pizza and pasta restaurant, one of the best in town. North of Bridge Street, it is cozy and welcoming. The kitchen brings a taste of Sicily to Stratford. Meals cost from £6 ($10.30), but could go far higher, depending on what you order. For example, one of the chef's specials is a grilled spring chicken flavored with herbs. There is also a wide range of pastas in various sauces (try the one with baby clams), along with the inevitable pizzas. Veal dishes are also good, and for dessert you might like a smooth zabaglione. Hours are daily, except Sunday, from noon to 2:30 p.m. and 6 to 11 p.m.

The **Vintner Wine Bar,** 5 Sheep St. (tel. 0789/297259), demonstrates why wine bar dining is all the rage in England, even in Stratford-upon-Avon. The Elizabethan decor is fitting in the town of Shakespeare, and the name comes from a wine merchant, John Smith, who occupied this address early in the 17th century. Around the corner from the Shakespeare Hotel, the popular drinking and dining spot offers meals from £6 ($10.50). Daily specials are posted on the blackboard. Many guests prefer one of the tempting cold plates at lunch. You can also order a vegetable dish of the day, a grilled sirloin, or a salmon steak. Hours are from 10:30 a.m. to 11:30 p.m. daily.

A TUDOR PUB

A black and white timbered Elizabethan pub, the **Garrick Inn,** High Street (tel. 0789/296816) was named after one of England's greatest actors, David Garrick. It has its own kind of unpretentious charm. The front bar is decked out with tapestry-covered settles, an old oak refectory table, and an open fireplace where the locals gravitate. The black bar has a circular fireplace with a copper hood—plus a buffet bar serving ploughman's lunches and steak-and-kidney pie, among other dishes. A buffet menu is served daily from 11:45 a.m. to 2:15 p.m., costing from £2.50 ($4.40). At night, regular pub hours are kept from 5:30 to 11 p.m. The Garrick is across from the Town Hall and next to Harvard House.

AT LOXLEY

The nearby village of Loxley, just 3½ miles from Stratford-upon-Avon, is an ancient community, boasting one of the oldest Saxon churches in England, the parish church of St. Nicholas. This quiet country village, claimed by some to be the original home of Robin Hood (Sir Robin of Loxley), is a quiet little place with a delightful old pub.

At historic **Loxley Farm,** Loxley, Warwickshire CV35 9JN (tel. 0789/840265), Roderick and Anne Horton live in a real dream of a thatched cottage with windows peeping from the thatch and creeper climbing up the old walls. The garden is full of apple blossoms, roses, and sweet-scented flowers. A stone path leads across the grass and into the flagstone hall, with nice old rugs and a roaring fire. Accommodations are in the main house and in the 17th-century half-timbered thatched barn nestling in the orchard. The barn has been remodeled to form two bedrooms with private baths, sitting room, and kitchen on the ground floor. There is one room with private bath in the main house. The Hortons charge from £15 ($26.25) per person nightly for a bed, a full English breakfast, and VAT. Breakfast is served in the house on a table made from a panel from the wall of the Royal Mint in London.

ELSEWHERE IN THE ENVIRONS

In the home village of Shakespeare's mother, Mary Arden, **Pear Tree Cottage,** Church Road, Wilmcote, Stratford-upon-Avon, Warwickshire CV37 9XJ (tel. 0789/205889), is a late 16th-century farmhouse (with later additions). Period charm has been preserved with exposed beams and antique furniture, while such things as modern plumbing and central heating add 20th-century comfort. No longer a farmhouse, the cottage stands in nearly an acre of lawn and gardens. Mr. and Mrs. Mander rent a total of seven rooms accommodating up to 15 guests at prices ranging from £12.50 ($21.90) to £14 ($24.50) nightly for units with private baths. However, the bathless rooms are the bargains at £11 ($19.25) per person. A sitting room for guests has color TV and comfortable chairs. Mary Arden's birthplace is visible across the field from the house.

A privately owned 16th-century inn, **Broom Hall Inn,** Broom, near Alcester, Warwickshire B50 4HE (tel. 0789/773757), stands in the little hamlet of Broom on the River Alne, shortly before it empties into the Avon. It's near Bidford-on-Avon, about six miles from Stratford-upon-Avon and ten miles from Broadway in the Cotswolds. The building is a black and white timbered Elizabethan structure in a rural location away from main roads. Steve Tavener owns and manages the inn, offering seven double- or twin-bedded rooms for £27.50 ($48.15) daily in a single and £40 ($70) in a twin, all prices including a full English breakfast and VAT. Mr. Tavener also operates a carvery restaurant serving a number of à la carte specialties. Meals cost from £7.50 ($13.15). A special Sunday lunch menu is also offered.

Templar House, Temple Grafton, near Alcester, Warwickshire B49 6NS (tel. 0789/490392), is five miles from Stratford-upon-Avon, between the A437 and the

A422 roads. The Fisher family rents three good-size rooms, charging £10 ($17.50) per person daily in a double, £16 ($28) in a single. A room with private bath costs £14 ($24.50) per person in a double. The tariffs include a full English breakfast and VAT. The farm is quite old, but the house has been modernized.

King's Lodge, Long Marston, Stratford-upon-Avon, Warwickshire CV37 8RL (tel. 0789/720705), lies six miles from Stratford-upon-Avon. From Stratford, take the A34 Oxford road; on the outskirts of town, fork right on to the B4632 Cheltenham road and continue for 4½ miles. Turn right at the signpost to Long Marston and proceed to a "T" junction, turning right. Once a manor house that has now partly disappeared, it was a place where Charles II hid out as a manservant after the Battle of Worcester. George and Angela Jenkins welcome guests to comfortably furnished and centrally heated bedrooms with hot and cold water basins. One bedroom features a traditional four-poster bed hewn from timber grown on the estate. Besides the bedrooms in the lodge, there are three self-contained apartments on the grounds equipped for self-catering, but when the other accommodations are full, the Jenkinses will rent any unoccupied apartments on a B&B basis to one couple or a party. The charges per night are from £24 ($42) for two persons, with a full English breakfast included. For £6.50 ($11.40), you can enjoy a three-course dinner with coffee at an oak table in what was once part of the manor's Great Hall. The restored room is dominated by a large stone inglenook fireplace. Mullioned windows frame vistas of green lawns and stately trees.

The Goodwins, Long Marston, Stratford-upon-Avon, Warwickshire CV37 8RQ (tel. 0789/720326), six miles from Stratford-upon-Avon and five miles from Chipping Campden, is where you can submerge yourself in the best traditional "Olde Worlde" England. A 17th-century stone farmhouse, with four front gables, beams throughout, and mullioned windows, this is a true gem in the Bard's countryside, complete with a pond, a gaggle of geese, and sheep grazing in the meadow. Mr. and Mrs. Hodges, the owners, have double- and twin-bedded rooms, each with a hot and cold water basin, TV, beverage-making facilities, and shaver points. The prices range from £12.50 ($21.90) per person daily, with a reduction for stays of three or more nights. There is a guest lounge with TV, where you can enjoy an English "cuppa." The farm aviation club offers gliding, parachute jumping, and ultralight flying at moderate prices, by prior arrangement. Other attractions at the farm are private trout fishing and a Sunday morning antique market. The local Equestrian Centre and Stratford and Broadway golf courses are nearby

Church Farm, Long Marston, Stratford-upon-Avon, Warwickshire CV37 8RH (tel. 0789/720275), lies about six miles from Stratford. The owner, Mrs. Wiggy Taylor, enjoys meeting people from other countries and welcomes children (she can provide babysitting services). You get not only a warm welcome at this family home, which is a 17th-century farmstead in a secluded garden, but good comfortable accommodations. You can rent a large comfortable twin-bedded room, with hot and cold running water, TV, and beverage-making equipment, at a rate of £12 ($21) a night.

AN ATTRACTION AT ALCESTER

A magnificent, 115-room Palladian country house, **Ragley Hall** (tel. 0789/762090), built in 1680, is the home of the Marquess and Marchioness of Hertford and their family, lying nine miles from Stratford-upon-Avon. The house has been lovingly restored and appears as it probably looked during the early 1700s. Great pains were taken to duplicate color patterns and in some cases even the original wallpaper patterns. Ragley Hall's vast and spacious rooms boast priceless pictures, furniture, and works of art that have been collected by ten generations of the Seymour family. While possessing a museum-like quality in the sense that its artifacts are properly displayed, lighted, and have great historical importance, Ragley Hall is indeed a private home.

Perhaps the most spectacular attraction is the lavishly painted south staircase hall. The present marquess commissioned muralist Graham Rust to paint the modern tromp l'oeil work on the subject of the Temptation, but this religious theme stops with the lavishly evil Devil offering a gold circlet to Christ in the central ceiling medallion.

The house is open from noon to 5:30 p.m., except Monday and Friday, from Easter Saturday to the end of September. The park, gardens, Adventure Wood, and Farm and Country Trail are open from noon to 5:30 p.m. in March, April, May, and September, and from 10 a.m. to 6 p.m. in June, July, and August. Admission to the house, garden, and park is £2.90 ($5.10) for adults, £1.90 ($3.35) for children. The garden, park, wood, and trail can be visited for £1.90 ($3.35) for adults, 90p ($1.65) for children.

Most travelers approach our next stopover, Warwick, via the A46 from Stratford-upon-Avon, eight miles away. The town is 92 miles from London and is on the Avon.

---

2. Warwick

Visitors seem to rush through here to see Warwick Castle; then they're off on their next adventure, traditionally to the ruins of Kenilworth Castle. But the historic center of medieval Warwick deserves to be treated with greater respect. It has far more to offer than a castle.

In 1694, a fire swept over the heart of Warwick, destroying large segments of the town, but it still retains a number of Elizabethan and medieval buildings, along with some fine Georgian structures from a later date. (Very few traces remain of the town walls except the East and West Gates.) Warwick looks to Ethelfleda, daughter of Alfred the Great, as its founder. But most of its history is associated with the Earls of Warwick, a title created by the son of William the Conqueror in 1088. The story of those earls—the Beaumonts, the Beauchamps (such figures as "Kingmaker" Richard Neville)—makes for an exciting episode in English history but is too complicated to document here.

WARWICK CASTLE

Perched on a rocky cliff above the Avon, this magnificent 14th-century fortress encloses a stately mansion in the grandest late 17th-century style.

The importance of the site has been recognized from earliest times. The first important work at Warwick was the Mound built by Ethelfleda, daughter of Alfred the Great, in A.D. 915. The same Mound was enlarged at the time of the Norman Conquest, and a Norman castle of the motte-and-bailey type was built. There are now no remains of the Norman castle, which was sacked by Simon de Montfort in the Barons' War of 1264.

The Beauchamp family, from which hailed the most illustrious medieval Earls of Warwick, was responsible for most of the castle as it is seen today, and much of the external structure remains unchanged from the mid-14th century. When the castle was granted to the ancestors of the Greville family in 1604, Sir Fulke Greville spent £20,000 constructing a mansion within the castle fortifications, although this has been much altered over the years. The Grevilles have held the Earl of Warwick title since 1759, when it passed from the Rich family.

The State Rooms and Great Hall house fine collections of paintings, furniture, arms, and armor. The armory, dungeon, torture chamber, ghost tower, clock tower, and Guy's tower give vivid insights into the castle's turbulent past and its important part in the history of England. The private apartments of Lord Brooke and his family, who in recent years sold the castle to Madame Tussaud's company (of waxworks fame) are open to visitors to display a carefully constructed Royal Weekend House Party of 1898. The major rooms contain wax models of celebrities of the time:

Winston Churchill, the Duchess of Devonshire, Winston's widowed mother, Jennie, and Clara Butt, the celebrated singer, along with the Earl and Countess of Warwick and their family. In the Kenilworth bedroom, the Prince of Wales, later to become King Edward VII, reads a letter, and in the red bedroom the Duchess of Marlborough prepares for her bath. Among the most lifelike of the figures is a little uniformed maid, bending over a bathtub into which the water is running, to test the temperature.

Surrounded by gardens, lawns, and woodland where peacocks roam freely, and skirted by the Avon, Warwick Castle was described by Sir Walter Scott in 1828 as "that fairest monument of ancient and chivalrous splendor which yet remains uninjured by time."

Don't miss the re-created Victorian Rose Garden, originally designed by Robert Marnock in 1868. It fell into disrepair, and a tennis court was built on the site among the trees. In 1980, it was decided to restore the garden, and as luck would have it, Marnock's original plans were discovered in the County Records Office. Close by the Rose Garden is a Victorian alpine rockery and water garden. The romantic castle is, throughout the year, host to various special events, colorful pageants such as those created by the members of the Sealed Knot and the French Foot Grenadiers. There are regular appearances of the magnificent Red Knight on his splendid warhorse, and international Morris Dancers perform on the lawns. Some form of live entertainment is presented almost every day on the grounds in summer.

Warwick Castle, Castle Hill (tel. 0926/495421), is open daily, except Christmas Day. From March 1 to October 31, hours are 10 a.m. to 5:30 p.m.; November 1 to February 28, 10 a.m. to 4:30 p.m. All-inclusive admission is £4.50 ($7.90) for adults, £3 ($5.25) for children.

OTHER SIGHTS

Other nearby sights worth exploring include the following:

St. Mary's Church

This church, on Old Square, was destroyed in part by the fire of 1694 and is characterized by its rebuilt battlemented tower and nave, considered among the finest examples of the work of the late 17th and early 18th centuries. The striking aspect of St. Mary's is that it's unusually lofty, dominating the surrounding countryside. The Beauchamp Chapel, spared from the flames, encases the Purbeck marble tomb of Richard Beauchamp, a well-known Earl of Warwick who died in 1439 and is commemorated by a gilded latten effigy. The most powerful man in the kingdom, not excepting Henry V, Beauchamp has a tomb considered one of the finest remaining examples of Perpendicular-Gothic as practiced in England in the mid-15th century. The tomb of Robert Dudley, Earl of Leicester, a favorite of Elizabeth I, is against the north wall. The choir, another survivor of the fire, dates from the 14th century. It too is built in the Perpendicular-Gothic style. The Norman Crypt is another fine example of this period, as is the 14th-century Chapter House. For more information, get in touch with the Parish Office, Old Square Warwick (tel. 0926/400771).

Lord Leycester Hospital

At the West Gate, this group of half-timbered almshouses was also spared from the Great Fire. The buildings were erected about 1400, and the hospital was founded in 1571 by Robert Dudley, the Earl of Leicester, as a home for old soldiers. It is still in use by ex-servicemen and their wives today. On top of the West Gate is the attractive little chapel of St. James, dating from the 12th century but much restored. The hospital, High Street (tel. 0926/491422), may be visited Monday to Saturday from 1 a.m. to 5:30 p.m. (it is closed Sunday) for £1.50 ($2.65) for adults, 50p

(90¢) for children. Off-season it closes at 4 p.m. Last admission is 15 minutes before closing.

Warwick Doll Museum

In one of the most charming Elizabethan buildings in Warwick, this doll museum, Oken's House, Castle Street (tel. 0926/495546), is near St. Mary's Church. Its seven rooms contain an extensive private collection of dolls in wood, wax, and porcelain. The house once belonged to Thomas Oken, a great benefactor of Warwick. The museum is open from 10 a.m. to 12:30 p.m. and 1:30 to 5 p.m. Monday to Saturday, and from 2 to 5 p.m. Sunday, from Easter to the end of September. Admission is 75p ($1.30) for adults, 50p (90¢) for children.

Warwickshire Museum

At the Market Place, this museum (tel. 0926/493431, ext. 2500) was established in 1836 to house a collection of geological remains, fossils, and a fine grouping of British amphibians from the Triassic period. There is also much for the natural historian. The history collections include church plate, coins, firearms, and the famous Sheldon tapestry map of Warwick. It is open Monday to Saturday from 10 a.m. to 5:30 p.m. and on Sunday in summer from 2:30 to 5 p.m. Admission is free.

St. John's House

At Coten End, not far from the castle gates, there is a display of domestic life and costumes. St. John's House, in which these exhibitions are displayed, is a thing of beauty itself, dating from the early 17th century. A Victorian schoolroom is furnished with original 19th-century school furniture and equipment. During term time, Warwickshire children dressed in replica costumes can be seen participating in Victorian-style lessons. Groups of children also use the Victorian parlor and the kitchen. As it is impossible to display more than a small amount at a time, a study room is available where you can see objects from the reserve collections. The costume collection is a particularly fine one, and visitors can study the drawings and photos that make up the costume catalogue. These facilities are available by prior appointment only. For more information and appointments, telephone the Keeper of Social History (tel. 0926/410410, ext. 2021).

Upstairs in St. John's House is a Military Museum tracing the history of the Royal Warwickshire Regiment from 1674 to the present day. The house is open Tuesday to Saturday from 10 a.m. to 12:30 p.m. and 1:30 to 5:30 p.m., and also on Sunday from 2:30 to 5 p.m., May to September. Admission is free.

BED AND BREAKFAST

A good B&B, **Warwick Lodge Guest House,** 82 Emscote Rd., Warwick, Warwickshire CV34 5QJ (tel. 0926/492927), is run by Grace and Bernard Smith. All rooms have color TV, tea- and coffee-making facilities, central heating, hot and cold running water, and comfortable beds. The cost of £15 ($26.25) per person nightly includes a full English breakfast. This is an informal place, close enough to Stratford-upon-Avon to be a base for touring Shakespeare Country. The area is full of pubs and restaurants that serve good "English fayre" at reasonable prices.

Penderrick, 26 Coten End, Warwick, Warwickshire CV34 4NP (tel. 0926/499399), was originally built in 1838. The architect carefully positioned it so it would not harm the enormous copper beech in the front yard. It was constructed of a blue-toned stone quarried near Birmingham, which had been procured from the ruins of a nearby prison. Today, the beech tree is bigger than ever, and the house has been transformed to receive paying guests. The Blackband family rent seven comfortably furnished bedrooms. Singles cost £24.50 ($42.90) daily, doubles £36 ($63) to £42 ($73.50), and a quad for £64 ($112), including breakfast and VAT. There's a long and narrow garden in back (the hotel actually occupies only half of the original house), and visitors can walk in the verdant St. Nicholas Park, whose entrance is just 50 yards from Penderrick. A fixed-price three-course dinner can be served at £9.50 ($16.35) to guests who request it in advance.

Cambridge Villa, 20a Emscote Rd., Warwick, Warwickshire CV34 4PL (tel. 0926/491169), lies within a four-minute walk west of Warwick Castle, but clients of this family-run hotel also appreciate an even more pleasant walk through St. Nicholas Park to reach it. Owned by the Greenfield family, the Cambridge Villa rents comfortably furnished rooms, the rates depending on the plumbing. Singles cost from £15.50 ($27.15) to £23 ($40.25) daily, with doubles going for £28 ($49) to £40 ($70), with an English breakfast included.

Westham Guest House, 76 Emscote Rd, Warwick, Warwickshire CV34 5QC (tel. 0926/491756), lies within a residential section of town along a busy road. This seven-bedroom B&B establishment is about a five-minute walk away from the center of Warwick. It is set behind canopies and a pleasant garden and is managed by the Donald family. With an English breakfast included, comfortably furnished singles rent for £11 ($19.25) daily, with doubles costing from £22 ($38.50) to £28 ($49), depending on the plumbing.

The Coach House, 40 The Butts, Warwick, Warwickshire CV34 4ST (tel. 0926/499585), is an excellent guesthouse lying in the heart of the city, near the Castle, St. Mary's Church, Eastgate, and the Avon River. Hundreds of years ago it was used by castle guards for archery practice. Nowadays it provides attractive and well-furnished accommodations for guests, each with a private bath. Sue Holland, its helpful owner, charges from £20 ($35) per person nightly for B&B. The breakfasts are good and home-cooked. Evening meals are also available, if required.

Tudor-House Inn & Restaurant, West Street, Warwick, Warwickshire CV34 6AW (tel. 0926/495447), was built in 1472. It's at the edge of town, on the main road from Stratford-upon-Avon leading to Warwick Castle. It is a black and white timbered inn, one of the few buildings to escape the fire that destroyed the High Street in 1694. Off the central hall are two large rooms, each of which could be the setting for an Elizabethan play. In the corner of the lounge is an open turning staircase, waiting for the entrance of a minstrel player. A regular meal in the restaurant and steak bar costs from £8 ($14). The inn has 12 bedrooms, all with washbasins and the majority with private baths or showers. The cost ranges from £20 ($35) to £48 ($84) per double room nightly. Two of the rooms have doors only four feet high. There's the usual resident ghost—an old man who gets up early in the morning, leaving the front door open and heading toward Stratford-upon-Avon without paying his bill to innkeeper Eddie Bush. In addition, the old priest's hiding hole has become the Priest Hole Bar.

The Old Rectory, Stratford Road, Sherbourne, near Warwick, Warwickshire CV35 8AB (tel. 0926/624562), is a 300-year-old farmhouse. It has been lovingly restored and decorated with antiques by the owners, Sheila and Martin Greenwood. There are seven double bedrooms, six of which have private baths or showers, in the main house, as well as a converted carriage house suitable for a family. Several bedroms have antique brass beds. The cost is £13 ($22.75) to £16 ($28) per person daily for B&B, and the English breakfast is bountiful. Just off the A46 between Warwick and Stratford-upon-Avon, the house lies less than three miles southwest of Warwick on the A429.

WHERE TO EAT

The pasta and pizza joint of Warwick is **Piccolino's,** 31 Smith St. (tel. 0929/491020), which is set beneath beamed ceilings and ringed with pictures and miniature spotlights. This Italian restaurant is informal and rather fun, serving a wide selection of pizzas, including a "red hot Mamma" with a zesty chili flavor. You can also order such really filling pasta dishes as tortellini à la crema and tagliatelle carbonara. Italian wine may be ordered by the glass. A full meal costs from £7 ($12.25) and is served from noon to 2:30 p.m., with dinner from 5 to either 10:30 or 11:30, depending on the night of the week.

Zaranoff's, 16 Market Pl. (tel. 0926/492708), is a dining oddity somewhat reminiscent of the restaurant run by the late Jack Dempsey in New York. Zaranoff is a former heavyweight wrestler whose origins are from Russia and Latvia. The walls are decorated with photographs of "half-naked men," in the words of one diner (actually pictures of British wrestlers). Meals are served from noon to 2 p.m. and 7:30 to 10:30 p.m. daily, except Sunday at lunch and all day Monday and Tuesday. A three-course meal costs from £10 ($17.50) to £12 ($21). The menu changes daily, and it features organically grown food. Typical dishes are likely to include Hungarian beef goulash, couscous with rabbit, and vegetarian specialties. The building has a medieval cellar.

Bar Roussel, 62a Market Pl. (tel. 0926/491983), is a bistro and wine bar that is open daily for lunch from noon to 2:15 p.m. (no lunch on Sunday) and for dinner from 7 to 9:45 p.m. daily. There is a choice of 53 wines, beers, and "spirits." Every day there is a freshly made soup followed by a homemade dish of the day, a hot casserole or a meat pie. The cheese board features nine different selections with crackers and bread. Meals cost from £5 ($8.75).

Nicolinis Bistro, 18 Jury St. (tel. 0926/495817), brings a touch of Italy and its savory cuisine to staid Warwick. Lynne and Nicky, as they are known, welcome you to their attractive restaurant, which is made most inviting with much greenery. Pause at the enclosed counter to check out the crisp salads and luscious Italian desserts. The lighting is also kind. You're faced with an array of appetizers, pizzas, pastas, salads, and desserts, and I haven't even gotten to the main courses. Pizzas come in sizes of 6½ to 9 inches, and Nicolinis Choice includes "everything." For a main course you can order chicken Kiev with potatoes, although the lasagne would be more typical. Full meals cost around £10 ($17.50). The restaurant serves Tuesday through Sunday from 9:30 a.m. to 10:30 p.m.

3. Kenilworth Castle

In magnificent ruins, this castle—the subject of Sir Walter's Scott's romance *Kenilworth*—once had walls that enclosed an area of seven acres. It lies five miles north of Warwick and 13 miles from Stratford-upon-Avon. In 1957, Lord Kenilworth presented the decaying castle to England, and limited restoration has since been carried out.

The castle dates back to the days of Henry I, having been built by one of his lieutenants, Geoffrey de Clinton. Of the original castle, only Caesar's Tower, with its 16-foot-thick walls, remains. Edward II was forced to abdicate at Kenilworth in 1327, before being carried off to Berkeley Castle in Gloucestershire, where he was undoubtedly murdered. Elizabeth I in 1563 gave the castle to her favorite, Robert Dudley, Earl of Leicester. The earl built the Gatehouse, which was visited on several occasions by the queen. After the Civil War, the Roundheads were responsible for breaching the outer walls and towers and blowing up the north wall of the keep. This was the only damage caused following the Earl of Monmouth's plea that it be "Slighted with as little spoil to the dwellinghouse as might be."

The castle is open daily from 10 a.m. to 6 p.m. Good Friday to September 30, and from 10 a.m. to 4 p.m. off-season; closed Monday. Admission is £1.10 ($1.95) for adults, 55p (95¢) for children. For information, phone 0926/52078.

WHERE TO STAY

One of the most preferred guesthouses in the area is **Abbey,** 41 Station Rd., Kenilworth, Warwickshire CV8 1JD (tel. 0926/512707), which has a certain old-fashioned Victorian aura that seems to delight many readers. Bedrooms have been well thought out, and everything is clean and well ordered. Seven bedrooms are rented, of which a trio contains private bath or shower. B&B charges go from £13.50 ($23.65) to £16 ($28) daily in a single, rising to £23 ($40.25) to £31 ($54.25) in a double. A good English dinner is served punctually at 7 p.m. Limited parking is available.

Enderley Guest House, 20 Queens Rd., Kenilworth, Warwickshire CV8 1JQ (tel. 0926/55388), is one of the best kept and most inviting guesthouses for those who'd like to stay over and savor some of the flavor of this town with its ruined 12th century castle. A family-operated place, it offers pleasant and comfortable bedrooms, only five in all. Guests of these accommodations share the two public baths. Bedrooms are well kept and inviting, and rates are reasonably priced at £14 ($24.50) to £17.50 ($30.65) daily in a single, going up to £25 ($43.75) to £28 ($49) in a double. The guesthouse lies within an easy reach of the heart of Kenilworth. In fact, you might choose to stay here and let the summer crowds fight it out in Stratford-upon-Avon, driving up only for the day.

The Priory Guest House, 58 Priory Rd., Kenilworth, Warwickshire CV8 1LQ (tel. 0926/56173), is a pleasant small Victorian guesthouse in the center of Kenilworth. Here you receive a warm welcome at the home of Nina and Richard Haynes. They offer comfortably furnished rooms with color TV, coffee-making equipment, and hot and cold running water. A double or twin-bedded room costs £22 ($38.50) per night, with singles ranging in price from £12 ($20) to £15 ($26.25). Many guests use this house as a base for exploring the countryside, including Stratford-upon-Avon and the Cotswolds.

WHERE TO DINE

If you're passing through on a sightseeing expedition for the day, try to get a seat for lunch at **George Rafters,** 42 Castle Hill (tel. 0926/52074), whose name is very similar to the old movie gangster, George Raft (remember *Some Like It Hot* with Marilyn Monroe?). Here, there is no relation. This is an intimate candlelit restaurant in the vicinity of Kenilworth Castle, and it's the obvious choice for lunch. It serves from noon to 2 p.m., with dinner from 7 to 10 p.m. Meals cost from £6 ($10.50) to £10 ($17.50), depending on what you order. Many of the dishes are continental in style or from the Cordon Bleu kitchen, while others depend on the imagination of the chef. Of course, good English food is always featured.

If you're in Kenilworth for the night, go over to **Ana's Bistro,** 121 Warwick Rd. (tel. 0926/53763), for dinner, any time from 7 to 10:30 p.m. (it is closed Sunday and Monday and for three weeks in August). Its location is downstairs under the Restaurant Diment (which some consider is the finest in Kenilworth for those willing to spend the extra money). However, at Ana's you get food that is almost equal in taste and flavor, but at a better price. The menu is wisely limited, and the hearty cookery is straightforward, with occasional innovations. Specials change daily based on the shopping for the day. Meals cost from £6.50 ($11.40) to £9.50 ($16.65).

Coventry is 19 miles from Stratford-upon-Avon, 11 from Warwick, and six from Kenilworth.

---

4. Coventry

Coventry has long been noted in legend as the ancient market town through which Lady Godiva made her famous ride, giving birth to a new name in English: Peeping Tom. The Lady Godiva story is clouded in such obscurity that the truth has probably been lost forever. It has been suggested that the good lady never appeared in the nude but was the victim of scandalmongers, who in their attempt to tarnish her image, unknowingly immortalized her.

THE SIGHTS

This Midlands city, home of motorcar and cycle manufacturing, is principally industrial, but you'll want to pay it a visit to see Sir Basil Spence's controversial **Coventry Cathedral,** consecrated in 1962. The city was partially destroyed during the blitz in the early '40s, but the rebuilding was miraculous. No city more than Coventry seems to symbolize England's power to bounce back from adversity.

The cathedral grew up on the same site as the 14th-century Perpendicular building. Many Coventry residents maintain that the foreign visitor is more disposed to admiring the structure than the Britisher, who perhaps is more tradition-laden in his concept of cathedral design.

Outside is Sir Jacob Epstein's bronze masterpiece, *St. Michael Slaying the Devil.* Inside, the oustanding feature is the 70-foot-high altar tapestry by Graham Sutherland, said to be the largest in the world. The floor-to-ceiling abstract stained-glass windows are the work of the Royal College of Art. The West Window is most interesting, with its engraved glass and rows of stylized saints and monarchs with jazzy angels flying around among them.

In the undercroft of the catehdral is a Visitor Centre, **The Spirit of Coventry.** There you can see the Walkway of Holograms, three-dimensional images created with laser light, depicting the Stations of the Cross. It is an exciting walk through sound, light, and special effects, tracing the history of Coventry and the cathedral from its foundation to the present day. The treasures of the cathedral are on show. An audio-visual on the city and church includes the fact that 450 aircraft dropped 40,000 firebombs on the city in one day.

The cathedral is open daily in summer from 8:30 a.m. to 7:30 p.m., closing at 5:30 p.m. in winter. The 14th-century tower of the old cathedral costs £1 ($1.75) for adults to visit, 50 p (90¢) for children 6 to 16.

After visiting the cathedral, you may want to have tea in Fraters Restaurant, nearby, listening to the chimes.

St. Mary's Guildhall, Bayley Lane (tel. 0203/225555), is up a flight of steps leading from a small yard off Bayley Lane. This is one of the most attractive medieval guildhalls in England, dating from 1342. It was originally built as a meeting place for the guilds of St. Mary, St. John the Baptist, and St. Catherine. It is now used for the solemn election of the lord mayors of the city and for banquets and civic ceremonies. Below the north window is an arras (tapestry), added in the 15th century, and a beautiful oak ceiling with its original 14th-century carved angels, which was rebuilt in the 1950s. There is a Minstrel's Gallery and a Treasury, and off the Armoury is Caesar's Tower, where Mary Queen of Scots was imprisoned in 1569. By appointment only, you can also see a magnificent collection of 42 original watercolors by H. E. Cox, depicting Coventry before the bombings of 1940. The guildhall is open from 10 a.m. to 5 p.m. Monday to Saturday, and from noon to 5 p.m. on Sunday, May to October. Admission is free. City pensioners conduct guided tours.

Ford's Hospital, Greyfriars Lane (tel. 0203/223838), is a house built in the very early 16th century to house the poor of the city. Today it is a wealth of old beams and mullioned windows restored during 1953. It is now the home once more of elderly Coventry residents. There is a beautiful inner courtyard surrounded by timbered walls hung with geraniums, ferns, and ivy in summer. It is open from 10 a.m. to 5 p.m. throughout the year and is well worth a visit. Admission is free.

The **Museum of British Road Transport,** St. Agnes Lane, Hales Street (tel. 0203/832425), is some five minutes' walk from Coventry Cathedral in the city center. It houses the largest municipally owned collection in the United Kingdom, possibly in the world. The oldest car is an original Daimler dating from 1897 (the first English Daimler was built in Coventry only one year before). The museum also displays some of the most antique vehicles still running—six of them are regular particpants in the annual London-Brighton run (only vehicles manufactured before 1905 are eligible). Curiosities include a 1910 Humber taxi whose mileage is listed at more than one million. Exhibits are diversified, as the museum has the ambitious task of covering the total history of transport in the Midlands, internationally recognized as the home of the British transport industry. Indeed, Coventry has been the home of some 124 individual motor vehicle manufacturers, many of which are represented in the collections. Among the military vehicles is the staff car in which Montgomery rode into Berlin after the defeat of the Nazis. Special exhibitions include a period street scene for the formative years of motoring (1895–1929); a "Royalty in the Road" display featuring both Queen Mary's 1935 limousine and King George IV's 1947 state landaulet; a history of the cycle from 1818–1987; and the most recent innovation, a hi-tech audio-visual display featuring *Thrust 2,* the current holder of the land-speed record, relating the entire history of this important story from 1898 to today. The museum is open daily throughout the summer (Easter to September) and on Friday, Saturday, and Sunday from October to March. Admission is £1 ($1.75) for adults, 75p ($1.30) for children.

WHERE TO STAY

A 12-bedroom licensed Victorian hostelry, **The Croft Hotel,** 23 Stoke Green, Coventry, West Midlands CV3 1FP (tel. 0203/457846), standing in three-quarters of an acre of mature garden, is just ten minutes from the city center and the cathedral. Owned by Mary and David Cadman, it's an all-purpose hotel where single travelers are as welcome as families. The daily rate is £18 ($31.50) in a basic single and £32 ($56) in a double or twin-bedded accommodation. A single with color TV and shower rents for £22 ($38.50), while a twin with those conveniences goes for £36 ($63). All rooms in this centrally heated hotel have radio-alarm clocks and tea- and coffee-makers. David prepares a hefty breakfast, and Mary offers evening meals costing from £7 ($12.25) per person. She also provides a selection of bar meals, which are served until 10:30 p.m. The garden supplies vegetables in season, and you are invited to use the gardens and solarium for relaxation.

Fairlight Guest House, 14 Regent St., off Queens Road, Coventry, West Midlands CV1 3EP (tel. 0203/224215), is a late Victorian three-story red-brick building with a courtyard decorated in summer with pots of bright flowers. Betty and Brian Smith provide 11 rooms where guests can stay for £12.50 ($21.90) daily in a single, £11.50 ($20.15) per person in a double for B&B. All rooms in this centrally heated establishment have tea- and coffee-makers and hot and cold water basins. Shower rooms with toilets are separate from the bedrooms. Color TV is provided in a pleasant lounge. The house is about five minutes from the city center.

At the **University of Warwick,** Gibbet Hill Road, Coventry, West Midlands CV4 7AL (tel. 0203/523279), David Wilson is the man to speak to if you want to stay at this modern university campus where rooms are available for summer rental when the students are gone. It is landscaped in beautiful Warwickshire farmland on the southern boundary of Coventry. Rooms are mostly single, but there are twins, some with private facilities. All units are well but simply furnished, with access to the usual student facilities, washing machines, dryers, swimming pool, tennis courts, and games room. The cost is from £15.50 ($27.15) per person daily, including a full breakfast, VAT, and service. If you're traveling with children and would like to stay four or more nights, ask about the self-catering flats, a five-bedroom unit being available at £25 ($43.75) per night.

WHERE TO EAT

A traditional dining place, **Ostlers Eating House,** 166 Spon St. (tel. 0203/226603), lies some five to eight minutes from the cathedral. This 17th-century building with a stone facade and all its original beams is unusual in that it wasn't destroyed in the bombing of Coventry during World War II. Spon Street itself is being restored to its original state as it was in medieval England, wtih some adjustments to the 20th century, of course. A satisfying meal will cost £8 ($14) to £10 ($17.50). You're presented with a choice of appetizer, then perhaps roast chicken with baked potato or a grilled steak with salad and potato. One section of the menu is reserved for "crock pots"—that is, selections that include chili con carne, lasagne, or vegetable goulash. Ostlers is open from 11 a.m. to 10:30 p.m. Monday to Thursday, closing at 11:30 p.m. on Friday and Saturday. Sunday hours are 7 to 10:30 p.m. The place is good for atmosphere in a city that has had to be almost totally rebuilt.

Remember dull vegetarian meals in health food restaurants where everything tastes bland? Forget that unfortunate memory here in Robert Jackson's **Trinity House Hotel and Herbs,** 28 Lower Holyhead Rd., Coventry, West Midlands, CV1 3AU (tel. 0203/555654). He turns vegetarian cookery into an art. In a small private hotel, the Trinity House Hotel and Herbs enjoys an enviable reputation, even among meat-eaters who visit to see what the excitement is about. Some of the sauces use wine and cream, and that enlivens the fare considerably. Only dinner from 6:30 to 9:30 p.m. (except Sunday) is served, with meals costing from £7.50 ($13.15). Everything is superfresh. Dishes include red lentil lasagne or pine nut loaf, and desserts are also luscious. If you like the place so much you'd like to stay over, ask about one of the good, clean basic bedrooms, seven in all, where the cost ranges from £15 ($26.25) daily in a single to £29 ($50.75) in a double.

Corks Wine Bar & Restaurant, 4-5 Whitefriars St. (tel. 0203/23628), is both a wine bar and bistro, plus an intimate à la carte restaurant. The wine bar evokes a stylized belle époque atmosphere with its dark colors and antique lighting fixtures. Daily fixed-price menus are displayed on chalkboards, costing anywhere from £1.80 ($3.15) to £3.50 ($6.15). From the handwritten à la carte menu you can select a filling meal of soup, pâté, salad, or lasagne, along with a dessert, for £5 ($8.75) and up. If you're really hungry for something to sink your teeth into, try the entrecôte bordelaise with a salad or french fries. In the more expensive restaurant, you can dine well for £12 ($21), perhaps beginning with frogs' legs in garlic butter, then going on to stuffed rainbow trout or sirloin steak with a pâté sauce. Monday to Saturday lunches are served from 11 a.m. to 2:30 p.m. Dinner is offered Monday to Thursday from 6 to 10:30 p.m., until 11 p.m. on Friday and Saturday, and on Sunday from 7 to 10:30 p.m.

---

5. Hereford and Worcester

The Wye Valley contains some of the most beautiful river scenery in Europe. The river cuts through agricultural country, and there is no population explosion in the sleepy villages. Wool used to be its staple business, and fruit growing and dairy farming are important today.

The old county of Herefordshire has now combined with Worcestershire to form "Hereford and Worcester"-shire. Worcestershire's name, of course, has become famous around the world because of its sauce familiar to gourmets. It is one of the most charming of Midland counties, covering a portion of the rich valleys of the Severn and Avon.

Herefordshire's Black Mountains border the Welsh Brecon Beacons National Park, and between the two cathedral cities of Hereford and Worcester the ridge of the Malverns rises from the Severn Plain.

The heart of England is the best point to travel to by train from Paddington Station in London if you wish to use your BritRail Pass. The train takes you through many of the previously mentioned towns and villages, and you can stop and visit Windsor, Henley-on-Thames, and Oxford, not to mention the numerous Cotswold villages, such as Chipping Campden. It must be one of the best train rides in the country, and you can also take a side trip by bus from Evesham to Stratford-upon-Avon too. Or else take the bus back from Stratford to Oxford via Woodstock, then the train back into London.

HEREFORD

One of the most colorful old towns of England, the ancient Saxon city of Hereford, on the Wye River, was the birthplace of both David Garrick and Nell Gwynne. Dating from 1079, the red sandstone **Hereford Cathedral** (tel. 0432/59880) contains all styles of architecture, from Norman to Perpendicular. One of its most interesting features is a library of chained books—more than 1600 copies—as well as one of the oldest maps in existence, the Mappa Mundi of 1290. There is also a Treasury in the crypt.

Hereford is surrounded by both orchards and rich pasturelands. Hence it has some of the finest cider in the world, best sampled in one of the city's mellow pubs. Hereford cattle sold here are some of the finest in the world too.

The Old House, High Street (tel. 0432/286121, ext. 207), is preserved as a Jacobean period museum, with the appropriate furnishings. The completely restored, half-timbered structure built in 1621 also contains superb 17th-century wall paintings and local history items. The house is open all year from Monday to Saturday. Summer hours are from 10 a.m. to 1 p.m. and 2 to 5:30 p.m. In winter, it is open only from 10 a.m. to 1 p.m. Admission is 50p (90¢) for adults, 25p (45¢) for children. A joint ticket costing 80p ($1.40) admits you to both The Old House and Churchill Gardens Museum.

The **Cider Museum & King Offa Cider Brandy Distillery,** Pomona Place, Whitecross Road (the A438 to Brecon; tel. 0432/354207), tells the story of traditional cider making right through to modern factory methods. Displays include orcharding, an enormous 17th-century French beam press, a cooper's shop, an old farm cider house, traveling cider makers' "tack" that used to be trundled from farm to farm, and the original champagne cider cellars with their tiers of bottles. Also on view are a 1920s press house and factory bottling line and the great oak vats of the Napoleonic period. The King Offa Distillery has been granted the first new license to distill cider brandy in the United Kingdom in more than 250 years, and visitors can see it being produced from the beautiful copper stills brought from Normandy. The museum shop sells cider, cider brandy, cider brandy liqueur, and Royal Cider, the real wine of Old England, as well as a good selection of gifts and souvenirs. The museum is open seven days a week from 10 a.m. to 5:30 p.m. April to the end of October, from 1 to 5 p.m. Monday to Saturday November to March. Admission is £1.20 ($2.10) for adults, 90p ($1.60) for children. The museum is five minutes' walk from the city center and a quarter of a mile from the city Ring Road on the A438 to Brecon.

Where to Stay

Alexander House Hotel, 61 Whitecross Rd., Hereford, Hereford and Worcester HR4 0DQ (tel. 0432/274882), offers moderately priced accommodations for 12 guests in a lovely house a half mile from the city center. It's on the A438 Hereford-Brecon road and easy to spot. Owners Doreen and Tony Lerigo charge £12 ($21) to £16 ($28) per person daily whether in a single or double. For an additional £6.50 ($11.40) to £8 ($14), you can have one of their home-produced dinners. The cooking is family-style, with fresh vegetables used whenever available. They are licensed for alcoholic beverages as well. They'll even prepare packed lunches for you. Each bedroom is commodious, with hot and cold running water, color TV, bedside lights, tea- and coffee-makers, and central heating. On each floor there is a bathroom with toilet and shower.

Ferncroft Hotel, Ledbury Road, Hereford, Hereford and Worcester HR1 2TB (tel. 0432/265538), is a simple, comfortable hotel with no pretensions, offering an economy accommodation. The B&B rate in a single is £17 ($29.75) daily, rising to £24 ($42) in a double. There is central heating, and each of the nicely furnished bedrooms contains hot and cold running water. The location is off St. Owens Street, a short walk from the railway station and the Wye River.

Bowes Guest House, 23 St. Martins St., Hereford, Hereford and Worcester HR2 7RD (tel. 0432/267202), is just across the River Wye, about a five-minute walk from the cathedral. John and Eileen Bowes own a nice old town house whose entrance leads straight from the street into the hallway. The 19th-century "listed" building was built by the Duke of Norfolk to accommodate his fishing retinue, and there is a large public park at the back. Parking is close by. There are 12 bedrooms with hot and cold running water and central heating. Baths and shower rooms are down the hall. Singles rent for £12 ($21) daily, with doubles and twins ranging from £20 ($35) to £21 ($36.75). These rates include a large breakfast that features haddock or kippers in addition to the regular bacon and eggs. They'll pack a picnic lunch for you if you give them warning. Eileen Bowes is a local person and will recommend tourist sights and give directions to places farther afield.

Westdene, 200 Whitecross Rd., Hereford, Hereford and Worcester HR4 0LT (tel. 0432/50438), is operated by Kate and Graham Wixey, who love the city and surrounding countryside and welcome guests into their comfortable home to share their enjoyment of the region. Their Victorian house is about five minutes from the center of the city by car, and there is a lounge with TV. They provide teas and light evening meals. Bed and a large English country breakfast, along with morning and evening coffee, cost £10 ($17.50) per person daily. The house is centrally heated.

Staying in the Environs

If you're motoring, you can seek a farmhouse accommodation. Gladys and Frank Lee own and run **Cwm Craig,** Little Dewchurch, Hereford, Hereford and Worcester HR2 6PS (tel. 0432/70250). This is a mixed farm, 180 acres around a solid Victorian farmhouse where bed and a farm breakfast costs £9 ($15.75) to £10 ($17.50) per person daily in rooms with hot and cold water basins. The large, spotless bedrooms have snug beds, and a bath and toilet facilities are down the passage. Guests can use the comfortable sitting room with TV, a grander drawing room, or, during the day, walk around the farm. Son Anthony provides an interesting guide when he's not away driving heavy trucks around the country. To get there from Hereford, take the Ross road, the A49, over the river and turn left at the traffic lights by the church. Follow this road to a pedestrian crossing, turning right and driving for four miles to the village. Once there, turn left. Cwm Craig is the first farm on the left.

The **Green Man Inn,** Fownhope, near Hereford, Hereford and Worcester HRL 4PE (tel. 043277/243), is an attractive country inn with black-and-white beams, gables, and leaded windows, lying in the center of this village outside Hereford. An archway leads into the inn yard. Dating from the 15th century, this inn was once known as the Naked Boy. It fulfilled its role as a hospice and inn during the Civil War when Colonel Birch and his Roundhead troops stayed here before occupying Hereford. In the 18th and 19th centuries, the Petty Sessional Court was held here, and you can still stay in the judge's room overlooking the courtyard (nowadays it has a modern shower and toilet). There is a four-poster room with bath, plus a garden room with bath that has views over the meadows and the River Wye. The bars are low beamed, and the dining room and sitting room also have low beams, cottage-style furnishings, wheelback chairs, and bench tables. The inn is run these days by Arthur and Margaret Williams, who offer good bar snacks and traditional English food in their dining room. A single goes for £26 ($45.50) daily, a double for £34 ($59.50), including a full English breakfast and VAT.

Apple Tree Cottage, Mansel Lacy, Hereford and Worcester HR4 7HH (tel. 098122/688), lies in a charming hamlet in the heart of beautiful country. This cottage in the Marches, near the Welsh border, is actually two farm cottages, one built in 1450 and the other in 1600, now joined and modernized inside to make for comfort but with the old beams and "cruck" construction still visible. It is centrally heated, and the two bedrooms contain facilities for making morning tea or coffee. Monica Barker offers B&B for £11.50 ($20.15) per person nightly, with an evening meal costing £8 ($14). Good home cooking is enhanced by use of fresh garden produce. To reach Mansel Lacy, take the A438 Brecon Road out of Hereford to the junction with the A480. Mansel Lacy is about 5 miles from the turn, just off the A480.

Food and Drink

Cathedral Restaurant, 17 Church St. (tel. 0432/265233), is, as its name suggests, quite close to Hereford Cathedral. Owners Neil and Helen Clarke run a relaxing place decorated in a light motif with a cozy cellar bar. Everything is freshly cooked, using local produce when available. The restaurant is open Tuesday to Saturday from 10:30 a.m. to 5:30 p.m., serving hot lunches from noon to 2:30 p.m. Dinner is from 6:30 to 9:30 p.m. Many patrons drop in for morning coffee or afternoon tea. In winter, evening meals are served only on Friday and Saturday nights. At lunch, specials change daily. You can order a three-course menu for £4.95 ($8.65) or else à la carte, and typical dishes include beef with beer, crab and prawn feuilletté, cream cheese and spinach crêpes, or else vegetarian dishes. Sunday lunch, also three courses, costs £6.95 ($12.15) and features the traditional roast beef with Yorkshire pudding. English desserts include the likes of treacle tart and "Spotted Dick." Evening meals cost from £12 ($21) per person and are likely to include such courses as stuffed breast of chicken, trout with white wine and cucumber, and magret with port and a red currant sauce. The service is polite and efficient.

Marches, 24 Union St. (tel. 0432/355712), is outstanding for the area. Reportedly, it is the biggest health food emporium in the country (in a health-conscious era), with not only a health food store but a dining room on two floors. Service is from 8:30 a.m. to 5:30 p.m., except Sunday. Meals cost from £5 ($8.75). The chef is a specialist in "whole-food cookery," and you're faced with a dozen different and tempting salads "made with good things." Vegetable flans are far better than the usual bland fare, and you can also order chicken and ham cold plates (it's not wholly vegetarian). Save room for one of the fruity pies.

Gaffers, 89 East St. (no phone), is a bright and cheerful vegetarian restaurant that displays the work of local artisans and artists. All food is homemade, and prices are reasonable: around £2.50 ($4.40) and up for a full meal. There are highchairs and changing facilities for young children, as well as open-air seating in summer. Smoking is not permitted from lunchtime on. Gaffers, a workers' cooperative, is open from 10 a.m. to 4:30 p.m. Monday to Saturday. A working jeweler is on the premises.

An Inn on the Border

The **Rhydspence Inn,** Whitney-on-Wye, near Hay-on-Wye, Hereford and Worcester HR3 6EU (tel. 04973/262), is a timbered inn right on the border of England and Wales, dating from the 16th century. It has a fascinating gabled porch through which you enter the gleaming bar where a log fire crackles in the chimney. Excellent meals and snacks prepared by the chef, Ray Grosvenor, are served, including thick homemade soups. Specialties are "hammy," a soup made with chopped ham and eggs, and "fishy," made with smoked haddock, anchovies, mushrooms, and cream. In addition to the bar food, there is a restaurant where the chef applies himself to grills, roasts, and tasty country dishes. Dinner costs about £9 ($15.75), and wine can be ordered by the glass. The hosts, Peter and Pamela Glover, have six rooms to rent, all with private bathrooms, color TV, beverage-making facilities, and central heating. For B&B, the charge is from £20 ($35) per person daily. The inn is open seven days a week, and you're assured of a warm welcome from the Glovers.

The local customers are friendly too, and you can join them in the bar in the evening for a game of darts or quoits. Try the local cider as an alternative to beer.

WORCESTER

This historic cathedral city, famous for its gloves and porcelain, lies 27 miles from Birmingham and 26 miles from Stratford-upon-Avon.

Offering views of the Malvern Hills, **Worcester Cathedral** stands high on the banks of the River Severn. Dating from 1084, it contains the Quire (rebuilt in 1224) that has sheltered King John's Tomb since 1216. The Chapter House, with its massive central supporting column, is considered one of the finest in England. A refreshment room and gift shop are in the cloisters. The cathedral is open from 7:45 a.m. to 7:30 p.m. in summer, 9 a.m. to 6 p.m. otherwise. There is no charge for entry, but donations are invited. You can usually climb the tower and see the view over the city and countryside. The tower door is open from 11 to 11:30 a.m., noon to 12:30 p.m., 2 to 2:30 p.m., and 3 to 3:30 p.m. The reason for the fixed times is that the traffic up and down has to be one way. Cost is 50p (90¢) for adults, 30p (55¢) for children.

A visit to the **Royal Worcester Porcelain Factory,** Severn Street (tel. 0905/23221) is worthwhile. There is a short tour for £2 ($3.50) for adults, £1 ($1.75) for children over 8, allowing you to see the craftspeople at work. Unfortunately it's necessary to book ahead if you wish to take a tour (for a "same day" tour, phone before 10 a.m.), but everyone can enjoy browsing in the shops at the factory. There you can buy examples of the craft. Many pieces are "seconds," all marked as such and sold at low prices. Most of the time you won't be able to tell why. There is a magnificent museum as well.

The city is rich in other sights, including the **Commandery** (tel. 0905/355071), founded in the 11th century as the Hospital of St. Wulstan and becoming over the years a fine 15th-century timber-frame structure that was the country home of the Wylde family. Charles II used the house as headquarters for the 1651 Battle of Worcester. The Great Hall has a hammerbeam roof and a minstrels' gallery. England's premier **Civil War Centre** is now situated here, with audio-visual displays and regular "living history" encampments with 17th-century costumes and crafts. The house is open from 10:30 a.m. to 5 p.m. Monday to Saturday and 2 to 5 p.m. on Sunday. Admission is £1.50 ($2.65) for adults, 75p ($1.31) for children, and £4 ($7) for a family ticket. The Commandery has canalside tea rooms, a picnic area, and a Garden of Fragrance.

You can also see **Queen Anne's Guildhall,** built in 1724, with statues honoring Charles I and Charles II that were erected by the Royalists. Walking tours of the city are offered in summer. Pump Room teas are available on certain dates. Ask at the **Tourist Information Centre** for details (tel. 0905/723471).

Food and Lodging

Talbot Hotel, 8 Barbourne Rd., Worcester, Hereford and Worcester WE1 1HT (tel. 0905/21206), is a bit of old England—a long, half-timbered coaching inn, with tiny dormers, a tower bay window, and leaded windows. All the bedrooms have private baths, intercoms, radios, and heating. Singles are rented for £18 ($31.50) nightly, doubles going for £28 ($49), and a triple costing £38 ($66.50). VAT and breakfast are included in the tariffs. Meals are served in the timbered, old-style dining room, with an à la carte dinner offered in the evening. Bar snacks are served in the pub lounge.

Chatsworth, 80 Barbourne Rd., Worcester, Hereford and Worcester WR1 1SD (tel. 0905/26410), is a good clean guesthouse with car parking, where an overnight stay will cost £12 ($21) per person nightly, including a full breakfast. All bedrooms have color TV and tea-and-coffee-makers. It's run by Patricia Grinnell, whose husband, Dennis, is a radio ham. His call sign is G4MKO, so if you care to make your advance reservations by radio, give him a call. Incidentally, a licensed ham will be allowed to use Dennis's equipment.

Park House, 12 Droitwich Rd., Worcester, Hereford & Worcester WR3 7LJ (tel. 0905/21816), is a neat Victorian guesthouse with a private car park and pleasantly decorated, centrally heated rooms, all with radio, TV, and hot and cold running water. Some units have private baths, and there is a TV lounge. John and Sheila Smith, the owners, charge £18 ($31.50) daily in a single and £35 ($61.25) in a double. Tariffs include a full English breakfast and VAT. The house has a license for serving residents alcoholic drinks, and the Smiths provide a good range of snacks and light meals. Dinner can be served by arrangement for £9 ($15.75).

For meals, I suggest **Bottles Wine Bar & Bistro,** 5 Friar St. (tel. 0905/21958), perhaps the favored rendezvous right in the historic center, popular with young and old alike. The decor is handsomely subdued, with mahogany tables, and the selection of cold foods is good. I usually prefer the vegetarian dish of the day preceded by one of the homemade soups, but you can choose from the roast joints, along with a crisp salad. The chef's specials are also recommended. You might choose to end your meal with Brie or Stilton. Main meals cost from £4 ($7). The wine bar is open from noon to 11 p.m. Monday to Saturday and 7 to 10:30 p.m. Sunday. Food is served from noon to 7:30 p.m. Monday to Saturday.

The **King Charles II Restaurant,** King Charles House, 29 New St. (tel. 0905/22449), is in a mellow black-and-white timber-frame building dating from the 15th century. Charles II hid here following the battle of Worcester and escaped through the back door as Cromwell's troops assembled outside. This was the starting point of his journey across England to exile in France. The dining room is elegantly decorated with oak paneling of the period. The ceiling has exposed large oak beams, and at one end of the room there is a dungeon you can view. The warmth and character of the room is completed by two open fireplaces with carved overmantels, one bearing the date 1634. Upstairs, the king's former bedchamber is now the restaurant's bar. The kitchen serves continental, mainly Italian, dishes prepared from the best ingredients. A fixed-price luncheon is a good value at £7.50 ($13.15), and an à la carte dinner costs from £15 ($26.25). Hours are from 12:15 to 1:45 p.m. and 7:30 to 9:45 p.m., except Sunday and bank holidays.

Museums on the Outskirts

Sir Edward Elgar's Birthplace, Crown East Lane, Lower Broadheath (tel. 090566/224), about three miles west of Worcester, is a brick cottage surrounded by stables and a coach house built by Sir Edward's father and uncle in the early 19th century. Nowadays the house contains a museum of photographs and drawings, original scores of Elgar's music, and mementos of his youth. Musicians and conductors come from afar to check his music and their interpretations of it. To reach the house, drive out of Worcester on the A44 toward Leominster. After two miles, turn off to the right at the sign. The house is in the village, a half mile along a side road. Admission is £2 ($3.50) for adults, 50p (90¢) for children. It is open daily, except Wednesday, from 10:30 a.m. to 6 p.m. in summer, and from 1:30 to 4:30 p.m. in winter. It's closed from mid-January to mid-February.

Avoncroft Museum of Buildings, Stoke Heath, Bromsgrove (tel. 0527/31886), is 11 miles from Worcester and 21 miles from Stratford-upon-Avon. It is open daily from 11 a.m. to 5:30 p.m. in June, July, and August. Hours are the same in April, May, September, and October, but it's closed Monday. In March and November, it's open from 11 a.m. to 4:30 p.m. daily, except Monday and Friday; it is closed altogether in December, January, and February. Admission is £2 ($3.50) for adults, £1 ($1.75) for children. A family ticket is offered for two adults and two children, costing £5.15 ($9).

The museum is an open-air site where a variety of historic buildings have been saved from destruction and reconstructed. Among them are a windmill in working order; a timber-frame merchant's house from the 15th century; an Elizabethan house; a cockfight theater, a stable, and a wagon shed, all from the 18th century; chain- and nail-making workshops; a blacksmith's forge; an ice house; and a three-hole outdoor toilet (earth closet). The displays give a fascinating insight into the construction of the buildings erected by English forefathers. The 14th-century Guesten Hall roof from Worcester is being reconstructed on a new building that, as well as displaying the roof, will serve as an exhibition hall for the museum. Free car parking is available, and there is also a picnic area.

The **Jinney Ring Craft Centre,** Hanbury, Bromsgrove (tel. 052784/272), is in the same area as Avoncroft Museum and Hanbury Hall, in the village of Hanbury on the B4091 from Bromsgrove, northeast of Worcester and only 15 miles from Stratford-upon-Avon. A number of old timbered farm buildings have been carefully restored by Richard and Jenny Greatwood into small studio workshops, housing a jeweler, an artist, a woodcarver, a leather worker, a fashion designer, and a stained-glass artist. Many examples of their work can be purchased from the Exhibition Gallery, which has art and craft work from all over Great Britain, and there is also a large gift shop. Coffee, tea, lunches, and evening meals are served in the 200-year-old Barn Restaurant. There is a display of old farm tools and implements, including the Jinney Ring from which the center gets its name. The ring was one of the first implements in the mechanization of farming. A series of complicated cogs and drives linked the cider press or the chaff-cutter with the patient horse who plodded ever onward around the ring to drive the grinding wheels. In season, there's a press for do-it-yourself cider making. Admission is free, and there's ample parking. The center is open from 10:30 a.m. to 5 p.m. Wednesday to Saturday and 2 to 5:30 p.m. on Sunday. Tasty lunchtime snacks are available from noon to 2:30 p.m., a light meal costing from £3 ($5.25).

Also in the area, **Hanbury Hall** (tel. 052784/214) is a Wren-style red-brick building erected in the early 18th century. It is remarkable for its outstanding painted ceilings and magnificent staircase by Thornhill. It is open from 2 to 5 p.m. Saturday and Sunday from April to October (including all of Easter weekend). From May to the end of September, hours are from 2 to 6 p.m. Wednesday to Sunday and bank holidays. Admission is £1.90 ($3.35) to 95p ($1.65) for children. Tea is served in the building.

THE MALVERNS

The beautiful, historic Malverns, once part of the ancient kingdom of Mercia, lie to the west of Worcester. Great Malvern became important in the 19th century as a spa town, and much of the Victorian splendor remains. The Malvern Hills stretch for nine miles, with six townships lying along their line, making this a splendid walking center for your visit to the shire of Hereford and Worcester. The Priory Church (the largest in the area) dates from the 15th century and has some fine stained glass. The monks' stalls have superb misericords and medieval titles. You can wander through Great Malvern, Malvern Link, West Malvern, Malvern Wells, Little Malvern, and several other hamlets on a walking tour.

Two miles out of Great Malvern, to the left as you leave on the Ledbury Road, is **St. Wulstan's Church,** where Sir Edward Elgar, who lived throughout his life in the Malvern area, is buried with his wife and daughter. There is a bronze bust of the composer in Priory Park, and he lived at Craeglea on the Malvern Wells Road and at Forli on Alexandra Road. It was here that he composed the *Enigma Variations, Sea Pictures,* and the *Dream of Gerontius.*

Water is still bottled at **Holy Well,** above Malvern Wells, and you can visit the place where monks are reputed to have wrapped the infirm in clothes steeped in the waters to cure their ills. St. Anne's Well is also open to view above the town, but you have to be hardy to climb the 200-odd steps to taste the waters.

Food and Lodging

Sidney House, 40 Worcester Rd., Great Malvern, Hereford and Worcester WR14 4AA (tel. 06845/4994), is a Georgian building whose owners rent seven attractive and comfortably furnished bedrooms, four of which contain private baths. B&B costs £14 ($24.50) to £20 ($35) daily in a single, £27 ($47.25) to £33 ($57.75) in a double. Half board can be arranged for £22.50 ($39.40) to £28.50 ($49.90) per person. It's a lovely place for a tranquil and relaxed stay, opening onto views of the countryside of Hereford & Worcester. Convenient to the town center, the hotel is run in an attentive and considerate manner.

Deacon's, 34 Worcester Rd., Malvern, Hereford and Worcester WR14 4AA (tel. 06845/66990), in the heart of this old resort, is a beautiful Georgian structure convenient to most everything. You receive a polite welcome here and are shown to one of the nine attractive and comfortably furnished bedrooms, of which six contain a private bath or shower. The single rate ranges from £21 ($36.75) to £26 ($45.50) nightly, with doubles costing £31 ($54.25) to £36 ($63). Dinners can also be arranged, but you should notify the owners in advance.

Trumps Hotel, 10 Victoria Rd., Malvern, Hereford and Worcester WR14 2TD (tel. 06845/5807), is one of the best of the small hotels of this town. Lying some 500 yards from the heart of this Victorian spa town, Trumps has a lot to offer—and all at a reasonable, price, too. Rooms are comfortably furnished and well maintained, and there are nearly a dozen in all, about half of which contain a private bath. Depending on your room assignment and plumbing, the single B&B rate ranges from £18.50 ($32.38) to £25 ($43.75) nightly, with doubles costing £30 ($52.50) to £37 ($64.75). You can also arrange to take dinner here, as the food is solid and reliable.

CAMBRIDGE AND EAST ANGLIA

1. CAMBRIDGE

2. ELY

3. THAXTED

4. SAFFRON WALDEN

5. FINCHINGFIELD

6. DEDHAM

7. NEWMARKET

8. CLARE

9. LONG MELFORD

10. LAVENHAM

11. WOODBRIDGE AND ALDEBURGH

12. EAST BERGHOLT

13. NORWICH

14. NORTH NORFOLK

The four counties of East Anglia—Essex, Suffolk, Norfolk, and Cambridgeshire—are essentially low-lying areas where the bucolic life still reigns supreme in parts.

East Anglia was an ancient Anglo-Saxon kingdom under heavy domination of the Danes for many a year. Beginning in the 12th century, it was the center of a great cloth industry that brought it prosperity, as the spires of some of its churches testify to this day. In part, it is a land of heaths, fens, marshes, and "broads" in Norfolk.

Cambridge is the most-visited city in East Anglia, but don't neglect to pass through Suffolk and Essex, the Constable country, containing some of the finest landscapes in England. Norwich, the seat of the Duke of Norfolk, is less visited, but the fortunate few who go that far toward the North Sea will be rewarded.

1. Cambridge

A young man and woman lying in an open green space between colleges, reading the romantic poets . . . rowing under the Bridge of Sighs . . . spires and turrets

... droopy willows that witness much punting ... dusty secondhand bookshops ... daffodils blowing in the meadows ... carol singing on Christmas Eve in King's College Chapel ... dancing till sunrise at the end-of-the-school-year balls ... the sounds of Elizabethan melodies from the throats of madrigal balladeers ... the purchase of horse brasses at a corner in the open market ... narrow lanes where Darwin, Newton, and Cromwell also trod ... a protest demonstration ... the Backs, where the lawns of the colleges sweep down to the Cam River ... the tattered black robe of an upperclassman, rebelliously hanging by a thread to his shoulder as it flies in the wind.

We're in the university city of Cambridge, which along with Oxford is one of the ancient seats of learning in Britain. The city on the banks of the Cam River is also the county town of Cambridgeshire, 55 miles northeast of London and 80 miles from Oxford. In many ways the stories of Oxford and Cambridge are similar, particularly the age-old conflict between "town and gown." But Oxford is an industrial city sheltering a thriving life beyond the campus. Cambridge has some industry too. Yet if the university were removed, I suspect it would revert to an unpretentious market town.

There is much to see and explore in Cambridge, so give yourself time to wander, even aimlessly. For those pressed, I'll offer more specific directions.

A *Word of Warning:* Unfortunately, because of the disturbances caused by the influx of tourists to the university, Cambridge has regretfully had to limit visitors and even exclude them from various parts of the university altogether, in some cases even charging a small fee for entrance. Small groups of up to six persons are generally admitted with no problem, and you can inquire from your local tourist office about visiting hours here.

A SELF-GUIDED TOUR

The center of Cambridge is closed to cars. There is good parking at the Anchor Pub in Silver Street, so why not leave your car there and then go for a walk around some of the colleges?

Cross Silver Street Bridge, and you'll see the entrance to Queens' College. Go into the college, crossing over the mathematical wooden bridge, so called because of its geometrical design. Then enter the older part of the college into the center of a quadrangle, and you'll see much of the Elizabethan architecture and also the doors around the quad leading to the "staircases" of tiny studies and bedrooms for undergraduates within the college itself. Those students who cannot get an accommodation here are boarded out around the city.

Exit through the fine Elizabethan arch into the new part of the college; turn right and, just past the Chapel, take the doorway that is open to the road. Turn left, and at the end of the road the archway leads to King's College Chapel and the college. Just inside is a very well-defined "staircase." This is also a beautiful college with lawns sweeping to the Cam. Visit the Chapel to see the *Adoration of the Magi* by Rubens hanging over the High Altar. You can attend evensong at King's almost every night at 5:30. There are services every Sunday at 10:30 a.m., 3:30 p.m., and again at 6 p.m.

Leave by the Porter's Lodge and walk to the Church Tower of the 800-year-old parish church of St. Edward Saint and Martyr. Within its walls the reformers of the 16th century preached and ministered the gospel. Turn right into the main Market Square, where there is a daily market for fruit, vegetables, and other produce.

From here, follow Wheeler Street, leading on to Benet Street. Opposite St. Bene't's Church in St. Bene't's Lane you will see two doors leading to a passage that will bring you to the Eagle Pub on the grounds of Corpus Christi, reputedly the only galleried inn in Cambridge. It is little known by visitors but much frequented by locals.

Without stops, this walk will take you about one hour of leisurely observation.

This tour is best done when the colleges aren't in session. Otherwise, many colleges at term time are closed in the morning.

GUIDED TOURS OF THE CAMBRIDGE COLLEGES

Leisurely walking tours of about two hours' duration take place daily all year. They start from the **Tourist Information Centre,** Wheeler Street (tel. 0223/ 322640). With a qualified and knowledgeable guide you will explore the small streets and courts of the major colleges. These are places of work, and at term time some of the buildings may be in use or closed. King's College Chapel, for example, may be in use for choir practice. Only Fellows and their guests may walk on the grass, and staircases lead to the accommodations of students and are private. The cost of these tours is £2.50 ($4.40) per person. Tours vary in direction but always contain as much of interest as is available at the time. Departure times also vary according to demand, but there are usually five departures a day during July and August, when the colleges are "down." Tickets should be booked at least a half hour in advance.

TOURS AND TOURIST SERVICES

A tourist reception center for Cambridge and Cambridgeshire is operated by **Guide Friday Ltd.** at Cambridge Railway Station (tel. 0223/62444). The center, on the concourse of the Railway Station, dispenses free maps and brochures of the city and area as well as operating tours. Also available is a full range of tourist services, including accommodation booking and car rental. In summer, the Tourism Centre is open daily from 9 a.m. to 6:30 p.m., closing at 4 p.m. in winter. Guided tours of Cambridge leave the center daily. In summer, aboard open-top double-decker buses, departures are every 15 minutes from 9 a.m. to 6 p.m. In winter, departures are hourly. The tour can be a one-hour panoramic ride, or you can get off at any of the many stops, such as King's College Chapel or the American Cemetery, then rejoin the tour when you wish. Tickets are valid all day for you to hop on and off the buses. The price of this tour is £3.50 ($6.15) per person.

CAMBRIDGE UNIVERSITY

Oxford University predates the one at Cambridge. But in the early 13th century, scholars began coming up to Cambridge. The choice of the market town as a seat of learning just happened, perhaps coming about because a core of important masters, dissatisfied with Oxford, elected to live near the fens. Eventually, Cambridge won partial recognition from Henry III, rising and slumping with the approval or disdain of subsequent English monarchs. In all, the University of Cambridge consists of 29 colleges. But if you have time for only one sight, then make it:

King's College Chapel

The teenage Henry VI founded the college on King's Parade in 1441. But most of its buildings today are from the 19th century. The Perpendicular chapel is not only its crowning glory but one of the architectural gems in England inherited from the Middle Ages. The chapel, owing to the altogether chaotic vicissitudes of English kings, wasn't completed until the early years of the 16th century. Its most characteristic features are its magnificent fan vaulting, all of stone, and its Great Windows, most of which were fashioned by Flemish artisans between 1515 and 1531 (the West Window, however, dates from the late Victorian period). The stained glass, in hues of blues, reds, and ambers, reflects biblical stories. The long range of the windows, reading from the first on the north side at the west end, right around the chapel back to the first on the south side, tell the story of the birth of the Virgin, the Annunciation, the Birth of Christ, the Life, Ministry, and Death of Christ, the Res-

CAMBRIDGE

KEY TO NUMBERED SIGHTS

1. Jesus College
2. Magdalen College
3. St. John's College
4. Trinity College
5. Sidney Sussex College
6. Christ's College
7. Clare College
8. King's College
9. Corpus Christi College
10. Emmanuel College
11. Selwyn College
12. Peterhouse College
13. Pembroke College
14. Downing College
15. Newnham College

urrection, the Ascension, the Acts of the Apostles, and the Assumption. The upper range contains Old Testament parallels to the New Testament stories—that is, the logic of the windows derives from the story of Christ. The rood screen is from the early 16th century. Henry James called King's College Chapel "the most beautiful in England."

It is open during vacation time Monday to Saturday from 9:30 a.m. to 5 p.m., and on Sunday from 10:30 a.m. to 5 p.m. During term time, the public is welcome to attend choral services, which are at 5:30 p.m. Monday to Saturday (service said on Monday) and at 10:30 a.m. and 3:30 p.m. on Sunday. In term the chapel is open to visitors from 9:30 a.m. to 3:45 p.m. on weekdays, from 2 to 3 p.m. and from the end of evensong (approximately 4:30) to 5:45 p.m. on Sunday. The chapel may be closed at other times of the year for special events. It is closed December 26 to January 4.

There is an exhibition in the seven northern side-chapels, showing why and how King's College Chapel was built. Admission to the exhibition is £1 ($1.75) for adults, 50p (90¢) for children.

Peterhouse

This college on Trumpington Street is visited largely because it is the oldest seat of learning at Cambridge, having been founded as early as 1284. The founding father was Hugo de Balsham, bishop of Ely. Of the original buildings, only the Hall remains. This was restored in the 19th century and now contains stained-glass windows by William Morris. Old Court was constructed in the 15th century but was refaced in 1754, and the Chapel dates from 1632. Parties of not more than 12 at a time may visit the college between 1 and 5 p.m. Ask at the porter's lodge.

Trinity College

On Trinity Street, Trinity College, the largest at Cambridge (not to be confused with Trinity Hall), was founded in 1546 by Henry VIII from a number of smaller colleges that had existed on the site. The Great Court is the most spacious court in Cambridge, built when Thomas Nevile was master. Sir Christopher Wren designed the Library. This college has Sir Isaac Newton, Lord Byron, and Prince Charles among its former students. For admission to the college, apply at the porter's lodge or telephone 0223/358201 for information.

Emmanuel College

On St. Andrew's Street, Emmanuel (tel. 0223/334200) was founded in 1584 by Sir Walter Mildmay, a chancellor of the exchequer to Elizabeth I. It is of interest at least to Harvard students, as John Harvard, founder of that university, studied here. With its attractive gardens, it makes for a good stroll. You might even visit the Chapel designed by Sir Christopher Wren and consecrated in 1677. Both the Chapel and college are open daily from 9:30 a.m. to 12:15 p.m. and 2 to 6 p.m.

Queens' College

On Queens' Lane, Queens' College (tel. 0223/335511) is considered by some old Cantabrigians as the loveliest in the architectural galaxy. Dating back to 1448, it was founded, then refounded, by two English queens—one the wife of Henry VI, the other the wife of Edward IV. Its second cloister is the most interesting, flanked by the half-timbered President's Lodge, dating from the first half of the 16th century. The college may be visited during the day from mid-March to mid-October. An admission fee of 40p (70¢) is charged and a short printed guide issued. Normally, individual visitors are admitted only from 1:45 to 4:30 p.m. daily, but during July, August, and September the college is also open to visitors from 10:15 a.m. to 12:45 p.m. daily. Entry and exit is by the Old Porters' Lodge in Queens' Lane only. The college is closed between mid-May and mid-June. The Old Hall and Chapel are normally open to the public when not in use.

St. John's College

On St. John's Street, this college was founded in 1511 by Lady Margaret, mother of Henry VIII. A few years earlier she had founded Christ's College. Before her intervention, an old monk-run hospital had stood on the site of St. John's. The impressive gateway bears the Tudor coat-of-arms, and Second Court is a fine example of late Tudor brickwork. But its best-known feature is the Bridge of Sighs, crossing the Cam, built as late as the 19th century and patterned after the bridge in Venice. It connects the older part of the college with New Court, a Gothic revival on the opposite bank from which there is an outstanding view of the famous Backs. Wordsworth was an alumnus of this college. The Bridge of Sighs is closed to visitors, but it can be viewed from the neighboring Wren Bridge. The Chapel is open from 9 a.m. to 4 p.m. Monday to Friday, and from 9 a.m. to noon Saturday. On Sunday, the Chapel is open to visitors attending the choral service. The college is closed to visitors from late April until late June.

Other College Sights

The preceding form only a representative selection of some of the more interesting-to-visit colleges. **Magdalene College** on Magdalene Street was founded in 1542; **Pembroke College** on Trumpington Street was founded in 1347; **Christ's College** on St. Andrew's Street was founded in 1505; and **Corpus Christi College** on Trumpington Street dates from 1352. Only someone planning to anchor in Cambridge for a long time will get around to them. Magdalene is open daily from 9 a.m. to 6:30 p.m.; Pembroke, daily till dusk; Christ's College, Monday to Saturday. For Corpus Christi times, inquire at the porter's lodge.

Colleges aren't the only thing to see in Cambridge, as you'll assuredly agree if you explore the following attractions:

THE FITZWILLIAM MUSEUM

On Trumpington Street, near Peterhouse, this museum (tel. 0223/332900) was the gift of the Viscount Fitzwilliam, who in 1816 gave Cambridge University his paintings and rare books, along with £100,000 to build the house in which to display them. He thereby knowingly or unknowingly immortalized himself. Other gifts have since been bequeathed to the museum, and now it is one of the finest in England. It is noted for its porcelain, old prints, archeological relics, and oils (works by such masters as Titian and Veronese). The museum is open Monday to Saturday from 10 a.m. to 5 p.m. and on Sunday from 2:15 till 5 p.m. However, only half of the exhibits are open in the morning, the other half in the afternoon, owing to the lack of staff. It is closed Monday, Good Friday, and December 24 to January 1, inclusive. Admission is free.

GREAT ST. MARY'S

Great St. Mary's (tel. 0223/350914), opposite King's College Chapel on King's Parade, is the university church. It is built on the site of an 11th-century church, but the present building dates largely from 1478. It was closely associated with events of the Reformation. The cloth that covered the hearse of King Henry VII is on display in the church. A fine view of Cambridge may be obtained from the top of the tower. Admission to the top of the church tower is 50p (90¢) for adults, 20p (35¢) for children.

BOAT RENTALS

Punting on the Cam (this has nothing to do with football) is a traditional pursuit of students and visitors in Cambridge, but there are other types of boating available if you don't trust yourself to stand up and pole a punt under and around the weeping willow trees. Upriver, you can go all the way to Grantchester, a distance of about 2 miles, made famous by Rupert Brooke. Downstream, you pass along the Backs behind the colleges of the university.

Scudamore's Boatyards, Granta Place (tel. 0223/359750), by the Anchor Pub, has been in business since 1910. All craft rent for £4 ($7) per hour, including punts, canoes, and rowboats. A £30 ($52.50) deposit, payable with cash or credit card, is required. There is a maximum of six persons per punt. Also offered is a chauffeured punt where a moonlighting student, dressed in a traditional punter's costume, rows you past the back view of several historic buildings, lecturing as he rows. The cost of this 45-minute guided tour is £3 ($5.25) per person.

BICYCLE RENTALS

The most popular way of getting around in Cambridge, next to walking, is bicycling. **Geoff's Bike Hire,** 65 Devonshire Rd. (tel. 0223/65629), has bicycles for rent for £3 ($5.25) per day or £8 ($14) per week. A deposit of £15 ($26.25) is required.

PERSONALIZED TOURS

The person to know if you're in the Cambridge area is Mrs. Isobel Bryant, who operates **Heritage Tours** from her 200-year-old cottage, Manor Cottage, Swaffham Prior (tel. 0638/741440). A highly qualified expert on the region, she will arrange tours starting from your hotel or Cambridge Railway Station to, for instance, Lavenham with its thatched and timbered houses, to the fine medieval churches of the Suffolk villages, to Ely Cathedral, and to one of the grand mansions nearby with their many treasures. The charge of £65 ($113.75) for the day covers up to three passengers and all travel expenses, including the services of the driver/guide. Lunch in a village pub and admission fees add £4 ($7) per person.

Mrs. Bryant can also arrange accommodation with local families in their country houses. The charges range from £28 ($49) to £50 ($87.50) for two persons per night in double rooms with private bath, these tariffs including a full English breakfast. Often dinner can be arranged at around £10 ($17.50) per person, including wine. Rooms without private bath rent from £12 ($21) per person.

There are also walking tours around the colleges of Cambridge, costing £18 ($31.50) for a family-size party and lasting about two hours. There is a fascinating trip to Newmarket, headquarters of the horse racing industry. That tour includes getting to watch training gallops, a visit to the Racing Museum or a stud stable, seeing the bloodstock-sales center, and being shown the Jockey Club. For a group of 12 or more persons, a whole-day tour costs £12 ($21) per person, a half-day tour going for £7 ($12.25) per person. A shorter tour can be arranged for individuals or a family group. If you want lunch at a private manor house with Cordon Bleu cooking, the cost will be £8.50 ($14.90) per person, with wine included, for groups of 12 or more. All prices include VAT.

ACCOMMODATIONS

During vacation periods, there are some 1000 rooms available for tourists that are used by students in term time. The **Tourist Office** (tel. 0223/322640), on Wheeler Street, opposite the Arts Theatre and behind the Guildhall on Market Place, will give you information on available accommodations through their booking service, charging £1 ($1.75) per person for finding a room in or around Cambridge. If you have no reservation and want to try it on your own, check your luggage at the train station and go to the beginning of Chesterton Road, knocking on front doors as you proceed.

I'll survey the pick of B&B lodgings scattered around the city.

Regent Hotel, 41 Regent St., Cambridge, Cambridgeshire CB2 1AB (tel.

0223/351470), reopened in 1985 to receive paying guests in its 19 attractive and comfortably furnished bedrooms, 14 of which contain private baths. All units have a color TV and radio. Only breakfast is served, but there's a cocktail bar on the street level. It's one of the nicest of the moderately priced small hotels of Cambridge. Depending on the plumbing, singles cost £24 ($42) to £33 ($57.75), daily, doubles or twins £35 ($61.25) to £45 ($78.75). Right in the city center, overlooking Parker's Piece, the house was built in the 1840s as the original site of Newham College. When the college outgrew its physical plant, the building became a hotel.

Ashley Hotel, 74 Chesterton Rd., Cambridge, Cambridgeshire CB4 1ER (tel. 0223/350059), is one of the best B&Bs in Cambridge. However, it rents only 10 rooms, so reserve early if you wish to stay here. Accommodations cost £18.50 ($32.40) daily in a single, £32 ($56)in a twin or double. It is within walking distance of the center of the university town and the colleges, lying near the River Cam and Jesus Green. While saving on room costs, guests of the Ashley can use the dining and drinking facilities of the nearby Arundel House Hotel at 53 Chesterton Rd.

Helen Hotel, 167-169 Hills Rd., Cambridge, Cambridgeshire CB2 2RJ (tel. 0223/246465), run by Gino and Helen (its namesake) Agodino, lies about a mile from the center of the university town. It's much bigger than most hotels considered in this section, containing a total of 29 well-furnished bedrooms. All have private showers, and 25 have toilets also. Accommodations contain phones and color TV as well. The single rate is £26 ($45.50) daily, a double or twin going for £40 ($70). The hotel has many amenities, including a pleasant garden along with a TV lounge and cocktail bar. You can also order dinner here for £10 ($15), the cooking a mixture of British and continental fare.

The Suffolk House Hotel, 69 Milton Rd., Cambridge, Cambridgeshire CB4 1XA (tel. 0223/352016), was once the home of a well-known local doctor, but it has long since been turned into one of the more winning B&Bs in Cambridge. This privately run licensed hotel stands a bit on the outskirts, but it is only about a 15-minute stroll to the heart of the colleges. In the back of this detached house there is a garden, and the location is peaceful. There are ten well-furnished bedrooms, six of which have a private shower. Guests are charged from £21 ($36.75) to £29 ($50.75) nightly, with doubles costing from £33 ($57.75) to £46 ($80.50). Nonsmokers may reserve a table for the well-prepared dinners served each night.

Fairways, 141-142 Cherry Hinton Rd., Cambridge, Cambridgeshire CB1 4BX (tel. 0223/246063), lies about a mile and a half from the heart of Cambridge. This handsomely restored Victorian-era house has 14 well-furnished and comfortable bedrooms, six of which contain a private bath. A trio of these accommodations are often rented as family rooms. B&B overnight rates range from £16 ($28) to £21 ($36.75) in a single, going up to £27 ($47.25) to £31 ($54.25) in a double. Rooms have extra amenities, such as beverage-making equipment and color TV. Guests meet in the lounge and seem to appreciate the locked car park at the rear of the house.

The Lensfield Hotel, 53 Lensfield Rd., Cambridge, Cambridgeshire CR2 1EN (tel. 0223/355017), has been acclaimed by some readers as "the best B&B hotel in the area." Actually more than a B&B, it has many of the amenities of a well-run small-town hotel. Within easy access to the colleges and the Cam River, it rents a total of 30 comfortably appointed bedrooms, 20 of which contain private baths or showers. Charges range from £26 ($45.50) to £34 ($59.50) daily for a single and from £41 ($71.75) to £43 ($75.25) for a double, a splurge many visitors find worthwhile. Other amenities in the rooms include radio, direct-dial phone, and TV. The hotel also has a good restaurant and a cozy bar, serving home-cooked meals often made of local produce.

Number Eleven, 11 Glisson Rd., Cambridge, Cambridgeshire CB1 2HA (tel. 0223/311890), is small but choice. Lying close to the heart of Cambridge, this 19th-century town house offers rather upmarket, well-decorated bedrooms that normally are found only in better hotels, and the breakfasts are substantial. The cost of a single ranges from £20 ($35) to £22 ($38.50), with doubles costing £28 ($49) to £32 ($56) daily. One room is suitable for families. Evening meals can also be arranged.

Dresden Villa Guest House, 34 Cherry Hinton Rd., Cambridge, Cambridgeshire CB1 4AA (tel. 0223/247539), has an Edwardian-era painted facade pierced with a quartet of sunny bay windows. Within a ten-minute walk of the Cambridge Railway Station, it is owned by the Ruggiero family, who came here many years ago from a village near Sorrento, Italy. The house contains eight comfortably furnished bedrooms, six of which offer a private shower and toilet. English or Italian fixed-course meals can be arranged in the evening for £7.50 ($13.15) per person. With breakfast and VAT included, the guesthouse charges from £16 ($28) nightly for a single, going up to £26 ($45.50) to £30 ($52.50) for a double- or twin-bedded room. The location is about 1¼ miles south of the Market Square in Cambridge.

Parkside Guest House, 25 Parkside, Cambridge, Cambridgeshire CB1 1JB (tel. 0223/311212), is one of the better guesthouses. This well-preserved, 1850 building in the city center has 11 rooms, each with its own phone, costing from £19.50 ($34.15) to £22 ($38.50) per person nightly (the higher price for a unit that has a private shower). A full breakfast and all taxes are included in the price. Packed lunches, snacks, and dinners are available on request. Adjacent to the dining room is a guest lounge and bar with reference books about the city and university. Laundry facilities are available.

Mr. and Mrs. D. Griffiths, 51 Jesus Lane, Cambridge, Cambridgeshire (tel. 0223/66801), welcome you into their home, charging £10 ($17.50) per person nightly for B&B. They offer clean, comfortable rooms with convenient facilities. Although accommodation is limited during university terms, a room is always kept for transient guests.

The **Suffolk House Hotel,** 69 Milton Rd., Cambridge, Cambridgeshire CB4 1XA (tel. 0223/352016), was built as the home of a well-known Cambridge doctor, but it has been converted into a contemporary private hotel with many modern conveniences. Most rooms have private baths, and all have outlets for electric razors, tea- and coffee-makers, color TV, and central heat. Singles rent for £26 ($45.50) nightly for B&B. Doubles go for £32 ($56) to £50 ($87.50), the latter for a room with a private bath. Children up to 10 sharing a double with their parents are charged £10 ($17.50). The helpful hosts will offer you their garden in the summer for tea or coffee.

The **Bridge Guest House,** 151-153 Hills Rd., Cambridge, Cambridgeshire CB2 2RJ (tel. 0223/247942), stands a mile south of the city center. It is composed of a pair of adjacent houses with a modern extension fitted onto the back. The 20 bedrooms, each with a private bath or shower, rent for £18 ($31.50) daily in a single and £30 ($52.52) in a double, with breakfast included. A fixed-price dinner is offered for £7.50 ($13.15) at this fully licensed house.

Miss M. A. Sampson, 7 Malcolm St., Cambridge, Cambridgeshire CB1 1LL (tel. 0223/353069), can accommodate tourists only when her university students go on vacation: that is, from mid-June till mid-September. Her home is a convenient place at which to stay in the center of Cambridge, just off Jesus Lane. Her B&B rate ranges from £10 ($17.50) per person nightly and you'll be nestling down at one of the finest lodging choices on this street.

Dykelands Guest House, 157 Mowbray Rd., Cambridge, Cambridgeshire CB1 4SP (tel. 0223/244300), is especially suited for travelers with small children. Built of red brick between the two world wars, this eight-room guesthouse lies on the south side of Cambridge, within a 30-minute walk of the center of town. It is most conveniently reached via buses 4, 44, or 197 from the center (ask to get off at Adkins Corner). An evening meal can be provided for £8 ($14). Rooms come with a wide variety of plumbing options, with singles costing from £18 ($31.50) to £22

($38.50) daily and doubles going for £28 ($49) to £32 ($56), with VAT and breakfast included.

WHERE TO EAT

Long a favorite at Oxford, **Browns,** 23 Trumpington St. (tel. 0223/461655), is now a sensation at Cambridge. Fronted with a neoclassical colonnade, it has all the grandeur of the Edwardian era. It was actually built in 1914 as the outpatient department of a hospital dedicated to Edward VII. Today it is the most lighthearted place for dining in the university city, with wicker chairs, high ceilings, pre–World War I woodwork, and a long bar laden with bottles of wine. Hours are Monday to Saturday from 11 a.m. to 11:30 p.m. (on Sunday from noon to 11:30 p.m.). The long bill of fare includes various renditions of spaghetti, fresh salads (even Mrs. Brown's vegetarian), several selections of meat and fish (from charcoal-grilled leg of lamb with rosemary to fresh fish in season), hot sandwiches, and the chef's daily specials posted on a blackboard. Meals range from £6 ($10.50) to £15 ($26.25). If you drop by in the afternoon, you can also order thick ice cream milk shakes or pure fruit juices.

At **Varsity Restaurant,** 35 St. Andrew's St. (tel. 0223/356060), the Greek dishes offered are eaten in a bare whitewashed room with black beams and pictures of boats and islands on the walls. Kebabs are served with rice and salad, and there are other Greek dishes, along with some continental ones for less adventurous palates. A meal, including a glass of wine and coffee, will cost about £6 ($10.50). Service is fast and cheerful, and hours are from noon to 3 p.m. and 5:30 to 11 p.m. daily.

Hobbs Pavilion, Park Terrace (tel. 0223/67480), opens onto Parker's Piece in the vicinity of the University Arms Hotel. A delightful place and deservedly popular, it is called "a crêperie with a difference" and is located in an historic brick-built Cricket Pavilion. You get a choice of nearly two dozen crêpes, both for a main course and as a dessert. The stuffings range from smoked haddock with egg to curried chicken. This savory list is backed up by a selection of freshly prepared soups and salads. Meals cost from £6 ($10.50) and up, and hours are Tuesday to Saturday, from noon to 2:30 p.m. and 7 to 10 p.m. (on Thursday it doesn't open until 8:30 p.m. for dinner). It is closed on Sunday and Monday and takes a vacation from mid-August to mid-September.

Shao Tao, 72 Regent St. (tel. 0223/353942), on a commercial street right near the center of town, is a specialist in the cuisine of Canton, Szechuan, and Peking. The menu, served in a choice of two inviting rooms, presents a wide array of dishes, including "three kinds of meat" soup, followed with beef with orange sauce and a host of other dishes. But if you're confused, you can order the "leave it to us feast" at £9.50 ($16.65) per person, and you are likely to be happily surprised. Hours are daily from noon to 2:30 p.m. and 6 to 11 p.m. (until 11:30 p.m. on Friday and Saturday).

Free Press, 7-9 Prospect Row (tel. 0223/68337), is a small back-street Victorian pub that is reputed to offer some of the best grub in town. After sampling its fare, I agree. Costing from £7 ($12.25), meals are served seven days a week from noon to 2 p.m. and 6 to 9 p.m. You get a good range of food here, freshly made soups, flavorsome meat pies, and a hot chef's special of the day, such as moussaka as well as some vegetarian meals. It's self-service, and the two outside tables go quickly in summer. Desserts are homemade and tempting as well. You can come back in the evening for a pint any time from 6 to 11:30 p.m. (until 10:30 p.m. on Sunday).

The Anchor, Silver Street (tel. 0223/353554), right beside the Silver Street Bridge, has a bar and terrace right on the banks of the River Cam. The Café Bar is open daily from 10 a.m. in summer, offering pastries and snacks with morning coffee, a selection of salads at lunch, and English teas in the afternoon. A single-course hot meal costs £2.70 ($4.75), with snacks tallying up at £1 ($1.75). The Riverview Saloon Bar, another popular place for drinks, opens at 11 a.m. daily (at noon on Sunday), offering a full lunchtime menu, including grills. During licensing hours, which last until 11 p.m., both bars offer an excellent selection of traditional hand-pulled beers, continental lagers, and fine wines.

Martin's Coffee House, 4 Trumpington St. (tel. 0223/361757), is just past the Fitzwilliam Museum. It's a small coffeehouse but has high standards, offering some of the best filled sandwiches in Cambridge. Whole-meal rolls are filled with turkey, ham, beef, salad, cheese, and eggs for a mouth-filling snack. Homemade cakes and doughnuts are also sold. You can have steak-and-kidney pie and two vegetables, as well as casseroles, curries, pâtés, and omelets. Meals cost from £4 ($7). All marketing is done daily so everything is fresh and wholesome. The place is open from 8:30 a.m. to 7:30 p.m. Monday to Friday, from 9 a.m. to 5:30 p.m. Saturday, and from 10 a.m. to 5:30 p.m. Sunday.

Pentagon and **Roof Garden,** 6 St. Edwards Passage (tel. 0223/355246), is in the center of Cambridge, overlooking medieval cottages and the historic churchyard. Cold buffet meals and four hot specialties are served daily at the Pentagon, with meals costing from £8.50 ($14.90). There is a fine wine list and fully licensed bar. Connected to and run by the Arts Theatre, the restaurant has a strong artistic atmosphere and is patronized by many stars of the English stage. It's open for lunch Monday to Saturday from noon to 3 p.m. and for supper from 6 to 10:30 p.m. The Roof Garden, perched above the theater, is popular in summer as it offers al fresco meals, self-service lunch, afternoon tea, and supper, with a view of the Cambridge spires. You select from an array of hot and cold buffet dishes, with meals averaging around £6 ($10.50). Wines are available by the glass, and there's a fully licensed bar. Local artists exhibit their work here. The Roof Garden is open Monday to Saturday from 9:30 a.m. to 8 p.m.

ENTERTAINMENT

An outstanding attraction in Cambridge is the **Arts Theatre,** adjacent to the city center and the Tourist Information Office and fitted into a maze of lodging houses and shops. It provides Cambridge and the surrounding area with its most important theatrical events. Almost all of the leading stars of the British stage have performed here at one time or another. Call 0223/352000 to find out what's playing. Seats for most productions are £7 ($12.25) to £7.50 ($13.15).

Cambridge Arms, 4 King St. (tel. 0223/359650), is a popular student haunt in the center of town. The place has plenty of atmosphere and doesn't neglect its food in favor of dispensing beer and ale. In fact, it has good lunchtime meals, including pâté as an appetizer and the chef's daily specials, such as grilled steaks and cold buffet dishes. Meals cost from £5 ($8.75) and hours are from 11 a.m. to 11 p.m. Monday to Saturday, and from noon to 3 p.m. and 7 to 10:30 p.m. Sunday. Jazz is a feature on Sunday through Tuesday nights. Ever played a game of shove-ha'penny?

Perhaps the most popular pub outing you can take from Cambridge is to the hamlet of Grantchester, lying two miles from the university city and reached by taking the A603. One of the most beautiful villages in the shire, Grantchester has an old church and gardens leading down to water meadows. It was made famous by Rupert Brooke, the famed pre–World War I English poet, who is best known today for his sonnet, *The Soldier.* He was a charming and romantic character, and his life, which ended prematurely in 1915, has inspired many books. Even if you've never heard of Brooke, you may enjoy spending a late afternoon here, wandering through the old church and then heading, as everybody does, including Cambridge students and their professors, to **The Green Man,** 59 High St., Grantchester (tel. 0223/841178), a coaching inn with a history of some four and a half centuries. On a winter's night, the mellow old pub welcomes you with an open fire. But in summer you may want to retreat to the beer garden in back, and from there you can stroll down to the river. If you're in Grantchester at lunch, you can enjoy a good spread, including fresh salads, pâtés, English cheese, and desserts, with filling meals costing from £5 ($8.75). Hours are from 11 a.m. to 2:30 p.m. and 6 to 11 p.m. Monday to Saturday, and from noon to 3 p.m. and 7 to 10:30 p.m. Sunday.

2. Ely

The top attraction in the fen country, outside of Cambridge, is **Ely Cathedral.** The small city of Ely lies 70 miles from London but only 16 miles north of Cambridge. Ely used to be known as the Isle of Ely, until the surrounding marshes and meres were drained, forcing the sea to recede. The last stronghold of Saxon England, Ely was defended by Hereward the Wake, until his capitulation to the Normans in 1071.

ELY CATHEDRAL

The near-legendary founder of the cathedral was Etheldreda, the wife of a Northumbrian king, who established a monastery on the spot in 673. But the present structure dates from 1083. Seen for miles around, the landmark octagonal lantern tower is the crowning glory of the cathedral. A remarkable engineering achievement, it was erected in 1322, following the collapse of the old tower. Four hundred tons of lead and wood hang in space, held there by timbers reaching to the eight pillars.

You enter the cathedral through the beautiful Galilee West Door, a good representation of the Early English style of architecture. The already-mentioned lantern tower and the Octagon are the most notable features inside, but don't fail to visit the Lady Chapel. Although this has lost much of its decoration over the centuries, it still is a handsome example of the Decorated style, having been completed in the mid-14th century. The cathedral is open daily from 7 a.m. to 7 p.m. in summer, and from 7:30 a.m. to 5 p.m. daily in winter. Visitors are asked to make a donation of £2 ($3.50) to help save the cathedral from ruin. The refectory and shop are open daily. For information, telephone 0353/667735).

FOOD AND LODGING

In a quiet residential section of Ely, **Nyton Guest House,** 7 Barton Rd., Ely, Cambridgeshire CB7 4HZ (tel. 0353/662459), is an attractive twin-gabled house surrounded by a two-acre flower garden with lawn and trees. Additional beauty is gained from the adjoining 18-hole golf course (on which reduced greens fees are available) with uninterrupted views over a wide area of fenland. The house is licensed for alcoholic drinks. B&B is provided, a double room costing £33 ($57.75) daily, and a single going for £23 ($40.25). Each bedroom has a private bath, hot beverage facilities, and a clock radio-alarm. Barton Road is easily accessible from the cathedral and railway station. It's on the A142 Ely-Newmarket road, off the A10 Ely road.

The Old Fire Engine House, St. Mary's Street (tel. 0353/662582), opposite St. Mary's Church, is one of the finer restaurants in East Anglia, worth a detour. It enjoys an interesting setting in a walled garden, in a complex of buildings with an art gallery. The restaurant was converted from a fire station. All the good English cooking is the result of the staff, who really care about food preparation. The ingredients are all fresh. Soups are served in huge bowls, and accompanying them is a coarse-grained crusty bread. Main dishes include duck with orange sauce, jugged hare, steak-and-kidney pie, baked stuffed pike, casserole of rabbit, and pigeon with bacon and black olives. Desserts include fruit pie and cream, although I'd recommend the syllabub. A meal costs from £12 ($21). In summer, you can dine outside in the garden, and even order a cream tea. It's open Monday to Saturday from 10:30 a.m. to 5:30 p.m. and 7:30 to 9 p.m. (last entry), and on Sunday from 12:30 to 5 p.m. Do try for a table if you're just passing, but this place is quite popular with locals and people coming out from Cambridge, especially on weekends, so it's better to make a reservation.

A TOUR TO GRIME'S GRAVES

On the B1108, off the main A1065 from Swaffham to Mildenhall Road east of Ely, you can visit Grime's Graves (tel. 0842/810656), three miles northeast of Brandon (Norfolkshire). This is well worth the short detour, as it is the largest group of Neolithic flint mines in the country. This is fir-wooded country with little population, and it's easy to imagine yourself transported back to ancient times.

The mines are well signposted, and you soon find yourself at a small parking lot presided over by a custodian who will open up one or several of the shafts, allowing you to enter ancient Britain.

Climb down the ladder of the pit and imagine what must have been going on even before the time of the Anglo-Saxons. Restoration has been carried out during the intervening years, and it is now possible to see where work took place and, if you're lucky, you may find a worked flint of your own to present to the custodian. It's best to have a flashlight handy. The climb down is perpendicular, so it's only for the stouthearted.

The mines are close to the air force bases so well known to countless American air crews during World War II. Hours are from 10 a.m. to 6 p.m. daily from Good Friday to September 30, and from 10 a.m. to 4 p.m. off-season; closed Monday. Admission is 80p ($1.40) for adults, 40p (70¢) for children.

AN AIRCRAFT MUSEUM

Part of the **Imperial War Museum** (tel. 0223/833963) is housed at Duxford Airfield on the A505 Newmarket-Royston road, a former Battle of Britain station and the U.S. Eighth Air Force base in World War II. In hangars that date from World War I, you'll find a huge collection of historic civil and military aircraft from both world wars, including the only B-29 Superfortress in Europe. Other exhibits include midget submarines, tanks, and a variety of field artillery pieces, as well as a special historical display on the U.S. Eighth Air Force.

The museum is open daily from 10:30 a.m. to 5:30 p.m. (or dusk if earlier) from mid-March to early November, and from 10:30 a.m. to 3:45 p.m. the remainder of the year. It is closed Christmas and New Year's Day. Admission is £3.50 ($6.15) for adults and £1.80 ($3.15) for children in summer, £2.50 ($4.40) for adults and £1.25 ($2.20) for children in winter. Special charges are made for special events. Parking is free.

ESSEX

Even though it borders London and is industrialized in places, Essex still contains unspoiled rural areas and villages. Most motorists pass through it on the way to Cambridge. What they find, after leaving Greater London, is a land of rolling fields. In the east are many seaside towns and villages, as Essex opens onto the North Sea.

The major city is Colchester in the east, known today for its oysters and roses. Fifty miles from London, it was the first Roman city in Britain, the oldest recorded town in the kingdom. It's a rather dull-appearing city today, although parts of its Roman fortifications remain. A Norman castle has been turned into a museum containing a fine collection of artifacts from Roman Britain. Among the former residents of Colchester were King Cole, immortalized in the nursery rhyme, and Cunobelinus, the warrior king known to Shakespearean scholars as "Cymbeline."

However, Colchester is not in the pathway of most visitors, so I have concentrated instead on three tiny villages in the western part of Essex—Saffron Walden, Thaxted, and Finchingfield, all three representative of the best of the shire. You can explore all of them quite easily on your way to Cambridge or on your return trip to

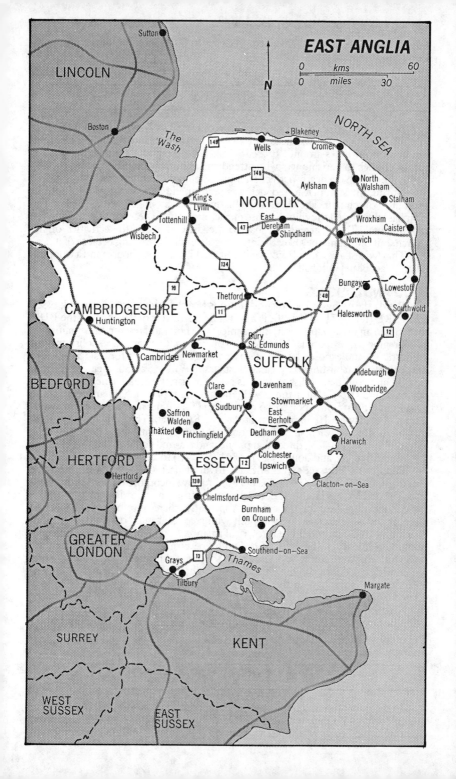

London. Roughly, they lie anywhere from 25 to 30 miles south of the university city.

3. Thaxted

Some 43 miles north of London, the Saxon town of Thaxted is set on the crest of a hill. It contains the most beautiful small church in England, whose graceful spire can be seen for miles around. Its bells are heard throughout the day, ringing out special chimes to parishioners who attend their church seriously. Dating back to 1340, the church is a nearly perfect example of religious architecture.

During the summer, folk dancing is performed by the townspeople, both in and out of the church. The London Philharmonic Orchestra comes up to play. The vicar has encouraged the church to use music, and you can hear both the old and the experimental. The denizens of Thaxted are divided about the activities of the church, but one thing they like: their town is alive and flourishing because of it.

Thaxted also has a number of well-preserved Elizabethan houses and a wooden-pillared Jacobean Guildhall.

FOOD AND LODGING

Beside the highway, the **Fox and Hounds Hotel,** Walden Road, Thaxted, Essex CM6 2RE (tel. 0371/830129), is a half mile northwest of Thaxted on the B184 road. Set in an isolated position, this comfortable hotel and restaurant contains one of the region's most popular bars. With an open brick-lined fireplace, polished brass knickknacks, and exposed beams, it serves as a gathering place for residents before they enter the establishment's pleasant restaurant. A £14 ($24.50) menu offers both English and continental dishes, such as pork Stroganoff, steak Diane, and steak au poivre. There's a tasty bar menu as well, including a variety of homemade pies. The restaurant is open from noon to 2 p.m. daily and for dinner from 7 to 10 p.m. Monday to Thursday (to 10:30 p.m. on Friday and Saturday). The hotel has nine comfortable bedrooms, each suitable for one or two occupants and equipped with a private shower, color TV, direct-dial phone, and tea- and coffee-maker. Singles cost £34 ($59.50) daily, and doubles go for £41 ($71.75) to £45 ($78.75).

Recorder's House Restaurant, 17 Town St. (tel. 0371/830438), near the Guildhall, was built in 1450 and is believed to have incorporated part of the medieval Thaxted Manor House. It derived its name from the recorder who used to live there, collecting taxes for the crown. Apparently, there were objections to these taxes, as the winding staircase was built with steps that pitch outward, so that an attacking swordsman would be thrown off balance. As you dine in front of an inglenook fireplace (where Edward IV did when he brought his queen here for their honeymoon), you'll surely be pleased with the linenfold paneling, the carefully preserved wide oak floors, and the candlelight at night. The food, reflecting a continental influence, is the best in the area. At luncheon, a three-course table d'hôte is offered from 12:30 to 2:30 p.m. for an inclusive price of £10.50 ($18.40). Dinner, from 7 to 9:30 p.m., includes fine steaks and seafood cooked on the charcoal broiler. Prices begin at £17.50 ($30.65) for a four-course meal. Specials could include roast haunch of venison.

4. Saffron Walden

In the northwestern corner of Essex, a short drive from Thaxted, is the ancient market town of Walden, renamed Saffron Walden because of the fields of autumn crocus that used to grow around it. It lies only 44 miles from London. Some residents of Cambridge, 15 miles to the north, escape to this old borough for their weekends.

One mile west of Saffron Walden (B1383 road) is **Audley End House** (tel. 0799/22842), considered one of the finest mansions in all of East Anglia. This Jacobean estate was built in 1603 by Sir Thomas Howard, treasurer to the king, on the foundation of a monastery. James I is reported to have said, "Audley End is too large for a king, though it might do for a Lord Treasurer." The house has many outstanding features, including an impressive Great Hall at whose north end is a screen dating from the early 17th century, considered one of the most ornamental in England. Rooms decorated by Robert Adam contain fine furniture and works of art. A "Gothick" chapel and a charming Victorian ladies' sitting room are among the other attractions. The park surrounding the house was landscaped by Capability Brown. It has a lovely rose garden, a river, and a cascade. In the stables built at the same time as the mansion is a collection of agricultural machinery, a Victorian coach, old wagons, and the estate fire engine. It's all open from Friday to the end of September daily from 1 to 6 p.m. for an admission of £2.50 ($4.40) for adults, £1.50 ($2.65) for children. The grounds are open from noon to 7 p.m.

Many of the houses in Saffron Walden are distinctive in England, in that the 16th- and 17th-century builders faced their houses with parget, a kind of plasterwork (sometimes made with cow dung) used for ornamental facades.

While Saffron Walden innkeepers charge fairly high prices, at least the buildings are romantic.

FOOD AND LODGING

Opposite the post office, **Cross Keys Hotel,** The High, Saffron Walden, Essex CB10 1AX (tel. 0799/22207), is a museum piece of black and white architecture built in 1449. Inside this pub hotel is an inglenook fireplace with a priest hole (a hiding place for fleeing priests). There are six renovated bedrooms, ranging in price from £35 ($61.25) to £55 ($96.25) per room, either single or double occupancy, with breakfast and tax included. The pub is open from 11 a.m. to 3 p.m. and 6 to 11 p.m. Monday to Saturday (noon to 3 p.m. and 7 to 10:30 p.m. on Sunday).

Eight Bells, 18 Bridge St., Saffron Walden, Essex, CB10 1BU (tel. 0799/22790), is right outside the center of Saffron Walden on the B184 in the direction of Cambridge. This black-and-white timbered Tudor building is both a restaurant and pub, the most frequented in town (Cambridge students often visit it). You can enjoy well-prepared meals here from noon to 2:30 p.m. and 6 to 9:30 p.m. Monday to Saturday and Sunday, noon to 1:45 p.m. and 7 to 9:30 p.m. For drinkers, however, the pub stays open until 11 p.m. Fresh fish is brought in and prepared in proper ways in the kitchen, along with poultry and meat dishes. Meals cost from £7 ($12.25) and are served in the bar areas or else in a candlelit restaurant, which is a timbered hall with oak furniture. Children are allowed into the pub's family room and the restaurant. The Eight Bells also rents two comfortable bedrooms, costing £21 ($36.75) daily in a single, £33 ($57.75) in a double. The bedrooms rest under a beamed ceiling, and the occupants share the bath.

5. Finchingfield

This little village only a short drive east of Thaxted, puts in a serious claim for being the model village of England. Even though you may have another personal favorite, you still must admit it's like a dream, surrounded by the quiet life of the countryside. If you're staying in either Saffron Walden or Thaxted, you might want to motor over here. It makes for an interesting jaunt.

FOOD AND LODGING

A small, six-bedroom guesthouse, the **Manse,** Finchingfield, Essex CM7 4JX (tel. 0371/810306), overlooks the village pond in the center of this pretty village. All rooms have central heating, hot and cold running water, TV, tea- and coffee-makers, and outlets for electric shavers. The cost, including VAT and a full English breakfast, is £14 ($24.50) per person per night.

The **Fox Inn** (tel. 0371/810151) also stands near the edge of the pond on the village green. It's an attractive 200-year-old pub with an authentic parget (raised plaster) design on the facade. You can order bar meals here costing around £5 ($8.75). They are served daily from noon to 2 p.m. and 7 to 9:30 p.m. (however, only lunches are offered on Sunday). Pub hours are Monday to Saturday from 10:30 a.m. to 3 p.m. and 6 to 11 p.m. (on Sunday from noon to 3 p.m. and 7 to 10:30 p.m.).

6. Dedham

Remember Constable's *Vale of Dedham?* In this little Essex village on the Stour River, you're in the heart of Constable country. Flatford Mill is only a mile farther down the river. The village, with its Tudor, Georgian, and Regency houses, is set in the midst of the water meadows of the Stour. Constable immortalized its church and tower. Dedham is right on the Essex-Suffolk border and makes a good center for exploring both North Essex and the Suffolk border country.

In the village is **Castle House** (tel. 0206/322127), home of Sir Alfred Munnings, the president of the Royal Academy (1944–1949) and painter extraordinaire of racehorses and other animals. The house and studio contain sketches and other works and are open from May to October on Wednesday and Sunday from 2 to 5 p.m. (also Thursday and Saturday in August), charging adults an admission of £1.50 ($2.65); children pay 25p (45¢).

LODGING

A half mile from the village, **Upper Park,** Coles Oak Lane, Dedham, Colchester, Essex CO7 6DN (tel. 0206/323197), is where Miss G. F. L. Watson offers B&B in her attractive private home with fine views over Constable country. To reach the place, you pass Dedham Church on your left, driving through the village and up the hill. Some 200 yards from the top of the hill by a letter box on the corner, which is signposted Coles Oak Lane, turn right. Travel another 100 yards, and Upper Park will be the first house on the right. The charge for B&B is £17 ($29.75) daily in a bathless single, £14 ($24.50) per person in a bathless twin-bedded room, and £17 ($29.75) per person in a twin with bath.

Burn Cottage, Long Road, West Dedham, Colchester, Essex CO7 6EH (tel. 0206/322339), receives guests to Constable country from April to October. This B&B is small, only four bedrooms, but it's in a desirable location, and the accommodations are comfortable and homelike. Guests share the one public bath, and rates range from £9.50 ($16.65) daily in a single to £17 ($29.75) and up in a double. The owners are helpful to visitors.

SUFFOLK

The easternmost county of England, a link in the four-county chain of East Anglia, is a refuge for artists, just as it was in the day of its famous native sons, Constable and Gainsborough. Many of the Suffolk landscapes have ended up on canvas.

A fast train can make it to East Suffolk from London in approximately an hour and a half. Still, its fishing villages, dozens of flint churches, historic homes, and national monuments remain relatively unvisited by overseas visitors.

The major towns of Suffolk are Bury St. Edmunds, the capital of West Suffolk, and Ipswich in the east, a port city on the Orwell River. But to capture the true charm of Suffolk, you must explore its little market towns and villages. Beginning at the Essex border, we'll strike out toward the North Sea, highlighting the most scenic villages as we move easterly across the shire.

7. Newmarket

This old Suffolk town 62 miles from London has been famous as a racing center since the time of King James I. Visitors can see Nell Gwynne's House, but mainly they come to visit Britain's first and only **National Horseracing Museum,** 99 High St. (tel. 0638/667333). The museum is housed in the old subscription rooms, early 19th-century rooms used for placing and settling bets, where visitors can see the history of horse racing over a 300-year period. There are fine paintings of famous horses, pictures on loan from Queen Elizabeth II, and copies of old Parliamentary Acts governing races. There is also a replica of a weighing-in room, plus explanations of the signs used by the ticktack men who keep the on-course bookies informed of changes in the price of bets. A continuous 53-minute audio-visual presentation shows races and racehorses.

In order to make history come alive for the museum visitor, popular tours of this historic town are offered. You are taken by a guide to watch morning gallops on the heath, proceeding through the town where you'll see bronzes of stallions from the past and other points of interest. An optional tour of a famous training establishment is offered, plus a visit to the Jockey Club Rooms, known for a fine collection of paintings. Reservations are necessary, but the tour, which lasts a whole morning, is always available.

At a shop at the entrance you can choose from an interesting collection of small souvenirs, along with books, tankards, a Derby chart showing the male descent line of every winner of the celebrated race since 1780, and silk scarves with equine motifs. The museum is open from 10 a.m. to 5 p.m. Tuesday to Saturday, and from 2 to 5 p.m. Sunday. It is closed Monday, except bank holidays and in August. Admission is £1.60 ($2.80) for adults, 80p ($1.40) for children. The museum is closed from December to March, but those with a special interest in seeing it during those months can telephone.

The National Stud (tel. 0638/663464), lying beside Newmarket's July Race Course two miles southwest of the town, is *the* place for those who wish to see some of the world's finest horseflesh, as well as watching a working thoroughbred breeding stud in operation. A tour lasting about 1¼ hours lets you see many mares and foals, plus horses in training for racing. Tours are possible at 11:15 a.m. and 2:30 p.m. Monday to Friday, as well as at 11:15 a.m. Saturday, when there is racing in Newmarket during the racing season, April to September. Reservations for tours must be made at the National Stud office from 9 a.m. to 1 p.m. or 2 to 5 p.m. Monday to Friday, or by phoning the number given above. Admission is £2.50 ($4.40) for adults, £1.25 ($2.20) for children.

WHERE TO STAY AND EAT

A gabled historic inn, the **White Hart Hotel,** High Street, Newmarket, Suffolk CB8 8JP (tel. 0638/663051), rises three stories in the center of town, opposite the Horseracing Museum. It was constructed on the site of an inn dating from the 1600s. The 23 well-furnished hotel rooms and the bars are decorated with racing pictures and prints. All the accommodations are tastefully furnished (you might even get a four-poster bed), and each has a private bath, direct-dial phone, color TV, hairdryer, trouser-press, and tea- and coffee-maker. Its B&B singles rent for £45 ($78.75) daily, with doubles costing from £60 ($105). Bar snacks are available from noon to 2 p.m. and 7 to 9 p.m. daily, with various hot and cold dishes costing from £1.25 ($2.20). The restaurant offers both à la carte and table d'hôte dining. A set lunch goes for £7.50 ($13.15), a table d'hôte dinner costs from £9.50 ($14.90). It is open from noon to 2 p.m. and 7 to 9 p.m. Monday to Thursday. On Friday, Saturday, and Sunday, hours are the same at lunch, but it closes at 9:30 p.m. Friday and Saturday and at 8:30 p.m. Sunday.

Rutland Arms Hotel, High Street, Newmarket, Suffolk CB8 8NB (tel. 0638/664251), is an imposing Georgian coaching inn dating in part from the reign of Charles II. The hotel is at the clock end of the High Street. There are 45 rooms, large and comfortably furnished. Its B&B prices are £46 ($80.50) daily for a single with bath, £57.50 ($100.60) for a double, also with bath; service and VAT are included. A good three-course lunch, costing £8.50 ($14.90), is served from 12:30 to 2 p.m., and a set dinner for £9 ($15.75) is available from 7 to 9:30 p.m.

---

8. Clare

Lying 58 miles from London but only 26 miles east from Cambridge, the small town of Clare holds to the old ways of East Anglia. Many of its houses are bathed in Suffolk pink, the facades of a few demonstrating the 16th- and 17th-century plaster-work technique of pargeting. The Stour River, which has its source a few miles away, flows by, marking the boundary of Suffolk and Essex. The little rail station has fallen to the economy axe. The nearest station is now at Sudbury, where Gainsborough was born. The journey by road from London takes about two hours, unless you succumb to the scenery and the countryside along the way.

The **Ancient House Museum** (tel. 0787/277865), directly across from the churchyard, is a splendid example of pargeting and has many notable architectural features. Its numerous fascinating exhibits give visitors an understanding and appreciation of the rural life of Suffolk. The museum is open from Easter to October from 2:30 to 4:30 p.m. Wednesday to Sunday and on bank holidays, as well as from 11 a.m. to 12:30 p.m. on Sunday. Admission is 60p ($1.05) for adults, 30p (55¢) for children.

FOOD AND LODGING

One of the oldest inns in England is the **Bell Hotel,** Market Hill, Clare, Suffolk CO10 8NN (tel. 0842/277741). Once known as the Green Dragon, it served the soldiers of Richard de Clare, one of William the Conqueror's barons. Later it became a posting house, but in time the old stable gave way to a car park. It's had a recent facelift and offers 20 bedrooms, 18 of which have private baths. B&B rates range from £32 ($56) daily for a single, £40 ($70) for a double, plus service and tax. The rooms have a fresh, pleasant style, and the beds are soft. The beamed dining room, with its high-back chairs and large fireplace, is ideal for winter dining. Lunch, from noon to 2 p.m., costs £8 ($14) and dinner, from 7 to 9:30 p.m., goes for around £12 ($21).

---

9. Long Melford

Long Melford has been famous since the days of the early clothmakers. Like its sister, Lavenham (coming up), it grew in prestige and importance in the Middle

Ages. Of the old buildings remaining, the village church is often called one of the glories of the shire. Along its High Street are many private homes erected by wealthy wool merchants of yore. While London seems far removed here, it is only 61 miles to the south.

Of special interest are Long Melford's two stately homes:

Melford Hall, standing with its back to the A134 road, was favored by Beatrix Potter. Her Jemima Puddleduck still occupies a chair in one of the bedrooms upstairs, and others of her figures are on display. Now a National Trust property, the house, built between 1554 and 1578, contains paintings, fine furniture, and Chinese porcelain. The principal rooms and gardens can be visited from May to the end of September from 2 to 6 p.m. Wednesday, Thursday, Saturday, Sunday, and bank holiday Mondays. From April to October, hours are from 2 to 6 p.m. only on Saturday and Sunday. Admission is £2 ($3.50) for adults, £1 ($1.75) for children.

Kentwell Hall, whose entrance is north of the green in Long Melford on the west side of the A134, about a half mile north of Melford Hall, has been restored by its owners, the barrister Patrick Phillips and his wife. At the end of an avenue of linden trees, the hall is a red-brick Tudor mansion surrounded by a broad moat. A 15th-century moat house, interconnecting gardens, a brick-paved maze, and a costume display are of interest, and there are also rare-breed farm animals to be seen. The public can visit this family home and its grounds over Easter weekend; on Sunday from mid-April to mid-June; and Wednesday to Sunday from mid-July to the end of September. Hours are 2 to 6 p.m. During bank holidays, when special rates apply, hours are from 11 a.m. to 6 p.m. Admission is £2.40 ($4.20) for adults, £1.40 ($2.45) for children.

EATING AND SLEEPING

If you're passing through, try to visit the **Bull Hotel** on Hall Street (tel. 0787/78494), one of the old (1540) inns of East Anglia. It was built by a wool merchant and is considered Long Melford's finest and best-preserved building. Incorporated into the general inn is a medieval weavers' gallery and an open hearth with Elizabethan brickwork. The dining room is the outstanding portion of the Bull, with its high-beamed ceilings, trestle tables, settles, and handmade chairs, as well as a ten-foot fireplace. You can order a set four-course lunch for £8.50 ($14.90) and a dinner for £12.50 ($21.90), all prices inclusive of VAT and service. On the dinner menu, you can expect such dishes as salmon-and-crayfish mousse, chilled vichyssoise, grilled Dover sole argenteuille, roast leg of lamb en croûte, and steak au poivre. Hours of food service are daily from noon to 2:30 p.m. and 6:30 to 9:30 p.m.

The **Countrymen Restaurant,** Hall Street (tel. 0787/79951), is a pretty Suffolk pink, 15th-century restaurant, standing on the main street. Inside, the dining room is oak beamed with a huge inglenook fireplace. Fixed-price menus are available for lunch and dinner, menus changing monthly. Prices range from £10 ($17.50) for lunch to £25 ($43.75) for the top-price gastronomic dinner menu, a justifiable splurge. All prices include VAT and unlimited coffee. A typical midweek lunch might include homemade soup, chicken chasseur with fresh garden vegetables, a choice of desserts from the chilled trolley, and coffee. A dinner, at £15 ($26.25), offers such specialties as deep-fried whitebait to start, a delicate poached filet of sole as a middle course, sirloin steak with a piquant sauce to follow, with fresh market vegetables or crisp salad, a choice of dessert or a selection of English and continental cheeses, and coffee. A recommendable traditional Sunday lunch with prime English roast beef is also offered. Food is served at the Countrymen from noon to 1:30 p.m. and 7 to 9 p.m. daily, except for dinner on Sunday. On Saturday, it remains open to 9:30 p.m.

If you're staying over, consider the following recommendation:

The **Crown Inn,** Hall Street, Long Melford, Suffolk CO10 9JL (tel. 0787/ 77666), is an attractive Suffolk inn on the main village road. Its restaurant and bed-rooms, all with private baths open onto a small but lovely garden kept private from the road by a high stone wall. While not ancient, the Crown has a country-cottage flavor, with a sitting room for guests that is filled with comfortable armchairs. The charge for B&B, including VAT, in one of the pleasantly furnished bedrooms ranges from £29.50 ($51.65) daily in a single, and from £39.50 ($69.15) to £45 ($78.75) per person in a twin or double. Fixed-price lunches and dinners cost £6.50 ($11.40), £9.50 ($16.65), and £13.50 ($23.65). You might have pâté, fish mousse, or crab, followed by trout meunière, supreme of salmon, or perhaps a slice of lamb, pork, or beef from a joint, washed down with real ale brewed locally. Many fine wines are stored in the pre-Tudor cellars. Lunch is served from noon to 2:30 p.m. and dinner from 6:30 to 9:30 p.m. Of special interest in the lounge is a stained-glass panel depicting a scene from Shakespeare's *A Midsummer Night's Dream.*

10. Lavenham

Once a great wool center, Lavenham is filled with a number of beautiful half-timbered Tudor houses, washed in the characteristic Suffolk pink. Be sure to visit the church, with its landmark tower, built in the Perpendicular style. Lavenham lies only seven miles from Sudbury and 11 miles from Bury St. Edmunds.

WHERE TO STAY

The best little B&B in town is the **Angel Hotel,** Market Place, Lavenham, Suf-folk CO10 9QZ (tel. 0787/247388), where a good bed and a bountiful breakfast the next morning all cost £16 ($28) per person nightly. It's also possible to order a three-course dinner from the inn's à la carte menu, paying from £6 ($10.50).

WHERE TO DINE

Popular with villagers and visitors alike, the **Timbers Restaurant,** High Street (tel. 0787/247218), provides traditional English meals in an agreeable setting. You can order such classic dishes as rack of English lamb flavored with rosemary, grilled trout, or beef Wellington. Desserts are rich and tempting. Lunches cost £5 ($8.75) and à la carte dinners from £10 ($17.50). A three-course fixed-price meal is offered at night for £7.95 ($13.90). The establishment is open from noon to 2 p.m. and 7:30 to 9:30 p.m., except Thursday evening and all day Saturday and Sunday. Call for a table.

FOOD AND LODGING IN THE ENVIRONS

Off the A11 road from Lavenham to Hadleigh, the **Bell Inn** at Kersey (tel. 0473/823229), is in an attractive village with a watersplash right in the middle of the main street. The inn, dating from the late 13th century, contains a blazing fire-place and ceiling beams. The Bell offers good bar snacks in the timbered bar with glinting horse brasses. In the grill room, lunches and dinners include a selection of main courses, good-tasting English fare such as steak-and-kidney pie (individually prepared), game pie, honey-roasted ham, or a filet steak. The grill serves daily from noon to 2:30 p.m. and 7 to 10 p.m. Lunches cost from £5 ($8.75), with dinners going for £10 ($17.50) and up. The actual pub serves bar meals during opening hours, from 11 a.m. to 3 p.m. and 6 to 11 p.m. Monday to Saturday, and from noon to 3 p.m. and 7 to 10:30 p.m. Sunday.

Also off the A1141, on the B1115, is Chelsworth, which is typical of the vil-lages of the area. There the **Peacock Inn,** The Street, Chelsworth, Suffolk IP7 7HU (tel. 0449/740758), spreads its feathers. This inn dates back to the 14th century, with genuine oak timbering, inglenook fireplaces, and its own unique character. It stands just across the road from the banks of the Brett River. At lunchtime they have a hot and cold table with a fresh soup, cold ham, chicken curry, homemade game pie, and salads, all from £4 ($7). A three-course evening dinner, beginning at £9 ($15.75), is also featured. Seasonal specialties are afternoon teas (from May onward) and beef roasted on a spit over an open log fire in winter. Most of the food is homemade on the premises and is available seven days a week. The Peacock also offers five bedrooms, consisting of four doubles and one single, each with hot and cold running water. All are furnished traditionally. The cost is £16 ($28) per person daily.

---

11. Woodbridge and Aldeburgh

WOODBRIDGE

A yachting center 12 miles from the North Sea, Woodbridge is a market town on a branch of the Deben River. Its best-known, most famous resident was Edward Fitzgerald, the Victorian poet and translator of the *Rubáiyàt* of Omar Khayyám (some critics consider the Englishman's version better than the original). The poet died in 1883 and was buried nearly four miles away at Boulge.

Woodbridge is a good base for exploring the East Suffolk coastline, particularly the small resort of Aldeburgh, noted for its Moot Hall. The town is also a good headquarters for excursions to Constable's Flatford Mill (coming up).

Where to Dine

The **Captain's Table,** 3 Quay St. (tel. 03943/3145), is a good choice for intimate dining. The food, mainly seafood, is well prepared, the atmosphere near the wharf colorful. The licensed restaurant serves a number of specialties, including Dover sole. Many of the main dishes are traditionally English, especially scallops cooked in butter with bacon and garlic. Vegetables are extra, and desserts are rich and good-tasting. A three-course bar lunch is likely to cost around £6.50 ($11.40), a dinner in the restaurant going for £14 ($24.50). The day's specials are written on a blackboard—oysters, sea salmon, turbot in lobster sauce, whatever. Hours are noon to 2 p.m. and 6:30 to 9:30 p.m. Tuesday to Saturday.

Land O'Gorman Wine Bar, 17 Thoro'fare (tel. 03943/2557), is a popular dining spot offering reasonably priced food. Food is home-cooked and based on seasonal produce. Many guests come here as well for a bottle of wine or a beer. You can order such typical dishes as sautéed duck liver with shallots, mushrooms, and a Madeira sauce; buttermilk and buckwheat blinis with smoked tuna and sour cream; or roast brace of quail stuffed with pecan nuts, celery, and mushrooms with a sauce of the meat juices. For dessert, you might select a caramelized apple tart or deep-fried choux buns with poached berries and a crème fraîche. Meals cost from £10 ($17.50) and are served daily, noon to 2:30 p.m. and 7 to 11 p.m. The wine bar is closed Sunday and Monday.

Lodgings at Orford

For lodgings, try the nearby village of Orford, which is known for the ruins of its 12th-century castle. At this ancient town, once a port, you can stay at the **King's Head Inn,** Front Street, Orford, near Woodbridge, Suffolk IP12 2LW (tel. 0394/450271), reputedly a 13th-century inn with a smuggling history, lying in the shadow of St. Bartholomew's Church. A wealth of old beams and a candlelit dining room add to the ambience of this small (five-bedroom) inn. Joy and Alistair Shaw rent the bathless units for £30 ($52.50) nightly in a double, with a full English breakfast and VAT included. Alistair, who is also the chef, prepares tasty evening meals, using fresh produce from the sea and locally caught game. Lunchtime bar snacks are available, and boat trips can be arranged by prior booking.

ALDEBURGH

Pressed against the North Sea, Aldeburgh is a favorite retreat of the in-the-know traveler, even attracting some Dutch people who make the sea crossing via Harwich, the British entrypoint for those coming from the Hook of Holland. Sir Benjamin Britten, the renowned composer (1913–1976) produced some of his most famous works while he lived here (*The Turn of the Screw, Gloriana,* and *Billy Budd*), but the festival he started at Aldeburgh in 1948 is now held at Snape in June, a short drive to the west. A second festival, sponsored by British Telecom, is now held in early autumn, featuring major international singers. Less than 100 miles from London, the resort was founded in Roman times, but legionnaires have been replaced by fishermen, boatmen, and fanciers of wildfowl. A bird sanctuary, Havergate Island, lies about six miles south of the town in the River Alde.

Constructed on a shelf of land at the level of the sea, the High or main street of town runs parallel to the often turbulent waterfront. This main street sits below a cliff face that rises some 55 feet. It has been turned in part into terraced gardens, which visitors can enter. Some take time out from their sporting activities (a golf course stretches 3½ miles) to visit the 16th-century **Moot Hall Museum** (tel. 072885/2158). The hall dates from the time of Henry VIII, but its tall, twin chimneys are Jacobean additions. The timber-frame structure contains old maps and prints. It's open from 2:30 to 5 p.m. on Saturday and Sunday only from Easter to June, and seven days a week, from July to September. Admission is 25p (55¢) for adults, free to children.

Aldeburgh also contains the nation's northernmost Martello tower, erected to protect the coast from a feared invasion by Napoleon.

In August, the time of a regatta and a carnival, accommodations tend to be fully booked.

Where to Stay

Uplands Hotel, Victoria Road, Aldeburgh, Suffolk LP15 5DX (tel. 072885/2420), is as untouristy a retreat as you are likely to find. It's more like a private home that takes in paying guests. The inn dates from the 18th century. At one time it was the childhood home of Elizabeth Garrett Anderson, the first woman doctor in England. Once inside the living room, you sense the informality and charm. The prices range from £21 ($36.75) per person daily for B&B. Half board costs from £30 ($43.75) to £42 ($73.50) per person. There are seven twin-bedded chalets in the garden, with private bath and TV. In the hotel are 12 individually designed units. The chef, who has won many cooking awards, offers an à la carte dinner for £12 ($21) and up. A typical meal might include escalope de veau "Uplands" or roast Aylesbury duck. You can have coffee in front of the fireplace or, in fair weather, in the garden.

Cotmandene Guest House, 6 Park Lane, Aldeburgh, Suffolk IP15 5HL (tel. 072885/3775), is considered the best guesthouse in the area (as opposed to the more expensive hotels). A Victorian double-fronted structure, it stands in a tranquil neighborhood. If you go for a walk before breakfast, you will undoubtedly be following not only in Britten's footsteps, but those of frequent visitor E. M. Forster, who liked Aldeburgh but called it—not very accurately—"a bleak little place, not beautiful." The owners of this pleasantly furnished and comfortable guesthouse rent six bedrooms with private baths. Amenities include hairdryers, shoe cleaning, and ironing facilities. The price is from £15 ($26.25) per person nightly for B&B. It's also possible to stay here on half-board terms for another £8 ($14) per person daily. The cookery is wholesome English.

Fish and Chips

Britten and his longtime friend Peter Pears used to bring visitors from London or America to **Aldeburgh Fish & Chip Shop,** 226 High St. (tel. 072885/2250), to sample locally caught fish, notably plaice and cod. You can get a generous portion for around £1.50 ($2.65). Many guests pick up their treat here and picnic on the seawall. The shop is open daily, except Sunday and Monday, from 11:45 a.m. to 1:45 p.m. and 5 to 9 p.m.

The Local Pub

Ye Olde Crosse Keys, Crabbe Street (tel. 0728/452637), is a genuine 16th-century pub with the real atmosphere of a Suffolk seaside local. In the summer, everyone takes his or her real English ale or lager out and sits on the seawall, sipping, talking, and thinking. The pub is favored by local artists, who in the cooler months sit beside an old brick fireplace and eat plates of oysters or smoked salmon. Meals cost from £5 ($8.75) and are served from 11 a.m. to 2:30 p.m. and 5:30 to 11 p.m. Monday to Saturday, and from noon to 3 p.m. and 7 to 10:30 p.m. Sunday.

---

12. East Bergholt

The English landscape painter John Constable (1776–1837) was born at East Bergholt. Near the village is **Flatford Mill,** subject of one of his most renowned canvases. The mill, in a scenic setting, was given to the National Trust in 1943 and since has been leased to the Fields Studies Council for use as a residential field center, which offers a wide-ranging program of week-long courses in all aspects of the countryside and the environment, including painting and photography. Visitors of all ages and degrees of experience are welcome to apply to attend these courses. Details can be obtained from The Warden, Field Studies Council, Flatford Mill Field Centre, East Bergholt, Colchester, Essex, CO7 6UL (tel. 0206/298283).

Nearby, the National Trust has furnished a 16th-century cottage with a display on the life and work of John Constable, plus a shop for refreshments.

THE LOCAL PUB

Cited by numerous writers as one of the unmarred inns of East Anglia, the **Red Lion Inn,** The Street (tel. 0206/298332), traces its ancestry back to around 1500. The family-run pub has an enclosed children's garden. There is a wide range of bar meals, costing from £1.75 ($3.05) to £5 ($8.75), including the best ploughman's lunch in the area. Steaks are offered in the evening. Hours are from noon to 3 p.m. and 7 to 11 p.m. Monday to Saturday, and from noon to 3 p.m. and 7 to 10:30 p.m. Sunday. A short stroll from Flatford Mill and the heart of Constable land, the inn is opposite a historic church with a bell cage on the ground, where the bells are hand-rung. The Red Lion is reached by turning off the A12 Colchester-Ipswich road.

NORFOLK

Bounded by the North Sea, Norfolk is the biggest of the East Anglian counties. It's a low-lying area, with fens, heaths, and salt marshes. An occasional dike or windmill makes you think you've been delivered to the Netherlands. One of the features of Norfolk is its network of "Broads," miles and miles of lagoons, shallow in parts, connected by streams.

Summer sportspeople flock to Norfolk to hire boats for sailing or fishing. From

Norwich, **Wroxham,** the capital of the Broads, is easily reached, being only eight miles to the northeast. Motorboats regularly leave from the resort, taking parties on short trips. Some of the best scenery of the Broads is to be found on the periphery of Wroxham.

---

13. Norwich

Some 20 miles from the North Sea, Norwich still holds to its claim as the capital city of East Anglia. The county town of Norfolk, Norwich is a charming and historic city, despite encroachments by industry.

Norwich is the most important shopping center in East Anglia and is well provided with hotels and entertainment. In addition to its cathedral, there are more than 30 medieval parish churches built of flint.

There are many interesting old houses in the narrow streets and alleyways, and there is a big open-air market, busy every weekday, where fruit, flowers, vegetables, and other goods are sold from stalls with colored canvas roofs.

The **Assembly House** (see below) is a Georgian building (1752) restored to provide a splendid arts and social center. The **Maddermarket Theatre,** the home of the Norwich Players, is an 18th-century chapel converted by Nugent Monck in 1921 to an Elizabethan-style theater. On the outskirts of the city, the buildings of the University of East Anglia are strikingly modern in design and include the Sainsbury Centre (1978).

There is a **Tourist Information Centre** at the Guildhall Gaol Hill (tel. 0603/666071).

THE SIGHTS

In the center of Norwich, on a partly artificial mound, sits **Norwich Castle,** formerly the county gaol (jail). Its huge 12th-century Norman keep and the later prison buildings are used as a civic museum and headquarters of the county-wide Norfolk Museums Service (tel. 0603/611277, ext. 279). The museum houses an impressive collection of pictures by artists of the Norwich School, of whom the most distinguished were John Crome, born 1768, and John Sell Cotman, born 1782. The castle museum also contains a fine collection of Lowestoft porcelain and Norwich silver. These are shown in the rotunda. There are two sets of dioramas, one showing Norfolk wildlife in its natural setting, the other illustrating scenes of Norfolk life from the Old Stone Age to the early days of Norwich Castle. You can also visit a geology gallery and a permanent exhibition in the keep, "Norfolk in Europe." The castle museum is open Monday to Saturday from 10 a.m. to 5 p.m. and on Sunday from 2 to 5 p.m. Adults pay 80p ($1.40) in summer, 40p (70¢) in winter, children being charged 10p (20¢) year-round. A licensed bar is open from 10:30 a.m. to 2:30 p.m. and a cafeteria from 10 a.m. to 4:30 p.m. Monday to Saturday.

Norwich Cathedral (tel. 0603/626290), principally of Norman design, dates from 1096. It is noted primarily for its long nave with lofty columns. Its spire, built in the late Perpendicular style, rises 315 feet and shares distinction with the keep of the castle as one of the significant landmarks on the Norwich skyline. On the vaulted ceiling are more than 300 bosses (knob-like ornamental projections) depicting biblical scenes. The impressive choir stalls with the handsome misericords date from the 15th century. Edith Cavell—"Patriotism is not enough"—the English nurse executed by the Germans in World War I, was buried on the cathedral's Life's Green. The quadrangular cloisters go back to the 13th century and are among the most spacious in England. The cathedral can be visited from 7:30 a.m. to 7 p.m. daily. A donation of 50p (90¢) is requested.

A short walk from the cathedral will take you to **Tombland,** one of the most interesting old squares in Norwich.

The **Sainsbury Centre for Visual Arts** (tel. 0603/592470) was the gift in 1973 of Sir Robert and Lady Sainsbury, who contributed their private collection to the University of East Anglia. Along with their son, David, they gave an endowment to provide a building to house the collection. The center, designed by Foster Associates, was opened in 1978, and since then the design has won many national and international awards. A feature of the structure is its flexibility, allowing solid and glass areas to be interchanged, and the superb quality of light, which allows optimum viewing of the works of art. The Sainsbury Collection is one of the foremost in the country, including modern, ancient, classical, and ethnographic art. It is especially strong in works by Francis Bacon, Alberto Giacometti, and Henry Moore. Other displays at the center include the Anderson Collection of art nouveau and the University aggregation of 20th-century abstract art and design. There is also a regular program of special exhibitions. The center is open from noon to 5 p.m. daily, except Monday. Admission is 50p (90¢) for adults, 25p (45¢) for children. The restaurant on the premises offers a self-service buffet from 10:30 a.m. to 2 p.m. and a carvery service from 12:30 to 2 p.m. Monday to Friday. A conservatory coffee bar serves light lunches and refreshments from noon to 4:30 p.m. Tuesday to Sunday.

The Victorian-style **Mustard Shop,** 3 Bridewell Alley (tel. 0603/627889), is a wealth of mahogany and shining brass. There is an old cash register to record your purchase, and the standard of service and pace of life also reflect the personality and courtesy of a bygone age. In the Mustard Museum is a series of displays illustrating the history of the Colman Company and the making of mustard, its properties and origins. There are old advertisements, as well as packages and "tins." You can browse in the shop, selecting whichever of the mustards you prefer. Really hot, English-type mustards are sold, as well as the continental blends. Besides mustard, the shop sells aprons, tea towels, chopping boards, pottery mustard pots, and mugs, all of which are also available by mail order from the attractive free brochure provided. The shop and museum are open from 9 a.m. to 5:30 p.m. Monday to Saturday (closed all day Thursday).

A Memorial Room honoring the **Second Air Division of the Eighth United States Army Air Force** is part of the Central Library, Bethel Street (tel. 0603/625038, ext. 27). A Memorial Fountain also honoring the United States airmen who were based in Norfolk and Suffolk in World War II, many losing their lives in the line of duty, is in the library courtyard. The fountain incorporates the insignia of the Second Air Division and a stone from each state of the United States. Books, audio-visual materials, and records of the various bomb groups are in the library. There is no admission charge, but contributions are used for the upkeep of the memorial.

Persons interested in a tour of the old air bases in East Anglia used by the Eighth United States Army Air Force during World War II should see **Tony North,** 62 Turner Rd. (tel. 0603/614041), who is connected to the Second Air Division Association, the Liberator Club, the American Aviation Historical Society, and the Eighth Air Force Historical Society. He greets visitors in the Memorial Room.

Before I begin my recommendations for finding lodgings, I'll lead off with a tip about how to find a room in a hurry.

ACCOMMODATIONS

Norwich is better equipped than most East Anglian cities to handle guests who arrive without reservations. The **Norwich City Tourist Information Centre** maintains an office at the Guildhall, Gaol Hill, opposite the market (tel. 0603/666071). Each year a new listing of accommodations is drawn up, including both licensed and unlicensed hotels, B&B houses, and even living arrangements on the outskirts.

A street called **Earlham Road** abounds in budget hotels and guesthouses. To drive there, go west along St. Giles Street from the north side of City Hall. The guesthouses here were mostly built at the turn of the century, and they offer widely varying prices.

Bed and Breakfast

Marlborough House Hotel, 22 Stracey Rd., Norwich, Norfolk NR1 1EZ (tel. 0603/628005), is a comfortable and welcoming centrally-heated hotel with 11 bedrooms, all with color TV and tea- and coffee-makers. Six have hot and cold running water, and five, including twins, doubles, and a family room, have private showers and toilets. The B&B tariff for a single goes from £12 ($21) daily, doubles and twins cost from £30 ($52.50), and the family room is priced from £38 ($66.50). Evening meals with home-style cooking, costing £3 ($5.25) and up, are served from 5:30 to 7 p.m. There is a comfortable TV lounge and a licensed bar. The hotel has a small car park as well as adequate parking facilities outside. It is centrally situated close to the railway station, Riverside Walk, the cathedral, and the central library.

Wedgewood Guest House, 42-44 St. Stephens Rd., Norwich, Norfolk NR1 3RE (tel. 0603/625730), in the vicinity of the bus station, is not only convenient for exploring many of the attractions of Norwich, it offers good rooms at a fair price. The hotel rents out 11 comfortably furnished bedrooms, eight of which contain private baths. The B&B rate in a single goes from £13.50 ($23.65) to £15 ($26.25) daily, in a double or twin from £26 ($45.50) to £31 ($54.25).

Heathcote Hotel, 19-23 Unthank Rd., Norwich, Norfolk NR2 2PA (tel. 0603/625639), established in 1904, is just a few minutes' walk from the city center. The heated rooms are well furnished and have hot and cold running water, color TV, radios, phones, and tea- and coffee makers. The charge, including service, in a single ranges from £18 ($31.50) to £25 ($43.75) nightly, and doubles go for £33 ($57.75) to £44 ($77), the latter with private baths. A three-course evening meal is available at £7.50 ($13.15). The hotel has a large car park.

Santa Lucia Hotel, 38-40 Yarmouth Rd., Norwich, Norfolk NR7 0EQ (tel. 0603/33207), is one of the best for value of the hotels outside Norwich, only 1½ miles from the center. The hotel offers not only an inexpensive accommodation, but an attractive setting by the river and an inviting atmosphere. You pay from £10 ($17.50) nightly for B&B. The food is quite good too, costing from £12.30 ($21.50) for half board. Each room has running water, color TV, and a clock radio. There are sun terraces for relaxing, modern bathrooms and showers, and plenty of parking space. Two buses pass by the door heading for the center of the city.

DINING IN NORWICH

In the heart of the old city, the **Briton Arms Coffee House,** Elm Hill (tel. 0603/623367), overlooks the most beautiful cobbled street in Norwich. Tracing its history back to the days of Edward III, it's now one of the least expensive eating places in Norwich, certainly one of the most intimate and informal. The coffeehouse has several rooms, including a back one with an inglenook. You'll find old beamed ceilings and Tudor benches. It is open daily, except Sunday, from 10 a.m. to 5 p.m. The procedure here is to go to the little counter, where you purchase your lunch and bring it to the table of your choice. Everything I've tried was well prepared, and the items are homemade. Every day a different kind of soup is offered. You're likely to pay about £4 ($7) for a substantial two-course meal. It's a good place to stop after your inspection of the cathedral, only a block away.

The **Assembly House,** Theatre Street (tel. 0603/626402), is a good example of Georgian architecture. You enter the building through a large front courtyard, which leads to the central hall with its columns, fine paneling, and crystal chandelier. The restaurant is administered by H. J. Sexton Norwich Arts Trust. On your left is a high-ceilinged room with paneling, fine paintings, and a long buffet table ready for self-service. After making your selection, take your plate to any one of the many tables. Often you'll share—perhaps with an artist. There is an unusually varied selection of hors d'oeuvres. A big bowl of homemade soup might get you started. Hot main courses are made with fresh ingredients. Meals cost from £5 ($8.75). The restaurant is open first for coffee, 10 a.m. to noon; then lunch, noon to 2 p.m. Teatime is from 2 to 5 p.m., and the supper hour is from 5 to 7:30 p.m. Service is daily. After dining, you may want to stroll through the rest of the building. Art exhibits are usually held regularly in the Ivory and Hobart Rooms, open from 10 a.m. to 5:30 p.m. Concerts are sponsored in the Music Room, with its chandeliers and sconces. There's even a little cinema.

Café la Tienda, 10 St. Gregory's Alley (tel. 0603/629122), is an informal two-story restaurant. Fresh, natural flavors are the hallmark of this place. Meals cost from £5 ($8.75). The café is open from 10 a.m. to 5 p.m. Monday to Saturday; closed Sunday.

Swelter's, Woburn Court, 8 Guildhall Hill (tel. 0603/612874), in terms of value is among the best establishments in Norwich. There are light meals during the day or more elaborate dinners, and service is from 11:30 a.m. to 2:30 p.m. and 5:30 to 10:30 p.m., except on certain closing days: all day Sunday, Monday, and Tuesday for dinner. You get substantial fare here, often using produce from the bountiful fields of Norfolk. The English cheese, the local pâté, and what the British call "raised pies" (usually with meat and vegetables, often ham and cheese) are justly praised, but you can also enjoy a daily special or two based on continental cookery. This wine bar is part of the new sophistication sweeping across this once-staid East Anglia city.

---

14. North Norfolk

This part is already well known by members of the American Eighth Air Force, as many Liberators and Flying Fortresses took off and landed from this corner of the country. Their captains and crews sampled most of the local hostelries at one time or another. Now it is mainly feathered birds that fly overhead, and the countryside is quiet and peaceful.

THE SIGHTS
The area is of considerable scenic interest, as the queen of England herself will surely agree. It's extremely convenient for a weekend out of London, as it lies only a three-hour drive away.

Sandringham Estate
In the Norfolk countryside, some 107 miles northeast of London, Sandringham Estate (tel. 0553/772675) is the famous country home in East Anglia where the British royal family spends many of its holidays. The gardens and a section of the interior are open to the public. The house and grounds are open from Easter Sunday until the last Thursday in September, inclusive, from Sunday through Thursday of each week. The house is closed for a certain period during the summer (normally the last two weeks in July and the first week in August). The house is open from 11 a.m. (noon on Sunday) to 4:45 p.m., and the grounds can be visited from 10:30 a.m. (11:30 a.m. on Sunday) to 5 p.m. For a combined ticket to the house and grounds, adults pay £2 ($3.50) and children are charged £1.20 ($2.10). The grounds are not open when the queen or any member of the royal family is in residence.

The house dates from the mid-19th century and stands on the site of one bought for Edward VII when he was Prince of Wales. There are picnic areas, a souvenir shop, a restaurant, and a cafeteria. The museum, first opened in 1973, includes cars and a fire engine, big-game trophies, and a gallery of local archeological finds.

The cars include a 1900 Daimler Tonneau of Edward VII's, which was the first car bought by a member of the royal family. It still works.

Traditionally, the royal family welcomes in the new year at Sandringham. Sandringham lies eight miles northeast of the ancient port and market town of King's Lynn.

Blickling Hall

A long drive, bordered by massive yew hedges towering above and framing your first view of this lovely old house, leads you to Blickling Hall, near Aylsham (tel. 0263/733084). Rose red and pinnacled, the hall is a near-perfect example of a historic English country house. The present building, erected during the reign of King James I by his chief justice, Sir Henry Hobart, has ornate State Rooms mainly in late 18th-century style. The long gallery houses a fine library and has an elaborate 17th-century ceiling. The Blickling Estate, given to the National Trust by Lord Lothian, once British ambassador to the United States, has an orangery with plants and statuary. The gardens are known for the great yew hedges and herbaceous borders, a Doric Temple, a woodland garden, and a secret garden. It is open from April to October from 1 to 5 p.m. daily, except Monday and Thursday. Admission to the house and gardens is £3.50 ($6.15) for adults, £1.75 ($3.05) for children; £2 ($3.50) for adults and £1 ($1.75) for children to the gardens only.

Norfolk Lavender Ltd.

At **Caley Mill** at Heacham (tel. 0485/70384), you can see how lavender is grown, the flowers harvested, and the essence distilled before appearing prettily packaged as perfume, aftershave, potpourri, and old-fashioned lavender bags to slip between your hankies. Much of the lavender is grown on the nearby Sandringham royal estate, so you may end up with a regal product. The grounds and shop are open all year. Hours are from 10 a.m. to 5 p.m. Monday to Friday from January to Easter; from 10 a.m. to 5:30 p.m. daily from Easter to October; and from 10 a.m. to 5 p.m. Monday to Saturday from November to Christmas. The tours cost 75p ($1.30) for adults and are free for children. The **Miller's Cottage Tea Room** serves cream teas, homemade cakes, and light lunches from Easter to the end of May in the afternoon only. From May to Christmas, the tea room is open at the same times as the shop. The best time to see the lavender in bloom is from late June to mid-August.

Sutton Windmill and Broads Museum

At Sutton (1½ miles southeast of Stalham off the A149) is the tallest mill in the country. But its main claim to fame, in a county where many of the windmills still work, is the exceptional quality and interest of the working machinery. Chris Nunn, who owns the mill, decided it was time he put something back into the country instead of taking it out. So he left the construction business and now devotes his days to restoring the mill. When money runs short, he works on North Sea oil rigs for a time. He hopes shortly to be grinding corn again, but the lower floors—there are nine in all—house a collection of bygones reflecting the mill's 100 years of history.

A recently constructed building on the car park houses the Broads Museum, based on the private collection of the Nunn family. Chris, Marian, and Robyn invite you to see the craft tools once used in woodworking, leather trades, farming, working the marshes, and cooperage. A large collection of kitchen and domestic memorabilia, animal traps, bank notes, and many more items from the past are displayed. In the tea rooms, you can enjoy tea, coffee, soft drinks, ice cream, and sorbets. The entire complex can be visited April to mid-May Sunday to Wednesday from 1:30 to 5:30 p.m., and mid-May to the end of September from 10 a.m. to 6 p.m. daily. Admission is £1.30 ($2.30) for adults, 65p ($1.15) for children. There is a telescope on the top floor, and the view over the countryside is magnificent. Crafts, pottery, books, and gifts are on sale. Telephone 0692/81195 for more information.

The Thursford Collection

Just off the A148 that runs from King's Lynn to Cromer, at **Laurel Farm,** Thursford Green, Thursford, near Fakenham (tel. 0328/77477), George Cushing has been collecting and restoring steam engines and organs for more years than you'd care to remember. His collection is now a trust, and the old painted giants are on display, a paradise of traction engines with impeccable pedigrees such as Burrells, Garretts, and the Ruston Proctors. There are some static steam engines, the sort that run merry-go-rounds at fairs, but the most flamboyant exhibits are the showman's organs, the Wurlitzers and concert organs with their brilliant decoration, moving figures, and mass of pipes. The organs play at 3 p.m. There is a children's play area and a Savages Venetian Gondola switchback ride with Gavoili organ, which operates daily. It was built at nearby King's Lynn, and Disneyland has been after it for years. On many days during the summer, the two-foot–gauge steam railway, the Cackler, will take you around the wooded grounds of the museum. There is a refreshment café and a souvenir shop where one can buy photographs, books, and records of the steam-organ music. The collection is open daily from 2 to 5:30 p.m. from the beginning of April until the end of October. In March, it is open on Sunday. Admission is £2.20 ($3.85) for adults and 95p ($1.65) for children. There are live Wurlitzer concerts every Tuesday evening at 8 p.m. from June to September.

The North Norfolk Railway

This steam railway plies from Sheringham to Weybourne. The station at Sheringham (tel. 0263/822045) opens daily at 10 a.m. from Easter to October. Admission to the station and museum is free between October and March. From Easter until the end of September, admission is 30p (55¢) for adults and 15p (25¢) for children. There are two museums of railway paraphernalia, steam locomotives, and historic rolling stock. The round-trip to Weybourne by steam train takes about 45 minutes through most attractive countryside. Days and times of departure vary, so you should telephone between 10 a.m. and 5 p.m. before you go there. A ride on a steam train between Weybourne and Sheringham is £2.20 ($3.85) for adults for a round-trip, £1.10 ($1.95) for children.

KING'S LYNN

This ancient port and market town on the banks of the Great Ouse has a wealth of historic buildings dating from as far back as the 14th century. In spite of modern buildings, it also has many quaint streets.

Food and Lodging

Russet House, 53 Goodwins Rd., King's Lynn, Norfolk PE30 5PE (tel. 0553/600250), is your best bet. Charm and economy go hand and hand here in this restored Victorian-era building standing on its own grounds in a tranquil area. You receive a warm welcome and are shown to one of nearly a dozen bedrooms, eight of which contain a private bath or shower. A trio of bedrooms is suitable for family occupancy. All the bedrooms are well maintained and have a number of comforts. The overnight B&B rate ranges from £23 ($40.25) to £30 ($52.50) daily in a single, rising to £25 ($43.75) to £32 ($56) in a double. When the weather's nippy, guests sit in front of an open fire. Solid and reliable East Anglia fare is served here, and nonsmokers may want to request an evening meal beginning at 7 p.m.

Antonio's Wine Bar, Baxters Plain (tel. 0553/772324), in the heart of King's Lynn, is a small, bistro-style wine bar offering a combination of fast service and simple but excellent food and wine. Antonio's Italian flair is reflected in the menu as well as the decor and congenial atmosphere. Appetizers include several home-smoked dishes and antipasto misto; main dishes are usually specials as well as outstanding fresh-dough pizzas and epicurean calzone. A good meal can be enjoyed here for less than £10 ($17.50). You can also partake of a drink at the bar or have a simple snack. The place is open from noon to 2 p.m. and 7 to 11:30 p.m. daily, except Sunday, Monday, and two weeks in August. This is the best watering hole for miles around, handy for visitors to Royal Sandringham and the Norfolk Lavender fields.

Staying on the Outskirts

Oakwood House, King's Lynn, Norfolk PE33 0RH on Route A10 near Tottenhill, just four miles south of King's Lynn (tel. 0553/810256), is a country house of Tudor origin with all the amenities of a modern hotel. The house was enlarged some 200 years ago and refaced with a typical Georgian exterior. Within a short drive of the Norfolk seacoast, Oakwood House offers visitors a peaceful alternative to the bustling seaside resorts and market towns. Nestled in its own two acres of gardens, the hotel and its annex have ten guest rooms with color TV, tea- and coffee-making facilities, hot and cold running water, individually controlled heating, and views over the Norfolk countryside and the gardens. Four rooms are equipped with private showers and toilets. There is a comfortably furnished guest lounge, and the spacious dining room adjoins the well-stocked bar. The menu is carefully chosen to make the best use of local and homegrown produce whenever possible. Rates per person for B&B begin at £15 ($26.25) daily. A two-course dinner costs £7.50 ($13.15), a three-course repast going for £8.50 ($14.90). VAT is included in the price, and there is no service charge. Ample parking facilities are within the grounds.

EAST MIDLANDS

1. NORTHAMPTONSHIRE
2. LEICESTERSHIRE
3. DERBYSHIRE
4. NOTTINGHAMSHIRE
5. LINCOLNSHIRE

The East Midlands contain several counties, widely varied both in character and scenery. This part of central England, for instance, offers miles of dreary industrial sections and their offspring row-type Victorian houses, yet the district is intermixed with some of Britain's noblest scenery, such as the Peak District National Park, centered in Derbyshire. Byron said that scenes there rivaled those of Switzerland and Greece. There are, in short, many pleasant surprises in store for you, from the tulip land of Lincoln to the 18th-century spa of Buxton in Derbyshire, from George Washington's ancestral home at Sulgrave Manor in Northamptonshire to what remains of Sherwood Forest.

1. Northamptonshire

Lying in the heart of the Midlands of England, the shire of which the city of Northampton has long been the administrative center has been inhabited since Paleolithic times. Traces have been found of the Beaker and other Bronze Age people, and a number of Iron Age hill-forts existed here, remains of which can still be seen. Two main Roman roads—Watling Street and Ermine Street—ran through the county, and relics of Roman settlements have been discovered at Towcester, Whilton, Irchester, and Castor. A racial mix was contributed by the invasion in the seventh century of West Saxons and Anglians. Also in that century, in 655, the first abbey was established at Medehamstede, now Peterborough.

The Danes took over late in the ninth century, and although their stay was not long as history goes, it was under their aegis that Northampton became the seat of administration for a borough with almost the same boundaries the shire has today and which are recorded in the *Domesday Book*.

In the Middle Ages, castles and manor houses dotted the country, which was rich in cattle and sheep farming and leatherwork, particularly the production of boots and shoes.

SULGRAVE MANOR

On your way from Oxford to visit the Warwickshire area of Stratford-upon-Avon, Warwick, and Coventry, if you take the A34 road north, you can visit Sulgrave

Manor, the ancestral home of George Washington. First, you'll come to Banbury (in Oxfordshire), a market town famed in the nursery rhyme immortalizing "a fine lady upon a white horse." The old Banbury Cross was destroyed by the Roundheads in the Civil War but was replaced in Victoria's day. Follow the A422 road east from Banbury into Northamptonshire, toward Brackley, but turn off to the left after a short distance onto the B4525 road, which will take you to the village of Sulgrave.

As part of Henry VIII's plan to dissolve monasteries, he sold the priory-owned manor in 1539 to Lawrence Washington, who had been mayor of Northampton. George Washington was a direct descendant of Lawrence (seven generations removed). The Washington family occupied Sulgrave for more than a century. In 1656, Colonel John Washington left for the New World.

In 1914, the manor was purchased by a group of English people in honor of the friendship between Britain and America. Over the years major restoration has taken place (a whole new wing had to be added), with an eye toward returning it as much as possible to its original state. The Colonial Dames have been largely responsible for raising the money. From both sides of the Atlantic the appropriate furnishings were donated, including a number of portraits—even a Gilbert Stuart original of the first president. On the main doorway is the Washington family coat-of-arms, two bars and a trio of mullets, which is believed to have been the inspiration for the "Stars and Stripes."

The manor is open from March to December daily, except Wednesday, from 10:30 a.m. to 1 p.m. and 2 to 5:30 p.m. (till 4 p.m. otherwise). Admission is £2 ($3.50) for adults, £1 ($1.75) for children. For more information, telephone 029576/205.

Food and Lodging

Across from Sulgrave Manor is the **Thatched House Hotel,** Manor Road, Sulgrave, near Banbury, Northamptonshire OX17 2SE (tel. 029576/232), a long, low group of 17th-century cottages, with a front garden full of flowers. Even if you're just passing through, it's a good place to stop for tea following your visit to Sulgrave Manor. Cream teas, served from 3:30 to 5:30 p.m. and costing £1.65 ($2.90), consist of scones with thick cream and jam and strawberries in season. Tea is served at a table in either the beamed living or dining room, furnished with antiques. For B&B stays, the bedrooms have been modernized with private baths in all the doubles. Each unit has TV and a tea- and coffee-maker. Depending on the plumbing, singles range from £23 ($40.25) to £30 ($52.50) daily, and doubles cost £50 ($90), including VAT. The hotel restaurant serves meals seven days a week. Lunches cost £6.50 ($11.40) Monday to Saturday, with a traditional English roast served at Sunday lunch, costing from £5.50 ($9.65) to £7.25 ($12.70). Dinner goes for £9.25 ($16.20), and you can feast on such dishes as medallion of English lamb flavored with herbs or roast guinea fowl in a sherry sauce. Food is served daily from noon to 2 p.m. and 7:30 to 9:30 p.m.

NORTHAMPTON

Fortified after 1066 by Simon de Senlis (St. Liz), the administrative and political center of Northamptonshire was a favorite meeting place of Norman and Plantagenet kings. Here King John was besieged by the barons trying to force the policy changes that finally resulted in the Magna Carta. During the War of the Roses, Henry VI was defeated and taken prisoner, and during the Civil War, Northampton stuck with Parliament and Cromwell. The town, on the River Nene, has long been an important center for the production of boots and shoes, as well as other leather craft, pursuits that are traced in two of the city's museums.

The **Central Museum & Art Gallery,** Guildhall Road (tel. 0604/39415), displays collections of footwear through the ages, plus a re-created cobbler's shop. It also houses local archeological artifacts tracing the history of Northampton up to the Great Fire, English Oriental ceramics, Old Masters, sculpture, and British 19th- and 20th-century art. It is open from 10 a.m. to 5 p.m. Monday to Saturday (to 9 p.m. Thursday). Admission is free.

The **Museum of Leathercraft**, The Old Blue Coat School, Bridge Street (tel. 0604/34881), traces the history of leather use from ancient Egyptian times to the present. Missal cases, 16th-century caskets, and modern saddles are displayed, with exhibits of costumes, luggage, and harnesses. It is open Monday to Saturday from 10 a.m. to 5 p.m., with no admission charge.

Where to Stay

Aarandale Regent Hotel & Guest House, 6-7 Royal Terrace, Barrack Road, Northampton, Northamptonshire NN1 3RF (tel. 0604/31096), is one of the best of the reasonably priced accommodations in this bustling Midlands town. It rents 14 comfortably furnished and well-maintained bedrooms, none with bath. The overnight B&B charge ranges from £17 ($29.75) to £19 ($33.25) in a single, from £28 ($49) to £30 ($52.50) in a double. Solid cooking with fresh produce is also served, and you can arrange to dine from 6 to 7:15 p.m. daily. There is limited parking.

The Coach House, 8-10 East Park Parade, Northampton, Northamptonshire NN1 4LA (tel. 0604/250981), lies slightly outside the heart of the city. Once it was a row of Victorian town houses, but now it has been turned into a well-run little hotel with a wide selection of rooms, including family accommodations. Those with private bath are more expensive, of course. The single rate ranges from £20 ($35) to £35 ($61.25) daily, and doubles cost from £30 ($52.50) to £50 ($87.50). Arrangements can be made for dinner. The location opens onto the old racecourse of the city, which is now a park.

Birchfields, 17 Hester St., Northampton, Northamptonshire NN2 6AP (tel. 0604/28199), is an immaculate guesthouse run by Mr. and Mrs. P. D. Darmanin. All rooms have color TV and facilities for making hot beverages, and the house's baths are modern, with warm showers. For a bed and full English breakfast, the charge is £13 ($22.75) daily in a single, £24 ($42) in a double.

Where to Eat

Sun Rise, 18 Kingsley Park Terrace (tel. 0604/711228), was built to attract business in a shopping complex about a mile from the heart of Northampton. But many "downtown diners" make the effort to drive out here, as they consider that this place serves some of the best food in the area. The Wan family, your hosts, welcome guests from noon to 2 p.m. and 5:30 to 11:30 p.m. seven days a week. A set lunch is offered at £3.50 ($6.15), a fantastic bargain, and you also get exceptional value if you order the table d'hôte dinner at only £8 ($14). You can also dine à la carte. Both the Peking and Canton kitchens are represented in the vast array of specialties. I find the duck and chicken preparations the most interesting. There's a modern decor.

Buddies New York Café, Old Mission School, Drychurch Lane (tel. 0604/20300), is inspired by life in these United States. That means big fresh salads, rib steaks, hamburgers done as you like 'em, milk shakes, and even Budweiser. The menu also offers hickory-smoked baby back ribs, a large range of club sandwiches, and foot-long hot dogs (with cheese, chili, and other toppings). At Buddies, the blackboard menus are always changing, against a backdrop of posters of the Manhattan skyline, Disney creatures, or whatever. Meals cost from £6 ($10.50), and hours are noon to 2 p.m. and 6 to 10:30 (it is open till 11 p.m. on Friday and Saturday but closed Sunday).

THE SPENCER HOME

The mansion that was the girlhood home of the Princess of Wales, **Althorp,** Northampton (no phone calls allowed), is the residence of the Earl and Countess Spencer, parents of the former Lady Diana Spencer who married Prince Charles. The entrance lodge is five miles northwest of Northampton, beyond the village of Harlestone. Althorp is about a 1½-hour drive from London on the A428 from Northampton to Rugby. Built in 1508 by Sir John Spencer, the house has undergone many alterations over the years.

It contains a collection of pictures by Van Dyck, Reynolds, Gainsborough, and Rubens, as well as fine and rare French and English furniture, along with Sèvres, Bow, and Chelsea porcelain. The collection is quite as magnificent as that in better-known stately homes. The house is open daily all year from 1 to 5 p.m., Wednesday being Connoisseurs' Day, when extra rooms are shown and the tour is longer. Admission to the house and grounds on regular days is £2.75 ($4.80) for adults, £1.75 ($3.05) for children, rising to £3.75 ($6.55) for adults and £2 ($3.50) for children on Connoisseurs' Day. The grounds and lake can be visited separately for 50p (90¢) for adults, 25p (45¢) for children. A gift shop, wine shop, and tea room are maintained at Althorp. The present countess helps in the gift shop, and Lord Spencer's own favorite sideline is the excellent cellar and wine store.

STOKE BRUERNE

On the Grand Union Canal, the **Waterways Museum** at Stoke Bruerne, near Towcester in Northamptonshire (tel. 0604/862229), is just south of the Blisworth Tunnel (take the A508 from the M1 junction 15 or the A5). The three-story grain warehouse has been lovingly restored and adapted to give an insight into the working lives of canal boatmen and their families. On display is a full-size replica of a "butty" boat cabin, complete with cooking range, brassware, and lace curtains, along with the traditional painted ware, tools, and teapots. There is also an early semidiesel Bolinder boat engine, a boat-weighing machine once used to determine canal toll charges, and a shop where you can buy posters, books, illustrations of canal life, hand-painted traditional canalware, models, and badges. The museum is open from 10 a.m. to 6 p.m. It is closed on Monday from October to Easter but open otherwise until 4 p.m. Admission is £1.20 ($2.10) for adults and 60p ($1.05) for children. A family ticket costs £2.75 ($4.80).

If you find yourself in the area, you'll be able to partake of one of the most delightful dining adventures in Northamptonshire.

The **Boat Inn,** Stoke Bruerne, near Towcester (tel. 0604/862428), started as a row of humble cottages in the 17th century and has gradually progressed without losing its original character. It is still a limestone building with a thatched roof overlooking the Grand Union Canal and the Stoke Bruerne Waterways Museum. The Public House is the oldest part, with stone floors and open fires, along with pictures depicting canal boats and life. Bar food includes the usual soup of the day, steak-and-kidney pie, and ploughman's lunch. You can also order sandwiches, salads, and basket meals. Count on spending around £5 ($8.75). Hours are daily from 11 a.m. to 3 p.m. and 6 to 11 p.m. Next to the pub is a traditional Northamptonshire skittles room where you can try your skill at throwing the "cheese," the flattened puck used to knock the skittles down.

The restaurant offers a full range of dishes, including smoked salmon, snails in garlic butter, and an interesting apple and Stilton soup. There are several fish dishes, including a whole lobster thermidor, and guinea fowl and grouse are served in season, along with such elegant continental dishes as tournedos Rossini or steak Diane. A three-course meal, finished off with a choice from the dessert trolley or the cheese board, then coffee and mints, will cost around £15 ($26.25), including VAT. That is, unless you started with poached oysters, followed by lobster thermidor, and rounded off with roast grouse. On Sunday they do a "Great Sunday Lunch," costing

£7.25 ($12.70) for adults and £4.95 ($8.65) for children. There is also a traditional cream tea in the afternoon, costing £2.25 ($3.95). The Woodward family has owned and run the Boat Inn since 1877.

Cruises are available on the Woodwards' narrow canal boat, *Indian Chief*. The boat has a fully stocked bar, soft drinks, tea, coffee, and snacks. A 25-minute trip to Blisworth Tunnel Mouth and back costs 75p ($1.30) for adults, 50p (90¢) for children. Other, longer cruises are offered, requiring a minimum of 30 persons.

BRACKLEY

This is an ancient market town mentioned in the *Domesday Book*. It lies on the A43 road about halfway between Oxford and Northampton. This is a handy base for touring such sights as Sulgrave Manor (six miles away) and Oxford (24 miles away).

If you're in the area, I suggest a stop at the **Old Crown Inn,** Market Square, Brackley, Northamptonshire NN13 5DP (tel. 0280/702210). This old-world posting house, parts of which date back to the 12th century, was a stopping place for the Duke of Wellington in 1814, a year before the Battle of Waterloo. Recent improvements have increased the size of the public rooms, but the original character of the Old Crown has been preserved. There are heavy, time-aged beams, open brick fireplaces, and oak paneling in the lounge. The bar has a Tudor-style fireplace. Each of the inn's 14 bedrooms has a private bathroom, color TV, a phone, and a radio. A single costs £36 ($63) daily and a double £53 ($92.75), including VAT and breakfast. Meals, served in the inn's dining room daily from noon to 2 p.m. and 7 to 9:30 p.m., include a traditional Sunday roast beef lunch. You can also have soup, steaks, and desserts in the bar.

---

2. Leicestershire

Virtually ignored by most North American tourists, this eastern Midland county was, according to legend, the home of King Lear. Whatever the truth of that, Leicestershire is rich in historical associations. It was at Bosworth Battlefield that the last of the Plantagenet kings, Richard III, was killed in 1485, irrevocably changing the course of English history.

LEICESTER

The county town is a busy industrial center, but it was once a Roman settlement and has a Roman wall and bath site that remind one of those days.

It also has a Norman castle-hall, a period museum, a costume museum in a late medieval building, a 15th-century Guildhall (Shakespeare is said to have played here), and many interesting gardens. On its abbey park and grounds are the remains of Leicester Abbey, Cardinal Wolsey's grave, a boating lake, paddling pool, riverside walks, ornamental gardens, and an aviary.

For details of guided tours and local excursions, ask at one of the **Tourism & Information Centres:** 2-6 St. Martin's Walk (tel. 0533/511300) or St. Margaret's Bus Station (tel. 0533/532353).

Where to Stay

Daval Hotel, 292 London Rd., Stoneygate, Leicester, Leicestershire LE2 2AG (tel. 0533/708234), is a historical building of architectural interest built in 1889 during the reign of Queen Victoria. There are rooms of all sizes: singles, doubles, twins, and family size. All are modern with hot and cold running water, outlets for electric razors, radio, intercom, and wall-to-wall carpeting. Charges, depending on the plumbing, are £17 ($29.75) to £20 ($35) daily in singles, £27.50 ($48.15) to £38 ($66.50) in doubles, all tariffs including a full English breakfast and taxes. There is a cozy restaurant where home-cooked evening meals are available, including steaks, chicken, duckling, scampi, and other dishes. The hotel has its own licensed bar with a TV lounge. The Daval is ideally situated for touring and visiting the Midlands. It is on the main A6 road. For those traveling by train or bus, it is just a few minutes' ride away from the stations.

Alexandra Hotel, 342 London Rd., Leicester, Leicestershire, LE2 2AG (tel. 0533/703056), is a modest hotel-B&B that offers a four-course dinner for £7.50 ($13.15) per person, as well as light snacks. Bedrooms have TV, baths with showers, and toilets. Singles begin at £16 ($28), doubles go for £25 ($43.75), and family rooms cost £36 ($63).

Where to Eat

Water Margin, 76-78 High St. (tel. 0533/56422), features a Canton kitchen from which comes an array of familiar and inventive dishes to intrigue you—everything from pork with plum sauce to eel prepared with flavor and skill. In other words, you can stick to the familiar here or else be a little adventurous with your palate. The business lunch at £3 ($5.25) is one of the food bargains of Leicester. At night count on spending from £8.50 ($14.90) and up. Some diners go here just for the selection of dim sum. Hours are daily from noon to 11:30 p.m.

Joe Rigatoni (don't you love that name?), 3 St. Martins Square (tel. 0533/533977), is a two-floor restaurant in a contemporary store complex. Bright and inviting, it serves some of the best Italian viands in town. Of course, most of the young diners come here for pizza and pasta, but you can get more substantial fare as well. Scampi and veal dishes are the most expensive items on the menu. You can eat for as little as £6 ($10.50), depending on what you order. Service is from noon to 2:30 p.m. and 6:30 to 11 p.m. Monday to Friday. On Saturday, however, it stays open until 2:30 a.m.; closed Sunday.

TOURING THE COUNTRY

As long as people continue to read Sir Walter Scott's *Ivanhoe,* they will remember **Ashby-de-la-Zouch,** a town that retains a pleasant country atmosphere. Mary Queen of Scots was imprisoned in an ancient castle here. Other places of interest are:

Belvoir Castle

On the northern border of Leicestershire, **Belvoir** (pronounced beaver) **Castle** overlooking the Vale of Belvoir has been the seat of the Dukes of Rutland since Henry VIII's time. Rebuilt by Wyatt in 1816, the castle contains paintings by Holbein, Reynolds, and Gainsborough, as well as tapestries in its magnificent State Rooms. The location is seven miles west-southwest of Grantham, between the A607 to Melton Mowbray and the A52 to Nottingham. The castle was the location of the films *Little Lord Fauntleroy* and Steven Spielberg's *Young Sherlock Holmes,* and in summer it is the site of medieval jousting tournaments. From late March to early October, it is open from 11 a.m. to 6 p.m. on Tuesday, Wednesday, Thursday, and Saturday, plus Friday in June, July, and August. On Sunday, hours are from 11 a.m. to 7 p.m. During October, it is open only on Saturday and Sunday, from noon to 6 p.m. Admission is £2.60 ($4.55) for adults, £1.50 ($2.65) for children. Further details are available from Jimmy Durrands, Estate Office, Belvoir Castle, Grantham, Lincolnshire NG31 6BR (tel. 0476/870262).

The Bosworth Battlefield

Bosworth Battlefield Visitor Centre & Country Park, Sutton Cheney, Market Bosworth, Leicestershire (tel. 0455/290429), lies between the M1 and the M6, close to Nuneaton. The 1485 battle it commemorates is considered one of England's three most important battles (the other two being the one at Hastings in 1066 and the Battle of Britain in 1940). The Battle of Bosworth ended the War of the Roses between the houses of York and Lancaster, ending with the death of King Richard III, last of the Plantagenets, and the proclamation of the victor, Henry Tudor, a Welsh nobleman who had been banished to France to thwart his ambition. Henry landed at Milford Haven and marched across country to Leicestershire where King Richard was encamped, defeated the monarch, and became King Henry VII, first of the Tudor dynasty. Today, the appropriate standards fly where the opponents had their positions, and in a three-quarters of a mile walk along the marked battle trails, you can see the whole scene of the fighting. In the center are exhibitions, models, book and gift shops, a cafeteria, and a film theater where an audio-visual introduction with an excerpt from the Lord Laurence Olivier film of Shakespeare's *Richard III* is presented.

The center is open from Easter to the end of October from 2 to 5:30 p.m. Monday to Saturday, and from 1 to 6 p.m. Sunday and bank holiday Mondays. Admission to the exhibition is £1.20 ($2.10) for adults, 80p ($1.40) for children. The battle trails can be visited all year without charge during daylight hours. Special medieval attractions are held in July, August, and September. Special charges apply on main event days

Melton Mowbray

Other interesting towns to visit in Leicestershire include **Melton Mowbray,** a fox-hunting center and market town that claims to be the original home of Stilton cheese and is renowned for its pork pies.

The **Melton Carnegie Museum,** Thorpe End (tel. 0664/69946), depicts the past and present life of the area, with special exhibits on Stilton cheese and Melton pork pies. It's open Easter to September from 10 a.m. to 5 p.m. Monday to Saturday, and from 2 to 5 p.m. on Sunday. October to Easter, opening is from 10 a.m. to 4:30 p.m. Monday to Friday and 10:30 a.m. to 4 p.m. on Saturday. It is closed Christmas Day, Boxing Day, January 1, and Good Friday.

---

3. Derbyshire

The most magnificent scenery in the Midlands is found within the borders of this county lying between Nottinghamshire and Staffordshire. Derbyshire has been less defaced by industry than its neighbors. The north of the county, containing the **Peak District National Park,** is by far the most exciting for touring. In the south the land is more level, and the look becomes, in places, one of pastoral meadows.

Some visitors avoid this part of the country because it is ringed by the industrial sprawl of Manchester, Leeds, Sheffield, and Derby. To do so, however, would be a pity, as this part of England contains the rugged peaks and leafy dales that merit a substantial detour, especially Dovedale, Chee Dale, and Millers Dale.

HISTORIC HOMES

Near Bakewell, ten miles north of Matlock, stands one of the great country houses of England, **Chatsworth,** the home of the 11th Duke of Devonshire and his duchess, the former Deborah Mitford (sister of Nancy and Jessica). With its lavishly decorated interiors and a wealth of art treasures, it comprises 175 rooms, the most spectacular of which are open to the public, who can visit daily from 11:30 a.m. to 4:30 p.m. March to October (tel. 024688/2204 for information). Admission to the house and garden is £3.75 ($6.55) for adults and £1.90 ($3.35) for children. The eccentric Bess of Hardwick built a house on this spot that eventually held Mary Queen of Scots prisoner upon orders of Queen Elizabeth I. Most of that structure was torn down, and the present building, with many, many additions, dates from 1686. Capability Brown (who seems to have been everywhere) worked on the landscaping at one time. But it was Joseph Paxton, the gardener to the sixth duke, who turned the garden into one of the most celebrated in Europe. Queen Victoria and Prince Albert were lavishly entertained here in 1843. The house contains a great library and such paintings as the *Adoration of the Magi* by Veronese and *King Uzziah* by Rembrandt. On the grounds you can see spectacular fountains, and there is a playground for children in the farmyard.

Hardwick Hall (tel. 0246/850430) lies 9½ miles southeast of Chesterfield. The approach from the M1 is at junction 29. The house was built in 1597 for the above-mentioned Bess of Hardwick, a woman who acquired four husbands and an estate from each of them. It is particularly noted for its architecture ("more glass than wall"). The High Great Chamber and Long Gallery crown an unparalleled series of late 16th-century interiors, including an important collection of tapestries, needlework, and furniture. The house is surrounded by a 300-acre country park that is open daily all year. Walled gardens, orchards, and an herb garden are just part of its attractions. The house is open from the first of April until the end of October on Wednesday, Thursday, Saturday, and Sunday from 1 to 5:30 p.m. Admission to the hall and garden is £4 ($7) for adults and £2 ($3.50) for children.

Melbourne Hall, at Melbourne (tel. 0332/862502), eight miles south of Derby, originally built by the Bishops of Carlisle (1133), stands in one of the most famous formal gardens in Britain. The ecclesiastical structure was restored in the 1600s by one of the cabinet ministers of Charles I and enlarged by Queen Anne's vice chamberlain. It was the home of Lord Melbourne, who was prime minister when Victoria ascended to the throne. He was born William Lamb, and Melbourne Hall was also the home of Lord Byron's friend, Lady Caroline Lamb. Lady Palmerston later inherited the house, which contains an important collection of pictures, antique furniture, and works of art. A special feature is the beautifully restored wrought-iron pergola by Robert Bakewell, noted 18th-century ironsmith. The house is open from 2 to 5 p.m. daily in August, except on August 7, 14, and 21. Admission is £1.50 ($2.65) for adults, 75p ($1.30) for children. The garden can be visited Wednesday, Saturday, Sunday, and bank holiday Mondays from 2 to 6 p.m. April to September. Admission to the garden is £1 ($1.75).

OTHER PLACES TO SEE

In addition to majestic scenery, you may want to seek out the following specific sights:

Royal Crown Derby Porcelain Co. Ltd., 194 Osmaston Rd., in Derby (tel. 0332/47051). In case this is your special favorite in the pottery world, I suggest a trip into the center of Derby to take the two-hour tour of the only factory allowed to use both the words "royal" and "crown" in its name, a double honor granted by George III and Queen Victoria. At the end of the tour, you can treat yourself to a bargain in the gift shop and visit the Royal Crown Derby Museum from 9 a.m. to 12:30 p.m. and 1:30 to 4 p.m. Monday to Friday. Tours take place at 10:30 a.m. and 1:45 p.m. Monday to Friday, costing £1.50 ($2.65). The factory shop is open Monday to Saturday from 9 a.m. to 4 p.m.

At **National Tramway Museum,** Crich, near Matlock (tel. 077385/2565), one young 65-year-old I know spends as much of his free time as his wife will allow in the paradise of vintage trams—electric, steam, and horse-drawn from home and overseas, including New York. Your admission ticket is £2.70 ($4.75) for adults and £1.50 ($2.65) for children. This ticket allows you unlimited rides on trams that make the two-mile round-trip to Glory Mine with scenic views over the Derwent Valley via Wakebridge, where a stop is made to visit the Peak District Mines Historical Society display of lead mining. It also includes admission to various tramway exhibitions and displays and to the tramway period street, which is an ongoing project. Hours are 10 a.m. to about 6 p.m. It's open Saturday, Sunday, and bank holidays from early April to November; Monday to Thursday from early May to early September; and on Friday from mid-July to early September.

Peak District Mining Museum, the Pavilion, Matlock Bath (tel. 0629/583834), is open year-round daily (except for Christmas) from 11 a.m. to 4 p.m.

Admission is 80p ($1.40) for adults and 50p (90¢) for children. The main exhibit of this display of 2000 years of Derbyshire lead mining is a giant water-pressure engine used to pump water from the mines, which was itself rescued from 360 feet underground by members of the society before being brought to the museum. The most popular feature is the children's climbing shaft, a twisting tunnel through which they crawl.

BUXTON

One of the loveliest towns in Britain, Buxton was developed in the 18th century to rival the spa at Bath. However, long before that, its waters were known to the Romans, whose settlement here was called *Aquae Arnemetiae*. The thermal waters were pretty much forgotten after that until the reign of Queen Elizabeth I, when the baths were reactivated, and even Mary Queen of Scots was brought here by her caretaker, the Earl of Shrewsbury, to "take the waters." Buxton today is mostly the result of the 18th-century development carried out under direction of the Duke of Devonshire.

The Crescent, modeled on the one in Bath but with more elegant classical lines, was originally a hotel complex, but it is now occupied by a hotel and the county library. The Pump Room of the spa has become the **Buxton Micrarium**, The Crescent (tel. 0298/78662), a world of microscopic animals and plants that is a popular attraction in The Crescent, open daily from 10 a.m. to 5 p.m. Admission is £1.80 ($3.15) for adults, 90p ($1.60) for children. Perhaps the most outstanding feature of recent restoration in Buxton is the Victorian opera house, for years the local movie palace, now restored in all its marble, velvet, and ornamental plaster opulence. The annual Opera Festival held here bids fair to become a rival of Glyndebourne.

The waters from the nine thermal wells are no longer available for spa treatment, except in the hydrotherapy pool at the Devonshire Royal Hospital. The water is also used in the swimming pool at the 23-acre **Pavilion Gardens**, but if you want a drink of spa water, you can purchase it at the Tourist Information Centre or help yourself at the public fountain across the street.

Poole's Cavern, Buxton Country Park, Green Lane, in Buxton (tel. 0298/6978), is a cave that was once inhabited by Stone Age man, who may have been the first to marvel at the natural vaulted roof bedecked with stalactites. Explorers walk through the spacious galleries, viewing the incredible horizontal cave, which is electrically illuminated. It is open daily from Easter until the first week in November, from 10 a.m. to 5 p.m., charging £2 ($3.50) for adults, £1.10 ($1.95) for children.

Some 20 minutes away in Grin Low Woods is **Solomon's Temple**, a folly built in 1895 on a tumulus which dates from the Neolithic Age. Climb the small spiral staircase inside the temple for impressive views over Buxton and the surrounding countryside.

The **Tourist Information Centre**, The Crescent, arranges guided walks lasting 1½ hours. You can take the Spa Heritage Trail around the conservation area of the town, including The Crescent, the Pavilion Gardens, and the Vera Britten Walk. Guides can also be booked for bus tours. Phone 0298/5106 for details.

Accommodations

Ashwood Park Hotel, Fairfield Road, Buxton, Derbyshire SK17 7DJ (tel. 0298/3416), is an impressive stone building in the heart of the spa, owned by M. Jean Howarth. It's set back from the busy roads, facing the well-tended public gardens with a small stream and lawns. It's more of a country inn, and the entire ground floor is a bar-lounge decorated in oranges and browns with a collection of glittering brass and copper. The charge for B&B in a double is £12 ($21) per person daily, and there are no evening meals. The hotel is open only from May 1 until the end of October.

The Old Manse, 6 Clifton Rd., Silverlands, Buxton Derbyshire SK17 6QL (tel.

0298/5638), is a spacious and interesting Victorian house quietly situated yet close to everything. For B&B, the charges are £10.50 ($18.40) to £11 ($19.25) daily. A three-course evening meal, the price is £7 ($12.25). For two or more nights, half-board is available for £16.50 ($28.90) per person. All the rooms have hot and cold water, outlets for electric razors, continental quilts, and tea- and coffee-makers. Some rooms with private baths cost £2.50 ($4.40) extra. The Old Manse offers comfort, service, a TV lounge, a small licensed bar, and a choice of menu for both breakfast and the evening meal, which is served from 6 to 7 p.m. The house is centrally heated, and there's space for parking cars.

Grove Hotel, Grove Parade, Buxton, Derbyshire SK17 6AJ (tel. 0289/3804), has a long history going back to the 1700s. It stands across from the old Spa Centre, near all the major attractions. This small, well-maintained hotel has many amenities and rents 21 comfortable bedrooms, seven of these with private bath. Depending on your room assignment and the plumbing (or lack of it), the overnight charge for B&B ranges from £19 ($33.25) to £29 ($50.75) in a single, rising to £31 ($54.25) to £39 ($68.25) in a double. The hotel also serves some of the most reasonably priced fare at the spa, so you may want to stick around for dinner.

Thorn Heyes Private Hotel, 137 London Rd., Buxton, Derbyshire SK17 9NW (tel. 0298/3539), is a solid Victorian stone house with a sweeping drive and large gardens. It has been much modernized to make comfortable bedrooms with central heating. All have showers, toilets, color TV, and beverage facilities. Rooms are prettily decorated with continental quilts and flowery curtains. Downstairs is a lounge overlooking the garden, plus a dining room where fresh local produce is served whenever possible. The hosts charge from £16 ($28), plus another £8.50 ($14.90) for dinner per person daily for B&B, VAT included.

On the Outskirts

Crewe & Harpur Arms Hotel, Longnor, near Buxton, Staffordshire SK17 0NS (tel. 029883/205), is set in a village in the hills of the Peak District, six miles from Buxton. The valleys of the Rivers Dove and Manifold are a couple of miles away. Located on the village square with its cobble street and market hall, at the crossing of the old wagon trails from Leicester to Liverpool, the hotel is tastefully furnished; all bedrooms have hot and cold water basins and showers. Ron King, the host, charges £15 ($26.25) per person daily for B&B. An evening meal costs from £6.50 ($11.40). You can also have bar meals if you wish. Fishing is available for £3 ($5.25) per day.

ASHBOURNE

This old market town has a 13th-century church, a 16th-century grammar school, and ancient almshouses.

For accommodations, I recommend—

The Green Man and Black Head's Royal Hotel, St. John Street, Ashbourne, Derbyshire DE6 1GH (tel. 0335/43861), in the town center, has many historical connections going back to 1710. In 1777, Dr. Samuel Johnson and his biographer, James Boswell, stayed here, and Boswell wrote: "I took my postchaise from the Green Man, a very good inn." In the Tap Room you can still see the chairs of Boswell and Johnson. Princess Victoria and her widowed mother, the Duchess of Kent, halted here and gave the inn the right to add "Royal" to its name. This red-brick posting inn has retained its traditional character, yet modern amenities have been added. There are 17 bedrooms, nine of which have private baths. Each is well decorated, and prices include a full English breakfast and early-morning tea or coffee, as well as VAT. The owner, John Clowes, charges from £20 ($35) to £22.50 ($39.40) daily in a single, from £30 ($52.50) to £35 ($61.25) in a double, the higher prices being for rooms with bath.

The Shrovetide Restaurant offers carvery meals at lunch, costing from £3 ($5.25) to £5 ($8.75), depending on what you select. At night, à la carte meals cost from £8 ($14) to £15 ($26.25). The budget bargain, however, is on Friday and Saturday night, when carvery dinners are served at lunchtime prices. The restaurant is open daily from noon to 2:30 p.m. and 7 to 9 p.m.

ALSTONFIELD

This is a pretty village on the edge of Dovedale, a perfect center from which to tour the Peaks and Dales. It lies off the A515 road from Ashbourne to Buxton, and it's actually just across the Derbyshire line in Staffordshire.

If you're in the neighborhood, drop in at the **George Inn** (tel. 033527/205), a 16th-century pub with oak beams and open fires right off the village green. It is the only place for locals to gather for an evening. Food is served daily from noon to 1:45 p.m. and 7 to 10 p.m., featuring such dishes as filet steak and fried plaice with french fries. Meals cost around £6 ($10.50). The bars, ringing with local chitchat, are open from 10:30 a.m. to 2:30 p.m. and 6 (7 in winter) to 11 p.m.

If you want to spend the night, try the following.

Overdale, near Ashbourne, Alstonfield, Derbyshire DE6 2FZ (tel. 033527/206), lies on the outskirts of the tiny village. This B&B is in a lovely Derbyshire house kept absolutely spotless and set on immaculate grounds. It has five bedrooms plus two family rooms, which are large and comfortable, costing from £10 ($17.50) per person daily. An extra charge of £5.50 ($9.65) gets you an evening meal of three courses with coffee.

---

4. Nottinghamshire

"Notts," as it is called, was the county of Robin Hood and Lord Byron. It is also Lawrence country, as the English novelist, author of *Sons and Lovers* and *Lady Chatterley's Lover,* was also from here, born at Eastwood.

Sherwood Forest is probably the most famous woodland in the world. It isn't the greenwood haven it used to be, but it did provide in its time excellent cover for its world-famous bandit and his band, Robin Hood and his Merry Men, including Friar Tuck and Little John. Actually very little of it was forest, even in its heyday. The area consists of woodland glades, fields, and agricultural land, along with villages and hamlets.

The **Sherwood Forest Visitor Centre,** Sherwood Forest Country Park at Edwinstowe, near Mansfield (tel. 0623/823202), stands in the area just by the Major Oak, popularly known as Robin Hood's tree. It's the center of many marked walks and footpaths through the woodland. There's an exhibition of life-size models of Robin Hood and the other well-known outlaws, as well as a shop with books, gifts, and souvenirs. The center, some 18 miles north of Nottingham city off the A614, will provide as much information as remains of Friar Tuck and Little John, along with Maid Marian and Alan-a-Dale, as well as the other Merry Men. Little John's grave can be seen at Hathersage, Will Scarlet's at Blidworth. Robin Hood is believed to have married Maid Marian at Edwinstowe Church, close to the Visitor Centre. Nearby is the Major Oak, 30 feet in circumference, where the outlaws could easily have hidden in the hollow trunk.

Robin Hood's Larder offers light snacks and meals. There is a full program of events taking place on the Centre site and in the area. The Centre also contains a Tourist Information Centre, one of the national network in England. It's open daily from 11 a.m. to 5 p.m. in April; May to September, hours are 11 a.m. to 5 p.m. Monday to Saturday, to 6:30 p.m. on Sunday. In March and October it's open Monday to Sunday from 11:30 a.m. to 4:30 p.m. November and December hours are Tuesday to Thursday and Saturday and Sunday from 11:30 a.m. to 4 p.m., while in January and February it is open only on Saturday and Sunday at those same hours.

The Larder is open at various hours, depending on the center opening days and times.

There is no admission charge to the Centre, which is on the B6034 north of Edwinstowe village, seven miles east of Mansfield. In summer, The Sherwood Forester bus service links Nottingham, the Visitor Centre, and other sights in the area, including Clumber Park and Rufford Country Park. In fine weather, several open-top buses are on the route, so you can get far closer to the atmosphere of the forest and Robin Hood.

Nottinghamshire is so rarely visited by foreign tourists that its beautiful landscapes could almost be called "undiscovered." British trippers, however, know of its hidden villages and numerous parks.

NOTTINGHAM

The county town is a busy industrial city 121 miles north of London. On the north bank of the Trent, Nottingham is one of the most pleasant cities in the Midlands.

Overlooking the city, **Nottingham Castle** (tel. 0602/483504) was built by the Duke of Newcastle on the site of a Norman fortress in 1679. After restoration in 1878, it was opened as a provincial museum, surrounded by a charmingly laid-out garden. See in particular the collection of medieval Nottingham alabaster carvings. The works of Nottingham-born artists are displayed in the first-floor gallery. The castle is open April to September daily from 10 a.m. to 5:45 p.m. Otherwise, its hours are daily from 10 a.m. to 4:45 p.m. Admission is free except on Sunday and bank holidays, when adults pay 20p (35¢) and children 10p (20¢); closed Christmas Day.

For 50p (90¢), you'll be taken on a tour conducted at the castle of Mortimer's Hole and underground passages. King Edward III is said to have led a band of noblemen through these secret passages, surprising Roger Mortimer and the queen, killing Mortimer, and putting his lady in prison. A statue of Robin Hood stands at the base of the castle. The museum shop has a wide range of British crafts.

The **Brewhouse Yard Museum,** Castle Boulevard, consists of five 17th-century cottages at the foot of Castle Rock, presenting a panorama of Nottingham life in a series of furnished rooms and shops. Some of them, open from cellar to attic, have much local historical material on display. The most interesting features are in a series of cellars cut into the rock of the castle instead of below the houses, plus an exhibition of a Nottingham shopping street, 1919–1939, with 11 shops for services that are local to the city. Open all year, the admission-free museum (tel. 0602/483504, ext. 48) may be visited daily from 10 a.m. to 5 p.m. It is closed Christmas Day. Donations to help with the upkeep are welcomed.

An elegant row of Georgian terraced houses, the **Museum of Costume and Textiles** at 51 Castle Gate (tel. 0602/411881) presents collections of costumes, textiles, and lace, one of the city's great industries. You'll see everything from the 1632 Eyre map tapestries of Nottingham to "fallals and frippery." The admission-free museum is open daily from 10 a.m. to 5 p.m.; closed Christmas Day.

On the outskirts of Nottingham, at Ravenshead, **Newstead Abbey** (tel. 0623/793557) was once Lord Byron's home. It lies 11 miles north of Nottingham on the A60 (the Mansfield road). Some of the original Augustinian priory, bought by Sir John Byron in 1540, still survives. In the 19th century, the mansion was given a neo-Gothic restoration. Mementos, including first editions and manuscripts, are displayed inside, and later you can explore a parkland of some 300 acres, with waterfalls, rose gardens, a Monk's Stew Pond, and a Japanese water garden. Admission to the grounds and gardens is 85p ($1.50) for adults, 40p (70¢) for children. To visit the abbey, the charge is £1.20 ($2.10) for adults, 20p (35¢) for children. The abbey is open from Good Friday to September 30 daily from 11:30 a.m. to 6 p.m. (last admissions at 5 p.m.). The gardens are open daily all year from 10 a.m. to dusk.

Also on the outskirts of Nottingham, **Wollaton Hall** (tel. 0602/281333) is a well-preserved Elizabethan mansion, the most ornate in England (finished in 1588), housing a natural history museum with lots of insects, invertebrates, and British mammals, along with reptiles and crustaceans, some a long way from their former home in the South Seas. The mansion is open from 10 a.m. to 7 p.m. Monday to Saturday and from 2 to 5 p.m. Sunday from April to September. From October to March hours are from 10 a.m. to dusk Monday to Saturday, from 1:30 to 4:30 p.m. Sunday; closed Christmas Day. Admission is free, except on Sunday and bank holidays, when a modest charge is made. The hall is surrounded by a Deer Park and gardens. See the camellia house with the world's earliest (1823) cast-iron front. The bird dioramas here are among the best in Britain.

Where to Stay

Fairhaven Private Hotel, 19 Meadow Rd., Beeston Rylands, Nottingham, Nottinghamshire NG9 1JP (tel. 0602/227509), is a good choice for motorists who don't want to drive into the center of town. Family operated, it is a small hotel with ten well-furnished and maintained bedrooms. As none of them has a private bath, guests share the three public baths. Prices are correspondingly low as well: from £13.50 ($23.65) to £17 ($29.75) daily in a single, rising to £19.50 ($34.15) to £24 ($42) in a double. You can also have a good Midlands meal at 6 p.m. if you make arrangements in advance.

Park Hotel, 7 Waverley St., Nottingham, Nottinghamshire NG7 4HP (tel. 0602/786299), is more convenient, especially if you're arriving by rail. It lies only a short walk from the heart of the city. The hotel is one of the best of the small properties of Nottingham, offering 16 comfortably furnished accommodations, 11 with private bath. The overnight B&B charge is from £17 ($29.75) in a single, going up to £27 ($47.25) in a double. Dinner is served from 7:30 to 10:30 p.m.

St. Andrews Guest House, 310 Queens Rd., Boeston, Nottingham, Nottinghamshire NG9 1JA (tel. 0602/254902), is another good possibility if you're arriving by rail. Family operated and within an easy walk of the train station, it is also convenient for exploring the major sights (previously described). The ten comfortably furnished bedrooms do not contain private baths. The B&B charges are among the least expensive in the city: from £15 ($26.25) daily in a single, going up to £22 ($38.50) in a double. Very reasonably priced dinners are available if you make arrangements in advance.

Food and Drink

At **Eviva Taverna,** 25 Victoria St. (tel. 0602/580243), the political squabbles between Greece and Britain are over, at least during a meal in this joyful tavern. Do you like to watch Greek dancing and smash plates? If so, this is the place, although you'll be charged extra for the plates demolished. Chef's specialties include stefado, a Greek stew of beef, onion, and herbs, cooked in wine vinegar; and kleftico, a thick piece of lamb cooked very slowly in the oven with herbs. Of course there are the inevitable dolmades, stuffed vine leaves. The owner, J. Kozakis, runs a kebab house above the tavern, offering kebabs of lamb, pork, and steak. A meal here will cost from £7.50 ($13.15), plus your wine—and plate smashing! Hours are Monday to Saturday evening from 7 p.m. to 2 a.m.

Ben Bowers Restaurant, 128 Derby Rd. (0602/413388), offers a complete range of meals and prices in its newly refurbished dining areas. Ben Bowers Piano Restaurant is candlelit and intimate, featuring an à la carte menu using local fresh herbs and produce. A resident pianist performs love songs and classical pieces Monday to Saturday. A meal costs around £16 ($28). The Ground Floor is a Victorian dining room offering two fixed-price three-course lunches, one for £4.50 ($7.90) including chef's seasonal specialties and another for £6.95 ($12.15). In the evening, there is a choice of à la carte or table d'hôte meals. Four courses cost about £10.50

($13.40). Hours for both eating places are from noon to 2 p.m. Monday to Friday, from 7 to 10:15 p.m. Monday to Thursday, and from 7 to 10:45 p.m. Friday and Saturday; closed Sunday.

Ye Olde Trip to Jerusalem, Brewhouse Yard, Castle Road (tel. 0302/473171), claims to be the oldest inn in England. It was a traditional stopover for the Crusaders on their way to the Holy Land. Founded in the 12th century, it was built right into the castle rock, and served, because of its coolness, as the castle brewery. Scientists can't fathom how the speaking tube, cut through the rocks, works—but it does. The two bars are literally cut out of the rocks, and the fireplace chimney is nearly 45 feet high, also cut out of the rock. The Trip specializes in real ales—that is, cask-conditioned beers drawn from the cellar by hand-pumps. The beers available are Ruddles Best, Marston's Pedigree, Samuel Smith's Old Brewery, and Ward's Sheffield Best Bitters, together with regular guest beers selected from different British breweries. They don't provide cooked lunches, but there is a selection of sandwiches at lunch, costing from £1 ($1.75). The pub is open from 11 a.m. to 3 p.m. and 5:30 to 11 p.m. Monday to Thursday; from 11 a.m. to 4 p.m. and 5:30 to 11 p.m. Friday and Saturday; and from noon to 3 p.m. and 7 to 10:30 p.m. Sunday.

About a half-hour drive from Lord Byron's Newstead Abbey leads to—

SOUTHWELL

This ancient market town is a good center for exploring the Robin Hood country. Byron once belonged to a local amateur dramatic society here. An unexpected gem is the old twin-spired cathedral, **Southwell Minster,** which many consider among the most beautiful churches in England. James I found that it held up with "any other kirk in Christendom." Look for the well-proportioned Georgian houses across from the cathedral.

East of Southwell, near the Lincolnshire border, is—

NEWARK-ON-TRENT

Here is an ancient riverside market town on the Roman Fosse Way, lying about 15 miles across flatlands from Nottingham. King John died at **Newark Castle** in 1216. Constructed between the 12th and 15th centuries, the castle survived three sieges by Cromwell's troops before falling into ruin in 1646. From its parapet you can look down on the Trent River and across to Nottingham. The delicately detailed parish church here is said to be the finest in the country. The town contains many ancient inns, reflecting its long history.

On the banks of the River Trent, a short walk from Newark Castle, is **Millgate Folk Museum** (tel. 0636/79403), in a building that housed a 19th-century oil-seed mill and then a warehouse. Today, it contains portrayals of social and industrial life in the area from the turn of the century to World War II. Agricultural, malting, and printing implements are displayed, and a series of furnished rooms depicts domestic life in those times. The museum, for which there is no admission fee, is open from 10 a.m. to 5 p.m. Monday to Friday and from 1 to 5 p.m. Saturday and Sunday.

On the outskirts, I'd suggest the following for food and lodgings:

Newcastle Arms Hotel, Market Place, Tuxford, near Newark-on-Trent, Nottingham NG22 0LA (tel. 0777/870208), has been a village inn since 1701, welcoming such guests as Margaret Tudor, Charles II, and Mr. Gladstone. It's a Georgian-style, two-story corner building with a plain facade, except for a pair of bay windows flanking the small pillared entrance. Furnishings are in the style of an English country inn. All B&B rooms contain private baths, direct-dial phones, color TV, and tea- and coffee-makers. From Monday to Thursday, a single room costs £30 ($52.50) daily, and a double is £35 ($61.25). On Friday, Saturday, and Sunday, the rates are £25 ($43.75) daily in a single, £30 ($52.50) in a double. All prices include VAT. The hotel is fully licensed and offers an extensive French cuisine, with an à la carte and a table d'hôte menu. Vegetarians are also accommodated. Lunches start at

£6.25 ($10.94) and dinner goes from £10.95 ($19.15). The hotel is on the A1, 12 miles north of Newark and 20 miles south of Doncaster.

THE DUKERIES

In the Dukeries, portions of Sherwood Forest legendarily associated with Robin Hood are still preserved. These are vast country estates on the edge of industrial towns. Most of the estates have disappeared, but the park at **Clumber,** covering some 4000 acres, is administered by the National Trust, which has preserved its 18th-century beauty, as exemplified by Lime Tree Avenue. Rolling heaths and a peaceful lake add to the charm. You can visit Clumber Chapel, built in 1886–1889 as a chapel for the seventh Duke of Newcastle. It is open from 10 a.m. to 5 p.m. daily, except Christmas Day. There is no admission charge, but entry costs £1.50 ($2.65) for cars, £2.50 ($4.40) for minibuses and house trailers. There are stables with a tower clock dated 1763, a classical bridge over the lake, lodges, and pleasure grounds, as well as fishing, bicycle rental, a shop, and a restaurant. The park is open all year. Clumber Park is five miles southeast of Clumber Park Stableyard, Workshop (tel. 0909/476592).

EASTWOOD

Because of the increased interest in D. H. Lawrence these days, many literary fans like to make a pilgrimage to Eastwood, his hometown. The English novelist was born there on September 11, 1885. Mrs. Brown, a member of the D. H. Lawrence Society, conducts parties of visitors around the "Lawrence country," hoping that at the end they'll make a donation to the society. If you're interested in taking a tour, write her in advance—Mrs. M. Brown, D. H. Lawrence Society, c/o 8a Victoria St., Eastwood, Nottingham NZ16 3GS (tel. 0773/718139).

The Victoria Street address is the Lawrence birthplace, which has been turned into the **D. H. Lawrence Information Centre and Museum** (tel. 0773/763312), now authentically depicting a miner's home as it was in 1885, with an audio-visual presentation. The Eastwood Library houses a unique collection of Lawrence's works and the headstone from his grave on the French Riviera. The museum is open daily April to October from 10 a.m. to 5 p.m., November to March from 10 a.m. to 4 p.m.; closed Christmas Eve to New Year's Day. Admission is 50p (90¢) for adults, 25p (45¢) for children.

SCROOBY

This is a tiny village of some 260 inhabitants where William Brewster, a leader of the Pilgrims, was born in 1566. His father was bailiff of the manor and master of the postes, so it may have been in the Manor House that the infant Brewster first saw the light of day. The original house dated from the 12th century, and the present manor farm, built on the site in the 18th century, has little except historical association to attract.

The village also contains Monks Hill on the River Ryton, now almost a backwater but once a navigable stream down which Brewster and his companions may have escaped to travel to Leyden in Holland and on to their eventual freedom.

In the 18th century, the turnpike ran through the village, and there are many stories of highwaymen, robberies, and murders. The body of John Spencer hung for more than 60 years as a reminder of the penalties of wrongdoing. He'd attempted to dispose of the bodies of the keeper of Scrooby toll-bar and his mother in the river.

Search for Pilgrim Roots

Many North Americans who trace their ancestry to the Pilgrims come to this part of England to see where it all started. The Separatist movement had its origin in an area north of Nottingham and south of York, and the towns from which its members came are all in a small area. They include **Blyth** (the one in Nottinghamshire,

not the one in Northumberland), **Scrooby, Austerfield, Bawtry,** and **Babworth.**
Pilgrim William Bradford's birthplace was a manor house in Austerfield, lived in
and well maintained today. It can be visited by arrangement with the occupant. The
churches at Scrooby and Babworth welcome North Americans.

Blyth is the most beautiful of the villages, with a green surrounded by well-kept
old houses, looking a lot like a New England village, which is no surprise. The parish
church was developed from the 11th-century nave of a Benedictine priory church.
On the green is a 12th-century stone building that was once the Hospital of St. John.

---

5. Lincolnshire

This large East Midlands county is bordered on one side by the North Sea. Its
most interesting section is Holland in the southeast, a land known for its fields of
tulips, its marshes and fens, and windmills reminiscent of the Netherlands. Much of
the shire is interesting to explore. Foreigners, particularly North Americans, generally cross the tulip fields, scheduling stopovers in the busy port of Boston before
making the swing north to the cathedral city of Lincoln, lying inland.

BOSTON

This old seaport in the riding of Holland has a namesake that has gone on to
greater glory, and perhaps for this reason it is visited by New Englanders. At Scotia
Creek, on a riverbank near Boston, is a memorial to the early Pilgrims who made an
unsuccessful attempt in 1607 to reach the promised land. They were imprisoned in
the Guildhall in cells that can be visited today. A company left again in 1620 and
fared better, as anybody who has ever been to Massachusetts will testify. Part of the
ritual here is climbing the Boston Stump, a church lantern tower with a view for
miles around of the all-encircling fens. In the 1930s, the people of Boston, U.S.A.,
paid for the restoration of the tower, known officially as St. Botolph's Tower. Actually, it's not recommended that you climb the tower, as the stairs aren't in good shape.
The tower, as it stands, was finished in 1460. The city fathers were going to add a
spire, making it the tallest in England. But because of the wind and the weight, they
feared the tower would collapse. Therefore, the tower became known as "the Boston
Stump." An elderly gentleman at the tower assured me it was the tallest in England
—that is, 272 feet tall. Boston is 116 miles north from London and 34 miles southeast of Lincoln.

Food and Lodging

At **Burton House,** Wainfleet Road, Boston, Lincolnshire PE21 9RW (tel.
0205/62307), most of this establishment's energies are directed toward the maintenance of its drinking and dining facilities on the ground floor. Upstairs, however,
comfortable bedrooms are available for overnight rentals. Two of the five rooms contain a private bath or shower. Singles range from £25 ($43.75) to £30 ($52.50) daily, with doubles costing £35 ($61.25) to £40 ($70), with breakfast and VAT
included. Meals are served in the Burton's grill room or its carvery. Depending on
the time of the week, as many as three bars might be in operation at the same time.
The stone-built house lies within a five-minute drive from the center of Boston, with
3½ acres of parkland.

Fairfield Guest House, 101 London Rd., Boston, Lincolnshire PE21 7EN
(tel. 0205/62869), is an economy oasis where you can spend the night in a stone
Victorian house set in its own garden. Built originally for a large family, it has been
adapted to receive overnight guests. Yet the personal quality hasn't been sacrificed.
At the edge of Boston, it is reached by a driveway leading to a formal entry. The
bedrooms have hot and cold running water and are centrally heated and pleasantly
furnished. For B&B, the owners, the Pages, charge £11 ($19.25) daily.

The Carving Table, New England Hotel, Wide Bargate (tel. 0205/65255), offers the best food value in town. In its carving room guests are invited to choose their main dish from a selection of freshly roasted joints of prime meat, carved by the hotel chef. The roast of the day costs from £7.25 ($12.70), and children are charged half price. An à la carte menu is also available. A choice of desserts from the trolley includes fruit salad and fruit pie, all served with fresh cream, but I found dessert almost unnecessary considering the amount of food offered at a fixed price. The Carving Table is open from noon to 2 p.m. and 7 to 10 p.m. seven days a week. The hotel also serves bar snacks all day every day.

LINCOLN

One of the most ancient cities in England, and only 135 miles north of London, Lincoln was known to the Romans as Lindum. Some of the architectural glory of the Roman Empire still stands to charm the present-day visitor. The renowned Newport Arch (the North Gate) is the last remaining arch left in Britain that still spans a principal highway. For a look at the Roman relics excavated in and around Lincoln, head for the **Greyfriars City & County Museum,** Broadgate (tel. 0522/30401), open daily from 10 a.m. to 5:30 p.m. (2:30 to 5 p.m. on Sunday). Admission is 25p (45¢) for adults, 10p (20¢) for children.

Two years after the Battle of Hastings, William the Conqueror built **Lincoln Castle** on the site of a Roman fortress. Used for administrative purposes today, parts of the castle still remain, including the walls, the 12th-century keep, and fragments of the gateway tower. In addition, you can visit the High Bridge over the Witham River, with its half-timbered houses (you can have a meal in one of them). This is one of the few medieval bridges left in England that has buildings nestling on it.

Visit also the **Museum of Lincolnshire Life,** Burton Road (tel. 0522/28448), the largest folk museum in the area, with displays ranging from a Victorian schoolroom to locally built steam engines. It's open daily from 10 a.m. to 5:30 p.m. (from 2 to 5:30 p.m. on Sunday). Admission is 75p ($1.30) for adults, 30p (55¢) for children.

Lincoln Cathedral

No other English cathedral dominates its surroundings as does Lincoln. Visible from up to 30 miles away, the minster's three towers are an arresting sight. The central tower is 271 feet high, making it the second tallest in England, giving just one foot to its near neighbor, Boston Stump, mentioned earlier. Monday to Saturday in summer, there are accompanied tower trips.

The original Norman cathedral was begun in 1072 and consecrated 20 years later. It sustained a major fire and then, in 1185, an earthquake. Only the central portion of the West Front and lower halves of the western towers survive from this period. The present cathedral represents the Gothic style, particularly the Early English and Decorated periods. The nave is 13th century, but the black font of tourni marble originates from the 12th century. In the Great North Transept is a rose medallion window known as the Dean's Eye. Opposite it, in the Great South Transept, is its cousin, the Bishop's Eye. East of the high altar is the Angel Choir consecrated in 1280 and so called after the sculpted angels high on the walls. The exquisite wood carving in St. Hugh's Choir dates from the 14th century. Lincoln's roof bosses, dating from the 13th and 14th centuries, are handsome. A mirror trolley assists visitors in their appreciation of these features that are some 70 feet above the floor. Easier to see are the oak bosses in the cloister.

In the Seamen's Chapel (Great North Transept) is a window commemorating Lincolnshire-born Captain John Smith, one of the pioneers of early settlement in America and the first governor of Virginia. The library and north walk of the cloister were built in 1674 to designs by Sir Christopher Wren. There are fine books and manuscripts, some of which may be on view in the adjoining Mediaeval Library (1422) together with one of the four remaining originals of the 1215 Magna Carta, although this document tours extensively throughout the world. The Cathedral Charter of 1072 and the Forester's Charter of 1225 are also extant.

In the Treasury, open from 2:30 to 4:30 p.m. Monday to Saturday from Easter to the end of September, there is fine gold and silver plate on display from the churches of the diocese.

The cathedral is open from 7:30 a.m. It closes at 8 p.m. Monday to Saturday in summer, at 6 p.m. Monday to Saturday in winter, and at 5 p.m. on Sunday in winter. The suggested donation to the cathedral is £1 ($1.75). Guided tours of about one hour are available Monday to Saturday in summer. For further details, phone 0522/544544.

Where to Stay

Hillcrest Hotel, 15 Lindum Terrace, Lincoln, Lincolnshire LN2 5RT (tel. 0522/510182), is a fine red-brick house built in 1871 as the private home of a local vicar. And although it has been converted into a comfortable small licensed hotel, it retains many of the features of its original use. It is suitable for those who appreciate a cozy atmosphere where personal tastes can be accommodated. It is in a quiet tree-lined road overlooking 26 acres of parkland, in the old high town and within easy walking distance of Lincoln Cathedral and the Roman remains. All B&B rooms have private baths, color TV, radios, and direct-dial phones. Monday to Thursday, singles cost £28 ($49) daily, and doubles go for £39 ($68.25). Friday to Sunday, the price of a single is £24 ($42), with doubles costing £36 ($63). Children are welcome, paying £5 ($8.75) to share with two adults. The Terrace Restaurant offers a wide variety of dishes cooked to order, with special menus for vegetarians and children.

Castle Hotel, Westgate, Lincoln, Lincolnshire LN1 3AS (tel. 0522/38801), constructed of red brick, rises three stories high, lying within a three-minute walk of the cathedral in Old Lincoln. When it was built around 1858, it was the North District National School, but it has been successfully converted into a hotel of character and comfort. The management rents 21 bedrooms, some of which are located within a nearby annex. Each is comfortably furnished, containing a private bath or shower. The charge for B&B in a single is £35 ($61.25) daily, rising to £48 ($84) in a double. A warmly masculine bar laden with Chesterfield-style leather sofas is located a few steps from the reception desk. Good English-style cooking is served in the Westgate Restaurant, where dinners cost from £10 ($17.50).

Duke William Hotel, 44 Bailgate, Lincoln, Lincolnshire LN1 3AP (tel. 0522/33351), is in the heart of historic Lincoln near the Roman arch, within walking distance of the cathedral. Although the structure has seen many architectural changes since its establishment in 1791, care has been taken to preserve the atmosphere of an 18th-century inn. Many of the 11 bedrooms still have their original heavy timbers. All of them contain TV. Singles cost from £28 ($49) to £38 ($66.50) daily with showers, and doubles go for £42 ($73.50) to £48 ($84) with showers. The hotel has both a good restaurant and a cozy bar. A tasty luncheon, costing from £5 ($8.75), is served from noon to 2:30 p.m. Monday to Saturday. Only cold snacks are served on Sunday, from noon to 1:45 p.m. Dinners are more elaborate, served Monday to Saturday from 7:30 to 9:30 p.m. An evening meal, with a main dish of rumpsteak, trout with almonds, or Mexican chicken, costs from £10 ($17.50).

Hollies Hotel, Carholme Road, Lincoln, Lincolnshire LN1 1RT (tel. 0522/22419), owned by the Colston family, provides clean, comfortable B&B accommodations at fair prices, including VAT. The rates are £14 ($24.50) nightly in a single, £25 ($43.75) in a double. Each room is centrally heated, with hot and cold running water and a radio. An evening meal is served. There's a free car park.

Fircroft Private Hotel, 396-398 Newark Rd., Lincoln, Lincolnshire LN6 8RX (tel. 0522/26522), is a clean and comfortable B&B house run by Val and Clive Hummerstone. All the heated rooms have color TV and tea- and coffee-making facilities and seven of the 15 accommodations have private toilets and showers. Depending on the plumbing, the B&B rates range from £18 ($31.50) to £25 ($42.75) daily in a single and from £29 ($50.75) to £35 ($61.25) in a double or twin, including VAT. There is a Tudor-style dining room and a small cocktail bar, serving an evening meal from Monday to Friday only for £7.50 ($13.15) per person. Sandwiches are usually available at most times when the dining room is closed.

Carline, 3 Carline Rd., Lincoln, Lincolnshire LN1 1HN (tel. 0522/530422), is considered among the finest B&B guesthouses in this cathedral city. Lying about a leisurely six-minute stroll from the cathedral, it has seven well-furnished and comfortable bedrooms with private baths or showers. Singles range from £12 ($21) to £18 ($31.50) daily, with doubles costing £21 ($36.75) to £24 ($42). There is limited parking. No dinner is provided, but Lincoln has several dining possibilities at night.

Tennyson, 7 South Park Ave., Lincoln, Lincolnshire LN5 8EN (tel. 0522/21624), is also a leading B&B house. It is really more a small hotel than a typical bed-and-breakfast establishment. Lying about a half mile from the cathedral precincts in the vicinity of South Park Common, Tennyson makes a good base for exploring the area, especially if you have a car. The eight bedrooms each have a private bath or shower. The overnight charge for B&B ranges from £24 ($42) to £26.50 ($46.40) in a single, going up to £38 ($66.50) to £41 ($71.75) in a double. Their food is good, and they serve dinner nightly from 6:30 to 8.

On the outskirts, you'll find **The Grassoes,** Hall Lane, Branston, Lincoln, Lincolnshire LN4 1PY (tel. 0522/791452), less than five miles from the center of Lincoln at Branston on the B1188. Mrs. Jean Stevenson offers B&B in her charming country house. A bed and a large, cooked-to-order breakfast goes for only £9 ($15.25) per person daily. An evening meal, a three-course family type, costs £5 ($8.75). Drive to Branston, then turn right at the Waggon and Horses and keep turning right for Mrs. Stevenson's house at the top of the hill.

Where to Dine

Wig & Mitre, 29 Steep Hill (tel. 0522/35190), run by Michael and Valerie Hope, is not only one of the best pubs in Old Lincoln, but it also serves a bill of fare better than that found in most restaurants. Sitting on the aptly named Steep Hill, it serves food daily from 8 a.m. to midnight. Decorated in an Old English atmosphere, the place operates throughout the day somewhat like a café-brasserie. The main restaurant, behind the drinking section on the second floor, has oak timbers, Victorian armchairs, and settees. This 14th-century pub, which has been much restored over the years, also has a summer beer garden. If the restaurant is full, all dishes can be served in the bar downstairs. Blackboard specials change daily, and you are likely to be offered such fare as roast rack of lamb resting on onion and sage purée, fricassee of guinea fowl, and breast of chicken wrapped in Parma ham and baked in phyllo pastry. A favorite dessert is chocolate rémoulade. Meals cost from £10 ($17.50).

Troff's, 35 Steep Hill (tel. 0522/510333), is operated by the town's finest restaurant, Harvey's, as a tag-along bistro to its more glamorous (and more expensive) parent. It sits next door to Harvey's, within a 200-year-old building offering views over Lincoln Cathedral. Its modern dining room is decorated with lithographs. Steaks are a popular item here, and other bistro-inspired food includes seafood lasagne and vegetarian burgers. Meals cost from £7 ($12.25). It is open Monday to Friday from 5 to 11 p.m. and on Saturday and Sunday from 11 a.m. to 11 p.m.

Brown's Pie Shop, 33 Steep Hill (tel. 0522/27330), is housed in a building dating from 1527, which bears the honor of having sheltered Lawrence of Arabia several times, when the house took in paying guests. Near the cathedral, it is today a beamed and rustic English dining room where you can order full meals from £5 ($8.75). Pies, as its name suggests, are the specialty, and they come in many varieties, including fish pies, vegetarian pies, steak-and-kidney pies, chicken-and-chestnut pies, and more. Don't like pies? Try the trout with almonds. Meals are served daily, except Sunday, from 11:30 a.m. to 5:30 p.m. for lunch and from 5:30 to 9:30 p.m. for dinner. Dinners are more expensive, costing from £9 ($15.75).

Stokes High Bridge Café, 207 High St. (tel. 0522/513825), is a 16th-century tea room built over the medieval bridge spanning the River Witham that is one of the sightseeing attractions of Lincoln. If you're seeking only tea and coffee, R. W. Stokes & Sons are specialists. The building is timbered with black-and-white beams. From the room on the top floor there is a view of the river and bridge. You reach the tea room by going through a little shop on the bridge level. Food here is a bargain. A complete luncheon, including a main course such as roast beef with Yorkshire pudding, vegetables, and a dessert (perhaps steamed blackberry and apple pudding), costs around £4 ($7). Lunch specials are served daily from 11:30 a.m. to 2 p.m. (no dinners).

Grand Hotel, St. Mary's Street (tel. 0522/24211), opens its restaurant to non-residents for good, well-prepared fare. From 7 to 9 p.m. daily, a four-course table d'hôte dinner is offered for £8.75 ($15.30). The food is not only typically English, but the portions are ample. The first course usually consists of a bowl of soup. Then comes the meat, poultry, or fish course, perhaps grilled rainbow trout with almonds or chicken chasseur. For dessert you can select desserts from the trolley. But that's not all: even cheese and biscuits (crackers) are included in the price. You can also lunch at the Grand from noon to 2 p.m. A buttery is open from 10:30 a.m. to 10 p.m.

Crust, 46 Broadgate (tel. 0522/540332), is a century-old building, an olde-worlde-style restaurant that occupies a site on the Old Roman Road. The chef-patron, Malta-born Victor Vella, has won a number of gold and silver medals for his cookery. He is assisted by his wife, Sylvia. They offer one of the best restaurant bargains in Lincoln, a fixed-price lunch for only £3 ($5.25). For that, you get three courses of well-prepared food. Other fixed-priced luncheon menus cost £5 ($8.75) to £6 ($10.50). The à la carte dinner menu is more elaborate, including such specialties as escalope of veal maréchale and steak Diane. You'll spend a lot more too, from £12 ($21) and up. A special luncheon menu, served from noon to 1:45 p.m. on Sunday, costs only £6 ($10.50) and includes the traditional roast beef and Yorkshire pudding. Morning coffee and cake are served from 10 a.m. to 2:30 p.m., lunch from 11:30 a.m. to 2:30 p.m., and dinner from 7 to 10:15 p.m. Tuesday to Thursday. On Friday and Saturday last orders are taken at 11:15 p.m. Sandwiches and bar snacks are served in the coffee lounge. The restaurant is closed Sunday evening and Monday.

STAMFORD

This is a charming stone market town lying 89 miles from London and visited chiefly for the following attraction.

Burghley House

This magnificent Elizabethan house (tel. 0780/52451), the home of the Marquess of Exeter, was built in the 16th century by William Cecil, the first Lord Burghley, who was lord high treasurer to Queen Elizabeth I. His descendants were created Earls of Exeter in 1605, and the house has remained in the family ever since. It contains a fabulous collection of Old Masters, but it is perhaps the marvelous painted ceilings for which the house is best known. The ceiling of the great drawing room and the ceiling and walls of the Heaven Room by Verrio are masterpieces of color and depth. Queen Elizabeth I's bedroom contains a four-poster bed covered in its original materials. The kitchens are in the oldest part of the house and have been restored and decorated exactly as they were originally. The house and the vast park around it—the latter landscaped by Capability Brown—are open daily April to September from 11 a.m. to 5 p.m. Admission to the Deer Park and a guided tour of the house and special exhibitions costs £3 ($5.25) for adults, £1.70 ($3) for children.

Food and Lodging

Crown Hotel, All Saints Place, Stamford, Lincolnshire PE9 2AG (tel. 0780/ 63136), is one of the best little town inns in the area. The owners rent 18 attractively furnished bedrooms, many quite generous in size. Nearly all of them contain private baths or showers. B&B charges are from £26 ($45.50) daily in a single, rising to £37 ($64.75) in a double. Guests gather in the intimate bar and a lounge with a stone wall, later enjoying some of the tasty fare served in the restaurant. You can order fish dishes and roast beef from the trolley.

If you're passing through for the day, consider a stopover at **Mr. Pips Coffee Shop and Restaurant,** 11 St. Mary St. (tel. 0708/65795), on the second floor of a building from the 16th century, above a china store near the heart of town. From 9:30 a.m. to 4:30 p.m. daily, except Sunday, you can get good-tasting food here, a meal costing £5 ($8.75) or even less. Some diners make a light lunch out of one of its stuffed potatoes, but you can get more substantial fare as well, including homemade soups, meat and poultry dishes, perhaps fresh fish. It's also a popular place for afternoon tea (also morning coffee), and one of the desserts might tempt you.

GRANTHAM

This market town stands in the middle of rich farming country. A corner site on North Parade was the childhood home of Britain's first woman prime minister, Margaret Thatcher. Her father, Alfred Roberts, ran a busy greengrocers shop on the ground floor, and the family lived in rooms above the business. Daughter Margaret was born here on October 13, 1925. The family moved to a nearby house in 1944, but Mr. Roberts continued with the store until he sold it in 1959.

In the Middle Ages, Grantham was a prosperous wool trade town. Isaac Newton attended King's School here in the 17th century, and his initials can still be seen on the wooden sill of the Old Schoolroom built of Ancaster stone. The 283-foot spire of St. Wulfram's Parish Church rises as a local landmark and can be seen for miles around. The town has many old inns and a medieval market cross. Its most important historic attraction is—

Belton House, a National Trust property 2½ miles north of Grantham (tel. 0476/66116), is one of the finest Restoration country houses in Britain, having been built in 1684 for Sir John Brownlow. The original architect was probably William Wynde, whose work resembles that of Wren. The house today appears very much as it did at its creation. The saloon and red drawing room are particularly finely carpeted, and the Tyrconnel room has a rare painted floor, apparently from the early 19th century. The library contains a fine barrel-vaulted ceiling by James Wyatt. Oriental porcelain and chinoiserie are part of the attractions. Throughout the house hang portraits of the family. It is open April to October, Wednesday to Sunday from 1 to 5:30 p.m., charging adults an admission of £3 ($5.25) and children, £1.50 ($2.65).

Food and Lodging

King's Hotel, 130 North Parade, Grantham, Lincolnshire NG31 8AU (tel. 0476/65881), stands on the street where Margaret Thatcher was born. Of the three major hotels in town, it is the best for the budget. It is small but well run, a Georgian-style private residence constructed in the 1880s. It has made a successful transformation to a small hotel of character, now offering 15 comfortably furnished bedrooms. Thirteen of these are equipped with private bath. The B&B rate in a single is £24 ($42) daily without bath, rising to £34 ($59.50) with bath. Doubles with private bath or shower cost from £49 ($85.75). Bar meals are popular at lunch, and you can eat in the hotel's Buttery daily from 7:30 a.m. to 11 p.m. (long hours have made it one of the most popular places in town). The hotel stands on the old A1, which in Dickens's day was known as the Great North Road leading out of town. However, there is a more modern A1 nowadays.

If you want an even better price, try the **Lanchester Guest House,** 84 Harrowby Rd., Grantham, Lincolnshire NG31 9DS (tel. 0476/74169), which is about the best B&B in town. It's small, only four rooms (one with private bath), and its prices are modest and appealing. The B&B rate ranges from £11 ($19.25) to £15.50 ($27.15) daily in a single, £20 ($35) to £25 ($43.75) in a double. The highest prices are for rooms with baths. The management is attentive at this Edwardian structure that was once a private home.

If you're looking for a good and reasonably priced place to eat, try **Knightingales,** Guildhall Court, Guildhall Street (tel. 0476/79243), which is open only during the day (9:30 a.m. to 4:30 p.m. daily, except Sunday). On a small back street, this is an attractive dining room specializing in vegetarian cookery. Instead of beef Stroganoff, you get mushroom Stroganoff, and nuts such as cashew are often used to give protein where meat might normally be used. The daily specials appear on the blackboard, and be assured that the chef insists that ingredients be fresh and good. You can also order certain fish and poultry dishes, including an excellent chicken liver pâté. A "carob slice" is a favorite, healthy dessert. Meals cost from £5 ($8.75) per person.

XVI

CHESHIRE, SHROPSHIRE, AND THE POTTERIES

1. CHESTER

2. NANTWICH

3. SHREWSBURY

4. STOKE-ON-TRENT

5. STAFFORD

6. LICHFIELD

Except for Chester, the cities, towns, and villages in this chapter were once little visited by tourists. But all that has changed now, and this section of western England is coming in for long overdue attention.

Chester is the capital of Cheshire—known for its cheese—and most visitors may want to anchor there because of its wealth of accommodations. Nantwich, an old salt town also previewed below, is another possibility.

Shropshire, on the border with Wales, has had a history of battles, sieges, and feuds. But the countryside is peaceful today and well worth a visit. One of the best centers for overnighting is Shrewsbury.

The county of Staffordshire lures because of its Potteries, which produce porcelain and china by such famous names as Spode and Wedgwood.

CHESHIRE

This county is low lying and largely agricultural. The name it gave to a cheese (Cheshire) has spread across the world. This northwestern county borders Wales, which accounts for its turbulent history. The towns and villages of Cheshire are peaceful and quiet, forming a good base for touring North Wales, the most beautiful part of that little country. For our headquarters in Cheshire, we'll locate at:

1. Chester

Chester is ancient, having been founded by a Roman legion on the Dee River in the first century A.D. It reached its pinnacle as a bustling port in the 13th and 14th centuries, declining thereafter following the gradual silting up of the river. The up-start Liverpudlians captured the sea-trafficking business. The other walls of medieval cities of England were either torn down or badly fragmented, but Chester still retains two miles of fortified city walls intact.

The main entrance into Chester is Eastgate, itself dating back to only the 18th century. Within the walls are half-timbered houses and shops. Of course, not all of them came from the days of the Tudors. Chester is freakish architecturally in that some of its builders kept to the black-and-white timbered facades even when erecting buildings during the Georgian and Victorian periods.

The Rows are double-decker layers of shops, one tier on the street level, the others stacked on top and connected by a footway. The upper tier is like a continuous galleried balcony. Shopping upstairs is much more adventurous than down on the street. Rain is never a problem. Thriving establishments operate in this traffic-free paradise: tobacco shops, restaurants, department stores, china shops, jewelers, and antique dealers. For the most representative look, take an arcaded walk on Watergate Street.

At noon and at 3 p.m. daily at the City Cross, the world's champion town crier issues his news (local stuff on sales, exhibitions, and attractions in the city) at the top of his not-inconsiderable voice, to the accompaniment of a hand bell, at the junction of Watergate, Northgate, and Bridge Streets.

After exploring The Rows, focus your attention on:

CHESTER CATHEDRAL

The present building, founded in 1092 as a Benedictine abbey, was created as a cathedral church in 1541. Considerable architectural restorations were carried out in the 19th century, but older parts have been preserved. Notable features include the fine range of monastic buildings, particularly the cloisters and refectory, the chapter house, and the superb medieval woodcarving in the choir (especially the misericords). Also worth attention are the long south transept with its various chapels, the consistory court, and the medieval roof bosses in the Lady Chapel. A free standing bell tower, the first to be built in England since the Reformation, was completed in 1975 and may be seen southeast of the main building. The cathedral is open daily from 7 a.m. to 6:30 p.m. There is a refectory, a bookshop, and an audio-visual presentation. For more information, phone 0244/324756.

DISCOVER CHESTER

In a big Victorian building opposite the amphitheater, the **Chester Visitor Centre,** Vicars Lane (tel. 0244/351609), only minutes from the city center, offers a number of services to visitors from 9 a.m. to 9 p.m. daily. A Tourist Information Centre, part of the national network, provides a wide range of services, including local and national accommodations booking, maps, free leaflets, guided tours, and reservations for local attractions. You are introduced to Chester by a map and print presentation on video film. A visit to a life-size Victorian street complete with sounds and smells helps your appreciation and orientation to Chester. The center has a gift shop, a licensed restaurant serving meals and snacks all day, and a currency exchange. Guided walking tours are also offered. Admission to the center is free, but a nominal charge is made for the video theater and exhibition areas.

A WALK ON THE WALL

In the center of town, you'll see an interesting old clock mounted on a wall. Climb the stairs near it, which lead up to the top of the city wall, and you can follow it on a walk looking down on Chester today from a path of the past. The wall passes through centuries of English history. You pass a cricket field, see the River Dee which was formerly a major trade artery, and get a look at many old buildings of the 18th century, some undergoing renovation. Flower-filled back gardens are lovely from this height. The wall also goes past some Roman ruins, and it is possible to leave the walkway to explore them. The walk is charming and free.

CHESTER ZOO

Just off the A41 on the outskirts of Chester, the Chester Zoo (tel. 0244/ 380280), two miles from the center of the city, is world famous for its wide collection of mammals, birds, reptiles, and fish, as well as for its 110 acres of gardens. Many rare and endangered species breed freely in spacious enclosures, and the zoo is particularly renowned for the most successful group of chimpanzees and orangutans in Europe. The gardens are worth seeing in any season, with 160,000 plants in the spring and summer bedding displays alone. A water bus, a popular summer feature, allows you to observe the hundreds of water birds who make their home here. The zoo has several facilities if you get hungry or thirsty during your visit: the licensed Oakfield Restaurant, the Jubilee self-service cafeteria, the Oasis snackbar, and the Rainbow kiosk, for either meals or snacks and drinks. The zoo is open daily from 10 a.m. to dusk, except Christmas Day. Admission is £3.80 ($6.65) for adults, £1.90 ($3.35) for children 3 to 15.

ACCOMMODATIONS

A well-restored and elegantly furnished Edwardian residence, the **Cavendish Hotel,** 44 Hough Green, Chester, Cheshire CH4 8JQ (tel. 0244/675100), is attractive and reasonable. It stands on the A549 coast road leading to North Wales. There is a large car park, and the city center is about a mile away. All 20 of the bedrooms contain color TV and direct-dial phones, and 16 have baths or showers. B&B costs £22.50 ($39.40) to £32.50 ($56.90) daily, and doubles go for £32.50 ($56.90) to £42.50 ($74.40). The lounge re-creates the mood of the Edwardian era, both in its decor and the antiques that furnish it. The dining room serves a limited but select menu, with dinner around £10 ($17.50), and packed lunches are available upon request. There's also a small residents bar. In all, it has a lot of cozy charm.

Ye Olde King's Head Hotel, 48-50 Lower Bridge St., Chester, Cheshire CH1 1RS (tel. 0244/324855), is a 16th-century museum piece of black-and-white architecture. From 1598 to 1707, it was occupied by the well-known Randle Holme family of Chester, noted heraldic painters and genealogists (some of their manuscripts have made it to the British Museum). Since 1717, the King's Head has been a licensed inn. The host rents out a dozen handsome bedrooms, all with private baths or showers, color TV, and facilities for making hot beverages. The place has central heating. The B&B charges are £39 ($68.25) daily in a single, £50 ($87.50) in a double or twin, and £59 ($103.25) in a double with a four-poster bed. Many of the walls and ceilings are sloped and highly pitched, with exposed beams. The dining room, Mrs. B's Restaurant, has a country farmhouse theme and serves wholesome dishes, including prime English roast, steak, or chicken. Meals cost from £10 ($17.50). The restaurant is open from noon to 2:30 p.m. and 7:30 to 10 p.m.

Riverside Recorder Hotel, 19 City Walls, Chester, Cheshire CH1 1SB (tel. 0244/311498), lies off Lower Bridge Street and is not to be confused with the Riverside Hotel nearby at 22 City Walls. A small ten-room guesthouse, one of the best B&Bs in town, it has been recently modernized. On the old Roman Wall, it enjoys an enviable location, within easy walking distance of the main attractions in the center of town. Some of the comfortably furnished accommodations open onto views of the River Dee, and the licensed hotel also has a garden in front (in the rear is a car park). Rates range from £15.50 ($27.15) to £22 ($38.50) daily in a single, £20.50 ($35.90) to £27 ($47.25) in a double. These accommodations have either private baths or showers.

The Redland Hotel, 64 Hough Green, Chester, Cheshire CH4 8JY (tel. 0244/671024), standing on its own grounds, is a Victorian town house of character and charm, with oak paneling and stained-glass windows. Open year-round except in January and February, it lies about a mile from the center of Chester in the direction of the Welsh border, and many guests use it as a base for exploring North Wales. Ten pleasant bedrooms are rented, all with private baths. The B&B charge is £24 ($42.75) nightly in a single, £35 ($61.25) to £45 ($78.75) in a double or twin. There is a residential license for serving alcohol.

The Eversley Hotel, 9 Eversley Park, Chester, Cheshire CH2 2AJ (tel. 0244/373744), lies off Liverpool Road, about a mile from the heart of old Chester. Bryn and Barbara Povey have fully modernized the select 11-bedroom hotel. Most units have private baths or showers, and all have color TV, hot beverage facilities, hot and cold water basins, razor sockets, and radios, as well as intercoms. The B&B charges are £18 ($31.50) daily in a single with shower, £32 ($56) in a double or twin with shower, and £34 ($59.50) in a double or twin with full bath. Evening meals are available in the candlelit dining room, and you can enjoy snacks in the Deva Bar. The hotel stands in a peaceful residential section.

Derry Raghan Guest House, 54 Hoole Rd., Chester, Cheshire CH2 3NL (tel. 0244/318740), lies about a mile from the heart of Chester and some three miles from the zoo. Bill and Doris Millar welcome guests to their pleasantly furnished rooms, charging them from £11 ($19.25) per person nightly. Each unit has a color TV and tea- and coffee-maker. Two double rooms have private baths. Drivers will find parking space.

WHERE TO EAT

For what some critics consider the best food in Chester, head for **Abbey Green,** 2 Abbey Green, Northgate Street (tel. 0244/313251). It just happens to be vegetarian. Some diehard meat-lovers, or so it is said, have been won over to the cause of vegetarian dining by eating at Abbey Green. The international influence prevails in many of the dishes, which often have zesty flavors that might be unfamiliar to you. For example, you might try, if featured, eggplant Szechuan (eggplant in Britain is called "aubergine"). The inventive menu is but a showcase of the fresh, well-prepared, and invariably good concoction of dishes. Phyllo pastry often wraps some delectable goodies from the kitchen. Desserts tend to be worth the trek across town, as exemplified by a hazelnut-flavored pastry flan stuffed with raspberries and freshly whipped cream, presumably from a fat, satisfied Cheshire cow. "The Abbey" serves daily, except it offers no dinner on Sunday or Monday. Otherwise, hours are from 11:30 a.m. to 3 p.m. and 6:30 to 10:15 p.m. Lunches cost from £5 ($8.75), with dinners going for £10 ($17.50).

Lilian's Downstairs Restaurant, 49 Lower Bridge St. (tel. 0244/321139). On the day Patricia Cowie opened the pretty little Upstairs Downstairs guesthouse she took over in Lower Bridge Street, a friend from the past, Lilian Rawlingson, stopped by to wish her luck, took her coat off, and stayed—to open this delightful restaurant in the vaulted basement of the house in what had been the Georgian below-stairs kitchen. A dancer by profession, Lilian had worked in many kitchens and restaurants while "resting" between engagements, and she used the time wisely to expand her natural gift for cooking. Appetizers here include shrimp with herbs, cream, and lemon cooked in garlic butter and served with crusty bread, roast spareribs with barbecue sauce, and pâté with hot toast. Among main dishes are two lamb cutlets with mint sauce and fresh vegetables, duckling à l'orange with dauphinoise potatoes, and beef Stroganoff with green salad or ratatouille. The vegetarian salad is served with a dip and crusty French bread and butter. A two-course steak and salad special at lunch goes for £5 ($8.75). Dinner is from £7.50 ($13.15) per person. The restaurant is so popular that unless you are a guest "Upstairs," you should make a reservation. The place is closed Monday, but otherwise service is from noon to 2 p.m. and 5:30 to 9:30 p.m.

The **Witches Kitchen,** 19 Frodsham St. (tel. 0244/311836), is in the center of town, just a short walk from the station. It seats 100 and has old-world charm and good service. The ground-floor restaurant is 15 yards from the city walls and Chester Cathedral. It is open every day for morning coffee from 9:30 to 11:30 a.m., for lunch from 11:30 to 2:30 p.m., for afternoon tea from 2:30 to 6 p.m., and for dinner from 6 to 10 p.m. Cheshire chicken is a favorite dish, and traditional roasts are served all day. Lunch costs around £6 ($10.50), and dinners go for £13 ($22.75) to £15 ($26.25). All meals are à la carte. The Kitchen is open seven days a week.

The **Gallery Restaurant,** 24 Paddock Row, Grosvenor Precinct (tel. 0244/47202), is festooned with masses of green plants, which make walking in here a little like going into an indoor garden. A varied menu is offered. Three courses with wine can be enjoyed for £6 ($10.50) to £11 ($19.25). Hours are 10 a.m. to 5 p.m. Monday to Saturday.

Claverton's Wine Bar, Lower Bridge Street (tel. 0244/319760), is very popular with the locals in the evening, a good way to see—if not to meet—the people of Chester. The imposing building of which Claverton's occupies the lower part began life as a private residence in 1715, becoming the Albion Hotel in 1818. Since then, the building has seen many changes. The wine bar is attractively decorated, the food good and reasonable, served throughout the day. However, many diners consider its best value to be from 12:30 to 2:30 p.m., when the buffet is served at a cost of £3 ($5.25) per person. You can begin with a soup, perhaps leek-and-potato, followed by a selection from the cold buffet. A popular dish is fish mousse. Full meals from the à la carte "snack menu" cost from £7 ($12.25). An unusual dish, at least to Americans, is the fresh trout stuffed with celery and nuts. Chicken roulade is a specialty. In addition to the regular mixed drinks, wines are available by the glass, as are "mocktails" for drivers or those nursing a hangover from the day before. In summer, the tables outside are popular. Claverton's is open Monday to Saturday from 11 a.m. to 11 p.m. From June to September, afternoon teas with fresh baked scones are served daily from 3:30 to 5:30 p.m.

Gibby's Restaurant, 12 Eastgate St. (tel. 0244/314669), is a bright and cheerful place for good simple food at low prices. Unelaborate service throughout the day starts at 8 a.m., lasting until 8 p.m. (on Sunday from 10 a.m. to 8 p.m.). You get such traditional English dishes as roast beef with Yorkshire pudding and home-baked steak-and-kidney pie. Fish dishes, hamburgers, salads, and a children's menu are also available. Expect to pay about £4.50 ($7.90) for a meal. Breakfast is served daily.

SOME LOCAL PUBS

One of the most famous pubs in Chester, the **Bear and Billet,** 94 Lower Bridge St. (tel. 0244/321272), was the former town house of the Earls of Shrewsbury, built in 1644. With its intricately timbered and highly decorative facade, this is one of the most photographed buildings in Chester. Full meals are served in the upstairs dining room daily from noon to 2:30 p.m. and 7 to 9 p.m. A three-course fixed-price menu costs £6 ($10.50) at midday, but your tab is likely to go up to £11 ($19.25) at night by ordering from an à la carte menu of good British cooking. Bar snacks are served at the street-level pub throughout the day. Pub hours are from 11 a.m. to 11 p.m. Monday to Saturday, and on Sunday from noon to 3 p.m. and 7 to 10:30 p.m.

An alternative for drinking is the **Boot Inn,** Eastgate Row (tel. 0244/314540), established in 1643, with timbered walls, high-back benches, and low ceilings. This is the smallest and most unspoiled pub in Chester, familiar only to oldtimers and those in the know. It's reached by entering a passageway along the upper Rows of Eastgate Street. The publican has a multitude of mementos cluttering the walls. Cold bar snacks here cost from £1.25 ($2.20). The Boot is open from 11 a.m. to 4 p.m. and 5 to 11 p.m. Monday to Friday, from 11 a.m. to 4 p.m. and 6 to 11 p.m. Saturday, and from noon to 3 p.m. and 7 to 10:30 p.m. Sunday.

2. Nantwich

The old market town on the Weaver River lies only 15 miles southeast of the county town of Chester and can easily be tied in with a visit to that city. The town is particularly outstanding because of its black-and-white timbered houses. The most spectacular one, Churche's Mansion, is a dining recommendation.

FOOD AND LODGING

The most enchanting old restaurant in Cheshire, **Churche's Mansion Restaurant,** 150 Hospital St. (tel. 0270/625933), lies in Nantwich at the junction of Newcastle Road and the Chester bypass. Many years ago, the late Dr. and Mrs. E. C. Myott learned that this historic home of a wealthy Elizabethan merchant had been advertised for sale in America and asked the town council to step in and save it. Alas, no English housewife wanted such a gloomy and dark home, so the Myotts attended the sale and outbid the American syndicate who wanted to transport it to the United States. They sought out the mysteries of the house: a window in the side wall, inlaid initials, a Tudor well in the garden, and a long-ago love knot with a central heart (a token of Richard Churche's affection for his young wife). Today the house is widely known and recommended for its quality meals. Lunch costs from £8.50 ($14.90) and dinners from £16.50 ($28.90). Tariffs include VAT and coffee. Hours are from noon to 2 p.m. and 7 to 9:30 p.m. daily. It is advisable but not absolutely necessary to make reservations.

For some two centuries, **Lamb Hotel,** Hospital Street, Nantwich, Cheshire CW5 5RH (tel. 0270/625286), a mellow old hotel in the heart of Nantwich, has been welcoming wayfarers to its 16 comfortably furnished bedrooms, 13 of which now contain private baths. Depending on the plumbing requested, the single rate ranges from £20 ($35) to £27.50 ($48.15) daily, the double from £31 ($54.25) to £40 ($70). There is ample parking outside as well. Visitors and locals alike mingle in the pub of the hotel, and meals are served daily. Pub fare is offered daily from noon to 2 p.m., with lunches costing from £5.50 ($9.65), and full dinners are served from 7:30 to 9:30 p.m. from £11.50 ($20.15). The cooking is both English and continental.

SHROPSHIRE

Immortalized by A. E. Housman's *A Shropshire Lad,* this hilly county borders Wales, which accounts for its turbulent history. The bloody battles are over today, and the towns, with their black-and-white timbered houses, are peaceful and quiet. It makes a good base for touring in the Welsh mountains.

When Parliament redistricted and even renamed some of the shires of England in 1973, the name of Shropshire was changed back to a much older name—Salop. However, in this case the name just didn't catch on, and you'll find the county still called Shropshire on recent maps and by most of its inhabitants.

3. Shrewsbury

Lying within a horseshoe bend of the Severn River, Shrewsbury is the capital of Shropshire. The river almost encloses the town. Known for its cakes and ale, Shrewsbury contains one of the best-known schools in England. It was also the birthplace of Charles Darwin.

Considered the finest Tudor town in England, Shrewsbury is noted for its black-and-white buildings of timber and plaster, including Abbot's House from 1450 and the tall-gabled Ireland's Mansion from 1575 standing on High Street. It also has a number of Georgian and Regency mansions, some old bridges, and handsome churches, including the Abbey Church of St. Peter and St. Mary's Church.

Shrewsbury Castle, built by the Norman Earl Roger de Montgomery in 1083, stands in a dominating position where the River Severn almost surrounds the town. It houses the Shropshire Regimental Museum, including the collections of the King's Shropshire Light Infantry, the Shropshire Yeomanry Cavalry, and the Shropshire Royal Horse Artillery. The collections represent more than 300 years of regimental service and include a lock of Napoleon's hair and an American flag captured when the Executive Mansion (called the White House after a subsequent paint job) was seized and burned in the War of 1812 (in 1814). The castle is open daily from 10 a.m. to 5 p.m. Admission is 60p ($1.05). For more information, phone 0743/52234.

Rowley's House Museum, Barker Street (tel. 0743/61196), is housed in a fine 16th-century timber-frame house and an adjoining brick mansion. This museum includes displays on art, local history, Roman and prehistoric archeology, geology, costumes, and natural history. The great treasures include the fine Hadrianic forum inscription and silver mirror, both from the nearby Roman city of Viroconium (Wroxeter). The museum is open Monday to Saturday from 10 a.m. to 5 p.m., as well as on Sunday from noon to 5 p.m. Easter to mid-September. Admission is 50p (90¢) for adults, 20p (35¢) for children.

Clive House Museum on College Hill (tel. 0743/54811), town house of Clive of India as Mayor of Shrewsbury in 1762, contains period rooms and splendid local pottery and porcelain, early watercolors and textiles, and a lovely garden. Hours are from 2 to 5 p.m. on Monday, and from 10 a.m. to 1 p.m. and 2 to 5 p.m. Tuesday to Saturday. Admission is 30p (55¢) for adults, 15p (25¢) for children.

At **Coleham Pumping Station,** Longden Coleham (tel. 0743/61196), you can see displayed compound rotative pumping engines from 1900. Open by appointment only, it charges an admission of 30p (55¢) for adults, 15p (25¢) for children.

WHERE TO STAY

A small, well-kept hotel, **Abbey Lodge Guest House,** 68 Abbey Foregate, Shrewsbury, Shropshire SY2 6BE (tel. 0743/235832), is a "listed" Georgian guesthouse, meaning its facade can't be altered. The owners rent nine comfortably furnished bedrooms, only five of which contain a private bath or shower. B&B charges for an overnight stay range from £11 ($19.25) to £18 ($31.50) per person. The house also serves good solid food, and you can arrange to have dinner here (but it must be ordered in advance).

The White House, Hanwood, Shrewsbury, Shropshire SY5 8LP (tel. 0743/860414), is a lovely half-timbered beamed country house supposedly dating back to the 16th century. It is to be found on the A488, 3½ miles from Shrewsbury near the Welsh border and famous Ironbridge with its museums. Mike and Gill Mitchell, the owners, charge £14 ($24.50) per person daily for bed and a full English breakfast. A three-course dinner costs £8.50 ($14.90). If you stay two or more nights, you can take half board for £18.50 ($32.40) per person per night. There are five guest bedrooms, a comfortable TV lounge, and a fully licensed bar. The bar and lounge are for the use of guests only. The hotel is centrally heated.

Glyndene, Abbey Foregate, Shrewsbury, Shropshire SY2 6BE (tel. 0743/52488), is an attractive guesthouse, providing B&B for £10 ($17.50) per person per night. Hot and cold running water, TV, and tea- and coffee-makers are in each room. A full English breakfast is served by the owner, Judy McRea.

WHERE TO DINE

A good place to find good food is the **Cavalier Restaurant,** Prince Rupert Hotel, Butcher Row (tel. 0743/236000). The hotel has three restaurants, of which the Cavalier is the most outstanding choice. White tablecloths, oil paintings, and a beamed ceiling live up to the tourist's conception of the heart of England. A fixed-price lunch menu, costing £8.90 ($15.60), includes a tempting choice of a well-prepared cuisine, such as a mortadella salad, followed by poached filet of plaice mornay, with potatoes and two vegetables, plus cheese. A fixed-price dinner might include smoked mackerel with horseradish sauce, poached sweetbreads mexicaine, along with vegetables and a freshly prepared dessert. This restaurant is popular with local residents as well as clients of the hotel. Lunch is daily from noon to 2:30 p.m. Dinner is served from 7 to 10:30 p.m. Guests can also patronize the Steak Bar and the Royalist Restaurant.

Delany's Vegetarian Restaurant, St. Julians Craft Centre, St. Alkmunds Square (tel. 0743/60602), is a whole-food vegetarian restaurant set in the vestry of a church that is now used as a craft center. The restaurant is open Monday to Saturday from 10:30 a.m. to 3:30 p.m., serving morning coffee, afternoon teas, and a selection of home-baked cakes and tasty fruit slices. At lunchtime, 11:30 a.m. to 2:30 p.m., a wide range of hot food is available. Spicy lentil and tomato soup with freshly baked bread and butter is a favorite. There is always a choice of a savory bake or a casserole. For example, Chilean marrow and sweet corn bake is a seasonal selection. There are also burgers, quiches, and loaves to choose from. To complement your choice of hot food, there are six fresh, crisp salads to try out, or try a combination of them. If there's any room left, the desserts are a delight. Pear and lemon cashew crumble or chocolate orange pudding may tempt you. Reasonably priced wine is available by the glass or bottle. Meals cost from £5 ($8.75).

Cornhouse, 59a Wyle Cop (tel. 0743/231991), is both a restaurant (on the second floor) and a wine bar (at ground level). A major rendezvous point in town, it attracts a flow of loyal patrons who walk down a steep street to partake of its fine food and drink. They do so daily from noon to 2:30 p.m. and 6:30 to 10:30 p.m. Many of the dishes, such as stuffed dolmades (vine leaves) and a Greek-inspired moussaka look to the Mediterranean kitchen for their inspiration. Daily specials are posted on a blackboard menu, with meals costing from £6 ($10.50).

WHITTINGTON

Many motorists in Shropshire drive across the county to eat at the **Whittington Inn,** at Whittington, near Stourbridge in West Midlands on the main Kidderminster-Wolverhampton road (tel. 0384/872496). The inn is the original manor house of Sir William de Whittington, Dick Whittington's grandfather, who built it in 1310. Dick Whittington, of course, was the enterprising lad from a merchant family who became one of the principal bankers to English kings and later lord mayor of London, elected three times between 1398 and 1420.

Today the ancestral home boasts a bistro and wine bar. The interior is white-painted brick, and the menu offers a selection from a cold buffet along with such hot food as chili con carne, cottage pie, and stews. You can also order sandwiches and a wide selection of English cheeses. Meals cost from £6 ($10.50). Hours Monday to Saturday are from 11 a.m. to 2:30 p.m. (on Sunday, noon to 3 p.m.) and 5:30 to 11 p.m. In addition to the bistro, the inn operates three oak-paneled and beamed bars with fires burning in winter, and a Tudor walled garden, where traditional real ale is served. The restaurant part of the operation is open from Monday to Saturday in the evening and for Sunday lunch, offering both a table d'hôte menu and a more expensive à la carte menu than that served in the wine bar. Families are welcome.

LUDLOW

Looking down on the Teme River, this is a mellow old town with a historic Norman castle. Many Georgian and Jacobean timbered buildings stand on its quiet lanes and courts. The most colorful street is known as "Broad," rising from the old Ludford Bridge to Broadgate, the one remaining gateway from walls erected in the Middle Ages. See, in particular, the Church of St. Laurence, Butter Cross, and Reader's House.

Bed and Breakfast

Wadboro Thatch, Thriftwicket Lane, Haytons Bent, Ludlow, Shropshire SY8 2AU (tel. 058475/249), is a genuine 16th-century thatched cottage. It is in a completely secluded position in beautiful countryside, yet only a five-minute drive from Ludlow, the historic market town with a castle. Take Fishmore Road out of Ludlow, turning left up a lane shortly after you pass a telephone kiosk (on the right).

The cottage has been fully restored, yet its original features have been maintained—in fact, it's a perfect example of an old English country cottage. Not large, it's very traditional, with its upper rooms tucked under the thatch, latticed windows, oak beams, and an inglenook fireplace with a bread oven. Accommodation comprises two doubles with private baths. Constructed of stone, the walls are nearly two feet thick. This, together with the thatch roof, keeps it cool in summer, warm in winter. The cottage is owned by Mrs. Pamela Allcock-Brown. She loves people and is very used to meeting them and making them feel at home. A room with bath and an English breakfast rents for £15 ($26.25) per night per person.

CRAVEN ARMS

A few miles north of Ludlow on the A49 is the small town of Craven Arms, in this "area of outstanding natural beauty" beside the River Onny.

Hillside, Twitchen, Clunbury, Shropshire SY7 0HN (tel. 05887/485), a short distance west of Craven Arms, just south of the B4368 road, is a good place to stay to explore the south Shropshire hills and visit major attractions of the area. Hillside is a 200-year-old stone country cottage, in which Mrs. Veronica Oates accommodates guests in one single room, one double, and two twin-bedded rooms. All have hot and cold water basins and facilities for making tea and coffee. There is one bathroom and two toilets. A comfortable sitting room has a large inglenook fireplace where log fires blaze in inclement weather. Maps and guides of the area are kept here for the use of guests. The charge for B&B is £9.50 ($16.65) per person daily. With dinner added, the rate goes up to £14 ($24.50) per person. In the dining room, at separate tables, Mrs. Oates serves either a light or a full English breakfast, depending on the desires of guests. A 50p (90¢) surcharge is asked of persons spending only one night here. Children are not accommodated.

IRONBRIDGE

Ironbridge Gorge is the birthplace of the Industrial Revolution and the location of an intriguing complex of museums.

The Iron Bridge was the first in the world made of that metal, which was cast at Coalbrookdale in 1779 and gave its name to the area. Abraham Darby I, ironmaster, first smelted iron using coke as a fuel at the Old Furnace in Coalbrookdale, thus paving the way for the first iron rails, iron bridge, iron boat, iron aqueduct, and iron-framed building. The Ironbridge Gorge Museum spreads over some six square miles of the Severn Gorge, encompassing a unique series of industrial monuments.

The **Ironbridge Gorge Museum,** Ironbridge, Telford (tel. 095245/3522), includes the Blists Hill Open Air Museum with a re-creation of a 19th-century town with costumed demonstrators; the Coalbrookdale Museum and Furnace of Iron with a sound-and-light display; the Coalport China Museum; the Jackfield Tile Museum; the Severn Warehouse (now the Museum of the River), and many other smaller museums, including the Bedlam Furnaces; the 1779 Iron Bridge (first in the world) with its original toll house; Rosehill House (the restored 19th-century home of the Darby family); the Long Warehouse Library and Archives; and the Elton Gallery with changing exhibitions. A ticket to all the attractions is £5.50 ($9.65) for adults, £3.50 ($6.15) for children. A family ticket for two adults and up to five children costs £17.50 ($30.65). All the sites are open from 10 a.m. to 6 p.m. daily from mid-February to the end of October. The Ironbridge Gorge was declared a World Heritage Site by UNESCO in 1987.

For an accommodation in the area, I suggest **The Hall,** Hope Bowdler, near Church Stretton, Shropshire SY6 7DD (tel. 0694/722041), which charges £12 ($21) daily per person for B&B. Hope Bowdler, on the B4371, is only 1½ miles from Church Stretton, an attractive small resort in the Shropshire Hills. Turn off the road in the village onto an unpaved lane leading past the church. The Hall entrance is on the left at the end of the lane. The house has been modernized, providing two twin-bedded and one single room for guests. There are two baths with showers, plus hot and cold running water and central heating in each unit. The house is really the home of the Inglis family, direct descendants of Bishop Charles Inglis, rector of New York's Trinity Church at the time of the War of Independence and later the first bishop of Nova Scotia. The house contains many interesting historical family pictures and possessions.

BRIDGNORTH/WORFIELD

The thriving town of Bridgnorth is accessible by a number of roads, chief among them being the A442 and the A458, as well as by the Severn Valley Railway. It is near the confluence of the Rivers Severn and Worfe. The Danes are known to have come to this area late in the ninth century, building a camp at Cwatford, which may be the present-day Quatbridge, a hamlet a short way down the Severn from Bridgnorth. At the beginning of the 10th century, a castle was erected here for King Alfred's daughter, Ethelfleda. Bridgnorth was first known to history when a castle was built here by Robert de Belleme at the end of the 11th century, but he was soon forced out by the army of King Henry I in 1102. The keep of the castle is all that remains, its tilted appearance reminiscent of the Leaning Tower of Pisa. The castle and the town that grew up around it, known as the High Town, were mainly destroyed during the Civil War, in the siege of 1646.

Surviving the depredations of war is the North Gate, dating from 1265 and now the site of **Bridgnorth Museum,** containing mainly local artifacts from Bronze Age tools to Civil War weapons and up to today. It is open from 2 to 4 p.m. April to September on Saturday, and mid-July to August and bank holidays on Monday, Tuesday, and Wednesday. Admission is free, but donations are welcomed.

In 1652, a new Town Hall, a little magpie half-timbered structure, was built over an archway in the middle of the wide main street. The Low Town is at the foot of the hill on the other side of the Severn, linked to the High Town by funicular.

At **Bridgnorth Station,** you can see railway sheds housing steam locomotives from the 1930s and 1940s restored and kept in working order by Severn Valley Railway buffs. In summer, it's possible to take a ride on a train pulled by one of the glistening engines operating daily.

For information on these and other sights in the area, see the **Bridgnorth Library and Information Centre,** Listley Street (tel. 07462/3358).

If you're seeking accommodation in the area, your best bet is **The Croft Hotel,** St. Mary's Street, Bridgnorth, Shropshire WV16 4DW (tel. 0746/767155). Many people use this hotel as their base for exploring not only Bridgnorth but the beautiful Severn Valley. And an excellent choice it is, renting out a dozen comfortable and pleasantly furnished bedrooms to paying guests. Of these, ten have private baths or showers. The charge for B&B, depending on the plumbing, ranges from £18 ($31.50) daily in a single, from £32 ($56) in a double. The hotel is one of character, with much charm, as reflected by its timeworn beams. The family who runs it are most welcoming and will guide you to attractions in their area, such as the Wenlock Edge, Wyre Forest, Ironbridge Gorge, and Clee Hills. Their food is good, and they will also quote half-board terms, ranging from £24 ($42) per person daily.

THE POTTERIES

In Staffordshire, Stoke-on-Trent is the name of the five towns called the Potteries, the "Five Towns" of Arnold Bennett's novels. The Potteries are known throughout the world for the excellence of their fine porcelain and china.

The so-called "Black Country" of steelworks and coal mines has almost disappeared, but you can visit a coal mine and descend in the "cage" to the worked-out seams.

Within easy reach of the industrial town of Dovedale is a valley with some of England's most beautiful scenery, forming part of the Peak District National Park.

4. Stoke-on-Trent

Because of the worldwide interest in the making of pottery, this Staffordshire town has found itself a tourist attraction. It's the home of the pottery made famous by Josiah Wedgwood, along with other well-known names such as Coalport, Minton, and Spode.

THE SIGHTS

An introduction to pottery making is provided at the **Wedgwood Visitor Centre,** at Barlaston (tel. 0782/204141), charging £1.75 ($3.05) for adults, £1 ($1.75) for children. It is open from 9 a.m. to 5 p.m. Monday to Friday and 10 a.m. to 4 p.m. Saturday, as well as from 10 a.m. to 4 p.m. on Sunday from Easter to October. It's closed only during the Christmas holidays and New Year's. In the demonstration hall you can watch the slip, the clay, built up on the potter's wheel, see how the raised motifs so well known on Wedgwood blue pottery are made and added to the pieces, and witness how delicate flowers are made and painted and plates turned and fired, then painted.

Craft operatives are happy to answer your questions about their special occupation. There's a continuous film show in the large cinema, and the beginning of the movie is announced on the public address system. In the shop you can see samples of all the sorts of items made at the factory and purchase souvenirs. Prices are the same as elsewhere, but they do sometimes have items of discontinued lines and some "seconds" available at reduced prices.

The fascinating museum was redesigned and enlarged in 1985 and features "living" displays, including Josiah Wedgwood's Etruria factory and his Victorian showroom. Other room settings can also be seen. When you need a rest, there is a lounge with a snack cafeteria where a selection of light refreshments can be had at reasonable prices. Here you can write your postcards home and have them franked with a special stamp to say they were mailed at the Wedgwood Centre.

At **Royal Doulton,** Nile Street, Burslem, near Stoke-on-Trent (tel. 0782/575454), you will walk for nearly a mile and negotiate some 250 steps during the tour of this pottery factory, but you will see exactly how plates, cups, and figures are made from basic raw materials. The gift shop has slightly imperfect articles on sale alongside quality goods, and you can browse through the Sir Henry Doulton Gallery, which traces the company's history since 1815 and contains a collection of Doulton's historical figures. Tours of the factory are at 10:15 a.m. and 2 p.m., costing £2 ($3.50). The gallery is open Monday to Friday from 9 a.m. to 4:15 p.m. Advance reservations are advisable. Call Sandra Baddeley, the tour organizer, at the number above.

Since 1896, the **John Beswick Studios** of Royal Doulton, Gold Street, Longton, near Stoke-on-Trent (tel. 0782/313041), have built a reputation for fine ceramic sculpture. Most renowned for its authentic studies of horses, birds, and animals, the studio also creates the famed Character and Toby Jugs of Royal Doulton. You may be lucky enough to see Peter Rabbit in the making during a tour. The 1½ hour tour ends in the factory shop so you can indulge your shopping whims. Tours depart at 10:15 a.m. and 2 p.m. Monday to Friday, costing £1.50 ($2.65). Advance reservations are essential (call Joan Barker).

It is recommended that you make reservations to visit any of the Royal Doulton facilities, either by writing or telephoning. All the premises date back to the 19th century and are not suitable for the elderly or disabled. Also, for safety reasons, they do not accommodate children under the age of 10.

Spode, Church Street, Stoke-on-Trent (tel. 0782/744011), is yet another factory that offers guided tours, available at 10 a.m. and 2 p.m. Monday to Thursday, and at 10 a.m. Friday. Again, advance reservations are essential. The cost is £1 ($1.75). The shop is open from 9 a.m. to 5 p.m. Monday to Thursday, from 9 a.m. to 4 p.m. Friday, and from 9 a.m. to 1 p.m. Saturday.

Coloroll Ceramics Division Factory Shop, Meir Park, Stoke-on-Trent (tel. 0782/315251), is the largest mug manufacturer in the world. It is open from 9:30 a.m. to 5:30 p.m. Monday to Saturday, offering a wide range of tableware, mugs, vases, pots, and ovenware. In addition to perfect examples, they also sell "seconds" where the flaws are so minor that the untrained eye can't detect them. And the prices are reasonable.

Moorcroft Pottery, W. Moorcroft Ltd., Sandbach Road, Burslem, Stoke-on-Trent (tel. 0782/24323), is an interesting alternative to the world-famous names. Founded in 1898 by William Moorcroft, who produced his own special brand of pottery and was his own exclusive designer until his death in 1945, the pottery is special in that decoration is part of the first firing, giving it a higher quality of color and brilliance than, say, Spode. Today, design is in the hands of William's son John, who carries on the personal traditions of the family firm, creating clear floral designs in bright, clear colors for what has been described as the art nouveau of the pottery world. There is much to admire and buy in the Factory Seconds Shop. The factory and the restored bottle oven is open Monday to Friday from 10 a.m. to 5 p.m. and on Saturday from 9:30 a.m. to 12:30 p.m. There is always someone around to explain the various processes and to show you around the museum, with its collections of early Moorcroft. Factory tours take place on Wednesday and cost £1 ($1.75).

Afterward, a visit to the past is in order. The **Gladstone Pottery Museum,** Uttoxeter Road at Longton (tel. 0782/319232), is a 19th-century pottery factory restored as a museum, with craftsmen demonstrating daily in original workshops. Galleries depict the rise of the Staffordshire pottery industry, tile history, sanitaryware with washstand bowls and jugs plus toilets of all shapes and sizes, and colors and decoration. There is a replica of a potter's house and a factory manager's office. Admission to the museum is £2 ($3.50) for adults, £1 ($1.75) for children. It is open from 10 a.m. to 4 p.m. Monday to Saturday and 2 to 4 p.m. Sunday. It's closed Monday in winter.

The **Stoke-on-Trent City Museum and Art Gallery,** on Bethesda Street in Hanley (tel. 0782/202173), surely must contain the most comprehensive collection of ceramics in the world. The enthusiastic curator tells me that they have eight times as much stored away as they can possibly show at any time. Even those who aren't museum buffs must find this a beautiful collection. There are also exhibitions of modern art as well as prehistoric local remains, all housed in a delightful contemporary building. The museum is open Monday to Saturday from 10:30 a.m. to 5 p.m., and Sunday from 2 to 5 p.m.

After all that, sustenance is required, and where better than at **Heath's Wine Bar,** Albion Street, at Hanley (tel. 0782/272472), almost opposite the museum? The long bar groans beneath great dishes of pâté, cold meats, pies (chicken, ham-and-mushroom, pork-and-apple, meat-and-potato), chili, casseroles, salads (several varieties), pasta dishes, and hot soup. Mounds of French bread and whole-meal rolls are stacked up, and jacket potatoes are a favorite item. For dessert, try hot fudge cake, cheesecake, or the rich "death by chocolate" cake. Everything is fresh, and all pies, quiches, and flans are homemade. Order and collect your meal and repair to one of the low coffee tables surrounded by sofas or the wheelback-chair–surrounded tables. The music is soft, the atmosphere warm and red. A two-course meal will cost around £3.50 ($6.15) and £4.50 ($7.90). A three-course luncheon with fresh filtered coffee ranges from £5 ($8.75) to £6 ($10.50). Only lunch is served, from 11:30 a.m. to 2:30 p.m.

The **Minton Museum** at London Road, Stoke-on-Trent (tel. 0782/744766), is the starting place for a 1½-hour tour through the major departments of the factory, where they specialize in heavily decorated work. A phone call or a letter in advance is needed to join the £1.50 ($2.65) tour, but your understanding of the processes will be complete when you have seen how to raise patterns and scour and burnish gold relief. It takes 45 minutes to finish the decoration on one plate, so you can see how much a dinner service would cost. Freehand painting from some 1800 patterns is also shown during the tour. It is here that you can get that unique souvenir, a personalized freehand-painted plate or other piece of china. Simply arrange to discuss with one of the artists the photo or picture you wish to have, and they'll do the rest. It'll take from two to 12 months to complete, depending on the demand for orders. But you'll have an elegant and totally different souvenir. For more information, see Mrs. Ann Hughes, the tour organizer.

The **Chatterley Whitfield Mining Museum,** at Tunstall, Stoke-on-Trent (tel. 0782/813337), is a unique museum of mining with an underground gallery showing the history of mining from early times to the modern day. Tours underground are led when possible by ex-miners who vividly relate their experiences working in a coal mine. Visitors are "kitted out" with lamp and helmet, and stout shoes are recommended. Chatterley Whitfield was the first colliery to produce one million tons of coal in a year. Coal was mined here for 140 years before its transformation into a museum in 1979. Other displays and attractions include a steam-winding engine, pit ponies, locomotives, and a colliery canteen and museum shop. Hours are from 10 a.m. to 4 p.m. daily. Tours cost £2.95 ($5.15) for adults, £1.85 ($3.25) for children.

WHERE TO STAY

Because of the long commercial history of Stoke-on-Trent, it has never been much of a tourist town so far as accommodations are concerned. However, there are several recommendations I can make within a radius of some ten or 12 miles from the heart of town where you might choose to settle in for your tours of the Potteries. Newcastle-under-Lyme, about three miles to the west of the main city, has some B&B places you might like, but the other suggestions I will make are to the east and north, toward the Peak National Park and along the valley of the River Churnet.

In the Environs

In the village of Cheddleton, on the A520 about six miles from Stoke-on-Trent, Mrs. Elaine Sutcliffe operates **Choir Cottage** and **Choir House,** Ostlers Lane, Cheddleton, near Leek, Staffordshire ST13 7HS (tel. 0538/360561), a guesthouse and adjoining restaurant, which is in the Sutcliffes' own home. The 300-year-old cottage was once used as a resting place for ostlers, caretakers of horses who traveled on Ostlers Lane when it was the main road between Alton and Manchester. The name "Choir Cottage" comes from the fact that this was at one stage used as a house for the choir at the local church. Mrs. Sutcliffe has well-furnished bedrooms with private showers and toilets, color TV, and beverage-making facilities. Two four-poster rooms are available. One twin-bedded room on the ground floor has a private patio with open countryside views. This and one of the four-poster-bedded rooms are ideal for people who cannot manage the stairs. All accommodations contain showers/toilets, color TV, phones, hairdryers, tea- and coffee-makers, individually controlled heating, and easy chairs. The charge for bed and a full English breakfast is £13.85 ($24.40) per person for one night, £12.95 ($22.65) per person for two or more nights. Meals are served in the Choir House, with evening dinner available on request.

The village of Cheddleton, on the River Churnet, has a Steam Railway Museum, a working flintmill, beautiful walkways, including the Deep Hayes Nature Park, and interesting waterways. It is a short distance from Leek.

Micklea Farm, Micklea Lane, Longsdon, near Leek, Stoke-on-Trent, Staffordshire ST9 9QA (tel. 0538/385006), is where Mrs. Barbara White welcomes paying guests, offering them good food and comfortable beds. The delightful stone house is furnished with taste, and the food is excellent. B&B costs from £9 ($15.25) per person nightly. Guests have use of the lounge and large garden. An evening meal will be served on request. Longsdon, not to be confused with Longton, which is larger and much closer to Stoke-on-Trent, is on the A53 road to the northeast about eight miles toward Leek. The farm is just off the A53.

In the same district, **Glenwood House Farm,** Ipstones, Stoke-on-Trent, Staffordshire ST10 2JP (tel. 053871/294), stands on the B5053 on the edge of the Peak National Park, with fine views over the Churnet Valley, yet it is still close enough to explore Stoke-on-Trent and the Potteries. This is the home of Joyce and Keith Brindley, and it is very much a working farm in the British tradition. Joyce has several rooms to rent, including a family one. The charge of £10.50 ($13.40) per person per night includes a large cooked breakfast. You'll pay another £7 ($12.25) if you want a three-course evening meal. If the color TV doesn't amuse, perhaps a games room with darts will. There is both a children's play area and tennis courts.

Between Stoke-on-Trent and Leek on the A53 road, Endon is a large village long famous for its Welldressing Festival. It is fast becoming a center for visitors spending a night or two for explorations of the Potteries, museums, the Staffordshire Moorlands, and Alton Towers, Britain's Disneyland. **The Hollies,** Clay Lake, Endon, Stoke-on-Trent, Staffordshire ST9 9DD (tel. 0782/503252), is a delightful Victorian house in a quiet location off the B5051, with a large secluded garden and ample space for parking. Mrs. Anne Hodgson rents three spacious bedrooms, one with a private bath and one with a shower. All have washbasins, shaver points, and tea- and coffee-makers. B&B costs from £10 ($17.50) to £12 ($21) per person nightly. The house is centrally heated and has a TV lounge and pleasant breakfast room. Smoking is prohibited.

Long known as a silk-manufacturing town, Leek lies in the River Churnet Valley, within easy reach of the Potteries, the Peak District, and Dovedale. The **Peak Weavers Hotel,** 21 King St., Leek, Staffordshire ST13 5NW (tel. 0538/383729), is a former convent now offering 11 comfortable rooms, many with private baths, costing £12.50 ($21.90) per person nightly for B&B, VAT included.

---

5. Stafford

The county town of Staffordshire was the birthplace of Izaak Walton, the British writer and celebrated fisherman. Long famous as a boot-making center, it contains many historic buildings, notably St. Chad's, the town's oldest church; St.

Mary's, with its unusual octagonal tower; and the Ancient High House, the largest timber-frame town house in England.

In the Staffordshire countryside, at Shallowford, between Stafford and Eccleshall, lies **Izaak Walton Cottage** (tel. 0785/760278). He is best remembered as the author of *The Compleat Angler*. The period garden of his cottage has been planted with 17th-century herbs, flowers, and plants, which are for sale. Admission is 25p (45¢) for adults, 15p (25¢) for children. It is open from 12:30 to 5:30 p.m. mid-March to October, Friday to Tuesday. In winter, it is open only on Saturday and Sunday, from 12:30 to 4:30 p.m.

FOOD AND LODGING

In the quiet part of the market town of Stafford, **The Vine Hotel,** Salter Street, Stafford, Staffordshire ST16 2JU (tel. 0785/44112), is believed to be the oldest licensed premises in the borough. The hostelry has an atmosphere enhanced by blackened beams and sloping floors. The 25 refurbished bedrooms rent for £30 ($52.50) daily in a single, depending on whether the bathroom has a shower or a tub, with doubles renting for £42 ($73.50). Each unit has color TV, a phone, beverage-making facilities, trouser-press, and hairdryer. Rates include a full English breakfast, VAT, and service. The hotel restaurant offers lunch Monday to Saturday from noon to 2 p.m. and dinner from 7 to 9 p.m., with a choice of a grill menu or table d'hôte meals. Steaks are a specialty. Expect to pay from £8.50 ($14.90) for a complete meal. The Vine's oak-beamed lounge bar is a good place to relax.

Albridge Private Hotel, 73 Wolverhampton Rd., Stafford, Staffordshire ST17 4AW (tel. 0785/54100), on the outskirts of town and suitable for motorists, offers some of the best values in the area. Guests exploring this part of the West Midlands seek out this little place, which has been restored. Family operated, it is a two-story structure built in the closing years of Victoria's reign. It enjoys a satellite location but yet is within an easy commute of the historic center of Stafford with its long history and half-timbered buildings. The location is about three miles from the M6 junction 13. Nearly 20 bedrooms are rented, about half of which offer a private bath. Rooms are comfortably furnished and well maintained, costing from £21 ($36.75) to £27 ($47.25) daily in a single, the tariff going up to £26 ($45.50) to £38 ($66.50) in a double, the difference in price depending on the plumbing. The hotel also provides good, reasonably priced food if you'd like to arrange to have dinner here.

6. Lichfield

Fans of Samuel Johnson pay a pilgrimage here to this historic city where he was born in 1709, son of an unsuccessful bookseller and parchment maker. The city is noted for its **Cathedral,** whose three spires are known as "Ladies of the Vale." The tallest spire rises more than 250 feet, and the west front of the cathedral was built about 1280. You can walk around the beautiful grounds and see a Bishop's Palace. Close, with its half-timbered houses, along with the 17th-century Vicars Close.

Dr. Johnson's Birthplace on Breadmarket Street (tel. 04972) contains mementos and pictures of the author and his contemporaries. It is open daily from 10 a.m. to 5 p.m. (to 4 p.m. January to March). Admission is 50p ($1.05) for adults, 30p (55¢) for children.

Across the street from Dr. Johnson's Birthplace, the **Heritage Centre & Treasury** in Lichfield's Market Square of Lichfield, 256611). The former parish church has been transformed into an exhibition room with coffeeshop and gift shop. The exhibition of the Civil War. The treasury displays civic, regimental, and church events, including an audiovisual, showing and the treasury displays examples of the s plate. It's open daily from 10 a.m. to 5 p.m. Admission is 70p ($1.25) for adults, 30p (55¢) for children.

You can also visit the **Guildhall** (across the road from Heritage Centre), built over the city dungeons dating from the Middle Ages. The Guildhall was rebuilt in 1846. Prisoners were jailed here before they were burned at the stake in Market Square.

Incidentally, market days are Friday and Saturday in Lichfield.

WHERE TO STAY

A modest town house of historic and architectural interest, **Mrs. Pauline Duval's Guest House,** 21-23 Dam St., Lichfield, Staffordshire WS13 6AE (tel. 0543/264303), is owned and kept tidy by its landlady. She charges £12 ($21) per person daily for B&B in her two single, two double, and two twin-bedded accommodations, all with hot and cold water basins, each with TV and beverage-making facilities. The house is centrally heated, with a separate residents' lounge. Off-street parking is available. Dam Street, which is for pedestrians only, was mentioned in the *Domesday Book* of 1086. Opposite the guesthouse stands Brooke House, where a general in Cromwell's army was shot in 1647. A plaque on the street commemorates where Johnson was taught English in 1714 at Dame Oliver's school.

Gaialands, 9 Gaiafields Rd., off Bulldog Lane, Lichfield, Staffordshire WS13 7LT (tel. 0543/263764), is a well-kept, small guesthouse within walking distance of the Cathedral and Minster Pool. Mr. and Mrs. Robert White give their guests a true Staffordshire welcome in a secluded environment. If you ask her, Mrs. White will prepare a home-cooked four-course dinner for £6.50 ($11.40). She charges £14 ($24.50) daily in a single, £12.50 ($21.90) per person in a twin-bedded unit for B&B. Units have central heating, pedestal hand basins, and the bathrooms are adjacent.

Oakleigh Hotel House, 25 St. Chad's Rd., Lichfield, Staffordshire WS13 7LZ (tel. 0543/262688), is a country house standing on its own grounds adjoining a sailing lake, Stowe Pool. The owners have improved the house both in decor and comfort. Visitors are assured a high standard of cleanliness and service. Guests are accommodated in the spacious rooms with full central heating. Rates are £28 ($49) daily in a single, from £40 ($70) to £44 ($77) in a double, depending on the plumbing. Oakleigh House serves the best dinners in Lichfield, and on that most locals agree. In fact, it is better known as a dining establishment than a place to stay. Dinners (for which you should make a reservation) cost from £16 ($28). No dinners are served on Sunday and Monday, however.

WHERE TO EAT

The town's best-known pub is **The Scales Inn,** Market Street (tel. 05432/24526). Guests enjoy the wood paneling while seated on leather seats or else retreat to the courtyard in back. While you drink your lager, stop to admire the collection of 2:3￼￼ftware. Bar food, with light meals costing from £4 ($7), are served from noon to day am. daily. Hearty soups and meat pies will tempt you, along with a roast of the You can ahly made salads. Or else you might settle for a sandwich or a hamburger. p.m. Monda. for traditional English beers and lager. The pub is open from 7 to 11 ￼turday, from 7 to 10:30 p.m. Sunday.

XVII

LIVERPOOL AND BLACKPOOL

1. LIVERPOOL
2. BLACKPOOL

The great industrial shadow of the 19th century cast such darkness over much of England's northwest that it has been relatively neglected by the foreign visitor. At best, Americans rush through it heading for the glories of the Lake District and Scotland. Cities such as Manchester have evoked grim, Victorian sprawls, the ugly scars left over from the Industrial Revolution.

However, the area is receiving some belated tourist attention. Chester, which is on the remote southwestern fringe of this district, is covered in another chapter, as is Derbyshire, which contains the great scenic beauty of the Peak District. Liverpool has done much in recent years to revitalize its tourist industry, and Blackpool, the resort to the north, has for decades been the place to which workers from the Midlands go to frolic along the seashore. It's like the old Atlantic City in New Jersey (before its gambling heyday), but with a distinctive English flavor.

The northwest, in spite of its industry and bleak commercial areas, also has much beauty for the tourist willing to seek it out. Manchester, Lancaster, Morecambe, and Southport—to name only a few—are all interesting cities with good-quality accommodations, and much of the countryside is beautiful, filled with inns, restaurants, and pubs, along with sightseeing attractions worth a visit. Because of space limitations, I will confine our visit to the two most popular destinations, Liverpool and Blackpool.

1. Liverpool

Liverpool, with its famous waterfront on the River Mersey, is a great shipping port and industrial center that gave the world everybody from the fictional Fannie Hill to the Beatles. King John launched it on its road to glory when he granted it a charter in 1207. Before that, it had been a tiny 12th-century fishing village, but it quickly became a port for shipping men and materials to Ireland. In the 18th century, its port grew to prominence as a result of the sugar, spice, and tobacco trade with the Americans. By the time Victoria came to the throne, Liverpool had become Britain's biggest commercial seaport. Recent refurbishing of the Albert Docks, establishment of a Maritime Museum, and the converting of warehouses into little stores similar to those in Ghirardelli Square in San Francisco, have made this an up-and-coming area once again, with many attractions for visitors.

Liverpudlians, as they are called, are rightly proud of their city with its new hotels, two cathedrals, shopping and entertainment complexes (as exemplified by St. John's Centre, a modern pedestrian precinct), and the parks and open spaces (2400 acres in and around the city, including Sefton Park with its Palm House). Liverpool's main shopping street, Church, is traffic free for most of the day.

Liverpool is easily reached by car, following the M1, the M6, the M62, and the A5080 from London right to the coast city in the west where the River Mersey joins the Irish Sea. Trains go from London's Euston or Kensington Olympia Stations, and the Rapide bus heads from Victoria Coach Station direct to Liverpool.

THE SIGHTS

Liverpool today has a wealth of things for the visitor to see and enjoy—major cathedrals, waterfront glories restored, cultural centers, even the places where the Beatles began their meteoric rise to fame and fortune.

The Cathedrals

Attracting many Liverpool visitors is the great new Anglican edifice, the **Cathedral Church of Christ,** Saint James Mount (tel. 051/709-6271), largely completed 74 years after it was begun in 1903. On a rocky eminence overlooking the Mersey River, the cathedral might possibly be the last Gothic-style one to be built on earth. Dedicated in the presence of Queen Elizabeth II in 1978, it is the largest church in the country (the fifth largest in the world). England's poet laureate, Sir John Betjeman, hailed it as "one of the great buildings of the world." Its vaulting under the tower is 175 feet high, the highest in the world, and its length of 619 feet is second only to that of St. Peter's in Rome. The architect, who won a competition in 1903 for the building's design, was Giles Scott. He later went on to rebuild the House of Commons, gutted by bombs after World War II. He personally laid the last stone on the highest tower pinnacle. The organ of the world's largest Anglican cathedral contains nearly 10,000 pipes, the biggest found in any church. The tower houses the highest (219 feet) and the heaviest (31 tons) ringing bells in the world, and the Gothic arches are the highest ever built.

In 1984, a Visitor Centre and Refectory was opened, the dominant feature being an aerial sculpture of 12 huge sails, with a ship's bell, clock, and lights that change color on an hourly basis. Full meals may be taken in the charming refectory. The cathedral can be visited from 9 a.m. to 6 p.m. daily. Tours of the tower are offered Monday to Saturday from 10:30 a.m. to 12:30 p.m. and 2 to 4:30 p.m., and on Sunday from 4 to 5 p.m. The tours cost adults £1.50 ($2.65), children (accompanied by an adult) 50p (90¢).

A half mile away from the Anglican cathedral stands the Roman Catholic **Metropolitan Cathedral of Christ the King,** Mount Pleasant (tel. 051/709-9222), but any notion that they glower at each other from that distance is dismissed by the name of the road that joins them: Hope Street. The sectarian strife of earlier generations has been ended, and a change in attitude, called by some the "Mersey Miracle," was illustrated clearly in 1982 when Pope John Paul II drove along Hope Street to pray in both cathedrals. The Metropolitan Cathedral is so called because Liverpool is, in Catholic terms, the mother city, the "metropolis" of the north of England. Construction of the cathedral to the design of Sir Edwin Lutyens was started in 1930, but when World War II halted progress in 1939, not even the granite and brick vaulting of the crypt was complete. At the end of the war it was estimated that the cost of completing the structure as Lutyens had designed it would be some £27 million. Architects throughout the world were invited to compete to design a more realistic project to cost about £1 million and to be completed in five years. Sir Frederick Gibberd won the competition and was commissioned to oversee construction of the circular cathedral in concrete and glass, pitched like a tent at one end of the piazza that covered all the original site, crypt included. Between 1962 and 1967 the construction was completed, providing seating for a congregation of more than 2000, all within 50 feet of the central altar. Above the altar rises a multicolored glass lantern weighing 2000 tons and rising to a height of 290 feet. It has been called a "space age" cathedral.

The Metropolitan Cathedral is open daily from 8 a.m. to 6 p.m. (to 5 p.m. on Sunday in winter). It has a bookshop, a tea room, and tour guides.

On the Waterfront

Albert Dock, Albert Dock Co. Ltd (tel. 051/709-9199), is the showpiece development on Liverpool's Waterfront. Built of brick, stone, and cast iron, it opened in 1846, saw a long period of decline, and has been renovated and refurbished so that the magnificent dockland warehouses now contain quality shops, restaurants, cafés, an English pub, and a cellar wine bar. One pavilion houses the main building of the Merseyside Maritime Museum (see below) and another is the home of the Tate Gallery Liverpool, the National Collection of modern art in the North of England (see below). Albert Dock is open daily from 10 a.m. to 8 p.m. There's no charge for going there and strolling around, and car parking is available.

Merseyside Maritime Museum, Albert Dock (tel. 051/207-0001), set in the historic heart of Liverpool's magnificent waterfront, is a large museum providing a unique blend of floating exhibits, craft demonstrations, working displays, and special events. In addition to restored waterfront buildings, exhibitions show the story of mass emigration through Liverpool in the last century, shipbuilding on Merseyside, and other aspects of Liverpool's maritime heritage. You can see a piermaster's house and a working cooperage. The museum is open daily from 10:30 a.m. to 5:30 p.m. (last entrance at 4:30 p.m.). Admission is £1 ($1.75) for adults, 50p (90¢) for children. A smörgåsbord restaurant, a waterfront café, gift shops, and ample parking space are among the facilities.

The **Tate Gallery** at Albert Dock (tel. 051/709-3223) opened in 1988, housing the National Collection of 20th century art in the north of England. It is the first gallery in England devoted entirely to modern art. The gallery was the result of a decision by the board of directors at the Tate Gallery in London to move more than 85% of its modern collections from vaults to the gallery in Liverpool, where all the world could see these "hidden treasures." Lack of space in London made it impossible to show the collection. So, this new "Tate Gallery of the North" came into being. Some of the world's greatest modern artists, such as Picasso, Dali, Magritte, and Rothko, are likely to be on display at any time, along with a changing array of temporary exhibitions and events. The gallery is open Tuesday to Sunday from 11 a.m. to 7 p.m., charging no admission. However, the price of special exhibitions is £1 ($1.75).

You can take a **Mersey Ferry** from the Pier Head to both Woodside and Seacombe, operating on a regular 20-minute schedule on Monday to Saturday and half-hourly on Sunday, from early morning to late evening. Special afternoon cruises are offered along Liverpool's historic waterfront in summer. For information about times and prices, get in touch with the **Merseyside Transport Ferries Office,** Victoria Place, Seacombe, Wallasey (tel. 051/630-1030).

Where the Beatles Began

Whether they're Beatles fans or not, most visitors who come to Liverpool want to take a look at where Beatlemania began in the Swinging '60s. Mathew Street is the heart of Beatleland, and **Cavern Walks** (tel. 051/236-9082) is a shopping development and tour service built on the site of the former Cavern Club, where the Beatles performed almost 300 times. John Doubleday's controversial statue of the group is in the central piazza of the Cavern complex, surrounded by shops and restaurants. The outside of Cavern Walks was decorated by Cynthia Lennon, John's first wife. Another controversial statue of John, Paul, George, and Ringo, this one by Liverpool sculptor Arthur Dooley, is opposite the building facade. Farther along Mathew Street is the John Lennon Memorial Club and the **Beatles Shop,** 31 Mathew St. (tel. 051/236-8066), open from 9:30 a.m. to 5:30 p.m. daily, except Sunday, when hours are from 10:30 a.m. to 4 p.m. Around the corner on Stanley Street is a statue of Eleanor Rigby, seated on a bench.

Tours

A daily £2 ($3.50) sightseeing tour gives a brief introduction to Liverpool, while for £3.50 ($6.15), Beatle fans can take a two-hour guided tour of famous locations, such as Penny Lane and Strawberry Fields. For those who prefer to "do it themselves," a Beatle map can be purchased for £1 ($1.75). Details are available from the **Merseyside Tourism Board's** two information centers: at 29 Lime St., in front of the main railway station (tel. 051/709-3631), and at the Albert Dock (tel. 051/708-8854). Both centers are open every day.

Other Sights

The **Museum of Labour History,** former County Sessions House, William Brown Street (tel. 051/207-0001, ext. 279), traces what it was like to live and work in Merseyside over the last 150 years, with people struggling for legal and political rights, establishing trade unions, and improving their working conditions. It is open from 10 a.m. to 5 p.m. Monday to Saturday, and 2 to 5 p.m. Sunday; closed New Year's Day, Good Friday, and the three Christmas holidays. Admission is free.

The **Liverpool Museum and Planetarium,** William Brown Street (tel. 051/207-0001), has displays on antiquities, archives, botany, decorative arts, geology, zoology, physical sciences, social industrial history, and a transport gallery, as well as an aquarium and a vivarium. It is open Monday to Saturday from 10 a.m. to 5 p.m., and Sunday from 2 to 5 p.m., except New Year's Day, Good Friday, and the Christmas holidays. The museum admission is free. To visit the planetarium, adults pay 80p ($1.40), children 40p (70¢).

The **Walker Art Gallery,** William Brown Street (tel. 051/207-0001), has one of the finest collections of paintings outside London. It is known for its European pictures and sculpture from 1300 to the present. Open from 10 a.m. to 5 p.m. Monday to Saturday, and 2 to 5 p.m. Sunday, it is closed New Year's Day, Good Friday, and for the Christmas holidays. Admission is free.

Among Liverpool's historic buildings, **St. George's Hall,** designed by a 24-year-old architect who never saw it realized, was completed in 1854. It has been called "England's finest public building." It contains law courts, and in the rear are pleasantly laid out gardens.

Speke Hall, The Walk, Speke (tel. 051/427-7231), on the north bank of the Mersey, seven miles from Liverpool's city center, is a National Trust property not far from Liverpool Airport. This lavishly furnished, half-timbered black-and-white Tudor house was built between 1490 and 1612. It is rich in ghost stories and priest holes, and two ancient yew trees stand in the courtyard. Hours are 1 to 5:30 p.m. Tuesday to Saturday (to 6 p.m. Sunday and bank holidays). It is closed Good Friday. From November to mid-December, hours are from 1 to 5 p.m. Saturday and Sunday. Admission is £1.80 ($3.15) for adults, 90p ($1.60) for children.

WHERE TO STAY

A well-kept B&B hotel, **Aplin House Private Hotel,** 35 Clarendon Rd., Garston, Liverpool, Merseyside L19 6PJ (tel. 051/427-5047), is run by Mr. and Mrs. Atherton, who have a good many repeat guests. Mrs. Atherton makes breakfast "as you want it." Her charges include VAT and service. Singles cost from £15 ($26.25) nightly, the rate in a twin-bedded room being from £11.50 ($20.15) to £12.50 ($21.90), rising to £13 ($22.75) to £14 ($24.50) per person in a large, double-bedded accommodation. Evening meals are offered, costing from £5.50

($9.65). The hotel is about ten minutes by train from the city center, two miles from Liverpool Airport, and 20 minutes by car from the Irish ferries.

New Manx Hotel, 39 Catherine St., Liverpool, Merseyside L8 7NE (tel. 051/708-6171), is a small, unlicensed hotel that seems to delight visitors. Families with children are especially welcomed here, as James Gilmour has an avocation of penning stories for them and is known for offering a Santa Claus letter service. About a 12-minute run from the center, the hotel has 12 bedrooms to rent, each comfortably furnished and well maintained. Only a few, however, contain private baths or showers. The overnight B&B charges are most reasonable, costing from £12.50 ($21.90) per person. Only breakfast is offered, and it's a generous meal.

Kensington Hotel, 111 Mount Pleasant, Liverpool, Merseyside L3 5TF (tel. 051/709-3823), is one of the best and most reasonably priced of the lesser-known hotels of Liverpool, which offer the best bargains. It is within an easy stroll from the city's heartland, and its bedrooms are up-to-date and comfortable, with a number of amenities. The owners of this inviting place rent ten bedrooms, six of which contain a private shower. Charges are from £14.50 ($25.40) to £18.50 ($32.40) daily in a single, the tariff rising to £26 ($45.50) to £30 ($52.50) in a double.

Aachen Hotel, 89-91 Mount Pleasant, Liverpool, Merseyside L3 5TB (tel. 051/709-3477), has a variety of rooms with a variety of plumbing. Singles range from £15 ($26.25) to £20 ($35) daily, and doubles cost from £26 ($45.50) to £34 ($59.50). You tip as you see fit. Mr. F. P. Wilson, the owner, provides complete English breakfasts. Each of his modernized bedrooms has hot and cold running water, hairdryer, color TV, in-house movies, radio alarm, beverage-making facilities, and trouser-press. The hotel has a bar. Mr. Wilson will help you with your Liverpool visit, as he knows the city well. The location is about five minutes from the center of the city.

EATING AND DRINKING

For some really good old-English cooking, go to the **Feathers Hotel,** 119-125 Mount Pleasant, Liverpool, Merseyside L3 5TF (tel. 051/709-9655), a long-standing favorite, moderately priced. Here you can sample the famous Lancashire hotpot, a casserole where the lamb chops are layered with onions and potatoes. It's traditionally eaten with pickled red cabbage. Meals costing from £7.50 ($13.15) are served in the Peacock Restaurant, which features "old English specialty menus." It's open daily from noon to 2 p.m. and 6:30 to 8:30 p.m. The Feathers also rents 100 comfortably furnished bedrooms. The more expensive rooms contain private baths or showers, as reflected by the difference in price structure: from £16 ($28) to £20 ($35) daily in a single and from £24.50 ($42.90) to £30 ($52.50) in a double.

La Grande Bouffe, 48a Castle St. (tel. 051/236-3375), continues to delight readers A French-like cellar bistro in the center of the city's commercial heartland, La Grande Bouffe maintains a strict value-for-money policy. Its set lunch of £7.50 ($13.15) is one of the best for the price in Liverpool. Some office workers come here just for sandwiches to take away and have with their tea. But I'd suggest you book a table and see what the chefs have planned for the day. The menu changes often but invariably uses fresh produce and handles the ingredients deftly. Dinners tend to be more relaxed, and also more expensive, with meals costing from £14 ($24.50). Hours are from noon to 2:30 p.m. and 6 to 10 p.m. (slightly later on Saturday). However, it is closed on Sunday and doesn't offer lunch on Saturday or dinner on Monday.

Liverpool is particularly famous for its Chinese restaurants, not surprising in a city that has one of the largest Chinese populations in Europe. **Mayflower,** 48 Duke St. (tel. 051/709-6339), is reported to be one of the finest Chinese dining rooms in town, serving excellent Cantonese fare. It also offers classic food from Beijing as well as fiery hot Szechuan dishes. Dozens and dozens of selections await your decision, which you can make daily, except for lunch on Saturday and Sunday, from noon to 4 a.m. (that's right: it's one of the latest dining rooms to close in the city). Its good, value-set lunches and dinners are among the best for the money in the city, costing from £3.50 ($6.15) at lunch and from £8.50 ($14.90) at dinner. Vegetarians will also find solace here.

St. George's Carvery, St. John's Precinct, Lime Street (tel. 051/709-7090), lies in one of the best-known hotels in the city center, a modern structure where you can enjoy a before-dinner drink in the Dragon Bar. Or, if you're in this bar from noon to 2 p.m. Monday to Saturday, you can make selections from a hot and cold buffet for only £2.25 ($3.95), truly one of the best food values in Liverpool. Or else you can go to the Carvery, where you can help yourself to excellent roasts, including beef, leg of lamb, and pork, along with seasonal specials and vegetarian dishes. On the cold table you'll find honey-baked ham and turkey. This special food bargain is served seven days a week from noon to 2 p.m. and 7 to 10 p.m. A two-course lunch costs £6.25 ($10.94), and you can order "the works" at night for £9.95 ($17.40).

Kismet Restaurant, 105 Bold St. (tel. 051/709-8469), is a well-patronized restaurant that has some of the best Indian food in Liverpool, specializing in tandoori dishes. Among these are their tandoori masala (lamb, chicken, or king prawns cooked in special gravy in the clay ovens). The Kismet special is a mild curry with prawns, chicken, meat, and pineapple with an omelet garnished with tomato, raisins, and coconut. Rogan josh (lamb spiced with herbs and cashew nuts) and sag gosht (beef cooked with fresh leaf spinach) are tasty selections. They also prepare English dishes. Lunch, served from noon to 2:30 p.m., costs from £4 ($7). Dinner, from 5:30 p.m. to midnight, comes to £8 ($14) and up. The Kismet is open seven days a week.

Bistro Everyman, 9 Hope St. (tel. 051/708-9545), is informal, crowded on weekends, fun, and prices are reasonable. A buffet is offered with a wide range of pâtés, quiche, pizzas, soups, meat and vegetarian main courses, seasonal salads, cheeses, desserts, and pastries. The menu is changed twice daily and is influenced by the season and the weather, with only fresh produce from the local market being used. A typical three-course meal might consist of carrot soup with French bread, chicken pie with new potatoes and green salad, strawberries in white wine with cream, and coffee, all costing from £6 ($10.50). On Sunday, only quiche, pizza, and salad are served, and live music predominates. The bistro is open from 10 a.m. to midnight Monday to Saturday, and from 7:30 to 11:30 p.m. Sunday. The bistro is part of the Everyman Theatre complex.

Everybody's favorite pub is at the **Philharmonic Hotel,** 36 Hope St. (tel. 051/709-1163), which has all those splendid turn-of-the-century architectural decorative features that are now so much in vogue—stained glass, carving, plasterwork, you name it. You pass through wrought-iron gates into a selection of several bars, some with rosewood paneling. Some of the rooms are named after famous composers, such as Liszt and Brahms. The heart of the pub is the Horseshoe Bar, with a mosaic floor and stained glass—fine Edwardian flamboyance. You can have a few pints and play dominoes. The feeling is like a private club, and almost any regular will advise a stranger what kind of local ale is good. The habitués refer to it as "The Phil," and it attracts art, drama, and music students as well as actors. If you're a man, I suggest you pay a visit to the gents' urinal, even if you don't need to go. It's a work of art. Hot and cold food is served in the cocktail lounge at lunch, with meals costing from £3.50 ($6.15). Hours are from 11 a.m. to 11 p.m. daily. Live music is presented four times a week.

---

2. Blackpool

The custom began in 1720 when wealthy families, complete with children, maiden aunts, cousins, and servants, arrived to breathe the sea air. Hotels were built to accommodate them, and Blackpool, north from Liverpool, began its long and often rocky history as a resort. It's had good times and bad times. Nowadays it's working hard to restore itself with a fresh new image and many more attractions.

It has survived because of its **beaches,** called "the magnificent seven" and stretching for seven miles. The most athletic of visitors walk the seven-mile stretch every day; others prefer to take an easier and shorter ride on one of the famous donkeys that go up and down the beachfront. The so-called Golden Mile stretches for only 500 yards, from the Tower of Blackpool south to the Foxhall Hotel. It takes in such pleasure centers as the Golden Mile, Coral Island, and the Palatine Precinct. It is a world of discos, dining spots, cabaret shows, and the inevitable Tussaud waxworks (Louis, not Madame).

Particularly in summer, there is always something going on at Blackpool, and it's trying hard to beef up its winter business, when the beaches are no longer a lure. Events range from strutting brass bands to dog shows and hockey tournaments. There's even an annual Coal Queen contest.

The landmark of Blackpool is its **Tower.** Soaring 519 feet into the air, it is illuminated at night by 10,000 lightbulbs. Brighton turned down the idea of such a tower, but in 1891 Blackpool went for it, and it's been a tradition every since. The plan was to erect a small Eiffel-like tower on the Lancashire coast. Under the giant four legs of the Tower is an indoor circus that is active both day and night. Its features include the Tower Ballroom (one of the great Victorian ballrooms of Britain), the Tower Circus, the Ocean Room cabaret, and a Tower Aquarium, plus many other amusements, some designed for children. Those who ascend the Tower are rewarded with a view of up to 60 miles on a clear day.

The best place for shopping is behind the Tower in the Hounds Hill Centre. In red brick, it has glass arcades as in the days of King Edward VII. You can see buskers perform here.

AMUSEMENTS

For Coney Island–type amusement, head for **Pleasure Beach,** built in 1904 and encompassing 40 acres of amusements, including what the English refer to as "white-knuckle" rides. Featured is a 360° "loop the loop" roller coaster. The Wonderful World Building is like an ocean liner with dining places, attractions, and a nightclub. You'll have an Atlantic City déjà vu as you walk along the seaside piers, three in all, each filled with restaurants (often selling fast food) and attractions to amuse.

And when you want to retreat from thriller rides and other amusements, there is **Stanley Park,** a 26-acre park filled with motor-and rowboats and such facilities as six bowling greens, 32 tennis courts, and two 18-hole putting greens (plus a special playground set aside for children).

If the seawater off the beach is too cool for your tastes, you can plunge into an Olympic-size pool at the **Derby Baths,** a large indoor pool standing adjacent to the Pembroke Hotel on the North Shore. It has saunas, massages, even vapor and aeratone baths.

The easiest way to see Blackpool is to ride along the sea in one of the single- or double-decker trams. Established in 1885, this is Britain's only city tramcar system.

Blackpool is famous for its **illuminations,** lasting from the end of August until the end of October. This razzle-dazzle attraction features hundreds of illuminated figures, such as butterflies, comprising 175 miles of wiring in all, with 375,000 lamps. Called the biggest single tourist attraction in the north of England, it draws some eight million visitors a year (hotel owners raise their prices at that time).

Some locals will tell you their **nightlife** outdazzles that of Las Vegas. In the past a lot of big names, such as Sarah Bernhardt, have performed at Blackpool. Today you are likely to see scantily clad showgirls in sequins and feathers. The major after-dark diversions take place at such establishments as the Horseshoe Bar at Pleasure Beach, the Gaiety Bar, the Yellow Submarine, and the Lion Showbar. Other nightlife attractions include the restored Grand Theatre, which was reopened by Prince Charles in 1981 after it had been allowed to become a Bingo hall. You can also attend a revue at the Ice Drome or patronize the modernized 1889 Opera House. Discos by the dozens are combined with lively pier shows and ballroom dancing. In all, there are some 50 cabaret spots and clubs.

Blackpool also has a modern **zoo,** with lions and elephants, along with a miniature railway and picnic areas.

It is also one of the least expensive places to go for a holiday in the United Kingdom.

WHERE TO STAY

Perhaps the finest of the small hotels at this sprawling fun resort of the north, **Sunray Hotel,** 42 Knowle Ave., Blackpool, Lancashire FY2 9TQ (tel. 0253/51937), wins my highest recommendation in terms of value for money. John and Jean Dodgson are your hosts, treating each guest with respect and dignity and housing them well. They offer nine well-furnished bedrooms with a number of amenities, such as color TV, phone, and electric blankets (even though there is full central heating). Most important, each of their bedrooms has a private bath or shower. Singles range from £17 ($29.75) to £22 ($38.50) daily for B&B, with doubles costing £33 ($57.75) to £39 ($68.25). The unlicensed hotel also has a small garden and is an inviting oasis lying off Queens Promenade. The Dodgson couple also serves good food, and you may want to arrange to have dinner here.

Alderley Hotel, 581 South Promenade, Blackpool, Lancashire FY4 1NG (tel. 0253/42173), is good for those seeking a central location close to the amusements of this Lancashire resort. The hotel offers many modern conveniences and rents a total of ten well-furnished and comfortable bedrooms, each with private bath. The overnight B&B charges range from £13.50 ($23.65) to £17.50 ($30.65) in a single, rising to £26 ($45.50) to £34 ($59.50) in a double. The standard of accommodation is high here, and you can also order good and reasonably priced meals.

The Seymour Hotel, 60-62 Queens Promenade, Blackpool, Lancashire FY2 9RP (tel. 0253/51463), is a red-brick building that occupies a prominent position overlooking the sea and cliffs. Of the 64 bedrooms, the majority have private baths and TV. All are centrally heated and have tea- and coffee-makers. B&B costs from £14.95 ($26.15) per person daily. If you prefer to take half board, the charge is from £17.25 ($30.20) per person. The hotel presents entertainment in high season. There are elevators to all floors, a games room, and a car park. The Seymour is licensed to serve alcoholic beverages.

The Sherwood Private Hotel, 414 North Promenade, Gynn, Blackpool, Lancashire FY1 2LB (tel. 0253/51898), is one of the best bets for a reasonably priced smaller hotel with a desirable position on the promenade. The dining room allows a sea view. Each of the 17 simple but comfortable modern bedrooms has central heating, and most of them have private bath. The charge is from £14 ($24.50) per person daily for B&B.

WHERE TO EAT

The place to go for fish and chips is **The Cottage,** 31 Newhouse Rd. (tel. 0253/64081). Some of the fish arrives on trawlers from the Irish Sea and the Faroes. You get a wide choice, including haddock, cod, hake, salmon, swordfish, and halibut, along with such delicacies as crab and prawns. Everything is reasonably priced and has a homemade taste. A basic three-course meal starts at £3.50 ($6.15), the price increasing according to the size of fish you order. They also serve other food if you don't want fish. Desserts are good too, including an English trifle. Food is served daily from noon to 2 p.m. Dinner is served from 5 p.m. to midnight (on Monday from 8 p.m.).

White Tower Restaurant, Balmoral Road (tel. 0253/46710), from its position high in the Wonderful World Building, offers both set meals and à la carte dinners, along with panoramic views. On Sunday, the only day lunch is served, you can have traditional roast beef carved from the trolley, a standard feature. Lunch is served from noon to 4 p.m., costing £7 ($12.25), and the place is likely to be crowded for this meal. When available, try one of the lobsters from the Isle of Man for dinner, served from 7 p.m. to midnight Tuesday to Saturday, costing from £13 ($22.75) to £20 ($35). The restaurant is closed all day Monday and Sunday night.

Robert's Oyster Bar, 92 Promenade (tel. 0253/21226), has long been a landmark on the dining scene. Grandparents who spent seaside holidays at Blackpool and ate here now take their grandchildren to sample the delights of the sea. Of course, oysters are the piéce de rèsistance, but you can also select from an array of cockles and mussels, in the best of the Cockney tradition, along with whelks. Many diners can be seen right on the Promenade, finger-sampling their favorite morsels and watching the passing parade. For £5 ($8.75) or so, you can get a good fill here any time from 9 a.m. to 10:30 p.m. daily (it closes at 5:30 p.m. off-season).

XVIII

THE LAKE DISTRICT

1. KENDAL

2. WINDERMERE

3. AMBLESIDE

4. RYDAL

5. GRASMERE

6. HAWKSHEAD AND CONISTON

7. KESWICK

8. BASSENTHWAITE

9. PENRITH

10. BORROWDALE

One of England's most popular summer retreats in Queen Victoria's day was the Lake District in the northwest. It enjoyed vogue during the flowering of the Lake Poets, including William Wordsworth, who was ecstatically moved by the rugged beauty of this area. In its time the district has lured such writers as Samuel Taylor Coleridge, Charles Lamb, Percy Bysshe Shelley, John Keats, Alfred Lord Tennyson, Matthew Arnold, and Charlotte Brontë.

The Lake District is a miniature Switzerland condensed into about 32 miles, principally in Cumbria, although it begins in the northern part of Lancashire.

The northwest of England is one of the special parts of the country, and more and more it is visited by foreign tourists, especially Americans, who view its remoteness as part of its charm. Have you ever seen one of those English-made films depicting the life of the Lake District? A soft mist hovers over the hills and dells, sheep graze contentedly on the slope of the pastures—and a foggy enchantment fills the air.

Driving in the wilds of this northwestern shire is fine for a start. But the best activity is walking, which is an art best practiced here by both young and old with a crooked stick. Don't go out without a warning, however. There is a great deal of rain and heavy mist, and sunny days are few. When the mist starts to fall, try to be near an old inn or pub, where you can drop in for a visit and warm yourself beside an open fireplace. You'll be carried back to the good old days, as many places in Cumbria have valiantly resisted change. If you strike up a conversation with a local, you must make sure you know something about hounds.

The far northwestern part of the shire, bordering Scotland, used to be called Cumberland. Now part of Cumbria, it is generally divided geographically into a trio of segments: the Pennines, dominating the eastern sector (loftiest point at Cross

Fell, nearly 3000 feet high); the Valley of Eden; and the lakes and secluded valleys of the west, by far the most interesting. The area, so beautifully described by the romantic Lake Poets, enjoys many literary associations. Wordsworth ("when all at once I saw a crowd, a host of golden daffodils") was a native son, born at Cockermouth.

The largest town is **Carlisle** in the north—not a very interesting tourist center, but a possible base for explorations to Hadrian's Wall. The wall stretches from Wallsend in the east to Bowness on the Solway, a distance of about 75 miles. It was built in the second century A.D. by the Romans.

Brockhole National Park Centre, between Ambleside and Windermere, is well worth a visit.

A traditional gateway to the district is from the south, approached via:

1. Kendal

A market town, Kendal contains the ruins of a castle where Catherine Parr, the last wife of Henry VIII, was born. With its 13th-century parish church, Kendal makes for a good stopover en route to the lakeside resort of Windermere, beginning about nine miles away. Kendal is 270 miles from London.

The town was also associated with George Romney, the 18th-century portrait painter (Lady Hamilton was his favorite subject), who used to travel all over the Lake District trying to get someone to sit for him. He held his first exhibition, married, and raised a family in Kendal. He deserted them in 1762, not returning until the end of his life. He died in Kendal in 1802.

Abbot Hall, Kirkland, a handsome stone Georgian mansion, houses the **Abbot Hall Art Gallery** and the **Museum of Lakeland Life and Industry** (tel. 0539/ 22646), operated by the Lake District Art Gallery and Museum Trust. The gallery, laid out in 18th-century rooms, contains portraits by Romney and Gardner and Lake District watercolors. The museum's exhibits include period rooms, costumes, printing, weaving, and local industries, as well as Queensgate, a reconstructed Victorian street scene, and a farming display. The gallery and museum are open Monday to Friday from 10:30 a.m. to 5:30 p.m., Saturday and Sunday from 2 to 5 p.m. They are closed for the Christmas holidays, New Year's Day, and Good Friday. Admission is £1.25 ($2.20) for adults, 65p ($1.15) for children.

The **Kendal Museum of Archaeology and Natural History,** Station Road (tel. 0539/21374), one of the oldest museums in Britain, now administered by the Abbot Hall Art Gallery, traces the story of people of the area since the Stone Age, as well as Kendal's development as a wool town. Realistic constructions take the visitor on a tour of the major wildlife habitats in the district. The museum also contains a world wildlife gallery with specimens of birds, animals, and insects, pointing out the ecological problems of the modern world. The museum is open Monday to Friday from 10:30 a.m. to 5 p.m., and on Saturday and Sunday from 2 to 5 p.m. From the spring bank holiday weekend to October 31, it is open from 10:30 a.m. to 5 p.m. Saturday. It's closed during the Christmas holidays, New Year's Day, and Good Friday. Admission is £1 ($1.75) for adults, 50p (90¢) for children. Family tickets at £2.50 ($4.40) are available.

FOOD AND LODGING

A comfortable guesthouse, **Hillside,** 4 Beast Banks, Kendal, Cumbria LA9 4JW (tel. 0539/22836), is just two blocks from the main street of Kendal. Carl and Brenda Denison are the gracious and helpful owners of this neat, clean accommodation. There is a lounge with color TV, and all rooms have beverage-making facilities and modern sinks with plenty of hot water. Some rooms have private showers. Depending on the plumbing, the B&B rates range from £11 ($19.25) to £15 ($25.25) per person nightly.

Brantholme, 7 Sedbergh Rd., Kendal, Cumbria LA9 6AD (tel. 0539/22340), is an interesting Victorian house standing on its own grounds. A Lake Country family welcomes you into their well-furnished accommodations, which include a room usually reserved for families. All rooms have private baths. The meals are so good here and so abundant that it's best to take the half-board rate, ranging from £17 ($29.75) to £19 ($33.25) per person nightly. There are no single accommodations. The house is owned and run by Cathryn and Leslie Bigland. Cathryn is a professionally trained chef. A finalist in the English Tourist Board's "Taste of Cumbria" competition, she takes delight in demonstrating her skills, and every evening she produces a superb three-course meal from fresh local produce. Brantholme is in some three-quarters of an acre of wooded garden in a secluded part of Kendal, within easy walking distance of both bus and rail terminals and the town center. There is private parking. The house does not receive guests in December.

The **Brewery Arts Centre,** Highgate (tel. 0539/25133), is set in a 150-year-old converted brewery and may be found just off Highgate. It is open daily. Morning coffee is served with freshly made scones from 10 a.m. in the restaurant and on the sun terrace in summer. Lunches, served between 11:30 a.m. and 2 p.m., cost from £5 ($8.75). In addition to a variety of fresh salads, the restaurant offers a range of hot dishes, plus a homemade dish of the day. The local specialty is Cumberland sausage. A warm welcome is always extended in the licensed Vats Bar, which is open lunchtime and in the evening. As its name suggests, the Vats Bar has been created out of the brewery's fermentation room, where the cedar-wood vats provide unique seating for that quiet drink. Not everybody can boast that they have had a drink *in* a vat. The pizzeria is open in the evening from 5:30 to 7:30, with regular entertainment, including music, dance, theater, and film.

The Cherry Tree, 24 Finkle St. (tel. 0539/20547), is a tucked-away restaurant that's worth the search to find. Ian English (how British can your name get?) runs this atmospheric 120-seat establishment, serving from 10 a.m. to 8 p.m. seven days a week. Appetizers are limited and the usual sort, but the fish dishes include a goodly assortment of scampi, rainbow trout, halibut, plaice, and haddock. The meat and poultry salads are made to order and are quite fine, especially the roast beef. He offers savory lunches and dinners from £6 ($10.50). For lighter appetites, snacks such as hamburgers or the local Cumberland sausages are served.

Outside Kendal

Garnett House Farm, Burneside, Kendal, Cumbria LA9 5SF (tel. 0539/24542), is a working farm with a large dairy herd and many sheep grazing the fells. The farmhouse, between Kendal and Windermere, dates from the 15th century, and its walls are thick, the beams low, and the windows deeply set. Guests enjoy an oak-paneled sitting room, and in a pleasant dining room Mrs. Beaty serves large country meals, using homegrown produce and fresh vegetables. One of the bedrooms is in the bell tower (the bell, once tolled to call farmhands to meals, is long gone). All have electric heat, hot and cold running water, and shaver points. The cost is from £9.50 ($16.65) per person nightly, including breakfast, and the set dinner goes for £4.25 ($7.45).

---

2. Windermere

The grandest of the lakes is Windermere, the largest one in England, whose shores wash up against the town of Bowness, with Windermere in close reach. Both of these resorts lie on the eastern shore of the lake. A ferry service connects Hawkshead and Bowness. Windermere, the resort, is the end of the railway line.

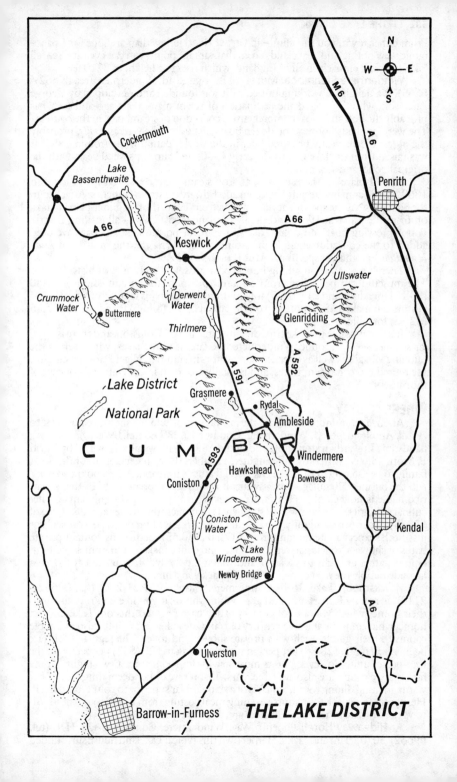

From either town, you can climb up **Orrest Head** in less than an hour for a panoramic view of England's lakeland. From that vantage point, you can even see **Scafell Pike,** the peak pinnacle in all of England, which rises to a height of 3210 feet.

Windermere Steamboat Museum, Rayrigg Road, Windermere (tel. 09662/5565), is a delightful working museum. It was founded and developed by George Pattinson, who discovered the fascination of steam many years ago and now has probably the best and most comprehensive collection of steamboats in the country. The wet boatsheds house some dozen boats, including the veteran *Dolly,* probably the oldest mechanically powered boat in the world, dating from around 1850. It was raised from the lake bed in the early 1960s and run for several years with the original boiler and steambox.

Also displayed is the *Esperance,* an iron steam yacht registered with Lloyds in 1869, as well as many elegant Victorian and Edwardian steam launches. Attached to the boathouses is the speedboat *Jane,* dating from 1938; the first glider-plane to take off from the water in 1943; and the hydroplane racer *Cookie*—all jostling Beatrix Potter's rowing boat and other Lakeland craft for position. Boats that have been added to the collection include the steam launch *Kittiwake,* the motorboat *Lady Hamilton,* and the fast speedboat *Miss Windermere IV.*

There's a small shop selling books, postcards, and souvenirs of historic craft. The museum can be visited from 10 a.m. to 5 p.m. for an admission of £1.80 ($3.15) for adults and £1 ($1.75) for children. The *Osprey* is regularly in steam, and visitors can make a 45-minute trip on the lake at £2.25 ($3.95) for adults and £1.35 ($2.35) for children.

It's also possible to make trips on Ullswater and on Coniston, and there is regular steamer service around Windermere, the largest of the lakes, which serves the outlying villages as well as operating for visitors in summer. Nigel Dalziel is curator. He retired there in recent times, and is totally absorbed in the craft and concept of the museum.

WHERE TO STAY

About a ten-minute walk from the railway station and the shops, **Willowsmere Hotel,** Ambleside Road, Windermere, Cumbria LA23 1ES (tel. 09662/3575), is a handsome Edwardian stone hotel along the A591. Willowsmere is owned by David F. Scott, who is assisted by his daughter, Heather, the fifth generation of the Scott family to be catering in the Lake District. Heather's husband, Alan Cook, also helps run the business. Regular guests say that it is most appropriate that Heather's married name is now Cook, as her father receives many glowing compliments on her culinary abilities. The best way to stay here is to request the dinner and B&B rate of £28 ($49) per person nightly. The evening meal is a well-prepared six-courser. For just B&B, expect a rate ranging from £17.50 ($30.65). Bedrooms contain private baths or showers, toilets, shaver points, tea- and coffee-makers, and unmetered heat. Guests gather at night to socialize and watch the "telly." If you want to go on a lakeside ramble the next day, Heather will pack you a lunch.

Hawksmoor, Lake Road, Windermere, Cumbria LA23 2EQ (tel. 09662/2110), is run by Robert and Barbara Tyson, who treat you like you're a visitor to their home (which you are, of course). They have restored this old Lake District home, which must be at least a century old, and they offer ten well-furnished double rooms to their guests, each with private shower and toilet. The regular B&B rate begins at £16.50 ($28.88) per person nightly, rising to £20 ($35) per person in the four-poster unit. However, guests must stay in this room at least two nights. Some family-style rooms are also available. Mrs. Tyson reveals her decorating flair in her warm, inviting dining room, which is of a standard far superior to your typical B&B. Here you can order a four-course evening meal costing from £8 ($14) per head. Always call or write in advance. Chances are, you'll be glad you did.

At **Hideaway Hotel,** Phoenix Way, Windermere, Cumbria LA23 1DB (tel. 09662/3070), Tim and Jackie Harper own this typical Lakeland house surrounded by neat lawns where tea is served on balmy summer evenings. The house is solid and comfortable, with a pleasant bar with an open fire and oak settles, along with a sitting room and an attractive dining room. The bedrooms are bright and lightly decorated. Dinner, bed, and breakfast in a room with private bath and toilet, color TV, radio, and tea- and coffee-making equipment costs from £25 ($43.75) per person daily. The hotel has a Switzerland-trained chef and has received awards for its cuisine, which includes roast meats, game pies, local trout, homemade soups, and exciting desserts. Breakfasts include Cumberland sausage, black pudding, and haggis.

Fir Trees, Lake Road, Windermere, Cumbria LA23 2EQ (tel. 09662), is by most accounts the finest guesthouse in Windermere, a place where the competition is keen. Here at this well-run place, you get hotel-like standards at B&B tariffs. Allene and Ira Fishman, the proprietors, enjoy a tranquil position and offer a warm welcome and a guarantee of a relaxing family hotel by the lakes. They rent seven well-furnished and beautifully maintained bedrooms, each with private bath or shower, color TV, beverage-making equipment, and other thoughtful amenities. Open year-round, they charge from £19.50 ($34.15) daily in a single, the tariff going up to £35 ($61.25) in a double. A generous English breakfast is also included in the rates.

Brendan Chase, College Road, Windermere, Cumbria LA23 1BU (tel. 09662/5638), has received the endorsement of many readers who stayed there. Mr. and Mrs. Graham welcome guests to their long-established Edwardian home and see to their comfort. They charge from £11.50 ($20.15) per person nightly for B&B in rooms that are comfortably furnished. A full English breakfast is included, and some of the rooms also contain private baths. In the center of the Lakeland resort, the guesthouse is nevertheless in a tranquil location yet convenient to the attractions. There is adequate parking adjacent to the guesthouse. Families are also welcomed and quoted special rates. The Grahams have proved helpful and courteous to their many visitors, who gather at night in the large color TV lounge.

Rockside Guest House, Ambleside Road, Windermere, Cumbria LA23 1AQ (tel. 09662/5343), is run by Neville and Mavis Fowles, who came to live in this area with their two daughters several years ago, thus achieving their ambition to live in "the most beautiful corner of England." They have since made Rockside one of the best establishments for B&B in the area. It is a guesthouse full of character, offering singles, twins, doubles, and family rooms from £11.50 ($20.15) to £17.50 ($30.65) per person nightly for B&B. The standard rooms have hot and cold running water basins, while those listed as "top choice" contain private showers and toilets, color TV, and beverage-making facilities. The house is centrally heated. Guests can choose from among six breakfasts big enough to start the day well whether you are walking or driving around the area. At the rear of the house is a car park for 12 vehicles, but Rockside is only two minutes' walk from the bus, train, or village of Windermere.

The Waverley Hotel, College Road, Windermere, Cumbria LA23 3AF (tel. 09662/5026), is conveniently situated on a quiet road close to the shops and public transport. It stands only a five-minute walk from the railway station and bus routes and has its own private car park. Erected in 1870 by a local builder, the Waverley retains much of its original Victorian charm, with spacious and well-furnished rooms. The bedrooms all have private baths, color TV, and tea- and coffee-makers. Family, double, twin, and single accommodations are offered. B&B costs £18 ($31.50) per person nightly, with half board available at £25 ($43.75) per person. The hotel has a comfortable TV lounge for the use of guests, and there is a licensed bar on the premises. The hotel is run by resident owners Bert and Elizabeth Nelson.

Kenilworth Guest House, Holly Road, Windermere, Cumbria LA23 2AF (tel. 09662/4004), is a house known for its cleanliness and comfort. Brian and Jean Gosling offer a good bargain in the centrally heated, pleasant bedrooms, each with hot and cold running water. One room has a private bath. Guests are received from March to October, paying £10.50 ($18.40) per person nightly for B&B. An informal atmosphere prevails. Prices include a full Lake Country breakfast, and an evening meal can be arranged upon request.

WHERE TO EAT

In the center of town, **Millers Restaurant,** 31-33 Crescent Rd. (tel. 09662/3877), has a simple tea-room decor and offers good, inexpensive food. Special lunches and dinners are offered for £4 ($7), including such dishes as homemade steak-and-kidney pie, two vegetables, new potatoes, and a choice of dessert. A three-course fish dinner is featured from £6 ($10.50). When available, char, a fish from Lake Windermere, is offered. The restaurant is owned and run by Mr. Lord, who is responsible for the carefully prepared, traditional dishes. It's best to go from noon to 9 p.m. daily.

Miller Howe Kaff, Lakeland Plastics, Station Precinct (tel. 09662/2255), was opened by former actor John Tovey, the celebrated owner of Miller Howe Hotel, a prestigious lakeside inn known for fine dining and recommended in our companion guide, *Frommer's England & Scotland.* That place is not for those on a budget. However, in an off-moment Mr. Tovey created this charming little place, where guests can enjoy dishes from his superb repertoire at very reasonable charges. It is open daily, except Sunday, from 10 a.m. to 4 p.m. and makes an ideal luncheon or afternoon tea stopover, with meals costing from £6 ($10.50) and up. The salads are remarkable, as are the "starters" (the British word for appetizers), and a main dish of the day, followed by such mouth-watering desserts as banana walnut. Vegetarians will also find solace here. No smoking is allowed, and tables are freely shared.

Village Pizza and Steak Restaurant, Victoria Street (tel. 09662/3429), stands near the railway station at the junction of Victoria and Cross Streets. The decor is pleasant and inviting, and fresh natural flavors are the hallmark of the kitchen of this place. Evening main meals cost from £3.50 ($6.15) for a pizza up to £8 ($14) for a juicy steak. You are also likely to be tempted by such selections as sautéed chicken chasseur, burgundy beef, lasagne, and moussaka. There is a small selection of vegetarian dishes also. The restaurant is open from 5:30 to 10 p.m. seven days a week in spring and summer, but only on Saturday and Sunday in winter.

BOWNESS-ON-WINDERMERE

A short way south of Windermere on Bowness Bay of the lake, the attractive town of Bowness has some interesting old architecture. This has been an important center for boating and fishing for a long time, and you can rent boats of all descriptions to explore the lake.

Lindeth Howe, Storrs Park, Bowness-on-Windermere, Cumbria LA23 3JF (tel. 09662/5759), is a country house hotel in a superb position above Lake Windermere, standing on six acres of lovely grounds. The house, part stone and part red brick with a roof of green Westmorland slate, was built for a wealthy mill-owner in 1879, but its most famous owner was Beatrix Potter, who installed her mother here while she lived across the lake at Sawrey. The present owners, Eileen and Clive Baxter, have furnished it in elegant style and offer 14 bedrooms, most of which have lake views. They are comfortably furnished, with private baths or showers, color TV, in-house movies, beverage-making facilities, and central heating. Two of them have handsome four-poster beds. Prices for B&B are from £20 ($35) to £23.50 ($41.15) per person daily, with half board costing from £29 ($50.75) to £33.50 ($58.65) per person. The dining room has two deep bay windows overlooking the lake. The lounge contains a brick fireplace with a solid oak mantel set in an oak-framed inglenook.

Lindeth Fell Hotel, Bowness-on-Windermere, Cumbria LA23 3JP (tel. 09662/3286), high above the town and the lake, is a traditional large Lakeland house of stone and brick, with many of its rooms overlooking the handsome gardens and the lake. The owners, the Kennedys, run the place more like a country house than a hotel, achieving an atmosphere of comfort in pleasingly furnished surroundings. For B&B, they charge from £25 ($43.75) per person nightly, the price going up to £35 ($61.25) to £37.50 ($65.65) per person for dinner, bed, and breakfast. All 15 bedrooms have private baths or showers, color TV, and beverage-making facilities. Prices include VAT. The cooking is under the supervision of Diana Kennedy and a resident chef, with local produce used when possible to prepare a variety of Lakeland and traditional English dishes. In pursuit of the country house atmosphere, the Kennedys offer tennis, croquet, and putting on the lawn, as well as a private tarn for fishing. The hotel is one mile south of Bowness on the A5074, the Lyth Valley road.

Belsfield Guest House, 4 Belsfield Terrace, Kendal Road, Bowness-on-Windermere, Cumbria LA23 3EQ (tel. 09662/5823), is a small, family-style guesthouse near the lake. It's owned by Peter and Anne Godfrey, who have modernized the house. Their welcome is personalized, and they offer cleanliness and an inviting atmosphere. Their B&B rate is from £12 ($21) to £15 ($26.25) per person per night, depending on the facilities and the season. All accommodations contain showers and color TV. The Godfreys offer family rooms, doubles, and twins.

Craig Foot Country House Hotel, Lake Road, Bowness-on-Windermere, Cumbria LA23 2EQ (tel. 09662/3902), is one of the stately homes in the area, dating from 1848, when it was built for a retired admiral. Standing on its own grounds, this Lake Country house opens onto views of the lake and the mountains in the distance. Most of its pleasantly furnished and comfortable bedrooms have private baths or showers. The resident proprietors, Audrey and Gordon Shore, charge £33 ($57.75) per person per night for dinner, bed, and a full English breakfast. All accommodations have TV and hot drink facilities. Most have views of the lake.

LAKE DISTRICT TOURS

To provide a true appreciation of the Lake District and its many attractions, try **Mountain Goat Holidays,** Victoria Street (tel. 09662/5161). Begun in 1972 by Chris Taylor, who had a strong desire to start his own business after spending some years in Australia, it has become firmly established in the Lake District for touring or walking holidays. Mountain Goat also runs daily minibus tours that take you to many of the otherwise inaccessible spots of the area.

These tours include trips to the Northern Lakes, Grasmere, Keswick, Buttermere, and Honister Pass, with a visit to Wordsworth's home in Grasmere, Rydal Mount. Cost: £13 ($22.75) per person.

An interesting day out is the tour up Hardknott and Wrynose Passes to Eskdale, following the old Roman route to Hardknott Roman fort. A pub lunch can be had in Eskdale. You can take a ride on the miniature Ravenglass-Eskdale railway before having tea at Ravenglass and returning over the fells to Duddon Bridge, Coniston, and Windermere. The cost is £14.50 ($25.40) per person. Other tours visit Hawkshead and the home of Beatrix Potter for £7.50 ($13.15) for a half day.

Also, there is a half-day tour, the Duddon Valley Picnic, for £10 ($17.50), and other half-day tours to Cartmel, Grange-over-Sands, and Dentdale for £7.50 ($13.15) per person. Mountain Goat also runs a regular bus service to York and back daily, except Tuesday, for £14 ($24.50) round-trip.

Mountain Goat Holidays run from Saturday to Saturday, or just for a short break of two or three nights. Based in Windermere or Keswick, they include dinner, bed, and breakfast in a hotel or guesthouse of your choice. All holidays in this category start at £220 ($385) per person.

3. Ambleside

A good and idyllic retreat, Ambleside is one of the major centers of the Lake District, attracting pony-trekkers, fell-hikers, and rock-scalers. The charms are here all year, even in late autumn, when it's fashionable to sport a mackintosh. Ambleside is superbly perched at the top of Lake Windermere. Traditions are entrenched, especially at the Rushbearing Festival, an annual event.

WHERE TO STAY

Nestled in the sheltered valley of the Rothay, the **Rothay Garth Hotel,** Rothay Road, Ambleside, Cumbria LA22 0EE (tel. 0966/32217), on the edge of Ambleside, is an elegant, century-old country house set in beautiful gardens. All bedrooms are tastefully decorated, warm, and comfortable, with private baths, color TV, phones, hairdryers, and tea- and coffee-makers. Doreen and David Clark charge £31 ($54.25) to £38 ($66.50) per person daily for dinner, bed, and breakfast. Superb and varied cuisine is served in the restaurant, and reduced half-board rates are quoted for two nights or more. For B&B, the charge is £22 ($38.50) to £29 ($50.75) per person. Prices depend on the season. Fresh flowers are arranged throughout the hotel daily, and guests can enjoy a sunny garden room or the cozy lounge with its seasonal log fire. A wide choice of connoisseur bar lunches are served all year in the Loughrigg Bar. The special ploughman's lunch has received much praise. Yachts, canoes, and sailboards can be rented. Tennis courts, a pitch and putt golf area, and a croquet lawn are adjacent to the hotel. Laundry and ironing facilities are available.

Crow How Hotel, Rydal Road, Ambleside, Cumbria LA22 9PN (tel. 0966/32193), along a private drive off the A591 north of Ambleside, is only a few minutes' walk from Rydal Water. This was originally a large farmhouse of Lakeland stone. The proprietors, Mark and Glenise Heywood, offer bedrooms with private baths (one room's private bath is along the corridor). Rates range from £18 ($31.50) to £19 ($33.25) per person daily, rising slightly higher in July and August. Note: there is a 10% surcharge for a single night booking. All the bedrooms have color TV, beverage-making facilities, and controllable heaters, while the public rooms are centrally heated. The hotel has a large guest lounge, a small but well-stocked bar, and two acres of gardens.

Queens Hotel, Market Place, Ambleside, Cumbria LA22 9BU (tel. 05394/32206), in the heart of the resort area, is an old-fashioned and long-established hotel where guests are housed and fed well. The hotel rents 28 comfortably furnished bedrooms, 23 of which contain private baths. The charge is £17 ($29.75) per person daily for a bed and full English breakfast. With a private bath or shower, there is a supplement of £2.50 ($4.40) per person. Since the hotel has two fully licensed bars and restaurants, you may want to dine here. The food is good and hearty, the portions generous. The Queens is centrally heated in winter.

WHERE TO EAT

For the ultimate in good wholesome Cumbria eating, head for **Sheila's Cottage,** The Slack (tel. 05394/33079), where you can order food that might have delighted those who remember a holiday here before the war. By that, I mean baked ham coated with sugar in the style of old Cumberland chefs, or Lakeland lemon bread and perhaps a Westmorland raisin-filled walnut tart. (Cumberland and Westmorland were the old names of the shires.) Meals cost from £8 ($14) and are served daily from 10:30 a.m. to 5:30 p.m., except Sunday. It might be hard to get a seat here for lunch unless you "book a table," as the English say.

Zeffirellis, Compston Road (tel. 0966/33845), is a drinking, dining, shopping, movie, and café complex right near the center of town. During the day you might enjoy its Garden Room downstairs or a pizzeria upstairs, ordering a selection of freshly made pastas or wheatmeal and sesame seed pizzas. A meal costs from £5 ($8.75). The Garden Room is open daily from 10 a.m. to 5:30 p.m., and the pizzeria and restaurant serves noon to 3 p.m. and 5 to 9:45 p.m. At night, against a Japanese art deco backdrop in the restaurant and pizzeria, you can order a three-course candlelit dinner for £9.95 ($17.40) that includes a reserved seat at the cinema. There is also a selection of French and Italian wines.

Apple Pie Eating House, Rydal Road (tel. 05394/33679), makes its own apple pie and does so exceedingly well, a thick slice with fresh cream. The cooks make very good quiches, including the Lorraine classic. Everything tastes better with their freshly ground coffee with cream. The homemade meat pies are also recommended. Lunches cost from £5 ($8.75). A licensed restaurant is upstairs, and out back there's a little terrace. The eating house is also a bakery, and the quality of the baking is so good you may want to take away with you some cakes, pastries, or scones. Hours are 9 a.m. to 5:30 p.m. Monday to Saturday, 10 a.m. to 5:30 p.m. on Sunday; closed in November.

Harvest Wholefood Vegetarian Restaurant, Compston Road (tel. 0966/33151), offers homemade fare, far better than some of the bland vegetarian restaurants opening in England. The home cooking is pure and simple, and fresh produce is used. Meals, eaten at simple, pine-sheathed tables, cost around £5 ($8.75). The restaurant is open daily from 10:30 a.m. to noon for morning coffee, noon to 2:30 p.m. for lunch, and 4 to 8:30 p.m. for dinner.

On the Outskirts

The **Britannia Inn,** Elterwater, Ambleside, Cumbria LA22 9HP (tel. 09667/210), just off the B5343 west of Ambleside, is a 400-year-old traditional village inn adjoining the green in the unspoiled village of Elterwater. Views from the inn are over the meadows to the three tarns making up Elterwater ("lake of the swan") and the fells beyond. Bar meals are served in the cozy bar where a log fire blazes in cool weather. David Fry, the innkeeper, rents ten well-appointed bedrooms all with tea- and coffee-makers and hairdryers. Four have private showers and toilets. Mr. Fry charges £19.75 ($34.55) to £22.25 ($38.95) per person daily for a bed and a full English breakfast in high season. Evening meals at £11 ($19.25) are served in a Victorian dining room. The inn receives guests all year, except Christmas. Guests enjoy staying in the whitewashed building with its low-beamed ceilings, stone fireplaces, and country bedrooms.

---

4. Rydal

Between Ambleside (the top of Lake Windermere) and Wordsworth's former retreat at Grasmere is Rydal, a small village on one of the smallest lakes, Rydal Water. **Rydal Mount** (tel. 0966/33002) was the home of William Wordsworth from 1813 until his death in 1850. Part of the house was built as a farmer's lake cottage around 1575. A descendant of Wordsworth's still owns the property, now a museum containing many portraits, furniture, and family possessions, as well as mementos and books of the poet. The 3½-acre garden was landscaped by Wordsworth and contains rare trees, shrubs, and other features of interest. The house is open daily from 9:30 a.m. to 5 p.m. from March to October, and from 10 a.m. to 4 p.m. from November to February. It is closed Tuesday in winter. Admission is £1.50 ($2.65) for adults, 50p (90¢) for children 5 to 16.

The village of Rydal is noted for its sheep-dog trials at the end of summer.

WHERE TO STAY

Beside the roadway between Ambleside and Grasmere, **Rydal Lodge,** Rydal, Ambleside, Cumbria LA22 9LR (tel. 0966/33208), is a good center for walking and touring the whole of the Lake District. The Rothay River runs beside the secluded gardens, and Rydal Water, a beautiful lake, is at the end of the garden. The family owners provide meals of high quality, and the menus are well planned. Strawberries and other fruit from the garden are provided in season, and the lodge has a license to serve wine with main meals. The bedrooms are equipped with hot and cold running water, shaving points, electric blankets, heaters, and innerspring mattresses. There are eight bedrooms as well as a private car park. Terms are from £19.50 ($34.15) per person daily for B&B, with dinner costing from £10 ($17.50), including VAT. Rydal Lodge is of historical interest. Matthew Arnold stayed here, and it is connected with Harriet Martineau. The older part of the house was an inn in 1655.

You may need good directions to find **Foxghyll,** Under Loughrigg, Rydal, near Ambleside, Cumbria LA23 2EQ (tel. 05394/33292), but if you succeed, you will have arrived at one of the best value small B&Bs in the Rydal and Ambleside district. You are welcomed by Timothy and Marjorie Mann, who seem only too happy to share this handsomely restored house that was once occupied by the writer Thomas de Quincey. They can only accept about six paying guests a night, so reservations are important. Much of the house has a decorative overlay familiar to Queen Victoria, but parts of the building are said to date from the 1600s. Three double bedrooms are decorated as in an affluent private home, and two have a private bath. The B&B charge per night ranges from £11 ($19.25) to £13.50 ($23.63). One room has a four-poster. The house stands on extensive grounds, which you can explore at leisure.

Nab Cottage, Rydal, Ambleside, Cumbria LA22 9SD (tel. 09665/311), is a 300-year-old cottage whose architectural facade is protected by the local building commission. That pleases the owners, Tim and Liz Melling, who maintain seven rooms for paying guests. Some of the accommodations contain a private bath, and the shared facilities are adequate. The cottage, dating from 1702, was once the residence of Hartley Coleridge, son of the famous poet, Samuel Taylor Coleridge. The writer Thomas de Quincey was also a resident. The cottage is well situated on the shore of Rydal Water about two miles outside of Grasmere, with views of the lake from many of the bedroom windows. The Mellings charge £13 ($22.75) daily for B&B, from £20 ($35) for a well-prepared half board. Much of the original character remains in the in-house pub, where a log fire wards off the cold-weather chill.

5. Grasmere

On a lake that bears its name, Grasmere was the home of Wordsworth from 1799 to 1808. He called this area "the loveliest spot that man hath ever known." The nature poet lived with his sister Dorothy (the writer and diarist) at **Dove Cottage,** which is now a museum administered by the Wordsworth Trust. Wordsworth, who followed Southey as poet laureate, died in the spring of 1850 and was buried in the graveyard of the village church at Grasmere. Another tenant of Dove Cottage was Thomas de Quincey *(Confessions of an English Opium Eater).* For a combined ticket costing £2.80 ($4.90) for adults, £1.20 ($2.10) for children, you can visit both Dove Cottage and the **Wordsworth Museum.** This houses the Wordsworth treasures, manuscripts, paintings, and memorabilia. There are also various special exhibitions throughout the year, exploring the art and literature of English Romanticism. The property is open daily from 9:30 a.m. to 5:30 p.m., except from mid-January to mid-February. For further information, phone 09665/544, 09665/268 for Dove Cottage Restaurant information.

WHERE TO STAY

Away from the traffic noise, **Titteringdales,** Pye Lane, Grasmere, Cumbria LA22 9RQ (tel. 09665/439), is a small private guesthouse. It opens onto views of Silverhow, Fairfield, and Helm Crag. Surrounded by its own gardens, the house is well run and comfortable, with full central heating. Children sharing accommodations with their parents are given one-third reductions in prices. The owners take pride in the English home cookery and personal service, trying and succeeding in achieving that home-away-from-home appeal. From April to October only, the seven bedrooms rent for £14.50 ($25.40) daily in a single, £35 ($61.25) in a double. An evening meal is provided for another £8 ($14). Packed lunches and afternoon teas are available on request.

Moss Grove Hotel, Grasmere, Cumbria LA22 9SW (tel. 09665/251), is an old Lakeland house in the center of town, owned and run by Ken and Shirley Wood. Mr. Wood used to work for a brewery, and Mrs. Wood is a physicist. Both loved the area and came here to make a life for themselves. The hotel is well furnished and warm. Singles cost from £20 ($35) to £28 ($49) nightly, with doubles priced from £23 ($40.25) to £28 ($49) per person, the difference in tariffs depending on the plumbing and the furnishings (some of the accommodations contain four-poster beds). A large, wholesome breakfast is included in the price. There are two lounges, one with TV, the other with a small bar. Dinner is a well-cooked meal, usually with a roast joint or poultry along with fresh vegetables. The hotel is open all year, but meals are served only from May to December.

How Foot Lodge, Town End, Grasmere, Cumbria LA22 9SQ (tel. 09665/366), a Victorian house that once belonged to Wordsworth's friends, lies just along the road from Dove Cottage and Rydal Mount. The bedrooms, which are quite elegant, all have private baths, color TV, radios, and tea- and coffee-makers. They cost from £19 ($33.25) per person daily for B&B. The house's lounges have open fires, comfortable chairs, and some antiques. John and Janet Timpson, your hosts, have a licensed bar in their gracious hotel.

Craigside House, Grasmere, Cumbria LA22 9SG (tel. 09665/292), is set in 1½ acres of garden, with views over the lake to the hills beyond. It's just above Dove Cottage, where Wordsworth lived. It was he who pointed out this site to the people who agreed with him that this was an ideal location for a house and built Craigside back in 1839. Ken and Shirley Wood, who operate the Moss Grove Hotel (previewed above), run this guesthouse as well, offering rooms with bath and breakfast from £17.50 ($30.65) per person nightly. One of the rooms has a Hepplewhite four-poster bed.

Ryelands, Grasmere, Cumbria LA22 9SU (tel. 09665/652), is a 19th-century country house of Lakeland stone in a tranquil spot looking south down the valley. Surrounding gardens and an adjacent paddock provide privacy and ample parking. The owners, Mr. and Mrs. Le Cornu, are interesting people with discriminating taste. The house is nonsmoking, light, airy, and welcoming. The comfortable bedrooms rent for £15.75 ($27.55) to £21.50 ($37.65) per person nightly for B&B in a shared double- or twin-bedded room, £27.75 ($48.55) to £36 ($63) for one person using a double room for single occupancy. The breakfast room is a calm oasis in which to begin the day. A traditional English breakfast is offered, but if you prefer, you can have a vegetarian meal.

Silver Lea, Easedale Road, Grasmere, Cumbria LA22 9QN (tel. 09665/657), is a small, well-run guesthouse operated by Ken and Olive Smith. The location is about a three-minute walk from the heart of Grasmere. Their stone house is well kept, and their rooms are comfortable, opening onto mountain views. Some of the accommodations have their own bath and toilet. The rate is from £20 ($35) per person nightly. Guests take delight in the Lakeland cookery of Mrs. Smith, who receives visitors from February to November.

At **Grasmere Hotel,** Broadgate, Grasmere, Cumbria LA22 9TA (tel. 09665/277), the main feature of this Lakeland hotel is the large, modern dining room at the rear where Ian and Annette Mansie provide mouth-watering evening meals for their guests. Prettily decorated tables cluster around the central buffet on which desserts are displayed along with a huge slate cheeseboard. Both Ian and Annette do the cooking, and their green-and-white kitchen is almost as popular a meeting place for guests as is the sitting room and bar. The four-course meals include such delectable dishes as lamb stuffed with apricots, celery, and walnuts. Upstairs, the pleasantly furnished bedrooms contain private baths or showers, color TV, radios, and direct-dial phones. Dinner, bed, and a full breakfast ranges from £29.50 ($51.65) to £36 ($63) per person daily.

WHERE TO EAT

A cheerful place offering good value, **Cumbria Carvery,** Stock Lane (tel. 09665/515), offers simple but good food at reasonable prices. Try, for example, Cumbrian lamb prepared Greek style, or else scallops, lake trout, salmon, steaks, or perhaps a vegetarian dish. The carvery is open daily from 10 a.m. to 10:30 p.m., with food being served continuously.

Baldry's, Red Lion Square (tel. 09665/301), serves good homemade food at prices most diners find appetizing. Elaine and Paul Nelson have brightened up the food situation in Grasmere. You can enjoy excellent cakes with your tea throughout the day, and desserts tend to be superb. If you're visiting at lunch, look for the daily specials. Vegetarians are catered to here, but meat-eaters will also be satisfied. Baldry's is open from 9:30 a.m. to 5:30 p.m. year-round (it remains open until 7:30 p.m. during the summer migration from the south). Sunday lunch here is a major event in town. Meals cost from £5 ($8.75) and up.

The Coffee Bean, Red Lion Square (tel. 09665/234), right in the center of Grasmere, offers soups, sandwiches (toasted or not), coffee, tea, chocolate, pastries, pies, and cookies, among other items. Food can be eaten here or taken away. They will fill flasks of hot tea or coffee for you. Everything is freshly made and much is home-baked. Light meals cost from £2.80 ($4.90). It's open from 9 a.m. to 5:30 p.m. daily in summer, and from 10 a.m. to 4 p.m. on Saturday and Sunday only, from November to mid-March.

---

6. Hawkshead and Coniston

Discover for yourself the village of Hawkshead, with its 15th-century grammar school where Wordsworth went to school for eight years (he carved his name on a desk that still remains). Near Hawkshead, in the vicinity of Esthwaite Water, is the 17th-century **Hill Top Farm,** former home of Beatrix Potter, the author of the Peter Rabbit books, who died during World War II.

At Coniston, four miles away from Hawkshead, you can visit the village famously associated with John Ruskin. Coniston is a good base for rock climbing. The Coniston "Old Man" towers in the background at 2633 feet, giving mountain climbers one of the finest views of the Lake District.

John Ruskin, poet, artist, and critic, was one of the great figures of the Victorian age and a prophet of social reform, inspiring such diverse men as Proust, Frank Lloyd Wright, and Gandhi. He moved to his home, **Brantwood** (tel. 05394/41396), on the east side of Coniston Water, in 1872 and lived there until his death in 1900. The house today is open for visitors to view much Ruskiniana, including some 200 pictures by him. Also displayed are his coach and boat, the *Jumping Jenny*. A video program tells the story of Ruskin's life and work.

An exhibition illustrating the work of W. J. Linton is laid out in his old printing room. Linton was born in England in 1812 and died at New Haven, Connecticut, in 1897. Well known as a wood engraver and for his private press, he lived at Brantwood, where he set up his printing business in 1853. He published *The English Republic,* a newspaper and review, before immigrating to America in 1866, where he set up his printing press in 1870. The house is owned and managed by the Education Trust, a self-supporting registered charity. It is open daily from mid-March to mid-November, and Wednesday to Sunday in winter, from 11 a.m. to 5:30 p.m. Admission is £2 ($3.50) for adults and £1 ($1.75) for children, with a family ticket costing £5.25 ($9.20). Part of the 250-acre estate is also open as a nature trail, costing 50p (90¢) for adults, 35p (60¢) for children, if the walk is taken separately.

The Brantwood stables, designed by Ruskin, have been converted into a tea room and restaurant called the Jumping Jenny. Also in the stable building is the Lakeland Guild Craft Gallery, which follows the Ruskin tradition in encouraging contemporary craft work of the finest quality.

There is also the **Ruskin Museum,** The Institute (tel. 0996/41387), where you can see Ruskin's personal possessions and relics, sketchbooks, letters, and a collection of mineral rocks he collected. It's open daily from 10 a.m. to 5:30 p.m. from Easter to October 31.

Literary fans may want to make a pilgrimage to the graveyard of the village church, where Ruskin was buried; his family turned down a chance to have him interred at Westminster Abbey.

HOTELS IN HAWKSHEAD

In a Georgian building, the **Ivy House Hotel,** Main Street, Hawkshead, near Ambleside, Cumbria LA22 0NS (tel. 09666/204), is an ideal headquarters from which to branch out for visits on Lake Windermere. All the 12 bedrooms are centrally heated and have hot and cold running water. Five have private baths. B&B costs from £21.25 ($37.20) to £22.75 ($39.80) per person daily. A modern, motel-type annex handles overflow guests. Log fires blaze in the lounge in early and late season. The hospitable proprietors, David and Jane Vaughan, are used to welcoming overseas visitors. Because of their charming house and lovely situation, they are heavily booked, so it's imperative to reserve well in advance. The house is open from March to November only.

Kings Arms, The Square, Hawkshead, near Ambleside, Cumbria LA22 0NZ (tel. 09666/372), is a crooked-fronted old coaching inn in the middle of the village, with leaded windows and sloping roofs. Inside, low beams and whitewashed walls complete the picture, along with a friendly bar patronized by the locals. There is also a neat buttery, and in the rear a room for bar games. The inn offers grills and steaks at mealtimes, and also experiments on the locals with national evenings, including Indian, Oriental, or Greek fare. Dinners start at £9 ($15.75). Nine bedrooms, five with private baths, are rented, costing £19 ($33.25) to £22 ($38.50) daily in a single, £30 ($52.50) to £37 ($64.75) in a double, depending on the plumbing.

On the outskirts, **Field Head House,** Outgate, Hawkshead, Cumbria LA22 0PY (tel. 09666/240), is a bit hard to find but worth the search. From Hawkshead, take the Ambleside road (B5286), then take the second turning on the left, a mile from Hawkshead (signposted Field Head). After about a quarter of a mile, Field Head is on your right. Once there, you will be welcomed by the Dutch-born owners, Eeke and Bob van Gulik, to this marvelous old Lake District home whose origins go back to the 1600s, when it was built as a hunting lodge for a duke. A friend of William Wordsworth, the artist John Harden lived in this house for about a decade from 1834. On its own six acres of wooded grounds and gardens, Field House offers eight different accommodations, all with private bath. Accommodations are homelike and well appointed, with B&B rates going from £20 ($35) to £25 ($43.75) per person daily.

Even if you can't stay here, you might call and see if you can have dinner with them, as their food is considered the best in the area. From 7:30, a superb five-course dinner is served for £15 ($26.25). The menu changes every night, but a typical meal might include a pear-and-Stilton savory, mushroom soup, roast shoulder of venison with five different fresh vegetables (often from their own garden), English cheese, and peaches and cream, followed by coffee. No dinner is served on Tuesday. It is imperative to make a reservation.

EATING AND DRINKING IN HAWKSHEAD

The most famous pub in the area is **Queen's Head,** Hawkshead, near Ambleside, Cumbria LA22 0NS (tel. 09666/271), in the center of this celebrated village. It's really more an inn than a pub, as it also rents out bedrooms. Behind a mock black-and-white timbered facade, it is a 17th-century structure of character, serving Hartley's Ulverston beer from the wood, a local favorite brew. Bar lunches, costing from £5.75 ($10.05), are served daily from noon to 2 p.m. Or else you can enjoy à la carte dinners from 7 to 9 p.m. for £8 ($14). Try a sizzling sirloin steak, grilled local rainbow trout, or perhaps pheasant in casserole. Eight comfortably old-fashioned bedrooms, half of which contain private baths or showers, cost from £21 ($36.75) daily in a single, from £33 ($57.75) in a double. Breakfast is included.

AN INN AT CONISTON

The most popular, traditional, and attractive pub, restaurant, and hotel in this Lakeland village is the **Coniston Sun Hotel,** Coniston, Cumbria LA21 8HQ (tel. 05394/41248). In reality it is a country-house hotel of much character, dating from 1902, although the inn attached to it is from the 16th century. Standing on its own beautiful grounds above the village, it lies at the foot of the Coniston "Old Man." Donald Campbell made this place his headquarters during his attempt on the world water speed record. Each of the 11 bedrooms is decorated with style and flair, and two of them contain four-posters. Each unit also has a private bath, color TV, and drink-making facilities. It's best to book in here on half-board terms, costing £43 ($75.25) per person nightly. Fresh local produce is used whenever possible in the candlelit restaurant. Log fires take the chill off a winter evening, and guests relax informally in the lounge, which is like a library. Many sports can be arranged.

A HOTEL AT FAR SAWREY

A welcoming old country inn, **The Sawrey Hotel,** Far Sawrey, near Ambleside, Cumbria LA22 0LQ (tel. 09662/3425), is in the village where Beatrix Potter lived the happiest years of her life. The inn was built of stone and "pebble-dash" (a form of stucco) as a coaching inn in the early 18th century. For single and double occupancy, charges are £20.50 ($35.90) daily in a bathless room and £24 ($42) in a room with bath, including bed, breakfast, and dinner. Nonresidents are welcome to come and dine on bar snacks at lunch from 11:30 a.m. to 2:30 p.m. and on a five-course, fixed-price dinner costing £9.75 ($17.05) every day from 7 to 8:45 p.m. David Brayshaw, the host, operates bars popular with locals and travelers alike.

---

7. Keswick

Lying 22 miles north of Windermere, Keswick opens onto Derwentwater, one of the loveliest lakes in the district. Robert Southey, poet laureate, lived for four decades at Greta Hall and was buried at Crosthwaite Church. Coleridge lived there too, depending on Southey for financial aid. Sir Hugh Walpole, the novelist, in a different era also resided near Keswick.

Keswick is the natural geographical starting point for car tours and walks of exploration in the northern Lake District, including the John Peel country to the north of Skiddaw (quiet and little known), Borrowdale, Buttermere, and Crummock Water, as well as Bassenthwaite, Thirlmere, and Ullswater.

And you too, following in the footsteps of Charles Lamb and Shelley, will seek out an accommodation.

WHERE TO STAY

Known to Southey and Coleridge, the **George Hotel,** St. John Street, Keswick, Cumbria CA12 5AZ (tel. 07687/72076), is a 400-year-old coaching inn, the oldest inn in town, once known as the George & Dragon. Still offering unvarnished charm, it lies in the middle of town near the market square, which comes alive on Saturday morning. For B&B, guests are charged from £15 ($26.25) per person daily, plus another £8 ($14) for dinner. The rooms are well appointed and maintained. The inn, particularly the two old-world bars, offers a relaxed atmosphere.

King's Arms Hotel, Main Street, Keswick, Cumbria CA12 5BL (tel. 0687/ 72083), is a coaching inn dating back more than 200 years to the time of George III. In the middle of town, it offers comfortably furnished bedrooms, all with private baths, color TV, in-house video, and tea- and coffee-makers. B&B costs £19 ($33.25) per person nightly. The Beefeater Restaurant offers an extensive à la carte menu, and snacks are served at lunchtime and in the evening in a charming oak-beamed bar and lounge. If you prefer, there is the Loose Box Pizzeria in the court-yard, which was the original stables. The Casablanca Piano Bar offers live music.

Linnett Hill Hotel, 4 Penrith Rd., Keswick, Cumbria CA12 4HF (tel. 07687/ 73109), has been thoroughly modernized, yet it retains oak beams and other typical characteristics. This private town house dates from 1812, and its decorations in the main are Victorian. Sylvia and Richard Harland offer seven bedrooms, most with private baths and all with hot and cold running water, TV, electric shaver points, and central heating. They cost from £11.50 ($20.15) per person daily for B&B, plus another £6 ($10.50) for an evening dinner. Meals are not only large, they're beauti-fully prepared and served. The hotel has a comfortable lounge, a small private bar, and a private car park. It is pleasantly situated opposite the River Greta and Fitz Park, with open views of Skiddaw Range and Latrigg, five minutes' walk to the lake shore.

Allerdale House, 1 Eskin St., Keswick, Cumbria CA12 4DH (tel. 07687/ 73891), is a large Victorian-era home close to the "center of everything" that might be ideal lodgings for your base near Derwentwater. Here you get real Lakeland hos-pitality, a warm welcome, and comfortable bedrooms. Rooms, a total of six in all, five with private bath or shower, are pleasantly furnished and well maintained. The B&B rate is also attractive, costing from £14.50 ($25.40) daily in a single, rising to £28 ($49) in a double. Guests are accepted year-round (except in December), and they can also arrange to have a real home-cooked dinner in the evening.

At **Crow Park Hotel,** The Heads, Keswick, Cumbria CA12 5ER (tel. 07687/ 72208), the Langfords' old gray-stone house makes a fine guesthouse only a short distance from the town center, where it overlooks Hope Park and opens onto views of the Borrowdale valley. All 25 well-furnished rooms have private showers or tubs and contain many amenities. B&B costs from £16.50 ($28.90) to £20 ($35) per person daily, and half board is £25 ($43.75) to £29 ($50.75). They close only for Christmas.

WHERE TO EAT

The most famous pub in Keswick is the **Dog & Gun,** Lake Road (tel. 07687/ 73463). Inside, there's warmth and character a-plenty, along with tasty bar snacks or full-size meals. A tavern with two rooms, it offers an atmosphere of low beams (at least in one section) and open fires in winter. Meals include such hearty fare as Hun-garian goulash and roast chicken. Service is daily from 11:30 a.m. to 2 p.m. and 6 to 9:30 p.m.; on Sunday from noon to 2 p.m. and 7 to 9:30 p.m. Meals cost from £3.90 ($6.85).

FOOD AND LODGING ON THE OUTSKIRTS

At the foot of Whinlatter Pass, west of Keswick in the village of Braithwaite, stands the **Coledale Inn,** Braithwaite, near Keswick, Cumbria CA12 5TN (tel. 059682/272), a typical Victorian Lakeland country inn that started life as a wool-len mill. It has a busy Georgian bar, circa 1824, a large lounge bar, a comfortable and quiet residents' lounge, and a restaurant. It is full of attractive Victorian prints and antique furnishings. A full bistro menu is available daily, including local specialties such as Flookburgh shrimp, Borrowdale trout, Cumberland sausage, and Cumbrian farmhouse cheese. Traditional English desserts with custard are also a treat. Up-stairs, the seven double, twin, or family bedrooms are spacious, all with mountain views, showers, and toilets. Stanley and Helen Hinde charge from £16 ($28) per person daily, including a full breakfast.

In the heart of Thornthwaite Forest close to the top of Whinlatter Pass is **Cottage in the Wood,** Whinlatter Pass, Keswick, Cumbria CA12 5TW (tel. 059682/409), which was once an old coaching inn providing a staging post for coaches and wagons traveling to and from the Cumbrian coast. Now it is a welcoming small country hotel with full central heating and cozy lounges containing deep armchairs and a warming fire. Comfortable bedrooms, decorated and furnished in cottage style, all have hot beverage-making facilities, and most have private baths. Bed and a full English breakfast cost from £15 ($26.25) to £17 ($29.75) per person nightly. Lunches from £2 ($3.50), and evening meals from £7 ($12.25), are served in the dining room, which has views of the Skiddaw mountain range. The emphasis is on traditional English cooking, with Lakeland specialties featured.

8. Bassenthwaite

With its fine stretch of water in the shadow of the 3053-foot Skiddaw, Bassenthwaite makes a good center for exploring the western Lakeland.

FOOD AND LODGING

A 16th-century inn, the **Pheasant,** Bassenthwaite Lake, near Cockermouth, Cumbria CA13 9YE (tel. 059681/234), has a neat exterior set against a wooded mountain backdrop. Inside, the bar is smoke-mellowed. Old hunting prints dot the walls, and real ale is on tap. The beamed dining room is bright and cheerful, with spotless white tablecloths and a menu of good-quality roasts, fish, and poultry with fresh vegetables. There are three pleasant lounges with open log fires, and fresh flowers when possible. The bedrooms are immaculate and bright with chintz. All 20 units have private baths. Prices are £33 ($57.75) daily in a single and £62 ($108.50) in a double, admittedly splurge prices but worth it for those who want to enjoy the charm of the place. Prices include VAT, service, and an English breakfast. There are three bedrooms in the annex, which is a bungalow on the grounds.

Ravenstone Hotel, Bassenthwaite, near Keswick, Cumbria CA12 4QG (tel. 059681/240), is a country house, one of the more inviting in the area, opening onto vistas over Bassenthwaite Lake. Personal service from the owners, the Stephenson family, is a hallmark of the well-run establishment. The house has much character and makes for a relaxed vacation. It is situated in its own grounds, and its accommodations open onto views of the Cumbrian countryside. Bedrooms, 15 in all, nine with private baths, have all the modern amenities and are well maintained. Depending on the plumbing and room assignment, the overnight B&B rate ranges from £18 ($31.50) to £21 ($36.75) in a single, rising to £35 ($61.25) to £41 ($71.75) in a double. The wholesome, homemade Lakeside cooking is another feature of the establishment, and you can arrange for meals served from 7 to 8 p.m. Ravenstone receives guests from March to October.

To keep costs low, your best bet is to stay at a local farm that receives paying guests during the summer months. Try **Bassenthwaite Hall Farm,** Bassenthwaite, Cumbria CA12 4QP (tel. 059681/393), dating from the 17th century. The centrally heated farmhouse on this 200-acre beef and sheep farm receives paying guests from February to November. Only two bedrooms, accommodating up to six persons, are available, both with hot and cold water basins. The hostess, Mrs. Trafford, charges from £10 ($17.50) per person daily for B&B. The farmhouse, brought up-to-date but keeping such features as its old oak beams, is in a village beside a stream.

The building is solidly constructed of stone daubed with rough-cast stucco "to keep the cold out."

---

9. Penrith

This is an old Lakeland border town with a turbulent history. See the red ruins of Penrith Castle and the ancient church with its Giant's Grave. It is a good area for exploring not only Hadrian's Wall but the rolling hills of the Lake District, the small and ancient stone hamlets that still carry Norse and Danish names—having been settled by the Vikings—and an occasional Norman tower.

In and around this area—but not in Penrith itself—I have selected a random sampling of accommodations in case you'd like to anchor in and do some exploring. This is an ideal stopping-off place en route to Scotland.

WHERE TO STAY

If you're driving past the Lake District without time to visit the better-known places, come off the M6 at Carlisle or Penrith and go east into the valley of the River Eden. There you can stay at **Nunnery House,** Staffield Kirkoswald, Penrith, Cumbria CA10 1EU (tel. 076883/537), the Armstrongs' 18th-century house built on the site of an ancient nunnery. Double or twin-bedded rooms, some with private baths and special features such as four-poster beds, cost from £15 ($26.25) to £20 ($35) per person nightly. However, bathless doubles or twins (with hot and cold running water) are a better bargain at only £12 ($21) per person. Ask about a family room housing two adults and two children at £35 ($61.25) nightly. There is a lounge and bar, so after a day's trek in the Nunnery Walks along the Eden and Croglin Rivers, you can sink into a chair with a well-earned drink at your elbow before enjoying an evening meal. For £6.75 ($11.80), you are served an appealing appetizer, then a meat or fish course with vegetables, followed by dessert. Vegetarian food is a specialty.

Nearer to Kendal, on the A685 in Gaisgill, is **Barbaras Cottage,** Gaisgill, Tebay, near Penrith, Cumbria CA10 3UA (tel. 05874/340). Mrs. Chrissy Hill owns this 17th-century cottage with open beams and roaring log fires. She provides comfortable overnight accommodations, where guests have their own baths with showers, dining room, and lounge with color TV. The overnight charge is £9 ($15.25) per person, including a full breakfast. The cottage is part of a small holding that provides fresh fruit and vegetables for the wholesome meals. The paddock is home to a herd of British Saanen dairy goats, hens, and ducks. Goat-milk products are made on the premises, including ice cream in several flavors. This is a good center for salmon fishing on the River Lune, bird-watching, fell walking, and sightseeing. Nearby is Appleby Castle with its perfect Norman keep, Langrigg Pottery at Winton, and Wetheriggs Country Pottery at Clifton Dykes.

Longthwaite Farm, Watermillock, near Penrith, Cumbria CA11 0LR (tel. 08536/584), with lake and fell views, was built in 1695. It has been modernized with hot and cold running water in the bedrooms, tea- and coffee-makers, and central heating. A separate bathroom has a shower and toilet. The house is in fine shape, with black oak floorboards and some of the original doors. The owner, Mrs. Brenda Ibbotson, receives a limited number of paying guests at any time of the year, charging £10 ($17.50) per person daily, including a full English breakfast. In fact, the farm is an ideal center for touring the English lakes. Mrs. Ibbotson will direct you to a number of old castles open to the public, as well as to festivals, exhibitions, and sheep-dog trials. If you're writing for reservations and an answer is required, send an International Reply Coupon.

10. Borrowdale

If you head south from Keswick for 3½ miles along the B5289, you come to one of the most charming spots in the Lake District. This beautiful Lakeland valley begins near Great Gable at a height of 2949 feet, opening out to enfold Derwentwater. Traditionally, it has been a center of rambling and rock climbing.

FOOD AND LODGING

One of the most charming guesthouses in the district, **Mrs. Patsy Hamilton's Ashness Cottage,** Ashness Bridge, Borrowdale, near Keswick, Cumbria CA12 5UN (tel. 059684/244), also lies within one of the most beautiful valleys. Originally built by Dame Edith Baxter in 1923 as a shooting lodge, it has witnessed crowds of Londoners flocking here for hunting and parties. It is sited ideally for views toward the lakes and mountains, and it is ringed with two acres of privately owned forest. Mrs. Hamilton runs the place, and in the words of reader Linda Wyman, she can "converse passionately and endearingly on subjects ranging from Mahler to sheep-dipping." With a copious English breakfast included, per person rates, single or double occupancy, are £9.50 ($16.35) nightly, with VAT included. No meals are served other than breakfast, but the restaurants and pubs of Keswick lie only 2½ miles to the north. The interior of the house is filled with carefully polished antiques, patterned chintzes, and mementos of a full and rich life. There are five rooms to rent, each cozy and charming, with access to shared bathrooms. To reach Ashness Cottage, take B5289 south from Keswick. Two miles from Keswick, turn at the sign pointing to Ashness Bridge/Watendlath. A few hundred yards from the bridge, you'll spot a sign on the right leading to the cottage.

The Yew Tree Country Restaurant, Seatoller, near Borrowdale (tel. 059684/634), dates from 1628. It has been turned into one of the best of the reasonably priced restaurants in the area. The setting, with an open fire, time-mellowed oak beams, and slate-covered floors, is inviting. The location is at the foot of Honister Pass. Jan and Andrew Lysser, the owners, now operate these Lakeland cottages, two in all, which they have tastefully decorated in the style of an old country inn. They also offer value for money with their good cuisine, using fresh produce, each dish handled with skill and served with a personal touch. Meals cost from £12 ($21), and service is from noon to 2:30 p.m. and 6 to 9:30 p.m. daily.

XIX

YORKSHIRE AND NORTHUMBRIA

1. YORK
2. NORTH YORKSHIRE
3. WEST YORKSHIRE
4. DURHAM
5. TYNE AND WEAR
6. NORTHUMBERLAND

For the connoisseur, the northeast of England is rich in attractions.

Yorkshire, known to readers of *Wuthering Heights* and *All Creatures Great and Small,* is the Texas of Britain, embracing both the moors of North Yorkshire and the Dales. With the radical changing of the old country boundaries, the shires are now divided into North Yorkshire (the most interesting from the tourist's point of view), West Yorkshire, South Yorkshire, and Humberside.

Away from the cities and towns that still carry the taint of the Industrial Revolution, the beauty is wild and remote. It's characterized by limestone crags, caverns along the Pennines, many peaks, mountainous uplands, rolling hills, the chalkland wolds, heather-covered moorlands, broad vales, lazy rivers, and tumbling streams.

Yorkshire lures not only in inland scenery, but with some 100 miles of shoreline, with its rocky headlands, cliffs, sandy bays, rock pools, sheltered coves, fishing villages, bird sanctuaries, former smugglers' dens, and yachting havens.

Across this vast region came the Romans, the Anglo-Saxons, the Vikings, the monks of the Middle Ages, kings of England, lords of the manor, craftsmen, hill farmers, and wool growers, each leaving his mark. You can still see Roman roads and pavements, great abbeys and castles, stately homes, open-air museums, and craft centers, along with parish churches, old villages, and cathedrals. In fact, Yorkshire's battle-scarred castles, Gothic abbeys, and great country manor houses (from all periods) are unrivaled anywhere in Britain.

Northumbria is made up of the counties of Northumberland, Cleveland, and Durham. Tyne and Wear is one of the more recently created counties, with Newcastle-upon-Tyne as its center.

The Saxons who came to northern England centuries ago carved out this kingdom, which at the time stretched from the Firth of Forth in Scotland to the banks of the Humber in Yorkshire. Vast tracts of that ancient kingdom remain natural and unspoiled. Again, this slice of England has more than its share of industrial towns, but you don't go here to see those. Set out to explore the wild hills and open spaces, crossing the dales of the eastern Pennines.

The whole area evokes ancient battles and bloody border raids. Castles, Saxon churches, and monastic ruins abound in Northumbria, none more notable than the Roman wall, one of the wonders of the Western world. The finest stretch of the wall lies within the Northumberland National Park between the stony North Tyne River and the county boundary at Gilsland.

1. York

Few cities in England are as rich in history as York. It is still encircled by its 13th- and 14th-century city walls—about 2½ miles long—with four gates. One of these, Micklegate, once grimly greeted visitors coming up from the south with the heads of traitors. To this day you can walk on the footpath of the walls of the Middle Ages.

The crowning achievement of York is its minster or cathedral, which makes the city an ecclesiastical center equaled only by Canterbury. In spite of this, York is one of the most overlooked cities on the cathedral circuit. Perhaps foreign visitors are intimidated by the feeling that the great city of northeastern England is too far north. Actually, it lies about 195 miles north of London on the Ouse River and can easily be tied in with a motor trip to Edinburgh. Or after visiting Cambridge, a motorist can make a swing through a too-often-neglected cathedral circuit: Ely, Lincoln, York, and Ripon.

There was a Roman York (Hadrian came this way), then a Saxon York, a Danish York, a Norman York (William the Conqueror slept here), a medieval York, a Georgian York, a Victorian York (the center of a flourishing rail business), and of course, a 20th-century York. A large amount of 18th-century York remains, including Richard Boyle's restored Assembly Rooms.

SEEING THE SIGHTS

The best way to see York is to go to the **Tourist Information Centre,** DeGrey Rooms, Exhibition Square (tel. 0904/621756), at 10:15 a.m. and 2:15 p.m. daily from April 1 to the end of October, where you'll be met by a voluntary guide who will take you on a 1½-hour walking tour of the city, revealing its history and lore through numerous intriguing stories. There is no charge. Additional tours are made at 7 p.m. daily during June, July, and August.

At some point in your exploration, you may want to visit **The Shambles,** once the meat-butchering center of York, dating back before the Norman Conquest. But this messy business has given way, and the ancient street survives. It is filled with jewelry stores, cafés, and buildings that huddle so closely together you can practically stand in the middle of the pavement, arms outstretched, and touch the houses on both sides of the street.

Recently, special interest has been focused on discoveries of the Viking era, from 867 to 1066, when the city was known as Jorvik, the Viking capital and major Scandinavian trade center. During excavations under York's Coppergate prior to development, a wealth of artifacts was unearthed in the late 1970s and early 1980s, including entire houses and workshops of the Viking age. For information on the period of history and treasures found in the excavations, inquire at the **Jorvik Viking Centre,** Coppergate (tel. 0904/643211).

Incidentally, the suffix *gate* for streets and sites in York is from the Scandinavian word for "street," a holdover from the era when the Vikings held sway here.

York Minster

One of the great cathedrals of the world, York Minster traces its origins back to the early 7th century. The present building, however, dates from the 13th century. Like the minster at Lincoln, York Cathedral is characterized by three towers, all built in the 15th century. The central tower is lantern-shaped, in the Perpendicular style.

Perhaps the distinguishing characteristic of the cathedral is its medley of stained glass from the Middle Ages—in glorious Angelico blues, ruby reds, forest greens, and ambers. See in particular the large East Window, the work of a 15th-century Coventry glass painter. In the North Transept is an architectural gem of the mid-13th century, the "Five Sisters," with its lancets. The choir screen, from the late 15th century, has an impressive lineup—everybody from William the Conqueror to the overthrown Henry VI.

The Chapter House is open Monday to Saturday from 10 a.m., costing adults 50p (90¢) and children 20p (35¢). The shop is open Monday to Saturday from 9 a.m. to 5 p.m. and on Sunday from 1:30 to 4 p.m. The refurbished Undercroft is open Monday to Saturday from 10 a.m. to dusk and on Sunday from 1 p.m. to dusk, costing £1.30 ($2.30) for adults, 60p ($1.05) for children. The Crypt is open during conducted tours only. At a party reception desk near the entrance to the Minster, parties can be put in touch with a guide, if one is available, for a conducted tour. Gifts toward the maintenance of the Minster are requested. For information, telephone 0904/624426.

From the top of the Central Tower on a clear day, there are unrivaled views of York and the Vale of York. It is a steep climb up a stone spiral staircase and not recommended for the very elderly, very young, or anyone with a heart condition or breathing difficulties. In winter, the Tower is only open on Saturday and Sunday, providing the weather is suitable. A climb costs adults £1 ($1.75), and children pay 50p (90¢).

The Treasurer's House

In the Minster Yard, the Treasurer's House (tel. 0904/624247) stands on a site where there's been a building since Roman times. The main part of the house was rebuilt in 1620 as the official residence of the treasurer of York Minster and was lived in as a private home until 1930. It has a magnificent series of rooms with fine furniture, glass, and china of the 17th and 18th centuries. An audio-visual program describes the work of the medieval treasurers and some of the personalities with which this York house is associated. The house has an attractive small garden. It is open from April until the end of October daily from 10:30 a.m. to 5 p.m. (last entry at 4:30 p.m.). Admission is £1.50 ($2.65) for adults, 75p ($1.30) for children. On some evenings in summer, the house is open from 7:30 to 9:30 p.m., when you can enjoy coffee by candlelight in the Great Hall. An attractive shop and licensed restaurant serving Yorkshire specialties are open the same hours as the house.

York Castle Museum

On the site of York's Castle, the York Castle Museum (tel. 0904/633932) is one of the finest folk museums in the country. Its unique feature is a re-creation of a Victorian cobbled street, "Kirkgate," named for the museum's founder, Dr. John Kirk. He acquired his large collection while visiting his patients in rural Yorkshire at the beginning of this century.

The period rooms range from a neoclassical Georgian dining room through an overstuffed and heavily adorned Victorian parlor, to the 1953 sitting room with a brand-new television set purchased to watch the coronation of Elizabeth II. In the Debtors' Prison, former prison cells display craft workshops. There is also a superb collection of arms and armor and a Costume Gallery, where displays are changed regularly to reflect the variety of the collection. Half Moon Court is an Edwardian

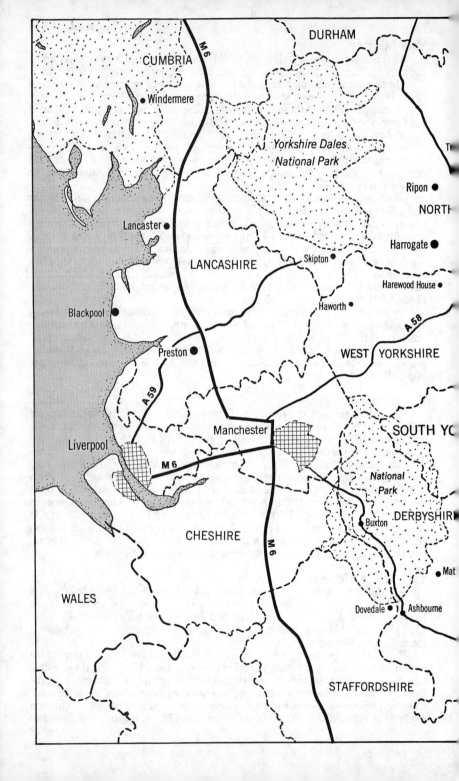

street, with a gypsy caravan and a pub (sorry, the bar's closed!). During the summer, you can visit a watermill on the bank of the River Foss.

The museum is open April to October from 9:30 a.m. to 6:30 p.m. Monday to Saturday (from 10 a.m. on Sunday). From November to March, hours are 9:30 a.m. to 5 p.m. Monday to Saturday (from 10 a.m. on Sunday). Last admission is one hour before closing, and it is recommended that you allow at least two hours for a visit to this museum. Admission is £2.50 ($4.40) for adults, £1.25 ($2.20) for children.

National Railway Museum

The first national museum to be built away from London, the National Railway Museum (tel. 0904/621261) has attracted millions of visitors since it opened in 1975. Adapted from an original steam locomotive depot, the museum gives visitors a chance to look under and inside steam locomotives or see how Queen Victoria traveled in luxury. In addition, there's a full-size collection of railway memorabilia, including an early 19th-century clock and penny machines for purchasing tickets on the railway platform. On display are more than 20 full-size locomotives. One, the *Agenoria,* dates from 1829 and is a contemporary of Stephenson's well-known *Rocket.* It's almost identical to the first American locomotive, the *Stourbridge Lion,* sent to the United States from England in 1828. Items on exhibition change from time to time, but there is always a fine selection of the beautifully colored British steam locomotives on display. *Mallard,* the fastest steam locomotive in the world, is in the museum when it's not at work on the railroad. Of several royal coaches, the most interesting is the century-old Royal Saloon, in which Queen Victoria rode until her death. It's like a small hotel, with polished wood, silk, brocade, and silver accessories.

The museum, on Leeman Road, can be visited Monday to Saturday from 10 a.m. to 6 p.m. and on Sunday from 11 a.m. to 6 p.m. It is closed on some public holidays. Admission is £2 ($3.50) for adults, £1 ($1.75) for children.

Jorvik Viking Centre

At Coppergate (tel. 0904/643211) is the Viking city discovered many feet below the present ground level. It was reconstructed exactly as it was in the year A.D. 948. In a "time car," you can travel back through the ages to 1067, when Normans sacked the city, and then ride slowly through the street market peopled by faithfully modeled Vikings. You can go through a house where a family lived and down to the river to see the ship-chandlers at work and a Norwegian cargo ship unloading. At the end of the ride you pass through the Finds Hut, where thousands of artifacts are displayed. The center is open from 9 a.m. to 7 p.m. daily (until 5:30 p.m. in summer). Admission is £2.75 ($4.80) for adults, £1.35 ($2.35) for children.

Theatre Royal

Theatre Royal, on St. Leonard's Place (tel. 0904/623568), is an old traditional theater building with modern additions to house the box office, bars, and restaurant. It is worth inquiring about the current production, as the Royal Shakespeare Company includes York in its tours. The Arts Council presents dance, drama, and opera, and visiting celebrities appear in classics. There is also an excellent resident repertory company.

Seat prices range from £3.50 ($6.15) to £6 ($10.50). The glass-walled, ground-floor snackbar serves coffee and tea along with low-cost fare. Upstairs in the Theatre Restaurant is a salad buffet and choice of hot dishes. A three-course meal will cost from £5 ($8.75). The restaurant is open daily from noon to 2:30 p.m. and 5 p.m. until curtain time. You don't have to buy a ticket to eat here, and it's quite a relaxing experience to sit outside with your drink and a snack, looking out on the world passing by.

An Unguided Walk-About

Starting from York Minster, walk down past Youngs Hotel, the reputed birth-place of Guy Fawkes. Turn right into Stonegate, a pedestrian area with old shops, a 12th-century house on the right, and some old coffeehouses. Continue across Davygate into St. Helen's Square to see the Guildhall and Mansion House, then go left into Coney Street, taking a right into Lower Ousegate.

At the beginning of Ouse Bridge, take the steps down to Kings Staithe, with a pub on the left for refreshment, before continuing on into South Esplanade and St. George's Gardens beside the river.

At the bridge, join the road again, turning left, and in front of you stand the Castle Museum, the Assize Courts, and Clifford's Tower. Walk up Tower Street and Clifford Street to Nessgate. Turn right into High Ousegate and continue across Parliament Street to the beginning of the Shambles on the left.

Walk up the Shambles past the attractive shops and ancient buildings to Kings Square, then bear right into Goodramgate. Walk down Goodramgate and, at the end, cross Deangate into College Street with St. William's College on the right. At the end a narrow road leads to the Treasurer's House.

You're now behind the east end of the Minster. Walk around to the west end and then up Bootham Bar, through the city gate, and turn left into Exhibition Square. The Art Gallery is on the right, the Tourist Information Centre to the left, and beside it, York's Theatre Royal. Continue down St. Leonard's Street to the crossroads, turning right into Museum Street. Cross the river and go right to join part of the old medieval wall, which you follow all the way to Skeldergate Bridge. Then follow the river's course upstream again to the center of York.

WHERE TO STAY

In a Georgian brick building, **Freshney's** (formerly Galtres Lodge), 54 Low Petergate, York, North Yorkshire YO1 2HZ (tel. 0904/622478), has cellars containing some beams believed to date back to the 13th century, as well as a beautiful Adam fireplace and three priest holes. It is owned by Mike and Janis Freshney. Janis used to work as a personal secretary to the Prime Minister at No. 10 Downing Street. There are 13 bedrooms, some of which open onto a view of the Rose Window of the Minster. A few contain private showers, toilets, and four-poster or half-tester beds. All accommodations have direct-dial phones, color TV, and hot beverage-making facilities. The tariff is from £14 ($24.50) to £24 ($42) per person daily for B&B, including VAT. Lunch and dinner are offered à la carte in the restaurant, and the lodge has a cozy, well-stocked bar and a separate guests' lounge. The hotel is in an excellent position, offering an ideal and centrally located base from which to explore the city, and it is within easy reach of the railway station.

Minster View, 2 Grosvenor Terrace, Bootham, York, North Yorkshire YO3 7AG (tel. 0904/655034), is a brick Victorian guesthouse run by the Atkinson family. The nine warm, comfortable bedrooms are well appointed, all with color TV, hot and cold water basins, and beverage-making facilities. Some have private baths. The charge, based on double occupancy, is £16 ($28) per person per night with bath, but only £13.50 ($23.65) per person without bath. Breakfast is included in the rates, and dinner costs £6.50 ($11.40). The excellent dinner menu and wine list will add to your pleasure of visiting York. The house has private parking, and it's about a 15-minute walk from the city center.

Arnot House, 17 Grosvenor Terrace, Bootham, York, North Yorkshire YO3 7AG (tel. 0904/641966), like other houses on the terrace, has views over Bootham Park, and in the distance you can see the Minster. Sue and Rupert Scott welcome guests to this Victorian house with its original fireplaces, cornices, and fine old staircase. The atmosphere is warm and comfortable. The bedrooms all have color TV, hot and cold water basins, and beverage-making facilities. Singles rent for £12.50 ($21.90) daily and twins or doubles for £24 ($42), with a full English breakfast (alternative on request) included. Price reductions are offered from November to March, costing £9.75 ($17.05) per person, including breakfast. A four-course set dinner is served in the candlelit dining room, costing £7.95 ($13.90). The house is licensed. Grosvenor Terrace is a 15- to 20-minute walk from the train station.

At **Craig-y-Don,** 3 Grosvenor Terrace, Bootham, York, North Yorkshire YO3 7AG (tel. 0904/637186). Mr. and Mrs. Oliver are two of the most hospitable hosts in the heart of York. They run an immaculately kept and most inviting home, serving a large Yorkshire breakfast. The inclusive rate is from £10 ($17.50) per person nightly. Mrs. Oliver also welcomes children.

Priory Hotel, 126 Fulford Rd., York, North Yorkshire YO1 4BE (tel. 0904/625280), stands on the main route into York from the south. Lying in a residential area, it has many double- and twin-bedded rooms. The rate for a good comfortable bed and one of their large breakfasts comes to £18 ($31.50) daily in a single, £34 ($59.50) in a double. A full English breakfast is served in the elegant period dining room. All 20 bedrooms have private showers and toilets. The hotel is on the A19. A riverside walk will take you to the heart of "monumental" York. Resident proprietors George and Barbara Jackson can offer helpful advice to the visitor.

The **Sycamore Hotel,** 19 Sycamore Pl., Bootham, York, North Yorkshire YO3 7DW (tel. 0904/624712), was built as a private dwelling in 1902, but has been carefully converted to maintain much of its original splendor. Now it's a family-owned and -run hotel, offering a high level of accommodation. All rooms have hot and cold running water (some have private baths), central heating, tea- and coffee-makers, and color TV. With private bath, the charge is £13 ($22.75) to £16 ($28) per person nightly, lowered to £11 ($19.25) to £12 ($21) per person if bathless. The location is close to the city center (a ten-minute walk to the Minster, a fifteen-minute walk to the rail station), yet it occupies a position in a quiet cul-de-sac. Keys are provided each guest, and car parking is available.

Dairy Wholefood Guest House, 3 Scarcroft Rd., York, North Yorkshire YO2 1ND (tel. 0904/639367), is a lovely house decorated throughout with ideas and furnishings in the "Habitat, Sanderson, Laura Ashley" style, with emphasis on pine and plants and an enclosed courtyard. It lies only 200 yards south of the medieval city walls, within easy access of car parking. Keith Jackman, proprietor, has some accommodations with private bath or shower. The charge for B&B is from £11 ($19.25) per person nightly. Breakfast choices range from traditional English to whole-food vegetarian. The lounge has a color TV and hot-drink facilities.

Gleneagles Lodge Guest House, 27 Nunthorpe Ave., York, North Yorkshire YO2 1PF (tel. 0904/637000), is a handsomely decorated, well-maintained, and comfortable guesthouse that is nicely furnished. On a quiet street, it is within walking distance of all York's historical attractions and is also near the train station and a number of restaurants serving good, reasonably priced food. The success of Gleneagles has everything to do with the hospitality of Michael and Wendy Cager, who go far out of their way to make your stay a memorable one. With them, good conversation comes easy, and they are kind and gracious, as well as sensitive to your needs. For B&B, the charge is from £11 ($19.25) per person nightly. Children are granted reductions. Don't be surprised if coffee and fresh scones are brought in to greet you on arrival.

At **Grasmead House Hotel,** 1 Scarcroft Hill, York, North Yorkshire YO2 1DF (tel. 0904/629996), one American guest departing was overheard to remark, "This hotel is just like an *Alice in Wonderland* place—so super inside." It doesn't have any white rabbits or mad hatters, but it does boast genuine four-poster beds in all the rooms. It's been refurbished with excellent fabrics and made comfortable with made-to-measure mattresses. Len and Eileen Spray, the resident owners, give you a real welcome and personal service. Their small family-run hotel lies within easy walking distance of the center, close to the Castle Museum. Some rooms look out toward the city walls and Minster. All units have their own private bath, with easy chairs, color TV, and tea- or coffee-making equipment. Prices are from £21 ($36.75) per person nightly, including an English breakfast and VAT.

Linden Lodge Hotel, 6 Nunthorpe Ave., Scarcroft Road, York, North Yorkshire YO2 1PF (tel. 0904/620107), is a 12-bedroom accommodation run by Joan and Bill Wharton. Their bedrooms are up-to-date, with hot and cold running water (some contain private baths). The charge for B&B begins at £11 ($19.25) per person nightly. The TV lounge is adjacent to the dining room and licensed bar.

Clifton Green Hotel, 8 Clifton Green, York, North Yorkshire YO3 6LN (tel. 0904/623523), about a 10-minute walk from Bootham Bar, the north gate of old York, is an immaculate small hotel fronting on a green. The seven bedrooms, rented by Ben and Gloria Braithwaite, are carpeted and have central heating, color TV, hot and cold water basins, hot-beverage facilities, bed-lights, wardrobes with hangers, dressing tables, nightstands, filled tissue dispensers, and other amenities to make a stay here rewarding. The B&B rates are from £14 ($24.50) daily in a single, from £25 ($43.75) in a double. Half board costs from £20 ($35) per person daily. The hotel offers private parking, some in covered spaces, and the no. 17 bus comes almost to the door. To find Clifton Green, take the A19 road toward Thirsk.

Adams House Hotel, 5 Main St., Fulford, York, North Yorkshire YO1 4HJ (tel. 0904/655413), is a family-owned business lying on the A19 York-Selby road, about a five-minute drive from the Minster. Sometimes guests have found accommodations here in the peak summer months when the hotels in the city center have been fully booked. Pat and David Johnson run this efficient hotel where the bedrooms are comfortably furnished, each with private bath. The charge, including VAT and a full breakfast, ranges from £13 ($22.75) to £17 ($29.75) per person nightly. The hotel has a residential license. Guests can enjoy the hotel's gardens as well as its proximity to the Fulford Golf Club.

Avenue House Guest House, 6 The Avenue, Clifton, York, North Yorkshire YO3 6AS (tel. 0904/620575), is a Victorian house, in a quiet residential area, run by Mr. and Mrs. Roberts and their family. All rooms have hot and cold running water and TV. There are two toilets, a shower room, and a bathroom. B&B costs from £10 ($17.50) per person daily, plus another £7 ($12.25) if you want dinner. Tea and cookies are served at 9:45 p.m. when you return from a theater performance.

Barrington House, 15 Nunthorpe Ave., Scarcroft Road, York, North Yorkshire YO2 1PF (tel. 0904/634539), is the small, family-run guesthouse of Jeff and Pauline Topham. They have a guest lounge, and each of their bedrooms has hot and cold running water, color TV, shaver points, and tea- and coffee-makers. Some rooms have private baths. Including a full English breakfast, the charge is from £11 ($19.25) per person daily. Evening meals can be served if arranged in advance. Jeff is a local tour guide, so he can be especially helpful to guests.

Feversham Lodge, 1 Feversham Crescent, York, North Yorkshire YO3 7HQ (tel. 0904/623882), was a 19th-century Methodist manse converted to receive guests. It still retains its lofty dining room and TV lounge. Bob and Jill Peacock charge from £10 ($17.50) to £11 ($19.25) per person daily for B&B in their neatly kept bedrooms, all of which have central heating and hot and cold running water.

Aberford House Hotel, 35-36 East Mount Rd., York, North Yorkshire YP2 2BD (tel. 0904/622694), is a family hotel belonging to Dick and Jean Tyson. It is just five minutes from the railway station, on a quiet road close to the great southern city gateway. There are 14 rooms, all with wash basins, shaver points, color TV, and tea- and coffee-makers. Some of the units have private showers, while others contain showers and toilets. B&B costs £13 ($22.75) per person nightly. The dining room has a good breakfast menu, and a five-course dinner with coffee is served at 7 p.m., if it is ordered in advance. The Tysons have a well-stocked cellar bar and a private car park.

Hazelwood, 24-25 Portland St., Gillygate, York, North Yorkshire YO3 7EH (tel. 0904/626548), lies an easy walk from York Minster. It is the domain of Joy and Peter Cox, who do a fine job of running a B&B. Their place is immaculately kept and well furnished, with rooms costing from £13 ($22.75) to £18 ($31.50) per person nightly, depending on the season. Their breakfast is large and well prepared, and they are always willing to answer your questions about touring in York and the surrounding moors and dales.

The **Railway King Hotel,** George Hudson Street, York, North Yorkshire YO1 1JL (tel. 0904/645161), is a good choice for those who want to pay slightly more to get the services of a hotel instead of the routine B&B. It is a short block from the bus station and about a seven-minute walk to York Minster and the Shambles. Charges in rooms with private baths, TV, and tea- and coffee-makers are £30 ($52.50) daily in a single, £40 ($70) in a double. On Saturday and Sunday prices are lowered to £20 ($35) in a single, £30 ($52.50) in a double or twin. A full English breakfast is included, and you have your choice of a morning paper brought to your door. The dining room serves good evening meals at reasonable prices.

Farthings Hotel, 5 Nunthorpe Ave., York, North Yorkshire YO2 1PF (tel. 0904/53545), is a handsomely rejuvenated Victorian-era private home now turned into a small hotel lying in a peaceful cul-de-sac about a ten-minute stroll from the heart of the historic district. Audrey and Robert Reid welcome guests to their pleasantly furnished bedrooms, seven in all (only one of which has a private bath). The overnight B&B rates are from £21 ($36.75) to £27 ($47.25) in a double. Guests meet in the lounge in the evening and chat with the Reids or fellow guests. There is a residential liquor license. Meals can also be arranged, given advance notice.

WHERE TO EAT

A good all-round eating house, **Bettys Café Tea Rooms,** St. Helens Square (tel. 0904/659142), is open from 9 a.m. to 9 p.m. daily. You can call in for a quick coffee and pastry or treat yourself to a full English breakfast, a Yorkshire cheese lunch, or a Yorkshire rarebit. Genteel afternoon teas with scones as well as fish-and-chips high teas are also firm favorites. A selection of healthy salads and whole-food quiches are also on offer. Bettys is famous for its cream cakes. The light suppers and wide variety of cooked and cold meals makes this a good place to stop in the evening. Families are made especially welcome, and customers drop in for anything from a cup of coffee to a substantial meal, costing from £6.50 ($11.40). You can make this the finishing point to a stroll through York or enjoy a pretheater supper, complete with fine Alsatian wine. A café concert entertains customers as they dine. The concerts range from lute duets to Palm Court trios. Bettys also has cafés in the heart of James Herriot Country, in Northallerton; in the Yorkshire Dales, at Ilkley in Wharfedale; and overlooking Montpellier Gardens in the old spa town of Harrogate.

St. Williams Restaurant, 3 College St. (tel. 0904/634830), lies within the shadow of the great East Window of the Minster. With its half-timbering and leaded-glass windows, it is a medieval and oak-beamed setting. It serves some of the best of the low-cost food of York. Lunch is offered from noon to 2:30 p.m. daily, costing from £5 ($8.75). Selections include much "olde English fayre," including roast rib of beef or one of the "raised pies" such as pork-and-apricot. A self-service cafeteria, St. Williams draws many young people to its precincts, as they know they get good value here. You can also visit for morning coffee daily from 10 a.m. to noon, and for afternoon tea from 2:30 to 5 p.m.

Dean Court Hotel, Duncombe Place (tel. 0904/625082), has a coffeeshop entered through the main door of the hotel and a bar with an entrance from a basement door just by the Minster. A sandwich and coffee are popular items, and they also provide hot foods, including a mug of hot soup, toast, Welsh rarebit, or chicken liver pâté. Desserts include peach and banana sundaes, and there is a good selection of afternoon tea specialties, such as scones with cream and strawberry jam. Service and VAT are included in the prices on the menu, so you know exactly what you're paying. Light meals cost from £3.50 ($6.15). The coffee shop is open daily from 10 a.m. to 10 p.m. in summer, and from 10 a.m. to 8 p.m. in winter.

Kooks Bistro, 108 Fishergate (tel. 0904/637553), is an informal, relaxed eating place run by the owner, Angie Cowl. Decorated in dark green with individually painted flamingos and a collection of memorabilia on the same theme given by customers, it features a varied and unusual menu of English, American, Mexican, French, and vegetarian food, with several dishes distinctive to Kooks. Most main courses include in the price a choice of baked potato, french fries, or side salad. Meats range from burgers to beef Stroganoff. The service is prompt and friendly and the atmosphere relaxed, with varied background music and a little fun in the form of handmade jigsaws and other puzzles and games on every table. Meals cost from £6 ($10.50). Kooks is fully licensed and open daily, except Monday, from 7 to 11 p.m., with last orders at 11 p.m. It is within walking distance of the city center, and there is plenty of easy parking.

Restaurant Bari, 15 The Shambles (tel. 0904/633807), stands in one of York's oldest and most colorful streets, originally the street of the butchers. It was mentioned in the *Domesday Book.* In a continental atmosphere, you can enjoy a quick single course or a full leisurely meal. Ten different pizzas are offered. Lasagne and cannelloni are popular. Lunch can cost as little as £6 ($10.50), and dinner starts at about £8.50 ($14.90). A main-dish specialty is escalope Sophia Loren (veal cooked with brandy and cheese with a rich tomato sauce). It is open seven days a week from 11:30 a.m. to 2:30 p.m. and 6 to 11 p.m.

Russel's Restaurants, at both 34 Stonegate (tel. 0904/641432) and at 26 Coppergate (tel. 0904/644330), are, in the words of one observer, "probably the only true British restaurants in York." Although this point may be arguable, Russell's does offer fresh food of a high standard. Many of its recipes are considered "just like mother used to make"—that is, if your mother came from northeast England. That means, among other items, roast beef with the inevitable Yorkshire pudding, along with roast potatoes and seasonal vegetables. A good range of appetizers is also offered, and the desserts are very English and very good, especially bread-and-butter pudding. Wine is available by the glass or bottle, and the kitchen always has a good selection of English cheese. A two-course menu costs £6.99 ($12.25), a three-course meal going for £8.99 ($15.75). Service is daily from noon to 2:30 p.m. and 6 to 10:30 p.m.

Raffles Tea Room, House of Tweed, Allenby House, 41 Stonegate (tel. 0904/629812), is above the House of Tweed shop. It's a traditional English tea room, offering morning coffee with pastries or toasted buns. Light lunches, including sandwiches, salads, chicken pie, and quiche, cost around £3.50 ($6.15). Afternoon teas are a specialty. You can enjoy warm scones with strawberry jam and clotted cream, with a choice of five blends of tea, for less than £3 ($5.25). Hours are from 9 a.m. to 5:30 p.m. Monday to Saturday; closed Sunday.

At **Taylors in Stonegate,** 46 Stonegate (tel. 0904/622865), the bow-windowed shop downstairs is filled with bags and jars of coffee. The old-fashioned till bears the prices of the 36 varieties of teas and coffees for sale. When you see the shop, you'll know that this is no idle boast. Teas come all the way from China and India, including exotic oolongs, souchongs, and passion fruit. Upstairs, the coffeeshop dispenses these same beverages. They advertise an English breakfast grill for £3.35 ($5.85) to £4 ($7). You can also order rarebits and omelets with various fillings, and a selection of salads, with meals costing from £5 ($8.75). Spiced Yorkshire tea cakes and cinnamon toast are also on the menu. Service is from 9 a.m. to 5:30 p.m. Monday to Saturday and most Sundays.

A PUB CRAWL

Known for the best location of any pub in York, the **Kings Arms,** King's Straithe (tel. 0904/659435), is a popular riverside pub. Right near the Ouse Bridge, the location is on the left bank of the River Ouse. This historic public house, one of charm, character, and intimacy, is filled with beamed ceilings, brick walls, and a mellow atmosphere. A board records flood levels of the Ouse. In summer, tables are placed outside along the river. Your hosts serve a full range of Samuel Smith's draft and bottled beers, traditionally brewed in Tadcaster, only ten miles from York. Bar meals cost from £4 ($7) and include such dishes as the "curry of the day" or roast chicken. Food is not served on Saturday evening, and the pub is open from 11 a.m. to 11 p.m. Monday to Saturday, and from noon to 3 p.m. and 7 to 10:30 p.m. Sunday.

The Black Swan, Peaseholme Green, York, North Yorkshire YO1 2PR (tel. 0904/625236), is a fine timbered frame house, the home of the lord mayor of York in 1417. The mother of General James Wolfe of Québec also lived here. One of the oldest inns in the city, it offers pub meals Monday to Saturday from noon to 2 p.m., costing £3 ($5.25). Open fires burn in winter, giving the place even more atmosphere. You can also go for drinks in the evening from 5:30 to 11. B&B is also available at £15 ($26.25) per person daily.

Olde Starre, Stonegate (tel. 0904/623063), lies on a pedestrian street in the heart of Old York. Considered York's oldest licensed pub, it serves hot and cold pub lunches from 11:30 a.m. to 2 p.m. It is also open for drinks in the evening from 5:30 to 11. Cod, plaice, and scampi appear regularly on the menu, along with chili con carne and shepherd's pie. Bar meals cost from £4 ($7). In fair weather, guests fill the tables in a courtyard. Inside, guests enjoy the old beams and the Edwardian benches.

2. North Yorkshire

For those seeking legendary untamed scenery, I recommend a tour of North Yorkshire, which also takes in the already-previewed historic cathedral city of York.

North Yorkshire contains England's most varied landscape. Its history has been turbulent, often bloody, and many relics of its rich past are still standing, including ruined abbeys. North Yorkshire is little known to the average North American visitor, but many an English traveler knows of its haunting moors, serene valleys, and windswept dales.

The hospitality of the people of North Yorkshire is world renowned, and if a pudding that originated there doesn't accompany a slab of roast beef, the plate looks naked to the British. The people of North Yorkshire, who speak an original twang often imitated in English cinema, are, in general, hardworking and industrious, perhaps a little contemptuous of the easy living of the south. But they are decidedly open to strangers, providing you speak to them first.

CASTLE HOWARD

In its dramatic setting of lakes, fountains, and extensive gardens, the 18th-century palace designed by Sir John Vanbrugh is undoubtedly the finest private residence in North Yorkshire. Principal location for the TV series "Brideshead Revisited," this was the first major achievement of the architect who later created the lavish Blenheim Palace near Oxford. Castle Howard was begun in 1699 for the third Earl of Carlisle, Charles Howard, whose descendants still call the place "home." The striking facade is topped by a painted and gilded dome, reaching more than 80 feet into the air. The interior boasts a 192-foot "Long Gallery," as well as a chapel with magnificent stained-glass windows by the 19th-century artist Sir Edward Burne-Jones. Besides the collections of antique furniture, porcelains, and sculpture, the castle contains a number of important paintings, including a portrait of Henry VIII by Holbein, and works by Rubens, Reynolds, and Gainsborough.

The seemingly endless grounds around the palace also offer the visitor some memorable sights, including the domed Temple of the Four Winds by Vanbrugh and the richly designed family mausoleum by Hawksmoor. There are two rose gardens, one with old-fashioned roses, the other featuring modern creations. The stable court houses the Costume Galleries, the largest private collection of 18th- to 20th-century costumes in Britain. The authentically dressed mannequins are exhibited in period settings. Castle Howard, just 15 miles northeast of York, is open to the public daily from March 20 to the end of October; the grounds are open from 10 a.m., the house and Costume Galleries from 11 a.m. to 5 p.m. (last entry at 4:30 p.m.). Admission is £4 ($7) for adults, £2 ($3.50) for children. There is a self-service cafeteria where you can order sandwiches and hot dishes, the latter for around £2.85 ($5). Good wines are served. The cafeteria opens at 10:30 a.m. For information, telephone 065384/333.

HARROGATE

If you head west from York for 20 miles, you reach Harrogate, North Yorkshire's second-largest town after York. In the 19th century, Harrogate was a fashionable spa. Most of the town center is surrounded by a 200-acre lawn called "The Stray." Boutiques and antique shops, which Queen Mary used to frequent, make Harrogate a shopping center of excellence, particularly along Montpellier Parade. Harrogate is called England's floral resort, deserving such a reputation because of its gardens, including Harlow Car Gardens and Valley Gardens. The former spa has an abundance of guesthouses and hotels, including the expensive Swan where Agatha Christie hid out during her mysterious disappearance—still unexplained—in the 1920s.

Where to Stay

Garden House Hotel, 14 Harlow Moor Dr., Harrogate, North Yorkshire HG2 0JX (tel. 0423/503059), is a handsomely restored Victorian house. It's really more an upmarket guesthouse than most B&Bs in Harrogate. With good car parking and peaceful surroundings, this is an ideal alternative to an accommodation in the heart of Harrogate, where parking can be a serious problem. All seven rooms have private baths or shower, color TV, and beverage-making facilities. The B&B charge ranges from £16 ($28) to £19 ($33.25) per person daily, and half board costs from £23 ($40.25) to £50 ($87.50) per person. Full English breakfasts incorporate all sorts of local and natural ingredients and are freshly prepared for guests. Evening meals are simple but tasty. Poultry or meat with a good sauce will be accompanied by crisp fresh vegetables. Meals are served at flexible hours to suit the guests.

Crescent Lodge Guest House, 20 Swan Rd., Harrogate, North Yorkshire HG1 2SA (tel. 0423/503688), is known for its charm and atmosphere, but since it takes only six guests, it might be hard to get in unless you reserve. This attractive early Victorian house overlooks Crescent Gardens and is only a short walk from the Royal Pump Room. The elegant drawing room has color TV, and a full English breakfast is served in the dining room. In your bedroom, you will find tea, coffee, mineral water, and fruit and flowers in season. B&B rates vary from £14.50 ($25.40) to £18.50 ($32.40) per person per night in accommodations with private shower and toilet. Help yourself to herbal and fruit teas, books, and magazines from the polished mahogany table on the landing leading to the bedrooms. A washing machine, dryer, iron, and hairdryer are available for use of guests. There is a quiet walled garden in the rear in which to relax.

Wessex Hotel, Harlow Moor Drive, Harrogate, North Yorkshire HG2 0JY (tel. 0423/565890), is in an attractive part of Harrogate overlooking (and with immediate access to) the Valley Gardens. It is only a ten-minute walk from the center of town. The family-run hotel provides hospitality in the Yorkshire style, combined with comfort and personal service, with special emphasis on good food served in their spacious dining room. There is central heating throughout the hotel, and all 15 bedrooms are equipped with radio and shaver points. All bedrooms have private showers and toilets and have been refurbished. A pleasantly decorated and well-furnished television lounge is available for relaxation after a busy day of sightseeing or shopping. Or you can have a drink in the comfortable bar lounge and unwind by getting to know your fellow guests. For £18 ($31.50) per person daily, you get a clean and airy room and an English breakfast. The proprietors, Mr. and Mrs. Terence Samuel, will be happy to direct you to the Valley Gardens with its beautiful floral displays; or to the facilities for tennis, or the 18-hole mini-golf course, or stables for horseback riding. And if you are a racing fan, there are four racecourses within easy distance of the hotel.

Ashley House Hotel, 36-40 Franklin Rd., Harrogate, North Yorkshire HG1 5EE (tel. 0423/507474), is a comfortable family-run licensed hotel with excellent food and an inviting atmosphere. There are 18 guest rooms, all equipped with coffee- and tea-making facilities, TV, and alarm-clock radios. Some rooms have private showers and toilets. A good selection of wines is available with meals in the spacious dining room, and in the evening guests may relax and meet fellow visitors in the cozy "olde worlde" bar. There are two lounges for guests, both with color TV, and there is full central heating throughout. The hotel is in a quiet residential part of town, yet it is only a five-minute walk to the center. It's a convenient site for visiting York and the Yorkshire Dales. Singles cost from £18 ($31.50) daily for B&B, with doubles going for £31 ($54.25), including a full English breakfast, VAT, and service. A four-course dinner is served each evening, costing from £8 ($14).

The Manor Hotel, 3 Clarence Dr., Harrogate, North Yorkshire HG1 2QE (tel. 0423/503916), is a solid Victorian stone concoction with complex architectural details—a square tower and off-balance gables—in the secluded Duchy area of Harrogate, yet within walking distance of the town center and the Valley Gardens. The hotel has been extensively modernized and provides a high standard of accommodation for guests in family surroundings. All bedrooms have private baths, remote-control color TV, radios, hot beverage facilities, and direct-dial phones. For B&B, the charge is from £24 ($42) per person daily in a double or twin to £29 ($50.75) in a single, VAT included. The restaurant offers table d'hôte and à la carte menus. There is an elevator to all floors, a bar and restaurant open to nonresidents, and a private car park.

Alvera Court Hotel, 76 Kings Rd., Harrogate, North Yorkshire HG1 5JX (tel. 0423/505735), is a fine Victorian stone residence that has been renovated and modernized. Charming architectural features of the Victorian era are enhanced by the furnishings and welcoming atmosphere. Lyn and Michael Haycock, owners and managers, offer bedrooms with private baths or showers, color TV, direct-dial phones, alarm-clock radios, in-house movies, and beverage-making facilities. Rents are £23.50 ($41.15) daily in a single and £22 ($38.50) per person in a double, with breakfast and VAT included. The hotel serves mainly traditional Yorkshire dishes. Dinner, which must be ordered by noon of the day required, costs £9.50 ($16.65). A restful lounge and a cocktail bar, plus a private car park, are among the Alvera's attractions. It's directly opposite the International Conference and Exhibition Centre. On warm days, you can sit on the front lawn and watch the world go by.

Where to Eat

Bettys Café Tea Room, 1 Parliament St. (tel. 0423/64659), one of four such places in Yorkshire, is in a Victorian building in the town center, marked by an iron canopy over the pavement and hanging baskets of flowers. Inside, the decor is Victorian with marquetry panels done by the man who decorated the *Queen Mary*. This was the first Bettys, founded by Fred Belmont, a Swiss confectioner who took a train to Highgate but ended up in Harrogate instead. The menu includes sandwiches, salads, toasted muffins, tea cakes, and scones served as a cream tea with masses of cream and strawberry jam. Hot dishes are offered, as well as rich fruit cakes with whipped cream or Wensleydale cheese. Several exotic brands of tea from India and China are available, or you might order a cafetère of coffee for one, choosing Jamaica Blue Mountain, Mexican Maragogipe, or Mocha Harrar Longberry from Ethiopia. James Herriot, the world-famous veterinarian (*All Creatures Great and Small*), has been a regular visitor to Bettys for a number of years. Bettys is open from 9 a.m. to 9 p.m. Monday to Saturday and 10 a.m. to 6 p.m. on Sunday. Soft music is played Thursday to Sunday. From the Verandah Café, you can look out over the flowers and lawns of the Montpellier Gardens as you enjoy a cup of coffee and one of Bettys cream cakes.

The **Open Arms Restaurant,** Royal Parade (tel. 0423/503034), is a neat little place with canopied ceilings, glinting wall lights, brass rails, and red curtains separating some of the tables into alcoves. The menu devised by Barry Holland over the past 20 years is truly a Taste of Yorkshire. Appetizers include Yorkshire pudding with onion gravy, served before the meat course to cut your appetite a bit. Among main dishes are the traditional roast beef and Yorkshire pudding; fried fish with chips; the chef's large golden Yorkshire puddings, which are served with vegetables and filled with beefsteak, onions, tomatoes, and mushrooms; country game in red wine sauce with celery, onions, and carrots; or seafood tidbits in white sauce. Of course, fillings vary with the seasons. Try apple pie with Wensleydale cheese for dessert. Meals cost from around £10 ($17.50). Hours are from noon to 2 p.m. Tuesday to Sunday and 6 to 9 p.m. Tuesday to Saturday (and Sunday in summer). It is closed Monday.

William & Victoria, 6 Cold Bath Rd., is a two-in-one dining selection, containing both a restaurant and bar (tel. 0423/521510) and a wine bar (tel. 0423/506883) in the basement. Look for the daily specials posted on the blackboard at the wine bar, where service is daily, except Saturday lunch and Sunday, from noon to 2 p.m. and 6:30 to 10 p.m. The restaurant upstairs serves only from 6:30 to 10 p.m., except Sunday. The food at both places is continental, with many well-prepared British specialties. Meals cost from £12 ($21), but you can do it for less, depending on what you order.

MOORS AND DALES

The rural landscape is pierced with ruins of once-great abbeys and castles. North Yorkshire is a land of green hills, valleys, and purple moors. Both the Yorkshire Dales and the Moors are wide-open spaces, making up two of Britain's finest national parks, with a combined area of some 1200 square miles. However, the term "national" can be misleading, as the land is managed by foresters, farmers, and private landowners. In fact, more than 90% of the land is in private ownership. The Dales rise toward Cumbria and Lancashire to the east, and the Moors stretch to the eastern coastline.

Of course, York, the major center, has already been previewed. But those with the time may want to explore deeper into the rural roots of England. From Harrogate, our last stopover, you can enjoy the wildest scenery of the region by heading out on day trips, anchoring at one of the inns coming up if you don't want to return to the old spa.

After leaving Harrogate, you can discover white limestone crags, drystone walls, fast-rushing rivers, and isolated sheep farms or clusters of sandstone cottages. **Malhamdale** receives more visitors annually than any dale in Yorkshire. Of the priories and castles to visit, two of the most interesting are the 12th-century ruins of **Bolton Priory** and the 14th-century pile, **Castle Bolton,** to the north in Wensleydale.

Richmond, the most frequently used town name in the world, stands here at the head of the Dales as the mother of them all. Here the Norman towers of Richmond Castle, the country's best-known fortress, dominate the cobbled market town. The Georgian Theatre here, which was constructed in 1788, has a resident amateur company of the highest quality.

In contrast, the Moors, on the other side of the Vale of York, have a wild beauty all their own, quite different from that of the Dales. They are bounded by the Cleveland and Hambleton Hills. The white horse of Kilburn can be seen hewn out of the landscape.

Both **Pickering** and **Northallerton,** two market towns, serve as gateways to the

Moors. Across the Moors are seen primordial burial grounds and stone crosses. The best-known trek in the moorlands is the 40-mile hike over bog, heather, and stream from Mount Grace Priory inland to Ravenscar on the seacoast. It's known as **Lyke Wake Walk.**

The beauty and seclusion along the southern border of today's park made this an area attractive to the founders of four great abbeys. The Cistercians established **Rievaulx** ecclesiastical community near Helmsley and **Fountains Abbey** near Ripon, both visited below, as well as **Byland Abbey** near the village of Wass. The Benedictines were also busy here, establishing **Ampleforth Abbey** near **Coxwold,** one of the most attractive villages in the Moors. Rievaulx, Fountains, and Byland Abbeys are in ruins, but Ampleforth still works as a monastery and well-known Roman Catholic boys' school. Much of Ampleforth comprises buildings of 19th- and 20th-century construction, however, although these contain artifacts from earlier monastic times.

Along North Yorkshire's 45 miles of coastline are such traditional seaside resorts as **Filey, Whitby,** and **Scarborough,** the latter claiming to be the oldest seaside spa in Britain, standing on the site of a Roman signaling station. It was founded in 1622, following the discovery of mineral springs with medicinal properties. In the 19th century, its Grand Hotel, a Victorian structure, was acclaimed as "the best in Europe." The Norman castle on big cliffs overlooks the twin bays.

In and Around Helmsley

This attractive market town, with a market every Friday, is a good center for exploring the surrounding area. It is called the key to Ryedale and is the mother town of the district, standing at the junction of the roads from York, Pickering, Malton, Stokesley, and Thirsk.

Helmsley is on the southern edge of the North Yorkshire Moors National Park and is well known as a center for walking and "potholing." It is an area among many places and things of interest: remains of Bronze and Iron Age existence on the moors; prehistoric highways; Roman roads; and, of course, the ruins of medieval castles and abbeys. Beyond the main square of the town are the ruins of its castle with an impressive keep. This castle was built between 1186 and 1227.

A good reason for selecting Helmsley as a stopover is because it is near York and well located, but the hotel rates are far below those of York.

Three miles to the north of Helmsley are the ruins of **Rievaulx** (pronounced "Reevo") **Abbey** (tel. 04396/228). The abbey was named for Rye Vallis, valley of the River Rye. It was the first Cistercian house in northern England and was founded in 1131 by monks who came over from Clairvaux in France. At its peak it housed 140 monks and 500 lay brothers. In its size, its architecture, and its setting, even its ruins are among the most impressive in the country. The land was given by Walter l'Espec, a Norman knight, who later entered the community as a novice and died and was buried here.

It is open from 10 a.m. to 6 p.m. daily, except Monday, from Good Friday to September 30, and from 10 a.m. to 4 p.m. off-season. Admission is £1.30 ($2.30) for adults, 65p ($1.15) for children.

Rievaulx Terrace, a property of the National Trust, is a landscaped grassy terrace about a half mile long, which was laid out in the mid-18th century by Thomas Duncombe of Duncombe Park. The visitor, after a woodland walk, emerges onto a wide lawn near a circular "temple," known as the Tuscan Temple. The walk along the terrace gives frequent views of the abbey ruins in the valley below. On a windy North Yorkshire spring day, this walk is truly a constitutional.

At the opposite end from the Tuscan Temple is the Ionic Temple, whose interior is beautifully decorated and furnished, with a classically painted ceiling and gilded wood and rose velvet upholstered furniture. In the basement are two rooms that were originally used by servants to prepare food for guests above. These rooms are now used to display exhibitions on English landscape design and architectural periods, using examples from the Duncombe family album. This temple was planned by Thomas Duncombe III as a banqueting house and a place of rest and refreshment after the long carriage ride from Duncombe Park. It is open from 10:30 a.m. to 6 p.m. daily from Good Friday to the end of October. Admission is £1.30 ($2.30) for adults and 60p ($1.05) for children. For information, phone 0439/340.

Crown Hotel, Market Square, Helmsley, North Yorkshire YO6 5BJ (tel. 0439/70297), is a 16th-century inn built of stone. The walls are covered by creepers, giving it charm. The owners, Mr. and Mrs. Mander, have spared no effort to make every room not only attractive but comfortable. Wherever possible in the restoration, old beams have been left exposed. Of the 14 bedrooms, 12 have private bath/showers and toilets, and all contain color TV and tea- and coffee-makers. The half-board rate ranges from £27 ($47.25) to £31 ($54.25) per person daily. The dining room is well furnished, the menus offering a roast, two different fresh East Coast fish, and at least three other main courses. The hotel has two living rooms and two bars, one public and a better-furnished one for residents.

At Hutton-le-Hole

Near Lastingham, Hutton-le-Hole is a village known as one of the prettiest in the North Yorkshire Moors—in fact, one of the prettiest in Great Britain. William Penn of Pennsylvania had close connections to the village, which was at the heart of the Quaker movement. The village, set in an area of natural beauty, has a well-documented history and a wealth of Elizabethan and Georgian properties.

Hammer & Hand, Hutton-le-Hole, Lastingham, North Yorkshire YO6 6UA (tel. 07515/300), run by John and Alison Wilkins, used to be the village beer house. Constructed in 1784 from timeworn Yorkshire stone, it lies in a tranquil spot on the east side of the village, opening onto the North Yorkshire Moors National Park. Mr. and Mrs. Wilkins will point out many attractions to explore on day trips, including Castle Howard. You are invited to share their world of stone fireplaces, cruck beams, and antiques, very "olde worlde" in style. Guests meet each other in a spacious sitting lounge with a beamed ceiling and a Georgian fireplace before an open log fire. Rooms are called by such names as "The Snug" or the "Hutton Room," the latter with a double bed, exposed beams, and a private shower room. Rates, depending on the room assignment, range from £12 ($21) to £14 ($24.50) per person nightly. The tariffs include a four-course Yorkshire breakfast, and for another £7 ($12.25) a four-course dinner will be prepared based on local produce and traditional dishes.

Near Skipton

The **Buck Inn,** Malham, near Skipton, North Yorkshire BD23 4DA (tel. 07293/317), is a Victorian stone inn where Dale explorers can find excellent ale, a comfortable and cozy room, and a good breakfast and dinner. There are two bars, one especially for hikers and the other for residents. The inn offers ten centrally heated bedrooms, most of which have private baths. The charge is from £22 ($38.50) per person daily for B&B, with VAT included. You can order bar snacks noon and evening if you don't want a full meal.

In and Around Richmond

Richmond, the most frequently used town name in the world, stands at the head of the Dales as the mother of them all. It's an old market town built beside the River Swale and dominated by the striking ruins of its Norman castle. In the center of the cobbled marketplace stands an ancient church and a tall stone pillar known as the Market Cross. It's a good touring center for the surrounding countryside.

The Georgian Theatre here, which was constructed in 1788, has a resident amateur company of the highest quality.

For an accommodation in the area, try the following recommendation:

Whashton Springs Farms, Richmond, North Yorkshire DL11 7JS (tel. 0748/2884), is a 300-acre mixed farm in the heart of Herriot country, three miles from Richmond set high in the hills. In the stone farmhouse, Fairlie and Gordon Turnbull receive guests, who are free to wander around the farm and enjoy the tranquil countryside. Bedrooms in the centrally heated house all have color TV and beverage-making facilities. They're all comfortably furnished, with wall-to-wall carpets. The six units in the stable courtyard have private baths or showers. For B&B, they charge £13 ($22.75) per person daily in bathless rooms, £15 ($26.25) per person in rooms with private plumbing. A four-poster accommodation with bath rents for £17 ($29.75). In the dining room, which has a bow window overlooking the moors, real Yorkshire farmhouse breakfasts and dinners are served (no evening meal on Thursday). On other days, half board costs from £21.50 ($37.65) to £23.50 ($41.15) per person, depending on whether the room you occupy has a bathroom. If you come into Richmond from the A1 South, turn right at a traffic light onto the Ravensworth Road, following it for three miles. Down a steep hill with woods on either side, you'll come upon the farm at the bottom on the left.

In and Around Bedale

Ainderby Myers, Bedale, North Yorkshire DL8 1PF (tel. 0609/748668), is a 16th-century manor house where Mrs. V. Anderson offers B&B, charging from £10.50 ($18.40) per person nightly. There are mentions of the manor in the *Domesday Book.* She offers four rooms with hot and cold running water and good heating, plus a lounge with TV. In the garden, you can sit and enjoy a view of the rolling Yorkshire countryside. An evening meal can be provided for £7.50 ($13.15), but there are some very good places to eat out in the area, of which Mrs. Anderson will furnish details if required. To reach the village, turn off the A1 at the Hackforth turning.

Elmfield Country House, Arrathorne, Bedale, North Yorkshire, DL8 1NE (tel. 0677/50558), is a lovely, spacious, and comfortable country-house estate with views over the surrounding Dales and Herriot country. Jim and Edith Lillie, the owners, will suggest such activities as pony trekking, riding, golf, fishing, and walking. All their nine bedrooms contain private baths and color TV. On the ground floor, two bedrooms are fully equipped for the disabled. One accommodation has a four-poster bed. Rates are £14 ($24.50) per person daily for B&B, with an evening meal costing £7 ($12.25). The house also has a solarium.

In and Around Ripon

Ripon has an ancient tradition of the watchman blowing a horn in the center of town every night, a custom dating back to 886. This cathedral city 27 miles north of Leeds by road was once a Saxon village where a Celtic monastery was founded in 651.

Beneath the central tower of **Ripon Cathedral,** a Norman cathedral dating from 1154, is the original crypt built by St. Wilfrid more than 1300 years ago. This is one of the oldest buildings in England, and the original plaster is still on the walls. It was built the same size and shape as was traditionally believed to be the layout of the tomb from which Jesus rose from the dead.

Archbishop Roger built the nave of the Norman cathedral, the North Transept, and part of the choir stalls. The twin towers of the West Front are Early English, from about 1216, and the Library (once the "Lady Loft") is from some time in the 14th century. The Canons' Stalls were hand-carved and were completed in 1495. Two sides of the Tower date from the original construction in 1220, but in 1450, an earthquake caused the other two to collapse. They were reconstructed, and the Central Tower and South Transept were added at the beginning of the 16th century. The completion of all the work was never carried out, as King Henry VIII took away all the Cathedral's endowments. Until 1664 the towers had tall spires, which were removed to prevent fires caused by lightning.

Today the cathedral is a lively Christian Centre, with a study center and a choir school. It is the mother church of the Diocese of Ripon, which spreads over most of the Yorkshire Dales to the fifth-largest city in England, Leeds. For further information, telephone 0765/4108.

Ripon Prison and Police Museum, St. Marygate (tel. 0765/3706), is an exhibition of the history of police work from the time of the wakeman of Ripon (the watchman of the town in the Middle Ages) up to the wonders of modern technology as they pertain to fighting crime. The building in which the museum is housed started life as a prison, built in 1815. In 1887, it became a police station and continued so until its retirement in 1956. Now it has displays of life in both phases of its existence, including some of the punishment devices so popular in Victorian days. The museum is open from 1:30 to 5 p.m. daily from May to the end of September, and Monday to Saturday in May, June, and September. In July and August, hours are 11 a.m. to 5 p.m. Monday to Saturday and bank holidays. Admission is 50p (90¢) for adults, 25p (45¢) for children.

Fountains Abbey and **Studley Royal,** Fountains, four miles southwest of Ripon off the B6265 (tel. 076586/333), stands on the banks of the River Skell. The abbey was founded by Cistercian monks in 1132 and is the largest monastic ruin in Britain. In 1987, it was awarded world heritage status. The ruins provide the focal point of the 18th-century landscape garden at Studley Royal, one of the few surviving examples of a Georgian green garden. It is known for its water gardens, ornamental temples, follies, and vistas. The garden is bounded at its northern edge by a lake and 400 acres of deer park. The abbey and gardens are open daily, except December 24 and 25 and Friday in November and December. From January through March and in November and December, it is open daily from 10 a.m. to 5 p.m. (or dusk). From April to June and in September, it is open daily from 10 a.m. to 7 p.m., and in July and August daily from 10 a.m. to 8 p.m. October sees daily openings from 10 a.m. to 6 p.m. (or dusk). Admission to the abbey and gardens is £1.90 ($3.35) for adults and 90p ($1.60) for children. A family ticket—two adults, two children—costs £4.70 ($8.25).

Newby Hall, lying on the northeast bank of the Ure River between Ripon (four miles away) and Boroughbridge (3½ miles away), is a famous Adam house set in 25 acres of grounds filled with sunken gardens, magnolias, azaleas, and countless flowering shrubs, along with many rare and unusual species. The house, built for Sir Edward Blackett, circa 1695, is in the style of Sir Christopher Wren. In the mid-18th century, Robert Adam redesigned the house, extending it to display the antique sculpture, tapestries, and furniture of its then owner, William Weddell, a connoisseur and art collector. Robin Compton is the present owner. Displayed are the Gobelin Tapestries, one of only five sets completed, with medallions by Boucher, who was appointed first painter to Louis XV.

On the grounds is a miniature railway, the Newby 10¼-inch gauge (providing rides for both children and adults); adventure gardens; a steamboat that sails on Sunday along the river; a gift shop; a licensed Garden Restaurant; a plant stall; and a Woodland Discovery Walk. From Easter to October, Newby Hall and its adjuncts are open daily, except Monday (open bank holidays). The house can be visited from noon to 5:30 p.m., with last admission at 5 p.m. The gardens and restaurant are open from 11 a.m. The train runs beginning at noon. Admission to the hall and gardens is £3.20 ($5.60) for adults, £1.60 ($2.80) for children. For information, phone 0423/322583.

Several attractive accommodations are available in the area:

The Nordale, 1-2 North Parade, North Road, Ripon, North Yorkshire HG4 1ES (tel. 0765/3557), is run by Peter and Sue Kerridge, who took over this long-established business and made substantial improvements. All their bedrooms, either single, double, or twin, are comfortable. Some bedrooms have a TV, although there is a TV lounge. Each unit has hot and cold running water, and a few contain private baths. The daily rate for B&B begins at £12 ($21) per person nightly, slightly higher with private bath. Food is considered excellent, and a home-cooked three-course meal is served at 7:30 nightly, costing £7.50 ($13.15) per person. The Nordale is a good center for touring the Yorkshire Dales, Herriot Country, the Moors, and for visiting York, Harrogate, Richmond, and many interesting abbeys and castles. Mrs. Kerridge was born locally and has a good knowledge of these places.

Eaglehurst Guest House, 9 Park St., Ripon, North Yorkshire HG4 2AX (tel. 0765/2081), is one of the best maintained guesthouses in the area. It is conveniently located close to the heart of this ancient city. This Georgian house has been converted to receive paying guests in three bedrooms, which share the one bath. The guesthouse makes a comfortable base for touring the attractions of North Yorkshire, and prices are reasonable as well. The overnight charge for B&B ranges from £13.50 ($23.65) to £15 ($26.25) in a single, going up to £21 ($36.75) to £25 ($43.75) in a double.

At Thirsk

This pleasant old market town north of York has a fine parish church lying in the Vale of Mowbray. But what makes it such a stopover for visitors is the fame brought to the village by James Herriot, author of *All Creatures Great and Small.* Mr. Herriot still practices in Thirsk, and visitors can photograph his office and perhaps get a picture of his partner standing in the door.

If you'd like to stay over, **Brook House,** Ingramgate, Thirsk, North Yorkshire YO7 1DD (tel. 0845/22240), is a large Victorian house set in two acres of land, some of which is filled with flower beds. It overlooks the open countryside, but a three-minute walk brings you to the Market Square. Mrs. Margaret McLauchlan charges from £13.50 ($23.65) per person daily for B&B, VAT included, and makes reductions for children. She is charming and kind, and has even been known to do a batch of washing for guests at no extra cost (however, I can't promise that). She serves a good Yorkshire breakfast, hearty and filling, plus an English tea in the afternoon. She has a spacious and comfortable living room with color TV, and her bedrooms are large and airy. For out-of-season visitors, the house is centrally heated, and in the guests' drawing room there is always an open log fire. One major benefit of staying at Brook House is the peace and quiet away from traffic and other noise. There is ample secluded parking for cars. The experience of knowing John and Margaret McLauchlan and enjoying their hospitality will remain long in your memory. They are acquaintanced with Mr. Herriot.

St. James House, 36 The Green, Thirsk, North Yorkshire YO7 1AQ (tel. 0845/22676), is a lovely three-story 18th-century Georgian brick house on the village green, near the former maternity home where James Herriot's children were born. The guesthouse, operated by Mrs. Liz Ogleby, is tastefully furnished, with some Regency antiques. (Mr. Ogleby is an antique dealer.) The attractive bedrooms have such touches as good bone china to use with the tea- and coffee-makers. They all have TV. In a room without bath, the B&B rate is £26 ($45.50) per person nightly. VAT is included in the prices. The house does not receive guests from November to March.

Among the B&B houses, you can try **Kirkgate Guest House,** 35 Kirkgate, Thirsk, North Yorkshire YO7 1PL (tel. 0845/25015), which is a three-story Georgian-era town house. In the center of this thriving market town with its cobbled square, Kirkgate is only a short walk from the veterinary clinic where James Herriot still practices. Guests receive personal attention and are well cared for, occupying a total of nine bedrooms, four of which have private showers. B&B charges are attractive to those on a budget, with overnight prices ranging from £16 ($28) to £21 ($36.75) in a single, going up to £25 ($43.75) to £26 ($45.50) in a double. If arranged in advance, dinner will be served.

Nearby stands **Lavender House,** 27 Kirkgate, Thirsk, North Yorkshire YO7 1PL (tel. 0845/22224), run by Mrs. Sue Dodds since 1985. She and her husband bought an old two-story house and rebuilt the interior, adding a cottage-like decor. The house has only two bedrooms reserved for guests, a twin and a double, and this allows Mrs. Dodds to give each guest her full attention. Charges in a double are from £25 ($43.75) nightly, making for a bargain stay in Thirsk.

HAWES

The natural center of the Yorkshire Dales National Park is Hawes, a market town in Wensleydale and home of the cheese of that name. It's on the Pennine Way, which is popular with hikers. Hawes lies on a good road, the A684, about midway between the A1 running on the east and the M6 on the west.

The **Upper Dales Folk Museum,** Station Yard (the old train station; tel. 09697/494), traces folk life in the area of the Upper Dales. Peat cutting and cheese making, among other occupations, are depicted. The museum is open from 11 a.m. to 5 p.m. Monday to Saturday and from 2 to 5 p.m. Sunday from March 20 to the end of July and during September. In August, hours are from 10 a.m. to 6 p.m. Monday to Saturday and from 2 to 5 p.m. Sunday. In October, it is open only from noon to 5 p.m.; closed in winter. Admission is 50p (90¢).

Rookhurst Georgian Country House, West End, Gayle, near Hawes, North Yorkshire DL8 3RT (tel. 0969667/454), is on the outskirts of the village of Gayle, about five minutes' walk from Hawes. Mrs. Iris VenDerSteen owns this handsome stone hotel fronting the Pennine Way. The bedrooms with views over the surrounding fells are individually furnished, all with unusual or antique beds, including a brass four-poster and a large mahogany four-poster. The Georgian rooms in part of the house, which was once named "West End" and was originally built in 1734 as a farmhouse, are heavily oak beamed. Those in the Victorian wing added in 1869 are larger and elegant. All rooms have private baths. B&B costs from £29 ($50.75) per person daily for double occupancy. Half board is from £38 ($66.50) double occupancy. Charges include a full English breakfast and VAT. A four-course dinner is served daily in the Mullion Restaurant for £9 ($15.25), coffee included, for residents only. Afternoon cream teas are offered on the patio in good weather.

You don't need to travel far from Rookhurst for beautiful Dales scenery. Gayle, originally a Celtic settlement, is divided by Duerley Beck, with two lovely waterfalls, a ford, and an old stone bridge beloved of artists and photographers.

At Thornton Rust

A little road to the south off the A684 between Worton and Aysgarth, east of Hawes, leads to the tiny hamlet of Thornton Rust, central to all the Yorkshire Dales. The post office for the village is Leyburn, to the east, but the village is much closer to Hawes.

Thornton Rust Hall, Thornton Rust, Leyburn, Wensleydale, North Yorkshire DL8 3AW (tel. 09693/569), is a handsome "listed" building of 17th- and 18th-century origin set in off-the-beaten-path Herriot country. The main house has been restored to provide a well-appointed country house with such features as exposed beam ceilings, a full-height arched stone fireplace in the paneled dining room, and a spacious billards/snooker room with a full-size table and a grand piano. The bedrooms, all with large private baths with antique brass fittings and bidets as well as tea- and coffee-makers, rent for £18 ($31.50) to £25 ($43.75) per person daily for B&B, depending on the room. Alan and Gillian Cooper serve home-cooked dinners for £12.50 ($21.90). The hall has an indoor heated swimming pool and a hard tennis court. The Coopers also have cottages, which they rent by the week to parties of two to four persons.

3. West Yorkshire

HAWORTH

In West Yorkshire, this ancient stone village lying on the high moors of the Pennines—45 miles west of York via Leeds and 21 miles west of Leeds—is world famous as the home of the Brontë family. The three sisters—Charlotte, Emily, and Anne—distinguished themselves as English novelists. They lived a life of imagination at a lonely parsonage at Haworth.

Anne wrote two novels, *The Tenant of Wildfell Hall* and *Agnes Grey*, and Charlotte's masterpiece was *Jane Eyre*, which depicted her experiences as a governess and enjoyed popular success in its day.

But, of course, it was Emily's fierce and tragic *Wuthering Heights* that made her surpass her sisters as she created a novel of such passion, intensity, and primitive power, with its scenes of unforgettable, haunting melancholy, that the book has survived to this day, appreciated by later generations far more than by those she'd written it for.

From Haworth (pronounced "How-worth"), you can walk to Withens, the "Wuthering Heights" of the immortal novel. In Haworth, Charlotte and Emily are buried in the family vault under the Church of St. Michael's.

The parsonage where they lived has been preserved as the **Brontë Parsonage Museum** (tel. 0535/42323), housing their furniture, personal treasures, pictures, books, and manuscripts. It may be visited daily from 11 a.m., closing at 5:30 p.m. April to September and at 4:30 p.m. October to March. It is closed the first three weeks in February and on December 24, 25, and 26. Admission is £1 ($1.75) for adults, 50p (90¢) for children.

Haworth is the second most visited literary shrine in England, after Stratford-upon-Avon. Frequent bus and train service is available from Haworth to Keighley and Bradford and Leeds in West Yorkshire. The popular Worth Valley Steam Railway is one of the best-preserved steam lines in England. At Keighley it connects with British Rail, running up the Worth Valley to Oxenhope via Haworth. From Haworth you can visit the tiny market town of Settle as well as Skipton with its canal and castle.

Food and Lodging

The **Tourist Information Centre,** 2-4 West Lane (tel. 0535/42329), offers an accommodation booking service for the local area and also a "book a bed ahead" service, but it cannot recommend individual establishments. The office is open daily from 9:30 a.m. to 5:30 p.m. Easter to the end of October, and from 10 a.m. to 5 p.m. November to March. If you don't avail yourself of this service, then you might stay at one of the recommendations below.

Ferncliffe, Hebden Road, Haworth, Keighley, West Yorkshire BD22 8RS (tel. 0535/43405), offers one of the most outstanding accommodations in the area. But be sure to reserve in advance as far as possible, as it offers only six bedrooms and Haworth proves popular in summer with Brontë fans. Modern and comfortable, the hotel and restaurant open onto views of the "Wuthering Heights" countryside. The hosts are gracious and give guests their personal attention. Each bedroom is comfortably and attractively furnished, renting for £16.50 ($28.90) to £18.50 ($32.40) daily in a single, the tariff rising to £32 ($56) to £34 ($59.50) in a double. The hotel also serves good Yorkshire cooking, and evening meals can be arranged beginning at 7 p.m. (but warn the staff that morning of your intention to eat in).

Moorfield Guest House, 80 West Lane, Haworth, Keighley, West Yorkshire BD22 8EN (tel. 0535/43689), in a rural setting on the edge of town overlooking the moors, is only a three-minute walk to downtown Haworth and the Brontë Parsonage. The owners of this Victorian house rent six well-furnished and comfortable bedrooms, five of which contain private showers. Overnight B&B charges range from £13.50 ($23.65) to £16 ($28) in a single, rising to £21 ($36.75) to £26 ($45.50) in a double. A four-course evening meal can also be arranged.

Eden Lodge, Spring Head, Lord Lane, Haworth, Keighley, West Yorkshire BD22 7RX (tel. 0535/44470), shelters Brontë pilgrims today as it once did Yorkshire mill hands centuries ago. One of the best bargains at this literary pilgrimage shrine, it offers four basic but comfortable bedrooms, the guests of which share two public baths. Overnight B&B charges are among the more reasonable in the area, only £10 ($17.50) per person.

Weaver's Restaurant, 15 West Lane (tel. 0535/43822), was once cottages for weavers, but it has now been turned into the best restaurant in the Brontë hometown. In the words of one satisfied diner, "It's the only game in town as far as food is concerned." British to the core, it not only has an inviting atmosphere but serves excellent food made with fresh ingredients. Jane Rushworth has a great talent in the kitchen, and you can sample her very English wares at dinner from 7 to 9:30 every evening. However, she doesn't offer dinner on Sunday and the restaurant is closed all day Monday. She also serves lunch in winter from 12:30 to 1:30 p.m., costing £8.50 ($14.90). Dinners, however, cost from £12 ($21) and up, and include such classic dishes as Yorkshire pudding with gravy. Try, if featured, one of the Gressingham ducks, which are widely praised in the U.K. for the quality of their meat. For your final course, you might select a Yorkshire cheese or one of the truly superb made-in-house desserts. The style of the place is informal. Mrs. Rushworth's place is likely to be closed for a certain time each summer for vacation, so call in advance to check. You should always reserve a table at any rate. The place tends to be popular, and with good reason.

On the Outskirts

On the Haworth moors stands a Brontë landmark, **Ponden Hall,** Stanbury, near Keighley, West Yorkshire BD22 0HR (tel. 0535/44154), a distance of some three miles from Haworth. A 400-year-old farmhouse, it lies about a third of a mile from the main road between Ponden Reservoir and the moors. The wide, rough track that is a part of the Pennine Way long-distance footpath leads to this Elizabethan farmhouse with its traditional hospitality to walkers, visitors by car, children, and pets. The hall was extended in 1801 and is reputedly the model for Thrushcross Grange, Catherine's home after her marriage to Edgar Linton in Emily Brontë's *Wuthering Heights.* Today it provides farmhouse accommodation that is spacious and homelike, with one double, a twin, and a family room. The dining hall has an open fire, traditional flagstone floor, original oak beams, timbered ceilings, and mullioned windows. B&B charges are £11 ($19.25) per person per night, and a home-cooked evening meal is offered at £7 ($12.25). Vegetarian and special diets are catered to.

HAREWOOD HOUSE AND BIRD GARDEN

In West Yorkshire, at junction A61/659, midway between Leeds and Harrogate and five miles from the A1 at Wetherby, stands the home of the Earl and Countess of Harewood. One of the "Magnificent Seven" homes of England, this 18th-century house was designed by John Carr and has always been owned by the Lascelles family. The fine Adam interior has superb ceilings and plasterwork, and furniture made especially for Harewood by Chippendale. There are also important collections of English and Italian paintings and Sèvres and Chinese porcelain.

The Capability Brown landscape includes a 4½-acre bird garden that borders the lake. It contains exotic species from all over the world, including penguins, macaws, flamingoes, and snowy owls, and there is an undercover extension. The spacious grounds offer terraces, lakeside and woodland walks, exhibitions, shops, and a restaurant and cafeteria. Car parking is free, and there is a picnic area, plus an adventure playground for the children.

Harewood is open daily from 10 a.m. to 5 p.m. from Easter to the end of October. The house, bird garden, and adventure playground are also open on Sunday in November, February, and March. Admission is £3.85 ($6.75) for adults, £1.60 ($2.80) for children. For further facts, phone Visitor Information (tel. 0532/886225).

---

4. Durham

This densely populated county of northeast England was once pictured as a dismal, foreboding place, with coalfields, ironworks, mining towns, and shipyards. Now its image has brightened considerably, as intrepid explorers have sought out its valleys of quiet charm and its regions of wild moors in the west. Therefore, if you have the time, it would be interesting to explore the Durham Dales, especially Teesdale with its waterfalls and rare wildflowers and Weardale with its brown sandstone villages.

DURHAM

The county town, which has the same name, is built on a sandstone peninsula. Its treasure is the **Durham Cathedral,** which ranks among the most beautiful buildings in the world. Its solid towers dominate the surrounding countryside from its sandstone pinnacle surrounded by the River Wear. Inside, the massive and bold incised piers in the nave and the ribbed vaults (this was the first great church in Northern Europe to develop this feature) give it a feeling of solidarity and security. The church was named for St. Cuthbert, the great North Country saint who was first buried at Lindisfarne in A.D. 687. After being hauled around for many years, his body was interred where it now lies behind the high altar in 1104 in the new construction begun in 1093. No admission is charged to visit the cathedral. However, to visit the Treasury, which houses relics connected with St. Cuthbert, as well as precious books and plate, you must pay 50p (90¢). It is open from 10 a.m. to 4:30 p.m. Monday to Saturday, and from 2 to 4:30 p.m. Sunday. The Monks' Dormitory is open from 11 a.m. to 3 p.m. Monday to Saturday, charging 25p (45¢) for adults, 10p (20¢) for children. The Audio-Visual Exhibition is also open from 11 a.m. to 3 p.m. Monday to Saturday, with adults paying 40p (70¢) and children 20p (35¢). During those same hours, you can visit the Tower, costing 50p (90¢) for adults, 25p (45¢) for children. You will have a magnificent view over the city and castle.

From Framweigate Bridge, below the massive church, is a peaceful riverside walk known locally as **The Banks.** It leads you through trees beneath the castle and then up a steep path to the cathedral. It's quite a challenge for the weak-hearted, but well worth the effort for the fit.

In the shadow of the cathedral is the Church of St. Mary le Bow, now containing the **Durham Heritage Centre,** which is open from May until the end of September from 2 to 4:30 p.m. daily. It presents changing exhibitions and audio-visual presentations of the city's past and history, plus rubbings of replicas of monumental brasses. Guided walking tours of the city are organized here daily at 2:30 and 3:30 p.m. when, for 50p (90¢) per person, you can join a fascinating and well-informed tour of the major sights, going through the Vennels, the narrow passages joining the old city streets.

Adjoining the cathedral is **Durham Castle** (tel. 091/386-5481), which was founded by the Normans and was the home of the prince-bishops until it was given to Durham University in 1832. Except on the occasion of university or other functions, the castle is open to visitors all year. From July to September, hours are 10 a.m. to noon and 2 to 4:30 p.m. Monday to Saturday. During the rest of the year it is open from 2 to 4 p.m. on Monday, Wednesday, and Saturday. Admission is £1 ($1.75) for adults, 50p (90¢) for children.

Where to Stay

Castle View Guest House, 4 Crossgate, Durham, County Durham DH1 4PS (tel. 091/386-8852), is on quite a steep road across the river from the cathedral, and Castle View has a magnificent view across the gorge. There is adequate parking in the street outside this large, 250-year-old house beside St. Margaret's Church. The house has been renovated, with old beams and woodwork uncovered in the process. Six rooms are rented, two of which have private showers. Overnight B&B charges are from £13 ($22.75) to £16 ($28) in a single, £25 ($43.75) to £31 ($54.25) in a double. A large breakfast is served, and there is a residents' lounge.

The **Georgian Town House,** 10 Crossgate, Durham, County Durham DH1 4PS (tel. 091/3868070), is an 18th-century town house owned and run by Jane Weil. It is a choice property, with six double bedrooms (three with double beds, three with twin beds, but all with private baths). The bedrooms are spacious, and some are large enough to accommodate a family of three. They are also centrally heated and furnished to a high standard. Two of them open onto a view of the Cathedral. The charge is from £17.50 ($30.63) per person nightly for B&B. There is a large sitting and dining room with a TV for residents. Tea or coffee is provided upon request, and a full English breakfast is offered. Special diets are catered to upon request.

Colebrick, 21 Crossgate, Durham, County Durham DH1 4PS (tel. 0385/49585), stands almost in the center of Durham City. It is a large, pink-painted, detached, and rather luxurious family home. The view from the house is of the Cathedral and Castle. Only three bedrooms are available to rent, and guests share one public bath. The rooms are attractively and comfortably furnished. It's really an upmarket B&B. The single overnight rate is £21 ($36.75), rising to £31 ($54.25) in a double. Dinner can also be ordered here if arranged in advance. You may find that the generous breakfast served will get you through to dinner with only a "spot of tea" and a crumpet in the afternoon.

Drumforke, 25 Crossgate, Durham, County Durham DH1 4PS (tel. 091/384-2966), is a modest guesthouse owned and run by Mrs. D. B. Greenwell, who for years has catered to small families. She asks £12 ($21) per person daily for a room, the rate including a hearty breakfast. She reduces the tariff for children sharing one of the good-size rooms with their parents.

Where to Eat

Undercroft Restaurant, The College (tel. 091/386-3721), is found under the ancient roof and arches of the Cathedral of Durham. It lies in the crypt beside the Treasury and is open Monday to Saturday from 9:30 a.m. to 5 p.m., and on Sunday from 11 a.m. to 5 p.m. In the midst of pine furnishings and stone walls, you can order a hot dish of the day, such as cottage pie and buttered cabbage, followed by apple pie and cream, or perhaps you'd prefer to choose from pastas, pâté, and quiches. You can also order wine by the glass. Meals cost from £4 ($7).

Almhouses, Palace Green (tel. 091/386-1054), occupies what used to be almhouses centuries ago. The vegetarian will call this place home, but meat-eaters will also find dishes to satisfy their desires. The place does some of the finest cooking in town and always uses fresh produce, which the kitchen uses expertly in turning out a number of often inventive dishes. Salads tend to be outstanding, as are the pastries and moist cakes. You can order wine by the glass, but the truly health-conscious will prefer a freshly squeezed juice instead. With meals costing from £6 ($10.50), this self-service cafeteria is open daily from 9 a.m. to 8 p.m. in summer (however, it closes at 5 p.m. in winter).

For the best Italian meal in Durham City, head for **Giovanni and Fabio Pizzeria,** 70 Claypath (tel. 0385/61643), where you can not only order pizza (as most diners do), but other typical trattoria dishes, including pasta. You don't get haute Italian cuisine here, but you wouldn't expect to at the price of £6.50 ($11.40) or so for a meal. University students here like it a lot, and they do so from 11:30 a.m. to 2 p.m. and 6:30 to 11:30 p.m., except on Monday. The kitchen always takes off Saturday at lunch and Sunday at lunch.

Three Tuns Hotel, New Elvet (tel. 091/386-4326), has a good bar buffet, serving baked ham, chili con carne, and baked potatoes, with meals costing from £4 ($7). The Tudor Restaurant, serving traditional and vegetarian menus, offers lunch costing from £5.50 ($9.65) and dinner from £10.50 ($18.40). Go for meals daily from noon to 2 p.m. and 6:30 to 9 p.m. The lower bar is noisy and crowded with students from the university discussing the latest fundraising "rag" event. But then they're the sort of people who know good value when they taste it.

The Swan and Three Cygnets, on Elvet Bridge (tel. 091/384-0242), is the domain of Debbie and Steve Gray, who serve Samuel Smith ale from Yorkshire's oldest brewery in a black-and-white timbered pub at the junction of the bridge and the pedestrian area leading to the Cathedral. At lunch, you can get "mince" and dumplings, along with steak-and-kidney pie, plus soups and desserts. Food is served from an open range, with meats costing £1.95 ($3.40) to £3 ($5.25). Also, there is a continental cheese and pâté bar in the conservatory overlooking the river. Hours are from noon to 2 p.m. daily for food service.

BARNARD CASTLE

Near the River Tees in the town of Barnard Castle stands the **Bowes Museum** (tel. 0833/690606) at the eastern end of town. It was built in 1869 by John Bowes and his wife, the Countess of Montalbo, to house and display their art collection. Here you'll find masterpieces by Goya and El Greco, plus many fine tapestries and porcelains. There are also collections of French and English furniture, superb costumes, musical instruments, a children's gallery, and many other things of interest. A tea room and ample parking are found on the premises. It is open from 10 a.m. to 5 p.m. Monday to Saturday, from 2 to 5 p.m. on Sunday, closing at 4 p.m. November to February. Admission is £1.50 ($2.65) for adults, 50p (90¢) for children.

Food and Lodging

Jersey Farm Hotel, West Town, Pasture Farm, Darlington Road, Barnard Castle, County Durham DL12 8TA (tel. 0833/38223), is the best place for food and lodgings in the area of this thriving market town. What started out as a 40-acre dairy farm might just end up a hotel after all. Opening onto views of the Teesdale country, the hotel offers 15 well-furnished bedrooms, each with private bath or shower. The accommodations are beautifully maintained with contemporary amenities. There are some suites (and more are planned) in stone-built cottages on the grounds. B&B rates are definitely upmarket at £31 ($54.25) to £36 ($63) daily in a single, rising to £39 ($68.25) to £47 ($82.25) in a double. You'll definitely want to take your meals here, as the farm offers an all-you-can-eat carvery of succulent roasts and other farm goodies.

George & Dragon Inn, Boldron, Barnard Castle, County Durham DL12 9RF (tel. 0833/38215), is a local favorite. This well-maintained old inn has a long tradition of welcoming wayfarers to the lovely Teesdale. It offers the traditions of a typical English country inn with the hospitality of the northeast and good food and ale. Management has only two rooms to rent, a double and a twin, and occupants share one bathroom. The charge is from £18 ($31.50) to £19 ($33.25) daily for two persons. It's also possible to book in here on a half-board rate of £13.50 ($23.65) per person. There is ample car parking.

Market Place Teashop, 29 Market Place (tel. 0833/690110), is a charming place for good-tasting meals, with a rustic interior and rugged stone walls. The building that houses it was built at the beginning of the 18th century. It's easy to

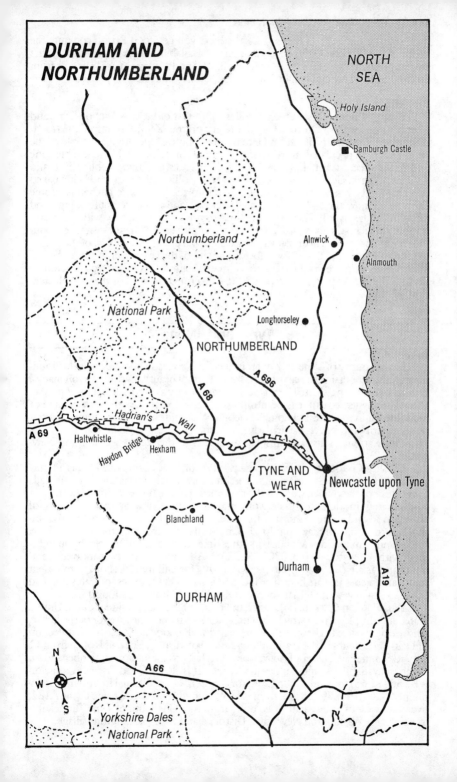

find, right in the heart of Barnard Castle. Here you get good British cooking, the menu changing constantly, depending on the availability of fresh produce. Hours are daily from 10 a.m. to 5:30 p.m. (it opens on Sunday at 3 p.m.). Meals cost from £6 ($10.50) and are amply filling with good, wholesome fare.

BEAMISH

West of Chester le Street, eight miles southwest of Newcastle-upon-Tyne and 12 miles northwest of Durham City, lying just off the A693, is Beamish, the **North of England Open Air Museum.** Here the way of life of the original people of the region has been re-created. You can take a tram ride into the past down a cobblestone Old Town Street to visit old shops, houses, printworks, a working public house, and a Victorian park. Go down a "drift" mine at the Colliery and see bread being baked in a coal-fired oven at the pit cottages. Step into the farmhouse kitchen at Home Farm to see how the farmer's wife spent her day, and meet the poultry, pigs, and cattle in the farmyard. There's a North Eastern Railway area, too, with a country station, signal box, goods yard, and steam locomotives. An average visit takes about four hours. Beamish is open daily from 10 a.m. to 5 p.m. from the first of the year to the end of March and from November to the end of the year. From April to the end of October, hours are from 10 a.m. to 6 p.m. (last entrance is always 4 p.m.). Admission is £3.30 ($5.80) for adults, £2.30 ($4.05) for children. For further information, phone 0207/231811.

---

5. Tyne and Wear

In the county of Tyne and Wear, industrial Newcastle-upon-Tyne is the dominant focus, yet outside the city there is much natural beauty. Cattle graze on many a grassed-over mining shaft. There is such scenic beauty as moors and hills of purple-blue. The rugged coastline is beautiful. Americans like to pass through because of their interest in the ancestral home of George Washington (see below), and Newcastle also merits a stopover, particularly from motorists heading to Scotland.

The National Trust administers two sights in the region surrounding Newcastle:

Gibside Chapel, built in the classical style of James Paine in 1760, is an outstanding example of Georgian church architecture. A stately oak-lined avenue leads to the door of the chapel, which is the mausoleum of the Bowes family. The interior is decorated in delicate plasterwork and is furnished with paneled pews of cherrywood and a rare mahogany three-tiered pulpit. The chapel is open Wednesday, Saturday, and Sunday from 1 to 5 p.m. April to the end of October (open Good Friday and bank holiday Mondays). Other times of year, it can be seen by appointment with the custodian (tel. 0207/542255). Admission to the car park avenue and the chapel is £1 ($1.75) for adults, 50p (90¢) for children. A shop, refreshment stand, and picnic area are here. The location is six miles southwest of Gateshead and 20 miles northwest of Durham between Rowlands Gill and Burnopfield.

Washington Old Hall is the ancestral home of the first president of the United States and the place from which the family took its name. The interior of the house, whose origins date back to 1183, is furnished with period antiques and a collection of Delftware. Relics of the Washingtons are also on display. The hall is open from 11 a.m. to 5 p.m. daily, except Friday, from March 24 to the end of September and on Wednesday, Saturday, and Sunday in October. It is closed Good Friday. Admission is £1.50 ($2.65) for adults, 50p (90¢) for children. For additional information, telephone 091/4166879. The location is in Washington on the east side of the A182, five miles west of Sunderland (two miles from the A1). South of Tyne Tunnel, follow signs for Washington New Town District 4 and then Washington Village.

NEWCASTLE-UPON-TYNE

An industrial city, Newcastle is graced with some fine streets and parks, as well as many old buildings. After crossing its best-known landmark, the Tyne Bridge, you enter a steep city that sweeps down to the Tyne, usually on narrow lanes called "chares." Once wealthy merchants built their town houses right on the quayside, and some of them remain.

For years Newcastle has been known as a shipbuilding and coal-exporting center, and the city gave rise to the expression suggesting the absurdity of shipping coals to Newcastle.

Dominating the skyline, **St. Nicholas Church of England Cathedral** rises to a soaring crown spire. It is England's most northerly cathedral and is situated close to the central station and the castle. The provost says that "the cathedral is one of the gems among the glorious churches of Northumberland." The present building is substantially from the 14th century, the spire being a 15th-century construction. The cathedral has a refectory open at lunchtime and also a gift shop.

The keep of the so-called New Castle built by Henry II in 1170 contains the **Keep Museum,** on St. Nicholas Street, with an interpretation of the history of the castle site. It's open April to September on Monday from 2 to 5 p.m. and Tuesday to Saturday 10 a.m. to 5 p.m. From October to March, its Monday hours are 2 to 4 p.m.; on Tuesday to Saturday 10 a.m. to 4 p.m.

Where to Stay

Chirton House Hotel, 46 Clifton Rd., Newcastle-upon-Tyne, Tyne and Wear NE4 6XH (tel. 091/273-0407), is a substantial hotel owned and managed by Captain and Mrs. Haggerty, who have set reasonable prices. Some of the rooms contain private baths, for which you pay more. Depending on the plumbing, singles range from £19 ($33.25) to £26 ($45.50) daily for B&B, with doubles costing £30 ($52.50) to £35 ($61.25). The accommodations are well maintained and comfortable. An evening meal can be prepared if requested in advance, costing £7.50 ($13.15). In the lounge, there's a color TV, and a bar serves residents. Chirton House is nicely located on a quiet street, yet it is close to the city.

Morrach Hotel, 82-86 Osborne Rd., Jesmond, Newcastle-upon-Tyne, Tyne and Wear NE2 2AP (tel. 091/2813361), is often cited as one of the best of the modestly priced hotels of Newcastle-upon-Tyne. A tranquil, family-managed establishment, it lies on the border of the city, on the Morpeth road or B1309, right off the A6125. The hotel was converted from a series of 19th-century private residences, and today it offers a total of 34 comfortably furnished bedrooms. Depending on the plumbing, the single B&B rate ranges from £19.50 ($34.15) to £34.50 ($60.40) daily, with doubles costing from £32 ($56) to £48 ($84). This two-story establishment has a Buttery Bar serving meals throughout the day and night and a more formal restaurant, which serves from noon to 2 p.m. and 7 to 9:30 p.m. Meals cost from £5 ($8.75) at lunch, £8 ($14) at dinner. Try, if featured, the Tweed salmon or one of the continental dishes such as coq au vin.

Food and Drink

Dennhofers Blackgate Restaurant, The Side, off Dean Street (tel. 091/2617356), offers a classical range of dishes, mainly European but prepared in a modern style. To please the health-conscious dining public of today, the owners offer no fried foods, with only small amounts of oil, cream, and butter used when necessary. Such main courses as fresh poached halibut, braised salmon, roast guinea fowl, and grilled steaks are served. Lunches change daily; dishes are listed on the blackboard. A fixed-price meal costs from £6 ($10.50) to £8 ($14) and is served from noon to 3 p.m. Dinner, with an à la carte menu changing seasonally, is served from 7:30 to 10:30 p.m., a table d'hôte meal priced from £10 ($17.50). The restaurant is open Monday to Friday for lunch and Tuesday to Saturday for dinner.

Newcastle-upon-Tyne enjoys quite a reputation in the northeast for its Chinese restaurants, of which **Great Wall,** 35-39 Bath Lane (tel. 091/232-0517), is one of the best known. Some of the wines came all the way from China, as the song goes. The kitchen offers one of the most genuine cuisines here, and you can order all your favorites, such as Peking (Beijing) duck. Try also chicken with cashews. Rice and noodle dishes are cheap and satisfying. The restaurant is open daily from noon to 2 p.m. and 6 to 11:30 p.m. (noon to 11 p.m. on Sunday). A set luncheon is a superb value at £3.50 ($6.15), with dinners costing from £10 ($17.50).

Mathers, 4 Old Eldon Square (tel. 091/232-4020), brings bistro-like cookery to this commercial and cultural center of the northeast. Many of the city's young people vacation regularly on the continent, and when they return home they are increasingly demanding the kind of food and service they got there. After all, Newcastle is no longer a place where the residents eat all stottie cake and chips. Mathers offers local produce, which is handled well in the kitchen, and when the dishes emerge they are well presented. In a casual basement setting, you can begin with one of the day's freshly made soups, then go on to a vegetarian specialty (if that is your health-conscious choice) or one of the meat dishes, finishing with something for your sweet tooth, likely to be one of the highlights of the menu. The bistro is open daily, except Sunday, from 9:30 a.m. to 10:30 p.m., with meals costing from £6 ($10.50) and up.

6. Northumberland

Unfortunately, most motorists zip through this far-northern county of England on their way to Scotland, missing the beauty and historic interest of the Border section. Because it is so close to Scotland, Northumberland was the scene of many a bloody skirmish. The county now displays a number of fortified castles that saw action in those battles. Inland are the valleys of the Cheviot Hills, lying mostly within the Northumberland National Park and the remainder of the Border Forest Park, Europe's largest man-made forest.

Northumberland's coast is one of Britain's best-kept secrets. Here are islands, castles, tiny fishing villages, miles of sands, as well as golf and fishing among the dunes, and bird-watching in the Farne Islands—in all, an area of outstanding natural beauty.

Wallington Hall, at Cambo, 12 miles west of Morpeth on the B6342 and six miles northwest of Belsey off the A696, dates from 1688, but the present building reflects the great changes brought about in the 1740s when Daniel Garrett completely refashioned the exterior of the house. The interior is decorated with rococo plasterwork and furnished with fine porcelains, furniture, and paintings. Travelers may also visit the museum and enjoy an extensive display of dollhouses. The Coach House contains an exhibit of ornate carriages. The main building is surrounded by 100 acres of woodlands and lakes, including a beautifully terraced walled garden and a conservatory restaurant, shop, and information center. The grounds are open all year; the house, April to October 29 from 1 to 5:30 p.m. daily, except Tuesday. Last admission is half an hour before closing time. Admission to the house and grounds is £2.80 ($4.90); to the grounds only, £1 ($1.75). Children pay half price. For more information, telephone 067074/283.

Seaton Delaval Hall (tel. 091/237-1493), the enormous country home of Lord Hastings near Whitley Bay, represents the architecture of Sir John Vanbrugh, builder of Blenheim Palace and Castle Howard. Many consider this English baroque hall the masterpiece of the playwright/architect. It looks like the stage settings for 14 Roman tragedies piled one on top of another. Walk over and look through a window, and you can almost imagine knights and wenches feasting at long tables and drinking mead. The house is open to view from May to September on Wednesday and Sunday from 2 to 6 p.m., charging adults an admission of £1 ($1.75); children, 50p (90¢). The hall is a half mile from the coast at Seaton Sluice between Blyth and Whitley Bay and ten miles from Newcastle, reached via Northumbrian bus routes 363 and 364 that run half-hourly.

The **Farne Islands** are a group of small islands off the Northumbria coast, which provide a summer home for at least 20 species of seabirds as well as for one of the largest British colonies of gray seals. St. Cuthbert died here in 687, and a chapel built in the 14th century is thought to be on the site of his original cell. Only Inner Farne and Staple Island are open to the public. Visiting season extends from April through September, but access is more controlled during the breeding season. From mid-May to mid-July, you can visit Staple Island from 10:30 a.m. to 1:30 p.m. each day, and Inner Farne from 2 to 5 p.m. daily. From April 1 to mid-May and from mid-July until the end of September, hours for both Staple Island and Inner Farne are from 10 a.m. to 6 p.m. Tickets are obtained on the island. During the peak season, the adults pay £2 ($3.50) and children are charged £1 ($1.75). During the rest of the season, the admission is £1.50 ($2.65), going up to £2 ($3.50) during the breeding season.

The best way to get to this most famous bird and animal sanctuary in the British Isles is to telephone or write Billy Shiel, the Farne Islands boatman, at 4 Southfield Ave., Seahouses, Northumberland NE68 7YT (tel. 0665/720308). He has been taking people in his licensed boat for the past 40 years, so he knows the tides and the best places to film seals, puffins, and guillemots. He runs 2½-hour trips in his 60-passenger craft at a cost of £3 ($5.25) per person.

Incidentally, these are the islands where Grace Darling and her father made their famous rescue of men from a foundered ship (see below).

HOLY ISLAND

The site of the Lindisfarne religious community during the Dark Ages, Holy Island is only accessible for ten hours of the day, high tides covering the causeway at other times. For crossing times, check with local information centers.

Lindisfarne Castle, on Holy Island, was built about 1550 as a fort to protect the harbor. In 1903, it was converted by Sir Edwin Lutyens into a comfortable home for Edward Hudson, the founder of *Country Life*. It is open from April to the end of September every day, except Friday (open Good Friday), 1 to 5:30 p.m. In October, also from 1 to 5:30 p.m., it's open only on Wednesday, Saturday, and Sunday. Admission is £2.50 ($4.40) in June, July, and August; £1.50 ($2.65) during the other months.

At Lindisfarne, you can stay at the **Lindisfarne Private Hotel,** Holy Island, Northumberland TD15 2SQ (tel. 0289/89273). This is a fine, substantial frame building with a trio of tall chimneys. It's run by members of the Massey family, who conduct it more like a private home than a hotel. Centrally heated bedrooms contain hot and cold running water (a few with private bath) and are decorated with personality, providing a homelike atmosphere. The charge ranges from £22 ($38.50) to £24 ($42) per person daily for bed, breakfast, and evening dinner. Boating excursions can be arranged to the Farnes.

BAMBURGH CASTLE

Guarding the British shore along the North Sea, the castle (tel. 06684/208) stands on a site that has been occupied since the 1st century B.C. The Craggy Citadel where it stands was a royal center by A.D. 547. The Norman keep has stood for eight centuries, the remainder of the castle having been restored toward the end of the 19th century. This was the first castle to succumb to artillery fire, the guns of Edward IV. You can visit the grounds and public rooms daily from April to early October. Hours are 1 to 5 p.m. in April, May, June, and September, 1 to 6 p.m. in July and August; and 1 to 4:30 p.m. in October. Admission is £1.70 ($3) for adults, 60p

($1.05) for children. There is a tea room. The castle is the home of Lord and Lady Armstrong and their family.

Nearby is the **Grace Darling Museum** (tel. 0665/720037), which has various mementos, pictures, and documents relating to the heroic Grace Darling, including the boat in which she and her father, who was keeper of the Longstone lighthouse in the Farne Islands, rescued nine people from the S.S. *Forfarshire* that foundered in 1838. It's open daily from Easter to mid-October from 11 a.m. to 6 p.m. Admission is free, but donations to the Royal National Lifeboat Institution are gratefully accepted.

HADRIAN'S WALL

This wall, which extends across the north of England for 73 miles, from the North Sea to the Irish Sea, is particularly interesting for a stretch of 3½ miles west of Housesteads. Only the lower courses of the wall are preserved intact; the rest were reconstructed in the 19th century with the original stones. From several vantage points along the wall, you have incomparable views north to the Cheviot Hills along the Scottish border, and south to the Durham moors.

The wall was built following a visit of the Emperor Hadrian in A.D. 122. He wanted to see the far frontier of the Roman Empire, and he also sought to build a dramatic line between the so-called civilized world and the barbarians. Legionnaires were ordered to build a wall across the width of the island of Britain, stretching for 73½ miles, going over hills and plains, beginning at the North Sea and ending at the Irish Sea.

The wall is a premier Roman attraction in Europe, ranking among many people with Rome's Colosseum. The western end can be reached from Carlisle, which has a good museum of Roman artifacts, and the eastern end can be reached from Newcastle-upon-Tyne (some remains are seen on the city outskirts and in a good museum at the university). South Shields, Chester, Corbridge, and Vindolanda are all good forts to visit in the area.

At Housesteads (English Heritage) you can visit a **Roman fort** (tel. 04984/363) built about A.D. 130 to house an infantry of 1000 men. Called Vercovicium in Latin, the fort held a full-scale military encampment, the remains of which can be seen today. The fort is open from 10 a.m. to 6 p.m. April to the end of September, to 4 p.m. October to the end of March; closed Monday and during the Christmas and New Year's holidays. Admission is £1.30 ($2.30) for adults, 60p ($1.05) for children.

Just west of Housesteads is **Vindolanda** (tel. 04984/277), another fort south of the wall at Chesterholm. The building is very well preserved, and there is also an excavated civilian settlement outside the fort with an interesting museum of artifacts of everyday Roman life. Hours are daily from 10 a.m. to 5 p.m. or dusk. Admission is £1.50 ($2.65) for adults, 80p ($1.40) for children.

Not far from Vindolanda is the **Roman Army Museum,** Carvoran, on Hadrian's Wall near Greenhead, which traces the growth and influence of Rome from her early beginnings to the development and expansion of the empire, with special emphasis on the role of the Roman army and the garrisons of Hadrian's Wall. A barracks room shows basic army living conditions. Realistic life-size figures make this a striking visual museum experience. Admission is £1.10 ($1.95) for adults, 60p ($1.05) for children. For information, phone 06972/485.

Within easy walking distance of the Roman Army Museum lies one of the most imposing and high-standing sections of Hadrian's Wall, Walltown Crags, where the height of the wall and magnificent views to north and south are impressive.

HALTWHISTLE

About 20 miles east of Carlisle lies the town of Haltwhistle. There the **Grey Bull Hotel,** Main Street, Haltwhistle, Northumberland NE49 0DL (tel. 0498/20298), is a good base of operations for seeing the best section of Hadrian's Wall and its

Roman garrisons. These include Housesteads, Vindolanda (the largest site in Europe), the Chesters, and the Carvoran Roman Army Museum, all within 15 minutes' drive from the hotel. The Grey Bull has been modernized and re-equipped. There are five bedrooms, each with its own washbasin with hot and cold running water. The inclusive price is £11 ($19.25) per person daily, including an English breakfast, service, and VAT. Packed lunches are available on request. The bar at the hotel is a lively gathering place for the local people. They serve lunches daily from noon to 2:30 p.m. and evening meals from 7:30 to 9:30 p.m. Specialties include homemade pies, such as rabbit or venison, and locally caught trout and salmon. They also smoke their own food, so you can have smoked salmon if you wish.

White Craig Farm, Shield Hill, Haltwhistle, Northumberland NE49 9NW (tel. 0498/20565), is a farmhouse just a mile up the hill north of Haltwhistle and about a mile from the major attraction, Hadrian's Wall. Mrs. J. W. Laidlow, a pleasant, accommodating person, rents rooms in an old house (part from the 17th century) with modern facilities and a good hillside view. Three bedrooms are offered, each with private bath or shower, color TV, and beverage-making equipment. The charge is from £15 ($26.15) per person nightly for B&B. There are no evening meals, but Mrs. Laidlow will recommend the local pub, which has a good restaurant, providing an unusual menu, including game dishes, at a discount to guests of White Craig Farm.

ALLENDALE

In the southwestern sector of the shire, this unspoiled country village is the geographic center of Great Britain. It is well known for its ancient Fire Festival on New Year's Eve in the Market Place. From a base here, some of the finest scenery of Northumbria—heather-clad hills, moor, and woodland—unfolds.

For the best food and lodging in the area, seek out **Bishopfield Farm,** Allendale, Hexham, Northumberland NE47 9EJ (tel. 043483/248), which remains open all year. On some 200 acres of rolling, lovely Northumberland countryside, this farm cum hotel traces its origins back to 1740. Keith and Kathy Fairless, the owners, are members of the family that have owned this homestead for several generations, and their welcome will take some of the chill off a gray day. They rent a total of 11 comfortably furnished and pleasantly equipped bedrooms. Each of these units contains a private shower or bath, and also has a phone and central heating. Two-thirds of the units lie in a courtyard of cobblestones. The most sensible way to book in here is to take half-board terms, costing £23 ($40.25) to £30 ($52.50) per person nightly. The food, one of the attractions of the place, is wholesome and fresh, the portions generous, and whenever possible the produce comes from Northumberland. The location is about a mile west of Allendale.

HEXHAM

Above the Tyne River, this historic old market town is characterized by its narrow streets, old Market Square, a fine abbey church, and its Moot Hall. It makes a good base for exploring Hadrian's Wall and the Roman supply base of Corstopitum at Corbridge-on-Tyne, the ancient capital of Northumberland. The **Tourist Office,** at Hallgate (tel. 0434/605225), has masses of information on the wall for walkers, drivers, campers, and picnickers.

The **Abbey Church of St. Wilfred** is full of ancient relics. The Saxon font, the misericord carvings on the choir stalls, Acca's Cross, and St. Wilfred's chair are well worth seeing.

For accommodations, try the **Beaumont Hotel,** Beaumont Street, Hexham, Northumberland NE46 3LT (tel. 0434/602331), in the town center overlooking the abbey and park. It offers excellent facilities, including two comfortable bars, a delightful restaurant, and pleasant bedrooms. Martin and Linda Owen have completely refurbished their 23 bedrooms, all with private bath or shower, direct-dial phone, and TV. Singles rent for £32 ($56) daily, and doubles or twins cost from

£45 ($78.75). All rates are inclusive of VAT and service. Dinner from an extensive à la carte menu costs from £10.50 ($18.40).

Royal Hotel, Priestpopple, Hexham, Northumberland NE46 1PQ (tel. 0434/602270), stands just off the Market Place with its "shambles" and Moot Hall. Two buildings are linked together by a central square tower and dome, and the car park is entered through the original coaching arch. Dinner in the restaurant goes from £9 ($15.75). A salad buffet is presented each day in the lounge bar. The 28 bedrooms are comfortable and well appointed, 20 with private bath and shower and tea- and coffee-making facilities. All have TV. Rates include a full English breakfast and VAT. Charges are from £30.50 ($53.40) daily in a single, from £45.50 ($79.65) in a double.

West Close Hotel, Hextol Terrace, Hexham, Northumberland NE46 2AD (tel. 0434/603307), is a detached 1920s residence tastefully refurbished, set in prize-winning secluded gardens in a quiet cul-de-sac with private parking. It is a half mile from Hexham (first left off the Allendale road, the B6305). Patricia Tomlinson welcomes guests into relaxed surroundings, where comfortable accommodations consist of four bedrooms with washbasins, heating, and tea- and coffee-makers. There's a bathroom with a separate shower, and guests can watch color TV in the dining room/lounge. The charge is from £10.75 ($18.80) per person daily. There is a choice of a full English or a continental breakfast, and packed lunches and light suppers are available on order.

CORBRIDGE-ON-TYNE

This is the ancient capital of Northumberland and a good base for exploring the eastern section of Hadrian's Wall. To the west of the historic village is Corstopitum (Corchester), dating from about A.D. 80 to A.D. 400, during which it was a supply town for the Roman wall. Extensive remains have been excavated. The town stood on Agricola's Road, the Dere Street York to the north. Corbridge was a Saxon town and in medieval days became a place of importance, sending two burgesses to the first English parliaments in the 13th century.

St. Andrew's Church is on the site of a 7th-century Saxon tower. The present bridge over the River Tyne, built in 1674, was the only Tyne bridge to survive the floods of 1771.

For accommodations, try **The Hayes,** Newcastle Road, Corbridge, Northumberland NE45 5LP (tel. 043471/2010), set in 7½ acres of gardens, neat lawns, and fenced-in pastureland, all owned by Mr. and Mrs. F. J. Matthews. You can stay here on B&B terms at £11 ($19.25) per person nightly, plus another £5.50 ($9.65) for dinner. Children are granted reductions according to age. On any arrangement, a cup of hot tea and cookies are provided at 10 p.m. In addition, families may want to inquire about two apartments for rent, a self-contained apartment sleeping four persons, and a comfortable caravan housing five.

Clive House, Appletree Lane, Corbridge-on-Tyne, Northumberland NE45 5PN (tel. 043460/2617), was once a boys' school that was divided into four homes. Mr. and Mrs. E. M. Clarke have made theirs a charming and interesting dwelling. Mr. Clarke was once a professor of art at a university where Mrs. Clarke also taught. Two double rooms contain four-poster beds, and all accommodations have private bath or shower rooms. Other amenities include color TV, direct-dial phones, and tea- and coffee-makers. The tariff is £35 ($61.25) daily in a double. No singles are available; however, single occupancy costs £25 ($43.75) per night. The hosts invite guests to relax in their living room around the fireplace. They will direct you to several good places to eat nearby.

Flags 2, 18 Front St. (tel. 043471/2536), is a late 18th-century building made of exposed local stonework. In the center of the village, the restaurant is open only from 7 to 10 p.m. every evening except Sunday. For about £11 ($19.25), you can order a four-course set menu. The cuisine is international, with dishes appearing from many parts of the Mediterranean, as well as China and South America. Special dishes can be arranged for vegetarians.

OTTERBURN

This mellow old village on the Rede River was the scene of the famous Battle of Otterburn in 1388. It makes a good base for touring the Cheviot Hills.

The **Percy Arms,** Otterburn, Northumberland NE19 1NR (tel. 0830/ 20261), is a fine English country inn for either food or lodging if you're touring the scenic route between Newcastle and Edinburgh. On the banks of the River Rede, the hotel is attractively furnished and decorated. Several of the rooms open onto views of the hotel gardens. Alice and Clive Emerson are your hosts, welcoming you to patronize their establishment for drinks, bar meals, or dinners in their Garden Restaurant, which most often features classic English specialties along with some local dishes. All their rooms contain private bath or shower, a single going for £30 ($52.50) daily, a double or twin ranging from £26 ($45.50) per person. Dinners cost from £13 ($22.75), but bar meals at lunch are much cheaper.

ALNMOUTH

A seaside resort on the Aln estuary, Alnmouth attracts sporting people who fish for salmon and trout in the Coquet River or play on its good golf course.

Lindores Guest House, 17 Argyle St., Alnmouth, Northumberland NE66 2SB (tel. 0665/830470), is one of the best guesthouses in this tranquil village at the mouth of the Aln River. Travelers journeying from London to Scotland might want to stop off and absorb some of the charms of Northumberland while based at this well-run little place. It offers only three bedrooms, the guests of whom share the two public baths. The B&B rate ranges from £11 ($19.25) to £13 ($22.75) daily in a single, going up to £21 ($36.75) to £25 ($43.75) in a double. The hotel is licensed (for residents only), and it's possible to order a dinner here, but it should be arranged in advance. Diners enjoy some of the fruits of Northumberland's field and water, including game in season and fresh crab and salmon.

Blue Dolphins, Riverside Road, Alnmouth, Northumberland NE66 2RS (tel. 0665/830893), was built in the Edwardian days. It opens onto vistas of the Aln. Across from a beach, this little guesthouse is a winner, attracting a clientele seeking value for pounds. The Blue Dolphins delivers, with its five well-furnished and comfortably appointed bedrooms, each with a private bath or shower. The overnight B&B charge ranges from £16 ($28) to £19 ($33.25) in a single, going up to £27 ($47.25) to £28 ($49) in a double. The guesthouse also serves tasty meals, which can be arranged in advance.

ALNWICK

Set in the peaceful countryside of Northumberland, this ancient market town has had a long history. A good center for touring an area of scenic beauty, Alnwick is visited chiefly today by travelers wanting to see—

Alnwick Castle

In the town of Alnwick, 35 miles north of Newcastle, Alnwick Castle (tel. 0665/510777), is the seat of the Duke of Northumberland. This border fortress dates from the 11th century, when the earliest parts of the present castle were constructed by Yvo de Vescy, the first Norman Baron of Alnwick. A major restoration was undertaken by the fourth duke in the mid-19th century, and Alnwick remains relatively unchanged to this day. The rugged medieval outer walls do not prepare the first-time visitor for the richness of the interior, decorated mainly in the style of the Italian Renaissance.

Most of the castle is open to the public during visiting hours. You can tour the principal apartments, including the Armory, Guard Chamber, and Library, where you can view portraits and landscapes painted by such masters as Titian, Canaletto, and Van Dyck. You may also visit the dungeons and the Museum of Early British and Roman Relics. From the terraces within the castle's outer walls, you can look across the broad landscape stretching over the River Aln.

Alnwick is open to the public daily, except Saturday (open Saturday on bank holiday weekends), from 1 to 5 p.m. May to September. Admission is £2 ($3.50) for adults and £1 ($1.75) for children. For an additional fee you can also visit the Regimental Museum of the Royal Northumberland Fusiliers, within the castle grounds.

Food and Lodging

The **Hotspur Hotel,** Bondgate Without, Alnwick, Northumberland NE66 1PR (tel. 0665/510101), started in the 16th century as a coaching inn and was well known as the favorite local rendezvous for the musicians when "Billy Bones," a famed piper to the Duchess of Northumberland, was host. Now it has been extensively modernized, providing much comfort. Percy's restaurant, decorated in the William and Mary style of dark oak, has a fine cuisine. The Cocktail Bar, also in the William and Mary style, is intimate and excellent for a before-dinner drink. The Billy Bones Buttery also has its own character, decorated in elm with Jacobean screens. It is both informal and intimate. You can drink or dine here as well as enjoy the music of Northumbrian folk singers. There are 28 comfortable bedrooms fitted with oak furniture, radio, and phone. Eighteen have private baths. Singles are £25 ($43.75) to £28 ($49) daily, with doubles costing £40 ($70) to £46 ($80.50), the higher prices being for chambers with private baths. Tariffs include an English breakfast, service, and VAT. A luncheon goes for £5 ($8.75) and up, dinners from £10 ($17.50). Last food orders are at 9 p.m. The cuisine includes such dishes as roast local beef and poached Bulmer salmon.

CRAGSIDE

Designed in the late 19th century by architect Norman Shaw for the first Lord Armstrong, Cragside at Rothbury is a grand estate stretching across 900 acres on the southern edge of the Alnwick Moor. Here groves of magnificent trees and fields of rhododendrons frequently give way to peaceful ponds and lakes. This Victorian house is open only for part of the season, but the grounds alone are worth the visit. At Rothbury, the house is just 13 miles southwest of Alnwick. The park is open from 10:30 a.m. to 6 p.m. daily from Good Friday to the end of September, to 5 p.m. daily in October, and to 4 p.m. on Saturday and Sunday from November to the end of March. Admission to the park only is £1.50 ($2.65) for adults and 75p ($1.30) for children. The house is open from 1 to 5:30 p.m. daily, except Monday, from April to the end of September, and from 1 to 5 p.m. on Wednesday, Saturday, and Sunday in October (last entry half an hour before closing). Admission to both house and park is £3 ($5.25) for adults, £1.50 ($2.65) for children. For more information, phone 0669/20333.

DUNSTANBURGH CASTLE

On the coast northeast of Alnwick, about 1½ miles east of Embleton (which is the castle's address), this castle was begun in 1316 by Thomas, Earl of Lancaster, and enlarged in the 14th century by John of Gaunt. The dramatic ruins of the gatehouse, towers, and curtain wall stand on a promontory high above the sea. You can reach the castle on foot only, either walking from Craster in the south or across the Dunstanburgh Golf Course from Embleton and Dunstan Steads in the north. The castle is open daily, except Monday, from 10 a.m. to 6 p.m. from Good Friday to September 30, and from 10 a.m. to 4 p.m. off-season. Admission is 80p ($1.40) for adults, 40p (70¢) for children.

INDEX

Abbey Church of St. Wilfred (Hexham), 549
Abbey Gardens (Tresco), 320
Abbey Museum (London), 119
Abbeys, 118–19, 288–9, 342, 355, 462, 532, 535
Abbot Hall Art Gallery (Kendal), 499
Adventure/wilderness travel, 33–4
Air travel, 9–12, 49
Albert Dock (Liverpool), 491
Alcester, 403–4
Aldeburgh, 442–3
Alfriston, 236
Allendale, 549
Alnmouth, 551
Alnwick, 551–2
Alstonfield, 461
Alternative/special-interest travel, 30–1, 33–7
Althorp (Northampton), 454
Alum Bay (Isle of Wight), 261
Ambleside, 505–7
American Museum (Bath), 357
Ancient House Museum (Clare), 438
Anne Hathaway Cottage (Stratford-Upon-Avon), 391, 393
Anne of Cleves House (Lewes), 237–8
Apsley House (London), 131–2
Arden's (Mary) House (Stratford-Upon-Avon), 393
Arlington Mill Museum (Bibury), 376
Arlington Row (Bibury), 376
Art museums:
  Barnard Castle, 542
  Kendal, 499
  Liverpool, 491, 492
  London, 120–7, 134–5
  Northampton, 452–3
  Northumberland, 548
  Shrewsbury, 479
  Stoke-on-Trent, 484–5
  Windsor, 175–6
Arundel, 243–5
Ascot, 183–4
Ashbourne, 460–1
Ashby-de-la-Zouch, 456
Assembly House (Norwich), 444
Athelhampton (Dorchester), 270
Audley End House (near Saffron Walden), 435
Avebury, 341
Avon, 331, 354–66
  Bath, 355–63
  Bristol, 363–6
Avoncroft Museum of Buildings (near Worcester), 417
Aylesbury, 200–1

Babysitters, 37
Backpacking, 17
Bamburgh Castle (Northumberland), 547–8

Banks, 37
Banks, The (Durham), 540
Banqueting House (London), 129
Barbara Hepworth Museum (St. Ives), 327
Barbican (Plymouth), 296
Barbican Centre (London), 154–5
Barnard Castle, 542–3
Bassenthwaite, 514
Bateman's (Kipling's home) (Sussex), 235
Bath, 355–63
Bath Abbey, 355–6
Bath International Festival, 356
Battersea Park (London), 166
Battle, 234–5
Bayswater (London), 67, 69–71, 108
Beamish, 544
Beauchamp Place (London), 141
Beaulieu Abbey-Palace House (near Southampton), 257–8
Bedale, 534
Bedfordshire, 203–5
Belgravia (London), 55–6, 99–100
Belton House (Grantham), 471
Belvoir Castle (Leicestershire), 456
Beswick (John) Studios (Stoke-on-Trent), 484
Bethnal Green Museum of Childhood (London), 167–8
Bibury, 376
Bickleigh, 284
Bicycles, 16
Big Ben (London), 129
Birdland (Bourton-on-the-Water), 379–80
Black Friars Refectory Room (Plymouth), 296
Blackheath (London), accommodations, 76–7
Blackpool, 494–7
Bleak House (Rochester), 207
Bledington, 379
Blenheim Palace (Woodstock), 196–7
Blickling Hall (North Norfolk), 448
Bloomsbury (London), 73–6, 99
Bluebell Railway, 238
Bodinnick-by-Fowey, 310
Bolton, Castle (North Yorkshire), 531
Bolventor, 330
Borrowdale, 516
Boston, 466–7
Bosworth Battlefield (Leicestershire), 456–7
Bournemouth, 265–8
Bourton-on-the-Water, 379–81
Bowes Museum (Barnard Castle), 542
Bowness-on-Windermere, 504–5
Brackley, 455
Brantwood (Coniston Water), 510–11
Brewhouse Yard Museum (Nottingham), 462
Bridgnorth/Worfield, 482
Bridport, 272–3
Brighton, 238–43

Bristol, 363–6
Britexpress card, 15–16
British Library (London), 121
British Museum (London), 120–1
British Road Transport, Museum of (Coventry), 410–11
BritRail passes, 12–13
Broadlands (Romsey), 255
Broads Museum (North Norfolk), 448
Broadway, 384–6
Brompton (London), accommodations, 61–2
Buckingham, 201
Buckingham Palace (London), 127
Buckinghamshire, 200–3
Buckler's Hard, 258
Bunyan Museum (Bedfordshire), 203
Burford, 174, 376–7
Burghley House (Stamford), 470–1
Burlington Arcade (London), 142–3
Buses, 15–16
Buxton, 459–60

Cabinet War Rooms (London), 128
Cambridge, 420–32
    accommodations, 426–9
    boat/bicycle rentals, 425–6
    map of, 423
    nightlife and entertainment, 430
    restaurants, 429–30
    tours and tourist services, 421–2, 426
Cambridge University, 422, 424–5
Camden Lock (London), 151
Camden Passage (London), 150–1
Canterbury, 17, 206, 213–19
Carisbrooke Castle (Isle of Wight), 260
Carlyle's House (London), 135
Carnaby Street (London), 143
Cars and driving, 14–15
Castle Combe, 342–3
Castle Drogo (near Chagford), 287–8
Castle Howard (North Yorkshire), 528–9
Castles and palaces:
    Devon, 280–1, 287–8
    East Midlands, 456, 462, 464
    Falmouth, 313–14
    Hampshire and Dorset, 253, 260, 276
    Kenilworth (near Warwick), 408–9
    Kent, Surrey, and Sussex: Arundel, 243–4; Deal, 221; Dover, 219–20; Hastings, 232; Hever Castle (near Edenbridge), 209–10; Leeds Castle (Maidstone), 212; Lympne Castle (Canterbury), 219; Walmer Castle and Gardens (Deal), 221–2
    London, 125, 127
    North Yorkshire, 528–9, 531
    Northumberland, 547–8
    Northumbria, 540–1, 551, 552
    Norwich, 444
    Shrewsbury, 479
    Sudeley (Winchcombe), 375
    Wiltshire, Somerset, and Avon, 338, 345–6
Cathedral Church of Christ (Liverpool), 490
Cathedral of Our Lady and St. Philip Howard (Arundel Cathedral), 244
Cave of Mendip (Somerset), 353–4
Cavern Walks (Liverpool), 491–2
Cenotaph (London), 128
Central Criminal Court (London), 130
Central Museum and Art Gallery (Northampton), 452–3
Ceremony of the Keys (London), 118
Chagford, 287–9
Chalfont St. Giles, 201–2
Changing of the Queen's Guard (London), 127
Chapter House (London), 119
Charmouth, 274
Charter flights, 11
Chartwell (Kent), 208
Chatsworth (near Bakewell), 457–8
Chatterley Whitfield Mining Museum (Stoke-on-Trent), 485
Chelsea (London), 63–4, 101–5
Cheltenham, 373–5
Cheshire, 473–8
Chester, 473–8
Chester Cathedral, 474
Chester Zoo, 475
Chewton Cheese Dairy (Somerset), 353–4
Chichester, 245–7
Chideock, 273–4
Chief Post Office (London), 53
Children's activities:
    Arundel Toy and Military Museum, 244
    Chester Zoo, 475
    Drusilla's Zoo Park (Alfriston), 236
    London, 164–8
    Pleasure Beach (Blackpool), 495
    Stanley Park (Blackpool), 495
    Thorpe Park (Surrey), 173
    Warwick Doll Museum, 406
    Whipsnade Wild Animal Park (Bedfordshire), 205
    Windsor Safari Park, 182
Chilham Castle Gardens (near Canterbury), 213
Chiltern Hills, 174
Chilterns, 174
Chipping Campden, 386–9
Chipping Norton, 378–9
Christ Church (Oxford), 187
Christ's College (Cambridge), 425
Churchill (Sir Winston), home of (Kent), 208
Cigarettes, 37
Cirencester, 370–2
City, the (London), 95–8, 163–4
Clare, 438
Climate, 37
Cliveden (Buckinghamshire), 200
Clive House (Northumberland), 550
Clive House Museum (Shrewsbury), 479
Clock Tower (St. Albans), 199
Clovelly, 300–1
Club Row (London), 111
Cockington, 289
Coleham Pumping Station (Shrewsbury), 479
Coleridge Cottage (Dunster), 346
College Garden (London), 119

Coloroll Ceramics Division Factory Shop (Stoke-on-Trent), 484
Combe Martin, 301
Combe Syndenham Hall (Dunster), 346
Companions, travel, 37
Coniston, 510, 512
Corbridge-on-Tyne, 550–1
Corinium Museum (Cirencester), 370–1
Cornwall, 304–30
  Bolventor, 330
  Falmouth, 313–15
  Fowey, 310
  Looe, 305–7
  map of, 282
  Newlyn, Mousehole, and Land's End, 322–4
  Penzance, 316–18
  Polperro, 307–9
  Port Isaac, 327–8
  St. Ives, 324–7
  St. Mawes, 312–13
  Tintagel, 328
  Truro, 311
Cornwall, 316–18
  Isles of Scilly, 318–22
Corpus Christi College (Cambridge), 425
Costume and Textiles, Museum of (Nottinham), 462
Cotswold Countryside Collection, 381
Cotswolds, 367–89
  Bibury, 376
  Bourton-on-the-Water, 379–81
  Broadway, 384–6
  Burford and Minster Lovell, 376–8
  Cheltenham, 373–5
  Chipping Campden, 386–9
  Chipping Norton, 378–9
  Cirencester and Painswick, 370–3
  Malmesbury, 369–70
  Moreton-in-Marsh, 383–4
  Shipton-under-Wychwood, 378
  Stow-on-the-Wold and Lower Swell, 381–3
  Sudeley Castle (Winchcombe), 375
  Tetbury, 369
  Wotton-under-Edge, 368
Courtauld Institute Galleries (London), 134–5
Covent Garden (London), 87–9, 144–6
Coventry, 409–12
Cowes (Isle of Wight), 260
Cragside, 552
Craven Arms, 481
Crime, 38
Currency exchange, 38
Customs, 38

Darling (Grace) Museum (Northumberland), 548
Dartington, 292–3
Dartmoor, 284–7
Dartmouth, 293–4
D-Day Museum (Portsmouth), 253
Deal Castle, 221, 222
Dedham, 436
Derby Baths (Blackpool), 495

Derbyshire, 457–61
  map of, 520–1
Devon, 278–303
  map of, 282
  North, 299–303; Clovelly, 300–1; Combe Martin and Lynton-Lynmouth, 301–3
  South, 279–81, 283–99; Chagford, 287–9; Dartmouth, 293–4; Dartmoor, 284–7; Exeter, 279–81, 283–4; Plymouth, 295–9; Salcombe, 294–5; Torbay (Torquay), 289–91; Totnes, 291–3
  transportation, 279
Dickens, Charles:
  House (London), 135–6
  Birthplace Museum (Portsmouth), 253
  Centre, Chalet, and Museum, 207
Didcot, 195–6
Doctors, 38
Documents for entry, 38
Doll Museum, Warwick, 406
Donyatt, 276
Dorchester, 270–2
Dorking, 227
Dorn, 384
Dorset, 249, 265–77
  Bournemouth, 265–8
  Bridport, 272–3
  Charmouth, 274
  Chideock, 273–4
  Donyatt, 276
  Dorchester, 270–2
  Lyme Regis, 274–5
  Shaftesbury, 268–9
  Sherborne, 276–7
  Wareham, 269
Dorset County Museum (Dorchester), 270
Dover, 219–22
Down House (Orpington), 209
Drake's (Sir Francis) House (Yelverton), 288–9
Drink and food, 28–30
Drugstores, 39
Dry cleaning and laundry, 39
Dukeries, the, 465
Dunstanburgh Castle, 552
Dunster, 345–7
Durham, 540–4
Dutch House (Kew Palace) (Kew), 170

Earl's Court (London), 60–1, 105
East Anglia:
  Essex, 432–6
  map of, 433
  Norfolk, 443–50
  Suffolk, 436–43
  See also Cambridge
East End (London), restaurants, 108–9
East Midlands:
  Derbyshire, 457–61
  Leicestershire, 455–7
  Lincolnshire, 466–72
  Northamptonshire, 451–5
  Nottinghamshire, 461–6

Eastwood, 465
Educational and study travel, 35–6
Electrical appliances, 39
Elgar's (Sir Edward) Birthplace (near Worcester), 417
Elham, 218
Elstow Moot Hall (Bedfordshire), 203
Ely, 431–2
Embassy and High Commission, 39
Emergencies, 39
Emmanuel College (Cambridge), 424
England:
    ABCs of, 37–42
    culture of, 24–8
    government, 24
    history of, 22–4
    map of, 32
English National Opera (London), 154
Essex, 432–6
Estates, manors, and mansions:
    Devon, 289, 296
    East Anglia, 435, 447–8
    East Midlands, 451–2, 454, 457–8, 470–1
    Gloucester, Worcester, and Warwick, 403–4, 406
    Hampshire and Dorset, 255, 257–8, 268, 270
    Kent, Surrey, and Sussex, 209–10
    Northumbria, 544, 546–7, 550
    Oxford, Windsor, and the Home Counties, 183, 197–9, 200, 202
    Wiltshire, Somerset, and Avon, 332–3, 338–41, 356–7
    Yorkshire and Northumbria, 535, 539–40
Eton (Windsor), 180–2
Exeter, 279–81, 283–4
Exford, 345
Exmoor National Park (Somerset), 343–5

Falmouth, 313–15
Farne Islands, 547
Far Sawrey, 512
Fax and telex, 42
Festivals and holidays, 39
Film, 39
Finchingfield, 435–6
Fishbourne Roman Palace and Museum, 248
Fitzwilliam Museum (Cambridge), 425
Flags 2 (Corbridge-on-Tyne), 550–1
Flatford Mill (East Bergholt), 443
Fleet Air Arm Museum and Concorde Exhibition (Somerset), 271–2
Food and drink, 28–30; see also Restaurants, and specific places
Ford's Hospital (Coventry), 410
Fortnum and Mason (London), 147
Fountains Abbey (Ripon), 535
Fowey, 310
Fox Talbot Museum (Lacock), 342
Freshwater Bay, 262
Freud Museum (London), 137
Fulham (London), restaurants, 105

Gardens: see Parks and gardens
Gatwick Airport (London), 49
    accommodations near, 78–9
Gibside Chapel (Tyne and Wear), 544
Gilbert and Sullivan entertainment (London), 155–6
Gladstone Pottery Museum (Stoke-on-Trent), 484
Glastonbury, 347–50
Gloucester, map of, 392
Gorhambury House (Hertfordshire), 199
Grantham, 471–2
Gray's Inn (London), 130
Great Barn Museum of Wiltshire Folk Life (Avebury), 341
Great Britain, S.S. (Bristol), 363–4
Great St. Mary's (Cambridge), 425
Green Park (London), 137
Greenwich, 171–2
Grime's Graves (Ely), 432
Grittleton, 343
Guildford, 226
Guildhall (London), 130

Hadrian's Wall, 548
Hairdressing, 39
Hall's Croft (Stratford-upon-Avon), 393
Haltwhistle, 548–9
Ham Common (Windsor), 177
Ham House (Richmond), 224
Hampshire, 249–69
Hampstead (London), 76, 136–7
Hampstead Heath (London), 110–11, 136, 168
Hampton Court (East Molesey), 169–70
Hardwick Hall (near Chesterfield), 458
Hardy's Cottage (Dorchester), 270
Harewood House and Bird Garden (West Yorkshire), 539–40
Harrods (London), 146
Harrogate, 529
Harvard House (Stratford-upon-Avon), 394
Haslemere, 225–7
Hastings, 231–4
Hatfield House (Hertfordshire), 197–8
Hathaway (Anne) Cottage (Stratford-upon-Avon), 391, 393
Hawes, 537
Hawkshead, 510–12
Haworth, 538–9
Hayes, The (Northumberland), 550
Hayward Gallery (London), 135
Health and fitness facilities, 36
Heathrow Airport (London), 49
    accommodations near, 77–8
Helmsley, 532–3
Henley-on-Thames, 174, 184–5
Hepworth (Barbara) Museum (St. Ives), 327
Hereford, 412–16
Heritage Centre and Treasury (Lichfield), 487–8
Hertford, 198–9
Hertfordshire, 197–8
Hever Castle (near Edenbridge), 209–10

Hexham, 549–50
High Commission and Embassy, 39
Higher Bockhampton (Dorchester), 270
Hill Top Farm (near Hawkshead), 510
Historical museums:
Beamish, 544
Cheshire, Shropshire, and the Potteries, 479, 481–2, 484, 485
Cornwall, 321, 327
Cotswolds, 376, 381
Dartmoor, 285–6
East Anglia, 425, 432, 438
East Midlands, 454, 457–9, 462, 464, 465
Eton (Windsor), 181
Gloucester, Worcester, and Warwick, 394, 406, 410–11
Hampshire and Dorset, 252–3, 270
Kendal, 499
Kent, Surrey, and Sussex, 214–15, 218, 228, 247–8
Kew, 170–1
Liverpool, 492
London, 119–21, 130–4, 137, 152–3, 167–8
Oxford, Windsor, and the Home Counties, 199, 203, 205
Wiltshire, Somerset, and Avon, 341, 342, 348, 357
Yorkshire and Northumbria, 519–20, 522, 535
Hitchhiking, 17
Holborn (London), restaurants, 98–9
Holidays and festivals, 39
Holland Park Open Air Theatre (London), 154
Holy Island, 547
Holy Trinity Church (Stratford-upon-Avon), 393–4
Home Counties, 174–5
Horse Guards Building (London), 128–9
Houses of Parliament, 119–20
Hove, 243
Hughenden Manor (Buckinghamshire), 202
Hutton-le-Hole, 533
Hyde Park (London), 137

Ightham Mote (Kent), 209
Imperial War Museum (Ely), 432
Imperial War Museum (London), 131
Inland waterways, 34
Ironbridge, 481–2
Ironbridge Gorge Museum, 481–2
Isle of Wight, 259–62
Isles of Scilly, 318–22
Iveagh Bequest, Kenwood House (London), 136–7

Jewel House (London), 116
Johnson (Samuel) House (London), 135
Johnson's (Samuel) Birthplace (Lichfield), 487
Jordans Village, 201
Jorvik Viking Centre (York), 518, 522
Jubilee Market (London), 151

Keat's House (London), 136
Kendal, 499–500
Kenilworth Castle (near Warwick), 408–9
Kennedy, John F., Memorial (Runnymede), 171
Kensington (London), 64–5, 67, 68, 105–7
Kensington Gardens (London), 137
Kensington Palace (London), 125
Kent, 206–23
Kent Battle of Britain Museum (Canterbury), 218
Kentwall Hall (Melford), 439
Kenwood House, Iveagh Bequest (London), 136–7
Keswick, 512–14
Kew (London), 170–1
Kew Bridge Stearn Museum, 170–1
Kew Gardens (Royal Botanic Gardens), 170
Kew Palace (Dutch House) (Kew), 170
King's College Chapel (Cambridge), 422, 424
King's Lynn, 449–50
King's Road (London), shopping, 148
Kingston Lacy (Bournemouth), 268
Kipling (Rudyard), home of (Sussex), 235
Kitchenham Farm (East Sussex), 235
Knightsbridge (London), 63, 100–3
Knole, 208–9

Labour History, Museum of (Liverpool), 492
Lacock, 342
Lake District, 498–516
map, 501
tours, 505
Lakeland Life and Industry, Museum of (Kendal), 499
Lamb House (Rye), 228
Lancaster, map of, 520–1
Land's End, 323–4
Laundry and dry cleaning, 39
Laurel Farm (North Norfolk), 449
Lavenham, 440–1
Lawrence (D. H.) Information Centre and Museum (Eastwood), 465
Leathercraft, Museum of (Northampton), 453
Leather Lane (London), 151
Leeds Castle (Maidstone), 212
Leicester, 455–6
Leicestershire, 455–7
Leicester Square (London), 73, 85–6
Lewes, 237–8
Leycester (Lord) Hospital (Warwick), 405–6
Liberty (London), 146
Libraries, 39
Lichfield, 487–8
Lincoln, 467–70
Lincoln's Inn (London), 129–30
Lincolnshire, 466–72
Lindisfarne Castle (Holy Island), 547
Liquor laws, 39–40
Little Venice, canal boats to, 164–5

Liverpool, 490–4
Liverpool Museum and Planetarium, 492
Lizard, 315
London, 17, 44–173
    accommodations, 54–7, 60–5, 67, 69–80; airport hotels, 77–9; bed-and-breakfast, 54; bed and breakfast, 79; Belgravia, 55–6; Blackheath, 76–7; Bloomsbury, 73–6; Chelsea, 63–4; Earl's Court, 60–1; on the fringe, 77; Hampstead, 76; Kensington, 64–5, 67; Knightsbridge, 63; Leicester Square, 73; Northern London, 72–77; Notting Hill Gate, 67; Paddington and Bayswater, 67, 69–71; reservations, 55; St. Marylebone, 71–2; Shepherd's Bush, 67; Southwest, 55–7, 60–4; staying with a family, 79; Victoria, 56–7, 60; West London, 64–7, 69–72; youth hostels, 79–80
    for children, 164–8
    excursions (one-day) from, 168–73; Greenwich, 171–2; Hampton Court, 169–70; Kew, 170–1; Runnymede, 171; Syon Park, 172–3; Thorpe Park, 173
    geography, 46–8
    history, 45–6
    maps of, 58–9; Chelsea/Knightsbridge, 102–3; the City, 97; Covent Garden, 145; Kensington, 68; Piccadilly, 84; Soho and Russell Square, 159; Underground, 117; West End, 66
    nightlife and entertainment, 151–63; concerts, 155; dancing, 161–2; discos, 158, 160; gambling, 162–3; gay, 156–7; Gilbert and Sullivan evenings, 155–6; jazz, 160–1; music halls, 156; nightclubs, 157–8; open-air entertainment, 154; opera and ballet, 154–5; Soho, 160; spectacles, 162; theaters, 152–3; vaudeville, 162
    orientation, 45
    parks and gardens, 137–8, 166
    practical facts, 51–2
    restaurants, pubs, and wine bars, 81–114; Belgravia and Knightsbridge, 99–101; Chelsea, 101, 104–5; the City, 95–6, 98; Covent Garden, 87–9; East End, 108–9; fish and chips, 112–13; Hampstead Heath, 110–11; Holborn and Bloomsbury, 98–9; Kensington, 105–7; Leicester Square, 85–86; Mayfair, 89–91; Piccadilly Circus, 83, 85; Pimlico, 95; Soho, 91–3; tea, 113–14; Thames, 111–12; Thames, South of the, 109–10; Trafalgar Square and the Strand, 86–7; Victoria Station, 94–5; West End, 83, 85–93; West London, 107–8; Westminster and St. James's, 93–4
    shopping, 140–4, 146–51; antique markets (for curios), 140–1; arts and crafts, 141; Beauchamp Place, 141; books, 141–2; brass rubbing, 142; British design, 142; Burlington Arcade, 142–3; Carnaby Street, 143; for children, 143; china, 143; chocolates, 143–4; Covent Garden, 144, 146; department stores, 146–7; designer clothing (secondhand), 147; groceries, 147; Irish wares, 147–8; jewelry, 148; King's Road, 148; maps and engravings, 149; men's clothing, 148; notions, 148–9; philately, 149; posters, 149; Princes Arcade, 149; St. Christopher's Place, 149; silver, 150; souvenirs, 150; street markets, 150–1; woolens, 151
    sights and attractions, 115–40; British Museum, 120–21; Galleries, 134–5; Hampstead, 136–7; homes of famous writers, 135–6; Houses of Parliament, 119–20; Kensington Palace, 125; landmark churches, 138; Madame Tussaud's, 122; National Gallery, 124–5; parks, 137–8; St. Paul's Cathedral, 125–6; Tate Gallery, 122–3; top ten, 115–16, 118–27; Tower of London, 115–16, 118; Victoria and Albert Museum, 126–7; Westminster Abbey, 118–19
    tourist information, 53–4
    tours, 163–5
    transportation, 48–51; map of the Underground, 117
London, Museum of, 132
London City Airport, 49
London Docklands, 140
London Dungeon, 166
London Planetarium, 122
London Transport Museum, 132–3
London Zoo, 167
Longleat House (near Warminster), 340
Long Melford, 438–40
Looe, 305–7
Loseley House (Guildford), 226
Lost property, 40
Lower Swell, 383
Loxley, 402
Ludlow, 481
Luggage storage, 40
Lyme Regis, 274–5
Lympne Castle (Canterbury), 219
Lynton-Lynmouth, 301–3

Madame Tussaud's (London), 122
Maddermarket Theatre (Norwich), 444
Magdalen College (Oxford), 187
Magdalene College (Cambridge), 425
Mail delivery, 40
Malhamdale (North Yorkshire), 531
Mall, The (London), 127
Malmesbury, 369–70
Malverns, 418–19
Mankind, Museum of (London), 121
Mapledurham House (Berkshire), 183
Maritime Museum (Buckler's Hard), 258
Maritime Museum (Exeter), 280
Marks & Spencer (London), 146

Mary Arden's House (Stratford-upon-Avon), 393
Mary Rose (Portsmouth), 252
Mayfair (London), restaurants, 89–91
Medical services, 40
Melbourne Hall (near Derby), 458
Melford Hall, 439
Melton Carnegie Museum (Melton Mowbray), 457
Melton Mowbray, 457
Mersey Ferry (Liverpool), 491
Merseyside Maritime Museum (Liverpool), 491
Merton College (Oxford), 187, 189
Metric system, 43
Metropolitan Cathedral of Christ the King (Liverpool), 490–1
Mileage between cities and towns, 18
Millgate Folk Museum (Newark-on-Trent), 464
Milton (John), home of, 201–2
Minack Theatre (Penzance), 316
Minster Lovell, 377–8
Minton Museum (Stoke-on-Trent), 485
MOMI (Museum of the Moving Image) (London), 152–3
Mompesson House and Garden (Salisbury), 332–3
Monks House (Rodmell), 238
Moorcroft Pottery (Stoke-on-Trent), 484
Moore, Cathedral of the (Dartmoor), 285
Moreton Hampstead, 285
Moreton-in-Marsh, 383–4
Mosquito Aircraft Museum (Hertfordshire), 199
Motorcycles, 16–17
Mousehole, 322–3

Nantwich, 478
Nash's House/New Place (Stratford-upon-Avon), 393
National Army Museum (London), 132
National Film Theatre (London), 152
National Gallery (London), 124–5
National Horseracing Museum (Newmarket), 437
National Maritime Museum (Greenwich), 172
National Portrait Gallery (London), 134
National Postal Museum (London), 133
National Railway Museum (York), 522
National Stud (Newmarket), 437
National Theatre (London), 152
National Tramway Museum (near Matlock), 458
Natural History Museum (London), 167
Nether Wallop, 339
Newark Castle (Newark-on-Trent), 464
Newark-on-Trent, 464–5
Newby Hall (Ripon), 535
New Caledonian Market (London), 150
Newcastle-upon-Tyne, 544
New College (Oxford), 189
New Forest, 257–9
Newlyn, 322
Newmarket, 437–8

New Place/Nash's House (Stratford-upon-Avon), 393
Newspapers, 40
Newstead Abbey (Nottingham), 462
Norfolk, 443–50
Normandy Way (Salcombe), 294–5
Northallerton, 531–2
Northampton, 452–3
Northamptonshire, 451–5
North Norfolk, 447–50
North of England Open Air Museum (Beamish), 544
Northumberland, 517–18, 543, 546–7
North Yorkshire
  accommodations, 529–30
  moors and dales, 531–7
  restaurants, 530–1
Norwich, 444–7
Nottingham, 462–4
Nottinghamshire, 461–6
Notting Hill Gate/Portobello (London), 67, 108
No. 1 Royal Crescent (Bath), 356–7

Office hours, 40
Old Bailey (London), 130
Old Bosham, 248
Old Curiosity Shop (London), 130
Old Royal Observatory (Greenwich), 172
Old Sarum (near Salisbury), 338
Old Vic, The (London), 153
Old Wardour Castle (near Salisbury), 338
Oldway (Paignton), 289
Opera tours, 36
Orford, 441–2
Osborne House (Isle of Wight), 260
Otterburn, 551
Overbecks Museum and Garden (Salcombe), 295
Oxford, 17, 174, 185–96
  accommodations, 189–92; nearby, 192–3
  cars and driving, 186
  excursion to Didcot, 195–6
  map of, 188
  restaurants and pubs, 193–5
  sights and attractions, 186–7, 189
  tours and tourist services, 186

Paddington (London), 67, 69–71, 108
Painswick, 372–3
Palace House–Beaulieu Abbey (near Southampton), 257–8
Palaces, see castles and palaces
Parks and gardens
  Birdland (Bourton-on-the-Water), 379–80
  East Midlands, 457, 459
  Exmoor, 343–5
  Kent, Surrey, and Sussex, 210, 212, 213, 224, 226–7
  Kew, 170
  London, 137–8, 166
  Salcombe, 295
  Swiss Garden (Bedfordshire), 203–4
  Syon, 172–3
  Tresco, 320

Parks·and gardens *(cont'd)*
  West Yorkshire, 539–40
  Windsor, 182
Parnham (Dorset), 272
Pavilion, the (Brighton), 239–40
Pavilion Gardens (Buxton), 459
Peak District Mining Museum (Matlock Bath), 458–9
Pembroke College (Cambridge), 425
Pendennis Castle (Falmouth), 313–14
Penrith, 515
Penshurst Place (near Tonbridge), 209–10
Penzance, 316–18
Peterhouse (Cambridge), 424
Pets, 40
Petticoat Lane (London), 111, 150
Piccadilly Circus (London), 83–5
Pickering, 531–2
Pilgrim roots, search for, Nottingham-shire, 465–6
Pilgrim's Way (Canterbury), 214–15
Pimlico (London), restaurants, 95
Pleasure Beach (Blackpool), 495
Plymouth, 295–9
Poldark Mine (near Helston), 315
Polesden Lacey (Dorking), 227
Police, 40
Polperro, 307–9
Poole's Cavern (Buxton), 459
Portchester Castle (Portsmouth), 253
Port Isaac, 327–8
Portloe, 313
Port Lympne Zoo Park, Mansion, and Gardens, 219
Portobello (London), restaurants, 108
Portobello Road Market (London), 150
Portsmouth, 250, 252–5
Postbridge (near Chagford), 287
Post office, 40
Potteries, the, 483–8
Powderham Castle, 280–1
Princes Arcade (London), 149
Prison and Police Museum, Ripon, 535
Prysten House (Plymouth), 296
Pump Room and Roman Baths (Bath), 356
Purcell Room (London), 155

Québec House (Westerham), 208
Queen Charlotte's Cottage (Kew), 170
Queen Elizabeth Hall (London), 155
Queen Mary's Dollhouse (Windsor), 176
Queens' College (Cambridge), 424–5
Queen's Gallery (London), 127

Radio and television, 41
Ragley Hall (Alcester), 403–4
Regent's Park (London), 137–8, 154
Regimental Museum (Salisbury), 333
Religious services, 41
Rest rooms, 41
Richmond, 224–5, 533–4
Rievaulx Abbey (near Helmsley), 532
Rievaulx Terrace (Helmsley), 532
Ripon, 534–5
Rochester, 207–8
Rodmell, 238

Roman Army Museum (Northumber-land), 548
Roman Baths, and Pump Room (Bath), 356
Roman fort (Northumberland), 548
Roman Pavement (Canterbury), 214
Romney, Hythe & Dymchurch Light Railway Co. (near Canterbury), 218–19
Rougemont House Museum of Costume and Lace (Exeter), 280
Rowley's House Museum (Shrewsbury), 479
Royal Academy of Arts (London), 131
Royal Air Force Museum (London), 133
Royal Albert Hall (London), 155
Royal Botanic Gardens (Kew Gardens), 170
Royal Courts of Justice (London), 129
Royal Court Theatre (London), 153
Royal Crown Derby Porcelain Co. Ltd. (Derby), 458
Royal Doulton (near Stoke-on-Trent), 483–4
Royal Festival Hall (London), 155
Royal Mews (London), 127–8
Royal Mews (Windsor), 176–7
Royal Naval College (Greenwich), 172
Royal Naval Museum (Portsmouth), 252–3
Royal Navy Submarine Museum (Ports-mouth), 254
Royal Opera House (London), 154
Royal Shakespeare Company (London), 153
Royal Shakespeare Theatre (Stratford-upon-Avon), 395
Royal Shakespeare Theatre Summer House (Stratford-upon-Avon), 394
Royal Tunbridge Wells, 222–3
Royalty and empire (Windsor), 177
Runnymede, 171
Ruskin Museum (Coniston Water), 511
Russell Square (London), map of, 159
Rydal, 507–10
Rydal Mount, 507
Ryde, 261
Rye, 228–31

Sadler's Wells Theatre (London), 153
Saffron Walden, 434–5
Sainsbury Centre for Visual Arts (Norwich), 445
St. Albans, 199
St. Christopher's Place (London), 149
St. Clement's Caves (Hastings), 233
St. Etheldreda's (London), 138
St. George's Chapel (Windsor), 176
St. George's Hall (Liverpool), 492
St. Ives, 324–7
St. James's Park (London), 137
St. James (London), restaurants, 93–4
St. John's College (Cambridge), 425
St. John's House (Warwick), 406
St. Katharine's Dock (London), 111
St. Lawrence, Church of (West Wycombe), 203

St. Leonards, 231–4
St. Martin-in-the-Fields (London), 138
St. Mary's, 318–22
St. Mary's Church (Warwick), 405
St. Mary's Guildhall (Coventry), 410
St. Marylebone (London), 71–2, 107
St. Mary Redcliffe (Bristol), 364
St. Mawes, 312–13
St. Michael's Mount (Penzance), 316
St. Nicholas Church of England Cathedral (Newcastle-upon-Tyne), 545
St. Nicholas Priory (Exeter), 280
St. Paul's Cathedral, 125–6
St. Wulstan's Church (Malverns), 418
Salcombe, 294–5
Salisbury, 332–42
  accommodations, 333, 335–6
  map of, 334
  restaurants, 336–8
  side trips from, 338–42
  tours, 333
Salisbury Cathedral, 332
Samuel Johnson's House (London), 135
Sandown (Isle of Wight), 260
Sandringham Estate (Norfolk), 447–8
Science Museum (London), 133–34
Science/technology museums, 172, 254, 271–2, 341, 463, 491, 492, 499
  London, 122, 133–4, 167
Scilly, Isles of: see Isles of Scilly
Scilly Museum (Isles of Scilly), 321
Scrooby, 465–6
Seaton Delaval Hall (Northumberland), 546–7
Second Air Division of the Eighth United States Army Air Force memorial (Norwich), 445
Selfridges (London), 146
Senior citizen vacations, 35
Senior discounts, 41
Shaftesbury, 268–9
Shakespeare's Birthplace (Stratford-upon-Avon), 391
Shakespeare Countryside Museum (Stratford-upon-Avon), 393
Shambles, The (York), 518
Shanklin, 261
Shanklin (Isle of Wight), 260
Shaw (George Bernard), home of (Ayot St. Lawrence), 200
Shepherd's Bush (London), accommodations, 67
Shepherd Market (London), restaurants, 90–1
Sherborne, 276–7
Sherwood Forest (Nottinghamshire), 461–2
Shipton-under-Wychwood, 378
Shoe repairs, 41
Shrewsbury, 479–80
Shropshire, 478–83
Shuttleworth Collection (Bedfordshire), 205
Simonsbath, 345
Simpson's (London), 147

Sissinghurst Castle Garden (near Cranbrook), 210, 212
Skipton, 533
Slapton Cellars (Salcombe), 295
Slaughter, Upper and Lower, 381
Soane, Sir John, Museum (London), 131
Soho (London), 91–3, 159, 160
Solomon's Temple (Buxton), 459
Somerset, 331, 343–54
Somerset Rural Life Museum (Glastonbury), 348
Southampton, 255–7
South Kensington (London), 61–2, 106–7
Southsea, 250, 252–5
Southsea Castle (Portsmouth), 253
Southwell, 464
Special-interest travel, 30–1, 33–7
Speke Hall (Liverpool), 492
Spencer Home (Northampton), 454
Spirit of Coventry (Coventry), 410
Spode (Stoke-on-Trent), 484
Squerryes Court (Westerham), 209
Stafford, 486–7
Stanley Park (Blackpool), 495
Staple Inn (London), 130
Stoke Bruerne (Northampton), 454–5
Stoke-on-Trent, 483–6
Stonehenge, 339
Store hours, 41
Stourhead, 340–1
Stow-on-the-Wold, 381–2
Strand, The (London), restaurants, 86–7
Stratfield Saye House (near Windsor), 182–3
Stratford-upon-Avon, 17, 390–1, 393–404
  accommodations, 396–9
  restaurants, 399–403
  sights and attractions, 391, 393–5
  tours and tourist services, 395
  transportation to, 394–5
Studley Royal (Ripon), 535
Study and educational travel, 35–6
Sudeley Castle (Winchcombe), 375
Suffolk, 436–43
Sulgrave Manor (Northamptonshire), 451–2
Surrey, 223–7
Surrey, map of, 211
Sussexes, The, 211, 227–8
Sutton Windmill (North Norfolk), 448
Swan Theatre (Stratford-upon-Avon), 395
Swiss Garden (Bedfordshire), 203–4
Syon Park, 172–3

Talbot (Fox) Museum (Lacock), 342
Tate Gallery (Liverpool), 491
Tate Gallery (London), 122–3
Taxes, 41
Telegrams, 41
Telephones, 42
Television and radio, 41
Telex and fax, 42
Temple, The (London), 129
Temple Church (London), 129

Tetbury, 369
Thames, River (London)
  boat cruises, 164, 178
  restaurants along, 111–12
  sights and attractions along the, 138–40
Thames Valley, 174
Thaxted, 434
Theatre Royal (Bath), 356
Theatre Royal (Bristol), 364
Theatre Royal (York), 522
Thirsk, 536–7
Thornton Rust, 537
Thorpe Park (Surrey), 173
Thursford Collection (North Norfolk), 449
Time, 42
Tintagel, 328
Tipping, 42
Torbay (Torquay), 289–91
Tors rock formations (Dartmoor), 284–5
Totland Bay, 262
Totnes, 291–3
Tourist information, 42
Tourist Trail pass, 16
Tours, 19; *see also specific places*
Tower Bridge (London), 138–9
Tower of London (London), 115–16, 118
Toy and Model Museum (London), 168
Trafalgar Square (London), 53, 86–7
Train travel, 12–14
Transportation, 9–19; *see also specific places and means of transportation*
Treasurer's House (York), 519
Tresco, 319–20
Tresillian, 311
Trinity College (Cambridge), 424
Truro, 311
Tyne, 544–6

Underground, the (London), 49–50, 117
University College (Oxford), 189

Valhalla (Tresco), 320
Ventnor, 261–2
Verulamium Museum, 199
Victoria (London), accommodations, 56–7, 60
Victoria and Albert Museum (London), 126–7
Victoria Station (London), restaurants near, 94–5
Victory, H.M.S. (Portsmouth), 252
Vindolanda (Northumberland), 548
Waddesdon Manor (near Aylebury), 200
Walker Art Gallery (Liverpool), 492
Wallace Collection (London), 134
Wallington Hall (Northumberland), 546
Walmer Castle and Gardens (Deal), 221–2
Walton (Izaak) Cottage (Stafford), 487
Wareham, 269
Warwick, 404–9
Warwickshire Museum (Warwick), 406
Washington Old Hall (Tyne and Wear), 544

Waterways Museum (Northampton), 454
Weald and Downland Open Air Museum (near Chichester), 247–8
Wear, 544
Weather, 42
Wedgwood Visitor Centre (Stoke-on-Trent), 483
Wellington Ducal Estate (near Windsor), 182–3
Wellington Museum, Apsley House (London), 131–2
Wells, 350–3
West Country, 17
West End (London), 66, 83, 85–93, 163–4
Westminster (London), restaurants, 93
Westminster Abbey (London), 118–19
Westminster Communications Center (London), 53
West Wycombe, 202–3
West Yorkshire, 538–40
Whimple, 284
Whipsnade Wild Animal Park (Bedfordshire), 205
Whitehall (London), 128
Whitehall Theatre (London), 153–4
White Tower (London), 116
Whittinghton, 480–1
Widecombe-in-the-Moor, 285
Wigmore Hall (London), 155
Wilderness/adventure travel, 33–4
Wilton House (near Salisbury), 338–9
Wiltshire, 331–43
Winchelsea, 228–9, 231
Winchester, 262–5
Windermere, 500, 502–3
Windsor, 175–83
Windsor Castle, 174, 175
Windsor Great Park (Windsor), 177
Windsor Safari Park, 182
Wisley Garden, 226–7
Withypool, 344–5
Woburn Abbey (Bedfordshire), 204–5
Wollaton Hall (Nottingham), 463
Woodbridge, 441
Woodstock (Blenheim Palace), 196–7
Wookey Hole (Cave of Mendip) (Somerset), 353
Wootten, 262
Worcester, 392, 412, 416–17
Worfield/Bridgnorth, 482
Wotton-under-Edge, 368

York, 518–19, 522–8
York Castle Museum, 519
York Minster, 519
Yorkshire, 517–40
  map of, 520–1
Young Vic, The (London), 153

Zoos, 167, 219, 236, 475

NOW, SAVE MONEY ON ALL YOUR TRAVELS!
Join Frommer's™ Dollarwise® Travel Club

Saving money while traveling is never a simple matter, which is why, over 29 years ago, the **Dollarwise Travel Club** was formed. Actually, the idea came from readers of the Frommer publications who felt that such an organization could bring financial benefits, continuing travel information, and a sense of community to value-conscious travelers all over the world.

In keeping with the money-saving concept, the annual membership fee is low—$18 (U.S. residents) or $20 U.S. (Canadian, Mexican, and other foreign residents)—and is immediately exceeded by the value of your benefits which include:

1. The latest edition of any TWO of the books listed on the following pages.
2. A copy of any one Frommer City Guide.
3. An annual subscription to an 8-page quarterly newspaper, *The Dollarwise Traveler,* which keeps you up-to-date on fast-breaking developments in good-value travel in all parts of the world—bringing you the kind of information you'd have to pay over $35 a year to obtain elsewhere. This consumer-conscious publication also includes the following columns:
    Hospitality Exchange—members all over the world who are willing to provide hospitality to other members as they pass through their home cities.
    Share-a-Trip—requests from members for travel companions who can share costs and help avoid the burdensome single supplement.
    Readers Ask . . . Readers Reply—travel questions from members to which other members reply with authentic firsthand information.
4. Your personal membership card, which entitles you to purchase through the club all Frommer publications for a third to a half off their regular retail prices during the term of your membership.

So why not join this hardy band of international Dollarwise travelers now and participate in its exchange of information and hospitality? Simply send $18 (U.S. residents) or $20 U.S. (Canadian, Mexican, and other foreign residents) along with your name and address to: Frommer's Dollarwise Travel Club, Inc., 15 Columbus Circle, New York, NY 10023. Remember to specify which *two* of the books in section (1) and which *one* in section (2) above you wish to receive in your initial package of member's benefits. Or tear out the next page, check off your choices, and send the page to us with your membership fee.

FROMMER BOOKS
PRENTICE HALL TRAVEL
15 COLUMBUS CIRCLE
NEW YORK, NY 10023

Date_____

Friends:
Please send me the books checked below:

FROMMER™ GUIDES

(Guides to sightseeing and tourist accommodations and facilities from budget to deluxe, with emphasis on the medium-priced.)

☐ Alaska	$14.95	☐ Japan & Hong Kong	$13.95
☐ Australia	$14.95	☐ Mid-Atlantic States	$14.95
☐ Austria & Hungary	$14.95	☐ New England	$14.95
☐ Belgium, Holland & Luxembourg	$14.95	☐ New York State	$14.95
☐ Bermuda & The Bahamas	$14.95	☐ Northwest	$14.95
☐ Brazil	$14.95	☐ Portugal, Madeira & the Azores	$13.95
☐ Canada	$14.95	☐ Skiing Europe	$14.95
☐ Caribbean	$14.95	☐ Skiing USA—East	$13.95
☐ Cruises (incl. Alaska, Carib, Mex, Hawaii, Panama, Canada & US)	$14.95	☐ Skiing USA—West	$13.95
☐ California & Las Vegas	$14.95	☐ South Pacific	$14.95
☐ England & Scotland	$14.95	☐ Southeast Asia	$14.95
☐ Egypt	$13.95	☐ Southern Atlantic States	$14.95
☐ Florida	$14.95	☐ Southwest	$14.95
☐ France	$14.95	☐ Switzerland & Liechtenstein	$14.95
☐ Germany	$14.95	☐ Texas	$13.95
☐ Italy	$14.95	☐ USA	$15.95

FROMMER $-A-DAY® GUIDES

(In-depth guides to sightseeing and low-cost tourist accommodations and facilities.)

☐ Europe on $40 a Day	$15.95	☐ New York on $60 a Day	$13.95
☐ Australia on $30 a Day	$12.95	☐ New Zealand on $40 a Day	$13.95
☐ Eastern Europe on $25 a Day	$13.95	☐ Scandinavia on $60 a Day	$13.95
☐ England on $50 a Day	$13.95	☐ Scotland & Wales on $40 a Day	$13.95
☐ Greece on $30 a Day	$13.95	☐ South America on $35 a Day	$13.95
☐ Hawaii on $60 a Day	$13.95	☐ Spain & Morocco on $40 a Day	$13.95
☐ India on $25 a Day	$12.95	☐ Turkey on $30 a Day	$13.95
☐ Ireland on $35 a Day	$13.95	☐ Washington, D.C. & Historic Va. on $40 a Day	$13.95
☐ Israel on $40 a Day	$13.95		
☐ Mexico on $35 a Day	$13.95		

FROMMER TOURING GUIDES

(Color illustrated guides that include walking tours, cultural & historic sites, and other vital travel information.)

☐ Australia	$9.95	☐ Paris	$8.95
☐ Egypt	$8.95	☐ Scotland	$9.95
☐ Florence	$8.95	☐ Thailand	$9.95
☐ London	$8.95	☐ Venice	$8.95

TURN PAGE FOR ADDITONAL BOOKS AND ORDER FORM.

A

FROMMER CITY GUIDES
(Pocket-size guides to sightseeing and tourist accommodations and facilities in all price ranges.)

☐ Amsterdam/Holland $5.95	☐ Minneapolis/St. Paul $5.95
☐ Athens. $5.95	☐ Montréal/Québec City $5.95
☐ Atlantic City/Cape May $5.95	☐ New Orleans $5.95
☐ Belgium $5.95	☐ New York $5.95
☐ Boston $5.95	☐ Orlando/Disney World/EPCOT. $5.95
☐ Cancún/Cozumel/Yucatán $5.95	☐ Paris. $5.95
☐ Chicago $5.95	☐ Philadelphia $5.95
☐ Dublin/Ireland. $5.95	☐ Rio. $5.95
☐ Hawaii $5.95	☐ Rome. $5.95
☐ Las Vegas $5.95	☐ San Francisco. $5.95
☐ Lisbon/Madrid/Costa del Sol $5.95	☐ Santa Fe/Taos/Albuquerque. $5.95
☐ London. $5.95	☐ Sydney $5.95
☐ Los Angeles. $5.95	☐ Washington, D.C. $5.95
☐ Mexico City/Acapulco $5.95	

SPECIAL EDITIONS

☐ A Shopper's Guide to the Caribbean $12.95	☐ Manhattan's Outdoor Sculpture $15.95
☐ Beat the High Cost of Travel. $6.95	☐ Motorist's Phrase Book (Fr/Ger/Sp) $4.95
☐ Bed & Breakfast—N. America $11.95	☐ Paris Rendez-Vous. $10.95
☐ California with Kids $14.95	☐ Swap and Go (Home Exchanging) $10.95
☐ Caribbean Hideaways $14.95	☐ The Candy Apple (NY with Kids) $12.95
☐ Guide to Honeymoon Destinations	☐ Travel Diary and Record Book $5.95
(US, Canada, Mexico & Carib). $12.95	

☐ Where to Stay USA (Lodging from $3 to $30 a night). $10.95

☐ Marilyn Wood's Wonderful Weekends (NY, Conn, Mass, RI, Vt, NH, NJ, Del,Pa) $11.95

☐ The New World of Travel (Annual sourcebook by Arthur Frommer previewing: new travel trends, new modes of
  travel, and the latest cost-cutting strategies for savvy travelers.) $14.95

SERIOUS SHOPPER'S GUIDES
(Illustrated guides listing hundreds of stores, conveniently organized alphabetically by category.)

☐ Italy $15.95	☐ Los Angeles. $14.95
☐ London. $15.95	☐ Paris. $15.95

GAULT MILLAU
(The only guides that distinguish the truly superlative from the merely overrated.)

☐ The Best of Chicago $15.95	☐ The Best of Los Angeles. $14.95
☐ The Best of France $16.95	☐ The Best of New England. $15.95
☐ The Best of Hong Kong $16.95	☐ The Best of New York $14.95
☐ The Best of Italy $16.95	☐ The Best of San Francisco. $14.95

☐ The Best of Washington, D.C. $14.95

ORDER NOW!

In U.S. include $2 shipping UPS for 1st book; $1 ea. add'l book. Outside U.S. $3 and $1, respectively.

Allow four to six weeks for delivery in U.S., longer outside U.S.

Enclosed is my check or money order for $_____

NAME _____

ADDRESS _____

CITY _____ STATE _____ ZIP _____

A